MyMarketingLab: Improves Student Engagement Before, During, and After Class

Prep and Engagement

- **NEW! VIDEO LIBRARY –** Robust video library with over 100 new book-specific videos that include easy-to-assign assessments, the ability for instructors to add YouTube or other sources, the ability for students to upload video submissions, and the ability for polling and teamwork.

- **Decision-making simulations – NEW and improved feedback for students.** Place your students in the role of a key decision-maker! Simulations branch based on the decisions students make, providing a variation of scenario paths. Upon completion students receive a grade, as well as a detailed report of the choices and the associated consequences of those decisions.

- **Video exercises – UPDATED with new exercises.** Engaging videos that bring business concepts to life and explore business topics related to the theory students are learning in class. Quizzes then assess students' comprehension of the concepts covered in each video.

- **Learning Catalytics –** A "bring your own device" student engagement, assessment, and classroom intelligence system helps instructors analyze students' critical-thinking skills during lecture.

- **Dynamic Study Modules (DSMs) – UPDATED with additional questions.** Through adaptive learning, students get personalized guidance where and when they need it most, creating greater engagement, improving knowledge retention, and supporting subject-matter mastery. Also available on mobile devices.

Decision Making

Critical Thinking

- **Writing Space – UPDATED with new commenting tabs, new prompts, and a new tool for students called Pearson Writer.** A single location to develop and assess concept mastery and critical thinking, the Writing Space offers automatic graded, assisted graded, and create your own writing assignments, allowing you to exchange personalized feedback with students quickly and easily.

  Writing Space can also check students' work for improper citation or plagiarism by comparing it against the world's most accurate text comparison database available from **Turnitin**.

- **Additional Features –** Included with the MyLab are a powerful homework and test manager, robust gradebook tracking, Reporting Dashboard, comprehensive online course content, and easily scalable and shareable content.

http://www.pearsonmylabandmastering.com

PEARSON

Marketing

An Introduction Thirteenth Edition

GARY ARMSTRONG
University of North Carolina

PHILIP KOTLER
Northwestern University

PEARSON

Boston   Columbus   Indianapolis   New York   San Francisco
Amsterdam   Cape Town   Dubai   London   Madrid   Milan   Munich
Paris   Montréal   Toronto   Delhi   Mexico City   São Paulo   Sydney
Hong Kong   Seoul   Singapore   Taipei   Tokyo

Vice President, Business Publishing: Donna Battista
Editor-in-Chief: Stephanie Wall
Program Manager Team Lead: Ashley Santora
Program Manager: Jennifer M. Collins
Editorial Assistant: Eric Santucci
Vice President, Product Marketing: Maggie Moylan
**Director of Marketing, Digital Services
and Products:** Jeanette Koskinas
**Executive Product Marketing
Manager:** Anne Fahlgren
Field Marketing Manager: Lenny Ann Kucenski
Team Lead, Project Management: Jeff Holcomb
Senior Project Manager: Jacqueline A. Martin
Operations Specialist: Carol Melville
**Vice President, Director of Digital
Strategy & Assessment:** Paul Gentile

Manager of Learning Applications: Paul Deluca
Digital Editor: Brian Surette
Director, Digital Studio: Sacha Laustsen
Digital Studio Manager: Diane Lombardo
Digital Studio Project Manager:
Monique Lawrence
Digital Studio Project Manager: Alana Coles
Digital Studio Project Manager:
Robin Lazrus
**Full-Service Project Management
and Composition:** Integra Software Services, Inc.
Cover Image: venimo/Shutterstock
Interior and Cover Designer: Integra Software
Services, Inc.
Printer/Binder: RR Donnelley/Menasha
Cover Printer: Phoenix Color/Hagerstown

Library of Congress Cataloging-in-Publication Data is on file with the Library of Congress

10 9 8 7 6 5 4 3 2 1

ISBN 10: 0-13-414953-X
ISBN 13: 978-0-13-414953-0

To Kathy, Betty, Mandy, Matt, KC, Keri,
Delaney, Molly, Macy, and Ben; Nancy, Amy, Melissa, and Jessica

About the Authors

As a team, Gary Armstrong and Philip Kotler provide a blend of skills uniquely suited to writing an introductory marketing text. Professor Armstrong is an award-winning teacher of undergraduate business students. Professor Kotler is one of the world's leading authorities on marketing. Together they make the complex world of marketing practical, approachable, and enjoyable.

GARY ARMSTRONG is Crist W. Blackwell Distinguished Professor Emeritus of Undergraduate Education in the Kenan-Flagler Business School at the University of North Carolina at Chapel Hill. He holds undergraduate and master's degrees in business from Wayne State University in Detroit, and he received his Ph.D. in marketing from Northwestern University. Dr. Armstrong has contributed numerous articles to leading business journals. As a consultant and researcher, he has worked with many companies on marketing research, sales management, and marketing strategy.

But Professor Armstrong's first love has always been teaching. His long-held Blackwell Distinguished Professorship is the only permanent endowed professorship for distinguished undergraduate teaching at the University of North Carolina at Chapel Hill. He has been very active in the teaching and administration of Kenan-Flagler's undergraduate program. His administrative posts have included Chair of Marketing, Associate Director of the Undergraduate Business Program, Director of the Business Honors Program, and many others. Through the years, he has worked closely with business student groups and has received several UNC campuswide and Business School teaching awards. He is the only repeat recipient of the school's highly regarded Award for Excellence in Undergraduate Teaching, which he received three times. Most recently, Professor Armstrong received the UNC Board of Governors Award for Excellence in Teaching, the highest teaching honor bestowed by the 16-campus University of North Carolina system.

PHILIP KOTLER is S. C. Johnson & Son Distinguished Professor of International Marketing at the Kellogg School of Management, Northwestern University. He received his master's degree at the University of Chicago and his Ph.D. at M.I.T., both in economics. Dr. Kotler is author of *Marketing Management* (Pearson), now in its 15th edition and the most widely used marketing textbook in graduate schools of business worldwide. He has authored dozens of other successful books and has written more than 50 books and 150 articles in leading journals. He is the only three-time winner of the coveted Alpha Kappa Psi award for the best annual article in the *Journal of Marketing*.

Professor Kotler was named the first recipient of four major awards: the *Distinguished Marketing Educator of the Year Award* and the *William L. Wilkie "Marketing for a Better World" Award*, both given by the American Marketing Association; the *Philip Kotler Award for Excellence in Health Care Marketing* presented by the Academy for Health Care Services Marketing; and the *Sheth Foundation Medal for Exceptional Contribution to Marketing Scholarship and Practice*. He is a charter member of the Marketing Hall of Fame, was voted the first Leader in Marketing Thought by the American Marketing Association, and was named the Founder of Modern Marketing Management in the Handbook of Management Thinking. His numerous other major honors include the Sales and Marketing Executives International *Marketing Educator of the Year Award;* the European Association of Marketing Consultants and Trainers *Marketing Excellence Award;* the *Charles Coolidge Parlin Marketing Research Award;* and the *Paul D. Converse Award,* given by the American Marketing Association to honor "outstanding contributions to science in marketing." A recent *Forbes* survey ranks Professor Kotler in the top 10 of the world's most influential business thinkers. And in a recent *Financial Times* poll of 1,000 senior executives across the world, Professor Kotler was ranked as the fourth "most influential business writer/ guru" of the twenty-first century.

Dr. Kotler has served as chairman of the College of Marketing of the Institute of Management Sciences, a director of the American Marketing Association, and a trustee of the Marketing Science Institute. He has consulted with many major U.S. and international companies in the areas of marketing strategy and planning, marketing organization, and international marketing. He has traveled and lectured extensively throughout Europe, Asia, and South America, advising companies and governments about global marketing practices and opportunities.

Brief Contents

Contents

4 Managing Marketing Information to Gain Customer Insights   98

5 Understanding Consumer and Business Buyer Behavior   132

8 Developing New Products and Managing the Product Life Cycle   236

11 Retailing and Wholesaling 332

12 Engaging Consumers and Communicating Customer Value: Advertising and Public Relations 364

13 Personal Selling and Sales Promotion   398

16 Sustainable Marketing: Social Responsibility and Ethics   488

Preface

The Thirteenth Edition of
Marketing: An Introduction!

Fresh. Proven. Practical. Engaging.

These are exciting times in marketing. Recent surges in digital technologies have created a new, more engaging, more connected marketing world. Beyond traditional tried-and-true marketing concepts and practices, today's marketers have added a host of new-age tools for engaging consumers, building brands, and creating customer value and relationships. In these digital times, sweeping advances in "the Internet of Things"—from social and mobile media, connected digital devices, and the new consumer empowerment to "big data" and new marketing analytics—have profoundly affected both marketers and the consumers they serve.

More than ever, the 13th edition of *Marketing: An Introduction* introduces the exciting and fast-changing world of marketing in a fresh yet proven, practical, and engaging way.

Marketing: Creating Customer Value and Engagement in the Digital and Social Age

Top marketers share a common goal: putting the consumer at the heart of marketing. Today's marketing is all about creating customer value and engagement in a fast-changing, increasingly digital and social marketplace.

Marketing starts with understanding consumer needs and wants, determining which target markets the organization can serve best, and developing a compelling value proposition by which the organization can attract and grow valued customers. Then, more than just making a sale, today's marketers want to *engage* customers and build deep customer relationships that make their brands a meaningful part of consumers' conversations and lives.

In this digital age, to go along with proven traditional marketing methods, marketers have a dazzling set of new online, mobile, and social media tools for engaging customers anytime, anyplace to jointly shape brand conversations, experiences, and community. If marketers do these things well, they will reap the rewards in terms of market share, profits, and customer equity. In the 13th edition of *Marketing: An Introduction,* you'll learn how *customer value* and *customer engagement* drive every good marketing strategy.

Marketing: An Introduction makes learning and teaching marketing more productive and enjoyable than ever. The 13th edition's streamlined approach strikes an effective balance between depth of coverage and ease of learning. The 13th edition builds on proven content developed over 12 previous editions, yet it has been thoroughly revised to provide the freshest insights into current marketing concepts and practices.

The 13th edition remains highly approachable, with an organization, writing style, and design well suited to beginning marketing students. Its learning design—with integrative features at the start and end of each chapter plus insightful author comments throughout—helps students to learn, link, and apply important concepts. The text presents the practical side of marketing, with engaging examples and illustrations throughout that help to bring marketing to life. And when combined with MyMarketingLab, our online homework and personalized study tool, *Marketing: An Introduction* ensures that students will come to class well prepared and leave class with a richer understanding of basic marketing concepts, strategies, and practices.

What's New in the 13th Edition?

Once again, we've thoroughly revised *Marketing: An Introduction* to provide the freshest coverage of the latest trends and forces that affect marketing. We've poured over every page, table, figure, fact, and example in order to keep this the best text from which to learn about and teach marketing. The new edition provides substantial new content, expanded coverage, and fresh examples throughout each chapter.

- The 13th edition adds fresh coverage in both traditional marketing areas and on fast-changing and trending topics such as customer engagement marketing, mobile and social media, big data and the new marketing analytics, omni-channel marketing and retailing, customer co-creation and empowerment, real-time customer listening and marketing, building brand community, marketing content creation and native advertising, B-to-B social media and social selling, tiered and dynamic pricing, consumer privacy, sustainability, global marketing, and much more.
- This new edition continues to build on its *customer engagement* framework—creating direct and continuous customer involvement in shaping brands, brand conversations, brand experiences, and brand community. New coverage and fresh examples throughout the text address the latest customer engagement tools, practices, and developments. See especially Chapter 1 (refreshed sections on *Customer Engagement and Today's Digital and Social Media* and *Consumer-Generated Marketing*); Chapter 4 (big data and real-time research to gain deeper customer insights); Chapter 5 (creating social influence and customer community through digital and social media marketing); Chapter 8 (customer co-creation and customer-driven new-product development); Chapter 11 (omni-channel retailing); Chapter 12 (marketing content curation and native advertising); Chapter 13 (salesforce social selling); and Chapter 14 (direct digital, online, social media, and mobile marketing).
- No area of marketing is changing faster than *online, mobile, social media, and other digital marketing technologies.* Keeping up with digital concepts, technologies, and practices has become a top priority and major challenge for today's marketers. The 13th edition of *Marketing: An Introduction* provides thoroughly refreshed, up-to-date coverage of these explosive developments in every chapter—from online, mobile, and social media engagement technologies discussed in Chapters 1, 5, 12, and 14 to "real-time listening" and "big data" research tools in Chapter 4, real-time dynamic pricing in Chapter 9, digitizing the in-store retail shopping experience in Chapter 11, and social selling in Chapter 13. A Chapter 1 section on *The Digital Age: Online, Mobile, and Social Media Marketing* introduces the exciting new developments in digital and social media marketing. Then a Chapter 14 section on *Direct, Online, Social Media, and Mobile Marketing* digs more deeply into digital marketing tools such as online sites, social media, mobile ads and apps, online video, email, blogs, and other digital platforms that engage consumers anywhere, anytime via their computers, smartphones, tablets, Internet-ready TVs, and other digital devices.
- The 13th edition continues to track fast-changing developments in *marketing communications* and the creation of *marketing content*. Marketers are no longer simply creating integrated marketing communications programs; they are joining with customers and media to curate customer-driven marketing content in paid, owned, earned, and shared media. You won't find fresher coverage of these important topics in any other marketing text.
- The 13th edition of *Marketing: An Introduction* continues to improve on its *innovative learning design*. The text's active and integrative presentation includes learning enhancements such as annotated chapter-opening stories, a chapter-opening objective outline, explanatory author comments on major chapter sections and figures, and Marketing at Work highlights that provide in-depth examples of marketing concepts and practices at

work. The chapter-opening layout helps to preview and position the chapter and its key concepts. Figures annotated with author comments help students to simplify and organize chapter material. New and substantially revised end-of-chapter features help to summarize important chapter concepts and highlight important themes, such as *marketing ethics, financial marketing analysis,* and *online, mobile, and social media marketing.* This innovative learning design facilitates student understanding and eases learning.

- The 13th edition provides 16 new end-of-chapter company cases by which students can apply what they learn to actual company situations. It also features 16 brand-new video cases, with brief end-of-chapter summaries and discussion questions. Finally, all of the chapter-opening stories, Marketing at Work highlights, and end-of-chapter features in the 13th edition are either new or substantially revised.

Five Major Customer Value and Engagement Themes

The 13th edition of *Marketing: An Introduction* builds on five major customer value and engagement themes:

1. *Creating value* **for** *customers in order to capture value* **from** *customers in return.* Today's marketers must be good at *creating customer value, engaging customers,* and *managing customer relationships.* Outstanding marketing companies understand the marketplace and customer needs, design value-creating marketing strategies, develop integrated marketing programs that engage customers and deliver value and satisfaction, and build strong customer relationships and brand community. In return, they capture value from customers in the form of sales, profits, and customer equity.

   This innovative *customer value and engagement framework* is introduced at the start of Chapter 1 in a five-step marketing process model, which details how marketing *creates* customer value and *captures* value in return. The framework is carefully developed in the first two chapters and then fully integrated throughout the remainder of the text.

2. *Customer engagement and today's digital and social media.* New digital and social media have taken today's marketing by storm, dramatically changing how companies and brands engage consumers and how consumers connect and influence each other's brand behaviors. The 13th edition thoroughly explores the contemporary concept of *customer engagement marketing* and the exciting new digital and social media technologies that help brands to engage customers more deeply and interactively. It starts with two major Chapter 1 sections: *Customer Engagement and Today's Digital and Social Media* and *The Digital Age: Online, Mobile, and Social Media Marketing.* A refreshed Chapter 14 on *Direct, Online, Social Media, and Mobile Marketing* summarizes the latest developments in digital engagement and relationship-building tools. Everywhere in between, you'll find revised and expanded coverage of the exploding use of digital and social tools to create customer engagement and build brand community.

3. *Building and managing strong, value-creating brands.* Well-positioned brands with strong brand equity provide the basis upon which to build customer value and profitable customer relationships. Today's marketers must position their brands powerfully and manage them well to create valued brand experiences. The 13th edition provides a deep focus on brands, anchored by a Chapter 7 section on *Branding Strategy: Building Strong Brands.*

4. *Measuring and managing return on marketing.* Especially in uneven economic times, marketing managers must ensure that their marketing dollars are being well spent. In the past, many marketers spent freely on big, expensive marketing programs, often without thinking carefully about the financial returns on their spending. But all that has changed rapidly. "Marketing accountability"—measuring and managing marketing return on investment—has now become an important part of strategic marketing decision making. This emphasis on marketing accountability is addressed in Chapter 2,

Appendix 3: *Marketing by the Numbers,* and end-of-chapter Marketing by the Numbers features and throughout the 13th edition.

5. ***Sustainable marketing around the globe***. As technological developments make the world an increasingly smaller and more fragile place, marketers must be good at marketing their brands globally and in sustainable ways. New material throughout the 13th edition emphasizes the concepts of global marketing and sustainable marketing— meeting the present needs of consumers and businesses while also preserving or enhancing the ability of future generations to meet their needs. The 13th edition integrates global marketing and sustainability topics throughout the text. It then provides focused coverage on each topic in Chapters 15 and 16, respectively.

An Emphasis on Real Marketing and Bringing Marketing to Life

Marketing: An Introduction, 13th edition, takes a practical marketing management approach, providing countless in-depth, real-life examples and stories that engage students with marketing concepts and bring modern marketing to life. In the 13th edition, every chapter has an engaging *First Stop* opening story plus *Marketing at Work* highlights that provide fresh insights into real marketing practices. Learn how:

- Netflix uses "big data" to personalize each customer's viewing experience. While Netflix subscribers are busy watching videos, Netflix is busy watching *them*—very, very closely.
- Wildly innovative Google has become an incredibly successful new product "moonshot factory," unleashing a seemingly unending flurry of diverse products, most of which are market leaders in their categories.
- Nike—by far the world's largest sports apparel company—does much more than just make and sell sports gear. The iconic brand creates customer value by building deep engagement and a sense of community with and between the Nike brand and its customers.
- Toy market leader LEGO uses innovative marketing research—lots and lots of it—to dig out fresh customer insights, then uses the insights to create irresistible play experiences for children around the world.
- Mighty Kellogg, the world's largest cereal maker, may be losing its snap, crackle, and pop as shifts in the marketing environment change how people today eat breakfast.
- Harley-Davidson's market dominance comes from a deep understanding of the emotions and motivations that underlie consumer behavior. Harley doesn't just sell motorcycles; it sells freedom, independence, power, and authenticity.
- Ultra low-price Spirit Airlines is thriving despite industry-low customer experience ratings. You don't get much when you fly Spirit. Then again, you don't pay for what you don't get.
- Marketers are now using real-time online, mobile, and social media marketing to engage customers in the moment, linking brands to trending topics, events, causes, personal occasions, or other happenings in their lives.
- Amazon has become the poster child for direct and digital marketing. Its passion for creating superb online customer experiences has made it one of the most powerful names on the Internet.
- Direct marketing insurance giant GEICO has gone from bit player to behemoth thanks to a big-budget advertising campaign featuring a smooth-talking gecko and an enduring "15 minutes could save you 15 percent" tagline.
- Outdoor apparel and gear maker Patagonia's "Conscious Consumption" mission takes sustainability to new extremes by telling consumers to buy *less* of its products.
- Cosmetics maker L'Oréal has become the "United Nations of Beauty" by achieving a global-local balance that adapts and differentiates brands in local markets while optimizing their impact across global markets.

Beyond such features, each chapter is packed with countless real, engaging, and timely examples that reinforce key concepts. No other text brings marketing to life like the 13th edition of *Marketing: An Introduction.*

Learning Aids That Create Value and Engagement

A wealth of chapter-opening, within-chapter, and end-of-chapter learning devices help students to learn, link, and apply major concepts:

- *Integrated Chapter-Opening Road Maps.* The active and integrative chapter-opening spread in each chapter features an *Objective Outline* that outlines chapter contents and learning objectives, a brief *Previewing the Concepts* section that introduces chapter concepts, and a *First Stop* opening vignette—an engaging, deeply developed, illustrated, and annotated marketing story that introduces the chapter material and sparks student interest.
- *Marketing at Work highlights.* Each chapter contains two carefully developed highlight features that provide an in-depth look at real marketing practices of large and small companies.
- *Author comments and figure annotations.* Throughout each chapter, author comments ease and enhance student learning by introducing and explaining major chapter sections and figures.
- *Reviewing and Extending the Concepts.* Sections at the end of each chapter summarize key chapter concepts and provide questions, exercises, and cases by which students can review and apply what they've learned. The *Chapter Review and Critical Thinking* section reviews major chapter concepts and links them to chapter objectives. It provides a helpful listing of chapter key terms by order of appearance with page numbers that facilitate easy reference. Finally, it provides discussion questions and critical thinking exercises that help students to keep track of and apply what they've learned in the chapter.

  The *Minicases and Applications* section at the end of each chapter provides brief *Marketing Ethics; Online, Mobile, and Social Media Marketing;* and *Marketing by the Numbers* applications cases that facilitate discussion of current issues and company situations in areas such as mobile and social marketing, ethics, and financial marketing analysis. It also includes a *Video Case* section that contains short vignettes with discussion questions to be used with a set of short videos that accompany the 13th edition. An end-of-chapter *Company Cases* section identifies which of the company cases found in Appendix 1 are best for use with each chapter.
- *Company Cases.* Appendix 1 contains 16 all-new company cases that help students to apply major marketing concepts to real company and brand situations.
- *Marketing Plan appendix.* Appendix 2 contains a sample marketing plan that helps students to apply important marketing planning concepts.
- *Marketing by the Numbers appendix.* An innovative Appendix 3 provides students with a comprehensive introduction to the marketing financial analysis that helps to guide, assess, and support marketing decisions. An exercise at the end of each chapter lets students apply analytical and financial thinking to relevant chapter concepts and links the chapter to the Marketing by the Numbers appendix.
- *Careers in Marketing.* Appendix 4 helps students to explore marketing career paths open to them and lays out a process for landing a marketing job that best matches their special skills and interests.

  More than ever before, the 13th edition of *Marketing: An Introduction* creates value and engagement for you—it gives you all you need to know about marketing in an effective and enjoyable total learning package!

A Total Teaching and Learning Package

A successful marketing course requires more than a well-written book. Today's classroom requires a dedicated teacher, well-prepared students, and a fully integrated teaching system.

A total package of teaching and learning supplements extends this edition's emphasis on creating value and engagement for both the student and instructor. The following aids support *Marketing: An Introduction,* 13th edition.

Instructor Resources

At the Instructor Resource Center, www.pearsonhighered.com/irc, instructors can easily register to gain access to a variety of instructor resources available with this text in downloadable format. If assistance is needed, our dedicated technical support team is ready to help with the media supplements that accompany this text. Visit http://247.pearsoned .com for answers to frequently asked questions and toll-free user support phone numbers.

The following supplements are available with this text:

- **Instructor's Resource Manual**
- **Test Bank**
- **TestGen® Computerized Test Bank**
- **PowerPoint Presentation**

Acknowledgments

No book is the work only of its authors. We greatly appreciate the valuable contributions of several people who helped make this new edition possible. As always, we owe extra-special thanks to Keri Jean Miksza for her dedicated and valuable contributions to *all* phases of the project and to her husband Pete and daughters Lucy and Mary for all the support they provide Keri during this very absorbing project.

We owe substantial thanks to Andy Norman of Drake University for his skillful help in developing chapter vignettes and highlights, company and video cases, and the Marketing Plan appendix. This and many previous editions have benefited greatly from Andy's assistance. We also thank Laurie Babin of the University of Louisiana at Monroe for her dedicated continued efforts in preparing end-of-chapter materials and for keeping our Marketing by the Numbers appendix fresh. Additional thanks also go to Jennifer Barr, Tony Henthorne, and Douglas Martin.

Many reviewers at other colleges and universities provided valuable comments and suggestions for this and previous editions. We are indebted to the following colleagues for their thoughtful inputs:

REVIEWERS

George Bercovitz, *York College*
Pari S. Bhagat, Ph.D., *Indiana University of Pennsylvania*
Sylvia Clark, *St. John's University*
Linda Jane Coleman, *Salem State University*
Mary Conran, *Temple University*
Datha Damron-Martinez, *Truman State University*
Lawrence K. Duke, *Drexel University*
Barbara S. Faries, MBA, *Mission College*
Ivan Filby, *Greenville College*
John Gaskins, *Longwood University*
Karen Halpern, *South Puget Sound Community College*
Jan Hardesty, *University of Arizona*
Hella-Ilona Johnson, *Olympic College*
David Koehler, *University of Illinois at Chicago*
Michelle Kunz, *Morehead State University*
Susan Mann, *University of Northwestern Ohio*
Thomas E. Marshall, M.B.E., *Owens Community College*

Nora Martin, *University of South Carolina*
Erika Matulich, *University of Tampa*
Marc Newman, *Hocking College*
John T. Nolan, *SUNY, Buffalo State*
Nikolai Ostapenko, *University of the District of Columbia*
Vic Piscatello, *University of Arizona*
Bill Rice, *California State University*
David Robinson, *University of California, Berkeley*
William M. Ryan, *University of Connecticut*
Elliot Schreiber, *Drexel University*
Lisa Simon, *Cal Poly, San Luis Obispo*
Robert Simon, *University of Nebraska, Lincoln*
Keith Starcher, *Indiana Wesleyan University*
John Talbott, *Indiana University*
Rhonda Tenenbaum, *Queens College*
Deborah Utter, *Boston University*
Tom Voigt, *Judson University*
Terry Wilson, *East Stroudsburg University*

We also owe a great deal to the people at Pearson Education who helped develop this book. Senior Acquisitions Editor Mark Gaffney provided resources and support during the revision. Senior Project Manager Jacqueline Martin and Program Manager Jennifer Collins provided valuable assistance and advice in guiding this complex revision project through development, design, and production. We'd also like to thank Stephanie Wall, Lenny Ann Kucenski, Judy Leale, Jeff Holcomb, and Eric Santucci for their able assistance along the way. We are proud to be associated with the fine professionals at Pearson. We also owe a mighty debt of gratitude to Charles Fisher and the team at Integra.

Finally, we owe many thanks to our families for all of their support and encouragement — Kathy, Betty, Mandy, Matt, KC, Keri, Delaney, Molly, Macy, and Ben from the Armstrong clan and Nancy, Amy, Melissa, and Jessica from the Kotler family. To them, we dedicate this book.

Gary Armstrong
Philip Kotler

Marketing

An Introduction Thirteenth Edition

1 Marketing
Creating Customer Value and Engagement

CHAPTER ROAD MAP | Objective Outline

OBJECTIVE 1-1 Define marketing and outline the steps in the marketing process. What Is Marketing? (4–5)

OBJECTIVE 1-2 Explain the importance of understanding the marketplace and customers and identify the five core marketplace concepts. Understanding the Marketplace and Customer Needs (6–8)

OBJECTIVE 1-3 Identify the key elements of a customer-value driven marketing strategy and discuss the marketing management orientations that guide marketing strategy. Designing a Customer-Driven Marketing Strategy (9–12) Preparing an Integrated Marketing Plan and Program (12–13)

OBJECTIVE 1-4 Discuss customer relationship management and identify strategies for creating value *for* customers and capturing value *from* customers in return. Engaging Customers and Managing Customer Relationships (13–20); Capturing Value from Customers (20–23)

OBJECTIVE 1-5 Describe the major trends and forces that are changing the marketing landscape in this age of relationships. The Changing Marketing Landscape (24–31)

Previewing the Concepts

This chapter introduces you to the basic concepts of marketing. We start with the question: What is marketing? Simply put, marketing is engaging customers and managing profitable customer relationships. The aim of marketing is to create value for customers in order to capture value from customers in return. Next we discuss the five steps in the marketing process—from understanding customer needs, to designing customer value-driven marketing strategies and integrated marketing programs, to building customer relationships and capturing value for the firm. Finally, we discuss the major trends and forces affecting marketing in this new age of digital, mobile, and social media. Understanding these basic concepts and forming your own ideas about what they really mean to you will provide a solid foundation for all that follows.

Let's start with a good story about marketing in action at Nike, the world's leading sports apparel company and one of the best-known brands on the planet. Nike's outstanding success results from much more than just making and selling good sports gear. It's based on a customer-focused marketing strategy by which Nike creates customer value through deep brand–customer engagement and close brand community with and among its customers.

First Stop

Nike's Customer Value-Driven Marketing:
Engaging Customers and Building Brand Community

The Nike "swoosh"—it's everywhere! Just for fun, try counting the swooshes whenever you pick up the sports pages or watch a basketball game or tune into a televised soccer match. Over the past 50 years, through innovative marketing, Nike has built the ever-present swoosh into one of the world's best-known brand symbols.

Product innovation has always been a cornerstone of Nike's success. Nike makes outstanding shoes, clothing, and gear, whether for basketball, football, and baseball or golf, skateboarding, wall climbing, bicycling, and hiking. But from the start, a brash, young Nike revolutionized sports marketing. To build image and market share, the brand lavishly outspent competitors on big-name endorsements, splashy promotional events, and big-budget, in-your-face "Just Do It" ads. Whereas competitors stressed technical performance, Nike built customer engagement and relationships.

Beyond shoes, Nike marketed a way of life, a genuine passion for sports, a "just-do-it" attitude. Customers didn't just wear their Nikes, they *experienced* them. As the company once stated on its Web page, "Nike has always known the truth—it's not so much the shoes but where they take you." Nike's mission isn't to "make better gear," it's to "connect with and inspire athletes around the world." Few brands have become more ever-present and valued than Nike in their customers' lives and conversations.

Whether customers connect with Nike through ads, in-person events at Niketown stores, a local Nike running club, or one of the company's profusion of community Web and social media sites, more and more people are bonding closely with the Nike brand. Connecting once required simply outspending competitors on big media ads and celebrity endorsers that talk *at* customers. But in these digital times, Nike is forging a new kind of brand–customer connection—a deeper, more personal, more engaging one. Nike still invests heavily in traditional advertising. But the brand now spends a lion's share of its marketing budget on cutting-edge digital and social media marketing that interacts *with* customers to build brand engagement and community.

Nike's innovative use of online, mobile, and social media recently earned the brand the title of "top genius" in "digital IQ" among 42 sportswear companies in one digital consultancy's rankings. Nike also placed first in creating brand "tribes"—large groups of highly engaged users—with the help of social media platforms such as Facebook, Twitter, Instagram, YouTube, and Pinterest. For example, the main Nike Facebook page has more than 42 million Likes. The Nike Soccer page adds another 35 million, the Nike Basketball page 7 million more, and Nike Running another 3 million. More than just numbers, Nike's social media presence engages customers at a high level, gets them talking with each other about the brand, and weaves the brand into their daily lives.

Nike excels at cross-media campaigns that integrate digital media with traditional tools to connect with customers. An example is Nike's recent "Risk Everything" World Cup soccer campaign. The Risk Everything campaign began with captivating four- to five-minute videos embedded in Nike social media sites and its own Risk Everything Web site. The campaign—featuring Nike-sponsored soccer superstars such as Portugal's Cristiano Ronaldo, England's Wayne Rooney, Brazil's Neymar, and a dozen others—was built around an intense, provocative World Cup story line of taking risks to gain the glory of succeeding against rival teams and nations.

In one Risk Everything video—"Winner Stays"—two teams of young men faced off on a local soccer field for a pickup game, pretending to be (then turning into) the superstars. The scene transformed into a legendary bout on a global stage. As the video ended, a young boy stepped in for Ronaldo and under immense pressure scored the winning goal. According to one analyst, the Risk Everything videos were "the perfect blend of product placement, provocative storytelling, and real-time marketing." Although the videos were filled with Nike swooshes, products, and stars, highly engaged viewers hardly realized that they were consuming ad content.

By the end of the final World Cup match, the Risk Everything videos had produced 372 million views, 22 million engagements (Likes, comments, shares), and 650,000 uses of #riskeverything. Nike reigned as the "most-viewed brand" of the World Cup in terms of online video, trouncing rival adidas. In fact, Nike's online views accounted for an incredible one-half of all the views attributed to the event's 97 World Cup marketing campaigns—and Nike wasn't even an official sponsor. Along with the Risk Everything videos, Nike ran a full array of traditional television, print, radio, cinema, and gaming

>> The Nike swoosh—it's everywhere. Nike has mastered social networking, both online and off, creating deep engagement and community with and among customers.

© Steve Hellerstein/Alamy

> Nike's outstanding success results from much more than just making good sports gear. The iconic brand delivers customer value by building deep engagement and a sense of community with and between the Nike brand and its customers.

3

advertising. Taken as a whole, across all media, the Risk Everything campaign generated more than 6 *billion* impressions in 35 countries. Now that's customer engagement.

Nike has also created customer value and brand community through groundbreaking mobile apps and technologies. For example, its Nike+ apps have helped Nike become a part of the daily fitness routines of millions of customers around the world. The Nike+ FuelBand device, for instance, converts just about every imaginable physical movement into NikeFuel, Nike's own universal activity metric. So whether your activity is running, jumping, baseball, skating, dancing, stacking sports cups, or chasing chickens, it counts for NikeFuel points. Everyday athletes can use NikeFuel to track their personal performance, then share and compare it across sports and locations with others in the global Nike community. The Nike+ mobile app lets users watch their progress, get extra motivation on the go, and stay connected with friends. Nike+ has engaged a huge global brand community. To date, more than 5 million Nike+ users worldwide have logged 1,118,434,247 miles. That's 44,914 trips around the world or 4,682 journeys to the moon and back.

Thus, Nike delivers customer value well beyond the products it makes. It has built a deep kinship and sense of community with and between the Nike brand and its customers. Whether it's through local running clubs, a performance-tracking app, primetime TV ads, videos, and other content in any of its dozens of brand Web sites and social media pages, the Nike brand has become a valued part of customers' lives and times.

As a result, Nike remains the world's largest sports apparel company, an impressive 44 percent larger than closest rival adidas. During the past decade, even as a sometimes-shaky economy left many sports footwear and apparel rivals gasping for breath, Nike's global sales and income have sprinted ahead by more than double. "Connecting used to be, 'Here's some product, and here's some advertising. We hope you like it,'" notes Nike's CEO. "Connecting today is a dialogue." Says Nike's chief marketing officer, "The engagement levels we have received…drive huge momentum for our brand. This is just the beginning of how we will connect with and inspire athletes around the world."[1]

T oday's successful companies have one thing in common: Like Nike, they are strongly customer focused and heavily committed to marketing. These companies share a passion for understanding and satisfying customer needs in well-defined target markets. They motivate everyone in the organization to help build lasting customer relationships based on creating value.

Customer relationships and value are especially important today. Facing dramatic technological advances and deep economic, social, and environmental challenges, today's customers are relating digitally with companies and each other, spending more carefully, and reassessing how they engage with brands. New digital, mobile, and social media developments have revolutionized how consumers shop and interact, in turn calling for new marketing strategies and tactics. In these fast-changing times, it's now more important than ever to build strong customer relationships based on real and enduring customer value.

We'll discuss the exciting new challenges facing both customers and marketers later in the chapter. But first, let's introduce the basics of marketing.

What Is Marketing?

Marketing, more than any other business function, deals with customers. Although we will soon explore more-detailed definitions of marketing, perhaps the simplest definition is this one: *Marketing is engaging customers and managing profitable customer relationships.* The twofold goal of marketing is to attract new customers by promising superior value and to keep and grow current customers by delivering satisfaction.

For example, Walmart has become the world's largest retailer—and the world's largest *company*—by delivering on its promise "Save Money. Live Better." Coca-Cola has earn a 49 percent global share of the carbonated beverage market—more than twice Pepsi's share—by fulfilling its "open happiness" motto with products that "spread smiles and open happiness every day all across the world." Facebook has attracted more than 1.4 billion active Web and mobile users worldwide by helping them to "connect and share with the people in their lives."[2]

Sound marketing is critical to the success of every organization. Large for-profit firms, such as Google, Target, Procter & Gamble, Coca-Cola, and Microsoft, use marketing. But so do not-for-profit organizations, such as colleges, hospitals, museums, symphony orchestras, and even churches.

You already know a lot about marketing—it's all around you. Marketing comes to you in the good old traditional forms: You see it in the abundance of products at your nearby shopping mall and the ads that fill your TV screen, spice up your magazines, or stuff your mailbox. But in recent years, marketers have assembled a host of new marketing approaches, everything from imaginative Web sites and smartphone apps to blogs, online videos, and social media. These new approaches do more than just blast out messages to the masses. They reach you directly, personally, and interactively. Today's marketers want to become a part of your life and enrich your experiences with their brands—to help you *live* their brands.

At home, at school, where you work, and where you play, you see marketing in almost everything you do. Yet there is much more to marketing than meets the consumer's casual eye. Behind it all is a massive network of people, technologies, and activities competing for your attention and purchases. This book will give you a complete introduction to the basic concepts and practices of today's marketing. In this chapter, we begin by defining marketing and the marketing process.

Marketing Defined

What *is* marketing? Many people think of marketing as only selling and advertising. We are bombarded every day with TV commercials, catalogs, spiels from salespeople, and online pitches. However, selling and advertising are only the tip of the marketing iceberg.

Today, marketing must be understood not in the old sense of making a sale—"telling and selling"—but in the new sense of *satisfying customer needs*. If the marketer engages consumers effectively, understands their needs, develops products that provide superior customer value, and prices, distributes, and promotes them well, these products will sell easily. In fact, according to management guru Peter Drucker, "The aim of marketing is to make selling unnecessary."[3] Selling and advertising are only part of a larger *marketing mix*—a set of marketing tools that work together to engage customers, satisfy customer needs, and build customer relationships.

Broadly defined, marketing is a social and managerial process by which individuals and organizations obtain what they need and want through creating and exchanging value with others. In a narrower business context, marketing involves building profitable, value-laden exchange relationships with customers. Hence, we define **marketing** as the process by which companies engage customers, build strong customer relationships, and create customer value in order to capture value from customers in return.[4]

Marketing
The process by which companies engage customers, build strong customer relationships, and create customer value in order to capture value from customers in return.

The Marketing Process

»» Figure 1.1 presents a simple, five-step model of the marketing process for creating and capturing customer value. In the first four steps, companies work to understand consumers, create customer value, and build strong customer relationships. In the final step, companies reap the rewards of creating superior customer value. By creating value *for* consumers, they in turn capture value *from* consumers in the form of sales, profits, and long-term customer equity.

In this chapter and the next, we will examine the steps of this simple model of marketing. In this chapter, we review each step but focus more on the customer relationship steps—understanding customers, engaging and building relationships with customers, and capturing value from customers. In Chapter 2, we look more deeply into the second and third steps—designing value-creating marketing strategies and constructing marketing programs.

This important figure shows marketing in a nutshell. By creating value *for* customers, marketers capture value *from* customers in return. This five-step process forms the marketing framework for the rest of the chapter and the remainder of the text.

Create value *for* customers and
build customer relationships

Capture value *from*
customers in return

| Understand the marketplace and customer needs and wants | → | Design a customer value-driven marketing strategy | → | Construct an integrated marketing program that delivers superior value | → | Engage customers, build profitable relationships, and create customer delight | → | Capture value from customers to create profits and customer equity |

»» Figure 1.1 The Marketing Process: Creating and Capturing Customer Value

Author Comment

Marketing is all about creating value for customers. So, as the first step in the marketing process, the company must fully understand consumers and the marketplace in which it operates.

Understanding the Marketplace and Customer Needs

As a first step, marketers need to understand customer needs and wants and the marketplace in which they operate. We examine five core customer and marketplace concepts: (1) *needs, wants, and demands*; (2) *market offerings (products, services, and experiences)*; (3) *value and satisfaction*; (4) *exchanges and relationships*; and (5) *markets*.

Customer Needs, Wants, and Demands

Needs
States of felt deprivation.

Wants
The form human needs take as they are shaped by culture and individual personality.

The most basic concept underlying marketing is that of human needs. Human **needs** are states of felt deprivation. They include basic *physical* needs for food, clothing, warmth, and safety; *social* needs for belonging and affection; and *individual* needs for knowledge and self-expression. Marketers did not create these needs; they are a basic part of the human makeup.

Wants are the form human needs take as they are shaped by culture and individual personality. An American *needs* food but *wants* a Big Mac, french fries, and a soft drink. A person in Papua, New Guinea, *needs* food but *wants* taro, rice, yams, and pork. Wants are shaped by one's society and are described in terms of objects that will satisfy those needs. When backed by buying power, wants become **demands**. Given their wants and resources, people demand products and services with benefits that add up to the most value and satisfaction.

Outstanding marketing companies go to great lengths to learn about and understand their customers' needs, wants, and demands. They conduct consumer research, analyze mountains of customer data, and observe customers as they shop and interact, offline and online. People at all levels of the company—including top management—stay close to customers:[5]

> Staying close to customers: Energetic new Target CEO Brian Collins makes regular unannounced visits to Target stores, accompanied by local moms and loyal Target shoppers.

Ackerman + Gruber

Target's energetic new CEO, Brian Cornell, makes regular unannounced visits to Target stores, accompanied by local moms and loyal Target shoppers. >> Cornell likes nosing around stores and getting a real feel for what's going on. It gives him "great, genuine feedback." Similarly, Boston Market CEO George Michel makes frequent visits to company restaurants, working in the dining room and engaging customers to learn about "the good, the bad, and the ugly." He also stays connected by reading customer messages on the Boston Market Web site and has even cold-called customers for insights. "Being close to the customer is critically important," says Michel. "I get to learn what they value, what they appreciate."

Market Offerings—Products, Services, and Experiences

Demands
Human wants that are backed by buying power.

Market offerings
Some combination of products, services, information, or experiences offered to a market to satisfy a need or want.

Consumers' needs and wants are fulfilled through **market offerings**—some combination of products, services, information, or experiences offered to a market to satisfy a need or a want. Market offerings are not limited to physical *products*. They also include *services*—activities or benefits offered for sale that are essentially intangible and do not result in the ownership of anything. Examples include banking, airline, hotel, retailing, and home repair services.

More broadly, market offerings also include other entities, such as *persons, places, organizations, information*, and *ideas*. For example, San Diego recently launched a $9 million "Happiness Is Calling" advertising campaign that invites visitors to come and enjoy the city's great weather and good times—everything from its bays and beaches to its downtown nightlife and urban scenes. And the Ad Council and

Marketing myopia
The mistake of paying more attention to the specific products a company offers than to the benefits and experiences produced by these products.

>> Marketing experiences: American Girl does more than just make and sell high-end dolls. It creates special experiences between the dolls and the girls who adore them.

the National Highway Traffic Safety Administration created a "Stop the Texts. Stop the Wrecks." campaign that markets the idea of eliminating texting while driving. The campaign points out that a texting driver is 23 times more likely to get into a crash than a non-texting driver.[6]

Many sellers make the mistake of paying more attention to the specific products they offer than to the benefits and experiences produced by these products. These sellers suffer from **marketing myopia**. They are so taken with their products that they focus only on existing wants and lose sight of underlying customer needs.[7] They forget that a product is only a tool to solve a consumer problem. A manufacturer of quarter-inch drill bits may think that the customer needs a drill bit. But what the customer *really* needs is a quarter-inch hole. These sellers will have trouble if a new product comes along that serves the customer's need better or less expensively. The customer will have the same *need* but will *want* the new product.

Smart marketers look beyond the attributes of the products and services they sell. By orchestrating several services and products, they create *brand experiences* for consumers. For example, you don't just visit Walt Disney World Resort; you immerse yourself and your family in a world of wonder, a world where dreams come true and things still work the way they should. "Let the magic begin!" says Disney. >> Similarly, Mattel's American Girl does much more than just make and sell high-end dolls. It creates special experiences between the dolls and the girls who adore them.[8]

To put more smiles on the faces of the girls who love their American Girl dolls, the company operates huge American Girl experiential stores in 20 major cities around the country. Each store carries an amazing selection of dolls plus every imaginable outfit and accessory. But more than just shopping spots, American Girl stores are exciting destinations unto themselves, offering wonderfully engaging experiences for girls, mothers, grandmothers, and even dads or grandpas. There's an in-store restaurant where girls, their dolls, and grown-ups can sit down together for brunch, lunch, afternoon tea, or dinner. There's even a doll hair salon where a stylist can give a doll a new hairdo. American Girl also offers "perfect parties" to celebrate a birthday or any day, as well as a full slate of special events, from crafts and activities to excursions. Much more than a store that sells dolls, says the company, "it's the place where imaginations can soar." A visit to American Girl creates "Fun today. Memories forever."

Customer Value and Satisfaction

Consumers usually face a broad array of products and services that might satisfy a given need. How do they choose among these many market offerings? Customers form expectations about the value and satisfaction that various market offerings will deliver and buy accordingly. Satisfied customers buy again and tell others about their good experiences. Dissatisfied customers often switch to competitors and disparage the product to others.

Marketers must be careful to set the right level of expectations. If they set expectations too low, they may satisfy those who buy but fail to attract enough buyers. If they set expectations too high, buyers will be disappointed. Customer value and customer satisfaction are key building blocks for developing and managing customer relationships. We will revisit these core concepts later in the chapter.

Exchanges and Relationships

Exchange
The act of obtaining a desired object from someone by offering something in return.

Marketing occurs when people decide to satisfy their needs and wants through exchange relationships. **Exchange** is the act of obtaining a desired object from someone by offering something in return. In the broadest sense, the marketer tries to bring about a response to some market offering. The response may be more than simply buying or trading products and services. A political candidate, for instance, wants votes; a church wants membership; an orchestra wants an audience; and a social action group wants idea acceptance.

Marketing consists of actions taken to create, maintain, and grow desirable exchange *relationships* with target audiences involving a product, service, idea, or other object. Companies want to build strong relationships by consistently delivering superior customer value. We will expand on the important concept of managing customer relationships later in the chapter.

Markets

Market
The set of all actual and potential buyers of a product or service.

The concepts of exchange and relationships lead to the concept of a market. A **market** is the set of actual and potential buyers of a product or service. These buyers share a particular need or want that can be satisfied through exchange relationships.

Marketing means managing markets to bring about profitable customer relationships. However, creating these relationships takes work. Sellers must search for and engage buyers, identify their needs, design good market offerings, set prices for them, promote them, and store and deliver them. Activities such as consumer research, product development, communication, distribution, pricing, and service are core marketing activities.

Although we normally think of marketing as being carried out by sellers, buyers also carry out marketing. Consumers market when they search for products, interact with companies to obtain information, and make their purchases. In fact, today's digital technologies, from online sites and smartphone apps to the explosion of social media, have empowered consumers and made marketing a truly two-way affair. Thus, in addition to customer relationship management, today's marketers must also deal effectively with *customer-managed relationships*. Marketers are no longer asking only "How can we influence our customers?" but also "How can our customers influence us?" and even "How can our customers influence each other?"

▶▶**Figure 1.2** shows the main elements in a marketing system. Marketing involves serving a market of final consumers in the face of competitors. The company and competitors research the market and interact with consumers to understand their needs. Then they create and exchange market offerings, messages, and other marketing content with consumers, either directly or through marketing intermediaries. Each party in the system is affected by major environmental forces (demographic, economic, natural, technological, political, and social/cultural).

Each party in the system adds value for the next level. The arrows represent relationships that must be developed and managed. Thus, a company's success at engaging customers and building profitable relationships depends not only on its own actions but also on how well the entire system serves the needs of final consumers. Walmart cannot fulfill its promise of low prices unless its suppliers provide merchandise at low costs. And Ford cannot deliver a high-quality car-ownership experience unless its dealers provide outstanding sales and service.

Arrows represent relationships that must be developed and managed to create customer value and profitable customer relationships.

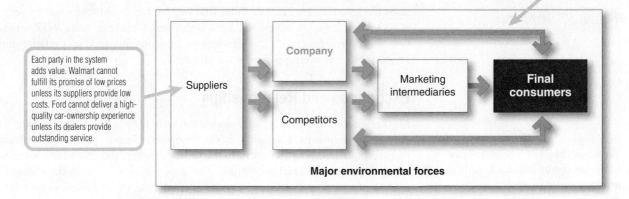

Each party in the system adds value. Walmart cannot fulfill its promise of low prices unless its suppliers provide low costs. Ford cannot deliver a high-quality car-ownership experience unless its dealers provide outstanding service.

Suppliers → Company / Competitors → Marketing intermediaries → **Final consumers**

Major environmental forces

▶▶ **Figure 1.2 A Modern Marketing System**

Author Comment
Once a company fully understands its consumers and the marketplace, it must decide which customers it will serve and how it will bring them value.

Designing a Customer Value-Driven Marketing Strategy

Once it fully understands consumers and the marketplace, marketing management can design a customer value-driven marketing strategy. We define **marketing management** as the art and science of choosing target markets and building profitable relationships with them. The marketing manager's aim is to engage, keep, and grow target customers by creating, delivering, and communicating superior customer value.

To design a winning marketing strategy, the marketing manager must answer two important questions: *What customers will we serve (what's our target market)?* and *How can we serve these customers best (what's our value proposition)?* We will discuss these marketing strategy concepts briefly here and then look at them in more detail in Chapters 2 and 6.

Marketing management
The art and science of choosing target markets and building profitable relationships with them.

Selecting Customers to Serve

The company must first decide *whom* it will serve. It does this by dividing the market into segments of customers (*market segmentation*) and selecting which segments it will go after (*target marketing*). Some people think of marketing management as finding as many customers as possible and increasing demand. But marketing managers know that they cannot serve all customers in every way. By trying to serve all customers, they may not serve any customers well. Instead, the company wants to select only customers that it can serve well and profitably. For example, Nordstrom profitably targets affluent professionals; Dollar General profitably targets families with more modest means.

Ultimately, marketing managers must decide which customers they want to target and on the level, timing, and nature of their demand. Simply put, marketing management is *customer management* and *demand management*.

Choosing a Value Proposition

The company must also decide how it will serve targeted customers—how it will *differentiate and position* itself in the marketplace. A brand's *value proposition* is the set of benefits or values it promises to deliver to consumers to satisfy their needs. JetBlue promises to put "You Above All" by bringing "humanity back to travel." By contrast, Spirit Airlines gives you "Bare Fare" pricing: "Less Money. More Go." >> Facebook helps you "connect and share with the people in your life," whereas Twitter's Vine app gives you "the best way to see and share life in motion" through "short, beautiful, looping videos in a simple and fun way for your friends and family to see."[9]

Such value propositions differentiate one brand from another. They answer the customer's question: "Why should I buy your brand rather than a competitor's?" Companies must design strong value propositions that give them the greatest advantage in their target markets.

>> **Value propositions: Vine gives you "the best way to see and share life in motion" through "short, beautiful, looping videos in a simple and fun way for your friends and family to see."**
Twitter, Inc.

Marketing Management Orientations

Marketing management wants to design strategies that will engage target customers and build profitable relationships with them. But what *philosophy* should guide these marketing strategies? What weight should be given to the interests of customers, the organization, and society? Very often, these interests conflict.

There are five alternative concepts under which organizations design and carry out their marketing strategies: the *production, product, selling, marketing,* and *societal marketing concepts.*

The Production Concept

Production concept
The idea that consumers will favor products that are available and highly affordable; therefore, the organization should focus on improving production and distribution efficiency.

The **production concept** holds that consumers will favor products that are available and highly affordable. Therefore, management should focus on improving production and distribution efficiency. This concept is one of the oldest orientations that guides sellers.

The production concept is still a useful philosophy in some situations. For example, both personal computer maker Lenovo and home appliance maker Haier dominate the highly competitive, price-sensitive Chinese market through low labor costs, high production efficiency, and mass distribution. However, although useful in some situations, the production concept can lead to marketing myopia. Companies adopting this orientation run a major risk of focusing too narrowly on their own operations and losing sight of the real objective—satisfying customer needs and building customer relationships.

The Product Concept

Product concept
The idea that consumers will favor products that offer the most quality, performance, and features; therefore, the organization should devote its energy to making continuous product improvements.

The **product concept** holds that consumers will favor products that offer the most in quality, performance, and innovative features. Under this concept, marketing strategy focuses on making continuous product improvements.

Product quality and improvement are important parts of most marketing strategies. However, focusing *only* on the company's products can also lead to marketing myopia. For example, some manufacturers believe that if they can "build a better mousetrap, the world will beat a path to their doors." But they are often rudely shocked. Buyers may be looking for a better solution to a mouse problem but not necessarily for a better mousetrap. The better solution might be a chemical spray, an exterminating service, a house cat, or something else that suits their needs even better than a mousetrap. Furthermore, a better mousetrap will not sell unless the manufacturer designs, packages, and prices it attractively; places it in convenient distribution channels; brings it to the attention of people who need it; and convinces buyers that it is a better product.

The Selling Concept

Selling concept
The idea that consumers will not buy enough of the firm's products unless the firm undertakes a large-scale selling and promotion effort.

Many companies follow the **selling concept**, which holds that consumers will not buy enough of the firm's products unless it undertakes a large-scale selling and promotion effort. The selling concept is typically practiced with unsought goods—those that buyers do not normally think of buying, such as life insurance or blood donations. These industries must be good at tracking down prospects and selling them on a product's benefits.

Such aggressive selling, however, carries high risks. It focuses on creating sales transactions rather than on building long-term, profitable customer relationships. The aim often is to sell what the company makes rather than to make what the market wants. It assumes that customers who are coaxed into buying the product will like it. Or, if they don't like it, they will possibly forget their disappointment and buy it again later. These are usually poor assumptions.

The Marketing Concept

Marketing concept
A philosophy in which achieving organizational goals depends on knowing the needs and wants of target markets and delivering the desired satisfactions better than competitors do.

The **marketing concept** holds that achieving organizational goals depends on knowing the needs and wants of target markets and delivering the desired satisfactions better than competitors do. Under the marketing concept, customer focus and value are the *paths* to sales and profits. Instead of a product-centered *make-and-sell* philosophy, the marketing concept is a customer-centered *sense-and-respond* philosophy. The job is not to find the right customers for your product but to find the right products for your customers.

>> **Figure 1.3** contrasts the selling concept and the marketing concept. The selling concept takes an *inside-out* perspective. It starts with the factory, focuses on the company's existing products, and calls for heavy selling and promotion to obtain profitable sales. It focuses primarily on customer conquest—getting short-term sales with little concern about who buys or why.

In contrast, the marketing concept takes an *outside-in* perspective. As Herb Kelleher, the colorful founder of Southwest Airlines, once put it, "We don't have a marketing department; we have a customer department." The marketing concept starts with a well-defined

>> Figure 1.3 **Selling and Marketing Concepts Contrasted**

market, focuses on customer needs, and integrates all the marketing activities that affect customers. In turn, it yields profits by creating relationships with the right customers based on customer value and satisfaction.

Implementing the marketing concept often means more than simply responding to customers' stated desires and obvious needs. *Customer-driven* companies research customers deeply to learn about their desires, gather new product ideas, and test product improvements. Such customer-driven marketing usually works well when a clear need exists and when customers know what they want.

In many cases, however, customers *don't* know what they want or even what is possible. As Henry Ford once remarked, "If I'd asked people what they wanted, they would have said faster horses."[10] For example, even 20 years ago, how many consumers would have thought to ask for now-commonplace products such as tablet computers, smartphones, digital cameras, 24-hour online buying, digital video and music streaming, and GPS systems in their cars and phones? Such situations call for *customer-driving* marketing—understanding customer needs even better than customers themselves do and creating products and services that meet both existing and latent needs, now and in the future. As an executive at 3M put it, "Our goal is to lead customers where they want to go before *they* know where they want to go."

The Societal Marketing Concept

Societal marketing concept
The idea that a company's marketing decisions should consider consumers' wants, the company's requirements, consumers' long-run interests, and society's long-run interests.

The **societal marketing concept** questions whether the pure marketing concept overlooks possible conflicts between consumer *short-run wants* and consumer *long-run welfare.* Is a firm that satisfies the immediate needs and wants of target markets always doing what's best for its consumers in the long run? The societal marketing concept holds that marketing strategy should deliver value to customers in a way that maintains or improves both the consumer's *and society's* well-being. It calls for *sustainable marketing,* socially and environmentally responsible marketing that meets the present needs of consumers and businesses while also preserving or enhancing the ability of future generations to meet their needs.

Even more broadly, many leading business and marketing thinkers are now preaching the concept of *shared value,* which recognizes that societal needs, not just economic needs, define markets.[11] The concept of shared value focuses on creating economic value in a way that also creates value for society. A growing number of companies known for their hard-nosed approaches to business—such as GE, Dow, Google, IBM, Intel, Johnson & Johnson, Nestlé, Unilever, and Walmart—are rethinking the interactions between society and corporate performance. They are concerned not just with short-term economic gains but with the well-being of their customers, the depletion of natural resources vital to their businesses, the viability of key suppliers, and the economic well-being of the communities in which they operate.

One prominent marketer calls this *Marketing 3.0.* "Marketing 3.0 organizations are values-driven," he says. "I'm not talking about being value-driven. I'm talking about 'values' plural, where values amount to caring about the state of the world." Another marketer calls it *purpose-driven marketing.* "The future of profit is purpose," he says.[12]

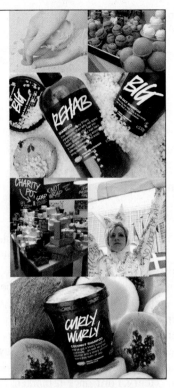

A LUSH LIFE
WE BELIEVE

... in making effective products from fresh organic* fruit and vegetables, the finest essential oils and safe synthetics.

We believe in buying ingredients only from companies that do not conduct or commission tests on animals and in testing our products on humans.

We invent our own products and fragrances, we make them fresh* by hand using little or no preservative or packaging, using only vegetarian ingredients and tell you when they were made.

We believe in happy people making happy soap, putting our faces on our products and making our mums proud.

We believe in long candlelit baths, sharing showers, massage, filling the world with perfume and in the right to make mistakes, lose everything and start again.

We believe our products are good value, that we should make a profit and that the customer is always right.

*We also believe words like 'Fresh' and 'Organic' have an honest meaning beyond marketing.

>> The societal marketing concept: Cosmetics retailer Lush does more than just make and sell premium body care products for profit. It also dedicates itself to doing right by customers, employees, the environment, and society.

Lush Fresh Handmade Cosmetics

As >>**Figure 1.4** shows, companies should balance three considerations in setting their marketing strategies: company profits, consumer wants, *and* society's interests. >>British-based cosmetics retailer Lush operates this way:[13]

Lush is known for "Fresh Handmade Cosmetics"—premium beauty products made by hand from the freshest possible natural ingredients. It sells products with evocative names such as Flying Fox shower gel, Angels on Bareskin cleanser, and Honey I Washed the Kids soap. But Lush does much more than just make and sell body care products for profit. It also dedicates itself to doing right by customers, employees, the environment, and society. Its do-good mission is spelled out in a seven-point statement titled "A Lush Life: We Believe...." For example, the company believes in inventing and making its own products from fresh organic fruits and vegetables using little or no preservatives or packaging. Lush has a strict policy against animal testing and supports fair-trade and community trade efforts. Each year, the company invests heavily in sustainable initiatives and support of grassroots charities. Lush takes care of its employees—"We believe in happy people making happy soap..." In fact, Lush seems to wish well to everyone, everywhere—"We believe in long candlelit baths, sharing showers, massage, filling the world with perfume, and the right to make mistakes, lose everything, and start again." Only in its final belief does Lush mention profits—"We believe our products are good value, that we should make a profit, and that the customer is always right." Thanks to its societal mission, Lush is thriving like fresh flowers in springtime. It now operates stores in 50 countries, with e-commerce sites in 27 countries. Its sales have nearly doubled in just the past three years, suggesting that doing good can benefit both the planet and the company.

Author Comment

The marketing strategy discussed in the previous section outlines which customers the company will serve and how. Now, the company develops marketing plans and programs—a marketing mix—that will deliver the intended customer value.

Preparing an Integrated Marketing Plan and Program

The company's marketing strategy outlines which customers it will serve and how it will create value for these customers. Next, the marketer develops an integrated marketing program that will actually deliver the intended value to target customers. The marketing program builds customer relationships by transforming the marketing strategy into action. It consists of the firm's *marketing mix*, the set of marketing tools the firm uses to implement its marketing strategy.

>> **Figure 1.4 Three Considerations Underlying the Societal Marketing Concept**

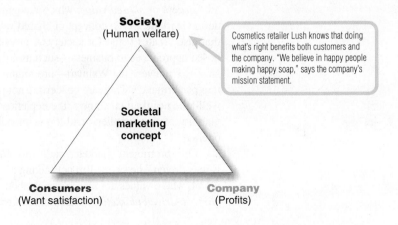

Cosmetics retailer Lush knows that doing what's right benefits both customers and the company. "We believe in happy people making happy soap," says the company's mission statement.

Society
(Human welfare)

Societal marketing concept

Consumers
(Want satisfaction)

Company
(Profits)

The major marketing mix tools are classified into four broad groups, called the *four Ps* of marketing: product, price, place, and promotion. To deliver on its value proposition, the firm must first create a need-satisfying market offering (product). It must then decide how much it will charge for the offering (price) and how it will make the offering available to target consumers (place). Finally, it must engage target consumers, communicate about the offering, and persuade consumers of the offer's merits (promotion). The firm must blend each marketing mix tool into a comprehensive integrated marketing program that communicates and delivers the intended value to chosen customers. We will explore marketing programs and the marketing mix in much more detail in later chapters.

 LINKING THE CONCEPTS

Stop here for a moment and stretch your mind. What have you learned so far about marketing? Set aside the more formal definitions we've examined and try to develop your own understanding of marketing.

- In *your own words*, what *is* marketing? Write down *your* definition. Does your definition include such key concepts as customer value, engagement, and relationships?
- What does marketing *mean* to you? How does it affect your daily life?
- What brand of athletic shoes did you purchase last? Describe your relationship with Nike, adidas, New Balance, Asics, Reebok, Puma, Converse, or whatever brand of shoes you purchased.

> **Author Comment**
> Doing a good job with the first three steps in the marketing process sets the stage for step four, building and managing customer relationships.

Engaging Customers and Managing Customer Relationships

The first three steps in the marketing process—understanding the marketplace and customer needs, designing a customer value-driven marketing strategy, and constructing a marketing program—all lead up to the fourth and most important step: engaging customers and managing profitable customer relationships. We first discuss the basics of customer relationship management. Then we examine how companies go about engaging customers on a deeper level in this age of digital and social marketing.

Customer Relationship Management

Customer relationship management
The overall process of building and maintaining profitable customer relationships by delivering superior customer value and satisfaction.

Customer relationship management is perhaps the most important concept of modern marketing. In the broadest sense, **customer relationship management** is the overall process of building and maintaining profitable customer relationships by delivering superior customer value and satisfaction. It deals with all aspects of acquiring, engaging, and growing customers.

Relationship Building Blocks: Customer Value and Satisfaction
The key to building lasting customer relationships is to create superior customer value and satisfaction. Satisfied customers are more likely to be loyal customers and give the company a larger share of their business.

Customer-perceived value
The customer's evaluation of the difference between all the benefits and all the costs of a market offering relative to those of competing offers.

Customer Value. Attracting and retaining customers can be a difficult task. Customers often face a bewildering array of products and services from which to choose. A customer buys from the firm that offers the highest **customer-perceived value**—the customer's evaluation of the difference between all the benefits and all the costs of a market offering relative to those of competing offers. Importantly, customers often do not judge values and costs "accurately" or "objectively." They act on *perceived* value.

To some consumers, value might mean sensible products at affordable prices. To other consumers, however, value might mean paying more to get more. For example,

>> Perceived value: Is a YETI cooler worth its premium price? To devoted YETI users, the answer is a resounding "yes." The "Wildly Stronger. Keep Ice Longer!" coolers are even certified as grizzly bear proof by the Interagency Grizzly Bear Committee.

Courtesy YETI Coolers and the Interagency Grizzly Bear Committee (IGBC)

what's a cooler worth—one of those insulated containers you take camping or haul to a picnic or tailgate party? If it's a YETI cooler, you can expect to pay from $229 to as much as $1,300 for the top-of-the-line Tundra model. However, despite their high prices and spare, boxy designs, YETI coolers have achieved an almost cult status among the field-and-stream set and on construction sites, ranches, and even military bases. The company's slogan—"YETI Coolers—Wildly Stronger. Keeps Ice Longer!"—suggests the reasons why. Devoted users will tell you that a YETI does keep things cooler—with a FatWall design (with twice the insulation of competitors) and an interlocking lid system with a gasket that keeps the cold in. And rugged YETI coolers are made to last—no more busted hinges, failed latches, or caved-in lids. >> They're even certified as grizzly bear resistant by the Interagency Grizzly Bear Committee. One reporter describes a YETI as "a cooler fit for the apocalypse," and the company claims it's "The cooler you've always wanted. The last cooler you'll ever need." So, is a YETI cooler worth the premium price compared with less expensive coolers made by Igloo or Rubbermaid? To many consumers, the answer is no. But to YETI's target buyers, the answer is a resounding yes.[14]

Customer satisfaction
The extent to which a product's perceived performance matches a buyer's expectations.

Customer Satisfaction. **Customer satisfaction** depends on the product's perceived performance relative to a buyer's expectations. If the product's performance falls short of expectations, the customer is dissatisfied. If performance matches expectations, the customer is satisfied. If performance exceeds expectations, the customer is highly satisfied or delighted.

Outstanding marketing companies go out of their way to keep important customers satisfied. Most studies show that higher levels of customer satisfaction lead to greater customer loyalty, which in turn results in better company performance. Companies aim to delight customers by promising only what they can deliver and then delivering more than they promise. Delighted customers not only make repeat purchases but also become willing marketing partners and "customer evangelists" who spread the word about their good experiences to others.

For companies interested in delighting customers, exceptional value and service become part of the overall company culture. For example, year after year, Ritz-Carlton ranks at or near the top of the hospitality industry in terms of customer satisfaction. >> Its passion for satisfying customers is summed up in the company's credo, which promises that its luxury hotels will deliver a truly memorable experience—one that "enlivens the senses, instills well-being, and fulfills even the unexpressed wishes and needs of our guests."[15]

>> Creating customer satisfaction: Ritz-Carlton hotels deliver a truly memorable experience, one that "enlivens the senses, instills well-being, and fulfills even the unexpressed wishes and needs of our guests."

Toronto Star via Getty Images

Check into any Ritz-Carlton hotel around the world, and you'll be amazed by the company's fervent dedication to anticipating even your slightest need. Without ever asking, they seem to know that you're allergic to peanuts and want a king-size bed, a hypoallergenic pillow, extra body gel, the blinds open when you arrive, and breakfast with decaffeinated coffee in your room. Each day, hotel staffers—from those at the front desk to those in maintenance and housekeeping—discreetly observe and record even the smallest guest preferences. Then, every morning, each hotel reviews the files of all new arrivals who have previously stayed at a Ritz-Carlton and prepares a list of suggested extra touches that might delight each guest. For example, according to one Ritz-Carlton manager, if the chain gets hold of a picture of a guest's pet, it will make a copy, have it framed, and display it in the guest's room in whatever Ritz-Carlton the guest visits.

Once they identify a special customer need, Ritz-Carlton employees go to legendary extremes to meet it. For instance, to serve the needs of a guest whose son had food allergies, a Ritz-Carlton chef in Bali located special eggs and milk in a small grocery store in another country and had them delivered to the hotel. In another case, when a businessman attending a conference at the Ritz-Carlton Orlando ordered his favorite soda during a dinner in a hotel ballroom, his banquet server told him that the hotel didn't serve that beverage but he would see what he could do. To no one's surprise, the server quickly returned with the requested beverage, and for the rest of the week he had the drink waiting for the guest. But here's the best part. A year later when the guest returned for the conference, as he sat in the ballroom waiting for dinner the first night, the same server walked up with his favorite drink in hand. As a result of such customer service heroics, an amazing 95 percent of departing guests report that their stay has been a truly memorable experience. More than 90 percent of Ritz-Carlton's delighted customers return.

Other companies that have become legendary for customer delight and their service heroics include Zappos.com, Amazon.com, Chick-Fil-A, Nordstrom department stores, and JetBlue Airways (see Marketing at Work 1.1). However, a company doesn't need to

---

MARKETING AT WORK   1.1

JetBlue: Delighting Customers and Bringing Humanity Back to Air Travel

There's an old adage in the airline industry: "You're not flying planes, you're flying people." These days, however, it seems that many big airlines overlook the people factor. Instead, they focus on moving their human cargo as efficiently as possible while charging as much as the traffic will bear. The American Customer Satisfaction Index rates the airline industry near the bottom among 47 industries in customer satisfaction, barely ahead of perennial cellar-dwellers subscription TV and Internet service providers.

Not so at JetBlue Airways. From the very beginning, young JetBlue (little more than 15 years old) has built a reputation for creating first-rate, customer-satisfying experiences. Its slogan—"YOU ABOVE ALL"—tells the JetBlue faithful that they are at the very heart of the company's strategy and culture. JetBlue is on a heartfelt mission to bring humanity back to air travel.

At JetBlue, customer care starts with basic amenities that exceed customer expectations, especially for a low-cost carrier. JetBlue's well-padded, leather-covered coach seats allow three inches more legroom than the average airline seat. Although the airline doesn't serve meals, it offers the best selection of free beverages and snacks to be found at 30,000 feet (including unexpected treats such as Terra Blues chips, Linden's chocolate chip cookies, and Dunkin' Donuts coffee). Every JetBlue seat has its own LCD entertainment system, complete with free 36-channel DirecTV and 100-plus channels of SiriusXM Radio. JetBlue rounds out the amenities with a recently launched industry first—Fly-Fi, an in-flight high-speed Internet service with free basic browsing on all equipped planes.

JetBlue continuously innovates to find new ways to delight customers. Its "Even More Space" seats give customers the option of going from "roomy to roomier," allow early boarding, and give early access to overhead bins. Its "Even More Speed" service provides VIP passage through airport security

screening. And JetBlue's Mint service puts a new spin on first-class air travel, offering front-of-the-plane, lie-flat "sweet seats," some of them in enclosed suites with their own doors. According to JetBlue, Mint services deliver "unexpected,

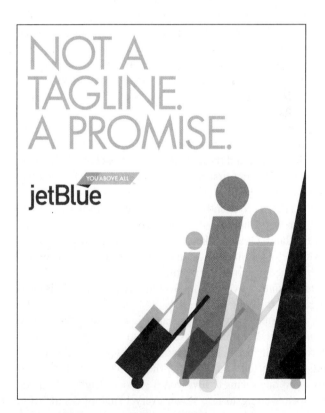

>> Creating customer satisfaction: JetBlue creates first-rate, customer-satisfying experiences. Its slogan—"JetBlue: YOU ABOVE ALL"—tells customers that they are at the very heart of JetBlue's strategy and culture.
JetBlue

individualized 'mo-mints' that revive and engage, keeping you in mint condition during your travels."

Such tangibles help keep JetBlue travelers satisfied. But former JetBlue CEO David Barger knows that the tangibles are only a small part of what really makes JetBlue special. "The hard product—airplanes, leather seats, satellite TVs—as long as you have a checkbook,…can be replicated," says Barger. "It's the JetBlue *culture* that can't be replicated. The *human* side of the equation is the most important part of what we're doing." It's that JetBlue culture—the near-obsessive focus on the customer flying experience—that creates not just satisfied JetBlue customers but *delighted* ones.

At JetBlue, developing a customer-centered corporate culture starts with hiring quality people whose personal values match JetBlue's values—from work-at-home part-time call center reservationists to baggage handlers to flight attendants and even pilots. By the time JetBlue employees are on board and trained, they not only *know* the company's core values—safety, integrity, caring, passion, and fun—they *live* them. It's those heartfelt values that result in outstanding customer experiences. And the outstanding customer experiences make JetBlue's customers the most satisfied and loyal in the industry.

Whereas passengers on most competing airlines regard flying as an experience just to be tolerated, many JetBlue customers actually look forward to flying. And customers themselves spread the good word about JetBlue with evangelistic zeal. Recently crowned a "social media all-star" by *Fortune* magazine, JetBlue has been a leader in using a full range of social media to engage customers and get them talking with each other about the brand. And whereas other airlines are just now discovering the power of customer dialogue, throughout its history, in ads and promotions, JetBlue has often let its customers do the talking.

For example, its "Experience JetBlue" Web site features authentic testimonials from some of the airline's most devoted fans, who were found through Twitter and Facebook. The customers give glowing first-person accounts about why they like flying JetBlue. "It's like an open bar for snacks," says one customer. "They're constantly walking around offering it, so I'm never thirsty or hungry." Another JetBlue fan, a 6'3" woman from Portland, Oregon, likes the seating: "I can stretch and sit crosslegged—no black-and-blue knees," she says. "The customer service is above and beyond," declares a third customer, a small business owner from Boston. "[Coach on] JetBlue is very similar to flying first class."

In a former advertising campaign called "Sincerely, JetBlue," actual customers gave voice to even deeper JetBlue experiences. In one ad, for example, customer Melissa confided, "Let me tell you, I wanted not to like you, if only because everyone seems to love you. I got on a flight with a pen and paper, waiting to take down every irritating detail." But, she continued, "two flights later, I was staring at the same blank piece of paper. You've done nothing wrong and everything more than right, if that's possible." After detailing all the right things the airline does, she mock-lamented, "JetBlue,

I wanted not to like you but it can't be done—at all. Sincerely, Melissa, Portland, Oregon."

In other Sincerely, JetBlue ads, customers recounted specific service heroics by dedicated JetBlue employees. For example, customer Ann recounted how, when her JetBlue flight was delayed by a snowstorm, the airline eased the long wait by providing pizza and even a live band. "My [three-year-old] son was dancing. I was dancing," she remembers. "It made a horrible experience really nice." And the Steins from Darien, Connecticut, told how they arrived late at night for a family vacation in Florida with their three very tired small children only to learn that their hotel wouldn't take them in. "Out of nowhere we heard a voice from behind us, go ahead, take my room," the Steins recalled. "A superhero in a JetBlue pilot's uniform, who sacrificed his room graciously, saved our night. And we slept like babies. Thank you, JetBlue."

Delighting customers has been good for JetBlue. Last year, the airline reported record revenues of $5.8 billion, up 75 percent in just the past five years, with profits soaring more than sixfold. Even during recent hard economic times, as many competing airlines were cutting routes, retiring aircraft, laying off employees, and losing money, JetBlue was adding planes, expanding into new cities, hiring thousands of new employees, and turning profits.

Perhaps even more important to future success, customers continue to adore their JetBlue. For nine straight years, the customer-centered company has topped the J. D. Power and Associates customer satisfaction rankings among major U.S. airlines. For the past five years, JetBlue has flip-flopped with fellow customer-service champ Southwest Airlines for the airline industry's highest customer loyalty scores in the respected Satmetrix Net Promoter rankings. Every year, more than 60 percent of customers have rated JetBlue 9 or 10 on a 0-to-10-point scale indicating the likelihood that they would recommend JetBlue to others.

So, JetBlue really means it when it tells customers YOU ABOVE ALL. "Above all else," says JetBlue's Customer Bill of Rights, "JetBlue Airways is dedicated to bringing humanity back to air travel. We strive to make every part of your experience as simple and as pleasant as possible." Adds JetBlue's senior VP of marketing: "[YOU ABOVE ALL] gets us back to our DNA, to our original mission."

Sources: "Industry Sector Reports: Airlines," Satmetrix, www.satmetrix .com/expertise/benchmarks-by-industry/travel-and-hospitality/, accessed June 2015; Iris Mansour, "Best in Customer Service," *Fortune*, August 29, 2013, http://money.cnn.com/gallery/technology/2013/08/29/social-media-all-stars .fortune/2.html; March Gunther, "Nothing Blue about JetBlue," *Fortune*, September 3, 2009, http://archive.fortune.com/2009/09/03/news/companies/ jetblue_airways_airline.fortune/index.htm; Kevin Randall, "Red, Hot, and Blue: The Hottest American Brand Is Not Apple," *Fast Company*, June 3, 2010, www.fastcompany.com/1656066/red-hot-and-blue-hottest-american-brand-not-apple; Rupal Parekh, "The Newest Marketing Buzzword? Human," *Advertising Age*, September 20, 2013, http://adage.com/print/244261/; "The American Customer Satisfaction Index: Benchmarks by Industry," www.theacsi.org/customer-satisfaction-benchmarks/benchmarks-by-industry, accessed September 2015; and http://experience.jetblue.com/, investor.jetblue .com; and www.jetblue.com/about/, accessed September 2015.

have over-the-top service to create customer delight. For example, no-frills grocery chain ALDI has highly satisfied customers, even though they have to bag their own groceries and can't use credit cards. ALDI's everyday very low pricing on good-quality products delights customers and keeps them coming back. Thus, customer satisfaction comes not just from service heroics but from how well a company delivers on its basic value proposition and helps customers solve their buying problems. "Most customers don't want to be 'wowed,'" says one marketing consultant. "They [just] want an effortless experience."[16]

Although a customer-centered firm seeks to deliver high customer satisfaction relative to competitors, it does not attempt to *maximize* customer satisfaction. A company can always increase customer satisfaction by lowering its prices or increasing its services. But this may result in lower profits. Thus, the purpose of marketing is to generate customer value profitably. This requires a very delicate balance: The marketer must continue to generate more customer value and satisfaction but not "give away the house."

Customer Relationship Levels and Tools

Companies can build customer relationships at many levels, depending on the nature of the target market. At one extreme, a company with many low-margin customers may seek to develop *basic relationships* with them. For example, Procter & Gamble's Tide detergent does not phone or call on all of its consumers to get to know them personally. Instead, Tide creates engagement and relationships through brand-building advertising, Web sites, and social media presence. At the other extreme, in markets with few customers and high margins, sellers want to create *full partnerships* with key customers. For example, P&G sales representatives work closely with Walmart, Kroger, and other large retailers that sell Tide. In between these two extremes, other levels of customer relationships are appropriate.

Beyond offering consistently high value and satisfaction, marketers can use specific marketing tools to develop stronger bonds with customers. For example, many companies offer *frequency marketing programs* that reward customers who buy frequently or in large amounts. Airlines offer frequent-flier programs, hotels give room upgrades to frequent guests, and supermarkets give patronage discounts to "very important customers." These days almost every brand has a loyalty rewards program. However, some innovative loyalty programs go a step beyond the usual. ≫Consider Walgreens:[17]

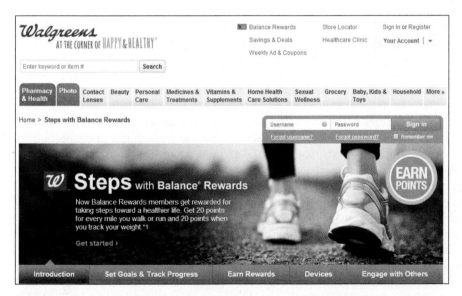

≫≫ **Relationship marketing tools: The innovative Walgreens Balance Rewards program builds stronger customer relationships and helps the brand by helping customers, befitting the chain's slogan: "Walgreens: At the corner of happy & healthy."**

Used with permission of Walgreen Co. Walgreens Balance® Rewards and "At the corner of healthy and happy®" are registered trademarks of Walgreen Co.

Members of Walgreens' Balance Rewards program earn points for in-store or online product purchases, redeemable for purchases in Walgreens stores or online. And members receive surprise offers and giveaways, everything from free movie passes to gift cards. But in line with the chain's mission "to keep our community happy and healthy," the unique Walgreens Balance Rewards program goes beyond just points for purchases. It also includes programs that reward customers for taking steps toward a happy, healthy, well-balanced life. The program has included giving members points for every mile they walk or run, every daily weigh-in as they track their weight, and every prescription and immunization. Walgreens even provides online and mobile tools that help members set healthy goals and track their progress, celebrating their achievements with milestone badges. Thus, the Walgreens Balance Rewards program builds stronger customer relationships and helps the brand by helping customers, befitting the chain's slogan: "Walgreens: At the corner of happy & healthy."

Other companies sponsor *club marketing programs* that offer members special benefits and create member communities. For example, Apple encourages customers to form local Apple user groups. More than 800 registered Apple user groups worldwide offer monthly meetings, a newsletter, advice on technical issues, training classes, product discounts, and a forum for swapping ideas and stories with like-minded Apple fans. Similarly, buy a Weber grill and you can join the Weber Nation—"the site for real people who love their Weber grills." Membership gets you exclusive access to online grilling classes, an interactive recipe box, grilling tips and 24/7 telephone support, audio and video podcasts, straight-talk forums for interacting with other grilling fanatics, and even a chance to star in a Weber TV commercial. "Become a spatula-carrying member today," says Weber.[18]

Engaging Customers

Significant changes are occurring in the nature of customer–brand relationships. Today's digital technologies—the Internet and the surge in online, mobile, and social media—have profoundly changed the ways that people on the planet relate to one another. In turn, these events have had a huge impact on how companies and brands connect with customers, and how customers connect with and influence each other's brand behaviors.

Customer Engagement and Today's Digital and Social Media

The digital age has spawned a dazzling set of new customer relationship-building tools, from Web sites, online ads and videos, mobile ads and apps, and blogs to online communities and the major social media, such as Twitter, Facebook, YouTube, Instagram, and Pinterest.

Customer-engagement marketing
Making the brand a meaningful part of consumers' conversations and lives by fostering direct and continuous customer involvement in shaping brand conversations, experiences, and community.

Yesterday's companies focused mostly on mass marketing to broad segments of customers at arm's length. By contrast, today's companies are using online, mobile, and social media to refine their targeting and to engage customers more deeply and interactively. The *old marketing* involved marketing brands *to* consumers. The *new marketing* is **customer-engagement marketing**—fostering direct and continuous customer involvement in shaping brand conversations, brand experiences, and brand community. Customer-engagement marketing goes beyond just selling a brand to consumers. Its goal is to make the brand a meaningful part of consumers' conversations and lives.

The burgeoning Internet and social media have given a huge boost to customer-engagement marketing. Today's consumers are better informed, more connected, and more empowered than ever before. Newly empowered consumers have more information about brands, and they have a wealth of digital platforms for airing and sharing their brand views with others. Thus, marketers are now embracing not only customer relationship management but also *customer-managed relationships,* in which customers connect with companies and with each other to help forge their own brand experiences.

Greater consumer empowerment means that companies can no longer rely on marketing by *intrusion*. Instead, they must practice marketing by *attraction*—creating market offerings and messages that engage consumers rather than interrupt them. Hence, most marketers now combine their mass-media marketing efforts with a rich mix of online, mobile, and social media marketing that promotes brand–consumer engagement and conversation.

For example, companies post their latest ads and videos on social media sites, hoping they'll go viral. They maintain an extensive presence on Twitter, YouTube, Facebook, Google+, Pinterest, Instagram, Vine, and other social media to create brand buzz. They launch their own blogs, mobile apps, online microsites, and consumer-generated review systems, all with the aim of engaging customers on a more personal, interactive level.

Take Twitter, for example. Organizations ranging from Dell, JetBlue, and Dunkin' Donuts to the Chicago Bulls, NASCAR, and the Los Angeles Fire Department have created Twitter pages and promotions. They use "Tweets" to start conversations with and between Twitter's more than 288 million active users, address customer service issues, research customer reactions, and drive traffic to relevant articles, Web and mobile marketing sites, contests, videos, and other brand activities.

Similarly, almost every company has something going on Facebook these days. Starbucks has more than 38 million Facebook "fans"; Coca-Cola has more than 94 million.

And every major marketer has a YouTube channel where the brand and its fans post current ads and other entertaining or informative videos. Instagram, LinkedIn, Pinterest, Snapchat, Vine—all have exploded onto the marketing scene, giving brands more ways to engage and interact with customers. Skilled use of social media can get consumers involved with and talking about a brand.

The key to engagement marketing is to find ways to enter consumers' conversations with engaging and relevant brand messages. Simply posting a humorous video, creating a social media page, or hosting a blog isn't enough. Successful engagement marketing means making relevant and genuine contributions to consumers' lives and interactions. ≫ Consider T-shirt and apparel maker Life is good:[19]

≫ **Engaging customers: Life is good starts with a deeply felt, engagement-worthy sense of purpose: spreading the power of optimism. Then it creates online and social media tools that let people engage and help co-author the brand's story.**

© WWPhotography/Alamy Stock Photo

For starters, Life is good has an authentic, engagement-worthy sense of purpose: spreading the power of optimism. The brand is about helping people to open up, create relationships, and connect with other people. The company's infectious philosophy is best represented by the "Life is good" slogan itself and by Jake—the familiar beret-wearing, happy-go-lucky stick figure who quickly became a pop-culture icon. Life is good backs its optimism philosophy with good deeds, donating 10 percent of its net profits each year to help kids in need.

Online and social media have become a perfect fit for sharing the Life is good message. Today, the brand fosters a thriving community of Optimists, with more than 2.5 million Facebook fans, 290,000 Twitter followers, 15,300 followers on Instagram, and an active YouTube channel. But the strongest engagement platform is the brand's own Web site, Lifeisgood.com, one of the most active customer-engagement sites found anywhere online. The site's "Live It" section gives brand fans a breath of "fresh share." It's a place where they share photos, videos, and stories showing the brand's role in their trials, triumphs, and optimism. To Life is good, true engagement is about deep meaningful relationships that go beyond the products it is selling. Says Life is good CEO Bert Jacobs: "You can't build a brand on your own; we have entered a world where customers co-author your story."

Consumer-Generated Marketing

Consumer-generated marketing
Brand exchanges created by consumers themselves—both invited and uninvited—by which consumers are playing an increasing role in shaping their own brand experiences and those of other consumers.

A growing form of customer-engagement marketing is **consumer-generated marketing**, by which consumers themselves are playing a bigger role in shaping their own brand experiences and those of others. This might happen through uninvited consumer-to-consumer exchanges in blogs, video-sharing sites, social media, and other digital forums. But increasingly, companies themselves are inviting consumers to play a more active role in shaping products and brand content.

Some companies ask consumers for new product and service ideas. For example, at its My Starbucks Idea site, Starbucks collects ideas from customers on new products, store changes, and just about anything else that might make their Starbucks experience better. "You know better than anyone else what you want from Starbucks," says the company at the Web site. "So tell us. What's your Starbucks idea? Revolutionary or simple—we want to hear it." The site invites customers to share their ideas, vote on and discuss the ideas of others, and see which ideas Starbucks has implemented.[20]

Other companies invite customers to play an active role in shaping ads. For example, for the past nine years, PepsiCo's Doritos brand has held a "Crash the Super Bowl" contest in which it invites 30-second ads from consumers and runs the best ones during the game. The consumer-generated ads have been a huge success. Last year, Doritos opened up the contest to people in all 46 countries where Doritos are sold. From more than 4,900 entries, Doritos aired two fan-produced ads during the Super Bowl. Past campaigns have produced numerous top-place finishers in *USA Today's* AdMeter rankings, earning their creators $1 million in cash prizes from PepsiCo's Frito-Lay division. In the recent campaign, the prizes were instead awarded based on fan votes at Doritos.

com. The winner, "Middle Seat"—a clever ad about a man who uses a bag of Doritos to entice a pretty woman to sit next to him on a plane flight only to find that she has a fussy baby in tow—earned its amateur creators the $1 million plus a "dream job" working at Universal Studios. The homemade commercial cost $2,000 to make and took just four hours to shoot.[21]

Despite the successes, however, harnessing consumer-generated content can be a time-consuming and costly process, and companies may find it difficult to glean even a little gold from all the garbage. Moreover, because consumers have so much control over social media content, inviting their input can sometimes backfire. For example, McDonald's famously launched a Twitter campaign using the hashtag #McDStories, hoping that it would inspire heartwarming stories about Happy Meals. Instead, the effort was hijacked by Twitter users, who turned the hashtag into a "bashtag" by posting less-than-appetizing messages about their bad experiences with the fast-food chain. McDonald's pulled the campaign within only two hours, but the hashtag was still churning weeks, even months later.[22]

As consumers become more connected and empowered, and as the boom in digital and social media technologies continues, consumer brand engagement—whether invited by marketers or not—will be an increasingly important marketing force. Through a profusion of consumer-generated videos, shared reviews, blogs, mobile apps, and Web sites, consumers are playing a growing role in shaping their own and other consumers' brand experiences. Engaged consumers are now having a say in everything from product design, usage, and packaging to brand messaging, pricing, and distribution. Brands must embrace this new consumer empowerment and master the new digital and social media relationship tools or risk being left behind.

Partner Relationship Management

When it comes to creating customer value and building strong customer relationships, today's marketers know that they can't go it alone. They must work closely with a variety of marketing partners. In addition to being good at *customer relationship management,* marketers must also be good at **partner relationship management**—working closely with others inside and outside the company to jointly engage and bring more value to customers.

Traditionally, marketers have been charged with understanding customers and representing customer needs to different company departments. However, in today's more connected world, every functional area in the organization can interact with customers. The new thinking is that—no matter what your job is in a company—you must understand marketing and be customer focused. Rather than letting each department go its own way, firms must link all departments in the cause of creating customer value.

Marketers must also partner with suppliers, channel partners, and others outside the company. Marketing channels consist of distributors, retailers, and others who connect the company to its buyers. The *supply chain* describes a longer channel, stretching from raw materials to components to final products that are carried to final buyers. Through *supply chain management,* companies today are strengthening their connections with partners all along the supply chain. They know that their fortunes rest on more than just how well they perform. Success at delivering customer value rests on how well their entire supply chain performs against competitors' supply chains.

Partner relationship management
Working closely with partners in other company departments and outside the company to jointly bring greater value to customers.

Author Comment
Look back at Figure 1.1. In the first four steps of the marketing process, the company creates value *for* target customers and builds strong relationships with them. If it does that well, it can capture value *from* customers in return, in the form of loyal customers who buy and continue to buy the company's brands.

Capturing Value from Customers

The first four steps in the marketing process outlined in Figure 1.1 involve engaging customers and building customer relationships by creating and delivering superior customer value. The final step involves capturing value in return in the form of sales, market share, and profits. By creating superior customer value, the firm creates highly satisfied customers who stay loyal and buy more. This, in turn, means greater long-run returns for the firm. Here, we discuss the outcomes of creating customer value: customer loyalty and retention, share of market and share of customer, and customer equity.

Creating Customer Loyalty and Retention

Good customer relationship management creates customer satisfaction. In turn, satisfied customers remain loyal and talk favorably to others about the company and its products. Studies show big differences in the loyalty of customers who are less satisfied, somewhat satisfied, and completely satisfied. Even a slight drop from complete satisfaction can create an enormous drop in loyalty. Thus, the aim of customer relationship management is to create not only customer satisfaction but also customer delight.

Customer lifetime value
The value of the entire stream of purchases a customer makes over a lifetime of patronage.

Keeping customers loyal makes good economic sense. Loyal customers spend more and stay around longer. Research also shows that it's five times cheaper to keep an old customer than acquire a new one. Conversely, customer defections can be costly. Losing a customer means losing more than a single sale. It means losing the entire stream of purchases that the customer would make over a lifetime of patronage. For example, here is a classic illustration of **customer lifetime value**:[23]

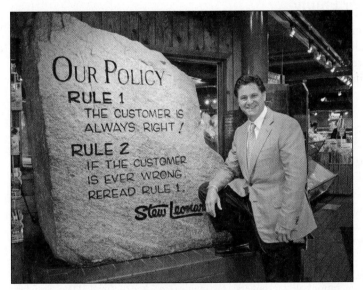

Stew Leonard, who operates a highly profitable four-store supermarket in Connecticut and New York, once said that he sees $50,000 flying out of his store every time he sees a sulking customer. Why? Because his average customer spends about $100 a week, shops 50 weeks a year, and remains in the area for about 10 years. If this customer has an unhappy experience and switches to another supermarket, Stew Leonard's has lost $50,000 in lifetime revenue. The loss can be much greater if the disappointed customer shares the bad experience with other customers and causes them to defect.

To keep customers coming back, Stew Leonard's has created what has been called the "Disneyland of Dairy Stores," complete with costumed characters, scheduled entertainment, a petting zoo, and animatronics throughout the store. From its humble beginnings as a small dairy store in 1969, Stew Leonard's has grown at an amazing pace. It's built 30 additions onto the original store, which now serves more than 300,000 customers each week. ≫ This legion of loyal shoppers is largely a result of the store's passionate approach to customer service. "Rule #1: The customer is always right. Rule #2: If the customer is ever wrong, reread rule #1."

≫ Customer lifetime value: To keep customers coming back, Stew Leonard's has created the "Disneyland of dairy stores." Rule #1—The customer is always right. Rule #2—If the customer is ever wrong, reread Rule #1.

Courtesy of Stew Leonard's

Stew Leonard is not alone in assessing customer lifetime value. Lexus, for example, estimates that a single satisfied and loyal customer is worth more than $600,000 in lifetime sales, and the estimated lifetime value of a Starbucks customer is more than $14,000.[24] In fact, a company can lose money on a specific transaction but still benefit greatly from a long-term relationship. This means that companies must aim high in building customer relationships. Customer delight creates an emotional relationship with a brand, not just a rational preference. And that relationship keeps customers coming back.

Growing Share of Customer

Share of customer
The portion of the customer's purchasing that a company gets in its product categories.

Beyond simply retaining good customers to capture customer lifetime value, good customer relationship management can help marketers increase their **share of customer**—the share they get of the customer's purchasing in their product categories. Thus, banks want to increase "share of wallet." Supermarkets and restaurants want to get more "share of stomach." Car companies want to increase "share of garage," and airlines want greater "share of travel."

To increase share of customer, firms can offer greater variety to current customers. Or they can create programs to cross-sell and up-sell to market more products and services to existing customers. For example, Amazon is highly skilled at leveraging relationships with its 244 million customers to increase its share of each customer's spending budget:[25]

Once they log onto Amazon.com, customers often buy more than they intend, and Amazon does all it can to help make that happen. The online giant continues to broaden its merchandise assortment, creating an ideal spot for one-stop shopping. And based on each customer's purchase and search history, the company recommends related products that might be of interest. This recommendation system influences perhaps a third of all sales. Amazon's ingenious Amazon Prime two-day shipping program has also helped boost its share of customers' wallets. For an annual fee of $99, Prime members receive delivery of all their purchases within two days, whether it's a single paperback book or a 60-inch HDTV. According to one analyst, the ingenious Amazon Prime program "converts casual shoppers, who gorge on the gratification of having purchases reliably appear two days after the order, into Amazon addicts." As a result, Amazon's 40 million Prime customers now account for more than half of its U.S. sales. On average, a Prime customer spends 2.4 times more a non-Prime customer.

Building Customer Equity

We can now see the importance of not only acquiring customers but also keeping and growing them. The value of a company comes from the value of its current and future customers. Customer relationship management takes a long-term view. Companies want to not only create profitable customers but also "own" them for life, earn a greater share of their purchases, and capture their customer lifetime value.

What Is Customer Equity?

Customer equity

The total combined customer lifetime values of all of the company's current and potential customers.

The ultimate aim of customer relationship management is to produce high *customer equity*.[26] **Customer equity** is the total combined customer lifetime values of all of the company's current and potential customers. As such, it's a measure of the future value of the company's customer base. Clearly, the more loyal the firm's profitable customers, the higher its customer equity. Customer equity may be a better measure of a firm's performance than current sales or market share. Whereas sales and market share reflect the past, customer equity suggests the future. ≫ Consider Cadillac:[27]

In the 1970s and 1980s, Cadillac had some of the most loyal customers in the industry. To an entire generation of car buyers, the name *Cadillac* defined "The Standard of the World." Cadillac's share of the luxury car market reached a whopping 51 percent in 1976, and based on market share and sales, the brand's future looked rosy. However, measures of customer equity would have painted a bleaker picture. Cadillac customers were getting older (average age 60), and average customer lifetime value was falling. Many Cadillac buyers were on their last cars. Thus, although Cadillac's market share was good, its customer equity was not.

Compare this with BMW. Its more youthful and vigorous image didn't win BMW the early market share war. However, it did win BMW younger customers (average age about 40) with higher customer lifetime values. The result: In the years that followed, BMW's market share and profits soared while Cadillac's fortunes eroded badly. BMW overtook Cadillac in the 1980s. In recent years, Cadillac has struggled to make the Caddy cool again with edgier, high-performance designs that target a younger generation of consumers. More recently, the brand has billed itself as "The New Standard of the World" with marketing pitches based on "power, performance, and design," attributes that position it more effectively against the likes of BMW and Audi. Recent ads invite consumers to "Dare Greatly" and "Drive the world forward." However, for the past decade, Cadillac's share of the luxury car market has stagnated. The moral: Marketers should care not just about current sales and market share. Customer lifetime value and customer equity are the name of the game.

≫ Managing customer equity: To increase customer equity, Cadillac is making the classic car cool again among younger buyers, encouraging consumers to "Dare Greatly."

General Motors

Building the Right Relationships with the Right Customers

Companies should manage customer equity carefully. They should view customers as assets that need to be managed and maximized. But not all customers, not even all loyal customers, are good investments. Surprisingly, some loyal customers can be unprofitable, and some disloyal customers can be profitable. Which customers should the company acquire and retain?

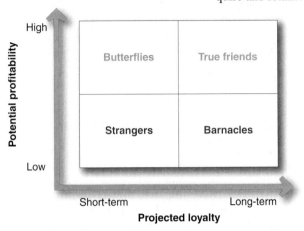

Figure 1.5 Customer Relationship Groups

The company can classify customers according to their potential profitability and manage its relationships with them accordingly. ▶▶ **Figure 1.5** classifies customers into one of four relationship groups, according to their profitability and projected loyalty.[28] Each group requires a different relationship management strategy. *Strangers* show low potential profitability and little projected loyalty. There is little fit between the company's offerings and their needs. The relationship management strategy for these customers is simple: Don't invest anything in them; make money on every transaction.

Butterflies are potentially profitable but not loyal. There is a good fit between the company's offerings and their needs. However, like real butterflies, we can enjoy them for only a short while and then they're gone. An example is stock market investors who trade shares often and in large amounts but who enjoy hunting out the best deals without building a regular relationship with any single brokerage company. Efforts to convert butterflies into loyal customers are rarely successful. Instead, the company should enjoy the butterflies for the moment. It should create satisfying and profitable transactions with them, capturing as much of their business as possible in the short time during which they buy from the company. Then it should move on and cease investing in them until the next time around.

True friends are both profitable and loyal. There is a strong fit between their needs and the company's offerings. The firm wants to make continuous relationship investments to delight these customers and nurture, retain, and grow them. It wants to turn true friends into *true believers*, who come back regularly and tell others about their good experiences with the company.

Barnacles are highly loyal but not very profitable. There is a limited fit between their needs and the company's offerings. An example is smaller bank customers who bank regularly but do not generate enough returns to cover the costs of maintaining their accounts. Like barnacles on the hull of a ship, they create drag. Barnacles are perhaps the most problematic customers. The company might be able to improve their profitability by selling them more, raising their fees, or reducing service to them. However, if they cannot be made profitable, they should be "fired."

The point here is an important one: Different types of customers require different engagement and relationship management strategies. The goal is to build the *right relationships* with the *right customers*.

 LINKING THE CONCEPTS

We've covered a lot of ground. Again, pause for a moment and develop *your own* thoughts about marketing.

- In *your own words*, what *is* marketing and what does it seek to accomplish?
- How well does JetBlue manage its relationships with customers? What customer relationship management strategy does it use? What relationship management strategy does Walmart use?
- Think of a company for which you are a "true friend." What strategy does this company use to manage its relationship with you?

Author Comment

Marketing doesn't take place in a vacuum. Now that we've discussed the five steps in the marketing process, let's look at how the ever-changing marketplace affects both consumers and the marketers who serve them. We'll look more deeply into these and other marketing environment factors in Chapter 3.

The Changing Marketing Landscape

Every day, dramatic changes are occurring in the marketplace. Richard Love of HP observed, "The pace of change is so rapid that the ability to change has now become a competitive advantage." Yogi Berra, the legendary New York Yankees catcher and manager, summed it up more simply when he said, "The future ain't what it used to be." As the marketplace changes, so must those who serve it.

In this section, we examine the major trends and forces that are changing the marketing landscape and challenging marketing strategy. We look at five major developments: the digital age, the changing economic environment, the growth of not-for-profit marketing, rapid globalization, and the call for sustainable marketing practices.

The Digital Age: Online, Mobile, and Social Media Marketing

The explosive growth in digital technology has fundamentally changed the way we live—how we communicate, share information, access entertainment, and shop. More than 3 billion people—42 percent of the world's population—are now online; 58 percent of all American adults own smartphones. These numbers will only grow as digital technology rockets into the future.[29]

Most consumers are totally smitten with all things digital. For example, according to one study, 44 percent of Americans keep their mobile phone next to them when they sleep—they say it's the first thing they touch when they get up in the morning and the last thing they touch at night. In just the past few years, people in the United States averaged more time per day with digital media (5.25 hours) than viewing traditional TV (4.5 hours).[30]

Digital and social media marketing
Using digital marketing tools such as Web sites, social media, mobile apps and ads, online video, email, and blogs to engage consumers anywhere, at any time, via their digital devices.

The consumer love affair with digital and mobile technology makes it fertile ground for marketers trying to engage customers. So it's no surprise that the Internet and rapid advances in digital and social media have taken the marketing world by storm. **Digital and social media marketing** involves using digital marketing tools such as Web sites, social media, mobile ads and apps, online video, email, blogs, and other digital platforms to engage consumers anywhere, anytime via their computers, smartphones, tablets, Internet-ready TVs, and other digital devices. These days, it seems that every company is reaching out to customers with multiple Web sites, newsy Tweets and Facebook pages, viral ads and videos posted on YouTube, rich-media emails, and mobile apps that solve consumer problems and help them shop.

At the most basic level, marketers set up company and brand Web sites that provide information and promote the company's products. Many companies also set up branded community sites, where customers can congregate and exchange brand-related interests and information. For example, Petco's Pet Talk Place site is a place where pet lovers can "connect, share, and learn" via discussions boards dedicated to dogs ("the bark"), cats ("the purr"), fish ("the splash"), birds ("the chirp"), reptiles ("the hiss"), and other types of pets. At cosmetics seller Sephora's Beauty Talk community site, like-minded members discuss, debate, and compare makeup, hair, fragrance, or skin care products to find the best match for them. And Sony's GreatnessAwaits.com site serves as a social hub for PlayStation PS4 game enthusiasts. It's a place where fans can follow social media posts about PS4, watch the latest PS4 videos, discover which PS4 games are trending on social networks, share content, and interact with other fans—all in real time. To date, GreatnessAwaits.com has earned more than 4.5 million page views, curated more than 3.3 million pieces of social content, and featured 75,000 fans.[31]

Beyond brand Web sites, most companies are also integrating social and mobile media into their marketing mixes.

Social Media Marketing

It's hard to find a brand Web site, or even a traditional media ad, that doesn't feature links to the brand's Facebook, Twitter, Google+, LinkedIn, YouTube, Instagram, Pinterest, or other social media sites. Social media provide exciting opportunities to extend customer engagement and get people talking about a brand. More than 90 percent of all U.S. companies now use social media as part of their marketing mixes, and 71 percent believe that social marketing is core to their business.[32]

Some social media are huge—Facebook has more than 1.2 billion active monthly members. Twitter has more than 232 million active users; Pinterest draws in 53 million users; and Instagram racks up an estimated 300 million active monthly visitors. Reddit, the online social news community, has nearly 174 million unique visitors each month from 185 countries. But more focused social media sites are also thriving, such as CafeMom, an online community of 20 million moms who exchange advice, entertainment, and commiseration at the community's online, Facebook, Twitter, Pinterest, YouTube, Google+, and mobile sites.

Online social media provide a digital home where people can connect and share important information and moments in their lives. As a result, they offer an ideal platform for *real-time marketing,* by which marketers can engage consumers in the moment by linking brands to important trending topics, real-world events, causes, personal occasions, or other important happenings in consumers' lives (see Marketing at Work 1.2).

Using social media might involve something as simple as a contest or promotion to garner Facebook Likes, Tweets, or YouTube postings. But more often these days, large organizations of all kinds use a wide range of carefully integrated social media. ≫For example, space agency NASA uses a broad mix of social media to educate the next generation of space explorers on its mission to "boldly go where no man has gone before." In all, NASA has more than 480 social media accounts spanning various topics and digital platforms. The agency has more than 10 million Facebook fans, 9 million Twitter followers, 2.5 million Instagram followers, and 30,000 YouTube subscribers. One of NASA's largest-ever social media campaigns supported the recent test launch of the Orion spacecraft, which will eventually carry humans to deep space destinations, such as Mars or an asteroid:[33]

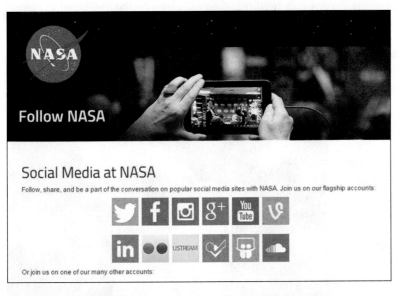

≫ **NASA uses an extensive array of social media to engage and educate the next generation of space explorers. The agency invites you to "follow, share, and be a part of the conversation on popular social media sites with NASA."**
NASA

The extensive campaign included a dozen or more YouTube "I'm On Board" videos starring actors from classic science-fiction TV shows, such as *Star Trek* and *The Incredible Hulk.* Even *Sesame Street*'s Elmo added his support, proudly displaying his "I'm On Board" boarding pass, chatting up astronauts, and relaying facts and launch information on the *Sesame Street* Twitter feed and other digital platforms. The campaign offered social media users a chance to put their names on a microchip aboard the space vehicle— more than a million people signed on. During the flight, NASA's social media team briefed the public through Twitter, Facebook, and Instagram posts. In all, it's a new NASA. People once followed NASA events from afar by gathering around their TV sets. Not anymore. Now, the space agency engages fans directly through interactive social media. "You can ask an astronaut a question," says NASA's social media manager. "You can…really be part of the experience in a much different way than ever before. It's not your father and grandfather's space agency anymore.

Mobile Marketing

Mobile marketing is perhaps the fastest-growing digital marketing platform. Four out of five smartphone users use their phones to shop—browsing product information through apps or the mobile Web, making in-store price comparisons, reading online product reviews, finding and redeeming coupons, and more.[34] Smartphones are ever present, always on, finely targeted, and highly personal. This makes them ideal for engaging customers anytime, anywhere as they move through the buying process. For example, Starbucks customers can use their mobile devices for everything from finding the nearest Starbucks and learning about new products to placing and paying for orders.

MARKETING AT WORK   1.2

Real-Time Marketing: Engaging Consumers in the Moment

A funny thing happened during Super Bowl XLVII in New Orleans. Early in the third quarter, the lights in the Mercedes-Benz Superdome suddenly went out. As 71,000 attendees and 106 million viewers restlessly bided their time and scratched their heads, engineers worked feverishly for a full 34 minutes to repair the power outage and bring the lights back on. But whereas the blackout was a disaster for Superdome management and CBS Sports, and an annoyance for players and fans, at least one marketer saw it as an opportunity. Shortly after the blackout began, Nabisco's Oreo brand tweeted out a simple message: "Power out? No problem. You can still dunk in the dark."

That now-famous single tweet, conceived and approved within just minutes, grabbed more attention for Oreo than the brand's extravagant first-quarter advertisement. Within an hour, the "dunk in the dark" message was retweeted nearly 16,000 times and racked up more than 20,000 Facebook likes, resulting in tens of millions of favorable exposures. In the following days, Oreo received tons of media coverage and was hailed as "The Brand That Won the Blackout Bowl." Those were pretty impressive results for a one-off joke by a cookie maker.

Oreo's successful Super Bowl one-liner triggered a surge in real-time marketing, and to this day it's hailed as the model for real-time success. Brands of all kinds are now trying to create their own "Oreo moments" by aligning marketing content with real-world events and trending topics through timely tweets, videos, blog entries, and social media posts. Done right, real-time marketing can engage consumers in the moment and make the brand more relevant.

Done poorly, however, real-time engagements can come off as little more than awkward or inappropriate intrusions. Too often, brands simply toss standalone, last-minute ads or messages into social channels, "hoping to catch lightning in a bottle." But hastily prepared or self-serving real-time messages can easily backfire, painting the brand as opportunistic or out of touch.

For example, after a video went viral showing Baltimore Ravens running back Ray Rice knocking his then-fiancée unconscious, thousands of women took to Twitter to discuss abusive relationships, referencing the hashtags #WhyIStayed and #WhyILeft. Jumping into the trending discussion, frozen pizza maker DiGiorno added three words: "#WhyIStayed You had pizza." As might be expected, the Twittersphere lit up with disgust at the insensitive pitch, leaving the number-one frozen pizza brand scrambling to explain itself. The best response it could muster was a feeble, "A million apologies. Did not read what the hashtag was about before posting."

Today, many real-time marketing efforts center on major media events, such as the Super Bowl, the Grammys, and the Academy Awards. These events let marketers engage huge, ready-made audiences. For example, when its blockbuster feature *The LEGO Movie* failed to win a nomination in the Best Animated Movie category at the recent Oscars, LEGO turned the snub into an opportunity to engage viewers in real time during the Academy Awards TV spectacular. During a performance of the movie's Oscar-nominated song—"Everything Is Awesome"—performers handed out Oscars made of golden LEGO bricks to celebrities in the audience. Simultaneously, the brand tweeted coordinated real-time images and the message "#EverythingIsAwesome at the #Oscars!" With pictures of stars such as Meryl Streep, Clint Eastwood, Oprah Winfrey, and Bradley Cooper posing with their LEGO Oscars, #LegoOscar became the number-one trending topic on Twitter.

Others companies attached real-time efforts to events in the competitive or natural environments. For example, with each new Apple iPhone model, at the very same time that Apple executives are on stage unveiling the features of the new phone, Samsung marketers are flooding social media with clever real-time "The next best thing is already here" responses. Starbucks, a social media powerhouse with nearly 36 million Facebook fans and more than 7 million Twitter followers, has long used real-time marketing to link the brand to current events important to its customers. For example, after Winter Storm Nemo hit the northeastern United States with heavy snowfall and hurricane-force winds in early 2013, Starbucks

>> Real-time marketing: Oreo's spectacularly successful "You can still dunk in the dark" tweet triggered a surge in real-time marketing, as brands of all kinds are now trying to create their own "Oreo moments" by aligning marketing content with real-world events and trending topics.

© Isabella Cassini/Alamy

Twitter and Facebook promotions offered "Snow Day" free coffee to customers in affected areas. "We wanted to make a grand [and timely] gesture," said a Starbucks digital marketer.

Minute-by-minute marketing strikes rarely succeed. Instead, to be consistently successful, real-time marketing must be part of a broader, carefully conceived strategy that makes the brand itself an engaging and relevant part of consumers' lives. According to one marketing strategist, brands must "evolve their entire plan to marketing in a real-time world." Today's smartphone-wielding, social media–saturated customers "are no longer just second-screen *viewing*—they are second-screen *living*." Smart brands build agile, ongoing real-time marketing programs that listen in on the social space and respond with relevant marketing content that blends smoothly with the dynamics of customers' real-time social sharing.

For example, although the Oreo "dunk in the dark" tweet might have seemed off the cuff, it was only the latest in a long series of real-time marketing efforts designed to make Oreo a part of consumers' daily discourse. In the months preceding the Super Bowl, Oreo had successfully carried out its "Daily Twist" campaign. Each day for 100 days, the brand posted consumer-inspired Oreo cookie art tied to a relevant event. There was a Mars Rover Landing Oreo (an open-face cookie with tire tracks through its red crème filling), an Elvis Week Oreo (with an Oreo profile of The King of Rock 'n' Roll), and a Shark Week Oreo (with a jagged bite taken out of it, of course). The groundbreaking Daily Twist campaign gave Oreo a fourfold increase in Facebook shares and boosted its Instagram following from 2,200 to more than 85,000.

Oreo wages an ongoing social media and mobile campaign to engage consumers in the moment, skillfully injecting the brand into consumers' lives and conversations. For example, there was the wildly popular "Twist, Lick, Dunk" mobile game app that had 4 million users dunking 4 billion virtual Oreo cookies. Then there was the catchy 90-second "Oreo Cookie Balls" rap video, tweeted and posted on YouTube and other social media, showing clever ideas for eating and serving cookie balls during the end-of-year holiday season—it quickly went viral with more than 1.6 million views on YouTube alone. And leading up to a recent Halloween season, Oreo Laboratorium, a series of brief stop-motion videos, showed different Oreo creatures and asked fans to "Name the Nomster." Such gems illustrate how Oreo keeps itself smack dab in the middle of the consumer consciousness by making real-time marketing an everyday event.

Whether connected to a social cause, a trending topic or event, a consumer's personal situation, or something else, the essential concept behind successful real-time marketing is pretty simple: Find or create ongoing connections between the brand and what's happening and important in consumers' lives, then engage consumers genuinely in the moment. One marketing executive suggests that real-time marketers should equate the practice to "meeting somebody in a social gathering—you don't accost them, instead you try to find a commonality of interest."

Sources: Georgia Christopher Heine, "Ads in Real Time, All the Time," *Adweek,* February 18, 2013, p. 9; David Griner, "DiGiorno Is Really, Really Sorry about Its Tweet Accidentally Making Light of Domestic Violence," *Adweek,* September 9, 2014, www.adweek.com/print/159998; Danielle Sacks, "The Story of Oreo: How an Old Cookie Became a Modern Marketing Personality," *Fast Company,* October 23, 2014, www.fastcocreate.com/3037068; Christopher Palmeri, "'Lego Movie' Picks Up Tweets Not Trophies at Academy Awards," *Businessweek,* February 23, 2015, www.bloomberg.com/news/articles/2015-02-23/lego-movie-picks-up-tweets-not-trophies-at-academy-awards-show; and www.360i.com/work/oreo-daily-twist/ and https://twitter.com/oreo/status/298246571718483968, accessed September 2015.

>> Mobile marketing: Redbox uses mobile marketing to engage its customers, personalize its service, and promote DVD rentals. Its "The 10 Days of Deals" mobile campaign generated nearly 1.5 million text messages, resulting in more than 200,000 new Redbox Text Club members.

AP Images for Redbox

Marketers use mobile channels to stimulate immediate buying, make shopping easier, enrich the brand experience, or all of these. >> Consider Redbox:[35]

Redbox DVD rental kiosks are unmanned, so the company has to find innovative ways to engage customers and personalize its service—most of which it does through its Web site and mobile app, text messaging, and email. Customers can use the Redbox mobile app to locate Redbox kiosks, check availability of movies and games, and reserve rentals for quick pickup. Mobile customers can also join the Redbox Text Club to receive texts about the latest Redbox news, releases, and members-only deals. Text Club members are Redbox's most valuable customers, so the company launched a 10-day-long mobile marketing campaign to increase membership. Using large call-to-action stickers on kiosks, a blast of email, and posts on its Facebook and other social media pages, Redbox offered discounts of between 10 cents and $1.50 on the next DVD rental to customers who texted the word "DEALS" to 727272. The campaign—called "The 10 Days of Deals"—generated nearly 1.5 million text messages from some 400,000 customers, resulting in more than 200,000 new Text Club members. "Mobile is like having a kiosk in your hand," explains Redbox's chief marketer. "It's an incredibly important part of our [marketing] strategy."

Although online, social media, and mobile marketing offer huge potential, most marketers are still learning how to use them effectively. The key is to blend the new digital approaches with traditional marketing to create a smoothly integrated marketing strategy and mix. We will examine digital, mobile, and social media marketing throughout the text—they touch almost every area of marketing strategy and tactics. Then, after we've covered the marketing basics, we'll look more deeply into digital and direct marketing in Chapter 14.

The Changing Economic Environment

The Great Recession of 2008 to 2009 and its aftermath hit American consumers hard. After two decades of overspending, new economic realities forced consumers to bring their consumption back in line with their incomes and rethink their buying priorities.

In today's post-recession era, consumer incomes and spending are again on the rise. However, even as the economy has strengthened, rather than reverting to their old free-spending ways, Americans are now showing an enthusiasm for frugality not seen in decades. Sensible consumption has made a comeback, and it appears to be here to stay. The new consumer spending values emphasize simpler living and more value for the dollar. Despite their rebounding means, consumers continue to buy less, clip more coupons, swipe their credit cards less, and put more in the bank.

Many consumers are reconsidering their very definition of the good life. "People are finding happiness in old-fashioned virtues—thrift, savings, do-it-yourself projects, self-improvement, hard work, faith, and community," says one consumer behavior expert. "We are moving from mindless to mindful consumption."[36] The new, more frugal spending values don't mean that people have resigned themselves to lives of deprivation. As the economy has improved, consumers are again indulging in luxuries and bigger-ticket purchases, just more sensibly.

In response, companies in all industries—from discounters such as Target to luxury brands such as Lexus—have realigned their marketing strategies with the new economic realities. More than ever, marketers are emphasizing the *value* in their value propositions. They are focusing on value for the money, practicality, and durability in their product offerings and marketing pitches.

For example, for years discount retailer Target focused increasingly on the "Expect More" side of its "Expect More. Pay Less." value proposition. Its carefully cultivated "upscale-discounter" image successfully differentiated it from Walmart's more hard-nosed "lowest-price" position. But when the economy soured, many consumers worried that Target's trendier assortments and hip marketing also meant higher prices. So Target has shifted its balance more toward the "Pay Less" half of the slogan, making certain that its prices are in line with Walmart's and that customers know it. Although still trendy, Target's marketing now emphasizes more practical price and savings appeals. Offering "more for your money" holds a prominent place in the Target mission. "We think a lot about your budget and how to give you the best value every time you shop with us," says the company.[37]

In adjusting to the new economy, companies may be tempted to cut their marketing budgets and slash prices in an effort to coax more frugal customers into opening their wallets. However, although cutting costs and offering selected discounts can be important marketing tactics, smart marketers understand that making cuts in the wrong places can damage long-term brand images and customer relationships. The challenge is to balance the brand's value proposition with the current times while also enhancing its long-term equity. Thus, rather than slashing prices in uncertain economic times, many marketers hold the line on prices and instead explain why their brands are worth it.

The Growth of Not-for-Profit Marketing

In recent years, marketing has also become a major part of the strategies of many not-for-profit organizations, such as colleges, hospitals, museums, zoos, symphony orchestras, foundations, and even churches. The nation's not-for-profits face stiff competition for support and membership. Sound marketing can help them attract membership, funds, and support.

For example, Alex's Lemonade Stand Foundation is a not-for-profit organization with a special mission: "Fighting childhood cancer, one cup at a time." It all started with a simple lemonade stand, run by four-year-old Alexandra "Alex" Scott, who was battling cancer. Alex wanted to raise money for doctors so that they could "help other kids, like they helped me." In its first summer, little Alex's lemonade stand raised $2,000. By age 8, with the help of founding sponsor Volvo and a nationwide network of volunteer-held lemonade stands, Alex had raised $1 million for pediatric cancer research. Although Alex has passed away, Alex's Lemonade Stand Foundation (ALSF) keeps her dream alive through a comprehensive marketing effort:[38]

>> Alex's Lemonade Stand Foundation's marketing revolves around a well-designed Web site (www.AlexsLemonade.org), which details the organization, its mission, sponsored research, a logo gifts and gear store, and special events such as National Lemonade Days, the Great Chefs Event, and Alex's Million Mile—Run, Walk, Ride. The site also gives detailed instructions for holding a successful local lemonade stand, backed by a fundraising kit containing ALSF-branded banners, signs, posters, and flyers. ALSF makes good use of social media. Its blog discusses issues of childhood cancer and shares stories about ALSF "heroes and amazing supporters." And its well-curated Facebook, Instagram, Twitter, YouTube, Pinterest, and LinkedIn sites have created an active community of dedicated fans.

Finally, ALSF has assembled a network of corporate marketing partners—from Volvo, Northwestern Mutual, and Toys "R" Us to Applebee's, Rita's Italian Ice, and A&P. For example, at Applebee's, if you donate to ALSF, you get a coupon for a free kid's meal or frozen lemonade. At Rita's, you can buy a paper lemon for $1 or text to a number to donate $5. Volvo holds raffles for new cars, with all proceeds going to ALSF. Northwestern Mutual supports ALSF's Family Travel Fund, which pays for gasoline and other expenses to help families get their children to and from treatment. Thus, Alex's one lemonade stand sparked a foundation that effectively markets her cause to raise funds to fight childhood cancer. Since 2005, Alex's Lemonade Stand Foundation has raised more than $100 million and funded more than 475 medical research projects.

>> Not-for-profit marketing: Alex's Lemonade Stand Foundation (ALSF) effectively markets its mission of "Fighting childhood cancer, one cup at a time." ALSF has raised more than $100 million for pediatric cancer research.

Alex's Lemonade Stand Foundation for Childhood Cancer

Government agencies have also shown an increased interest in marketing. For example, the U.S. military has a marketing plan to attract recruits to its different services, and various government agencies are now designing social marketing campaigns to encourage energy conservation and concern for the environment or discourage smoking, illegal drug use, and obesity. Even the once-stodgy U.S. Postal Service has developed innovative marketing to sell commemorative stamps, promote its Priority Mail services, and lift its image as a contemporary and competitive organization. In all, the U.S. government is the nation's 39th largest advertiser, with an annual advertising budget of more than $980 million.[39]

Rapid Globalization

As they are redefining their customer relationships, marketers are also taking a fresh look at the ways in which they relate with the broader world around them. Today, almost every company, large or small, is touched in some way by global competition. A neighborhood florist buys its flowers from Mexican nurseries, and a large U.S. electronics manufacturer competes in its home markets with giant Korean rivals. A fledgling Internet retailer finds itself receiving orders from all over the world at the same time that an American consumer goods producer introduces new products into emerging markets abroad.

American firms have been challenged at home by the skillful marketing of European and Asian multinationals. Companies such as Toyota, Nestlé, and Samsung have often outperformed their U.S. competitors in American markets. Similarly, U.S. companies in a wide range of industries have developed truly global operations, making and selling their products worldwide. Quintessentially American McDonald's now serves 70 million customers daily in more than 36,000 local restaurants in more than 100 countries worldwide—68 percent of its corporate revenues come from outside the United States. Similarly, Nike markets in 190 countries, with non-U.S. sales accounting for 52 percent of its worldwide sales.[40] Today, companies are not just selling more of their locally produced goods in international markets; they are also sourcing more supplies and components abroad and developing new products for specific markets around the world.

Thus, managers in countries around the world are increasingly taking a global, not just local, view of the company's industry, competitors, and opportunities. They are asking: What is global marketing? How does it differ from domestic marketing? How do global competitors and forces affect our business? To what extent should we "go global"? We will discuss the global marketplace in more detail in Chapter 15.

Sustainable Marketing—The Call for More Environmental and Social Responsibility

Marketers are reexamining their relationships with social values and responsibilities and with the very Earth that sustains us. As the worldwide consumerism and environmentalism movements mature, today's marketers are being called on to develop *sustainable marketing* practices. Corporate ethics and social responsibility have become hot topics for almost every business. And few companies can ignore the renewed and very demanding environmental movement. Every company action can affect customer relationships. Today's customers expect companies to deliver value in a socially and environmentally responsible way.

The social responsibility and environmental movements will place even stricter demands on companies in the future. Some companies resist these movements, budging only when forced by legislation or organized consumer outcries. Forward-looking companies, however, readily accept their responsibilities to the world around them. They view sustainable marketing as an opportunity to do well by doing good. They seek ways to profit by serving immediate needs and the best long-run interests of their customers and communities.

Some companies, such as Patagonia, Timberland, Method, Ben & Jerry's, and others, practice *caring capitalism*, setting themselves apart by being civic minded and responsible. They build social and environmental responsibility into their company value and mission statements. >> For example, Ben & Jerry's, a division of Unilever, has long prided itself on being a "values-led business," one that creates "linked prosperity" for everyone connected to the brand—from suppliers to employees to customers and communities:[41]

>> Sustainable marketing: Ben & Jerry's three-part "linked prosperity" mission drives it to make fantastic ice cream (product mission), manage the company for sustainable financial growth (economic mission), and use the company "in innovative ways to make the world a better place" (social mission).

© ZUMA Press, Inc/Alamy

Under its three-part mission, Ben & Jerry's wants to make fantastic ice cream (product mission), manage the company for sustainable financial growth (economic mission), and use the company "in innovative ways to make the world a better place" (social mission). Ben & Jerry's backs its mission with actions. For example, the company is committed to using wholesome, natural, non-GMO, fair-trade-certified ingredients and buys from local farms. It employs business practices "that respect the earth and the environment," investing in wind energy, solar usage, travel offsets, and carbon neutrality. Its Caring Dairy program helps farmers develop more sustainable practices on the farm ("Caring Dairy means happy cows, happy farmers, and a happy planet"). The Ben & Jerry's Foundation awards nearly $2 million annually in grassroots grants to community service organizations and projects in communities across the nation. Ben & Jerry's also operates 14 PartnerShops, scoop shops that are independently owned and operated by community-based not-for-profit organizations. The company waives standard franchise fees for these shops.

Sustainable marketing presents both opportunities and challenges for marketers. We will revisit the topic of sustainable marketing in greater detail in Chapter 16.

So, What Is Marketing? Pulling It All Together

At the start of this chapter, Figure 1.1 presented a simple model of the marketing process. Now that we've discussed all the steps in the process, ≫**Figure 1.6** presents an expanded model that will help you pull it all together. What is marketing? Simply put, marketing is the process of engaging customers and building profitable customer relationships by creating value for customers and capturing value in return.

The first four steps of the marketing process focus on creating value for customers. The company first gains a full understanding of the marketplace by researching customer needs and managing marketing information. It then designs a customer-driven marketing strategy based on the answers to two simple questions. The first question is "What

Author Comment

Remember Figure 1.1 outlining the marketing process? Now, based on everything we've discussed in this chapter, we'll expand that figure to provide a road map for learning marketing throughout the remainder of the text.

This expanded version of Figure 1.1 at the beginning of the chapter provides a good road map for the rest of the text. The underlying concept of the entire text is that marketing creates value for customers in order to capture value from customers in return.

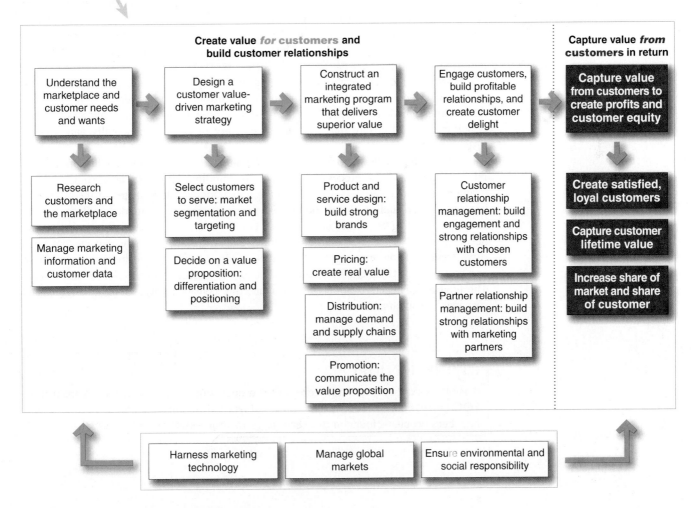

≫ **Figure 1.6 An Expanded Model of the Marketing Process**

consumers will we serve?" (market segmentation and targeting). Good marketing companies know that they cannot serve all customers in every way. Instead, they need to focus their resources on the customers they can serve best and most profitably. The second marketing strategy question is "How can we best serve targeted customers?" (differentiation and positioning). Here, the marketer outlines a value proposition that spells out what values the company will deliver to win target customers.

With its marketing strategy chosen, the company now constructs an integrated marketing program—consisting of a blend of the four marketing mix elements, the four Ps—that transforms the marketing strategy into real value for customers. The company develops product offers and creates strong brand identities for them. It prices these offers to create real customer value and distributes the offers to make them available to target consumers. Finally, the company designs promotion programs that engage target customers, communicate the value proposition, and persuade customers to act on the market offering.

Perhaps the most important step in the marketing process involves building value-laden, profitable relationships with target customers. Throughout the process, marketers practice customer relationship management to create customer satisfaction and delight. They engage customers in the process of creating brand conversations, experiences, and community. In creating customer value and relationships, however, the company cannot go it alone. It must work closely with marketing partners both inside the company and throughout its marketing system. Thus, beyond practicing good customer relationship management and customer-engagement marketing, firms must also practice good partner relationship management.

The first four steps in the marketing process create value *for* customers. In the final step, the company reaps the rewards of its strong customer relationships by capturing value *from* customers. Delivering superior customer value creates highly satisfied customers who will buy more and buy again. This helps the company capture customer lifetime value and greater share of customer. The result is increased long-term customer equity for the firm.

Finally, in the face of today's changing marketing landscape, companies must take into account three additional factors. In building customer and partner relationships, they must harness marketing technologies in the new digital age, take advantage of global opportunities, and ensure that they act sustainably in an environmentally and socially responsible way.

Figure 1.6 provides a good road map to future chapters of this text. Chapters 1 and 2 introduce the marketing process, with a focus on building customer relationships and capturing value from customers. Chapters 3 through 5 address the first step of the marketing process—understanding the marketing environment, managing marketing information, and understanding consumer and business buyer behavior. In Chapter 6, we look more deeply into the two major marketing strategy decisions: selecting which customers to serve (segmentation and targeting) and determining a value proposition (differentiation and positioning). Chapters 7 through 14 discuss the marketing mix variables one by one. The final two chapters examine special marketing considerations: global marketing and sustainable marketing.

MyMarketingLab

If assigned by your instructor, complete the questions marked with the ⭐ from the EOC Discussion Questions section in the MyLab. To complete the Marketing by the Numbers problems found in this section, go to your Assignments in the MyLab.

REVIEWING AND EXTENDING THE CONCEPTS

CHAPTER REVIEW AND CRITICAL THINKING

Objectives Review

Today's successful companies—whether large or small, for-profit or not-for-profit, domestic or global—share a strong customer focus and a heavy commitment to marketing. The goal of marketing is to engage customers and manage profitable customer relationships.

 OBJECTIVE 1-1 Define marketing and outline the steps in the marketing process. (pp 4–5)

Marketing is the process by which companies create value for customers and build strong customer relationships in order to capture value from customers in return. The marketing process involves five steps. The first four steps create value *for* customers. First, marketers need to understand the marketplace and customer needs and wants. Next, marketers design a customer-driven marketing strategy with the goal of getting, engaging, and growing target customers. In the third step, marketers construct a marketing program that actually delivers superior value. All of these steps form the basis for the fourth step: engaging customers, building profitable customer relationships, and creating customer delight. In the final step, the company reaps the rewards of strong customer relationships by capturing value *from* customers.

 OBJECTIVE 1-2 Explain the importance of understanding the marketplace and customers and identify the five core marketplace concepts. (pp 6–8)

Outstanding marketing companies go to great lengths to learn about and understand their customers' *needs, wants,* and *demands.* This understanding helps them to design want-satisfying market offerings and build value-laden customer relationships by which they can capture *customer lifetime value* and greater *share of customer.* The result is increased long-term *customer equity* for the firm.

The core marketplace concepts are needs, wants, and demands; market offerings (products, services, and experiences); value and satisfaction; exchange and relationships; and markets. Companies address needs, wants, and demands by putting forth a value proposition, a set of benefits that they promise to consumers to satisfy their needs. The value proposition is fulfilled through a market offering, which delivers customer value and satisfaction, resulting in long-term exchange relationships with customers.

 OBJECTIVE 1-3 Identify the key elements of a customer value-driven marketing strategy and discuss the marketing management orientations that guide marketing strategy. (pp 9–13)

To design a winning marketing strategy, the company must first decide whom it will serve. It does this by dividing the market into segments of customers (*market segmentation*) and selecting which segments it will cultivate (*target marketing*). Next, the company must decide *how* it will serve targeted customers (how it will *differentiate and position* itself in the marketplace).

Marketing management can adopt one of five competing market orientations. The *production concept* holds that management's task is to improve production efficiency and bring down prices. The *product concept* holds that consumers favor products that offer the most in quality, performance, and innovative features; thus, little promotional effort is required. The *selling concept* holds that consumers will not buy enough of an organization's products unless it undertakes a large-scale selling and promotion effort. The *marketing concept* holds that achieving organizational goals depends on determining the needs and wants of target markets and delivering the desired satisfactions more effectively and efficiently than competitors do. The *societal marketing concept* holds that generating customer satisfaction *and* long-run societal well-being through sustainable marketing strategies is key to both achieving the company's goals and fulfilling its responsibilities.

 OBJECTIVE 1-4 Discuss customer relationship management and identify strategies for creating value *for* customers and capturing value *from* customers in return. (pp 13–23)

Broadly defined, *customer relationship management* is the process of engaging customers and building and maintaining profitable customer relationships by delivering superior customer value and satisfaction. *Customer-engagement marketing* aims to make a brand a meaningful part of consumers' conversations and lives through direct and continuous customer involvement in shaping brand conversations, experiences, and community. The aim of customer relationship management and customer engagement is to produce high *customer equity,* the total combined customer lifetime values of all of the company's customers. The key to building lasting relationships is the creation of superior *customer value* and *satisfaction*. In return for creating value *for* targeted customers, the company captures value *from* customers in the form of profits and customer equity.

 OBJECTIVE 1-5 **Describe the major trends and forces that are changing the marketing landscape in this age of relationships. (pp 24–31)**

Dramatic changes are occurring in the marketing arena. The digital age has created exciting new ways to learn about and relate to individual customers. As a result, advances in digital and social media have taken the marketing world by storm. Online, mobile, and social media marketing offer exciting new opportunities to target customers more selectively and engage them more deeply. The key is to blend the new digital approaches with traditional marketing to create a smoothly integrated marketing strategy and mix.

The Great Recession caused consumers to rethink their buying priorities and bring their consumption back in line with their incomes. Even as the post-recession economy has strengthened, Americans are now showing an enthusiasm for frugality not seen in decades. The challenge is to balance a brand's value proposition with current times while also enhancing its long-term equity.

In recent years, marketing has become a major part of the strategies for many not-for-profit organizations, such as colleges, hospitals, museums, zoos, symphony orchestras, foundations, and even churches. Also, in an increasingly smaller world, many marketers are now connected *globally* with their customers, marketing partners, and competitors. Finally, today's marketers are also reexamining their ethical and societal responsibilities. Marketers are being called on to take greater responsibility for the social and environmental impacts of their actions.

Pulling it all together, as discussed throughout the chapter, the major new developments in marketing can be summed up in a single concept: *engaging customers and creating and capturing customer value*. Today, marketers of all kinds are taking advantage of new opportunities for building value-laden relationships with their customers, their marketing partners, and the world around them.

Key Terms

Objective 1-1
Marketing (p 5)

Objective 1-2
Needs (p 6)
Wants (p 6)
Demands (p 6)
Market offerings (p 6)
Marketing myopia (p 7)
Exchange (p 7)
Market (p 8)

Objective 1-3
Marketing management (p 9)
Production concept (p 10)
Product concept (p 10)
Selling concept (p 10)
Marketing concept (p 10)
Societal marketing concept (p 11)

Objective 1-4
Customer relationship
    management (p 13)

Customer-perceived value (p 13)
Customer satisfaction (p 14)
Customer-engagement marketing (p 18)
Consumer-generated marketing (p 19)
Partner relationship management (p 20)
Customer lifetime value (p 21)
Share of customer (p 21)
Customer equity (p 22)

Objective 1-5
Digital and social media
    marketing (p 24)

Discussion Questions

1-1. Define marketing and outline the steps in the marketing process. (AASCB: Communication)

1-2. Describe how the *marketing concept* differs from the other marketing management orientations. (AACSB: Communication; Reflective Thinking)

⭐ 1-3. What is customer-engagement marketing and how is it related to the surge in digital and social media technologies? (AACSB: Communication; Reflective Thinking)

⭐ 1-4. When implementing customer relationship management, why might a business desire fewer customers over more customers? Shouldn't the focus of marketing be to acquire as many customers as possible? (AACSB: Communication; Reflective Thinking)

1-5. Discuss how technology is affecting marketing. (AACSB: Communication)

Critical Thinking Exercises

1-6. Select three companies competing in the same product or service category. How does each differentiate and position itself, and how do they execute these strategies in their marketing mixes? Which competitor is most successful? Which element(s) of that competitor's marketing mix has contributed to its success? (AACSB Communication; Analytic Reasoning)

1-7. Go to a company, organization, or specific brand Web site that has a link to Facebook, Google+, YouTube, Twitter, and/or Pinterest. Click on the links and describe how that company is using social media to market its products or services. Evaluate its effectiveness in creating customer engagement. (AACSB: Communication; Use of IT; Reflective Thinking)

1-8. In a small group, create a presentation about careers in marketing. Search the Internet for information regarding the different career options available in marketing and the skills, education, and experience necessary to advance in the field of marketing. Then select a company and describe the marketing career opportunities available there. (AACSB: Communication; Use of IT; Reflective Thinking)

MINICASES AND APPLICATIONS

Online, Mobile, and Social Media Marketing   Do Us A Flavor

Two Lay's chip flavors—Cheesy Garlic Bread and Kettle Cooked Wasabi Ginger—were created by consumers as part of Frito-Lay's wildly successful "Do Us A Flavor" marketing campaign (www.dousaflavor.com). Launched in July 2012 in a pop-up shop in New York's Times Square, the event took on new dimensions in 2015 by incorporating real-time marketing. In response to interesting Tweets during the three-month-long submission period, digital shop Deep Focus produced 20 one-minute YouTube clips featuring two potato puppets named Marvin and Duncan (also known as the Taste Spuds). Google has now developed the "Flavorcast Heat Map" showing trending ingredients for each state, and consumers can see state-versus-state contests in the Flavor Showdown Gallery on the Web site. Consumers submit their flavor's name, up to three ingredients, and a chip style. They can also vote online at the Web site or via social media, and finalists' flavors are developed and shipped to stores a few months later, where they can be purchased and then voted upon. The creator of the winning flavor receives $1 million. But Lay's is the big winner of this campaign. The first contest's goal was 1.2 million submissions, but Lay's received 3.8 million submissions, 22.5 million Facebook visits a week, and a 12 percent increase in sales.

⭐ **1-9.** Some have argued that real-time marketing success is luck-based, whereas responsive marketing is more strategy-based. Research these two concepts and support or refute this statement. (AACSB: Communication; Reflective Thinking)

1-10. Select a brand in a different product category and create a responsive campaign that incorporates online, mobile, and social media to create customer engagement. How would you measure the success of your campaign? (AACSB: Communication; Reflective Thinking)

Marketing Ethics   Extreme Baby Monitoring

Every parent's fear when putting an infant to sleep is Sudden Infant Death Syndrome (SIDS)—the sudden unexplainable death of an otherwise healthy baby. In the United States, about 2,000 infants die each year of SIDS, the third leading cause of infant death. For $199, parents can buy monitors that track babies' vital signs, such as respiration, heart rate, skin temperature, sleeping position, and quality of sleep. The Mimo Smart Baby Monitor is a cute clip-on turtle that attaches to a special organic cotton onesie, and the Owlet Baby Monitor is a smart sock that looks like a little toeless boot. If parents don't want to attach these devices on their little ones, they can opt for the SafeToSleep Breathing Monitor sheet with a built-in monitor. All of these devices stream data to parents' smartphones. Manufacturers of these devices promote them to parents for "your baby's health" or to give "that extra assurance" to protect against SIDS. However, several government agencies such as the Food and Drug Administration, the Consumer Product Safety Commission, the Centers for Disease Control and Prevention, and the National Institutes of Health as well as the American Academy of Pediatrics all agree that these devices cannot protect a baby from SIDS. But fear sells, and most of these manufacturers cannot keep up with the demand for their products.

1-11. Is it right for marketers to play on parents' fear to sell products that experts conclude are not necessary or effective? (AACSB: Communication; Ethical Reasoning; Reflective Thinking)

1-12. Discuss other examples of marketers using emotion to sell products. Are they ethical? (AACSB: Communication; Ethical Reasoning)

Marketing by the Numbers   What's a Customer Worth?

How much are you worth to a given company if you continue to purchase its brand for the rest of your life? Many marketers are grappling with that question, but it's not easy to determine how much a customer is worth to a company over his or her lifetime. Calculating customer lifetime value can be very complicated. Intuitively, however, it can be a fairly simple net present value calculation, which incorporates the concept of the time value of money. To determine a basic customer lifetime value, each stream of profit (C, the net cash flow after costs are subtracted) is discounted back to its present value (PV) and then summed. The basic equation for calculating net present value (NPV) is:

$$NPV = \sum_{t=0}^{N} \frac{C_t}{(1 + r)^t}$$

Where,

t = time of the cash flow

N = total customer lifetime

r = discount rate

C_t = net cash flow (the profit) at time t (The initial cost of acquiring a customer would be a negative net cash flow at time 0.)

NPV can be calculated easily on most financial calculators or by using one of the calculators available on the Internet, such as the one found at www.investopedia.com/calculator/NetPresentValue.aspx.

1-13. Assume that a customer shops at a local grocery store spending an average of $200 a week, resulting in a retailer profit of $10 each week from this customer. Assuming the shopper visits the store all 52 weeks of the year, calculate the customer lifetime value if this shopper remains loyal over a 10-year life span. Also assume a 5 percent annual interest rate and no initial cost to acquire the customer. (AACSB: Communication; Analytic Reasoning)

1-14. Describe ways marketers can increase the lifetime value of a customer. (AACSB: Communication; Reflective Thinking)

Video Case   Eskimo Joe's

Since 1975, Eskimo Joe's has been a popular watering hole in Stillwater, Oklahoma. Through word of mouth and a popular logo spread via T-shirts, it rapidly became a favorite place to grab a beer for students at Oklahoma State. But what started as a basic beer joint has grown into something much more.

When the drinking age changed from 18 to 21 in the 1980s, Eskimo Joe's had to decide how it would move forward. That challenge helped the company to recognize that its product is much more than just a cold mug of beer. Instead, people flocked to Eskimo Joe's for the fun atmosphere and customer-friendly service. This realization led to an expansion into different businesses that have now spread the Eskimo Joe's logo all over the planet.

After viewing the video featuring Eskimo Joe's, answer the following questions:

1-15. Describe Eskimo Joe's market offering.

1-16. What is Eskimo Joe's value proposition? How does its value proposition relate to its market offering?

1-17. How does Eskimo Joe's build long-term customer relationships?

Company Cases   1 FedEx/4 Campbell's/14 Alibaba

See Appendix 1 for cases appropriate for this chapter. **Case 1, FedEx: Making Every Customer Experience Outstanding.** From the time FedEx opened for business over 40 years ago, the company strategy has been built on a foundation of obsessive customer focus. **Case 4, Campbell's: Watching What You Eat.** Through extensive marketing research, Campbell's maintains its customer focus. **Case 14, Alibaba: The World's Largest E-Tailer Is Not Amazon.** Alibaba is on track to hit $700 billion in annual revenues within two years by providing everything customers need and desire.

MyMarketingLab

If assigned by your instructor, complete these writing sections from your Assignments in the MyLab.

1-18. Compare and contrast needs, wants, and demands. Which one(s) can marketers influence? (AACSB: Communication; Reflective Thinking)

1-19. Is it fair to single out specific products for restrictions such as when New York City proposed size cap on soft drinks? Discuss this argument from all sides of this issue: government, soft drink marketers, and consumers. (AACSB: Written and Oral Communication; Reflective Thinking)

2 Company and Marketing Strategy
Partnering to Build Customer Engagement, Value, and Relationships

CHAPTER ROAD MAP Objective Outline

▶ OBJECTIVE 2-1 **Explain company-wide strategic planning and its four steps.** Company-Wide Strategic Planning: Defining Marketing's Role (40–43)

▶ OBJECTIVE 2-2 **Discuss how to design business portfolios and develop growth strategies.** Designing the Business Portfolio (43–48)

▶ OBJECTIVE 2-3 **Explain marketing's role in strategic planning and how marketing works with its partners to create and deliver customer value.** Planning Marketing: Partnering to Build Customer Relationships (48–50)

▶ OBJECTIVE 2-4 **Describe the elements of a customer value-driven marketing strategy and mix and the forces that influence it.** Marketing Strategy and the Marketing Mix (50–56)

▶ OBJECTIVE 2-5 **List the marketing management functions, including the elements of a marketing plan, and discuss the importance of measuring and managing marketing return on investment.** Managing the Marketing Effort (56–60); Measuring and Managing Marketing Return on Investment (60–61)

Previewing the Concepts

In the first chapter, we explored the marketing process by which companies create value for customers to capture value from them in return. In this chapter, we dig deeper into steps two and three of that process: designing customer value-driven marketing strategies and constructing marketing programs. First, we look at the organization's overall strategic planning, which guides marketing strategy and planning. Next, we discuss how, guided by the strategic plan, marketers partner closely with others inside and outside the firm to engage customers and create value for them. We then examine marketing strategy and planning—how marketers choose target markets, position their market offerings, develop a marketing mix, and manage their marketing programs. Finally, we look at the important step of measuring and managing marketing return on investment (marketing ROI).

First, let's look at Starbucks, a good company and a good marketing strategy story. Starbucks met with enormous early success by focusing not just on coffee, but on the coffee-drinking experience. The company has since taken a bumpy ride from boom to bust and back to boom again. Along the way, it learned that good marketing strategy means more than just growth, sales, and profits. It means skillfully engaging customers and creating value for them. At its core, Starbucks doesn't sell just coffee, it sells "The Starbucks Experience."

First Stop

Starbucks's Customer Value-Driven Marketing Strategy: Delivering "The Starbucks Experience"

More than 30 years ago, Howard Schultz transformed the coffee industry by bringing a European-style coffeehouse to America. He believed that people needed to slow down—to "smell the coffee" and to enjoy life a little more. The result was Starbucks, founded with a whole new strategy for engaging customers and creating customer value.

Starbucks didn't sell just coffee, it sold "The Starbucks Experience"—"an uplifting experience that enriches people's lives one moment, one human being, one extraordinary cup of coffee at a time." Starbucks gave customers what it calls a "third place"—a place away from home and away from work. At Starbucks, the smells, the sound of beans grinding, watching baristas blend and brew the brand's specialty coffees—all became as much or more a part of the customer experience as the coffee itself.

Over the next two decades, customers flocked to Starbucks cafés. By 2007, some 15,000 Starbucks stores dotted the nation and globe, and the company's sales and profits rose like steam off a mug of hot java. However, Starbucks's enormous success drew a host of competitors. It seemed that every rival—from independent coffeehouses to fast-food restaurants—was peddling its own brand of premium coffee.

To maintain its phenomenal growth in the increasingly overcaffeinated marketplace, Starbucks brewed up an ambitious growth strategy. It opened new stores at a breakneck pace, seemingly *everywhere*. For example, one three-block stretch in Chicago contained six of the trendy coffee bars. In New York City, there were two Starbucks in one Macy's store. In fact, cramming so many stores so close together caused one satirical publication to run this headline: "A New Starbucks Opens in the Restroom of Existing Starbucks." The company also blanketed the country with Starbucks kiosks and coffee stands in everything from Target stores and supermarkets to hotel lobbies, and service businesses from airlines to car dealerships proclaimed "We proudly serve Starbucks coffee."

The more Starbucks grew, however, the more it drifted away from the core mission and values that had made it so successful. The company's almost obsessive focus on growth for growth's sake began to take a toll on the prized Starbucks Experience. Far from its roots as a warm and intimate coffeehouse, Starbucks began to evolve into more of a caffeine filling station. More and more, the premium brand found itself competing with the likes of—gasp!—McDonald's for many of the same customers.

Founder Howard Schultz, who had stepped down as CEO in 2000, expressed concern. In a 2007 memo to Starbucks management, Schultz lamented that the company's push for growth had "led to the watering down of the Starbucks Experience" and that Starbucks was "losing its soul." Schultz was right that something was wrong. By early 2008, when Schultz reassumed his role as Starbucks president and CEO, the company found itself in hot water. For the first time ever, the average number of transactions per U.S. store fell off and same-store sales growth slowed. Within just the previous two years, Starbucks's stock had tumbled nearly 80 percent. According to one analyst, "The financial vultures circled. Obituaries were drafted."

>> More than just coffee, Starbucks sells the Starbucks Experience, one that "enriches people's lives one moment, one human being, one extraordinary cup of coffee at a time."
Associated Press

Instead of presiding over the brand's demise, however, Schultz reacted quickly to restore its luster. He cooled the pace of Starbucks's growth, closed underperforming locations, and replaced most of the company's top executives. Most important, Schultz laid plans to reestablish the brand's core mission and values and to refocus the company on giving customers the authentic Starbucks Experience. "As we grew rapidly and had phenomenal success," Shultz announced, "we started to lose sight of our focus on the customer and our commitment to continually and creatively enhance the Starbucks Experience." Starbucks needed to shift its focus back to customers—to "reignite the emotional attachment with customers."

To emphasize the point, at a cost of $30 million, Schultz transported 10,000 Starbucks store managers to a morale-building reorientation in New Orleans. A short time later, Starbucks dramatically closed all of its U.S. locations for three hours to conduct nationwide employee training on the basics of producing satisfying customer experiences.

Those early actions began a process of continual renewal by which Starbucks has reignited the Starbucks customer experience through new products, innovative store formats, and new platforms for engaging customers. Beyond improvements in its signature coffee products, Starbucks has developed new products that take the Starbucks Experience into new areas. For example, a few years ago, Starbucks successfully launched Via, an instant coffee that's as good at home as fresh-brewed is in stores. More recently, Starbucks added Fizzio to its menu—freshly carbonated and handcrafted sodas in classic flavors.

> Starbucks has become America's—the world's—largest coffeehouse by skillfully engaging customers and delivering superior customer value. At its core, Starbucks doesn't sell just coffee. It sells "The Starbucks Experience."

The company is also experimenting with new store formats, such as the new high-end Starbucks Reserve Roastery and Tasting Room in Seattle that's part café, part shrine, and part working roastery. Schultz describes the new interactive store as "Niketown meets Apple meets Starbucks"—think of it as the Starbucks Experience on steroids. In another big move, Starbucks purchased Teavana—a specialty tea retailer with more than 400 locations in five countries. Schultz sees the Teavana acquisition as pivotal to Starbucks's renewal and reinvention. Tea is "a $90 billion global category, ripe for innovation," he says. "We're going to do for tea what we've done for coffee."

Starbucks's renewal extends the Starbucks Experience well beyond employee relearning, new products, and innovative stores formats. Over the past decade, as much as any brand, Starbucks has built customer engagement and brand community through digital and mobile platforms. Its highly successful mobile payments app, My Starbucks Rewards loyalty program, and prepaid Starbucks Cards now give Starbucks "a direct, real-time, personalized, two-way digital relationship with its customers," says the company's chief digital officer. The Starbucks Rewards mobile payment app has 12 million active users, and digital products now account for roughly 35 percent of payments at Starbucks's North American stores.

Today, a rejuvenated Starbucks is once again fully engaged with customers and delivering the one-of-a-kind Starbucks Experience. And once again, sales and profits are really perking. Every week, Starbucks serves more than 70 million customers face to face in 20,200 stores in 64 countries. Over the past six years, revenues have increased 70 percent, profits have shot up fivefold, and Starbucks's stock price has skyrocketed by a factor of 12.

The moral of the Starbucks story: Good marketing strategy means keeping your eye squarely on delivering customer value. The objective isn't just growth or sales or profits; it's engaging customers in a meaningful way and creating value for them. If a company takes care of customer engagement and value, good performance will result. "It's not just about ringing a register and performing a task," says Schultz. "It's also about creating an emotional, enduring relationship and connection with our...customers. At our core, we celebrate the interaction between us and our customers through the coffee experience. Life happens over coffee."[1]

Strategic planning
The process of developing and maintaining a strategic fit between the organization's goals and capabilities and its changing marketing opportunities.

Company-Wide Strategic Planning: Defining Marketing's Role

Each company must find the game plan for long-run survival and growth that makes the most sense given its specific situation, opportunities, objectives, and resources. This is the focus of **strategic planning**—the process of developing and maintaining a strategic fit between the organization's goals and capabilities and its changing marketing opportunities.

Strategic planning sets the stage for the rest of planning in the firm. Companies usually prepare annual plans, long-range plans, and strategic plans. The annual and long-range plans deal with the company's current businesses and how to keep them going. In contrast, the strategic plan involves adapting the firm to take advantage of opportunities in its constantly changing environment.

At the corporate level, the company starts the strategic planning process by defining its overall purpose and mission (see >> **Figure 2.1**). This mission is then turned into detailed supporting objectives that guide the entire company. Next, headquarters decides what portfolio of businesses and products is best for the company and how much support to give each one. In turn, each business and product develops detailed marketing and other departmental plans that support the company-wide plan. Thus, marketing planning occurs at the business-unit, product, and market levels. It supports company strategic planning with more detailed plans for specific marketing opportunities.

Company-wide strategic planning guides marketing strategy and planning.

Business unit, product, and market level

Corporate level

Like the marketing strategy, the broader company strategy must be customer focused.

Defining the company mission → Setting company objectives and goals → Designing the business portfolio → **Planning marketing and other functional strategies**

>> Figure 2.1 Steps in Strategic Planning

Defining a Market-Oriented Mission

An organization exists to accomplish something, and this purpose should be clearly stated. Forging a sound mission begins with the following questions: What *is* our business? Who is the customer? What do consumers value? What *should* our business be? These simple-sounding questions are among the most difficult the company will ever have to answer. Successful companies continuously raise these questions and answer them carefully and completely.

Mission statement
A statement of the organization's purpose—what it wants to accomplish in the larger environment.

Many organizations develop formal mission statements that answer these questions. A **mission statement** is a statement of the organization's purpose—what it wants to accomplish in the larger environment. A clear mission statement acts as an "invisible hand" that guides people in the organization.

Some companies define their missions myopically in product or technology terms ("We make and sell furniture" or "We are a chemical-processing firm"). But mission statements should be *market oriented* and defined in terms of satisfying basic customer needs. Products and technologies eventually become outdated, but basic market needs may last forever. For example, social scrapbooking site Pinterest doesn't define itself as just an online place to post pictures. Its mission is to give people a social media platform for collecting, organizing, and sharing things they love. And Chipotle's mission isn't to sell burritos. Instead, the restaurant promises "Food with Integrity," highlighting its commitment to the immediate and long-term welfare of customers and the environment. To back its mission, Chipotle serves only the very best natural, sustainable, local ingredients. **≫ Table 2.1** provides several examples of product-oriented versus market-oriented business definitions.[2]

Mission statements should be meaningful and specific yet motivating. Too often, mission statements are written for public relations purposes and lack specific, workable guidelines. Instead, they should emphasize the company's strengths and tell forcefully how it intends to win in the marketplace. For example, Google's mission isn't to be the world's best search engine. It's to give people a window into the world's information, wherever it might be found.[3]

≫ Table 2.1	**Product- versus Market-Oriented Business Definitions**	
Company	**Product-Oriented Definition**	**Market-Oriented Definition**
Chipotle	We sell burritos and other Mexican food.	We give customers "Food With Integrity," served with a commitment toward the long-term welfare of customers and the environment.
Facebook	We are an online social network.	We connect people around the world and help them share important moments in their lives.
Home Depot	We sell tools and home repair and improvement items.	We empower consumers to achieve the homes of their dreams.
NASA	We explore outer space.	We reach for new heights and reveal the unknown so that what we do and learn will benefit all humankind.
Revlon	We make cosmetics.	We sell lifestyle and self-expression; success and status; memories, hopes, and dreams.
Ritz-Carlton Hotels & Resorts	We rent rooms.	We create "The Ritz-Carlton experience,"—a memorable stay that far exceeds guests' already high expectations.
Starbucks	We sell coffee and snacks.	We sell "The Starbucks Experience," one that enriches people's lives one moment, one human being, one extraordinary cup of coffee at a time.
Walmart	We run discount stores.	We deliver low prices every day and give ordinary folks the chance to buy the same things as rich people. "Save Money. Live Better."

Finally, as we discovered in the chapter-opening Starbucks story, a company's mission should not be stated as making more sales or profits; profits are only a reward for creating value for customers. Instead, the mission should focus on customers and the customer experience the firm seeks to create. >> Thus, the fast-growing Buffalo Wild Wings restaurant chain's mission isn't just to sell the most wings at a profit:[4]

>> Customer-focused mission: The fast-growing Buffalo Wild Wings chain's mission is to provide a total eating and social environment that "fuels the sports fan experience." As a result, it creates in-store and online experiences that promote brand fan engagement.

Reprinted with permission of Buffalo Wild Wings, Inc.

Customers do, in fact, come to Buffalo Wild Wings ("B-Dubs" to regulars) to eat wings and drink beer, but they also come to watch sports, trash talk, cheer on their sports teams, and meet old friends and make new ones—that is, a total eating and social experience. "We realize that we're not just in the business of selling wings," says the company. "We're something much bigger. We're in the business of fueling the sports fan experience. Our mission is to WOW people every day!" Each table has two types of servers, a food-order server and a "guest experience captain," whose job is to make sure that guests can see whatever game they came to watch on one of the 40 to 60 screens lining the walls, over the bar, and about everywhere else. True to that broader mission, Buffalo Wild Wings creates in-store and online promotions that inspire camaraderie. "It's about giving them tools to not just be spectators but advocates of the brand," says the chain. For example, the brand's very active Web site draws 3 million visitors per month; its Facebook page has more than 12 million fans. Pursuing a customer-focused mission has paid big dividends for Buffalo Wild Wings. The wing joint's sales and profits have both jumped 250 percent in the past four years, and the company brags that it's the number-one brand in its industry for fan engagement. The chain's "hottest wing coating available comes with a warning to B-Dubs customers: 'keep away from eyes, pets, and children.' The sauce is called Blazin'," says one analyst. "That term also happens to be a good description of the stock's performance lately."

Setting Company Objectives and Goals

The company needs to turn its broad mission into detailed supporting objectives for each level of management. Each manager should have objectives and be responsible for reaching them. For example, most Americans know CVS as a chain of retail pharmacies selling prescription and over-the-counter medicines, personal care products, and a host of convenience and other items. But CVS—recently renamed CVS Health—has a much broader mission. >> It views itself as a "pharmacy innovation company," one that is "helping people on their path to better health." The company's motto: "Health is everything."[5]

CVS Health's broad mission leads to a hierarchy of objectives, including business objectives and marketing objectives. CVS Health's overall business objective is to increase access, lower costs, and improve the quality of care. It does this through the products it sells at its retail pharmacies and by taking a more active role in overall health-care management through research, consumer outreach and education, and support of health-related programs and organizations. However, such activities are expensive and must be funded through improved profits, so improving profits becomes another major objective for CVS Health. Profits can be improved by increasing sales or by reducing costs. Sales can be increased by improving customer engagement and raising the company's share of the health-care market. These goals then become the company's current marketing objectives.

Marketing strategies and programs must be developed to support these marketing objectives. To increase customer

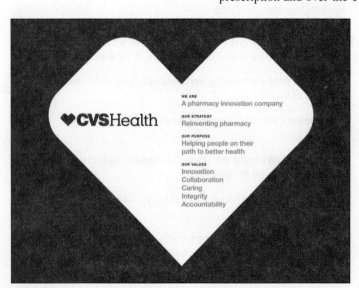

>> CVS Health's overall mission is to be a "pharmacy innovation company" that "helps people on their way to better health." Its marketing strategies and programs must support this mission.

CVS Caremark Corporation

engagement, sales, and market share, CVS Health has reshaped and broadened its lines of products and services. For example, it recently stopped selling tobacco products, items not compatible with its "better health" mission. And it has placed CVS MinuteClinic locations in nearly 1,000 of its more than 7,800 stores, providing walk-in medical care in more than 23 million patient visits since 2000. CVS Health has also broadened its range of customer contact activities to include tailored advising to customers managing chronic and specialty health conditions.

These are CVS Health's broad marketing strategies. Each marketing strategy must then be defined in greater detail. For example, the company's rapidly expanding MinuteClinic services will require more advertising and promotional efforts, and such efforts will need to be spelled out carefully. In this way, CVS Health's broad mission is translated into a set of specific short-term objectives and marketing plans.

Designing the Business Portfolio

Business portfolio
The collection of businesses and products that make up the company.

Guided by the company's mission statement and objectives, management now must plan its **business portfolio**—the collection of businesses and products that make up the company. The best business portfolio is the one that best fits the company's strengths and weaknesses to opportunities in the environment.

Most large companies have complex portfolios of businesses and brands. Strategic and marketing planning for such business portfolios can be a daunting but critical task. For example, ESPN's brand portfolio consists of more than 50 business entities, ranging from multiple ESPN cable channels to ESPN Radio, ESPN.com, *ESPN The Magazine*, and even ESPN Zone sports-themed restaurants. In turn, ESPN is just one unit in the even more complex portfolio of its parent company, The Walt Disney Company. Through skillful portfolio management, however, ESPN has built a cohesive brand, unified powerfully under its mission to serve sports enthusiasts "wherever sports are watched, listened to, discussed, debated, read about, or played" (see Marketing at Work 2.1).

Similarly, GE is a giant $149 billion conglomerate operating in dozens of consumer and business markets, with a broad portfolio of products that "move, power, build, and cure the world." Most consumers know GE for its home appliance and lighting products, part of the company's GE Home & Business Solutions unit. But that's just the beginning for GE. Other company units—such as GE Transportation, GE Aviation, GE Energy Management, GE Power & Water, GE Gas & Oil, GE Healthcare, and others—offer products and services ranging from jet engines, diesel-electric locomotives, wind turbines, and off-shore drilling solutions to aerospace systems and medical imaging equipment. GE Capital offers a breadth of business financial products and services. Successfully managing such a broad portfolio takes plenty of management skill and—as GE's long-running corporate slogan suggests—lots of "Imagination at work."[6]

Business portfolio planning involves two steps. First, the company must analyze its *current* business portfolio and determine which businesses should receive more, less, or no investment. Second, it must shape the *future* portfolio by developing strategies for growth and downsizing.

Analyzing the Current Business Portfolio

Portfolio analysis
The process by which management evaluates the products and businesses that make up the company.

The major activity in strategic planning is business **portfolio analysis**, whereby management evaluates the products and businesses that make up the company. The company will want to put strong resources into its more profitable businesses and phase down or drop its weaker ones.

Management's first step is to identify the key businesses that make up the company, called *strategic business units* (SBUs). An SBU can be a company division, a product line within a division, or sometimes a single product or brand. The company next assesses the attractiveness of its various SBUs and decides how much support each deserves. When designing a business portfolio, it's a good idea to add and support products and businesses that fit closely with the firm's core philosophy and competencies.

MARKETING AT WORK   2.1

ESPN: Skillfully Managing a Complex Brand Portfolio

When you think about ESPN, you probably think of it as a cable TV network, or a magazine, or maybe a Web site. ESPN is all of those things. But over the years, ESPN has grown to become a huge and complex brand portfolio consisting of more than 50 different entities. Thanks to skillful portfolio management, however, ESPN is much more than just a haphazard collection of media entities. Instead, it's an immersive brand experience—a meaningful part of customers' lives. ESPN is synonymous with sports entertainment, inexorably linked with customers' sports memories, realities, and anticipations.

In 1979, entrepreneur Bill Rasmussen took a daring leap and founded the round-the-clock sports network ESPN (Entertainment and Sports Programming Network). Despite many early skeptics—seriously, a 24-hour sports network?—ESPN is now a multibillion-dollar sports empire and a "can't-live-without-it" part of the daily routines of hundreds of millions of people worldwide. Today, ESPN is as much recognized and revered as iconic megabrands such as Coca-Cola, Nike, Apple, and Google. No matter who you are, chances are good that ESPN has touched you in some meaningful way. And no matter what the sport or where, ESPN seems to be everywhere at once.

Here's a brief summary of the incredible variety of entities tied together as part of the ESPN portfolio:

Television: From its original groundbreaking cable network, the ESPN brand has sprouted eight additional U.S. networks—ESPN3D, ESPN2, ESPN Classic, ESPNEWS, ESPNU, ESPN Deportes (Spanish language), the Longhorn Network, and the SEC Network. With its signal now flowing into almost 115 million U.S. households at an industry-topping cost of $6 per household per month—TNT is a distant second at $1.48—ESPN is by far the most-sought cable network. Additionally, ESPN International serves fans through 26 international networks in 61 countries on all seven continents. ESPN is the home of the NBA Finals, WNBA, MLB, Monday Night Football, IndyCar, the NHRA, college football, college basketball, tennis's Grand Slam events, golf's Masters and British Open, the Little League World Series, and more. This list grows every year as ESPN continues to outbid the major broadcast networks to capture the rights to major sports events. For 14 straight years, American men have named ESPN their favorite channel.

Radio: Sports radio is thriving, and ESPN Radio is the largest sports radio network, broadcasting more than 8,500 hours of content annually to 23 million listeners through nearly 500 U.S. affiliates. Overseas, ESPN has radio and syndicated radio programs in 11 countries. ESPN Radio extends its reach even further through Sirius XM, digital distributors Slacker Radio and Tune In, and its own ESPNRadio.com.

Online: ESPN Digital Media is composed of 19 U.S. Web sites, including the flagship ESPN.com. These digital destinations capture some 75 million unique visitors and 6.8 billion minutes of usage every month. ESPN accounts for 31 percent of all online

>> ESPN is much more than just a haphazard collection of media entities. It's a skillfully managed brand portfolio that delivers an immersive sports entertainment experience, inexorably linked with customers' sports memories, realities, and anticipations.
© R Heyes Design/Alamy

sports activity, more than the combined totals of its two closest competitors. ESPNRadio.com is the world's most-listened-to online sports destination. And ESPN's Podcasts are downloaded more than 369 million times per year.

With access to its own content from television, radio, and print, ESPN has a plentiful supply of material to feed its digital efforts. But ESPN also leads the game in the exploding mobile arena. It employs a "mobile first" strategy, in which it orients all of its Web sites around mobile, thus optimizing performance. ESPN delivers mobile sports content via all major U.S. wireless providers—including real-time scores, stats, late-breaking news, and video-on-demand. Its mobile sites and apps lead the sports category in unique visitors and average audience per minute. The digital strategy has led to ESPN3, a multi-screen live 24/7 sports network available at no cost to tens of millions of homes that receive their high-speed Internet connection from an affiliated service provider.

Publishing: When ESPN first published *ESPN The Magazine* in 1998, critics gave it little chance against mighty *Sports Illustrated*. Yet, with its bold look, bright colors, and unconventional format, the ESPN publication now serves more than 15 million readers each month and is the leading publication among men ages 18 to 34. Digital-only consumption of *ESPN The Magazine* is soaring, whereas a relatively stagnate *Sports Illustrated* is struggling to make the shift to a digital world.

Even More: As if all this weren't enough, ESPN also manages events, including the X Games, the Winter X Games, the Bassmaster Classic, the Jimmy V Classic, and several football bowl games. It also develops ESPN-branded consumer products and services, including DVDs, video games, apparel, and even golf schools. If reading all this makes you hungry, you may be near an ESPN Zone, which includes a sports-themed restaurant, interactive games, and sports-related merchandise sales. You'll now find ESPN content in airports and on planes, in health clubs, and even on gas station video panels. All this translates into annual revenues of $11 billion, making ESPN more important to its parent The Walt Disney Company than the Disneyland and Disney World theme parks combined.

What ties this huge collection of ESPN entities together? The brand's customer-focused mission: It wants to serve sports enthusiasts "wherever sports are watched, listened to, discussed, debated, read about, or played." ESPN has a philosophy known as "best available screen." It knows that when fans are at home, they'll watch the big 60-inch flat-screen. But during the morning hours, smartphones light up more. During the day, desktops dominate, and in the evening, tablet activity increases. ESPN is on a crusade to know when, where, and under what conditions fans will reach for which device, and to provide the most seamless, high-quality experience for them.

It's no surprise, then, that sports fans around the world love their ESPN. To consumers everywhere, ESPN means sports. Tech savvy, creative, and often irreverent, the well-managed, ever-extending yet carefully integrated brand portfolio continues to build meaningful customer engagement and experiences. If it has to do with your life and sports—large or small—ESPN covers it for you, anywhere you are, 24/7. Perhaps the company should rename ESPN to stand for Every Sport Possible—Now.

Sources: Dorothy Pomerantz, "Are You Willing to Pay $36 per Month for ESPN?" *Forbes*, March 25, 2015, www.forbes.com/sites/dorothypomerantz/2015/03/25/are-you-willing-to-pay-36-per-month-for-espn/; Anthony Kosner, "Mobile First: How ESPN Delivers to the Best Available Screen," *Forbes*, January 30, 2012, www.forbes.com/sites/anthonykosner/2012/01/30/mobile-first-how-espn-delivers-to-the-best-available-screen/2/; Derek Thompson, "The Global Dominance of ESPN," *The Atlantic*, August 14, 2013, www.theatlantic.com/magazine/archive/2013/09/the-most-valuable-network/309433/; and information from http://espnmediazone.com/us/espn-inc-fact-sheet/ and www.espn.com, accessed September 2015.

The purpose of strategic planning is to find ways in which the company can best use its strengths to take advantage of attractive opportunities in the environment. For this reason, most standard portfolio analysis methods evaluate SBUs on two important dimensions: the attractiveness of the SBU's market or industry and the strength of the SBU's position in that market or industry. The best-known portfolio-planning method was developed by the Boston Consulting Group, a leading management consulting firm.[7]

The Boston Consulting Group Approach. Using the now-classic Boston Consulting Group (BCG) approach, a company classifies all its SBUs according to the **growth-share matrix**, as shown in ≫ **Figure 2.2**. On the vertical axis, *market growth rate* provides a measure of market attractiveness. On the horizontal axis, *relative market share* serves as a measure of company strength in the market. The growth-share matrix defines four types of SBUs:

Growth-share matrix
A portfolio-planning method that evaluates a company's SBUs in terms of market growth rate and relative market share.

1. *Stars.* Stars are high-growth, high-share businesses or products. They often need heavy investments to finance their rapid growth. Eventually their growth will slow down, and they will turn into cash cows.
2. *Cash cows.* Cash cows are low-growth, high-share businesses or products. These established and successful SBUs need less investment to hold their market share. Thus, they produce a lot of the cash that the company uses to pay its bills and support other SBUs that need investment.

≫ **Figure 2.2 The BCG Growth-Share Matrix**

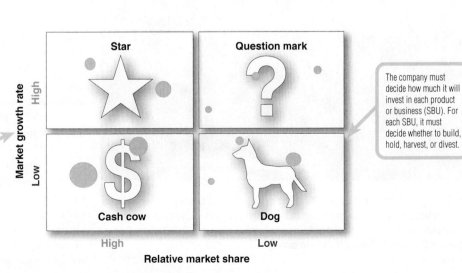

Under the classic BCG portfolio planning approach, the company invests funds from mature, successful products and businesses (cash cows) to support promising products and businesses in faster-growing markets (stars and question marks), hoping to turn them into future cash cows.

The company must decide how much it will invest in each product or business (SBU). For each SBU, it must decide whether to build, hold, harvest, or divest.

Market growth rate — High / Low

Relative market share — High / Low

Star   Question mark

Cash cow   Dog

3. *Question marks.* Question marks are low-share business units in high-growth markets. They require a lot of cash to hold their share, let alone increase it. Management has to think hard about which question marks it should try to build into stars and which should be phased out.

4. *Dogs.* Dogs are low-growth, low-share businesses and products. They may generate enough cash to maintain themselves but do not promise to be large sources of cash.

The 10 circles in the growth-share matrix represent the company's 10 current SBUs. The company has two stars, two cash cows, three question marks, and three dogs. The area of each circle is proportional to the SBU's dollar sales. This company is in fair shape, although not in good shape. It wants to invest in the more promising question marks to make them stars and maintain the stars so that they will become cash as their markets mature. Fortunately, it has two good-sized cash cows. Income from these cash cows will help finance the company's question marks, stars, and dogs. The company should take some decisive action concerning its dogs and its question marks.

Once it has classified its SBUs, the company must determine what role each will play in the future. It can pursue one of four strategies for each SBU. It can invest more in the business unit to *build* its share. Or it can invest just enough to *hold* the SBU's share at the current level. It can *harvest* the SBU, milking its short-term cash flow regardless of the long-term effect. Finally, it can *divest* the SBU by selling it or phasing it out and using the resources elsewhere.

As time passes, SBUs change their positions in the growth-share matrix. Many SBUs start out as question marks and move into the star category if they succeed. They later become cash cows as market growth falls and then finally die off or turn into dogs toward the end of the life cycle. The company needs to add new products and units continuously so that some of them will become stars and, eventually, cash cows that will help finance other SBUs.

Problems with Matrix Approaches. The BCG and other formal methods revolutionized strategic planning. However, such centralized approaches have limitations: They can be difficult, time consuming, and costly to implement. Management may find it difficult to define SBUs and measure market share and growth. In addition, these approaches focus on classifying current businesses but provide little advice for future planning.

Because of such problems, many companies have dropped formal matrix methods in favor of more customized approaches that better suit their specific situations. Moreover, unlike former strategic planning efforts that rested mostly in the hands of senior managers at company headquarters, today's strategic planning has been decentralized. Increasingly, companies are placing responsibility for strategic planning in the hands of cross-functional teams of divisional managers who are close to their markets. In this digital age, such managers have rich and current data at their fingertips and can adapt their plans quickly to meet changing conditions and events in their markets.

Portfolio planning can be challenging. For example, think about The Walt Disney Company. >> Most people think of Disney as theme parks and wholesome family entertainment. But in the mid-1980s, Disney set up a powerful, centralized strategic planning group to guide its direction and growth. Over the next two decades, the strategic planning group turned The Walt Disney Company into a huge and diverse collection of media and entertainment businesses. The sprawling company grew to include everything from theme

>> Managing the business portfolio: Most people think of Disney as theme parks and wholesome family entertainment, but over the past two decades, it's become a sprawling collection of media and entertainment businesses that requires big doses of the famed "Disney Magic" to manage.

Martin Beddall/Alamy

resorts and film studios (Walt Disney Pictures, Touchstone Pictures, Pixar Animation, and Marvel Studios) to media networks (ABC Television plus ESPN, Disney Channel, parts of A&E and the History Channel, and a half dozen others) to consumer products (from apparel and toys to interactive games) and a cruise line.

The newly transformed company proved hard to manage and performed unevenly. To improve company performance, Disney disbanded the centralized strategic planning unit, decentralizing its functions to Disney division managers. For example, although carefully coordinated with other Disney units, in many respects ESPN runs autonomously. As a result of such decisions, The Walt Disney Company retains its position at the head of the world's media conglomerates. And even through the recently uneven economy, Disney's sound strategic management of its broad mix of businesses, plus a touch of the famed Disney magic, has helped it fare better than rival media companies.[8]

Developing Strategies for Growth and Downsizing

Beyond evaluating current businesses, designing the business portfolio involves finding businesses and products the company should consider in the future. Companies need growth if they are to compete more effectively, satisfy their stakeholders, and attract top talent. At the same time, a firm must be careful not to make growth itself an objective. The company's objective must be to manage "profitable growth."

Marketing has the main responsibility for achieving profitable growth for the company. Marketing needs to identify, evaluate, and select market opportunities and lay down strategies for capturing them. One useful device for identifying growth opportunities is the **product/market expansion grid**, shown in ➤➤ **Figure 2.3**.[9] We apply it here to performance sports apparel maker Under Armour:[10]

> Less than 20 years ago, Under Armour introduced its innovative line of comfy, moisture-wicking performance shirts and shorts with the mission "to make all athletes better through passion, design, and the relentless pursuit of innovation." Since then, it has grown at a torrid pace. In just the past five years, Under Armour's sales have quadrupled. Its earnings have grown at a blistering rate of 20 percent in every quarter during that five-year period. Under Armour is now the nation's second-best-selling apparel brand behind Nike. Looking forward, the company must look for new ways to keep growing.

First, Under Armour might consider whether the company can achieve deeper **market penetration**—making more sales in its current product lines and markets. It can spur growth through marketing mix improvements—adjustments to its product design, advertising, pricing, and distribution efforts. For example, Under Armour offers an ever-increasing range of styles and colors in its original apparel lines. And it boosted its spending on advertising and professional athlete and team endorsements last year by 35 percent over the previous year. The company has also added direct-to-consumer distribution channels, including its own retail stores and sales Web sites. Direct-to-consumer sales have tripled over the past seven years and now account for some 30 percent of total revenues.

Second, Under Armour might consider possibilities for **market development**—identifying and developing new markets for its current products. Under Armour can review new *demographic markets*. ➤➤ For instance, the company recently stepped up its marketing to women consumers, with new products and a highly acclaimed $15 million women-focused promotion campaign called "I Will What I Want." Under Armour can also pursue

---

Product/market expansion grid A portfolio-planning tool for identifying company growth opportunities through market penetration, market development, product development, or diversification.

Market penetration Company growth by increasing sales of current products to current market segments without changing the product.

Market development Company growth by identifying and developing new market segments for current company products.

➤➤ **Figure 2.3 The Product/Market Expansion Grid**

Companies can grow by developing new markets for existing products. For example, Under Armour recently stepped up its marketing to women consumers and is expanding rapidly in international markets.

	Existing products	New products
Existing markets	Market penetration	Product development
New markets	Market development	Diversification

Through diversification, companies can grow by starting or buying businesses outside their current product/markets. For example, Under Armour has entered the digital personal health and fitness market by acquiring three fitness app companies.

>> **Strategies for growth:** Under Armour has grown at a blistering rate under its multipronged growth strategy. In recent years, the brand has stepped up its marketing to women, as in its highly acclaimed "I Will" advertising campaign.

UNDER ARMOUR, INC.

Product development
Company growth by offering modified or new products to current market segments.

Diversification
Company growth through starting up or acquiring businesses outside the company's current products and markets.

new *geographical markets*. For example, the brand is rapidly making a name for itself in international markets, including Japan, Europe, Canada, and Latin America. It recently opened its first-ever brand store in China. Although Under Armour's international sales grew 94 percent last year, they still account for only 12 percent of total sales, leaving plenty of room for international growth.

Third, Under Armour can consider **product development**—offering modified or new products to current markets. For example, the company added athletic shoes to its apparel lines in 2006, and it continues to introduce innovative new athletic-footwear products, such as the recently added Under Armour SPEEDFORM line. Sneaker sales rose 44 percent last year yet still account for only about 13 percent of total sales, again leaving plenty of growth potential.

Finally, Under Armour can consider **diversification**—starting up or buying businesses outside of its current products and markets. For example, the company recently expanded into the digital personal health and fitness tracking market by acquiring three fitness app companies—MapMyFitness, MyFitnessPal, and Endomondo. Under Armour might also consider moving into nonperformance leisurewear or begin making and marketing Under Armour fitness equipment. When diversifying, companies must be careful not to overextend their brands' positioning.

Companies must develop not only strategies for growing their business portfolios but also strategies for *downsizing* them. There are many reasons that a firm might want to abandon products or markets. A firm may have grown too fast or entered areas where it lacks experience. The market environment might change, making some products or markets less profitable. For example, in difficult economic times, many firms prune out weaker, less-profitable products and markets to focus their more limited resources on the strongest ones. Finally, some products or business units simply age and die.

When a firm finds brands or businesses that are unprofitable or that no longer fit its overall strategy, it must carefully prune, harvest, or divest them. For example, over the past several years, P&G has sold off dozens of major brands—from Crisco, Folgers, Jif, and Pringles to Duracell batteries, Right Guard deodorant, Aleve pain reliever, CoverGirl and Max Factor cosmetics, Wella and Clairol hair care products, and its Iams and other pet food brands—allowing the company to focus on household care and beauty and grooming products. And in recent years, GM has pruned several underperforming brands from its portfolio, including Oldsmobile, Pontiac, Saturn, Hummer, and Saab. Weak businesses usually require a disproportionate amount of management attention. Managers should focus on promising growth opportunities, not fritter away energy trying to salvage fading ones.

Author Comment
Marketing can't go it alone in creating customer value. Under the company-wide strategic plan, marketing must work closely with other departments to form an effective internal company value chain and with other companies in the marketing system to create an external value delivery network that jointly serves customers.

Planning Marketing: Partnering to Build Customer Relationships

The company's strategic plan establishes what kinds of businesses the company will operate and its objectives for each. Then, within each business unit, more detailed planning takes place. The major functional departments in each unit—marketing, finance, accounting, purchasing, operations, information systems, human resources, and others—must work together to accomplish strategic objectives.

Marketing plays a key role in the company's strategic planning in several ways. First, marketing provides a guiding *philosophy*—the marketing concept—that suggests the company strategy should revolve around creating customer value and building profitable relationships with important consumer groups. Second, marketing provides *inputs* to strategic planners by helping to identify attractive market opportunities and assessing the firm's potential to take advantage of them. Finally, within individual business units, marketing designs *strategies* for reaching the unit's objectives. Once the unit's objectives are set, marketing's task is to help carry them out profitably.

Customer engagement and value are the key ingredients in the marketer's formula for success. However, as noted in Chapter 1, although marketing plays a leading role, it alone cannot produce engagement and superior value for customers. It can be only a partner in attracting, engaging, and growing customers. In addition to *customer relationship management*, marketers must also practice *partner relationship management*. They must work closely with partners in other company departments to form an effective internal *value chain* that serves customers. Moreover, they must partner effectively with other companies in the marketing system to form a competitively superior external *value delivery network*. We now take a closer look at the concepts of a company value chain and a value delivery network.

Partnering with Other Company Departments

Value chain

The series of internal departments that carry out value-creating activities to design, produce, market, deliver, and support a firm's products.

Each company department can be thought of as a link in the company's internal **value chain**.[11] That is, each department carries out value-creating activities to design, produce, market, deliver, and support the firm's products. The firm's success depends not only on how well each department performs its work but also on how well the various departments coordinate their activities.

For example, True Value Hardware's goal is to create customer value and satisfaction by providing shoppers with the hardware and home improvement products they need at affordable prices along with top-notch customer service. Marketers at the retail-owned cooperative play an important role. They learn what customers need and help the 3,500 independent True Value retailers stock their store shelves with the desired products at competitive prices. They prepare advertising and merchandising programs and assist shoppers with customer service. Through these and other activities, True Value marketers help deliver value to customers.

However, True Value's marketers, both at the home office and in stores, need help from the company's other functions. True Value's ability to help you "Start Right. Start Here." depends on purchasing's skill in developing the needed suppliers and buying from them at low cost. True Value's information technology people must provide fast and accurate information about which products are selling in each store. And its operations people must provide effective, low-cost merchandise handling and delivery.

A company's value chain is only as strong as its weakest link. Success depends on how well each group performs its work of adding customer value and on how the company coordinates the activities of various functions. ≫ True Value's recent marketing campaign—"Behind Every Project Is a True Value"—recognizes the importance of having everyone in the organization—from in-store managers and employees to home-office operations

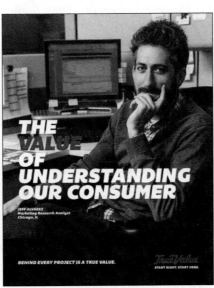

≫ The value chain: These True Value ads recognize that everyone in the organization—from operations managers Tom Statham (left) to marketing research analyst Jeff Alvarez (right)—must contribute to helping the chain's customers handle their home improvement projects. They form the foundation for the brand's "Behind Every Project Is a True Value" positioning.

True Value and Start Right. Start Here. are registered trademarks of True Value Company. The print ads and images are copyrighted works of authorship of True Value Company.

managers and marketing research analysts—understand the needs and aspirations of the chain's do-it-yourself customers and help them handle home improvement projects.

Ideally, then, a company's different functions should work in harmony to produce value for consumers. But, in practice, interdepartmental relations are full of conflicts and misunderstandings. The marketing department takes the consumer's point of view. But when marketing tries to improve customer satisfaction, it can cause other departments to do a poorer job *in their terms*. Marketing department actions can increase purchasing costs, disrupt production schedules, increase inventories, and create budget headaches. Thus, other departments may resist the marketing department's efforts.

Yet marketers must find ways to get all departments to "think consumer" and develop a smoothly functioning value chain. One marketing expert puts it this way: "True market orientation...means that the entire company obsesses over creating value for the customer and views itself as a bundle of processes that profitably define, create, communicate, and deliver value to its target customers.... Everyone must do marketing regardless of function or department." Says another, "Engaging customers today requires commitment from the entire company. We're all marketers now."[12] Thus, whether you're an accountant, an operations manager, a financial analyst, an IT specialist, or a human resources manager, you need to understand marketing and your role in creating customer value.

Partnering with Others in the Marketing System

In its quest to engage customers and create customer value, the firm needs to look beyond its own internal value chain and into the value chains of its suppliers, its distributors, and, ultimately, its customers. Consider McDonald's. People do not swarm to McDonald's only because they love the chain's hamburgers. Consumers flock to the McDonald's *system*, not only to its food products. Throughout the world, McDonald's finely tuned value delivery system delivers a high standard of QSCV—quality, service, cleanliness, and value. McDonald's is effective only to the extent that it successfully partners with its franchisees, suppliers, and others to jointly create "our customers' favorite place and way to eat."

More companies today are partnering with other members of the supply chain—suppliers, distributors, and, ultimately, customers—to improve the performance of the customer **value delivery network**. Competition no longer takes place only between individual competitors. Rather, it takes place between the entire value delivery network created by these competitors. Thus, Ford's performance against Toyota depends on the quality of Ford's overall value delivery network versus Toyota's. Even if Ford makes the best cars, it might lose in the marketplace if Toyota's dealer network provides a more customer-satisfying sales and service experience.

Value delivery network
A network composed of the company, suppliers, distributors, and, ultimately, customers who partner with each other to improve the performance of the entire system in delivering customer value.

 LINKING THE CONCEPTS

Pause here for a moment to apply what you've read in the first part of this chapter.

- Why are we talking about company-wide strategic planning in a marketing text? What *does* strategic planning have to do with marketing?
- What are Starbucks's strategy and mission? What role does marketing play in helping Starbucks to accomplish its strategy and mission?
- What roles do other Starbucks departments play, and how can the company's marketers partner with these departments to maximize overall customer value? What roles do Starbucks's suppliers play?

Author Comment
Now that we've set the context in terms of company-wide strategy, it's time to discuss customer value-driven marketing strategies and programs.

Marketing Strategy and the Marketing Mix

The strategic plan defines the company's overall mission and objectives. Marketing's role is shown in ❯❯ **Figure 2.4**, which summarizes the major activities involved in managing a customer-driven marketing strategy and the marketing mix.

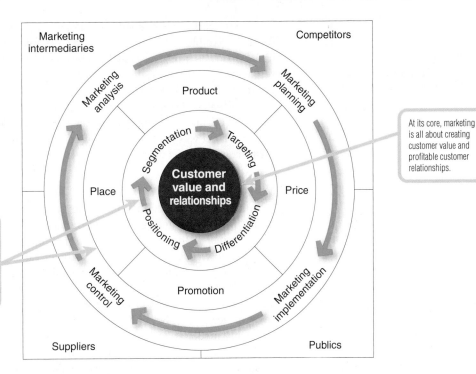

>> Figure 2.4 Managing Marketing Strategies and the Marketing Mix

At its core, marketing is all about creating customer value and profitable customer relationships.

Marketing strategy involves two key questions: Which customers will we serve (segmentation and targeting)? and How will we create value for them (differentiation and positioning)? Then the company designs a marketing program—the four *P*s—that delivers the intended value to targeted consumers.

Marketing strategy

The marketing logic by which the company hopes to create customer value and achieve profitable customer relationships.

Consumers are in the center. The goal is to create value for customers and build profitable customer relationships. Next comes **marketing strategy**—the marketing logic by which the company hopes to create this customer value and achieve these profitable relationships. The company decides which customers it will serve (segmentation and targeting) and how (differentiation and positioning). It identifies the total market and then divides it into smaller segments, selects the most promising segments, and focuses on serving and satisfying the customers in these segments.

Guided by marketing strategy, the company designs an integrated *marketing mix* made up of factors under its control—product, price, place, and promotion (the four *P*s). To find the best marketing strategy and mix, the company engages in marketing analysis, planning, implementation, and control. Through these activities, the company watches and adapts to the actors and forces in the marketing environment. We will now look briefly at each activity. In later chapters, we will discuss each one in more depth.

Customer Value-Driven Marketing Strategy

To succeed in today's competitive marketplace, companies must be customer centered. They must win customers from competitors and then engage and grow them by delivering greater value. But before it can satisfy customers, a company must first understand customer needs and wants. Thus, sound marketing requires careful customer analysis.

Companies know that they cannot profitably serve all consumers in a given market—at least not all consumers in the same way. There are too many different kinds of consumers with too many different kinds of needs. Most companies are in a position to serve some segments better than others. Thus, each company must divide up the total market, choose the best segments, and design strategies for profitably serving chosen segments. This process involves *market segmentation, market targeting, differentiation*, and *positioning*.

Market Segmentation

Market segmentation

Dividing a market into distinct groups of buyers who have different needs, characteristics, or behaviors and who might require separate marketing strategies or mixes.

The market consists of many types of consumers, products, and needs. The marketer must determine which segments offer the best opportunities. Consumers can be grouped and served in various ways based on geographic, demographic, psychographic, and behavioral factors. The process of dividing a market into distinct groups of buyers who have different needs, characteristics, or behaviors and who might require separate marketing strategies or mixes is called **market segmentation**.

Market segment
A group of consumers who respond in a similar way to a given set of marketing efforts.

Every market has segments, but not all ways of segmenting a market are equally useful. For example, Tylenol would gain little by distinguishing between low-income and high-income pain-relief users if both respond the same way to marketing efforts. A **market segment** consists of consumers who respond in a similar way to a given set of marketing efforts. In the car market, for example, consumers who want the biggest, most comfortable car regardless of price make up one market segment. Consumers who care mainly about price and operating economy make up another segment. It would be difficult to make one car model that was the first choice of consumers in both segments. Companies are wise to focus their efforts on meeting the distinct needs of individual market segments.

Market Targeting

Market targeting
The process of evaluating each market segment's attractiveness and selecting one or more segments to enter.

After a company has defined its market segments, it can enter one or many of these segments. **Market targeting** involves evaluating each market segment's attractiveness and selecting one or more segments to enter. A company should target segments in which it can profitably generate the greatest customer value and sustain it over time.

A company with limited resources might decide to serve only one or a few special segments or market niches. Such nichers specialize in serving customer segments that major competitors overlook or ignore. For example, Ferrari sells only 2,200 of its very-high-performance cars in North America each year but at very high prices—such as its Ferrari California model at $198,000 or the 740-horsepower F-12 Berlinetta at an eye-opening $318,000. Most nichers aren't quite so exotic. Profitable low-cost airline Allegiant Air avoids direct competition with larger major airline rivals by targeting smaller, neglected markets and new flyers. Nicher Allegiant "goes where they ain't." And small online-search startup DuckDuckGo thrives among privacy-minded users in the shadows of search giants Google and Microsoft's Bing (see Marketing at Work 2.2).

Alternatively, a company might choose to serve several related segments—perhaps those with different kinds of customers but with the same basic wants. Gap Inc., for example, targets different age, income, and lifestyle clothing and accessory segments with six different store and online brands: Gap, Banana Republic, Old Navy, Piperlime, Athleta, and INTERMIX. The Gap store brand breaks its segment down into even smaller niches, including Gap, GapKids, babyGap, GapMaternity, and GapBody.[13] Or a large company (for example, car companies like Honda and Ford) might decide to offer a complete range of products to serve all market segments.

Most companies enter a new market by serving a single segment; if this proves successful, they add more segments. For example, Nike started with innovative running shoes for serious runners. Large companies eventually seek full market coverage. Nike now makes and sells a broad range of sports apparel and equipment for just about anyone and everyone, in about every sport. It designs different products to meet the special needs of each segment it serves.

Market Differentiation and Positioning

Positioning
Arranging for a product to occupy a clear, distinctive, and desirable place relative to competing products in the minds of target consumers.

Differentiation
Actually differentiating the market offering to create superior customer value.

Marketing mix
The set of tactical marketing tools—product, price, place, and promotion—that the firm blends to produce the response it wants in the target market.

After a company has decided which market segments to enter, it must determine how to differentiate its market offering for each targeted segment and what positions it wants to occupy in those segments. A product's *position* is the place it occupies relative to competitors' products in consumers' minds. Marketers want to develop unique market positions for their products. If a product is perceived to be exactly like others on the market, consumers would have no reason to buy it.

Positioning is arranging for a product to occupy a clear, distinctive, and desirable place relative to competing products in the minds of target consumers. Marketers plan positions that distinguish their products from competing brands and give them the greatest advantage in their target markets.

Audi promises "Truth in Engineering"; Subaru is "Confidence in Motion." Coke is all about "open happiness"; Pepsi says "live for now." Del Monte is "Bursting with Life"; Cascadian Farm products are "Certified Organic. Guaranteed Delicious." At Panera, you can "Live Consciously, Eat Deliciously; at Wendy's, "Quality Is Our Recipe."

Such deceptively simple statements form the backbone of a product's marketing strategy. For example, from its founding, Southwest Airlines has positioned itself as "The LUV Airline," a positioning recently reinforced by the colorful heart in its new logo and plane

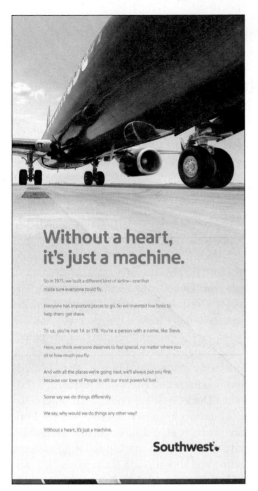

Without a heart, it's just a machine.

So in 1971, we built a different kind of airline—one that made sure everyone could fly.

Everyone has important places to go. So we invented low fares to help them get there.

To us, you're not 1A or 17B. You're a person with a name, like Steve.

Here, we think everyone deserves to feel special, no matter where you sit or how much you fly.

And with all the places we're going next, we'll always put you first, because our love of People is still our most powerful fuel.

Some say we do things differently.

We say, why would we do things any other way?

Without a heart, it's just a machine.

Southwest

>> Positioning: Southwest's positioning as "The LUV Airline" is reinforced by the colorful heart in its new logo and plane redesign. Southwest has "always put heart in everything it does."

Southwest Airlines Co.

graphics design. >> As recent Southwest advertising affirms, "Without a heart, it's just a machine." The airline has "always put Heart in everything it does."

In positioning its brand, a company first identifies possible customer value differences that provide competitive advantages on which to build the position. A company can offer greater customer value by either charging lower prices than competitors or offering more benefits to justify higher prices. But if the company *promises* greater value, it must then *deliver* that greater value. Thus, effective positioning begins with **differentiation**—actually *differentiating* the company's market offering to create superior customer value. Once the company has chosen a desired position, it must take strong steps to deliver and communicate that position to target consumers. The company's entire marketing program should support the chosen positioning strategy.

Developing an Integrated Marketing Mix

After determining its overall marketing strategy, the company is ready to begin planning the details of the **marketing mix**, one of the major concepts in modern marketing. The marketing mix is the set of tactical marketing tools that the firm blends to produce the response it wants in the target market. The marketing mix consists of everything the firm can do to engage consumers and deliver customer value. The many possibilities can be collected into four groups of variables—the four *P*s. >> **Figure 2.5** shows the marketing tools under each *P*.

- *Product* means the goods-and-services combination the company offers to the target market. Thus, a Ford Escape consists of nuts and bolts, spark plugs, pistons, headlights, and thousands of other parts. Ford offers several Escape models and dozens of optional features. The car comes fully serviced and with a comprehensive warranty that is as much a part of the product as the tailpipe.
- *Price* is the amount of money customers must pay to obtain the product. For example, Ford calculates suggested retail prices that its dealers might charge for each Escape. But Ford dealers rarely charge the full sticker price. Instead, they negotiate the price with each customer, offering discounts, trade-in allowances, and credit terms. These actions adjust prices for the current competitive and economic situations and bring them into line with the buyer's perception of the car's value.
- *Place* includes company activities that make the product available to target consumers. Ford partners with a large body of independently owned dealerships that sell the company's many different models. Ford selects its dealers carefully and strongly

>> Figure 2.5 The Four *P*s of the Marketing Mix

The marketing mix—or the four *P*s—consists of tactical marketing tools blended into an integrated program that actually engages target customers and delivers the intended customer value.

MARKETING AT WORK | 2.2

DuckDuckGo: Google's Tiniest, Fiercest Competitor

Google dominates global online search with its massive 67 percent market share. Three other giants—Microsoft's Bing, Yahoo!, and China-based Baidu—combine for another 31 percent of the market. That leaves a precious 2 percent sliver of the market for dozens of other search engines trying to get a foothold. What's more, Google and the other search giants have deep pockets from their non-search businesses, letting them spend abundantly to hold and grow market share. So how does a small search engine wannabe compete against global powerhouses? The best answer: It doesn't—at least not directly. Instead, it finds a unique market niche and runs where the big dogs don't.

Enter DuckDuckGo, a plucky search engine start-up that's carving out its own special market niche. Instead of battling Google and other giants head-on, DuckDuckGo provides a customer benefit that the market leaders can't—privacy. Then it energizes its unique niche with brand personality and user community. One look at DuckDuckGo's icon—a quirky bow-tied duck—gives you the sense that, like the small locomotive in the classic children's story, this might be "the little engine that could."

DuckDuckGo isn't just surviving in its niche, it's exploding. The company is still comparatively tiny—it averages about 9 million daily searches compared with Google's nearly 6 billion. But DuckDuckGo's daily search volume has surged nearly tenfold in just the past three years, whereas Google's volume growth has lagged a bit.

When Gabriel Weinberg first launched DuckDuckGo seven years ago, most people questioned his sanity. How could a small upstart challenge the likes of mighty Google? But rather than simply mimicking Google, Weinberg went a different direction, developing a quality search engine with a key differentiating feature. DuckDuckGo now positions itself strongly on "Smarter Search. Less Clutter. Real Privacy."

DuckDuckGo focuses only on search. It offers a streamlined, clutter-free, customizable user interface with far fewer sponsored ads. As with other search engines, a DuckDuckGo query returns link-by-link search results based on third-party sources, but the results are filtered and reorganized to reduce spam. And beyond the usual search-result links, for many searches, DuckDuckGo provides direct "Instant Answers" in the form of zero-click information boxes above the search results. "When you do a search, you generally want an answer," says Weinberg. "It's our job to try to get an answer." With Instant Answers, DuckDuckGo can "help you get where you want to go in fewer clicks."

The Instant Answer feature is a good one, so good in fact that it has now been copied by Google and Bing. For example, run a Google search for "davinci" or "how long is the great wall" and along with the familiar list of blue links you'll get a white box containing a mini-biography of Leonardo Da Vinci or displaying the length of the Great Wall of China (5,500.3 miles) and other interesting facts about it.

DuckDuckGo would tell you that its Instant Answers are often better. Its answers rely not just on third-party data sources but also on the deep and diverse knowledge of its active, growing, and loyal community of users and developers. DuckDuckGo's community provides additional power behind its searches. In a Wikipedia-like fashion, DuckDuckGo users come up with ideas about what the answers should be, suggest sources, and even develop answers themselves. "DuckDuckGo is a search engine driven by community—you're on the team!" says the company. "We're not just servers and an algorithm. We're so much more."

Still, even though DuckDuckGo had Instant Answers long before Google, Google's response illustrates a typical nicher dilemma. Market leaders usually have huge resources and can quickly copy the start-up's most popular features. "At any point," notes one analyst, "the Googles or Facebooks or Apples of the world can just mimic what made you different, slam-dunking your shattered dreams into the waste bin of tech history."

Fortunately for DuckDuckGo, it has one crucial differentiator that the Googles of the world simply can't mimic. Real privacy. Google's entire model is built around personalization for customers and behaviorally targeted marketing for advertisers. That requires collecting and sharing data about users and their searches. When you search on Google, the company knows and retains in detail who you are, what you've searched for, and when you've searched. It then integrates your online identity and data with its services.

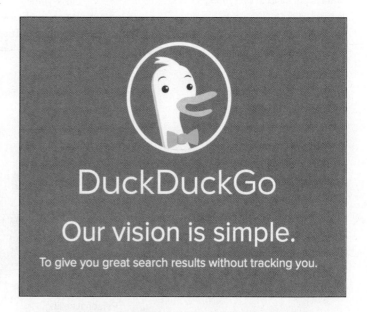

>> **Niche marketing:** DuckDuckGo thrives in the shadows of giant search engine competitors by giving its user community something the Googles of the world can't mimic—real privacy.

Duck Duck Go, Inc.

By contrast, DuckDuckGo is specifically designed to be less invasive and less creepy than its competitors. DuckDuckGo doesn't know who you are. It doesn't log user IP addresses or use cookies to track users over time or other online locations. Users don't have accounts. In fact, DuckDuckGo doesn't even save user search histories. Perhaps most important, when users click on DuckDuckGo's search results links, the linked Web sites don't receive any information generated by the search engine. As one privacy advocate puts it, "DuckDuckGo is a solid search engine that lets you surf the Web without leaving behind a bunch of bread crumbs for Uncle Sam or anyone else to follow.... The sites you visit are being kept at arm's length."

So DuckDuckGo has become the preferred search engine for people concerned about online privacy, and that's a fast-growing group. "If you look at the logs of people's search sessions, they're the most personal thing on the Internet," Weinberg says. "Unlike Facebook, where you choose what to post, with search you're typing in medical and financial problems and all sorts of other things." Today, more and more people are thinking about the privacy implications of their search histories. "It was extreme at the time," says Weinberg of DuckDuckGo's early privacy positioning. But today, he adds, "It's become obvious why people don't want to be tracked."

How does DuckDuckGo make money? Last year, Google made almost all of its $66 billion of revenue from search-related advertising, and most of that business involved large-scale, behaviorally targeted advertising that relies on the very tracking tools that DuckDuckGo shuns. However, even without tracking users, smaller DuckDuckGo can be profitable. It simply focuses on the other part of Google's business—delivering contextual search ads based on the topic of the search itself. So when users search for "curved OLED TVs," DuckDuckGo shows ads and links for TV manufacturers and retailers who've paid for the associated key words.

Thus, in many ways, DuckDuckGo is David to Google's Goliath. But unlike David, DuckDuckGo isn't out to slay the giant. It knows that it can't compete head-on with the Googles and Bings of the world—it doesn't even try. Then again, given the depth of consumer engagement and loyalty that DuckDuckGo engenders in its own small corner of the online search market, Google and the other giants may find it difficult to compete with DuckDuckGo for privacy-minded users. DuckDuckGo is currently the nation's 11th-most-popular search engine based on unique monthly visitors. And as privacy grows in importance, so will DuckDuckGo.

That's what niche marketing is all about—a well-defined brand engaging a focused customer community with meaningful brand relationships that even large and resourceful competitors can't crack. Smart niching has made DuckDuckGo "Google's tiniest, fiercest competitor," says the analyst. "Our vision is simple," says DuckDuckGo. "To give you great search results without tracking you."

Sources: John Paul Titlow, "Inside DuckDuckGo, Google's Tiniest, Fiercest Competitor," *Fast Company*, February 20, 2014, www.fastcompany .com/3026698/inside-duckduckgo-googles-tiniest-fiercest-competitor; "DuckDuckGo Direct Queries per Day," https://duckduckgo.com/traffic.html, accessed June 2015; "Privacy, DuckDuckGo, and the Battle for Search Market Share," *Perioncodefuel*, February 13, 2015, www.codefuel.com/blog/privacy-duckduckgo-battle-search-market-share/; "Top 15 Most Popular Search Engines—April 2015," www.ebizmba.com/articles/search-engines, accessed September 2015; and https://duckduckgo.com/about and www.netmarketshare .com, accessed September 2015.

supports them. The dealers keep an inventory of Ford automobiles, demonstrate them to potential buyers, negotiate prices, close sales, and service the cars after the sale.

- *Promotion* refers to activities that communicate the merits of the product and persuade target customers to buy it. Ford spends nearly $2.6 billion each year on U.S. advertising to tell consumers about the company and its many products.[14] Dealership salespeople assist potential buyers and persuade them that Ford is the best car for them. Ford and its dealers offer special promotions—sales, cash rebates, and low financing rates—as added purchase incentives. And Ford's Facebook, Twitter, YouTube, Instagram, and other social media platforms engage consumers with the brand and with other brand fans.

An effective marketing program blends the marketing mix elements into an integrated marketing program designed to achieve the company's marketing objectives by engaging consumers and delivering value to them. The marketing mix constitutes the company's tactical tool kit for establishing strong positioning in target markets.

Some critics think that the four *P*s may omit or underemphasize certain important activities. For example, they ask, "Where are services? Just because they don't start with a *P* doesn't justify omitting them." The answer is that services, such as banking, airline, and retailing services, are products too. We might call them *service products*. "Where is packaging?" the critics might ask. Marketers would answer that they include packaging as one of many product decisions. All said, as Figure 2.5 suggests, many marketing activities that might appear to be left out of the marketing mix are included under one of the four *P*s. The issue is not whether there should be four, six, or ten *P*s so much as what framework is most helpful in designing integrated marketing programs.

There is another concern, however, that is valid. It holds that the four *P*s concept takes the seller's view of the market, not the buyer's view. From the buyer's viewpoint, in this age of customer value and relationships, the four *P*s might be better described as the four *A*s:[15]

Four *P*s	Four *A*s
Product	Acceptability
Price	Affordability
Place	Accessibility
Promotion	Awareness

Under this more customer-centered framework, *acceptability* is the extent to which the product exceeds customer expectations; *affordability* the extent to which customers are willing and able to pay the product's price; *accessibility* the extent to which customers can readily acquire the product; and *awareness* the extent to which customers are informed about the product's features, persuaded to try it, and reminded to repurchase. The four *A*s relate closely to the traditional four *P*s. Product design influences acceptability, price affects affordability, place affects accessibility, and promotion influences awareness. Marketers would do well to think through the four *A*s first and then build the four *P*s on that platform.

Author Comment
So far we've focused on the *marketing* in marketing management. Now, let's turn to the *management*.

Managing the Marketing Effort

In addition to being good at the *marketing* in marketing management, companies also need to pay attention to the *management*. Managing the marketing process requires the five marketing management functions shown in ≫ **Figure 2.6**—*analysis, planning, implementation, organization,* and *control*. The company first develops company-wide strategic plans and then translates them into marketing and other plans for each division, product, and brand. Through implementation and organization, the company turns the plans into actions. Control consists of measuring and evaluating the results of marketing activities and taking corrective action where needed. Finally, marketing analysis provides the information and evaluations needed for all the other marketing activities.

Marketing Analysis

SWOT analysis
An overall evaluation of the company's strengths (S), weaknesses (W), opportunities (O), and threats (T).

Managing the marketing function begins with a complete analysis of the company's situation. The marketer should conduct a **SWOT analysis** (pronounced "swat" analysis), by which it evaluates the company's overall strengths (S), weaknesses (W), opportunities (O),

≫ **Figure 2.6 Managing Marketing: Analysis, Planning, Implementation, and Control**

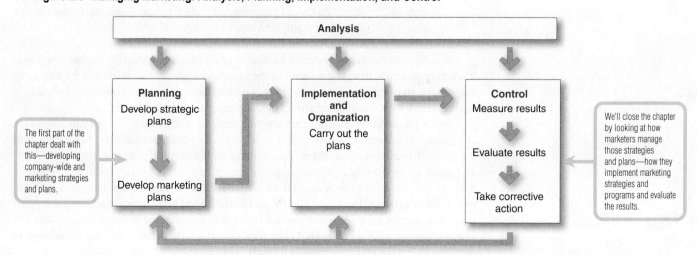

» Figure 2.7 SWOT Analysis: Strengths (S), Weaknesses (W), Opportunities (O), and Threats (T)

The goal of SWOT analysis is to match the company's strengths to attractive opportunities in the environment while eliminating or overcoming the weaknesses and minimizing the threats.

Internal

External

Strengths	Weaknesses
Internal capabilities that may help a company reach its objectives	Internal limitations that may interfere with a company's ability to achieve its objectives

Opportunities	Threats
External factors that the company may be able to exploit to its advantage	Current and emerging external factors that may challenge the company's performance

Positive   **Negative**

Hang on to this figure! SWOT analysis (pronounced "swat" analysis) is a widely used tool for conducting a situation analysis. You'll find yourself using it a lot in the future, especially when analyzing business cases.

and threats (T) (see **» Figure 2.7**). Strengths include internal capabilities, resources, and positive situational factors that may help the company serve its customers and achieve its objectives. Weaknesses include internal limitations and negative situational factors that may interfere with the company's performance. Opportunities are favorable factors or trends in the external environment that the company may be able to exploit to its advantage. And threats are unfavorable external factors or trends that may present challenges to performance.

The company should analyze its markets and marketing environment to find attractive opportunities and identify threats. It should analyze company strengths and weaknesses as well as current and possible marketing actions to determine which opportunities it can best pursue. The goal is to match the company's strengths to attractive opportunities in the environment while simultaneously eliminating or overcoming the weaknesses and minimizing the threats. Marketing analysis provides inputs to each of the other marketing management functions. We discuss marketing analysis more fully in Chapter 3.

Marketing Planning

Through strategic planning, the company decides what it wants to do with each business unit. Marketing planning involves choosing marketing strategies that will help the company attain its overall strategic objectives. A detailed marketing plan is needed for each business, product, or brand. What does a marketing plan look like? Our discussion focuses on product or brand marketing plans.

» Table 2.2 outlines the major sections of a typical product or brand marketing plan. (See Appendix 2 for a sample marketing plan.) The plan begins with an executive summary that quickly reviews major assessments, goals, and recommendations. The main section of the plan presents a detailed SWOT analysis of the current marketing situation as well as potential threats and opportunities. The plan next states major objectives for the brand and outlines the specifics of a marketing strategy for achieving them.

A *marketing strategy* consists of specific strategies for target markets, positioning, the marketing mix, and marketing expenditure levels. It outlines how the company intends to engage target customers and create value in order to capture value in return. In this section, the planner explains how each strategy responds to the threats, opportunities, and critical issues spelled out earlier in the plan. Additional sections of the marketing plan lay out an action program for implementing the marketing strategy along with the details of a supporting *marketing budget*. The last section outlines the controls that will be used to monitor progress, measure return on marketing investment, and take corrective action.

Marketing Implementation

Marketing implementation
Turning marketing strategies and plans into marketing actions to accomplish strategic marketing objectives.

Planning good strategies is only a start toward successful marketing. A brilliant marketing strategy counts for little if the company fails to implement it properly. **Marketing implementation** is the process that turns marketing *plans* into marketing *actions* to

» Table 2.2   Contents of a Marketing Plan

Section	Purpose
Executive summary	Presents a brief summary of the main goals and recommendations of the plan for management review, helping top management find the plan's major points quickly.
Current marketing situation	Describes the target market and the company's position in it, including information about the market, product performance, competition, and distribution. This section includes the following: ● A *market description* that defines the market and major segments and then reviews customer needs and factors in the marketing environment that may affect customer purchasing. ● A *product review* that shows sales, prices, and gross margins of the major products in the product line. ● A review of *competition* that identifies major competitors and assesses their market positions and strategies for product quality, pricing, distribution, and promotion. ● A review of *distribution* that evaluates recent sales trends and other developments in major distribution channels.
Threats and opportunities analysis	Assesses major threats and opportunities that the product might face, helping management to anticipate important positive or negative developments that might have an impact on the firm and its strategies.
Objectives and issues	States the marketing objectives that the company would like to attain during the plan's term and discusses key issues that will affect their attainment.
Marketing strategy	Outlines the broad marketing logic by which the business unit hopes to engage customers, create customer value, and build customer relationships, plus the specifics of target markets, positioning, and marketing expenditure levels. How will the company create value for customers in order to capture value from customers in return? This section also outlines specific strategies for each marketing mix element and explains how each responds to the threats, opportunities, and critical issues spelled out earlier in the plan.
Action programs	Spells out how marketing strategies will be turned into specific action programs that answer the following questions: *What* will be done? *When* will it be done? *Who* will do it? *How* much will it cost?
Budgets	Details a supporting marketing budget that is essentially a projected profit-and-loss statement. It shows expected revenues and expected costs of production, distribution, and marketing. The difference is the projected profit. The budget becomes the basis for materials buying, production scheduling, personnel planning, and marketing operations.
Controls	Outlines the controls that will be used to monitor progress, allow management to review implementation results, and spot products that are not meeting their goals. It includes measures of return on marketing investment.

accomplish strategic marketing objectives. Whereas marketing planning addresses the *what* and *why* of marketing activities, implementation addresses the *who, where, when,* and *how*.

Many managers think that "doing things right" (implementation) is as important as, or even more important than, "doing the right things" (strategy). The fact is that both are critical to success, and companies can gain competitive advantages through effective implementation. One firm can have essentially the same strategy as another yet win in the marketplace through faster or better execution. Still, implementation is difficult—it is often easier to think up good marketing strategies than it is to carry them out.

In an increasingly connected world, people at all levels of the marketing system must work together to implement marketing strategies and plans. At John Deere, for example, marketing implementation for the company's residential, commercial, agricultural, and industrial equipment requires day-to-day decisions and actions by thousands of people both inside and outside the organization. Marketing managers make decisions about target segments, branding, product development, pricing, promotion, and distribution. They talk with engineering about product design, with manufacturing about production and inventory levels, and with finance about funding and cash flows. They also connect with outside people, such as advertising agencies to plan ad campaigns and the news media to obtain publicity support. The sales force urges and supports independent John Deere dealers and large retailers like Lowe's in their efforts to convince residential, agricultural, and industrial customers that "Nothing Runs Like a Deere."

Marketing Department Organization

The company must design a marketing organization that can carry out marketing strategies and plans. If the company is very small, one person might do all the research, selling, advertising, customer service, and other marketing work. As the company expands, however, a marketing department emerges to plan and carry out marketing activities. In large companies, this department contains many specialists—product and market managers, sales managers and salespeople, market researchers, and advertising and social media experts, among others.

To head up such large marketing organizations, many companies have now created a *chief marketing officer* (or CMO) position. This person heads up the company's entire marketing operation and represents marketing on the company's top management team. The CMO position puts marketing on equal footing with other "C-level" executives, such as the chief operating officer (COO) and the chief financial officer (CFO). As a member of top management, the CMO's role is to champion the customer's cause—to be the "chief customer officer." To that end, British Airways even went so far as to rename its top marketing position as Director of Customer Experience.[16]

Modern marketing departments can be arranged in several ways. The most common form of marketing organization is the *functional organization*. Under this organization, different marketing activities are headed by a functional specialist—a sales manager, an advertising manager, a marketing research manager, a customer service manager, or a new product manager. A company that sells across the country or internationally often uses a *geographic organization*. Its sales and marketing people are assigned to specific countries, regions, and districts. Geographic organization allows salespeople to settle into a territory, get to know their customers, and work with a minimum of travel time and cost. Companies with many very different products or brands often create a *product management organization*. Using this approach, a product manager develops and implements a complete strategy and marketing program for a specific product or brand.

For companies that sell one product line to many different types of markets and customers who have different needs and preferences, a *market* or *customer management organization* might be best. A market management organization is similar to the product management organization. Market managers are responsible for developing marketing strategies and plans for their specific markets or customers. This system's main advantage is that the company is organized around the needs of specific customer segments. Many companies develop special organizations to manage their relationships with large customers. For example, companies such as P&G and Stanley Black & Decker have created large teams, or even whole divisions, to serve large customers, such as Walmart, Target, Kroger, or Home Depot.

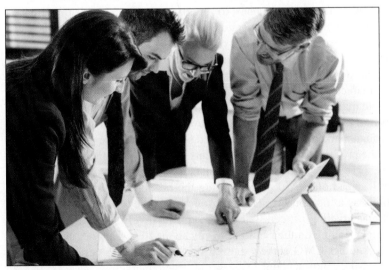

>> **Marketers must continually plan their analysis, implementation, and control activities.**

Kzenon/Shutterstock

Large companies that produce many different products flowing into many different geographic and customer markets usually employ some *combination* of the functional, geographic, product, and market organization forms.

Marketing organization has become an increasingly important issue in recent years. More and more, companies are shifting their brand management focus toward *customer management*—moving away from managing only product or brand profitability and toward managing customer profitability and customer equity. They think of themselves not as managing portfolios of brands but as managing portfolios of customers. And rather than managing the fortunes of a brand, they see themselves as managing customer-brand engagement, experiences, and relationships.

Marketing Control

Marketing control

Measuring and evaluating the results of marketing strategies and plans and taking corrective action to ensure that the objectives are achieved.

Because many surprises occur during the implementation of marketing strategies and plans, marketers must practice constant **marketing control**—measuring and evaluating results and taking corrective action to ensure that the objectives are attained. Marketing control involves four steps. Management first sets specific marketing goals. It then measures its performance in the marketplace and evaluates the causes of any differences between expected and actual performance. Finally, management takes corrective action to close the gaps between goals and performance. This may require changing the action programs or even changing the goals.

Operating control involves checking ongoing performance against the annual plan and taking corrective action when necessary. Its purpose is to ensure that the company achieves the sales, profits, and other goals set out in its annual plan. It also involves determining the profitability of different products, territories, markets, and channels. *Strategic control* involves looking at whether the company's basic strategies are well matched to its opportunities. Marketing strategies and programs can quickly become outdated, and each company should periodically reassess its overall approach to the marketplace.

Author Comment

Measuring marketing return on investment has become a major emphasis. But it can be difficult. For example, a Super Bowl ad reaches more than 100 million consumers but may cost more than $4 million for 30 seconds of airtime. How do you measure the return on such an investment in terms of sales, profits, and building customer engagement and relationships? We'll look at this question again in Chapter 12.

Measuring and Managing Marketing Return on Investment

Marketing managers must ensure that their marketing dollars are being well spent. In the past, many marketers spent freely on big, expensive marketing programs and flashy advertising campaigns, often without thinking carefully about the financial returns on their spending. Their goal was often a general one—to "build brands and consumer preference." They believed that marketing produces intangible creative outcomes, which do not lend themselves readily to measures of productivity or return.

Marketing return on investment (or marketing ROI)

The net return from a marketing investment divided by the costs of the marketing investment.

In today's tighter economic times, however, all that has changed. The free-spending days have been replaced by a new era of marketing measurement and accountability. More than ever, today's marketers are being held accountable for linking their strategies and tactics to measurable marketing performance outcomes. One important marketing performance measure is **marketing return on investment** (or **marketing ROI**). *Marketing ROI* is the net return from a marketing investment divided by the costs of the marketing investment. It measures the profits generated by investments in marketing activities.

In one recent survey, 64 percent of senior marketers rated accountability as a top three concern, well ahead of the 50 percent rating the hot topic of integrated marketing communications as a top concern. However, another survey found that only about 36 percent of chief marketing officers felt able to quantitatively prove the short-term impact of marketing spending on their business; only about 29 percent felt able to prove long-term impact. Another CMO survey showed that a startling 57 percent of CMOs don't take ROI measures into account when setting their marketing budgets, and an even more startling 28 percent said they base their marketing budgets on "gut instinct." Clearly, marketers must think more strategically about the marketing performance returns of their marketing spending.[17]

>> **Figure 2.8**
Marketing Return on Investment

Source: Adapted from Roland T. Rust, Katherine N. Lemon, and Valerie A. Zeithaml, "Return on Marketing: Using Consumer Equity to Focus Marketing Strategy," *Journal of Marketing*, January 2004, p. 112. Used with permission.

Beyond measuring marketing return on investment in terms of standard performance measures such as sales or market share, many companies are using customer relationship measures, such as customer satisfaction, engagement, retention, and equity. These are more difficult to measure but capture both current and future performance.

Marketing ROI can be difficult to measure. In measuring financial ROI, both the *R* and the *I* are uniformly measured in dollars. For example, when buying a piece of equipment, the productivity gains resulting from the purchase are fairly straightforward. As of yet, however, there is no consistent definition of marketing ROI. For instance, returns such as engagement, advertising, and brand-building impact aren't easily put into dollar returns.

A company can assess marketing ROI in terms of standard marketing performance measures, such as brand awareness, sales, or market share. Many companies are assembling such measures into *marketing dashboards*—meaningful sets of marketing performance measures in a single display used to monitor strategic marketing performance. Just as automobile dashboards present drivers with details on how their cars are performing, the marketing dashboard gives marketers the detailed measures they need to assess and adjust their marketing strategies. For example, VF Corporation uses a marketing dashboard to track the performance of its more than 30 lifestyle apparel brands—including Wrangler, Lee, The North Face, Vans, Nautica, 7 For All Mankind, Timberland, and others. VF's marketing dashboard tracks brand equity and trends, share of voice, market share, online sentiment, and marketing ROI in key markets worldwide, not only for VF brands but also for competing brands.[18]

Increasingly, however, beyond standard performance measures, marketers are using customer-centered measures of marketing impact, such as customer acquisition, customer engagement, customer retention, customer lifetime value, and customer equity. These measures capture not only current marketing performance but also future performance resulting from stronger customer relationships. >> **Figure 2.8** views marketing expenditures as investments that produce returns in the form of more profitable customer relationships.[19] Marketing investments result in improved customer value, engagement, and satisfaction, which in turn increase customer attraction and retention. This increases individual customer lifetime values and the firm's overall customer equity. Increased customer equity, in relation to the cost of the marketing investments, determines return on marketing investment.

Regardless of how it's defined or measured, the marketing ROI concept is here to stay. In good times or bad, marketers will be increasingly accountable for the performance outcomes of their activities.

MyMarketingLab

If assigned by your instructor, complete the questions marked with the ⭐ from the EOC Discussion Questions section in the MyLab. To complete the Marketing by the Numbers problems found in this section, go to your Assignments in the MyLab.

REVIEWING AND EXTENDING THE CONCEPTS

CHAPTER REVIEW AND CRITICAL THINKING

Objectives Review

In Chapter 1, we defined marketing and outlined the steps in the marketing process. In this chapter, we examined company-wide strategic planning and marketing's role in the organization. Then we looked more deeply into marketing strategy and the marketing mix and reviewed the major marketing management functions. So you've now had a pretty good overview of the fundamentals of modern marketing.

 OBJECTIVE 2-1   Explain company-wide strategic planning and its four steps. (pp 40–43)

Strategic planning sets the stage for the rest of the company's planning. Marketing contributes to strategic planning, and the overall plan defines marketing's role in the company.

Strategic planning involves developing a strategy for long-run survival and growth. It consists of four steps: (1) defining the company's mission, (2) setting objectives and goals, (3) designing a business portfolio, and (4) developing functional plans. The company's mission should be market oriented, realistic, specific, motivating, and consistent with the market environment. The mission is then transformed into detailed supporting goals and objectives, which in turn guide decisions about the business portfolio. Then each business and product unit must develop detailed marketing plans in line with the company-wide plan.

 OBJECTIVE 2-2   Discuss how to design business portfolios and develop growth strategies. (pp 43–48)

Guided by the company's mission statement and objectives, management plans its business portfolio, or the collection of businesses and products that make up the company. The firm wants to produce a business portfolio that best fits its strengths and weaknesses to opportunities in the environment. To do this, it must analyze and adjust its current business portfolio and develop growth and downsizing strategies for adjusting the future portfolio. The company might use a formal portfolio-planning method. But many companies are now designing more-customized portfolio-planning approaches that better suit their unique situations.

 OBJECTIVE 2-3   Explain marketing's role in strategic planning and how marketing works with its partners to create and deliver customer value. (pp 48–50)

Under the strategic plan, the major functional departments—marketing, finance, accounting, purchasing, operations, information systems, human resources, and others—must work together to accomplish strategic objectives. Marketing plays a key role in the company's strategic planning by providing a marketing concept philosophy and inputs regarding attractive market opportunities. Within individual business units, marketing designs strategies for reaching the unit's objectives and helps to carry them out profitably.

Marketers alone cannot produce superior value for customers. Marketers must practice partner relationship management, working closely with partners in other departments to form an effective *value chain* that serves the customer. And they must also partner effectively with other companies in the marketing system to form a competitively superior value delivery network.

 OBJECTIVE 2-4   Describe the elements of a customer value-driven marketing strategy and mix and the forces that influence it. (pp 50–56)

Customer engagement, value, and relationships are at the center of marketing strategy and programs. Through market segmentation, targeting, differentiation, and positioning, the company divides the total market into smaller segments, selects segments it can best serve, and decides how it wants to bring value to target consumers in the selected segments. It then designs an integrated marketing mix to produce the response it wants in the target market. The marketing mix consists of product, price, place, and promotion decisions (the four *P*s).

 OBJECTIVE 2-5   List the marketing management functions, including the elements of a marketing plan, and discuss the importance of measuring and managing marketing return on investment. (pp 56–61)

To find the best strategy and mix and to put them into action, the company engages in marketing analysis, planning, implementation, and control. The main components of a marketing plan are the executive summary, the current marketing situation, threats and opportunities, objectives and issues, marketing strategies, action programs, budgets, and controls. Planning good strategies is often easier than carrying them out. To be successful, companies must also be effective at implementation—turning marketing strategies into marketing actions.

Marketing departments can be organized in one way or a combination of ways: functional marketing organization, geographic organization, product management organization, or market management organization. In this age of customer relationships, more and more companies are now changing their organizational focus from product or territory management to customer relationship management. Marketing organizations carry out marketing control, both operating control and strategic control.

More than ever, marketing accountability is the top marketing concern. Marketing managers must ensure that their marketing dollars are being well spent. In a tighter economy, today's marketers face growing pressures to show that they are adding value in line with their costs. In response, marketers are developing better measures of marketing return on investment. Increasingly, they are using customer-centered measures of marketing impact as a key input into their strategic decision making.

Key Terms

Objective 2-1
Strategic planning (p 40)
Mission statement (p 41)

Objective 2-2
Business portfolio (p 43)
Portfolio analysis (p 43)
Growth-share matrix (p 45)
Product/market expansion grid (p 47)
Market penetration (p 47)
Market development (p 47)

Product development (p 48)
Diversification (p 48)

Objective 2-3
Value chain (p 49)
Value delivery network (p 50)

Objective 2-4
Marketing strategy (p 51)
Market segmentation (p 51)
Market segment (p 52)

Market targeting (p 52)
Positioning (p 52)
Differentiation (p 53)
Marketing mix (p 53)

Objective 2-5
SWOT analysis (p 56)
Marketing implementation (p 57)
Marketing control (p 60)
Marketing return on investment
  (marketing ROI) (p 60)

Discussion Questions

2-1. Define *strategic planning* and briefly describe the four steps that lead managers and the firm through the strategic planning process. Discuss the role marketing plays in this process. (AASCB: Communication)

2-2. Name and define the four product/market growth strategies. (AACSB: Communications; Reflective Thinking)

⭐ **2-3.** Define each of the four *P*s. What insights might a firm gain by considering the four *A*s rather than the four *P*s? (AACSB: Communication; Reflective Thinking)

2-4. How are marketing departments organized? Which organization is best? (AACSB: Communication, Reflective Thinking)

2-5. Why must marketers practice marketing control, and how is it done? (AACSB: Communication)

Critical Thinking Exercises

2-6. Form a small group and conduct a SWOT analysis for your school, a group that you are a member of, a publicly traded company, a local business, or a nonprofit organization. Based on your analysis, suggest a strategy from the product/market expansion grid and an appropriate marketing mix to implement that strategy. (AACSB: Communication; Reflective Thinking)

2-7. The Boston Consulting Group (BCG) Matrix is a useful strategic tool. Another classic portfolio planning method useful to marketers is the GE/McKinsey Matrix (see

www.quickmba.com/strategy/matrix/ge-mckinsey/). How is the GE/McKinsey Matrix similar to and different from the BCG matrix? (AACSB: Communication; Reflective Thinking)

⭐ **2-8.** Create a mission statement for a nonprofit organization you would be interested in starting. Have another student evaluate your mission statement while you evaluate the other student's statement, suggesting areas of improvement. (AACSB: Communication; Reflective Thinking)

MINICASES AND APPLICATIONS

Online, Mobile, and Social Media Marketing   Google's Mission

Founded in 1998 as an Internet search engine, Google's mission statement remains the same to this day: to "organize the world's information and make it universally accessible and useful." Google is certainly successful, with revenues growing from $3.2 billion in 2002 to $66 billion in 2014, 90 percent of which comes from advertisers. Google is expanding rapidly into other areas well beyond its search engine, such as self-driving cars, smart contact lenses that measure a person's blood sugar levels, Internet-bearing balloons to create Internet hotspots anywhere on earth, and even magnetic nanoparticles to search for disease within the human bloodstream. Google has been on a buying frenzy recently, purchasing security, biotech, and robotic companies in a quest to capitalize on the Internet of Things (IoT) phenomenon. Experts predict there will be 25 million connected devices in our homes and workplaces by 2020. Google recently announced its new IoT operating system, dubbed Brillo (after the Brillo scrubbing pad

because it is a scrubbed-down version of its Android operating system), targeted to developers of smart products connected to the Internet, such as ovens, thermostats, and even toothbrushes. It has also developed Weave, the corresponding IoT language that will allow smart products to speak to each other. Perhaps one day you will be sitting in your Google self-driving car, streaming the news, checking your blood sugar, and cooling your home by turning down your thermostat on the way home from work.

2-9. Conduct research on Google to learn more about its products and services. Some say the time has come for Google to create a new mission statement. Do you agree? Explain. (AACSB: Communication; Reflective Thinking)

2-10. Create a new mission statement for Google that will take it through the rest of this century. (AACSB: Communication; Reflective Thinking)

Marketing Ethics   Family Feud

Otsuka Kagu, a well-known furniture store in Japan, made news recently because of an ugly family feud between the founding father and his daughter. Mr. Otsuka started the store in 1969 and built it into one of Japan's leading furniture retailers, now a publicly traded company. Mr. Otsuka's business model focused on high-end customers using a membership system, large showrooms, customer advisors, and strong relationships with a wide range of suppliers. This strategy worked until the 2008 worldwide financial crisis, when the company started experiencing losses as customers sought out lower-priced rivals like IKEA. As a result, Mr. Otsuka put his daughter in charge as president of the company. Ms. Otsuka cut prices, renovated stores, and created a line of lower-priced walk-in stores, bringing the company back to profitability. Although customers

apparently approved of Ms. Otsuka's actions, her father and many employees did not. So Mr. Otsuka fired his daughter and reverted to the company's original strategy. Mr. Otsuka even went so far as to call his daughter a "bad child" and label her marketing actions "terrorism." When the company's profitability once again suffered, shareholders voted to bring back Ms. Otsuka as president of the company.

2-11. Do you think Mr. Otsuka's demands to continue focusing on high-end customers are reasonable? (AACSB: Communication; Ethical Reasoning)

2-12. Discuss an example of a company that successfully changed its marketing strategy. (AACSB: Communication; Reflective Thinking)

Marketing by the Numbers   Apple Versus Microsoft

In 2014, Apple reported profits of more than $50 billion on sales of $182 billion. For that same period, Microsoft posted a profit of almost $30 billion on sales of $88 billion. So Apple is a better marketer, right? Sales and profits provide information to compare the profitability of these two competitors, but between these numbers is information regarding the efficiency of marketing efforts in creating those sales and profits. Appendix 3, Marketing by the Numbers, discusses other marketing profitability measures beyond the return on marketing investment (marketing ROI) measure described in this chapter. Review the Appendix 2 to answer the questions using the following information from the two companies' incomes statements (all numbers are in thousands):

	Apple	**Microsoft**
Sales	$182,795,000	$86,833,000
Gross Profit	$70,537,000	$59,899,000
Marketing Expenses	$8,994,750	$15,474,000
Net Income (Profit)	$52,503,000	$27,759,000

2-13. Calculate profit margin, net marketing contribution, marketing return on sales (or marketing ROS), and marketing return on investment (or marketing ROI) for each company. Which company is performing better? (AACSB: Communication; Use of IT; Analytic Thinking)

2-14. Go to Yahoo! Finance (http://finance.yahoo.com/) and find the income statements for two other competing companies. Perform the same analyses for these companies that you performed for the previous question. Which company is doing better overall and with respect to marketing? For marketing expenses, use 75 percent of the company's reported "Selling General and Administrative" expenses, as not all of the expenses in that category are marketing expenses. (AACSB: Communication; Analytic Reasoning; Reflective Thinking)

Video Case   Konica Minolta

Konica Minolta has been in business since 1873. For decades, it was a successful photo company selling cameras, equipment, and supplies primarily to final consumers. But dramatic changes in the marketing environment forced the company to reevaluate its marketing strategy and ultimately to abandon what had been its primary industry.

Today, Konica Minolta has a successful business-to-business strategy centered on office equipment and print products for commercial printers. The company has also developed a health-care and medical group, an optics group, and a division that produces components for mobile phones and televisions. With the advent and growth of social media, Konica Minolta's marketing strategy continues to evolve.

After viewing the video featuring Konica Minolta, answer the following questions:

2-15. What is Konica Minolta's mission?

2-16. What market conditions led Konica Minolta to reevaluate its marketing strategy?

2-17. How has Konica Minolta modified its marketing mix? Are these changes in line with its mission?

Company Cases   2 Samsung/1 FedEx/3 Sony

See Appendix 1 for cases appropriate for this chapter. **Case 2, Samsung: A Strategic Plan for Success.** Once an off-brand, strategic planning has made Samsung the number one consumer electronics company. **Case 1, FedEx: Making Every Customer Experience Outstanding.** From the time FedEx opened for business over 40 years ago, the company strategy has been built on a foundation of obsessive customer focus. **Case 3, Sony: Battling the Marketing Environment's "Perfect Storm."** Where Samsung has succeeded through sound strategic planning, Sony is struggling due to the lack thereof.

MyMarketingLab

If assigned by your instructor, complete these writing sections from your Assignments in the MyLab.

2-18. Explain the roles of market segmentation, market targeting, differentiation, and positioning in implementing an effective marketing strategy. (AACSB: Communication)

2-19. Marketers are increasingly held accountable for demonstrating marketing success. Research the various marketing metrics, in addition to those described in the chapter and Appendix 3, used by marketers to measure marketing performance. Write a brief report of your findings. (AACSB: Written and Oral Communication; Reflective Thinking)

3 Analyzing the Marketing Environment

CHAPTER ROAD MAP | Objective Outline

OBJECTIVE 3-1 **Describe the environmental forces that affect the company's ability to serve its customers.** The Microenvironment (68–72); The Macroenvironment (72)

OBJECTIVE 3-2 **Explain how changes in the demographic and economic environments affect marketing decisions.** The Demographic Environment (72–80); The Economic Environment (80–81)

OBJECTIVE 3-3 **Identify the major trends in the firm's natural and technological environments.** The Natural Environment (81–82); The Technological Environment (82–85)

OBJECTIVE 3-4 **Explain the key changes in the political and cultural environments.** The Political and Social Environment (85–88); The Cultural Environment (88–91)

OBJECTIVE 3-5 **Discuss how companies can react to the marketing environment.** Responding to the Marketing Environment (91–93)

Previewing the Concepts

So far, you've learned about the basic concepts of marketing and the steps in the marketing process for engaging and building profitable relationships with targeted consumers. Next, we'll begin digging deeper into the first step of the marketing process—understanding the marketplace and customer needs and wants. In this chapter, you'll see that marketing operates in a complex and changing environment. Other actors in this environment—suppliers, intermediaries, customers, competitors, publics, and others—may work with or against the company. Major environmental forces—demographic, economic, natural, technological, political, and cultural—shape marketing opportunities, pose threats, and affect the company's ability to engage customers and build customer relationships. To develop effective marketing strategies, a company must first understand the environment in which marketing operates.

To start, let's look at Kellogg, the world's largest cereal maker and one of its most recognized and respected brands. Kellogg's cereals have been staples in American homes for generations. However, as demographic, cultural, lifestyle, and other environmental shifts have changed how people eat breakfast, mighty Kellogg has had difficulty adapting. The storied company now finds itself battling to bring modern breakfast eaters back to its table.

First Stop

Kellogg: Losing Its Snap, Crackle, and Pop?

For more than 109 years, ever since the Kellogg brothers of Battle Creek, Michigan, first perfected the process of making toasted corn flakes, the morning bowl of cereal has been a daily ritual in U.S. homes. Generations of sleepy-eyed Americans have bellied up to the breakfast table, filled a bowl with crunchy goodness, and munched their way through enough fuel to fortify them until lunch.

That morning ritual has made Kellogg the world's largest cereal maker. For more than a century, the company's storied brands—such as Kellogg's Corn Flakes, Frosted Flakes, Froot Loops, Rice Krispies, Frosted Mini-Wheats, Raisin Bran, and Special K—have helped define the American breakfast experience.

From its origins, Kellogg has capitalized on environmental trends and shifts, even led them. Before Kellogg, most people ate leftovers for breakfast, a sure-fire path to late-morning indigestion. Then John and Will Kellogg patented the process for making a healthy alternative, "flaked cereal," leading to their first successful product, Kellogg's Corn Flakes. When television appeared in 1950s, Kellogg pioneered the pairing of its cereal brands with familiar animated mascots, such as Tony the Tiger for Frosted Flakes; Toucan Sam for Froot Loops; and Snap, Crackle, and Pop for Rice Krispies. And when cereal sales waned in the 1980s, Kellogg almost single-handedly grew the entire cereal category by 50 percent in just five years by targeting baby boomers with products positioned on nutrition and convenience.

But in recent years, amid a flurry of demographic, cultural, and lifestyle changes, Kellogg's bowl-of-cereal breakfast has lost a lot of its allure. Today, as people increasingly reach for granola bars or Greek yogurt, cold cereal consumption has dipped. As breakfast-eating behavior has changed, however, Kellogg has not. As a result, in recent years, Kellogg's overall revenues and profits have lost their snap, crackle, and pop. Its morning-foods sales—which account for the lion's share of its overall revenues—have been hardest hit. Last year, for example, sales of 19 of Kellogg's 25 top cereals dropped by as much as 14 percent.

Americans simply aren't eating as much cereal these days. Gone are the times when families gathered around the breakfast table before Dad headed off to work while Mom stayed home, made lunches, and got the kids off to school. Cold cereal fit well with that routine. But now, with both parents often working, it's a grab-and-go breakfast world, with little time to linger over a bowl of Raisin Bran and the morning newspaper. "For a while, breakfast cereal was convenience food," says one food historian. "But convenience is relative. It's more convenient [now] to grab a breakfast bar, yogurt, a piece of fruit, or a breakfast sandwich at some fast-food place than to eat a bowl of breakfast cereal." Kellogg does market some grab-and-go breakfast lines—such as Eggo frozen waffles, Pop-Tarts toaster pastries, and Nutri-Grain cereal bars. But the modest gains in those products have done little to offset the bigger losses from Kellogg's powerhouse cereals.

There's another major lifestyle trend affecting Kellogg's cereal business—Americans have become more health-conscious. Increasingly, consumers are looking for food with attributes such as "low-carb,"

>> For generations, Kellogg's storied cereal brands have helped to define the American breakfast experience. But as modern American lifestyles and breakfast-eating behaviors have changed, Kellogg has lost some of its snap, crackle, and pop.

Associated Press

"gluten-free," "organic," and "non-GMO" (genetically modified organisms). That presents a big problem for Kellogg, which churns out box after box of carb-heavy, processed foods made from corn, oats, wheat, and rice.

Increased health concerns also add new weight to long-standing claims by food activists that the cereal industry is peddling junk food to children. "Many of the kid-oriented cereals have a fair amount of sugar in them," says one Kellogg critic. "Their Eggo waffles are mostly white flour. Pop-Tarts are white flour and sugar. For a company that started out as a health-food company, they've turned into something very different." For some discerning breakfast eaters, says one analyst, "Tony the Tiger and Toucan Sam may seem less like friendly childhood avatars and more like malevolent sugar traffickers."

Kellogg has responded to some of these concerns. Over the years it has lowered the amount of sugar in its top-selling children's cereals, added gluten-free and GMO-free cereal varieties, and added healthier extensions such as Raisin Bran with Cranberries and Special K Red Berries, a current best seller. In 2000, Kellogg also purchased Kashi, a California-based health-food cereal brand known for natural and organic ingredients. Leveraging Kellogg's resources and know-how, Kashi's annual revenues grew from $25 million to more than $600 million in less than a decade.

But moves toward a healthier Kellogg have been compromised by decisions that seemed at odds with shifting customer lifestyles and preferences. For example, at the same time that Kellogg was adding healthier options to its mainstream brands, it was weighing

> Kellogg is the world's largest cereal maker. But as demographic, cultural, lifestyle, and other shifts in the marketing environment change how people eat breakfast, mighty Kellogg finds itself battling to bring modern breakfast eaters back to its table.

down its more wholesome brands like Special K and Kashi with less-than-healthy extensions—such as Special K Chocolately Pretzel Bars, Special K Fudge Brownie Bites, Kashi GoLean Vanilla Graham Clusters cereal, and Kashi Blueberry Frozen Waffles—all processed foods loaded with carbs and calories. Kashi also now sells cookies, crackers, pizzas, and frozen entrees in addition to breakfast foods. As a result, these "healthier" Kellogg brands have suffered setbacks. Last year, some Special K versions posted double-digit declines. And the Kashi brand is now struggling with both its identity and its sales. "Kashi is a brand that has lost its way," says an analyst. "Many of its varieties are not organic. Many have GMOs."

Kellogg has plans to reenergize its breakfast sales, such as restoring Kashi's credibility among health-food shoppers and repositioning Special K from a diet brand to one with broader appeal to health-conscious consumers. And the company is busy developing new on-trend breakfast products. Kellogg has also reduced its reliance on cereals with the acquisitions of big snack brands such as Pringles and Keebler—cereal now accounts for 45 percent of its business, down from 70 percent 15 years ago.

Still, some analysts wonder if Kellogg's heart is really into keeping up with new health and lifestyle trends. For example, its recent unveiling of a new gluten-free Special K was largely overshadowed by the enthusiastic introduction of peanut butter and jelly Pop-Tarts, a product largely out of sync with where the U.S. food culture is heading. And although Kellogg has already put 15 new GMO-free cereals on supermarket shelves, behind the scenes the company is spending millions to defeat ballot initiatives in three Western states that would require companies to identify GMO ingredients on their labels. Finally, the Pringles and Keebler acquisitions were more off-trend than on, and they moved the company farther away from its breakfast-foods core.

Despite its recent woes, Kellogg remains a strong, iconic brand. Kellogg's CEO doesn't seem all that worried: "The company has been around for 109 years," he says. "We have the time. We have a plan to turn it around." Some analysts, however, paint a more ominous picture. "Carbs, sugar, and stubbornness are killing Kellogg," says one. Whatever their views, all observers agree that Kellogg is at a critical juncture. As consumers change, Kellogg must change with them. The company's difficulties provide a cautionary tale of what can happen when a company—even a dominant market leader—fails to adapt to its changing marketing environment. Companies that understand and adapt well to their environments can thrive. Those that don't risk their very survival.[1]

A company's **marketing environment** consists of the actors and forces outside marketing that affect marketing management's ability to build and maintain successful relationships with target customers. Like Kellogg, companies must constantly watch and adapt to the changing environment—or, in many cases, lead those changes.

More than any other group in the company, marketers must be environmental trend trackers and opportunity seekers. Although every manager in an organization should watch the outside environment, marketers have two special aptitudes. They have disciplined methods—marketing research and marketing intelligence—for collecting information and developing insights about the marketing environment. They also spend more time in customer and competitor environments. By carefully studying the environment, marketers can adapt their strategies to meet new marketplace challenges and opportunities.

The marketing environment consists of a *microenvironment* and a *macroenvironment*. The **microenvironment** consists of the actors close to the company that affect its ability to engage and serve its customers—the company, suppliers, marketing intermediaries, customer markets, competitors, and publics. The **macroenvironment** consists of the larger societal forces that affect the microenvironment—demographic, economic, natural, technological, political, and cultural forces. We look first at the company's microenvironment.

The Microenvironment

Marketing management's job is to build relationships with customers by creating customer value and satisfaction. However, marketing managers cannot do this alone. >> **Figure 3.1** shows the major actors in the marketer's microenvironment. Marketing success requires building relationships with other company departments, suppliers, marketing intermediaries, competitors, various publics, and customers, which combine to make up the company's value delivery network.

The Company

In designing marketing plans, marketing management takes other company groups into account—groups such as top management, finance, research and development (R&D), purchasing, operations, human resources, and accounting. All of these interrelated groups

Author Comment

The microenvironment includes all the actors close to the company that affect, positively or negatively, its ability to create value for and relationships with customers.

>> Figure 3.1 Actors in the Microenvironment

In creating value for customers, marketers must partner with other firms in the company's value delivery network.

Marketers must work in harmony with other company departments to create customer value and relationships.

Customers are the most important actors in the company's microenvironment. The aim of the entire value delivery system is to serve target customers and create strong relationships with them.

form the internal environment. Top management sets the company's mission, objectives, broad strategies, and policies. Marketing managers make decisions within these broader strategies and plans. Then, as we discussed in Chapter 2, marketing managers must work closely with other company departments. With marketing taking the lead, all departments—from manufacturing and finance to legal and human resources—share the responsibility for understanding customer needs and creating customer value.

Suppliers

Suppliers form an important link in the company's overall customer value delivery network. They provide the resources needed by the company to produce its goods and services. Supplier problems can seriously affect marketing. Marketing managers must watch supply availability and costs. Supply shortages or delays, natural disasters, and other events can cost sales in the short run and damage customer satisfaction in the long run. Rising supply costs may force price increases that can harm the company's sales volume.

Most marketers today treat their suppliers as partners in creating and delivering customer value. For example, Honda knows the importance of building close relationships with its extensive network of suppliers, who furnish everything from fuel tanks, brake controls, and seating systems to production equipment and office supplies.[2]

>> In the United States alone, American Honda purchases $23 billion worth of auto parts and materials annually from 530 strategic suppliers in 34 states. It spends billions of dollars more on maintenance, repair, and operations (MRO) supplies and services from another 13,900 suppliers. Outside purchases represent about 75 percent of the cost of making a Honda vehicle. So Honda views strategic suppliers as key players in its success and develops deep relationships and teamwork with them. "These suppliers are literally considered extensions of Honda," says one insider.

For example, Honda requires that strategic suppliers open up their books and give Honda full access to their financial information. This helps Honda purchasing associates, Honda engineers, and supplier engineers work as a team to achieve target costs and quality standards, often improving suppliers' performance and profit margins in the process. Supplier personnel also participate in Honda training programs on leadership, finance, quality, and other topics. And Honda meets formally each year with strategic suppliers to review the previous year's results and set goals for the coming year. As a result of such teamwork, Honda has developed healthy, long-term supplier relationships. "Almost 100 percent of the original suppliers selected in the late 1980s are still Honda suppliers today," says the insider. In a recent industry survey, automotive suppliers rated Honda the "most preferred" customer among the world's top six auto manufacturers.

>> Suppliers: Through close teamwork, Honda has developed healthy, long-term supplier relationships. Strategic suppliers are considered extensions of Honda, to the benefit of both partners.

(right) © Ian Dagnall/Alamy Stock Photo (left) Bloomberg via Getty Images

Marketing Intermediaries

Marketing intermediaries help the company promote, sell, and distribute its products to final buyers. They include resellers, physical distribution firms, marketing services agencies, and financial intermediaries. *Resellers* are distribution channel firms that help the company find customers or make sales to them. These include wholesalers and retailers that buy and resell merchandise. Selecting and partnering with resellers is not easy. No longer do manufacturers have many small, independent resellers from which to choose. They now face large and growing reseller organizations, such as Walmart, Target, Home Depot, Costco, and Best Buy. These organizations frequently have enough power to dictate terms or even shut smaller manufacturers out of large markets.

Physical distribution firms help the company stock and move goods from their points of origin to their destinations. *Marketing services agencies* are the marketing research firms, advertising agencies, media firms, and marketing consulting firms that help the company target and promote its products to the right markets. *Financial intermediaries* include banks, credit companies, insurance companies, and other businesses that help finance transactions or insure against the risks associated with the buying and selling of goods.

Like suppliers, marketing intermediaries form an important component of the company's overall value delivery network. In its quest to create satisfying customer relationships, the company must do more than just optimize its own performance. It must partner effectively with marketing intermediaries to optimize the performance of the entire system.

Thus, today's marketers recognize the importance of working with their intermediaries as partners rather than simply as channels through which they sell their products. >> For example, when Coca-Cola signs on as the exclusive beverage provider for a fast-food chain, such as McDonald's, Wendy's, or Subway, it provides much more than just soft drinks. It also pledges powerful marketing support:[3]

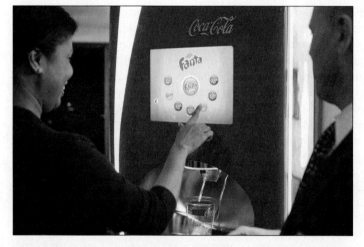

>> **Partnering with intermediaries: Coca-Cola provides its retail partners with much more than just soft drinks. It also pledges powerful marketing support.**
Bloomberg via Getty Images

Coca-Cola assigns cross-functional teams dedicated to understanding the finer points of each retail partner's business. It conducts a staggering amount of research on beverage consumers and shares these insights with its partners. It analyzes the demographics of U.S. zip code areas and helps partners determine which Coke brands are preferred in their areas. Coca-Cola has even studied the design of drive-through menu boards to better understand which layouts, fonts, letter sizes, colors, and visuals induce consumers to order more food and drink. Based on such insights, the Coca-Cola Foodservice group develops marketing programs and merchandising tools that help its retail partners improve their beverage sales and profits. Its Web site, www.CokeSolutions.com, provides retailers with a wealth of information, business solutions, merchandising tips, advice on digital and social media marketing, and techniques on how to go green. "At Coca-Cola we always strive to be our customers' most valued partner," says Coca-Cola's vice president of Foodservice Customer Marketing. Such intense partnering has made Coca-Cola a runaway leader in the U.S. fountain-soft-drink market.

Competitors

The marketing concept states that, to be successful, a company must provide greater customer value and satisfaction than its competitors do. Thus, marketers must do more than simply adapt to the needs of target consumers. They also must gain strategic advantage by positioning their offerings strongly against competitors' offerings in the minds of consumers.

No single competitive marketing strategy is best for all companies. Each firm should consider its own size and industry position compared with those of its competitors. Large firms with dominant positions in an industry can use certain strategies that smaller firms cannot afford. But being large is not enough. There are winning strategies for large firms, but there are also losing ones. And small firms can develop strategies that give them better rates of return than large firms enjoy.

Publics

Public
Any group that has an actual or potential interest in or impact on an organization's ability to achieve its objectives.

The company's marketing environment also includes various publics. A **public** is any group that has an actual or potential interest in or impact on an organization's ability to achieve its objectives. We can identify seven types of publics:

- *Financial publics.* This group influences the company's ability to obtain funds. Banks, investment analysts, and stockholders are the major financial publics.
- *Media publics.* This group carries news, features, editorial opinions, and other content. It includes television stations, newspapers, magazines, and blogs and other social media.
- *Government publics.* Management must take government developments into account. Marketers must often consult the company's lawyers on issues of product safety, truth in advertising, and other matters.
- *Citizen-action publics.* A company's marketing decisions may be questioned by consumer organizations, environmental groups, minority groups, and others. Its public relations department can help it stay in touch with consumer and citizen groups.
- *Local publics.* This group includes neighborhood residents and community organizations. Large companies usually work to become responsible members of the local communities in which they operate. ≫ For example, Office Depot serves its communities through the Office Depot Foundation, an independent, nonprofit foundation that serves as Office Depot's primary charitable giving arm. The foundation supports a variety of programs that give children tools to succeed in school and in life, build the capacity of nonprofit organizations, and help communities prepare for and overcome disasters. The company backs its "Listen Learn Care" mission with several key community programs supporting children, parents, and teachers. Since 2001, the foundation's National Backpack Program has donated new backpacks containing essential school supplies to more than 3.3 million deserving children. The Office Depot Foundation works with the Kids In Need Foundation to fund Ready, Steady, GO! teacher grants that inspire innovative hands-on learning projects in primary and secondary classrooms. And the company's Be The Difference: Speak Up Against Bullying initiative sponsors school assemblies for students, along with anti-bullying education sessions for parents, teachers, and administrators conducted by nationally known experts.[4]
- *General public.* A company needs to be concerned about the general public's attitude toward its products and activities. The public's image of the company affects its buying behavior.
- *Internal publics.* This group includes workers, managers, volunteers, and the board of directors. Large companies use newsletters and other means to inform and motivate their internal publics. When employees feel good about the companies they work for, this positive attitude spills over to the external publics.

≫ **Publics:** The Office Depot Foundation's "Listen Learn Care" mission calls for giving children tools to succeed in school...and in life. Its National Backpack Program has donated new backpacks containing essential school supplies to more than 3.3 million deserving children.
Office Depot Foundation

A company can prepare marketing plans for these major publics as well as for its customer markets. Suppose the company wants a specific response from a particular public, such as goodwill, favorable word of mouth and social sharing, or donations of time or money. The company would have to design an offer to this public that is attractive enough to produce the desired response.

Customers

Customers are the most important actors in the company's microenvironment. The aim of the entire value delivery network is to engage target customers and create strong relationships with them. The company might target any or all of five types of customer markets. *Consumer markets* consist of individuals and households that buy goods and services for personal consumption. *Business markets* buy goods and services for further processing or use in their production processes, whereas *reseller markets* buy goods and services to resell at a profit. *Government markets* consist of government agencies that buy goods and services to produce public services or transfer the goods and services to others who need them. Finally, *international markets* consist of these buyers in other countries, including consumers, producers, resellers, and governments. Each market type has special characteristics that call for careful study by the seller.

Author Comment
The macroenvironment consists of broader forces that affect the actors in the microenvironment.

Demography
The study of human populations in terms of size, density, location, age, gender, race, occupation, and other statistics.

Author Comment
Changes in demographics mean changes in markets, so they are very important to marketers. We first look at the biggest demographic trend—the changing age structure of the population.

The Macroenvironment

The company and all of the other actors operate in a larger macroenvironment of forces that shape opportunities and pose threats to the company. >> **Figure 3.2** shows the six major forces in the company's macroenvironment. Even the most dominant companies can be vulnerable to the often turbulent and changing forces in the marketing environment. Some of these forces are unforeseeable and uncontrollable. Others can be predicted and handled through skillful management. Companies that understand and adapt well to their environments can thrive. Those that don't can face difficult times. One-time dominant market leaders such as Xerox, Sears, and Sony have learned this lesson the hard way. In the remaining sections of this chapter, we examine these forces and show how they affect marketing plans.

The Demographic Environment

Demography is the study of human populations in terms of size, density, location, age, gender, race, occupation, and other statistics. The demographic environment is of major interest to marketers because it involves people, and people make up markets. The world population is growing at an explosive rate. It now exceeds 7.2 billion people and is expected to grow to more than 8 billion by the year 2030.[5] The world's large and highly diverse population poses both opportunities and challenges.

>> **Figure 3.2 Major Forces in the Company's Macroenvironment**

Changes in the world demographic environment have major implications for business. Thus, marketers keep a close eye on demographic trends and developments in their markets. They analyze changing age and family structures, geographic population shifts, educational characteristics, and population diversity. Here, we discuss the most important demographic trends in the United States.

The Changing Age Structure of the Population

The U.S. population currently stands at nearly 321 million and may reach almost 364 million by 2030.[6] The single most important demographic trend in the United States is the changing age structure of the population. Primarily because of falling birthrates and longer life expectancies, the U.S. population is rapidly getting older. In 1980, the median age was 23; by 2050, it is estimated to be 38.[7] This aging of the population will have a significant impact on markets and those who service them.

The U.S. population contains several generational groups. Here, we discuss the four largest groups—the baby boomers, Generation X, the Millennials, and Generation Z—and their impact on today's marketing strategies.

Baby boomers

The 78 million people born during the years following World War II and lasting until 1964.

The Baby Boomers.   The post–World War II baby boom produced 78 million **baby boomers**, who were born between 1946 and 1964. Over the years, the baby boomers have been one of the most powerful forces shaping the marketing environment. The youngest boomers are now in their fifties; the oldest are in their late sixties and well into retirement.

The baby boomers are the wealthiest generation in U.S. history, what one analyst calls "a marketer's dream." Today's baby boomers account for about 35 percent of the U.S. population but control an estimated 70 percent of the nation's disposable income and half of all consumer spending.[8] The boomers constitute a lucrative market for financial services, new housing and home remodeling, new cars, travel and entertainment, eating out, health and fitness products, and just about everything else.

In a recent campaign aimed at convincing companies to advertise in its magazine, the AARP (formerly the American Association of Retired Persons) advises that brands focusing on younger demographics groups are missing a big opportunity. The AARP ads feature people in their 50s and 60s, with headlines such as "I may be creased, but my money is crisp" and "I may be gray, but my money is as green as it gets." The ads continue: "Why is it all about 18–34, when they barely have a dime of their own? The story is simple, AARP…reaches the best boomers, and 68 percent of those over 50 give money to their adult kids."

It would be a mistake to think of the older boomers as phasing out or slowing down. For example, the titles of many magazines targeting boomers suggest that these consumers are anything but the stereotypical faded, poverty-struck shut-ins. >> With titles such as *Everything Zoomer, WatchBoom,* and *BOOM! Magazine,* they appeal to an active boomer generation that is redefining the meaning of growing older:[9]

> *BOOM! Magazine* targets active 50-plus consumers, with an appeal to Live Smart—Live Well—Live Large." The magazine bills itself as "a lifestyle resource for active adults [that] inspires, educates, motivates, and delights readers with a vigorous new image of phase-two living." Monthly topics include health and wellness, travel and leisure, food and wine, history, visual and performing arts, and financial planning. Each issue features local personalities in a *Fifty & Fabulous* spotlight. Fodder for old folks? You won't find much of that in *BOOM! Magazine* or its online newsletter *Boom! Blast.*

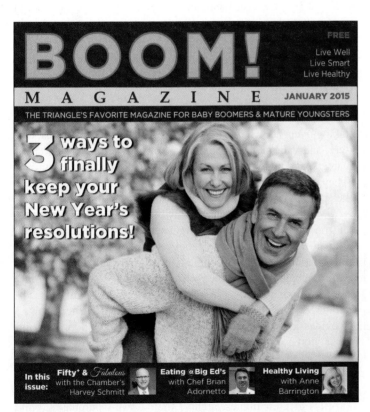

>> **Targeting baby boomers:** *BOOM! Magazine* targets active 50-plus consumers, urging them to "Live Smart—Live Well—Live Large."

Boom! Magazine

Rather than viewing themselves that way, many of today's boomers see themselves as entering new life phases. The more active boomers—sometimes called zoomers—have no intention of abandoning their youthful lifestyles as they age. For example, adults over 50 now account for 80 percent of luxury travel spending in America. Boomers are also digitally active and increasingly social media savvy. They are the fastest-growing demographic online, and nine out of 10 boomers have made an online purchase. They are also the fastest-growing social media users, with an 80 percent surge in Facebook usage over the past four years.[10]

Thus, although the boomers buy lots of products that help them deal with issues of aging—from vitamins to blood pressure monitors to Good Grips kitchen tools—they also constitute a lucrative market for products and services that help them live life to the fullest. For example, Amazon created a site dedicated to customers over 50—called "50+ Active & Healthy Living." The site features four sections catering to health-care, medical, and dietary needs but five sections focused on products for travel and leisure, exercise and fitness, personal care, beauty, and entertainment.

Generation X. The baby boom was followed by a "birth dearth," creating another generation of 49 million people born between 1965 and 1976. Author Douglas Coupland calls them **Generation X** because they lie in the shadow of the boomers.

Considerably smaller than the boomer generation that precedes them and the Millennials who follow, the Generation Xers are a sometimes overlooked consumer group. Although they seek success, they are less materialistic than the other groups; they prize experience, not acquisition. For many of the Gen Xers who are parents, family comes first—both children and their aging parents—and career second. From a marketing standpoint, the Gen Xers are a more skeptical bunch. They tend to research products heavily before they consider a purchase, prefer quality to quantity, and tend to be less receptive to overt marketing pitches. They are more likely to be receptive to irreverent ad pitches that make fun of convention and tradition.

The first to grow up in the Internet era, Generation X is a connected generation that embraces the benefits of new technology. Some 60 percent use a smartphone daily compared with 42 percent of baby boomers. Of the Xers on the Internet, 74 percent use the Internet for banking, 72 percent use it for researching companies or products, and 81 percent have made purchases online. Nearly two-thirds of Xers used Facebook in the last month and 30 percent use Pinterest.[11]

The Gen Xers, now middle-aged, have grown up and are taking over. They have increasingly displaced the lifestyles, culture, and values of the baby boomers. They are firmly into their careers, and many are proud homeowners with growing families. They are the most educated generation to date, and they possess hefty annual purchasing power.

With so much potential, many brands and organizations focus on Gen Xers as a prime target segment. For example, a full 82 percent of Gen Xers own their own homes, making them an important segment for home-and-hearth marketers. ≫ Home improvement retailer Lowe's markets heavily to Gen X homeowners, urging them to "Never Stop Improving." Through ads, online videos, and a substantial social media presence, Lowe's provides ideas and advice on a wide range of indoor and outdoor home improvement projects and problems, providing solutions that make life simpler for busy Gen X homeowners and their families. Its myLowe's app is like a 24/7 home improvement concierge that lets customers build room-by-room profiles of their homes, archive their Lowe's purchases, build product lists with photos, receive reminders for things like changing furnace filters, and even consult with store employees online as they plan out home improvement projects.[12]

Generation X
The 49 million people born between 1965 and 1976 in the "birth dearth" following the baby boom.

≫ **Targeting Gen Xers: Lowe's markets heavily to Gen X homeowners with ideas and advice on home improvement projects and problems, urging them to "Never Stop Improving." The Lowe's Pinterest page is loaded with tips for Gen Xers.**

LOWE'S, the Gable Mansard Design, and NEVER STOP IMPROVING are trademarks or registered trademarks of LF, LLC.

Millennials (or Generation Y)
The 83 million children of the baby boomers born between 1977 and 2000.

Millennials. Both the baby boomers and Gen Xers will one day be passing the reins to the **Millennials** (also called **Generation Y** or the echo boomers). Born between 1977 and 2000, these children of the baby boomers number 83 million or more, dwarfing the Gen Xers and becoming larger even than the baby boomer segment. In the postrecession era, the Millennials are the most financially strapped generation. Facing higher unemployment and saddled with more debt, many of these young consumers have near-empty piggy banks. Still, because of their numbers, the Millennials make up a huge and attractive market, both now and in the future.

One thing that all Millennials have in common is their comfort with digital technology. They don't just embrace technology; it's a way of life. The Millennials were the first generation to grow up in a world filled with computers, mobile phones, satellite TV, iPods and iPads, and online social media. As a result, they engage with brands in an entirely new way, such as with mobile or social media. More than sales pitches from marketers, Millennials seek authenticity and opportunities to shape their own brand experiences and share them with others. One AT&T marketer identifies what she calls "universal Millennial truths: being transparent, authentic, immediate and versatile."[13]

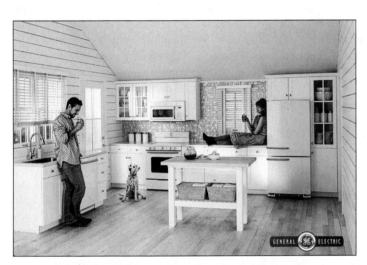

Many brands are now fielding specific products and marketing campaigns aimed at Millennial needs and lifestyles. ⟫ For example, GE has created a new entry-level line of stylish but affordable home appliances called GE Artistry. GE has traditionally focused its marketing and design on consumers ages 45 to 60, who boast fatter wallets and fancier kitchens. However, the GE Artistry line is designed to capture the fast-growing segment of tech-design-savvy but price-conscious Millennials who are buying and equipping their first homes.[14]

Similarly, Marriott and IKEA recently joined forces to launch a new European hotel chain called Moxy Hotels. The innovative lifestyle hotel chain targets the fast-emerging market of young Millennial travelers by combining contemporary design, approachable service, high-tech features, and—perhaps most important—reasonable prices. Moxy hotels offer stylish, no-frills accommodations to keep prices down. But they feature plenty of the technologies that young Millennials favor, such as checking in via mobile devices, big-screen TVs, plenty of built-in USB ports in rooms, free Wi-Fi, and "Plug and Meet" common areas furnished with state-of-the-art computers, writing walls, and large TV screens for presentations.[15]

⟫ **Targeting Millennials: GE's Artistry appliance line is designed to capture the fast-growing segment of tech-design-savvy but price-conscious Millennials who are buying and equipping their first homes.**
GE

Generation Z
People born after 2000 (although many analysts include people born after 1995) who make up the kids, tweens, and teens markets.

Generation Z. Hard on the heels of the Millennials is **Generation Z**, young people born after 2000 (although many analysts include people born after 1995 in this group). The approximately 72 million Gen Zers make up important kids, tweens, and teens markets. They spend an estimated $44 billion annually of their own money and influence a total of almost $200 billion of their own and parents' spending.[16] These young consumers also represent tomorrow's markets—they are now forming brand relationships that will affect their buying well into the future.

Even more than the Millennials, the defining characteristic of Gen Zers is their utter fluency and comfort with digital technologies. Generation Z take smartphones, tablets, Internet-connected game consoles, wireless Internet, and digital and social media for granted—they've always had them—making this group highly mobile, connected, and social. On average, connected Gen Zers receive more than 3,000 texts per month. "If they're awake, they're online," quips one analyst. They have "digital in their DNA," says another.[17]

Gen Zers blend the online and offline worlds seamlessly as they socialize and shop. According to recent studies, despite their youth, more than half of all Generation Z tweens and teens do product research before buying a product or having their parents buy it for them. Of those who shop online, more than half *prefer* shopping online in categories ranging from electronics, books, music, sports equipment, and beauty products to clothes, shoes, and fashion accessories.

>> Targeting Generation Z: By themselves, U.S. "tweens" number 20 million girls and boys who spend billions of dollars annually of their own money and influence billions more of their parents' spending.

© Blend Images/Alamy

>> Companies in almost all industries market products and services aimed at Generation Z. For example, many retailers have created special lines or even entire stores appealing to Gen Z buyers and their parents—consider Abercrombie Kids, Gap Kids, Old Navy Kids, and Pottery Barn Kids. The Justice chain targets tween girls, with apparel and accessories laser-focused on their special preferences and lifestyles. Although these young buyers often have their mothers in tow, "the *last* thing a 10- or 12-year-old girl wants is to look like her mom," says Justice's CEO. Justice's stores, Web site, and social media pages are designed with tweens in mind. "You have to appeal to their senses," says the CEO. "They love sensory overload—bright colors, music videos, a variety of merchandise, the tumult of all of that." Justice now outsells even Walmart and Target in girl's apparel (that's impressive considering that Walmart has almost 4,000 U.S. stores compared with Justice's 1,000).[18]

Marketing to Gen Zers and their parents presents special challenges. Traditional media are still important to this group. Magazines such as J-14 and *Twist* are popular with some Gen Z segments, as are TV channels such as Nickelodeon and the Disney Channel. But marketers know they must meet Gen Zers where they hang out and shop. Increasingly, that's in the online and mobile worlds. Although the under-13 set remains barred from social media such as Facebook and Instagram, at least officially, the social media will play a crucial marketing role as the kids and tweens grow into teens.

Today's kids are notoriously fickle and hard to pin down, and they have short attention spans. The key is to engage these young consumers and let them help to define their brand experiences. Another Generation Z concern involves children's privacy and their vulnerability to marketing pitches. Companies marketing to this group must do so responsibly or risk the wrath of parents and public policy makers.

Generational Marketing. Do marketers need to create separate products and marketing programs for each generation? Some experts warn that marketers need to be careful about turning off one generation each time they craft a product or message that appeals effectively to another. Others caution that each generation spans decades of time and many socioeconomic levels. For example, marketers often split the baby boomers into three smaller groups—leading-edge boomers, core boomers, and trailing-edge boomers—each with its own beliefs and behaviors. Similarly, they split Generaton Z into kids, tweens, and teens.

Thus, marketers need to form more precise age-specific segments within each group. More important, defining people by their birth date may be less effective than segmenting them by lifestyle, life stage, or the common values they seek in the products they buy. We will discuss many other ways to segment markets in Chapters 5 and 6.

The Changing American Family

The traditional household consists of a husband, wife, and children (and sometimes grandparents). Yet the historic American ideal of the two-child, two-car suburban family has lately been losing some of its luster.

In the United States, fewer than half of today's households contain married couples, down from 76 percent in 1940. Married couples with children under 18 represent only 19 percent of the nation's 123 million households. Married couples without children represent 23 percent and single parents are another 14 percent. A full 34 percent are nonfamily households—singles living alone or unrelated adults of one or both sexes living together.[19]

More people are divorcing or separating, choosing not to marry, marrying later, remarrying, or marrying without intending to have children. One in 12 married couples is interracial. The number of same-sex couples raising children has increased 75 percent since 2000. >> The changing composition of today's modern American families is increasingly reflected in popular movies and televisions shows, such as *Modern Family*, the award-winning TV sitcom about an extended nontraditional family.

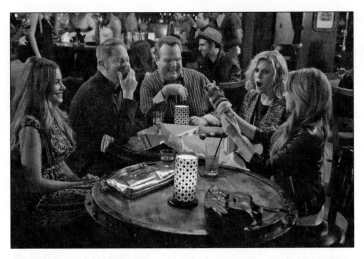

>> The American family: The changing composition of American families is increasingly reflected in popular movies and television shows, such as *Modern Family*, the award-winning TV sitcom about an extended nontraditional family.

Mitch Haddad/Getty Images

Marketers must consider the special needs of nontraditional households because they are now growing more rapidly than traditional households. Each group has distinctive needs and buying habits.

The number of working women has also increased greatly, growing from under 40 percent of the U.S. workforce in the late 1950s to 69 percent today. American women now make up 40 percent of primary family breadwinners. Among households made up of married couples with children, 60 percent are dual-income households; only the husband works in 28.5 percent. Meanwhile, more men are staying home with their children and managing the household while their wives go to work. Four percent of the stay-at-home-parent families have a full-time stay-at-home dad.[20]

Companies are now adapting their marketing to reflect the changing dynamics of American families. For example, whereas fathers were once ignored or portrayed as dolts in family-oriented ads, today's advertisers are showing more caring and capable dads. One recent Samsung Galaxy phone ad, for instance, features a dad swaddling and calming his newborn son while Mom runs errands. When the anxious mom calls home to check in, the newly minted swaddle master replies, "We're having a dudes' day here. We're fiiiiine. You take the *weekend* if you want to."

Other ads reflect the evolving diversity in modern American households. For instance, one ad for Honey Maid graham crackers takes family diversity to a whole new level:[21]

A single 30-second Honey Maid commercial features everything from a same-sex couple bottle-feeding their son, to an interracial couple and their three kids holding hands, to a Hispanic mother and an African-American father with their three mixed-race children. There's even a father covered in body tattoos. The century-old Honey Maid brand—owned by Mondelez, which also makes Oreos, Ritz, and Chips Ahoy—is reinventing itself as a wholesome but relevant snack for today's families. "No matter how things change," says the narrator in the ad, "what makes wholesome never will." The ad concludes: "Honey Maid everyday wholesome snacks. For every wholesome family." Says a Mondelez marketer, no matter what their skin color or sexual orientation, "these families that we portray all have wonderful parent and child connections. This is a recognition that the family dynamic in America is evolving…and we've evolved, too."

Geographic Shifts in Population

This is a period of great migratory movements between and within countries. Americans, for example, are a mobile people, with about 12 percent of all U.S. residents moving each year and 35 percent or more moving every five years. Over the past two decades, the U.S. population has shifted toward the Sunbelt states. The West and South have grown, whereas the Midwest and Northeast states have lost population.[22] Such population shifts interest marketers because people in different regions buy differently. For example, people in the Midwest buy more winter clothing than people in the Southeast.

Also, for more than a century, Americans have been moving from rural to metropolitan areas. In the 1950s, they made a massive exit from the cities to the suburbs. Today, the migration to the suburbs continues. And more and more Americans are moving to "micropolitan areas," small cities located beyond congested metropolitan areas, such as Minot, North Dakota; Boone, North Carolina; Traverse City, Michigan; and Concord, New Hampshire. These smaller micros offer many of the advantages of metro areas—jobs, restaurants, diversions, community organizations—but without the population crush, traffic jams, high crime rates, and high property taxes often associated with heavily urbanized areas. Ten percent of the U.S. population now resides in micropolitan areas.[23]

The shift in where people live has also caused a shift in where they work. For example, the migration toward micropolitan and suburban areas has resulted in a rapid increase in the number of people who "telecommute"—work at home or in a remote office and conduct business by phone or the Internet. This trend, in turn, has created a booming SOHO

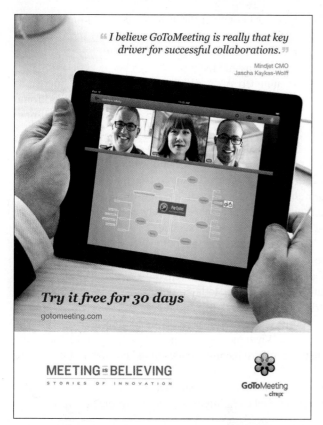

" I believe GoToMeeting is really that key driver for successful collaborations. "

Mindjet CMO
Jascha Kaykas-Wolff

Try it free for 30 days
gotomeeting.com

MEETING IS BELIEVING
S T O R I E S   O F   I N N O V A T I O N

GoToMeeting
by CITRIX

≫ **Telecommuting: Applications like Citrix's GoToMeeting help people meet and collaborate online via computer, tablet, or smartphone, no matter what their work location.**

Citrix Systems, Inc.

(small office/home office) market. Increasing numbers of people are working from home with the help of electronic conveniences such as PCs, smartphones, and broadband Internet access. One recent study estimates that 24 percent of employed individuals do some or all of their work at home.[24]

Many marketers are actively courting the lucrative telecommuting market. ≫ For example, online applications such as Citrix's GoToMeeting and Cisco's WebEx help connect people who telecommute or work remotely. With such applications, people can meet and collaborate online via computer, tablet, or smartphone, no matter what their work location. And companies ranging from Salesforce.com to Google and IBM offer cloud computing applications that let people collaborate anywhere and everywhere through the Internet and mobile devices.[25]

Additionally, for telecommuters who can't work fully at home, companies such as NextSpace, Grind, and Regus rent out fully equipped shared office space. For a daily, monthly, or yearly fee, telecommuters who work away from a main office can rent shared space that includes the same amenities of regular office, from networked computers, printers, and copiers to conference rooms and lounge spaces.[26]

A Better-Educated, More White-Collar, More Professional Population

The U.S. population is becoming better educated. For example, in 2012, 88 percent of the U.S. population over age 25 had completed high school and 32 percent had a bachelor's degree or better, compared with 66 percent and 16 percent, respectively, in 1980.[27] The workforce also is becoming more white collar. Job growth is now strongest for professional workers and weakest for manufacturing workers. Between 2010 and 2020, of 30 detailed occupations projected to have the fastest employment growth, 17 require some type of postsecondary education.[28] The rising number of educated professionals will affect not just what people buy but also how they buy.

Increasing Diversity

Countries vary in their ethnic and racial makeup. At one extreme is Japan, where almost everyone is Japanese. At the other extreme is the United States, with people from virtually all national origins. The United States has often been called a melting pot, where diverse groups from many nations and cultures have melted into a single, more homogenous whole. Instead, the United States seems to have become more of a "salad bowl" in which various groups have mixed together but have maintained their diversity by retaining and valuing important ethnic and cultural differences.

Marketers now face increasingly diverse markets, both at home and abroad, as their operations become more international in scope. The U.S. population is about 62.2 percent non-Hispanic white, with Hispanics at 17.4 percent and African Americans at 13.2 percent. The U.S. Asian American population now totals more than 5.4 percent of the total U.S. population, with the remaining groups being Native Hawaiian, Pacific Islander, American Indian, Eskimo, or Aleut. Moreover, one in eight people living in the United States—more than 13 percent of the population—was born in another country. The nation's ethnic populations are expected to explode in coming decades. By 2060, Hispanics will be about 28 percent of the population, African Americans will be about 14 percent, and Asian Americans will increase to 9 percent.[29]

Most large companies, from P&G, Walmart, Allstate, and Wells Fargo to McDonald's and Southwest Airlines, now target specially designed products, ads, and promotions to one or more of these groups. For example, Southwest Airlines' outreach to Asian Americans includes being the title sponsor for the Chinese New Year Festival and Parade in San Francisco, the biggest nighttime parade in the United States and the second-biggest in North America after the Macy's Thanksgiving Day parade:[30]

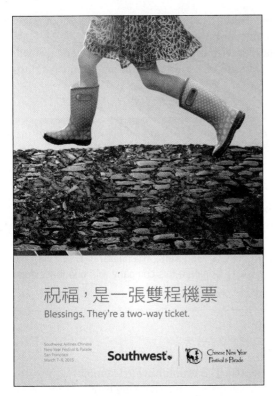

San Francisco's Chinese New Year Festival and Parade typically draws hundreds of thousands of spectators and is broadcast on English- and Asian-language TV stations to viewers around the world. Consumers in the affluent, fast-growing Asian American segment travel often. And they are concentrated in a few key areas such as California and New York, making them easy to pinpoint. That makes them an ideal target for Southwest. The Chinese New Year Festival and Parade event also aligns well with Southwest's preference for grassroots marketing programs that position it as a hometown carrier targeting local "passion points," in this case a cultural and family-related celebration. >> To support its title sponsorship, Southwest ties its brand to the Lunar New Year though promotional efforts ranging from floats and ticket-giveaway contests to "cleverly constructed well wishes and cheerful nods to the community" on street pole banners, bus shelters, billboards, and traditional broadcast and print ads. Something must be working right—Southwest has been the event's title sponsor for more than 15 years.

祝福，是一張雙程機票

Blessings. They're a two-way ticket.

Southwest Airlines Chinese
New Year Festival & Parade
San Francisco
March 7-8, 2015

Southwest | Chinese New Year Festival & Parade

>> **Serving diverse customer communities:** Southwest Airlines reaches out to Asian American consumers through its title sponsorship of San Francisco's Chinese New Year Festival and Parade and through ads like this one, which pass along "cleverly constructed well wishes and cheerful nods to the community."

Southwest Airlines Co.

Diversity goes beyond ethnic heritage. For example, many major companies explicitly target gay and lesbian consumers. According to one estimate, the 6 to 7 percent of U.S. adults who identify themselves as lesbian, gay, bisexual, or transgender (LGBT) have buying power of more than $830 billion.[31] As a result of TV shows such as *Modern Family,* movies like *Brokeback Mountain* and *The Perks of Being a Wallflower,* and openly gay celebrities and public figures such as Neil Patrick Harris, Ellen DeGeneres, David Sedaris, and Apple CEO Tim Cook, the LGBT community has increasingly emerged in the public eye.

Numerous media now provide companies with access to this market. For example, Planet Out Inc., a leading global media and entertainment company that exclusively serves the LGBT community, offers several successful magazines (*Out, The Advocate, Out Traveler*) and Web sites (*Gay.com* and *PlanetOut.com*). In addition, media giant Viacom's MTV Networks offers LOGO, a cable television network aimed at gays and lesbians and their friends and family. LOGO is now available in more than 51 million U.S. households, and its Web site is number one in the LGBT category of digital, mobile, and video streaming. More than 100 mainstream marketers have advertised on LOGO, including Ameriprise Financial, Toyota, Anheuser-Busch, Dell, Levi Strauss, eBay, J&J, Orbitz, Sears, Sony, and Subaru.

Brands in a wide range of industries are now targeting the LGBT community with gay-specific ads and marketing efforts—from Amazon, American Airlines, Allstate, and Apple to luxury jewelry retailer Tiffany. Allstate recently ran an "Everyone deserves to be in good hands" campaign with ads featuring same-sex couples and the hashtag #OutHoldingHands. Brands ranging from Axe to Tiffany have sponsored similar ads. American Airlines has a dedicated LGBT "Rainbow Team," sponsors gay and lesbian community events, and offers a special Web site (www.aa.com/rainbow), Facebook pages, and a Twitter feed featuring LGBT-oriented travel deals, information, and discussion. The airline's focus on gay consumers has earned it double-digit revenue growth from the LGBT community each year for more than a decade.[32]

Another attractive diversity segment is the 57 million U.S. adults with disabilities—a market larger than African Americans or Hispanics—representing anywhere from $200 to $500 billion in annual spending power. Most individuals with disabilities are active consumers. For example, one study found that the segment spends $13.6 billion on 31.7 million business or leisure trips every year. And if certain needs were met, the amount spent on travel could double to $27 billion annually.[33]

How are companies trying to reach consumers with disabilities? Many marketers now recognize that the worlds of people with disabilities and those without disabilities are one in the same. Marketers such as McDonald's, Verizon Wireless, Nike, Samsung, Nordstrom, and Toyota have featured people with disabilities in their mainstream marketing. For instance, a recent Toyota Super Bowl commercial featured Paralympic snowboarder Amy Purdy (also a popular recent finalist on *Dancing with the Stars*) persevering as she trains on the slopes, performs on the dance floor, and poses for a photo shoot, using special prosthetic legs for each task. And, of course, she drives a Toyota.[34]

As the population in the United States grows more diverse, successful marketers will continue to diversify their marketing programs to take advantage of opportunities in fast-growing segments.

 ## LINKING THE CONCEPTS

Stop here and think about how deeply these demographic factors affect all of us and, as a result, marketing strategies.

- Apply these demographic developments to your own life. Discuss some specific examples of how changing demographic factors affect you and your buying behavior.
- Identify a specific company that has done a good job of reacting to the shifting demographic environment—generational segments (baby boomers, Gen Xers, Millennials, or Gen Zers), the changing American family, and increased diversity. Compare this company with one that's done a poor job.

Author Comment

The economic environment can offer both opportunities and threats. For example, in the post–Great Recession era of more sensible consumer spending, "value" has become the marketing watchword.

Economic environment
Economic factors that affect consumer purchasing power and spending patterns.

The Economic Environment

Markets require buying power as well as people. The **economic environment** consists of economic factors that affect consumer purchasing power and spending patterns. Economic factors can have a dramatic effect on consumer spending and buying behavior. For example, until fairly recently, American consumers spent freely, fueled by income growth, a boom in the stock market, rapid increases in housing values, and other economic good fortunes. They bought and bought, seemingly without caution, amassing record levels of debt. However, the free spending and high expectations of those days were dashed by the Great Recession of 2008–2009.

As a result, as discussed in Chapter 1, consumers have now adopted a back-to-basics sensibility in their lifestyles and spending patterns that will likely persist for years to come. They are buying less and looking for greater value in the things they do buy. In turn, *value marketing* has become the watchword for many marketers. Marketers in all industries are looking for ways to offer today's more financially frugal buyers greater value—just the right combination of product quality and good service at a fair price.

You'd expect value pitches from the sellers of everyday products. ❯❯ For example, as Target has shifted emphasis toward the "Pay Less" side of its "Expect More. Pay Less." slogan, the once-chic headlines at the Target.com Web site have been replaced by more practical appeals such as "Our lowest prices of the season," "Fun, sun, save," and "Free shipping, every day." However, these days, even luxury-brand marketers are emphasizing good value. For example, Tiffany has long been known for selling high-end "fine jewelry" and "statement jewelry" at prices of $5,000 to $50,000 or more. However, when the Great Recession eroded Tiffany's high-end sales, the company began offering affordable luxury items—what it calls "fashion jewelry"—priced at as little as $100 to $500. Such relatively affordable items now account for about one-quarter of the Tiffany's sales.[35]

Marketers should pay attention to *income distribution* as well as income levels. Over the past several decades, the rich have grown richer, the middle class has shrunk, and the poor have remained poor. The top 5 percent of American earners get more than 22 percent of the country's adjusted gross income, and the top 20 percent of earners capture 51 percent of all

❯❯ **Economic environment: To serve the tastes of today's more financially frugal buyers, companies like Target are emphasizing the "pay less" side of their value propositions.**
Associated Press

Natural environment
The physical environment and the natural resources that are needed as inputs by marketers or that are affected by marketing activities.

income. In contrast, the bottom 40 percent of American earners get just 11.5 percent of the total income.[36]

This distribution of income has created a tiered market. Many companies—such as Nordstrom and Neiman Marcus—aggressively target the affluent. Others—such as Dollar General, Five Below, and Family Dollar—target those with more modest means. In fact, dollar stores are now the fastest-growing retailers in the nation. Still other companies tailor their marketing offers across a range of markets, from the less affluent to the very affluent. For example, Ford offers cars ranging from the low-priced Ford Fiesta, starting at $13,965, to the luxury Lincoln Navigator SUV, starting at $61,920.

Changes in major economic variables, such as income, cost of living, interest rates, and savings and borrowing patterns, have a large impact on the marketplace. Companies watch these variables by using economic forecasting. Businesses do not have to be wiped out by an economic downturn or caught short in a boom. With adequate warning, they can take advantage of changes in the economic environment.

Author Comment
Today's enlightened companies are developing environmentally sustainable strategies in an effort to create a world economy that the planet can support indefinitely.

The Natural Environment

The **natural environment** involves the physical environment and the natural resources that are needed as inputs by marketers or that are affected by marketing activities. At the most basic level, unexpected happenings in the physical environment—anything from weather to natural disasters—can affect companies and their marketing strategies. For example, during a recent cold winter—in which the term *polar vortex* gusted into the American vocabulary—sales suffered across a wide range of businesses, from florists and auto dealers to restaurants, airlines, and tourist destinations. In contrast, the severe weather boosted demand for products such as salt, snow blowers, winter clothing, and auto repair centers.

Although companies can't prevent such natural occurrences, they should prepare for dealing with them. For example, shipping companies such as FedEx and UPS maintain corps of meteorologists on their staffs to anticipate weather conditions that might inhibit on-time deliveries around the world. "Someone awaiting a package in Bangkok doesn't care if it snowed in Louisville, Kentucky," says a UPS meteorologist. "They want their stuff."[37]

At a broader level, environmental sustainability concerns have grown steadily over the past three decades. In many cities around the world, air and water pollution have reached dangerous levels. World concern continues to mount about the possibilities of global warming, and many environmentalists fear that we soon will be buried in our own trash.

Marketers should be aware of several trends in the natural environment. The first involves growing *shortages of raw materials*. Air and water may seem to be infinite resources, but some groups see long-run dangers. Air pollution chokes many of the world's large cities, and water shortages are already a big problem in some parts of the United States and the world. By 2030,

>> **Natural environment: Companies must prepare for unexpected happenings in the natural environment. For example, FedEx and UPS employ large staffs of meteorologists to anticipate weather conditions that might inhibit on-time deliveries around the world.**

PAUL J. RICHARDS/AFP/GettyImages

more than one in three people in the world will not have enough water to drink.[38] Renewable resources, such as forests and food, also have to be used wisely. Nonrenewable resources, such as oil, coal, and various minerals, pose a serious problem. Firms making products that require these scarce resources face large cost increases even if the materials remain available.

A second environmental trend is *increased pollution*. Industry will almost always damage the quality of the natural environment. Consider the disposal of chemical and nuclear wastes; the dangerous mercury levels in the ocean; the quantity of chemical pollutants in the soil and food supply; and the littering of the environment with nonbiodegradable bottles, plastics, and other packaging materials.

A third trend is *increased government intervention* in natural resource management. The governments of different countries vary in their concern and efforts to promote a clean environment. Some, such as the German government, vigorously pursue environmental quality. Others, especially many poorer nations, do little about pollution, largely because they lack the needed funds or political will.

In the United States, the Environmental Protection Agency (EPA) was created in 1970 to create and enforce pollution standards and conduct pollution research. In the future, companies doing business in the United States can expect continued strong controls from government and pressure groups. Instead of opposing regulation, marketers should help develop solutions to the materials and energy problems facing the world.

Concern for the natural environment has spawned an **environmental sustainability** movement. Today, enlightened companies go beyond what government regulations dictate. They are developing strategies and practices that create a world economy that the planet can support indefinitely. Environmental sustainability means meeting present needs without compromising the ability of future generations to meet their needs.

Many companies are responding to consumer demands with more environmentally responsible products. Others are developing recyclable or biodegradable packaging, recycled materials and components, better pollution controls, and more energy-efficient operations. For example, Timberland's mission is about more than just making rugged, high-quality boots, shoes, clothes, and other outdoor gear. The VF brand is about doing everything it can to reduce the environmental footprint of its products and processes:[39]

> Timberland is on a mission to develop processes and products that cause less harm to the environment and to enlist consumers in the cause. For example, it has a solar-powered distribution center in California and a wind-powered factory in the Dominican Republic. It has installed energy-efficient lighting and equipment retrofits in its facilities and is educating workers about production efficiency. Timberland is constantly looking for and inventing innovative materials that allow it to reduce its impact on the planet while at the same time making better gear. Its Earthkeepers line of boots is made from recycled and organic materials, and the brand has launched footwear collections featuring outsoles made from recycled car tires. Plastic from recycled soda bottles goes into its breathable linings and durable shoe laces. Coffee grounds find a place in its odor-resistant jackets. Organic cotton without toxins makes it into its rugged canvas. To inspire consumers to make more sustainable decisions, Timberland puts Green Index tags on its products that rate each item's ecological footprint in terms of climate impact, chemicals used, and resources consumed. To pull it all together, Timberland launched an Earthkeepers campaign, an online social media effort that seeks to inspire people to take actions to lighten their environmental footprints.

Companies today are looking to do more than just good deeds. More and more, companies are making environmental sustainability a part of their core missions. And they are learning that what's good for customer well-being and the planet can also be good business. For example, Chipotle Mexican Grill has built a thriving business around an environmentally responsible mission of providing "Food With Integrity" (see Marketing at Work 3.1).

Environmental sustainability
Developing strategies and practices that create a world economy that the planet can support indefinitely.

Technological environment
Forces that create new technologies, creating new product and market opportunities.

The Technological Environment

The **technological environment** is perhaps the most dramatic force now shaping our destiny. Technology has released such wonders as antibiotics, robotic surgery, smartphones, and the Internet. It also has released such horrors as nuclear missiles and assault rifles. It has released such mixed blessings as the automobile, television, and credit cards. Our attitude toward technology depends on whether we are more impressed with its wonders or its blunders.

New technologies can offer exciting opportunities for marketers. For example, what would you think about having tiny little transmitters implanted in all the products you buy that would allow tracking of the products from their point of production through use and disposal? Or how about a bracelet with a chip inserted that would let you make and pay for purchases, receive personalized specials at retail locations, or even track your whereabouts or those of friends? On the one hand, such technology would provide many advantages to both buyers and sellers. On the other hand, it could be a bit scary. Either way, with the advent of radio-frequency identification (RFID) transmitters, it's already happening.

Author Comment
Technological advances are perhaps the most dramatic forces affecting today's marketing strategies. Just think about the tremendous impact on marketing of digital technologies—which have exploded in recent years. You'll see examples of the fast-growing world of online, mobile, and social media marketing throughout every chapter, and we'll discuss them in detail in Chapter 14.

MARKETING AT WORK | 3.1

Chipotle's Environmental Sustainability Mission: Food With Integrity

Envision this. You're sitting in a restaurant where the people—from the CEO on down to the kitchen crew—obsess over using only the finest ingredients. They come to work each morning inspired by all the "fresh produce and meats they have to marinate, rice they have to cook, and fresh herbs they have to chop," says the CEO. The restaurant prefers to use sustainable, naturally raised ingredients sourced from local family farms. It's on a mission not just to serve its customers good food but to change the way its entire industry produces food. This sounds like one of those high-falutin', gourmet specialty restaurants, right? Wrong. It's your neighborhood Chipotle Mexican Grill. That's right, it's a fast-food restaurant.

In an age when many fast-feeders seem to be using ever-cheaper ingredients and centralization of food preparation to cut costs and keep prices low, Chipotle is doing just the opposite. The chain's core sustainable mission is to serve "Food With Integrity." What does that mean? The company explains it this way:

> Chipotle is committed to finding the very best ingredients raised with respect for animals, the environment, and farmers. It means serving the very best sustainably raised food possible with an eye to great taste, great nutrition, and great value. It means that we support and sustain family farmers who respect the land and the animals in their care. It means that whenever possible we use meat from animals raised without the use of antibiotics or added hormones. And it means that we source organic and local produce when practical, and that we use dairy from cows raised without the use of synthetic hormones. In other words, "integrity" is kind of a funny word for "good."

When founder and CEO Steve Ells opened the first Chipotle in Denver in 1993, his primary goal was to make the best gourmet burrito around. However, as the chain grew, Ells found that he didn't like the way the ingredients Chipotle used were raised and processed. So, in 2000, Chipotle began developing a supply chain with the goal of producing and using naturally raised, organic, hormone-free, non–genetically modified ingredients. Pursuing this healthy-food mission was no easy task. As the fast-food industry increasingly moved toward low-cost, efficient food processing, factory farms were booming, whereas independent farms producing naturally raised and organic foods were in decline.

To obtain the ingredients it needed, Chipotle had to develop many new sources by supporting family farming and encouraging sustainable farming practices. Such efforts have paid off. For example, when Chipotle first started serving naturally raised pork in 2000, there were only 60 to 70 farms producing meat for the Niman Ranch pork cooperative, an important Chipotle supplier. Now, there are more than 700.

Today, 100 percent of Chipotle's pork and beef comes from producers that meet or exceed its "naturally raised" standards (the animals are raised in a humane way, fed a vegetarian diet, never given hormones, and allowed to display their natural tendencies). Chipotle's goal is to meet that same 100 percent mark for its chicken, its dairy, and even its produce. It then plans to tighten its standards even more.

Sourcing such natural and organic ingredients not only serves Chipotle's sustainability mission, it results in one of the most nutritious, best-tasting fast-food burritos on the market—something the company can brag about to customers. Whereas some fast-food companies intentionally obscure the sometimes less-than-appetizing truths about their ingredients, Chipotle doesn't play that game. Instead, it commits fast-food heresy: Proudly telling customers what's really inside its burritos.

Chipotle chose the "Food With Integrity" slogan because it sends the right message in an appetizing way. "Saying that we don't buy dairy from cows that are given the hormone rBGH is not an appetizing message," says Ells. So the company is building its marketing campaign around the more positive message that food production should be healthier and more ethical. Chipotle communicates this positioning via an integrated mix of traditional and digital promotion venues, ranging from its Farm Team invitation-only loyalty program—by which

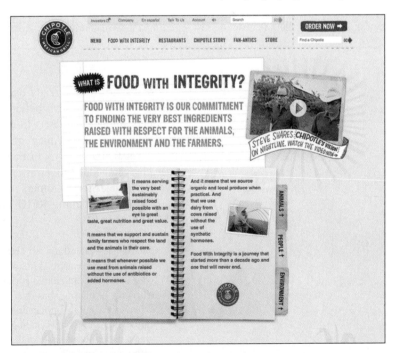

>> Environmental sustainability: What's good for customer well-being and the planet can also be good for business. Chipotle is thriving under its environmentally responsible mission of providing "Food With Integrity."
© Chipotle Mexican Grill, Inc.

customers earn rewards based not on frequent buying but on knowledge about food and how it is produced—to its Pasture Pandemonium smartphone app, where players try to get their pig across a pasture without getting trapped in pens or pricked by antibiotic needles.

While Chipotle doesn't spend much on traditional media advertising, the company uses both traditional and nontraditional promotional methods to broadcast its message. Chipotle made a big splash a few years ago during the broadcast for the Grammy Awards with its first-ever national television ad, "Back to the Start"—a two-and-a-half-minute stop-motion animation film showing the negative effects of industrialized farming. The ad received critical acclaim and racked up millions of views online.

As a follow-up, Chipotle released "The Scarecrow," another animated video indicting the industrial food industry. Accompanied by Fiona Apple's cover of "Pure Imagination," the star character leaves his job at a factory farm and opens his own little shop selling freshly prepared food under the banner "Cultivate a better world." The online ad directed people to the campaign's centerpiece—an arcade-style game app. So far, the video has racked up more than 14 million views on YouTube and more than 9 million people have downloaded the app. Today, Chipotle has moved well beyond ads. The eco-conscious burrito maker is now producing sitcoms with a message. For example, it partnered with Hulu for the original comedy series *Farmed and Dangerous,* attacking the sins of big agriculture.

Companies with a socially responsible business model often struggle to grow and make profits. But Chipotle is proving that a company can do both. Last year, its 45,000 employees chopped, sliced, diced, and grilled their way to $4.1 billion in revenues and $445 million in profits at Chipotle's almost 1,800 U.S. restaurants. And the chain is growing fast, opening a new restaurant about every two days. In the past five years, Chipotle's stock price surged sixfold, suggesting that the company's investors are as pleased as its fast-growing corps of customers.

Founder and CEO Ells wants Chipotle to grow and make money. But ultimately, on a larger stage, he wants to change the way fast food is produced and sold—not just by Chipotle but by the entire industry. "We think the more people understand where their food comes from and the impact that has on independent family farmers [and] animal welfare, the more they're going to ask for better ingredients," says Ells. Whether customers stop by Chipotle's restaurants to support the cause, gobble down the tasty food, or both, it all suits Ells just fine. Chipotle's sustainability mission isn't an add-on, created just to position the company as "socially responsible." Doing good "is the company's ethos and ingrained in everything we do," says Chipotle's director of communications. "Chipotle is a very different kind of company where the deeper you dig into what's happening, the more there is to like and feel good about."

Sources: Based on information and quotes from Denise Lee Yohn, "How Chipotle Changed American Fast Food Forever," *Fast Company,* March 14, 2014, www.fastcompany.com/3027647/lessons-learned/how-chipotle-changed-american-fast-food-forever; Danielle Sacks, "Chipotle: For Exploding All the Rules of Fast Food," *Fast Company,* March 2012, pp. 125–126; John Trybus, "Chipotle's Chris Arnold and the Food With Integrity Approach to Corporate Social Responsibility," *The Social Strategist,* March 22, 2012, https://blogs.commons.georgetown.edu/socialimpact/2012/03/22/the-social-strategist-part-xvi-chipotle%E2%80%99s-chris-arnold-and-the-food-with-integrity-approach-to-corporate-social-responsibility/; Emily Bryson York, "Chipotle Ups the Ante on Its Marketing," *Chicago Tribune,* September 30, 2011, http://articles.chicagotribune.com/2011-09-30/business/ct-biz-chipotle-profile-20110930_1_chipotle-plans-executive-steve-ells-chipotle-founder; Kyle Stock and Venesa Wong, "Chipotle: The Definitive Oral History," *Bloomberg Business,* www.bloomberg.com/graphics/2015-chipotle-oral-history/, accessed June, 2015; and information from www.chipotle.com and www.chipotle.com/en-US/fwi/fwi.aspx, accessed September 2015.

Many firms are already using RFID technology to track products and customers at various points in the distribution channel. For example, Walmart has strongly encouraged suppliers shipping products to its distribution centers to apply RFID tags to their pallets. And retailers such as American Apparel, Macy's, and Bloomingdales are now installing item-level RFID systems in their stores. Fashion and accessories maker Burberry even uses chips imbedded in items and linked to smartphones to provide personalized, interactive experiences for customers in its stores and at runway shows.[40]

>> Disney is taking RFID technology to new levels with its cool new MagicBand RFID wristband:[41]

Wearing a MagicBand at The Walt Disney World Resort opens up a whole new level of Disney's famed magic. After registering for cloud-based MyMagic+ services, with the flick of your wrist you can enter a park or attraction, buy dinner or souvenirs, or even unlock your hotel room. But Disney has only begun to tap the MagicBand's potential for personalizing guest experiences. Future applications could be truly magical. Imagine, for example, the wonder of a child who receives a warm hug from Mickey Mouse or a bow from Prince Charming, who then greets the child by name and wishes her a happy birthday. Imagine animatronics that interact with nearby guests based on personal information supplied in advance. You get separated from family or friends? No problem. A quick scan of your MagicBand at a nearby directory could pinpoint the locations of your entire party. Linked to your Disney phone app, the MagicBand could trigger in-depth information about park features, ride wait times, FastPass check-in alerts, and your reservations schedule. Of course, the MagicBand also offers Disney a potential mother lode of digital data on guest activities and movements in minute detail, helping to improve guest logistics, services, and sales. If all this seems too big-brotherish, there will be privacy options—for example, letting parents opt out of things like characters knowing children's names. In all, such digital technologies promise to enrich the Disney experience for both guests and the company.

>> **Marketing technology: Disney is taking RFID technology to new levels with its cool new MagicBand RFID wristband.**

Bob Croslin

The technological environment changes rapidly, creating new markets and opportunities. However, every new technology replaces an older technology. Transistors hurt the vacuum-tube industry, digital photography hurt the film business, and digital downloads and streaming are hurting the CD and DVD businesses. When old industries fight or ignore new technologies, their businesses decline. Thus, marketers should watch the technological environment closely. Companies that do not keep up will soon find their products outdated. If that happens, they will miss new product and market opportunities.

As products and technologies become more complex, the public needs to know that these items are safe. Thus, government agencies investigate and ban potentially unsafe products. In the United States, the Food and Drug Administration (FDA) has created complex regulations for testing new drugs. The Consumer Product Safety Commission (CPSC) establishes safety standards for consumer products and penalizes companies that fail to meet them. Such regulations have resulted in much higher research costs and longer times between new product ideas and their introduction. Marketers should be aware of these regulations when applying new technologies and developing new products.

Author Comment

Even the strongest free-market advocates agree that the system works best with at least some regulation. But beyond regulation, most companies *want* to be socially responsible. We'll dig deeper into marketing and social responsibility in Chapter 16.

Political environment

Laws, government agencies, and pressure groups that influence or limit various organizations and individuals in a given society.

The Political and Social Environment

Marketing decisions are strongly affected by developments in the political environment. The **political environment** consists of laws, government agencies, and pressure groups that influence or limit various organizations and individuals in a given society.

Legislation Regulating Business

Even the strongest advocates of free-market economies agree that the system works best with at least some regulation. Well-conceived regulation can encourage competition and ensure fair markets for goods and services. Thus, governments develop *public policy* to guide commerce—sets of laws and regulations that limit business for the good of society as a whole. Almost every marketing activity is subject to a wide range of laws and regulations.

Legislation affecting business around the world has increased steadily over the years. The United States and many other countries have many laws covering issues such as competition, fair-trade practices, environmental protection, product safety, truth in advertising, consumer privacy, packaging and labeling, pricing, and other important areas (see >> **Table 3.1**).

Understanding the public policy implications of a particular marketing activity is not a simple matter. In the United States, there are many laws created at the national, state, and local levels, and these regulations often overlap. For example, aspirin products sold in Dallas are governed by both federal labeling laws and Texas state advertising laws. Moreover, regulations are constantly changing; what was allowed last year may now be prohibited, and what was prohibited may now be allowed. Marketers must work hard to keep up with changes in regulations and their interpretations.

Business legislation has been enacted for a number of reasons. The first is to *protect companies* from each other. Although business executives may praise competition, they sometimes try to neutralize it when it threatens them. Therefore, laws are passed to define and prevent unfair competition. In the United States, such laws are enforced by the Federal Trade Commission (FTC) and the Antitrust Division of the Attorney General's office.

>> Table 3.1   Major U.S. Legislation Affecting Marketing

Legislation	Purpose
Sherman Antitrust Act (1890)	Prohibits monopolies and activities (price-fixing, predatory pricing) that restrain trade or competition in interstate commerce.
Federal Food and Drug Act (1906)	Created the Food and Drug Administration (FDA). It forbids the manufacture or sale of adulterated or fraudulently labeled foods and drugs.
Clayton Act (1914)	Supplements the Sherman Act by prohibiting certain types of price discrimination, exclusive dealing, and tying clauses (which require a dealer to take additional products in a seller's line).
Federal Trade Commission Act (1914)	Established the Federal Trade Commission (FTC), which monitors and remedies unfair trade methods.
Robinson-Patman Act (1936)	Amends the Clayton Act to define price discrimination as unlawful. Empowers the FTC to establish limits on quantity discounts, forbid some brokerage allowances, and prohibit promotional allowances except when made available on proportionately equal terms.
Wheeler-Lea Act (1938)	Makes deceptive, misleading, and unfair practices illegal regardless of injury to competition. Places advertising of food and drugs under FTC jurisdiction.
Lanham Trademark Act (1946)	Protects and regulates distinctive brand names and trademarks.
National Traffic and Safety Act (1958)	Provides for the creation of compulsory safety standards for automobiles and tires.
Fair Packaging and Labeling Act (1966)	Provides for the regulation of the packaging and labeling of consumer goods. Requires that manufacturers state what the package contains, who made it, and how much it contains.
Child Protection Act (1966)	Bans the sale of hazardous toys and articles. Sets standards for child-resistant packaging.
Federal Cigarette Labeling and Advertising Act (1967)	Requires that cigarette packages contain the following statement: "Warning: The Surgeon General Has Determined That Cigarette Smoking Is Dangerous to Your Health."
National Environmental Policy Act (1969)	Establishes a national policy on the environment. The 1970 Reorganization Plan established the Environmental Protection Agency (EPA).
Consumer Product Safety Act (1972)	Establishes the Consumer Product Safety Commission (CPSC) and authorizes it to set safety standards for consumer products as well as exact penalties for failing to uphold those standards.
Magnuson-Moss Warranty Act (1975)	Authorizes the FTC to determine rules and regulations for consumer warranties and provides consumer access to redress, such as the class-action suit.
Children's Television Act (1990)	Limits the number of commercials aired during children's programs.
Nutrition Labeling and Education Act (1990)	Requires that food product labels provide detailed nutritional information.
Telephone Consumer Protection Act (1991)	Establishes procedures to avoid unwanted telephone solicitations. Limits marketers' use of automatic telephone dialing systems and artificial or prerecorded voices.
Americans with Disabilities Act (1991)	Makes discrimination against people with disabilities illegal in public accommodations, transportation, and telecommunications.
Children's Online Privacy Protection Act (2000)	Prohibits Web sites or online services operators from collecting personal information from children without obtaining consent from a parent and allowing parents to review information collected from their children.
Do-Not-Call Implementation Act (2003)	Authorizes the FTC to collect fees from sellers and telemarketers for the implementation and enforcement of a national Do-Not-Call Registry.
CAN-SPAM Act (2003)	Regulates the distribution and content of unsolicited commercial email.
Financial Reform Law (2010)	Created the Bureau of Consumer Financial Protection, which writes and enforces rules for the marketing of financial products to consumers. It is also responsible for enforcement of the Truth-in-Lending Act, the Home Mortgage Disclosure Act, and other laws designed to protect consumers.

The second purpose of government regulation is to *protect consumers* from unfair business practices. Some firms, if left alone, would make shoddy products, invade consumer privacy, mislead consumers in their advertising, and deceive consumers through their packaging and pricing. Rules defining and regulating unfair business practices are enforced by various agencies.

The third purpose of government regulation is to *protect the interests of society* against unrestrained business behavior. Profitable business activity does not always create a better quality of life. Regulation arises to ensure that firms take responsibility for the social costs of their production or products.

International marketers will encounter dozens, or even hundreds, of agencies set up to enforce trade policies and regulations. In the United States, Congress has established federal regulatory agencies, such as the FTC, the FDA, the Federal Communications Commission, the Federal Energy Regulatory Commission, the Federal Aviation Administration, the Consumer Product Safety Commission, the Environmental Protection Agency, and hundreds of others. Because such government agencies have some discretion in enforcing the laws, they can have a major impact on a company's marketing performance.

New laws and their enforcement will continue to increase. Business executives must watch these developments when planning their products and marketing programs. Marketers need to know about the major laws protecting competition, consumers, and society. They need to understand these laws at the local, state, national, and international levels.

Increased Emphasis on Ethics and Socially Responsible Actions

Written regulations cannot possibly cover all potential marketing abuses, and existing laws are often difficult to enforce. However, beyond written laws and regulations, business is also governed by social codes and rules of professional ethics.

Socially Responsible Behavior. Enlightened companies encourage their managers to look beyond what the regulatory system allows and simply "do the right thing." These socially responsible firms actively seek out ways to protect the long-run interests of their consumers and the environment.

Almost every aspect of marketing involves ethics and social responsibility issues. Unfortunately, because these issues usually involve conflicting interests, well-meaning people can honestly disagree about the right course of action in a given situation. Thus, many industrial and professional trade associations have suggested codes of ethics. And more companies are now developing policies, guidelines, and other responses to complex social responsibility issues.

The boom in online, mobile, and social media marketing has created a new set of social and ethical issues. Critics worry most about online privacy issues. There has been an explosion in the amount of personal digital data available. Users themselves supply some of it. They voluntarily place highly private information on social media sites, such as Facebook or LinkedIn, or on genealogy sites that are easily searched by anyone with a computer or a smartphone.

However, much of the information is systematically developed by businesses seeking to learn more about their customers, often without consumers realizing that they are under the microscope. Legitimate businesses track consumers' online browsing and buying behavior and collect, analyze, and share digital data from every move consumers make at their online sites. Critics worry that these companies may now know *too* much and might use digital data to take unfair advantage of consumers. Although most companies fully disclose their Internet privacy policies and most try to use data to benefit their customers, abuses do occur. As a result, consumer advocates and policy makers are taking action to protect consumer privacy. In Chapters 4 and 16, we discuss these and other societal marketing issues in greater depth.

Cause-Related Marketing. To exercise their social responsibility and build more positive images, many companies are now linking themselves to worthwhile causes. These days, every product seems to be tied to some cause. For example, the P&G "Tide Loads of Hope" program provides mobile laundromats and loads of clean laundry to families in disaster-stricken

>> **Cause-related marketing: AT&T joined forces with competitors Verizon, Sprint, and T-Mobile to spearhead the "It Can Wait" campaign, which urges people of all ages to take the pledge to never text and drive.**

areas—P&G washes, dries, and folds clothes for these families for free. Shake Shack runs an annual Great American Shake Sale: If you donate at least $2 at the register to Share Our Strength's No Kid Hungry program dedicated to ending child hunger in America, you get a $5 shake free on your next visit. >> And AT&T joined forces with competitors Verizon, Sprint, and T-Mobile to spearhead the "It Can Wait" campaign, which addresses the texting-while-driving epidemic by urging people of all ages to take the pledge to never text and drive. The campaign's cause-related message: "No text is worth the risk. It can wait."[42]

Some companies are founded on cause-related missions. Under the concept of "values-led business" or "caring capitalism," their mission is to use business to make the world a better place. For example, Warby Parker—the online marketer of low-priced prescription eyewear—was founded with the hope of bringing affordable eyewear to the masses. The company sells "eyewear with a purpose." For every pair of glasses Warby Parker sells, it distributes a free pair to someone in need. The company also works with not-for-profit organizations that train low-income entrepreneurs to sell affordable glasses. "We believe that everyone has the right to see," says the company.[43]

Cause-related marketing has become a primary form of corporate giving. It lets companies "do well by doing good" by linking purchases of the company's products or services with benefiting worthwhile causes or charitable organizations. Beyond being socially admirable, Warby Parker's Buy a Pair, Give a Pair program also makes good economic sense, for both the company and its customers. "Companies can do good in the world while still being profitable," says Warby Parker co-founder Neil Blumenthal. "A single pair of reading glasses causes, on average, a 20 percent increase in income. Glasses are one of the most effective poverty alleviation tools in the world."[44]

Cause-related marketing has also stirred some controversy. Critics worry that cause-related marketing is more a strategy for selling than a strategy for giving—that "cause-related" marketing is really "cause-exploitative" marketing. Thus, companies using cause-related marketing might find themselves walking a fine line between increased sales and an improved image and facing charges of exploitation. However, if handled well, cause-related marketing can greatly benefit both the company and the cause. The company gains an effective marketing tool while building a more positive public image. The charitable organization or cause gains greater visibility and important new sources of funding and support. Spending on cause-related marketing in the United States skyrocketed from only $120 million in 1990 to $1.92 billion in 2015.[45]

The Cultural Environment

The **cultural environment** consists of institutions and other forces that affect a society's basic values, perceptions, preferences, and behaviors. People grow up in a particular society that shapes their basic beliefs and values. They absorb a worldview that defines their relationships with others. The following cultural characteristics can affect marketing decision making.

The Persistence of Cultural Values

People in a given society hold many beliefs and values. Their core beliefs and values have a high degree of persistence. For example, most Americans believe in individual freedom, hard work, getting married, and achievement and success. These beliefs shape more specific attitudes and behaviors found in everyday life. *Core* beliefs and values are passed on from parents to children and are reinforced by schools, businesses, religious institutions, and government.

Secondary beliefs and values are more open to change. Believing in marriage is a core belief; believing that people should get married early in life is a secondary belief.

Cultural environment
Institutions and other forces that affect a society's basic values, perceptions, preferences, and behaviors.

Marketers have some chance of changing secondary values but little chance of changing core values. For example, family-planning marketers could argue more effectively that people should get married later than not get married at all.

Shifts in Secondary Cultural Values

Although core values are fairly persistent, cultural swings do take place. Consider the impact of popular music groups, movie personalities, and other celebrities on young people's hairstyle and clothing norms. Marketers want to predict cultural shifts to spot new opportunities or threats. The major cultural values of a society are expressed in people's views of themselves and others, as well as in their views of organizations, society, nature, and the universe.

People's Views of Themselves. People vary in their emphasis on serving themselves versus serving others. Some people seek personal pleasure, wanting fun, change, and escape. Others seek self-realization through religion, recreation, or the avid pursuit of careers or other life goals. Some people see themselves as sharers and joiners; others see themselves as individualists. People use products, brands, and services as a means of self-expression, and they buy products and services that match their views of themselves.

>> **People's self-views: Yogi appeals to tea drinkers with a more spiritual view of themselves, their lives, and their teas. Yogi Sweet Tangerine Positive Energy tea "energizes and elevates mood." "How good can you feel?"**

Courtesy Yogi Tea. Photo in ad: Mark Laita, Absodels/Getty Images

For example, ads for Tetley tea focus on taste, appealing to tea drinkers with a more practical view and telling them to "Brew Up Something Brilliant." Its Classic Blend black tea offers "a deep amber color and delicious tea flavor." By contrast, Yogi Tea Company appeals to tea drinkers with a more transcendent, holistic view of themselves, their lives, and their teas. The brand offers more than 100 herbs and botanicals, blended "for both flavor and purpose." >>Yogi's slogan, "How Good Can You Feel?," suggests that its teas not only taste good but also make you feel well, both physically and mentally. For example, Yogi Stress Relief tea is "a delicious, all-natural blend that helps soothe your body and mind." Yogi Sweet Tangerine Positive Energy tea "is a harmonizing and aromatic blend that energizes and elevates mood." A recent post at the Yogi Community online site invited everyone to have a "Happy Feel-Good Friday and a Happy Spring!"[46]

People's Views of Others. People's attitudes toward and interactions with others shift over time. In recent years, some analysts have voiced concerns that the digital age would result in diminished human interaction, as people buried themselves in social media pages or emailed and texted rather than interacting personally. Instead, today's digital technologies seem to have launched an era of what one trend watcher calls "mass mingling." Rather than interacting less, people are using social media and mobile communications to connect more than ever. Basically, the more people meet, network, Tweet, and socialize online, the more likely they are to eventually meet up with friends and followers in the real world.

However, these days, even when people are together, they are often "alone together." Groups of people may sit or walk in their own little bubbles, intensely connected to tiny screens and keyboards. One expert describes the latest communication skill as "maintaining eye contact with someone while you text someone else; it's hard but it can be done," she says. "Technology-enabled, we are able to be with one another, and also elsewhere, connected to wherever we want to be."[47] Thus, whether the new technology-driven communication is a blessing or a curse is a matter of much debate.

This new way of interacting strongly affects how companies market their brands and communicate with customers. Consumers increasingly tap digitally into networks of friends and online brand communities to learn about and buy products and to shape and share brand experiences. As a result, it is important for brands to participate in these networks too.

People's Views of Organizations. People vary in their attitudes toward corporations, government agencies, trade unions, universities, and other organizations. By and large, people are willing to work for major organizations and expect them, in turn, to carry out society's work.

The past two decades have seen a sharp decrease in confidence in and loyalty toward America's business and political organizations and institutions. In the workplace, there has been an overall decline in organizational loyalty. Waves of company downsizings bred cynicism and distrust. In just the past decade, major corporate scandals, rounds of layoffs resulting from the Great Recession, the financial meltdown triggered by Wall Street bankers' greed and incompetence, and other unsettling activities have resulted in a further loss of confidence in big business. Many people today see work not as a source of satisfaction but as a required chore to earn money to enjoy their nonwork hours. This trend suggests that organizations need to find new ways to win consumer and employee confidence.

People's Views of Society. People vary in their attitudes toward their society—patriots defend it, reformers want to change it, and malcontents want to leave it. People's orientation to their society influences their consumption patterns and attitudes toward the marketplace.

American patriotism has been increasing gradually for the past two decades. Marketers respond with renewed "Made in America" pitches and patriotic products and promotions, offering everything from orange juice to computers to cars with patriotic themes. For example, Chrysler's patriotic "Imported from Detroit" campaign, which declared that "the world's going to hear the roar of our engines," resonated strongly with Americans consumers. And Apple recently kicked off a $100 million "Made in America" push with the introduction of a new high-end Mac Pro personal computer. The Mac Pro, "the most powerful Mac ever," is built in Austin, Texas, with components made domestically.[48]

Although most such marketing efforts are tasteful and well received, waving the red, white, and blue can sometimes prove tricky. Flag-waving promotions can be viewed as corny or as token attempts to cash in on the nation's emotions. For example, some critics note that, so far, Apple's "Made in America" push hasn't had much real impact. The Mac Pro contributes less than 1 percent of Apple's total revenues. More than 70 percent of the company's revenues come from its iPhone and iPad products, both built in China. Marketers must take care when appealing to patriotism and other strong national emotions.

People's Views of Nature. People vary in their attitudes toward the natural world—some feel ruled by it, others feel in harmony with it, and still others seek to master it. A long-term trend has been people's growing mastery over nature through technology and the belief that nature is bountiful. More recently, however, people have recognized that nature is finite and fragile; it can be destroyed or spoiled by human activities.

This renewed love of things natural has created a sizable market of consumers who seek out everything from natural, organic, and nutritional products to fuel-efficient cars and alternative medicines. These consumers make up a sizable and growing market. For example, food producers have also found fast-growing markets for natural and organic products. In total, the U.S. organic/natural food market generated $53.5 billion in retail sales last year, more than doubling over the past five years.[49]

Annie's Homegrown, a General Mills company, caters to this market with sustainable, all-natural food products—from mac and cheese to pizzas, pastas, snacks, and salad dressings—made and sold in a sustainable way:[50]

>> Annie's mission is "to cultivate a healthier and happier world by spreading goodness through nourishing foods, honest words, and conduct that is considerate and forever kind to the planet." Annie's products are made from simple, natural ingredients grown by its farm partners. The products contain "no artificial anything," says the company. "If it's not real, it's

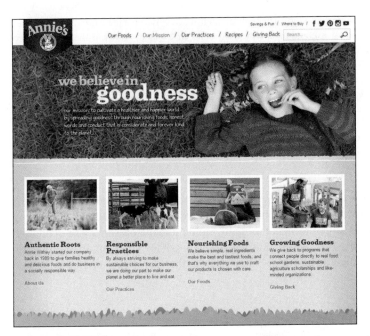

not Annie's." The company works closely with its food supply-system partners to jointly raise the bar for sustainability and organics. Annie's also makes sustainable practices a top priority with its packaging—more than 90 percent of Annie's packaging by weight is recyclable. Finally, Annie's gives back to the community through programs such as sustainable agriculture scholarships, school garden programs, and support for like-minded organizations dedicated to making the planet a better place to live and eat.

People's Views of the Universe. Finally, people vary in their beliefs about the origins of the universe and their place in it. Although most Americans practice religion, religious conviction and practice have been dropping off gradually through the years. According to a recent poll, one-fifth of Americans now say they are not affiliated with any particular faith, double the percentage in 1990. Among Americans ages 18 to 29, one-third say they are not currently affiliated with any particular religion.[51]

However, the fact that people are dropping out of organized religion doesn't mean that they are abandoning their faith. Some futurists have noted a renewed interest in spirituality, perhaps as a part of a broader search for a new inner purpose. People have been moving away from materialism and dog-eat-dog ambition to seek more permanent values—family, community, earth, faith—and a more certain grasp of right and wrong. Rather than calling it "religion," they call it "spirituality."[52] This changing spiritualism affects consumers in everything from the television shows they watch and the books they read to the products and services they buy.

Author Comment
Rather than simply watching and reacting to the marketing environment, companies should take proactive steps.

Responding to the Marketing Environment

Someone once observed, "There are three kinds of companies: those who make things happen, those who watch things happen, and those who wonder what's happened." Many companies view the marketing environment as an uncontrollable element to which they must react and adapt. They passively accept the marketing environment and do not try to change it. They analyze environmental forces and design strategies that will help the company avoid the threats and take advantage of the opportunities the environment provides.

Other companies take a *proactive* stance toward the marketing environment. Rather than assuming that strategic options are bounded by the current environment, these firms develop strategies to change the environment. Companies and their products often create and shape new industries and their structures, products such as Ford's Model T car, Apple's iPod and iPhone, and Google's search engine.

Even more, rather than simply watching and reacting to environmental events, proactive firms take aggressive actions to affect the publics and forces in their marketing environment. Such companies hire lobbyists to influence legislation affecting their industries and stage media events to gain favorable press coverage. They take to the social media and run blogs to shape public opinion. They press lawsuits and file complaints with regulators to keep competitors in line, and they form contractual agreements to better control their distribution channels.

By taking action, companies can often overcome seemingly uncontrollable environmental events. For example, whereas some companies try to hush up negative talk about their products, others proactively counter false information. McDonald's did this when a photo went viral showing unappetizing "mechanically separated chicken" (also known as "pink goop") and associating it with the company's Chicken McNuggets:[53]

McDonald's quickly issued statements disclaiming the pink goop photo as a hoax and noting that McNuggets are made using only boneless white breast meat chicken in a process that never produces anything remotely resembling the weird pink substance. But McDonald's took its response an important step further. It created its own nearly three-minute social media video giving a tour of a company processing plant in Canada, showing the step-by-step process by which McNuggets are made. In the process, fresh chicken breasts are ground and seasoned, stamped into four nugget shapes (balls, bells, boots, and bow ties), battered, flash-fried, frozen, packaged, and shipped out to local McDonald's restaurants where they are fully cooked. There's not a trace of the gross pink goop anywhere in the process. The proactive video itself went viral, garnering more than 3.5 million YouTube views in less than six weeks. As a follow-up, McDonald's launched an "Our Food. Your Questions." campaign inviting consumers to submit questions about its food-making processes via Facebook, Twitter, YouTube, and other social media. It then addressed the top concerns in a series of "behind-the-scenes" Webisodes.

Marketing management cannot always control environmental forces. In many cases, it must settle for simply watching and reacting to the environment. For example, a company would have little success trying to influence geographic population shifts, the economic environment, or major cultural values. But whenever possible, smart marketing managers take a *proactive* rather than *reactive* approach to the marketing environment (see Marketing at Work 3.2).

MARKETING AT WORK | 3.2

In the Social Media Age: When the Dialogue Gets Nasty

Marketers have hailed the Internet and social media as the great new way to engage customers and nurture customer relationships. In turn, today's more-empowered consumers use the new digital media to share their brand experiences with companies and with each other. All of this back and forth helps both the company and its customers. But sometimes, the dialogue can get nasty. Consider the following examples:

- Upon receiving a severely damaged computer monitor via FedEx, YouTube user goobie55 posts footage from his security camera. The video clearly shows a FedEx delivery man hoisting the monitor package over his head and tossing it over goobie55's front gate without ever attempting to ring the bell, open the gate, or walk the package to the door. The video—with FedEx's familiar purple and orange logo prominently displayed on everything from the driver's shirt to the package and the truck—goes viral, with 5 million hits in just five days. TV news and talk shows go crazy discussing the clip.
- A young creative team at Ford's ad agency in India produces a Ford Figo print ad and releases it to the Internet without approval. The ad features three women—bound, gagged, and scantily clad—in the hatch of a Figo, with a caricature of a grinning Silvio Berlusconi (Italy's sex-scandal-plagued ex-prime minister) at the wheel. The ad's tagline: "Leave your worries behind with Figo's extra-large boot (trunk)." Ford quickly pulls the ad, but not before it goes viral. Within days, millions of people around the world have viewed the ad, causing an online uproar and giving Ford a global black eye.

- When 8-year-old Harry Winsor sends a crayon drawing of an airplane he's designed to Boeing with a suggestion that the company might want to manufacture it, the company responds with a stern, legal-form letter. "We do not accept unsolicited ideas," the letter states. "We regret to inform you that we have disposed of your message and retain no

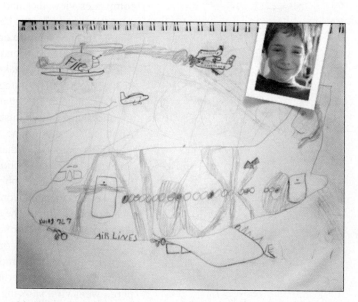

>> Today's empowered consumers: Boeing's embarrassing blunder over young Harry Winsor's airplane design made instant national news. However, Boeing quickly took responsibility and turned the potential PR disaster into a positive.

John Winsor

copies." The embarrassing blunder would probably go unnoticed were it not for the fact that Harry's father—John Winsor, a prominent ad exec—blogs and tweets about the incident, making it instant national news.

Extreme events? Not anymore. The Internet and social media have turned the traditional power relationship between businesses and consumers upside down. In the good old days, disgruntled consumers could do little more than bellow at a company service rep or shout out their complaints from a street corner. Now, armed with only a laptop or smartphone, they can take it public, airing their gripes to millions on blogs, social media sites, or even hate sites devoted exclusively to their least favorite corporations. "A consumer's megaphone is now [sometimes] more powerful than a brand's," says one ad agency executive. "Individuals can bring a huge company to its knees...simply by sharing their experiences and opinions on Facebook, Yelp, Twitter, Instagram, or other social forums."

"I hate" and "sucks" sites are almost commonplace. These sites target some highly respected companies with some highly disrespectful labels: Walmartblows.com, PayPalSucks.com (aka NoPayPal), IHateStarbucks.com, DeltaREALLYsucks. com, and UnitedPackageSmashers.com (UPS), to name only a few. "Sucks" videos on YouTube and other video sites also abound. For example, a search of "Apple sucks" on YouTube turns up more than 600,000 videos; a search for Microsoft finds 143,000 videos. An "Apple sucks" search on Facebook links to hundreds of groups. If you don't find one you like, try "Apple suks" or "Apple sux" for hundreds more.

Some of these sites, videos, and other online attacks air legitimate complaints that should be addressed. Others, however, are little more than anonymous, vindictive slurs that unfairly ransack brands and corporate reputations. Some of the attacks are only a passing nuisance; others can draw serious attention and create real headaches.

How should companies react to online attacks? The real quandary for targeted companies is figuring out how far they can go to protect their images without fueling the already raging fire. One point on which all experts seem to agree: Don't try to retaliate in kind. "It's rarely a good idea to lob bombs at the fire starters," says one analyst. "Preemption, engagement, and diplomacy are saner tools." Such criticisms are often based on real consumer concerns and unresolved anger. Hence, the best strategy might be to proactively monitor these sites and respond honestly to the concerns they express.

For example, Boeing quickly took responsibility for mishandling aspiring Harry Winsor's designs, turning a potential PR disaster into a positive. It called and invited young Harry to visit Boeing's facilities. On its corporate Twitter site, it confessed, "We're experts at airplanes but novices in social media. We're learning as we go." In response to its Figo ad fiasco, Ford's chief marketing officer issued a deep public apology,

citing that Ford had not approved the ads and that it had since modified its ad review process. Ford's ad agency promptly fired the guilty creatives.

Similarly, FedEx drew praise by immediately posting its own YouTube video addressing the monitor-smashing incident. In the video, FedEx Senior Vice President of Operations Matthew Thornton stated that he had personally met with the aggrieved customer, who had accepted the company's apology. "This goes directly against all FedEx values," declared Thornton. The FedEx video struck a responsive chord. Numerous journalists and bloggers responded with stories about FedEx's outstanding package handling and delivering record.

Many companies have now created teams of specialists that monitor online conversations and engage unhappy consumers. For example, the social media team at Southwest Airlines includes a chief Twitter officer who tracks Twitter comments and monitors Facebook groups, an online representative who checks facts and interacts with bloggers, and another person who takes charge of the company's presence on sites such as YouTube, Instagram, Flickr, and LinkedIn. So if someone posts an online comment, the company can respond promptly in a personal way.

Not long ago, Southwest's team averted what could have been a major PR catastrophe when a hole popped open in a plane's fuselage on a flight from Phoenix to Sacramento. The flight had Wi-Fi, and the first passenger tweet about the incident, complete with a photo, was online in only nine minutes—11 minutes before Southwest's official dispatch channel report. But Southwest's monitoring team picked up the social media chatter and was able to craft a blog post and other social media responses shortly after the plane made an emergency landing in Yuma, Arizona. By the time the story hit the major media, the passenger who had tweeted initially was back on Twitter praising the Southwest crew for its professional handling of the situation.

Thus, by monitoring and proactively responding to seemingly uncontrollable events in the environment, companies can prevent the negatives from spiraling out of control or even turn them into positives. Who knows? With the right responses, Walmartblows.com might even become Walmartrules.com. Then again, probably not.

Sources: Quotes, excerpts, and other information based on Matt Wilson, "How Southwest Airlines Wrangled Four Social Media Crises," *Ragan .com*, February 20, 2013, www.ragan.com/Main/Articles/How_Southwest_ Airlines_wrangled_four_social_media_46254.aspx#; Vanessa Ko, "FedEx Apologizes after Video of Driver Throwing Fragile Package Goes Viral," *Time*, December 23, 2011, http://newsfeed.time.com/2011/12/23/fedex-apologizes-after-video-of-driver-throwing-fragile-package-goes-viral/; Michelle Conlin, "Web Attack," *BusinessWeek*, April 16, 2007, pp. 54–56; "Boeing's Social Media Lesson," May 3, 2010, http://mediadecoder.blogs .nytimes.com/2010/05/03/boeings-social-media-lesson/; Brent Snavely, "Ford Marketing Chief Apologizes for Ads," *USA Today*, March 27, 2013; David Angelo, "CMOs, Agencies: It's Time to Live Your Brands," *Advertising Age*, October 2, 2013, http://adage.com/print/244524; and www.youtube.com/ watch?v=C5uIH0VTg_o, accessed September 2015.

MyMarketingLab

If assigned by your instructor, complete the questions marked with the ⭐ from the EOC Discussion Questions section in the MyLab. To complete the Marketing by the Numbers problems found in this section, go to your Assignments in the MyLab.

REVIEWING AND EXTENDING THE CONCEPTS

CHAPTER REVIEW AND CRITICAL THINKING

Objectives Review

In this and the next two chapters, you'll examine the environments of marketing and how companies analyze these environments to better understand the marketplace and consumers. Companies must constantly watch and manage the *marketing environment* to seek opportunities and ward off threats. The marketing environment consists of all the actors and forces influencing the company's ability to transact business effectively with its target market.

 OBJECTIVE 3-1   Describe the environmental forces that affect the company's ability to serve its customers. (pp 68–72)

The company's *microenvironment* consists of actors close to the company that combine to form its value delivery network or that affect its ability to serve customers. It includes the company's *internal environment*—its several departments and management levels—as it influences marketing decision making. *Marketing channel firms*—suppliers, marketing intermediaries, physical distribution firms, marketing services agencies, and financial intermediaries—cooperate to create customer value. *Competitors* vie with the company in an effort to serve customers better. Various *publics* have an actual or potential interest in or impact on the company's ability to meet its objectives. Finally, five types of customer *markets* exist: consumer, business, reseller, government, and international markets.

The *macroenvironment* consists of larger societal forces that affect the entire microenvironment. The six forces making up the company's macroenvironment are demographic, economic, natural, technological, political/social, and cultural forces. These forces shape opportunities and pose threats to the company.

 OBJECTIVE 3-2   Explain how changes in the demographic and economic environments affect marketing decisions. (pp 72–81)

Demography is the study of the characteristics of human populations. Today's *demographic environment* shows a changing age structure, shifting family profiles, geographic population shifts, a better-educated and more white-collar population, and increasing diversity. The *economic environment* consists of factors that affect buying power and patterns. The economic environment is

characterized by more frugal consumers who are seeking greater value—the right combination of good quality and service at a fair price. The distribution of income also is shifting. The rich have grown richer, the middle class has shrunk, and the poor have remained poor, leading to a two-tiered market.

 OBJECTIVE 3-3   Identify the major trends in the firm's natural and technological environments. (pp 81–85)

The *natural environment* shows three major trends: shortages of certain raw materials, higher pollution levels, and more government intervention in natural resource management. Environmental concerns create marketing opportunities for alert companies. The *technological environment* creates both opportunities and challenges. Companies that fail to keep up with technological change will miss out on new product and marketing opportunities.

 OBJECTIVE 3-4   Explain the key changes in the political and cultural environments. (pp 85–91)

The *political environment* consists of laws, agencies, and groups that influence or limit marketing actions. The political environment has undergone changes that affect marketing worldwide: increasing legislation regulating business, strong government agency enforcement, and greater emphasis on ethics and socially responsible actions. The *cultural environment* consists of institutions and forces that affect a society's values, perceptions, preferences, and behaviors. The environment shows trends toward new technology-enabled communication, a lessening trust of institutions, increasing patriotism, greater appreciation for nature, a changing spiritualism, and the search for more meaningful and enduring values.

 OBJECTIVE 3-5   Discuss how companies can react to the marketing environment. (pp 91–93)

Companies can passively accept the marketing environment as an uncontrollable element to which they must adapt, avoiding threats and taking advantage of opportunities as they arise. Or they can take a *proactive* stance, working to change the environment rather than simply reacting to it. Whenever possible, companies should try to be proactive rather than reactive.

Key Terms

Objective 3-1
Marketing environment (p 68)
Microenvironment (p 68)
Macroenvironment (p 68)
Marketing intermediaries (p 70)
Public (p 71)

Objective 3-2
Demography (p 72)
Baby boomers (p 73)

Generation X (p 74)
Millennials (Generation Y) (p 75)
Generation Z (p 75)
Economic environment (p 80)

Objective 3-3
Natural environment (p 81)
Environmental sustainability (p 82)
Technological environment (p 82)

Objective 3-4
Political environment (p 85)
Cultural environment (p 88)

Discussion Questions

3-1. Name and describe the types of publics in a company's marketing environment. (AASCB: Communication)

⭐ **3-2.** Who are the Millennials, and why are they of so much interest to marketers? (AACSB: Communication; Reflective Thinking)

3-3. Describe Generation Z. What differentiates it from other demographic groups, such as baby boomers, Generation X, and Millennials? (AACSB: Communication; Reflective Thinking)

3-4. Compare and contrast core beliefs/values and secondary beliefs/values. Provide an example of each and discuss the potential impact marketers have on each. (AACSB: Communication; Reflective Thinking)

⭐ **3-5.** How should marketers respond to the changing environment? (AACSB: Communication)

Critical Thinking Exercises

3-6. In 1965, more than 40 percent of American adults were smokers. That percentage has now fallen to less than 18 percent. Tobacco companies have dealt with this threat by developing new markets overseas and also developing alternative nicotine products such as electronic cigarettes (e-cigarettes). Research this product and the regulatory environment regarding this product, then write a report advising tobacco companies on the opportunities and threats posed by this technology. (AACSB: Communication; Reflective Thinking)

3-7. Form a small group and discuss cultural trends in the United States. Research one of them in depth and create a presentation on the trend's impact on marketing. (AACSB: Communication; Reflective Thinking)

3-8. Visit www.causemarketingforum.com to learn about companies that have won Halo Awards for outstanding cause-related marketing programs. Present an award-winning case study to your class. (AACSB: Communication; Use of IT)

MINICASES AND APPLICATIONS

Online, Mobile, and Social Media Marketing   Sharing Economy

Changes in the technological environment have created amazing opportunities for new business models while at the same time threatening traditional ones. For example, Airbnb has shaken up the hospitality industry by allowing people to rent out spare rooms or their entire homes to strangers. The Uber and Lyft ride-sharing businesses allow consumers to find a ride from people looking to earn extra money with their vehicles. And with Uber you don't have to worry about having enough cash or giving your credit card to the

driver—payments and tips are all done through the Uber app. Traditional hotel and cab companies are crying foul, claiming that these businesses are not playing by the same regulatory rules to which they are subject. Others are concerned about safety amid reports of riders allegedly being attacked, kidnappings, and driver accidents, questioning the thoroughness of background checks of the 160,000-plus Uber drivers around the world. Some countries, states, and cities have banned Uber because of these issues.

⭐ **3-9.** Describe how Uber's business model works and the role technology has played in its success. What are the arguments for banning these types of businesses? What are the arguments for defending them? (AACSB: Communication; Use of IT; Reflective Thinking)

3-10. Describe examples of two other businesses based on the sharing economy model and create a new business idea based on this concept. (AACSB: Communication; Reflective Thinking)

Marketing Ethics   Mutant Loophole

Genetically modifying seeds to produce herbicide-resistant plants that increase crop yields has revolutionized modern agriculture. However, genetically modified organisms (GMOs) have come under fire in recent years, with consumer groups calling for mandatory GMO labeling on all food packages that contain GMO ingredients. GMO labeling laws have been in force in the European Union and other countries for several years, but the threat to the U.S. food industry is only now surfacing. Although bills requiring GMO labeling have been introduced in many state legislatures, Vermont is the only state where such a law has so far withstood the first round of legal battles from the industry. Leading chemical companies, including Monsanto, BASF, and DuPont, are the world's largest suppliers of seeds that grow the food that feeds the world. To counter the GMO labeling threat, they now are turning to mutagenesis as an alternative technique to create herbicide-resistant crops. Mutagenesis mimics the sun's irradiation of plants to create similar results to GMO techniques but with virtually no regulation. Some scientists claim mutant crops created from this process are likely to create even greater health risks than genetic modification. Seed companies see it as a way around the threat of GMO labeling requirements as consumer package-goods marketers put pressure on suppliers for non-GMO ingredients.

3-11. Debate whether it is ethical for seed manufacturers to replace one controversial technique (genetic engineering) with another (mutagenesis) to avoid regulatory threats. (AACSB: Communication; Reflective Thinking; Ethical Reasoning)

3-12. Is it wise for GMO manufacturers to fight mandatory labeling? Debate this issue. (AACSB: Communication; Reflective Thinking)

Marketing by the Numbers   Demographic Trends

Marketers are interested in demographic trends related to variables such as age, ethnicity, and population. The U.S. Census Bureau provides considerable demographic information that is useful for marketers. For example, the following table provides a sample of such population data (see www.censusscope.org/2010Census/PDFs/RaceEth-States.pdf):

State	2000		2010	
	Total	Hispanic	Total	Hispanic
Georgia	8,186,453	435,227	9,687,653	853,689
Michigan	9,938,444	323,877	9,883,640	436,358
California	33,871,648	10,966,556	37,253,956	14,013,719

3-13. What percentage change in the total and Hispanic populations occurred in each state between 2000 and 2010? What conclusions can be drawn from this analysis? (AACSB: Communication; Analytical Reasoning; Reflective Thinking)

3-14. Research another demographic trend and create a presentation to marketers regarding the significance of the trend you analyzed. (AACSB: Communication; Reflective Thinking)

Video Case   Burger King

In the fast-food burgers business, french fries are perhaps more important than the burgers themselves. System-wide, Burger King sells 56 million orders of french fries every month—one order of fries for every two customers. But nothing is exempt from the impact of marketing environment forces. As health trends drove some companies to cut back on fatty foods, Burger King saw its french fry sales dip.

So Burger King decided to let people have their fries and eat them to. To bring health-conscious customers back to the counter, Burger King introduced Satisfries—french fries with 30 percent less fat and 20 percent fewer calories than its regular fries. In a product category that has seen little if any innovation, Satisfries could be a big game changer. Still, reduced fat and calories may not be enough to make a difference to health-food lovers. And at 30 to 40 cents more per item, Satisfries may end up as little more than a fry fiasco.

After viewing the video featuring Burger King, answer the following questions:

3-15. Considering marketing environment forces, describe how Burger King went about developing its new Satisfries.

3-16. With Satisfries, has Burger King truly created customer value, or is it just chasing trends? Explain.

Company Cases   3 Sony/7 Target/9 Coach

See Appendix 1 for cases appropriate for this chapter. **Case 3, Sony: Battling the Marketing Environment's "Perfect Storm."** The many forces of the marketing environment have converged to take Sony from the global leader in consumer electronics to a company that is struggling to remain relevant. **Case 7, Target: Where Store Brands Offer More Than Low Prices.**

In addition to carrying popular national brands, Target caters to current trends in consumer desire by building a portfolio of store brands. **Case 9, Coach: Riding the Wave of Premium Pricing.** Coach grew from a premium niche brand into a $5 billion powerhouse by pursuing popular trends of selling through outlet stores at a discount. But such tactics are taking a toll.

MyMarketingLab

If assigned by your instructor, complete these writing sections from your Assignments in the MyLab.

3-17. What is environmental sustainability and why has it grown in importance for marketers? (AACSB: Communication)

3-18. Discuss a recent change in the technological environment that impacts marketing. How has it affected buyer behavior and how has it changed marketing? (AACSB: Written and Oral Communication; Reflective Thinking)

4 Managing Marketing Information
to Gain Customer Insights

| CHAPTER ROAD MAP | Objective Outline |

▶ OBJECTIVE 4-1 **Explain the importance of information in gaining insights about the marketplace and customers.** Marketing Information and Customer Insights (100–101)

▶ OBJECTIVE 4-2 **Define the marketing information system and discuss its parts.** Assessing Marketing Information Needs (102); Developing Marketing Information (102–106)

▶ OBJECTIVE 4-3 **Outline the steps in the marketing research process.** Marketing Research (106–118)

▶ OBJECTIVE 4-4 **Explain how companies analyze and use marketing information.** Analyzing and Using Marketing Information (118–123)

▶ OBJECTIVE 4-5 **Discuss the special issues some marketing researchers face, including public policy and ethics issues.** Other Marketing Information Considerations (123–127)

Previewing the Concepts

In this chapter, we continue our exploration of how marketers gain insights into consumers and the marketplace. We look at how companies develop and manage information about important marketplace elements: customers, competitors, products, and marketing programs. To succeed in today's marketplace, companies must know how to turn mountains of marketing information into fresh customer insights that will help them deliver greater value to customers.

Let's start with a story about marketing research and customer insights in action. Over the past decade, The LEGO Group has used innovative marketing research to gain deep insights into how children really play and then used those insights to create compelling play experiences for children all over the world. In the process, it has rescued itself from near bankruptcy to become the world's biggest toy maker. As one analyst puts it, The LEGO Group has now become "the Apple of Toys."

First Stop

The LEGO Group: Digging Out Fresh Customer Insights

Classic LEGO plastic bricks have been fixtures in homes around the world for more than 65 years. Last year, The LEGO Group (TLG) produced a record 55 *billion* LEGO bricks, enough to construct a continuous line stretching around the world more than 20 times. More than 78 million LEGO sets found their way into the eager hands of customers in 130 countries. TLG is now the world's second-largest toy company, ahead of Hasbro and neck and neck with market leader Mattel. And whereas Mattel and Hasbro are facing flat or declining sales, TLG's sales are exploding. In the past 10 years, its revenues have quadrupled to nearly $5 billion, up 25 percent last year alone.

But only a decade ago, TLG was near bankruptcy, spiraling downward and losing money at a rate of $1 million a day. The problem: The classic toy company had fallen out of touch with its customers. In the age of the Internet, video games, mobile devices, and high-tech playthings, traditional toys such as LEGO bricks had been pushed to the back of the closet. So, in 2004, the company set out to rebuild its aging products and approaches, brick by brick.

The LEGO makeover, however, didn't start with engineers working in design labs. First, TLG had to reconnect with customers. So it started with marketing research—lots and lots of it—listening to customers and learning in depth how children around the world really play. It created a Global Insights Team, a group of marketing researchers charged with finding innovative new ways to dig out fresh customer insights.

Beyond traditional research methods and data analytics, TLG used innovative immersive research approaches to understand the deeper motivations underlying LEGO purchases and play. For example, TLG research teams conducted up-close-and-personal ethnographic studies. They embedded researchers with families, observed children at play, interviewed their parents, shopped with families, and studied the inside workings of toy stores. This immersive research produced a lot of "Aha! Moments," customer insights that shattered many of the brand's decades-old traditions.

For example, TLG had long held fast to a "keep it simple" mantra. From the beginning, it had offered only basic play sets—bricks, building bases, beams, doors, windows, wheels, and slanting roof tiles—with few or no instructions. The philosophy was that giving children unstructured building sets would stimulate their imaginations and foster creativity. But the research showed that this concept just wasn't cutting it in today's modern, tech-rich world. Today's children get bored easily, and in the current fast-moving environment, they are exposed to many more characters, themes, and technologies. However, counter to previous assumptions that kids seek only instant gratification, TLG found that today's children welcome challenging tasks, such as putting together complex LEGO sets.

Responding to such insights, TLG shifted toward more-specialized, more-structured play experiences. It now churns out a seemingly endless assortment of themed product lines and specific building projects, complete with detailed instructions. So instead of

» The LEGO Group's innovative marketing research produced lots of "Aha! Moments," helping the brand to recast its classic, colorful bricks into modern, tech-rich play experiences for children around the world.

just buying a set of basic square LEGO bricks and building their own houses or cars, children can now buy specialized kits to construct anything from fire trucks and helicopters to crave-worthy ninja castles. To add variety and familiarity, TLG also offers an ever-changing assortment of licensed lines based on everything from *Star Wars* and *DC Comics* to *Marvel Super Heroes* and *Disney Princesses*. And to satisfy children's needs for skill-mastery challenges, TLG has developed involving play experiences such as LEGO MINDSTORMS, a series of building sets complete with hardware and software for making customizable robots that are programmable from a smartphone app. The latest incarnation of LEGO MINDSTORMS, EV3, is a 601-piece kit that includes software, motors, and sensors that control robot movements and speech.

Another customer insight that emerged from the ethnographic research is that kids no longer draw meaningful distinctions between digital and physical play. "To them, it's not two separate worlds," says a LEGO Group product designer. "It's one world that blends together." This insight led to TLG's "One Reality" products, which combine digital and real-world play experiences that involve building with LEGO bricks alongside software running on a phone or tablet app. For example, the LEGO Fusion line lets children build physical models with actual LEGO bricks, scan their creations using a phone or tablet app, and bring them to life in a virtual world. In LEGO Fusion Town Master, for instance, kids create a miniature virtual LEGO city, then run the city as its mayor in an app. Town Master was one of last year's hottest-selling Christmas toys.

> The LEGO Group uses innovative marketing research—lots and lots of it—to dig out fresh customer insights, then uses the insights to create irresistible play experiences for children around the world. LEGO is now neck and neck with Mattel as the world's number-one toy maker.

TLG's marketing researchers have also discovered important differences between how boys and girls play, leading to the launch of girl-focused lines such as LEGO Friends. Both boys and girls like the construction aspects of LEGO bricks. However, boys tend to be more drawn to narrative—as reflected in popular boy-focused, story-based product lines such as Ninjago and Legends of Chima. In contrast, girls tend to use their sets for role-play, as reflected in the pink- and purple-accented LEGO Friends, which focuses on community and friendship themes. The development of LEGO Friends took four years, based on research involving 3,500 girls and their mothers around the world, seeking to understand what girls who had not previously played with LEGO products might want in a construction toy. LEGO Friends has been a major hit with girls in markets ranging from the United States and Germany to China.

Of course, kids aren't the only ones playing with LEGO bricks. The classic brick sets have a huge fan base of adults who never got over the toys of their youth. Hundreds of thousands of AFOLs (Adult Fans of LEGO) around the globe spend large sums on LEGO products. These adults maintain thousands of LEGO fan sites and blogs and organize get-togethers such as the annual BrickFest fan festival. TLG actively taps into the AFOL community for new customer insights and ideas. It has created a roster of customer ambassadors who provide regular input, and it even invites customers to participate directly in the product-development process. For example, it once invited 250 LEGO train-set enthusiasts to visit its New York office to assess new designs. The result was the LEGO Santa Fe Super Chief set, which sold out the first 10,000 units in less than two weeks with virtually no marketing. Similarly, TLG used customer co-creation to develop its most popular product ever, LEGO MINDSTORMS.

Thus, over the past decade, thanks to customer insight-driven marketing research, The LEGO Group has reconnected with both its customers and the times. TLG probably knows as much about how children play as any organization on earth, and it has parlayed that knowledge into compelling, profitable play experiences for the world's children. As one analyst concludes, "In the last 10 years, LEGO has grown into nothing less than the Apple of Toys: a profit-generating, design-driven miracle built around premium, intuitive, highly covetable [play experiences that its young] fans can't get enough of."[1]

As the LEGO story highlights, good products and marketing programs begin with good customer information. Companies also need an abundance of information on competitors, resellers, and other actors and marketplace forces. But more than just gathering information, marketers must *use* the information to gain powerful *customer and market insights*.

Author Comment
Marketing information by itself has little value. The value is in the *customer insights* gained from the information and how marketers use these insights to make better decisions.

Marketing Information and Customer Insights

To create value for customers and build meaningful relationships with them, marketers must first gain fresh, deep insights into what customers need and want. Such customer insights come from good marketing information. Companies use these customer insights to develop a competitive advantage.

For example, when it began five years ago, social media site Pinterest needed to differentiate itself from the dozens, even hundreds, of existing social networking options.[2]

> Pinterest's research uncovered a key customer insight: Many people want more than just Twitter- or Facebook-like places to swap messages and pictures. They want a way to collect, organize, and share things on the Internet related to their interests and passions. So Pinterest created a social scrapbooking site, where people can create and share digital pinboards—theme-based image collections on things that inspire them. "Pinterest is your own little Internet of only the things you love," says the company.
> ≫ Thanks to this unique customer insight, Pinterest has been wildly popular. Today, more than 70 million Pinterest users collectively pin more than 5 million articles a day and view more than 2.5 billion Pinterest pages a month. In turn, more than a half-million businesses use Pinterest to engage and inspire their customer communities. Nordstrom, for example, has more than 4.4 million Pinterest followers. Some 47 percent of U.S. online shoppers have purchased something as a result of a Pinterest recommendation.

Although customer and market insights are important for building customer value and engagement, these insights can be very difficult to obtain. Customer needs and buying motives are often anything but obvious—consumers themselves usually can't tell you exactly what they need and why they buy. To gain good customer insights, marketers must effectively manage marketing information from a wide range of sources.

>> Key customer insights have helped make social scrapbooking site Pinterest wildly successful with its 70 million users. In turn, more than a half-million brands use Pinterest to engage and inspire their customer communities.

Pinterest

Big data
The huge and complex data sets generated by today's sophisticated information generation, collection, storage, and analysis technologies.

Customer insights
Fresh marketing information-based understandings of customers and the marketplace that become the basis for creating customer value, engagement, and relationships.

Marketing information system (MIS)
People and procedures dedicated to assessing information needs, developing the needed information, and helping decision makers to use the information to generate and validate actionable customer and market insights.

Marketing Information and Today's "Big Data"

With the recent explosion of information technologies, companies can now generate and find marketing information in great quantities. The marketing world is filled to the brim with information from innumerable sources. Consumers themselves are now generating tons of marketing information. Through their smartphones, PCs, and tablets via online browsing and blogging, apps and social media interactions, texting and video, and geolocation data, consumers now volunteer a tidal wave of bottom-up information to companies and to each other.

Far from lacking information, most marketing managers are overloaded with data and often overwhelmed by it. This problem is summed up in the concept of **big data**. The term *big data* refers to the huge and complex data sets generated by today's sophisticated information generation, collection, storage, and analysis technologies. Every year, the people and systems of the world generate about a trillion gigabytes of information. That's enough data to fill 2.47 trillion good old CD-ROMs, a stack tall enough to go to the moon and back four times. A full 90 percent of all the data in the world has been created in just the past two years.[3]

Big data presents marketers with both big opportunities and big challenges. Companies that effectively tap this glut of big data can gain rich, timely customer insights. However, accessing and sifting through so much data is a daunting task. For example, when a large consumer brand such as Coca-Cola or Apple monitors online discussions about its brand in Tweets, blogs, social media posts, and other sources, it might take in a stunning 6 million public conversations a day, more than 2 billion a year. That's far more information than any manager can digest. Thus, marketers don't need *more* information; they need *better* information. And they need to make better *use* of the information they already have.

Managing Marketing Information

The real value of marketing information lies in how it is used—in the **customer insights** that it provides. Based on such thinking, companies ranging from Coca-Cola, Starbucks, and McDonald's to Google and GEICO are restructuring their marketing information and research functions. They are creating *customer insights teams*, headed by a senior marketing executive with representatives from all of the firm's functional areas. For example, GEICO's Customer Insights team analyzes data from dozens of sources to gain insights into the GEICO customer experience and then works with functional leaders across the organization to find ways to improve that experience.[4]

Customer insights groups collect customer and market information from a wide variety of sources, ranging from traditional marketing research studies to mingling with and observing consumers to monitoring social media conversations about the company and its products. They mine big data from sources far and wide. Then they *use* this information to develop important customer insights from which the company can create more value for its customers.

Thus, companies must design effective marketing information systems that give managers the right information, in the right form, at the right time and help them to use this information to create customer value, engagement, and stronger customer relationships. A **marketing information system (MIS)** consists of people and procedures dedicated to assessing information needs, developing the needed information, and helping decision makers use the information to generate and validate actionable customer and market insights.

>> **Figure 4.1** shows that the MIS begins and ends with information users—marketing managers, internal and external partners, and others who need marketing information. First, it interacts with these information users to assess information needs. Next, it interacts with the marketing environment to develop needed information through internal company databases, marketing intelligence activities, and marketing research. Finally, the MIS helps users to analyze and use the information to develop customer insights, make marketing decisions, and manage customer engagement and relationships.

» Figure 4.1
The Marketing
Information System

This chapter is all about managing marketing information to gain customer insights. And this important figure organizes the entire chapter. Marketers start by assessing user information needs. Then they develop the needed information using internal data, marketing intelligence, and marketing research processes. Finally, they make the information available to users in the right form at the right time.

Assessing Marketing Information Needs

The marketing information system primarily serves the company's marketing and other managers. However, it may also provide information to external partners, such as suppliers, resellers, or marketing services agencies. For example, Walmart's Retail Link system gives key suppliers access to information on everything from customers' buying patterns and store inventory levels to how many items they've sold in which stores in the past 24 hours.[5]

A good marketing information system balances the information users would *like* to have against what they really *need* and what is *feasible* to offer. Some managers will ask for whatever information they can get without thinking carefully about what they really need. And in this age of big data, some managers will want to collect and store vast amounts of digital data simply because technology lets them. But too much information can be as harmful as too little. In contrast, other managers may omit things they ought to know, or they may not know to ask for some types of information they should have. The MIS must monitor the marketing environment to provide decision makers with information they should have to make key marketing decisions.

Finally, the costs of obtaining, analyzing, storing, and delivering information can mount quickly. The company must decide whether the value of insights gained from additional information is worth the costs of providing it, and both value and cost are often hard to assess.

Developing Marketing Information

Marketers can obtain the needed information from *internal data, marketing intelligence,* and *marketing research.*

Internal Data

Many companies build extensive **internal databases**, collections of consumer and market information obtained from data sources within the company's network. Information in an internal database can come from many sources. The marketing department furnishes information on customer characteristics, in-store and online sales transactions, and Web and social media site visits. The customer service department keeps records of customer satisfaction or service problems. The accounting department provides detailed records of sales, costs, and cash flows. Operations reports on production, shipments, and inventories. The sales force reports on reseller reactions and competitor activities, and marketing channel

Internal databases
Collections of consumer and market information obtained from data sources within the company network.

partners provide data on sales transactions. Harnessing such information can provide powerful customer insights and competitive advantage.

>> For example, as part of its MyMacy's customer-centricity program, Macy's uses its huge internal database to glean customer insights and personalize customer engagements:[6]

>> Through its MyMacy's program, Macy's digs deeply into its huge customer database and uses the resulting insights to hyper-personalize its customers' shopping experiences.

Bloomberg/Getty Images

Macy's has assembled a vast shopper database containing reams of information on 33 million customer households and 500 million shopper transactions a year. Individual customer data include demographics, in-store and online purchases, style preferences and personal motivations, and even browsing patterns at Macy's Web, mobile, and social media sites. Macy's then analyzes the data intensely and uses the resulting insights to coordinate and hyper-personalize each customer's shopping experiences.

For example, Macy's now sends out up to 500,000 unique versions of a single direct mail catalogue. "My book might look very different from [someone else's]," says Macy's chief marketer. "I'm not such a great homemaker, but I am a cosmetic, shoe, and jewelry person, so what you might see in my book would be all of those categories." Similarly, under its "Intelligent Display" initiative, Macy's can track what customers browse on the company Web or mobile sites, then have relevant display ads appear as they are browsing on other sites. Future MyMacy's actions will include data-informed email, mobile, and Web and social media site customizations. The ultimate goal of the massive internal database effort is to "put the customer at the center of all decisions."

Internal databases usually can be accessed more quickly and cheaply than other information sources, but they also present some problems. Because internal information is often collected for other purposes, it may be incomplete or in the wrong form for making marketing decisions. Data also age quickly; keeping the database current requires a major effort. Finally, managing and mining the mountains of information that a large company produces requires highly sophisticated equipment and techniques.

Competitive Marketing Intelligence

Competitive marketing intelligence
The systematic monitoring, collection, and analysis of publicly available information about consumers, competitors, and developments in the marketplace.

Competitive marketing intelligence is the systematic monitoring, collection, and analysis of publicly available information about consumers, competitors, and developments in the marketplace. The goal of competitive marketing intelligence is to improve strategic decision making by understanding the consumer environment, assessing and tracking competitors' actions, and providing early warnings of opportunities and threats. Marketing intelligence techniques range from observing consumers firsthand to quizzing the company's own employees, benchmarking competitors' products, online research, and monitoring social media buzz.

Good marketing intelligence can help marketers gain insights into how consumers talk about and engage with their brands. Many companies send out teams of trained observers to mix and mingle personally with customers as they use and talk about the company's products. Other companies—such as Dell, PepsiCo, Kraft, and MasterCard—have set up sophisticated digital command centers that routinely monitor brand-related online consumer and marketplace activity (see Marketing at Work 4.1).

Companies also need to actively monitor competitors' activities. They can monitor competitors' Web and social media sites. For example, Amazon's Competitive Intelligence arm routinely purchases merchandise from competing sites to analyze and compare their assortment, speed, and service quality. Companies can use the Internet to search specific competitor names, events, or trends and see what turns up. And tracking consumer conversations about competing brands is often as revealing as tracking conversations about the company's own brands.

Firms use competitive marketing intelligence to gain early insights into competitor moves and strategies and to prepare quick responses. For example, Samsung routinely

MARKETING AT WORK | 4.1

Social Media Command Centers: Listening to and Engaging Customers in Social Space

Today's social space is alive with buzz about brands and related happenings and trends. As a result, many companies are now setting up state-of-the-art social media command centers with which they track or even help shape the constant barrage of social media activity surrounding their brands.

Some social media command centers are event-specific. For example, Jaguar set up "The Villain's Lair," a social media command center for the express purpose of managing engagement with its Super Bowl ads featuring famous movie villains. But many other organizations, ranging from financial institutions and consumer products companies to not-for-profit organizations, have opened permanent digital command centers to help them harness the power of today's burgeoning social media chatter.

For example, MasterCard's digital intelligence command center—called the Conversation Suite—monitors, analyzes, and responds in real time to millions of online conversations around the world. It monitors online brand-related conversations across 56 markets and 27 languages. It tracks social networks, blogs, online and mobile video, and traditional media—any and every digital place that might contain relevant content or commentary on MasterCard and its competitors.

At MasterCard's Purchase, New York, headquarters, Conversation Suite staff huddle with managers from various MasterCard departments and business units in front of a giant 40-foot LED screen that displays summaries of ongoing global brand conversations, refreshed every four minutes. A rotating group of marketing and customer service people spends two or three hours a day in the command center. "It's a real-time focus group," says a MasterCard communications executive. "We track all mentions of MasterCard and any of our products, plus the competition."

MasterCard uses what it sees, hears, and learns in the Conversation Suite to improve its products and marketing, track brand performance, and spark meaningful customer conversations and engagement. MasterCard is even training "social ambassadors," who can join online conversations and engage customers and brand influencers directly. "Today, almost everything we do [across the company] is rooted in insights we're gathering from the Conversation Suite," says another manager. "[It's] transforming the way we do business."

PepsiCo's Gatorade was one of the first brands to set up a social media command center, called Gatorade Mission Control. The center conducts extensive real-time monitoring of brand-related social media activity. Whenever someone mentions anything related to Gatorade (including competitors, Gatorade athletes, and sports nutrition–related topics) on major social media or blogs, it pops up in various visualizations and dashboards on one of six big screens. Gatorade Mission Control staffers also monitor digital ad, Web, and mobile site traffic, producing a consolidated picture of the brand's Internet image. Gatorade uses what it sees and learns at the center to improve its products, marketing, and interactions with customers.

Gatorade Mission Control also lets the brand engage consumers in real time, sometimes adding to or even shaping the online discourse. For example, during Game One of the 2014 NBA Finals, when then-Miami Heat forward LeBron James was carried off the court with leg cramps, Twitter exploded with comments that Gatorade had failed to prevent James's cramps. Although the former Gatorade spokesman had recently switched to rival Powerade, a Coca-Cola brand, most fans still associated King James with Gatorade. However, at the same time that fans were Tweeting concerns about the brand, the Gatorade Mission Control team was countering with its own humorous responses, such as "The person cramping isn't our client. Our athletes can take the Heat." When one fan Tweet asked where Gatorade was when LeBron James needed it, the team replied, "Waiting on the sidelines, but he prefers to drink something else." Thus, real-time social media monitoring

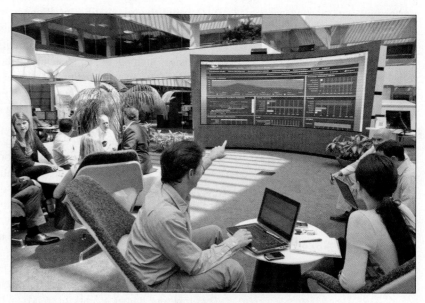

>> Competitive marketing intelligence: MasterCard's digital intelligence command center—called the Conversation Suite—monitors, analyzes, and responds in real time to millions of brand-related conversations across 56 markets and 27 languages around the world.

MasterCard

helped Gatorade turn potentially negative online chatter into a game-winning shot at the buzzer.

All kinds of organizations are now setting up social media command centers, even not-for-profits. For example, the American Red Cross partnered with Dell to create its Digital Operations Center in Washington, DC, which helps the humanitarian relief organization improve its responses to emergencies and natural disasters. The Red Cross got serious about monitoring social media after an opinion poll revealed that 80 percent of Americans expect emergency responders to monitor social networks, and one-third presumed that they could get help during a disaster within an hour if they posted or Tweeted a request. Modeled after Dell's own iconic social media center, the Red Cross Digital Operations Center broke new ground with an innovative digital volunteer program, adding thousands of trained volunteers around the country to help handle the massive volume of social media traffic that occurs during a disaster.

The Digital Operations Center helps improve the Red Cross's everyday relief efforts, such as responses to an apartment fire in a large metropolitan area. "Not only are we scanning the social media landscape looking for actionable intelligence," says a Red Cross manager, "we are also scanning the social space to see if there are people out there who need information and emotional support."

But it's the major disasters that highlight the center's biggest potential. For example, during the week of Hurricane Sandy, one of the biggest natural disasters in U.S. history, the Digital Operations Center played a crucial role in directing Red Cross relief efforts. In addition to the usual data from government partners, on-the-ground assessments, and damage reports from traditional media, the center pored through and acted on millions Tweets, Facebook posts, blog entries, and photos posted online. In all, it tracked more than 2 million posts and responded directly to thousands of people. In at least 88 cases, social media posts had a direct effect on

Red Cross actions. "We put trucks in areas where we saw a greater need, we moved cots to a shelter where we needed more supplies," says the Red Cross manager. Even a lack of social media activity was an important indicator. A social media "black hole" in a specific area probably meant that factors were preventing people in that area from Tweeting and that they needed help.

So whether it's MasterCard, Gatorade, or the American Red Cross, a social media command center can help marketers scour the digital environment, analyze brand-related conversations in real time to gain marketing insights, and respond quickly and appropriately. Ultimately, social media listening gives consumers another voice, to the benefit of both customers and the brand. "It enables us to give the public a seat at our response table," says the Red Cross manager. Wells Fargo's Director of Social Media agrees: "Consumers want to be a part of how companies serve them," she says. "Our nirvana is that if someone offers us an idea, tip, or feedback that really helps us, we respond directly."

Sources: "MasterCard Conversation Suite Video," http://newsroom.mastercard .com/videos/mastercard-conversation-suite-video/, accessed September 2015; Sheila Shayon, "MasterCard Harnesses the Power of Social with Innovative Conversation Suite," *brandchannel,* May 7, 2013, www.brandchannel.com/ home/post/2013/05/07/MasterCard-Conversation-Suite-050713.aspx; Giselle Abramovich, "Inside Mastercard's Social Command Center," *Digiday,* May 9, 2013, http://digiday.com/brands/inside-mastercards-social-command-center/; Anthony Shop, "Social Media Lessons from Gatorade Mission Control," *Socialmediadriver.com,* August 28, 2013, http://socialdriver.com/2013/08/28/ social-media-lessons-from-gatorade-mission-control/; Evan Hanson, "PepsiCo Drinks In Gatorade's Social Media Performance at Game One of NBA Finals," *24/7 Wallstreet,* June 7, 2014, http://247wallst.com/general/2014/06/07/ pepsico-drinks-in-gatorades-social-media-performance-at-game-one-of-nba-finals/#ixzz3O6SWtQJt; Ariel Schwartz, "How the Red Cross Used Tweets to Save Lives during Hurricane Sandy," *Fast Company,* October 31, 2013, www.fastcoexist.com/3020923/how-the-red-cross-used-tweets-to-save-lives-during-hurricane-sandy; and Scott Gulbransen, "Taking Back the Social-Media Command Center," *Forbes,* January 22, 2014, www.forbes.com/sites/ onmarketing/2014/01/22/taking-back-the-social-media-command-center/.

monitors real-time social media activity surrounding the introduction of Apple's latest iPhones to quickly shape marketing responses for its own Galaxy S smartphones and tablets.[7]

At the same time that Apple CEO Tim Cook is on stage unveiling the latest much-anticipated new iPhone, Samsung marketing strategists are huddled around screens in a war room hundreds of miles away watching the introduction unfold. They carefully monitored not only each new iPhone feature as it is presented but also the gush of online consumer commentary flooding blogs and social media channels. Even as the real-time consumer and competitive data surge in, the Samsung team is drafting a response. Within only a few days, just as the new iPhones are hitting store shelves, Samsung is already airing TV, print, and social media response ads that rechannel the excitement surrounding the iPhone debut toward its own Galaxy line.

For example, during the iPhone 5 roll-out, Samsung launched an ad mocking iPhone fans lined up outside Apple stores buzzing about the features of the new iPhone, only to be upstaged by passersby and their Samsung Galaxy smartphones ("The next big thing is already here"). Lines in the ad were based on thousands of actual Tweets and other social media interactions concerning specific iPhone features. The real-time-insights-based ad became the tech-ad sensation of the year (grabbing more than 70 million online views). Similarly, during the iPhone 6 debut, Samsung quickly launched a series of "It doesn't take a genius" ads poking fun at various iPhone features announced at Apple's release event.

Much competitor intelligence can be collected from people inside the company—executives, engineers and scientists, purchasing agents, and the sales force. The company can also obtain important intelligence information from suppliers, resellers, and key customers. Intelligence seekers can also pour through any of thousands of online databases. Some are free. For example, the U.S. Security and Exchange Commission's database provides a huge stockpile of financial information on public competitors, and the U.S. Patent Office and Trademark database reveals patents that competitors have filed. For a fee, companies can also subscribe to any of the more than 3,000 online databases and information search services, such as Hoover's, LexisNexis, and Dun & Bradstreet. Today's marketers have an almost overwhelming amount of competitor information only a few keystrokes away.

The intelligence game goes both ways. Facing determined competitive marketing intelligence efforts by competitors, most companies take steps to protect their own information. One self-admitted corporate spy advises that companies should try conducting marketing intelligence investigations of themselves, looking for potentially damaging information leaks. They should start by "vacuuming up" everything they can find in the public record, including job postings, court records, company advertisements and blogs, Web pages, press releases, online business reports, social media postings by customers and employees, and other information available to inquisitive competitors.[8]

The growing use of marketing intelligence also raises ethical issues. Some intelligence-gathering techniques may involve questionable ethics. Clearly, companies should take advantage of publicly available information. However, they should not stoop to snoop. With all the legitimate intelligence sources now available, a company does not need to break the law or accepted codes of ethics to get good intelligence.

Marketing Research

Author Comment

Whereas marketing intelligence involves actively scanning the general marketing environment, marketing research involves more focused studies to gain customer insights relating to specific marketing decisions.

Marketing research

The systematic design, collection, analysis, and reporting of data relevant to a specific marketing situation facing an organization.

In addition to marketing intelligence information about general consumer, competitor, and marketplace happenings, marketers often need formal studies that provide customer and market insights for specific marketing situations and decisions. For example, Starbucks wants to know how customers would react to a new breakfast menu item. Yahoo! wants to know how Web searchers will react to a proposed redesign of its site. Or Samsung wants to know how many and what kinds of people will buy its next-generation, ultrathin televisions. In such situations, managers will need marketing research.

Marketing research is the systematic design, collection, analysis, and reporting of data relevant to a specific marketing situation facing an organization. Companies use marketing research in a wide variety of situations. For example, marketing research gives marketers insights into customer motivations, purchase behavior, and satisfaction. It can help them to assess market potential and market share or measure the effectiveness of pricing, product, distribution, and promotion activities.

Some large companies have their own research departments that work with marketing managers on marketing research projects. In addition, these companies—like their smaller counterparts—frequently hire outside research specialists to consult with management on specific marketing problems and to conduct marketing research studies. Sometimes firms simply purchase data collected by outside firms to aid in their decision making.

The marketing research process has four steps (see ≫ **Figure 4.2**): defining the problem and research objectives, developing the research plan, implementing the research plan, and interpreting and reporting the findings.

This first step is probably the most difficult but also the most important one. It guides the entire research process. It's frustrating and costly to reach the end of an expensive research project only to learn that you've addressed the wrong problem!

≫ **Figure 4.2 The Marketing Research Process**

Defining the Problem and Research Objectives

Marketing managers and researchers must work together closely to define the problem and agree on research objectives. The manager best understands the decision for which information is needed, whereas the researcher best understands marketing research and how to obtain the information. Defining the problem and research objectives is often the hardest step in the research process. The manager may know that something is wrong without knowing the specific causes.

After the problem has been defined carefully, the manager and the researcher must set the research objectives. A marketing research project might have one of three types of objectives. The objective of **exploratory research** is to gather preliminary information that will help define the problem and suggest hypotheses. The objective of **descriptive research** is to describe things, such as the market potential for a product or the demographics and attitudes of consumers who buy the product. The objective of **causal research** is to test hypotheses about cause-and-effect relationships. For example, would a 10 percent decrease in tuition at a private college result in an enrollment increase sufficient to offset the reduced tuition? Managers often start with exploratory research and later follow with descriptive or causal research.

The statement of the problem and research objectives guides the entire research process. The manager and the researcher should put the statement in writing to be certain that they agree on the purpose and expected results of the research.

Exploratory research
Marketing research to gather preliminary information that will help define problems and suggest hypotheses.

Descriptive research
Marketing research to better describe marketing problems, situations, or markets, such as the market potential for a product or the demographics and attitudes of consumers.

Causal research
Marketing research to test hypotheses about cause-and-effect relationships.

Developing the Research Plan

Once researchers have defined the research problem and objectives, they must determine the exact information needed, develop a plan for gathering it efficiently, and present the plan to management. The research plan outlines sources of existing data and spells out the specific research approaches, contact methods, sampling plans, and instruments that researchers will use to gather new data.

Research objectives must be translated into specific information needs. For example, suppose that ≫ Chipotle Mexican Grill wants to know how consumers would react to the addition of drive-thru service to its restaurants. U.S. fast-food chains generate an estimated 24 percent of sales through drive-thrus. However, Chipotle—the sustainability-minded fast-casual restaurant that positions itself on "Food With Integrity"—doesn't offer drive-thru service. Adding drive-thrus might help Chipotle leverage its strong brand position and attract new sales. The proposed research might call for the following specific information:

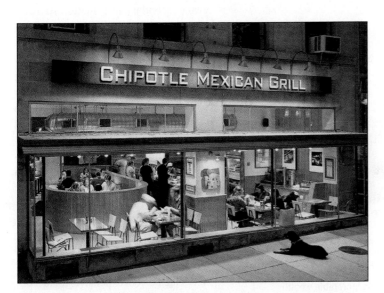

≫ **A decision by Chipotle Mexican Grill to add drive-thru service would call for marketing research that provides lots of specific information.**

Chipotle Mexican Grill, Inc.

- The demographic, economic, and lifestyle characteristics of current Chipotle customers: Do current counter-service customers also use drive-thrus? Are drive-thrus consistent with their needs and lifestyles? Or would Chipotle need to target a new segment of consumers?
- The characteristics and usage patterns of the broader population of fast-food and fast-casual diners: What do they need and expect from such restaurants? Where, when, and how do they use them, and what existing quality, price, and service levels do they value? The new Chipotle service would require trong, relevant, and distinctive positioning in the crowded fast-food market.
- Impact on the Chipotle customer experience: Would drive-thrus be consistent with a higher-quality fast-casual experience like the one Chipotle offers?
- Chipotle employee reactions to drive-thru service: Would restaurant employees support drive-thrus? Would adding drive-thrus disrupt operations and their ability to deliver high-quality food and service to inside customers?

- Forecasts of both inside and drive-thru sales and profits: Would the new drive-thru service create new sales and customers or simply take sales away from current operations?

Chipotle's marketers would need these and many other types of information to decide whether to introduce drive-thru service and, if so, the best way to do it.

The research plan should be presented in a *written proposal*. A written proposal is especially important when the research project is large and complex or when an outside firm carries it out. The proposal should cover the management problems addressed, the research objectives, the information to be obtained, and how the results will help management's decision making. The proposal also should include estimated research costs.

To meet the manager's information needs, the research plan can call for gathering secondary data, primary data, or both. **Secondary data** consist of information that already exists somewhere, having been collected for another purpose. **Primary data** consist of information collected for the specific purpose at hand.

Secondary data
Information that already exists somewhere, having been collected for another purpose.

Primary data
Information collected for the specific purpose at hand.

Gathering Secondary Data

Researchers usually start by gathering secondary data. The company's internal database provides a good starting point. However, the company can also tap into a wide assortment of external information sources.

Companies can buy secondary data from outside suppliers. For example, Nielsen sells shopper insight data from a consumer panel of more than 250,000 households in 25 countries worldwide, with measures of trial and repeat purchasing, brand loyalty, and buyer demographics. Experian Simmons carries out a full spectrum of consumer studies that provide a comprehensive view of the American consumer. The U.S. Yankelovich MONITOR service by The Futures Company sells information on important social and lifestyle trends. These and other firms supply high-quality data to suit a wide variety of marketing information needs.[9]

Using *commercial online databases*, marketing researchers can conduct their own searches of secondary data sources. >> General database services such as ProQuest and LexisNexis put an incredible wealth of information at the fingertips of marketing decision makers. Beyond commercial services offering information for a fee, almost every industry association, government agency, business publication, and news medium offers free information to those tenacious enough to find their Web sites or apps.

Internet search engines can also be a big help in locating relevant secondary information sources. However, they can also be very frustrating and inefficient. For example, a Chipotle marketer Googling "fast-food drive-thru" would come up with more than 2.8 million hits. Still, well-structured, well-designed online searches can be a good starting point to any marketing research project.

Secondary data can usually be obtained more quickly and at a lower cost than primary data. Also, secondary sources can sometimes provide data an individual company cannot collect on its own—information that either is not directly available or would be too expensive to collect. For example, it would be too expensive for a consumer products brand such as Coca-Cola or Tide to conduct a continuing retail store audit to find out about the

>> General database services such as ProQuest and LexisNexis put an incredible wealth of information at the fingertips of marketing decision makers.

market shares, prices, and displays of its own and competitors' brands. But those marketers can buy the InfoScan service from SymphonyIRI Group, which provides this information based on scanner and other data from 34,000 retail stores in markets around the nation.[10]

Secondary data can also present problems. Researchers can rarely obtain all the data they need from secondary sources. For example, Chipotle will not find existing information regarding consumer reactions about new drive-thru service that it has not yet installed. Even when data can be found, the information might not be very usable. The researcher must evaluate secondary information carefully to make certain it is *relevant* (fits the research project's needs), *accurate* (reliably collected and reported), *current* (up-to-date enough for current decisions), and *impartial* (objectively collected and reported).

Primary Data Collection

Secondary data provide a good starting point for research and often help to define research problems and objectives. In most cases, however, the company must also collect primary data. ≫ Table 4.1 shows that designing a plan for primary data collection calls for a number of decisions on *research approaches, contact methods*, the *sampling plan*, and *research instruments*.

Research Approaches

Research approaches for gathering primary data include observation, surveys, and experiments. We discuss each one in turn.

Observational research
Gathering primary data by observing relevant people, actions, and situations.

Observational Research. **Observational research** involves gathering primary data by observing relevant people, actions, and situations. For example, food retailer Trader Joe's might evaluate possible new store locations by checking traffic patterns, neighborhood conditions, and the locations of competing Whole Foods, Fresh Market, and other retail chains.

Researchers often observe consumer behavior to glean customer insights they can't obtain by simply asking customers questions. For instance, Fisher-Price has established an observation lab in which it can observe the reactions little tots have to new toys. The Fisher-Price Play Lab is a sunny, toy-strewn space where lucky kids get to test Fisher-Price prototypes under the watchful eyes of designers who hope to learn what will get them worked up into a new-toy frenzy. In the lab, some 3,500 kids participate each year testing 1,200 products annually. "Our designers watch and learn from how [children] play," says a Fisher-Price child research manager. "It really helps us make better products."[11]

Marketers not only observe what consumers do but also observe what consumers are saying. As discussed earlier, marketers now routinely listen in on consumer conversations on blogs, social networks, and Web sites. Observing such naturally occurring feedback can provide inputs that simply can't be gained through more structured and formal research approaches.

Ethnographic research
A form of observational research that involves sending trained observers to watch and interact with consumers in their "natural environments."

A wide range of companies now use **ethnographic research**. Ethnographic research involves sending observers to watch and interact with consumers in their "natural environments." The observers might be trained anthropologists and psychologists or company

≫ Table 4.1	Planning Primary Data Collection		
Research Approaches	**Contact Methods**	**Sampling Plan**	**Research Instruments**
Observation	Mail	Sampling unit	Questionnaire
Survey	Telephone	Sample size	Mechanical instruments
Experiment	Personal	Sampling procedure	
	Online		

researchers and managers. For example, Coors insights teams frequent bars and other locations in a top-secret small-town location—they call it the "Outpost"—within a day's drive of Chicago. The researchers use the town as a real-life lab, hob-knobbing anonymously with bar patrons, supermarket shoppers, restaurant diners, convenience store clerks, and other townspeople to gain authentic insights into how middle American consumers buy, drink, dine, and socialize around Coors and competing beer brands.[12]

Global branding firm Landor launched Landor Families, an ongoing ethnographic study that has followed 11 French families intensely for the past seven years. »Landor researchers visit the families twice a year in their homes, peeking into their refrigerators and diving deeply into both their refrigerators and their food shopping behaviors and opinions. The researchers also shop with the families at their local supermarkets and look over their shoulders while they shop online. The families furnish monthly online reports detailing their shopping behaviors and opinions. The Landor Families study provides rich behavioral insights for Landor clients such as Danone, Kraft Foods, and Procter & Gamble. Today's big data analytics can provide important insights into the whats, whens, and wheres of consumer buying. The Landor Families program is designed to explore the whys. According to Landor, "There is no better way to understand people than to observe them in real life."[13]

Beyond conducting ethnographic research in physical consumer environments, many companies now routinely conduct *Netnography* research—observing consumers in a natural context in the Internet and mobile space. Observing people as they interact and move about in the online world can provide useful insights into both online and offline buying motives and behavior. And observing people's shopping patterns by tracking their mobile movement, both within and between stores, can provide retailers with valuable marketing information.

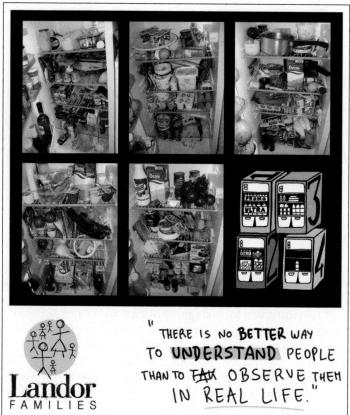

» The Landor Families ongoing ethnographic study has followed 11 French families intensely for the past seven years, diving deeply into both their refrigerators and their food shopping behaviors. Says Landor, "There is no better way to understand people than to observe them in real life."
Landor

Observational and ethnographic research often yields the kinds of details that just don't emerge from traditional research questionnaires or focus groups. Whereas traditional quantitative research approaches seek to test known hypotheses and obtain answers to well-defined product or strategy questions, observational research can generate fresh customer and market insights that people are unwilling or unable to provide. It provides a window into customers' unconscious actions and unexpressed needs and feelings.

However, some things simply cannot be observed, such as attitudes, motives, or private behavior. Long-term or infrequent behavior is also difficult to observe. Finally, observations can be very difficult to interpret. Because of these limitations, researchers often use observation along with other data collection methods.

Survey research
Gathering primary data by asking people questions about their knowledge, attitudes, preferences, and buying behavior.

Survey Research. **Survey research**, the most widely used method for primary data collection, is the approach best suited for gathering descriptive information. A company that wants to know about people's knowledge, attitudes, preferences, or buying behavior can often find out by asking them directly.

The major advantage of survey research is its flexibility; it can be used to obtain many different kinds of information in many different situations. Surveys addressing almost any marketing question or decision can be conducted by phone or mail, in person, or online.

However, survey research also presents some problems. Sometimes people are unable to answer survey questions because they cannot remember or have never thought about what they do and why they do it. People may be unwilling to respond to unknown interviewers or about things they consider private. Respondents may answer survey questions even when they do not know the answer just to appear smarter or more informed. Or they may try to help the interviewer by giving pleasing answers. Finally, busy people may not take the time, or they might resent the intrusion into their privacy.

Experimental Research. Whereas observation is best suited for exploratory research and surveys for descriptive research, **experimental research** is best suited for gathering causal information. Experiments involve selecting matched groups of subjects, giving them different treatments, controlling unrelated factors, and checking for differences in group responses. Thus, experimental research tries to explain cause-and-effect relationships.

For example, before adding a new sandwich to its menu, McDonald's might use experiments to test the effects on sales of two different prices it might charge. It could introduce the new sandwich at one price in one city and at another price in another city. If the cities are similar and if all other marketing efforts for the sandwich are the same, then differences in sales in the two cities could be related to the price charged.

Contact Methods

Information can be collected by mail, telephone, personal interview, or online. >> Table 4.2 shows the strengths and weaknesses of each contact method.

Mail, Telephone, and Personal Interviewing. *Mail questionnaires* can be used to collect large amounts of information at a low cost per respondent. Respondents may give more honest answers to more personal questions on a mail questionnaire than to an unknown interviewer in person or over the phone. Also, no interviewer is involved to bias respondents' answers.

However, mail questionnaires are not very flexible; all respondents answer the same questions in a fixed order. Mail surveys usually take longer to complete, and the response rate—the number of people returning completed questionnaires—is often very low. Finally, the researcher often has little control over the mail questionnaire sample. Even with a good mailing list, it is hard to control *who* at a particular address fills out the questionnaire. As a result of the shortcomings, more and more marketers are now shifting to faster, more flexible, and lower-cost email, online, and mobile phone surveys.

Telephone interviewing is one of the best methods for gathering information quickly, and it provides greater flexibility than mail questionnaires. Interviewers can explain difficult questions and, depending on the answers they receive, skip some questions or probe on others. Response rates tend to be higher than with mail questionnaires, and interviewers can ask to speak to respondents with the desired characteristics or even by name.

However, with telephone interviewing, the cost per respondent is higher than with mail, online, or mobile questionnaires. Also, people may not want to discuss personal questions

Experimental research
Gathering primary data by selecting matched groups of subjects, giving them different treatments, controlling related factors, and checking for differences in group responses.

>> Table 4.2	Strengths and Weaknesses of Contact Methods			
	Mail	**Telephone**	**Personal**	**Online**
Flexibility	Poor	Good	Excellent	Good
Quantity of data that can be collected	Good	Fair	Excellent	Good
Control of interviewer effects	Excellent	Fair	Poor	Fair
Control of sample	Fair	Excellent	Good	Excellent
Speed of data collection	Poor	Excellent	Good	Excellent
Response rate	Poor	Poor	Good	Good
Cost	Good	Fair	Poor	Excellent

Source: Based on Donald S. Tull and Del I. Hawkins, *Marketing Research: Measurement and Method,* 7th ed. (New York: Macmillan Publishing Company, 1993). Adapted with permission of the authors.

with an interviewer. The method introduces interviewer bias—the way interviewers talk, how they ask questions, and other differences that may affect respondents' answers. Finally, in this age of do-not-call lists and promotion-harassed consumers, potential survey respondents are increasingly hanging up on telephone interviewers rather than talking with them.

Personal interviewing takes two forms: individual interviewing and group interviewing. *Individual interviewing* involves talking with people in their homes or offices, on the street, or in shopping malls. Such interviewing is flexible. Trained interviewers can guide interviews, explain difficult questions, and explore issues as the situation requires. They can show subjects actual products, packages, advertisements, or videos and observe reactions and behavior. However, individual personal interviews may cost three to four times as much as telephone interviews.

Group interviewing consists of inviting small groups of people to meet with a trained moderator to talk about a product, service, or organization. Participants normally are paid a small sum for attending. A moderator encourages free and easy discussion, hoping that group interactions will bring out actual feelings and thoughts. At the same time, the moderator "focuses" the discussion—hence the name **focus group interviewing**.

In traditional focus groups, researchers and marketers watch the focus group discussions from behind a one-way mirror and record comments in writing or on video for later study. Focus group researchers often use videoconferencing and Internet technology to connect marketers in distant locations with live focus group action. Marketing executives in far-off locations can look in and listen, even participate, as a focus group progresses.

Along with observational research, focus group interviewing has become one of the major qualitative marketing research tools for gaining fresh insights into consumer thoughts and feelings. In focus group settings, researchers not only hear consumer ideas and opinions, they also can observe facial expressions, body movements, group interplay, and conversational flows. However, focus group studies present some challenges. They usually employ small samples to keep time and costs down, and it may be hard to generalize from the results. Moreover, consumers in focus groups are not always open and honest about their real feelings, behavior, and intentions in front of other people.

To overcome these problems, many researchers are tinkering with the focus group design. Some companies are changing the environments in which they conduct focus groups to help consumers relax and elicit more authentic responses. For example, Lexus hosts "An Evening with Lexus" dinners in customers' homes with groups of luxury car buyers to learn up close and personal why they did or did not buy a Lexus. Other companies use *immersion groups*—small groups of consumers who interact directly and informally with product designers without a focus group moderator present. ≫ Research and innovation consultancy The Mom Complex uses such immersion groups to help brand marketers from companies such as Unilever, Johnson & Johnson, Kimberly-Clark, Kellogg, Playskool, and Walmart understand and connect with their "mom customers":[14]

Focus group interviewing
Personal interviewing that involves inviting small groups of people to gather for a few hours with a trained interviewer to talk about a product, service, or organization. The interviewer "focuses" the group discussion on important issues.

≫ **New focus group designs: The Mom Complex uses "Mom Immersion Sessions" to help brand marketers understand and connect directly with their "mom customers" on important brand issues.**
© caia image/Alamy

According to The Mom Complex, America's 80 million moms control 85 percent of household purchases, yet three out of four moms say marketers have no idea what it's like to be a mother. To change that, The Mom Complex arranges "Mom Immersion Sessions," in which brand marketers interact directly with groups of mothers, who receive $100 in compensation for a two-hour session. Rather than the usual focus group practice of putting the marketers behind a one-way mirror to observe groups of moms discussing their brands, the participants and marketers sit in the same room. Guided by a discussion facilitator, the moms begin by educating the marketers about the realities of motherhood—"the raw, real ugly truth about being a mom." Then the moms and marketers work together to address specific brand issues—whether it's new product ideas, current product problems, or positioning and communications strategy. The goal is to "turn the challenges of motherhood into growth opportunities for brands."

Individual and focus group interviews can add a personal touch as opposed to more numbers-oriented, big data research. They can provide rich insights into the motivations and feelings behind the numbers and analytics. "Focus groups are the most widely used qualitative research tool," says one analyst, "and with good reason. They foster fruitful discussion and can provide unique insight into customers' and potential customers' needs, wants, thoughts, and feelings." Things really come to life when you hear people say them.[15]

Online marketing research
Collecting primary data online through Internet surveys, online focus groups, Web-based experiments, or tracking of consumers' online behavior.

Online Marketing Research. The Internet has had a dramatic impact on how marketing research is conducted. Increasingly, researchers are collecting primary data through **online marketing research**: Internet and mobile surveys, online panels, experiments, and online focus groups and brand communities.

Online research can take many forms. A company can use the Internet or mobile technology as a survey medium: It can include a questionnaire on its Web or social media sites or use email or mobile devices to invite people to answer questions. It can create online panels that provide regular feedback or conduct live discussions or online focus groups. Researchers can also conduct online experiments. They can experiment with different prices, headlines, or product features on different Web or mobile sites or at different times to learn the relative effectiveness of their offers. They can set up virtual shopping environments and use them to test new products and marketing programs. Or a company can learn about the behavior of online customers by following their click streams as they visit the online site and move to other sites.

The Internet is especially well suited to *quantitative* research—for example, conducting marketing surveys and collecting data. More than 87 percent of all Americans now use the Internet, making it a fertile channel for reaching a broad cross-section of consumers.[16] As response rates for traditional survey approaches decline and costs increase, the Internet is quickly replacing mail and the telephone as the dominant data collection methodology.

Internet-based survey research offers many advantages over traditional phone, mail, and personal interviewing approaches. The most obvious advantages are speed and low costs. By going online, researchers can quickly and easily distribute surveys to thousands of respondents simultaneously via email or by posting them on selected online and mobile sites. Responses can be almost instantaneous, and because respondents themselves enter the information, researchers can tabulate, review, and share research data as the information arrives.

Online research also usually costs much less than research conducted through mail, phone, or personal interviews. Using the Internet eliminates most of the postage, phone, interviewer, and data-handling costs associated with the other approaches. Moreover, sample size and location have little impact on costs. Once the questionnaire is set up, there's little difference in cost between 10 respondents and 10,000 respondents on the Internet, or between local or globally distant respondents.

Its low cost puts online research well within the reach of almost any business, large or small. In fact, with the Internet, what was once the domain of research experts is now available to almost any would-be researcher. >> Even smaller, less sophisticated researchers can use online survey services such as Snap Surveys (www.snapsurveys.com) and SurveyMonkey (www.surveymonkey.com) to create, publish, and distribute their own custom online or mobile surveys in minutes.

Internet-based surveys also tend to be more interactive and engaging, easier to complete, and less intrusive

>> **Online research: Thanks to survey services such as Snap Surveys, almost any business, large or small, can create, publish, and distribute its own custom online or mobile surveys in minutes.**

Reproduced with permission from Snap Surveys. www.snapsurveys.com

than traditional phone or mail surveys. As a result, they usually garner higher response rates. The Internet is an excellent medium for reaching the hard-to-reach consumer—for example, the often-elusive teen, single, affluent, and well-educated audiences. It's also good for reaching people who lead busy lives, from working mothers to on-the-go executives. Such people are well represented online, and they can respond in their own space and at their own convenience.

Just as marketing researchers have rushed to use the Internet for quantitative surveys and data collection, they are now also adopting *qualitative* Internet-based research approaches, such as online focus groups, blogs, and social networks. The Internet can provide a fast, low-cost way to gain qualitative customer insights.

A primary qualitative Internet-based research approach is **online focus groups**. For example, online research firm FocusVision offers its InterVu service, which harnesses the power of the Internet to conduct focus groups with participants at remote locations, anywhere in the world, at any time. Using their own Webcams, InterVu participants can log on to focus sessions from their homes or offices and see, hear, and react to each other in real-time, face-to-face discussions.[17] Such focus groups can be conducted in any language and viewed with simultaneous translation. They work well for bringing together people from different parts of the country or world at low cost. Researchers can view the sessions in real time from just about anywhere, eliminating travel, lodging, and facility costs. Finally, although online focus groups require some advance scheduling, results are almost immediate.

Online focus groups
Gathering a small group of people online with a trained moderator to chat about a product, service, or organization and gain qualitative insights about consumer attitudes and behavior.

Although growing rapidly, both quantitative and qualitative Internet-based research have some drawbacks. One major problem is controlling who's in the online sample. Without seeing respondents, it's difficult to know who they really are. To overcome such sample and context problems, many online research firms use opt-in communities and respondent panels. Alternatively, many companies have now developed their own custom social networks and are using them to gain customer inputs and insights. For example, in its relentless "Pursuit of Perfection," Lexus has built an extensive online research community called the Lexus Advisory Board, which consists of 20,000 invitation-only Lexus owners representing a wide range of demographics, psychographics, and model ownership. ≫ Similarly, NASCAR has built an online community of 12,000 core fans called the NASCAR Fan Council. Both companies survey these online communities regularly to obtain quick and relevant feedback from customers about everything from brand perceptions to proposed marketing initiatives.[18]

≫ NASCAR has built an online research community of 12,000 core fans called the NASCAR Fan Council, which it surveys regularly for inputs and insights.
NASCAR

Online Behavioral and Social Tracking and Targeting. Thus, in recent years, the Internet has become an important tool for conducting research and developing customer insights. But today's marketing researchers are going even further—well beyond online surveys, focus groups, and Internet communities. Increasingly, they are listening to and watching consumers by actively mining the rich veins of unsolicited, unstructured, "bottom-up" customer information already coursing around the Internet. Whereas traditional marketing research provides more logical consumer responses to structured and intrusive research questions, online listening provides the passion and spontaneity of unsolicited consumer opinions.

Tracking consumers online might be as simple as scanning customer reviews and comments on the company's brand site or on shopping sites such as Amazon.com or BestBuy.com. Or it might mean using sophisticated online-analysis tools to deeply analyze the mountains of consumer brand–related comments and messages found in blogs or on social media sites, such as Facebook, Yelp, YouTube, Instagram, or Twitter. Listening to and engaging customers online can provide valuable insights into what consumers are saying or feeling about a brand. It can also provide opportunities for building positive brand experiences and relationships. Many companies now excel at listening online and responding quickly and appropriately. As noted previously, more and more companies are setting up social media command centers with which they scour the digital environment and analyze brand-related comments and conversations to gain marketing insights.

Information about what consumers do while trolling the vast digital expanse—what searches they make, the online and mobile sites they visit, how they shop, and what they buy—is pure gold to marketers. And today's marketers are busy mining that gold. Then, in a practice called **behavioral targeting**, marketers use the online data to target ads and offers to specific consumers. For example, if you place an Apple iPad in your Amazon.com shopping cart but don't buy it, you might expect to see some ads for that very type of tablet the next time you visit your favorite ESPN site to catch up on the latest sports scores.

The newest wave of Web analytics and targeting takes online eavesdropping even further—from *behavioral* targeting to *social* targeting. Whereas behavioral targeting tracks consumer movements across online sites, social targeting also mines individual online social connections and conversations from social networking sites. Research shows that consumers shop a lot like their friends and are much more likely to respond to ads from brands friends use. So, instead of just having a Zappos.com ad for running shoes pop up because you've recently searched online for running shoes (behavioral targeting), an ad for a specific pair of running shoes pops up because a friend that you're connected to via Twitter just bought those shoes from Zappos.com last week (social targeting).

Online listening, behavioral targeting, and social targeting can help marketers to harness the massive amounts of consumer information swirling around the Internet. However, as marketers get more adept at trolling blogs, social networks, and other Internet and mobile domains, many critics worry about consumer privacy. ≫At what point does sophisticated online research cross the line into consumer stalking? Proponents claim that behavioral and social targeting benefit more than abuse consumers by feeding back ads and products that are more relevant to their interests. But to many consumers and public advocates, following consumers online and stalking them with ads feels more than just a little creepy.

Regulators and others are stepping in. The Federal Trade Commission (FTC) has recommended the creation of a "Do Not Track" system (the online equivalent to the "Do Not Call" registry)—which would let people opt out of having their actions monitored online. However, progress has been mixed. Meanwhile, many major Internet browsers and social media have heeded the concerns by adding extended privacy features to their services.[19]

Behavioral targeting
Using online consumer tracking data to target advertisements and marketing offers to specific consumers.

≫ **Marketers watch what consumers say and do online, then use the resulting insights to personalize online shopping experiences. Is it sophisticated online research or "just a little creepy"?**

Andresr/Shutterstock.com

Sampling Plan

Marketing researchers usually draw conclusions about large groups of consumers by studying a small sample of the total consumer population. A **sample** is a segment of the population selected for marketing research to represent the population as a whole. Ideally, the sample should be representative so that the researcher can make accurate estimates of the thoughts and behaviors of the larger population.

Designing the sample requires three decisions. First, *who* is to be studied (what *sampling unit*)? The answer to this question is not always obvious. For example, to learn about the decision-making process for a family automobile purchase, should the subject be the husband, the wife, other family members, dealership salespeople, or all of these? Second, *how many* people should be included (what *sample size*)? Large samples give more reliable results than small samples. However, larger samples usually cost more, and it is not necessary to sample the entire target market or even a large portion to get reliable results.

Finally, *how* should the people in the sample be *chosen* (what *sampling procedure*)? ≫**Table 4.3** describes different kinds of samples. Using *probability samples*, each population member has a known chance of being included in the sample, and researchers can calculate confidence limits for sampling error. But when probability sampling costs too much or takes too much time, marketing researchers often take *nonprobability samples* even though their sampling error cannot be measured. These varied ways of drawing samples have different costs and time limitations as well as different accuracy and statistical properties. Which method is best depends on the needs of the research project.

Sample
A segment of the population selected for marketing research to represent the population as a whole.

» Table 4.3	**Types of Samples**

Probability Sample

Simple random sample	Every member of the population has a known and equal chance of selection.
Stratified random sample	The population is divided into mutually exclusive groups (such as age groups), and random samples are drawn from each group.
Cluster (area) sample	The population is divided into mutually exclusive groups (such as blocks), and the researcher draws a sample of the groups to interview.

Nonprobability Sample

Convenience sample	The researcher selects the easiest population members from which to obtain information.
Judgment sample	The researcher uses his or her judgment to select population members who are good prospects for accurate information.
Quota sample	The researcher finds and interviews a prescribed number of people in each of several categories.

Research Instruments

In collecting primary data, marketing researchers have a choice of two main research instruments: *questionnaires* and *mechanical devices*.

Questionnaires. The questionnaire is by far the most common instrument, whether administered in person, by phone, by email, or online. Questionnaires are very flexible—there are many ways to ask questions. Closed-ended questions include all the possible answers, and subjects make choices among them. Examples include multiple-choice questions and scale questions. Open-ended questions allow respondents to answer in their own words. In a survey of airline users, Southwest Airlines might simply ask, "What is your opinion of Southwest Airlines?" Or it might ask people to complete a sentence: "When I choose an airline, the most important consideration is. . . ." These and other kinds of open-ended questions often reveal more than closed-ended questions because they do not limit respondents' answers.

Open-ended questions are especially useful in exploratory research, when the researcher is trying to find out *what* people think but is not measuring *how many* people think in a certain way. Closed-ended questions, on the other hand, provide answers that are easier to interpret and tabulate.

Researchers should also use care in the *wording* and *ordering* of questions. They should use simple, direct, and unbiased wording. Questions should be arranged in a logical order. The first question should create interest if possible, and difficult or personal questions should be asked last so that respondents do not become defensive.

Mechanical Instruments. Although questionnaires are the most common research instrument, researchers also use mechanical instruments to monitor consumer behavior. Nielsen Media Research attaches people meters to television sets, cable boxes, and satellite systems in selected homes to record who watches which programs. Retailers use checkout scanners to record shoppers' purchases. Mondelez International—maker of Chips Ahoy!, Ritz crackers, Oreos, and other goodies—is even building supermarket "smart shelves." »The shelves use sensors to analyze facial structures and other characteristics that identify a shopper's age and sex and determine if and when the shopper selects a product off the shelf. Along with supplying a wealth of insights into consumer shopping behavior, based on who's buying what, the smart shelves allow marketers to deliver real-time, personalized promotions via video screens on the shelves.[20]

>> **Using mechanical instruments to monitor consumers: Some marketers are building supermarket "smart shelves" that track shopper demographics and purchases, supplying a wealth of insights into consumer shopping behavior.**

Associated Press

Other mechanical devices measure subjects' physical responses to marketing offerings. Consider this example:[21]

> Time Warner's MediaLab at its New York headquarters looks more like a chic consumer electronics store than a research lab. But the lab employs a nifty collection of high-tech observation techniques to capture the changing ways that today's viewers are using and reacting to television and Web content. The MediaLab uses biometric measures to analyze every show subjects watch, every site they visit, and every commercial they skip. Meanwhile, mechanical devices assess viewer engagement via physiological measures of skin temperature, heart rate, sweat level, leaning in, and facial and eye movements. Observers behind two-way mirrors or using cameras that peer over each subject's shoulder make real-time assessments of Web browsing behavior. In all, the deep consumer insights gained from MediaLab observations are helping Time Warner prepare for marketing in today's rapidly changing digital media landscape.

Still other researchers apply *neuromarketing*, measuring brain activity to learn how consumers feel and respond. Marketing scientists using MRI scans and EEG devices have learned that tracking brain electrical activity and blood flow can provide companies with insights into what turns consumers on and off regarding their brands and marketing.

Companies ranging from PepsiCo and Disney to Google and Microsoft now hire neuromarketing research companies such as Neurons Inc., Sands Research, and Nielsen NeuroFocus to help figure out what people are really thinking. For example, PepsiCo's Frito-Lay worked with Nielsen NeuroFocus to assess consumer motivations underlying the success of its Cheetos snack brand. After scanning the brains of carefully chosen consumers, Nielsen NeuroFocus learned that part of what makes Cheetos a junk-food staple is the messy orange cheese dust—that's right, the neon stuff that gloms onto your fingers and then smears on your shirt or the couch cushions. As it turns out, the icky coating triggers a powerful brain response: a sense of "giddy subversion" that makes the messiness more than worth the trouble it causes. Using this finding, Frito-Lay successfully framed an entire advertising campaign—called "The Orange Underground"—around the mess Cheetos make. For its part, Nielsen NeuroFocus won an award for outstanding advertising research.[22]

Although neuromarketing techniques can measure consumer involvement and emotional responses second by second, such brain responses can be difficult to interpret. Thus, neuromarketing is usually used in combination with other research approaches to gain a more complete picture of what goes on inside consumers' heads.

Implementing the Research Plan

The researcher next puts the marketing research plan into action. This involves collecting, processing, and analyzing the information. Data collection can be carried out by the company's marketing research staff or outside firms. Researchers should watch closely to make sure that the plan is implemented correctly. They must guard against problems with data collection techniques and technologies, data quality, and timeliness.

Researchers must also process and analyze the collected data to isolate important information and insights. They need to check data for accuracy and completeness and code them for analysis. The researchers then tabulate the results and compute statistical measures.

Interpreting and Reporting the Findings

The market researcher must now interpret the findings, draw conclusions, and report them to management. The researcher should not try to overwhelm managers with numbers and fancy statistical techniques. Rather, the researcher should present important findings and insights that are useful in the major decisions faced by management.

However, interpretation should not be left only to researchers. Although they are often experts in research design and statistics, the marketing manager knows more about the problem and the decisions that must be made. The best research means little if the manager blindly accepts faulty interpretations from the researcher. Similarly, managers may be biased. They might tend to accept research results that show what they expected and reject those that did not expect or hope for. In many cases, findings can be interpreted in different ways, and discussions between researchers and managers will help point to the best interpretations. Thus, managers and researchers must work together closely when interpreting research results, and both must share responsibility for the research process and resulting decisions.

LINKING THE CONCEPTS

Whew! We've covered a lot of territory. Hold up a minute, take a breather, and see if you can apply the marketing research process you've just studied.

- What specific kinds of research do Chipotle Mexican Grill's marketing managers use to learn more about its customers' preferences and buying behaviors? Sketch out a brief research plan for assessing potential reactions to a new drive-thru service.
- Could you use the marketing research process to analyze your career opportunities and job possibilities? (Think of yourself as a "product" and employers as potential "customers.") If so, what would your research plan look like?

Author Comment
We've talked generally about managing customer relationships throughout the book. But here, "customer relationship management" (CRM) has a much narrower data-management meaning. It refers to capturing and using customer data from all sources to manage customer interactions, engage customers, and build customer relationships.

Analyzing and Using Marketing Information

Information gathered from internal databases, competitive marketing intelligence, and marketing research usually requires additional analysis. Managers may need help applying the information to gain customer and market insights that will improve their marketing decisions. This help may include advanced analytics to learn more about the relationships within sets of data. Information analysis might also involve the application of analytical models that will help marketers make better decisions.

Once the information has been processed and analyzed, it must be made available to the right decision makers at the right time. In the following sections, we look deeper into analyzing and using marketing information.

Customer Relationship Management (CRM)

The question of how best to analyze and use individual customer data presents special problems. In the current *big data* era, most companies are awash in information about their customers and the marketplace. Still, smart companies capture information at every possible customer *touch point*. These touch points include customer purchases, sales force contacts, service and support calls, Web and social media site visits, satisfaction surveys, credit and payment interactions, market research studies—every contact between a customer and a company.

Unfortunately, this information is usually scattered widely across the organization or buried deep in separate company databases. To overcome such problems, many companies are now turning to **customer relationship management (CRM)** to manage detailed information about individual customers and carefully manage customer touch points to maximize customer loyalty.

CRM consists of sophisticated software and analysis tools from companies such as Salesforce.com, Oracle, Microsoft, and SAS that integrate customer and marketplace information from all sources, analyze it, and apply the results to build stronger customer relationships. CRM integrates everything that a company's sales, service, and marketing

Customer relationship management (CRM)
Managing detailed information about individual customers and carefully managing customer touch points to maximize customer loyalty.

teams know about individual customers, providing a 360-degree view of the customer relationship. For example, MetLife recently developed a CRM system that it calls "The MetLife Wall":[23]

> One of the biggest customer service challenges for MetLife's sales and service reps used to be quickly finding and getting to customer information—different records, transactions, and interactions stored in dozens of different company data locations and formats. The MetLife Wall solves that problem. The Wall uses a Facebook-like interface to serve up a consolidated view of each MetLife customer's service experience. The innovative CRM system draws customer data from 70 different MetLife systems containing 45 million customer agreements and 140 million transactions. It puts all of a given customer's information and related links into a single record on a single screen, updated in near real time. Now, thanks to The MetLife Wall—with only a single click instead of the 40 clicks it used to take—sales and service reps can see a complete view of a given customer's various policies, transactions, and claims filed and paid, along with a history of all the interactions the customer has had with MetLife across the company's many touch points, all on a simple timeline. The Wall has given a big boost to MetLife's customer service and cross-selling efforts. According to a MetLife marketing executive, it's also had "a huge impact on customer satisfaction."

By using CRM to understand customers better, companies can provide higher levels of customer service and develop deeper customer relationships. They can use CRM to pinpoint high-value customers, target them more effectively, cross-sell the company's products, and create offers tailored to specific customer requirements.

Big Data and Marketing Analytics

Today's big data can yield big results. But simply collecting and storing huge amounts of data has little value. Marketers must sift through the mountains of data to mine the gems—the bits that yield customer insights. As one marketing executive puts it, "It's actually [about getting] *big insights* from big data. It's throwing away 99.999 percent of that data to find things that are actionable." Says another data expert, "*right* data trumps *big* data."[24] That's the job of *marketing analytics*.

Marketing analytics consists of the analysis tools, technologies, and processes by which marketers dig out meaningful patterns in big data to gain customer insights and gauge marketing performance.[25] Marketers apply marketing analytics to the large and complex sets of data they collect from Web, mobile, and social media tracking; customer transactions and engagements; and other big data sources. For example, Netflix maintains a bulging customer database and uses sophisticated marketing analytics to gain insights, which it then uses to fuel recommendations to subscribers, decide what programming to offer, and even develop its own exclusive content in the quest to serve its customers better (see Marketing at Work 4.2).

Another good example of marketing analytics in action comes from food products giant Kraft, whose classic brands—from JELL-O, Miracle Whip, and Kraft Macaroni and Cheese to Oscar Meyer, Philadelphia Cream Cheese, Lunchables, and Planters nuts—are found in 98 percent of all North American households:[26]

> Kraft has a treasure trove of marketing data, gathered from years of interactions with customers and from its social media monitoring hub called Looking Glass. Looking Glass tracks consumer trends, competitor activities, and more than 100,000 brand-related conversations daily in social media and on blogs. Kraft also reaps data from customer interactions with its *Kraft Food & Family* magazine, email communications, and the more than 100 Web and social media sites that serve its large brand portfolio. In all, Kraft has 18 years' worth of customer data across 22,000 different attributes.

Marketing analytics
The analysis tools, technologies, and processes by which marketers dig out meaningful patterns in big data to gain customer insights and gauge marketing performance.

>> **Marketing analytics: Food products giant Kraft reaps a treasure trove of data from customers of its classic brands, then applies high-level marketing analytics to mine nuggets of customer insights.**

Bloomberg/Getty Images

MARKETING AT WORK   4.2

Netflix Streams Success with Big Data and Marketing Analytics

Americans now watch more movies and TV programs streamed online than they watch on DVDs and Blu-ray discs. And with its rotating library of more than 60,000 titles, Netflix streams more movie and program content by far than any other video service. Netflix's 62 million paid subscribers watch more than 3.3 billion hours of movies and TV programs every month. During peak hours on any given day, a remarkable one-third of all downloads on the non-mobile Internet are devoted to streamed programming from Netflix.

All of this comes as little surprise to avid Netflixers. But members might be startled to learn that while they are busy watching Netflix videos, Netflix is busy watching *them*—watching them very, very closely. Netflix tracks and analyzes heaps of customer data in excruciating detail. Then it uses the big data insights to give customers exactly what they want. Netflix knows in depth what its audience wants to watch, and it uses this knowledge to fuel recommendations to subscribers, decide what programming to offer, and even develop its own exclusive content.

No company knows its customers better than Netflix. The company has mind-boggling access to real-time data on member viewing behavior and sentiments. Every day, Netflix tracks and parses member data on tens of millions of searches, ratings, and "plays." Netflix's bulging database contains every viewing detail for each individual subscriber—what shows they watch, at what time of day, on what devices, at what locations, even when they hit the pause, rewind, or fast-forward buttons during programs.

Netflix supplements this already-massive database with consumer information purchased from Nielsen, Facebook, Twitter, and other sources. Finally, the company employs experts to classify each video on hundreds of characteristics, such as talent, action, tone, genre, color, volume, scenery, and many, many others. Using this rich base of big data, Netflix builds detailed subscriber profiles based on individual viewing habits and preferences. It then uses these profiles to personalize each customer's viewing experience. According to Netflix, there are 53 million different versions of Netflix, one for each individual subscriber worldwide.

For example, Netflix uses data on viewing history to make personalized recommendations. Wading through 60,000 titles to decide what to watch can be overwhelming. So when new customers sign up, Netflix asks them to rate their interest in movie and TV genres and to rate specific titles they have already seen. It then cross-references what people like with other similar titles to predict additional movies or programs customers will enjoy.

But that's just the beginning. As customers watch and rate more and more video content, and as Netflix studies the details of their viewing behavior, the predictions become more and more accurate. Netflix often comes to know individual customer viewing preferences better than customers themselves do. How accurate are Netflix's recommendations? Seventy-five percent of viewing activity results from these suggestions. That's important. The more subscribers watch, the more likely they are to stay with Netflix—viewers who watch at least 15 hours of content each month are 75 percent less likely to cancel. Accurate recommendations increase average viewing time, keeping subscribers in the fold.

Increased viewing also depends on offering the right content in the first place. But adding new programming is expensive—content licensing fees constitute the lion's share of Netflix's cost of goods sold. With so many new and existing movies and TV programs on the market, Netflix must be very selective in what it adds to its content inventory. Once again, it's big data and marketing analytics to the rescue. Just as Netflix analyzes its database to come up with subscriber recommendations, it uses the data to assess what additional titles customers might enjoy and how much each is worth. The goal is to maximize subscriber "happiness-per-dollar-spent" on new titles. "We always use our in-depth knowledge about what our members love to watch to decide what's available on Netflix," says a Netflix marketer. "If you keep watching, we'll keep adding more of what you love."

>> Netflix, big data, and CRM: While members are busy watching Netflix videos, Netflix is busy watching *them*—watching them very, very closely. Then it uses the big data insights to give customers exactly what they want.

© OJO Images Ltd/Alamy (photo); PR NEWSWIRE (logo)

To get even more viewers watching even more hours, Netflix uses its extensive big data insights to add its own exclusive video content—things you can see only on Netflix. In its own words, Netflix wants "to become HBO faster than HBO can become Netflix." For example, Netflix stunned the media industry when it outbid both HBO and AMC by paying a stunning $100 million for exclusive rights to air the first two seasons of *House of Cards*, a U.S. version of a hit British political drama produced by Hollywood bigwigs David Fincher and Kevin Spacey.

To outsiders, the huge investment in *House of Cards* seemed highly risky. However, using its powerful database, Netflix was able to predict accurately which and how many existing members would watch the new *House of Cards* regularly and how many new members would sign up because of the show. Netflix also used its viewer knowledge to pinpoint and personalize promotion of the exclusive new series to just the right members. Before *House of Cards* premiered, based on their profiles, selected subscribers saw one of 10 different trailers of the show aimed at their specific likes and interests.

Thanks to Netflix's big data and marketing analytics prowess, *House of Cards* was a smash hit. It brought in 3 million new subscribers in only the first three months. These new subscribers alone covered almost all of the $100 million investment. More important, a Netflix survey revealed that for the average *House of Cards* viewer, 86 percent were less likely to cancel because of the new program. Such success came as no surprise to Netflix. Its data had predicted that the program would be a hit before the director ever shouted "action."

Since then, *House of Cards* has become Netflix's hottest program. Based on its success, Netflix developed a number of other original series, including *Hemlock Grove, Lillyhammer, Orange Is the New Black, Bad Samaritans, Marco Polo,* and the animated series *BoJack Horseman*. For traditional broadcast networks, the average success rate for new television shows is 35 percent. In contrast, Netflix is batting almost 70 percent. To continue the momentum, Netflix has committed $300 million a year to developing new original content.

The digital video giant now has 12 exclusive or original shows on the air, with another 24 scheduled for the next two years, including drama series, comedy specials, movies, and documentaries.

Netflix's success has thrown a scare into competitors such as leading cable-subscription network HBO. Although Netflix still lags HBO in profits, its U.S. online-only membership has reached 36 million compared with HBO's 30 million cable subscribers, and Netflix recently passed HBO in U.S. revenues. Such numbers, along with its unconventional methods for producing content, have earned Netflix the nickname "The Red Menace" among competitors. It's no surprise, then, that HBO announced that it will soon start selling online-only subscriptions.

As more and more high-quality video streams out of Netflix, more success streams in. Netflix's sales have surged 53 percent during the past two years. Last year alone, membership grew by more than 20 percent. Netflix thrives on using big data and marketing analytics to know and serve its customers. The company excels at helping customers figure out just what they want to watch and offering just the right content profitably. Says Netflix's chief communications officer, "Because we have a direct relationship with consumers, we *know* what people like to watch, and that helps us [immeasurably]."

Sources: Nicole Laporte, "Netflix: The Red Menace," *Fast Company*, January 7, 2014, www.fastcompany.com/3024158/netflix-the-red-menace; Anders Bylund, "Netflix, Inc. Is Paying Huge Sums to Produce Original Shows," *Motley Fool*, October 6, 2014, www.fool.com/investing/general/2014/10/06/netflix-inc-is-paying-huge-sums-to-produce-origina.aspx; David Carr, "Giving Viewers What They Want," *New York Times*, February 25, 2013, p. B1; Zach Bulygo, "How Netflix Uses Analytics to Select Movies, Create Content, and Make Multimillion Dollar Decisions," *Kissmetrics*, September 6, 2013, blog.kissmetrics.com/how-netflix-uses-analytics/; Craig Smith, "By the Numbers: 40 Amazing Netflix Statistics and Facts," *Expanded Ramblings*, October 24, 2014, http://expandedramblings.com/index.php/netflix_statistics-facts/; Marcus Wohlsen, "Netflix Is Beating HBO in Revenue, but It's Still the Underdog," *Wired*, August 7, 2014, www.wired.com/2014/08/netflix-is-beating-hbo-in-revenue-but-its-still-the-underdog/; Lisa Richwine, "Netflix Beats Forecasts with 62 Million Streaming Subscribers," *Reuters*, April 15, 2015, http://www.reuters.com/article/2015/04/15/us-netflix-results-idUSKBN0N62HC20150415; and www.netflix.com, accessed September 2015.

Kraft applies high-level marketing analytics to this wealth of data to mine nuggets of customer insight. Then it uses these insights to shape big data–driven marketing strategies and tactics, from developing new products to creating more focused and personalized Web, mobile, and social media content. For example, Kraft's analytics have identified more than 500 custom target segments. Within these segments, Kraft knows in detail what consumers need and like. Says one analyst, it knows "their dietary [characteristics and] restrictions—gluten free, a diabetic, low calorie, big snacks, feeding a big family, whether they are new cooks." Kraft uses this knowledge to personalize digital interactions with individual customers, down to the fine details. "If Kraft knows you're not a bacon user," says the analyst, "you will never be served a bacon ad." Thus, sophisticated analytics let Kraft target the right customer with the right message in the right medium at the right moment.

The benefits of customer relationship management and big data analytics don't come without costs or risks. The most common mistake is to view CRM and marketing analytics as technology processes only. Yet technology alone cannot build profitable customer relationships. Companies can't improve customer relationships by simply installing some new software. Instead, marketers should start with the fundamentals of managing customer relationships and *then* employ high-tech data and analytics solutions. They should focus first on the R—it's the *relationship* that CRM is all about.

Distributing and Using Marketing Information

Marketing information has no value until it is used to make better marketing decisions. Thus, the marketing information system must make information readily available to managers and others who need it, when they need it. In some cases, this means providing managers with regular performance reports, intelligence updates, and reports on the results of research studies.

But marketing managers may also need access to nonroutine information for special situations and on-the-spot decisions. For example, a sales manager having trouble with a large customer may want a summary of the account's sales and profitability over the past year. Or a brand manager may want to get a sense of the amount of the social media buzz surrounding the recent launch of a new product. These days, therefore, information distribution involves making information available in a timely, user-friendly way.

Many firms use company *intranet* and internal CRM systems to facilitate this process. These systems provide ready access to research and intelligence information, customer transaction and experience information, shared reports and documents, and more. For example, the CRM system at phone and online gift retailer 1-800-Flowers.com gives customer-facing employees real-time access to customer information. When a repeat customer calls, the system immediately pulls up data on previous transactions and other contacts, helping reps make the customer's experience easier and more relevant. For instance, if a customer usually buys tulips for his wife, the rep can talk about the best tulip selections and related gifts. Such connections result in greater customer satisfaction and loyalty and greater sales for the company. "We can do it in real time," says a 1-800-Flowers.com executive, "and it enhances the customer experience."[27]

In addition, companies are increasingly allowing key customers and value-network members to access account, product, and other data on demand through *extranets*. Suppliers, customers, resellers, and select other network members may access a company's extranet to update their accounts, arrange purchases, and check orders against inventories to improve customer service. ≫ For example, online shoes and accessories retailer Zappos considers suppliers to be "part of the Zappos family" and a key component in its quest to deliver "WOW" through great customer service. So it treats suppliers as valued partners, including sharing information with them. Through its ZUUL extranet (Zappos Unified User Login), thousands of suppliers are given full access to brand-related Zappos' inventory levels, sales figures, and even profitability. Suppliers can also use ZUUL to interact with the Zappos creative team and to enter suggested orders for Zappos buyers to approve.[28]

Thanks to modern technology, today's marketing managers can gain direct access to a company's information system at any time and from virtually anywhere. They can tap into the system from a home office, customer location, airport, or the local Starbucks—anyplace they can connect on a laptop, tablet, or smartphone. Such systems allow managers to get the information they need directly and quickly and tailor it to their own needs.

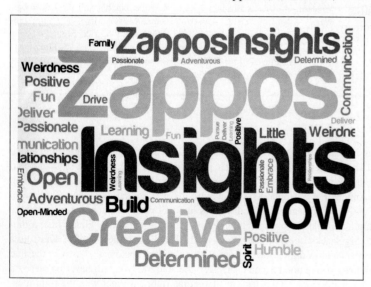

≫ **Extranets: Zappos shares marketing information and insights with suppliers through its ZUUL extranet. It considers suppliers to be "part of the Zappos family."**

Zappos

LINKING THE CONCEPTS

Let's stop here, think back, and be certain that you've got the "big picture" concerning marketing information systems.

- What's the overall goal of a marketing information system? How are the individual components linked, and what does each contribute? Take another look at Figure 4.1—it provides a good organizing framework for the entire chapter.
- Apply the MIS framework to Converse (a Nike company). How might Converse go about assessing marketing managers' information needs, developing the needed information, and helping managers to analyze and use the information to gain actionable customer and market insights?

Author Comment
We finish this chapter by examining three special marketing information topics.

Other Marketing Information Considerations

This section discusses marketing information in two special contexts: marketing research in small businesses and nonprofit organizations and international marketing research. Then we look at public policy and ethics issues in marketing research.

Marketing Research in Small Businesses and Nonprofit Organizations

Just like larger firms, small organizations need market information and the customer insights that it can provide. Managers of small businesses and not-for-profit organizations often think that marketing research can be done only by experts in large companies with big research budgets. True, large-scale research studies are beyond the budgets of most small organizations. However, many of the marketing research techniques discussed in this chapter also can be used by smaller organizations in a less formal manner and at little or no expense. ≫Consider how one small business owner conducted market research on a shoestring before even opening his doors:[29]

≫ **Before opening Bibbentuckers dry cleaner, owner Robert Byerley conducted research to gain insights into what customers wanted. First on the list: quality.**

Bibbentuckers

After a string of bad experiences with his local dry cleaner, Robert Byerley decided to open his own dry-cleaning business. But before jumping in, he conducted plenty of market research. He needed a key customer insight: How would he make his business stand out from the others? To start, Byerley spent an entire week online, researching the dry-cleaning industry. To get input from potential customers, using a local marketing firm, Byerley held focus groups on the store's name, look, and brochure. He also took clothes to the 15 best competing cleaners in town and had focus group members critique their work. Based on his research, he made a list of features for his new business. First on his list: quality. His business would stand behind everything it did. Not on the list: cheap prices. Creating the perfect dry-cleaning establishment simply didn't fit with a discount operation.

With his research complete, Byerley opened Bibbentuckers, a high-end dry cleaner positioned on high-quality service and convenience. It featured a bank-like drive-through area with curbside delivery. A computerized barcode system read customer cleaning preferences and tracked clothes all the way through the cleaning process. Byerley added other differentiators, such as decorative awnings, TV screens, and refreshments (even "candy for the kids and a doggy treat for your best friend"). "I wanted a place…that paired five-star service and quality with an establishment that didn't look like a dry cleaner," he says. The market research yielded results. Today, Bibbentuckers is a thriving eight-store operation.

Thus, small businesses and not-for-profit organizations can obtain good marketing insights through observation or informal surveys using small convenience samples. Also, many associations, local media, and government agencies provide special help to small organizations. For example, the U.S. Small Business Administration offers dozens of free publications and a Web site (www.sba.gov) that give advice on topics ranging from starting, financing, and expanding a small business to ordering business cards. Other excellent research resources for small businesses include the U.S. Census Bureau (www.census.gov) and the Bureau of Economic Analysis (www.bea.gov). Finally, small businesses can collect a considerable amount of information at very little cost online. They can check out online product and service review sites, use Internet search engines to research specific companies and issues, and scour competitor and customer Web, mobile, and social media sites.

In summary, secondary data collection, observation, surveys, and experiments can all be used effectively by small organizations with small budgets. However, although these informal research methods are less complex and less costly, they still must be conducted with care. Managers must think carefully about the objectives of the research, formulate questions in advance, recognize the biases introduced by smaller samples and less skilled researchers, and conduct the research systematically.[30]

International Marketing Research

International marketing research has grown tremendously over the past few decades. International researchers follow the same steps as domestic researchers, from defining the research problem and developing a research plan to interpreting and reporting the results. However, these researchers often face more and different problems. Whereas domestic researchers deal with fairly homogeneous markets within a single country, international researchers deal with diverse markets in many different countries. These markets often vary greatly in their levels of economic development, cultures and customs, and buying patterns.

In many foreign markets, the international researcher may have a difficult time finding good secondary data. Whereas U.S. marketing researchers can obtain reliable secondary data from dozens of domestic research services, many countries have almost no research services at all. Some of the largest international research services operate in many countries. ≫ For example, The Nielsen Company (the world's largest marketing research company) has offices in more than 100 countries, from Schaumburg, Illinois, to Hong Kong to Nicosia, Cyprus.[31] However, most research firms operate in only a relative handful of countries. Thus, even when secondary information is available, it usually must be obtained from many different sources on a country-by-country basis, making the information difficult to combine or compare.

Because of the scarcity of good secondary data, international researchers often must collect their own primary data. However, obtaining primary data may be no easy task. For example, it can be difficult simply to develop good samples. U.S. researchers can use current telephone directories, email lists, census tract data, and any of several sources of socioeconomic data to construct samples. However, such information is largely lacking in many countries.

Once the sample is drawn, the U.S. researcher usually can reach most respondents easily by phone, by mail, online, or in person. However, reaching respondents is often not so easy in other parts of the world. Researchers in Mexico cannot rely on phone, Internet, and mail data collection—most data collection is conducted door to door and concentrated in three or four of the largest cities. In some

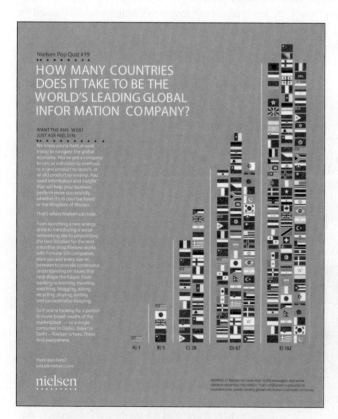

≫ Some of the largest research services firms have large international organizations. Nielsen has offices in more than 100 countries.

countries, few people have computers, let alone Internet access. For example, whereas there are 84 Internet users per 100 people in the United States, there are only 43 Internet users per 100 people in Mexico. In Madagascar, the number drops to 2 Internet users per 100 people. In some countries, the postal system is notoriously unreliable. In Brazil, for instance, an estimated 30 percent of the mail is never delivered; in Russia, mail delivery can take several weeks. In many developing countries, poor roads and transportation systems make certain areas hard to reach, making personal interviews difficult and expensive.[32]

Cultural differences from country to country cause additional problems for international researchers. Language is the most obvious obstacle. For example, questionnaires must be prepared in one language and then translated into the languages of each country researched. Responses then must be translated back into the original language for analysis and interpretation. This adds to research costs and increases the risks of error. Even within a given country, language can be a problem. For example, in India, English is the language of business, but consumers may use any of 14 "first languages," with many additional dialects.

Translating a questionnaire from one language to another is anything but easy. Many idioms, phrases, and statements mean different things in different cultures. For example, a Danish executive noted, "Check this out by having a different translator put back into English what you've translated from English. You'll get the shock of your life. I remember [an example in which] 'out of sight, out of mind' had become 'invisible things are insane.'"[33]

Consumers in different countries also vary in their attitudes toward marketing research. People in one country may be very willing to respond; in other countries, nonresponse can be a major problem. Customs in some countries may prohibit people from talking with strangers. In certain cultures, research questions often are considered too personal. For example, in many Muslim countries, mixed-gender focus groups are taboo, as is videotaping female-only focus groups. In some countries, even when respondents are *willing* to respond, they may not be *able* to because of high functional illiteracy rates.

Despite these problems, as global marketing grows, global companies have little choice but to conduct these types of international marketing research. Although the costs and problems associated with international research may be high, the costs of not doing it—in terms of missed opportunities and mistakes—might be even higher. Once recognized, many of the problems associated with international marketing research can be overcome or avoided.

Public Policy and Ethics in Marketing Research

Most marketing research benefits both the sponsoring company and its consumers. Through marketing research, companies gain insights into consumers' needs, resulting in more satisfying products and services and stronger customer relationships. However, the misuse of marketing research can also harm or annoy consumers. Two major public policy and ethics issues in marketing research are intrusions on consumer privacy and the misuse of research findings.

Intrusions on Consumer Privacy
Many consumers feel positive about marketing research and believe that it serves a useful purpose. Some actually enjoy being interviewed and giving their opinions. However, others strongly resent or even mistrust marketing research. They don't like being interrupted by researchers. They worry that marketers are building huge databases full of personal information about customers. Or they fear that researchers might use sophisticated techniques to probe our deepest feelings, track us as we use our mobile devices or browse and interact on the Internet, or peek over our shoulders as we shop and then use this knowledge to manipulate our buying. A recent survey showed that more than 90 percent of Americans feel that they have lost control over the collection and use by companies of their personal data and information they share on social media sites.[34]

For example, Target made some of its customers very uneasy recently when it used their buying histories to figure out that they had a baby on the way, including eerily accurate estimates of child gender and due date:[35]

> Target gives every customer a Guest ID number, tied to his or her name, credit card, or email address. It then tracks the customer's purchases in detail, along with demographic information

>> Consumer privacy: Target made some customers uneasy when it used their buying histories to figure out things about them that even their family and friends didn't know. The chain's bulls-eye logo may now "send a shiver...down the closely-watched spines of some Target shoppers.

© Jonathan Larsen/Diadem Images/Alamy Stock Photo

from other sources. By studying the buying histories of women who'd previously signed up for its baby registries, Target found that it could develop a "pregnancy prediction" score for each customer based on her purchasing patterns across 25 product categories. It used this score to start sending personalized books of coupons for baby-related items to expectant parents, keyed to their pregnancy stages.

The strategy seemed to make good marketing sense—by hooking parents-to-be, Target could turn them into loyal buyers as their families developed. However, the strategy hit a snag when an angry man showed up at his local Target store, complaining that his high school–aged daughter was receiving Target coupons for cribs, strollers, and maternity clothes. "Are you trying to encourage her to get pregnant?" he demanded. The Target store manager apologized. But when he called to apologize again a few days later, he learned that Target's marketers had, in fact, known about the young woman's pregnancy before her father did. It turns out that many other customers were creeped out that Target knew about their pregnancies before they'd told even family and close friends. And they wondered what else Target might be tracking and profiling. As one reporter concluded: >> "The store's bulls-eye logo may now send a shiver... down the closely-watched spines of some [Target shoppers]."

When mining customer information, marketers must be careful not to cross over the privacy line. But there are no easy answers when it comes to marketing research and privacy. For example, is it a good or bad thing that marketers track and analyze consumers' online browsing or buying patterns to send them personalized promotions? Should we worry when marketers track consumer locations via their mobile phones to issue location-based information, ads, and offers? Should we care that some retailers use mannequins with cameras hidden in one eye to record customer demographics and shopping behavior? Similarly, should we applaud or resent companies that monitor consumer posts on Facebook, Twitter, Instagram, YouTube, or other social media in an effort to be more responsive?[36]

Increasing consumer privacy concerns have become a major problem for the marketing research industry. Companies face the challenge of unearthing valuable but potentially sensitive consumer data while also maintaining consumer trust. At the same time, consumers wrestle with the trade-offs between personalization and privacy. They want to receive relevant, personalized offers that meet their needs, but they worry or resent that companies may track them too closely. The key question: When does a company cross the line in gathering and using customer data? One recent study shows that nearly half of U.S. adults worry that they have little or no control over the personal information that companies gather about them online. Another survey found that 86 percent of Internet users have taken steps to remove or mask their digital footprints, such as removing cookies or encrypting email.

Failure to address privacy issues could result in angry, less cooperative consumers and increased government intervention. As a result, the marketing research industry is considering several options for responding to intrusion and privacy issues. One example is the Marketing Research Association's "Your Opinion Counts" and "Respondent Bill of Rights" initiatives to educate consumers about the benefits of marketing research and distinguish it from telephone selling and database building. The industry also has considered adopting broad standards, perhaps based on the International Chamber of Commerce's International Code of Marketing and Social Research Practice. This code outlines researchers' responsibilities to respondents and the general public. For example, it urges that researchers make their names and addresses available to participants and be open about the data they are collecting.[37]

Most major companies—including Facebook, Apple, Microsoft, IBM, American Express, and even the U.S. government—have now appointed a chief privacy officer (CPO), whose job is to safeguard the privacy of consumers who do business with the company. In the end, however, if researchers provide value in exchange for information, customers will gladly provide it. For example, Amazon.com's customers don't mind if the firm builds a database of products they buy as a way to provide future product recommendations. This saves time and provides value. The best approach is for researchers to ask only for the information they need, use it responsibly to provide customer value, and avoid sharing information without the customer's permission.

Misuse of Research Findings

Research studies can be powerful persuasion tools; companies often use study results as claims in their advertising and promotion. Today, however, many research studies appear to be little more than vehicles for pitching the sponsor's products. In fact, in some cases, research surveys appear to have been designed just to produce the intended effect. For example, a Black Flag survey once asked: "A roach disk...poisons a roach slowly. The dying roach returns to the nest and after it dies is eaten by other roaches. In turn these roaches become poisoned and die. How effective do you think this type of product would be in killing roaches?" Not surprisingly, 79 percent said effective.

However, few advertisers openly rig their research designs or blatantly misrepresent the findings—most abuses tend to be more subtle "stretches." Or disputes arise over the validity and use of research findings. >> Consider this example:

> The FTC recently charged POM Wonderful—the pomegranate juice sold in the distinctive curvy bottle—and its parent company with making false and unsubstantiated health claims in its advertising. The disputed ads suggest that POM Wonderful Pomegranate Juice can prevent or treat heart disease, prostate cancer, and even erectile dysfunction. For instance, one ad boasted that POM has "Super Health Powers!" while another proclaimed, "I'm off to saveprostates!" POM has stood behind its ad claims, asserting that they are backed by $35 million worth of company research showing that antioxidant-rich pomegranate products are good for you. The brand even retaliated during two years of legal wrangling with ads disputing the FTC and its allegations. But the FTC isn't buying the research behind POM's claims—it recently issued a final ruling ordering the brand to refrain from making claims that its products could improve a user's health unless backed by more stringent research. "When a company touts scientific research in its advertising, the research must squarely support the claims made," says the agency. "Contrary to POM Wonderful's advertising, the available scientific information does not prove that POM Juice...effectively treats or prevents these illnesses." POM Wonderful is currently appealing the FTC ruling.[38]

>> **Use of research findings: The FTC recently ruled against POM Wonderful's research-based advertising claims that the brand could improve a user's health. POM is appealing the ruling.**

Christopher Schall | Impact Photo

Recognizing that marketing research can be abused, several associations—including the American Marketing Association, the Marketing Research Association, and the Council of American Survey Research Organizations (CASRO)—have developed codes of research ethics and standards of conduct. For example, the CASRO Code of Standards and Ethics for Survey Research outlines researcher responsibilities to respondents, including confidentiality, privacy, and avoidance of harassment. It also outlines major responsibilities in reporting results to clients and the public.[39]

In the end, however, unethical or inappropriate actions cannot simply be regulated away. Each company must accept responsibility for policing the conduct and reporting of its own marketing research to protect consumers' best interests and its own.

MyMarketingLab

If assigned by your instructor, complete the questions marked with the ⭐ from the EOC Discussion Questions section in the MyLab. To complete the Marketing by the Numbers problems found in this section, go to your Assignments in the MyLab.

REVIEWING AND EXTENDING THE CONCEPTS

CHAPTER REVIEW AND CRITICAL THINKING

Objectives Review

To create value for customers and build meaningful relationships with them, marketers must first gain fresh, deep insights into what customers need and want. Such insights come from good marketing information. As a result of the recent explosion of "big data" and marketing technology, companies can now obtain great quantities of information, sometimes even too much. Consumers themselves are now generating a tidal wave of bottom-up information through their smartphones, PCs, and tablets via online browsing and blogging, apps and social media interactions, and texting and video. The challenge is to transform today's vast volume of consumer information into actionable customer and market insights.

 OBJECTIVE 4-1 Explain the importance of information in gaining insights about the marketplace and customers. (pp 100–101)

The marketing process starts with a complete understanding of the marketplace and consumer needs and wants. Thus, the company needs to turn sound consumer information into meaningful *customer insights* by which it can produce superior value for its customers. The company also requires information on competitors, resellers, and other actors and forces in the marketplace. Increasingly, marketers are viewing information not only as an input for making better decisions but also as an important strategic asset and marketing tool.

 OBJECTIVE 4-2 Define the marketing information system and discuss its parts. (pp 102–106)

The *marketing information system* (MIS) consists of people and procedures for assessing information needs, developing the needed information, and helping decision makers use the information to generate and validate actionable customer and market insights. A well-designed information system begins and ends with users.

The MIS first *assesses information needs*. The MIS primarily serves the company's marketing and other managers, but it may also provide information to external partners. Then the MIS *develops information* from internal databases, marketing intelligence activities, and marketing research. *Internal databases* provide information on the company's own operations and departments. Such data can be obtained quickly and cheaply but often need to be adapted for marketing decisions. *Marketing intelligence* activities supply everyday information about developments in the external marketing environment, including listening and responding to the vast and complex digital environment. *Market research* consists of collecting information relevant to a specific marketing problem faced by the company.

Last, the marketing information system helps users analyze and use the information to develop customer insights, make marketing decisions, and manage customer relationships.

 OBJECTIVE 4-3 Outline the steps in the marketing research process. (pp 106–118)

The first step in the marketing research process involves *defining the problem and setting the research objectives*, which may be exploratory, descriptive, or causal research. The second step consists of *developing a research plan* for collecting data from primary and secondary sources. The third step calls for *implementing the marketing research plan* by gathering, processing, and analyzing the information. The fourth step consists of *interpreting and reporting the findings*. Additional information analysis helps marketing managers apply the information and provides them with sophisticated statistical procedures and models from which to develop more rigorous findings.

Both *internal* and *external* secondary data sources often provide information more quickly and at a lower cost than primary data sources, and they can sometimes yield information that a company cannot collect by itself. However, needed information might not exist in secondary sources. Researchers must also evaluate secondary information to ensure that it is *relevant, accurate, current*, and *impartial*.

Primary research must also be evaluated for these features. Each primary data collection method—*observational, survey*, and *experimental*—has its own advantages and disadvantages. Similarly, each of the various research contact methods—mail, telephone, personal interview, and online—has its own advantages and drawbacks.

 OBJECTIVE 4-4 Explain how companies analyze and use marketing information. (pp 118–123)

Information gathered in internal databases and through marketing intelligence and marketing research usually requires more analysis. To analyze individual customer data, many companies have now acquired or developed special software and analysis techniques—called *customer relationship management* (CRM)—that integrate, analyze, and apply the mountains of individual customer data to gain a 360-degree view of customers and build stronger the customer relationships. They apply *marketing analytics* to dig out meaningful patterns in big data and gain customer insights and gauge marketing performance.

Marketing information has no value until it is used to make better marketing decisions. Thus, the MIS must make the information available to managers and others who make marketing decisions or deal with customers. In some cases, this means providing regular reports and updates; in other cases, it means making nonroutine information available for special situations and on-the-spot decisions. Many firms use company intranets and extranets to facilitate this process. Thanks to modern technology, today's marketing managers can gain direct access to marketing information at any time and from virtually any location.

 OBJECTIVE 4-5 **Discuss the special issues some marketing researchers face, including public policy and ethics issues. (pp 123–127)**

Some marketers face special marketing research situations, such as those conducting research in small business,

not-for-profit, or international situations. Marketing research can be conducted effectively by small businesses and non-profit organizations with limited budgets. International marketing researchers follow the same steps as domestic researchers but often face more and different problems. All organizations need to act responsibly concerning major public policy and ethical issues surrounding marketing research, including issues of intrusions on consumer privacy and misuse of research findings.

Key Terms

Objective 4-1
Big data (p 101)
Customer insights (p. 101)
Marketing information system
  (MIS) (p. 101)

Objective 4-2
Internal databases (p 102)
Competitive marketing intelligence
  (p 103)

Objective 4-3
Marketing research (p 106)
Exploratory research (p 107)
Descriptive research (p 107)
Causal research (p 107)
Secondary data (p 108)
Primary data (p 108)
Observational research (p 109)
Ethnographic research (p 109)
Survey research (p 110)

Experimental research (p 111)
Focus group interviewing (p 112)
Online marketing research (p 113)
Online focus groups (p 114)
Behavioral targeting (p 115)
Sample (p 115)

Objective 4-4
Customer relationship management
  (CRM) (p 118)
Marketing analytics (p 119)

Discussion Questions

4-1. What is *big data,* and what opportunities and challenges does it provide for marketers? (AACSB: Communication; Reflective Thinking)

4-2. What is a marketing information system (MIS), and what characteristics should it possess? (AACSB: Communication)

⭐ **4-3.** Name and describe the three types of research objectives and give an example of a research study for each. (AACSB: Communication; Reflective Thinking)

4-4. What impact has the Internet had on how marketing research is conducted? What advantages does the Internet provide over traditional marketing data collection methods? (AACSB: Communication)

4-5. Why are marketing analytics so important in the age of big data? (AACSB: Communication)

Critical Thinking Exercises

⭐ **4-6.** In a small group, identify a problem faced by a local business or charitable organization and propose a research project addressing that problem. Develop a research proposal that implements each step of the marketing research process. Discuss how the research results will help the business or organization. (AACSB: Communication; Reflective Thinking)

4-7. Go to www.bized.co.uk/learn/business/marketing/research/index.htm and review the various resources

available. Select one activity and present what you learned from that activity. (AACSB: Communication; Use of IT; Reflective Thinking)

4-8. Research the marketing research industry and develop a presentation describing various marketing research jobs and compensation for those jobs. Create a graphical representation to communicate your findings. (AACSB: Communication; Use of IT; Reflective Thinking)

MINICASES AND APPLICATIONS

Online, Mobile, and Social Media Marketing   Social Data

People have been using Twitter's social media platform to Tweet short bursts of information in 140 characters or less since 2006 and now average 500 million Tweets a day. The full stream of Tweets is referred to as Twitter's fire hose. Various firms analyze data from the fire hose and sell the information gleaned from that analysis to other companies. Twitter recently purchased Gnip, the world's largest social data provider and one of the few companies that had access to the fire hose. Gnip also mines public data from Facebook, Google+, Tumblr, and other social media platforms. Analyzing social data has become a big business because companies such as PepsiCo, Warner Brothers, and General Motors pay to learn about consumers' sentiments toward them. According to the CEO of social media analysis company BrandWatch, "We're at the bottom of the foothills in terms of the kind of global demand for social data." Twitter

alone earned more than $70 million last year from licensing its data. Perhaps Mark Twain's character, Mulberry Sellers, summed it up nicely—"There's gold in them thar hills"—and Twitter and other social media platforms and data analytic companies are mining that gold.

4-9. Discuss the value of social data for marketers. (AACSB: Communication; Reflective Thinking)

4-10. A "dark social channel" refers to a private channel or a channel difficult to match with other digital channels. An example of a dark channel is email. However, Google routinely mines its roughly half-billion Gmail users' emails. Research how Google scans email data and the fallout from those actions, then summarize your findings. (AACSB: Communication; Use of IT; Reflective Thinking)

Marketing Ethics   Metadata

Everyone generates metadata as they use technologies such as computers and mobile devices to search, post, Tweet, play, text, and talk. What many people don't realize, however, is that this treasure trove of date, time, and location information can be used to identify them without their knowledge. For example, in analyzing more than a million anonymous credit card transactions, researchers at the Massachusetts Institute of Technology were able to link 90 percent of the transactions to specific users with just four additional bits of metadata, such as user locations based on apps such as Foursquare, the timing of an activity such as a Tweet on Twitter, or playing a mobile game. Since there are more mobile devices than there are people in

the United States and 60 percent of purchases are made with a credit card, marketing research firms are gobbling up all sorts of metadata that will let them tie a majority of purchase transactions to specific individuals.

4-11. Describe at least four applications you use that provide location, time, and date information that can be tied to your identity. (AACSB Communication; Reflective Thinking)

⭐**4-12.** Debate whether it is ethical for marketers to use metadata to link individual consumers with specific credit card transactions. (AACSB: Communication; Ethical Reasoning)

Marketing by the Numbers   The Value of Information

Conducting research is costly, and the costs must be weighed against the value of the information gathered. Consider a company faced with a competitor's price reduction. Should the company also reduce price in order to maintain market share, or should the company maintain its current price? The company has conducted some preliminary research showing the financial outcomes of each decision under two competitor responses: the competition maintains its price or the competition lowers its price further. The company feels pretty confident that the competitor cannot lower its price further and assigns that outcome a probability (p) of 0.7, which means the other outcome would have only a 30 percent chance of occurring ($1 - p = 0.3$). These outcomes are shown in the table below:

	Competitive Response	
Company action	**Maintain Price** $p = 0.7$	**Reduce Price** $(1 - p) = 0.3$
Reduce Price	$160,000	$120,000
Maintain Price	$180,000	$100,000

For example, if the company reduces its price and the competitor maintains its price, the company would realize $160,000, and so on. From this information, the expected monetary value (EMV) of each company action (reduce price or maintain price) can be determined using the following equation:

$$EMV = (p)(\text{financial outome}_p)$$
$$+ (1 - p)(\text{financial outcome}_{(1-p)})$$

The company would select the action expected to deliver the greatest EMV. More information might be desirable, but is it worth the cost of acquiring it? One way to assess the value of additional information is to determine the expected value of perfect information (EMV_{PI}), calculated using the following equation:

$$EMV_{PI} = EMV_{certainty} - EMV_{best\ alternative}$$

where

$$EMV_{certainty} = (p)\ (\text{highest financial outcome}_p)$$
$$+ (1 - p)\ (\text{highest financial outcome}_{(1-p)})$$

If the value of perfect information is more than the cost of conducting the research, then the research should be undertaken (that is, $EMV_{PI} >$ cost of research). However, if the value of the additional information is less than the cost of obtaining more information, the research should not be conducted.

4-13. Calculate the expected monetary value (EMV) of both company actions. Which action should the company take? (AACSB: Communication; Analytical Reasoning)

4-14. What is the expected value of perfect information (EMV_{PI})? Should the research be conducted? (AACSB: Communication; Analytical Reasoning)

Video Case   Nielsen

Most people know Nielsen as the TV ratings company. In reality, however, Nielsen is a multiplatform market research company that has constantly been evolving since 1923. Its goal is to measure and track a wide range of consumer activity in order to establish a 360-degree view of individuals and market segments. To accomplish this, Nielsen has to follow consumers wherever they may be—watching TV, online, in their homes, or in stores.

How does Nielsen track all this activity? The veteran research firm has established effective methods of recording consumer activity, from retail scanner data to household panels to monitoring social networks. As data are captured, they are transferred to a Nielsen data warehouse, where they are matched to the right individual and added to the terabytes of information Nielsen already possesses. Through data sorting and analytics, Nielsen cuts through billions of daily transactions to deliver clear consumer insights to clients.

After viewing the video featuring Nielsen, answer the following questions:

4-15. What is Nielsen's expertise?

4-16. Providing a real-world example, describe how Nielsen might discover a consumer insight.

4-17. What kinds of partnerships might Nielsen need to form with other companies in order to accomplish its goals?

Company Cases   4 Campbell's/8 3M/14 Alibaba

See Appendix 1 for cases appropriate for this chapter.

Case 4, Campbell's: Watching What You Eat. The pillar of product development at Campbell's is deep dive research—field research where observations lead to consumer insight.

Case 8, 3M: Where Innovation Is a Way of Life. Few companies provide more support for research-based product development than 3M.

Case 14, Alibaba: The World's Largest E-Tailer Is Not Amazon. The largest customer base provides ecommerce giant with the largest database and endless possibilities.

MyMarketingLab

If assigned by your instructor, complete these writing sections from your Assignments in the MyLab.

4-18. What is neuromarketing and how is it useful in marketing research? Why is this research approach usually combined with other approaches? (AACSB: Communication)

4-19. Describe an example in which marketing research could cause harm to participants. Many companies have a review process similar to that required for following the government's "Common Rule." Write a brief report explaining this rule and how you would apply it to your example. (AACSB: Written and Oral Communication; Reflective Thinking)

5 Understanding Consumer and Business Buyer Behavior

CHAPTER ROAD MAP | Objective Outline

▶ **OBJECTIVE 5-1** **Understand the consumer market and the major factors that influence consumer buyer behavior.** Consumer Markets and Consumer Buyer Behavior (134); Model of Consumer Behavior (134–135); Characteristics Affecting Consumer Behavior (135–148)

▶ **OBJECTIVE 5-2** **Identify and discuss the stages in the buyer decision process.** The Buyer Decision Process (149–151)

▶ **OBJECTIVE 5-3** **Describe the adoption and diffusion process for new products.** The Buyer Decision Process for New Products (151–153)

▶ **OBJECTIVE 5-4** **Define the business market and identify the major factors that influence business buyer behavior.** Business Markets and Business Buyer Behavior (154); Business Markets (154–156); Business Buyer Behavior (156–159)

▶ **OBJECTIVE 5-5** **List and define the steps in the business buying decision process.** The Business Buying Process (159–161); E-Procurement and Online Purchasing (162); Business-to-Business Digital and Social Media Marketing (162–163)

Previewing the Concepts

You've studied how marketers obtain, analyze, and use information to develop customer insights and assess marketing programs. In this chapter, we take a closer look at the most important element of the marketplace—customers. The aim of marketing is to engage customers and affect how they think and act. To affect the *whats*, *whens*, and *hows* of buyer behavior, marketers must first understand the *whys*. We first look at *final consumer* buying influences and processes and then at the buyer behavior of *business customers*. You'll see that understanding buyer behavior is an essential but very difficult task.

To get a better sense of the importance of understanding consumer behavior, we begin by looking at Harley-Davidson, maker of the nation's top-selling heavyweight motorcycles. Who rides these big Harley "Hogs"? What moves them to tattoo their bodies with the Harley-Davidson bar and shield logo, abandon home and hearth for the open road, and flock to Harley rallies by the hundreds of thousands? You might be surprised by the answers to these questions, but Harley-Davidson knows them *very* well.

First Stop

Harley-Davidson: Selling Freedom, Independence, Power, and Authenticity

Few brands engender such intense loyalty as that found in the hearts of Harley-Davidson owners. Harley buyers are granitelike in their devotion to the brand. You don't see people tattooing "Yamaha" on their bodies, or "Kawasaki" or "Honda." Harley-Davidson riders don't want just any motorcycle—it's *got* to be a Harley. The iconic Harley-Davidson brand is that strong.

In August 2013, an estimated 100,000 to 200,000 people flocked to Harley-Davidson's 110th anniversary celebration in Milwaukee, the city where it all began. One reporter described the epic event's opening parade as "one of the greatest spectacles in America, . . . a thunder of Harley-Davidson pride you could literally feel as nearly 7,000 [riders] rolled through downtown Milwaukee." During the three days of rumbling fun, bikers from across the nation lounged on their low-slung Harley's, swapped biker tales, and sported T-shirts proclaiming things like "Screw it, let's ride!" and "I'd rather push a Harley than ride a Yamaha."

>> **For Harley-Davidson enthusiasts, it's all about the experience. More than just bikes, the iconic company is selling self-expression, lifestyle, aspirations, and dreams.**

Scott Olson/Getty images

Riding such intense emotions, Harley-Davidson has long dominated the U.S. motorcycle market. The brand captures 30 percent of all U.S. bike sales and nearly 55 percent of the heavyweight segment, and its sales and profits are growing at a smooth-riding pace. Over the past three years, sales have grown more than 20 percent and profits have jumped sixfold.

Harley-Davidson's marketers have spent a great deal of time thinking about customers and their buying behavior. They want to know who their customers are, what they think and how they feel, and why they buy a Harley-Davidson Softail rather than a Yamaha or a Kawasaki or a big Honda Gold Wing. What is it that makes Harley buyers so fiercely loyal? These are difficult questions; even Harley owners themselves don't know exactly what motivates their buying. But Harley-Davidson management puts top priority on understanding customers and what makes them tick.

Who rides a Harley-Davidson? You might be surprised. It's not the outlaw bad-boy biker that some people still associate with Harleys. The brand's motorcycles attract a different breed of bikers—older, more affluent, and better educated. Remove the helmets and the leathers of a hard-core Harley enthusiast, and there's no telling whom you'll find. It might be a guy with tattoos and unruly hair, but it's just as likely to be a CEO, investment banker, or gourmet chef.

The average Harley customer is a 50-something male with a median household income of $87,000. More than 12 percent of Harley purchases today are made by women. "Harley brings together all walks of life," says Harley's chief marketing officer. "You'll find a neurosurgeon talking and riding with a janitor. It's a family." And a big family it is. The Harley Owners Group (H.O.G.)—the official riding club of "Harley owners around the world, bound by a passion to ride"—has more than a million members. The brand's Facebook site counts more the 7 million Likes.

In recent years, the company has been extending the Harley-Davidson family beyond the core segment of older Caucasian males who now account for about two-thirds of buyers. It has crafted products and programs specifically designed to attract what it calls "outreach customers," segments such as young adults ages 18 to 34, women, African Americans, and Hispanics. Last year, sales to those outreach groups grew at more than twice the rate of sales to its traditional core customers. For example, to broaden its reach, Harley-Davidson recently introduced its first all-new motorcycle platform in 13 years—its Street models—smaller, lighter, more agile, and more efficient motorcycles designed for the riding needs of young urban riders. Though smaller, these new motorcycles still carry the Harley mystique. "These new bikes are leaner, yet still have a mean streak," says Harley's CMO. "They're the real deal, made of real steel."

Harley-Davidson makes good bikes, and to keep up with its shifting market, the company has upgraded its showrooms and sales approaches. But Harley customers are buying a lot more than just a quality bike and a smooth sales pitch. To gain a better understanding of customers' deeper motivations, over the years Harley-Davidson has conducted seemingly endless surveys, focus groups, and interpretive studies that plumb the depths of customers' feelings about their Harleys. Beyond research, everyone connected with the Harley-Davidson brand—from the CEO and CMO to ad agency copywriters—attend biker events and immerse themselves deeply in the biker culture. They spend countless hours in the saddle to gain a first-hand understanding of what moves and motivates core customers.

All of the research yields strong and consistent results. No matter who they are, what they do, or where they come from, Harley-Davidson disciples share a common, deeply held attraction to the brand. The universal Harley appeals are these: freedom,

> Harley-Davidson's market dominance market comes from a deep understanding of the emotions and motivations that underlie consumer behavior. Harley doesn't just sell motorcycles; its sells freedom, independence, power, and authenticity.

independence, power, and authenticity. Harley-Davidson doesn't just sell motorcycles. It sells self-expression, lifestyles, aspirations, and dreams. "It's all about the *experience*," says an analyst, "one forged in heavy metal thunder, living free and peeling wheel down Route 66. It's an experience that allows middle-aged accountants to don black, studded leather and forget about debits and credits for a little while."

To hard-core enthusiasts, a Harley is much more than a machine. It's a part of who they are and where they want to go in life. A Harley renews your spirits and announces your freedom and independence. A popular line at Harley-Davidson is that "Thumbing the starter of a Harley does a lot more than fire the engine. It fires the imagination." The classic look, the throaty sound, the very idea of a Harley—all contribute to its mystique. Owning this "American legend" makes you a part of something bigger, a member of the Harley-Davidson family.

The strong emotions and motivations underlying Harley consumer behavior are captured in a classic old Harley-Davidson print advertisement. The ad shows a close-up of an arm, the bicep adorned with a Harley-Davidson tattoo. The headline asks, "When was the last time you felt this strongly about anything?" The ad copy outlines the problem and suggests a solution: "Wake up in the morning and life picks up where it left off. . . . What once seemed exciting has now become part of the numbing routine. It all begins to feel the same. Except when you've got a Harley-Davidson. Something strikes a nerve. The heartfelt thunder rises up, refusing to become part of the background. Suddenly things are different. Clearer. More real. As they should have been all along. Riding a Harley changes you from within. The effect is permanent. Maybe it's time you started feeling this strongly. Things are different on a Harley."[1]

Author Comment

In some ways, consumer and business markets are similar in their buyer behavior. But in many other ways, they differ a lot. We start by digging into consumer buyer behavior. Later in the chapter, we'll tackle business buyer behavior.

The Harley-Davidson example shows that factors at many levels affect consumer buying behavior. Buying behavior is never simple, yet understanding it is an essential task of marketing management. First we explore the dynamics of the consumer market and the consumer buyer behavior. We then examine business markets and the business buyer process.

Consumer Markets and Consumer Buyer Behavior

Consumer buyer behavior refers to the buying behavior of final consumers—individuals and households that buy goods and services for personal consumption. All of these final consumers combine to make up the **consumer market**. The American consumer market consists of more than 320 million people who consume more than $11 trillion worth of goods and services each year, making it one of the most attractive consumer markets in the world.[2]

Consumers around the world vary tremendously in age, income, education level, and tastes. They also buy an incredible variety of goods and services. How these diverse consumers relate with each other and with other elements of the world around them affects their choices among various products, services, and companies. Here we examine the fascinating array of factors that affect consumer behavior.

Consumer buyer behavior
The buying behavior of final consumers—individuals and households that buy goods and services for personal consumption.

Model of Consumer Behavior

Consumers make many buying decisions every day, and the buying decision is the focal point of the marketer's effort. Most large companies research consumer buying decisions in great detail to answer questions about what consumers buy, where they buy, how and how much they buy, when they buy, and why they buy. Marketers can study actual consumer purchases to find out what they buy, where, and how much. But learning about the *whys* behind consumer buying behavior is not so easy—the answers are often locked deep within the consumer's mind. Often, consumers themselves don't know exactly what influences their purchases.

The central question for marketers is this: How do consumers respond to various marketing efforts the company might use? The starting point is the stimulus-response model of buyer behavior shown in **Figure 5.1**. This figure shows that marketing and other stimuli enter the consumer's "black box" and produce certain responses. Marketers must figure out what is in the buyer's black box.

Marketing stimuli consist of the four *P*s: product, price, place, and promotion. Other stimuli include major forces and events in the buyer's environment: economic, technological, social, and cultural. All these inputs enter the buyer's black box,

Author Comment

Despite the simple-looking model in Figure 5.1, understanding the *whys* of buying behavior is very difficult. Says one expert, "The mind is a whirling, swirling, jumbled mass of neurons bouncing around. . . ."

Consumer market
All the individuals and households that buy or acquire goods and services for personal consumption.

»» Figure 5.1 The Model of Buyer Behavior

Environment		Buyer's black box	Buyer responses
Marketing stimuli	**Other**	Buyer's characteristics	Buying attitudes and preferences
Product	Economic	Buyer's decision process	Purchase behavior: what the buyer buys, when, where, and how much
Price	Technological		Brand engagements and relationships
Place	Social		
Promotion	Cultural		

We can measure the whats, wheres, and whens of consumer buying behavior. But it's very diffcult to "see" inside the consumer's head and figure out the whys of buying behavior (that's why it's called the black box). Marketers spend a lot of energy and dollars trying to figure out what makes customers tick.

where they are turned into a set of buyer responses—the buyer's attitudes and preferences, brand engagements and relationships, and what he or she buys, when, where, and how much.

Marketers want to understand how the stimuli are changed into responses inside the consumer's black box, which has two parts. First, the buyer's characteristics influence how he or she perceives and reacts to the stimuli. Second, the buyer's decision process itself affects his or her behavior. We look first at buyer characteristics as they affect buyer behavior and then discuss the buyer decision process.

Characteristics Affecting Consumer Behavior

Author Comment
Many levels of factors affect our buying behavior—from broad cultural and social influences to motivations, beliefs, and attitudes lying deep within us. For example, why did you buy that specific phone you're carrying?

Consumer purchases are influenced strongly by cultural, social, personal, and psychological characteristics, as shown in **»» Figure 5.2**. For the most part, marketers cannot control such factors, but they must take them into account.

Cultural Factors

Cultural factors exert a broad and deep influence on consumer behavior. Marketers need to understand the role played by the buyer's *culture*, *subculture*, and *social class*.

Culture
The set of basic values, perceptions, wants, and behaviors learned by a member of society from family and other important institutions.

Culture. **Culture** is the most basic cause of a person's wants and behavior. Human behavior is largely learned. Growing up in a society, a child learns basic values, perceptions, wants, and behaviors from his or her family and other important institutions. A child in the United States normally is exposed to the following values: achievement and success, freedom, individualism, hard work, activity and involvement, efficiency and practicality, material comfort, youthfulness, and fitness and health. Every group or society has a culture, and cultural influences on buying behavior may vary greatly from both county to county and country to country.

Many brands now target specific subcultures—such as Hispanic American, African American, and Asian American consumers—with marketing programs tailored to their specific needs and preferences.

Cultural	Social	Personal	Psychological	
Culture	Groups and social networks	Age and life-cycle stage	Motivation	**Buyer**
Subculture	Family	Occupation	Perception	
		Economic situation	Learning	
		Lifestyle	Beliefs and attitudes	
Social class	Roles and status	Personality and self-concept		

People's buying decisions reflect and contribute to their lifestyles—their whole pattern of acting and interacting in the world. For example, KitchenAid sells much more than just kitchen appliances. It sells an entire cooking and entertainment lifestyle to "Kitchenthusiasts."

Our buying decisions are affected by an incredibly complex combination of external and internal influences.

»» Figure 5.2 Factors Influencing Consumer Behavior

Marketers are always trying to spot *cultural shifts* so as to discover new products that might be wanted. For example, the cultural shift toward greater concern about health and fitness has created a huge industry for health-and-fitness services, exercise equipment and clothing, organic foods, and a variety of diets.

Subculture

A group of people with shared value systems based on common life experiences and situations.

Subculture. Each culture contains smaller **subcultures**, or groups of people with shared value systems based on common life experiences and situations. Subcultures include nationalities, religions, racial groups, and geographic regions. Many subcultures make up important market segments, and marketers often design products and marketing programs tailored to their needs. Examples of three such important subculture groups are African American, Hispanic American, and Asian American consumers.

The U.S. *African American* population is growing in affluence and sophistication. The nation's more than 42 million black consumers wield almost $1.2 trillion in annual buying power. Although more price conscious than other segments, blacks are also strongly motivated by quality and selection. Brands are important. African American consumers are heavy users of digital and social media, providing access through a rich variety of marketing channels.[3]

Many companies develop special products, appeals, and marketing programs for African American consumers—from carmakers like Ford and Hyundai to consumer products companies like P&G to even not-for-profits and government agencies such as the U.S. Forest Service. »For example, the U.S. Forest Service and the Ad Council recently joined forces to create the "Discover the Forest" public service campaign to raise awareness among families of the benefits for children of getting outside and enjoying nature. One round of the campaign specifically targeted the parents of African American tweens:[4]

Although more than 245 million Americans live within 100 miles of a national forest or grassland, research shows that a majority of children in some population segments are not spending active time outdoors. For example, only 37 percent of African American children ages six to twelve participate frequently in outdoor activities compared with 67 percent of the broader U.S. population in that age group. To help close that gap, the U.S. Forest Service and the Ad Council created the "Discover the Forest" campaign, a series of public service messages ranging from billboards and radio commercials to interactive social media and Web site content. With headlines such as "Unplug," "Where curiosity blooms," and "Where imagination sprouts," the ads targeting African American families promote the discovery and imagination wonders of connecting with the great outdoors and the resulting physical, mental health, and emotional well-being benefits. "The forest is one of those amazing places where kids can flex their imagination muscles through exploration and discovery," says a marketer associated with the campaign.

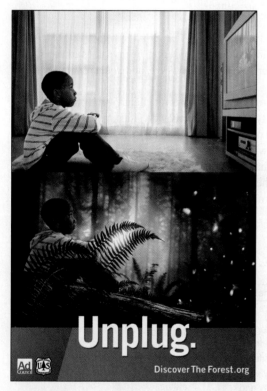

» **Targeting African American consumers: The U.S. Forest Service and Ad Council joined forces to create the "Discover the Forest" public service campaign to raise awareness among African American families of the benefits for children of getting outside and enjoying nature.**

The Forest Service, an agency of the U.S. Department of Agriculture and the Ad Council.

Hispanics represent a large, fast-growing market. The nation's more than 55 million Hispanic consumers (almost one out of every six Americans) have total annual buying power of $1.7 trillion. The U.S. Hispanic population will surge to more than 120 million by 2060, close to one-third of the total U.S. population.[5] Within the Hispanic market, there exist many distinct subsegments based on nationality, age, income, and other factors. A company's product or message may be more relevant to one nationality over another, such as Mexicans, Costa Ricans, Argentineans, or Cubans.

Although Hispanic consumers share many characteristics and behaviors with the mainstream buying public, there are also distinct differences. They tend to be deeply family oriented and make shopping a family affair—children have a big say in what brands they buy. Older, first-generation Hispanic consumers tend to be very brand loyal and to favor brands and sellers who show special interest in them. Younger Hispanics, however, have shown increasing price sensitivity in recent years and a willingness to switch to store brands. Hispanics are more active on mobile and social networks than other segments, making digital media ideal for reaching this segment.[6]

Companies such as P&G, McDonald's, Walmart, State Farm, Chrysler, Google, and many others have developed special targeting efforts for this fast-growing consumer segment. For example, Walmart and Target both spend heavily to cultivate the Hispanic market. Both use Spanish-language ads and social media, place bilingual signs in stores, and stock their shelves with products that appeal to the special preferences of Hispanics. And Chrysler's successful three-year "A Todo, Con Todo" campaign markets the company's Ram trucks to the important Hispanic segment:[7]

Pickup trucks are Ram's biggest market, and Hispanics are crucial to the brand's success in that segment. The "A Todo, Con Todo" Ram truck campaign targets Hispanic pickup-truck owners with Spanish- and English-language TV, magazine, radio, and digital ads in major Hispanic markets, such as Albuquerque, Miami, Phoenix, New York, Los Angeles, Denver, and numerous Texas communities. "A Todo, Con Todo"—which translates as "To everything, with everything" (or "Give it all you've got")—appeals to authentic Hispanic values. The first ads in the series featured two Hispanic truck owners—Ascension Banuelos and Arturo Barcelo—who use their Ram trucks day in and day out for work and recreation. Banuelos manages a horse training ranch in Jacksboro, Texas, and owns a Ram 3500; Barcelo drives a Ram 1500 and owns a home-improvement construction company in Dallas. In the ads, these truck owners give unscripted, real-life testimonials about values that are important to them and how their Ram trucks fit those values. An announcer concludes: "Finding a way to rise above, to push our limits further. The Ram 1500. Because success is not a destination, it's our journey. Ram. A Todo, Con Todo." Thanks largely to this campaign, Ram pickup-truck sales to the important Hispanics segment were up 33 percent last year.

Asian Americans are the most affluent U.S. demographic segment. A relatively well-educated segment, they now number more than 18 million (5 percent of the population), with annual buying power expected to approach $1 trillion by 2017. Asian Americans are the second-fastest-growing subsegment after Hispanic Americans. And like Hispanic Americans, they are a diverse group. Chinese Americans constitute the largest group, followed by Filipinos, Asian Indians, Vietnamese, Korean Americans, and Japanese Americans. Yet, unlike Hispanics who all speak various dialects of Spanish, Asians speak many different languages. For example, ads for the 2010 U.S. Census ran in languages ranging from Japanese, Cantonese, Khmer, Korean, and Vietnamese to Thai, Cambodian, Hmong, Hinglish, and Taglish.[8]

Total market strategy
Integrating ethnic themes and cross-cultural perspectives within a brand's mainstream marketing, appealing to consumer similarities across subcultural segments rather than differences.

As a group, Asian American consumers shop frequently and are the most brand conscious of all the ethnic groups. They can be fiercely brand loyal. As a result, many firms now target the Asian American market. >> AT&T learned that young Asian Americans are more than just a lucrative technology market in themselves—they also influence other consumers. So it created an innovative marketing campaign aimed at improving perceptions in this influential young segment:[9]

To raise perceptions of AT&T as an innovative and preferred brand among Asian-American youth, key influencers in its tech markets, AT&T created an engaging crowd-sourced, boy-meets-girl Web series called "Away We Happened." The low-cost series featured popular Asian youth celebrities Victor Kim and Jen Chae of Frmheadtotoe. AT&T partnered with Asian YouTube producer Wong Fu Productions to create the first episode. It then encouraged viewers to visit a Facebook app to submit their ideas for what happened next and vote on the best ideas for future episodes. The Effie-winning, six-episode series went viral, grabbing more than 13 million views over its six-week run and raising AT&T brand perceptions by 50 percent among young Asian American consumers.

>> **Targeting Asian American consumers: To improve perceptions among young Asian Americans, key influencers in its tech markets, AT&T created an engaging crowd-sourced, boy-meets-girl Web series called "Away We Happened."**

Courtesy of AT&T Intellectual Property, interTrend Communications, Wong Fu Productions, Inc., and Rezonate Media. Female talent: Jen Chae (Jen of FrmHeadtoToe). Used with permission.

Beyond targeting segments such as Hispanics, African Americans, and Asian Americans with specially tailored efforts, many marketers now embrace a **total market strategy**—the practice of integrating ethnic themes and cross-cultural perspectives within their mainstream marketing. An example is general-market commercials for Cheerios and Swiffer that feature interracial families.[10] A total market strategy appeals to consumer similarities across subcultural segments rather than differences.

Many marketers are finding that insights gleaned from ethnic consumer segments can influence their broader markets. For example, today's youth-oriented lifestyle is influenced heavily by Hispanic and African American entertainers. So it follows that consumers expect to see many different cultures and ethnicities represented in the advertising and products they consume. For instance, McDonald's takes cues from African Americans, Hispanics, and Asians to develop menus and advertising in hopes of encouraging mainstream consumers to buy smoothies, mocha drinks, and snack wraps as avidly as they consume hip-hop and rock'n' roll. Or McDonald's might take an ad primarily geared toward African Americans and run it in general-market media.

Social class

Relatively permanent and ordered divisions in a society whose members share similar values, interests, and behaviors.

Social Class. Almost every society has some form of social class structure. **Social classes** are society's relatively permanent and ordered divisions whose members share similar values, interests, and behaviors. Social scientists have identified the seven American social classes: upper upper class, lower upper class, upper middle class, middle class, working class, upper lower class, and lower lower class.

Social class is not determined by a single factor, such as income, but is measured as a combination of occupation, income, education, wealth, and other variables. In some social systems, members of different classes are reared for certain roles and cannot change their social positions. In the United States, however, the lines between social classes are not fixed and rigid; people can move to a higher social class or drop into a lower one.

Marketers are interested in social class because people within a given social class tend to exhibit similar buying behavior. Social classes show distinct product and brand preferences in areas such as clothing, home furnishings, travel and leisure activity, financial services, and automobiles.

Social Factors

A consumer's behavior also is influenced by social factors, such as the consumer's *small groups, social networks, family*, and *social roles and status*.

Group

Two or more people who interact to accomplish individual or mutual goals.

Groups and Social Networks. Many small **groups** influence a person's behavior. Groups that have a direct influence and to which a person belongs are called *membership groups*. In contrast, *reference groups* serve as direct (face-to-face interactions) or indirect points of comparison or reference in forming a person's attitudes or behavior. People often are influenced by reference groups to which they do not belong. For example, an *aspirational group* is one to which the individual wishes to belong, as when a young basketball player hopes to someday emulate basketball star LeBron James and play in the NBA.

Marketers try to identify the reference groups of their target markets. Reference groups expose a person to new behaviors and lifestyles, influence the person's attitudes and self-concept, and create pressures to conform that may affect the person's product and brand choices. The importance of group influence varies across products and brands. It tends to be strongest when the product is visible to others whom the buyer respects.

Word-of-mouth influence

The impact of the personal words and recommendations of trusted friends, family, associates, and other consumers on buying behavior.

Word-of-mouth influence can have a powerful impact on consumer buying behavior. The personal words and recommendations of trusted friends, family, associates, and other consumers tend to be more credible than those coming from commercial sources, such as advertisements or salespeople. One recent study showed that 92 percent of consumers trust recommendations from friends and family above any form of advertising.[11] Most word-of-mouth influence happens naturally: Consumers start chatting about a brand they use or feel strongly about one way or the other. Often, however, rather than leaving it to chance, marketers can help to create positive conversations about their brands.

Opinion leader

A person within a reference group who, because of special skills, knowledge, personality, or other characteristics, exerts social influence on others.

Marketers of brands subjected to strong group influence must figure out how to reach **opinion leaders**—people within a reference group who, because of special skills, knowledge, personality, or other characteristics, exert social influence on others. Some experts call this group the *influentials* or *leading adopters*. When these influentials talk, consumers listen. Marketers try to identify opinion leaders for their products and direct marketing efforts toward them.

>> **Creating word of mouth:** Mercedes-Benz's "Take the Wheel" influencer campaign really got people buzzing about its all-new CLA model, helping to create millions of positive social conversations and record sales.

© Courtesy of Daimler AG

Online social networks

Online communities—blogs, social networking Web sites, and other online communities—where people socialize or exchange information and opinions.

Buzz marketing involves enlisting or even creating opinion leaders to serve as "brand ambassadors" who spread the word about a company's products. Consider Mercedes-Benz's award-winning "Take the Wheel" influencer campaign:[12]

>> Mercedes-Benz wanted get more people talking about its all-new, soon-to-be-launched 2014 CLA model, priced at $29,900 and aimed at getting a new generation of younger consumers into the Mercedes brand. So it challenged five of Instagram's most influential photographers—everyday Gen Y consumers whose stunning imagery had earned them hundreds of thousands of fans—to each spend five days behind the wheel of a CLA, documenting their journeys in photos shared via Instagram. The photographer who got the most Likes got to keep the CLA. The short campaign really got people buzzing about the car, earning 87 million social media impressions and more than 2 million likes. Ninety percent of the social conversation was positive. And when Mercedes launched the CLA the following month, it broke sales records.

Sometimes, everyday customers become a brand's best evangelists. For instance, Alan Klein loves the McDonald's McRib—a sandwich made of a boneless pork patty molded into a rib-like shape, slathered in BBQ sauce and topped with pickles and onion. The McRib is sold for only short time periods each year at McDonald's restaurants around the nation. Klein loves it so much that he created the McRib Locator app and Web site (mcriblocator.com), where McRib fans buzz about locations where they've recently sighted the coveted sandwich.[13]

Over the past several years, a new type of social interaction has exploded onto the scene—online social networking. **Online social networks** are online communities where people socialize or exchange information and opinions. Social networking communities range from blogs (Consumerist, Gizmodo, Zenhabits) and message boards (Craigslist) to social media sites (Facebook, Twitter, YouTube, Pinterest, and LinkedIn) and even communal shopping sites (Amazon.com and Etsy). These online forms of consumer-to-consumer and business-to-consumer dialogue have big implications for marketers.

Marketers are working to harness the power of these new social networks and other "word-of-Web" opportunities to promote their products and build closer customer relationships. Instead of throwing more one-way commercial messages at consumers, they hope to use the digital, mobile, and social media to *interact* with consumers and become a part of their conversations and lives.

For example, Red Bull has an astounding 46 million friends on Facebook; Twitter and Facebook are the primary ways it communicates with college students. JetBlue listens in on customers on Twitter and often responds; one consumer recently Tweeted "Thanks for taking me home for the holidays @JetBlue. And thanks to the crew in Austin for giving me a row to myself so I can sleep!" JetBlue Tweeted back "You're most welcome, Nancy! Thanks for letting us be your ride! Happy Holidays to you and your family! #VIPTreatmentForNancy." Even the Mayo Clinic uses social media extensively. It maintains Facebook, Pinterest, and Twitter pages; a YouTube channel; smartphone patient apps that "put Mayo in your pocket wherever you are"; and a Sharing Mayo Clinic blog on which patients share their Mayo Clinic experiences and employees offer a behind-the-scenes view.

Most brands have built a comprehensive social media presence. We will dig deeper into online and social media as marketing tools in Chapter 14. However, although much of the current talk about tapping social influence focuses on the digital, mobile, and social media, most brand conversations still take place the old-fashioned way—face to face. So most effective word-of-mouth marketing programs begin with generating person-to-person brand conversations and integrating both offline and online social influence strategies. The goal is to create opportunities for customers to get involved with brands and then help them share their brand passions and experiences with others in both their real and digital worlds (see Marketing at Work 5.1).

MARKETING AT WORK   5.1

Word-of-Mouth Marketing: Sparking Brand Conversations and Helping Them Catch Fire

People love talking with others about things that make them happy—including their favorite products and brands. Say you really like JetBlue Airways—it flies with flair and gets you there at an affordable price. Or you just plain love your new little GoPro HERO4 Black Edition video camera—it's too cool to keep to yourself. So you spread the good word about your favorite brands to anyone who will listen. In the old days, you'd have chatted up these brands with a few friends and family members. But these days, thanks to the online, mobile, and social media, anyone can share brand experiences with thousands, even millions, of other consumers digitally.

In response, marketers are now feverishly working to harness today's technologies and get people interacting with each other about their brands, both online and offline. The aim is to inspire, nurture, and amplify brand conversations. Whether it entails seeding a product among high-potential consumers to get them talking, creating brand ambassadors, tapping into existing influentials and the social media, or developing conversation-provoking events and videos, the idea is to get people involved with and talking about the brand.

Generating successful word of mouth might be as simple as prompting Facebook Likes and Shares, Twitter streams, Pinterest boards, online reviews, blog commentaries, or YouTube videos. Even companies with small budgets can earn global exposure in the social media. For example, little-known start-up DollarShaveClub.com—which ships quality razors directly to customers for as little as $1 a month—became an overnight sensation thanks largely to a single YouTube video. Founder Michael Dubin scraped together $4,500 to produce a clever video featuring himself, some corny props, a guy in a bear suit, and very salty language to pitch the new service. "Are the blades any good?" Dubin asked in the video. "No. Our blades are f***ing great," he answered. "So stop forgetting where you're going to buy your blades every month and start deciding where you're going to stack all those dollar bills I'm saving you." The edgy video went viral, and the word-of-mouth firestorm earned DollarShaveClub.com more than 17 million YouTube views, 60,000 Twitter followers, 1.5 million Likes on Facebook, dozens of response videos, and $10 million in venture capital funding. DollarShaveClub's success has even prompted giant Gillette to begin its own blade subscription program.

But most successful social influence campaigns go well beyond a YouTube video or Facebook Likes.

For example, many companies start by creating their own brand evangelists. That's what Ford did to introduce its Fiesta subcompact model in the United States. Under its now-classic Fiesta Movement campaign, Ford handed out Fiestas to 100 young Millennial drivers—the target audience for the car—selected from 4,000 applicants. These "Fiesta Agents" lived with their cars for six months, all the while sharing their experiences via blogs, Tweets, Facebook updates, and YouTube and Flickr posts. The highly successful Fiesta Movement campaign generated 58 percent prelaunch brand awareness among Fiesta's under-30 target consumers. The Fiesta ambassadors posted 50,000 items, generating 28 million social media views, 52,000 test drives, and 10,000 online vehicle reservations. The Fiesta Movement was so successful that Ford created similar social media evangelist campaigns for the Ford Escape ("Escape Routes") and the Ford Fusion ("Random Acts of Fusion").

Beyond creating their own ambassadors, companies looking to harness influence can work with the army of self-made influencers already plying the Internet—independent bloggers. Believe it or not, there are now almost as many people making a living as bloggers as there are lawyers. No matter what the interest area, there are probably hundreds of bloggers covering it. Moreover, research shows that 90 percent of bloggers post about their favorite and least favorite brands.

» Sparking word of mouth: Chubbies spreads its "shorts revolution" manifesto through both a booming social media presence and an army of face-to-face brand ambassadors on college campuses.
Chubbies Shorts

As a result, most companies try to form relationships with influential bloggers and online personalities. The key is to find bloggers who have strong networks of relevant readers, a credible voice, and a good fit with the brand. For example, companies ranging from P&G and McDonald's to Walmart work closely with influential "mommy bloggers." And you'll no doubt cross paths with the likes of climbers and skiers blogging for Patagonia, bikers blogging for Harley-Davidson, and foodies blogging for Whole Foods Market or Trader Joe's. Sometimes, bloggers and other social media mavens focus exclusively on a given brand. For example, StarbucksMelody.com is "an unofficial fan site for any and all Starbucks enthusiasts everywhere." TUAW is "The Unofficial Apple Weblog—a resource for all things Apple and beyond." Thanks to their independence, such blogs often generate more trustworthy buzz than a company's own blogs or online sites can.

Much of the word-of-mouth marketing frenzy today seems to center on creating online buzz. However, the majority of brand conversations still take place offline. According to one expert, some 93 percent of brand conversations still happen in the real world rather than the virtual one. So many marketers look beyond the digital world to create good old face-to-face brand conversations.

For example, Chubbies is a small but trendy and fast-growing startup that targets young men with a line of "anti-cargo shorts" (and a retro 5 1/2-inch inseam). So far, the brand has marketed itself only through its social media presence. Avid Chubsters actively swap influence via pictures, videos, and stories on YouTube, Facebook, Twitter, Instagram, Pinterest, and the Chubbies Web site and ChubsterNation blog. But now, Chubbies is building an army of face-to-face influencers in the form of 250 student ambassadors at college campuses across the country. The ambassadors—what it calls "thigh-liberating patriots"—spread the Chubster manifesto that "We don't do pants. We don't do cargos. We don't do capris. We do shorts and only shorts." "Pants are for work," they preach. Chubbies "are for having fun, or jumping off rocks, or playing beer pong, or climbing Everest." The ambassadors personally rally the faithful at tailgate parties and other campus events, expanding the ChubsterNation and sparking even more word of mouth for the irreverent brand.

Whether offline, online, or both, effective word-of-mouth marketing isn't something that just happens. And it's more than just building a following on Facebook. Marketers must build comprehensive programs that spark person-to-person brand conversations and then help them catch fire. The goal of word-of-mouth marketing is to find the company's best customers, give them opportunities to become more involved, and help them spread their brand passion and enthusiasm within their in-person and digital networks. It's all about sparking brand conversations and helping them catch fire.

Sources: Jefferson Graham, "Dollar Shave Club's Dubin: From YouTube Star to CEO," June 14, 2014, www.usatoday.com/story/money/business/2014/06/09/ceo-profile-dollar-shave-clubs-michael-dubin/9993045/; Giselle Abramovich, "Why Ford Credits Social Media in Turnaround," *Digiday*, October 10, 2012, www.digiday.com/brands/why-ford-credits-social-media-in-turnaround/; Iris Mansour, "The New Face of Word-of-Mouth," *CNNMoney*, August 2013, http://management.fortune.cnn.com/2013/08/28/word-of-mouth-marketing/; Nellie Bowles, "Chubbies Shorts Popular with Troops," June 28, 2013, www.sfgate.com/style/article/Chubbies-shorts-popular-with-troops-4634821.php; Jim Dougherty, "9 Ways to Improve Word-of-Mouth Communications," *Cision*, January 5, 2015, www.cision.com/us/2015/01/9-ways-to-improve-word-of-mouth-communication/; www.chubbiesshorts.com/pages/manifesto, www.dollarshaveclub.com, and www.chubbiesshorts.com/, accessed September 2015.

Family. Family members can strongly influence buyer behavior. The family is the most important consumer buying organization in society, and it has been researched extensively. Marketers are interested in the roles and influence of the husband, wife, and children on the purchase of different products and services.

Husband–wife involvement varies widely by product category and by stage in the buying process. Buying roles change with evolving consumer lifestyles. For example, in the United States, the wife traditionally has been considered the main purchasing agent for the family in the areas of food, household products, and clothing. But with 71 percent of all mothers now working outside the home and the willingness of husbands to do more of the family's purchasing, all this has changed in recent years. Recent surveys of men show that nearly half do at least 50 percent of their household's grocery shopping, 39 percent handle most of their household's laundry, and about one-quarter say they are responsible for all of their household's cooking. At the same time, today women outspend men three to two on new technology purchases and influence more than 80 percent of all new car purchases.[14]

Such shifting roles signal a new marketing reality. Marketers in industries that have traditionally sold their products to only women or only men—from groceries and personal care products to cars and consumer electronics—are now carefully targeting the opposite sex. Other companies are showing their products in "modern family" contexts. For example, ≫ one General Mills ad shows a father packing Go-Gurt yogurt in his son's lunch as the child heads off to school in the morning, with the slogan "Dads who get it, get Go-Gurt." And the recent General Mills "How to Dad" campaign for Cheerios presents a

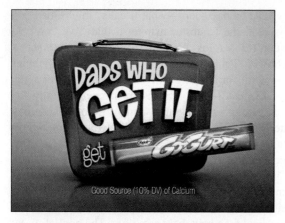

>> Changing family buying influences: One Go-Gurt ad shows a father packing Go-Gurt yogurt in his son's lunch as the child heads off to school. "Dads who get it, get Go-Gurt."

Use with permission of General Mills Marketing Inc. (GMMI).

dad as a multitasking superhero around the house, a departure from the bumbling dad stereotypes often shown in food ads. This dad does all the right things, including feeding this children healthy Cheerios breakfasts. "Being a dad is awesome," he proclaims in one ad. "Just like Cheerios are awesome. That's why it's the Official Cereal of Dadhood."[15]

Children may also have a strong influence on family buying decisions. The nation's kids and tweens influence up to 80 percent of all household purchases, to the tune of $1.2 trillion of spending annually. Kids significantly influence family decisions about everything from clothing, cars, and entertainment to where they eat out and take vacations.[16]

Roles and Status. A person belongs to many groups—family, clubs, organizations, online communities. The person's position in each group can be defined in terms of both role and status. A role consists of the activities people are expected to perform according to the people around them. Each role carries a status reflecting the general esteem given to it by society.

People usually choose products appropriate to their roles and status. Consider the various roles a working mother plays. In her company, she may play the role of a brand manager; in her family, she plays the role of wife and mother; at her favorite sporting events, she plays the role of avid fan. As a brand manager, she will buy the kind of clothing that reflects her role and status in her company. At the game, she may wear clothing supporting her favorite team.

Personal Factors

A buyer's decisions also are influenced by personal characteristics such as the buyer's *occupation, age and life-cycle stage, economic situation, lifestyle*, and *personality and self-concept*.

Occupation. A person's occupation affects the goods and services bought. Blue-collar workers tend to buy more rugged work clothes, whereas executives buy more business suits. Marketers try to identify the occupational groups that have an above-average interest in their products and services. A company can even specialize in making products needed by a given occupational group. For example, Duluth Trading Company makes rugged, durable work clothes with a "no-bull" guarantee. From its "Ballroom Jeans" that give you "room to crouch without singing soprano" to its "Longtail T-shirts" that fix your "plumber's butt," Duluth's products are designed and tested by tradesmen. "Taking care of working guys is priority #1 at Duluth," says the company.

Age and Life Stage. People change the goods and services they buy over their lifetimes. Tastes in food, clothes, furniture, and recreation are often age related. Buying is also shaped by the stage of the family life cycle—the stages through which families might pass as they mature over time. Life-stage changes usually result from demographics and life-changing events—marriage, having children, purchasing a home, divorce, children going to college, changes in personal income, moving out of the house, and retirement. Marketers often define their target markets in terms of life-cycle stage and develop appropriate products and marketing plans for each stage.

One of the leading life-stage segmentation systems is the Nielsen PRIZM Lifestage Groups system. PRIZM classifies every American household into one of 66 distinct life-stage segments, which are organized into 11 major life-stage groups, based on affluence, age, and family characteristics. The classifications consider a host of demographic factors such as age, education, income, occupation, family composition, ethnicity, and housing; and behavioral and lifestyle factors, such as purchases, free-time activities, and media preferences.

The major PRIZM Lifestage groups carry names such as "Striving Singles," "Midlife Success," "Young Achievers," "Sustaining Families," "Affluent Empty Nests," and "Conservative Classics," which in turn contain subgroups such as "Brite Lites, Li'l City," "Kids & Cul-de-Sacs," "Gray Power," and "Big City Blues." The "Young Achievers" group consists of hip, single 20-somethings who rent apartments in or close to metropolitan neighborhoods. Their incomes range from working class to well-to-do, but the entire group tends to be politically liberal, listen to alternative music, and enjoy lively nightlife.[17]

Different life-stage groups exhibit different buying behaviors. Life-stage segmentation provides a powerful marketing tool for marketers in all industries to better find, understand, and engage consumers. Armed with data about the makeup of consumer life stages, marketers can create targeted, actionable, personalized campaigns based on how people consume and interact with brands and the world around them.

Economic Situation. A person's economic situation will affect his or her store and product choices. Marketers watch trends in spending, personal income, savings, and interest rates. In today's more value-conscious times, most companies have taken steps to create more customer value by redesigning, repositioning, and repricing their products and services. For example, in recent years, upscale discounter Target has put more emphasis on the "Pay Less" side of its "Expect More. Pay Less." positioning promise.

Similarly, in line with worldwide economic trends, smartphone makers who once offered only premium-priced phones are now offering lower-priced models for consumers both at home and in the world's emerging economies. Microsoft's Nokia division recently targeted emerging markets with lower-end Lumia models priced well under $100. And Apple introduced a lower-end, lower-priced version of its iPhone, the iPhone 5C. As their more affluent Western markets have become saturated and more competitive, the phone makers hope that their lower-priced phones will help them to compete effectively and grow in less-affluent emerging Eastern markets such as China and Southeast Asia.[18]

Lifestyle. People coming from the same subculture, social class, and occupation may have quite different lifestyles. **Lifestyle** is a person's pattern of living as expressed in his or her psychographics. It involves measuring consumers' major AIO dimensions—*activities* (work, hobbies, shopping, sports, social events), *interests* (food, fashion, family, recreation), and *opinions* (about themselves, social issues, business, products). Lifestyle captures something more than the person's social class or personality. It profiles a person's whole pattern of acting and interacting in the world.

When used carefully, the lifestyle concept can help marketers understand changing consumer values and how they affect buyer behavior. Consumers don't just buy products; they buy the values and lifestyles those products represent. For example, you may know KitchenAid by its high-performance mixers and other kitchen appliances. ≫ But KitchenAid sells much more than just appliances. It sells an entire cooking and entertainment lifestyle:[19]

> KitchenAid cultivates "Kitchenthusiasts"—a lifestyle community of "hosts with the most" who thrive on cooking and entertainment challenges. Its Kitchenthusiast blog, Facebook pages, and 11 Pinterest boards are brimming with recipes, cooking challenges, tips and techniques, and coverage of the latest cooking lifestyle news and events by key contributors. KitchenAid's "There's So Much More to Make" marketing campaign highlights how the brand's appliances contribute to the lifestyles of passionate Kitchenthusiasts. Says one ad: "When entertaining elates you, when every machine does incredible things, there's so much more to make."

Marketers look for lifestyle segments with needs that can be served through special products or marketing approaches. Such segments might be defined by anything from family characteristics or outdoor interests to the foods people eat. For example, fast-food chain Taco Bell recently repositioned itself as an experience brand, consistent with the lifestyles of its primary target customers, Millennials (see Marketing at Work 5.2).

Lifestyle
A person's pattern of living as expressed in his or her activities, interests, and opinions.

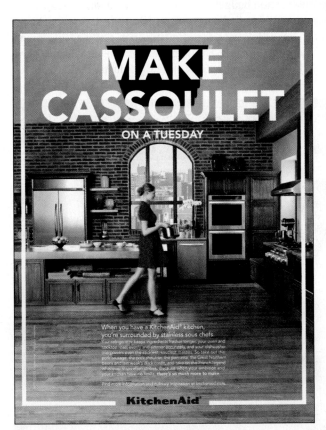

≫ Lifestyles: KitchenAid sells much more than just high-performance kitchen appliances. It sells an entire cooking and entertainment lifestyle to "Kitchenthusiasts."

Courtesy of Whirlpool Corporation. Photo © Melanie Acevedo/Stockland Martel

Taco Bell: More than Just Tacos, a "Live Más" Lifestyle

Years ago, Taco Bell practically invented the fast-food "value menu," with its "59¢-79¢-99¢" pricing structure. With slogans such as "The Cure for the Common Meal," "Make a Run for the Border," and "Think Outside the Bun," Taco Bell firmly established its affordable Mexican-inspired fare as a unique, "more-for-your-money" alternative to the mostly burgers and fries offered by dominant McDonald's and other fast-food competitors.

In the early 2000s, however, consumer tastes began to change. Americans were looking for fresher, better-tasting, healthier eating options and more contemporary fast-casual atmospheres. Taco Bell's "food-as-fuel" marketing philosophy—its "fill them up, move them out" thinking—made the chain seem out of step with the times. After three straight years of flat sales, Taco Bell ended 2011 with a 1.4-percent decline in systemwide revenues. These dire results called for a shift in Taco Bell's strategy.

The shift began with the realization that customers want more from a fast-food restaurant than just lots of food on the cheap. More than "calories per dollar," they are seeking a food-eating experience, one that fits with and enhances their lifestyles. So in early 2012, Taco Bell shifted its positioning from "food as fuel" to "food as experience and lifestyle." It crafted a new tagline—"Live Más" ("más" is Spanish for "more"). As part of its $280 million annual marketing budget, the "Live Más" slogan is designed as a lifestyle rallying cry for Taco Bell's core customers, Millennials—young adults who consume a disproportionate share of fast and fast-casual food.

Taco Bell's aspirational "Live Más" message is crafted to inspire Millennials to try new things and to live life to the fullest. The first "Live Más" ad, called "Pockets," showed a hip, 20-something man coming into a dim apartment as dawn breaks. He emptied his pockets onto a table as he thought back over the night he'd had. Along with the standard wallet, keys, and smartphone, he tossed out a concert ticket stub, a matchbook from a 24-hour psychic, a pair of Kanji dice, and a strip of photo-booth images of himself with a young woman. The last item he pulled out was a blister pack of Taco Bell Fire Sauce, adorned with the new "Live Más" logo and the message "You have chosen wisely." It was this last item that brought a smile to his face.

Support for the "Live Más" lifestyle tagline goes well beyond just advertising. For example, it includes new menu items aimed to please Millennial palates. In early 2012, Taco Bell unveiled cobranded Doritos Locos Tacos, like a standard Taco Bell taco or Taco Supreme but wrapped in a tasty shell made from Nacho Cheese Doritos. Hungry Millennials gobbled up 100 million Doritos Locos Tacos in just the first 10 weeks, at the time making it the most successful new-product launch in the company's 50-year history. The brand quickly added Cool Ranch and Fiery versions.

Recognizing that customers who want to "Live Más" might be looking to eat at just about any time of day, Taco Bell has focused on more day parts. For example, after a long absence from morning hours, Taco Bell has rolled out a 7 am (or earlier) to 11 am breakfast menu. Initial options included breakfast burritos, waffle tacos, the A.M. Crunchwrap, the A.M. Grilled Taco, and bite-size Cinnabon Delights. Similarly, Taco Bell's "Happier Hour" initiative targets between-meal-snack appetites from 2 pm to 5 pm daily, featuring new Mountain Dew Baja Blast and Dr Pepper frozen beverages and $1 Loaded Grillers. And for the late-night "Live Más" crowd, there's Fourthmeal, as in "You're out. You're hungry. You're doing Fourthmeal." In one ad—titled "After-Wedding Party"—a newlywed couple feasts on Taco Bell fare in the back of a limo along with their groomsmen and bridesmaids. The announcer concludes, "Fourthmeal—sometimes the best dinner is after the dinner."

To better engage targeted Millennials, Taco Bell now reaches them where they hang out—online, digital, and mobile. Befitting the Millennial lifestyle, it recently added a new mobile ordering app. And a significant portion of the "Live Más" promotion budget goes to social media, digital tools, and other nontraditional channels. Beyond the usual Facebook and Twitter, Taco Bell uses social media such as Vine, Instagram, and Snapchat for buzz-building announcements, limited-time promotions, and sneak peeks at new products. The revitalized

>> Taco Bell's innovative "Live Más" positioning targets the lifestyles of the brand's key target customers, Millennials.

Taco Bell Corporation

chain watches and participates in online brand conversations with its "Fishbowl"—Taco Bell's own command center for monitoring social media and generating digital dialogue. For example, the brand achieved more than 600 million social-media impressions for Cool Ranch Doritos Locos Tacos alone before the product even officially launched.

Some analysts suggest that with "Live Más," Taco Bell is stretching too far beyond its core affordable fast-food positioning. "They're trying to suggest a lifestyle aspiration, but this seems an overreach for Taco Bell," says one restaurant-marketing consultant. "A tagline should embrace the DNA of the brand, which for Taco Bell is extraordinary value." Not so, says Taco Bell. Rather than abandoning the brand's "value" roots, says the company, the new tagline and other elements of "Live Más" underscore brand values dating back to its founding—"value, quality, relevance, and an exceptional experience." The "value" message still resonates in the tagline, but "Live Más" also energizes the "relevance" and "experience" aspects of Taco Bell's long-standing value proposition.

The early results suggest that Taco Bell is right on track with the "Live Más" lifestyle positioning. The year following the introduction of the tagline saw sales soar 8 percent, more than twice the gain of industry leader McDonald's. And ad industry magazine *Advertising Age* recently named Taco Bell its Marketer of the Year for going "into innovation overdrive, churning out a string of hot new products, game-changing menus, and an aggressive mix of traditional, social, and digital media that's hitting the mark with Millennials."

But for Taco Bell, becoming an experience and lifestyle brand isn't just about reversing sales declines and reaping marketing honors. It's about building for the future. Taco Bell recently announced plans to nearly double its business to $14 billion by 2022 with 8,000 restaurants domestically. Accomplishing that lofty objective will have both Taco Bell's customers *and* Taco Bell marketers shouting "Live Más!"

Sources: Kate Taylor, "KFC, Pizza Hut, and Taco Bell Want Even More Millennial Customers in 2015," *Entrepreneur,* December 11, 2014, www.entrepreneur.com/article/240835; Maureen Morrison, "Sales Are Going Loco at Taco Bell, Ad Age's Marketer of the Year," *Advertising Age*, September 2, 2013, p. 2; Shirley Brady, "Taco Bell Promotes New 'Live Más' Tagline in New Campaign," *Brand Channel*, February 24, 2012, www.brandchannel.com/home/post/2012/02/24/Taco-Bell-Live-Mas-Doritos-Locos-Tacos-Spots-022412.aspx; Maureen Morrison, "Taco Bell to Exchange 'Think Outside the Bun' for 'Live Más,'" *Advertising Age*, February 21, 2012, adage.com/print/232849; Mark Brandau, "Yum Plans to Double U.S. Taco Bell Sales," *Restaurant News*, May 22, 2013, nrn.com/quick-service/analysts-yum-plans-double-us-taco-bell-sales; and various pages at www.tacobell.com and www.tacobell.com/livemas, accessed September 2015.

Personality
The unique psychological characteristics that distinguish a person or group.

Personality and Self-Concept. Each person's distinct personality influences his or her buying behavior. **Personality** refers to the unique psychological characteristics that distinguish a person or group. Personality is usually described in terms of traits such as self-confidence, dominance, sociability, autonomy, defensiveness, adaptability, and aggressiveness. Personality can be useful in analyzing consumer behavior for certain product or brand choices.

The idea is that brands also have personalities, and consumers are likely to choose brands with personalities that match their own. A *brand personality* is the specific mix of human traits that may be attributed to a particular brand. One researcher identified five brand personality traits: *sincerity* (down-to-earth, honest, wholesome, and cheerful), *excitement* (daring, spirited, imaginative, and up-to-date), *competence* (reliable, intelligent, and successful), *sophistication* (glamorous, upper class, charming), and *ruggedness* (outdoorsy and tough). "Your personality determines what you consume, what TV shows you watch, what products you buy, and [most] other decisions you make," says one consumer behavior expert.[20]

Most well-known brands are strongly associated with one particular trait: the Ford F150 with "ruggedness," Apple with "excitement," the *Washington Post* with "competence," Method with "sincerity," and Gucci with "class and sophistication." Hence, these brands will attract persons who are high on the same personality traits. JetBlue projects a "human" personality. Its recent "Air on the Side of Humanity" marketing campaign affirms that the airline cares about people. The airline is committed to award-winning customer service "for everyone, at every stage of the flying experience." »» It has been "inspiring humanity since 2000."[21]

»» Brand personality: Customers are likely to choose brands with personalities that match their own. JetBlue projects a "human" personality. It's been "inspiring humanity since 2000."

JetBlue

Many marketers use a concept related to personality—a person's *self-concept* (also called *self-image*). The idea is that people's possessions contribute to and reflect their identities—that is, "we are what we consume." Thus, to understand consumer behavior, marketers must first understand the relationship between consumer self-concept and possessions.

Psychological Factors

A person's buying choices are further influenced by four major psychological factors: *motivation, perception, learning,* and *beliefs and attitudes*.

Motivation. A person has many needs at any given time. Some are biological, arising from states of tension such as hunger, thirst, or discomfort. Others are psychological, arising from the need for recognition, esteem, or belonging. A need becomes a motive when it is aroused to a sufficient level of intensity. A **motive** (or **drive**) is a need that is sufficiently pressing to direct the person to seek satisfaction. Psychologists have developed theories of human motivation. Two of the most popular—the theories of Sigmund Freud and Abraham Maslow—carry quite different meanings for consumer analysis and marketing.

Sigmund Freud assumed that people are largely unconscious about the real psychological forces shaping their behavior. His theory suggests that a person's buying decisions are affected by subconscious motives that even the buyer may not fully understand. Thus, an aging baby boomer who buys a sporty BMW convertible might explain that he simply likes the feel of the wind in his thinning hair. At a deeper level, he may be trying to impress others with his success. At a still deeper level, he may be buying the car to feel young and independent again.

Consumers often don't know or can't describe why they act as they do. Thus, many companies employ teams of psychologists, anthropologists, and other social scientists to carry out *motivation research* that probes the subconscious motivations underlying consumers' emotions and behaviors toward brands. One ad agency routinely conducts one-on-one, therapy-like interviews to delve the inner workings of consumers. Another company asks consumers to describe their favorite brands as animals or cars (say, a Mercedes versus a Chevy) to assess the prestige associated with various brands. Still others rely on hypnosis, dream therapy, or soft lights and mood music to plumb the murky depths of consumer psyches.

Such projective techniques might seem pretty goofy, and some marketers dismiss such motivation research as mumbo jumbo. But many marketers use such touchy-feely approaches, now sometimes called *interpretive consumer research*, to dig deeper into consumer psyches and develop better marketing strategies.

Abraham Maslow sought to explain why people are driven by particular needs at particular times. Why does one person spend a lot of time and energy on personal safety and another on gaining the esteem of others? Maslow's answer is that human needs are arranged in a hierarchy, as shown in ≫ **Figure 5.3**, from the most pressing at the bottom to the least pressing at the top.[22] They include *physiological* needs, *safety* needs, *social* needs, *esteem* needs, and *self-actualization* needs.

A person tries to satisfy the most important need first. When that need is satisfied, it will stop being a motivator, and the person will then try to satisfy the next most important need. For example, starving people (physiological need) will not take an interest in the latest happenings in the art world (self-actualization needs) nor in how they are seen or esteemed by others (social or esteem needs) nor even in whether they are breathing clean air (safety needs). But as each important need is satisfied, the next most important need will come into play.

Perception. A motivated person is ready to act. How the person acts is influenced by his or her own perception of the situation. All of us learn by the flow of information through our five senses: sight, hearing, smell, touch, and taste. However, each of us receives, organizes, and interprets this sensory information in an individual way. **Perception** is the process by which people select, organize, and interpret information to form a meaningful picture of the world.

People can form different perceptions of the same stimulus because of three perceptual processes: selective attention, selective distortion, and selective retention. People are exposed to a great amount of stimuli every day. For example, individuals are exposed to an estimated 3,000 to 5,000 ad messages daily. The cluttered digital environment adds 30 billion online display ads shown each day, 500 million Tweets sent daily, 144,000 hours of

---

Motive (drive)
A need that is sufficiently pressing to direct the person to seek satisfaction.

Perception
The process by which people select, organize, and interpret information to form a meaningful picture of the world.

>> Figure 5.3 Maslow's Hierarchy of Needs

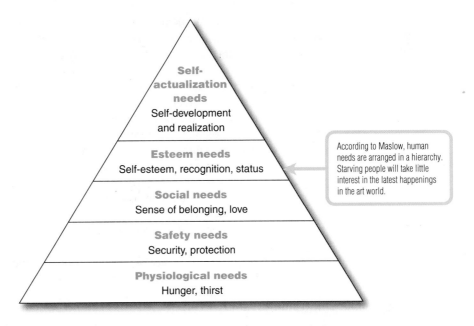

According to Maslow, human needs are arranged in a hierarchy. Starving people will take little interest in the latest happenings in the art world.

video uploaded daily on YouTube, and 4.75 billion pieces of content shared on Facebook every day.[23] People can't possibly pay attention to all the competing stimuli surrounding them. *Selective attention*—the tendency for people to screen out most of the information to which they are exposed—means that marketers must work especially hard to attract the consumer's attention.

Even noticed stimuli do not always come across in the intended way. Each person fits incoming information into an existing mindset. *Selective distortion* describes the tendency of people to interpret information in a way that will support what they already believe. People also will forget much of what they learn. They tend to retain information that supports their attitudes and beliefs. *Selective retention* means that consumers are likely to remember good points made about a brand they favor and forget good points made about competing brands. Because of selective attention, distortion, and retention, marketers must work hard to get their messages through.

Interestingly, although most marketers worry about whether their offers will be perceived at all, some consumers worry that they will be affected by marketing messages without even knowing it—through *subliminal advertising*. More than 50 years ago, a researcher announced that he had flashed the phrases "Eat popcorn" and "Drink Coca-Cola" on a screen in a New Jersey movie theater every five seconds for 1/300th of a second. He reported that although viewers did not consciously recognize these messages, they absorbed them subconsciously and bought 58 percent more popcorn and 18 percent more Coke. Suddenly advertisers and consumer-protection groups became intensely interested in subliminal perception. Although the researcher later admitted to making up the data, the issue has not died. Some consumers still fear that they are being manipulated by subliminal messages.

Numerous studies by psychologists and consumer researchers have found little or no link between subliminal messages and consumer behavior. Recent brain-wave studies have found that in certain circumstances, our brains may register subliminal messages. However, it appears that subliminal advertising simply doesn't have the power attributed to it by its critics. >> One classic ad from the American Association of Advertising Agencies pokes fun at subliminal advertising. "So-called 'subliminal advertising' simply doesn't exist," says the ad. "Overactive imaginations, however, most certainly do."

>> This classic ad from the American Association of Advertising Agencies pokes fun at subliminal advertising. "So-called 'subliminal advertising' simply doesn't exist," says the ad. "Overactive imaginations, however, most certainly do."

American Association of Advertising Agencies

Learning
Changes in an individual's behavior arising from experience.

Learning. When people act, they learn. **Learning** describes changes in an individual's behavior arising from experience. Learning theorists say that most human behavior is learned. Learning occurs through the interplay of drives, stimuli, cues, responses, and reinforcement.

A *drive* is a strong internal stimulus that calls for action. A drive becomes a motive when it is directed toward a particular *stimulus object*. For example, a person's drive for self-actualization might motivate him or her to look into buying a camera. The consumer's response to the idea of buying a camera is conditioned by the surrounding cues. *Cues* are minor stimuli that determine when, where, and how the person responds. For example, the person might spot several camera brands in a shop window, hear of a special sale price, or discuss cameras with a friend. These are all cues that might influence a consumer's *response* to his or her interest in buying the product.

Suppose the consumer buys a Nikon camera. If the experience is rewarding, the consumer will probably use the camera more and more, and his or her response will be *reinforced*. Then the next time he or she shops for a camera, or for binoculars or some similar product, the probability is greater that he or she will buy a Nikon product. The practical significance of learning theory for marketers is that they can build up demand for a product by associating it with strong drives, using motivating cues, and providing positive reinforcement.

Belief
A descriptive thought that a person holds about something.

Attitude
A person's relatively consistently favorable or unfavorable evaluations, feelings, and tendencies toward an object or idea.

Beliefs and Attitudes. Through doing and learning, people acquire beliefs and attitudes. These, in turn, influence their buying behavior. A **belief** is a descriptive thought that a person holds about something. Beliefs may be based on real knowledge, opinion, or faith and may or may not carry an emotional charge. Marketers are interested in the beliefs that people formulate about specific products and services because these beliefs make up product and brand images that affect buying behavior. If some of the beliefs are wrong and prevent purchase, the marketer will want to launch a campaign to correct them.

People have attitudes regarding religion, politics, clothes, music, food, and almost everything else. **Attitude** describes a person's relatively consistent evaluations, feelings, and tendencies toward an object or idea. Attitudes put people into a frame of mind of liking or disliking things, of moving toward or away from them. Our camera buyer may hold attitudes such as "Buy the best," "The Japanese make the best camera products in the world," and "Creativity and self-expression are among the most important things in life." If so, the Nikon camera would fit well into the consumer's existing attitudes.

Attitudes are difficult to change. A person's attitudes fit into a pattern; changing one attitude may require difficult adjustments in many others. Thus, a company should usually try to fit its products into existing attitude patterns rather than attempt to change attitudes. Of course, there are exceptions. For example, trying to convince parents that their children would actually like onions—that's right, onions—seems like an uphill battle against prevailing attitudes. Convincing the children themselves seems like an even bigger challenge. However, the Vidalia Onion Committee (VOC), formed to promote one of Georgia's most important agricultural products, managed to do just that:[24]

> It can be hard selling children on the idea of eating onions. Onions have a strong smell, they can make you cry, and many kids simply refuse to eat them. So to help change these attitudes, the ⟩⟩ VOC employed Shrek, the famous ogre from the hugely popular animated films. The inspiration came from a scene in the first Shrek film, in which Shrek explains ogres to his friend, Donkey. "Onions have layers, ogres have layers," says Shrek. "Ogres are like onions. End of story." The result was a national now-classic "Ogres and Onions" marketing campaign, launched to coincide with both the onion harvest and the premiere of the latest Shrek film. The campaign featured giant Shrek placards in grocery store aisles alongside bags of Vidalia onions on which Shrek asked, "What do ogres and onions have in common?" At the VOC Web site, Shrek offered kid-friendly Vidalia onion recipes. The award-winning campaign soon had kids clamoring for onions, and surprised and delighted parents responded. Sales of bagged Vidalia onions increased almost 30 percent for the season.

⟩⟩ Attitudes and beliefs are difficult to change; however, the Vidalia Onion Committee's award-winning Ogres and Onions campaign made believers of children and their delighted parents. Sales of bagged Vidalia onions shot up 30 percent.

Vidalia Onion Committee. Vidalia® is a registered certification mark of Georgia Department of Agriculture.

We can now appreciate the many forces acting on consumer behavior. The consumer's choice results from the complex interplay of cultural, social, personal, and psychological factors.

Author Comment
The actual purchase decision is part of a much larger buying process—from recognizing a need through how you feel after making the purchase. Marketers want to be involved throughout the entire buyer decision process.

The Buyer Decision Process

Now that we have looked at the influences that affect buyers, we are ready to look at how consumers make buying decisions. ≫**Figure 5.4** shows that the buyer decision process consists of five stages: *need recognition, information search, evaluation of alternatives,* the *purchase decision*, and *postpurchase behavior*. Clearly, the buying process starts long before the actual purchase and continues long after. Marketers need to focus on the entire buying process rather than on the purchase decision only.

Figure 5.4 suggests that consumers pass through all five stages with every purchase in a considered way. But buyers may pass quickly or slowly through the buying decision process. And in more routine purchases, consumers often skip or reverse some of the stages. Much depends on the nature of the buyer, the product, and the buying situation. A person buying a regular brand of toothpaste would recognize the need and go right to the purchase decision, skipping information search and evaluation. However, we use the model in Figure 5.4 because it shows all the considerations that arise when a consumer faces a new and complex purchase situation.

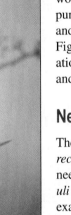

Need Recognition

The buying process starts with *need recognition*—the buyer recognizes a problem or need. The need can be triggered by *internal stimuli* when one of the person's normal needs—for example, hunger or thirst—rises to a level high enough to become a drive. ≫A need can also be triggered by *external stimuli*. For example, an advertisement or a discussion with a friend might get you thinking about buying a new car. At this stage, the marketer should research consumers to find out what kinds of needs or problems arise, what brought them about, and how they led the consumer to this particular product.

≫ **Need recognition: This ad for *National Geographic Kids* reminds parents that, in these days of game consoles and social networking sites, they need to be certain that their children "make room for nature."**

Courtesy National Geographic Society, Fox P2 Advertising, and Lung Animation

Information Search

An interested consumer may or may not search for more information. If the consumer's drive is strong and a satisfying product is near at hand, he or she is likely to buy it then. If not, the consumer may store the need in memory or undertake an *information search* related to the need. For example, once you've decided you need a new car, at the least, you will probably pay more attention to car ads, cars owned by friends, and car conversations. Or you may actively search online, talk with friends, and gather information in other ways.

Consumers can obtain information from any of several sources. These include *personal sources* (family, friends, neighbors, acquaintances), *commercial sources* (advertising, salespeople, dealer and manufacturer Web and mobile sites, packaging, displays), *public sources* (mass media, consumer rating organizations, social media, online searches,

The buying process starts long before the actual purchase and continues long after. In fact, it might result in a decision not to buy. Therefore, marketers must focus on the entire buying process, not just the purchase decision.

≫ **Figure 5.4 Buyer Decision Process**

and peer reviews), and *experiential sources* (examining and using the product). The relative influence of these information sources varies with the product and the buyer.

Traditionally, consumers have received the most information about a product from commercial sources—those controlled by the marketer. The most effective sources, however, tend to be personal. Commercial sources normally *inform* the buyer, but personal sources *legitimize* or *evaluate* products for the buyer. Few advertising campaigns can be as effective as a next-door neighbor leaning over the fence and raving about a wonderful experience with a product you are considering.

Increasingly, that "neighbor's fence" is a digital one. Today, consumers share product opinions, images, and experiences freely across social media. And buyers can find an abundance of user-generated reviews alongside the products they are considering at sites ranging from Amazon.com or BestBuy.com to Yelp, TripAdvisor, Epinions, and Epicurious. Although individual user reviews vary widely in quality, an entire body of reviews often provides a reliable product assessment—straight from the fingertips of people like you who've actually purchased and experienced the product.

As more information is obtained, the consumer's awareness and knowledge of the available brands and features increase. In your car information search, you may learn about several brands that are available. The information might also help you to drop certain brands from consideration. A company must design its marketing mix to make prospects aware of and knowledgeable about its brand. It should carefully identify consumers' sources of information and the importance of each source.

Evaluation of Alternatives

We have seen how consumers use information to arrive at a set of final brand choices. Next, marketers need to know about *alternative evaluation*, that is, how consumers process information to choose among alternative brands. Unfortunately, consumers do not use a simple and single evaluation process in all buying situations. Instead, several evaluation processes are at work.

How consumers go about evaluating purchase alternatives depends on the individual consumer and the specific buying situation. In some cases, consumers use careful calculations and logical thinking. At other times, the same consumers do little or no evaluating. Instead, they buy on impulse and rely on intuition. Sometimes consumers make buying decisions on their own; sometimes they turn to friends, online reviews, or salespeople for buying advice.

Suppose you've narrowed your car choices to three brands. And suppose that you are primarily interested in four attributes—price, style, operating economy, and performance. By this time, you've probably formed beliefs about how each brand rates on each attribute. Clearly, if one car rated best on all the attributes, the marketer could predict that you would choose it. However, the brands will no doubt vary in appeal. You might base your buying decision mostly on one attribute, and your choice would be easy to predict. If you wanted style above everything else, you would buy the car that you think has the most style. But most buyers consider several attributes, each with different importance. By knowing the importance that you assigned to each attribute, the marketer could predict and affect your car choice more reliably.

Marketers should study buyers to find out how they actually evaluate brand alternatives. If marketers know what evaluative processes go on, they can take steps to influence the buyer's decision.

Purchase Decision

In the evaluation stage, the consumer ranks brands and forms purchase intentions. Generally, the consumer's *purchase decision* will be to buy the most preferred brand, but two factors can come between the purchase *intention* and the purchase *decision*. The first factor is the *attitudes of others*. If someone important to you thinks that you should buy the lowest-priced car, then the chances of you buying a more expensive car are reduced.

The second factor is *unexpected situational factors*. The consumer may form a purchase intention based on factors such as expected income, expected price, and expected product benefits. However, unexpected events may change the purchase intention. For example, the economy might take a turn for the worse, a close competitor might drop its price, or a friend might report being disappointed in your preferred car. Thus, preferences and even purchase intentions do not always result in an actual purchase choice.

Postpurchase Behavior

The marketer's job does not end when the product is bought. After purchasing the product, the consumer will either be satisfied or dissatisfied and will engage in *postpurchase behavior* of interest to the marketer. What determines whether the buyer is satisfied or dissatisfied with a purchase? The answer lies in the relationship between the *consumer's expectations* and the product's *perceived performance*. If the product falls short of expectations, the consumer is disappointed; if it meets expectations, the consumer is satisfied; if it exceeds expectations, the consumer is delighted. The larger the negative gap between expectations and performance, the greater the consumer's dissatisfaction. This suggests that sellers should promise only what their brands can deliver so that buyers are satisfied.

Cognitive dissonance
Buyer discomfort caused by postpurchase conflict.

Almost all major purchases, however, result in **cognitive dissonance**, or discomfort caused by postpurchase conflict. After the purchase, consumers are satisfied with the benefits of the chosen brand and are glad to avoid the drawbacks of the brands not bought. However, every purchase involves compromise. So consumers feel uneasy about acquiring the drawbacks of the chosen brand and about losing the benefits of the brands not purchased. Thus, consumers feel at least some postpurchase dissonance for every purchase.

Why is it so important to satisfy the customer? Customer satisfaction is a key to building profitable relationships with consumers—to keeping and growing consumers and reaping their customer lifetime value. Satisfied customers buy a product again, talk favorably to others about the product, pay less attention to competing brands and advertising, and buy other products from the company. >> Many marketers go beyond merely *meeting* the expectations of customers—they aim to *delight* customers.

A dissatisfied consumer responds differently. Bad word of mouth often travels farther and faster than good word of mouth. It can quickly damage consumer attitudes about a company and its products. But companies cannot simply wait for dissatisfied customers to volunteer their complaints. Most unhappy customers never tell the company about their problems. Therefore, a company should measure customer satisfaction regularly. It should set up systems that *encourage* customers to complain. In this way, the company can learn how well it is doing and how it can improve.

>> Postpurchase cognitive dissonance: Postpurchase customer satisfaction is a key to building profitable customer relationships. Most marketers go beyond merely *meeting* the customer expectations—they aim to *delight* customers.

Dusit/Shutterstock

New product
A good, service, or idea that is perceived by some potential customers as new.

By studying the overall buyer decision process, marketers may be able to find ways to help consumers move through it. For example, if consumers are not buying a new product because they do not perceive a need for it, marketing might launch advertising messages that trigger the need and show how the product solves customers' problems. If customers know about the product but are not buying because they hold unfavorable attitudes toward it, marketers must find ways to change either the product or consumer perceptions.

Author Comment
Here we look at some special considerations in *new product* buying decisions.

The Buyer Decision Process for New Products

We now look at how buyers approach the purchase of new products. A **new product** is a good, service, or idea that is perceived by some potential customers as new. It may have been around for a while, but our interest is in how consumers learn about products for the

Adoption process
The mental process through which an individual passes from first hearing about an innovation to final adoption.

first time and make decisions on whether to adopt them. We define the **adoption process** as the mental process through which an individual passes from first learning about an innovation to final adoption. *Adoption* is the decision by an individual to become a regular user of the product.[25]

Stages in the Adoption Process

Consumers go through five stages in the process of adopting a new product:

Awareness. The consumer becomes aware of the new product but lacks information about it.

Interest. The consumer seeks information about the new product.

Evaluation. The consumer considers whether trying the new product makes sense.

Trial. The consumer tries the new product on a small scale to improve his or her estimate of its value.

Adoption. The consumer decides to make full and regular use of the new product.

This model suggests that marketers should think about how to help consumers move through these stages. ≫ For example, if SodaStream finds that many consumers are evaluating its home soda makers favorably but are still tentative about buying one, it might work with Bed Bath & Beyond and other retailers to offer a sale price that gets consumers over the decision hump.

To help car buyers past purchase-decision hurdles following the economic meltdown in 2008, Hyundai offered a unique Hyundai Assurance Plan. It promised buyers who financed or leased new Hyundais that they could return them at no cost and with no harm to their credit rating if they lost their jobs or incomes within a year. Sales of the Hyundai Sonata surged 85 percent in the month following the start of the campaign.

Individual Differences in Innovativeness

People differ greatly in their readiness to try new products. In each product area, there are "consumption pioneers" and early adopters. Other individuals adopt new products much later. People can be classified into the adopter categories shown in ≫ **Figure 5.5**.[26] As shown by the curve, after a slow start, an increasing number of people adopt the new product. As successive groups of consumers adopt the innovation, it eventually reaches its cumulative saturation level. Innovators are defined as the first 2.5 percent of buyers to adopt a new idea (those beyond two standard deviations from mean adoption time); the early adopters are the next 13.5 percent (between one and two standard deviations); and then come early mainstream, late mainstream, and lagging adopters.

The five adopter groups have differing values. *Innovators* are venturesome—they try new ideas at some risk. *Early adopters* are guided by respect—they are opinion leaders in their communities and adopt new ideas early but carefully. *Early mainstream* adopters are deliberate—although they rarely are leaders, they adopt new ideas before the average person. *Late mainstream* adopters are skeptical—they adopt an innovation only after a majority of people have tried it. Finally, *lagging adopters* are tradition bound—they are suspicious of changes and adopt the innovation only when it has become something of a tradition itself.

This adopter classification suggests that an innovating firm should research the characteristics of innovators and early adopters in their product categories and direct initial marketing efforts toward them.

≫ **The adoption process: To help get tentative consumers over the buying decision hump, SodaStream offers sales at retail, rebates, and other buying incentives—here a $20 cashback rebate offer.**

Image courtesy of SodaStream

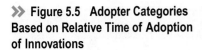

»» Figure 5.5 Adopter Categories Based on Relative Time of Adoption of Innovations

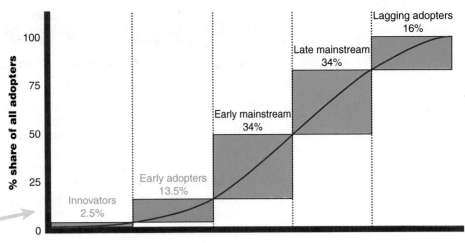

New product marketers often target innovators and early adopters, who in turn influence later adopters.

Influence of Product Characteristics on Rate of Adoption

The characteristics of the new product affect its rate of adoption. Some products catch on almost overnight. For example, Apple's iPod, iPhone, and iPad flew off retailers' shelves at an astounding rate from the day they were first introduced. Others take a longer time to gain acceptance. For example, all-electric cars were first introduced in the United States in 2010, led by models such as the Nissan Leaf and the Tesla Model S. However, electric vehicles still account for far less than 1 percent of total U.S. automobile sales. It will likely be years or even decades before they replace the gasoline-powered cars.[27]

Five characteristics are especially important in influencing an innovation's rate of adoption. For example, consider the characteristics of all-electric vehicles in relation to their rate of adoption:

Relative advantage. The degree to which the innovation appears superior to existing products. All-electric cars require no gas and use clean, less costly energy. This accelerated their rate of adoption. However, they have limited driving range before recharging and cost more initially, which will slow the adoption rate.

Compatibility. The degree to which the innovation fits the values and experiences of potential consumers. Electric cars are driven the same way as gas-powered cars. However, they are not compatible with the nation's current refueling network. Plug-in electric charging stations are few and far between. Increased adoption will depend on the development of a national network of recharging stations, which may take considerable time.

Complexity. The degree to which the innovation is difficult to understand or use. Electric cars are not different or complex to drive, which will help to speed up adoption. However, the "conceptual complexity" of the new technologies and concerns about how well they will likely work slow down the adoption rate.

Divisibility. The degree to which the innovation may be tried on a limited basis. Consumers can test-drive electric cars, a positive for the adoption rate. However, current high prices to own and fully experience these new technologies will likely slow adoption.

Communicability. The degree to which the results of using the innovation can be observed or described to others. To the extent that electric cars lend themselves to demonstration and description, their use will spread faster among consumers.

Other characteristics influence the rate of adoption, such as initial and ongoing costs, risk and uncertainty, and social approval. The new product marketer must research all these factors when developing the new product and its marketing program.

LINKING THE CONCEPTS

Here's a good place to pause and apply the concepts you've examined in the first part of this chapter.

- Think about a specific major purchase you've made recently. What buying process did you follow? What major factors influenced your decision?
- Pick a company or brand that we've discussed in a previous chapter—Nike, Starbucks, Netflix, Apple, JetBlue, or another. How does the company you chose use its understanding of customers and their buying behavior to build better customer relationships?
- Think about a company such as Intel, which sells its products to computer makers and other businesses rather than to final consumers. How would Intel's marketing to business customers differ from Apple's marketing to final consumers? The second part of the chapter deals with this issue.

> **Author Comment**
> Now that we've looked at consumer markets and buyer behavior, let's dig into business markets and buyer behavior. Thinking ahead, how are they the same? How are they different?

Business buyer behavior
The buying behavior of organizations that buy goods and services for use in the production of other products and services that are sold, rented, or supplied to others.

Business buying process
The process by which business buyers determine which products and services their organizations need to purchase and then find, evaluate, and choose among alternative suppliers and brands.

Business Markets and Business Buyer Behavior

In one way or another, most large companies sell to other organizations. Companies such as Boeing, DuPont, IBM, Caterpillar, and countless other firms sell *most* of their products to other businesses. Even large consumer-products companies, which make products used by final consumers, must first sell their products to other businesses. For example, General Mills makes many familiar consumer brands—Big G cereals (Cheerios, Wheaties, Trix, Chex, Total, Fiber One), baking products (Pillsbury, Betty Crocker, Bisquick, Gold Medal flour), snacks (Nature Valley, Bugles, Chex Mix), Yoplait yogurt, Häagen-Dazs ice cream, and many others. But to sell these products to consumers, General Mills must first sell them to its wholesaler and retailer customers, who in turn serve the consumer market.

Business buyer behavior refers to the buying behavior of organizations that buy goods and services for use in the production of other products and services that are sold, rented, or supplied to others. It also includes the behavior of retailing and wholesaling firms that acquire goods to resell or rent to others at a profit. In the **business buying process**, business buyers determine which products and services their organizations need to purchase and then find, evaluate, and choose among alternative suppliers and brands.

Business-to-business (B-to-B) marketers must do their best to understand business markets and business buyer behavior. Then, like businesses that sell to final buyers, they must engage business customers and build profitable relationships with them by creating superior customer value.

> **Author Comment**
> Business markets operate "behind the scenes" to most consumers. Most of the things you buy involve many sets of business purchases before you ever see them.

Business Markets

The business market is *huge*. In fact, business markets involve far more dollars and items than do consumer markets. For example, think about the large number of business transactions involved in the production and sale of a single set of Goodyear tires. Various suppliers sell Goodyear the rubber, steel, equipment, and other goods that it needs to produce tires. Goodyear then sells the finished tires to retailers, which in turn sell them to consumers. Thus, many sets of *business* purchases were made for only one set of *consumer* purchases. In addition, Goodyear sells tires as original equipment to manufacturers that install them on new vehicles and as replacement tires to companies that maintain their own fleets of company cars, trucks, or other vehicles.

In some ways, business markets are similar to consumer markets. Both involve people who assume buying roles and make purchase decisions to satisfy needs. However, business markets differ in many ways from consumer markets. The main differences are in *market structure and demand*, the *nature of the buying unit*, and the *types of decisions and the decision process* involved.

Market Structure and Demand

The business marketer normally deals with *far fewer but far larger buyers* than the consumer marketer does. Even in large business markets, a few buyers often account for most of the purchasing. For example, when Goodyear sells replacement tires to final consumers, its potential market includes millions of car owners around the world. But its fate in business markets depends on getting orders from only a handful of large automakers.

Further, many business markets have *inelastic and more fluctuating demand*. The total demand for many business products is not much affected by price changes, especially in the short run. A drop in the price of leather will not cause shoe manufacturers to buy much more leather unless it results in lower shoe prices that, in turn, increase consumer demand for shoes. And the demand for many business goods and services tends to change more—and more quickly—than does the demand for consumer goods and services. A small percentage increase in consumer demand can cause large increases in business demand.

Finally, business demand is **derived demand**—it ultimately derives from the demand for consumer goods. For example, demand for Gore-Tex fabrics derives from consumer

Derived demand
Business demand that ultimately comes from (derives from) the demand for consumer goods.

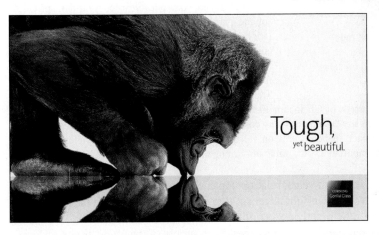

purchases of outdoor apparel brands made from Gore-Tex. And consumers buy Corning's Gorilla Glass only when they buy laptops, tablets, and smartphones with Gorilla Glass screens from producers such as Apple, Samsung, Lenovo, Dell, HP, Sony, and Microsoft. If consumer demand for these end products increases, so does the demand for the Gore-Tex fabrics and the Gorilla Glass they contain.

Therefore, B-to-B marketers sometimes promote their products directly to final consumers to increase business demand. >> For example, Corning's long-running "Tough, yet beautiful" consumer marketing campaign features a family of gorillas who are out to convince final buyers that it makes sense to choose digital devices with screens made of Gorilla Glass rather than a less-tough competitor. Such advertising benefits both Corning and the partner brands that incorporate its durable, scratch-resistant glass. Thanks in part to the consumer marketing campaign, Corning's Gorilla Glass has to date been featured in more than 40 major brands and more than 3 billion devices worldwide.[28]

>> **Derived demand: Corning's long-running "Tough, yet beautiful" consumer marketing campaign convinces final users that it makes sense to buy devices with screens made of Gorilla Glass, to the benefit of both Corning and its partner brands.**
Photo courtesy Corning Incorporated.

Nature of the Buying Unit

Compared with consumer purchases, a business purchase usually involves *more decision participants* and a *more professional purchasing effort*. Often, business buying is done by trained purchasing agents who spend their working lives learning how to buy better. The more complex the purchase, the more likely it is that several people will participate in the decision-making process. Buying committees composed of technical experts and top management are common in the buying of major goods. Beyond this, B-to-B marketers now face a new breed of higher-level, better-trained supply managers. Therefore, companies must have well-trained marketers and salespeople to deal with these well-trained buyers.

Types of Decisions and the Decision Process

Business buyers usually face *more complex* buying decisions than do consumer buyers. Business purchases often involve large sums of money, complex technical and economic considerations, and interactions among people at many levels of the buyer's organization. The business buying process also tends to be *longer* and *more formalized*. Large business purchases usually call for detailed product specifications, written purchase orders, careful supplier searches, and formal approval.

Finally, in the business buying process, the buyer and seller are often much *more dependent* on each other. B-to-B marketers may roll up their sleeves and work closely with customers during all stages of the buying process—from helping customers define problems to finding solutions to supporting after-sale operation. In the short run, sales go to suppliers who meet buyers' immediate product and service needs. In the long run,

>> **Business buyer decision process: In selling locomotives with an average list price of $2.2 million, GE's real challenge is to win buyers' business by building day-in, day-out, year-in, year-out partnerships with them based on close collaboration.**

GE Transportation

however, business-to-business marketers keep customers by meeting current needs *and* by partnering with them to help solve their problems. >> For example, consider the buying process for GE's diesel locomotives:[29]

> GE locomotives might not seem glamorous to you, but they are beautiful brutes to those who buy and use them. Performance plays an important role in the locomotive buyer's decision, and GE locomotives outperform competing engines on most important dimensions. But performance is only part of the buying equation. Selling locomotives with an average list price of $2.2 million involves a tortuously long buying process, dozens or even hundreds of decision makers, and layer upon layer of subtle and not-so-subtle buying influences.
>
> GE's real challenge is to win buyers' business by building day-in, day-out, year-in, year-out, problem-solving partnerships with them based on close collaboration. More than just "selling locomotives," GE wins contracts by partnering strategically with customers to help them translate performance into moving passengers and freight more efficiently and reliably. For example, CSX Transportation (CSXT), one of GE's largest customers, has purchased hundreds of GE locomotives in recent years. According to a CSXT purchasing executive, the company "evaluates many cost factors before awarding...a locomotive contract. Environmental impact, fuel consumption, reliability, serviceability [are] all key elements in this decision." But as important is "the value of our ongoing partnership with GE."

Supplier development
Systematic development of networks of supplier-partners to ensure a dependable supply of products and materials for use in making products or reselling them to others.

As in GE's case, in recent years, relationships between most customers and suppliers have been changing from downright adversarial to close and chummy. In fact, many customer companies are now practicing **supplier development**, systematically developing networks of supplier-partners to ensure a dependable supply of the products and materials that they use in making their own products or reselling to others. For example, Walmart doesn't have a "Purchasing Department"; it has a "Supplier Development Department." The giant retailer knows that it can't just rely on spot suppliers who might be available when needed. Instead, Walmart manages a huge network of supplier-partners that help provide the hundreds of billions of dollars of goods that it sells to its customers each year.

Business Buyer Behavior

Author Comment
Business buying decisions can range from routine to incredibly complex, involving only a few or very many decision makers and buying influences.

At the most basic level, marketers want to know how business buyers will respond to various marketing stimuli. >> **Figure 5.6** shows a model of business buyer behavior. In this model, marketing and other stimuli affect the buying organization and produce certain buyer responses. To design good marketing strategies, marketers must understand what happens within the organization to turn stimuli into purchase responses.

Within the organization, buying activity consists of two major parts: the *buying center*, composed of all the people involved in the buying decision, and the *buying decision process*. The model shows that the buying center and the buying decision process are influenced by internal organizational, interpersonal, and individual factors as well as external environmental factors.

The model in Figure 5.6 suggests four questions about business buyer behavior: What buying decisions do business buyers make? Who participates in the business buying process? What are the major influences on buyers? How do business buyers make their buying decisions?

Major Types of Buying Situations

Straight rebuy
A business buying situation in which the buyer routinely reorders something without any modifications.

There are three major types of buying situations.[30] In a **straight rebuy**, the buyer reorders something without any modifications. It is usually handled on a routine basis by the purchasing department. To keep the business, "in" suppliers try to maintain customer

>> **Figure 5.6 A Model of Business Buyer Behavior**

In some ways, business markets are similar to consumer markets—this model looks a lot like the model of consumer buyer behavior presented in Figure 5.1. But there are some major differences, especially in the nature of the buying unit, the types of decisions made, and the decision process.

The environment		The buying organization	Buyer responses
Marketing stimuli	**Other stimuli**	**The buying center**	Product or service choice
Product	Economic	**Buying decision process**	Supplier choice
Price	Technological		Order quantities
Place	Political		Delivery terms and times
Promotion	Cultural	(Interpersonal and individual influences)	Service terms
	Competitive	(Organizational influences)	Payment

Modified rebuy

A business buying situation in which the buyer wants to modify product specifications, prices, terms, or suppliers.

New task

A business buying situation in which the buyer purchases a product or service for the first time.

Systems selling (or **solutions selling**)

Buying a complete solution to a problem from a single seller, thus avoiding all the separate decisions involved in a complex buying situation.

engagement and product and service quality. "Out" suppliers try to find new ways to add value or exploit dissatisfaction so that the buyer will consider them.

In a **modified rebuy**, the buyer wants to modify product specifications, prices, terms, or suppliers. The "in" suppliers may become nervous and feel pressured to put their best foot forward to protect an account. "Out" suppliers may see the modified rebuy situation as an opportunity to make a better offer and gain new business.

A company buying a product or service for the first time faces a **new task** situation. In such cases, the greater the cost or risk, the larger the number of decision participants and the greater the company's efforts to collect information. The new task situation is the marketer's greatest opportunity and challenge. The marketer not only tries to reach as many key buying influences as possible but also provides help and information. The buyer makes the fewest decisions in the straight rebuy and the most in the new task decision.

Many business buyers prefer to buy a complete solution to a problem from a single seller rather than buying separate products and services from several suppliers and putting them together. The sale often goes to the firm that engages business customers deeply and provides the most complete *system* for meeting a customer's needs and solving its problems. Such **systems selling** (or **solutions selling**) is often a key business marketing strategy for winning and holding accounts. Consider IBM and its customer Six Flags Entertainment Corporation:[31]

>> **Solutions selling: Delivering a fun and safe experience for Six Flags guests requires careful and effective management of thousands of park assets across its 19 regional theme parks. IBM works hand in hand with Six Flags to provide not just software but a complete solution.**

Mathew Imaging/WireImage/Getty Images

Six Flags operates 19 regional theme parks across North America featuring exciting rides and water attractions, world-class roller coasters, and special shows and concerts. >> To deliver a fun and safe experience for guests, Six Flags must carefully and effectively manage thousands of park assets—from rides and equipment to buildings and other facilities. Six Flags needed a tool for managing all those assets efficiently and effectively across its far-flung collection of parks. So it turned to IBM, which has software—called Maximo Asset Management software—that handles that very problem well.

But IBM didn't just hand the software over to Six Flags with best wishes for happy implementation. Instead, IBM's Maximo Professional Services group combined the software with an entire set of services designed to get and keep the software up and running. IBM worked hand in hand with Six Flags to customize the application and strategically implement and run it across Six Flags's far-flung facilities, along with on-site immersion training and planning workshops. Thus, IBM isn't just selling the software; it's selling a complete solution to Six Flags's complex asset management problem.

Participants in the Business Buying Process

Who does the buying of the trillions of dollars' worth of goods and services needed by business organizations? The

Buying center
All the individuals and units that play a role in the purchase decision-making process.

decision-making unit of a buying organization is called its **buying center**. It consists of all the individuals and units that play a role in the business purchase decision-making process. This group includes the actual users of the product or service, those who make the buying decision, those who influence the buying decision, those who do the actual buying, and those who control buying information.

The buying center is not a fixed and formally identified unit within the buying organization. It is a set of buying roles assumed by different people for different purchases. Within the organization, the size and makeup of the buying center will vary for different products and for different buying situations. For some routine purchases, one person—say, a purchasing agent—may assume all the buying center roles and serve as the only person involved in the buying decision. For more complex purchases, the buying center may include 20 or 30 people from different levels and departments in the organization.

The buying center concept presents a major marketing challenge. The business marketer must learn who participates in the decision, each participant's relative influence, and what evaluation criteria each decision participant uses. This can be difficult.

The buying center usually includes some obvious participants who are involved formally in the buying decision. For example, the decision to buy a corporate jet will probably involve the company's CEO, the chief pilot, a purchasing agent, some legal staff, a member of top management, and others formally charged with the buying decision. It may also involve less obvious, informal participants, some of whom may actually make or strongly affect the buying decision. Sometimes, even the people in the buying center are not aware of all the buying participants. For example, the decision about which corporate jet to buy may actually be made by a corporate board member who has an interest in flying and who knows a lot about airplanes. This board member may work behind the scenes to sway the decision. Many business buying decisions result from the complex interactions of ever-changing buying center participants.

Major Influences on Business Buyers

Business buyers are subject to many influences when they make their buying decisions. Some marketers assume that the major influences are economic. They think buyers will favor the supplier who offers the lowest price or the best product or the most service. They concentrate on offering strong economic benefits to buyers. Such economic factors are very important to most buyers, especially in a tough economy. However, business buyers actually respond to both economic and personal factors. Far from being cold, calculating, and impersonal, business buyers are human and social as well. They react to both reason and emotion.

Today, most B-to-B marketers recognize that emotion plays an important role in business buying decisions. Consider this example:[32]

>> Emotions play a role in business buying. Ads like this one from USG's "It's Your World. Build It." corporate marketing campaign pack a decidedly emotional wallop.
USG Corportion

>> USG Corporation is a leading manufacturer of gypsum wallboard and other building materials for the construction and remodeling industries. Given its construction contractor, architect, and builder audience, you might expect USG's B-to-B ads to focus heavily on performance features and benefits, such as strength, impact resistance, ease of installation, and costs. USG does promote these benefits. However, it's most recent corporate marketing campaign, built around its new "It's Your World. Build It." positioning, packs a decidedly more emotional wallop. The campaign focuses not on how USG's products perform but on what the company and its products stand for and mean. For example, one split-image ad shows excited children building a sand castle on one side and a worker at a construction site, hard hat in hand, on the other. The headline states: "As children we imagine great kingdoms. Build them." As one analyst concludes, "Building materials and emotion aren't something you would link immediately, but the [USG] campaign captures a powerful sentiment about the human need to build."

▶▶Figure 5.7 lists various groups of influences on business buyers—environmental, organizational, interpersonal, and individual. Business buyers are heavily influenced by factors in the current and expected *economic environment*, such as the level of primary demand, the economic outlook, and the cost of money. Another environmental factor is the *supply* of key materials. Business buyers also are affected by *supply, technological, political,* and *competitive* developments in the environment. Finally, *culture and customs* can strongly influence business buyer reactions to the marketer's behavior and strategies, especially in the international marketing environment. The business buyer must watch these factors, determine how they will affect the buyer, and try to turn these challenges into opportunities.

Organizational factors are also important. Each buying organization has its own objectives, strategies, structure, systems, and procedures, and the business marketer must understand these factors well. Questions such as these arise: How many people are involved in the buying decision? Who are they? What are their evaluative criteria? What are the company's policies and limits on its buyers?

The buying center usually includes many participants who influence each other, so *interpersonal factors* also influence the business buying process. However, it is often difficult to assess such interpersonal factors and group dynamics. Buying center participants do not wear tags that label them as "key decision maker" or "not influential." Nor do buying center participants with the highest rank always have the most influence. Participants may influence the buying decision because they control rewards and punishments, are well liked, have special expertise, or have a special relationship with other important participants. Interpersonal factors are often very subtle. Whenever possible, business marketers must try to understand these factors and design strategies that take them into account.

Each participant in the business buying decision process brings in personal motives, perceptions, and preferences. These *individual factors* are affected by personal characteristics such as age, income, education, professional identification, personality, and attitudes toward risk. Also, buyers have different buying styles. Some may be technical types who make in-depth analyses of competitive proposals before choosing a supplier. Other buyers may be intuitive negotiators who are adept at pitting the sellers against one another for the best deal.

The Business Buyer Decision Process

▶▶Figure 5.8 lists the eight stages of the business buyer decision process.[33] Buyers who face a new task buying situation usually go through all stages of the buying process. Buyers making modified or straight rebuys, in contrast, may skip some of the stages. We will examine these steps for the typical new task buying situation.

Problem Recognition. The buying process begins when someone in the company recognizes a problem or need that can be met by acquiring a specific product or service. *Problem recognition* can result from internal or external stimuli. Internally, the company may decide to launch a new product that requires new production equipment and materials. Or a machine may break down and need new parts. Perhaps a purchasing manager is unhappy with a current supplier's product quality, service, or prices. Externally, the buyer may get

▶▶ Figure 5.7 Major Influences on Business Buyer Behavior

Like consumer buying decisions in Figure 5.2, business buying decisions are affected by an incredibly complex combination of environmental, interpersonal, and individual influences, but with an extra layer of organizational factors thrown into the mix.

>> **Figure 5.8 Stages of the Business Buyer Decision Process**

Buyers facing new, complex buying decisions usually go through all of these stages. Those making rebuys often skip some of the stages. Either way, the business buyer decision process is usually much more complicated than this simple flow diagram suggests.

| Problem recognition | General need description | Product specification | Supplier search |

| Proposal solicitation | Supplier selection | Order-routine specification | Performance review |

some new ideas at a trade show, see an ad or Web site, or receive a call from a salesperson who offers a better product or a lower price.

In fact, in their advertising, business marketers often alert customers to potential problems and then show how their products and services provide solutions. >> For example, consulting firm Accenture's award-winning "High Performance. Delivered." B-to-B ads do this. One Accenture ad points to the urgent need for a business to get up to speed with digital technology. "Accenture Digital can help you attract more customers." the ad states, showing moths drawn to a brightly lit smartphone screen. Accenture's solution: "Our industry expertise, coupled with our integrated capabilities across interactive, analytics, and mobility, can help you take advantage of the opportunity to innovate and compete." Other ads in the series tell success stories of how Accenture has helped client companies recognize and solve a variety of other problems.[34]

>> **Problem recognition: This Accenture ad alerts customers to the problem of getting up to speed with digital technology, then suggests a solution. It promises "High Performance. Delivered."**

Accenture

General Need Description. Having recognized a need, the buyer next prepares a *general need description* that describes the characteristics and quantity of the needed item. For standard items, this process presents few problems. For complex items, however, the buyer may need to work with others—engineers, users, consultants—to define the item. The team may want to rank the importance of reliability, durability, price, and other attributes desired in the item. In this phase, the alert business marketer can help the buyers define their needs and provide information about the value of different product characteristics.

Product Specification. The buying organization next develops the item's technical *product specifications*, often with the help of a value analysis engineering team. *Product value analysis* is an approach to cost reduction in which components are studied carefully to determine if they can be redesigned, standardized, or made by less costly methods of production. The team decides on the best product characteristics and specifies them accordingly. Sellers, too, can use value analysis as a tool to help secure a new account. By showing buyers a better way to make an object, outside sellers can turn straight rebuy situations into new task situations that give them a chance to obtain new business.

Supplier Search. The buyer now conducts a *supplier search* to find the best vendors. The buyer can compile a small list of qualified suppliers by reviewing trade directories, doing online searches, or phoning other companies for recommendations. Today, more and more companies are turning to the Internet to find suppliers. For marketers, this has leveled the playing field—the Internet gives smaller suppliers many of the same advantages as larger competitors.

The newer the buying task and the more complex and costly the item, the greater the amount of time the buyer will spend searching for suppliers. The supplier's task is to get listed in major directories and build a good reputation in the marketplace. Salespeople should watch for companies in the process of searching for suppliers and make certain that their firm is considered.

Proposal Solicitation. In the *proposal solicitation* stage of the business buying process, the buyer invites qualified suppliers to submit proposals. In response, some suppliers will refer the buyer to its Web site or promotional materials or send a salesperson to call on the prospect. However, when the item is complex or expensive, the buyer will usually require detailed written proposals or formal presentations from each potential supplier.

Business marketers must be skilled in researching, writing, and presenting proposals in response to buyer proposal solicitations. Proposals should be marketing documents, not just technical documents. Presentations should inspire confidence and should make the marketer's company stand out from the competition.

Supplier Selection. The members of the buying center now review the proposals and select a supplier or suppliers. During *supplier selection*, the buying center often will draw up a list of the desired supplier attributes and their relative importance. Such attributes include product and service quality, reputation, on-time delivery, ethical corporate behavior, honest communication, and competitive prices. The members of the buying center will rate suppliers against these attributes and identify the best suppliers.

Buyers may attempt to negotiate with preferred suppliers for better prices and terms before making the final selections. In the end, they may select a single supplier or a few suppliers. Many buyers prefer multiple sources of supplies to avoid being totally dependent on one supplier and to allow comparisons of prices and performance of several suppliers over time. Today's supplier development managers want to develop a full network of supplier-partners that can help the company bring more value to its customers.

Order-Routine Specification. The buyer now prepares an *order-routine specification*. It includes the final order with the chosen supplier or suppliers and lists items such as technical specifications, quantity needed, expected delivery time, return policies, and warranties. In the case of maintenance, repair, and operating items, buyers may use blanket contracts rather than periodic purchase orders. A blanket contract creates a long-term relationship in which the supplier promises to resupply the buyer as needed at agreed prices for a set time period.

Many large buyers now practice *vendor-managed inventory*, in which they turn over ordering and inventory responsibilities to their suppliers. Under such systems, buyers share sales and inventory information directly with key suppliers. The suppliers then monitor inventories and replenish stock automatically as needed. For example, most major suppliers to large retailers such as Walmart, Target, Home Depot, and Lowe's assume vendor-managed inventory responsibilities.

Performance Review. In this stage, the buyer reviews supplier performance. The buyer may contact users and ask them to rate their satisfaction. The *performance review* may lead the buyer to continue, modify, or drop the arrangement. The seller's job is to monitor the same factors used by the buyer to make sure that the seller is giving the expected satisfaction.

In all, the eight-stage buying-process model shown in Figure 5.8 provides a simple view of the business buying as it might occur in a new task buying situation. However, the actual process is usually much more complex. In the modified rebuy or straight rebuy situation, some of these stages would be compressed or bypassed. Each organization buys in its own way, and each buying situation has unique requirements.

Different buying center participants may be involved at different stages of the process. Although certain buying-process steps usually do occur, buyers do not always follow them in the same order, and they may add other steps. Often, buyers will repeat certain stages of the process. Finally, a customer relationship might involve many different types of purchases ongoing at a given time, all in different stages of the buying process. The seller must manage the total *customer relationship*, not just individual purchases.

Engaging Business Buyers with Digital and Social Marketing

As in every other area of marketing, the explosion of information technologies and online, mobile, and social media has changed the face of the B-to-B buying and marketing process. In the following sections, we discuss two important technology advancements: *e-procurement and online purchasing* and *B-to-B digital and social media marketing*.

E-procurement and Online Purchasing

E-procurement

Purchasing through electronic connections between buyers and sellers—usually online.

Advances in information technology have dramatically affected the face of the B-to-B buying process. Online and electronic purchasing, often called **e-procurement**, has grown rapidly in recent years. Virtually unknown two decades ago, online purchasing is standard procedure for most companies today. In turn, business marketers can connect with customers online to share marketing information, sell products and services, provide customer support services, and maintain ongoing customer relationships.

Companies can do e-procurement in any of several ways. They can conduct *reverse auctions*, in which they put their purchasing requests online and invite suppliers to bid for the business. Or they can engage in online *trading exchanges*, through which companies work collectively to facilitate the trading process. Companies also can conduct e-procurement by setting up their own *company buying sites*. For example, GE operates a company trading site on which it posts its buying needs and invites bids, negotiates terms, and places orders. Or companies can create *extranet links* with key suppliers. For instance, they can create direct procurement accounts with suppliers such as Dell or Staples through which company buyers can purchase equipment, materials, and supplies directly. >> Staples operates a business-to-business procurement division called Staples Advantage, which serves the office supplies and services buying needs of businesses of any size, from 20 employees to the *Fortune* 1000.

Business-to-business e-procurement yields many benefits. First, it shaves transaction costs and results in more efficient purchasing for both buyers and suppliers. E-procurement reduces the time between order and delivery. And an online-powered purchasing program eliminates the paperwork associated with traditional requisition and ordering procedures and helps an organization keep better track of all purchases. Finally, beyond the cost and time savings, e-procurement frees purchasing people from a lot of drudgery and paperwork. Instead, they can focus on more-strategic issues, such as finding better supply sources and working with suppliers to reduce costs and develop new products.

The rapidly expanding use of e-procurement, however, also presents some problems. For example, at the same time that the Internet makes it possible for suppliers and customers to share business data and even collaborate on product design, it can also erode decades-old customer–supplier relationships. Many buyers now use the power of the Internet to pit suppliers against one another and search out better deals, products, and turnaround times on a purchase-by-purchase basis.

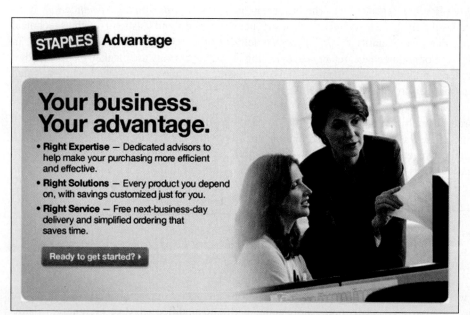

>> Online buying: Staples operates a business-to-business procurement division called Staples Advantage, which serves the office supplies and services buying needs of business customers of any size.

Staples the Office Superstore, LLC

Business-to-Business Digital and Social Media Marketing

In response to customers' rapid shift toward online buying, today's B-to-B marketers are now using a wide range of digital and social media marketing approaches—from Web sites, blogs, mobile apps, e-newsletters, and proprietary online networks to mainstream social media such as Facebook, LinkedIn, YouTube, Google+, and Twitter—to engage customers and manage customer relationships anywhere, any time. The use of digital and social media channels in business marketing isn't just growing, it's exploding. Digital and social media marketing have rapidly become *the* new space for engaging business customers. Consider Makino, a leading manufacturer of metal cutting and machining technology:

>> There's a hot new video on YouTube these days, featured at the Makino Machine Tools YouTube channel. It shows Makino's D500 five-axis vertical machining center in action, with metal chips flying as the machinery mills a new industrial part. Sound exciting? Probably not to you. But to the right industrial customer, the video is downright spellbinding. The video has been viewed more than 33,000 times, mostly by current or prospective Makino customers. For B-to-B marketer Makino, that's great exposure.[35]

Makino employs a wide variety of digital and social media initiatives to engage customers. For example, it hosts an ongoing series of industry-specific webinars that position the company as an industry thought leader. It produces about three webinars each month and offers a library of more than 100 on topics ranging from optimizing machine tool performance to discovering new metal-cutting processes. The Webinars help to build Makino's customer database, generate leads, build customer relationships, and prepare the way for salespeople by providing relevant information and educating customers online. Makino also uses Twitter, Facebook, Google+, and YouTube extensively to engage customers and prospects with the latest Makino innovations and events and to vividly demonstrate the company's machines in action.

>> B-to-B social media: Machining tool manufacturer Makino engages its business customers through extensive digital and social marketing—everything from proprietary online communities and webinars to Facebook, YouTube, and Twitter.

Courtesy of Makino

Compared with traditional media and sales approaches, digital and social media can create greater customer engagement and interaction. B-to-B marketers know that they aren't really targeting *businesses,* they are targeting *individuals* in those businesses who affect buying decisions. And today's business buyers are always connected via their digital devices—whether it's PCs, tablets, or smartphones.

Digital and social media play an important role in engaging these always-connected business buyers in a way that personal selling alone cannot. Instead of the old model of sales reps calling on business customers at work or maybe meeting up with them at trade shows, the new digital approaches facilitate anytime, anywhere connections between a wide range of people in the selling and customer organizations. It gives both sellers and buyers more control of and access to important information. B-to-B marketing has always been social network marketing, but today's digital environment offers an exciting array of new networking tools and applications.

MyMarketingLab

If assigned by your instructor, complete the questions marked with the ★ from the EOC Discussion Questions section in the MyLab. To complete the Marketing by the Numbers problems found in this section, go to your Assignments in the MyLab.

REVIEWING AND EXTENDING THE CONCEPTS

CHAPTER REVIEW AND CRITICAL THINKING

Objectives Review

This chapter is the last of three chapters that address understanding the marketplace and consumers. Here, we've looked closely at *consumer* and *business buyer behavior.* The American consumer market consists of more than 320 million people who consume more than $11 trillion worth of goods and services each year, making it one of the most attractive consumer markets in the world. The business market involves even more dollars and items than the consumer market. Understanding buyer behavior is one of the biggest challenges marketers face.

 OBJECTIVE 5-1   Understand the consumer market and the major factors that influence consumer buyer behavior. (pp 134–148)

The *consumer market* consists of all the individuals and households that buy or acquire goods and services for personal consumption. A simple model of consumer behavior suggests that marketing stimuli and other major forces enter the consumer's "black box." This black box has two parts: buyer characteristics and the buyer's decision process. Once in the black box, the inputs result in buyer responses, such as buying attitudes and preferences and purchase behavior.

Consumer buyer behavior is influenced by four key sets of buyer characteristics: cultural, social, personal, and psychological. Understanding these factors can help marketers to identify interested buyers and to shape products and appeals to serve consumer needs better. *Culture* is the most basic determinant of a person's wants and behavior. People in different cultural, subcultural, and social class groups have different product and brand preferences. *Social factors*—such as small group, social network, and family influences—strongly affect product and brand choices, as do *personal characteristics,* such as age, life stage, occupation, economic circumstances, lifestyle, and personality. Finally, consumer buying behavior is influenced by four major sets of *psychological factors*—motivation, perception, learning, and beliefs and attitudes. Each of these factors provides a different perspective for understanding the workings of the buyer's black box.

 OBJECTIVE 5-2   Identify and discuss the stages in the buyer decision process. (pp 149–151)

When making a purchase, the buyer goes through a decision process consisting of need recognition, information search, evaluation of alternatives, purchase decision, and postpurchase behavior. During *need recognition*, the consumer recognizes a problem or need that could be satisfied by a product or service.

Once the need is recognized, the consumer moves into the *information search* stage. With information in hand, the consumer proceeds to *alternative evaluation* and assesses brands in the choice set. From there, the consumer makes a *purchase decision* and actually buys the product. In the final stage of the buyer decision process, *postpurchase behavior,* the consumer takes action based on satisfaction or dissatisfaction. The marketer's job is to understand the buyer's behavior at each stage and the influences that are operating.

 OBJECTIVE 5-3   Describe the adoption and diffusion process for new products. (pp 151–153)

The product *adoption process* is made up of five stages: awareness, interest, evaluation, trial, and adoption. New product marketers must think about how to help consumers move through these stages. With regard to the *diffusion process* for new products, consumers respond at different rates, depending on consumer and product characteristics. Consumers may be innovators, early adopters, early mainstream, late mainstream, or lagging adopters. Each group may require different marketing approaches. Marketers often try to bring their new products to the attention of potential early adopters, especially those who are opinion leaders.

 OBJECTIVE 5-4   Define the business market and identify the major factors that influence business buyer behavior. (pp 154–159)

The *business market* is composed of all organizations that buy goods and services for use in the production of other products and services or for the purpose of reselling or renting them to others at a profit. Compared with consumer markets, business markets usually have fewer, larger buyers who are more geographically concentrated. Business demand is derived demand, and the business buying decision usually involves more, and more professional, buyers.

Business buyers make decisions that vary with the three types of *buying situations:* straight rebuys, modified rebuys, and new tasks. The decision-making unit of a buying organization—the *buying center*—can consist of many different persons playing many different roles. The business marketer needs to know the following: Who are the major buying center participants? In what decisions do they exercise influence and to what degree? What evaluation criteria does each decision participant use? The business marketer also needs to understand the major environmental, organizational, interpersonal, and individual influences on the buying process.

OBJECTIVE 5-5 **List and define the steps in the business buyer decision process. (pp 159–163)**

The *business buyer decision process* itself can be quite involved, with eight basic stages: problem recognition, general need description, product specification, supplier search, proposal solicitation, supplier selection, order-routine specification, and performance review. Buyers who face a new task buying situation usually go through all stages of the buying process. Buyers making modified or straight rebuys may skip some of the stages. Companies must manage the overall customer relationship, which often includes many different buying decisions in various stages of the buying decision process. Recent advances in information and digital technology have given birth to "e-procurement," by which business buyers are purchasing all kinds of products and services online. Business marketers are increasingly connecting with customers online and through digital, mobile, and social media to engage customers, share marketing information, sell products and services, provide customer support services, and maintain ongoing customer relationships.

Key Terms

Objective 5-1
Consumer buyer behavior (p 134)
Consumer market (p 134)

Objective 5-2
Culture (p 135)
Subculture (p 136)
Total market strategy (p 137)
Social class (p 138)
Group (p 138)
Word-of-mouth influence (p 138)
Opinion leader (p 138)
Online social networks (p 139)
Lifestyle (p 143)
Personality (p 145)

Motive (drive) (p 146)
Perception (p 146)
Learning (p 148)
Belief (p 148)
Attitude (p 148)
Cognitive dissonance (p 151)

Objective 5-3
New product (p 151)
Adoption process (p 152)

Objective 5-4
Business buyer behavior (p 154)
Business buying process (p 154)

Derived demand (p 155)
Supplier development (p 156)
Straight rebuy (p 156)
Modified rebuy (p 157)
New task (p 157)
Systems selling (solutions selling) (p 157)
Buying center (p 158)

Objective 5-5
E-procurement (p 162)

Discussion Questions

5-1. Discuss the stages of the consumer buyer decision process and describe how you or your family used this process to make a purchase. (AACSB: Communication; Reflective Thinking)

5-2. Name and describe the stages in the adoption process and discuss the importance of this model for marketers. (AACSB: Communication; Reflective Thinking)

5-3. How does the market structure and demand faced by business marketers differ from that faced by consumer marketers? (AACSB: Communication)

5-4. Compare and contrast the types of business buying situations. (AACSB: Communication; Reflective Thinking)

5-5. Describe how business-to-business marketers use digital and social media channels to engage customers, market their products, and manage customer relationships anywhere. (AACSB: Communication)

Critical Thinking Exercises

5-6. Researchers study the role of personality on consumer purchase behavior. One research project—Beyond the Purchase—offers a range of surveys consumers can take to learn more about their own personalities in general and their consumer personalities in particular. Register at www.beyondthepurchase.org/ and take the "Spending Habits" surveys along with any of the other surveys that interest you. What do these surveys tell you about your general and consumer personality? Do you agree with the findings? Why or why not? (AACSB: Communication; Use of IT; Diversity; Reflective Thinking)

5-7. *Kaizen. Seiri. Seiton. Seiso. Seiketsu. Shitsako. Jishuken.* These Japanese words are related to continuous quality improvement and are applied in supplier development programs, particularly Toyota's. Research Toyota's Production System (TPS) and describe how these concepts are applied in supplier development. (AACSB: Communication; Multicultural and Diversity)

5-8. Business buying occurs worldwide, so marketers need to be aware of cultural factors influencing business customers. In a small group, select a country and develop a multimedia presentation on proper business etiquette and manners, including appropriate appearance, behavior, and communication. Include a map showing the location of the country as well as a description of the country in terms of its demographics, culture, and economic history. (AACSB: Communication; Multicultural and Diversity; Use of IT)

MINICASES AND APPLICATIONS

Online, Mobile, and Social Media Marketing   Digital Influencers

Jen Hsieh is a college student with a love for fashion who shares outfits and fashion sense on Jennifhsieh, her fashion blog. Her social influence earned her an invitation to Kate Spade's New York fashion week presentation, after which she blogged, "I had to keep myself from drooling" when describing the collection. Digital influencers like Jen are often paid to write product reviews on their blogs and to post pictures of themselves on sites such as Pinterest and Instagram wearing clothes given to them by the sponsor. Some are given all-expenses-paid trips to events. For example, Olivia Lopez, a personal-style blogger with a site called Lust for Life, was invited by Samsung to the South by Southwest and Lollapalloza music festivals and provided a phone with which to post pictures for her 90,000 Instagram followers. The hashtag "#thenextbigthing," which is used in Samsung's product promotions, was included in her posts. Otherwise, Olivia included no indication that Samsung provided sponsorship.

5-9. Find an example of a blog on a topic that interests you. Are there advertisements on the blog? Does the blogger appear to be sponsored by any companies? Is there information regarding sponsorship? Write a brief report of your observations. (AACSB: Use of IT; Communication; Reflective Thinking)

5-10. Summarize the FTC's disclosure rules on using social media to promote products and services. Does the blogger you reviewed in the previous question follow these rules? Explain. (AACSB: Communication; Reflective Thinking)

Marketing Ethics   Business-to-Business Commercial Bribery

The CEO of FalconStor Software directed employees to bribe B-to-B customer JPMorgan Chase executives with more than $300,000 worth of stock options, golf-related perks, gift cards, and gambling vouchers in return for lucrative licensing contracts totaling more than $13 million that pumped up the company's stock price 22 percent. The Department of Justice filed charges under the Travel Act against FalconStor because a FalconStor sales representative traveled with a JPMorgan executive on a lavish entertainment and gambling junket to Hong Kong and Macau. FalconStor must pay $5.8 million in fines and institute corporate compliance reforms before criminal charges can be dropped. But that's not the end of it. The Securities and Exchange Commission (SEC) also filed a complaint claiming FalconStor misled investors by claiming the contracts with customer JPMorgan Chase as vindication of the quality of the company's product. In addition, since the bribery expenses were disguised as employee performance bonuses, promotional expenses, and entertainment expenses, the SEC filed charges under the Foreign Corrupt Practices Act (FCPA).

5-11. Research the Travel Act and the FCPA. Explain how the SEC could file charges under the FCPA if this was not a bribery case involving a foreign government. (AACSB: Communication; Reflective Thinking)

5-12. What would you do if your supervisor directed you to bribe other businesses to obtain contracts? Is there legal protection for employees who report employers' illegal behavior? (AACSB: Communication; Ethical Reasoning)

Marketing by the Numbers   Evaluating Alternatives

One way consumers can evaluate alternatives is to identify important attributes and assess how purchase alternatives perform on those attributes. Consider the purchase of a tablet. Each attribute, such as screen size, is given a weight to reflect its level of importance to that consumer. Then the consumer evaluates each alternative on each attribute. For example, in the table below, price (weighted at 0.5) is the most important attribute for this consumer. The consumer believes that brand C performs best on price, rating it 7 (higher ratings indicate higher performance). Brand B is perceived as performing the worst on this attribute (rating of 3). Screen size and available apps are the consumer's next most important attributes. Operating system is least important.

Attributes	Importance Weight (e)	Alternative Brands		
		A	B	C
Screen size	0.2	4	6	2
Price	0.5	6	3	7
Operating system	0.1	5	5	4
Apps available	0.2	4	6	7

A score can be calculated for each brand by multiplying the importance weight for each attribute by the brand's score on that attribute. These weighted scores are then summed to

determine the score for that brand. For example, $Score_{Brand\ A} = (0.2 \times 4) + (0.5 \times 6) + (0.1 \times 5) + (0.2 \times 4) = 0.8 + 3.0 + 0.5 + 0.8 = 5.1$. This consumer will select the brand with the highest score.

5-13. Calculate the scores for brands B and C. Which brand would this consumer likely choose? (AACSB: Communication; Analytic Reasoning)

5-14. Which brand is this consumer least likely to purchase? Discuss two ways the marketer of this brand can enhance consumer likelihood of purchasing its brand. (AACSB: Communication; Reflective Thinking; Analytic Reasoning)

Video Case IMG Worldwide

IMG Worldwide is the world's largest sports entertainment media company. In years past, IMG was all about professional golf and tennis marketing. But today, IMG handles sales and marketing activities for 70 to 80 colleges, making college sports marketing the company's highest-growth business. In short, IMG handles anything and everything that touches the college sports consumer short of actually playing games on the court or field.

Although you might think that all college sports fans are created equal, IMG finds that nothing could be further from the truth. How different fans consume sports and sports-related activities is affected by geographical, generational, and institutional factors. IMG focuses on comprehensively understanding

the process that consumers go through to view or attend a sporting event. It then connects with consumers at each and every stage.

After viewing the video featuring IMG Worldwide, answer the following questions:

5-15. What "product" is a college athletics department selling?

5-16. Discuss how a college sports fan might go through the buying decision process, providing examples for each stage.

5-17. Of the four sets of factors affecting consumer behavior, which most strongly affects how college sports fans consume a sport?

Company Cases 5 UPS/1 FedEx/7 Target

See Appendix 1 for cases appropriate for this chapter. **Case 5, UPS: "We Love Logistics"—Put UPS to Work for You and You'll Love Logistics Too.** Business buying decisions are influenced by numerous factors that go way beyond dollars and cents. UPS recognizes the value business clients place on providing full-service logistics solutions. **Case 1, FedEx: Making Every Customer Experience Outstanding.** Businesses and consumers have various needs when it comes to shipping

letters and packages. From the time FedEx opened for business more than 40 years ago, the company strategy has been built on a foundation of obsessive customer focus and meeting those needs at every stage. **Case 7, Target: Where Store Brands Offer More Than Low Prices.** So many factors influence the decisions consumers make. Target understands this and has focused on making the purchase decision easy with a comprehensive strategy based on store brands.

MyMarketingLab

If assigned by your instructor, complete these writing sections from your Assignments in the MyLab.

5-18. Discuss how lifestyle influences consumers' buying behavior and how marketers measure lifestyle. (AACSB: Communication; Reflective Thinking)

5-19. Describe the characteristics of a new product that affect its rate of adoption. Which characteristics will affect how quickly the new digital and social media services described above will be accepted by consumers in the United States? (AACSB: Written and Oral Communication; Reflective Thinking)

6 Customer Value-Driven Marketing Strategy
Creating Value for Target Customers

Previewing the Concepts

So far, you've learned what marketing is and about the importance of understanding
consumers and the marketplace. With that as a background, you're now ready to delve deeper
into marketing strategy and tactics. This chapter looks further into key customer value-
driven marketing strategy decisions—dividing up markets into meaningful customer groups
(*segmentation*), choosing which customer groups to serve (*targeting*), creating market offerings that best serve targeted customers (*differentiation*), and positioning the offerings in the
minds of consumers (*positioning*). The chapters that follow explore the tactical marketing
tools—the four Ps—by which marketers bring these strategies to life.

To open our discussion of segmentation, targeting, differentiation, and positioning, let's
look at Dunkin' Donuts. Dunkin' has expanded rapidly in recent years into a national powerhouse, on par with Starbucks. But Dunkin' is no Starbucks. In fact, it doesn't want to be. It
targets a very different kind of customer with a very different value proposition. Grab yourself
a cup of coffee and read on.

First Stop

Dunkin' Donuts: Targeting the Average Joe

A few years back, Dunkin' Donuts paid dozens of faithful customers in cities around the country $100 a week to buy coffee at Starbucks instead. At the same time, the coffee chain paid Starbucks customers to make the opposite switch. When it later debriefed the two groups, Dunkin' says it found them so polarized that company researchers dubbed them "tribes," each of which loathed the very things that made the other tribe loyal to their coffee shop. Dunkin' fans viewed Starbucks as pretentious and trendy, whereas Starbucks loyalists saw Dunkin' as plain and unoriginal. "I don't get it," one Dunkin' regular told researchers after visiting Starbucks. "If I want to sit on a couch, I stay at home."

Dunkin' Donuts has rapidly expanded into a national coffee powerhouse, on par with Starbucks, the nation's largest coffee chain. But the research confirmed a simple fact: Dunkin' is *not* Starbucks. In fact, it doesn't want to be. To prosper, Dunkin' must have its own clear vision of just which customers it wants to serve and how. Dunkin' and Starbucks target very different customers who want very different things from their favorite coffee shops. Starbucks is strongly positioned as a sort of high-brow "third place"—outside the home and office—featuring couches, eclectic music, and art-splashed walls. Dunkin' has a decidedly more low-brow, "everyman" kind of appeal.

Dunkin' Donuts's research showed that its brand fans were largely bewildered and turned off by the atmosphere at Starbucks. They groused that crowds of laptop users made it difficult to find a seat. They didn't like Starbucks's "tall," "grande," and "venti" lingo for small, medium, and large coffees. And they couldn't understand why anyone would pay so much for a cup of coffee. "It was almost as though they were a group of Martians talking about a group of Earthlings," says an executive from Dunkin's advertising agency. The Starbucks customers that Dunkin' paid to switch were equally uneasy in Dunkin' shops. "The Starbucks people couldn't bear that they weren't special anymore," says the ad executive.

Such opposing opinions aren't surprising, given the differences in the two stores' customers. Dunkin's customers include more middle-income blue- and white-collar workers across all age, race, and income demographics. By contrast, Starbucks targets a higher income, more professional group. But Dunkin' researchers concluded that it was more the ideal, rather than income, that set the two tribes apart: Dunkin's tribe members want to be part of a crowd, whereas members of the Starbucks tribe want to stand out as individuals. "You could open a Dunkin' Donuts right next to Starbucks and get two completely different types of consumers," says one retailing expert.

Dunkin' Donuts built its positioning on serving simple fare at reasonable prices to working-class customers. It gained a reputation as a morning pit stop where everyday folks could get their daily donut and caffeine fix. But in recent years, to broaden its appeal and fuel expansion, the chain has been moving upscale—a bit, but not too far. It has spiffed up its stores and added new menu items, such as lattes and non-breakfast items like a steak sandwich and breaded chicken sandwich with barbecue sauce. Dunkin' has also made dozens of store and atmosphere redesign changes, big and small, ranging from adding free Wi-Fi, digital menu boards, and more electrical outlets for laptops and smartphones to playing relaxing background music. And Dunkin' franchisees can now redecorate their stores in any of four Starbucks-esque color schemes, including "Dark Roast," "Cappuccino Blend," and "Jazz Brew," which features "dark orange and brown cozy booth seating, as well as hanging light fixtures that lend a soft glow to wall murals printed with words such as 'break,' 'fresh' and 'quality.'"

As it inches upscale, however, Dunkin' Donuts is being careful not to alienate its traditional customer base. There are no couches in the remodeled stores. Dunkin' even renamed a new hot sandwich a "stuffed melt" after customers complained that calling it a "panini" was too fancy; it then dropped it altogether when faithful customers thought it was too messy. "We're walking [a fine] line," says the chain's vice president of consumer insights. "The thing about the Dunkin' tribe is, they see through the hype."

Over the past several years, both Dunkin' Donuts and Starbucks have grown rapidly, each targeting its own tribe of customers and riding the wave of America's growing thirst for coffee. Now, both are looking for more growth by convincing "grab-and-go" morning customers to visit later in the day and stick around longer. Although still smaller than Starbucks—which captures a 36 percent U.S. market share versus Dunkin's roughly 24 percent share—Dunkin' is currently the nation's fastest-growing snack and coffee chain. It hopes that the recent repositioning and upgrades will help keep that momentum going. Dunkin' plans to add at least 4,000 more U.S. stores in by 2020.

» **Dunkin' Donuts targets everyday Joes who just don't get what Starbucks is all about. Its targeting and positioning are pretty well summed up in its long-running ad slogan "America Runs on Dunkin'."**
Tim Boyle/Getty Images

> Dunkin' Donuts targets the "Dunkin' tribe"—not the Starbucks coffee snob but the average Joe. Dunkin' isn't like Starbucks; it doesn't want to be.

Again, however, in refreshing its stores and positioning, Dunkin' Donuts has stayed true to the needs and preferences of the Dunkin' tribe. Dunkin' is "not going after the Starbucks coffee snob," says one analyst, it's "going after the average Joe." So far so good. For seven years running, Dunkin' Donuts has ranked number one in the coffee category in a leading customer loyalty and engagement survey, ahead of number-two Starbucks. According to the survey, Dunkin' Donuts was the top brand for consistently meeting or exceeding customer expectations with respect to taste, quality, and customer service.

Dunkin' Donuts' targeting and positioning are pretty well summed up in its long-running ad slogan "America Runs on Dunkin'." No longer just a morning pit stop, Dunkin now bills itself as America's favorite all-day, everyday stop for coffee and baked goods. "We remain committed to keeping America running with our great coffee, baked goods, and snacks served in a friendly environment at a great value," says Dunkin's chief global marketing officer. Nothing too fancy—just meeting the everyday, all-day needs of the Dunkin' tribe.[1]

Market segmentation
Dividing a market into distinct groups of buyers who have different needs, characteristics, or behaviors and who might require separate marketing strategies or mixes.

Market targeting (targeting)
Evaluating each market segment's attractiveness and selecting one or more segments to serve.

Differentiation
Actually differentiating the market offering to create superior customer value.

Positioning
Arranging for a market offering to occupy a clear, distinctive, and desirable place relative to competing products in the minds of target consumers.

C ompanies today recognize that they cannot appeal to all buyers in the marketplace—or at least not to all buyers in the same way. Buyers are too numerous, widely scattered, and varied in their needs and buying practices. Moreover, companies themselves vary widely in their abilities to serve different market segments. Instead, like Dunkin' Donuts, companies must identify the parts of the market they can serve best and most profitably. They must design customer-driven marketing strategies that build the right relationships with the right customers. Thus, most companies have moved away from mass marketing and toward *target marketing:* identifying market segments, selecting one or more of them, and developing products and marketing programs tailored to each.

>> **Figure 6.1** shows the four major steps in designing a customer value-driven marketing strategy. In the first two steps, the company selects the customers that it will serve. **Market segmentation** involves dividing a market into distinct groups of buyers who have different needs, characteristics, or behaviors and who might require separate marketing strategies or mixes. The company identifies different ways to segment the market and develops profiles of the resulting market segments. **Market targeting** (or **targeting**) consists of evaluating each market segment's attractiveness and selecting one or more market segments to serve.

In the final two steps, the company decides on a value proposition—how it will create value for target customers. **Differentiation** involves actually differentiating the firm's market offering to create superior customer value. **Positioning** consists of arranging for a market offering to occupy a clear, distinctive, and desirable place relative to competing products in the minds of target consumers. We discuss each of these steps in turn.

Market Segmentation

Buyers in any market differ in their wants, resources, locations, buying attitudes, and buying practices. Through market segmentation, companies divide large, diverse markets into smaller segments that can be reached more efficiently and effectively with products and services that match their unique needs. In this section, we discuss four important segmentation topics: segmenting consumer markets, segmenting business markets, segmenting international markets, and the requirements for effective segmentation.

>> **Figure 6.1 Designing a Customer Value-Driven Market Strategy**

In concept, marketing boils down to two questions: (1) Which customers will we serve? and (2) How will we serve them? Of course, the tough part is coming up with good answers to these simple-sounding yet difficult questions. The goal is to create more value for the customers we serve than competitors do.

Select customers to serve

Segmentation
Divide the total market into smaller segments

Targeting
Select the segment or segments to enter

Create value for targeted customers

Decide on a value proposition

Differentiation
Differentiate the market offering to create superior customer value

Positioning
Position the market offering in the minds of target customers

Segmenting Consumer Markets

There is no single way to segment a market. A marketer has to try different segmentation variables, alone and in combination, to find the best way to view market structure. **>> Table 6.1** outlines variables that might be used in segmenting consumer markets. Here we look at the major *geographic, demographic, psychographic,* and *behavioral* variables.

Geographic Segmentation

Geographic segmentation calls for dividing the market into different geographical units, such as nations, regions, states, counties, cities, or even neighborhoods. A company may decide to operate in one or a few geographical areas or operate in all areas but pay attention to geographical differences in needs and wants. Moreover, many companies today are localizing their products, services, advertising, promotion, and sales efforts to fit the needs of individual regions, cities, and neighborhoods.

Geographic segmentation
Dividing a market into different geographical units, such as nations, states, regions, counties, cities, or even neighborhoods.

>> Geographic segmentation: Target is now opening smaller-format, conveniently located CityTarget and TargetExpress stores designed to fit into densely packed urban neighborhoods.
ZUMA Press, Inc/Alamy

For example, many large retailers—from Target and Walmart to Kohl's and Staples—are now opening smaller-format stores designed to fit the needs of densely packed urban neighborhoods not suited to their typical large suburban superstores. >>Target's CityTarget stores average about half the size of a typical Super Target; its TargetExpress stores are even smaller at about one-fifth the size of a big-box outlet. These smaller, conveniently located stores carry a more limited assortment of goods that meet the needs of urban residents and commuters, such as groceries, home essentials, beauty products, and consumer electronics. They also offer pick-up-in-store services and a pharmacy.[2]

Beyond adjusting store size, many retailers also localize product assortments and services. For example, department store chain Macy's has a localization program called MyMacy's in which merchandise is customized under 69 different geographical districts. At stores around the country, Macy's sales clerks record local shopper requests and pass them along to district managers. In turn, blending the customer requests with store transaction data, the district managers customize the mix of merchandise in their stores. So, for instance, Macy's stores in Michigan stock more locally made Sanders chocolate candies. In Orlando, Macy's carries more swimsuits in stores near waterparks and more twin bedding in stores near condominium rentals. The chain stocks extra coffee percolators in its Long Island stores, where it sells more of the 1960s must-haves than anywhere else in the country. In all, the "MyMacy's" strategy is to meet the needs of local markets, making the giant retailer seem smaller and more in touch.[3]

>> Table 6.1	Major Segmentation Variables for Consumer Markets

Segmentation Variable	Examples
Geographic	Nations, regions, states, counties, cities, neighborhoods, population density (urban, suburban, rural), climate
Demographic	Age, life-cycle stage, gender, income, occupation, education, religion, ethnicity, generation
Psychographic	Social class, lifestyle, personality
Behavioral	Occasions, benefits, user status, usage rate, loyalty status

Demographic Segmentation

Demographic segmentation divides the market into segments based on variables such as age, life-cycle stage, gender, income, occupation, education, religion, ethnicity, and generation. Demographic factors are the most popular bases for segmenting customer groups. One reason is that consumer needs, wants, and usage rates often vary closely with demographic variables. Another is that demographic variables are easier to measure than most other types of variables. Even when marketers first define segments using other bases, such as benefits sought or behavior, they must know a segment's demographic characteristics to assess the size of the target market and reach it efficiently.

Demographic segmentation
Dividing the market into segments based on variables such as age, life-cycle stage, gender, income, occupation, education, religion, ethnicity, and generation.

Age and Life-Cycle Stage. Consumer needs and wants change with age. Some companies use **age and life-cycle segmentation**, offering different products or using different marketing approaches for different age and life-cycle groups. For example, Kraft's Oscar Mayer brand markets Lunchables, convenient prepackaged lunches for children. To extend the substantial success of Lunchables, however, Oscar Mayer later introduced Lunchables Uploaded, a version designed to meet the tastes and sensibilities of teenagers. Most recently, the brand launched an adult version, but with the more adult-friendly name P3 (Portable Protein Pack). Now, consumers of all ages can enjoy what is rapidly becoming one of America's favorite noontime meals.

Age and life-cycle segmentation
Dividing a market into different age and life-cycle groups.

Other companies offer brands that target specific age or life-stage groups. For example, whereas most tablet makers have been busy marketing their devices to grown-ups, Amazon has spotted a tinier tablet market. Feedback from parents suggested that they were handing their entertainment-packed Kindle Fire tablet over to their young children for entertainment, education, and babysitting purposes. To tap this young-family market, Amazon introduced FreeTime Unlimited, a multimedia subscription service targeted toward three- to eight-year-olds. Complete with parental controls, the service features "Endless kid stuff. No grownup stuff." It provides access to a treasure trove of G-rated movies, games, and books, including premium content from Nickelodeon, Disney, Sesame Street, and DC Comics. Not only does FreeTime Unlimited generate revenues for Amazon, it helps sell more Kindle Fire tablets to young families.[4]

Marketers must be careful to guard against stereotypes when using age and life-cycle segmentation. For example, although some 80-year-olds fit the stereotypes of doddering shut-ins with fixed incomes, others ski and play tennis. Similarly, whereas some 40-year-old couples are sending their children off to college, others are just beginning new families. Thus, age is often a poor predictor of a person's life cycle, health, work or family status, needs, and buying power.

Gender segmentation
Dividing a market into different segments based on gender.

Gender. **Gender segmentation** has long been used in marketing clothing, cosmetics, toiletries, toys, and magazines. For example, P&G was among the first to use gender segmentation with Secret, a deodorant brand specially formulated for a woman's chemistry, packaged and advertised to reinforce the female image.

More recently, the men's personal care industry has exploded, and many cosmetics brands that previously catered mostly to women—from L'Oréal, Nivea, and Sephora to Unilever's Dove brand—now successfully market men's lines. For example, Dove's Men+Care line calls itself "The authority on man maintenance." The brand provides a full line of body washes ("skin care built in"), body bars ("fight skin dryness"), antiperspirants ("tough on sweat, not on skin"), face care ("take better care of your face"), and hair care ("3X stronger hair").[5]

Going in the other direction, GoldieBlox markets a collection of engineering toys for girls. >> Designed by a female engineer from Stanford University, the brand's goal is "to get

>> Gender segmentation: GoldieBlox markets engineering toys for girls. "Move over Barbie, there's a new girl in town. And she's wearing overalls and construction boots."
GoldieBlox, Inc.

girls building" and to inspire a future generation of female engineers. Aimed at girls 5 to 9 years old, GoldieBlox consists of storybooks and construction sets that require young girls to solve a series of construction challenges. Initially funded by more than $250,000 raised via crowdfunding platform Kickstarter, the innovative product has recently won two Toy Industry Foundation Toy of the Year awards—Educational and People's Choice. As one writer notes, "Move over Barbie, there's a new girl in town. And she's wearing overalls and construction boots."[6]

Income segmentation
Dividing a market into different income segments.

Income. The marketers of products and services such as automobiles, clothing, cosmetics, financial services, and travel have long used **income segmentation**. Many companies target affluent consumers with luxury goods and convenience services. Other marketers use high-touch marketing programs to court the well-to-do. Upscale retailer Saks Fifth Avenue provides exclusive services to its elite clientele of Fifth Avenue Club members, some of whom spend as much as $150,000 to $200,000 a year on clothing and accessories from Saks alone. For example, Fifth Avenue Club members have access to a Saks Personal Stylist. The fashion-savvy, well-connected personal consultant gets to know and helps to shape each client's personal sense of style, then guides her "through the maze of fashion must-haves." The Personal Stylist puts the customer first. For example, if Saks doesn't carry one of those must-haves that the client covets, the personal stylist will find it elsewhere at no added charge.[7]

However, not all companies that use income segmentation target the affluent. For example, many retailers—such as the Dollar General, Family Dollar, and Dollar Tree store chains—successfully target low- and middle-income groups. The core market for such stores is represented by families with incomes under $30,000. When Family Dollar real estate experts scout locations for new stores, they look for lower-middle-class neighborhoods where people wear less-expensive shoes and drive old cars that drip a lot of oil. With their low-income strategies, dollar stores are now the fastest-growing retailers in the nation.

Psychographic Segmentation

Psychographic segmentation
Dividing a market into different segments based on social class, lifestyle, or personality characteristics.

Psychographic segmentation divides buyers into different segments based on social class, lifestyle, or personality characteristics. People in the same demographic group can have very different psychographic characteristics.

In Chapter 5, we discussed how the products people buy reflect their *lifestyles*. As a result, marketers often segment their markets by consumer lifestyles and base their marketing strategies on lifestyle appeals. For example, retailer Anthropologie, with its whimsical, "French flea market" store atmosphere, sells a Bohemian-chic lifestyle to which its young women customers aspire. ≫ And VF Corporation offers a closet full of more than 30 premium lifestyle brands that "fit the lives of consumers the world over, from commuters to cowboys, surfers to soccer moms, sports fans to rock bands."[8]

VF is the nation's number-one jeans maker, with brands such as Lee, Riders, Rustler, and Wrangler. But jeans are not the only focus for VF. The company's brands are carefully separated into five major lifestyle segments—Jeanswear, Imagewear (workwear), Outdoor and Action Sports, Sportswear, and Contemporary. The North Face and Timberland brands, both part of the Outdoor unit, offer top-of-the-line gear and apparel for outdoor enthusiasts. From the Sportswear unit, Nautica focuses on people who enjoy high-end casual apparel inspired by sailing and the sea. Vans began as a skate shoemaker, and Reef features surf-inspired footwear and apparel. In the Contemporary unit, Lucy features upscale activewear, whereas 7 for All Mankind supplies premium denim and accessories sold in boutiques and

≫ Differentiated marketing: VF Corporation offers a closet full of more than 30 premium lifestyle brands, each of which "taps into consumer aspirations to fashion, status, and well-being" in a well-defined segment.
VF Corporation

high-end department stores such as Saks and Nordstrom. At the other end of the spectrum, Horace Small, part of the Imagewear unit, markets uniforms for police and fire departments and other first responders. No matter who you are, says the company, "We fit your life."

Marketers also use *personality* variables to segment markets. For example, different soft drinks target different personalities. On the one hand, Mountain Dew projects a youthful, rebellious, adventurous, go-your-own-way personality. Its ads remind customers that "It's different on the Mountain." By contrast, Coca-Cola Zero appears to target more mature, practical, and cerebral but good-humored personality types. Its subtly humorous ads promise "Real Coca-Cola taste and zero calories."

Marketers sometimes refer to brand-focused psychographic segments as *brand "tribes"*—communities of core customers with shared characteristics, brand experiences, and strong affinities for a particular brand.[9] For example, outfitter REI's core customers are passionate about the great outdoors and share this belief as members of the REI tribe. The Apple tribe consists of stylish, tech-savvy nonconformists. Home Depot targets a core psychographic segment of dedicated do-it-yourself enthusiasts; the Nike tribe consists of high-performance athletes. Often, brands in the same product category target very different tribes. For example, as discussed in the chapter-opening story, although both Dunkin' Donuts and Starbucks are snack and coffee shops, their brand tribes are as different as day and night.

Behavioral Segmentation

Behavioral segmentation divides buyers into segments based on their knowledge, attitudes, uses, or responses concerning a product. Many marketers believe that behavior variables are the best starting point for building market segments.

Occasions. Buyers can be grouped according to occasions when they get the idea to buy, actually make their purchases, or use the purchased items. **Occasion segmentation** can help firms build up product usage. Campbell's advertises its soups more heavily in the cold winter months. And for more than a decade, Starbucks has welcomed the autumn season with its Pumpkin Spice Latte (PSL). Sold only in the fall, to date, the coffee chain has sold more than 200 million cups of the eagerly anticipated concoction. "I've never been happier about burning my tongue with a hot beverage," Tweeted a Starbucks customer recently.[10]

Still other companies try to boost consumption by promoting usage during nontraditional occasions. For example, most consumers drink orange juice in the morning, but orange growers have promoted drinking orange juice as a cool, healthful refresher at other times of the day. Similarly, whereas consumers tend to drink soft drinks later in the day, Mountain Dew introduced Mtn Dew A.M. (a mixture of Mountain Dew and orange juice) to increase morning consumption. And Taco Bell's First Meal campaign attempts to build business by promoting Mtn Dew A.M. (available only at Taco Bell) along with the chain's A.M. Crunchwrap and other breakfast items as a great way to start the day.

Benefits Sought. A powerful form of segmentation is grouping buyers according to the different *benefits* that they seek from a product. **Benefit segmentation** requires finding the major benefits people look for in a product class, the kinds of people who look for each benefit, and the major brands that deliver each benefit.

For example, people buying bicycles are looking for any number of benefits, from competitive racing and sports performance to recreation, fitness, touring, transportation, and just plain fun. To meet varying benefit preferences, Schwinn makes affordable, quality bikes in seven major benefit groups: cruisers, hybrid, bike path, mountain, road, urban, and kids. *Bike path* bikes are "Perfect for riders who want a comfortable and easy-riding bike with convenient features for casual riding over all surfaces." ≫ Schwinn's *urban*

Behavioral segmentation
Dividing a market into segments based on consumer knowledge, attitudes, uses of a product, or responses to a product.

Occasion segmentation
Dividing the market into segments according to occasions when buyers get the idea to buy, actually make their purchase, or use the purchased item.

Benefit segmentation
Dividing the market into segments according to the different benefits that consumers seek from the product.

≫ **Benefit segmentation: Schwinn makes bikes for every benefit segment. For example, Schwinn's urban bikes are "for riders who want a functional, durable, and stylish bike to commute or ride casually in urban areas."**
Schwinn Bicycles

bikes are "for riders who want a functional, durable, and stylish bike to commute or ride casually in urban areas."

In all, Schwinn makes more than 50 different lines of bikes, each designed for a specific benefit segment or subsegment. For example, Schwinn's Lakeshore bike (priced at an affordable $170 to $220) is a steel frame classic cruiser bike with coaster brakes that sells at mass retailers. It allows for "relaxing exercise" and comes with a rack on the back, handy for running errands. In contrast, the high-tech Vestige bike (priced at $1,470) is a sustainably designed urban bike, with a frame made of natural, biodegradable flax fibers and coated in water-soluble paint. The Vestige's fenders and grips are made of bamboo, and the bike can be purchased only through select dealers. The Schwinn Vestige combines style with function and has a low carbon footprint.

User Status. Markets can be segmented into nonusers, ex-users, potential users, first-time users, and regular users of a product. Marketers want to reinforce and retain regular users, attract targeted nonusers, and reinvigorate relationships with ex-users. Included in the potential users group are consumers facing life-stage changes—such as new parents and newlyweds—who can be turned into heavy users. For example, to get new parents off to the right start, P&G makes certain that its Pampers Swaddlers are the diaper most U.S. hospitals provide for newborns and then promotes them as "the #1 choice of hospitals."

Usage Rate. Markets can also be segmented into light, medium, and heavy product users. Heavy users are often a small percentage of the market but account for a high percentage of total consumption. For instance, Carl's Jr. and Hardee's restaurants, both owned by parent company CKE Restaurants, focus on a target of "young, hungry men." These young male customers, ages 18 to 34, fully embrace the chain's "If you're gonna eat, eat like you mean it" positioning. That means they wolf down a lot more Thickburgers and other indulgent items featured on the chains' menus. >> To attract this audience, the company is known for its steamy hot-models-in-bikinis commercials, featuring models such as Kate Upton, Padma Lakshmi, Nina Agdal, and Hannah Ferguson to heat up the brands' images. Such ads clearly show "what our target audience of young, hungry guys like," says CKE's chief executive.[11]

>> Targeting heavy users: Sister chains Hardee's and Carl's, Jr. use steamy hot-models-in-bikinis commercials to attract an audience of "young, hungry men," who wolf down a lot more of the chains' featured Thickburgers and other indulgent items than consumers in other segments.

Audrina Patridge/CKE Restaurants/Splash News/Newscom

Loyalty Status. A market can also be segmented by consumer loyalty. Consumers can be loyal to brands (Tide), stores (Target), and companies (Apple). Buyers can be divided into groups according to their degree of loyalty. Some consumers are completely loyal—they buy one brand all the time and can't wait to tell others about it. For example, whether they own a MacBook Pro, an iPhone, or an iPad, Apple devotees are granitelike in their devotion to the brand. At one end are the quietly satisfied Apple users, folks who own one or several Apple devices and use them for browsing, texting, email, and social networking. At the other extreme, however, are the Apple zealots—the so-called MacHeads or Macolytes—who can't wait to tell anyone within earshot of their latest Apple gadget. Such loyal Apple devotees helped keep Apple afloat during the lean years a decade ago, and they are now at the forefront of Apple's huge iPhone, iPad, iPod, and iTunes empire.

Other consumers are somewhat loyal—they are loyal to two or three brands of a given product or favor one brand while sometimes buying others. Still other buyers show no loyalty to any brand—they either want something different each time they buy, or they buy whatever's on sale.

A company can learn a lot by analyzing loyalty patterns in its market. It should start by studying its own loyal customers. Highly loyal customers can be a real asset. They often promote the brand through personal word of mouth and social media. Some companies actually put loyalists to work for the brand. For example, Patagonia relies on its most tried-and-true customers—what it calls Patagonia ambassadors—to field-test products in harsh environments, provide input for "ambassador-driven" lines of apparel and gear, and share their product experiences with others.[12] In contrast, by studying its less-loyal buyers, a company can detect which brands are most competitive with its own. By looking at customers who are shifting away from its brand, the company can learn about its marketing weaknesses and take actions to correct them.

Using Multiple Segmentation Bases

Marketers rarely limit their segmentation analysis to only one or a few variables. Rather, they often use multiple segmentation bases in an effort to identify smaller, better-defined target groups. Several business information services—such as Nielsen, Acxiom, Esri, and Experian—provide multivariable segmentation systems that merge geographic, demographic, lifestyle, and behavioral data to help companies segment their markets down to zip codes, neighborhoods, and even households.

One of the leading consumer segmentation systems is Experian's Mosaic USA system. ≫ It classifies U.S. households into one of 71 lifestyle segments and 19 levels of affluence, based on specific consumer demographics, interests, behaviors, and passions. Mosaic USA segments carry exotic names such as Birkenstocks and Beemers, Bohemian Groove, Sports Utility Families, Colleges and Cafes, Heritage Heights, Small Town Shallow Pockets, and True Grit Americans.[13] Such colorful names help bring the segments to life.

For example, the Birkenstocks and Beemers group is located in the Middle Class Melting Pot level of affluence and consists of 40- to 65-year-olds who have achieved financial security and left the urban rat race for rustic and artsy communities located near small cities. They find spirituality more important than religion. Colleges and Cafes consumers are part of the Singles and Starters affluence level and are mainly white, under-35 college graduates who are still finding themselves. They are often employed as support or service staff related to a university. They don't make much money and tend to not have any savings.

Mosaic USA and other such systems can help marketers to segment people and locations into marketable groups of like-minded consumers. Each segment has its own pattern of likes, dislikes, lifestyles, and purchase behaviors. For example, Bohemian Groove consumers, part of the Significant Singles group, are urban singles ages 45 to 65 living in apartments in smaller cities such as Sacramento, CA, and Harrisburg, PA. They tend to be laid back, maintain a large circle of friends, and stay active in community groups. They enjoy music, hobbies, and the creative arts. When they go out to eat, they choose places such as the Macaroni Grill or Red Robin. Their favorite TV channels are Bravo, Lifetime, Oxygen, and TNT, and they watch two times more CSI than the average American. Using the Mosaic system, marketers can paint a surprisingly precise picture of who you are and what you might buy.

Such rich segmentation provides a powerful tool for marketers of all kinds. It can help companies identify and better understand key customer segments, reach them more efficiently, and tailor market offerings and messages to their specific needs.

≫ Using Experian's mosaic USA segmentation system, marketers can paint a surprisingly precise picture of who you are and what you might buy. Mosiac USA segments carry colorful names such as Colleges and Cafes, Birkenstocks and Beemers, Bohemian Groove, Rolling the Dice, Small Town Shallow Pockets, and True Grit Americans that help bring the segments to life.

Zeljkodan/Shutterstock

Segmenting Business Markets

Consumer and business marketers use many of the same variables to segment their markets. Business buyers can be segmented geographically, demographically (industry, company size), or by benefits sought, user status, usage rate, and loyalty status. Yet business marketers also use some additional variables, such as customer *operating characteristics, purchasing approaches, situational factors*, and *personal characteristics*.

Almost every company serves at least some business markets. For example, Starbucks has developed distinct marketing programs for each of its two business segments: the office coffee segment and the food service segment. In the office coffee and vending segment, Starbucks Office Coffee Solutions markets a variety of workplace coffee services to businesses of any size, helping them to make Starbucks coffee and related products available to their employees in their workplaces. Starbucks helps these business customers design the best office solutions involving its coffees (the Starbucks or Seattle's Best brands), teas (Tazo), syrups, and branded paper products and methods of serving them—portion packs, single cups, or vending. The Starbucks Foodservice division teams up with businesses and other organizations—ranging from airlines, restaurants, colleges, and hospitals to baseball stadiums—to help them serve the well-known Starbucks brand to their own customers. Starbucks provides not only the coffee, tea, and paper products to its food service partners but also equipment, training, and marketing and merchandising support.[14]

Many companies establish separate systems for dealing with larger or multiple-location customers. For example, Steelcase, a major producer of office furniture systems, first divides customers into several segments: health-care, education, hospitality, legal, U.S. and Canadian governments, and state and local governments. Next, company salespeople work with independent Steelcase dealers to handle smaller, local, or regional Steelcase customers in each segment. But many national, multiple-location customers, such as ExxonMobil or IBM, have special needs that may reach beyond the scope of individual dealers. Therefore, Steelcase uses national account managers to help its dealer networks handle national accounts.

Segmenting International Markets

Few companies have either the resources or the will to operate in all, or even most, of the countries that dot the globe. Although some large companies, such as Coca-Cola or Unilever, sell products in more than 200 countries, most international firms focus on a smaller set. Different countries, even those that are close together, can vary greatly in their economic, cultural, and political makeup. Thus, just as they do within their domestic markets, international firms need to group their world markets into segments with distinct buying needs and behaviors.

Companies can segment international markets using one or a combination of several variables. They can segment by *geographic location*, grouping countries by regions such as Western Europe, the Pacific Rim, South Asia, or Africa. Geographic segmentation assumes that nations close to one another will have many common traits and behaviors. Although this is sometimes the case, there are many exceptions. For example, some U.S. marketers lump all Central and South American countries together. However, the Dominican Republic is no more like Brazil than Italy is like Sweden. Many Central and South Americans don't even speak Spanish, including more than 200 million Portuguese-speaking Brazilians and the millions in other countries who speak a variety of Indian dialects.

World markets can also be segmented based on *economic factors*. Countries might be grouped by population income levels or by their overall level of economic development. A country's economic structure shapes its population's product and service needs and therefore the marketing opportunities it offers. For example, many companies are now targeting the BRIC countries—Brazil, Russia, India, and China—which are fast-growing developing economies with rapidly increasing buying power.

Countries can also be segmented by *political and legal factors* such as the type and stability of government, receptivity to foreign firms, monetary regulations, and amount of bureaucracy. *Cultural factors* can also be used, grouping markets according to common languages, religions, values and attitudes, customs, and behavioral patterns.

Segmenting international markets based on geographic, economic, political, cultural, and other factors presumes that segments should consist of clusters of countries. However, as new communications technologies, such as satellite TV and online and social media, connect consumers around the world, marketers can define and reach segments of like-minded consumers no matter where in the world they are. Using **intermarket segmentation** (also called **cross-market segmentation**), they

Intermarket (cross-market) segmentation
Forming segments of consumers who have similar needs and buying behaviors even though they are located in different countries.

>> **Intermarket segmentation: Coca-Cola targets teens the world over through universal teen themes, such as music.**

Shirlaine Forrest/Getty Images

form segments of consumers who have similar needs and buying behaviors even though they are located in different countries.

For example, retailer H&M targets fashion-conscious but frugal shoppers in 43 countries with its low-priced, trendy apparel and accessories. >> And Coca-Cola creates special programs to target teens, core consumers of its soft drinks the world over. By 2020, one-third of the world's population—some 2.5 billion people—will be under 18 years of age. Coca-Cola reaches this important market through the universal teen themes, such as music. For example, it joined forces with Spotify to provide a global music network that helps teens discover new music, connect with other music-loving teens, and share their experiences with friends worldwide both online and offline. And it's teen-focused "The Aah Effect" digital campaign serves up "snackable pieces of content"—games, videos, and music—designed to engage the world's teens with the Coca-Cola brand.[15]

Requirements for Effective Segmentation

Clearly, there are many ways to segment a market, but not all segmentations are effective. For example, buyers of table salt could be divided into blonde and brunette customers. But hair color obviously does not affect the purchase of salt. Furthermore, if all salt buyers bought the same amount of salt each month, believed that all salt is the same, and wanted to pay the same price, the company would not benefit from segmenting this market.

To be useful, market segments must be

- *Measurable.* The size, purchasing power, and profiles of the segments can be measured.
- *Accessible.* The market segments can be effectively reached and served.
- *Substantial.* The market segments are large or profitable enough to serve. A segment should be the largest possible homogeneous group worth pursuing with a tailored marketing program. It would not pay, for example, for an automobile manufacturer to develop cars especially for people whose height is greater than seven feet.
- *Differentiable.* The segments are conceptually distinguishable and respond differently to different marketing mix elements and programs. If men and women respond similarly to marketing efforts for soft drinks, they do not constitute separate segments.
- *Actionable.* Effective programs can be designed for attracting and serving the segments. For example, although one small airline identified seven market segments, its staff was too small to develop separate marketing programs for each segment.

 LINKING THE CONCEPTS

Pause for a bit and think about segmentation. How do the companies you do business with employ the segmentation concepts you're reading about here?

- Can you identify specific companies, other than the examples already mentioned, that practice the different types of segmentation just discussed?
- Using the segmentation bases you've just read about, segment the U.S. footwear market. Describe each of the major segments and subsegments. Keep these segments in mind as you read the next section on market targeting.

Author Comment
After dividing the market into segments, it's time to answer that first seemingly simple marketing strategy question we raised in Figure 6.1: Which customers will the company serve?

Market Targeting

Market segmentation reveals the firm's market segment opportunities. The firm now has to evaluate the various segments and decide how many and which segments it can serve best. We now look at how companies evaluate and select target segments.

Evaluating Market Segments

In evaluating different market segments, a firm must look at three factors: segment size and growth, segment structural attractiveness, and company objectives and resources. First, a company wants to select segments that have the right size and growth characteristics. But "right size and growth" is a relative matter. The largest, fastest-growing segments are not always the most attractive ones for every company. Smaller companies may lack the skills and resources needed to serve larger segments. Or they may find these segments too competitive. Such companies may target segments that are smaller and less attractive, in an absolute sense, but that are potentially more profitable for them.

The company also needs to examine major structural factors that affect long-run segment attractiveness.[16] For example, a segment is less attractive if it already contains many strong and aggressive *competitors* or if it is easy for *new entrants* to come into the segment. The existence of many actual or potential *substitute products* may limit prices and the profits that can be earned in a segment. The relative *power of buyers* also affects segment attractiveness. Buyers with strong bargaining power relative to sellers will try to force prices down, demand more services, and set competitors against one another—all at the expense of seller profitability. Finally, a segment may be less attractive if it contains *powerful suppliers* that can control prices or reduce the quality or quantity of ordered goods and services.

Even if a segment has the right size and growth and is structurally attractive, the company must consider its own objectives and resources. Some attractive segments can be dismissed quickly because they do not mesh with the company's long-run objectives. Or the company may lack the skills and resources needed to succeed in an attractive segment. For example, the economy segment of the automobile market is large and growing. But given its objectives and resources, it would make little sense for luxury-performance carmaker Mercedes-Benz to enter this segment. A company should only enter segments in which it can create superior customer value and gain advantages over its competitors.

Selecting Target Market Segments

After evaluating different segments, the company must decide which and how many segments it will target. A **target market** consists of a set of buyers who share common needs or characteristics that the company decides to serve. Market targeting can be carried out at several different levels. >> **Figure 6.2** shows that companies can target very broadly (*undifferentiated marketing*), very narrowly (*micromarketing*), or somewhere in between (*differentiated or concentrated marketing*).

Undifferentiated Marketing

Using an **undifferentiated marketing** (or **mass marketing**) strategy, a firm might decide to ignore market segment differences and target the whole market with one offer. Such a

Target market
A set of buyers sharing common needs or characteristics that the company decides to serve.

Undifferentiated (mass) marketing
A market-coverage strategy in which a firm decides to ignore market segment differences and go after the whole market with one offer.

This figure covers a broad range of targeting strategies, from mass marketing (virtually no targeting) to individual marketing (customizing products and programs to individual customers). An example of individual marketing: At mymms.com you can order a batch of M&M's with your face and personal message printed on each little candy.

Targeting broadly

Undifferentiated (mass) marketing → Differentiated (segmented) marketing → Concentrated (niche) marketing → Micromarketing (local or individual marketing)

Targeting narrowly

>> **Figure 6.2 Market-Targeting Strategies**

strategy focuses on what is *common* in the needs of consumers rather than on what is *different*. The company designs a product and a marketing program that will appeal to the largest number of buyers.

As noted earlier in the chapter, most modern marketers have strong doubts about this strategy. Difficulties arise in developing a product or brand that will satisfy all consumers. Moreover, mass marketers often have trouble competing with more-focused firms that do a better job of satisfying the needs of specific segments and niches.

Differentiated Marketing

Differentiated (segmented) marketing
A market-coverage strategy in which a firm decides to target several market segments and designs separate offers for each.

Using a **differentiated marketing** (or **segmented marketing**) strategy, a firm decides to target several market segments and designs separate offers for each. For example, P&G markets at least six different laundry detergent brands in the United States (Tide, Gain, Cheer, Era, Dreft, and Bold), which compete with each other on supermarket shelves. Then P&G further segments each detergent brand to serve even narrower niches. ≫ For example, you can buy any of dozens of versions of Tide—from Tide Original, Tide Coldwater, or Tide Pods to Tide Free & Gentle, Tide Vivid White + Bright, Tide Colorguard, Tide plus Febreze, or Tide with a Touch of Downy.

By offering product and marketing variations to segments, companies hope for higher sales and a stronger position within each market segment. Developing a stronger position within several segments creates more total sales than undifferentiated marketing across all segments. Thanks to its differentiated approach, P&G is really cleaning up in the $15 billion U.S. laundry detergent market. Incredibly, by itself, the Tide family of brands captures a 38 percent share of all North American detergent sales; the Gain brand pulls in another 15 percent. Even more incredible, all P&G detergent brands combined capture a 60 percent U.S. market share.[17]

≫ **Differentiated marketing: P&G markets multiple laundry detergent brands, then further segments each brand to service even narrower niches. As a result, it's really cleaning up in the U.S. laundry detergent market, with an almost 60 percent market share.**

© Torontonian/Alamy Stock Photo

But differentiated marketing also increases the costs of doing business. A firm usually finds it more expensive to develop and produce, say, 10 units of 10 different products than 100 units of a single product. Developing separate marketing plans for separate segments requires extra marketing research, forecasting, sales analysis, promotion planning, and channel management. And trying to reach different market segments with different advertising campaigns increases promotion costs. Thus, the company must weigh increased sales against increased costs when deciding on a differentiated marketing strategy.

Concentrated Marketing

Concentrated (niche) marketing
A market-coverage strategy in which a firm goes after a large share of one or a few segments or niches.

When using a **concentrated marketing** (or **niche marketing**) strategy, instead of going after a small share of a large market, a firm goes after a large share of one or a few smaller segments or niches. For example, Whole Foods Market has little more than 400 stores and about $14 billion in sales, compared with goliaths such as Kroger (more than 2,600 stores and sales of $98 billion) and Walmart (more than 11,000 stores and sales of $476 billion).[18] Yet, over the past five years, the smaller, more upscale retailer has grown faster and more profitably than either of its giant rivals. Whole Foods thrives by catering to affluent customers who the Walmarts of the world can't serve well, offering them "organic, natural, and gourmet foods, all swaddled in Earth Day politics." In fact, a typical Whole Foods customer is more likely to boycott the local Walmart than to shop at it.

Through concentrated marketing, the firm achieves a strong market position because of its greater knowledge of consumer needs in the niches it serves and the special reputation it acquires. It can market more *effectively* by fine-tuning its products, prices, and programs to the needs of carefully defined segments. It can also market more *efficiently*, targeting its products or services, channels, and communications programs toward only consumers that it can serve best and most profitably.

Niching lets smaller companies focus their limited resources on serving niches that may be unimportant to or overlooked by larger competitors. Many companies start as nichers to get a foothold against larger, more resourceful competitors and then grow into broader competitors. For example, Southwest Airlines began by serving intrastate, no-frills commuters in Texas but is now one of the nation's largest airlines. And Enterprise Rent-A-Car began by building a network of neighborhood offices rather than competing with Hertz and Avis in airport locations. Enterprise is now the nation's largest car rental company.

Today, the low cost of setting up shop on the Internet makes it even more profitable to serve seemingly small niches. Small businesses, in particular, are realizing riches from serving niches on the Web. >> Consider online women's fashion retailer Stitch Fix:[19]

> Stitch Fix offers affordable personal styling services online to busy women on the go. It positions itself as "Your partner in personal style." Although "personal service" and "online" might seem a contradiction, Stitch Fix pulls it off with a team of more than 1,500 personal stylists who apply a sophisticated algorithm to determine each customer's unique sense of style. A customer begins by filling out a detailed style profile that goes far beyond the usual sizing charts. It probes personal preferences with questions such as "What do you like to flaunt?" and "How adventurous do you want your Fix selections to be?" (One answer choice: "Frequently: Adventure is my middle name, bring it on!") The customer also rates photo montages of different fashions and can even submit links to her own Pinterest pages or other social media.
>
> Combining the algorithm with large doses of human judgment (the stylist may completely override the algorithm), the personal stylist assembles and ships the customer's first fashion "Fix"—a box containing five clothing or accessory items pegged to the customer's special tastes. "Our professional stylists will pick out items they think you'll love—sometimes a little out of your comfort zone, but that's part of the fun," says the company. The customer keeps what she likes and returns the rest, along with detailed feedback. The first Fix is the hardest because the stylist and algorithm are still learning. But after that, the Stitch Fix experience becomes downright addictive for many shoppers. Thanks to the power and personalization qualities of the Internet, Stitch Fix is attracting attention and growing fast. The online nicher has inspired a virtual army of pro-Stitch Fix blog and social media posters, and its revenues have skyrocketed.

>> **Concentrated marketing: Thanks to the power and personalization characteristics of online marketing, online women's fashion retailer Stitch Fix is attracting attention and growing fast.**

STITCH FIX and FIX are trademarks of Stitch Fix, Inc.

Concentrated marketing can be highly profitable. At the same time, it involves higher-than-normal risks. Companies that rely on one or a few segments for all of their business will suffer greatly if the segment turns sour. Or larger competitors may decide to enter the same segment with greater resources. In fact, many large companies develop or acquire niche brands of their own. For example, Coca-Cola's Venturing and Emerging Brands unit markets a cooler full of niche beverages. Its brands include Honest Tea (the nation's number-one organic bottled tea brand), NOS (an energy drink popular among auto enthusiasts), FUZE (a fusion of tea, fruit, and other flavors), Zico (pure premium coconut water), Odwalla (natural beverage and bars that "bring goodness to your life"), Core Power (milk-based protein drink), and many others. Such brands let Coca-Cola compete effectively in smaller, specialized markets, and some will grow into future powerhouse brands.[20]

Micromarketing

Differentiated and concentrated marketers tailor their offers and marketing programs to meet the needs of various market segments and niches. At the same time, however, they do not customize their offers to each individual customer. **Micromarketing** is the practice of tailoring products and marketing programs to suit the tastes of specific individuals and locations. Rather than seeing a customer in every individual, micromarketers see the individual in every customer. Micromarketing includes *local marketing* and *individual marketing*.

Micromarketing
Tailoring products and marketing programs to the needs and wants of specific individuals and local customer segments; it includes *local marketing* and *individual marketing*.

Local marketing
Tailoring brands and marketing to the needs and wants of local customer segments—cities, neighborhoods, and even specific stores.

Local Marketing. **Local marketing** involves tailoring brands and promotions to the needs and wants of local customers. For example, Marriott's Renaissance Hotels has rolled out its Navigator program, which hyper-localizes guest experiences at each of its 155 lifestyle hotels around the world:[21]

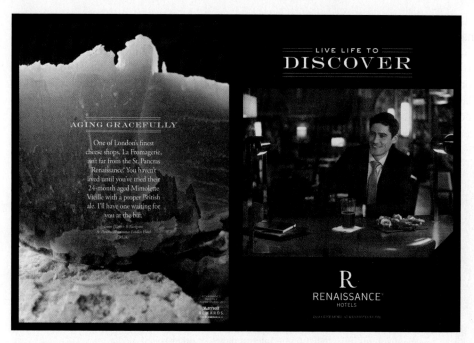

>> **Geographic segmentation:** Marriott's Renaissance Hotels' Navigators and "Live Life to Discover" programs help guests to experience "the hidden gems around the unique neighborhood of each hotel through the eyes of those who know it best."

Renaissance Hotels/Marriott International/Marriott Rewards

Renaissance Hotels' Navigator program puts a personal and local face on each location by "micro-localizing" recommendations for guests' food, shopping, entertainment, and cultural experiences at each destination. The program is anchored by on-site Renaissance Hotels "Navigators" at each location. Whether it's Omar Bennett, a restaurant-loving Brooklynite at the Renaissance New York Times Square Hotel, or James Elliott at the St. Pancras Renaissance London Hotel, a history buff and local pub expert, Navigators are extensively trained locals who are deeply passionate about the destination and often have a personal connection to the locale. >> Based on their own personal experiences and ongoing research, they work with guests personally to help them experience "the hidden gems throughout the neighborhood of each hotel through the eyes of those who know it best."

In addition, Renaissance Hotels engages locals in each city to participate by inviting them to follow their local Navigator via social media as well as adding their own favorites to the system, creating each hotel's own version of Yelp. Navigators then cull through submitted tips and feature the best recommendations alongside their own for sharing within the hotel lobby or on its Web, mobile, and social media channels. Since introducing the hyper-localized Navigator program as part of Renaissance Hotels' "Live Life to Discover" campaign two years ago, the hotel's Web site traffic has grown more than 80 percent, Facebook Likes have exploded from 40,000 to more than 970,000, and Twitter followers have surged from 5,000 to 100,000.

Advances in communications technology have given rise to new high-tech versions of location-based marketing. Thanks to the explosion in smartphones and tablets that integrate geo-location technology, companies can now track consumers' whereabouts closely and engage them on the go with localized deals and information fast, wherever they may be. It's called *SoLoMo (social+local+mobile)* marketing. Services such as Foursquare and Shopkick and retailers ranging from REI and Starbucks to Walgreens and Macy's have jumped onto the SoLoMo bandwagon, primarily in the form of smartphone and tablet apps. Consider Shopkick:[22]

Mobile app Shopkick excels at SoLoMo. It sends special offers and rewards to shoppers simply for checking into client stores such as Target, Macy's, Best Buy, Old Navy, or Crate & Barrel and buying brands from Shopkick partners such as P&G, Unilever, Disney, Kraft, and L'Oréal. When shoppers are near a participating store, the Shopkick app on their phone picks up a signal from the store and spits out store coupons, deal alerts, and product information. When Shopkickers walk into their favorite retail stores, the app automatically checks them in and they rack up rewards points or "kicks." If they buy something, they get even more kicks. Users can use their kicks for discounted or free merchandise of their own choosing. Shopkick helps users get the most out of their efforts by mapping out potential kicks in a given geographic area. Shopkick has grown quickly to become one of the nation's top shopping apps, with more than 6 million users than and 200 brand partners.

Local marketing has some drawbacks, however. It can drive up manufacturing and marketing costs by reducing the economies of scale. It can also create logistics problems as companies try to meet the varied requirements of different local markets. Still, as companies face increasingly fragmented markets and as new supporting digital technologies develop, the advantages of local marketing often outweigh the drawbacks.

Individual marketing

Tailoring products and marketing programs to the needs and preferences of individual customers.

Individual Marketing. In the extreme, micromarketing becomes **individual marketing**—tailoring products and marketing programs to the needs and preferences of individual customers. Individual marketing has also been labeled one-to-one marketing, mass customization, and markets-of-one marketing.

The widespread use of mass marketing has obscured the fact that for centuries consumers were served as individuals: The tailor custom-made a suit, the cobbler designed shoes for an individual, and the cabinetmaker made furniture to order. Today, new technologies are permitting many companies to return to customized marketing. Detailed databases, robotic production and flexible manufacturing, and interactive technologies such as smartphones and online and social media have combined to foster mass customization. *Mass customization* is the process by which firms interact one to one with masses of customers to design products, services, and marketing programs tailor-made to individual needs.

Individual marketing has made relationships with customers more important than ever. Just as mass production was the marketing principle of the twentieth century, interactive marketing is becoming a marketing principle for the twenty-first century. The world appears to be coming full circle—from the good old days when customers were treated as individuals to mass marketing when nobody knew your name and then back again.

Companies these days are hyper-customizing everything from food to artwork, earphones, sneakers, and motorcycles:[23]

> **Individual marketing: The PUMA Factory sneaker customization Web site lets customers tailor their PUMA shoes to taste. "You know what works—what styles, what textures, what colors. Customize your sneakers whatever way you want."**
PUMA SE

At mymms.com, candy lovers can buy M&M's embossed with images of their kids or pets; at mixmyown.com, nutrition-minded folks can create their own healthy cereal mix. JH Audio in Orlando makes music earphones based on molds of customers' ears to provide optimized fit and better and safer sound. The company even laser prints designs on the tiny ear buds—some people request a kid for each ear; others prefer a dog. >> The PUMA Factory sneaker customization Web site lets customers pick their own fabrics and tailor their PUMA shoes to taste. "It's a place for you to match your shoes to your favorite team or oldest t-shirt, paint by numbers, and innovate outside the lines," says PUMA. On a much larger scale, Harley-Davidson's H-D1 customization program lets customers go online, design their own Harley, and get it in as little as four weeks. It invites customers to explore some 8,000 ways to create their own masterpiece. "You dream it. We build it," says the company.

Beyond customizing products, marketers also customize their marketing messages to engage customers on a one-to-one basis. For example, Nike collected data on its most enthusiastic customers, those who train using FuelBands and apps such as Nike+ Running. It then used the data to create 100,000 customized animated videos based on each individual's actual workout activities. For example, one video might feature an animation of a person in Los Angeles running past the Hollywood sign; another might show a New Yorker running in the rain along the East River. Nike then emailed the unique customized videos to each of the 100,000 Nike+ users, challenging them to achieve new heights in the coming year. The videos not only engaged Nike's biggest fans, they also spread to the broader Nike community. "These are some of the most social people on the planet," says one campaign manager. "They share like crazy. So that becomes a pretty awesome flagship marketing move for Nike."[24]

Choosing a Targeting Strategy

Companies need to consider many factors when choosing a market-targeting strategy. Which strategy is best depends on the company's resources. When the firm's resources are limited, concentrated marketing makes the most sense. The best strategy also depends on the degree of product variability. Undifferentiated marketing is more suited for uniform products, such as grapefruit or steel. Products that can vary in design, such as cameras and cars, are more suited to differentiation or concentration. The product's life-cycle stage also must be considered. When a firm introduces a new product, it may be practical to launch one version only, and undifferentiated marketing or concentrated marketing may make the most sense. In the mature stage of the product life cycle, however, differentiated marketing often makes more sense.

Another factor is *market variability*. If most buyers have the same tastes, buy the same amounts, and react the same way to marketing efforts, undifferentiated marketing is appropriate. Finally, *competitors' marketing strategies* should be considered. When competitors use differentiated or concentrated marketing, undifferentiated marketing can be suicidal. Conversely, when competitors use undifferentiated marketing, a firm can gain an advantage by using differentiated or concentrated marketing, focusing on the needs of buyers in specific segments.

Socially Responsible Target Marketing

Smart targeting helps companies become more efficient and effective by focusing on the segments that they can satisfy best and most profitably. Targeting also benefits consumers—companies serve specific groups of consumers with offers carefully tailored to their needs. However, target marketing sometimes generates controversy and concern. The biggest issues usually involve the targeting of vulnerable or disadvantaged consumers with controversial or potentially harmful products.

For example, fast-food chains have generated controversy over the years by their attempts to target inner-city minority consumers. They've been accused of pitching their high-fat, salt-laden fare to low-income, urban residents who are much more likely than suburbanites to be heavy consumers. Similarly, big banks and mortgage lenders have been criticized for targeting consumers in poor urban areas with attractive adjustable-rate home mortgages that they can't really afford.

Children are seen as an especially vulnerable audience. Marketers in a wide range of industries—from cereal, soft drinks, and fast food to toys and fashion—have been criticized for their marketing efforts directed toward children. Critics worry that enticing premium offers and high-powered advertising appeals will overwhelm children's defenses. In recent years, for instance, McDonald's has been criticized by various health advocates and parent groups concerned that its popular Happy Meals offers—featuring trinkets and other items tied in with popular children's movies and TV shows—create a too-powerful connection between children and the often fat- and calorie-laden meals. Some critics have even asked McDonald's to retire its iconic Ronald McDonald character. McDonald's has responded by putting the Happy Meal on a diet, cutting the overall calorie count by 20 percent, adding fruit to every meal, and promoting Happy Meals only with milk, water, and juice. And for a two-week span during each of the past two years, McDonald's has replaced the toys in its Happy Meals with children's books.[25]

The digital era may make children even more vulnerable to targeted marketing messages. In all, according to one source, kids ages 2 to 11 see an average of 25,600 ads a year.[26] Traditional child-directed TV and print ads usually contain obvious pitches that are easily detected and controlled by parents. However, marketing in digital media may be subtly embedded within the content and viewed by children on personal, small-screen devices that are beyond even the most watchful parent's eye. Such marketing might take the form of immersive "advergames"—video games specifically designed to engage children with products. Or they might consist of embedded ads, quizzes, or product placements that let marketers cross-promote branded products, TV shows, popular characters, or other marketable entities.

>> **Socially responsible targeting:** McDonald's has responded to the concerns of parents and children's health advocates by putting the Happy Meal on a diet, cutting the calorie count by 20 percent, adding fruit, and promoting Happy Meals only with milk, water, and juice.

Michael Neelon/Alamy

For example, free video games offered at Barbie.com let children help Barbie "build 'n style" her "perf mansion" or play "princess charm school games" with her. At Nickelodeon's The Club—an "online virtual world for kids"—young children can create an avatar and immerse themselves in "Super Spongy Square Games" with SpongeBob SquarePants or browse the Power Rangers Samurai store. Kraft's free "Jiggle-It" app engages kids by letting them watch a JELL-O cube dance to their favorite songs; the brand's "Dinner, Not Art" app lets them create digital macaroni art, helping to promote the company's Kraft Macaroni and Cheese. Some watchers see such marketing as adding value for both the children and the marketers—promoting child creativity and entertainment while engaging the child in brand-related experiences. Others, however, worry that it constitutes "stealth marketing" that takes advantage of children who can't yet tell the difference between commercial and entertainment or educational content.[27]

To encourage responsible children's advertising, the Children's Advertising Review Unit, the advertising industry's self-regulatory agency, has published extensive children's advertising guidelines that recognize the special needs of child audiences. Still, critics feel that more should have been done, especially concerning online and digital marketing. Some have even called for a complete ban on advertising to children.

Not all attempts to target children, minorities, or other special segments draw such criticism. In fact, most provide benefits to targeted consumers. For example, Pantene markets Relaxed and Natural hair products to women of color. Samsung markets the Jitterbug, an easy-to-use phone, directly to seniors who need a simpler mobile phone with bigger buttons, large screen text, and a louder speaker. And Colgate makes a large selection of toothbrush shapes and toothpaste flavors for children—from Colgate SpongeBob SquarePants Mild Bubble Fruit toothpaste to Colgate Dora the Explorer character toothbrushes. Such products help make tooth brushing more fun and get children to brush longer and more often.

More broadly, the growth of the Internet, smartphones, and other carefully targeted direct media has raised fresh concerns about potential targeting abuses. The Internet and mobile marketing allow more precise targeting, letting the makers of questionable products or deceptive advertisers zero in on the most vulnerable audiences. Unscrupulous marketers can now send tailor-made, deceptive messages by email directly to millions of unsuspecting consumers. For example, the Federal Bureau of Investigation's Internet Crime Complaint Center Web site alone received more than 263,000 complaints last year.[28]

Today's marketers are also using sophisticated analytical techniques to track consumers' digital movements and to build detailed customer profiles containing highly personal information. Such profiles can then be used to hypertarget individual consumers with personalized brand messages and offers. Hypertargeting can benefit both marketers and consumers, getting the right brand information into the hands of the right customers. However, taken too far or used wrongly, hypertargeting can harm consumers more than benefit them. Marketers must use these new targeting tools responsibly (see Marketing at Work 6.1).

Thus, in target marketing, the issue is not really *who* is targeted but rather *how* and for *what*. Controversies arise when marketers attempt to profit at the expense of targeted segments—when they unfairly target vulnerable segments or target them with questionable products or tactics. Socially responsible marketing calls for segmentation and targeting that serve not just the interests of the company but also the interests of those targeted.

 ## LINKING THE CONCEPTS

It's time to pause and take stock.

- At the last Linking the Concepts, you segmented the U.S. footwear market. Refer to Figure 6.2 and select two companies that serve the footwear market. Describe their segmentation and targeting strategies. Can you come up with a company that targets many different segments versus another that focuses on only one or a few segments?
- How does each company you chose differentiate its market offering and image? Has each done a good job of establishing this differentiation in the minds of targeted consumers? The final section in this chapter deals with such positioning issues.

MARKETING AT WORK   6.1

Hypertargeting: Walking a Fine Line between Serving Customers and Stalking Them

How well does your smartphone know you? What stories could your laptop tell? In truth, your digital devices probably know more about you than you know about yourself. Smartphones and other digital equipment have become fundamental extensions of our lives. Whatever you do—at work, at play, socializing, shopping—your phone, tablet, laptop, or desktop is almost always a part of the action. These devices go where you go, entertain you, connect you with friends, take you browsing and shopping, feed you news and information, and listen in on even your most intimate voice, text, and email conversations. They know where you live, with whom you interact, what you search for, what you buy, and what you do for fun. And more and more, these devices are sharing all that personal information with marketers, who in turn use it to create hypertargeted brand messages and promotions crafted just for you.

In the old days (really only a year or two ago) marketers gathered information about consumers' digital doings using cookies—those small bits of data sent from Web sites or third parties and stored in users' Web browsers. But cookies don't work with mobile devices and apps. So as mobile and app usage has soared and as cookie-blocking technologies have improved, marketers have sought new ways to track consumers as they move about digitally.

As a result, companies have now developed sophisticated new ways to extract intimate insights about consumers that border on wizardry. For example, a string of high-tech mobile advertising service start-ups—with intriguing names such as Drawbridge, Flurry, Velti, and SessionM—are developing technologies that can put together amazingly detailed profiles of smartphone users—who they are, where they go, what they do, whom they know, and what they like and don't like. For brands and marketers, such information is pure gold.

These mobile advertising companies use different methods to track consumers. Drawbridge creates partnerships with online publishers and advertising exchanges to track online activity—every time a user visits a Web site or uses a mobile app, the partners send a notification to Drawbridge. In contrast, Flurry works with publishers to embed its software directly into their apps—so far, its software can be found in 350,000 apps on

more than 1.2 billion devices. The companies then apply statistical modeling to analyze the mountain of data they collect, assign identifiers to individual users, and ferret out user characteristics and behavior patterns.

And here's the real wizardry: By tracking individual digital activity, the services can link several different devices—a smartphone, home computer, work computer, and tablet—to the same person, even if the devices themselves aren't connected. Every person's data profile is unique—kind of like a fingerprint. So Drawbridge, Flurry, and the other services can use the profiles to identify individuals no matter what device they are using.

For example, suppose that you regularly check your Snapchat Snaps in bed every morning from your smartphone. Then, while eating breakfast at the kitchen table, you use your laptop to browse the latest entertainment news on TMZ and to check a few social media sites. Between your morning classes, you use your phone to text friends and your tablet to do a little online browsing. In the afternoon, during breaks at your job, you use a company desktop to monitor your favorite sites and make a purchase at Amazon.com. At home that evening, you catch up on your favorite TV shows, exchange messages with friends, and do some online research for a class project, jumping back and forth between your phone, tablet, and laptop.

>> Hypertargeting: Marketers have developed sophisticated new ways to extract intimate insights about consumers that border on wizardry. But hypertargeting walks a fine line between "serving" consumers and "stalking" them.

Andrew Bret Wallis/Photographer's Choice RF/Getty Images

The entire time, chances are good that the information brokers are peering over your shoulder. Based on your unique pattern of browsing and carousing, one of the data services may well have identified your unique digital fingerprint. Not surprisingly, when you're signed into Google, Facebook, or Amazon.com, those companies can track your activities on their sites across devices. But companies like Drawbridge, once they've figured you out, can follow you across all activities and devices even if you aren't logged in.

This uncanny ability to follow unique users across devices lets mobile advertising services like Drawbridge and Flurry help marketers craft mobile ads and promotions that reach carefully targeted users with exactly the right message at just the right moment. So if you use your work computer to check on airline tickets to travel home for the holidays, that night you might see an Expedia ad on your phone offering a low price on a ticket for that same route and date. Drawbridge can define user profiles so precisely that it can often distinguish between different family members using the same devices and then target ads accordingly. Such targeting accuracy has attracted a host of blue chip brands to Drawbridge and similar services, from Expedia, Ford, and Fidelity Investments to Quiznos and Groupon.

Marketers argue that all of this up-close-and-personal information and hypertargeting better serve both customers and a company. Customers receive tailored, relevant information and offers from brands that really interest them. However, many consumer privacy advocates are concerned that such intimate information in the hands of unscrupulous marketers or other parties could result in more harm or concern than benefit to consumers. Even responsible marketers worry that customers will be put off by what they view less as "getting to know me better to serve me better" and more as "stalking" and "profiling." Companies like Drawbridge are careful in how they position their services. They don't call it tracking. "Tracking is a dirty word," says a Drawbridge executive. Instead, Drawbridge is "observing your behaviors and connecting your profile to mobile devices," he says elliptically. Drawbridge's CEO talks more grandly about "trying to democratize identity so that rivals like Facebook aren't the only firms with access to consumers."

Some information seems far too sensitive for use in hypertargeting. For example, targeting based on health, financial, or personal activity profiles could cause consumers embarrassment, discomfort, or damage. Consider revelations about certain prescription drug medications, financial planning or debt counseling, or private leisure activities. For instance, imagine having a taboo ad pop up on your work computer while your boss is looking over your shoulder or while you are making a presentation to colleagues. Or consider that someone targeting customized ads based on your travel plans also knows when your home will likely be unattended. And who's to protect the privacy of children and other vulnerable groups and shield them from the advances of overzealous marketers? Although most consumers are willing to share some personal information if it means getting better service or deals, many consumers worry that marketers might go too far.

Thus, with today's super-sophisticated behavioral targeting tools, marketers walk a fine line between serving consumers and stalking them. Most marketers want to do the right thing with hypertargeting—focusing on the right customers with personalized offers that meet their exacting needs. They want to build trusted relationships with customers by serving them, not harming them. But responsible hypertargeting calls for proactively guarding the rights and sensitivities of those being targeted. Marketers who cross the line risk the wrath of advocates, legislators, and consumers themselves.

Sources: Kate Kay, "Three Big Privacy Changes to Plan for in 2014," *Advertising Age,* January 3, 2014, http://adage.com/print/290885/; Claire Cain Miller and Somini Sengupta, "Selling Secrets of Phone Users to Advertisers," *New York Times,* October 6, 2013, p. A1; George Fox, "When Online Marketers Target Mobile Device Users, Nothing's Out of Bounds," *ECN Magazine,* October 28, 2013, www.ecnmag.com/blogs/2013/10/when-online-marketers-target-mobile-device-users-nothing's-out-bounds; Katy Bachman, "FTC's Ad Regulator Plans to Focus Heavily on Native and Mobile," *Adweek,* January 5, 2014, www.adweek.com/print/154693; "12 Stars of Ad Tech Who Are Building the Future of the Industry Right Now," *Adweek,* November 2, 2014, www.adweek.com/news-gallery/advertising-branding/12-stars-ad-tech-who-are-building-future-industry-right-now-161164; and www.flurry.com/solutions/analytics and www.drawbrid.ge, accessed September 2015.

Author Comment

While a company is answering the first simple-sounding question (Which customers will we serve?), it must be asking the second question (How will we serve them?).

Differentiation and Positioning

Beyond deciding which segments of the market it will target, the company must decide on a *value proposition*—how it will create differentiated value for targeted segments and what positions it wants to occupy in those segments. A **product position** is the way a product is *defined by consumers* on important attributes—the place the product occupies in consumers' minds relative to competing products. Products are made in factories, but brands happen in the minds of consumers.

Method laundry detergent is positioned as a smarter, easier, and greener detergent; Tide is "a washing miracle," an all-purpose, heavy-duty family detergent that gets out grime and tough stains. At IHOP, you "Come hungry. Leave happy"; at Buffalo Wild Wings it's "Wings. Beer. Sports." In the automobile market, the Honda Fit and Nissan Versa are positioned on economy, Mercedes and Cadillac on luxury, and Porsche and BMW on

Product position

How a product is defined by consumers on important attributes—the place a product occupies in consumers' minds relative to competing products.

>> Positioning: IKEA does more than just sell affordable home furnishings; it's the "Life improvement store."

Used with the permission of Inter IKEA Systems B.V.

performance. Home-improvement store Lowe's helps you "Never stop improving." >> And IKEA does more than just sell affordable home furnishings; it's the "Life improvement store."

Consumers are overloaded with information about products and services. They cannot reevaluate products every time they make a buying decision. To simplify the buying process, consumers organize products, services, and companies into categories and "position" them in their minds. A product's position is the complex set of perceptions, impressions, and feelings that consumers have for the product compared with competing products.

Consumers position products with or without the help of marketers. But marketers do not want to leave their products' positions to chance. They must *plan* positions that will give their products the greatest advantage in selected target markets, and they must design marketing mixes to create these planned positions.

Positioning Maps

In planning their differentiation and positioning strategies, marketers often prepare *perceptual positioning maps* that show consumer perceptions of their brands versus those of competing products on important buying dimensions. >> **Figure 6.3** shows a positioning map for the U.S. large luxury SUV market.[29] The position of each circle on the map indicates the brand's perceived positioning on two dimensions: price and orientation (luxury versus performance). The size of each circle indicates the brand's relative market share.

Thus, customers view the market-leading Cadillac Escalade as a moderately priced, large, luxury SUV with a balance of luxury and performance. The Escalade is positioned on urban luxury, and, in its case, "performance" probably means power and safety performance. You'll find no mention of off-road adventuring in an Escalade ad.

By contrast, the Range Rover and the Land Cruiser are positioned on luxury with nuances of off-road performance. For example, the Toyota Land Cruiser began in 1951 as a four-wheel-drive, jeep-like vehicle designed to conquer the world's most grueling terrains and climates. In recent years, the Land Cruiser has retained this adventure and performance positioning but with luxury added. Its Web site brags of "legendary off-road capability," with off-road technologies such as an Acoustic Control Induction System to get the most out of the RPMs, "so you can make molehills out of mountains." Despite its

>> **Figure 6.3 Positioning Map: Large Luxury SUVs**

Source: Based on data provided by WardsAuto.com and Edmunds.com, 2015.

The location of each circle shows where consumers position a brand on two dimensions: price and luxury-performance orientation. The size of each circle indicates the brand's relative market share in the segment. Thus, Toyota's Land Cruiser is a niche brand that is perceived to be relatively expensive and more performance oriented.

- Cadillac Escalade
- Infiniti QX
- Lexus LX570
- Lincoln Navigator
- Toyota Land Cruiser
- Land Rover Range Rover

ruggedness, however, the company notes that "its Bluetooth hands-free technology, DVD entertainment, and a sumptuous interior have softened its edges."

Choosing a Differentiation and Positioning Strategy

Some firms find it easy to choose a differentiation and positioning strategy. For example, a firm well known for quality in certain segments will go after this position in a new segment if there are enough buyers seeking quality. But in many cases, two or more firms will go after the same position. Then each will have to find other ways to set itself apart. Each firm must differentiate its offer by building a unique bundle of benefits that appeal to a substantial group within the segment.

Above all else, a brand's positioning must serve the needs and preferences of well-defined target markets. For example, as discussed in the chapter-opening story, although both Dunkin' Donuts and Starbucks are coffee and snack shops, they target very different customers who want very different things from their favorite coffee seller. Starbucks targets more upscale professionals with more high-brow positioning. In contrast, Dunkin' Donuts targets the "average Joe" with a decidedly more low-brow, "everyman" kind of positioning. Yet each brand succeeds because it creates just the right value proposition for its unique mix of customers.

The differentiation and positioning task consists of three steps: identifying a set of differentiating competitive advantages on which to build a position, choosing the right competitive advantages, and selecting an overall positioning strategy. The company must then effectively communicate and deliver the chosen position to the market.

Identifying Possible Value Differences and Competitive Advantages

To build profitable relationships with target customers, marketers must understand customer needs and deliver more customer value better than competitors do. To the extent that a company can differentiate and position itself as providing superior customer value, it gains **competitive advantage**.

Competitive advantage

An advantage over competitors gained by offering greater customer value, either by having lower prices or providing more benefits that justify higher prices.

But solid positions cannot be built on empty promises. If a company positions its product as *offering* the best quality and service, it must actually differentiate the product so that it *delivers* the promised quality and service. Companies must do much more than simply shout out their positions with slogans and taglines. They must first *live* the slogan. For example, online shoes and accessories seller Zappos' "powered by service" positioning would ring hollow if not backed by truly outstanding customer care. Zappos aligns its entire organization and all of its people around providing the best possible customer service. The online seller's number-one core value: "Deliver WOW through service."[30]

To find points of differentiation, marketers must think through the customer's entire experience with the company's product or service. An alert company can find ways to differentiate itself at every customer contact point. In what specific ways can a company differentiate itself or its market offer? It can differentiate along the lines of *product, services, channels, people,* or *image.*

Through *product differentiation,* brands can be differentiated on features, performance, or style and design. Thus, premium audio brand Bose positions its audio products on the innovative, high-quality listening experiences it gives users. Bose promises "better sound through research." And SodaStream positions itself as an alternative to bottled carbonated waters and soft drinks. It promises a simple, convenient, ecofriendly process for turning home tap water into fresh, homemade soda with no heavy bottles to carry, store, and recycle. SodaStream gives you "Smart. Simple. Soda."

Beyond differentiating its physical product, a firm can also differentiate the services that accompany the product. Some companies gain *services differentiation* through speedy, convenient service. ⟫ Jimmy John's doesn't just offer fast food; its gourmet sandwiches come "Freaky Fast." Other firms promise high-quality customer service. For example, in an age where customer satisfaction with airline service is in constant decline, Singapore Airlines sets itself apart through extraordinary customer care and the grace of its flight attendants.

>> Services differentiation: Jimmy John's doesn't just offer fast food; its gourmet sandwiches come "Freaky Fast."

Jimmy John's Sandwiches

Firms that practice *channel differentiation* gain competitive advantage through the way they design their channel's coverage, expertise, and performance. Amazon.com and GEICO, for example, set themselves apart with their smooth-functioning direct channels. Companies can also gain a strong competitive advantage through *people differentiation*—hiring and training better people than their competitors do. People differentiation requires that a company select its customer-contact people carefully and train them well. For example, East Coast supermarket chain Wegmans has long been recognized as a customer service champ with a cult-like loyalty among its shoppers. The secret to its extraordinary customer service lies in its carefully selected, superbly trained, happy employees, who personify Wegmans' commitment to customers: "Everyday You Get Our Best." For example, the chain's cashiers aren't allowed to interact with customers until they've had at least 40 hours of training. "Our employees are our number one asset," says the chain's vice president for human resources.[31]

Even when competing offers look the same, buyers may perceive a difference based on company or brand *image differentiation*. A company or brand image should convey a product's distinctive benefits and positioning. Developing a strong and distinctive image calls for creativity and hard work. A company cannot develop an image in the public's mind overnight by using only a few ads. If Ritz-Carlton means quality, this image must be supported by everything the company is, says, and does.

Symbols, such as the McDonald's golden arches, the colorful Google logo, the Twitter bird, the Nike swoosh, or Apple's "bite mark" logo, can provide strong company or brand recognition and image differentiation. The company might build a brand around a famous person, as Nike did with its Michael Jordan, Kobe Bryant, and LeBron James basketball shoe and apparel collections. Some companies even become associated with colors, such as Coca-Cola (red), IBM (blue), or UPS (brown). The chosen symbols, characters, and other image elements must be communicated through advertising that conveys the company's or brand's personality.

Choosing the Right Competitive Advantages

Suppose a company is fortunate enough to discover several potential differentiations that provide competitive advantages. It now must choose the ones on which it will build its positioning strategy. It must decide how many differences to promote and which ones.

How Many Differences to Promote. Many marketers think that companies should aggressively promote only one benefit to the target market. Former advertising executive Rosser Reeves, for example, said a company should develop a *unique selling proposition (USP)* for each brand and stick to it. Each brand should pick an attribute and tout itself as "number one" on that attribute. Buyers tend to remember number one better, especially in this overcommunicated society. Thus, Walmart promotes its unbeatable low prices and Burger King promotes personal choice—"have it your way."

Other marketers think that companies should position themselves on more than one differentiator. This may be necessary if two or more firms are claiming to be best on the same attribute. For example, with its "Expect More. Pay Less." positioning, Targets sets itself apart from Walmart by adding a touch of class to its low prices. >> And Microsoft differentiates its innovative Surface tablet as being both a laptop and tablet in one. It's the "One device for everything in your life"—lighter and thinner than a laptop but with a click-in keyboard and fuller features than competing tablets. It's "Powerful as a laptop, lighter than Air." Microsoft's challenge is to convince buyers that it's one brand can do it all.

Today, in a time when the mass market is fragmenting into many small segments, companies and brands are trying to broaden their positioning strategies to appeal to more segments. Today, in a time when the mass market is fragmenting into many small segments, companies and brands are trying to broaden their positioning strategies to appeal to more segments.

>> **Positioning on multiple competitive advantages: Microsoft's innovative Surface is positioned as "Powerful as a laptop, lighter than Air.**

Microsoft Corporation

Which Differences to Promote. Not all brand differences are meaningful or worthwhile, and each difference has the potential to create company costs as well as customer benefits. A difference is worth establishing to the extent that it satisfies the following criteria:

- *Important.* The difference delivers a highly valued benefit to target buyers.
- *Distinctive.* Competitors do not offer the difference, or the company can offer it in a more distinctive way.
- *Superior.* The difference is superior to other ways that customers might obtain the same benefit.
- *Communicable.* The difference is communicable and visible to buyers.
- *Preemptive.* Competitors cannot easily copy the difference.
- *Affordable.* Buyers can afford to pay for the difference.
- *Profitable.* The company can introduce the difference profitably.

Many companies have introduced differentiations that failed one or more of these tests. When the Westin Stamford Hotel in Singapore once advertised itself as the world's tallest hotel, it was a distinction that was not important to most tourists; in fact, it turned many off. Similarly, Coca-Cola's now classic product failure—New Coke—failed the superiority and importance tests among core Coca-Cola drinkers:

> Extensive blind taste tests showed that 60 percent of all soft drink consumers chose a new, sweeter Coca-Cola formulation over the original Coke, and 52 percent chose it over Pepsi. So the brand dropped its original-formula Coke and, with much fanfare, replaced it with New Coke, a sweeter, smoother version. However, in its research, Coca-Cola overlooked the many intangibles that have made Coca-Cola so popular for 125 years. To loyal Coke drinkers, the original beverage stands alongside baseball, apple pie, and the Statue of Liberty as an American institution. As it turns out, Coca-Cola differentiates its brand not just by taste but by tradition. By dropping the original formula, Coca-Cola trampled on the sensitivities of the huge core of loyal Coke drinkers who loved Coke just the way it was. After only three months, the company brought the classic Coke back.

Thus, choosing competitive advantages on which to position a product or service can be difficult, yet such choices are crucial to success. Choosing the right differentiators can help a brand stand out from the pack of competitors.

Selecting an Overall Positioning Strategy

The full positioning of a brand is called the brand's **value proposition**—the full mix of benefits on which a brand is differentiated and positioned. It is the answer to the customer's question "Why should I buy your brand?" BMW's "ultimate driving machine" value proposition hinges on performance but also includes luxury and styling, all for a price that is higher than average but seems fair for this mix of benefits.

>> **Figure 6.4** shows possible value propositions on which a company might position its products. In the figure, the five green cells on the top and right represent winning value propositions—differentiation and positioning that give the company a competitive advantage. The cells at the lower left, however, represent losing value propositions. The center cell represents at best a marginal proposition. In the following sections, we discuss the five winning value propositions: more for more, more for the same, the same for less, less for much less, and more for less.

More for More. *More-for-more* positioning involves providing the most upscale product or service and charging a higher price to cover the higher costs. A more-for-more market offering not only offers higher quality, it also gives prestige to the buyer. It symbolizes status and a loftier lifestyle. Four Seasons hotels, Rolex watches, Starbucks

Value proposition
The full positioning of a brand—the full mix of benefits on which it is differentiated and positioned.

>> Figure 6.4 Possible Value
Propositions

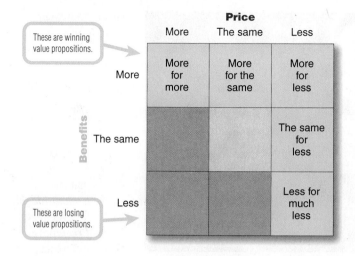

coffee, Louis Vuitton handbags, Mercedes automobiles, SubZero appliances—each claims superior quality, craftsmanship, durability, performance, or style and therefore charges a higher price.

Similarly, the marketers of >> Hearts On Fire diamonds have created a more-for-more niche as "The World's Most Perfectly Cut Diamond." Hearts On Fire diamonds have a unique "hearts and arrow" design. When viewed under magnification from the bottom, a perfect ring of eight hearts appears; from the top comes a perfectly formed Fireburst of light. Hearts On Fire diamonds aren't for everyone, says the company. "Hearts On Fire is for those who expect more and give more in return." The brand commands a 15 to 20 percent price premium over comparable competing diamonds.[32]

Although more-for-more can be profitable, this strategy can also be vulnerable. It often invites imitators who claim the same quality but at a lower price. For example, more-for-more brand Starbucks now faces "gourmet" coffee competitors ranging from Dunkin' Donuts to McDonald's. Also, luxury goods that sell well during good times may be at risk during economic downturns when buyers become more cautious in their spending. The recent gloomy economy hit premium brands, such as Starbucks, the hardest.

More for the Same. A company can attack a competitor's value proposition by positioning its brand as offering more for the same price. For example, Target positions itself as the "upscale discounter." It claims to offer more in terms of store atmosphere, service, stylish merchandise, and classy brand image but at prices comparable to those of Walmart, Kohl's, and other discounters.

The Same for Less. Offering *the same for less* can be a powerful value proposition—everyone likes a good deal. Discount stores such as Walmart and "category killers" such as Best Buy, PetSmart, David's Bridal, and DSW Shoes use this positioning. They don't claim to offer different or better products. Instead, they offer many of the same brands as department stores and specialty stores but at deep discounts based on superior purchasing power and lower-cost operations. Other companies develop imitative but lower-priced brands in an effort to lure customers away from the market leader. For example, Amazon offers a line of Kindle Fire tablets, which sell for less than 40 percent of the price of the Apple iPad or Samsung Galaxy tablet. Amazon claims that it offers "Premium products at non-premium prices."

Less for Much Less. A market almost always exists for products that offer less and therefore cost less. Few people need, want, or can afford "the very

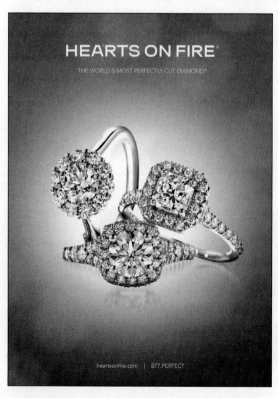

>> More-for-more positioning: Hearts On Fire diamonds have created a more-for-more niche as "The World's Most Perfectly Cut Diamond—for those who expect more and give more in return."

best" in everything they buy. In many cases, consumers will gladly settle for less-than-optimal performance or give up some of the bells and whistles in exchange for a lower price. For example, many travelers seeking lodgings prefer not to pay for what they consider unnecessary extras, such as a pool, an attached restaurant, or mints on the pillow. Hotel chains such as Ramada Limited, Holiday Inn Express, and Motel 6 suspend some of these amenities and charge less accordingly.

Less-for-much-less positioning involves meeting consumers' lower performance or quality requirements at a much lower price. For example, Costco warehouse stores offer less merchandise selection and consistency and much lower levels of service; as a result, they charge rock-bottom prices. And under Spirit Airlines' "Bare Fare" pricing, you don't get much when you fly Spirit. Then again, with its super-cheap fares, you don't pay for what you don't get (see Marketing at Work 6.2).

More for Less. Of course, the winning value proposition would be to offer *more for less*. Many companies claim to do this. And, in the short run, some companies can actually achieve such lofty positions. For example, when it first opened for business, Home Depot had arguably the best product selection, the best service, *and* the lowest prices compared with local hardware stores and other home-improvement chains.

Yet in the long run, companies will find it very difficult to sustain such best-of-both positioning. Offering more usually costs more, making it difficult to deliver on the "for-less" promise. Companies that try to deliver both may lose out to more focused competitors. For example, facing determined competition from Lowe's stores, Home Depot must now decide whether it wants to compete primarily on superior service or on lower prices.

All said, each brand must adopt a positioning strategy designed to serve the needs and wants of its target markets. *More for more* will draw one target market, *less for much less* will draw another, and so on. In any market, there is usually room for many different companies, each successfully occupying different positions. The important thing is that each company must develop its own winning positioning strategy, one that makes the company special to its target consumers.

Developing a Positioning Statement

Positioning statement

A statement that summarizes company or brand positioning using this form: To (target segment and need) our (brand) is (concept) that (point of difference).

Company and brand positioning should be summed up in a **positioning statement**. The statement should follow the form: To (target segment and need) our (brand) is (concept) that (point of difference).[33] >> Here is an example using the popular digital information management application Evernote: "To busy multitaskers who need help remembering things, Evernote is a digital content management application that makes it easy to capture and remember moments and ideas from your everyday life using your computer, phone, tablet, and the Web."

Note that the positioning statement first states the product's membership in a category (digital content management application) and then shows its point of difference from other members of the category (easily capture moments and ideas and remember them later). Evernote helps you "remember everything" by letting you take notes, capture photos, create to-do lists, and record voice reminders and then makes them easy to find and access using just about any device, anywhere—at home, at work, or on the go.

Placing a brand in a specific category suggests similarities that it might

>> Positioning statement: Evernote is positioned as a digital content management application that helps busy people to capture and remember moments and ideas and find them fast later.

Evernote Corporation

MARKETING AT WORK   6.2

Spirit Airlines: Getting Less but Paying Much Less for It

"@SpiritAirlines worst, most devious, nickel-and-diming I've ever experienced. I will NEVER fly with you again. #lessonlearned."

This Tweet, and a flood of similar social media comments posted regularly by dissatisfied Spirit Airlines customers, isn't the kind of feedback most companies want to hear. What's more, adding to such negative social media testimonials, Spirit Airlines also recently earned the dubious distinction of being *Consumer Reports'* lowest-rated airline for the customer experience, receiving one of the lowest-ever overall scores given by the organization.

So Spirit Airlines must be headed down the path to bankruptcy and ruin, right? To the contrary—Spirit is one of the nation's fastest-growing carriers. It fills almost every available seat on every flight. And it turns a healthy profit every quarter—a difficult feat in the up-and-down airline industry. How does Spirit Airlines do it? By mastering the art and science of its less-for-much-less value proposition. Spirit's positioning promise: "Less money. More go."

Spirit Airlines is an unrivaled "ultra low-cost carrier," resulting in prices much lower than those of competitors—up to 90 percent lower in some cases. But to cash in on such rock-bottom fares, customers must accept less in return. Buying a ticket on a Spirit flight gets you one thing and one thing only—a seat on a plane to your destination. If you want more, you pay for it. Under what it calls "Bare Fare" pricing, Spirit charges extra for everything. *Everything.* You get only what you pay for—and not one peanut more.

For example, whereas most airlines provide free beverages, Spirit charges $3 for a bottle of water or can of soda. Want a pillow or a blanket? Glad to oblige—that'll be $7, please. Spirit offers no on-board entertainment or Wi-Fi. Getting a seat assignment costs $15, and it will cost you $10 extra to have a check-in agent print out your boarding pass. A full-size carry-on bag runs another $50. Adding insult to injury, seats on Spirit flights are crammed much closer together (what Spirit calls "a little cozier seating"), and the seats don't recline. If you do want a little more breathing room—you guessed it—for a fee you can get an exit row or front-row seat.

Spirit refers to its pricing practices as "Frill Control," claiming that it gives customers more control over what they pay for. It points out that the so-called free sodas and extra legroom on other airlines aren't really free. Customers pay for them in the ticket price whether they want them or not. On Spirit, passengers have the option. Although this approach sounds refreshing, some customers view it as cheap nickel-and-diming or, worse, as unfair and deceitful. The

social media are filled with tales of unwary customers who say they ended up paying more for extras than they saved on the initial ticket.

Spirit Airlines takes a hardline approach in responding to customer complaints. When customers request pricing exceptions, Spirit agents stand their ground. The extra charges are optional, not mandatory, the airline explains. The base ticket price includes everything passengers need to get to their destinations. "We've rejected, for example, charging for bathrooms," says Spirit's CEO. "We're never going to do that. That's not an optional thing."

Rather than hiding from its poor customer service record, Spirit Airlines seems almost to wear it as a badge of honor. When one recent study showed that Spirit ranked dead last in complaints made to the U.S. Department of Transportation, Spirit turned it into bragging rights. Over the five years of the study, the airline averaged only eight complaints per 100,000 customers. Spirit celebrated by offering $24 discounts. "That's right, over 99.99 percent of our customers did not file a complaint with the Department of Transportation," Spirit declared in a press release. "To the 0.01 percent—that's OK, we know we aren't the airline for everyone (though we'd love for you to save by flying with us again!)."

The company further defends its pricing by noting that, for customers who take the time to look, it provides plenty

>> **Less-for-much-less positioning:** Fast-growing Spirit Airlines thrives on giving customers less but charging them much less for it. You don't pay for what you don't get.

Spirit Airlines

of up-front information about what its fares cover. In fact, Spirit's online site offers "Spirit 101: Your Simple Guide to the Way We Fly," a detailed guide on what you get for what you pay and how to make the Spirit Bare Fare system work to your advantage. Despite the angst of the vocal few who think they are being fleeced, most Spirit customers seem to know exactly what they are getting and are happy with that. When asked if she resented paying $3 for water on a Spirit flight, one passenger replied, "Not at all. They're trying to cover their costs." That attitude is shared by most Spirit customers, who seem more than happy to give up the extras to get the super-cheap fares.

To see what all the fuss was about, one airline analyst put Spirit Airlines to the test, eyes wide open. After paying only $63 for a one-way flight from Detroit to LaGuardia—roughly $300 less than the same fare offered by Delta, American, or United—he reported on his experience. "After we landed I turned to my friend and said, 'I don't get it—what...are people complaining about?'" He concluded that most dissatisfaction stems from misconceptions—that if people are aware of Spirits' policies ahead of time, they can avoid unpleasant surprises and add-ons they don't want. If you want entertainment, he suggests, bring along your own on a mobile device. Plan ahead and buy snacks and beverages before boarding. Think ahead and add in the fees for carry-ons or checked bags to calculate the true fare. Or pack light and jam everything into a small carry-on bag or backpack you can take on for free. And prepare yourself mentally that you might "be able to determine the shampoo used by the person in the row ahead of you." For flights no longer than three hours, being a little squished isn't all that bad.

For those customers who complain that the extras add up to more than the savings, official numbers suggest otherwise. Spirit's total flight price (all fees included) is still the lowest in the industry—an average of 40 percent below competitors' prices. Even at those super-low prices, thanks to its industry-lowest cost per seat-mile, Spirit Airlines still reaps industry-leading profit margins. For example, Spirit's total revenue per passenger is less than half of what United Airlines needs per passenger just to break even. Over the past four years, Spirit's annual revenues shot up 46 percent to $1.7 billion; net income soared 250 percent.

Thus, Spirit Airlines is thriving with its less-for-much-less positioning approach. True, you don't get much when you fly Spirit. Then again, you don't pay for what you don't get. If paying for the extras bothers you, don't buy them. Or just fly another airline and pay the full up-front fare. But Spirit won't be giving away those extras for free anytime soon. "[We won't] add costs for things that most customers don't value as much as our low fares just to reduce the complaints of a few customers," says the CEO. "Doing that would raise prices for everyone, compromising our commitment to what our customers have continuously told us they truly value—the lowest possible price."

Sources: Based on information from "If Spirit Airlines Is So Unpopular, Why Are Its Flights So Full?" *CBS News*, March 23, 2014, www.cbsnews .com/news/if-spirit-airlines-is-so-unpopular-why-are-its-flights-so-full/; Justin Bachman, "Spirit Airlines Sees All Those Passenger Complaints as Mere Misunderstandings," *Bloomberg Businessweek*, April 18, 2014, www.business week.com/articles/2014-04-18/spirit-airlines-passenger-complaints-part-of-its-business-model; Jared Blank, "3 Myths about Spirit Airlines," *Online Travel Review*, September 10, 2012, www.onlinetravelreview.com/2012/09/10/3-myths-about-spirit-airlines-or-my-flight-on-spirit-was-perfectly-fine-really/; Adam Levine-Weinberg, "Why Houston Is Spirit Airlines' Next Big Growth Market," *The Motley Fool*, November 20, 2014, www.fool.com/investing/general/2014/11/20/why-houston-is-spirit-airlines-next-big-growth-mar.aspx; "Value Airline of the Year—Spirit Airlines," ATW, January 23, 2015, http:// atwonline.com/airlines/value-airline-year-spirit-airlines; and http://marketing .spirit.com/how-to-fly-spirit-airlines/en/ and www.spirit.com, accessed September 2015.

share with other products in the category. But the case for the brand's superiority is made on its points of difference. For example, the U.S. Postal Service ships packages just like UPS and FedEx, but it differentiates its Priority Mail from competitors with convenient, low-price, flat-rate shipping boxes and envelopes. "If it fits, it ships," promises the Post Office.

Communicating and Delivering the Chosen Position

Once it has chosen a position, the company must take strong steps to deliver and communicate the desired position to its target consumers. All the company's marketing mix efforts must support the positioning strategy.

Positioning the company calls for concrete action, not just talk. If the company decides to build a position on better quality and service, it must first *deliver* that position. Designing the marketing mix—product, price, place, and promotion—involves working out the tactical details of the positioning strategy. Thus, a firm that seizes on a more-for-more position knows that it must produce high-quality products, charge a high price, distribute through high-quality dealers, and advertise in high-quality media. It must hire and train more service people, find retailers that have a good reputation for service, and develop sales and advertising messages that broadcast its superior service. This is the only way to build a consistent and believable more-for-more position.

Companies often find it easier to come up with a good positioning strategy than to implement it. Establishing a position or changing one usually takes a long time. In contrast, positions that have taken years to build can quickly be lost. Once a company has built the desired position, it must take care to maintain the position through consistent performance and communication. It must closely monitor and adapt the position over time to match changes in consumer needs and competitors' strategies. However, the company should avoid abrupt changes that might confuse consumers. Instead, a product's position should evolve gradually as it adapts to the ever-changing marketing environment.

MyMarketingLab

If assigned by your instructor, complete the questions marked with the ⭐ from the EOC Discussion Questions section in the MyLab. To complete the Marketing by the Numbers problems found in this section, go to your Assignments in the MyLab.

REVIEWING AND EXTENDING THE CONCEPTS

CHAPTER REVIEW AND CRITICAL THINKING

Objectives Review

In this chapter, you learned about the major elements of a customer value-driven marketing strategy: segmentation, targeting, differentiation, and positioning. Marketers know that they cannot appeal to all buyers in their markets—or at least not to all buyers in the same way. Therefore, most companies today practice *target marketing*—identifying market segments, selecting one or more of them, and developing products and marketing mixes tailored to each.

 OBJECTIVE 6-1 Define the major steps in designing a customer value-driven marketing strategy: market segmentation, targeting, differentiation, and positioning. (p 170)

A customer value-driven marketing strategy begins with selecting which customers to serve and determining a value proposition that best serves the targeted customers. It consists of four steps. *Market segmentation* is the act of dividing a market into distinct groups of buyers who have different needs, characteristics, or behaviors and who might require separate marketing strategies or mixes. Once the groups have been identified, *market targeting* evaluates each market segment's attractiveness and selects one or more segments to serve. *Differentiation* involves actually differentiating the market offering to create superior customer value. *Positioning* consists of positioning the market offering in the minds of target customers. A customer value-driven marketing strategy seeks to build the *right relationships* with the *right customers*.

 OBJECTIVE 6-2 List and discuss the major bases for segmenting consumer and business markets. (pp 170–178)

There is no single way to segment a market. Therefore, the marketer tries different variables to see which give the best segmentation opportunities. For consumer marketing, the major segmentation variables are geographic, demographic, psychographic, and behavioral. In *geographic segmentation*, the market is divided into different geographical units, such as nations, regions, states, counties, cities, or even neighborhoods. In *demographic segmentation*, the market is divided into groups based on demographic variables, including age, life-cycle stage, gender, income, occupation, education, religion, ethnicity, and generation. In *psychographic segmentation*, the market is divided into different groups based on social class, lifestyle, or personality characteristics. In *behavioral segmentation*, the market is divided into groups based on consumers' knowledge, attitudes, uses, or responses concerning a product.

Business marketers use many of the same variables to segment their markets. But business markets also can be segmented by business *demographics* (industry, company size), *operating characteristics, purchasing approaches, situational factors,* and *personal characteristics*. The effectiveness of the segmentation analysis depends on finding segments that are *measurable, accessible, substantial, differentiable,* and *actionable*.

OBJECTIVE 6-3 **Explain how companies identify attractive market segments and choose a market-targeting strategy. (pp 179–185)**

To target the best market segments, the company first evaluates each segment's size and growth characteristics, structural attractiveness, and compatibility with company objectives and resources. It then chooses one of four market-targeting strategies—ranging from very broad to very narrow targeting. The seller can ignore segment differences and target broadly using *undifferentiated* (or *mass*) *marketing*. This involves mass producing, mass distributing, and mass promoting the same product in about the same way to all consumers. Or the seller can adopt *differentiated marketing*—developing different market offers for several segments. *Concentrated marketing* (or *niche marketing*) involves focusing on one or a few market segments only. Finally, *micromarketing* is the practice of tailoring products and marketing programs to suit the tastes of specific individuals and locations. Micromarketing includes *local marketing* and *individual marketing*. Which targeting strategy is best depends on company resources, product variability, product life-cycle stage, market variability, and competitive marketing strategies.

 OBJECTIVE 6-4 **Discuss how companies differentiate and position their products for maximum competitive advantage. (pp 187–196)**

Once a company has decided which segments to enter, it must decide on its *differentiation and positioning strategy*. The differentiation and positioning task consists of three steps: identifying a set of possible differentiations that create competitive advantage, choosing advantages on which to build a position, and selecting an overall positioning strategy.

The brand's full positioning is called its *value proposition*—the full mix of benefits on which the brand is positioned. In general, companies can choose from one of five winning value propositions on which to position their products: more for more, more for the same, the same for less, less for much less, or more for less. Company and brand positioning are summarized in positioning statements that state the target segment and need, the positioning concept, and specific points of difference. The company must then effectively communicate and deliver the chosen position to the market.

Key Terms

Objective 6-1
Market segmentation (p 170)
Market targeting (targeting) (p 170)
Differentiation (p 170)
Positioning (p 170)

Objective 6-2
Geographic segmentation (p 171)
Demographic segmentation (p 172)
Age and life-cycle segmentation (p 172)
Gender segmentation (p 172)

Income segmentation (p 173)
Psychographic segmentation (p 173)
Behavioral segmentation (p 174)
Occasion segmentation (p 174)
Benefit segmentation (p 174)
Intermarket (cross-market) segmentation (p 177)

Objective 6-3
Target market (p 179)
Undifferentiated (mass) marketing (p 179)

Differentiated (segmented) marketing (p 180)
Concentrated (niche) marketing (p 180)
Micromarketing (p 181)
Local marketing (p 181)
Individual marketing (p 183)

Objective 6-4
Product position (p 187)
Competitive advantage (p 189)
Value proposition (p 191)
Positioning statement (p 193)

Discussion Questions

6-1. Name and briefly describe the four major steps in designing a customer value-driven marketing strategy. (AACSB: Communication)

6-2. How can marketers use behavioral segmentation in consumer markets? Give an example for each method of behavioral segmentation. (AACSB: Communication; Reflective Thinking)

6-3. Discuss the three factors firms consider when evaluating market segments. Which is most important? (AACSB: Communication; Reflective Thinking)

6-4. How can a company gain competitive advantage through differentiation? Describe an example of a company that illustrates each type of differentiation discussed in the chapter. (AACSB: Communication)

6-5. Discuss the criteria that should be evaluated in determining which differences a company should promote in its products. (AACSB: Communication)

Critical Thinking Exercises

6-6. The chapter describes many companies' individual marketing efforts that customize products for individual customers, such as M&Ms, PUMA, and Harley-Davidson. Find and describe another example and discuss whether the cost of customizing is worth the value provided to consumers. (AACSB: Communication; Reflective Thinking)

⭐ **6-7.** *Manfluencers* is a term that describes a new marketing trend. To what does this refer? Describe two examples of how marketers have responded to the manfluencers trend. (AACSB: Communication; Reflective Thinking)

6-8. In a small group, create an idea for a new business. Using the steps described in the chapter, develop a customer value-driven marketing strategy. Describe your strategy and conclude with a positioning statement for this business. (AACSB: Communication; Reflective Thinking)

MINICASES AND APPLICATIONS

Online, Mobile, and Social Media Marketing   SoLoMo (social+local+mobile)

Imagine walking into a retail store that has very little merchandise on display. Technology company Hointer is allowing retailers to do just that. For example, the company's store in Seattle has only one of every style of clothing hanging on display, seemingly floating in the air. With the store app, customers simply scan the tag to get information about each product, read reviews by others, access media clips, and request that the product be added to their fitting room. Once in the fitting room, customers can request other sizes or styling advice via a tablet on the wall or through the mobile app on their phones. Customers return products they don't want through one chute and another size is delivered through another chute in about 30 seconds. With one click, customers can check out on a mobile device or at the sales counter, and they can share their purchases with others on Instagram, Facebook, or Twitter. Sales associates still exist, but they are likely using the associate's tools to monitor customers' choices and suggest matching items of clothing and accessories. All this is possible with Hointer's suite of SoLoMo tools for retailers—eTag, Digital Connections, Omnicart, Associate Tools, and Whoosh Fitting Room.

6-9. Search the Internet to find other examples of retailers using SoLoMo to target and engage potential customers, or describe how you have used a retailer's app in this manner. (AACSB: Communication; Use of IT; Reflective Thinking)

6-10. Do manufacturers use SoLoMo? Find examples of or make suggestions as to how manufacturers can use this type of targeting. (AACSB: Communication; Reflective Thinking)

Marketing Ethics   Unrealistic Bodies

With more than a third of American children and adolescents overweight, you would think that Mattel's slender Barbie doll would be a good role model for little girls. Not so, according to some critics. If Barbie was a real woman, she would have less than 17 percent body fat, a neck too thin to hold her head up, a waist too small to house a full liver and intestines, and ankles and feet too tiny to walk. One group of researchers estimated the likelihood of a woman having Barbie's body at one in 100,000. Yet some women strive for impossible bodies, with more than 20 million suffering from eating disorders such as anorexia and bulimia. Other research has shown that 40 to 60 percent of preadolescent girls are concerned about their weight, and almost 70 percent of elementary-age girls who read magazines say the pictures of thin models influence their perceptions of an ideal weight. Statistics like these cause consumer advocacy groups such as the Campaign for a Commercial-Free Childhood (CCFC) to call for action, especially when targeting young girls. For example, the CCFC is concerned about Mattel's Barbie Be Anything, Do Everything partnership with the Girl Scouts, in which Daisy and Brownie scouts (that is, kindergarten through third-graders) can play an interactive game on the Girl Scouts' Web site and earn Barbie participation badges to wear on their uniforms.

⭐ **6-11.** Do you think it is wrong for Mattel and other doll manufacturers to market dolls with unrealistic body proportions to young girls? Explain why you think that way. Discuss other examples of marketers targeting females with unrealistic body concepts. (AACSB: Communication; Ethical Reasoning)

6-12. Give an example of a company that is countering this trend by offering more realistic dolls for young girls. (AACSB: Communication; Reflective Thinking)

Marketing by the Numbers　USAA

USAA is a financial services company formed in 1922 by 25 Army officers who came together to insure each other's automobiles because they were deemed too high-risk to insure. USAA now has almost 25,000 employees and more than 9 million member customers. It consistently ranks in the top 10 automobile insurance companies and offers other types of insurance as well as banking, investment, retirement, and financial planning services. USAA practices a niche marketing strategy—it targets only active and former military personnel and their immediate families. Members earn the right to be customers by serving in the military and can pass that on to their spouses and children. The company was originally even more restrictive, targeting only military officers. However, in 1996, eligibility was extended to enlisted personnel and is now extended to anyone who served and was honorably discharged from the military and their immediate family members. The potential market represents all active duty military members, all veterans, and their families. According to the U.S. Department of Defense, as of December 31, 2014, there were 1,361,755 active duty personnel in all armed services. The veteran population totaled 21 million at the end of 2014.

6-13. Assuming the average cost of life insurance is $700 per year and that potential customers purchase one policy per year, use the chain ratio method described in Appendix 3: Marketing by the Numbers to calculate the market potential for life insurance in the military market.

6-14. Discuss the factors used to evaluate the usefulness of the military segment. (AACSB: Communication; Reflective Thinking)

Video Case　Sprout

In the world of children's television programming, Sprout is a relative newcomer. Owned by NBCUniversal, Sprout airs PBS Kids programming as well as additional acquired material. A true multi-platform network, Sprout can be accessed as regular cable programming, as on-demand programming through Comcast, and online through Sproutonline.com.

Sprout does not target only kids, however. It targets preschool families—households that have one or more preschool-age children. Parents need to be involved with their children's viewing of interactive content, multiple access points, and 24-hour programming. For this reason, Sprout's promotional efforts are geared toward parents as well as children.

After viewing the video featuring Sprout, answer the following questions:

6-15. Why does Sprout target preschool families rather than focusing solely on children? Give examples.

6-16. Which target marketing strategy best describes Sprout's efforts? Support your choice.

6-17. How does Sprout use differentiation and positioning to build relationships with target customers?

Company Cases　6 Virgin America/7 Target/11 Sears

See Appendix 1 for cases appropriate for this chapter. **Case 6, Virgin America: Flight Service for the Tech Savvy.** Fighting since 2007 for a place in the air travel market, Virgin America has found a profitable niche by providing exceptional customer service for Silicon Valley clientele. **Case 7, Target: Where Store Brands Offer More than Low Prices.** In addition to carrying popular national brands, Target has built its own house for brands by moving store brands upscale. **Case 11, Sears: Why Should You Shop There?** Once "Where America Shops," the former largest retailer is struggling to find its place among Millennials and other shoppers in today's market.

MyMarketingLab

If assigned by your instructor, complete these writing sections from your Assignments in the MyLab.

6-18. Describe how marketers segment international markets. What is intermarket segmentation? (AACSB: Communication)

6-19. Discuss ideas for applications of the Google Glass device among the business and institutional markets. How can these applications be incorporated into online, mobile, and social media marketing? (AACSB: Written and Oral Communication; Information Technology; Reflective Thinking)

7 Products, Services, and Brands
Building Customer Value

Previewing the Concepts

After examining customer value-driven marketing strategy, we now take a deeper look at the marketing mix: the tactical tools that marketers use to implement their strategies, engage customers, and deliver superior customer value. In this and the next chapter, we will study how companies develop and manage products, services, and brands. Then, in the chapters that follow, we look at pricing, distribution, and marketing communication tools. The product and brand are usually the first and most basic marketing consideration. We start with a seemingly simple question: What *is* a product? As it turns out, the answer is not so simple.

To dig a little deeper into the question of "What is a product?", we begin by looking at GoPro. You may never have heard of GoPro, the fast-growing company that makes tiny, wearable HD video cameras. Yet few brands can match the avid enthusiasm and loyalty that GoPro has created in the hearts and minds of its customers. GoPro knows that, deep down, its products are much more than just durable little cameras. More than that, it gives customers a way to share action-charged moments and emotions with friends.

First Stop

GoPro: Be a HERO

A growing army of GoPro customers—many of them extreme sports enthusiasts—are now strapping amazing little GoPro cameras to their bodies or mounting them on anything from the front bumpers of race cars to the heels of skydiving boots in order to capture the extreme moments of their lives and lifestyles. Then they can't wait to share those emotion-packed GoPro moments with friends. In fact, the chances are good that you've seen many GoPro-created videos on YouTube, Facebook, and Instagram or even on TV.

Maybe it's the video shot by the skier who sets off an avalanche in the Swiss Alps and escapes by parachuting off a cliff—that amateur video received 2.6 million YouTube views in nine months. Or maybe you saw the one where a seagull picks up a tourist's camera and takes off with it, capturing a bird's-eye view of a castle in Cannes, France (3 million views in seven months). Or what about the video of the mountain biker in Africa who is ambushed by a full-grown gazelle (more than 13 million views in four months)? One promotional video featuring 5 minutes of video clips captured by fans with the latest GoPro model snared more than 16 million YouTube videos in only three months.

GoPro's avid customers have become evangelists for the brand. On average, they upload three new videos to YouTube every minute. In turn, the videos inspire new GoPro customers and even more video sharing. As a result, GoPro has become the world's hottest camera company. GoPro holds a 21.5 percent share of the digital camcorder market and an estimated 70 to 90 percent share of the wearable-camera market. The company went public in mid-2014, and its sales soared to an estimated $1.2 billion in 2015, a fivefold increase in only four years.

What makes GoPro so successful? Part of the formula is the physical product itself: GoPro cameras are marvels of technology, especially given their affordable starting price of only $200 to $400. A GoPro HD video camera looks like little more than a small gray box. But the lightweight, wearable or mountable GoPro is extremely versatile, and it packs amazing power for capturing stunning HD-quality video. A removable housing makes GoPro cameras waterproof to depths of 130 feet. And GoPro cameras are drop-proof from 3,000 feet (so claims one skydiver).

But GoPro knows that it sells much more than just a small metal box that takes action-sports videos. GoPro users don't just want to take videos. More than that, they want to tell the stories and share the adrenaline-pumped emotions of the extreme moments in their lives. "Enabling you to share your life through incredible photos and video is what we do," says GoPro. We "help people capture and share their lives' most meaningful experiences with others—to celebrate them together."

When people view a stunning GoPro video clip—like the one of New Zealand's Jed Mildon landing the first-ever BMX triple backflip captured by his helmet camera—to some degree, they experience what the subject experiences. They feel the passion and adrenaline. And when that happens, GoPro creates an emotional connection between the GoPro storyteller and the audience.

▶▶ GoPro's amazing little cameras let even the rankest video amateurs take stunning videos, giving them a way to celebrate the action-charged moments and emotions of their lives with others.

Used with permission of Mike Basich

Thus, making good cameras is only the start of GoPro's success. GoPro founder Nick Woodman, himself an extreme sports junkie, talks about helping customers through four essential steps in their storytelling and emotion-sharing journeys: capture, creation, broadcast, and recognition. *Capture* is what the cameras do—shooting pictures and videos. *Creation* is the editing and production process that turns raw footage into compelling videos. *Broadcast* involves distributing the video content to an audience. *Recognition* is the payoff for the content creator. Recognition might come in the form of YouTube views or Likes and Shares on Facebook. More probably, it's the enthusiastic oohs and ahs that their videos evoke from friends and family. The company's slogan sums up what it's really selling: "GoPro: Be a HERO."

Initially, GoPro focused primarily on the capture step of the customer storytelling experience. It offers a seemingly endless supply of rigs, mounts, harnesses, straps, and other accessories that make GoPro cameras wearable or mountable just about anywhere. Users can strap the little cameras to their wrists or mount them on helmets. They can attach them to the tip of a snow ski, the bottom of a skateboard, or the underside of an RC helicopter. In fact, rumor has it that GoPro will soon make drones that will let GoPro enthusiasts take breathtaking videos from on high. The handy little GoPro lets even the rankest video amateur capture some pretty incredible footage.

But Woodman knows that to keep growing, GoPro must broaden its offer to address the full range of customer needs and motivations—not just capture, but also creation, broadcast, and

> GoPro's runaway success comes from a deep-down understanding that it's selling much more than just tiny, wearable sports-action video cameras. GoPro helps people capture, share, and celebrate with others the most meaningful experiences in their lives.

recognition. For example, on the creation side, GoPro offers free GoPro Studio software that makes it easier for users to create professional-quality videos from their GoPro content. On the broadcast side, with the GoPro app, users can view and play back photos and videos, then share their favorites with friends on the GoPro Channel, which is already distributed though social media platforms such as YouTube, Facebook, Twitter, Instagram, Vimeo, Pinterest, and GoPro.com/Channels. As for recognition, GoPro now airs TV commercials created from the best videos submitted by customers at its Web site. GoPro's future lies in enabling and integrating the full user experience, from capturing video to sharing stories and life's emotions with others.

GoPro's rich understanding of what product it's really selling is serving the company well. Its enthusiastic customers are among the most loyal and engaged of any brand. For example, GoPro's Facebook fan base is more than 8.4 million and growing fast. To put that in perspective, much larger Canon USA has only 1.2 million Facebook followers. Beyond uploading nearly half a million videos a year, GoPro fans interact heavily across a broad range of social media. "I think we have the most socially engaged online audience of any consumer brand in the world," claims Woodman.

All that customer engagement and enthusiasm has made GoPro the world's fastest-growing camera company. Today GoPro cameras are available in more than 35,000 stores in more than 100 countries, from small sports-enthusiast shops to REI, Best Buy, and Amazon.com. GoPro's remarkable little cameras have also spread beyond amateurs. They have become standard equipment for many professional filmmakers—whether it's the Discovery Channel or a news show team filming rescues, wildlife, and storms or the production crew of hit reality-TV shows such as *Deadliest Catch* taking pictures of underwater crab pots or the sides of ships in heavy seas. When stuntman Felix Baumgartner made his breathtaking 128,000-foot jump from the edge of space, he was wearing five GoPros. The use of GoPro equipment by professionals lends credibility that fuels even greater consumer demand.

The moral of this story: GoPro knows that it doesn't just sell cameras. More than that, it enables customers to share important moments and emotions. Says Woodman: "We spent a lot of time recently thinking about, What are we really doing here? We know that our cameras are arguably the most socially networked consumer devices of our time, so it's clear we're not just building hardware." The company sums it up this way: "Dream it. Do it. Capture it with your GoPro. Capture and share your world."[1]

As the GoPro story shows, in their quest to create customer relationships, marketers must build and manage products and brands that connect with customers. This chapter begins with a deceptively simple question: *What is a product?* After addressing this question, we look at ways to classify products in consumer and business markets. Then we discuss the important decisions that marketers make regarding individual products, product lines, and product mixes. Next, we examine the characteristics and marketing requirements of a special form of product—services. Finally, we look into the critically important issue of how marketers build and manage product and service brands.

Author Comment
As you'll see, this is a deceptively simple question with a very complex answer. For example, think back to the opening GoPro story. What is the GoPro "product"?

Product
Anything that can be offered to a market for attention, acquisition, use, or consumption that might satisfy a want or need.

Service
An activity, benefit, or satisfaction offered for sale that is essentially intangible and does not result in the ownership of anything.

What Is a Product?

We define a **product** as anything that can be offered to a market for attention, acquisition, use, or consumption that might satisfy a want or need. Products include more than just tangible objects, such as cars, computers, or mobile phones. Broadly defined, *products* also include services, events, persons, places, organizations, and ideas or a mixture of these. Throughout this text, we use the term *product* broadly to include any or all of these entities. Thus, an Apple iPhone, a Toyota Camry, and a Caffé Mocha at Starbucks are products. But so are a trip to Las Vegas, Schwab online investment services, your Pinterest page, and advice from your family doctor.

Because of their importance in the world economy, we give special attention to services. **Services** are a form of product that consists of activities, benefits, or satisfactions offered for sale that are essentially intangible and do not result in the ownership of anything. Examples include banking, hotel, airline travel, retail, wireless communication, and home-repair services. We will look at services more closely later in this chapter.

Products, Services, and Experiences

Products are a key element in the overall *market offering*. Marketing mix planning begins with building an offering that brings value to target customers. This offering becomes the basis on which the company builds profitable customer relationships.

A company's market offering often includes both tangible goods and services. At one extreme, the market offer may consist of a *pure tangible good*, such as soap, toothpaste, or salt; no services accompany the product. At the other extreme are *pure services*, for which the market offer consists primarily of a service. Examples include a doctor's exam and financial services. Between these two extremes, however, many goods-and-services combinations are possible.

Today, as products and services become more commoditized, many companies are moving to a new level in creating value for their customers. To differentiate their offers, beyond simply making products and delivering services, they are creating and managing customer *experiences* with their brands or companies.

Experiences have always been an important part of marketing for some companies. Disney has long manufactured dreams and memories through its movies and theme parks—it wants theme park cast members to deliver a thousand "small wows" to every customer. And Nike has long declared, "It's not so much the shoes but where they take you." Today, however, all kinds of firms are recasting their traditional goods and services to create experiences. For example, newly redesigned Verizon Wireless Smart Stores don't just sell phones. They create lifestyle experiences that encourage customers to visit more often, hang around, and experience the wonders of mobile technology:[2]

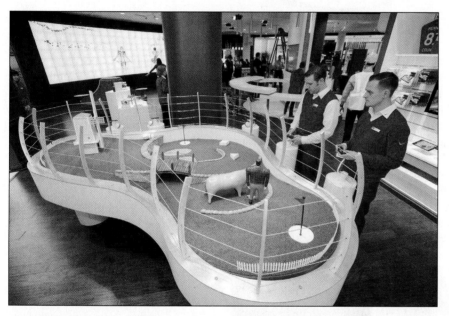

>> **Creating customer experiences: Verizon's redesigned Smart Stores don't just sell phones. They create lifestyle experiences—a kind of "rec room for geeks" in which customers can hang around and experience the wonders of mobile technology.**

Craig Lassig/AP Images

You probably don't much look forward to visiting your wireless carrier's retail store—you maybe stop by every few years to upgrade your phone in exchange for extending your contract. But Verizon Wireless is trying to change all that. >> It's remodeling some 1,700 retail stores nationwide, turning them into "Smart Stores"—what one observer calls "rec rooms for geeks." The aim is to create a new retail experience, one that helps customers to discover how Verizon technology can enhance their mobile lifestyles. These wireless lifestyle stores are organized into interactive mobile lifestyle zones where customers can try out gadgets, apps, and gear relevant to their lifestyle needs running on the Verizon network. For example, a "Get Fit" zone caters to active sports and fitness buffs; a "Have Fun" zone focuses on gamers; a "Home and On the Go" zone is for folks interested in home monitoring and energy management. In the "Workshop" area, Verizon specialists hold classes in front of a large digital display screen and share tips about getting the most out of mobile devices and Verizon's services. With the new stores, Verizon hopes to build deeper brand engagement and customer relationships by serving as a guide for its wireless customers. "We want to talk with them about all the ways they can use their devices," says a Verizon executive.

Levels of Product and Services

Product planners need to think about products and services on three levels (see >> **Figure 7.1**). Each level adds more customer value. The most basic level is the *core customer value*, which addresses the question: *What is the buyer really buying?* When designing products, marketers must first define the core, problem-solving benefits or services that consumers seek. A woman buying lipstick buys more than lip color. Charles Revson of Revlon saw this early: "In the factory, we make cosmetics; in the store, we sell hope." >> And people who buy an Apple iPad are buying much more than just a tablet computer. They are buying entertainment, self-expression, productivity, and connectivity with friends and family—a mobile and personal window to the world.

At the second level, product planners must turn the core benefit into an *actual product*. They need to develop product and service features, a design, a quality level, a brand

>> **Figure 7.1 Three Levels of Product**

At the most basic level, the company asks, "What is the customer really buying?" For example, people who buy an Apple iPad are buying more than just a tablet computer. They are buying entertainment, self-expression, productivity, and connectivity—a mobile and personal window to the world.

name, and packaging. For example, the iPad is an actual product. Its name, parts, styling, operating system, features, packaging, and other attributes have all been carefully combined to deliver the core customer value of staying connected.

Finally, product planners must build an *augmented product* around the core benefit and actual product by offering additional consumer services and benefits. The iPad is more than just a digital device. It provides consumers with a complete connectivity solution. Thus, when consumers buy an iPad, Apple and its resellers also might give buyers a warranty on parts and workmanship, quick repair services when needed, and Web and mobile sites to use if they have problems or questions. Apple also provides access to a huge assortment of apps and accessories, along with an iCloud service that integrates buyers' photos, music, documents, apps, calendars, contacts, and other content across all of their devices from any location.

Consumers see products as complex bundles of benefits that satisfy their needs. When developing products, marketers first must identify the *core customer value* that consumers seek from the product. They must then design the *actual* product and find ways to *augment* it to create customer value and a full and satisfying brand experience.

Product and Service Classifications

Products and services fall into two broad classes based on the types of consumers who use them: *consumer products* and *industrial products*. Broadly defined, products also include other marketable entities such as experiences, organizations, persons, places, and ideas.

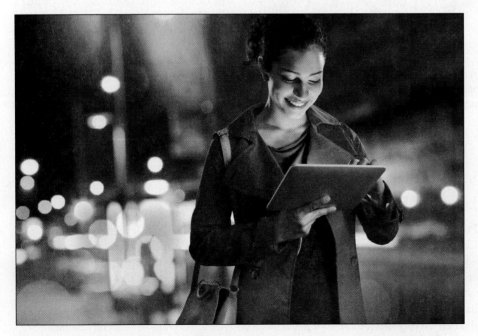

>> Core, actual, and augmented product: People who buy an iPad are buying much more than a tablet computer. They are buying entertainment, self-expression, productivity, and connectivity—a mobile and personal window to the world.

Betsie Van der Meer/Stone/Getty Images

Consumer Products

Consumer products are products and services bought by final consumers for personal consumption. Marketers

Consumer product
A product bought by final consumers for personal consumption.

Convenience product
A consumer product that customers usually buy frequently, immediately, and with minimal comparison and buying effort.

Shopping product
A consumer product that the customer, in the process of selecting and purchasing, usually compares on such attributes as suitability, quality, price, and style.

Specialty product
A consumer product with unique characteristics or brand identification for which a significant group of buyers is willing to make a special purchase effort.

Unsought product
A consumer product that the consumer either does not know about or knows about but does not normally consider buying.

usually classify these products and services further based on how consumers go about buying them. Consumer products include *convenience products, shopping products, specialty products,* and *unsought products.* These products differ in the ways consumers buy them and, therefore, in how they are marketed (see >> Table 7.1).

Convenience products are consumer products and services that customers usually buy frequently, immediately, and with minimal comparison and buying effort. Examples include laundry detergent, candy, magazines, and fast food. Convenience products are usually low priced, and marketers place them in many locations to make them readily available when customers need or want them.

Shopping products are less frequently purchased consumer products and services that customers compare carefully on suitability, quality, price, and style. When buying shopping products and services, consumers spend much time and effort in gathering information and making comparisons. Examples include furniture, clothing, major appliances, and hotel services. Shopping product marketers usually distribute their products through fewer outlets but provide deeper sales support to help customers in their comparison efforts.

Specialty products are consumer products and services with unique characteristics or brand identifications for which a significant group of buyers is willing to make a special purchase effort. Examples include specific brands of cars, high-priced photography equipment, designer clothes, gourmet foods, and the services of medical or legal specialists. A Lamborghini automobile, for example, is a specialty product because buyers are usually willing to travel great distances to buy one. Buyers normally do not compare specialty products. They invest only the time needed to reach dealers carrying the wanted products.

Unsought products are consumer products that the consumer either does not know about or knows about but does not normally consider buying. Most major new innovations are unsought until the consumer becomes aware of them through advertising. Classic examples of known but unsought products and services are life insurance, preplanned funeral services, and blood donations to the Red Cross. By their very nature, unsought products require a lot of advertising, personal selling, and other marketing efforts.

>> **Table 7.1** | **Marketing Considerations for Consumer Products**

	Type of Consumer Product			
Marketing Considerations	Convenience	Shopping	Specialty	Unsought
Customer buying behavior	Frequent purchase; little planning, little comparison or shopping effort; low customer involvement	Less frequent purchase; much planning and shopping effort; comparison of brands on price, quality, and style	Strong brand preference and loyalty; special purchase effort; little comparison of brands; low price sensitivity	Little product awareness or knowledge (or, if aware, little or even negative interest)
Price	Low price	Higher price	High price	Varies
Distribution	Widespread distribution; convenient locations	Selective distribution in fewer outlets	Exclusive distribution in only one or a few outlets per market area	Varies
Promotion	Mass promotion by the producer	Advertising and personal selling by both the producer and resellers	More carefully targeted promotion by both the producer and resellers	Aggressive advertising and personal selling by the producer and resellers
Examples	Toothpaste, magazines, and laundry detergent	Major appliances, televisions, furniture, and clothing	Luxury goods, such as Rolex watches or fine crystal	Life insurance and Red Cross blood donations

Industrial Products

Industrial products are those products purchased for further processing or for use in conducting a business. Thus, the distinction between a consumer product and an industrial product is based on the *purpose* for which the product is purchased. If a consumer buys a lawn mower for use around home, the lawn mower is a consumer product. If the same consumer buys the same lawn mower for use in a landscaping business, the lawn mower is an industrial product.

The three groups of industrial products and services are materials and parts, capital items, and supplies and services. *Materials and parts* include raw materials as well as manufactured materials and parts. Raw materials consist of farm products (wheat, cotton, livestock, fruits, vegetables) and natural products (fish, lumber, crude petroleum, iron ore). Manufactured materials and parts consist of component materials (iron, yarn, cement, wires) and component parts (small motors, tires, castings). Most manufactured materials and parts are sold directly to industrial users. Price and service are the major marketing factors; branding and advertising tend to be less important.

Capital items are industrial products that aid in the buyer's production or operations, including installations and accessory equipment. Installations consist of major purchases such as buildings (factories, offices) and fixed equipment (generators, drill presses, large computer systems, elevators). Accessory equipment includes portable factory equipment and tools (hand tools, lift trucks) and office equipment (computers, fax machines, desks). These types of equipment have shorter lives than do installations and simply aid in the production process.

The final group of industrial products is *supplies and services*. Supplies include operating supplies (lubricants, coal, paper, pencils) and repair and maintenance items (paint, nails, brooms). Supplies are the convenience products of the industrial field because they are usually purchased with a minimum of effort or comparison. Business services include maintenance and repair services (window cleaning, computer repair) and business advisory services (legal, management consulting, advertising). Such services are usually supplied under contract.

Organizations, Persons, Places, and Ideas

In addition to tangible products and services, marketers have broadened the concept of a product to include other market offerings: organizations, persons, places, and ideas.

Organizations often carry out activities to "sell" the organization itself. *Organization marketing* consists of activities undertaken to create, maintain, or change the attitudes and behavior of target consumers toward an organization. Both profit and not-for-profit organizations practice organization marketing.

Business firms sponsor public relations or *corporate image marketing* campaigns to market themselves and polish their images. ≫ For example, GE's long-running "Imagination at Work" campaign markets the industrial giant as a company whose imaginative products and technologies are making a difference in the world. Consider one recent award-winning TV spot, called "Childlike Imagination." The whimsical ad brings GE's products—from jet engines and diesel locomotives to giant wind turbines and hospital diagnostics machines—to life through the eyes of an amazed young girl whose mom works at GE. GE is "Building, powering, moving, and curing the world," says the company. "Not just imagining. Doing. GE works."[3]

≫ **Organization marketing: GE's long-running Imagination at Work campaign markets the industrial giant as a company whose imaginative products and technologies are making a difference in the world.**

General Electric Company

People can also be thought of as products. *Person marketing* consists of activities undertaken to create, maintain, or change attitudes or behavior toward particular people. People ranging from presidents, entertainers, and sports figures to professionals such as doctors, lawyers, and architects use person marketing to build their reputations. And businesses, charities, and other organizations use well-known personalities to help sell their products or causes. For example, P&G's Cover Girl brand is represented by well-known celebrities such as Katy Perry, Janelle, and Sofia Vergara. The skillful use of marketing can turn a person's name into a powerhouse brand. For example, The Food Network's celebrity chef Rachael Ray is a one-woman marketing phenomenon, with her own daytime talk show, cookware and cutlery brands, dog food brand (Nutrish), and even her own brand of EVOO (extra virgin olive oil, for those not familiar with Rayisms).

Place marketing involves activities undertaken to create, maintain, or change attitudes or behavior toward particular places. Cities, states, regions, and even entire nations compete to attract tourists, new residents, conventions, and company offices and factories. The New Orleans city Web site shouts "Go NOLA" and markets annual events such as Mardi Gras festivities and the New Orleans Jazz and Heritage Festival. Tourism Australia advertises that "There's Nothing Like Australia" and provides a Web site and smartphone app complete with videos, holiday ideas, destination information, and about anything else travelers might need to plan an Australian vacation.[4]

Ideas can also be marketed. In one sense, all marketing is the marketing of an idea, whether it is the general idea of brushing your teeth or the specific idea that Crest toothpastes create "healthy, beautiful smiles for life." Here, however, we narrow our focus to the marketing of *social ideas*. This area has been called **social marketing** and consists of using traditional business marketing concepts and tools to create behaviors that will create individual and societal well-being.

Social marketing programs cover a wide range of issues. The Ad Council of America (www.adcouncil.org), for example, has developed dozens of social advertising campaigns involving issues ranging from health care, education, and environmental sustainability to human rights and personal safety. But social marketing involves much more than just advertising. It involves a broad range of marketing strategies and marketing mix tools designed to bring about beneficial social change.[5]

Social marketing
Using traditional business marketing concepts and tools to create behaviors that will create individual and societal well-being.

Product and Service Decisions

Author Comment
Now that we've answered the "What is a product?" question, we dig into the specific decisions that companies must make when designing and marketing products and services.

Marketers make product and service decisions at three levels: individual product decisions, product line decisions, and product mix decisions. We discuss each in turn.

Individual Product and Service Decisions

>> **Figure 7.2** shows the important decisions in the development and marketing of individual products and services. We will focus on decisions about *product attributes, branding, packaging, labeling,* and *product support services.*

Product and Service Attributes
Developing a product or service involves defining the benefits that it will offer. These benefits are communicated and delivered by product attributes such as *quality, features,* and *style and design.*

>> **Figure 7.2 Individual Product Decisions**

Don't forget Figure 7.1. The focus of all of these decisions is to create core customer value.

Product attributes → Branding → Packaging → Labeling → Product support services

Product quality
The characteristics of a product or service that bear on its ability to satisfy stated or implied customer needs.

Product Quality. **Product quality** is one of the marketer's major positioning tools. Quality affects product or service performance; thus, it is closely linked to customer value and satisfaction. In the narrowest sense, quality can be defined as "no defects." But most marketers go beyond this narrow definition. Instead, they define quality in terms of creating customer value and satisfaction. The American Society for Quality defines quality as the characteristics of a product or service that bear on its ability to satisfy stated or implied customer needs. Similarly, Siemens defines quality this way: "Quality is when our customers come back and our products don't."[6]

Total quality management (TQM) is an approach in which all of the company's people are involved in constantly improving the quality of products, services, and business processes. For most top companies, customer-driven quality has become a way of doing business. Today, companies are taking a *return-on-quality* approach, viewing quality as an investment and holding quality efforts accountable for bottom-line results.

Product quality has two dimensions: level and consistency. In developing a product, the marketer must first choose a *quality level* that will support the product's positioning. Here, product quality means *performance quality*—the product's ability to perform its functions. For example, a Rolls-Royce provides higher performance quality than a Chevrolet: It has a smoother ride, lasts longer, and provides more hand craftsmanship, luxury, and "creature comforts." Companies rarely try to offer the highest possible performance quality level; few customers want or can afford the high levels of quality offered in products such as a Rolls-Royce automobile, a Viking range, or a Rolex watch. Instead, companies choose a quality level that matches target market needs and the quality levels of competing products.

Beyond quality level, high quality also can mean high levels of quality consistency. Here, product quality means *conformance quality*—freedom from defects and consistency in delivering a targeted level of performance. All companies should strive for high levels of conformance quality. In this sense, a Chevrolet can have just as much quality as a Rolls-Royce. Although a Chevy doesn't perform at the same level as a Rolls-Royce, it can just as consistently deliver the quality that customers pay for and expect.

» Similarly, the Chick-fil-A fast-food chain doesn't aspire to provide gourmet dining experiences. However, by consistently meeting or exceeding customers' quality expectations, the chain has earned a trophy case full of awards for top food and service quality.[7] Last year, for instance, the chain was the only restaurant named to *24/7 Wall Street's* Customer Service Hall of Fame, based on a survey of 2,500 adults asked about the quality of customer service at 150 of America's best-known companies across 15 industries. Chick-fil-A placed fourth overall, alongside the likes of Amazon, Marriott, and Apple. Although it doesn't try to be Ritz-Carlton, it does send its managers to the Ritz-Carlton quality training program, where they learn things such as how to greet customers and how to probe for and serve unexpressed needs. Such consistency in meeting quality expectations has helped Chick-fil-A build a following of fiercely loyal customers.

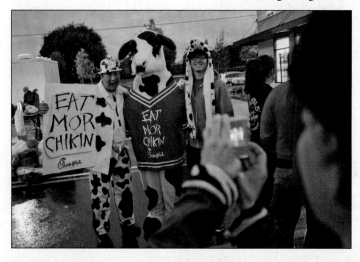

» By consistently meeting or exceeding customers' quality expectations, Chick-fil-A has won a trophy case full of awards for top food and service quality, helping it build a fierce following of loyal customers.
Bloomberg/Getty Images

Product Features. A product can be offered with varying features. A stripped-down model, one without any extras, is the starting point. The company can then create higher-level models by adding more features. Features are a competitive tool for differentiating the company's product from competitors' products. Being the first producer to introduce a valued new feature is one of the most effective ways to compete.

How can a company identify new features and decide which ones to add to its product? It should periodically survey buyers who have used the product and ask these questions: How do you like the product? Which specific features of the product do you like most? Which features could we add to improve the product? The answers to these questions provide the company with a rich list of feature ideas. The company can then assess each feature's *value* to customers versus its *cost* to the company. Features that customers value highly in relation to costs should be added.

Product Style and Design. Another way to add customer value is through distinctive *product style and design*. Design is a larger concept than style. *Style* simply describes the appearance of a product. Styles can be eye catching or yawn producing. A sensational style may grab attention and produce pleasing aesthetics, but it does not necessarily make the product *perform* better. Unlike style, *design* is more than skin deep—it goes to the very heart of a product. Good design contributes to a product's usefulness as well as to its looks.

Good design doesn't start with brainstorming new ideas and making prototypes. Design begins with observing customers, understanding their needs, and shaping their product-use experience. Product designers should think less about technical product specifications and more about how customers will use and benefit from the product. For example, using smart design based on consumer needs, Sonos created a wireless, Internet-enabled speaker system that's easy to use and fills a whole house with great sound.

In the past, setting up a whole-house entertainment or sound system required routing wires through walls, floors, and ceilings, creating a big mess and lots of expense. And if you moved, you couldn't take it with you. Enter Sonos, which took home-audio and theater systems to a new level worthy of the digital age. The innovative company created a wireless speaker system that's not just stylish but also easy to set up, easy to use, and easy to move to meet changing needs. With Sonos, you can stream high-quality sound through a variety of stylish speakers anywhere in your home with just an app and a tap on your smartphone. Smart design has paid off handsomely for Sonos. Founded in 2002, over just the past two years the company's sales have nearly tripled to an estimated $1 billion a year.[8]

Branding

Perhaps the most distinctive skill of professional marketers is their ability to build and manage brands. A **brand** is a name, term, sign, symbol, or design or a combination of these that identifies the maker or seller of a product or service. Consumers view a brand as an important part of a product, and branding can add value to a consumer's purchase. Customers attach meanings to brands and develop brand relationships. As a result, brands have meaning well beyond a product's physical attributes. >> Consider this story:[9]

One Tuesday evening in January, Joshua Bell, one of the world's finest violinists, played at Boston's stately Symphony Hall before a packed audience who'd paid an average of $100 a seat. Based on the well-earned strength of the "Joshua Bell brand," the talented musician routinely drew standing-room-only audiences at all of his performances around the world. Three days later, however, as part of a *Washington Post* social experiment, Bell found himself standing in a Washington, DC, metro station, dressed in jeans, a T-shirt, and a Washington Nationals baseball cap. As morning commuters streamed by, Bell pulled out his $4 million Stradivarius violin, set the open case at his feet, and began playing the same revered classics he'd played in

Brand

A name, term, sign, symbol, or design or a combination of these that identifies the products or services of one seller or group of sellers and differentiates them from those of competitors.

>> The meaning of a strong brand: The "branded" and "unbranded" Joshua Bell. The premier musician packs concert halls at an average of $100 or more a seat but made only $32 as a street musician at a Washington, DC, metro station.

(left) NBCUniversal/Getty Images; (right) The Washington Post/Getty Images

Boston. During the next 45 minutes, some 1,100 people passed by but few stopped to listen. Bell earned a total of $32. No one recognized the "unbranded" Bell, so few appreciated his artistry. What does that tell you about the meaning of a strong brand?

Branding has become so strong that today hardly anything goes unbranded. Salt is packaged in branded containers, common nuts and bolts are packaged with a distributor's label, and automobile parts—spark plugs, tires, filters—bear brand names that differ from those of the automakers. Even fruits, vegetables, dairy products, and poultry are branded—Cuties mandarin oranges, Dole Classic salads, Horizon Organic milk, Perdue chickens, and Eggland's Best eggs.

Branding helps buyers in many ways. Brand names help consumers identify products that might benefit them. Brands also say something about product quality and consistency—buyers who always buy the same brand know that they will get the same features, benefits, and quality each time they buy. Branding also gives the seller several advantages. The seller's brand name and trademark provide legal protection for unique product features that otherwise might be copied by competitors. Branding helps the seller to segment markets. For example, rather than offering just one general product to all consumers, Toyota can offer the different Lexus, Toyota, and Scion brands, each with numerous subbrands—such as Avalon, Camry, Corolla, Prius, Yaris, Tundra, and Land Cruiser.

Finally, a brand name becomes the basis on which a whole story can be built about a product's special qualities. For example, the Cuties brand of pint-sized mandarins sets itself apart from ordinary oranges by promising "Kids love Cuties because Cuties are made for kids." They are a healthy snack that's "perfect for little hands": sweet, seedless, kid-sized, and easy to peel.[10] Building and managing brands are perhaps the marketer's most important tasks. We will discuss branding strategy in more detail later in the chapter.

Packaging

Packaging
The activities of designing and producing the container or wrapper for a product.

Packaging involves designing and producing the container or wrapper for a product. Traditionally, the primary function of the package was to hold and protect the product. In recent times, however, packaging has become an important marketing tool as well. Increased competition and clutter on retail store shelves means that packages must now perform many sales tasks—from attracting buyers to communicating brand positioning to closing the sale. Not every customer will see a brand's advertising, social media pages, or other promotions. However, all consumers who buy and use a product will interact regularly with its packaging. Thus, the humble package represents prime marketing space.

Companies are realizing the power of good packaging to create immediate consumer recognition of a brand. For example, an average supermarket stocks about 44,000 items; the average Walmart supercenter carries 142,000 items. The typical shopper makes three out of four purchase decisions in stores and passes by some 300 items per minute. In this highly competitive environment, the package may be the seller's best and last chance to influence buyers. So the package itself has become an important promotional medium.[11]

Poorly designed packages can cause headaches for consumers and lost sales for the company. Think about all those hard-to-open packages, such as DVD cases sealed with impossibly sticky labels, packaging with finger-splitting wire twist-ties, or sealed plastic clamshell containers that cause "wrap rage" and send thousands of people to the hospital each year with lacerations and puncture wounds. Another packaging issue is overpackaging—as when a tiny USB flash drive in an oversized cardboard and plastic display package is delivered in a giant corrugated shipping carton. Overpackaging creates an incredible amount of waste, frustrating those who care about the environment.

>> Distinctive packaging may become an important part of a brand's identity. An otherwise plain brown carton imprinted with only the familiar curved arrow from the Amazon.com logo—variously interpreted as "a to z" or even a smiley face—leaves no doubt as to who shipped the package sitting at your doorstep.

Lux Igitur/Alamy

Amazon now offers Frustration-Free Packaging to alleviate both wrap rage and over-packaging. The online retailer works with more than 2,000 companies, such as Fisher-Price, Mattel, Unilever, Microsoft, and others, to create smaller, easy-to-open, recyclable packages that use less packaging material and no frustrating plastic clamshells or wire ties. It currently offers more than 200,000 such items and to date has shipped more than 75 million of them to 175 countries. In the process, the initiative has eliminated nearly 60 million square feet of cardboard and 25 million pounds of packaging waste.[12]

Innovative packaging can give a company an advantage over competitors and boost sales. Distinctive packaging may even become an important part of a brand's identity. ≫ For example, an otherwise plain brown carton imprinted with the familiar curved arrow from the Amazon.com logo—variously interpreted as "a to z" or even a smiley face—leaves no doubt as to who shipped the package sitting at your doorstep. And Tiffany's distinctive blue boxes have come to embody the exclusive jewelry retailer's premium legacy and positioning. As the company puts it, "Glimpsed on a busy street or resting in the palm of a hand, Tiffany Blue Boxes make hearts beat faster and epitomize Tiffany's great heritage of elegance, exclusivity, and flawless craftsmanship."[13]

In recent years, product safety has also become a major packaging concern. We have all learned to deal with hard-to-open "childproof" packaging. Due to the rash of product tampering scares in the 1980s, most drug producers and food makers now put their products in tamper-resistant packages. In making packaging decisions, the company also must heed growing environmental concerns. Fortunately, many companies have gone "green" by reducing their packaging and using environmentally responsible packaging materials.

Labeling

Labels range from simple tags attached to products to complex graphics that are part of the packaging. They perform several functions. At the very least, the label *identifies* the product or brand, such as the name Sunkist stamped on oranges. The label might also *describe* several things about the product—who made it, where it was made, when it was made, its contents, how it is to be used, and how to use it safely. Finally, the label might help to *promote* the brand and engage customers. For many companies, labels have become an important element in broader marketing campaigns.

Labels and brand logos can support the brand's positioning and add personality to the brand. In fact, brand labels and logos can become a crucial element in the brand–customer connection. Customers often become strongly attached to logos as symbols of the brands they represent. Consider the feelings evoked by the logos of companies such as Coca-Cola, Google, Twitter, Apple, and Nike.

Logos must be redesigned from time to time. ≫ For example, brands ranging from Yahoo!, eBay, and Southwest Airlines to Wendy's, Pizza Hut, Black+Decker, and Hershey have successfully adapted their logos to keep them contemporary and to meet the needs of new interactive media such as the Web and mobile apps and browsers. Although important, such changes are often subtle and may even go largely unnoticed by customers.

However, companies must take care when changing such important brand symbols. Customer often form strong connections to the visual representations of their brands and may react strongly to changes. For example, a few years ago when Gap introduced a more contemporary redesign of its familiar old logo—the well-known white text on a blue square—customers went ballistic and imposed intense online pressure. Gap reinstated the old logo after only one week.

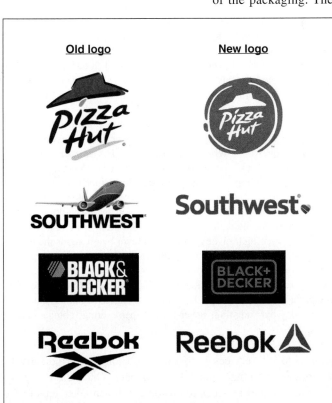

≫ **Brand logos must be redesigned from time to time to keep them contemporary with the brand's positioning and to meet the needs of new digital media. The above brands recently made seemingly small but important logo changes.**

Pizza Hut, Inc.; The Hershey Company; Southwest Airlines Co.; Reebok International Ltd; Black & Decker

Along with the positives, there has been a long history of legal concerns about packaging and labels. The Federal Trade Commission Act of 1914 held that false, misleading, or deceptive labels or packages constitute unfair competition. Labels can mislead customers, fail to describe important ingredients, or fail to include needed safety warnings. As a result, several federal and state laws regulate labeling. The most prominent is the Fair Packaging and Labeling Act of 1966, which set mandatory labeling requirements, encouraged voluntary industry packaging standards, and allowed federal agencies to set packaging regulations in specific industries. The Nutritional Labeling and Educational Act of 1990 requires sellers to provide detailed nutritional information on food products, and recent sweeping actions by the Food and Drug Administration (FDA) regulate the use of health-related terms such as *low fat, light, high fiber,* and *organic.* Sellers must ensure that their labels contain all the required information.

Product Support Services

Customer service is another element of product strategy. A company's offer usually includes some support services, which can be a minor part or a major part of the total offering. Later in this chapter, we will discuss services as products in themselves. Here, we discuss services that augment actual products.

Support services are an important part of the customer's overall brand experience. For example, L.L.Bean—the iconic American outdoor apparel and equipment retailer—knows good marketing doesn't stop with making the sale. Keeping customers happy *after* the sale is the key to building lasting relationships.[14]

NOTICE

I do not consider a sale complete until goods are worn out and customer still satisfied.

We will thank anyone to return goods that are not perfectly satisfactory.

Should the person reading this notice know of anyone who is not satisfied with our goods, I will consider it a favor to be notified.

Above all things we wish to avoid having a dissatisfied customer.

L.L.Bean

>> Customer service: For more than 100 years, L.L.Bean has been going the extra mile for customers. As founder Leon Leonwood Bean put it: "I do not consider a sale complete until goods are worn out and customer still satisfied."

L.L.Bean Inc.

Year after year, L.L.Bean lands in the top 10 of virtually every list of top service companies, including J.D. Power's most recent list of "customer service champions." The customer-service culture runs deep at L.L.Bean. >> More than 100 years ago, Leon Leonwood Bean founded the company on a philosophy of complete customer satisfaction, expressed in the following guarantee: "I do not consider a sale complete until [the] goods are worn out and [the] customer [is] still satisfied." To this day, customers can return any item, no questions asked, even decades after purchase.

The company's customer-service philosophy is perhaps best summed up in founder L.L.'s answer to the question "What is a customer?" His answer still forms the backbone of the company's values: "A customer is the most important person ever in this company—in person or by mail. A customer is not dependent on us, we are dependent on him. A customer is not an interruption of our work, he is the purpose of it. We are not doing a favor by serving him, he is doing us a favor by giving us the opportunity to do so. A customer is not someone to argue or match wits with. Nobody ever won an argument with a customer. A customer is a person who brings us his wants. It is our job to handle them profitably to him and to ourselves." Adds former L.L.Bean CEO Leon Gorman: "A lot of people have fancy things to say about customer service, but it's just a day-in, day-out, ongoing, never-ending, persevering, compassionate kind of activity."

The first step in designing support services is to survey customers periodically to assess the value of current services and obtain ideas for new ones. Once the company has assessed the quality of various support services to customers, it can take steps to fix problems and add new services that will both delight customers and yield profits to the company.

Many companies now use a sophisticated mix of phone, email, online, social media, mobile, and interactive voice and data technologies to provide support services that were not possible before. For example, home improvement store Lowe's offers a vigorous dose of customer service at both its store and online locations that makes shopping easier, answers customer questions, and handles problems. Customers can access Lowe's extensive support by phone, email (CareTW@lowes.com), Web site, mobile app, and Twitter via @LowesCares. The Lowe's Web site and mobile app link to a buying guide and how-to library. In its stores, Lowe's has equipped employees with 42,000 iPhones filled with custom apps and add-on hardware, letting them perform service tasks such as checking inventory at nearby stores, looking up specific customer purchase histories, sharing how-to videos, and checking competitor prices—all without leaving the customer's side. Lowe's is even experimenting with putting interactive, talking, moving robots in stores that can greet customers as they enter, answer even their most vexing questions, and guide them to whatever merchandise they are seeking.[15]

Product Line Decisions

Product line

A group of products that are closely related because they function in a similar manner, are sold to the same customer groups, are marketed through the same types of outlets, or fall within given price ranges.

Beyond decisions about individual products and services, product strategy also calls for building a product line. A **product line** is a group of products that are closely related because they function in a similar manner, are sold to the same customer groups, are marketed through the same types of outlets, or fall within given price ranges. For example, Nike produces several lines of athletic shoes and apparel, and Marriott offers several lines of hotels.

The major product line decision involves *product line length*—the number of items in the product line. The line is too short if the manager can increase profits by adding items; the line is too long if the manager can increase profits by dropping items. Managers need to analyze their product lines periodically to assess each item's sales and profits and understand how each item contributes to the line's overall performance.

A company can expand its product line in two ways: by *line filling* or *line stretching*. *Product line filling* involves adding more items within the present range of the line. There are several reasons for product line filling: reaching for extra profits, satisfying dealers, using excess capacity, being the leading full-line company, and plugging holes to keep out competitors. However, line filling is overdone if it results in cannibalization (eating up sales of the company's own existing products) and customer confusion. The company should ensure that new items are noticeably different from existing ones.

Product line stretching occurs when a company lengthens its product line beyond its current range. The company can stretch its line downward, upward, or both ways. Companies located at the upper end of the market can stretch their lines *downward*. A company may stretch downward to plug a market hole that otherwise would attract a new competitor or to respond to a competitor's attack on the upper end. Or it may add low-end products because it finds faster growth taking place in the low-end segments. Companies can also stretch their product lines *upward*. Sometimes, companies stretch upward to add prestige to their current products. Or they may be attracted by a faster growth rate or higher margins at the higher end.

>> Over the past few years Samsung has both stretched and filled its Galaxy line of premium smartphone and tablet mobile devices:

Samsung started the Galaxy line with a 4" smartphone, then quickly added a 10.1" tablet. It now offers a bulging Galaxy line that includes a size for any need or preference. The basic Galaxy smartphones come with 5" screens. The popular Galaxy Note "phablet" comes with a 5.7" screen in what Samsung calls "the best of both" between a phone and tablet. Galaxy Tab buyers can now choose among any

>> **Product line stretching and filling: Samsung's bulging Galaxy mobile devices line now offers a size for any need or preference, including smartphones, "phablets," tablets, and even a wristwatch-like wearable smartphone, the Galaxy Gear.**

Oleksiy Maksymenko Photography/Alamy

of four sizes—7", 8", 10" and 12". To top things off, Samsung offers the Galaxy Gear, a wristwatch-like wearable Galaxy smartphone, and the Galaxy Fit, a wearable activity-tracking device. The Galaxy line still caters heavily to the top end of its markets. But to address the fastest-growing smartphone segment—phones that sell for less than $300 contract-free—Samsung is rumored to have lower-priced Galaxy J1 models in the works. As a result, through artful stretching and filling, Samsung's successful Galaxy line has broadened its appeal, improved its competitive position, and boosted growth.

Product Mix Decisions

Product mix (or product portfolio)
The set of all product lines and items that a particular seller offers for sale.

An organization with several product lines has a product mix. A **product mix** (or **product portfolio**) consists of all the product lines and items that a particular seller offers for sale. For example, The Clorox Company is best known for its CLOROX bleach. But, in fact, Clorox is a $5.6 billion firm that makes and markets a full product mix consisting of dozens of familiar lines and brands. Clorox divides its overall product mix into five major lines: Cleaning, Household, Lifestyle, Professional, and International.[16] Each product line consists of many brands and items.

A company's product mix has four important dimensions: width, length, depth, and consistency. Product mix *width* refers to the number of different product lines the company carries. ≫ For example, Clorox has a fairly contained product mix that fits its mission to "make everyday life better, every day." By contrast, GE manufactures as many as 250,000 items across a broad range of categories, from lightbulbs to medical equipment, jet engines, and diesel locomotives.

Product mix *length* refers to the total number of items a company carries within its product lines. Clorox carries several brands within each line. For example, its cleaning line includes CLOROX, FORMULA 409, LIQUID PLUMBER, SOS, PINE-SOL, TILEX, HANDI-WIPES, and others. The lifestyle line contains the KC MASTERPIECE, BRITA, HIDDEN VALLEY, and BURT'S BEES brands, among others.

Product mix *depth* refers to the number of versions offered for each product in the line. The Clorox brand contains a deep assortment of items and varieties, including disinfecting wipes, floor cleaners, stain removers, and bleach products. Each variety comes in a number of product forms, formulations, scents, and sizes. For example, you can buy CLOROX Regular Bleach, CLOROX Scented Bleach, CLOROX Bleach Foamer, CLOROX High Efficiency Bleach, CLOROX UltimateCare Bleach (gentle for delicate fabrics), or any of a dozen other varieties.

Finally, the *consistency* of the product mix refers to how closely related the various product lines are in end use, production requirements, distribution channels, or some other aspect. The Clorox Company's product lines are consistent insofar as they are primarily consumer products and go through the same distribution channels. The lines are less consistent insofar as they perform different functions for buyers.

These product mix dimensions provide the handles for defining the company's product strategy. A company can increase its business in four ways. It can add new product lines, widening its product mix. In this way, its new lines build on the company's reputation in its other lines. A company can lengthen its existing product lines to become a more full-line company. It can add more versions of each product and thus deepen its product mix. Finally, a company can pursue more product line consistency—or less—depending on whether it wants to have a strong reputation in a single field or in several fields.

From time to time, a company may also have to streamline its product mix to pare out marginally performing lines and to regain its focus. For example, P&G pursues a megabrand strategy built around 23 billion-dollar-plus brands in the household care and beauty and grooming categories. During the past decade, the consumer products giant has sold off dozens of major brands that no longer fit either its evolving focus or the billion-dollar threshold, ranging from Jif peanut butter, Crisco shortening, Folgers coffee, Pringles snack chips, and Sunny Delight drinks to Noxzema skin

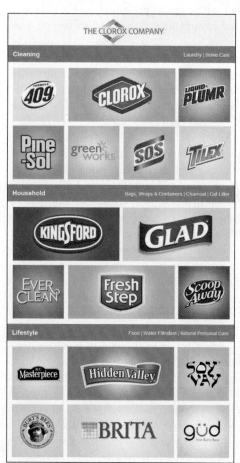

≫ The product mix: The Clorox Company has a nicely contained product mix consistent with its mission to "make everyday life better, every day."

care products, Right Guard deodorant, and Aleve pain reliever. In its most dramatic product pruning move yet, P&G announced plans to cut or sell off as many as 90 to 100 of its remaining brands, resulting in the recent unloading of headliner brands such as Duracell batteries, CoverGirl and Max Factor cosmetics, Wella and Clairol hair care products, and its Iams and other pet food brands. These divestments will allow P&G to focus investment and energy on the 70 to 80 core brands that yield 90 percent of its sales and more than 95 percent of profits. "Less will be much more," says P&G's CEO.[17]

LINKING THE CONCEPTS

Slow down for a minute. To get a better sense of how large and complex a company's product offering can become, investigate Procter & Gamble's product mix.

- Using P&G's Web site (www.pg.com), its annual report, or other sources, develop a list of all the company's product lines and individual products. What surprises you about this list of products?
- Is P&G's product mix consistent? What products has P&G dropped or sold recently? What overall strategy or logic appears to have guided the shaping of this product mix?

Services Marketing

Author Comment
As noted at the start of this chapter, services are "products," too—intangible ones. So all the product topics we've discussed so far apply to services as well as to physical products. However, in this section, we focus on the special characteristics and marketing needs that set services apart.

Services have grown dramatically in recent years. Services now account for 80 percent of the U.S. gross domestic product (GDP). Services are growing even faster in the world economy, making up almost 64 percent of the gross world product.[18]

Service industries vary greatly. *Governments* offer services through courts, employment services, hospitals, military services, police and fire departments, the postal service, and schools. *Private not-for-profit organizations* offer services through museums, charities, churches, colleges, foundations, and hospitals. In addition, a large number of *business organizations* offer services—airlines, banks, hotels, insurance companies, consulting firms, medical and legal practices, entertainment and telecommunications companies, real estate firms, retailers, and others.

The Nature and Characteristics of a Service

A company must consider four special service characteristics when designing marketing programs: intangibility, inseparability, variability, and perishability (see >> **Figure 7.3**).

Service intangibility
Services cannot be seen, tasted, felt, heard, or smelled before they are bought.

Service intangibility means that services cannot be seen, tasted, felt, heard, or smelled before they are bought. For example, people undergoing cosmetic surgery cannot see the result before the purchase. Airline passengers have nothing but a ticket and a promise that they and their luggage will arrive safely at the intended destination, hopefully

>> **Figure 7.3 Four Service Characteristics**

Although services are "products" in a general sense, they have special characteristics and marketing needs. The biggest differences come from the fact that services are essentially intangible and that they are created through direct interactions with customers. Think about your experiences with an airline or Google versus Nike or Apple.

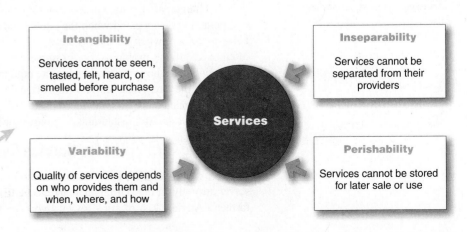

Intangibility
Services cannot be seen, tasted, felt, heard, or smelled before purchase

Inseparability
Services cannot be separated from their providers

Services

Variability
Quality of services depends on who provides them and when, where, and how

Perishability
Services cannot be stored for later sale or use

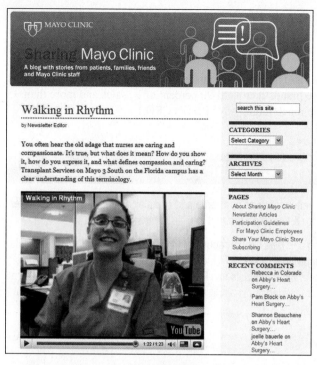

>> By providing customers with organized, honest evidence of
its capabilities, the Mayo Clinic has built one of the most powerful
brands in health care. Its Sharing Mayo Clinic blog lets you hear
directly from those who have been to the clinic or who work there.
Mayo Clinic

at the same time. To reduce uncertainty, buyers look for *signals* of
service quality. They draw conclusions about quality from the place,
people, price, equipment, and communications that they can see.

Therefore, the service provider's task is to make the service tangible in one or more ways and send the right signals about quality.
>> The Mayo Clinic does this well:[19]

> When it comes to hospitals, most patients can't really judge "product
> quality." It's a very complex product that's hard to understand, and you
> can't try it out before buying it. So when considering a hospital, most
> people unconsciously search for evidence that the facility is caring,
> competent, and trustworthy. The Mayo Clinic doesn't leave these things
> to chance. Rather, it offers patients organized and honest evidence of its
> dedication to "providing the best care to every patient every day."
>
> Inside, staff is trained to act in a way that clearly signals Mayo
> Clinic's concern for patient well-being. For example, doctors regularly
> follow up with patients at home to see how they are doing, and they
> work with patients to smooth out scheduling problems. The clinic's
> physical facilities also send the right signals. They've been carefully
> designed to offer a place of refuge, show caring and respect, and signal
> competence. Looking for external confirmation? Go online and hear
> directly from those who've been to the clinic or work there. The Mayo
> Clinic uses social networking—everything from blogs to Facebook,
> Twitter, YouTube, and Pinterest—to enhance the patient experience.
> For example, on the Sharing Mayo Clinic blog (http://sharing
> .mayoclinic.org), patients and their families retell their Mayo experi-
> ences, and Mayo employees offer behind-the-scenes views. The result?
> Highly loyal customers who willingly spread the good word to others,
> building one of the most powerful brands in health care.

Service inseparability

Services are produced and consumed at
the same time and cannot be separated
from their providers.

Physical goods are produced, then stored, then later sold, and then still later consumed. In contrast, services are first sold and then produced and consumed at the same
time. **Service inseparability** means that services cannot be separated from their providers,
whether the providers are people or machines. If a service employee provides the service,
then the employee becomes a part of the service. And customers don't just buy and use a
service; they play an active role in its delivery. Customer coproduction makes *provider–
customer interaction* a special feature of services marketing. Both the provider and the
customer affect the service outcome.

Service variability

The quality of services may vary
greatly depending on who provides
them and when, where, and how they
are provided.

Service variability means that the quality of services depends on who provides them
as well as when, where, and how they are provided. For example, some hotels—say,
Marriott—have reputations for providing better service than others. Still, within a given
Marriott hotel, one registration-counter employee may be cheerful and efficient, whereas
another standing just a few feet away may be grumpy and slow. Even the quality of a
single Marriott employee's service varies according to his or her energy and frame of mind
at the time of each customer encounter.

Service perishability

Services cannot be stored for later sale
or use.

Service perishability means that services cannot be stored for later sale or use. Some
doctors charge patients for missed appointments because the service value existed only at
that point and disappeared when the patient did not show up. The perishability of services
is not a problem when demand is steady. However, when demand fluctuates, service firms
often have difficult problems. For example, because of rush-hour demand, public transportation companies have to own much more equipment than they would if demand were even
throughout the day. Thus, service firms often design strategies for producing a better match
between demand and supply. Hotels and resorts charge lower prices in the off-season to attract more guests. And restaurants hire part-time employees to serve during peak periods.

Marketing Strategies for Service Firms

Just like manufacturing businesses, good service firms use marketing to position themselves strongly in chosen target markets. FedEx promises to take your packages "faster,
farther"; Angie's List offers "Reviews you can trust." At Hampton, "We love having you

here." And St. Jude Children's Hospital is "Finding cures. Saving children." These and other service firms establish their positions through traditional marketing mix activities. However, because services differ from tangible products, they often require additional marketing approaches.

The Service Profit Chain

In a service business, the customer and the front-line service employee *interact* to co-create the service. Effective interaction, in turn, depends on the skills of front-line service employees and on the support processes backing these employees. Thus, successful service companies focus their attention on both their customers and their employees. They understand the **service profit chain**, which links service firm profits with employee and customer satisfaction. This chain consists of five links:[20]

Service profit chain
The chain that links service firm profits with employee and customer satisfaction.

- *Internal service quality.* Superior employee selection and training, a quality work environment, and strong support for those dealing with customers, which results in...
- *Satisfied and productive service employees.* More satisfied, loyal, and hardworking employees, which results in...
- *Greater service value.* More effective and efficient customer value creation, engagement, and service delivery, which results in...
- *Satisfied and loyal customers.* Satisfied customers who remain loyal, make repeat purchases, and refer other customers, which results in...
- *Healthy service profits and growth.* Superior service firm performance.

For example, supermarket chain Wegmans—a perennial customer service champion—has developed a cult-like customer following by putting its employees first. Wegmans believes that happy, superbly trained employees create a superior customer experience. The resulting happy customers become tremendously loyal, give the firm more business, and convince other customers to do the same. That, in turn, results in happy investors. "Our employees are our number one asset, period," says a Wegmans executive. "The first question [we] ask is 'Is this the best thing for employees?'"[21] Similarly, customer-service all-star Zappos.com—the online shoes, clothing, and accessories retailers—knows that happy customers begin with happy, dedicated, energetic employees (see Marketing at Work 7.1).

Internal marketing
Orienting and motivating customer-contact employees and supporting service employees to work as a team to provide customer satisfaction.

Services marketing requires more than just traditional external marketing using the four Ps. >> **Figure 7.4** shows that services marketing also requires *internal marketing* and *interactive marketing*. **Internal marketing** means that the service firm must orient and motivate its customer-contact employees and supporting service people to work as a team to provide customer satisfaction. Marketers must get everyone in the organization to be customer centered. In fact, internal marketing must *precede* external marketing. For example, Zappos starts by hiring the right people and carefully orienting and inspiring them to give unparalleled customer service. The idea is to make certain that employees themselves believe in the brand so that they can authentically deliver the brand's promise to customers.

>> **Figure 7.4 Three Types of Services Marketing**

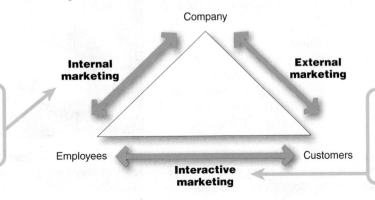

Service firms must sell customer-contact employees on the importance of delighting customers. At Zappos.com, the No. 1 core value is "Deliver WOW through service."

Company

Internal marketing

External marketing

Employees

Customers

Interactive marketing

Then service firms must help employees master the art of interacting with customers. Every employee at Zappos.com, from the CEO down, goes through four weeks of customer loyalty training.

MARKETING AT WORK   7.1

Zappos.com: Taking Care of Those Who Take Care of Customers

Imagine a retailer with service so good its customers wish it would take over the Internal Revenue Service or start up an airline. It might sound like a marketing fantasy, but this scenario is a reality for customer-service all-star Zappos.com. At Zappos, the customer experience really does come first—it's a daily obsession. Says Zappos's understated CEO Tony Hsieh (pronounced "Shay"), "Our whole goal at Zappos is for the Zappos brand to be about the very best customer service and customer experience." Zappos is "Powered by Service."

From the start, the scrappy online retailer of shoes, clothing, handbags, and accessories made customer service a cornerstone of its marketing. As a result, Zappos grew astronomically. In fact, Zappos's online success and passion for customers made it an ideal match for another highly successful, customer-obsessed online retailer, Amazon.com, which purchased Zappos a few years ago and has allowed it to operate as an independent division.

At Zappos, customer care starts with a deep-down, customer-focused culture. How does Zappos turn this culture into a customer reality? It all starts with the company's customer-service reps—what the company calls its Customer Loyalty Team. Most of Zappos.com's business is driven by word-of-mouth and customer interactions with company employees. And Zappos knows that happy *customers* begin with happy, dedicated, and energetic *employees*. So the company starts by hiring the right people, training them thoroughly in customer-service basics, and inspiring them to new heights in taking care of customers.

"Getting customers excited about the service they had at Zappos has to come naturally," says one Zappos marketing executive. "You can't teach it; you have to hire for it." Hiring the right people starts with the application process. The invitation to apply on the Zappos Web site suggests the kind of people Zappos seeks:

> Please check out the Zappos Family's 10 Core Values before applying! They are the heart and soul of our culture and central to how we do business. If you are "fun and a little weird"—and think the other 9 Core Values fit you too—please take a look at our openings! PS: At the Zappos Family of Companies, over-sized egos are not welcome. Over-sized Eggos, however, are most welcome and appreciated!

Once hired, to make sure Zappos's customer obsession permeates the entire organization, each new employee—everyone from the CEO and chief financial officer to the children's footwear buyer—is required to go through four weeks of customer loyalty training. In fact, in an effort to weed out the half-hearted, Zappos actually bribes people to quit. During the four weeks of customer-service training, it offers employees a full month's pay in cash plus payment for the time worked if they *leave* the company. The theory goes that those willing to take the money and run aren't right for Zappos' culture anyway.

Once in place, Zappos treats employees as well as it treats customers. "It's not so much about what the company provides externally," says CEO Hsieh. "It's what the employees ultimately feel internally." The Zappos family culture emphasizes "a satisfying and fulfilling job...and a career you can be proud of. Work hard. Play hard. All the time!" Hsieh continues, "We think it's important for employees to have fun...it drives employee engagement." Zappos creates a relaxed, fun-loving, and close-knit family atmosphere, complete with free meals, a nap room, Nerf gun wars, and Oreo eating contests, not to mention full benefits, a 40 percent employee discount on all Zappos.com merchandise, and even a full-time life coach—all of which make it a great place to work. In fact, Zappos appears annually on *Fortune* magazine's "100 Best Companies to Work For" list.

The result is what one observer calls "1,550 perpetually chipper employees." Every year, the company publishes a "culture book," filled with unedited, often gushy testimonials from Zapponians about what it's like to work there. "Oh my gosh,"

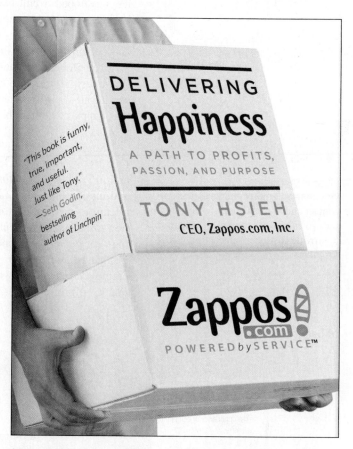

>> Zappos knows that delivering customer happiness begins with happy, dedicated, energetic employees. Zappos is "Powered by Service."
Zappos

says one employee, "this is my home away from home.... It's changed my life.... Our culture is the best reason to work here." Says another, "The most surprising thing about coming to work here is that there are no limits. So pretty much anything you are passionate about is possible." And what are the things about which Zapponians are most passionate? The Zappos family's No. 1 core value: "Deliver WOW through service."

Such enthusiastic employees, in turn, make outstanding brand ambassadors. Whereas many Web sites bury contact information several links deep because they don't really want to hear from customers, Zappos.com puts the number at the top of every single Web page and staffs its call center 24/7. Hsieh sees each customer contact as an opportunity: "We actually want to talk to our customers," he says. "If we handle the call well, we have an opportunity to create an emotional impact and lasting memory."

Hsieh insists that reps be helpful with anything that customers might call about—and he really means it. One customer called in search of a pizza joint open after midnight in Santa Monica, CA. Two minutes later, the Zappos rep found him one. And Zappos doesn't hold its reps accountable for call times. Its longest phone call lasted 10 hours. Another call, from a customer who wanted the rep's help while she looked at what seemed like thousands of pairs of shoes, lasted almost six hours.

At Zappos, each employee is like a little marketing department. Relationships—inside and outside the company—mean everything at Zappos. Hsieh and many other employees stay in direct touch with customers, with each other, and with just about anyone else interested in the company. They use social networking tools such as Facebook, Twitter, Pinterest, and blogs to share information, both good and bad. Such openness might worry some retailers, but Zappos embraces it.

Zappos even features employees in its marketing. For example, it uses associates in short videos to describe and explain its products. In one recent year, it turned out 100,000 such videos of staff—not professional models—showing off shoes, bags, and clothing. Zappos found that when the product includes a personal video explanation, purchases rise and returns decrease.

The moral: Just as the service-profit chain suggests, taking good care of customers begins with taking good care of those who take care of customers. The Zappos customer-driven philosophy is perhaps best summed up by the title of CEO Hsieh's book—*Delivering Happiness: A Path to Profits, Passion, and Purpose*. Zappos's enthusiasm and culture are infectious. Put Zappos happy reps together with happy customers and good things will result. "We've actually had customers ask us if we would please start an airline or run the IRS," Hsieh says, adding, "30 years from now I wouldn't rule out a Zappos airline that's all about the very best service."

Sources: Portions based on http://about.Zappos.com/jobs, accessed March 2015; and Natalie Zmuda, "Zappos: Customer Service First—and a Daily Obsession," *Advertising Age*, October 20, 2008, p. 36; with additional information and quotes from Jim Edwards, "Check Out the Insane Lengths Zappos Customer Service Reps Will Go To," *Business Insider*, January 9, 2012, www.businessinsider.com/zappos-customer-service-crm-2012-1; Tony Hsieh, "Zappos's CEO on Going to Extremes for Customers," *Harvard Business Review*, July–August 2010, pp. 41–44; "Zappos Corporate Culture: Innovating for Employees, Clients, and the Ecosystem," *Innovation Is Everywhere*, www .innovationiseverywhere.com/zappos-corporate-culture-innovating-employees-clients-ecosystem/, accessed March 2015; "100 Best Companies to Work For," *Fortune*, http://money.cnn.com/magazines/fortune/best-companies/, accessed September 2015; and www.youtube.com/users/zappos and www.zappos.com, accessed September 2015.

Interactive marketing
Training service employees in the fine art of interacting with customers to satisfy their needs.

Interactive marketing means that service quality depends heavily on the quality of the buyer–seller interaction during the service encounter. In product marketing, product quality often depends little on how the product is obtained. But in services marketing, service quality depends on both the service deliverer and the quality of delivery. Service marketers, therefore, have to master interactive marketing skills. Thus, Zappos selects only people with an innate "passion to serve" and instructs them carefully in the fine art of interacting with customers to satisfy their every need. All new hires—at all levels of the company—complete a four-week customer-loyalty training regimen.

Today, as competition and costs increase and as productivity and quality decrease, more services marketing sophistication is needed. Service companies face three major marketing tasks: They want to increase their *service differentiation, service quality*, and *service productivity*.

Managing Service Differentiation

In these days of intense price competition, service marketers often complain about the difficulty of differentiating their services from those of competitors. To the extent that customers view the services of different providers as similar, they care less about the provider than the price. The solution to price competition is to develop a differentiated offer, delivery, and image.

The *offer* can include innovative features that set one company's offer apart from competitors' offers. For example, some retailers differentiate themselves with offerings that take you well beyond the products they stock. »Apple's highly successful stores offer a Genius Bar for technical support and a host of free workshops on everything from iPhone, iPad, and

Mac basics to the intricacies of using iMovie to turn home movies into blockbusters. At some Dick's Sporting Goods, customers can sample shoes on Dick's indoor footwear track, test golf clubs with an on-site golf swing analyzer and putting green, shoot bows in its archery range, and receive personalized fitness product guidance from an in-store team of fitness trainers.

Service companies can differentiate their service *delivery* by having more able and reliable customer-contact people, developing a superior physical environment in which the service product is delivered, or designing a superior delivery process. For example, many grocery chains now offer online shopping and home delivery as a better way to shop than having to drive, park, wait in line, and tote groceries home. And most banks offer mobile phone apps that allow you to more easily transfer money and check account balances. Many even allow mobile check deposits. "Sign, snap a photo, and submit a check from anywhere," says one Citibank ad. "It's easier than running to the bank."

Finally, service companies also can work on differentiating their *images* through symbols and branding. Aflac adopted the duck as its advertising symbol. Today, the duck is immortalized through stuffed animals, golf club covers, and free ringtones and screensavers. The well-known Aflac duck helped make the big but previously unknown insurance company memorable and approachable. Other well-known service characters and symbols include the GEICO gecko, Progressive Insurance's Flo, McDonald's golden arches, Allstate's "good hands," the Twitter bird, and the freckled, red-haired, pig-tailed Wendy's girl. Mr. Clean has amassed more than 1 million Facebook fans.

Managing Service Quality

A service firm can differentiate itself by delivering consistently higher quality than its competitors provide. Like manufacturers before them, most service industries have now joined the customer-driven quality movement. And like product marketers, service providers need to identify what target customers expect in regard to service quality.

Unfortunately, service quality is harder to define and judge than product quality. For instance, it is harder to agree on the quality of a haircut than on the quality of a hair dryer. Customer retention is perhaps the best measure of quality; a service firm's ability to hang onto its customers depends on how consistently it delivers value to them.

Top service companies set high service-quality standards. They watch service performance closely, both their own and that of competitors. They do not settle for merely good service—they strive for 100 percent defect-free service. A 98 percent performance standard may sound good, but using this standard, the U.S. Postal Service would lose or misdirect 361,000 pieces of mail each hour, and U.S. pharmacies would misfill 1.5 million prescriptions each week.[22]

Unlike product manufacturers who can adjust their machinery and inputs until everything is perfect, service quality will always vary, depending on the interactions between employees and customers. As hard as they may try, even the best companies will have an occasional late delivery, burned steak, or grumpy employee. However, good *service recovery* can turn angry customers into loyal ones. In fact, good recovery can win more customer purchasing and loyalty than if things had gone well in the first place.

For example, Southwest Airlines has a proactive customer communications team whose job is to find the situations in which something went wrong—a mechanical delay, bad weather, a medical emergency, or a berserk passenger—then remedy the bad experience quickly, within 24 hours if possible.[23] The team's communications to passengers, usually emails these days, have three basic components: a sincere apology, a brief explanation of what happened, and a gift to make it up, usually a voucher in dollars that can be used on their next Southwest flight. Surveys show that when Southwest handles a delay situation well, customers score it 14 to 16 points higher than on regular on-time flights.

These days, social media such as Facebook and Twitter can help companies root out and remedy customer dissatisfaction with service. As discussed in Chapter 4, many companies now monitor the digital space to spot customer issues quickly and respond in real time. A quick and thoughtful response can turn a dissatisfied customer into a brand advocate.[24]

Managing Service Productivity

With their costs rising rapidly, service firms are under great pressure to increase service productivity. They can do so in several ways. They can train current employees better or hire new ones who will work harder or more skillfully. Or they can increase the quantity of their service by giving up some quality. Finally, a service provider can harness the power of technology. Although we often think of technology's power to save time and costs in manufacturing companies, it also has great—and often untapped—potential to make service workers more productive.

However, companies must avoid pushing productivity so hard that doing so reduces quality. Attempts to streamline a service or cut costs can make a service company more efficient in the short run. But that can also reduce its longer-run ability to innovate, maintain service quality, or respond to consumer needs and desires. ≫For example, some airlines have learned this lesson the hard way as they attempt to economize in the face of rising costs. Passengers on most airlines now encounter "time-saving" check-in kiosks rather than personal counter service. And most airlines have stopped offering even the little things for free—such as in-flight snacks—and now charge extra for everything from checked luggage to aisle seats. The result is a plane full of disgruntled customers. In their attempts to improve productivity, many airlines have mangled customer service.

Thus, in attempting to improve service productivity, companies must be mindful of how they create and deliver customer value. They should be careful not to take *service* out of the service. In fact, a company may purposely lower service productivity in order to improve service quality, in turn allowing it to maintain higher prices and profit margins.

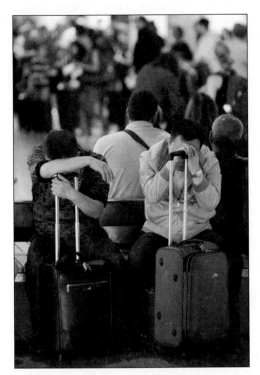

≫ **Managing service productivity: Companies should be careful not to take things too far. For example, in their attempts to improve productivity, some airlines have mangled customer service.**

DPA/Stringer/Getty Images

 LINKING THE CONCEPTS

Let's pause here for a moment. We've said that although services are "products" in a general sense, they have special characteristics and marketing needs. To get a better grasp of this concept, select a traditional product brand, such as Nike or Honda. Next, select a service brand, such as JetBlue Airlines or McDonald's. Then compare the two.

- How are the characteristics and marketing needs of the product and service brands you selected similar?
- How do the characteristics and marketing needs of the two brands differ? How are these differences reflected in each brand's marketing strategy? Keep these differences in mind as we move into the final section of the chapter.

Author Comment
A brand represents everything that a product or service *means* to consumers. As such, brands are valuable assets to a company. For example, when you hear someone say "Coca-Cola," what do you think, feel, or remember? What about "Target"? Or "Google"?

Branding Strategy: Building Strong Brands

Some analysts see brands as *the* major enduring asset of a company, outlasting the company's specific products and facilities. John Stewart, former CEO of Quaker Oats, once said, "If this business were split up, I would give you the land and bricks and mortar, and I would keep the brands and trademarks, and I would fare better than you." A former CEO of McDonald's declared, "If every asset we own, every building, and every piece of equipment were destroyed in a terrible natural disaster, we would be able to borrow all the money to replace it very quickly because of the value of our brand.... The brand is more valuable than the totality of all these assets."[25]

Thus, brands are powerful assets that must be carefully developed and managed. In this section, we examine the key strategies for building and managing product and service brands.

Brand Equity and Brand Value

Brands are more than just names and symbols. They are a key element in the company's relationships with consumers. Brands represent consumers' perceptions and feelings about a product and its performance—everything that the product or the service *means* to consumers. In the final analysis, brands exist in the heads of consumers. As one well-respected marketer once said, "Products are created in the factory, but brands are created in the mind."[26]

A powerful brand has high *brand equity*. **Brand equity** is the differential effect that knowing the brand name has on customer response to the product and its marketing. It's a measure of the brand's ability to capture consumer preference and loyalty. A brand has positive brand equity when consumers react more favorably to it than to a generic or unbranded version of the same product. It has negative brand equity if consumers react less favorably than to an unbranded version.

Brands vary in the amount of power and value they hold in the marketplace. Some brands—such as Coca-Cola, Nike, Disney, GE, McDonald's, Harley-Davidson, and others—become larger-than-life icons that maintain their power in the market for years, even generations. Other brands—such as Google, Apple, ESPN, Instagram, and Wikipedia—create fresh consumer excitement and loyalty. These brands win in the marketplace not simply because they deliver unique benefits or reliable service. Rather, they succeed because they forge deep connections with customers. People really do have relationships with brands. >> For example, to devoted Vespa fans around the world, the brand stands for much more than just a scooter. It takes them places, physically and emotionally. It stands for "La Vespa Vita," a carefree, stylish lifestyle. Colorful, cute, sleek, nimble, efficient—the Vespa brand represents the freedom to roam wherever you wish and "live life with passion."[27]

Ad agency Young & Rubicam's BrandAsset Valuator measures brand strength along four consumer perception dimensions: *differentiation* (what makes the brand stand out), *relevance* (how consumers feel it meets their needs), *knowledge* (how much consumers know about the brand), and *esteem* (how highly consumers regard and respect the brand).

Brand equity
The differential effect that knowing the brand name has on customer response to the product and its marketing.

Brands with strong brand equity rate high on all four dimensions. The brand must be distinct, or consumers will have no reason to choose it over other brands. However, the fact that a brand is highly differentiated doesn't necessarily mean that consumers will buy it. The brand must stand out in ways that are relevant to consumers' needs. Even a differentiated, relevant brand is far from a shoe-in. Before consumers will respond to the brand, they must first know about and understand it. And that familiarity must lead to a strong, positive consumer–brand connection.[28]

Thus, positive brand equity derives from consumer feelings about and connections with a brand. Consumers sometimes bond *very* closely with specific brands. As perhaps the ultimate expression of brand devotion, a surprising number of people—and not just Harley-Davidson fans—have their favorite brand tattooed on their bodies.

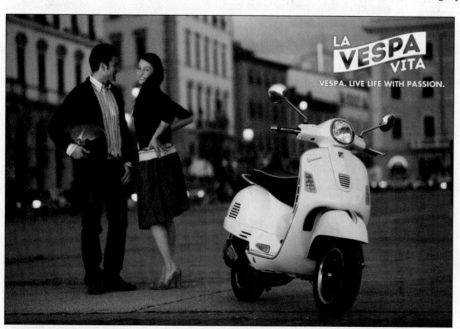

>> Consumers' relationship with brands: To devoted Vespa fans, the brand stands for much more than just a scooter. It stands for "La Vespa Vita"—living life with passion.
Courtesy of Piaggio Group

Whether it's contemporary new brands such as Facebook or Amazon or old classics like Harley or Converse, strong brands are built around an ideal of engaging consumers in some relevant way.

A brand with high brand equity is a very valuable asset. **Brand value** is the total financial value of a brand. Measuring such value is difficult. However, according to one estimate, the brand value of Google is a whopping $159 billion, with Apple at $148 billion, IBM at $108 billion, Microsoft at $90 billion, McDonald's at $86 billion, and Coca-Cola at $81 billion. Other brands rating among the world's most valuable include AT&T, China Mobile, GE, Walmart, and Amazon.[29]

High brand equity provides a company with many competitive advantages. A powerful brand enjoys a high level of consumer brand awareness and loyalty. Because consumers expect stores to carry the particular brand, the company has more leverage in bargaining with resellers. Because a brand name carries high credibility, the company can more easily launch line and brand extensions. A powerful brand also offers the company some defense against fierce price competition and other competitor marketing actions.

Above all, however, a powerful brand forms the basis for building strong and profitable customer engagement and relationships. The fundamental asset underlying brand equity is *customer equity*—the value of customer relationships that the brand creates. A powerful brand is important, but what it really represents is a profitable set of loyal customers. The proper focus of marketing is building customer equity, with brand management serving as a major marketing tool. Companies need to think of themselves not as portfolios of brands but as portfolios of customers.

Building Strong Brands

Branding poses challenging decisions to the marketer. **≫ Figure 7.5** shows that the major brand strategy decisions involve *brand positioning, brand name selection, brand sponsorship*, and *brand development*.

Brand Positioning

Marketers need to position their brands clearly in target customers' minds. They can position brands at any of three levels.[30] At the lowest level, they can position the brand on *product attributes*. For example, P&G invented the disposable diaper category with its Pampers brand. Early Pampers marketing focused on attributes such as fluid absorption, fit, and disposability. In general, however, attributes are the least desirable level for brand positioning. Competitors can easily copy attributes. More important, customers are not interested in attributes as such—they are interested in what the attributes will do for them.

A brand can be better positioned by associating its name with a desirable *benefit*. Thus, Pampers can go beyond technical product attributes and talk about the resulting containment and baby skin-health benefits from staying dry. Some successful brands positioned on benefits are FedEx (guaranteed on-time delivery), Nike (performance), Walmart (save money), and Instagram (capturing and sharing moments).

The strongest brands go beyond attribute or benefit positioning. They are positioned on strong *beliefs and values,* engaging customers on a deep, emotional level. For example, to parents, Pampers mean much more than just containment and dryness. The Pampers Web site (www.pampers.com) positions Pampers as a "love, sleep, and play" brand that's concerned about happy babies, parent–child relationships, and total baby care. Says a former

Brand value
The total financial value of a brand.

Brands are powerful assets that must be carefully developed and managed. As this figure suggests, building strong brands involves many challenging decisions.

≫ **Figure 7.5 Major Brand Strategy Decisions**

P&G executive, "Our baby care business didn't start growing aggressively until we changed Pampers from being about dryness to helping mom with her baby's development."[31]

Successful brands engage customers on a deep, emotional level. Advertising agency Saatchi & Saatchi suggests that brands should strive to become *lovemark*s, products or services that "inspire loyalty beyond reason." Brands ranging from Apple, Disney, Nike, and Coca-Cola to Trader Joe's, Google, and Pinterest have achieved this status with many of their customers. Lovemark brands pack an emotional wallop. Customers don't just like these brands; they have strong emotional connections with them and love them unconditionally.[32] Brands don't have to be big or legendary to be classified as lovemarks. Consider Shake Shack, which began 11 years ago as a lowly hot dog cart in Manhattan and grew into a small burger chain with a big, almost cult-like following. The occasionally epic lines at local Shake Shacks testify to its status as a lovemark brand.

When positioning a brand, the marketer should establish a mission for the brand and a vision of what the brand must be and do. A brand is the company's promise to deliver a specific set of features, benefits, services, and experiences consistently to buyers. The brand promise must be clear, simple, and honest. Motel 6, for example, offers clean rooms, low prices, and good service but does not promise expensive furnishings or large bathrooms. In contrast, the Ritz-Carlton offers luxurious rooms and a truly memorable experience but does not promise low prices.

>> Brands don't have to be big or legendary to be classified as lovemarks. The occasionally epic lines at local Shake Shacks testify to its lovemark status.

Chuck Solomon/Getty Images

Brand Name Selection

A good name can add greatly to a product's success. However, finding the best brand name is a difficult task. It begins with a careful review of the product and its benefits, the target market, and proposed marketing strategies. After that, naming a brand becomes part science, part art, and a measure of instinct.

Desirable qualities for a brand name include the following: (1) It should suggest something about the product's benefits and qualities: Beautyrest, Slimfast, Snapchat, Pinterest. (2) It should be easy to pronounce, recognize, and remember: iPad, Tide, Jelly Belly, Twitter, JetBlue. (3) The brand name should be distinctive: Panera, Swiffer, Zappos, Nest. (4) It should be extendable—Amazon.com began as an online bookseller but chose a name that would allow expansion into other categories. (5) The name should translate easily into foreign languages. The official name of Microsoft's Bing search engine in China is *bi ying,* which literally means "very certain to respond" in Chinese.[33] (6) It should be capable of registration and legal protection. A brand name cannot be registered if it infringes on existing brand names.

Choosing a new brand name is hard work. After a decade of choosing quirky names (Yahoo!, Google) or trademark-proof made-up names (Novartis, Aventis, Accenture), today's style is to build brands around names that have real meaning. For example, names like Silk (soy milk), Method (home products), Smartwater (beverages), and Snapchat (photo messaging app) are simple and make intuitive sense. But with trademark applications soaring, *available* new names can be hard to find. Try it yourself. Pick a product and see if you can come up with a better name for it. How about Moonshot? Tickle? Vanilla? Treehugger? Simplicity? Mindbender? Google them and you'll find that they are already taken.

Once chosen, the brand name must be protected. Many firms try to build a brand name that will eventually become identified with the product category. Brand names such as Kleenex, JELL-O, BAND-AID, Scotch Tape, Velcro, Formica, Magic Marker, Post-it Notes, and Ziploc have succeeded in this way. However, their very success may threaten

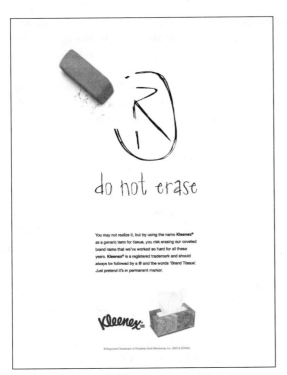

do not erase

You may not realize it, but by using the name Kleenex® as a generic term for tissue, you risk erasing our coveted brand name that we've worked so hard for all these years. Kleenex® is a registered trademark and should always be followed by a ® and the words 'Brand Tissue'. Just pretend it's in permanent marker.

Kleenex®

®Registered Trademark of Kimberly-Clark Worldwide, Inc. ©2015 KCWW.

>> **Protecting the brand name: This ad asks advertisers and others to always add the registered trademark symbol and the words "Brand Tissue" to the Kleenex name, helping to keep from "erasing our coveted brand name that we've worked so hard for all these years."**

Kimberly-Clark Worldwide, Inc. Reprinted with permission.

Store brand (or **private brand**)
A brand created and owned by a reseller of a product or service.

the company's rights to the name. Many originally protected brand names—such as cellophane, aspirin, nylon, kerosene, linoleum, yo-yo, trampoline, escalator, thermos, and shredded wheat—are now generic names that any seller can use.

>> To protect their brands, marketers present them carefully using the word *brand* and the registered trademark symbol, as in "BAND-AID® Brand Adhesive Bandages." Even the long-standing "I am stuck on BAND-AID 'cause BAND-AID's stuck on me" jingle has now become "I am stuck on BAND-AID brand 'cause BAND-AID's stuck on me." Similarly, a recent Kleenex ad advises advertisers and others that the name Kleenex should always be followed by the registered trademark symbol and the words "Brand Tissue." "You may not realize it, but by using the name Kleenex® as a generic term for tissue," says the ad, "you risk erasing our coveted brand name that we've worked so hard for all these years."

Brand Sponsorship

A manufacturer has four sponsorship options. The product may be launched as a *national brand* (or *manufacturer's brand*), as when Samsung and Kellogg sell their output under their own brand names (the Samsung Galaxy tablet or Kellogg's Frosted Flakes). Or the manufacturer may sell to resellers who give the product a *private brand* (also called a *store brand* or *distributor brand*). Although most manufacturers create their own brand names, others market licensed brands. Finally, two companies can join forces and *co-brand* a product. We discuss each of these options in turn.

National Brands versus Store Brands. National brands (or manufacturers' brands) have long dominated the retail scene. In recent times, however, increasing numbers of retailers and wholesalers have created their own **store brands** (or **private brands**). Store brands have been gaining strength for more than two decades, but recent tighter economic times have created a store-brand boom. Studies show that consumers are now buying even more private brands, which on average yield a 38 percent savings.[34] More frugal times give store brands a boost as consumers become more price-conscious and less brand-conscious.

In fact, store brands have grown much faster than national brands in recent years. Private labels now account for almost 17 percent of drugstore dollar sales and 20 percent of supermarket dollar sales. One of every four supermarket products sold is private label. Similarly, for apparel sales, department store private-label brands have shot up. At Kohl's, for example, private label sales grew from 42 percent to 52 percent over the past five years.[35]

Many large retailers skillfully market a deep assortment of store-brand merchandise. >> For example, Kroger's private brands—the Kroger house brand, Private Selection, Heritage Farm, Simple Truth (natural and organic), Psst and Check This Out (savings), and others—add up to a whopping 25 percent of the giant grocery retailer's sales, nearly $25 billion worth annually. At thrifty grocery chain ALDI, more than 90 percent of sales come from private brands such as Baker's Choice, Friendly Farms, Simply Nature, and Mama Cozzi's Pizza Kitchen. Even online retailer Amazon has developed a stable of private brands, including Amazon Elements (diapers and other everyday essentials), AmazonBasics (electronics), Pinzon (kitchen gadgets), Strathwood (outdoor furniture), Pike Street (bath and home products), and Denali (tools).[36]

Once known as "generic" or "no-name" brands, today's store brands are shedding their image as cheap knockoffs of national brands. Store brands now offer much greater selection, and they are rapidly achieving name-brand quality.

>> **Store Brands: Kroger's store brands—from Private Selection to Simple Truth—account for 25 percent of the grocery retailer's sales.**

Al Behrman/AP Images

In fact, retailers such as Target and Trader Joe's are out-innovating many of their national-brand competitors. Kroger even offers a Kroger brand guarantee—"Try it, like it, or get the national brand free." As a result, consumers are becoming loyal to store brands for reasons besides price. Recent research showed that 9 out of 10 consumers believe that several store brands are just as good as national brands. "Sometimes I think they don't actually know what is a store brand," says one retail analyst.[37] In some cases, consumers are even willing to pay more for store brands that have been positioned as gourmet or premium items.

In the so-called *battle of the brands* between national and private brands, retailers have many advantages. They control what products they stock, where they go on the shelf, what prices they charge, and which ones they will feature in local promotions. Retailers often price their store brands lower than comparable national brands and feature the price differences in side-by-side comparisons on store shelves. Although store brands can be hard to establish and costly to stock and promote, they also yield higher profit margins for the reseller. And they give resellers exclusive products that cannot be bought from competitors, resulting in greater store traffic and loyalty. Fast-growing retailer Trader Joe's, which carries 85 percent store brands, largely controls its own brand destiny rather than relying on producers to make and manage the brands it needs to serve its customers best.[38]

To compete with store brands, national brands must sharpen their value propositions, especially when appealing to today's more frugal consumers. Many national brands are fighting back by rolling out more discounts and coupons to defend their market share. In the long run, however, leading brand marketers must compete by investing in new brands, new features, and quality improvements that set them apart. They must design strong advertising programs to maintain high awareness and preference. And they must find ways to partner with major distributors to find distribution economies and improve joint performance.

For example, in response to the surge in private-label sales, consumer product giant Procter & Gamble has redoubled its efforts to develop and promote new and better products, particularly at lower price points. "We invest $2 billion a year in research and development, $400 million on consumer knowledge, and about 10 percent of sales on advertising," says P&G's CEO. "Store brands don't have that capacity." As a result, P&G brands still dominate in their categories. For example, its Tide, Gain, Cheer, and other premium laundry detergent brands capture a combined 60 percent of the $7 billion U.S. detergent market.[39]

Licensing. Most manufacturers take years and spend millions to create their own brand names. However, some companies license names or symbols previously created by other manufacturers, names of well-known celebrities, or characters from popular movies and books. For a fee, any of these can provide an instant and proven brand name. For example, consider the Kodak brand with its familiar red and yellow colors, which has retained its value even after the company went bankrupt and discontinued its consumer products:[40]

Consumer products carrying the Kodak name are no longer made by Eastman Kodak, which now focuses exclusively on printing-related commercial equipment and technology following its bankruptcy a few years ago. But the Kodak brand name and associated "Kodak moments" still resonate powerfully with consumers. So even though Eastman Kodak has dropped its consumer lines, we'll still be seeing a lot of Kodak-branded consumer products made by other companies under licensing agreements with Eastman Kodak. For example, Sakar International now makes Kodak cameras and accessories, and the Bullitt Group will soon launch a variety of Kodak electronics, including an Android smartphone and a tablet computer. Video monitoring company Seedonk makes and sells a Kodak Baby Monitoring System.

Thus, the venerable old Kodak name still has value to both Eastman Kodak and the licensees who put it on their products. For Kodak, brand licensing agreements earn the company upwards of $200 million a year. In turn, licensees get a name that's immediately familiar and trusted—it will be a lot easier to market a Kodak phone than a Bullitt phone or a Kodak baby monitoring system than a Seedonk one. "It was difficult to find a brand that resonated—family values, taking care of loved ones," says a Seedonk executive. "Then the Kodak opportunity came up. Kodak Moments, these are things that are important to our customers."

Licensing: Nickelodeon has developed a stable full of hugely popular characters—such as SpongeBob SquarePants—that generate billions of dollars of retail sales each year.

AF Archive/Alamy

Apparel and accessories sellers pay large royalties to adorn their products—from blouses to ties and linens to luggage—with the names or initials of well-known fashion innovators such as Calvin Klein, Tommy Hilfiger, Gucci, or Armani. Sellers of children's products attach an almost endless list of character names to clothing, toys, school supplies, linens, dolls, lunch boxes, cereals, and other items. Licensed character names range from classics such as Sesame Street, Disney, Barbie, Star Wars, Scooby Doo, Hello Kitty, SpongeBob SquarePants, and Dr. Seuss characters to the more recent Doc McStuffins, Monster High, Angry Birds, and Ben 10. And currently, numerous top-selling retail toys are products based on television shows and movies.

Name and character licensing has grown rapidly in recent years. Annual retail sales of licensed products worldwide have grown from only $4 billion in 1977 to $55 billion in 1987 and more than $252 billion today. Licensing can be a highly profitable business for many companies. For example, Nickelodeon's hugely popular SpongeBob SquarePants character by itself has generated some $12 billion worth of endorsement deals over the past 15 years. Disney is the world's biggest licensor with a studio full of hugely popular characters, from the Disney Princesses and Disney Fairies to heroes from *Toy Story* and *Cars* and classic characters such as Mickey and Minnie Mouse. Disney characters reaped a reported $41 billion in worldwide merchandise sales last year.[41]

Co-branding

The practice of using the established brand names of two different companies on the same product.

Co-branding. **Co-branding** occurs when two established brand names of different companies are used on the same product. Co-branding offers many advantages. Because each brand operates in a different category, the combined brands create broader consumer appeal and greater brand equity. For example, Benjamin Moore and Pottery Barn joined forces to create a special collection of Benjamin Moore paint colors designed to perfectly coordinate with Pottery Barn's unique furnishings and accents. Taco Bell and Doritos teamed up to create the Doritos Locos Taco. Taco Bell sold more than 100 million of the tacos in just the first 10 weeks and quickly added Cool Ranch and Fiery versions and has since sold more than a billion. More than just co-branding, these companies are "co-making" these products.[42]

Co-branding can take advantage of the complementary strengths of two brands. It also allows a company to expand its existing brand into a category it might otherwise have difficulty entering alone. For example, Nike and Apple co-branded the Nike+iPod Sport Kit, which lets runners link their Nike shoes with their iPods to track and enhance running performance in real time. The Nike+iPod arrangement gave Apple a presence in the sports and fitness market. At the same time, it helps Nike bring new value to its customers.

Co-branding can also have limitations. Such relationships usually involve complex legal contracts and licenses. Co-branding partners must carefully coordinate their advertising, sales promotion, and other marketing efforts. Finally, when co-branding, each partner must trust that the other will take good care of its brand. If something damages the reputation of one brand, it can tarnish the co-brand as well.

Brand Development

A company has four choices when it comes to developing brands (see **Figure 7.6**). It can introduce *line extensions, brand extensions, multibrands,* or *new brands.*

Line extension

Extending an existing brand name to new forms, colors, sizes, ingredients, or flavors of an existing product category.

Line Extensions. **Line extensions** occur when a company extends existing brand names to new forms, colors, sizes, ingredients, or flavors of an existing product category. For example, over the years, KFC has extended its "finger lickin' good" chicken lineup well beyond original recipe, bone-in Kentucky fried chicken. It now offers grilled chicken, boneless fried chicken, chicken tenders, hot wings, chicken bites, and, most recently, KFC Go Cups—chicken and potato wedges in a handy car-cup holder that lets customers snack on the go.

>> **Figure 7.6 Brand Development Strategies**

Product category

	Existing	New
Existing	Line extension	Brand extension
New	Multibrands	New brands

(Brand name on vertical axis)

> This is a very handy framework for analyzing brand development opportunities. For example, what strategy did Toyota use when it introduced the Toyota Camry Hybrid? When it introduced the Toyota Prius? The Scion?

A company might introduce line extensions as a low-cost, low-risk way to introduce new products. Or it might want to meet consumer desires for variety, use excess capacity, or simply command more shelf space from resellers. However, line extensions involve some risks. An overextended brand name might cause consumer confusion or lose some of its specific meaning.

For example, in its efforts to offer something for everyone—from basic burger buffs to practical parents to health-minded fast-food seekers—McDonald's has created a menu bulging with options. Some customers find the crowded menu a bit overwhelming, and offering so many choices has complicated the chain's food assembly process and slowed service at counters and drive-throughs. McDonald's has extended its menu by more than 40 percent in the past seven years, and average drive-thru wait times are the longest they've been in 15 years. As a result, McDonald's recently announced plans to cut items and simplify its menu.[43]

Brand extension

Extending an existing brand name to new product categories.

At some point, additional extensions might add little value to a line. For instance, the original Doritos Tortilla Chips have morphed into a U.S. roster of more than 20 different types of chips and flavors, plus dozens more in foreign markets. Flavors include everything from Nacho Cheese and Pizza Supreme to Blazin' Buffalo & Ranch, Fiery Fusion, and Salsa Verde. Or how about duck-flavored Gold Peking Duck Chips or wasabi-flavored Mr. Dragon's Fire Chips (Japan)? Although the line seems to be doing well with global sales of nearly $5 billion, the original Doritos chips now seem like just another flavor.[44] And how much would adding yet another flavor steal from Doritos' own sales versus those of competitors? A line extension works best when it takes sales away from competing brands, not when it "cannibalizes" the company's other items.

>> **Brand extensions:** Nest is now extending its brand to include "Works with Nest," applications developed with a variety of partners that let its smart devices interact with and control everything from video monitoring devices, smart door locks, and home lighting systems to home appliances and fitness tracking bands.

Nest Labs

Brand Extensions. A **brand extension** extends a current brand name to new or modified products in a new category. For example, Nest—the maker of stylish, connected, learning thermostats that can be controlled remotely from a phone—extended its line with an equally smart and stylish Nest Protect home smoke and carbon monoxide alarm. >> It's now extending the Nest line to include "Works with Nest," applications developed with a variety of partners that let its smart devices interact with and control everything from video monitoring devices, smart door locks, and home lighting systems to home appliances and fitness tracking bands. All of the extensions fit together under Nest's smart homes mission.[45]

A brand extension gives a new product instant recognition and faster acceptance. It also saves the high advertising costs usually required to build a new brand name. At the same time, a brand extension strategy involves some risk. The extension may confuse the image of the main brand—for example, how about Zippo perfume or Dr Pepper marinades? Brand extensions such as Cheetos lip balm, Heinz pet food, and Life Savers gum met early deaths.[46] And if a brand extension fails, it may harm consumer attitudes toward other products carrying the same brand name. Furthermore, a brand name may not be appropriate to a particular new product, even if it is well made and satisfying—would you consider flying on Hooters Air or wearing an Evian water-filled padded bra (both failed)? Thus, before transferring a brand name to a new product, marketers must research how well the extension fits the parent brand's associations as well as how much the parent brand will boost the extension's market success (see Marketing at Work 7.2).

Multibrands. Companies often market many different brands in a given product category. For example, in the United States, PepsiCo markets at least eight brands of soft drinks (Pepsi, Sierra Mist, Mountain Dew, Manzanita Sol, Mirinda, IZZE, Tropicana Twister, and Mug root beer), three brands of sports and energy drinks (Gatorade, AMP Energy, Starbucks Refreshers), four brands of bottled teas and coffees (Lipton, SoBe, Starbucks, and Tazo), three brands of bottled waters (Aquafina, H2OH!, and SoBe), and nine brands of fruit drinks (Tropicana, Dole, IZZE, Lipton, Looza, Ocean Spray, and others). Each brand includes a long list of sub-brands. For instance, SoBe consists of SoBe Teas & Elixers, SoBe Lifewater, SoBe Lean, and SoBe Lifewater with Coconut Water. Aquafina includes regular Aquafina, Aquafina Flavorsplash, and Aquafina Sparkling.

Multibranding offers a way to establish different features that appeal to different customer segments, lock up more reseller shelf space, and capture a larger market share. For example, although PepsiCo's many brands of beverages compete with one another on supermarket shelves, the combined brands reap a much greater overall market share than any single brand ever could. Similarly, by positioning multiple brands in multiple segments, Pepsi's eight soft drink brands combine to capture much more market share than any single brand could capture by itself.

A major drawback of multibranding is that each brand might obtain only a small market share, and none may be very profitable. The company may end up spreading its resources over many brands instead of building a few brands to a highly profitable level. These companies should reduce the number of brands they sell in a given category and set up tighter screening procedures for new brands. This happened to GM, which in recent years has cut numerous brands from its portfolio, including Saturn, Oldsmobile, Pontiac, Hummer, and Saab. Similarly, as part of its recent turnaround, Ford dropped its Mercury line, sold off Volvo, and pruned the number of Ford nameplates from 97 to fewer than 20.

New Brands. A company might believe that the power of its existing brand name is waning, so a new brand name is needed. Or it may create a new brand name when it enters a new product category for which none of its current brand names are appropriate. For example, Toyota created the separate Lexus brand aimed at luxury car consumers and the Scion brand, targeted toward Millennial consumers.

As with multibranding, offering too many new brands can result in a company spreading its resources too thin. And in some industries, such as consumer packaged goods, consumers and retailers have become concerned that there are already too many brands with too few differences between them. Thus, P&G, PepsiCo, Kraft, and other large marketers of consumer products are now pursuing megabrand strategies—weeding out weaker or slower-growing brands and focusing their marketing dollars on brands that can achieve the number-one or number-two market share positions with good growth prospects in their categories.

Managing Brands

Companies must manage their brands carefully. First, the brand's positioning must be continuously communicated to consumers. Major brand marketers often spend huge amounts on advertising to create brand awareness and build preference and loyalty. For example, worldwide, Coca-Cola spends almost $3 billion annually to advertise its many brands, GM spends nearly $3.4 billion, Unilever spends $7.9 billion, and P&G spends an astounding $11.5 billion.[47]

Such advertising campaigns can help create name recognition, brand knowledge, and perhaps even some brand preference. However, the fact is that brands are not maintained

MARKETING AT WORK   7.2

Brand Extensions: Consumers Say "Yeah!" or "Huh?"

These days, a large majority of new products—tens of thousands of them every year—are extensions of already-successful brands. Compared with building new brands, extensions can create immediate new-product familiarity and acceptance. For example, it's not just any new wireless charging mat for your mobile devices, it's a Duracell Powermat. And it's not just a new, no-name over-the-counter sleep-aid, it's Vicks ZzzQuil. Extensions such as the Duracell Powermat and Vicks ZzzQuil make good sense—they connect well with the core brand's values and build on its strengths.

But for every sensible and successful brand extension, there are puzzlers that leave you scratching your head and asking, "Huh? What were they thinking?" For example, how about Gerber food for adults (including a lip-smacking pureed sweet-and-sour pork and chicken Madeira)? Or how would you feel about quaffing a can of Exxon fruit punch or Kodak quencher? Other misbegotten attempts to stretch a good name include Cracker Jack cereal, Smucker's premium ketchup, Carnation pet food, and Fruit of the Loom laundry detergent. Not only were these extensions epic flops themselves, they threatened to sully the reputations of the base brands they extended. Huh? Really. What *were* they thinking?

What separates brand extension hits from misses? According to brand extension consultancy Parham | Santana, the success of a brand extension rests on three pillars: The extension should have a logical fit with the parent brand; the parent brand should give the extension a competitive advantage in a new category; and the extension should offer significant sales and profit potential.

It's the "fit factor" that seems to drive the other two pillars. The value of any brand is its good name, which it earns over time. People become loyal to it; they trust it to deliver a consistent set of attributes. You can't just take a familiar brand name and slap it on a product in another category. Instead, a good extension should fit logically with its parent brand. But brands are complex perceptual and emotional entities, so fit can be hard to define. One way to ensure fit is to focus on the brand's core product portfolio.

Consider the recent introduction of Planters Peanut Butter. For more than 100 years, the Planters brand has focused on one type of product—nuts. Cashews, almonds, pistachios, walnuts, sunflower seeds, and, of course, peanuts. No brand is more strongly associated with America's favorite nut. The company's mascot—the 100-year-old, monocled Mr. Peanut—is one of the best-known icons in advertising history. Given Planters' focus on nuts in general and on peanuts in particular, extending the brand to include peanut butter seems obvious. Consumers appear to agree. Only nine months after its introduction, Planters Peanut Butter had achieved a profitable, mid-single-digit share in a mature and highly competitive market.

Other well-known brands, however, have squandered consumer trust by attaching their good names to something totally out of character. For example, Louis Sherry No Sugar Added Gorgonzola Cheese Dressing was everything that the Louis Sherry brand—known for its rich chocolate candies and ice cream—shouldn't be: sugarless, cheese, and salad dressing. Similarly, Zippo, the company that's been making quality refillable lighters for more than 80 years, recently extended its brand with a perfume, named Zippo The Woman. The perfume has an attractive fruity and floral fragrance, and it comes in a frosted pink container that looks like a lighter, complete with the classic Zippo flip top. Unfortunately, however, no matter how good it smells, perfume has little to do with the Zippo brand's core competency of "all things flame." As a result, in a recent Parham | Santana survey, consumers voted Zippo The Woman as the worst brand extension of the past year. Zippo, what were you thinking?

Even when a new product seems to associate well with a brand's core values, consumers may not make the connection. For example, back in the early 1990s, Clorox investigated several cleaning-related extensions, from laundry detergents to carpet cleaners. That seemed to make sense, given Clorox's

›› Brand extensions: A good brand extension should fit the parent brand, and the parent brand should give the extension competitive advantage in its new category. Above, it's not just a new, no-name over-the-counter sleep-aid, it's Vicks ZzzQuil.

The Procter & Gamble Company

association with cleaning. But consumers rejected these new-product concepts, worried that cleaning products from a bleach company might damage the colors in their clothes or carpets. More than just "cleaning," consumers associated the Clorox brand with "cleaning, disinfecting, and stain fighting." So rather than trying to change those brand perceptions, Clorox leveraged them with products such as Clorox Toilet Bowl Cleaner, now the bestselling brand in its category with a 35 percent market share. Other successful brand extensions include Clorox Disinfecting Wipes, Clorox Clean-Up (designed to clean and disinfect stains on a variety of surfaces), and Clorox OxiMagic (a multi-purpose stain remover spray that works on both laundry and household stains).

Good fit goes both ways. Just as an extension should fit the parent brand, the parent brand should give the extension competitive advantage in its new category. The result is sales and profit success. For example, consumers have long associated the Vicks NyQuil brand with relieving cold symptoms so that they could get a better night's sleep. So the Vicks ZzzQuil name gave the extension a substantial boost in the sleep-aids segment. Similarly, when FedEx created FedEx TechConnect, a service that handles technology configuring, repairing, and refurbishing for businesses, the FedEx brand's established reputation for speed, reliability, and accessibility gave the new service immediate credibility over competitors.

Of course, when it comes to brand extensions, most consumers don't stop to think about the "three pillars" or other factors of success. Instead, they simply react. And according to Parham Santana's president, consumers usually have instantaneous, almost visceral responses to brand extensions. An extension either makes sense or it doesn't. In his words, "Some folks say 'Yeah!' and some just say 'Huh?'" What were they thinking?

Sources: Based on information from Robert Klara, "The Best (and Worst) Brand Extensions," *Adweek*, February 4, 2013, pp. 26–27; Robert Klara, "Best and Worst Brand Extension: Connecting with Consumers in a Meaningful Way," *Adweek*, January 14, 2014, www.adweek.com/news-gallery/advertising-branding/best-brand-extensions-2013-154948#intro; Brad Tuttle, "Why Some Brand Extensions Are Brilliant and Others Are Just Awkward," *Time*, February 7, 2013, http://business.time.com/2013/02/07/why-some-brand-extensions-are-brilliant-and-others-are-just-awkward/; Gary Belsky, "These Companies Stretched Their Brands to Make Even Bigger Bucks," *Time*, March 13, 2012, http://business.time.com/2012/03/14/the-10-best-brand-extensions-ever-according-to-me/; Denise Lee Yohn, "Great Brands Aim for Customers' Hearts, Not Their Wallets," *Forbes*, January 2014, www.forbes.com/sites/onmarketing/2014/01/08/great-brands-aim-for-customers-hearts-not-their-wallets/; and www.clorox.com/products, www.duracellpowermat.com, and www.zzzquil.com, accessed September 2015.

by advertising but by customers' *engagement* with brands and customers' *brand experiences*. Today, customers come to know a brand through a wide range of contacts and touch points. These include advertising but also personal experience with the brand, word of mouth and social media, company Web pages and mobile apps, and many others. The company must put as much care into managing these touch points as it does into producing its ads. ❯❯ As one former Disney top executive put it: "A brand is a living entity, and it is enriched or undermined cumulatively over time, the product of a thousand small gestures."[48]

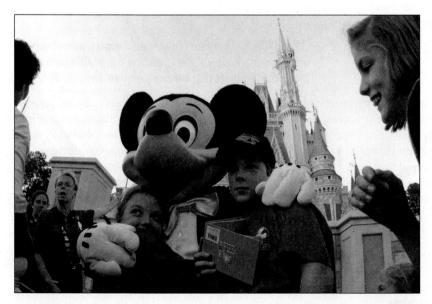

❯❯ Managing brands requires managing touch points. Says a former Disney executive: "A brand is a living entity, and it is enriched or undermined cumulatively over time, the product of a thousand small gestures."

Joe Raedle/Getty Images

The brand's positioning will not take hold fully unless everyone in the company lives the brand. Therefore, the company needs to train its people to be customer centered. Even better, the company should carry on internal brand building to help employees understand and be enthusiastic about the brand promise. Many companies go even further by training and encouraging their distributors and dealers to serve their customers well.

Finally, companies need to periodically audit their brands' strengths and weaknesses. They should ask: Does our brand excel at delivering benefits that consumers truly value? Is the brand properly positioned? Do all of our consumer touch points support the brand's positioning? Do the brand's managers understand what the brand means to consumers? Does the brand receive proper, sustained support? The brand audit may turn up brands that need more support, brands that need to be dropped, or brands that must be rebranded or repositioned because of changing customer preferences or new competitors.

REVIEWING AND EXTENDING THE CONCEPTS

CHAPTER REVIEW AND CRITICAL THINKING

Objectives Review

A product is more than a simple set of tangible features. Each product or service offered to customers can be viewed on three levels. The *core customer value* consists of the core problem-solving benefits that consumers seek when they buy a product. The *actual product* exists around the core and includes the quality level, features, design, brand name, and packaging. The *augmented product* is the actual product plus the various services and benefits offered with it, such as a warranty, free delivery, installation, and maintenance.

▶ **OBJECTIVE 7-1 Define *product* and describe the major classifications of products and services. (pp 202–207)**

Broadly defined, a *product* is anything that can be offered to a market for attention, acquisition, use, or consumption that might satisfy a want or need. Products include physical objects but also services, events, persons, places, organizations, ideas, or mixtures of these entities. *Services* are products that consist of activities, benefits, or satisfactions offered for sale that are essentially intangible, such as banking, hotel, tax preparation, and home-repair services.

Products and services fall into two broad classes based on the types of consumers who use them. *Consumer products*—those bought by final consumers—are usually classified according to consumer shopping habits (convenience products, shopping products, specialty products, and unsought products). *Industrial products*—those purchased for further processing or for use in conducting a business—include materials and parts, capital items, and supplies and services. Other marketable entities—such as organizations, persons, places, and ideas—can also be thought of as products.

▶ **OBJECTIVE 7-2 Describe the decisions companies make regarding their individual products and services, product lines, and product mixes. (pp 207–215)**

Individual product decisions involve product attributes, branding, packaging, labeling, and product support services. *Product* *attribute* decisions involve product quality, features, and style and design. *Branding* decisions include selecting a brand name and developing a brand strategy. *Packaging* provides many key benefits, such as protection, economy, convenience, and promotion. Package decisions often include designing *labels*, which identify, describe, and possibly promote the product. Companies also develop *product support services* that enhance customer service and satisfaction and safeguard against competitors.

Most companies produce a product line rather than a single product. A *product line* is a group of products that are related in function, customer-purchase needs, or distribution channels. All product lines and items offered to customers by a particular seller make up the *product mix*. The mix can be described by four dimensions: width, length, depth, and consistency. These dimensions are the tools for developing the company's product strategy.

▶ **OBJECTIVE 7-3 Identify the four characteristics that affect the marketing of services and the additional market- ing considerations that services require. (pp 215–221)**

Services are characterized by four key aspects: they are *intangi- ble, inseparable, variable,* and *perishable.* Each characteristic poses problems and marketing requirements. Marketers work to find ways to make the service more tangible, increase the productivity of providers who are inseparable from their prod- ucts, standardize quality in the face of variability, and improve demand movements and supply capacities in the face of service perishability.

Good service companies focus attention on *both* custom- ers and employees. They understand the *service profit chain,* which links service firm profits with employee and customer satisfaction. Services marketing strategy calls not only for ex- ternal marketing but also for *internal marketing* to motivate employees and *interactive marketing* to create service delivery skills among service providers. To succeed, service marketers must create *competitive differentiation,* offer high *service qual- ity,* and find ways to increase *service productivity.*

OBJECTIVE 7-4 **Discuss branding strategy—the decisions companies make in building and managing their brands. (pp 221–231)**

Some analysts see brands as *the* major enduring asset of a company. Brands are more than just names and symbols; they embody everything that the product or the service *means* to consumers. *Brand equity* is the positive differential effect that knowing the brand name has on customer response to the product or the service. A brand with strong brand equity is a very valuable asset.

In building brands, companies need to make decisions about brand positioning, brand name selection, brand sponsorship, and brand development. The most powerful *brand positioning* builds around strong consumer beliefs and values. *Brand name selection* involves finding the best brand name based on a careful review of product benefits, the target market, and proposed marketing strategies. A manufacturer has four *brand sponsorship* options: it can launch a *national brand* (or manufacturer's brand), sell to resellers that use a *private brand*, market *licensed brands*, or join forces with another company to *co-brand* a product. A company also has four choices when it comes to developing brands. It can introduce *line extensions, brand extensions, multibrands,* or *new brands*.

Companies must build and manage their brands carefully. The brand's positioning must be continuously communicated to consumers. Advertising can help. However, brands are not maintained by advertising but by customers' *brand experiences*. Customers come to know a brand through a wide range of contacts and interactions. The company must put as much care into managing these touch points as it does into producing its ads. Companies must periodically audit their brands' strengths and weaknesses.

Key Terms

Objective 7-1
Product (p 202)
Service (p 202)
Consumer product (p 204)
Convenience product (p 205)
Shopping product (p 205)
Specialty product (p 205)
Unsought product (p 205)
Industrial product (p 206)
Social marketing (p 207)

Objective 7-2
Product quality (p 208)
Brand (p 209)
Packaging (p 210)
Product line (p 213)
Product mix (product portfolio)
(p 214)

Objective 7-3
Service intangibility (p 215)
Service inseparability (p 216)
Service variability (p 216)

Service perishability (p 216)
Service profit chain (p 217)
Internal marketing (p 217)
Interactive marketing (p 219)

Objective 7-4
Brand equity (p 222)
Brand value (p 223)
Store brand (private brand) (p 225)
Co-branding (p 227)
Line extension (p 227)
Brand extension (p 228)

Discussion Questions

7-1. What is a product? Name, describe, and give an example of each type of consumer product. (AACSB: Communication; Reflective Thinking)

7-2. Compare and contrast the two dimensions of product quality. (AACSB: Communication)

7-3. What is a product line? Discuss the various product line decisions marketers make and how a company can expand its product line. (AACSB: Communication)

7-4. What is a product mix? Name and describe the four important dimensions of a product mix. (AACSB: Communication)

7-5. Discuss the four special characteristics of services. In terms of these characteristics, how do the services offered by a doctor's office differ from those offered by a bank? (AACSB: Communication, Reflective Thinking)

Critical Thinking Exercises

7-6. The Food and Drug Administration recently announced a proposal to change the standard nutrition label on food items. In a small group, research the proposed changes and create a report explaining them. Include history on nutrition labels in your presentation. (AACSB: Communication; Use of IT; Reflective Thinking)

7-7. List the names of the store brands found in the following stores: Walmart, Best Buy, and Whole Foods.

Identify the private label brands of another retailer of your choice and compare the price and quality of one of the products to a comparable national brand. (AACSB: Communication; Reflective Thinking)

7-8. What is "genericide"? Discuss a recent case and make recommendations regarding how marketers can avoid it. (AACSB: Communication; Reflective Thinking)

MINICASES AND APPLICATIONS

Online, Mobile, and Social Media Marketing   Keeping Tabs on Fido's Health

Want to monitor your dog's health and fitness? Now you can with devices like Whistle and Voyce, wearable bands placed around a dog's neck like a regular collar. Only this is no regular collar. It monitors your pooch's vital signs, such as heart and respiratory rates and calories burned. You can also learn if your dog is active or sleeps most of the day. Unlike humans, dogs do not exhibit symptoms and it is often too late when you notice something is wrong. Voyce gives dogs a "voice" by letting owners "connect the dots" to reveal anything that's amiss. Although the monitoring will not set off alarm bells, owners can track vital stats through a monthly subscription service synced with a computer, tablet, or smartphone and share those data with a veterinarian. Over time, the device gets to know a dog and sends owners customized articles, tips, and advice. Using a mobile device, owners can remotely access their pet's data anytime through www.MyDogsVoyce.com. Voyce also makes it easy to share your pup's milestones with friends and family through social media. Such devices are not cheap, however, ranging from $129.95 for similar product Whistle to $299 for Voyce in addition to a monthly service fee. The makers of Voyce also hope to introduce a device to fit even the smallest dogs, cats, and horses.

7-9. Describe the core, actual, and augmented levels of product associated with this product. What level does the monitoring service represent? Explain. (AACSB: Communication; Reflective Thinking)

7-10. Discuss two examples of similar types of wearable technology for humans. (AACSB: Communication; Reflective Thinking)

Marketing Ethics   Geographical Indication (GI)

Scotch Whiskey, Champagne Sparkling Wine, Parmesan Cheese, Dijon Mustard—what do all of these have in common? They are not brand names but rather geographical indicators (GIs) of the origins of these foodstuffs. Europe has a long history of gastronomical delicacies that the European Union has been eager to protect for economic reasons. For example, not just any sparkling wine can be labeled *champagne* because only sparkling wine produced in the Champagne region of France can put that on the label. The British government is launching a registry of Scottish whiskey makers to protect its $4 billion industry from imitators who label their whiskey as Scotch. True Scotch must be aged in oak casks in Scotland for at least three years. Dijon mustard must be produced in Dijon, France, with chardonnay wine from the Burgundy wine region. Parmesan cheese was developed more than 2,000 years ago in Parma, Italy, which also boasts Parma ham (Prosciutto di Parma). True Swiss cheeses, such as Emmental, Gruyere, and other varieties, are produced in Switzerland following strict rules to guarantee purity, and the authorities there identify counterfeits with DNA fingerprinting based on the 10,000 strains of milk bacteria that are used for authentic Swiss cheeses. All of these come with a higher price tag for consumers. For example, Portugal Algarve Salt and French Fleur De Sel sea salt cost about $80 per pound compared with 30¢ per pound for regular table salt.

7-11. Do you think products with geographical indications are actually superior to other similar ones not originating from that geographical region? Is it ethical for makers of these products to command higher prices when others can make or grow them just as well? (AACSB: Communication; Reflective Thinking; Ethical Reasoning)

7-12. Do geographical indications (GIs) offer benefits to consumers? Are there disadvantages for sellers? Explain. (AACSB: Communication; Reflective Thinking)

Marketing by the Numbers   Pop-Tarts Gone Nutty!

Kellogg's, maker of Pop-Tarts, recently introduced Pop-Tarts Gone Nutty! The new product includes flavors such as peanut butter and chocolate peanut butter. Although the new Gone Nutty! product will reap a higher wholesale price for the company ($1.20 per eight-count package of the new product versus $1.00 per package for the original product), it also comes with higher variable costs ($0.55 per eight-count package for the new product versus $0.30 per eight-count package for the original product).

7-13. What brand development strategy is Kellogg's undertaking? (AACSB: Communication; Reflective Thinking)

7-14. Assume the company expects to sell 5 million packages of Pop-Tarts Gone Nutty! in the first year after introduction but expects that 80 percent of those sales will come from buyers who would normally purchase existing Pop-Tart flavors (that is, cannibalized sales). Assuming the sales of regular Pop-Tarts are normally

300 million packages per year and that the company will incur an increase in fixed costs of $500,000 during the first year to launch Gone Nutty!, will the new product be profitable for the company? Refer to the discussion of cannibalization in Appendix 3: Marketing by the Numbers for an explanation regarding how to conduct this analysis. (AACSB: Communication; Analytical Reasoning)

Video Case   Plymouth Rock Assurance

Plymouth Rock Assurance is an insurance company with a branding tale to tell. What started as a single Massachusetts-based auto insurance company in the early 1980s quickly grew into a group of separate companies that write and manage property and casualty insurance in various states. To streamline operations, cut costs, and better serve customers, the company undertook a rebranding process to combine three distinct auto insurance brands—Plymouth Rock, High Point, and Palisades—into one.

Rather than remaking the brand overnight, the company carried out a gradual transformation that retained existing brand equity and put customers' minds at ease. With Plymouth Rock as the parent brand and High Point and Palisades as sub-brands, the company transitioned the three into a single brand in incremental steps

After viewing the video featuring Plymouth Rock Assurance, answer the following questions:

7-15. What value proposition lies at the core of Plymouth Rock Assurance?)

7-16. What was the reasoning behind the decision to rebrand the three auto insurance brands as one brand?)

7-17. Describe the process that Plymouth Rock Assurance used to rebrand the company. How does this process differ from other options it could have pursued?

Company Cases   7 Target/10 Apple Pay/16 Adidas

See Appendix 1 for cases appropriate for this chapter. **Case 7, Target: Where Store Brands Offer More Than Low Prices**. In addition to carrying popular national brands, Target has built its own house for brands by moving store brands upscale. **Case 10, Apple Pay: Taking Mobile Payments Mainstream**.

Apple may succeed where Google, Paypal, Visa, and others have failed in making mobile payments the go-to way to pay. **Case 16, Adidas: Athletic Apparel with Purpose**. Not just fashionable shoes and apparel, adidas is making a difference by focusing on a strategy of sustainability.

MyMarketingLab

If assigned by your instructor, complete these writing sections from your Assignments in the MyLab.

7-18. Describe how marketers manage service differentiation, other than through pricing, and describe an example of a service provider that has successfully differentiated its offering from competitors. (AACSB: Communication, Reflective Thinking)

7-19. A product's package must satisfy many criteria, such as sustainability, convenience, safety, efficiency, functionality, and marketing. Research "packaging awards" and develop a presentation analyzing an award-winning product packaging effort. Describe the organization hosting the award competition, the criteria for selecting winners, and one of the award-winning packages. (AACSB: Written and Oral Communication; Information Technology)

8 Developing New Products
and Managing the Product Life Cycle

CHAPTER ROAD MAP | Objective Outline

▶ OBJECTIVE 8-1 **Explain how companies find and develop new product ideas.** New Product Development Strategy (238–239)

▶ OBJECTIVE 8-2 **List and define the steps in the new product development process and the major considerations in managing this process.** The New Product Development Process (239–247); Managing New Product Development (247–249)

▶ OBJECTIVE 8-3 **Describe the stages of the product life cycle and how marketing strategies change during a product's life cycle.** Product Life-Cycle Strategies (249–256)

▶ OBJECTIVE 8-4 **Discuss two additional product issues: socially responsible product decisions and international product and services marketing.** Additional Product and Service Considerations (256–258)

Previewing the Concepts

In the previous chapter, you've learned how marketers manage and develop products and brands. In this chapter, we examine two additional product topics: developing new products and managing products through their life cycles. New products are the lifeblood of an organization. However, new product development is risky, and many new products fail. So, the first part of this chapter lays out a process for finding and growing successful new products. Once introduced, marketers then want their products to enjoy long and happy lives. In the second part of this chapter, you'll see that every product passes through several life-cycle stages, and each stage poses new challenges requiring different marketing strategies and tactics. Finally, we wrap up our product discussion by looking at two additional considerations: social responsibility in product decisions and international product and services marketing.

For openers, consider Google, one of the world's most innovative companies. Google seems to come up with an almost unending flow of knock-your-eye-out new technologies and services. If it has to do with finding, refining, or using information, there's probably an innovative Google solution for it. At Google, innovation isn't just a process; it's in the very spirit of the place.

First Stop

Google: The New Product Moonshot Factory

Google is wildly innovative. Over the past decade, it has become a top five fixture in every list of most-innovative companies. Google simply refuses to get comfortable with the way things are. Instead, it innovates constantly, plunging into new markets and taking on new competitors.

As a result, Google is also spectacularly successful. Despite formidable competition from giants such as Microsoft and Yahoo!, Google's U.S. share in its core business—online search—stands at a decisive 75 percent, more than six times the market shares of its next two competitors combined. The company also dominates in paid online and mobile search-related and other online and mobile advertising revenue, which accounted for 90 percent of Google's $66 billion in revenues last year. And Google is growing at a blistering rate—its revenues have more than doubled in just the past four years.

But Google has rapidly become much more than just an online search and advertising company. Google's mission is "to organize the world's information and make it universally accessible and useful." In Google's view, information is a kind of natural resource—one to be mined, refined, and universally distributed. That idea unifies what would otherwise appear to be a widely diverse set of Google projects, such as mapping the world, creating wearable computer technology, amassing the world's largest video library, or even developing a fleet of stratospheric balloons to blanket the world with Internet access. If it has to do with harnessing and using information, Google's got it covered in some innovative way.

Google knows how to innovate. At many companies, new product development is a cautious, step-by-step affair that might take years to unfold. In contrast, Google's freewheeling new product development process moves at the speed of light. The nimble innovator implements major new products and services in less time than it takes competitors to refine and approve an initial idea. As one Google executive explains, "The hardest part about indoctrinating people into our culture is when engineers show me a prototype and I'm like, 'Great, let's go!' They'll say, 'Oh, no, it's not ready.' I tell them, 'The Googly thing is to launch it early [as a beta product] and then to iterate, learning what the market wants—and making it great.'"

When it comes to new product development at Google, there are no two-year plans. The company's new product planning looks ahead only four to five months. Google would rather see projects fail quickly than see a carefully planned, drawn-out project fail. As one Google executive puts it, "Why put off failing until tomorrow or next week if you can fail now?" Whereas even highly innovative companies such as Apple prefer the safety of a "perfect-it-before-you-sell-it" approach, at Google, it's all about "launching and iterating." When Google developers face two paths and aren't sure which one to take, they invariably take the quickest one.

Google's famously chaotic innovation process has unleashed a seemingly unending flurry of diverse products, most of which are market leaders in their categories. These include an email service (Gmail), a digital media store (Google Play), an online payment service (Google Wallet), a photo sharing service (Google Picasa), a mobile operating system (Google Android), an online social network

>> **Google is wildly innovative. Its innovation machine is renowned for producing new product "moonshots," futuristic longshots that, if successful, will profoundly change how people live.**
Guy Corbishley/Alamy

(Google+), an ultrahigh-speed residential broadband network (Google Fiber), a cloud-friendly Internet browser (Chrome), affordable laptops with a browser for an operating system (Chromebooks), and even projects for mapping and exploring the world (Google Maps and Google Earth).

Google's most recent innovations are taking it well beyond simply organizing and searching for information. The company is now leading the way in harnessing the potential of the Internet to connect virtually everything in people's lives. For example, Google recently paid an eyeball-bending $3.2 billion—twice what it paid for YouTube—to acquire Nest Labs, a maker of smart thermostats and smoke alarms. Nest has reimagined these lowly home appliances into connected, digital devices worthy of the smartphone age, making them fun, easy, and efficient to use. And the fast-growing Nest is now moving quickly into the exploding "smart homes" arena with "Works with Nest" applications by which its devices interact with and control video monitoring devices, smart door locks, appliances, garage doors, and just about anything else around the house. Although it may seem like Google paid a lot for a little with Nest, with Google's substantial resources and innovation prowess, Nest may soon be helping you run your entire home, a huge potential market.

> Google's famously chaotic, wild-eyed innovation process has unleashed a seemingly unending flurry of diverse new products. But at Google, innovation is more than a process. It's part of the company's DNA. "Where does innovation happen at Google? It happens everywhere."

If the concept of Internet-connected smart homes seems a bit far-fetched for Google, that's pretty tame next to some of the company's other grand ideas. Google's innovation machine is renowned for "moonshots"— futuristic, breathtakingly idealistic long shots that, if successful, will profoundly change how people live. To foster moonshots, Google created Google X—a secretive innovation lab and kind of nerd heaven charged with developing things that seem audacious even for Google. "Anything which is a huge problem for society we'll sign up for," says the innovation unit's director, whose official title is Captain of Moonshots.

Google X's most notable innovations so far have been in wearable smart devices, such as Google Glass virtual-reality eyewear, which jump-started the wearable technology trend. But behind the secret curtain are numerous other futuristic projects, such as those high-altitude Wi-Fi balloons, glucose-monitoring contact lenses, and Google's self-driving car—a project once thought to be pure science fiction but now surprisingly close to reality. Imagine buying something online, then having an automated Google Car pull up to your home and a Google Humanoid jump out to deliver the package to your door. Seem far-fetched? Maybe not. Google is now a leading robotics developer.

Google is open to new product ideas from just about any source. But the company also places responsibility for innovation on every employee. Google is famous for its Innovation Time-Off program, which encourages engineers and developers to spend 20 percent of their time—one day a week—developing their own "cool and wacky" new product ideas. In the end, at Google, innovation is more than a process—it's part of the company's DNA. "Where does innovation happen at Google? It happens everywhere," says a Google research scientist.

Talk to Googlers at various levels and departments, one powerful theme emerges: These people feel that their work can change the world. The marvel of Google is its ability to continue to instill a sense of creative fearlessness and ambition in its employees. Prospective hires are often asked, "If you could change the world using Google's resources, what would you build?" But here, this isn't a goofy or even theoretical question: Google wants to know because thinking—and building—on that scale is what Google does. When it comes to innovation, Google is different. But the difference isn't tangible. It's in the air—in the spirit of the place.[1]

As the Google story suggests, companies that excel at developing and managing new products reap big rewards. Every product seems to go through a life cycle: It is born, goes through several phases, and eventually dies as newer products come along that create new or greater value for customers.

This product life cycle presents two major challenges: First, because all products eventually decline, a firm must be good at developing new products to replace aging ones (the challenge of *new product development*). Second, a firm must be good at adapting its marketing strategies in the face of changing tastes, technologies, and competition as products pass through stages (the challenge of *product life-cycle strategies*). We first look at the problem of finding and developing new products and then at the problem of managing them successfully over their life cycles.

New Product Development Strategy

A firm can obtain new products in two ways. One is through *acquisition*—by buying a whole company, a patent, or a license to produce someone else's product. The other is through the firm's own **new product development** efforts. By *new products* we mean original products, product improvements, product modifications, and new brands that the firm develops through its own research and development (R&D) efforts. In this chapter, we concentrate on new product development.

New products are important to both customers and the marketers who serve them: They bring new solutions and variety to customers' lives, and they are a key source of growth for companies. In today's fast-changing environment, many companies rely on new products for the majority of their growth. For example, new products have almost completely transformed Apple in recent years. The iPhone and iPad—neither of which was available a decade ago—are now the company's two biggest-selling products, with the latest iPhone model bringing in more than two-thirds of Apple's total revenues shortly after its introduction.[2]

Yet innovation can be very expensive and very risky. New products face tough odds. For example, by one estimate, 60 percent of all new consumer packaged products introduced by established companies fail; two-thirds of new product concepts are never even launched.[3] Why do so many new products fail? There are several reasons. Although an idea may be good, the company may overestimate market size. The actual product may be poorly designed. Or it might be incorrectly positioned, launched at the wrong time, priced too high, or poorly advertised. A high-level executive might push a favorite idea despite poor marketing research findings. Sometimes the costs of product development are higher than expected, and sometimes competitors fight back harder than expected.

New product development
The development of original products, product improvements, product modifications, and new brands through the firm's own product development efforts.

238

So, companies face a problem: They must develop new products, but the odds weigh heavily against success. To create successful new products, a company must understand its consumers, markets, and competitors and develop products that deliver superior value to customers.

The New Product Development Process

Rather than leaving new products to chance, a company must carry out strong new product planning and set up a systematic, customer-driven *new product development process* for finding and growing new products. **≫ Figure 8.1** shows the eight major steps in this process.

Idea Generation

Idea generation
The systematic search for new product ideas.

New product development starts with **idea generation**—the systematic search for new product ideas. A company typically generates hundreds—even thousands—of ideas to find a few good ones. Major sources of new product ideas include internal sources and external sources such as customers, competitors, distributors and suppliers, and others.

Internal Idea Sources

Using *internal sources*, the company can find new ideas through formal R&D. For example, Ford operates an innovation and mobility center in Silicon Valley staffed by engineers, app developers, and scientists working on everything from driverless cars to Works with Nest apps that let consumers control home heating, lighting, and appliances from their vehicles. Chick-fil-A set up a large innovation center called Hatch, where its staff and partners explore new ideas in food, design, and service. Hatch is a place to "ideate, explore, and imagine the future," to hatch new food and restaurant ideas and bring them to life.[4]

Beyond its internal R&D process, a company can pick the brains of its own people—from executives to salespeople to scientists, engineers, and manufacturing staff. Many companies have developed successful internal social networks and *intrapreneurial* programs that encourage employees to develop new product ideas. For example, Google's Innovation Time-Off program has resulted in blockbuster product ideas ranging from Gmail and Ad Sense to Google News. A similar program at 3M, called Dream Days, has long encouraged employees to spend 15 percent of their working time on their own projects, resulting in Post-it Notes and many other successful products.[5]

Tech companies such as Facebook and Twitter sponsor periodic "hackathons," in which employees take a day or a week away from their day-to-day work to develop new ideas. LinkedIn, the 300 million–member professional social media network, holds "hack-days," a Friday each month when it encourages employees to work on whatever they want that will benefit the company. LinkedIn takes the process a step further with its InCubator program, under which employees can form teams each quarter that pitch innovative new ideas to LinkedIn executives. If approved, the team gets up to 90 days away from its regular work to develop the idea into reality.[6]

New product development starts with good new product ideas—lots of them. For example, Cisco's I-Prize crowdsourcing challenge attracted 824 ideas from 2,900 innovators representing more than 156 countries.

The remaining steps reduce the number of ideas and develop only the best ones into profitable products. Of the 824 ideas from Cisco's I-Prize challenge, only a handful are being developed.

≫ Figure 8.1 Major Stages in New Product Development

External Idea Sources

Companies can also obtain good new product ideas from any of a number of external sources. For example, *distributors and suppliers* can contribute ideas. Distributors are close to the market and can pass along information about consumer problems and new product possibilities. Suppliers can tell the company about new concepts, techniques, and materials that can be used to develop new products.

Competitors are another important source. Companies watch competitors' ads to get clues about their new products. They buy competing new products, take them apart to see how they work, analyze their sales, and decide whether they should bring out a new prod-

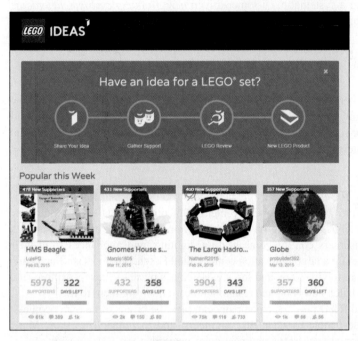

New product ideas from customers: The LEGO Ideas Web site invites customer to submit and vote on new product ideas. So far, LEGO Ideas has resulted in 10 major new products.

LEGO and the LEGO logo are trademarks of the LEGO Group of Companies, used here by permission. © 2015 The LEGO Group, all rights reserved.

uct of their own. Other idea sources include trade magazines, shows, Web sites, and seminars; government agencies; advertising agencies; marketing research firms; university and commercial laboratories; and inventors.

Perhaps the most important sources of new product ideas are *customers* themselves. The company can analyze customer questions and complaints to find new products that better solve consumer problems. Or it can invite customers to share suggestions and ideas. For example, the LEGO Group, maker of the classic LEGO® plastic bricks that have been fixtures in homes around the world for more than 60 years, systematically taps users for new product ideas and input via the LEGO Ideas Web site:[7]

> At the LEGO Ideas Web site, the giant toy maker turns user ideas into new LEGO building sets. The site invites customers to submit their ideas and to evaluate and vote on the ideas of others. Ideas supported by 10,000 votes head to the LEGO Review Board for an internal review by various departments including marketing and design. Ideas passing the review are made into official LEGO products. Customers whose ideas reach production earn 1 percent of total net sales of the product and receive credit as the LEGO Ideas set creator inside every set sold. So far, LEGO Ideas has resulted in 10 major new products, including the likes of LEGO Minecraft, LEGO Birds, LEGO *Big Bang Theory*, LEGO *Ghostbusters*, and LEGO *Back to the Future* DeLorean Time Machine.

Crowdsourcing

Crowdsourcing

Inviting broad communities of people—customers, employees, independent scientists and researchers, and even the public at large—into the new product innovation process.

More broadly, many companies are now developing crowdsourcing or open-innovation new product idea programs. Through **crowdsourcing**, a company invites broad communities of people—customers, employees, independent scientists and researchers, and even the public at large—into the innovation process. Tapping into a breadth of sources—both inside and outside the company—can produce unexpected and powerful new ideas (see Marketing at Work 8.1).

Companies large and small, across all industries, are crowdsourcing product innovation ideas rather than relying only on their own R&D labs. For example, Samsung recently launched an Open Innovation Program, which breaks down the walls surrounding Samsung's own innovation process and opens the doors to fresh new product and technology ideas from outside the company. Through the program, Samsung creates alliances with top industry and university researchers around the world, participates actively in industry-wide forums, works with suppliers on innovation, and seeks out and invests in promising start-up companies. "In the 21st century, no company can do all the research alone," says a Samsung executive, "and we see it as critically important to partner with [others] across the world to build and strengthen a vibrant research community."[8]

Rather than creating and managing their own crowdsourcing platforms, companies can use third-party crowdsourcing networks, such as InnoCentive, TopCoder, and jovoto. For example, organizations ranging from Audi, Microsoft, and Nestlé to Swiss Army Knife maker Victorinox have tapped into jovoto's network of 50,000 creative professionals for

MARKETING AT WORK | 8.1

Crowdsourcing: Throwing the Innovation Doors Wide Open

Today, crowdsourcing is big business. You're probably most familiar with consumer-generated marketing efforts in which companies invite customers to help them create new advertising or product ideas. PepsiCo's Frito-Lay division is well known for doing this. For example, its annual Doritos Crash the Super Bowl ad competition generates award-winning, consumer-produced Super Bowl ads every year. And its Frito-Lay "Do Us a Flavor" competition invites consumers to submit and vote on new flavors for Lays potato chips. These highly successful crowdsourcing campaigns generate heaps of customer involvement and buzz. Last year's "Do Us a Flavor" contest alone produced more than 4 million new flavor ideas.

But today's crowdsourcing is about much more than just clever consumer contests that build buzz. Companies ranging from giants like P&G and Under Armour to small manufacturing start-ups like Quirky are throwing the innovation doors wide open, inviting broad communities of people—customers, employees, independent scientists and researchers, and even the public at large—into the new product innovation process. Consider the following examples.

Procter & Gamble

P&G has long set the gold standard for breakthrough innovation and new product development in its industry. P&G's Tide detergent was the first synthetic laundry detergent for automatic washing machines, its Pampers brand was the first successful disposable diaper, and P&G's Febreze was the first air freshener that eliminated odors rather than just covering them up. Such breakthrough innovations have been pivotal in P&G's incredible growth and success.

Until recently, most of P&G's innovations came from its own R&D labs. P&G employs more than 8,000 R&D researchers in 26 facilities around the globe, some of the best research talent in the world. But P&G's research labs alone simply can't provide the quantity of innovation required to meet the growth needs of the $84 billion company.

So about 12 years ago, P&G began inviting outside partners to help develop new products and technologies. It launched P&G Connect + Develop, a major crowdsourcing program that invites entrepreneurs, scientists, engineers, and other researchers—even consumers themselves—to submit ideas for new technologies, product designs, packaging, marketing models, research methods, engineering, or promotion—anything that has the potential to create better products that will help P&G meet its goal of "improving more consumers' lives."

P&G isn't looking to replace its 8,000 researchers; it wants to leverage them better. Through careful crowdsourcing, it can extend its inside people with millions of brilliant minds outside. Through Connect + Develop, says the company, "Together, we can do more than either of us could do alone."

Today, thanks to Connect + Develop, P&G has a truly global open-innovation network. More than 50 percent of its innovations involve some kind of external partner. So far, the program has resulted in more than 2,000 successful agreements. The long list of successful Connect + Develop products includes, among others, Tide Pods, Tide Total Care, Olay Regenerist, Swiffer Dusters, Glad ForceFlex Bags, CoverGirl Eyewear, the Oral B Pulsonic toothbrush, and Mr. Clean Magic Eraser. P&G Connect + Develop is "at the heart of how P&G innovates."

Under Armour

Sports apparel maker Under Armour knows that no matter how many top-notch developers it has inside, sometimes the only way to produce good outside-the-box ideas is by going outside the company. So Under Armour sponsors a semiannual Future Show Innovation Challenge, a competition that is part crowdsourcing and part new product *American Idol* but all business in its quest to find the Next Big Thing. The Future Show invites inventors from around the nation to submit new product ideas. From thousands of entries, an Under Armour team culls 12 finalists, who go before a panel of seven judges to pitch their products in a splashy, *Shark Tank*–like reality TV setting. The winner earns $50,000 and a contract to work with Under Armour to help develop the winning product.

Quirky

Products invented by real people just like Jake.

Sign up to join the community, or start shopping.

» **Crowdsourcing: New product start-up Quirky best illustrates the raw power of crowdsourcing in its purest form. "Nobody is innovating at the pace that Quirky is."**
Quirky

Under Armour founder and CEO Kevin Plank started the company with his innovative idea for a shirt that pulled moisture away from the body to keep athletes dry. Since then, the now-$2.3-billion-a-year company has built its reputation on innovative but pricy sports gear. The Future Show is one more way to keep Under Armour on the cutting edge of innovation. "We don't have all the good ideas," says Plank. The goal of the Future Show Challenge is to "cajole top innovators to come to Under Armour first with gee-whizzers."

The first winner, and Plank's favorite so far, is a made-for-athletes zipper—the UA MagZip—that can be zipped easily with only one hand. Under Armour's internal R&D team had been trying to develop a better zipper for two years, but "we couldn't get it to work," says the company's innovation chief. The crowdsourced zipper has now shown up in stores on Under Armour jackets and could eventually be used in all Under Armour outerwear. That simple zipper is just one of dozens of creative new product ideas from Future Show. But by itself, it makes the entire crowdsourcing effort worthwhile.

Quirky

It's not just big companies such as P&G and Under Armour that use crowdsourcing. Quirky is a promising $100 million company built solely around crowdsourcing. Based on the notion that ordinary people have extraordinary ideas, Quirky manufactures products from everyday inventors. It taps into an online community of 600,000 members—what one writer calls an "invention mob"—who submit inventive new product ideas in the form of "a napkin sketch, a sentence, or a fully baked product." The company receives more than 4,000 ideas a week. The community then votes for its favorites, and each week, in a live Webcast from Quirky's New York headquarters, company executives, industry experts, and community members debate the merits of submitted ideas and select three or four for development.

Quirky then handles all of the difficult design, production, legal, and marketing details in turning chosen ideas into marketable products. Crowdsourcing plays a role throughout—the Quirky community provides input on everything from design to the product's name, packaging, tagline, and price. Products that make it through development are shipped off to one of five global distribution centers, then to any of more than 35,000 retail locations, including Target, Bed Bath & Beyond, Home Depot, Best Buy, Amazon.com, Quirky's own Internet store, and even QVC.

Inventors whose ideas become products and people who contribute to improving those products share in royalties based on product sales. Of the more than 400 products that Quirky has put on store shelves in its brief history, not one has lost money. The company's top seller to date is a clever pivoting power strip called Pivot Power. Sales of the Pivot Power quickly surpassed a million units, making its young amateur inventor more than $1 million in royalties last year alone.

The P&Gs, PepsiCos, and Under Armours of the world operate on a scale that dwarfs the Quirkys. Yet small Quirky perhaps best illustrates the raw power of crowdsourcing, the democratization of product development in its purest form. As one Target representative concludes, "Nobody is innovating at the pace that Quirky is."

Sources: Based on information from Dale Buss, "P&G Enhances Connect + Develop Innovation Pipeline," *BrandChannel,* February 13, 2013, www.brandchannel.com/home/post/2013/02/13/PG-Connect-Develop-Website-021313.aspx; Larry Huston and Nabil Sakkab, "Connect and Develop: Inside Procter & Gamble's New Model for Innovation," *Harvard Business Review,* March 2006, pp. 2–9; Bruce Horovitz, "Under Armour Seeks Ideas for Its Next Big Thing," *USA Today,* October 20, 2013; Josh Dean, "Is This the World's Most Creative Manufacturer?" *Inc.,* October 2013, pp. 95–114; Kyle Stock, "Under Armour Holds a Game Show to Find Its Future," *Bloomberg Businessweek,* October 13, 2014, www.businessweek.com/articles/2014-10-13/under-armour-holds-a-game-show-to-find-its-future; Steve Lohr, "The Invention Mob, Brought to You by Quirky," *New York Times,* February 15, 2015, p. BU1; and www.pgconnectdevelop.com and www.quirky.com, accessed October 2015.

VICTORINOX
SWISS ARMY

» **Victorinox used third-party crowdsourcing network jovoto to capture creative designs for limited fashion editions of its venerable Swiss Army Knife. The crowdsourced designed models had 20 percent better sales success than any previous internally created limited editions.**

Victorinox AG

ideas and solutions, offering prizes of $100 to $100,000. » For the past three years, Victorinox has used jovoto to capture new designs for a limited fashion edition of its Swiss Army Knife. The aim of the fashion designs is to attract younger buyers to the venerable old product. The first year, more than 1,000 artists submitted designs via jovoto. The limited edition, consisting of 10 designs selected after review by jovoto community members and voting on Facebook by Victorinox brand fans, had 20 percent better sales success than any previous internally created limited edition models.[9]

Crowdsourcing can produce a flood of innovative ideas. In fact, opening the floodgates to anyone and everyone can overwhelm the company with ideas—some good and some bad. For example, when Cisco Systems sponsored an open-innovation effort called I-Prize, soliciting ideas from external sources, it received more than 820 distinct ideas from more than 2,900 innovators from 156 countries. "The evaluation process was far more labor-intensive than we'd anticipated," says Cisco's chief technology officer. It required "significant investments of time, energy, patience, and imagination...to discern the gems hidden within rough stones." In the end, a team of six Cisco people worked full-time for three months to carve out 32 semifinalist ideas, as well as nine teams representing 14 countries in six continents for the final phase of the competition.[10]

Truly innovative companies don't rely only on one source or another for new product ideas. Instead, they develop extensive innovation networks that capture ideas and inspiration from every possible source, from employees and customers to outside innovators and multiple points beyond.

Idea Screening

Idea screening
Screening new product ideas to spot good ones and drop poor ones as soon as possible.

The purpose of idea generation is to create a large number of ideas. The purpose of the succeeding stages is to *reduce* that number. The first idea-reducing stage is **idea screening**, which helps spot good ideas and drop poor ones as soon as possible. Product development costs rise greatly in later stages, so the company wants to go ahead only with those product ideas that will turn into profitable products.

Many companies require their executives to write up new product ideas in a standard format that can be reviewed by a new product committee. The write-up describes the product or the service, the proposed customer value proposition, the target market, and the competition. It makes some rough estimates of market size, product price, development time and costs, manufacturing costs, and rate of return. The committee then evaluates the idea against a set of general criteria.

One marketing expert describes an R-W-W ("real, win, worth doing") new product screening framework that asks three questions. First, *Is it real?* Is there a real need and desire for the product, and will customers buy it? Is there a clear product concept, and will such a product satisfy the market? Second, *Can we win?* Does the product offer a sustainable competitive advantage? Does the company have the resources to make such a product a success? Finally, *Is it worth doing?* Does the product fit the company's overall growth strategy? Does it offer sufficient profit potential? The company should be able to answer yes to all three R-W-W questions before developing the new product idea further.[11]

Concept Development and Testing

Product concept
A detailed version of the new product idea stated in meaningful consumer terms.

An attractive idea must then be developed into a **product concept**. It is important to distinguish between a product idea, a product concept, and a product image. A *product idea* is an idea for a possible product that the company can see itself offering to the market. A *product concept* is a detailed version of the idea stated in meaningful consumer terms. A *product image* is the way consumers perceive an actual or potential product.

Concept Development

Suppose a car manufacturer has developed a practical battery-powered, all-electric car. Its initial model is a sleek, sporty roadster convertible that sells for more than $100,000.[12] ≫ However, in the near future it plans to introduce more-affordable, mass-market versions that will compete with recently introduced hybrid-electric or all-electric cars such as the Nissan Leaf, Chevy Volt, KIA Soul EV, and Chevy Bolt EV. This 100 percent plug-in electric car will accelerate from 0 to 60 miles per hour in four seconds, travel up to 300 miles on a single charge, recharge in 45 minutes from a normal 120-volt electrical outlet, and cost about one penny per mile to power.

≫ **All-electric cars: This is Tesla's initial all-electric roadster. Later, more-affordable mass-market models will travel more than 300 miles on a single charge, recharge in 45 minutes from a normal 120-volt electrical outlet, and cost about one penny per mile to power.**

Tesla

Looking ahead, the marketer's task is to develop this new product into alternative product concepts, find out how attractive each concept is to customers, and choose the best one. It might create the following product concepts for this all-electric car:

- *Concept 1.* An affordably priced midsize car designed as a second family car to be used around town for running errands and visiting friends.
- *Concept 2.* A mid-priced sporty compact appealing to young singles and couples.
- *Concept 3.* A "green" car appealing to environmentally conscious people who want practical, no-polluting transportation.
- *Concept 4.* A high-end midsize utility vehicle appealing to those who love the space SUVs provide but lament the poor gas mileage.

Concept Testing

Concept testing calls for testing new product concepts with groups of target consumers. The concepts may be presented to consumers symbolically or physically. Here, in more detail, is concept 3:

> An efficient, fun-to-drive, battery-powered compact car that seats four. This 100 percent electric wonder provides practical and reliable transportation with no pollution. It goes 300 miles on a single charge and costs pennies per mile to operate. It's a sensible, responsible alternative to today's pollution-producing gas-guzzlers. Its fully equipped base price is $28,800.

Many firms routinely test new product concepts with consumers before attempting to turn them into actual new products. For some concept tests, a word or picture description might be sufficient. However, a more concrete and physical presentation of the concept will increase the reliability of the concept test. After being exposed to the concept, consumers then may be asked to react to it by answering questions similar to those in **≫ Table 8.1**.

The answers to such questions will help the company decide which concept has the strongest appeal. For example, the last question asks about the consumer's intention to buy. Suppose 2 percent of consumers say they "definitely" would buy and another 5 percent say "probably." The company could project these figures to the full population in this target group to estimate sales volume. Even then, however, the estimate is uncertain because people do not always carry out their stated intentions.

Marketing Strategy Development

Suppose the carmaker finds that concept 3 for the electric car tests best. The next step is **marketing strategy development**, designing an initial marketing strategy for introducing this car to the market.

Concept testing
Testing new product concepts with a group of target consumers to find out if the concepts have strong consumer appeal.

Marketing strategy development
Designing an initial marketing strategy for a new product based on the product concept.

≫ Table 8.1	Questions for the All-Electric Car Concept Test

1. Do you understand the concept of a battery-powered electric car?
2. Do you believe the claims about the car's performance?
3. What are the major benefits of an all-electric car compared with a conventional car?
4. What are its advantages compared with a hybrid gas-electric car?
5. What improvements in the car's features would you suggest?
6. For what uses would you prefer an all-electric car to a conventional car?
7. What would be a reasonable price to charge for the car?
8. Who would be involved in your decision to buy such a car? Who would drive it?
9. Would you buy such a car (definitely, probably, probably not, definitely not)?

The *marketing strategy statement* consists of three parts. The first part describes the target market; the planned value proposition; and the sales, market-share, and profit goals for the first few years. Thus:

> The target market is younger, well-educated, moderate- to high-income individuals, couples, or small families seeking practical, environmentally responsible transportation. The car will be positioned as more fun to drive and less polluting than today's internal combustion engine or hybrid cars. The company will aim to sell 50,000 cars in the first year, at a loss of not more than $15 million. In the second year, the company will aim for sales of 90,000 cars and a profit of $25 million.

The second part of the marketing strategy statement outlines the product's planned price, distribution, and marketing budget for the first year:

> The battery-powered all-electric car will be offered in three colors—red, white, and blue—and will have a full set of accessories as standard features. It will sell at a base retail price of $28,800, with 15 percent off the list price to dealers. Dealers who sell more than 10 cars per month will get an additional discount of 5 percent on each car sold that month. A marketing budget of $50 million will be split 40-30-30 among a national media campaign, online and social media marketing, and local event marketing. Advertising, the Web and mobile sites, and various social media content will emphasize the car's fun spirit and low emissions. During the first year, $100,000 will be spent on marketing research to find out who is buying the car and what their satisfaction levels are.

The third part of the marketing strategy statement describes the planned long-run sales, profit goals, and marketing mix strategy:

> We intend to capture a 3 percent long-run share of the total auto market and realize an after-tax return on investment of 15 percent. To achieve this, product quality will start high and be improved over time. Price will be raised in the second and third years if competition and the economy permit. The total marketing budget will be raised each year by about 10 percent. Marketing research will be reduced to $60,000 per year after the first year.

Business Analysis

Business analysis
A review of the sales, costs, and profit projections for a new product to find out whether these factors satisfy the company's objectives.

Once management has decided on its product concept and marketing strategy, it can evaluate the business attractiveness of the proposal. **Business analysis** involves a review of the sales, costs, and profit projections for a new product to find out whether they satisfy the company's objectives. If they do, the product can move to the product development stage.

To estimate sales, the company might look at the sales history of similar products and conduct market surveys. It can then estimate minimum and maximum sales to assess the range of risk. After preparing the sales forecast, management can estimate the expected costs and profits for the product, including marketing, R&D, operations, accounting, and finance costs. The company then uses the sales and cost figures to analyze the new product's financial attractiveness.

Product Development

Product development
Developing the product concept into a physical product to ensure that the product idea can be turned into a workable market offering.

For many new product concepts, a product may exist only as a word description, a drawing, or perhaps a crude mock-up. If the product concept passes the business test, it moves into **product development**. Here, R&D or engineering develops the product concept into a physical product. The product development step, however, now calls for a huge jump in investment. It will show whether the product idea can be turned into a workable product.

The R&D department will develop and test one or more physical versions of the product concept. R&D hopes to design a prototype that will satisfy and excite consumers and that can be produced quickly and at budgeted costs. Developing a successful prototype can take days, weeks, months, or even years depending on the product and prototype methods.

Often, products undergo rigorous tests to make sure that they perform safely and effectively or that consumers will find value in them. Companies can do their own product testing or outsource testing to other firms that specialize in testing.

>> **Product testing: Carhartt has enlisted an army of Groundbreakers, volunteers who take part in live chats with Carhartt designers, review new product concepts, and field-test products that they helped to create.**
Carhartt, Inc.

Marketers often involve actual customers in product development and testing. >> For example, Carhartt, maker of durable workwear and outerwear, has enlisted an army of Groundbreakers, "hard working men and women to help us create our next generation of products." These volunteers take part in live chats with Carhartt designers, review new product concepts, and field-test products that they helped to create.[13]

A new product must have the required functional features and also convey the intended psychological characteristics. The all-electric car, for example, should strike consumers as being well built, comfortable, and safe. Management must learn what makes consumers decide that a car is well built. To some consumers, this means that the car has "solid-sounding" doors. To others, it means that the car is able to withstand a heavy impact in crash tests. Consumer tests are conducted in which consumers test-drive the car and rate its attributes.

Test Marketing

Test marketing
The stage of new product development at which the product and its proposed marketing program are tested in realistic market settings.

If the product passes both the concept test and the product test, the next step is **test marketing**, the stage at which the product and its proposed marketing program are introduced into realistic market settings. Test marketing gives the marketer experience with marketing a product before going to the great expense of full introduction. It lets the company test the product and its entire marketing program—targeting and positioning strategy, advertising, distribution, pricing, branding and packaging, and budget levels.

The amount of test marketing needed varies with each new product. When introducing a new product requires a big investment, when the risks are high, or when management is not sure of the product or its marketing program, a company may do a lot of test marketing. For instance, Taco Bell took three years and 45 prototypes before introducing Doritos Locos Tacos, now the most successful product launch in the company's history. And Starbucks spent 20 years developing Starbucks VIA instant coffee—one of its most risky product rollouts ever—and several months testing the product in Starbucks shops in Chicago and Seattle before releasing it nationally. The testing paid off. The Starbucks VIA line now accounts for more than $300 million in sales annually.[14]

>> **Companies sometimes shorten or skip test marketing to take advantage of fast-changing market developments, as Starbucks did with its hugely successful mobile payments app.**
Kevin Schafer/Moment Mobile/Getty Images

However, test marketing costs can be high, and testing takes time that may allow market opportunities to slip by or competitors to gain advantages. A company may do little or no test marketing when the costs of developing and introducing a new product are low or when management is already confident about the new product. For example, companies often do not test-market simple line extensions or copies of competitors' successful products.

Companies may also shorten or skip testing in the face of fast-changing market developments. >> For example, to take advantage of digital and mobile trends, Starbucks quickly introduced a less-than-perfect mobile payments app, then worked out the flaws during the six months after launch. The Starbucks app now accounts for 6 million transactions per week. "We don't think it is okay if things aren't perfect," says Starbucks' chief digital officer, "but we're willing to innovate and have speed to market trump a 100 percent guarantee that it'll be perfect."[15]

As an alternative to extensive and costly standard test markets, companies can use controlled test markets or simulated test markets. In *controlled test markets*, such as SymphonyIRI's BehaviorScan, new products and tactics are tested among controlled panels of shoppers and stores.[16] By combining information on each test consumer's purchases with consumer demographic and TV viewing information, BehaviorScan can provide store-by-store, week-by-week reports on the sales of tested products and the impact of in-store and in-home marketing efforts. Using *simulated test markets*, researchers measure consumer responses to new products and marketing tactics in laboratory stores or simulated online shopping environments. Both controlled test markets and simulated test markets reduce the costs of test marketing and speed up the process.

Commercialization

Commercialization

Introducing a new product into the market.

Test marketing gives management the information needed to make a final decision about whether to launch the new product. If the company goes ahead with **commercialization**—introducing the new product into the market—it will face high costs. For example, the company may need to build or rent a manufacturing facility. And, in the case of a major new consumer product, it may spend hundreds of millions of dollars for advertising, sales promotion, and other marketing efforts in the first year. For instance, to introduce the Surface tablet, Microsoft spent close to $400 million on an advertising blitz that spanned TV, print, radio, outdoor, the Internet, events, public relations, and sampling. Similarly, Tide spent $150 million on a campaign to launch Tide Pods in the highly competitive U.S. laundry detergent market.[17]

A company launching a new product must first decide on introduction *timing*. If the new product will eat into the sales of other company products, the introduction may be delayed. If the product can be improved further or if the economy is down, the company may wait until the following year to launch it. However, if competitors are ready to introduce their own competing products, the company may push to introduce its new product sooner.

Next, the company must decide *where* to launch the new product—in a single location, a region, the national market, or the international market. Some companies may quickly introduce new models into the full national market. Companies with international distribution systems may introduce new products through swift global rollouts. For example, Apple launched its iPhone 6 and iPhone 6 Plus phones in its fastest-ever global rollout, making them available in 115 countries within less than three months of initial introduction.[18]

Author Comment

Above all else, new product development must focus on creating customer value. Says a senior Samsung executive, "We get our ideas from the market. The market is the driver."

Managing New Product Development

The new product development process shown in Figure 8.1 highlights the important activities needed to find, develop, and introduce new products. However, new product development involves more than just going through a set of steps. Companies must take a holistic approach to managing this process. Successful new product development requires a customer-centered, team-based, and systematic effort.

Customer-Centered New Product Development

Customer-centered new product development

New product development that focuses on finding new ways to solve customer problems and create more customer-satisfying experiences.

Above all else, new product development must be customer centered. When looking for and developing new products, companies often rely too heavily on technical research in their R&D laboratories. But like everything else in marketing, successful new product development begins with a thorough understanding of what consumers need and value. **Customer-centered new product development** focuses on finding new ways to solve customer problems and create more customer-satisfying experiences.

One study found that the most successful new products are ones that are differentiated, solve major customer problems, and offer a compelling customer value proposition. Another study showed that companies that directly engage their customers in the new product innovation process had twice the return on assets and triple the growth in operating income of firms that did not. Thus, customer involvement has a positive effect on the new product development process and product success.[19]

Intuit—maker of financial software such as TurboTax, QuickBooks, and Quicken—is a strong proponent of customer-driven new product development:[20]

> Intuit follows a "Design for Delight (D4D)" development philosophy that says products should delight customers by providing experiences that go beyond their expectations. ≫Design for Delight starts with customer empathy—knowing customers better than they know themselves.

HOW WE INNOVATE

DEEP CUSTOMER EMPATHY

DELIGHT

GO BROAD TO GO NARROW

RAPID EXPERIMENTS WITH CUSTOMERS

intuit. simplify the business of life

✓ TurboTax   QuickBooks   Q Quicken   Mint

>> **Customer-centered new product development: Financial software maker Intuit follows a "Design for Delight" philosophy that says products should delight customers by providing experiences that go beyond their expectations.**

Team-based new product development
New product development in which various company departments work closely together, overlapping the steps in the product development process to save time and increase effectiveness.

To that end, each year, Intuit conducts 10,000 hours of what it calls "follow-me-homes," in which design employees observe firsthand how customers use its products at home and at work. They look to understand problems and needs that even customers themselves might not recognize. Based on customer observations, the next D4D step is to "go broad, go narrow"—developing many customer-driven product ideas, then narrowing them down to one or a few great ideas for products that will solve customer problems. The final D4D step involves turning the great ideas into actual products and services that create customer delight, collecting customer feedback steadily throughout the development process.

Intuit works relentlessly to embed Design for Delight concepts deeply into its culture. "You've got to feel it," says the company's vice president of design innovation. "It can't be in your head. It's got to be in your heart. It's got to be in your gut. And we want to put it in our products." Thanks to customer-centered new product development, Intuit's revenues have grown to $4.5 billion annually, a 45 percent increase in just the past five years.

Thus, today's innovative companies get out of the research lab and connect with customers in search of fresh ways to meet customer needs. Customer-centered new product development begins and ends with understanding customers and involving them in the process.

Team-Based New Product Development

Good new product development also requires a total-company, cross-functional effort. Some companies organize their new product development process into the orderly sequence of steps shown in Figure 8.1, starting with idea generation and ending with commercialization. Under this *sequential product development* approach, one company department works individually to complete its stage of the process before passing the new product along to the next department and stage. This orderly, step-by-step process can help bring control to complex and risky projects. But it can also be dangerously slow. In fast-changing, highly competitive markets, such slow-but-sure product development can result in product failures, lost sales and profits, and crumbling market positions.

To get their new products to market more quickly, many companies use a **team-based new product development** approach. Under this approach, company departments work closely together in cross-functional teams, overlapping the steps in the product development process to save time and increase effectiveness. Instead of passing the new product from department to department, the company assembles a team of people from various departments that stays with the new product from start to finish. Such teams usually include people from the marketing, finance, design, manufacturing, and legal departments and even supplier and customer companies. In the sequential process, a bottleneck at one phase can seriously slow an entire project. In the team-based approach, however, if one area hits snags, it works to resolve them while the team moves on.

The team-based approach does have some limitations, however. For example, it sometimes creates more organizational tension and confusion than the more orderly sequential approach. However, in rapidly changing industries facing increasingly shorter product life cycles, the rewards of fast and flexible product development far exceed the risks. Companies that combine a customer-centered approach with team-based new product development gain a big competitive edge by getting the right new products to market faster.

Systematic New Product Development

Finally, the new product development process should be holistic and systematic rather than compartmentalized and haphazard. Otherwise, few new ideas will surface, and many good ideas will sputter and die. To avoid these problems, a company can install an *innovation management system* to collect, review, evaluate, and manage new product ideas.

The company can appoint a respected senior person to be its innovation manager. It can set up Web-based idea management software and encourage all company stakeholders—employees, suppliers, distributors, dealers—to become involved in finding and developing new products. It can assign a cross-functional innovation management committee to evaluate proposed new product ideas and help bring good ideas to market. It can also create recognition programs to reward those who contribute the best ideas.

The innovation management system approach yields two favorable outcomes. First, it helps create an innovation-oriented company culture. It shows that top management supports, encourages, and rewards innovation. Second, it will yield a larger number of new product ideas, among which will be found some especially good ones. The good new ideas will be more systematically developed, producing more new product successes. No longer will good ideas wither for the lack of a sounding board or a senior product advocate.

Thus, new product success requires more than simply thinking up a few good ideas, turning them into products, and finding customers for them. It requires a holistic approach for finding new ways to create valued customer experiences, from generating and screening new product ideas to creating and rolling out want-satisfying products to customers.

More than this, successful new product development requires a whole-company commitment. At companies known for their new product prowess, such as Google, Samsung, Apple, 3M, P&G, and GE, the entire culture encourages, supports, and rewards innovation. ≫ Consider Samsung:[21]

≫ Samsung's entire culture encourages and supports innovation. Every product has to pass the customer "Wow!" test, or it goes straight back to development.

Julie Jacobson/AP Images

Not many years ago, Samsung was a copycat consumer electronics brand you bought if you couldn't afford Sony, then the world's most coveted consumer electronics brand. In the mid-1990s, however, Samsung made an inspired decision. It turned its back on cheap knockoffs and set out to overtake rival Sony. To dethrone the consumer electronics giant, however, Samsung first had to change its entire culture, from copycat to leading edge. To out-*sell* Sony, Samsung first had to out-*innovate* Sony.

To make that happen, Samsung hired a crop of fresh, young designers and managers who unleashed a torrent of new products—not humdrum, me-too products but sleek, bold, and beautiful products targeted to high-end users. Samsung called them "lifestyle works of art." Every new product had to pass the "Wow!" test: If it didn't get a "Wow!" reaction during market testing, it went straight back to development. Beyond innovative technology and stylish designs, Samsung put the customer at the core of its innovation movement. Its primary goal was to improve the customer experience and bring genuine change to people's lives in everything it did.

Today, thanks to its whole-company culture of innovation, the Samsung brand holds a high-end, cutting-edge aura that rivals or even exceeds that of Apple, long considered to be the keeper of all things cool. Samsung is now by far the world's largest consumer electronics company, with sales two and a half times those of Sony and 25 percent greater than Apple's.

Product life cycle (PLC)
The course of a product's sales and profits over its lifetime.

Author Comment
A company's products are born, grow, mature, and then decline, just as living things do. To remain vital, the firm must continually develop new products and manage them effectively throughout their life cycles.

Product Life-Cycle Strategies

After launching the new product, management wants that product to enjoy a long and happy life. Although it does not expect the product to sell forever, the company wants to earn a decent profit to cover all the effort and risk that went into launching it. Management is aware that each product will have a life cycle, although its exact shape and length is not known in advance.

≫ **Figure 8.2** shows a typical **product life cycle (PLC)**, the course that a product's sales and profits take over its lifetime. The PLC has five distinct stages:

1. *Product development* begins when the company finds and develops a new product idea. During product development, sales are zero, and the company's investment costs mount.

>> Figure 8.2 Sales and Profits over the Product's Life from Inception to Decline

Some products die quickly; others stay in the mature stage for a long, long time. For example, TABASCO sauce has been around for more than 140 years. Even then, to keep the product young, the company has added a full line of flavors (such as Sweet & Spicy and Chipotle) and a kitchen cabinet full of new TABASCO products (such as salsas, marinades, and a chili mix).

2. **Introduction** is a period of slow sales growth as the product is introduced in the market. Profits are nonexistent in this stage because of the heavy expenses of product introduction.
3. **Growth** is a period of rapid market acceptance and increasing profits.
4. **Maturity** is a period of slowdown in sales growth because the product has achieved acceptance by most potential buyers. Profits level off or decline because of increased marketing outlays to defend the product against competition.
5. **Decline** is the period when sales fall off and profits drop.

Not all products follow all five stages of the PLC. Some products are introduced and die quickly; others stay in the mature stage for a long, long time. Some enter the decline stage and are then cycled back into the growth stage through strong promotion or repositioning. It seems that a well-managed brand could live forever. Venerable brands like Coca-Cola, Gillette, Budweiser, Guinness, American Express, Wells Fargo, Kikkoman, and TABASCO® sauce, for instance, are still going strong after more than 100 years. >> Guinness beer has been around for more than 250 years, Life Savers Mints recently celebrated "100 years of keeping mouths feeling fresh," and TABASCO sauce brags that it's "over 140 years old and still able to totally whup your butt!"

The PLC concept can describe a *product class* (gasoline-powered automobiles), a *product form* (SUVs), or a *brand* (the Ford Escape). The PLC concept applies differently in each case. Product classes have the longest life cycles; the sales of many product classes stay in the mature stage for a long time. Product forms, in contrast, tend to have the standard PLC shape. Product forms such as dial telephones, VHS tapes, and film cameras passed through a regular history of introduction, rapid growth, maturity, and decline.

A specific brand's life cycle can change quickly because of changing competitive attacks and responses. For example, although laundry soaps (product class) and powdered detergents (product form) have enjoyed fairly long life cycles, the life cycles of specific brands have tended to be much shorter. Today's leading U.S. brands of powdered laundry soap are Tide and Gain; the leading brands 100 years ago were Fels-Naptha, Octagon, and Kirkman.

The PLC concept also can be applied to what are known as styles, fashions, and fads. Their special life cycles are shown in >> **Figure 8.3**. A **style** is a basic and distinctive mode of expression. For example, styles appear in homes (colonial, ranch, transitional), clothing (formal, casual), and art (realist, surrealist, abstract). Once a style is invented, it may last for generations, passing in and out of vogue. A style has a cycle showing several periods of renewed interest.

A **fashion** is a currently accepted or popular style in a given field. For example, the more formal "business attire" look of corporate dress of the 1980s and 1990s gave way to the "business casual" look of the 2000s and 2010s. Fashions tend to grow slowly, remain popular for a while, and then decline slowly.

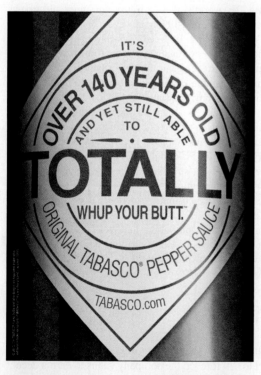

>> Product life cycle: Some products die quickly; others stay in the mature stage for a long, long time. TABASCO® sauce is "over 140 years old and yet still able to totally whup your butt!"

TABASCO® is a registered trademark for sauces and other goods and services; TABASCO, the TABASCO bottle design and label designs are the exclusive property of and licensed by McIlhenny Company, Avery Island, Louisiana 70513. www.TABASCO.com

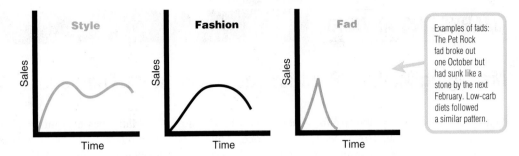

Figure 8.3 Styles, Fashions, and Fads

Examples of fads: The Pet Rock fad broke out one October but had sunk like a stone by the next February. Low-carb diets followed a similar pattern.

Style
A basic and distinctive mode of expression.

Fashion
A currently accepted or popular style in a given field.

Fad
A temporary period of unusually high sales driven by consumer enthusiasm and immediate product or brand popularity.

Fads are temporary periods of unusually high sales driven by consumer enthusiasm and immediate product or brand popularity.[22] A fad may be part of an otherwise normal life cycle, as in the case of recent surges in the sales of poker chips and accessories. Or the fad may comprise a brand's or product's entire life cycle. Pet Rocks are a classic example. Upon hearing his friends complain about how expensive it was to care for their dogs, advertising copywriter Gary Dahl joked about his pet rock. He soon wrote a spoof of a dog-training manual for it, titled *The Care and Training of Your Pet Rock*. Soon Dahl was selling some 1.5 million ordinary beach pebbles at $4 a pop. Yet the fad, which broke one October, had sunk like a stone by the next February. Dahl's advice to those who want to succeed with a fad: "Enjoy it while it lasts." Other examples of fads include Silly Bandz, Furbies, and Pogs.[23]

Marketers can apply the product life-cycle concept as a useful framework for describing how products and markets work. And when used carefully, the PLC concept can help in developing good marketing strategies for the different life-cycle stages. However, using the PLC concept for forecasting product performance or developing marketing strategies presents some practical problems. For example, in practice, it is difficult to forecast the sales level at each PLC stage, the length of each stage, and the shape of the PLC curve. Using the PLC concept to develop marketing strategy also can be difficult because strategy is both a cause and a result of the PLC. The product's current PLC position suggests the best marketing strategies, and the resulting marketing strategies affect product performance in later stages.

Moreover, marketers should not blindly push products through the traditional product life-cycle stages. Instead, marketers often defy the "rules" of the life cycle and position or reposition their products in unexpected ways. By doing this, they can rescue mature or declining products and return them to the growth phase of the life cycle. Or they can leapfrog obstacles that slow consumer acceptance and propel new products forward into the growth phase.

The moral of the product life cycle is that companies must continually innovate; otherwise, they risk extinction. No matter how successful its current product lineup, a company must skillfully manage the life cycles of existing products for future success. And to grow, the company must develop a steady stream of new products that bring new value to customers. Toy maker Mattel is learning this lesson the hard way. It has long dominated the world toy industry with classic brands such as Barbie, Hot Wheels, Fisher-Price, and American Girl. In recent years, however, as its core brands have matured, Mattel's sales have stagnated at the hands of nimbler, more innovative competitors (see Marketing at Work 8.2).

We looked at the product development stage of the PLC in the first part of this chapter. We now look at strategies for each of the other life-cycle stages.

Introduction Stage

Introduction stage
The PLC stage in which a new product is first distributed and made available for purchase.

The **introduction stage** starts when a new product is first launched. Introduction takes time, and sales growth is apt to be slow. Well-known products such as frozen foods and HDTVs lingered for many years before they entered a stage of more rapid growth.

In this stage, as compared to other stages, profits are negative or low because of the low sales and high distribution and promotion expenses. Much money is needed to attract distributors and build their inventories. Promotion spending is relatively high to inform

MARKETING AT WORK 8.2

Managing Mattel's Product Life Cycle: More Than Just Fun and Games

Mattel has ruled the toy industry for generations, with classic brands such as Barbie, Hot Wheels, Fisher-Price, American Girl, and a host of others. For more than 50 years, Mattel's toys have topped the wish lists of children across America.

Recently, however, Mattel's sales have fallen off as its core brands have matured. Venerable Barbie, now in her mid-50s, has experienced double-digit sales dips in each of the past two years. Sagging Fisher-Price and American Girl sales suggest that today's toy buyers are less enamored with those storied brands than previous generations were. And Mattel's Hot Wheels brand, while holding its own, now seems coveted more by nostalgic dads than by their young sons.

Mattel could blame its slump on broader toy industry trends—declining birthrates, rising costs, unfavorable economic conditions, and the boom in digital technologies that make many traditional toys now seem like relics from the past. The global toy industry has stagnated in recent years, with market leaders such as Mattel and Hasbro taking the biggest hits. Yet none of that has slowed Mattel's hottest competitor, The LEGO Group. In the past 10 years, despite the toy industry's doldrums, LEGO revenues have quadrupled, up 25 percent last year alone. LEGO recently surged past Mattel and Hasbro to become the world's largest toy maker.

LEGO's success suggests that Mattel's problems go beyond just industry ups and downs. Rather, the company appears to have a product life-cycle problem—lots of good old products but too few good new ones. In an industry facing a barrage of hot new playthings, Mattel has lagged in product development and failed to adapt to rapidly changing toy trends and tastes.

Consider Barbie, Mattel's biggest and oldest brand. Born in 1959, Barbie quickly became a must-have for young girls everywhere. By the late 1970s, 90 percent of U.S. girls between the ages of 5 and 10 owned at least one Barbie. For more than five decades, Barbie has remained Mattel's number-one moneymaker, accounting for as much as 30 percent of its revenues. But during the past few years, Barbie's popularity has spiraled downward. Although still one of the world's largest toy brands, Barbie's current annual revenues of $1 billion are little more than half of what they were at her peak. Barbie sales dropped a stomach-churning 16 percent last year, prompting one analyst to suggest that "it might be time for Mattel to roll out Retirement Barbie."

That won't happen anytime soon. But like many other Mattel brands, Barbie is showing her age. Designers work tirelessly on new Barbie models and features. An example is Entrepreneur Barbie, the first Barbie with her own smartphone and LinkedIn profile. Still, Barbie continues to lose relevance alongside trendier toy aisle juggernauts like Disney's *Frozen* line of toys and play sets.

Mattel has also misfired in some of its marketing attempts to modernize Barbie. For example, the Barbie "Unapologetic" campaign—with its "If you can dream it, you can be it" slogan—tried to strike a blow for female empowerment. Yet despite the fact that it targets 3- to 12-year-old girls and even after decades of criticism concerning Barbie's unrealistic figure and the standard of beauty she sets, Mattel kicked the campaign off by featuring Barbie on an advertising wrap on the cover of 1,000 issues of the 50th anniversary *Sports Illustrated* swimsuit edition. That move incurred the wrath of countless mothers across the nation.

Over the years, as Barbie has aged, Mattel has tried to round out its product portfolio with new, younger lines of dolls. In the late 1990s, the company purchased the wildly popular, premium-priced American Girl line. And more recently, it created runaway hit Monster High—a line of dolls and accessories composed of characters such as Draculaura, Ghoulia Yelps, and Abbey Bominable. However, much like Barbie, both American Girl and Monster High are now maturing and experiencing sales declines. Critics blame Mattel's uninspired designs, conservative innovation mindset, and inability to keep the brands fresh and relevant to the times.

With most of its core brands in mature or declining life-cycle stages, Mattel is fighting an uphill battle. Take Hot Wheels, long the market leader in toy cars. Mattel has had modest success in revitalizing the mature brand by taking it

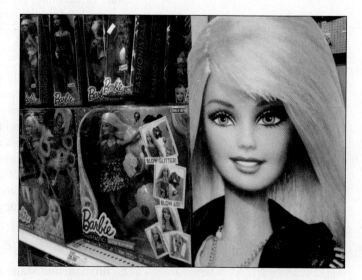

» Product life-cycle management: Like many other Mattel brands, Barbie is showing her age. Beyond revitalizing its classic brands, Mattel must create a steady stream of exciting new ones that stay ahead of changing consumer trends and tastes.

Mike Blake/Reuters

into hot pockets of the market. For example, as the popularity of remote control helicopters and drones has soared in recent years, Hot Wheels launched the Street Hawk, a flying remote control car. Street Hawk became one of the biggest hits during its first holiday season. Still, the hits have been too few and too far between. Even with its avid cross-generational collector base, the Hot Wheels brand is barely holding its own against the onslaught of new-age products from competitors with more inspired innovation processes.

As its own core brands have aged, Mattel has injected new life into its product lines by licensing hot characters from popular movies, TV shows, and comic books. Specifically, Mattel has made a small fortune with licensed Disney Princess and *Frozen* dolls and toys. It recently launched a line of Star Wars Hot Wheels cars, and it has partnered with Warner Bros. Entertainment on 10 upcoming films based on DC Comics characters. Although profitable, however, such licensed products can't compensate for Mattel's inability to revitalize its own brands and develop new ones. For example, Mattel recently lost its Disney character rights to rival Hasbro, leaving a huge revenue hole to fill.

Thus, to regain its prowess in today's turbulent, fast-changing toy market, Mattel must develop a faster, more nimble, more customer-focused process for developing relevant new products and guiding them profitably through their product life cycles. Beyond reinvigorating its classic brands, Mattel must create a steady stream of exciting new ones that stay ahead of changing consumer trends and tastes. For Mattel, mastering the product life cycle is more than just fun and games. It's a matter of growth, prosperity, and even long-run survival.

Sources: Jens Hansegard, "Oh, Snap! Lego Pushes Ahead of Mattel in Sales," *Wall Street Journal*, September 5, 2014, p. D5; Paul Ziobro, "Floundering Mattel Tries to Make Things Fun Again," *Wall Street Journal*, December 23, 2014, p. A1; Alexandra Petri, "The End of (Doll) History," *Washington Post*, May 4, 2013, P. A13; Shan Li, "Mattel's CEO Resigns as Toy Maker Struggles," *Los Angeles Times*, January 27, 2015, p. A1; John Kell, "Mattel's Barbie Sales Down for Third Consecutive Year," *Fortune,* January 30, 2015, http://fortune.com/2015/01/30/mattels-barbie-sales-drop-third-year/; "Shake-Up at Mattel as Barbie Loses Her Appeal," *New York Times,* January 27, 2015, p. B1; Laura Stampler, "Bye, Bye Barbie: 2015 Is the Year We Abandon Unrealistic Beauty Ideals," *Time,* January 30, 2015, http://time.com/3667580/mattel-barbie-earnings-plus-size-body-image/; and www.barbie.com and http://corporate.mattel.com, accessed October 2015.

consumers of the new product and get them to try it. Because the market is not generally ready for product refinements at this stage, the company and its few competitors produce basic versions of the product. These firms focus their selling on those buyers who are the most ready to buy.

A company, especially the *market pioneer*, must choose a launch strategy that is consistent with the intended product positioning. It should realize that the initial strategy is just the first step in a grander marketing plan for the product's entire life cycle. If the pioneer chooses its launch strategy to make a "killing," it may be sacrificing long-run revenue for the sake of short-run gain. The pioneer has the best chance of building and retaining market leadership if it plays its cards correctly from the start.

Growth Stage

Growth stage
The PLC stage in which a product's sales start climbing quickly.

If the new product satisfies the market, it will enter a **growth stage** in which sales will start climbing quickly. The early adopters will continue to buy, and later buyers will start following their lead, especially if they hear favorable word of mouth. Attracted by the opportunities for profit, new competitors will enter the market. They will introduce new product features, and the market will expand. The increase in competitors leads to an increase in the number of distribution outlets, and sales jump just to build reseller inventories. Prices remain where they are or decrease only slightly. Companies keep their promotion spending at the same or a slightly higher level. Educating the market remains a goal, but now the company must also meet the competition.

Profits increase during the growth stage as promotion costs are spread over a large volume and as unit manufacturing costs decrease. The firm uses several strategies to sustain rapid market growth as long as possible. It improves product quality and adds new product features and models. It enters new market segments and new distribution channels. It shifts some advertising from building product awareness to building product conviction and purchase, and it lowers prices at the right time to attract more buyers.

In the growth stage, the firm faces a trade-off between high market share and high current profit. By spending a lot of money on product improvement, promotion, and distribution, the company can capture a dominant position. In doing so, however, it gives up maximum current profit, which it hopes to make up in the next stage.

Maturity Stage

At some point, a product's sales growth will slow down, and it will enter the **maturity stage**. This maturity stage normally lasts longer than the previous stages, and it poses strong challenges to marketing management. Most products are in the maturity stage of the life cycle, and therefore most of marketing management deals with the mature product.

The slowdown in sales growth results in many producers with many products to sell. In turn, this overcapacity leads to greater competition. Competitors begin marking down prices, increasing their advertising and sales promotions, and upping their product development budgets to find better versions of the product. These steps lead to a drop in profit. Some of the weaker competitors start dropping out, and the industry eventually contains only well-established competitors.

Although many products in the mature stage appear to remain unchanged for long periods, most successful ones are actually evolving to meet changing consumer needs. Product managers should do more than simply ride along with or defend their mature products—a good offense is the best defense. They should consider modifying the market, product offering, and marketing mix.

In *modifying the market*, the company tries to increase consumption by finding new users and new market segments for its brands. For example, brands such as Harley-Davidson and Axe fragrances, which have typically targeted male buyers, are introducing products and marketing programs aimed at women. Conversely, Weight Watchers and Bath & Body Works, which have typically targeted women, have created products and programs aimed at men.

The company may also look for ways to increase usage among present customers. For example, 3M recently ran a marketing campaign to inspire more usage of its Post-it products:[24]

> The Post-it Brand's "Go Ahead" campaign aimed to convince customers that the sticky pieces of paper are good for much more than just scribbling temporary notes and reminders. Instead, it positioned Post-it Notes as a means of self-expression by showing creative, nontraditional ways that consumers around the world use them. In the past, 3M promoted mostly functional uses of Post-it products, but research showed that consumers have a surprisingly strong emotional relationship with the brand. "They're using it to communicate, using it to collaborate, using it to organize themselves," says a 3M marketing executive. The "Go Ahead" campaign was motivated by customers' "quirky and inspired uses of our product."
>
> An initial ad showed people on a college campus blanketing a wall outside a building with Post-it Notes answering the question "What inspires you?" "Share on a real wall," the announcer explained. Other scenes showed a young man filling a wall with mosaic artwork created from multiple colors of Post-it Notes, teachers using Post-it Notes to enliven their classrooms, and a man posting a "Morning, beautiful" note on the bathroom mirror as his wife is brushing her teeth. "Go ahead," said the announcer, "keep the honeymoon going." The ad ended with a hand peeling Post-it Notes off a pad one by one to reveal new, unexpected uses: "Go ahead, Connect," "Go ahead, Inspire," and "Go ahead, Explore."

The company might also try *modifying the product*—changing characteristics such as quality, features, style, packaging, or technology platforms to retain current users or attract new ones. Thus, to freshen up their products for today's technology-obsessed children, many classic toy and game makers are creating new digital versions or add-ons for old favorites. For example, the venerable Crayola brand has souped up its product line to meet the technology tastes of the new generation. With the Crayola My Virtual Fashion Show drawing kit and app, for instance, children first design fashions using the provided color pencils and sketchpad. They then take photos of the designs with their smartphones or tablets and watch their original creations magically come to life inside the app on 3D models who walk virtual runways in Milan, New York, and Paris.[25]

Finally, the company can try *modifying the marketing mix*—improving sales by changing one or more marketing mix elements. The company can offer new or improved services to buyers. It can cut prices to attract new users and competitors' customers. It can launch a better advertising campaign or use aggressive sales promotions—trade deals, cents-off, premiums, and contests. In addition to pricing and promotion, the company can also move into new marketing channels to help serve new users.

>> **Managing the product life cycle:** Thanks to the "Quaker Up" campaign, 137-year-old Quaker now has a more contemporary appeal as a lifestyle brand that helps give young families the fuel and energy needed to get through the day.

Provided courtesy of The Quaker Oat Company.

Decline stage
The PLC stage in which a product's sales fade away.

PepsiCo used all of these market, product, and marketing mix modification approaches to reinvigorate its 137-year-old Quaker brand and keep it from sinking into decline. >> To reawaken the brand, Quaker launched a major new "Quaker Up" marketing campaign, supported by an estimated $100 million budget:[26]

The "Quaker Up" campaign targets a new market of young mothers under 35, positioning Quaker's lines of hot and cold cereals, snack bars, cookies, and other products as healthy lifestyle choices that help give a young family the fuel and energy needed to get through the day. The campaign advises families to "Quaker Up—with Quaker's good energy for the moments that matter." As part of the retargeting and repositioning effort, Quaker has modernized every element of the brand, from products and packaging to in-store displays and ad platforms. To start, it slimmed down the iconic Quaker man by 20 pounds and gave him a facelift to make him look healthier, stronger, and more contemporary. The brand added new energy-packed products, such as Quaker Medleys—a hearty blend of oats and grains with real fruit and nuts; Quaker Soft Baked Bars—high in fiber, protein, and B vitamins; and Quaker Protein—protein-packed instant oatmeal and baked energy bars. Befitting the more mobile and connected lifestyles of today's young parents, the "Quaker Up" campaign also incorporates and healthy dose of digital media, including banner ads, YouTube videos, a Facebook app, a Quaker Up community Web site, and a full slate of other digital content. In all, despite its age, the reenergized Quaker brand now has a much younger appeal. "People know the brand, people love the brand, but we needed to forge a stronger connection with contemporary moms," says Quaker's chief marketing officer.

Decline Stage

The sales of most product forms and brands eventually dip. The decline may be slow, as in the cases of stamps and oatmeal cereal, or rapid, as in the cases of VHS tapes. Sales may plunge to zero, or they may drop to a low level where they continue for many years. This is the **decline stage**.

Sales decline for many reasons, including technological advances, shifts in consumer tastes, and increased competition. As sales and profits decline, some firms withdraw from the market. Those remaining may prune their product offerings. In addition, they may drop smaller market segments and marginal trade channels, or they may cut the promotion budget and reduce their prices further.

Carrying a weak product can be very costly to a firm, and not just in profit terms. There are many hidden costs. A weak product may take up too much of management's time. It often requires frequent price and inventory adjustments. It requires advertising and sales-force attention that might be better used to make "healthy" products more profitable. A product's failing reputation can cause customer concerns about the company and its other products. The biggest cost may well lie in the future. Keeping weak products delays the search for replacements, creates a lopsided product mix, hurts current profits, and weakens the company's foothold on the future.

For these reasons, companies must identify products in the decline stage and decide whether to maintain, harvest, or drop them. Management may decide to *maintain* its brand, repositioning or reinvigorating it in hopes of moving it back into the growth stage of the product life cycle. P&G has done this with several brands, including Mr. Clean and Old Spice. Over the past decade, P&G has retargeted, repositioned, revitalized, and extended both of these old brands, taking each from near extinction to billion-dollar-brand status.

Management may decide to *harvest* the product, which means reducing various costs (plant and equipment, maintenance, R&D, advertising, sales force), hoping that sales hold up. If successful, harvesting will increase the company's profits in the short run. Finally, management may decide to *drop* the product from its line. The company can sell the product to another firm or simply liquidate it at salvage value. If the company plans to find a buyer, it will not want to run down the product through harvesting. In recent years, P&G has sold off several declining brands and brands that no longer fit strategically, such as Folgers coffee, Crisco oil, Comet cleanser, Sure deodorant, Duncan Hines cake mixes, Jif peanut butter, Duracell batteries, and Iams pet foods.[27]

>> **Table 8.2** summarizes the key characteristics of each stage of the PLC. The table also lists the marketing objectives and strategies for each stage.[28]

Author Comment
Let's look at just a few more product topics, including regulatory and social responsibility issues and the special challenges of marketing products internationally.

Additional Product and Service Considerations

We wrap up our discussion of products and services with two additional considerations: social responsibility in product decisions and issues of international product and services marketing.

Product Decisions and Social Responsibility

Marketers should carefully consider public policy issues and regulations regarding acquiring or dropping products, patent protection, product quality and safety, and product warranties.

Regarding new products, the government may prevent companies from adding products through acquisitions if the effect threatens to lessen competition. Companies dropping products must be aware that they have legal obligations, written or implied, to their suppliers, dealers, and customers who have a stake in the dropped product. Companies

>> **Table 8.2** | **Summary of Product Life-Cycle Characteristics, Objectives, and Strategies**

	Introduction	Growth	Maturity	Decline
Characteristics				
Sales	Low sales	Rapidly rising sales	Peak sales	Declining sales
Costs	High cost per customer	Average cost per customer	Low cost per customer	Low cost per customer
Profits	Negative	Rising profits	High profits	Declining profits
Customers	Innovators	Early adopters	Mainstream adopters	Lagging adopters
Competitors	Few	Growing number	Stable number beginning to decline	Declining number
Marketing objectives				
	Create product engagement and trial	Maximize market share	Maximize profit while defending market share	Reduce expenditure and milk the brand
Strategies				
Product	Offer a basic product	Offer product extensions, service, and warranty	Diversify brand and models	Phase out weak items
Price	Use cost-plus	Price to penetrate market	Price to match or beat competitors	Cut price
Distribution	Build selective distribution	Build intensive distribution	Build more intensive distribution	Go selective: phase out unprofitable outlets
Advertising	Build product awareness among early adopters and dealers	Build engagement and interest in the mass market	Stress brand differences and benefits	Reduce to level needed to retain hard-core loyals
Sales Promotion	Use heavy sales promotion to entice trial	Reduce to take advantage of heavy consumer demand	Increase to encourage brand switching	Reduce to minimal level

Source: Based on Philip Kotler and Kevin Lane Keller, *Marketing Management,* 15th ed. (Upper Saddle River, NJ: Pearson Education, 2016), p. 358. © 2016. Printed and Electronically reproduced by permission of Pearson Education, Inc., Upper Saddle River, New Jersey.

must also obey U.S. patent laws when developing new products. A company cannot make its product illegally similar to another company's established product.

Manufacturers must comply with specific laws regarding product quality and safety. The Federal Food, Drug, and Cosmetic Act protects consumers from unsafe and adulterated food, drugs, and cosmetics. Various acts provide for the inspection of sanitary conditions in the meat- and poultry-processing industries. Safety legislation has been passed to regulate fabrics, chemical substances, automobiles, toys, and drugs and poisons. The Consumer Product Safety Act of 1972 established the Consumer Product Safety Commission, which has the authority to ban or seize potentially harmful products and set severe penalties for violation of the law.

If consumers have been injured by a product with a defective design, they can sue manufacturers or dealers. A recent survey of manufacturing companies found that product liability was the second-largest litigation concern, behind only labor and employment matters. Tens of thousands of product liability suits are now tried in U.S. district courts each year. Although manufacturers are found to be at fault in only a small percentage of all product liability cases, when they are found guilty, awards can run into the tens or even hundreds of millions of dollars. Class-action suits can run into the billions. For example, after it recalled 11 million vehicles for acceleration pedal–related issues, Toyota faced more than 100 class-action and individual lawsuits and ended up paying a $1.6 billion settlement to compensate owners for financial losses associated with the defect.[29]

This litigation phenomenon has resulted in huge increases in product liability insurance premiums, causing big problems in some industries. Some companies pass these higher rates along to consumers by raising prices. Others are forced to discontinue high-risk product lines. Some companies are now appointing *product stewards*, whose job is to protect consumers from harm and the company from liability by proactively ferreting out potential product problems.

International Product and Services Marketing

International product and services marketers face special challenges. First, they must figure out what products and services to introduce and in which countries. Then they must decide how much to standardize or adapt their products and services for world markets.

On the one hand, companies would like to standardize their offerings. Standardization helps a company develop a consistent worldwide image. It also lowers the product design, manufacturing, and marketing costs of offering a large variety of products. On the other hand, markets and consumers around the world differ widely. Companies must usually respond to these differences by adapting their product offerings. For example, by carefully tailoring its products to local tastes in China, PepsiCo has become the largest snack-and-beverage company in the world's second-biggest economy:[30]

PepsiCo has found that success in China's huge beverage and snack markets depends on carefully adapting its many brands—such as Pepsi, Lay's, Gatorade, and Quaker—to the tastes of Chinese consumers. Its large food-and-beverage innovation center in Shanghai employs consumer and food researchers, product developers, experimental kitchens, and even a pilot manufacturing plant, all devoted to pinpointing and pinging the unique palates of Chinese consumers. And before new product concepts ever hit the market, they are sampled extensively by local taste testers—often local homemakers. While not likely to be favorites in Western markets, PepsiCo's Chinese lineup includes lip-smackers such as hot and sour fish soup potato chips, white fungus oatmeal, and blueberry Gatorade. Lay's famously funky Chinese chip flavors include cucumber (a best-seller), iced lemon tea, "Numb & Spicy Hot Pot," and "Sha La Cui,"a concoction designed to taste like a baked salad.

>> **Global product adaptation: Lay's famously funky Chinese chip flavors include cucumber (a best-seller), iced lemon tea, "Numb & Spicy Hot Pot," and "Sha La Chui," a concoction that tastes like a baked salad.**

Frito-Lay, Inc.

The Chinese market holds huge potential for PepsiCo. For example, China's 1.35 billion people now consume an average of only about one small bag of potato chips every two to four weeks, compared with 15 bags in that period in the United States. Skillful product adaptation has helped PepsiCo achieve double-digit growth in this important market.

Service marketers also face special challenges when going global. Some service industries have a long history of international operations. For example, the commercial banking industry was one of the first to grow internationally. Banks had to provide global services to meet the foreign exchange and credit needs of their home-country clients who wanted to sell overseas. In recent years, many banks have become truly global. Germany's Deutsche Bank, for example, serves more than 28 million customers through 2,900 branches in more than 70 countries. For its clients around the world who wish to grow globally, Deutsche Bank can raise money not only in Frankfurt but also in Zurich, London, Paris, Tokyo, and Moscow.[31]

Professional and business services industries, such as accounting, management consulting, and advertising, have also globalized. The international growth of these firms followed the globalization of the client companies they serve. For example, as more clients employ worldwide marketing and advertising strategies, advertising agencies have responded by globalizing their own operations. McCann Worldgroup, a large U.S.-based advertising and marketing services agency, operates in 120 countries. It serves international clients such as Coca-Cola, GM, ExxonMobil, Microsoft, MasterCard, Johnson & Johnson, and Unilever in markets ranging from the United States and Canada to Korea and Kazakhstan. Moreover, McCann Worldgroup is one company in the Interpublic Group of Companies, an immense, worldwide network of advertising and marketing services companies.[32]

Retailers are among the latest service businesses to go global. As their home markets become saturated, American retailers such as Walmart, Office Depot, and Saks Fifth Avenue are expanding into faster-growing markets abroad. For example, Walmart now serves 250 million customers weekly in 27 countries; its international division's sales account for nearly 29 percent of total sales. Foreign retailers are making similar moves. Asian shoppers can now buy American products in French-owned Carrefour stores. Carrefour—the world's fourth-largest retailer behind Walmart, Costco, and the UK's Tesco—now operates more than 10,000 stores in 34 countries. It is the leading retailer in Europe, Brazil, and Argentina and the largest foreign retailer in China.[33]

The trend toward growth of global service companies will continue, especially in banking, airlines, telecommunications, and professional services. Today, service firms are no longer simply following their manufacturing customers. Instead, they are taking the lead in international expansion.

MyMarketingLab

If assigned by your instructor, complete the questions marked with the ⭐ from the EOC Discussion Questions section in the MyLab. To complete the Marketing by the Numbers problems found in this section, go to your Assignments in the MyLab.

REVIEWING AND EXTENDING THE CONCEPTS

CHAPTER REVIEW AND CRITICAL THINKING

Objectives Review

A company's current products face limited life spans and must be replaced by newer products. But new products can fail—the risks of innovation are as great as the rewards. The key to successful innovation lies in a customer-focused, holistic, total-company effort; strong planning; and a systematic new product development process.

OBJECTIVE 8-1   **Explain how companies find and develop new product ideas. (pp 238–239)**

Companies find and develop new product ideas from a variety of sources. Many new product ideas stem from *internal sources*. Companies conduct formal R&D, or they pick the brains of their employees, urging them to think up and develop new product ideas. Other ideas come from *external sources*. Companies track *competitors'* offerings and obtain ideas from *distributors and suppliers* who are close to the market and can pass along information about consumer problems and new product possibilities.

Perhaps the most important sources of new product ideas are *customers* themselves. Companies observe customers, invite them to submit their ideas and suggestions, or even involve customers in the new product development process. Many companies are now developing *crowdsourcing* or *open-innovation* new product idea programs, which invite broad communities of people—customers, employees, independent scientists and researchers, and even the general public—into the new product innovation process. Truly innovative companies do not rely only on one source for new product ideas.

 OBJECTIVE 8-2   **List and define the steps in the new product development process and the major considerations in managing this process. (pp 239–249)**

The new product development process consists of eight sequential stages. The process starts with *idea generation*. Next comes *idea screening,* which reduces the number of ideas based on the company's own criteria. Ideas that pass the screening stage continue through *product concept development,* in which a detailed version of the new product idea is stated in meaningful consumer terms. This stage includes *concept testing,* in which new product concepts are tested with a group of target consumers to determine whether the concepts have strong consumer appeal. Strong concepts proceed to *marketing strategy development,* in which an initial marketing strategy for the new product is developed from the product concept. In the *business-analysis* stage, a review of the sales, costs, and profit projections for a new product is conducted to determine whether the new product

is likely to satisfy the company's objectives. With positive results here, the ideas become more concrete through *product development* and *test marketing* and finally are launched during *commercialization.*

New product development involves more than just going through a set of steps. Companies must take a systematic, holistic approach to managing this process. Successful new product development requires a customer-centered, team-based, systematic effort.

 OBJECTIVE 8-3   **Describe the stages of the product life cycle and how marketing strategies change during a product's life cycle. (pp 249–256)**

Each product has a *life cycle* marked by a changing set of problems and opportunities. The sales of the typical product follow an S-shaped curve made up of five stages. The cycle begins with the *product development* stage in which the company finds and develops a new product idea. *The introduction stage* is marked by slow growth and low profits as the product is distributed to the market. If successful, the product enters a *growth stage,* which offers rapid sales growth and increasing profits. Next comes a *maturity stage* in which the product's sales growth slows down and profits stabilize. Finally, the product enters a *decline stage* in which sales and profits dwindle. The company's task during this stage is to recognize the decline and decide whether it should maintain, harvest, or drop the product. The different stages of the PLC require different marketing strategies and tactics.

 OBJECTIVE 8-4   **Discuss two additional product issues: socially responsible product decisions and international product and services marketing. (pp 256–258)**

Marketers must consider two additional product issues. The first is *social responsibility.* This includes public policy issues and regulations involving acquiring or dropping products, patent protection, product quality and safety, and product warranties. The second involves the special challenges facing international product and services marketers. International marketers must decide how much to standardize or adapt their offerings for world markets.

Key Terms

Objective 8-1
New product development (p 238)

Objective 8-2
Idea generation (p 239)
Crowdsourcing (p 240)
Idea screening (p 243)
Product concept (p 243)
Concept testing (p 244)

Marketing strategy development (p 244)
Business analysis (p 245)
Product development (p 245)
Test marketing (p 246)
Commercialization (p 247)
Customer-centered new product
  development (p 247)
Team-based new product development
  (p 248)

Objective 8-3
Product life cycle (PLC) (p 249)
Style (p 250)
Fashion (p 250)
Fad (p 251)
Introduction stage (p 251)
Growth stage (p 253)
Maturity stage (p 254)
Decline stage (p 255)

Discussion Questions

8-1. Define crowdsourcing and describe an example not already presented in the chapter. (AACSB: Communication; Reflective Thinking)

⭐ **8-2.** What activities are performed in the marketing strategy development step of the new product development process? What is required in a good marketing strategy statement? (AACSB: Communication; Reflective Thinking)

8-3. What is performed in the business analysis step of the new product development process? How does a business carry out this step? (AACSB: Communication)

8-4. How can companies adopt a holistic approach to managing new product development? (AACSB: Communication).

8-5. Describe the options available to marketers of products in the decline stage of the product life cycle. (AACSB: Communication)

Critical Thinking Exercises

8-6. It appears that the sky is the limit regarding ideas for smartphone/tablet apps. In a small group, create an idea for new apps related to (1) business, (2) health, (3) education, (4) sports, and (5) shopping. (AACSB: Communication; Use of IT; Reflective Thinking)

⭐ **8-7.** Find an example of a company that launched a new consumer product within the past five years. Develop a presentation showing how the company implemented the 4*P*s in launching the product and report on the product's success since the launch. (AACSB: Communication; Reflective Thinking)

⭐ **8-8.** The "Internet of Things"—a term that refers to everyday objects being connected to the Internet—is growing. Thermostats, ovens, cars, toothbrushes, and even baby clothes are connecting to the Internet. Research this phenomenon and suggest five innovative product ideas connected to the Internet of Things. (AACSB: Communication; Use of IT; Reflective Thinking)

MINICASES AND APPLICATIONS

Online, Mobile, and Social Media Marketing   Telemedicine

With the majority of health-care costs spent for the treatment of chronic diseases and the reason for most emergency room visits being nonemergencies, the time is ripe for telemedicine. Patients are tapping their phones, tablets, and keyboards instead of making an office visit or trip to the emergency room. Technology makes it possible for doctors to consult with patients through Skype or FaceTime on smartphones, access medical tests via electronic medical records, and send a prescription to a patient's local pharmacy—all from miles away. The telemedicine industry is still in its infancy, earning only $200 million in annual revenue, but it is predicted to increase to an almost $2 billion industry in just a few years. Technology isn't the only reason for this industry's growth. The HITECH Act encouraging electronic medical records is also adding fuel to this fire.

⭐ **8-9.** Research the telemedicine industry and describe two companies offering services. What are the pros and cons of offering medical services this way, and is there governmental or industry guidance for this industry? (AACSB: Communications; Reflective Thinking)

8-10. In what stage of the product life cycle is telemedicine? What role has mobile technology played in evolution of this industry? Explain (AACSB: Communication; Reflective Thinking)

Marketing Ethics   Put On Your Thinking Caps!

For years, electrical current has been used to treat brain disorders such as depression, Parkinson's disease, and epilepsy. Traditional electrical treatment methods are invasive and require sending large currents or implanting devices in users' brains to achieve positive results. Recent studies have shown, however, that sending noninvasive low-dose electric current powered by a nine-volt battery through the brains of adults and children helps them to learn math and languages better.

For as little as $55, you can purchase your own transcranial direct-current stimulation (tDCS) device to get better grades in school. The Brain Stimulator tDCS Basic Kit allows users to select between four different current levels and a nice blue headband or cap to hold the electrodes next to your skull. The buyer should beware, however, because these devices have been neither reviewed nor approved by the Food and Drug Administration as medical devices.

8-11. Discuss the ethical issues surrounding this type of product. Is there substantial research to support the claims and safety of these new products? (AACSB: Communication; Ethical Reasoning)

8-12. What is the Food and Drug Administration's stance on these types of devices and other products, such as herbal supplements, marketed as cognitive enhancers? (AACSB: Communication; Reflective Thinking)

Marketing by the Numbers   Dental House Calls

With the population aging and patients who dread sitting in a sterile dental office, dentists are finding an opportunity in dental house calls. The Blende Dental Group has taken its service on the road in San Francisco and New York City, performing everything from routine exams and cleanings to root canals. Some patients are wealthy and prefer the personal service, whereas others are elderly homebounds who cannot get out to the dentist's office. Recreating a dental office in a home requires additional equipment, such as a portable X-ray machine that looks like a ray gun, sterile water tanks, a dental drill, lights, and a laptop. A portable X-ray machine alone costs $8,000. Refer to Appendix 3: Marketing by the Numbers to answer the following questions.

8-13. What types of fixed costs are associated with this service? Assuming fixed costs of adding this mobile service will increase by $20,000 and a desired contribution margin of 40 percent, determine the amount of sales necessary to break even on this increase in fixed costs to offer this additional service. (AACSB: Communication; Analytical Thinking)

8-14. What other factors must a dentist consider before offering this service in addition to his or her in-office service? (AACSB: Communication; Reflective Thinking)

Video Case   Day2Night Convertible Heels

Many women love the fashionable looks and heightening effects of high-heeled shoes. But every woman knows the problems associated with wearing them. For example, they are very uncomfortable for anything more than light walking for short distances. For other activities, you'd better be packing a second pair of shoes.

That's where Day2Night Convertible Heels comes in. Created by a woman who had an epiphany after a hard night of dancing, Day2Night's shoes instantly convert to any one of four heel sizes, from low-heeled pumps to spiked-heeled stilettos. An interchangeable heel makes these high heels a high-tech proposition. Beyond launching a line of shoes,

Day2Night is looking to license the technology to other shoe manufacturers.

After viewing the video featuring Day2Night Convertible Heels, answer the following questions:

8-15. Based on the stages of new product development, discuss how Day2Night was likely developed.

8-16. What stage of the product life cycle best applies to Day2Night's shoe line? As the company attempts to launch the shoes, how should it market them?

8-17. What challenges does Day2Night face?

Company Cases   8 3M/2 Samsung/10 Apple Pay

See Appendix 1 for cases appropriate for this chapter. **Case 8, 3M: Where Innovation Is a Way of Life**. Generally not considered high-tech, 3M is consistently one of the most innovative companies due to a culture of innovation. **Case 2, Samsung: A Strategic Plan for Success.** One of the most innovative companies in the world, Samsung consistently raises the bar with

cutting-edge new products in numerous categories. **Case 10, Apple Pay: Taking Mobile Payments Mainstream.** While the Apple Watch was a highly anticipated new product, the real new product story may be Apple Pay—the mobile payment system that was initially seen as merely a feature of Apple's flashy hardware.

MyMarketingLab

If assigned by your instructor, complete these writing sections from your Assignments in the MyLab.

8-18. Discuss how a company can maintain success for products in the mature stage of the product life cycle and give examples not already described in the chapter. (AACSB: Communication)

8-19. What decisions must be made once a company decides to go ahead with commercialization for a new product? (AACSB: Written and Oral Communication)

9 Pricing
Understanding and Capturing Customer Value

Previewing the Concepts

In this chapter, we look at the second major marketing mix tool—pricing. If effective product development, promotion, and distribution sow the seeds of business success, effective pricing is the harvest. Firms successful at creating customer value with the other marketing mix activities must still capture some of this value in the prices they earn. In this chapter, we discuss the importance of pricing, dig into three major pricing strategies, and look at internal and external considerations that affect pricing decisions. Finally we examine some additional pricing considerations and approaches.

For openers, let's examine the importance of pricing in online retailing. In case you haven't noticed, there's a war going on—between Walmart, by far the world's largest retailer, and Amazon, the planet's largest online merchant. Each combatant brings an arsenal of potent weapons to the battle. For now, the focus is on price. But in the long run, it'll take much more than low prices to win this war. The spoils will go to the company that delivers the best overall online customer experience and value for the price.

First Stop

Amazon versus Walmart: A Price War for Online Supremacy

"Walmart to Amazon: Let's Rumble" read the headline. Ali had Frazier. Coke has Pepsi. The Yankees have the White Sox. And now, the two retail heavyweights are waging a war all their own. The objective? Online supremacy. The weapon of choice? Prices, at least for now—not surprising, given the two combatants' long-held low-cost positions.

Each side is formidable in its own right. Walmart dominates offline retailing. It's price-driven "Save money. Live better." positioning has made it far and away the world's biggest retailer, and the world's largest company to boot. In turn, Amazon is the "Walmart of the Web"—our online general store. Although Walmart's yearly sales total an incredible $487 billion, more than 5.3 times Amazon's $89 billion annually, Amazon's online sales are 7.5 times greater than Walmart's online sales. By one estimate, Amazon captures a full one-third of all U.S. online buying.

Why does Walmart worry about Amazon? After all, online sales currently account for only about 5 percent of total U.S. retail sales. Walmart captures most of its business through its 11,000 brick-and-mortar stores—online buying accounts for only a trifling 2.7 percent of its total sales. But this battle isn't about now, it's about the future. Although still a small market by Walmart's standards, online sales are growing at three times the rate of physical-world sales. Within the next decade, online and mobile buying will capture as much as a third of all retail sales. Because Amazon owns online, its revenues have soared 20 percent or more annually over the past three years. Meanwhile, Walmart's earthbound sales have grown at less than 5 percent a year during that period. At that rate, Amazon's revenues will reach $100 billion within the next year, reaching that mark faster than any other company in history.

Amazon has shown a relentless ambition to offer more of almost everything online. It started by selling only books but now sells everything from books, movies, and music to consumer electronics, home and garden products, clothing, jewelry, toys, tools, and even groceries. Thus, Amazon's online prowess now looms as a significant threat to Walmart. If Amazon's expansion continues and online sales spurt as predicted, the digital merchant will eat further and further into Walmart's bread-and-butter store sales.

But Walmart isn't about to let that happen without a fight. Instead, it's taking the battle to Amazon's home territory—the Internet and mobile buying. It started with the tactics it knows best—low costs and prices. Through aggressive pricing, Walmart is now fighting for every dollar consumers spend online. If you compare prices at Walmart.com and Amazon.com, you'll find a price war raging across a broad range of products.

In a price war, Walmart would seem to have the edge. Low costs and prices are in the company's DNA. Through the years, Walmart has used its efficient operations and immense buying power to slash prices and thrash one competitor after another. But Amazon is not like most other competitors. Its network is optimized for online shopping, and the Internet seller isn't saddled with the costs of running physical stores. As a result, Amazon has been able to match or even beat Walmart at its own pricing game online. The two giants now seem

>> **Walmart versus Amazon online:** Achieving online supremacy will take more than just waging and winning an online price war. The spoils will go to the company that delivers the best overall online customer experience and value for the price.

(top) Andrew Harrer/Bloomberg/Getty Images; (bottom) Digitallife/Alamy

pretty much stalemated on low prices, giving neither much of an advantage there. In fact, in the long run, reckless price cutting will likely do more damage than good to both Walmart and Amazon. So, although low prices will be crucial, they won't be enough to win over online buyers. Today's online shoppers want it all, low prices *and* selection, speed, convenience, and a satisfying overall shopping experience.

> Walmart, the world's largest retailer, and Amazon, the world's largest online merchant, are fighting a war for online supremacy. The weapon of choice? Prices, at least for now. But in the long run, winning the war will take much more than low prices.

For now, Amazon seems to have the upper hand on most of the important nonprice buying factors. Its made-for-online distribution network speeds orders to buyers' homes quickly and efficiently—including same-day delivery in some markets. Amazon's online assortment outstrips even Walmart's, and the online and mobile shopping wizard is now moving into groceries, an area that currently accounts for 55 percent of Walmart's sales. As for Amazon's lack of physical stores—no problem. Amazon's heavily used mobile app lets customers shop Amazon.com even as they are browsing

Walmart's stores. Finally, Amazon's unmatched, big data–driven customer interface creates personalized, highly satisfying online buying experiences. Amazon regularly rates among the leaders in customer satisfaction across all industries.

By contrast, Walmart came late to online selling. It's still trying to figure out how to efficiently deliver goods into the hands of online shoppers. As its online sales have grown, the store-based giant has patched together a makeshift online distribution network out of unused corners of its store distribution centers. And the still–mostly store retailer has yet to come close to matching Amazon's online customer buying experience. So even with its impressive low-price legacy, Walmart finds itself playing catch-up online.

To catch up, Walmart is investing heavily to create a next-generation fulfillment network. Importantly, it's taking advantage of a major asset that Amazon can't match—an opportunity to integrate online buying with its massive network of brick-and-mortar stores. For example, Walmart now fulfills more than a fifth of Walmart.com orders more quickly and cheaply by having workers in stores pluck and pack items and mail or deliver them to customers' homes. Two-thirds of the U.S. population lives within five miles of a Walmart store, offering the potential for 30-minute delivery.

And by combining its online and offline operations, Walmart can provide some unique services, such as free and convenient pickup and returns of online orders in stores (Walmart.com gives you three buying options: "online," "in-store," and "site-to-store"). Using Walmart's Web site and mobile app can also smooth in-store shopping. They let customers prepare shopping lists in advance, locate products by aisle to reduce wasted shopping time, and use their smartphones at checkout with preloaded digital coupons applied automatically. Customers who pick up online orders in the store can pay with cash, opening up online shopping to the 20 percent of Walmart customers who don't have bank accounts or credit cards. For customers who do pay online, Walmart is testing in-store lockers where customers can simply go to an assigned locker for pickup.

Who will win the battle for the hearts and dollars of online buyers? Certainly, low prices will continue to be important. But achieving online supremacy will involve much more than just waging and winning an online price war. It will require delivering low prices *plus* selection, convenience, and a world-class online buying experience—something that Amazon perfected long ago. For Walmart, catching and conquering Amazon online will require time, resources, and skills far beyond its trademark everyday low prices. As Walmart's president of global e-commerce puts it, the important task of winning online "will take the rest of our careers and as much as we've got [to invest]. This isn't a project. It's about the future of the company."[1]

Price
The amount charged for a product or service, or the sum of the values that customers exchange for the benefits of having or using the product or service.

C ompanies today face a fierce and fast-changing pricing environment. Value-seeking customers have put increased pricing pressure on many companies. Thanks to tight economic times in recent years, the pricing power of the Internet, and value-driven retailers such as Walmart, today's more frugal consumers are pursuing spend-less strategies. In response, it seems that almost every company has been looking for ways to cut prices.

>> Yet cutting prices is often not the best answer. Reducing prices unnecessarily can lead to lost profits and damaging price wars. It can cheapen a brand by signaling to customers that price is more important than the customer value a brand delivers. Instead, in both good economic times and bad, companies should sell value, not price. In some cases, that means selling lesser products at rock-bottom prices. But in most cases, it means persuading customers that paying a higher price for the company's brand is justified by the greater value they gain.

What Is a Price?

In the narrowest sense, **price** is the amount of money charged for a product or a service. More broadly, price is the sum of all the values that customers give up to gain the benefits of having or using a product or service. Historically, price has been the major factor affecting buyer choice. In recent decades, however, nonprice factors have gained increasing importance. Even so, price remains one of the most important elements that determine a firm's market share and profitability.

Price is the only element in the marketing mix that produces revenue; all other elements represent costs. Price is also one of the most flexible marketing mix elements. Unlike product features and channel commitments, prices can be changed quickly. At the same time, pricing is the number-one problem facing many marketing executives, and many companies do not handle pricing well. Some managers view pricing as a big headache, preferring instead to focus on other marketing mix elements.

However, smart managers treat pricing as a key strategic tool for creating and capturing customer value. Prices have a direct impact on a firm's bottom line. A small percentage improvement in price can generate a large percentage increase in profitability. More important, as part of a company's overall value proposition, price plays a key role in creating customer value and building customer relationships. So, instead of shying away from pricing, smart marketers are embracing it as an important competitive asset.[2]

Major Pricing Strategies

The price the company charges will fall somewhere between one that is too low to produce a profit and one that is too high to produce any demand. **» Figure 9.1** summarizes the major considerations in setting prices. Customer perceptions of the product's value set the ceiling for its price. If customers perceive that the product's price is greater than its value, they will not buy the product. Likewise, product costs set the floor for a product's price. If the company prices the product below its costs, the company's profits will suffer. In setting its price between these two extremes, the company must consider several external and internal factors, including competitors' strategies and prices, the overall marketing strategy and mix, and the nature of the market and demand.

Figure 9.1 suggests three major pricing strategies: customer value-based pricing, cost-based pricing, and competition-based pricing.

Customer Value-Based Pricing

In the end, the customer will decide whether a product's price is right. Pricing decisions, like other marketing mix decisions, must start with customer value. When customers buy a product, they exchange something of value (the price) to get something of value (the benefits of having or using the product). Effective customer-oriented pricing involves understanding how much value consumers place on the benefits they receive from the product and setting a price that captures that value.

Customer value-based pricing uses buyers' perceptions of value as the key to pricing. Value-based pricing means that the marketer cannot design a product and marketing program and then set the price. Price is considered along with all other marketing mix variables *before* the marketing program is set.

Customer value-based pricing
Setting price based on buyers' perceptions of value rather than on the seller's cost.

» Figure 9.2 compares value-based pricing with cost-based pricing. Although costs are an important consideration in setting prices, cost-based pricing is often product driven. The company designs what it considers to be a good product, adds up the costs of making the product, and sets a price that covers costs plus a target profit. Marketing must then convince buyers that the product's value at that price justifies its purchase. If the price turns out to be too high, the company must settle for lower markups or lower sales, both resulting in disappointing profits.

Value-based pricing reverses this process. The company first assesses customer needs and value perceptions. It then sets its target price based on customer perceptions of value. The targeted value and price drive decisions about what costs can be incurred and the

» Figure 9.1 Considerations in Setting Price

If customers perceive that a product's price is greater than its value, they won't buy it. If the company prices the product below its costs, profits will suffer. Between the two extremes, the "right" pricing strategy is one that delivers both value to the customer and profits to the company.

>> **Figure 9.2 Value-Based Pricing versus Cost-Based Pricing**

Costs play an important role in setting prices. But like everything else in marketing, good pricing starts with the customer.

Cost-based pricing

Design a good product → Determine product costs → Set price based on cost → Convince buyers of product's value

Value-based pricing

Assess customer needs and value perceptions → Set target price to match customer perceived value → Determine costs that can be incurred → Design product to deliver desired value at target price

resulting product design. As a result, pricing begins with analyzing consumer needs and value perceptions, and the price is set to match perceived value.

It's important to remember that "good value" is not the same as "low price." >> For example, some owners consider a luxurious Patek Philippe watch a real bargain, even at eye-popping prices ranging from $20,000 to $500,000:[3]

>> **Perceived value: Some owners consider a luxurious Patek Philippe watch a real bargain, even at eye-popping prices ranging from $20,000 to $500,000. Every Patek Philippe watch is handmade by Swiss watchmakers and can take more than a year to make.**
Fabrice Coffrini/AFP/Getty Images

Listen up here, because I'm about to tell you why a certain watch costing $20,000, or even $500,000, isn't actually expensive but is in fact a tremendous value. Every Patek Philippe watch is handmade by Swiss watchmakers from the finest materials and can take more than a year to make. Still not convinced? Beyond keeping precise time, Patek Philippe watches are also good investments. They carry high prices but retain or even increase their value over time. Many models achieve a kind of cult status that makes them the most coveted timepieces on the planet. But more important than just a means of telling time or a good investment is the sentimental and emotional value of possessing a Patek Philippe. Says the company's president: "This is about passion. I mean—it really is a dream. Nobody needs a Patek." These watches are unique possessions steeped in precious memories, making them treasured family assets. According to the company, "The purchase of a Patek Philippe is often related to a personal event—a professional success, a marriage, or the birth of a child—and offering it as a gift is the most eloquent expression of love or affection." A Patek Philippe watch is made not to last just one lifetime but many. Says one ad: "You never actually own a Patek Philippe, you merely look after it for the next generation." That makes it a real bargain, even at twice the price.

A company will often find it hard to measure the value customers attach to its product. For example, calculating the cost of ingredients in a meal at a fancy restaurant is relatively easy. But assigning value to other measures of satisfaction such as taste, environment, relaxation, conversation, and status is very hard. Such value is subjective; it varies both for different consumers and different situations.

Still, consumers will use these perceived values to evaluate a product's price, so the company must work to measure them. Sometimes, companies ask consumers how much they would pay for a basic product and for each benefit added to the offer. Or a company might conduct experiments to test the perceived value of different product offers. According to an old Russian proverb, there are two fools in every market—one who asks too much and one who asks too little. If the seller charges more than the buyers' perceived value, the company's sales will suffer. If the seller charges less, its products will sell very well, but they will produce less revenue than they would if they were priced at the level of perceived value.

We now examine two types of value-based pricing: *good-value pricing* and *value-added pricing*.

The art of seduction. At a price reduction.

The Concept Style Coupe set the auto show circuit abuzz with its dramatic design and athletic presence. Showgoers had only one request: Build it. The CLA brings an international sensation to life with nothing lost in translation, from its diamond-block grille to its frameless door glass to its sweeping taillamps, all at a down-to-earth price.

>> **Good-value pricing: Even premium brands can launch good-value versions. The Mercedes CLA Class gives customers "The Art of Seduction. At a price reduction."**

Courtesy of Daimler AG.

Good-value pricing
Offering just the right combination of quality and good service at a fair price.

Value-added pricing
Attaching value-added features and services to differentiate a company's offers and charging higher prices.

Good-Value Pricing

The Great Recession of 2008 to 2009 caused a fundamental and lasting shift in consumer attitudes toward price and quality. In response, many companies have changed their pricing approaches to bring them in line with changing economic conditions and consumer price perceptions. More and more, marketers have adopted the strategy of **good-value pricing**—offering the right combination of quality and good service at a fair price.

In many cases, this has involved introducing less-expensive versions of established brand name products or new lower-price lines. For example, Walmart launched an extreme-value store brand called Price First. Priced even lower than the retailer's already-low-priced Great Value brand, Price First offer thrift-conscious customers rock-bottom prices on grocery staples. Good-value prices are a relative thing—even premium brands can launch value versions. >> Mercedes-Benz recently released its CLA Class, entry-level models starting at $31,500. From its wing-like dash and diamond-block grille to its 208-hp turbo inline-4 engine, the CLA Class gives customers "The Art of Seduction. At a price reduction."[4]

In other cases, good-value pricing involves redesigning existing brands to offer more quality for a given price or the same quality for less. Some companies even succeed by offering less value but at very low prices. For example, the ALDI supermarket chain has established an impressive good-value pricing position by which it gives customers "more 'mmm' for the dollar" (see Marketing at Work 9.1).

ALDI practices an important type of good-value pricing at the retail level called *everyday low pricing* (*EDLP*). EDLP involves charging a constant, everyday low price with few or no temporary price discounts. Other retailers such as Costco and Lumber Liquidators practice EDLP. However, the king of EDLP is Walmart, which practically defined the concept. Except for a few sale items every month, Walmart promises everyday low prices on everything it sells. In contrast, *high-low pricing* involves charging higher prices on an everyday basis but running frequent promotions to lower prices temporarily on selected items. Department stores such as Kohl's and Macy's practice high-low pricing by having frequent sale days, early-bird savings, and bonus earnings for store credit-card holders.

Value-Added Pricing

Value-based pricing doesn't mean simply charging what customers want to pay or setting low prices to meet competition. Instead, many companies adopt **value-added pricing** strategies. Rather than cutting prices to match competitors, they attach value-added features and services to differentiate their offers and thus support their higher prices. >> For example, even as frugal consumer spending habits linger, some movie theater chains are *adding* amenities and charging *more* rather than cutting services to maintain lower admission prices:[5]

> Some theater chains are turning their multiplexes into smaller, roomier luxury outposts. The premium theaters offer value-added features such as online reserved seating, high-backed leather executive or rocking chairs with armrests and footrests, the latest in digital sound and super-wide screens, dine-in restaurants serving fine food and drinks, and even valet parking. For example, AMC Theatres (the second-largest American theater chain) operates more than 75 theaters with some kind of enhanced food and beverage amenities, including Fork & Screen (upgraded leather seating, seat-side service, extensive menu including dinner offerings, beer, wine, and cocktails) and

>> **Value-added pricing: Rather than cutting services to maintain lower admission prices, premium theaters such as AMC's Cinema Suites are adding amenities and charging more. "Once people experience it,...they don't want to go anywhere else."**

Courtesy of AMC Theaters.

MARKETING AT WORK | 9.1

ALDI: Impressively High Quality at Impossibly Low Prices, Every Day

When asked to name the world's largest grocery chains, you'd probably come up with Walmart, the world's largest retailer; and maybe Kroger, the largest U.S. grocery-only merchant. One name that probably wouldn't come to mind is Germany-based discount grocer ALDI. Yet, surprisingly, with more than $81 billion in annual revenues and more than 10,000 stores in 17 countries, ALDI is the world's eighth-largest retailer overall and the second-largest grocery-only retailer behind Kroger. What's more, ALDI is taking the United States and other country markets by storm, growing faster than any of its larger rivals.

How does ALDI do it? Its simple formula for success is no secret. In fact, it's almost a cliché: Give customers a basic assortment of good-quality everyday items at everyday extra low prices. These days, many grocers brag about low prices. But at ALDI, they are an absolute fact. The rapidly expanding chain promises customers "Simply Smarter Shopping," driven by a long list of "ALDI Truths" by which it delivers "impressively high quality at impossibly low prices." (ALDI Truth #1: When deciding between eating well and saving money, always choose both.)

ALDI has redesigned the food shopping experience to reduce costs and give customers prices that it claims are up to 50 percent lower than those of rival supermarkets. To keep costs and prices down, ALDI operates smaller, energy-saving stores (about one-third the size of traditional supermarkets), and each store carries only about 1,800 of the fastest-moving grocery items (the typical supermarket carries about 40,000 items). Almost 95 percent of its items are ALDI store brands. So, ALDI claims, customers are paying for the product itself, not national brand advertising and marketing. Also, ALDI does no promotional pricing or price matching—it just sticks with its efficient everyday very low prices (ALDI Truth #12: We don't match other stores' prices because that would mean raising ours).

In trimming costs and passing savings along to customers, ALDI leaves no stone unturned. Even customers themselves help to keep costs low: They bring their own bags (or purchase them from ALDI for a small charge), bag their own groceries (ALDI provides no baggers), return shopping carts on their own (to get back a 25-cent deposit), and pay with cash or a debit card (no credit cards accepted at most ALDI stores). But to ALDI fans, the savings make it all worthwhile (ALDI Truth #14: You can't eat frills, so why pay for them?).

Whereas ALDI cuts operating costs to the bone, it doesn't scrimp on quality. With its preponderance of store brands, ALDI exercises complete control over the quality of the products on its shelves, and the chain promises that everything it sells is certifiably fresh and tasty. ALDI Truth #60—We make delicious cost a lot less—makes it clear that the chain promises

more than just low prices. ALDI backs this promise with a Double Guarantee on all items: "If for any reason you are not 100-percent satisfied with any product, we will gladly replace the product AND refund your money."

To improve the quality of its assortment, ALDI has progressively added items that aren't usually associated with "discounted" groceries. Beyond the typical canned, boxed, and frozen food basics, ALDI carries fresh meat, baked goods, and fresh produce. It also carries an assortment of regular and periodic specialty goods, such as Mama Cozzi's Pizza Kitchen Meat Trio Focaccia, Appetitos Spinach Artichoke Dip, and All Natural Mango Salsa. ALDI even offers a selection of organic foods. With such items, and with its clean, bright stores, ALDI targets not just low-income customers, but frugal middle-class and upper-middle-class customers as well.

None of this is news to German shoppers, who have loved ALDI for decades. In Germany, the chain operates more than 4,200 stores, accounting for more than 28 percent of the market. That might explain why Walmart gave up in Germany just

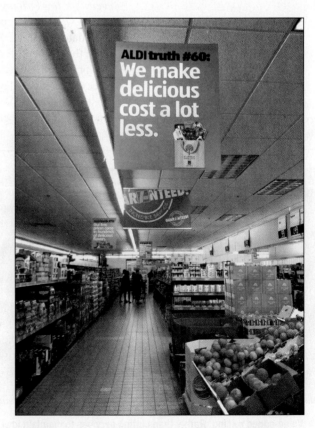

>> Good-value pricing: ALDI keeps costs low so that it can offer customers "impressively high quality at impossibly low prices" every day.

Keri Miksza

nine years after entering the market. Against competitors like ALDI, Walmart's normally low prices were just too expensive for frugal German consumers.

ALDI's no-frills basic approach isn't for everyone. Whereas some shoppers love the low prices, basic assortments, and simple store atmosphere, others can't imagine life without at least some of the luxuries and amenities offered by rivals. But most people who shop at ALDI quickly become true believers. Testimonials from converts litter the Internet. "I just recently switched to ALDI from a 'premium' grocery store … and the savings blow me away!" proclaims one customer. "Shoot, I wish I had some pom-poms, because I am so totally team ALDI!" Says another fervent fan:

> I will probably never grocery shop anywhere else! As a family of three on a very strict budget, I usually scour the sale papers and coupons looking to save. I usually make two or three different stops on my grocery trips and do my shopping every two weeks. We budget $200 a month for groceries and I usually come in right under that amount. Today at ALDI I got everything on my list, plus about 20 extra items not on the list, and my total was only $86! I cannot believe how much I saved! ALDI is now my immediate go-to grocery store!

Many customers also wax enthusiastic about their favorite ALDI products, items they can't live without and can't get anywhere else.

With tradition behind it and its can't-lose operating and marketing model, ALDI plans for rapid U.S. expansion. The company has quickly grown to more than 1,300 stores in 32 states. That's a huge accomplishment compared with, say, British discount chain Tesco, the world's second-largest retailer, which exited the U.S. market with heavy losses after only seven years. ALDI still has plenty of room for more growth. It has a $3 billion plan to open 130 U.S. stores a year, expanding by 50 percent to 1,950 stores by 2018. With its proven everyday extra low pricing strategy, ALDI will likely accomplish or even exceed that goal. That's good news for the company but also for customers. When ALDI comes to your neighborhood, "Your wallet and taste buds are in for a treat" (ALDI Truth #34).

Sources: Walter Loeb, "Why Aldi and Lidl Have What It Takes to Beat the Best and the Biggest," *Forbes*, October 30, 2013, www.forbes.com/sites/walterloeb/2013/10/30/why-aldi-and-lidl-have-what-it-takes-to-beat-the-best-and-the-biggest/; Leslie Patton, "Aldi Plans to Expand U.S. Store Count by 50% in Next Five Years," *Businessweek*, December 20, 2013, www.businessweek.com/news/2013-12-20/aldi-plans-to-expand-u-dot-s-dot-store-count-by-50-percent-in-next-five-years; Bill Bishop, "ALDI Offers the Thrill of Discovery," *Supermarket News,* October 20, 2014, http://supermarketnews.com/limited-assortment/aldi-offers-thrill-discovery; "Top 250 Global Powers of Retailing 2015," Deloitte, https://nrf.com/2015/global250-table; and www.aldi.us, www.aldi.us/en/new-to-aldi/aldi-truths/, and www.aldi.us/en/new-to-aldi/switch-save/, accessed October 2015.

Cinema Suites (additional upscale food offerings in addition to premium cocktails and an extensive wine list, seat-side service, red leather reclining chairs, and eight to nine feet of spacing between rows).

So at the Cinema Suites at the AMC Easton 30 with IMAX in Columbus, Ohio, bring on the mango margaritas! For $9 to $15 a ticket (depending on the time and day), moviegoers are treated to reserved seating, a strict 21-and-over-only policy, reclining leather seats, and the opportunity to pay even more to have dinner and drinks brought to their seats. Such theaters are so successful that AMC plans to add more. "Once people experience it," says a company spokesperson, "more often than not they don't want to go anywhere else."

Cost-Based Pricing

Cost-based pricing
Setting prices based on the costs of producing, distributing, and selling the product plus a fair rate of return for effort and risk.

Whereas customer value perceptions set the price ceiling, costs set the floor for the price that the company can charge. **Cost-based pricing** involves setting prices based on the costs of producing, distributing, and selling the product plus a fair rate of return for the company's effort and risk. A company's costs may be an important element in its pricing strategy.

Some companies, such as Walmart or Spirit Airlines, work to become the *low-cost producers* in their industries. Companies with lower costs can set lower prices that result in smaller margins but greater sales and profits. However, other companies—such as Apple, BMW, and Steinway—intentionally pay higher costs so that they can add value and claim higher prices and margins. For example, it costs more to make a "handcrafted" Steinway piano than a Yamaha production model. But the higher costs result in higher quality, justifying an average $87,000 price. To those who buy a Steinway, prices is nothing; the Steinway experience is everything. The key is to manage the spread between costs and prices—how much the company makes for the customer value it delivers.

Types of Costs

Fixed costs (overhead)
Costs that do not vary with production or sales level.

A company's costs take two forms: fixed and variable. **Fixed costs** (also known as **overhead**) are costs that do not vary with production or sales level. For example, a company must pay each month's bills for rent, heat, interest, and executive salaries regardless

Variable costs
Costs that vary directly with the level of production.

Total costs
The sum of the fixed and variable costs for any given level of production.

of the company's level of output. **Variable costs** vary directly with the level of production. Each PC produced by HP involves a cost of computer chips, wires, plastic, packaging, and other inputs. Although these costs tend to be the same for each unit produced, they are called variable costs because the total varies with the number of units produced. **Total costs** are the sum of the fixed and variable costs for any given level of production. Management wants to charge a price that will at least cover the total production costs at a given level of production.

The company must watch its costs carefully. If it costs the company more than its competitors to produce and sell a similar product, the company will need to charge a higher price or make less profit, putting it at a competitive disadvantage.

Author Comment
Costs set the floor for price, but the goal isn't always to *minimize* costs. In fact, many firms invest in higher costs so that they can claim higher prices and margins (think back about Patek Philippe watches). The key is to manage the *spread* between costs and prices—how much the company makes for the customer value it delivers.

Cost-plus pricing (markup pricing)
Adding a standard markup to the cost of the product.

Break-even pricing (target return pricing)
Setting price to break even on the costs of making and marketing a product or setting price to make a target return.

Cost-Plus Pricing

The simplest pricing method is **cost-plus pricing (or markup pricing)**—adding a standard markup to the cost of the product. For example, an electronics retailer might pay a manufacturer $20 for a flash drive and mark it up to sell at $30, a 50 percent markup on cost. The retailer's gross margin is $10. If the store's operating costs amount to $8 per flash drive sold, the retailer's profit margin will be $2. The manufacturer that made the flash drive probably used cost-plus pricing, too. If the manufacturer's standard cost of producing the flash drive was $16, it might have added a 25 percent markup, setting the price to the retailers at $20.

Does using standard markups to set prices make sense? Generally, no. Any pricing method that ignores consumer demand and competitor prices is not likely to lead to the best price. Still, markup pricing remains popular for many reasons. First, sellers are more certain about costs than about demand. By tying the price to cost, sellers simplify pricing. Second, when all firms in the industry use this pricing method, prices tend to be similar and price competition is minimized.

Another cost-oriented pricing approach is **break-even pricing,** or a variation called **target return pricing**. The firm tries to determine the price at which it will break even or make the target return it is seeking. Target return pricing uses the concept of a *break-even chart*, which shows the total cost and total revenue expected at different sales volume levels. **»Figure 9.3** shows a break-even chart for the flash drive manufacturer discussed previously. Fixed costs are $6 million regardless of sales volume, and variable costs are $5 per unit. Variable costs are added to fixed costs to form total costs, which rise with volume. The slope of the total revenue curve reflects the price. Here, the price is $15 (for example, the company's revenue is $12 million on 800,000 units, or $15 per unit).

At the $15 price, the manufacturer must sell at least 600,000 units to *break even* (break-even volume = fixed costs ÷ [price − variable costs] = $6,000,000 ÷ [$15 − $5] = 600,000). That is, at this level, total revenues will equal total costs of $9 million, producing no profit. If the flash drive manufacturer wants a target return of $2 million, it must sell at least 800,000 units to obtain the $12 million of total revenue needed to cover the costs of $10 million plus the $2 million of target profits. In contrast, if the company charges a higher price, say, $20, it will not need to sell as many units to break even or to achieve its target profit. In fact, the higher the price, the lower the manufacturer's break-even point will be.

The major problem with this analysis, however, is that it fails to consider customer value and the relationship between price and demand.

»Figure 9.3 Break-Even Chart for Determining Target Return Price and Break-Even Volume

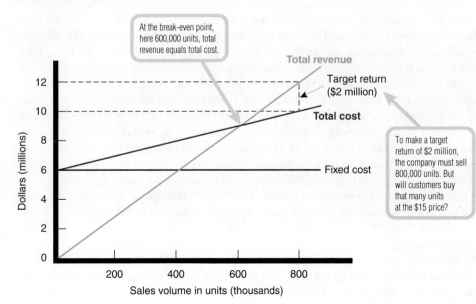

At the break-even point, here 600,000 units, total revenue equals total cost.

Total revenue

Target return ($2 million)

Total cost

Fixed cost

To make a target return of $2 million, the company must sell 800,000 units. But will customers buy that many units at the $15 price?

Dollars (millions)

Sales volume in units (thousands)

As the *price* increases, *demand* decreases, and the market may not buy even the lower volume needed to break even at the higher price. For example, suppose the flash drive manufacturer calculates that, given its current fixed and variable costs, it must charge a price of $30 for the product in order to earn its desired target profit. But marketing research shows that few consumers will pay more than $25. In this case, the company must trim its costs in order to lower the break-even point so that it can charge the lower price consumers expect.

Thus, although break-even analysis and target return pricing can help the company to determine the minimum prices needed to cover expected costs and profits, they do not take the price–demand relationship into account. When using this method, the company must also consider the impact of price on the sales volume needed to realize target profits and the likelihood that the needed volume will be achieved at each possible price.

Author Comment

In setting prices, the company must also consider competitors' prices. No matter what price it charges—high, low, or in between—the company must be certain to give customers superior value for that price.

Competition-based pricing

Setting prices based on competitors' strategies, prices, costs, and market offerings.

Competition-Based Pricing

Competition-based pricing involves setting prices based on competitors' strategies, costs, prices, and market offerings. Consumers will base their judgments of a product's value on the prices that competitors charge for similar products.

In assessing competitors' pricing strategies, the company should ask several questions. First, how does the company's market offering compare with competitors' offerings in terms of customer value? If consumers perceive that the company's product or service provides greater value, the company can charge a higher price. If consumers perceive less value relative to competing products, the company must either charge a lower price or change customer perceptions to justify a higher price.

Next, how strong are current competitors, and what are their current pricing strategies? If the company faces a host of smaller competitors charging high prices relative to the value they deliver, it might charge lower prices to drive weaker competitors from the market. If the market is dominated by larger, lower-price competitors, a company may decide to target unserved market niches by offering value-added products and services at higher prices.

Importantly, the goal is not to match or beat competitors' prices. Rather, the goal is to set prices according to the relative value created versus competitors. If a company creates greater value for customers, higher prices are justified. >> For example, Caterpillar makes high-quality, heavy-duty construction and mining equipment. It dominates its industry despite charging higher prices than competitors such as Komatsu. When a commercial customer once asked a Caterpillar dealer why it should pay $500,000 for a big Caterpillar bulldozer when it could get an "equivalent" Komatsu dozer for $420,000, the Caterpillar dealer famously provided an analysis like the following:

$420,000	the Caterpillar's price if equivalent to the competitor's bulldozer
$50,000	the value added by Caterpillar's superior reliability and durability
$40,000	the value added by Caterpillar's lower lifetime operating costs
$40,000	the value added by Caterpillar's superior service
$20,000	the value added by Caterpillar's longer parts warranty
$570,000	the total value-added price for Caterpillar's bulldozer
−$70,000	discount
$500,000	final price

>> **Pricing versus competitors: Despite Caterpillar's premium prices. Customers believe that Caterpillar gives them a lot more value for the price over the lifetime of its machines.**

Kristoffer Tripplaar/Alamy

Thus, although the customer pays an $80,000 price premium for the Caterpillar bull-dozer, it's actually getting $150,000 in added value over the product's lifetime. The customer chose the Caterpillar bulldozer.

What principle should guide decisions about what price to charge relative to those of competitors? The answer is simple in concept but often difficult in practice: No matter what price you charge—high, low, or in between—be certain to give customers superior value for that price.

Other Internal and External Considerations Affecting Price Decisions

Beyond customer value perceptions, costs, and competitor strategies, the company must consider several additional internal and external factors. Internal factors affecting pricing include the company's overall marketing strategy, objectives, and marketing mix as well as other organizational considerations. External factors include the nature of the market and demand and other environmental factors.

Overall Marketing Strategy, Objectives, and Mix

Price is only one element of the company's broader marketing strategy. So, before setting price, the company must decide on its overall marketing strategy for the product or service. Sometimes, a company's overall strategy is built around its price and value story. For example, grocery retailer Trader Joe's unique price-value positioning has made it one of the nation's fastest-growing, most popular food stores:

> Trader Joe's has put its own special twist on the food price-value equation—call it "cheap gourmet." It offers gourmet-caliber, one-of-a-kind products at bargain prices, all served up in a festive, vacation-like atmosphere that makes shopping fun. Trader Joe's is a gourmet foodie's delight, featuring everything from kettle corn cookies, organic strawberry lemonade, creamy Valencia peanut butter, and fair-trade coffees to kimchi fried rice and triple-ginger ginger snaps. If asked, almost any customer can tick off a ready list of Trader Joe's favorites that he or she just can't live without—a list that quickly grows.
>
> The assortment is uniquely Trader Joe's—more than 85 percent of the store's brands are private labels. The prices aren't all that low in absolute terms, but they're a real bargain compared with what you'd pay for the same quality and coolness elsewhere. "It's not complicated," says Trader Joe's. "We just focus on what matters—great food + great prices = value. So you can afford to be adventurous without breaking the bank." Trader Joe's inventive price-value positioning has earned it an almost cult-like following of devoted customers who love what they get from Trader Joe's for the prices they pay.[6]

If a company has selected its target market and positioning carefully, then its marketing mix strategy, including price, will be fairly straightforward. For example, Amazon positions its Kindle Fire tablet as offering the same (or even more) for less and prices it at 40 percent less than Apple's iPads and Samsung's Galaxy tablets. It recently began targeting families with young children, positioning the Kindle Fire as the "perfect family tablet," with models priced as low as $99, bundled with Kindle FreeTime, an all-in-one subscription service starting at $2.99 per month that brings together books, games, educational apps, movies, and TV shows for kids ages 3 through 8. Thus, the Kindle pricing strategy is largely determined by decisions on market positioning.

Pricing may play an important role in helping to accomplish company objectives at many levels. A firm can set prices to attract new customers or profitably retain existing ones. It can set prices low to prevent competition from entering the market or set prices at competitors' levels to stabilize the market. It can price to keep the loyalty and support of resellers or avoid government intervention. Prices can be reduced temporarily to create excitement for a brand. Or one product may be priced to help the sales of other products in the company's line.

Price decisions must be coordinated with product design, distribution, and promotion decisions to form a consistent and effective integrated marketing mix program. Decisions made for other marketing mix variables may affect pricing decisions. For example, a decision to position the product on high-performance quality will mean that the seller must charge a higher price to cover higher costs. And producers whose resellers are expected to support and promote their products may have to build larger reseller margins into their prices.

Companies often position their products on price and then tailor other marketing mix decisions to the prices they want to charge. Here, price is a crucial product-positioning factor that defines the product's market, competition, and design. Many firms support such price-positioning strategies with a technique called **target costing**. Target costing reverses the usual process of first designing a new product, determining its cost, and then asking, "Can we sell it for that?" Instead, it starts with an ideal selling price based on customer value considerations and then targets costs that will ensure that the price is met. For example, when Honda initially designed the Honda Fit, it began with a $13,950 starting price point and highway mileage of 33 miles per gallon firmly in mind. It then designed a stylish, peppy little car with costs that allowed it to give target customers those values.

Other companies deemphasize price and use other marketing mix tools to create *nonprice* positions. Often, the best strategy is not to charge the lowest price but rather to differentiate the marketing offer to make it worth a higher price. >> For example, luxury smartphone maker Vertu puts very high value into its products and charges premium prices to match that value. Vertu phones are made from high-end materials such as titanium and sapphire crystal, and each phone is hand-assembled by a single craftsman in England. Phones come with additional services such as Vertu Concierge, which helps create personal, curated user experiences and recommendations. Vertu phones sell for an average price of $6,000, with top models going for more than $20,000. But target customers recognize Vertu's very high quality and are willing to pay more to get it. With Vertu, "Every moment makes for an extraordinary story."[7]

Thus, marketers must consider the total marketing strategy and mix when setting prices. But again, even when featuring price, marketers need to remember that customers rarely buy on price alone. Instead, they seek products that give them the best value in terms of benefits received for the prices paid.

Organizational Considerations

Management must decide who within the organization should set prices. Companies handle pricing in a variety of ways. In small companies, prices are often set by top management rather than by the marketing or sales departments. In large companies, pricing is typically handled by divisional or product managers. In industrial markets, salespeople may be allowed to negotiate with customers within certain price ranges. Even so, top management sets the pricing objectives and policies, and it often approves the prices proposed by lower-level management or salespeople.

In industries in which pricing is a key factor (airlines, aerospace, steel, railroads, oil companies), companies often have pricing departments to set the best prices or help others set them. These departments report to the marketing department or top management. Others who have an influence on pricing include sales managers, production managers, finance managers, and accountants.

Target costing
Pricing that starts with an ideal selling price, then targets costs that will ensure that the price is met.

VERTU

NOTHING WILL EVER
FEEL THE SAME

THE CLARITY OF THE SAPPHIRE SCREEN, THE STRENGTH
AND LIGHTNESS OF THE TITANIUM CASING, THE HARMONY OF THE
SYMPHONIC SOUND, TOGETHER WITH OUR UNIQUELY CURATED SERVICES.

SEE | TOUCH | HEAR | THE NEW VERTU Ti

HANDMADE IN ENGLAND. POWERED BY ANDROID™

>> **Nonprice positioning: Luxury smartphone maker Vertu puts very high value into its products and charges sky-high prices to match that value. Average price: nearly $6,000.**
Vertu

The Market and Demand

As noted earlier, good pricing starts with an understanding of how customers' perceptions of value affect the prices they are willing to pay. Both consumer and industrial buyers balance the price of a product or service against the benefits of owning it. Thus, before setting prices, the marketer must understand the relationship between price and demand for the company's product. In this section, we take a deeper look at the price–demand relationship and how it varies for different types of markets. We then discuss methods for analyzing the price–demand relationship.

Pricing in Different Types of Markets

The seller's pricing freedom varies with different types of markets. Economists recognize four types of markets, each presenting a different pricing challenge.

Under *pure competition*, the market consists of many buyers and sellers trading in a uniform commodity, such as wheat, copper, or financial securities. No single buyer or seller has much effect on the going market price. In a purely competitive market, marketing research, product development, pricing, advertising, and sales promotion play little or no role. Thus, sellers in these markets do not spend much time on marketing strategy.

Under *monopolistic competition*, the market consists of many buyers and sellers trading over a range of prices rather than a single market price. A range of prices occurs because sellers can differentiate their offers to buyers. Because there are many competitors, each firm is less affected by competitors' pricing strategies than in oligopolistic markets. Sellers try to develop differentiated offers for different customer segments and, in addition to price, freely use branding, advertising, and personal selling to set their offers apart. Thus, Wrigley sets its Skittles candy brand apart from the profusion of other candy brands not by price but by brand building—clever "Taste the Rainbow" positioning built through quirky advertising and a heavy presence in social media such as Tumblr, Instagram, YouTube, Facebook, and Twitter. The social media-savvy brand boasts nearly 27 million Facebook Likes and 258,000 Twitter followers.

Under *oligopolistic competition*, the market consists of only a few large sellers. >> For example, only a handful of providers—Comcast, Time Warner, AT&T, and Dish Network—control a lion's share of the cable/satellite television market. Because there are few sellers, each seller is alert and responsive to competitors' pricing strategies and marketing moves. In the battle for subscribers, price becomes a major competitive tool. For example, to woo customers away from Comcast, TimeWarner, and other cable companies, AT&T's DirecTV unit offers low-price "Cable Crusher" offers, lock-in prices, and free HD. In a *pure monopoly*, the market is dominated by one seller. The seller may be a government monopoly (the U.S. Postal Service), a private regulated monopoly (a power company), or a private unregulated monopoly (De Beers and diamonds). Pricing is handled differently in each case.

>> Pricing in oligopolistic markets: Price is an important competitive tool for AT&T's DirecTV unit and other cable/satellite television providers. Here, DirecTV woos cable customers with low lock-in prices and free HD.

NetPhotos/Alamy Stock Photo

Analyzing the Price–Demand Relationship

Each price the company might charge will lead to a different level of demand. The relationship between the price charged and the resulting demand level is shown in the **demand curve** in >> **Figure 9.4**. The demand curve shows the number of units the market will buy in a given time period at different prices that might be charged. In the normal case, demand and price are inversely related—that is, the higher the price, the lower the demand. Thus, the company would sell less if it raised its price from P_1 to P_2. In short, consumers with limited budgets probably will buy less of something if its price is too high.

Demand curve
A curve that shows the number of units the market will buy in a given time period at different prices that might be charged.

>> **Figure 9.4 Demand Curve**

Price and demand are related—no big surprise there. Usually, higher prices result in lower demand.

Quantity demanded per period

Understanding a brand's price–demand curve is crucial to good pricing decisions. ConAgra Foods learned this lesson when pricing its Banquet frozen dinners:[8]

> When ConAgra tried to cover higher commodity costs by raising the list price of Banquet dinners from $1 to $1.25, consumers turned up their noses to the higher price. Sales dropped, forcing ConAgra to sell off excess dinners at discount prices. It turns out that "the key component for Banquet dinners—the key attribute—is you've got to be at $1," says ConAgra's CEO Gary Rodkin. "Everything else pales in comparison to that." Banquet dinner prices are now back to a buck a dinner. To make money at that price, ConAgra has done a better job of managing costs by shrinking portions and substituting less expensive ingredients for costlier ones. More than just Banquet dinners, ConAgra prices all of its frozen and canned products at under $1 per serving. Consumers are responding well to the brand's efforts to keep prices down. After all, where else can you find dinner for $1?

Most companies try to measure their demand curves by estimating demand at different prices. The type of market makes a difference. In a monopoly, the demand curve shows the total market demand resulting from different prices. If the company faces competition, its demand at different prices will depend on whether competitors' prices stay constant or change with the company's own prices.

Price Elasticity of Demand

Price elasticity

A measure of the sensitivity of demand to changes in price.

Marketers also need to know **price elasticity**—how responsive demand will be to a change in price. If demand hardly changes with a small change in price, we say demand is *inelastic*. If demand changes greatly, we say the demand is *elastic*.

If demand is elastic rather than inelastic, sellers will consider lowering their prices. A lower price will produce more total revenue. This practice makes sense as long as the extra costs of producing and selling more do not exceed the extra revenue. At the same time, most firms want to avoid pricing that turns their products into commodities. In recent years, forces such as deregulation and the instant price comparisons afforded by the Internet and other technologies have increased consumer price sensitivity, turning products ranging from phones and computers to new automobiles into commodities in some consumers' eyes.

The Economy

Economic conditions can have a strong impact on the firm's pricing strategies. Economic factors such as a boom or recession, inflation, and interest rates affect pricing decisions because they affect consumer spending, consumer perceptions of the product's price and value, and the company's costs of producing and selling a product.

In the aftermath of the Great Recession of 2008 to 2009, many consumers rethought the price–value equation. They tightened their belts and become more value conscious. Consumers have continued their thriftier ways well beyond the economic recovery. As a result, many marketers have increased their emphasis on value-for-the-money pricing strategies.

The most obvious response to the new economic realities is to cut prices and offer discounts. Thousands of companies have done just that. Lower prices make products more affordable and help spur short-term sales. However, such price cuts can have undesirable long-term consequences. Lower prices mean lower margins. Deep discounts may cheapen a brand in consumers' eyes. And once a company cuts prices, it's difficult to raise them again when the economy recovers.

Rather than cutting prices on their main-market brands, many companies have instead developed "price tiers," adding both more affordable lines and premium lines that span the varied means and preferences of different customer segments. For example, for cost-conscious customers with tighter budgets, P&G has added lower-price versions of its brands, such as "Basic" versions of Bounty and Charmin and a lower-priced version of Tide called Tide Simply Clean and Fresh. At the same time, at the higher end, P&G has launched upscale versions of some of its brands, such as Bounty DuraTowel and Cascade Platinum dishwasher detergent, which offer superior performance at up to twice the price of the middle-market versions.

Other companies are holding their price positions but redefining the "value" in their value propositions. >> Consider upscale grocery retailer Whole Foods Market:[9]

Whole Foods Market practically invented the upscale, socially responsible supermarket concept, and it grew rapidly and profitably under its "Whole Foods. Whole People. Whole Planet." mission. However, the high-margin chain faced setbacks following the 2008 financial crisis, as even well-heeled consumers cut their food budgets. It also felt increasing price pressures from swarms of new, lower-priced competitors—from specialty supermarkets such as Trader Joe's and Sprouts Farmers Market to traditional chains such as Walmart and Kroger—that rushed to add organics to their shelves.

In response, Whole Foods has worked to shed its "Whole Foods. Whole Paycheck." image. The chain has reduced costs, passed the savings along to customers, and subtly increased its emphasis on affordable options. At the same time, however, Whole Foods has reinforced its core up-market positioning by convincing shoppers that, when it comes to quality food, bargain prices aren't everything. Whole Foods' new marketing campaign—called Values Matter—emphasizes that "value" is inseparable from "values." When shopping at Whole Foods, customers can be confident about "where their food comes from and how it was grown, raised, or made." The retailer's produce is "responsibly grown." Thus, Whole Foods Market is meeting pricing challenges in a way that preserves what has made it special to customers through the years. "We have the ability to compete on price, and we will do that," says the chain's co-CEO. "But this is not just a race to the bottom. We are also going to start a new race to the top, with better-quality food, higher standards, richer experiences for our customers, and new levels of transparency and accountability in the marketplace." Even if that means a little higher prices.[10]

>> Whole Foods Market's new "Values Matter" campaign emphasizes that there is more to value than just bargain prices. "Value" is inseparable from "values."

Justin Sullivan/Getty Images

Remember, even in tough economic times, consumers do not buy based on prices alone. They balance the price they pay against the value they receive. For example, despite selling its shoes for as much as $150 a pair, Nike commands the highest consumer loyalty of any brand in the footwear segment. Customers perceive the value of Nike's products and the Nike ownership experience to be well worth the price. Thus, no matter what price they charge—low or high—companies need to offer great *value for the money*.

Other External Factors

Beyond the market and the economy, the company must consider several other factors in its external environment when setting prices. It must know what impact its prices will have on other parties in its environment. How will *resellers* react to various prices? The company should set prices that give resellers a fair profit, encourage their support, and help them to sell the product effectively. The *government* is another important external influence on pricing decisions. Finally, *social concerns* may need to be taken into account. In setting prices, a company's short-term sales, market share, and profit goals may need to be tempered by broader societal considerations. We will examine public policy issues later in this chapter.

LINKING THE CONCEPTS

The concept of customer value is critical to good pricing and to successful marketing in general. Pause for a minute and be certain that you appreciate what value really means.

- An earlier example states that although the average Steinway piano costs $87,000, to those who own one, a Steinway is a great value. Does this fit your idea of value?
- Pick two competing brands from a familiar product category (watches, perfume, consumer electronics, restaurants)—one low-priced and the other high-priced. Which, if either, offers the greatest value?
- Does "value" mean the same thing as "low price"? How do these concepts differ?

New Product Pricing Strategies

Pricing strategies usually change as the product passes through its life cycle. The introductory stage is especially challenging. Companies bringing out a new product face the challenge of setting prices for the first time. They can choose between two broad strategies: *market-skimming pricing* and *market-penetration pricing*.

Market-Skimming Pricing

Market-skimming pricing (price skimming)
Setting a high price for a new product to skim maximum revenues layer by layer from the segments willing to pay the high price; the company makes fewer but more profitable sales.

Many companies that invent new products set high initial prices to *skim* revenues layer by layer from the market. Apple frequently uses this strategy, called **market-skimming pricing** (or **price skimming**). When Apple first introduced the iPhone, its initial price was as high as $599 per phone. The phones were purchased only by customers who really wanted the sleek new gadget and could afford to pay a high price for it. Six months later, Apple dropped the price to $399 for an 8-GB model and $499 for the 16-GB model to attract new buyers. Within a year, it dropped prices again to $199 and $299, respectively, and you can now get a basic 8-GB model for free with a wireless phone contract. In this way, each new iPhone model starts at a high price, then works its way down as new models are introduced. Apple skims the maximum amount of revenue from the various segments of the market.

Market skimming makes sense only under certain conditions. First, the product's quality and image must support its higher price, and enough buyers must want the product at that price. Second, the costs of producing a smaller volume cannot be so high that they cancel the advantage of charging more. Finally, competitors should not be able to enter the market easily and undercut the high price.

Market-Penetration Pricing

Market-penetration pricing
Setting a low price for a new product in order to attract a large number of buyers and a large market share.

Rather than setting a high initial price to skim off small but profitable market segments, some companies use **market-penetration pricing**. Companies set a low initial price to *penetrate* the market quickly and deeply—to attract a large number of buyers quickly and win a large market share. The high sales volume results in falling costs, allowing companies to cut their prices even further. For example, Samsung has used penetration pricing to quickly build demand for its mobile devices in fast-growing emerging markets:[11]

> In Kenya, Nigeria, and other African countries, Samsung recently unveiled an affordable yet full-function Samsung Galaxy Pocket Neo model that sells for only about $113 with no contract. ≫ The Samsung Pocket is designed and priced to encourage millions of first-time

>> **Penetration pricing: Samsung has used low initial prices to make quick and deep inroads into emerging mobile device markets such as Africa and India.**

Trevor Snapp/Bloomberg/Getty Images

African buyers to trade up to smartphones from their more basic handsets. Samsung also offers a line of Pocket models in India, selling for as little as $87. Through penetration pricing, the world's largest smartphone maker hopes to make quick and deep inroads into India's exploding mobile device market, which consists of mostly first-time users and accounts for nearly one-quarter of all smartphones sold globally each year. Low prices are also required in emerging markets to compete with supercheap phones from competitors such as Chinese phone maker Xiaomi. Samsung's penetration pricing has set off price wars with Apple, which has responded in emerging markets with heavy discounts and more affordable models of its own. Apple iPhones have typically sold for more than $300 in India, limiting Apple's market share to only about 2 percent there.

Several conditions must be met for this low-price strategy to work. First, the market must be highly price sensitive so that a low price produces more market growth. Second, production and distribution costs must decrease as sales volume increases. Finally, the low price must help keep out the competition, and the penetration pricer must maintain its low-price position. Otherwise, the price advantage may be only temporary.

Product Mix Pricing Strategies

Author Comment
Most individual products are part of a broader product mix and must be priced accordingly. For example, Gillette prices its Fusion razors low. But once you buy the razor, you're a captive customer for its higher-margin replacement cartridges.

The strategy for setting a product's price often has to be changed when the product is part of a product mix. In this case, the firm looks for a set of prices that maximizes its profits on the total product mix. Pricing is difficult because the various products have related demand and costs and face different degrees of competition. We now take a closer look at the five product mix pricing situations summarized in >> **Table 9.1**: *product line pricing, optional-product pricing, captive-product pricing, by-product pricing*, and *product bundle pricing*.

Product Line Pricing

Product line pricing
Setting the price steps between various products in a product line based on cost differences between the products, customer evaluations of different features, and competitors' prices.

Companies usually develop product lines rather than single products. In **product line pricing**, management must determine the price steps to set between the various products in a line. The price steps should take into account cost differences between products in the line. More important, they should account for differences in customer perceptions of the value of different features.

For example, at a Mr. Clean car wash, you can choose from any of six wash packages, ranging from a basic exterior-clean-only "Bronze" wash for $5; to an exterior clean, shine,

>> **Table 9.1**	**Product Mix Pricing**
Pricing Situation	**Description**
Product line pricing	Setting prices across an entire product line
Optional-product pricing	Pricing optional or accessory products sold with the main product
Captive-product pricing	Pricing products that must be used with the main product
By-product pricing	Pricing low-value by-products to get rid of or make money on them
Product bundle pricing	Pricing bundles of products sold together

and protect "Gold" package for $12; to an interior-exterior "Signature Shine" package for $27 that includes the works, from a thorough cleaning inside and out to a tire shine, underbody rust inhibitor, surface protectant, and even air freshener. The car wash's task is to establish perceived value differences that support the price differences.

Optional-Product Pricing

Optional-product pricing
The pricing of optional or accessory products along with a main product.

Many companies use **optional-product pricing**—offering to sell optional or accessory products along with the main product. For example, a car buyer may choose to order a navigation system and premium entertainment system. Refrigerators come with optional ice makers. And when you order a new computer, you can select from a bewildering array of processors, hard drives, docking systems, software options, and service plans. Pricing these options is a sticky problem. Companies must decide which items to include in the base price and which to offer as options.

Captive-Product Pricing

Captive-product pricing
Setting a price for products that must be used along with a main product, such as blades for a razor and games for a video-game console.

Companies that make products that must be used along with a main product are using **captive-product pricing**. Examples of captive products are razor blade cartridges, video games, printer cartridges, single-serve coffee pods, and e-books. Producers of the main products (razors, video-game consoles, printers, single-cup coffee brewing systems, and tablet computers) often price them low and set high markups on the supplies. For example, Amazon makes little or no profit on its Kindle readers and tablets. It hopes to more than make up for thin margins through sales of digital books, music, movies, subscription services, and other content for the devices. "We want to make money when people use our devices, not when they buy our devices," declares Amazon CEO Jeff Bezos.[12]

By-product pricing
Setting a price for by-products in order to make the main product's price more competitive.

Captive products can account for a substantial portion of a brand's sales and profits. >> For example, only a relatively small percentage of Keurig's revenues come from the sale of its single-cup brewing systems. The bulk of the brand's revenues—nearly 77 percent—comes from captive sales of its K-Cup portion packs.[13] However, companies that use captive-product pricing must be careful. Finding the right balance between the main-product and captive-product prices can be tricky. Even more, consumers trapped into buying expensive captive products may come to resent the brand that ensnared them.

For example, customers of single-cup coffee brewing systems may cringe at what they must pay for those handy little coffee portion packs. Although they might seem like a bargain when compared on a cost-per-cup basis versus Starbucks, the pods' prices can seem like highway robbery when broken down by the pound. One investigator calculated the cost of pod coffee at a shocking $51 per pound.[14] At those prices, you'd be better off cost-wise brewing a big pot of premium coffee and pouring out the unused portion. For many buyers, the convenience and selection offered by single-cup brewing systems outweigh the extra costs. However, such captive product costs might make others avoid buying the device in the first place or cause discomfort during use after purchase.

In the case of services, captive-product pricing is called *two-part pricing*. The price of the service is broken into a *fixed fee* plus a *variable usage rate*. Thus, at Six Flags and other amusement parks, you pay a daily ticket or season pass charge plus additional fees for food and other in-park features.

>> Captive product pricing: Nearly 77 percent of Keurig's sales come from its K-Cup portion packs. The brand must find the right balance between main-product and captive-product prices.

Toby Talbot/AP Images

By-Product Pricing

Producing products and services often generates by-products. If the by-products have no value and if getting rid of them is costly, this will affect the pricing of the main product. Using **by-product pricing**, the company seeks a market for these by-products to help offset the costs of disposing of them and help make the price of the main product more competitive.

The by-products themselves can even turn out to be profitable—turning trash into cash. For example, cheese makers in Wisconsin have discovered a use for their leftover brine, a salt solution used in the cheese-making process. Instead of paying to have it disposed of, they now sell it to local city and county highway departments, which use it in conjunction with salt to melt icy roads. It doesn't stop there. In New Jersey, pickle makers sell their leftover brine for similar uses. In Tennessee, distilleries sell off potato juice, a by-product of vodka distillation. And on many highways across the nation, highway crews use a product called Beet Heet, which is made from—you guessed it—beet juice brine by-products. The only side effect of these brine solutions is a slight odor. Says one highway department official about cheese brine, "If you were behind a snow plow, you'd immediately smell it."[15]

Product Bundle Pricing

Product bundle pricing
Combining several products and offering the bundle at a reduced price.

Using **product bundle pricing**, sellers often combine several products and offer the bundle at a reduced price. For example, fast-food restaurants bundle a burger, fries, and a soft drink at a "combo" price. Bath & Body Works offers "three-fer" deals on its soaps and lotions (such as three antibacterial soaps for $10). And Comcast, AT&T, Verizon, and other telecommunications companies bundle TV service, phone service, and high-speed Internet connections at a low combined price. Price bundling can promote the sales of products consumers might not otherwise buy, but the combined price must be low enough to get them to buy the bundle.

Price Adjustment Strategies

Author Comment
Setting the base price for a product is only the start. The company must then adjust the price to account for customer and situational differences. When was the last time you paid the full suggested retail price for something?

Companies usually adjust their basic prices to account for various customer differences and changing situations. Here we examine the seven price adjustment strategies summarized in ≫ Table 9.2: *discount and allowance pricing, segmented pricing, psychological pricing, promotional pricing, geographical pricing, dynamic pricing,* and *international pricing.*

Discount and Allowance Pricing

Most companies adjust their basic price to reward customers for certain responses, such as paying bills early, volume purchases, and off-season buying. These price adjustments—called *discounts* and *allowances*—can take many forms.

≫ Table 9.2	Price Adjustments

Strategy	Description
Discount and allowance pricing	Reducing prices to reward customer responses such as volume purchases, paying early, or promoting the product
Segmented pricing	Adjusting prices to allow for differences in customers, products, or locations
Psychological pricing	Adjusting prices for psychological effect
Promotional pricing	Temporarily reducing prices to spur short-run sales
Geographical pricing	Adjusting prices to account for the geographic location of customers
Dynamic pricing	Adjusting prices continually to meet the characteristics and needs of individual customers and situations
International pricing	Adjusting prices for international markets

Discount
A straight reduction in price on purchases during a stated period of time or of larger quantities.

Allowance
Promotional money paid by manufacturers to retailers in return for an agreement to feature the manufacturer's products in some way.

Segmented pricing
Selling a product or service at two or more prices, where the difference in prices is not based on differences in costs.

One form of **discount** is a *cash discount*, a price reduction to buyers who pay their bills promptly. A typical example is "2/10, net 30," which means that although payment is due within 30 days, the buyer can deduct 2 percent if the bill is paid within 10 days. A *quantity discount* is a price reduction to buyers who buy large volumes. A seller offers a *functional discount* (also called a *trade discount*) to trade-channel members who perform certain functions, such as selling, storing, and record keeping. A *seasonal discount* is a price reduction to buyers who buy merchandise or services out of season.

Allowances are another type of reduction from the list price. For example, *trade-in allowances* are price reductions given for turning in an old item when buying a new one. Trade-in allowances are most common in the automobile industry, but they are also given for other durable goods. *Promotional allowances* are payments or price reductions that reward dealers for participating in advertising and sales-support programs.

Segmented Pricing

Companies will often adjust their basic prices to allow for differences in customers, products, and locations. In **segmented pricing**, the company sells a product or service at two or more prices, even though the difference in prices is not based on differences in costs.

Segmented pricing takes several forms. Under *customer-segment pricing*, different customers pay different prices for the same product or service. Museums and movie theaters, for example, may charge a lower admission for students and senior citizens. Under *product form pricing*, different versions of the product are priced differently but not according to differences in their costs. For instance, a round-trip economy seat on a flight from New York to London might cost $1,100, whereas a business-class seat on the same flight might cost $3,400 or more. Although business-class customers receive roomier, more comfortable seats and higher-quality food and service, the differences in costs to the airlines are much less than the additional prices to passengers. ≫However, to passengers who can afford it, the additional comfort and services are worth the extra charge.

Using *location-based pricing*, a company charges different prices for different locations, even though the cost of offering each location is the same. For instance, state universities charge higher tuition for out-of-state students, and theaters vary their seat prices because of audience preferences for certain locations. Finally, using *time-based pricing*, a firm varies its price by the season, the month, the day, and even the hour. For example, movie theaters charge matinee pricing during the daytime, and resorts give weekend and seasonal discounts.

For segmented pricing to be an effective strategy, certain conditions must exist. The market must be segmentable, and segments must show different degrees of demand. The costs of segmenting and reaching the market cannot exceed the extra revenue obtained from the price difference. Of course, the segmented pricing must also be legal.

Most important, segmented prices should reflect real differences in customers' perceived value. Consumers in higher price tiers must feel that they're getting their extra money's worth for the higher prices paid. By the same token, companies must be careful not to treat customers in lower price tiers as second-class citizens. Otherwise, in the long run, the practice will lead to customer resentment and ill will. For example, in recent years, the airlines have incurred the wrath of frustrated customers at both ends of the airplane. Passengers paying full fare for business- or first-class seats often feel that they are being gouged. At the same time, passengers in lower-priced coach seats feel that they're being ignored or treated poorly.

≫ **Product-form pricing: A roomier business-class seat on a flight from New York to London is several times the price of an economy seat on the same flight. To customers who can afford it, the extra comfort and service are worth the extra charge.**

Stewart Cohen/Photolibrary/Getty Images

Psychological Pricing

Psychological pricing
Pricing that considers the psychology of prices and not simply the economics; the price is used to say something about the product.

Price says something about the product. For example, many consumers use price to judge quality. A $100 bottle of perfume may contain only $3 worth of scent, but some people are willing to pay the $100 because this price indicates something special.

In using **psychological pricing**, sellers consider the psychology of prices, not simply the economics. For example, consumers usually perceive higher-priced products as having higher quality. When they can judge the quality of a product by examining it or by calling on past experience with it, they use price less to judge quality. But when they cannot judge quality because they lack the information or skill, price becomes an important quality signal. For instance, who's the better lawyer, one who charges $50 per hour or one who charges $500 per hour? You'd have to do a lot of digging into the respective lawyers' credentials to answer this question objectively; even then, you might not be able to judge accurately. Most of us would simply assume that the higher-priced lawyer is better.

Reference prices
Prices that buyers carry in their minds and refer to when they look at a given product.

Another aspect of psychological pricing is **reference prices**—prices that buyers carry in their minds and refer to when looking at a given product. The reference price might be formed by noting current prices, remembering past prices, or assessing the buying situation. Sellers can influence or use these consumers' reference prices when setting price. For example, a grocery retailer might place its store brand of bran flakes and raisins cereal priced at $2.49 next to Kellogg's Raisin Bran priced at $3.79. Or a company might offer more expensive models that don't sell very well to make its less expensive but still-high-priced models look more affordable by comparison. For example, Williams-Sonoma once offered a fancy bread maker at the steep price of $279. However, it then added a $429 model. The expensive model flopped, but sales of the cheaper model doubled.[16]

For most purchases, consumers don't have all the skill or information they need to figure out whether they are paying a good price. They don't have the time, ability, or inclination to research different brands or stores, compare prices, and get the best deals. Instead, they may rely on certain cues that signal whether a price is high or low. Interestingly, such pricing cues are often provided by sellers, in the form of sales signs, price-matching guarantees, loss-leader pricing, and other helpful hints.

Promotional pricing
Temporarily pricing products below the list price, and sometimes even below cost, to increase short-run sales.

Even small differences in price can signal product differences. A 9 or 0.99 at the end of a price often signals a bargain. You see such prices everywhere. For example, browse the online sites of top discounters such as Target, Best Buy, or Overstock.com, where almost every price ends in 9. In contrast, high-end retailers might favor prices ending in a whole number (for example, $6, $25, or $200). Others use 00-cent endings on regularly priced items and 99-cent endings on discount merchandise.

>> Although actual price differences might be small, the impact of such psychological tactics can be big. For example, in one study, people were asked how likely they were to choose among LASIK eye surgery providers based only on the prices they charged: $299 or $300. The actual price difference was only $1, but the study found that the psychological difference was much greater. Preference ratings for the providers charging $300 were much higher. Subjects perceived the $299 price as significantly less, but the lower price also raised stronger concerns about quality and risk. Some psychologists even argue that each digit has symbolic and visual qualities that should be considered in pricing. Thus, eight (8) is round and even and creates a soothing effect, whereas seven (7) is angular and creates a jarring effect.[17]

>> Psychological pricing: What do the prices marked on these tags suggest about the products and buying situations?
Jamie Grill/Tetra Images/Alamy

Promotional Pricing

With **promotional pricing**, companies will temporarily price their products below list price—and sometimes even below cost—to create buying excitement and urgency. Promotional pricing takes several forms. A seller may simply offer *discounts* from normal prices to increase sales and reduce inventories. Sellers also use *special-event pricing* in certain seasons to draw more customers. Thus, TVs and other consumer electronics are promotionally priced in November and

December to attract holiday shoppers into the stores. *Limited-time offers*, such as online *flash sales*, can create buying urgency and make buyers feel lucky to have gotten in on the deal.

Manufacturers sometimes offer *cash rebates* to consumers who buy the product from dealers within a specified time; the manufacturer sends the rebate directly to the customer. Rebates have been popular with automakers and producers of mobile phones and small appliances, but they are also used with consumer packaged goods. Some manufacturers offer *low-interest financing, longer warranties*, or *free maintenance* to reduce the consumer's "price." This practice has become another favorite of the auto industry.

>> Promotional pricing: To Encourage Apple customers to switch from their Apple laptops to its Surface tablets, Microsoft recently offered buyers up to $650 toward a Surface Pro 3 when they traded in a MacBook Air. Such aggressive price promotions can provide powerful buying incentives.

Microsoft

Promotional pricing can help move customers over humps in the buying decision process. >> For example, to encourage Apple customers to switch from their Apple laptops to its Surface tablets, Microsoft recently offered buyers up to $650 toward a Surface Pro 3 when they traded in a MacBook Air. Such aggressive price promotions can provide powerful buying and switching incentives.

Promotional pricing, however, can have adverse effects. During most holiday seasons, for example, it's an all-out bargain war. Marketers carpet-bomb consumers with deals, causing buyer wear-out and pricing confusion. Used too frequently, price promotions can create "deal-prone" customers who wait until brands go on sale before buying them. In addition, constantly reduced prices can erode a brand's value in the eyes of customers.

Marketers sometimes become addicted to promotional pricing, especially in tight economic times. They use price promotions as a quick fix instead of sweating through the difficult process of developing effective longer-term strategies for building their brands. Consider JCPenney:

Over the past two decades, JCPenney has steadily lost ground to discounters and department store rivals such as Walmart, Kohl's, and Macy's on the one hand and to nimbler specialty store retailers on the other. To compete, the 110-year-old retailer increasingly relied on deep and frequent discounts to drive sales, even at the expense of profitability. By 2012, almost 75 percent of JCPenney's merchandise was being sold at discounts of 50 percent or more, and less than 1 percent was sold at full price. To reverse declining sales and profits, Penney's implemented a bold new everyday-low-pricing strategy, called "Fair and Square" pricing. It ditched deep discounts and endless rounds of sales, instead cutting regular retail prices by 40 percent across the board. The goal was to offer fair, predictable prices for the value received while at the same time boosting the chain's margins. However, the new pricing strategy turned out to be an absolute disaster. JCPenney's deal-prone core customers, accustomed to deep discounts, didn't want just "fair" prices; they wanted rock-bottom prices. Penney's sales plunged to the lowest levels in 25 years. To win back core customers, JCPenney soon reverted to pricing as usual, once again featuring regular sale prices, discounts, and coupons. Moving forward, as sales and profits continue to suffer, JCPenney faces a desperate struggle to find the right pricing formula. It can't live with sale prices, but it can't live without them, either.[18]

Geographical Pricing

A company also must decide how to price its products for customers located in different parts of the United States or the world. Should the company risk losing the business of more-distant customers by charging them higher prices to cover the higher shipping costs? Or should the company charge all customers the same prices regardless of location? We will look at five *geographical pricing* strategies for the following hypothetical situation:

The Peerless Paper Company is located in Atlanta, Georgia, and sells paper products to customers all over the United States. The cost of freight is high and affects the companies from which customers buy their paper. Peerless wants to establish a geographical pricing policy. It is trying to determine how to price a $10,000 order to three specific customers: Customer A (Atlanta), Customer B (Bloomington, Indiana), and Customer C (Compton, California).

One option is for Peerless to ask each customer to pay the shipping cost from the Atlanta factory to the customer's location. All three customers would pay the same factory price of $10,000, with Customer A paying, say, $100 for shipping; Customer B, $150; and Customer C, $250. Called *FOB-origin pricing*, this practice means that the goods are placed *free on board* (hence, FOB) a carrier. At that point, the title and responsibility pass to the customer, who pays the freight from the factory to the destination. Because each customer picks up its own cost, supporters of FOB pricing feel that this is the fairest way to assess freight charges. The disadvantage, however, is that Peerless will be a high-cost firm to distant customers.

Uniform-delivered pricing is the opposite of FOB pricing. Here, the company charges the same price plus freight to all customers, regardless of their location. The freight charge is set at the average freight cost. Suppose this is $150. Uniform-delivered pricing therefore results in a higher charge to the Atlanta customer (who pays $150 freight instead of $100) and a lower charge to the Compton customer (who pays $150 instead of $250). Although the Atlanta customer would prefer to buy paper from another local paper company that uses FOB-origin pricing, Peerless has a better chance of capturing the California customer.

Zone pricing falls between FOB-origin pricing and uniform-delivered pricing. The company sets up two or more zones. All customers within a given zone pay a single total price; the more distant the zone, the higher the price. For example, Peerless might set up an East Zone and charge $100 freight to all customers in this zone, a Midwest Zone in which it charges $150, and a West Zone in which it charges $250. In this way, the customers within a given price zone receive no price advantage from the company. For example, customers in Atlanta and Boston pay the same total price to Peerless. The complaint, however, is that the Atlanta customer is paying part of the Boston customer's freight cost.

Using *basing-point pricing*, the seller selects a given city as a "basing point" and charges all customers the freight cost from that city to the customer location, regardless of the city from which the goods are actually shipped. For example, Peerless might set Chicago as the basing point and charge all customers $10,000 plus the freight from Chicago to their locations. This means that an Atlanta customer pays the freight cost from Chicago to Atlanta, even though the goods may be shipped from Atlanta. If all sellers used the same basing-point city, delivered prices would be the same for all customers, and price competition would be eliminated.

Finally, the seller who is anxious to do business with a certain customer or geographical area might use *freight-absorption pricing*. Using this strategy, the seller absorbs all or part of the actual freight charges to get the desired business. The seller might reason that if it can get more business, its average costs will decrease and more than compensate for its extra freight cost. Freight-absorption pricing is used for market penetration and to hold on to increasingly competitive markets.

Dynamic and Online Pricing

Throughout most of history, prices were set by negotiation between buyers and sellers. *Fixed-price* policies—setting one price for all buyers—is a relatively modern idea that arose with the development of large-scale retailing at the end of the nineteenth century. Today, most prices are set this way. However, some companies are now reversing the fixed-pricing trend. They are using **dynamic pricing**—adjusting prices continually to meet the characteristics and needs of individual customers and situations.

Dynamic pricing
Adjusting prices continually to meet the characteristics and needs of individual customers and situations.

Dynamic pricing is especially prevalent online, where the Internet seems to be taking us back to a new age of fluid pricing. Such pricing offers many advantages for marketers. For example, online sellers such as L.L.Bean, Amazon.com, and Dell can mine their databases to gauge a specific shopper's desires, measure his or her means, check out competitors' prices, and instantaneously tailor offers to fit that shopper's situation and behavior, pricing products accordingly.

Services ranging from retailers, airlines, and hotels to sports teams change prices on the fly according to changes in demand, costs, or competitor pricing, adjusting what they charge for specific items on a daily, hourly, or even continuous basis. Done well, dynamic pricing can help sellers to optimize sales and serve customers better. However, done poorly, it can trigger margin-eroding price wars and damage customer relationships and trust. Companies must be careful not to cross the fine line between smart dynamic pricing strategies and damaging ones (see Marketing at Work 9.2).

MARKETING AT WORK   9.2

Dynamic Pricing: The Wonders and Woes of Real-Time Price Adjustments

These days, it seems every seller knows what prices competitors are charging—for anything and everything it sells, minute by minute, and down to the penny. What's more, today's technologies give sellers the flexibility to adjust their own prices on the fly. This often results in some pretty zany pricing dynamics.

For example, during a recent Black Friday weekend, the prices charged for the latest version of an Xbox game, Dance Central, experienced some head-spinning dips and dives. The day before Thanksgiving, Amazon marked the game down to $49.96, matching Walmart's price and beating Target's price by three cents. On Thanksgiving Day, Amazon slashed that price in half to just $24.99, matching Best Buy's Thanksgiving Day special. Walmart responded quickly with a rock-bottom price of $15, which Amazon matched immediately. "What kind of pricing lunacy is this?" you ask. Welcome to the wonders and woes of dynamic pricing.

On the plus side, dynamic pricing can help sellers optimize sales and serve customers better by aligning prices with market conditions. For example, airlines routinely use dynamic pricing to constantly adjust fares for specific flights, depending on competitor pricing and anticipated seat availability. As any frequent flyer knows, if you call now to book a seat on a flight to sunny Florida next week, you'll get one price. Try again an hour later and you'll get a different price—maybe higher, maybe lower. Book the same seat a month in advance, and you'll probably pay a lot less.

Dynamic pricing isn't just about sellers optimizing their returns. It also puts pricing power into the hands of consumers, as alert shoppers take advantage of the constant price skirmishes among sellers. By using online price checkers and shopping apps to monitor prices, consumers can snap up good deals or leverage retailer price-matching policies. In fact, today's fluid pricing sometimes gives buyers too much of an upper hand. With price checking and online ordering now at the shopper's fingertips, even giant retailers such as Target, Walmart, and Best Buy have fallen victim to "showrooming"—whereby shoppers check merchandise and prices in store-retailer showrooms, then buy the goods online.

Stores like Best Buy are in turn using dynamic pricing to combat showrooming or even turn it into an advantage. For example, Best Buy Canada provides its sales associates with mobile price checkers of their own that they can use with every transaction to check the competing prices in real time. Associates can often show customers that Best Buy actually has the best prices on most items. When Best Buy's price isn't lowest, associates are instructed to beat the lower-priced competitor—online or offline—by 10 percent. Once it has neutralized price as a buying factor, Best Buy reasons, it can convert showroomers into in-store buyers with its nonprice advantages of service, immediacy, convenient locations, and easy returns.

As the Best Buy example illustrates, dynamic pricing doesn't just happen in the fast-shifting online environment. For example, discount department store Kohl's has replaced static price tags with digital ones. These digital tags can be centrally controlled to change prices dynamically on individual items within a given store or across the entire chain. The technology lets Kohl's apply Internet-style dynamic pricing, changing prices as conditions dictate without the time and costs of changing physical tags.

Beyond using dynamic pricing to match competitors, many sellers use it to adjust prices based on customer characteristics or buying situations. Some sellers vary prices they charge different customers based on customer purchase histories or personal data. Some companies offer special discounts to customers with more items in their shopping carts. Online travel agent Orbitz has even been reported to charge higher prices to Mac and iPad users because Apple fans have higher average household incomes.

Most consumers are surprised to learn that it's perfectly legal under most circumstances to charge different prices to different customers based on their buying behaviors. In fact, one survey found that two-thirds of online shoppers thought the practice was illegal. When they learned that it was not illegal, nearly nine out of ten thought it should be.

Legal or not, dynamic pricing doesn't always sit well with customers. Done poorly, it can cause customer confusion, frustration, or even resentment, damaging hard-won customer relationships. For example, according to one source, Amazon's automated dynamic pricing system changes the price on as

>> **Dynamic pricing:** Amazon's automated dynamic pricing system reportedly changes the price on as many as 80 million items on its site in a given day based on a host of marketplace factors.

Webpics/Alamy

many as 80 million items on its site throughout a given day, based on a host of marketplace factors. Consider this Amazon shopper's experience:

> Nancy Plumlee had just taken up mahjong, a Chinese game of tiles similar to rummy. She browsed Amazon.com and, after sifting through several pages of options, settled on a set for $54.99. She placed it in her [shopping cart] and continued shopping for some scorecards and game accessories. A few minutes later, she scanned the cart and noticed the $54.99 had jumped to $70.99. Plumlee thought she was going crazy. She checked her computer's viewing history and, indeed, the game's original price was listed at $54.99. Determined, she cleared out the cart and tried again. [This time,] the game's price jumped from $54.99 to $59.99. "That just doesn't feel like straight-up business honesty. Shame on Amazon," said Plumlee, who called [Amazon] and persuaded the online retailer to refund her $5.

It is sometimes difficult to locate the fine line between a smart dynamic pricing strategy and one that crosses the line, doing more damage to customer relationships than good to the company's bottom line. Consider Uber, an app-based car dispatch service serving many major U.S. cities that lets customers summon taxis, cars, or other transportation using texts or the company's phone app:

> Uber uses a form of dynamic pricing called "surge pricing." Under normal circumstances, Uber customers pay reasonable fares. However, using Uber in periods of surging demand can result in shocking price escalations. For example, on one recent stormy, holiday-Saturday night in Manhattan, Uber charged—and got— fares that were more than eight times the usual. Although Uber's app warned customers of heightened fares before processing their requests, many customers were outraged. One customer shared an Instagram photo of a taxi receipt for $415. "That is robbery!"

Tweeted another. However, despite the protests, Uber experienced no subsequent drop in demand in the New York City area. It seems that, to most people who can afford Uber, convenience and prestige are the deciding factors, not price.

Thus, used well, dynamic pricing can help sellers to optimize sales and profits by keeping track of competitor pricing and quickly adjusting to marketplace changes. Used poorly, however, it can trigger margin-eroding price wars and damage customer relationships and trust. Too often, dynamic pricing takes the form of a pricing "arms race" among sellers, putting too much emphasis on prices at the expense of other important customer value-building elements. Companies must be careful to keep pricing in balance. As one Best Buy marketer states, pricing—dynamic or otherwise—remains "just one part of the equation. There's the right assortment, convenience, expedited delivery, customer service, warranty. All of these things matter to the customer."

Sources: Andrew Nusca, "The Future of Retail Is Dynamic Pricing. So Why Can't We Get It Right?," *ZDNet,* October 2, 2013, www.zdnet.com/the-future-of-retail-is-dynamic-pricing-so-why-cant-we-get-it-right-7000021444/;   Laura Gunderson, "Amazon's 'Dynamic' Prices Get Some Static," *The Oregonian,* May 5, 2012, http://blog.oregonlive.com/complaintdesk/2012/05/amazons_dynamic_prices_get_som.html; David P; Schulz, "Changing Direction," *Stores,* March 2013, www.stores.org/STORES%20Magazine%20March%202013/changing-direction; Jessi Hempel, "Why Surge-Pricing Fiasco Is Great for Uber," *CNNMoney,* December 30, 2013, http://tech.fortune.cnn.com/2013/12/30/why-the-surge-pricing-fiasco-is-great-for-uber/; Alison Griswold, "Everybody Hates Surge Pricing," *Slate,* April 24, 2014, www.slate.com/articles/business/moneybox/2014/04/uber_style_surge_pricing_does_the_system_make_sense_for_d_c_cabs.html; and Mike Murphy, "Amazon Changed the Price of the Bible Over 100 Times in Five Years," *Quartz,* January 21, 2015, http://qz.com/327835/amazon-dynamic-pricing-changed-the-price-of-the-bible-over-100-times-in-five-years/.

In the extreme, some companies customize their offers and prices based on the specific characteristics and behaviors of individual customers, mined from online browsing and purchasing histories. These days, online offers and prices might well be based on what specific customers search for and buy, how much they pay for other purchases, and whether they might be willing and able to spend more. For example, a consumer who recently went online to purchase a first-class ticket to Paris or customize a new Mercedes coupe might later get a higher quote on a new Bose Wave Radio. By comparison, a friend with a more modest online search and purchase history might receive an offer of 5 percent off and free shipping on the same radio.[19]

Although such dynamic pricing practices seem legally questionable, they're not. Dynamic pricing is legal as long as companies do not discriminate based on age, gender, location, or other similar characteristics. Dynamic pricing makes sense in many contexts—it adjusts prices according to market forces and consumer preferences. But marketers need to be careful not to use dynamic pricing to take advantage of certain customer groups, thereby damaging important customer relationships.

The practice of online pricing, however, goes both ways, and consumers often benefit from online and dynamic pricing. Thanks to the Internet, the centuries-old art of haggling is suddenly back in vogue. For example, consumers can negotiate prices at online auction sites and exchanges. Want to sell that antique pickle jar that's been collecting dust for generations? Post it on eBay or Craigslist. Want to name your own price for a hotel room or rental car? Visit Priceline.com or another reverse auction site. Want to bid on a ticket to a hot show or sporting event? Check out Ticketmaster.com, which offers an online auction service for event tickets.

>> **Dynamic and Internet pricing: Using mobile apps such as Amazon's Price Check, consumers can get instant product and price comparisons. Just "Scan it," "Snap it," or "Say it."**

Andrew Harrer/Bloomberg/Getty Images

>> Also thanks to the Internet, consumers can get instant product and price comparisons from thousands of vendors at price comparison sites such as Yahoo! Shopping, Epinions.com, and PriceGrabber.com or using mobile apps such as TheFind, eBay's RedLaser, or Amazon's Price Check. For example, the RedLaser mobile app lets customers scan barcodes or QR codes (or search by voice or image) while shopping in stores. It then searches online and at nearby stores to provide thousands of reviews and comparison prices, and even offers buying links for immediate online purchasing. Armed with this information, consumers can often negotiate better in-store prices.

In fact, many retailers are finding that ready online access to comparison prices is giving consumers *too much* of an edge. Store retailers ranging from Target and Best Buy to Brookstone and GNC are now devising strategies to combat the consumer practice of *showrooming*. Consumers armed with smartphones now routinely come to stores to see an item, compare prices online while in the store, and then buy the item online at a lower price. Such behavior is called showrooming because consumers use retailers' stores as de facto "showrooms" for online resellers such as Amazon.com.

This past holiday season, Best Buy launched an advertising campaign—called "Your Ultimate Holiday Showroom"—designed to directly combat showrooming:[20]

In the campaign, a host of popular celebrities pitched Best Buy as a better shopping experience than buying from online-only retailers like Amazon.com. They touted Best Buy advantages, such as assistance by well-trained associates, the ability to order online and pick up in store, and Best Buy's low-price guarantee. "Showrooming … is not the ideal experience," says a Best Buy marketer, "…to do research at home, go to the store, do more research, then hit pause, go home and order and hope it arrives on time. There's a better way." That better way would be shopping and buying at Best Buy, the ultimate holiday showroom. Most consumers reacted positively to the light-hearted campaign, which helped lift holiday store traffic. However, the real challenge for Best Buy is to convert shoppers to buyers. Some customers remained skeptics. As one consumer Tweeted regarding the "Ultimate Showroom" ads: "Dear Best Buy, I'm glad you know your place as a showroom. Love, everyone who shops at Amazon."

International Pricing

Companies that market their products internationally must decide what prices to charge in different countries. In some cases, a company can set a uniform worldwide price. For example, Boeing sells its jetliners at about the same price everywhere, whether the buyer is in the United States, Europe, or a third-world country. However, most companies adjust their prices to reflect local market conditions and cost considerations.

The price that a company should charge in a specific country depends on many factors, including economic conditions, competitive situations, laws and regulations, and the nature of the wholesaling and retailing system. Consumer perceptions and preferences also may vary from country to country, calling for different prices. Or the company may have different marketing objectives in various world markets, which require changes in pricing strategy. For example, Apple introduces sophisticated, feature-rich, premium smartphones in carefully segmented mature markets in highly developed countries using a market-skimming pricing strategy. By contrast, it's now under pressure to discount older models and develop cheaper, more basic phone models for sizable but less affluent markets in developing countries, where even discounted older Apple phones sell at prices three to five times those of those of competing low-price models.

Costs play an important role in setting international prices. Travelers abroad are often surprised to find that goods that are relatively inexpensive at home may carry outrageously higher price tags in other countries. A pair of Levi's selling for $30 in the United States might go for $63 in Tokyo and $88 in Paris. A McDonald's Big Mac selling for a modest $4.20 in the United States might cost $7.85 in Norway or $5.65 in Brazil, and an Oral-B toothbrush selling for $2.49 at home may cost $10 in China. Conversely, a Gucci handbag going for only $140 in Milan, Italy, might fetch $240 in the United States.

In some cases, such *price escalation* may result from differences in selling strategies or market conditions. In most instances, however, it is simply a result of the higher costs of selling in another country—the additional costs of operations, product modifications, shipping and insurance, exchange-rate fluctuations, and physical distribution. Import tariffs and taxes can also add to costs. >> For example, China imposes duties as high as 25 percent on imported Western luxury products such as watches, designer dresses, shoes, and leather handbags. It also levies consumption taxes of 30 percent for cosmetics and 20 percent on high-end watches. As a result, Western luxury goods bought in mainland China carry prices as much as 50 percent higher than in Europe.[21]

>> International prices: Travelers are often surprised to find that product price tags vary greatly from country to country. For example, thanks to Chinese import tariffs and consumption taxes, Western luxury goods bought in mainland China carry prices as much as 50 percent higher than in Europe.

James McCauley/Harrods/Getty Images

Price has become a key element in the international marketing strategies of companies attempting to enter less affluent emerging markets. Typically, entering such markets has meant targeting the exploding middle classes in developing countries such as China, India, Russia, and Brazil, whose economies have been growing rapidly. More recently, however, as the weakened global economy has slowed growth in both domestic and emerging markets, many companies are shifting their sights to include a new target—the so-called "bottom of the pyramid," the vast untapped market consisting of the world's poorest consumers.

Not long ago, the preferred way for many brands to market their products in developing markets—whether consumer products or cars, computers, and smartphones—was to paste new labels on existing models and sell them at higher prices to the privileged few who could afford them. However, such a pricing approach put many products out of the reach of the tens of millions of poor consumers in emerging markets. As a result, many companies developed smaller, more basic and affordable product versions for these markets. For example, Unilever—the maker of such brands as Dove, Sunsilk, Lipton, and Vaseline—shrunk its packaging and set low prices that even the world's poorest consumers could afford. It developed single-use packages of its shampoo, laundry detergent, face cream, and other products that it could sell profitably for just pennies a pack. As a result, today, more than half of Unilever's revenues come from emerging economies.[22]

Although this strategy has been successful for Unilever, most companies are learning that selling profitably to the bottom of the pyramid requires more than just repackaging or stripping down existing products and selling them at low prices. Just like more well-to-do consumers, low-income buyers want products that are both functional *and* aspirational. Thus, companies today are innovating to create products that not only sell at very low prices but also give bottom-of-the-pyramid consumers more for their money, not less.

International pricing presents many special problems and complexities. We discuss international pricing issues in more detail in Chapter 15.

Author Comment
When and how should a company change its price? What if costs rise, putting the squeeze on profits? What if the economy sags and customers become more price sensitive? Or what if a major competitor raises or drops its prices? As Figure 9.5 suggests, companies face many price-changing options.

Price Changes

After developing their pricing structures and strategies, companies often face situations in which they must initiate price changes or respond to price changes by competitors.

Initiating Price Changes

In some cases, the company may find it desirable to initiate either a price cut or a price increase. In both cases, it must anticipate possible buyer and competitor reactions.

Initiating Price Cuts

Several situations may lead a firm to consider cutting its price. One such circumstance is excess capacity. Another is falling demand in the face of strong price competition or a weakened economy. In such cases, the firm may aggressively cut prices to boost sales and market share. But as the airline, fast-food, automobile, retailing, and other industries have learned in recent years, cutting prices in an industry loaded with excess capacity may lead to price wars as competitors try to hold on to market share.

A company may also cut prices in a drive to dominate the market through lower costs. Either the company starts with lower costs than its competitors, or it cuts prices in the hope of gaining market share that will further cut costs through larger volume. For example, computer and electronics maker Lenovo uses an aggressive low-cost, low-price strategy to increase its share of the PC market in developing countries. Similarly, Chinese low-price phone maker Xiaomi has now become China's smartphone market leader, and the low-cost producer is making rapid inroads into India and other emerging markets.

Initiating Price Increases

A successful price increase can greatly improve profits. For example, if the company's profit margin is 3 percent of sales, a 1 percent price increase will boost profits by 33 percent if sales volume is unaffected. A major factor in price increases is cost inflation. Rising costs squeeze profit margins and lead companies to pass cost increases along to customers. Another factor leading to price increases is over-demand: When a company cannot supply all that its customers need, it may raise its prices, ration products to customers, or both—consider today's worldwide oil and gas industry.

When raising prices, the company must avoid being perceived as a *price gouger*. For example, when gasoline prices rise rapidly, angry customers often accuse the major oil companies of enriching themselves at the expense of consumers. Customers have long memories, and they will eventually turn away from companies or even whole industries that they perceive as charging excessive prices. In the extreme, claims of price gouging may even bring about increased government regulation.

There are some techniques for avoiding these problems. One is to maintain a sense of fairness surrounding any price increase. Price increases should be supported by company communications telling customers why prices are being raised.

Wherever possible, the company should consider ways to meet higher costs or demand without raising prices. For example, it might consider more cost-effective ways to produce or distribute its products. It can "unbundle" its market offering, removing features, packaging, or services and separately pricing elements that were formerly part of the offer. Or it can shrink the product or substitute less-expensive ingredients instead of raising the price. P&G recently did this with Tide by holding price while shrinking 100-ounce containers to 92 ounces and 50-ounce containers to 46 ounces, creating a more than 8 percent price increase per ounce without changing package prices. Similarly, Kimberly-Clark raised Kleenex prices by "desheeting"— reducing the number of sheets of toilet paper or facial tissues in each package. And a regular Snickers bar now weighs 1.86 ounces, down from 2.07 ounces in the past, effectively increasing prices by 11 percent.[23]

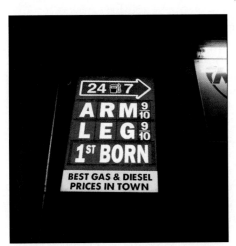

>> Initiating price increases: When gasoline prices rise rapidly, angry consumers often accuse the major oil companies of enriching themselves by gouging customers.

Jerry/Marcy Monkman/EcoPhotography.com/Alamy

Buyer Reactions to Price Changes

Customers do not always interpret price changes in a straightforward way. A price *increase*, which would normally lower sales, may have some positive meanings for buyers. For example, what would you think if Rolex *raised* the price of its latest watch model? On the one hand, you might think that the watch is even more exclusive or better made. On the other hand, you might think that Rolex is simply being greedy by charging what the traffic will bear.

Similarly, consumers may view a price *cut* in several ways. For example, what would you think if Rolex were to suddenly cut its prices? You might think that you are getting a better deal on an exclusive product. More likely, however, you'd think that quality had been reduced, and the brand's luxury image might be tarnished. A brand's price and image are often closely linked. A price change, especially a drop in price, can adversely affect how consumers view the brand.

Competitor Reactions to Price Changes

A firm considering a price change must worry about the reactions of its competitors as well as those of its customers. Competitors are most likely to react when the number of firms involved is small, when the product is uniform, and when the buyers are well informed about products and prices.

How can the firm anticipate the likely reactions of its competitors? The problem is complex because, like the customer, the competitor can interpret a company price cut in many ways. It might think the company is trying to grab a larger market share or that it's doing poorly and trying to boost its sales. Or it might think that the company wants the whole industry to cut prices to increase total demand.

The company must assess each competitor's likely reaction. If all competitors behave alike, this amounts to analyzing only a typical competitor. In contrast, if the competitors do not behave alike—perhaps because of differences in size, market shares, or policies—then separate analyses are necessary. However, if some competitors will match the price change, there is good reason to expect that the rest will also match it.

Responding to Price Changes

Here we reverse the question and ask how a firm should respond to a price change by a competitor. The firm needs to consider several issues: Why did the competitor change the price? Is the price change temporary or permanent? What will happen to the company's market share and profits if it does not respond? Are other competitors going to respond? Besides these issues, the company must also consider its own situation and strategy and possible customer reactions to price changes.

>> **Figure 9.5** shows the ways a company might assess and respond to a competitor's price cut. Suppose a company learns that a competitor has cut its price and decides that this price cut is likely to harm its sales and profits. It might simply decide to hold its current price and profit margin. The company might believe that it will not lose too much market share or that it would lose too much profit if it reduced its own price. Or it might decide that it should wait and respond when it has more information on the effects of the competitor's price change. However, waiting too long to act might let the competitor get stronger and more confident as its sales increase.

If the company decides that effective action can and should be taken, it might make any of four responses. First, it could *reduce its price* to match the competitor's price. It may decide that the market is price sensitive and that it would lose too much market share to the lower-priced competitor. However, cutting the price will reduce the company's profits in the short run. Some companies might also reduce their product quality, services,

>> **Figure 9.5 Responding to Competitor Price Changes**

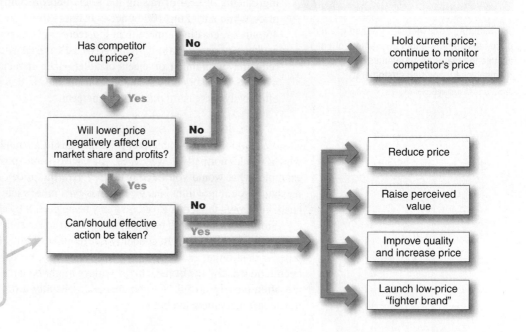

When a competitor cuts prices, a company's first reaction may be to drop its prices as well. But that is often the wrong response. Instead, the firm may want to emphasize the "value" side of the price–value equation.

Has competitor cut price? — No → Hold current price; continue to monitor competitor's price

Yes ↓

Will lower price negatively affect our market share and profits? — No →

Yes ↓

Can/should effective action be taken? — No →

Yes →

Reduce price

Raise perceived value

Improve quality and increase price

Launch low-price "fighter brand"

and marketing communications to retain profit margins, but this will ultimately hurt long-run market share. The company should try to maintain its quality as it cuts prices.

Alternatively, the company might maintain its price but *raise the perceived value* of its offer. It could improve its communications, stressing the relative value of its product over that of the lower-price competitor. The firm may find it cheaper to maintain price and spend money to improve its perceived value than to cut price and operate at a lower margin. Or the company might *improve quality* and *increase price*, moving its brand into a higher price–value position. The higher quality creates greater customer value, which justifies the higher price. In turn, the higher price preserves the company's higher margins.

>> Fighter brands: Starbucks has positioned its Seattle's Best Coffee unit to compete more directly with the "mass-premium" brands sold buy Dunkin' Donuts, McDonald's, and other lower-priced competitors.
Curved Light USA/Alamy

Finally, the company might launch a *low-price "fighter brand"*—adding a lower-price item to the line or creating a separate lower-price brand. This is necessary if the particular market segment being lost is price sensitive and will not respond to arguments of higher quality. >> Starbucks did this when it acquired Seattle's Best Coffee, a brand positioned with working-class, "approachable-premium" appeal compared to the more professional, full-premium appeal of the main Starbucks brand. Seattle's Best coffee is generally cheaper than the parent Starbucks brand. As such, at retail, it competes more directly with Dunkin' Donuts, McDonald's, and other mass-premium brands through its franchise outlets and through partnerships with Subway, Burger King, Delta, AMC theaters, Royal Caribbean cruise lines, and others. On supermarket shelves, it competes with store brands and other mass-premium coffees such as Folgers Gourmet Selections and Millstone.

To counter store brands and other low-price entrants in a tighter economy, P&G turned a number of its brands into fighter brands. Luvs disposable diapers give parents "premium leakage protection for less than pricier brands." And P&G offers popular budget-priced basic versions of several of its major brands. For example, Charmin Basic "holds up at a great everyday price," and Puffs Basic gives you "Everyday softness. Everyday value." Tide Simply Clean & Fresh is about 35 percent cheaper than regular Tide detergent. However, companies must use caution when introducing fighter brands, as such brands can tarnish the image of the main brand. In addition, although they may attract budget buyers away from lower-priced rivals, they can also take business away from the firm's higher-margin brands.

Author Comment
Pricing decisions are often constrained by social and legal issues. For example, think about the pharmaceuticals industry. Are rapidly rising prescription drug prices justified? Or are the drug companies unfairly lining their pockets by gouging consumers who have few alternatives? Should the government step in?

Public Policy and Pricing

Price competition is a core element of our free-market economy. In setting prices, companies usually are not free to charge whatever prices they wish. Many federal, state, and even local laws govern the rules of fair play in pricing. In addition, companies must consider broader societal pricing concerns. In setting their prices, for example, pharmaceutical firms must balance their development costs and profit objectives against the sometimes life-and-death needs of drug consumers.

The most important pieces of legislation affecting pricing are the Sherman Act, the Clayton Act, and the Robinson-Patman Act, initially adopted to curb the formation of monopolies and regulate business practices that might unfairly restrain trade. Because these federal statutes can be applied only to interstate commerce, some states have adopted similar provisions for companies that operate locally.

>> **Figure 9.6 Public Policy Issues in Pricing**

Source: Adapted from Dhruv Grewal and Larry D. Compeau, "Pricing and Public Policy: A Research Agenda and Overview of the Special Issue," *Journal of Public Policy and Marketing,* Spring 1999, pp. 3–10.

Major public policy issues in pricing take place at two levels: pricing practices within a given channel level ...

... and pricing practices across channel levels.

Producer A

Price-fixing
Predatory pricing

Producer B

Retail price maintenance

Discriminatory pricing

Retailer 1

Price-fixing
Predatory pricing

Retailer 2

Deceptive pricing

Consumers

Deceptive pricing

>> **Figure 9.6** shows the major public policy issues in pricing. These include potentially damaging pricing practices within a given level of the channel (price-fixing and predatory pricing) and across levels of the channel (retail price maintenance, discriminatory pricing, and deceptive pricing).[24]

Pricing within Channel Levels

Federal legislation on *price-fixing* states that sellers must set prices without talking to competitors. Otherwise, price collusion is suspected. Price-fixing is illegal per se—that is, the government does not accept any excuses for price-fixing. As such, companies found guilty of these practices can receive heavy fines. Recently, governments at the state and national levels have been aggressively enforcing price-fixing regulations in industries ranging from gasoline, insurance, and concrete to credit cards, CDs, computer chips, and e-books. For example, in recent years, the U.S. Department of Justice has brought charges against Apple for colluding with publishers to fix prices on e-books. Price-fixing is also prohibited in many international markets. For example, Apple was recently fined $670,000 on price-fixing charges for its iPhones in Taiwan.[25]

Sellers are also prohibited from using *predatory pricing*—selling below cost with the intention of punishing a competitor or gaining higher long-run profits by putting competitors out of business. This protects small sellers from larger ones that might sell items below cost temporarily or in a specific locale to drive them out of business. The biggest problem is determining just what constitutes predatory pricing behavior. Selling below cost to unload excess inventory is not considered predatory; selling below cost to drive out competitors is. Thus, a given action may or may not be predatory depending on intent, and intent can be very difficult to determine or prove.

In recent years, several large and powerful companies have been accused of predatory pricing. However, turning an accusation into a lawsuit can be difficult. >> For example, many publishers and booksellers have expressed concerns about Amazon.com's predatory practices, especially its book pricing:[26]

>> **Predatory pricing:** Some industry critics have accused Amazon.com of pricing books at fire-sale prices that harm competing booksellers. But is it predatory pricing or just plain good competitive marketing?

Iain Masterton/Alamy

Many booksellers and publishers complain that Amazon's book pricing policies are destroying their industry. During past holiday seasons, Amazon has sold top 10 best-selling hardback books as loss leaders at cut-rate prices of less than $10 each. And Amazon now sells e-books at fire-sale prices in order to win customers for its Kindle e-reader. Such very low book prices have caused considerable damage to competing booksellers, many of whom view Amazon's pricing actions as predatory. Says one observer, "The word 'predator' is pretty strong, and I don't use it loosely, but ... I could have sworn we had laws against predatory pricing. I just don't understand why [Amazon's pricing] is not an issue." Still, no predatory pricing charges have ever been filed against Amazon. It would be extremely difficult to prove that such loss-leader pricing is purposefully predatory as opposed to just plain good competitive marketing.

Pricing across Channel Levels

The Robinson-Patman Act seeks to prevent unfair *price discrimination* by ensuring that sellers offer the same price terms to customers at a given level of trade. For example, every retailer is entitled to the same price terms from a given manufacturer, whether the retailer is REI or a local bicycle shop. However, price discrimination is allowed if the seller can prove that its costs are different when selling to different retailers—for example, that it costs less per unit to sell a large volume of bicycles to REI than to sell a few bicycles to the local dealer.

The seller can also discriminate in its pricing if the seller manufactures different qualities of the same product for different retailers. The seller has to prove that these differences are proportional. Price differentials may also be used to "match competition" in "good faith," provided the price discrimination is temporary, localized, and defensive rather than offensive.

Laws also prohibit *retail (or resale) price maintenance*—a manufacturer cannot require dealers to charge a specified retail price for its product. Although the seller can propose a manufacturer's *suggested* retail price to dealers, it cannot refuse to sell to a dealer that takes independent pricing action, nor can it punish the dealer by shipping late or denying advertising allowances. For example, the Florida attorney general's office investigated Nike for allegedly fixing the retail price of its shoes and clothing. It was concerned that Nike might be withholding items from retailers who were not selling its most expensive shoes at prices the company considered suitable.

Deceptive pricing occurs when a seller states prices or price savings that mislead consumers or are not actually available to consumers. This might involve bogus reference or comparison prices, as when a retailer sets artificially high "regular" prices and then announces "sale" prices close to its previous everyday prices. For example, Overstock.com came under scrutiny for inaccurately listing manufacturer's suggested retail prices, often quoting them higher than the actual prices. Such comparison pricing is widespread.

Although comparison pricing claims are legal if they are truthful, the Federal Trade Commission's "Guides against Deceptive Pricing" warn sellers not to advertise (1) a price reduction unless it is a savings from the usual retail price, (2) "factory" or "wholesale" prices unless such prices are what they are claimed to be, and (3) comparable value prices on imperfect goods.[27]

Other deceptive pricing issues include *scanner fraud* and price confusion. The widespread use of scanner-based computer checkouts has led to increasing complaints of retailers overcharging their customers. Most of these overcharges result from poor management, such as a failure to enter current or sale prices into the system. Other cases, however, involve intentional overcharges.

Many federal and state statutes regulate against deceptive pricing practices. For example, the Automobile Information Disclosure Act requires automakers to attach a statement on new vehicle windows stating the manufacturer's suggested retail price, the prices of optional equipment, and the dealer's transportation charges. However, reputable sellers go beyond what is required by law. Treating customers fairly and making certain that they fully understand prices and pricing terms are an important part of building strong and lasting customer relationships.

MyMarketingLab

If assigned by your instructor, complete the questions marked with the ⭐ from the EOC Discussion Questions section in the MyLab. To complete the Marketing by the Numbers problems found in this section, go to your Assignments in the MyLab.

REVIEWING AND EXTENDING THE CONCEPTS

CHAPTER REVIEW AND CRITICAL THINKING

Objectives Review

Price can be defined as the sum of all the values that customers give up in order to gain the benefits of having or using a product or service. Pricing decisions are subject to an incredibly complex array of company, environmental, and competitive forces.

 OBJECTIVE 9-1 Identify the three major pricing strategies and discuss the importance of understanding customer-value perceptions, company costs, and competitor strategies when setting prices. (pp 264–272)

The three major pricing strategies include customer value-based pricing, cost-based pricing, and competition-based pricing. Good pricing begins with a complete understanding of the value that a product or service creates for customers and setting a price that captures that value.

Customer perceptions of the product's value set the ceiling for prices. If customers perceive that the price is greater than the product's value, they will not buy the product. At the other extreme, company and product costs set the floor for prices. If the company prices the product below its costs, its profits will suffer. Between these two extremes, consumers will base their judgments of a product's value on the prices that competitors charge for similar products. Thus, in setting prices, companies need to consider all three factors: customer perceived value, costs, and competitors pricing strategies.

Costs are an important consideration in setting prices. However, cost-based pricing is often product driven. The company designs what it considers to be a good product and sets a price that covers costs plus a target profit. If the price turns out to be too high, the company must settle for lower markups or lower sales, both resulting in disappointing profits. Value-based pricing reverses this process. The company assesses customer needs and value perceptions and then sets a target prices to match targeted value. The targeted value and price then drive decisions about product design and what costs can be incurred. As a result, price is set to match customers' perceived value.

 OBJECTIVE 9-2 Identify and define the other important external and internal factors affecting a firm's pricing decisions. (pp 272–277)

Other *internal* factors that influence pricing decisions include the company's overall marketing strategy, objectives, and marketing mix as well as organizational considerations. Price is only one element of the company's broader marketing strategy. If the company has selected its target market and positioning carefully, then its marketing mix strategy, including price, will

be fairly straightforward. Common pricing objectives might include customer retention and building profitable customer relationships, preventing competition, supporting resellers and gaining their support, or avoiding government intervention. Price decisions must be coordinated with product design, distribution, and promotion decisions to form a consistent and effective marketing program. Finally, in order to coordinate pricing goals and decisions, management must decide who within the organization is responsible for setting price.

Other *external* pricing considerations include the nature of the market and demand and environmental factors such as the economy, reseller needs, and government actions. Ultimately, the customer decides whether the company has set the right price. The customer weighs the price against the perceived values of using the product—if the price exceeds the sum of the values, consumers will not buy. So the company must understand concepts like demand curves (the price-demand relationship) and price elasticity (consumer sensitivity to prices).

Economic conditions can have a major impact on pricing decisions. The Great Recession caused consumers to rethink the price-value equation. Marketers have responded by increasing their emphasis on value-for-the-money pricing strategies. Even in tight economic times, however, consumers do not buy based on prices alone. Thus, no matter what price they charge—low or high—companies need to offer superior value for the money.

 OBJECTIVE 9-3 Describe the major strategies for pricing new products. (pp 277–278)

Pricing is a dynamic process. Companies design a *pricing structure* that covers all their products. They change this structure over time and adjust it to account for different customers and situations. Pricing strategies usually change as a product passes through its life cycle. In pricing innovative new products, a company can use *market-skimming pricing* by initially setting high prices to "skim" the maximum amount of revenue from various segments of the market. Or it can use *market-penetrating pricing* by setting a low initial price to penetrate the market deeply and win a large market share.

 OBJECTIVE 9-4 Explain how companies find a set of prices that maximizes the profits from the total product mix. (pp 278–280)

When the product is part of a product mix, the firm searches for a set of prices that will maximize the profits from the total mix. In *product line pricing*, the company decides on price steps for the entire set of products it offers. In addition, the company must set prices for *optional products* (optional or accessory products included with the main product), *captive products* (products that are required for use of the main product), *by-products* (waste or residual products produced when making the main product), and *product bundles* (combinations of products at a reduced price).

 OBJECTIVE 9-5 Discuss how companies adjust their prices to take into account different types of customers and situations. (pp 280–288)

Companies apply a variety of *price adjustment strategies* to account for differences in consumer segments and situations. One is *discount and allowance pricing*, whereby the company establishes cash, quantity, functional, or seasonal discounts or varying types of allowances. A second strategy is *segmented pricing*, where the company sells a product at two or more prices to accommodate different customers, product forms, locations, or times. Sometimes companies consider more than economics in their pricing decisions, using *psychological pricing* to better communicate a product's intended position. In *promotional pricing*, a company offers discounts or temporarily sells a product below list price as a special event, sometimes even selling below cost as a loss leader. Another approach is *geographical pricing*, whereby the company decides how to

price to near or distant customers. In *dynamic pricing*, companies adjust prices continually to meet the characteristics and needs of individual customers and situations. Finally, *international pricing* means that the company adjusts its price to meet different conditions and expectations in different world markets.

 OBJECTIVE 9-6 Discuss the key issues related to initiating and responding to price changes. (pp 288–293)

When a firm considers initiating a *price change*, it must consider customers' and competitors' reactions. There are different implications to *initiating price cuts* and *initiating price increases*. Buyer reactions to price changes are influenced by the meaning customers see in the price change. Competitors' reactions flow from a set reaction policy or a fresh analysis of each situation.

There are also many factors to consider in responding to a competitor's price changes. The company that faces a price change initiated by a competitor must try to understand the competitor's intent as well as the likely duration and impact of the change. If a swift reaction is desirable, the firm should pre-plan its reactions to different possible price actions by competitors. When facing a competitor's price change, the company might sit tight, reduce its own price, raise perceived quality, improve quality and raise price, or launch a fighting brand.

Key Terms

Objective 9-1
Price (p 264)
Customer value-based pricing (p 265)
Good-value pricing (p 267)
Value-added pricing (p 267)
Cost-based pricing (p 269)
Fixed costs (overhead) (p 269)
Variable costs (p 270)
Total costs (p 270)
Cost-plus pricing (markup pricing) (p 270)
Break-even pricing (target return pricing) (p 270)
Competition-based pricing (p 271)

Objective 9-2
Target costing (p 273)
Demand curve (p 274)
Price elasticity (p 275)

Objective 9-3
Market-skimming pricing (price skimming) (p 277)
Market-penetration pricing (p 277)

Objective 9-4
Product line pricing (p 278)
Optional-product pricing (p 279)
Captive-product pricing (p 279)

By-product pricing (p 279)
Product bundle pricing (p 280)

Objective 9-5
Discount (p 281)
Allowance (p 281)
Segmented pricing (p 281)
Psychological pricing (p 282)
Reference prices (p 282)
Promotional pricing (p 282)
Dynamic pricing (p 284)

Discussion Questions

9-1. Name and describe the two types of value-based pricing methods. (AACSB: Communication)

9-2. Name and describe the four types of markets and the challenges they pose with respect to setting prices. (AACSB: Communication)

⭐ **9-3.** What is captive-product pricing? What is this pricing tactic called in the case of services? Give examples. (AACSB: Communication; Reflective Thinking)

9-4. Name and describe the two broad new product pricing strategies. When would each be appropriate? (AACSB: Communication)

⭐ **9-5.** Compare and contrast price discounts and allowances, describing the types of each. (AACSB: Communication)

Critical Thinking Exercises

9-6. If you've ever traveled to another country, such as Germany, you may have noticed that the price on a product is the total amount you actually pay when you check out. That is, no sales tax is added to the purchase price at the checkout as it is in the United States. That is because many countries impose a Value Added Tax (VAT). In a small group, research value added taxes and debate whether such taxes benefit consumers. Do marketers support or dislike these types of taxes? (AACSB: Communication; Reflective Thinking)

9-7. In a small group, research the legal requirements regarding orders resulting from an online pricing mistake. Must sellers honor such orders? Write a report of what you learned. Then describe an example of an online pricing glitch and summarize what the company did to respond to the glitch. (AACSB: Communication; Reflective Thinking)

9-8. Bridgestone Corporation, the world's largest tire and rubber producer, recently agreed to plead guilty to price-fixing along with 25 other automotive suppliers. What is price-fixing? Discuss other recent examples of price-fixing. (AACSB: Communication; Reflective Thinking)

MINICASES AND APPLICATIONS

Online, Mobile, and Social Media Marketing   Online Price Tracking

Got your eye on a new 32-inch Samsung television? Well, you better not purchase it in December—that's when the price was highest on Amazon.com ($500 versus $400 in November or February). Most consumers know that prices fluctuate throughout the year, but did you know they even fluctuate hourly? You probably can't keep up with that, but there's an app that can. Camelcamelcamel is a tool that tracks Amazon's prices for consumers and sends alerts when a price hits the sweet spot. This app allows users to import entire Amazon wishlists and to set desired price levels at which emails or tweets are sent to inform them of the prices. All of this is free. Camel makes its money from an unlikely partner—Amazon—which funnels price data directly to Camel. Camel is a member of Amazon's Affiliate program, kicking back 8.5 percent of sales for each customer Camel refers. It would seem that Amazon would want customers to buy when prices

are higher, not lower. But the online behemoth sees this as a way to keep the bargain hunters happy while realizing more profitability from less price-sensitive customers. This is an improvement over Amazon's earlier pricing tactics, which charged different customers different prices based on their buying behavior.

9-9. Go to http://us.camelcamelcamel.com/ and set up a free account. Track 10 products that interest you. Did any of the products reach your desired price? Write a report on the usefulness of this type of app for consumers. (AACSB: Communication; Use of IT)

9-10. Camel is not the only Amazon tracking or online price-tracking application. Find and describe an example of another online price-tracking tool for consumers. (AACSB: Communication; Use of IT)

Marketing Ethics   Psychology of Mobile Payments

Consumers love to play games on their mobile devices, and Japanese consumers seem to be the most passionate. Mobile game publishers in Japan have mastered the art of getting as much revenue as possible from players—some earning more than $4 million per day. The makers of Puzzle & Dragons have seemingly cracked the revenue code by using the psychology of mobile payments to squeeze more revenue by encouraging players to play longer. One Puzzle & Dragons secret was to issue its own virtual currency, called magic stones, so consumers don't feel like they are spending real money for chances to enhance play. Then the game offers a little reward at the end with a reminder of what is lost if the player doesn't take the offer. Limited-time sales offer monsters to use in battle for just a few magic stones, and if players run out of space, the game reminds them that they will lose their monsters if they don't purchase more space. All the while, mathematicians and statisticians

work behind the scenes to track game play and make it easier or more challenging to keep players engaged and spending. One expert called Puzzle & Dragons "truly diabolical" in convincing players to pay and play more. These and other game producers' tactics have propelled Japan's game revenue alone to exceed revenue from all apps in the United States.

9-11. Is it ethical for game producers to use game-playing data to encourage consumers to spend more? Explain why or why not. (AACSB: Communication; Ethical Reasoning)

9-12. Is this similar to the "freemium" model used by many U.S. game producers? Explain the "freemium" model and discuss examples of games that use this model. (AACSB: Communication; Reflective Thinking; Ethical Reasoning)

Marketing by the Numbers   Breakeven on Price Reduction

Abercrombie & Fitch, once the favorite of loyal teens, is considering lowering prices on all items it sells in an effort to win them back after several years of sales declines. A&F's total sales were $4 billion last year, but they have been declining in the face of a weak economy and an intensively competitive retail environment. Price reductions are often effective in increasing sales, but marketers need to analyze how much sales must go up before a price reduction pays off and increases revenue enough to make the it worth doing. Refer to Appendix 3: Marketing by the Numbers to answer the following questions.

9-13. Assuming A&F's gross profit margin is 60 percent and cost of goods sold represents the only variable cost, by how much must sales increase to maintain the same gross profit margin in terms of absolute dollars if A&F lowers prices by 10 percent? (AACSB: Communication; Analytical Reasoning)

9-14. By what percentage must costs decrease if A&F wants to maintain the gross margin percentage of 60 percent? (AACSB: Communication; Analytical Reasoning)

Video Case   Fast-Food Discount Wars

Fast-food chains are locked in a fierce battle that has them practically giving food away. McDonald's, Wendy's, Burger King, and others are constantly trying to lure customers at the low end of the price spectrum with tempting menu options that can serve as a snack or a meal. Although this technique is nothing new, it's more popular today than ever. The tactic has even found its way into full-service restaurant chains such as Olive Garden.

But are bargain-basement options a sustainable path for restaurant chains? This video takes a look at the various ways discount menus are executed. It also considers the reasons for using discount menu tactics as well as the possible negative outcomes.

After viewing the video featuring restaurant discount menu wars, answer the following questions:

9-15. Can discount menu strategies like those featured in the video be classified as "value pricing"? Explain.

9-16. Discuss why a restaurant chain might employ a discount menu as a pricing option.

9-17. What are the possible negative outcomes of employing a discount menu strategy?

Company Cases   9 Coach/11 Sears

See Appendix 1 for cases appropriate for this chapter. **Case 9, Coach: Riding the Wave of Premium Pricing.** After years of high-growth revenues, discount tactics are taking a toll on this premium brand. **Case 11, Sears: Why Should You Shop There?** Sears is a perfect example of why it takes more than low prices to succeed in discount retail.

MyMarketingLab

If assigned by your instructor, complete these writing sections from your Assignments in the MyLab.

9-18. Describe the cost-plus pricing method and discuss why marketers use it even if it is not the best method for setting prices. (AACSB: Communication)

9-19. Compare and contrast fixed costs and variable costs and discuss their importance in setting prices. (AACSB: Written and Oral Communication; Reflective Thinking)

10 Marketing Channels
Delivering Customer Value

CHAPTER ROAD MAP   Objective Outline

▶ **OBJECTIVE 10-1   Explain why companies use marketing channels and discuss the functions these channels perform.** Supply Chains and the Value Delivery Network (300–301); The Nature and Importance of Marketing Channels (301–303)

▶ **OBJECTIVE 10-2   Discuss how channel members interact and how they organize to perform the work of the channel.** Channel Behavior and Organization (304–311)

▶ **OBJECTIVE 10-3   Identify the major channel alternatives open to a company.** Channel Design Decisions (311–315)

▶ **OBJECTIVE 10-4   Explain how companies select, motivate, and evaluate channel members.** Channel Management Decisions (315–318); Public Policy and Distribution Decisions (319)

▶ **OBJECTIVE 10-5   Discuss the nature and importance of marketing logistics and integrated supply chain management.** Marketing Logistics and Supply Chain Management (319–326)

Previewing the Concepts

We now look at the third marketing mix tool—distribution. Companies rarely work alone in creating value for customers and building profitable customer relationships. Instead, most are only a single link in a larger supply chain and marketing channel. As such, a firm's success depends not only on how well *it* performs but also on how well its *entire marketing channel* competes with competitors' channels. The first part of this chapter explores the nature of marketing channels and the marketer's channel design and management decisions. We then examine physical distribution—or logistics—an area that has grown dramatically in importance and sophistication. In the next chapter, we'll look more closely at two major channel intermediaries: retailers and wholesalers.

We start by looking at Uber, the fast-growing, app-based car-hailing service that has recently sprouted up in cities around the world. Uber has radically reinvented urban transportation channels, posing a serious threat to conventional taxi cab and car service companies. As Uber grows, traditional competitors must innovate or risk being pushed aside.

First Stop

Uber: Radically Reshaping Urban Transportation Channels

It's rare. But every now and then a company comes along that completely disrupts the traditional ways of distributing a product or service. FedEx revolutionized small package delivery channels; Amazon.com radically transformed online selling; and Apple's iTunes and iPod turned music distribution on its ear. Now comes Uber, the app-based ride service that is revolutionizing urban transportation. Fast-growing Uber is giving conventional taxi cab and car services a real ride for their money. In just five short years, Uber has revved up operations in 270 major cities in 55 countries, already booking more than $1 billion in rides annually.

Why are so many customers around the world bypassing good old taxi cabs in favor of newcomer Uber? It's all about convenience, ease of use, and peace of mind. No more stepping out into busy city streets to wave down a passing cab. Instead, Uber's smartphone app lets passengers hail the nearest cab or limo from any location with the touch of a button, then track the vehicle on a map as it approaches. The Uber app gives riders an accurate estimate in advance of the fare to their destinations (usually less than that charged by a regular cab), eliminating guesswork and uncertainty. After the ride, passengers simply exit and walk away. Uber automatically pays the driver (including tip) from the passenger's prepaid Uber account, eliminating the often inconvenient and awkward moment of payment. And it's the same process all over the world, from San Francisco, London, Paris, or Abu Dhabi to Ashville, North Carolina, or Athens, Georgia.

Compare the Uber experience to the uncertain and often unsettling experience of using a standard taxi cab. One business reporter describes waiting in line at a taxi stand while a driver tried to convince another would-be passenger—a total stranger—to share the cab, thereby increasing his fare. The cab itself was ancient and filthy, with ripped and worn seats. During the entire ride, the cabbie carried on a phone conversation in a foreign language via his headset, causing safety concerns while distractedly navigating busy city streets. The driver spoke only poor, hard-to-understand English. "That turned out to be a good thing," says the reporter, "because I couldn't understand what he was trying to say when he insulted me for not tipping him enough." The reporter's conclusion: "I stepped out of the taxi in front of my house and realized I just don't have to put up with this garbage anymore. Uber has changed my life, and as God is my witness, [wherever Uber is available] I will never take a taxi again."

Uber actually began as a ride-sharing service. Current Uber drivers range from professional drivers who've switched over from conventional cab and transportation companies to regular people looking for a little adventure and some extra income in their spare time. All Uber drivers go through an orientation that requires proficiency in a market area's dominant language, ensuring that they can communicate effectively with customers. Uber vehicles must be at least 2007-year models or newer, and customers can often choose the type of car they want, from an entry-level Prius to a stretch Mercedes S-Class. A two-way rating system—by which riders rate drivers and drivers rate riders in return—helps keep both sides on

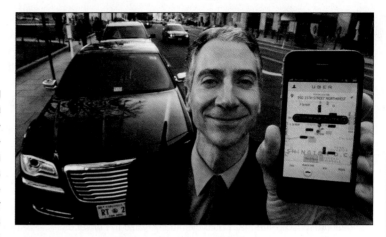

>> **Uber lets passengers hail the nearest cab from any location using its smartphone app, then track the vehicle on a map as it approaches.**
PAUL J. RICHARDS/AFP/Getty Images

their best behavior. Poorly rated drivers risk being rejected by future passengers; poorly rated passengers risk rejection by drivers, who can choose which fares they accept.

Uber's disruptive innovation has brought a breath of fresh air to an industry begging for change. Urban transportation channels have long been characterized by cartel-like relationships between cab companies and local governments, high fixed fares, poor service, and little accountability. As one economics professor points out, the taxi cab industry "was ripe for entry [by startups] because everybody hates it." The business reporter puts it more plainly: "If service at Starbucks was as routinely disappointing as service from taxis, Starbucks would have gone out of business long ago."

Like any innovator, upstart Uber faces some significant challenges. For example, Uber has been criticized for exercising too little control over driver quality and security. So far, the company has ridden beneath the radar of industry regulators by not directly employing drivers (all Uber drivers are independent contractors) and not owning any vehicles (all vehicles are driver-owned). However, although some municipalities have passed ordinances favorable to Uber's operations, others are imposing new regulatory restrictions and licensing requirements.

> **Uber—the fast-growing app-based ride service—is revolutionizing urban transportation channels in cities around the globe. As Uber grows, traditional taxi cab services must innovate or risk extinction.**

Uber has also been criticized for its "surge pricing" practices—a dynamic pricing mechanism that kicks in to raise prices when demand exceeds supply, sometimes resulting in shockingly high fares and accusations of price gouging. Uber justifies surge pricing by pointing to the very foundation of its business model—allowing the forces of supply and demand to work. Surge pricing provides an incentive for more drivers to be available during periods when passengers need them most. According to Uber, if a passenger faces a higher-than-normal fare because of surge pricing, the alternative without Uber would more than likely be no taxi at all. Moreover, Uber informs passengers in advance what the fares will be. If they don't like the fare, they can find another cab, take public transportation, or walk.

As Uber expands within a given market, Uber founder and CEO Travis Kalanick envisions the increased likelihood of what he calls "a perfect day"—a day when there is a ride available for everyone who needs one and no surge pricing results. Such a scenario is no pipe dream. In New York City recently, Uber riders experienced seven such "perfect days" in a row.

Uber's huge success has attracted a garage full of competitors, such as Lyft, Sidecar, Gett, Carma, and Curb. Even Google (itself a major Uber investor) is rumored to be readying the launch of its own ride-sharing service, one that would eventually utilize the driverless vehicles Google is developing. Uber still has a huge first-to-market advantage. It has an estimated seven times the riders and 12 times the revenues of nearest competitor Lyft, and it's adding new customers at an estimated five times faster.

Beyond the numbers, however, for now, Uber has little to fear from like-minded competitors. In fact, the more competitors adopt the new model, the more the revolutionary channel will grow and thrive versus traditional channels, creating opportunities for all new entrants. Instead, the new distribution model poses the biggest threat to traditional taxi cab and car-for-hire companies, who are now losing both customers and drivers to Uber and its competitors.

Uber-mania is even catching on in other industries. It seems like there's an app-based on-demand "Uber" for almost anything these days—laundry and dry cleaning (Washio), in-home massage (Zeel), 24/7 delivery services (Postmates), and even booze (Minibar). In fact, CEO Kalanick sees no end of future applications for Uber's services, well beyond just delivering people to their destinations. Once Uber has established a dense network of cars in every city, he predicts using the network to deliver everything from packages from retailers to takeout food. As Kalanick puts it, "Once you're delivering cars in five minutes, there are a lot of other things you can deliver in five minutes."[1]

As the Uber story shows, good distribution strategies can contribute strongly to customer value and create competitive advantage for a firm. But firms cannot bring value to customers by themselves. Instead, they must work closely with other firms in a larger value delivery network.

Author Comment

These are pretty hefty terms for a really simple concept: A company can't go it alone in creating customer value. It must work within a broader network of partners to accomplish this task. Individual companies and brands don't compete; their entire value delivery networks do.

Supply Chains and the Value Delivery Network

Producing a product or service and making it available to buyers requires building relationships not only with customers but also with key suppliers and resellers in the company's *supply chain*. This supply chain consists of upstream and downstream partners. Upstream from the company is the set of firms that supply the raw materials, components, parts, information, finances, and expertise needed to create a product or service. Marketers, however, have traditionally focused on the downstream side of the supply chain—the *marketing channels* (or *distribution channels*) that look toward the customer. Downstream marketing channel partners, such as wholesalers and retailers, form a vital link between the firm and its customers.

The term *supply chain* may be too limited, as it takes a *make-and-sell* view of the business. It suggests that raw materials, productive inputs, and factory capacity should serve as the starting point for market planning. A better term would be *demand chain* because it suggests a *sense-and-respond* view of the market. Under this view, planning starts by identifying the needs of target customers, to which the company responds by organizing a chain of resources and activities with the goal of creating customer value.

Yet, even a demand chain view of a business may be too limited because it takes a step-by-step, linear view of purchase-production-consumption activities. Instead, most large companies today are engaged in building and managing a complex, continuously evolving value delivery network. As defined in Chapter 2, a **value delivery network** is made up of the company, suppliers, distributors, and, ultimately, customers who "partner" with each other to improve the performance of the entire system. ›› For example, Pepsi makes great beverages. But to make and market just one of its many lines—say, its classic colas—Pepsi manages a huge network of people

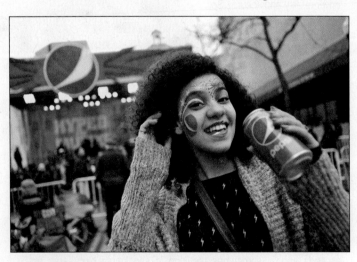

›› **Value delivery network:** In making and marketing even just its classic colas, Pepsi manages a huge network of people within the company plus thousands of outside suppliers, bottlers, retailers, and marketing service firms that must work together to create customer value and establish the brand's "Pepsi: Live for Now" positioning.

Vasiliy Baziuk/AP Images

Value delivery network
A network composed of the company, suppliers, distributors, and, ultimately, customers who partner with each other to improve the performance of the entire system in delivering customer value.

within the company, from marketing and sales people to folks in finance and operations. It also coordinates the efforts of thousands of suppliers, bottlers, retailers ranging from Kroger and Walmart to Papa John's Pizza, and advertising agencies and other marketing service firms. The entire network must function together to create customer value and establish the brand's "Pepsi: Live for Now" positioning.

This chapter focuses on marketing channels—on the downstream side of the value delivery network. We examine four major questions concerning marketing channels: What is the nature of marketing channels, and why are they important? How do channel firms interact and organize to do the work of the channel? What problems do companies face in designing and managing their channels? What role do physical distribution and supply chain management play in attracting and satisfying customers? In the next chapter, we will look at marketing channel issues from the viewpoints of retailers and wholesalers.

Author Comment
In this section, we look at the downstream side of the value delivery network—the marketing channel organizations that connect the company and its customers. To understand their value, imagine life without retailers—say, without grocery stores or department stores.

The Nature and Importance of Marketing Channels

Few producers sell their goods directly to final users. Instead, most use intermediaries to bring their products to market. They try to forge a **marketing channel** (or **distribution channel**)—a set of interdependent organizations that help make a product or service available for use or consumption by the consumer or business user.

Marketing channel (distribution channel)
A set of interdependent organizations that help make a product or service available for use or consumption by the consumer or business user.

A company's channel decisions directly affect every other marketing decision. Pricing depends on whether the company works with national discount chains, uses high-quality specialty stores, or sells directly to consumers online. The firm's sales force and communications decisions depend on how much persuasion, training, motivation, and support its channel partners need. Whether a company develops or acquires certain new products may depend on how well those products fit the capabilities of its channel members.

Companies often pay too little attention to their distribution channels—sometimes with damaging results. In contrast, many companies have used imaginative distribution systems to gain a competitive advantage. Enterprise Rent-A-Car revolutionized the car-rental business by setting up off-airport rental offices. Apple turned the retail music business on its head by selling music for the iPod via the Internet on iTunes. FedEx's creative and imposing distribution system made it a leader in express package delivery. And Amazon.com forever changed the face of retailing and became the Walmart of the Internet by selling anything and everything without using physical stores.

Distribution channel decisions often involve long-term commitments to other firms. For example, companies such as Ford, McDonald's, or Nike can easily change their advertising, pricing, or promotion programs. They can scrap old products and introduce new ones as market tastes demand. But when they set up distribution channels through contracts with franchisees, independent dealers, or large retailers, they cannot readily replace these channels with company-owned stores or Internet sites if the conditions change. Therefore, management must design its channels carefully, with an eye on both today's likely selling environment and tomorrow's as well.

How Channel Members Add Value

Why do producers give some of the selling job to channel partners? After all, doing so means giving up some control over how and to whom they sell their products. Producers use intermediaries because they create greater efficiency in making goods available to target markets. Through their contacts, experience, specialization, and scale of operation, intermediaries usually offer the firm more than it can achieve on its own.

>> **Figure 10.1** shows how using intermediaries can provide economies. Figure 10.1A shows three manufacturers, each using direct marketing to reach three customers. This system requires nine different contacts. Figure 10.1B shows the three manufacturers working through one distributor, which contacts the three customers. This system requires only

Marketing channel intermediaries make buying a lot easier for consumers. Again, think about life without grocery retailers. How would you go about buying that 12-pack of Coke or any of the hundreds of other items that you now routinely drop into your shopping cart?

A. Number of contacts without a distributor

B. Number of contacts with a distributor

>> **Figure 10.1 How a Distributor Reduces the Number of Channel Transactions**

six contacts. In this way, intermediaries reduce the amount of work that must be done by both producers and consumers.

From the economic system's point of view, the role of marketing intermediaries is to transform the assortments of products made by producers into the assortments wanted by consumers. Producers make narrow assortments of products in large quantities, but consumers want broad assortments of products in small quantities. Marketing channel members buy large quantities from many producers and break them down into the smaller quantities and broader assortments desired by consumers.

For example, Unilever makes millions of bars of Lever 2000 hand soap each week. However, you most likely only want to buy a few bars at a time. Therefore, big food, drug, and discount retailers, such as Safeway, Walgreens, and Target, buy Lever 2000 by the truckload and stock it on their stores' shelves. In turn, you can buy a single bar of Lever 2000 along with a shopping cart full of small quantities of toothpaste, shampoo, and other related products as you need them. Thus, intermediaries play an important role in matching supply and demand.

In making products and services available to consumers, channel members add value by bridging the major time, place, and possession gaps that separate goods and services from those who use them. Members of the marketing channel perform many key functions. Some help to complete transactions:

- *Information.* Gathering and distributing information about consumers, producers, and other actors and forces in the marketing environment needed for planning and aiding exchange.
- *Promotion.* Developing and spreading persuasive communications about an offer.
- *Contact.* Finding and engaging customers and prospective buyers.
- *Matching.* Shaping offers to meet the buyer's needs, including activities such as manufacturing, grading, assembling, and packaging.
- *Negotiation.* Reaching an agreement on price and other terms so that ownership or possession can be transferred.

Others help to fulfill the completed transactions:

- *Physical distribution.* Transporting and storing goods.
- *Financing.* Acquiring and using funds to cover the costs of the channel work.
- *Risk taking.* Assuming the risks of carrying out the channel work.

The question is not *whether* these functions need to be performed—they must be—but rather *who* will perform them. To the extent that the manufacturer performs these functions, its costs go up; therefore, its prices must be higher. When some of these functions are shifted to intermediaries, the producer's costs and prices may be lower, but the intermediaries must charge more to cover the costs of their work. In dividing the work of the channel, the various functions should be assigned to the channel members that can add the most value for the cost.

Number of Channel Levels

Channel level
A layer of intermediaries that performs some work in bringing the product and its ownership closer to the final buyer.

Direct marketing channel
A marketing channel that has no intermediary levels.

Indirect marketing channel
A marketing channel containing one or more intermediary levels.

Companies can design their distribution channels to make products and services available to customers in different ways. Each layer of marketing intermediaries that performs some work in bringing the product and its ownership closer to the final buyer is a **channel level**. Because both the producer and the final consumer perform some work, they are part of every channel.

The *number of intermediary levels* indicates the *length* of a channel. ≫ **Figure 10.2** shows both consumer and business channels of different lengths. Figure 10.2A shows several common consumer distribution channels. Channel 1, called a **direct marketing channel**, has no intermediary levels—the company sells directly to consumers. For example, Mary Kay Cosmetics and Amway sell their products through home and office sales parties and online Web sites and social media; companies ranging from GEICO insurance to Omaha Steaks sell directly to customers via the Internet, mobile, and telephone. The remaining channels in Figure 10.2A are **indirect marketing channels**, containing one or more intermediaries.

Figure 10.2B shows some common business distribution channels. The business marketer can use its own sales force to sell directly to business customers. Or it can sell to various types of intermediaries, which in turn sell to these customers. Although consumer and business marketing channels with even more levels can sometimes be found, these are less common. From the producer's point of view, a greater number of levels means less control and greater channel complexity. Moreover, all the institutions in the channel are connected by several types of *flows*. These include the *physical flow* of products, the *flow of ownership*, the *payment flow*, the *information flow*, and the *promotion flow*. These flows can make even channels with only one or a few levels very complex.

≫ **Figure 10.2 Consumer and Business Marketing Channels**

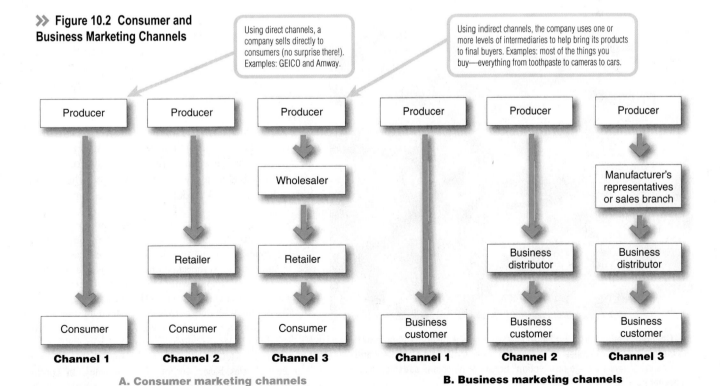

A. Consumer marketing channels

B. Business marketing channels

Author Comment
Channels are made up of more than just boxes and arrows on paper. They are behavioral systems consisting of real companies and people who interact to accomplish their individual and collective goals. Like groups of people, sometimes they work well together and sometimes they don't.

Channel Behavior and Organization

Distribution channels are more than simple collections of firms tied together by various flows. They are complex behavioral systems in which people and companies interact to accomplish individual, company, and channel goals. Some channel systems consist of only informal interactions among loosely organized firms. Others consist of formal interactions guided by strong organizational structures. Moreover, channel systems do not stand still—new types of intermediaries emerge and whole new channel systems evolve. Here we look at channel behavior and how members organize to do the work of the channel.

Channel Behavior

A marketing channel consists of firms that have partnered for their common good. Each channel member depends on the others. For example, a Ford dealer depends on Ford to design cars that meet customer needs. In turn, Ford depends on the dealer to engage customers, persuade them to buy Ford cars, and service the cars after the sale. Each Ford dealer also depends on other dealers to provide good sales and service that will uphold the brand's reputation. In fact, the success of individual Ford dealers depends on how well the entire Ford marketing channel competes with the channels of Toyota, GM, and other auto manufacturers.

Each channel member plays a specialized role in the channel. For example, Samsung's role is to produce electronics products that consumers will covet and create demand through national advertising. Best Buy's role is to display these Samsung products in convenient locations, answer buyers' questions, and complete sales. The channel will be most effective when each member assumes the tasks it can do best.

Ideally, because the success of individual channel members depends on the overall channel's success, all channel firms should work together smoothly. They should understand and accept their roles, coordinate their activities, and cooperate to attain overall channel goals. However, individual channel members rarely take such a broad view. Cooperating to achieve overall channel goals sometimes means giving up individual company goals. Although channel members depend on one another, they often act alone in their own short-run best interests. They often disagree on who should do what and for what rewards. Such disagreements over goals, roles, and rewards generate **channel conflict**.

Horizontal conflict occurs among firms at the same level of the channel. For instance, some Ford dealers in Chicago might complain that other dealers in the city steal sales from them by pricing too low or advertising outside their assigned territories. Or Holiday Inn franchisees might complain about other Holiday Inn operators overcharging guests or giving poor service, hurting the overall Holiday Inn image.

Vertical conflict, conflict between different levels of the same channel, is even more common. ≫ For example, McDonald's has recently faced growing conflict with its corps of almost 3,000 independent franchisees:[2]

Channel conflict
Disagreements among marketing channel members on goals, roles, and rewards—who should do what and for what rewards.

≫ Channel conflict: Growing McDonald's franchisee discontent may explain the increasing lack of smiles on the faces of both McDonald's cashiers and customers. "There's a huge connection" between franchisee satisfaction and customer service.

Seth Perlman/AP Images

In a recent company Webcast, based on rising customer complaints that service isn't fast or friendly enough, McDonald's told its franchisees that their cashiers need to smile more. At the same time, it seems, the franchisees weren't very happy with McDonald's, either. A recent survey of franchise owners reflected growing franchisee discontent with the corporation. Much of the conflict stems from a recent slowdown in systemwide sales that has both sides on edge. The most basic conflicts are financial. McDonald's makes its money from franchisee royalties based on total system sales. In contrast, franchisees make money on margins—what's left over after their costs.

To reverse the sales slump, McDonald's has increased emphasis on Dollar Menu items, a strategy that increases corporate sales but squeezes franchisee margins. Franchisees are also grumbling about adding popular but more complex menu items, such as Snack Wraps, that increase the top line for McDonald's but add preparation and staffing costs for franchisees while slowing down service. McDonald's is also asking franchisees to make costly restaurant upgrades and overhauls. As one survey respondent summarized, there's "too much reliance on price-pointing and discounting to drive top-line sales, which is where the corporate cow feeds." In all, the survey rates McDonald's current franchisee relations at a decade-low 1.93 out of a possible 5, in the "fair" to "poor" range. That fact might explain both the lack of smiles and the increasing customer complaints. According to one restaurant consultant, "there's a huge connection" between franchisee satisfaction and customer service.

Some conflict in the channel takes the form of healthy competition. Such competition can be good for the channel; without it, the channel could become passive and non-innovative. For example, the McDonald's conflict with its franchisees might represent normal give-and-take over the respective rights of the channel partners. However, severe or prolonged conflict can disrupt channel effectiveness and cause lasting harm to channel relationships. McDonald's should manage the channel conflict carefully to keep it from getting out of hand.

Vertical Marketing Systems

Conventional distribution channel
A channel consisting of one or more independent producers, wholesalers, and retailers, each a separate business seeking to maximize its own profits, perhaps even at the expense of profits for the system as a whole.

Vertical marketing system (VMS)
A channel structure in which producers, wholesalers, and retailers act as a unified system. One channel member owns the others, has contracts with them, or has so much power that they all cooperate.

For the channel as a whole to perform well, each channel member's role must be specified, and channel conflict must be managed. The channel will perform better if it includes a firm, agency, or mechanism that provides leadership and has the power to assign roles and manage conflict.

Historically, *conventional distribution channels* have lacked such leadership and power, often resulting in damaging conflict and poor performance. One of the biggest channel developments over the years has been the emergence of *vertical marketing systems* that provide channel leadership. ≫ **Figure 10.3** contrasts the two types of channel arrangements.

A **conventional distribution channel** consists of one or more independent producers, wholesalers, and retailers. Each is a separate business seeking to maximize its own profits, perhaps even at the expense of the system as a whole. No channel member has much control over the other members, and no formal means exists for assigning roles and resolving channel conflict.

In contrast, a **vertical marketing system (VMS)** consists of producers, wholesalers, and retailers acting as a unified system. One channel member owns the others, has

≫ **Figure 10.3 Comparison of Conventional Distribution Channel with Vertical Marketing System**

Vertical marketing system—here's another fancy term for a simple concept. It's simply a channel in which members at different levels (hence, vertical) work together in a unified way (hence, system) to accomplish the work of the channel.

contracts with them, or wields so much power that they must all cooperate. The VMS can be dominated by the producer, the wholesaler, or the retailer.

We look now at three major types of VMSs: *corporate, contractual,* and *administered.* Each uses a different means for setting up leadership and power in the channel.

Corporate VMS

Corporate VMS

A vertical marketing system that combines successive stages of production and distribution under single ownership—channel leadership is established through common ownership.

A **corporate VMS** integrates successive stages of production and distribution under single ownership. Coordination and conflict management are attained through regular organizational channels. For example, Sherwin-Williams, the largest U.S. coatings manufacturer, sells its Sherwin-Williams-branded products exclusively through more than 4,000 company-owned retail paint stores. And grocery giant Kroger owns and operates 38 manufacturing plants—17 dairies, 6 bakery plants, 5 grocery plants, 2 frozen dough plants, 2 beverage plants, 2 cheese plants, 2 ice cream plants, and 2 meat plants—that give it factory-to-store channel control over 40 percent of the more than 11,000 private-label items found on its shelves.[3]

Contractual VMS

A vertical marketing system in which independent firms at different levels of production and distribution join together through contracts.

Integrating the entire distribution chain—from its own design and manufacturing operations to distribution through its own managed stores—has turned Spanish clothing chain Zara into the world's fastest-growing fast-fashion retailer:[4]

> In recent years, fashion retailer Zara has attracted an army of loyal shoppers swarming to buy its "cheap chic"—stylish designs that resemble those of big-name fashion houses but at moderate prices. However, Zara's amazing success comes not just from *what* it sells but from *how fast* its cutting-edge distribution system *delivers* what it sells. Zara delivers fast fashion—*really* fast fashion. Thanks to vertical integration, Zara can take a new fashion concept through design, manufacturing, and store-shelf placement in as little as three weeks, whereas competitors such as H&M, Gap, or Benetton often take six months or more. And the resulting low costs let Zara offer the very latest midmarket chic at downmarket prices.

Franchise organization

A contractual vertical marketing system in which a channel member, called a franchisor, links several stages in the production-distribution process.

> Speedy design and distribution allow Zara to introduce a copious supply of new fashions—at three times the rate of competitor introductions. Then Zara's distribution system supplies its stores with small shipments of new merchandise twice a week, compared with competing chains' outlets, which get large shipments seasonally, usually just four to six times per year. The combination of a large number of timely new fashions delivered in frequent small batches gives Zara stores a continually updated merchandise mix that brings customers back more often. Fast turnover also results in less outdated and discounted merchandise. Rather than guessing about tomorrow's fashions, Zara can wait to see what customers are actually buying and then make that.

Contractual VMS

A **contractual VMS** consists of independent firms at different levels of production and distribution that join together through contracts to obtain more economies or sales impact than each could achieve alone. Channel members coordinate their activities and manage conflict through contractual agreements.

The **franchise organization** is the most common type of contractual relationship. In this system, a channel member called a *franchisor* links several stages in the production-distribution process. In the United States alone, some 780,000 franchise outlets account for more than $889 billion of economic output. Industry analysts estimate that a new franchise outlet opens somewhere in the United States every eight minutes and that about one out of every 12 retail business outlets is a franchised business.[5]

Almost every kind of business has been franchised—from motels and fast-food restaurants to dental centers and dating services, from wedding consultants and handyman services to funeral homes, fitness centers, and moving services. For example, through franchising, Two Men and a Truck moving services—"Movers Who Care"—grew quickly from two high school students looking to make extra money with a pickup truck to an international network of 330 franchise locations that's experienced record growth over the past six years and completed more than 5.5 million moves.[6]

There are three types of franchises. The first type is the *manufacturer-sponsored retailer franchise system*—for example, Ford and its network of

>> Franchising systems: Through franchising, Two Men and a Truck—"Movers Who Care"—grew quickly from two high school students with a pickup truck to an international network of 330 franchise locations that's experienced record growth over the past six years.

Two Men and a Truck International

independent franchised dealers. The second type is the *manufacturer-sponsored whole-saler franchise system*—Coca-Cola licenses bottlers (wholesalers) in various world markets that buy Coca-Cola syrup concentrate and then bottle and sell the finished product to retailers locally. The third type is the *service-firm-sponsored retailer franchise system*—for example, Burger King and its nearly 12,100 franchisee-operated restaurants around the world. Other examples can be found in everything from auto rentals (Hertz, Avis), apparel retailers (The Athlete's Foot, Plato's Closet), and motels (Holiday Inn, Hampton Inn) to supplemental education (Huntington Learning Center, Mathnasium) and personal services (Great Clips, Mr. Handyman, Anytime Fitness).

The fact that most consumers cannot tell the difference between contractual and corporate VMSs shows how successfully the contractual organizations compete with corporate chains. The next chapter presents a fuller discussion of the various contractual VMSs.

Administered VMS

Administered VMS
A vertical marketing system that coordinates successive stages of production and distribution through the size and power of one of the parties.

In an **administered VMS**, leadership is assumed not through common ownership or contractual ties but through the size and power of one or a few dominant channel members. Manufacturers of a top brand can obtain strong trade cooperation and support from resellers. For example, GE, P&G, and Apple can command unusual cooperation from many resellers regarding displays, shelf space, promotions, and price policies. In turn, large retailers such as Walmart, Home Depot, Kroger, and Walgreens can exert strong influence on the many manufacturers that supply the products they sell.

For example, in the normal push and pull between Walmart and its consumer goods suppliers, giant Walmart—the biggest grocer in the United States with nearly 30 percent share of all U.S. grocery sales—usually gets its way. Take supplier Clorox, for instance. Although The Clorox Company's strong consumer brand preference gives it significant negotiating power, Walmart simply holds more cards. Sales to Walmart make up 26 percent of Clorox's sales, whereas Clorox products account for only one-third of 1 percent of Walmart's purchases, making Walmart by far the dominant partner. Things get even worse for Cal-Maine Foods and its Eggland's Best brand, which relies on Walmart for nearly one-third of its sales but tallies only about one-tenth of 1 percent of Walmart's volume. For such brands, maintaining a strong relationship with the giant retailer is crucial.[7]

Horizontal marketing system
A channel arrangement in which two or more companies at one level join together to follow a new marketing opportunity.

Horizontal Marketing Systems

Another channel development is the **horizontal marketing system**, in which two or more companies at one level join together to follow a new marketing opportunity. By working together, companies can combine their financial, production, or marketing resources to accomplish more than any one company could alone.

Companies might join forces with competitors or noncompetitors. They might work with each other on a temporary or permanent basis, or they may create a separate company. For example, competing big media companies Fox Broadcasting, Disney-ABC, and NBCUniversal (Comcast) jointly own and market Hulu, the successful online subscription service that provides on-demand streaming of TV shows, movies, and other video content. Together, they compete more effectively against digital streaming competitors such as Netflix. Walmart partners with noncompetitor McDonald's to place "express" versions of McDonald's restaurants in Walmart stores. McDonald's benefits from Walmart's heavy store traffic, and Walmart keeps hungry shoppers from needing to go elsewhere to eat.

Such channel arrangements also work well globally. For example, competitors General Mills and Nestlé operate a joint venture—Cereal Partners Worldwide—to market General Mills Big G cereal brands in 130 countries outside North America. General Mills supplies a kitchen

Horizontal marketing systems: General Mills and Nestlé operate a joint venture—Cereal Partners Worldwide—that markets General Mills Big G cereal brands outside North America.

Sonny Meddle/Rex Features/Presselect/Alamy

cabinet full of quality cereal brands, whereas Nestlé contributes its extensive international distribution channels and local market knowledge. The 25-year-old alliance produces $1.1 billion in revenues for General Mills.[8]

Multichannel Distribution Systems

Multichannel distribution system
A distribution system in which a single firm sets up two or more marketing channels to reach one or more customer segments.

In the past, many companies used a single channel to sell to a single market or market segment. Today, with the proliferation of customer segments and channel possibilities, more and more companies have adopted **multichannel distribution systems**. Such multichannel marketing occurs when a single firm sets up two or more marketing channels to reach one or more customer segments.

>> **Figure 10.4** shows a multichannel marketing system. In the figure, the producer sells directly to consumer segment 1 using catalogs, online, and mobile channels and reaches consumer segment 2 through retailers. It sells indirectly to business segment 1 through distributors and dealers and to business segment 2 through its own sales force.

These days, almost every large company and many small ones distribute through multiple channels. For example, John Deere sells its familiar green-and-yellow lawn and garden tractors, mowers, and outdoor power products to consumers and commercial users through several channels, including John Deere retailers, Lowe's home improvement stores, and online. It sells and services its tractors, combines, planters, and other agricultural equipment through its premium John Deere dealer network. And it sells large construction and forestry equipment through selected large, full-service John Deere dealers and their sales forces.

Multichannel distribution systems offer many advantages to companies facing large and complex markets. With each new channel, the company expands its sales and market coverage and gains opportunities to tailor its products and services to the specific needs of diverse customer segments. But such multichannel systems are harder to control, and they can generate conflict as more channels compete for customers and sales. For example, when John Deere first began selling selected consumer products through Lowe's home improvement stores, many of its independent dealers complained loudly. To avoid such conflicts in its online marketing channels, the company routes all of its online sales to John Deere dealers.

Changing Channel Organization

Disintermediation
The cutting out of marketing channel intermediaries by product or service producers or the displacement of traditional resellers by radical new types of intermediaries.

Changes in technology and the explosive growth of direct and online marketing are having a profound impact on the nature and design of marketing channels. One major trend is toward **disintermediation**—a big term with a clear message and important consequences.

>> **Figure 10.4 Multichannel Distribution System**

Most large companies distribute through multiple channels. For example, you could buy a familiar green-and-yellow John Deere lawn tractor from a neighborhood John Deere dealer or from Lowe's. A large farm or forestry business would buy larger John Deere equipment from a premium full-service John Deere dealer and its sales force.

Disintermediation occurs when product or service producers cut out intermediaries and go directly to final buyers or when radically new types of channel intermediaries displace traditional ones.

Thus, in many industries, traditional intermediaries are dropping by the wayside, as is the case with online marketers taking business from traditional brick-and-mortar retailers.

 Disintermediation: Streaming music services such as Spotify are rapidly disintermediating both traditional music-store retailers and even music download services such as iTunes.

Dado Ruvic/Reuters/Corbis

For example, online music download services such as iTunes and Amazon MP3 have pretty much put traditional music-store retailers out of business. ≫In turn, streaming music services such as Spotify and Vevo are now disintermediating digital download services—digital downloads peaked last year while music streaming increased 32 percent.

Disintermediation presents both opportunities and problems for producers and resellers. Channel innovators who find new ways to add value in the channel can displace traditional resellers and reap the rewards. In turn, traditional intermediaries must continue to innovate to avoid being swept aside. For example, when Netflix pioneered online DVD-by-mail video rentals, it sent traditional brick-and-mortar video stores such as Blockbuster into ruin. Then Netflix itself faced disintermediation threats from an even hotter channel—video streaming. But instead of simply watching developments, Netflix has led them (see Marketing at Work 10.1).

Similarly, superstore booksellers Borders and Barnes & Noble pioneered huge book selections and low prices, shutting down most small independent bookstores. Then along came Amazon.com, which threatened even the largest brick-and-mortar bookstores. Amazon.com almost single-handedly bankrupted Borders in less than 10 years. Now, both offline and online sellers of physical books are being threatened by digital book downloads and e-readers. Rather than yielding to digital developments, however, Amazon.com is leading them with its highly successful Kindle e-readers and tablets. By contrast, Barnes & Noble—the giant that put so many independent bookstores out of business—was a latecomer with its struggling Nook e-reader and now finds itself locked in a battle for survival.[9]

Like resellers, to remain competitive, product and service producers must develop new channel opportunities, such as the Internet and other direct channels. However, developing these new channels often brings them into direct competition with their established channels, resulting in conflict. To ease this problem, companies often look for ways to make going direct a plus for the entire channel.

For example, Volvo Car Group (now owned by Chinese car maker Geeley) recently announced plans to start selling Volvo vehicles online in all of its markets. Some 80 percent of Volvo buyers already shop online for other goods, so cars seem like a natural extension. Few auto makers have tried selling directly, with the exception of Tesla, which sells its all-electric cars online, bypassing dealers altogether. Other car companies worry that selling directly would alienate their independent dealer networks. "If you say e-commerce, initially dealers get nervous," says Volvo's head of marketing. So, to avoid channel conflicts, Volvo will pass all online sales through established dealers for delivery. In that way, boosting sales through direct marketing will benefit both Volvo and its channel partners.[10]

LINKING THE CONCEPTS

Stop here for a moment and apply the distribution channel concepts we've discussed so far.

- Compare the Zara and Ford channels. Draw a diagram that shows the types of intermediaries in each channel. What kind of channel system does each company use?
- What are the roles and responsibilities of the members in each channel? How well do these channel members work together toward overall channel success?

MARKETING AT WORK 10.1

Netflix: Disintermediate or Be Disintermediated

Baseball great Yogi Berra, known more for his mangled phrasing than for his baseball prowess, once said, "The future ain't what it used to be." For Netflix, the world's largest video subscription service, no matter how you say it, figuring out the future is challenging and a bit scary. Netflix faces dramatic changes in how video entertainment will be distributed. The question is: Will Netflix be among the disintermediators or among the disintermediated?

Time and again, Netflix has innovated its way to the top in the distribution of video entertainment. In the early 2000s, Netflix's revolutionary DVD-by-mail service put all but the most powerful movie-rental stores out of business. In 2007, Netflix's then-groundbreaking move into digital streaming once again revolutionized how people accessed movies and other video content. Now, with Netflix leading the pack, video distribution has become a roiling pot of emerging technologies and high-tech competitors, one that offers both mind-bending opportunities and stomach-churning risks.

Just ask Blockbuster. Less than a decade ago, the giant brick-and-mortar movie-rental chain flat-out owned the industry. Then along came Netflix, the fledgling DVD-by-mail service. First thousands, then millions, of subscribers were drawn to Netflix's innovative distribution model. In 2010, as Netflix surged, once-mighty Blockbuster fell into bankruptcy.

The Blockbuster riches-to-rags disintermediation story underscores the turmoil that typifies today's video distribution business. In only the past few years, a glut of video access options has materialized. At the same time that Netflix ascended and Blockbuster plunged, Coinstar's Redbox came out of nowhere to build a novel national network of $1-a-day DVD-rental kiosks. Then high-tech start-ups such as Hulu—with its high-quality, ad-supported free access to movies and current TV shows—began pushing digital streaming via the Internet.

All along the way, Netflix has acted boldly to stay ahead of the competition. For example, by 2007, Netflix had mailed out its one-billionth DVD. But rather than rest on success, Netflix and its CEO, Reed Hastings, set their sights on a then-revolutionary new video distribution model: Deliver Netflix to any and every Internet-connected screen—from laptops to Internet-ready TVs to smartphones and other Wi-Fi–enabled devices. Netflix launched a new Watch Instantly service, which let members stream movies to their computers as part of their monthly fee, even if it came at the expense of the company's still-hot DVD-by-mail business.

Although Netflix didn't pioneer digital streaming, it poured resources into improving the technology and building the largest streaming library. It built a huge subscriber base, and sales and profits soared. With its massive physical DVD library and a streaming library of more than 20,000

high-definition movies accessible via 200 different Internet-ready devices, it seemed that nothing could stop Netflix.

But Netflix's stunning success drew a slew of resourceful competitors. Video giants such as Google's YouTube and Apple's iTunes began renting movie downloads, and Hulu introduced subscription-based Hulu Plus. To stay ahead, even to survive, Netflix needed to keep the innovation pedal to the metal. So in the summer of 2011, in an ambitious but risky move, CEO Hastings made an all-in bet on digital streaming. He split off Netflix's still-thriving DVD-by-mail service into a separate business named Qwikster and required separate subscriptions for DVD rentals and streaming (at a startling 60 percent price increase for customers using both). The Netflix name would now stand for nothing but digital streaming, which would be the primary focus of the company's future growth.

Although perhaps visionary, Netflix's abrupt changes didn't sit well with customers. Some 800,000 subscribers dropped the service, and Netflix's stock price plummeted by almost two-thirds. Within only weeks, Netflix admitted its blunder and reversed its decision to set up a separate Qwikster operation. Despite the setback, however, Netflix retained its separate, higher pricing for DVDs by mail. The company rebounded quickly, soon replacing all of its lost subscribers and then some. What's more, with a 60 percent higher price, revenues and profits rose as well. Netflix's stock price was once again skyrocketing.

Now more than ever, Netflix's focus is on streaming video. Although customers can still access Netflix's world's-biggest DVD library, the DVD operation is now located at a separate DVD.Netflix Web site, with a separate subscription fee. Nearly

>> Netflix's innovative distribution strategy: From DVDs by mail to Watch Instantly to video streaming on almost any device, Netflix has stayed ahead of the howling pack by doing what it does best—revolutionize distribution. What's next?
Mike Blake/Reuters

80 percent of Netflix's revenues now come from streaming. Its current 62 million paid subscribers stream an astounding 3.3 billion hours of movies and TV programs every month. On an average weeknight, Netflix commands more than a third of all Internet traffic in North American homes.

Despite its continuing success, Netflix knows that it can't rest its innovation machine. Competition continues to move at a blurring rate. For example, Amazon's Prime Instant Video offers streaming of thousands of movies and TV shows to Amazon Prime members at no extra cost. Google has moved beyond its YouTube rental service with Google Play, an all-media entertainment portal for movies, music, e-books, and apps. Comcast offers Xfinity Streampix, which lets subscribers stream older movies and television programs via their TVs, laptops, tablets, or smartphones. And Apple and Samsung are creating smoother integration with streaming content via smart TVs.

Moving ahead, as the industry settles into streaming as the main delivery model, content—not just delivery—will be a key to distancing Netflix from the rest of the pack. Given its head start, Netflix remains well ahead in the content race. However, Amazon, Hulu Plus, and other competitors are working feverishly to sign contracts with big movie and TV content providers. But so is Netflix. It recently scored a big win with a Disney exclusive—soon, Netflix will be the only place viewers can stream Disney's deep catalog and new releases from Walt Disney Animation, Marvel, Pixar, and Lucasfilm.

But as content-licensing deals with movie and television studios become harder to get, in yet another innovative video distribution twist, Netflix and its competitors are now developing their own original content at a feverish pace. Once again, Netflix appears to have the upper hand. For example, it led the way with the smash hit *House of Cards,* a U.S. version of a hit British political drama series produced by Hollywood bigwigs David Fincher and Kevin Spacey. Based on its huge success with *House of Cards,* Netflix developed a number of other original series, including *Hemlock Grove, Lillyhammer, Marco Polo,* and *Orange Is the New Black*, its most successful release to date. Such efforts have left the rest of the video industry scrambling to keep up. And Netflix is just getting started. It plans to invest $300 million a year in developing new original content, adding at least five original titles annually.

Thus, from DVDs by mail, to Watch Instantly, to video streaming on almost any device, to developing original content, Netflix has stayed ahead of the howling pack by doing what it does best—innovate and revolutionize distribution. What's next? No one really knows. But one thing seems certain: Whatever's coming, if Netflix doesn't lead the change, it risks being left behind—and quickly. Netflix must continue to disintermediate its own distribution model before competitors can. As Netflix's slower-moving competitors have learned the hard way, it's disintermedi*ate* or be disintermedi*ated*.[i]

[i] See Susan Young, "2014 SUCCESS Achiever of the Year: Reed Hastings," SUCCESS, February 10, 2015, www.success.com/article/2014-success-achiever-of-the-year-reed-hastings; Brian Stelter, "Netflix Grabs a Slice of Star Wars," *CNNMoney,* February 13, 2014, http://money.cnn.com/2014/02/13/technology/netflix-star-wars/; Mike Snider, "Netflix, Adding Customers and Profits, Will Raise Prices," *USA Today,* April 22, 2014, www.usatoday.com/story/tech/2014/04/21/netflix-results/7965613/; Michael Leidtke, "With 'House of Cards,' Netflix Got a Winning Hand," *Boston Globe,* February 27, 2015, www.bostonglobe.com/business/2015/02/27/house-cards-dealt-netflix-winning-hand/M5kBWc916HP1XMQyjdAd8N/story.html; Lisa Richwine, "Netflix Beats Forecasts with 62 Million Streaming Subscribers," *Reuters,* April 15, 2015, http://www.reuters.com/article/2015/04/15/us-netflix-results-idUSKBN0N62HC20150415; and annual reports and information at www.netflix.com, accessed October 2015.

Channel Design Decisions

Author Comment
Like everything else in marketing, good channel design begins with analyzing customer needs. Remember, marketing channels are really *customer value delivery networks*.

We now look at several channel design decisions manufacturers face. In designing marketing channels, manufacturers struggle between what is ideal and what is practical. A new firm with limited capital usually starts by selling in a limited market area. In this case, deciding on the best channels might not be a problem: The problem might simply be how to convince one or a few good intermediaries to handle the line.

If successful, the new firm can branch out to new markets through existing intermediaries. In smaller markets, the firm might sell directly to retailers; in larger markets, it might sell through distributors. In one part of the country, it might grant exclusive franchises; in another, it might sell through all available outlets. Then it might add an online store that sells directly to hard-to-reach customers. In this way, channel systems often evolve to meet market opportunities and conditions.

For maximum effectiveness, however, channel analysis and decision making should be more purposeful. **Marketing channel design** calls for analyzing consumer needs, setting channel objectives, identifying major channel alternatives, and evaluating those alternatives.

Analyzing Consumer Needs

Marketing channel design
Designing effective marketing channels by analyzing customer needs, setting channel objectives, identifying major channel alternatives, and evaluating those alternatives.

As noted previously, marketing channels are part of the overall *customer value delivery network*. Each channel member and level adds value for the customer. Thus, designing the marketing channel starts with finding out what target consumers want from the channel. Do consumers want to buy nearby, or are they willing to travel to more centralized locations? Would customers rather buy in person, by phone, or online? Do they value breadth of assortment, or do they prefer specialization? Do consumers want many add-on services (delivery, installation, repairs), or will they obtain these services elsewhere? The faster the delivery, the greater the assortment provided, and the more add-on services supplied, the greater the channel's service level.

Providing the fastest delivery, the greatest assortment, and the most services, however, may not be possible, practical, or desired. The company and its channel members may not have the resources or skills needed to provide all the desired services. Also, higher levels of service result in higher costs for the channel and higher prices for consumers. The success of modern discount retailing shows that consumers often accept lower service levels in exchange for lower prices.

>> Meeting customers' channel service needs: Ace Hardware positions itself as "The helpful place." To loyal Ace customers, the convenience of smaller stores and the personal service they receive are well worth Ace's somewhat higher prices.

ZUMA Press, Inc/Alamy

Many companies, however, position themselves on higher service levels, and customers willingly pay the higher prices. >> For example, your local independently owned Ace Hardware store probably provides more personalized service, a more convenient location, and less shopping hassle than the nearest huge Home Depot or Lowe's store. As a result, it also charges somewhat higher prices. To loyal Ace customers, the convenience and higher service levels are well worth the price. Ace positions itself as "The helpful place." Says the company: "While others have become large and impersonal, at Ace, we've remained small and very personal. That's why we say a visit to Ace is like a visit to your neighbor." In his review on Yelp, one loyal Ace customer agrees:[11]

I have become a convert from Lowe's/Home Depot to Ace for two reasons. For one, it's much easier to get in and out of and it's closer to my house. Second, and most importantly, upon entering the store a knowledgeable employee will greet me and ask how they may help. Then they will lead me to where I need to go and boom, I'm done. At Lowe's I end up wandering around the caverns of that building—back and forth, is it here? down there? did I pass it?—until I'm exhausted. At Ace, the time and energy saved more than makes up for an increase in cost. Plus, they're very friendly.

Thus, companies must balance consumer needs not only against the feasibility and costs of meeting these needs but also against customer price preferences.

Setting Channel Objectives

Companies should state their marketing channel objectives in terms of targeted levels of customer service. Usually, a company can identify several segments wanting different levels of service. The company should decide which segments to serve and the best channels to use in each case. In each segment, the company wants to minimize the total channel cost of meeting customer service requirements.

The company's channel objectives are also influenced by the nature of the company, its products, its marketing intermediaries, its competitors, and the environment. For example, the company's size and financial situation determine which marketing functions it can handle itself and which it must give to intermediaries. Companies selling perishable products, for example, may require more direct marketing to avoid delays and too much handling.

In some cases, a company may want to compete in or near the same outlets that carry competitors' products. For example, Maytag and other appliance makers want their products displayed alongside competing brands to facilitate comparison shopping. In other cases, companies may avoid the channels used by competitors. The Pampered Chef, for instance, sells high-quality kitchen tools directly to consumers through its corps of more than 60,000 consultants worldwide rather than going head-to-head with other kitchen tool makers for scarce positions in retail stores. And Stella & Dot sells quality jewelry through more than 30,000 independent reps—called stylists—who hold Tupperware-like in-home "trunk shows."[12] GEICO and USAA primarily market insurance and banking products to consumers via phone and Internet channels rather than through agents.

Finally, environmental factors such as economic conditions and legal constraints may affect channel objectives and design. For example, in a depressed economy, producers will want to distribute their goods in the most economical way, using shorter channels and dropping unneeded services that add to the final price of the goods.

Identifying Major Alternatives

When the company has defined its channel objectives, it should next identify its major channel alternatives in terms of the *types* of intermediaries, the *number* of intermediaries, and the *responsibilities* of each channel member.

Types of Intermediaries

A firm should identify the types of channel members available to carry out its channel work. Most companies face many channel member choices. For example, until recently, Dell sold directly to final consumers and business buyers only through its sophisticated phone and online marketing channel. It also sold directly to large corporate, institutional, and government buyers using its direct sales force. However, to reach more consumers and match competitors such as Samsung and Apple, Dell now sells indirectly through retailers such as Best Buy, Staples, and Walmart. It also sells indirectly through *value-added resellers*, independent distributors and dealers that develop computer systems and applications tailored to the special needs of small and medium-sized business customers.

Using many types of resellers in a channel provides both benefits and drawbacks. For example, by selling through retailers and value-added resellers in addition to its own direct channels, Dell can reach more and different kinds of buyers. However, these are more difficult to manage and control. In addition, the direct and indirect channels compete with each other for many of the same customers, causing potential conflict. In fact, Dell often finds itself "stuck in the middle," with its direct sales reps complaining about competition from retail stores, whereas its value-added resellers complain that the direct sales reps are undercutting their business.

Number of Marketing Intermediaries

Intensive distribution
Stocking the product in as many outlets as possible.

Companies must also determine the number of channel members to use at each level. Three strategies are available: intensive distribution, exclusive distribution, and selective distribution. Producers of convenience products and common raw materials typically seek **intensive distribution**—a strategy in which they stock their products in as many outlets as possible. These products must be available where and when consumers want them. For example, toothpaste, candy, and other similar items are sold in millions of outlets to provide maximum brand exposure and consumer convenience. Kraft, Coca-Cola, Kimberly-Clark, and other consumer goods companies distribute their products in this way.

Exclusive distribution
Giving a limited number of dealers the exclusive right to distribute the company's products in their territories.

By contrast, some producers purposely limit the number of intermediaries handling their products. The extreme form of this practice is **exclusive distribution**, in which the producer gives only a limited number of dealers the exclusive right to distribute its products in their territories. Exclusive distribution is often found in the distribution of luxury brands. Breitling watches—positioned as "Instruments for Professionals" and selling at prices from $5,000 to more than $100,000—are sold by only a few authorized dealers in any given market area. For example, the brand sells through only one jeweler in Chicago and only six jewelers in the entire state of Illinois. Exclusive distribution enhances Breitling's distinctive positioning and earns greater dealer support and customer service.

Selective distribution
The use of more than one but fewer than all of the intermediaries that are willing to carry the company's products.

Between intensive and exclusive distribution lies **selective distribution**—the use of more than one but fewer than all of the intermediaries who are willing to carry a

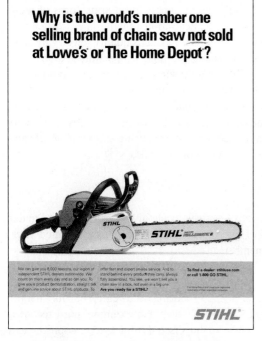

Why is the world's number one selling brand of chain saw not sold at Lowe's or The Home Depot?

>> **Selective distribution: STIHL sells its chain saws, blowers, hedge trimmers, and other products through a select corps of independent hardware and lawn and garden retailers. "We count on them every day and so can you."**

STIHL Incorporated

company's products. Most consumer electronics, furniture, and home appliance brands are distributed in this manner. >> For example, outdoor power equipment maker STIHL doesn't sell its chain saws, blowers, hedge trimmers, and other products through mass merchandisers such as Lowe's, Home Depot, or Sears. Instead, it sells through a select corps of independent hardware and lawn and garden dealers. By using selective distribution, STIHL can develop good working relationships with dealers and expect a better-than-average selling effort. Exclusive distribution also enhances the STIHL brand's image and allows for higher markups resulting from greater value-added dealer service. "We count on our select dealers every day and so can you," says one STIHL ad.

Responsibilities of Channel Members

The producer and intermediaries need to agree on the terms and responsibilities of each channel member. They should agree on price policies, conditions of sale, territory rights, and the specific services to be performed by each party. The producer should establish a list price and a fair set of discounts for the intermediaries. It must define each channel member's territory, and it should be careful about where it places new resellers.

Mutual services and duties need to be spelled out carefully, especially in franchise and exclusive distribution channels. For example, McDonald's provides franchisees with promotional support, a record-keeping system, training at Hamburger University, and general management assistance. In turn, franchisees must meet company standards for physical facilities and food quality, cooperate with new promotion programs, provide requested information, and buy specified food products.

Evaluating the Major Alternatives

Suppose a company has identified several channel alternatives and wants to select the one that will best satisfy its long-run objectives. Each alternative should be evaluated against economic, control, and adaptability criteria.

Using *economic criteria*, a company compares the likely sales, costs, and profitability of different channel alternatives. What will be the investment required by each channel alternative, and what returns will result? The company must also consider *control issues*. Using intermediaries usually means giving them some control over the marketing of the product, and some intermediaries take more control than others. Other things being equal, the company prefers to keep as much control as possible. Finally, the company must apply *adaptability criteria*. Channels often involve long-term commitments, yet the company wants to keep the channel flexible so that it can adapt to environmental changes. Thus, to be considered, a channel involving long-term commitments should be greatly superior on economic and control grounds.

Designing International Distribution Channels

International marketers face many additional complexities in designing their channels. Each country has its own unique distribution system that has evolved over time and changes very slowly. These channel systems can vary widely from country to country. Thus, global marketers must usually adapt their channel strategies to the existing structures within each country.

In some markets, the distribution system is complex, competitive, and hard to penetrate. For example, many Western companies find India's distribution system difficult to navigate. Large discount, department store, and supermarket retailers still account for only a small portion of the huge Indian market. >> Instead, most shopping is done in small neighborhood stores called *kirana* shops, run by their owners and popular because they offer personal service and credit. In addition, large Western retailers have difficulty dealing with India's complex government regulations and poor infrastructure.

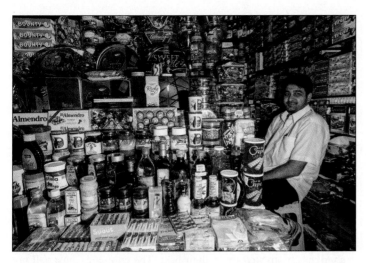

International distribution: In the huge Indian market, most shopping is done in small neighborhood stores call *kirana* shops, run by their owners and popular because they offer personal service and credit.

Frank Bienewald/imageBROKER/Alamy

Distribution systems in developing countries may be scattered, inefficient, or altogether lacking. For example, China's rural markets are highly decentralized, made of many distinct submarkets, each with its own subculture. And, because of inadequate distribution systems, most companies can profitably access only the small portion of China's massive population located in affluent cities. China's distribution system is so fragmented that logistics costs to wrap, bundle, load, unload, sort, reload, and transport goods amount to 18 percent of the nation's GDP, far higher than in most other countries. (In comparison, U.S. logistics costs account for about 8.5 percent of the nation's GDP.) After years of effort, even Walmart executives admit that they have been unable to assemble an efficient supply chain in China.[13]

Sometimes local conditions can greatly influence how a company distributes products in global markets. For example, in low-income neighborhoods in Brazil where consumers have limited access to supermarkets, Nestlé supplements its distribution with thousands of self-employed salespeople who sell Nestlé products from refrigerated carts door to door. And in big cities in Asia and Africa, where crowded streets and high real estate costs make drive-thrus impractical, fast-food restaurants such as McDonald's and KFC offer delivery. Legions of motorbike delivery drivers in colorful uniforms dispense Big Macs and buckets of chicken to customers who call in. More than 30 percent of McDonald's total sales in Egypt and 12 percent of its Singapore sales come from delivery. Similarly, for KFC, delivery accounts for nearly half of all sales in Kuwait and a third of sales in Egypt.[14]

Thus, international marketers face a wide range of channel alternatives. Designing efficient and effective channel systems between and within various country markets poses a difficult challenge. We discuss international distribution decisions further in Chapter 15.

Channel Management Decisions

Once the company has reviewed its channel alternatives and determined the best channel design, it must implement and manage the chosen channel. **Marketing channel management** calls for selecting, managing, and motivating individual channel members and evaluating their performance over time.

Selecting Channel Members

Marketing channel management
Selecting, managing, and motivating individual channel members and evaluating their performance over time.

Producers vary in their ability to attract qualified marketing intermediaries. Some producers have no trouble signing up channel members. For example, when Toyota first introduced its Lexus line in the United States, it had no trouble attracting new dealers. In fact, it had to turn down many would-be resellers.

At the other extreme are producers that have to work hard to line up enough qualified intermediaries. For example, when Timex first tried to sell its inexpensive watches through regular jewelry stores, most jewelry stores refused to carry them. The company then managed to get its watches into mass-merchandise outlets. This turned out to be a wise decision because of the rapid growth of mass merchandising.

Even established brands may have difficulty gaining and keeping their desired distribution, especially when dealing with powerful resellers. For example, you won't find Marlboro, Winston, Camel, or any other cigarette brand at your local CVS pharmacy store. CVS Caremark recently announced that it will no longer sell cigarettes in its stores, despite the resulting loss of more than $2 billion in annual sales. "This is the right thing to do," says the company. "We came to the decision that cigarettes and providing healthcare

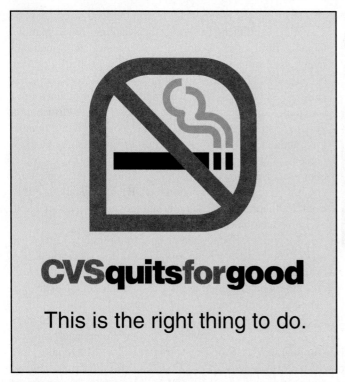

CVSquitsforgood

This is the right thing to do.

>> **Selecting channels: Even established brands may have difficulty keeping desired channels. CVS Caremark's decision to stop selling cigarettes leaves tobacco companies seeking new sales channels.**

CVS Caremark Corporation

just don't go together in the same setting." Target dropped cigarettes nearly 20 years ago, and public advocates are pressuring Walmart to do the same. If the major discount stores and other drugstore chains such as Walgreens and Rite Aid follow suit, Philip Morris, R.J. Reynolds, and other tobacco companies will have to seek new channels for selling their brands.[15]

When selecting intermediaries, the company should determine what characteristics distinguish the better ones. It will want to evaluate each channel member's years in business, other lines carried, location, growth and profit record, cooperativeness, and reputation.

Managing and Motivating Channel Members

Once selected, channel members must be continuously managed and motivated to do their best. The company must sell not only *through* the intermediaries but also *to* and *with* them. Most companies see their intermediaries as first-line customers and partners. They practice strong *partner relationship management* to forge long-term partnerships with channel members. This creates a value delivery system that meets the needs of both the company *and* its marketing partners.

In managing its channels, a company must convince suppliers and distributors that they can succeed better by working together as a part of a cohesive value delivery system. Companies must work in close harmony with others in the channel to find better ways to bring value to customers. Thus, Amazon and P&G work closely to accomplish their joint goal of selling consumer package goods profitably online. Through its Vendor Flex program, Amazon operates within P&G warehouses to reduce distribution costs and speed up delivery, benefiting both the partnering companies and the customers they jointly serve (see Marketing at Work 10.2).

Similarly, heavy-equipment manufacturer Caterpillar works hand-in-hand with its superb dealer network—together they dominate the world's construction, mining, and logging equipment business:

> Heavy-equipment manufacturer Caterpillar produces innovative, high-quality industrial equipment products. But ask anyone at Caterpillar, and they'll tell you that the most important reason for Caterpillar's dominance is its outstanding distribution network of 189 independent dealers in more than 180 countries. Dealers are the ones on the front line. Once the product leaves the factory, the dealers take over. They're the ones that customers see. So rather than selling to or through its dealers, Caterpillar treats dealers as inside partners. When a big piece of Caterpillar equipment breaks down, customers know that they can count on both Caterpillar and its dealer network for support. A strong dealer network makes for a strong Caterpillar, and the other way around. On a deeper level, dealers play a vital role in almost every aspect of Caterpillar's operations, from product design and delivery to service and support. As a result of its close partnership with dealers, the big Cat is purring. Caterpillar dominates the world's markets for heavy construction, mining, and logging equipment. Its familiar yellow tractors, crawlers, loaders, bulldozers, and trucks capture well over a third of the worldwide heavy-equipment business, more than twice that of number-two Komatsu.

Many companies are now installing integrated high-tech partnership relationship management (PRM) systems to coordinate their whole-channel marketing efforts. Just as they use customer relationship management (CRM) software systems to help manage relationships with important customers, companies can now use PRM and supply chain management (SCM) software to help recruit, train, organize, manage, motivate, and evaluate relationships with channel partners.

MARKETING AT WORK | 10.2

Amazon and P&G: Taking Channel Partnering to a New Level

Until recently, if you ordered Bounty paper towels, Pampers diapers, Charmin toilet paper, or any of the dozens of other P&G consumer products from Amazon.com, they probably came to your doorstep by a circuitous distribution route. The paper towels, for example, might well have been produced in P&G's large northeastern Pennsylvania factory and shipped by the trailer-truck load to its nearby Tunkhannock warehouse, where they were unloaded and repacked with other P&G goods and shipped to Amazon's Dinwiddie, Virginia, fulfillment center. At the fulfillment center, they were unloaded and shelved and then finally picked and packed by Amazon employees for shipment to you via UPS, FedEx, or the USPS.

But these days, in a move that could turn consumer package goods distribution upside down, Amazon and P&G are quietly blazing a new, simpler, lower-cost distribution trail for such goods. Now, for example, at the Pennsylvania warehouse, rather than reloading truckloads of P&G products and shipping them to Amazon fulfillment centers, P&G employees simply cart the goods to a fenced-off area inside their own warehouse. The fenced-in area is run by Amazon. From there, Amazon employees pack, label, and ship items directly to customers who've ordered them online. Amazon calls this venture Vendor Flex—and it's revolutionizing how people buy low-priced, low-margin everyday household products.

Amazon's Vendor Flex program offers big potential for both Amazon and supplier–partners like P&G. Americans currently buy only about 2 percent of their nonfood consumer package goods online. Boosting online sales of these staples to 6 percent—the percentage that the Internet now captures of overall retail sales—would give Amazon an additional $10 billion a year in revenues, up from the current $2 billion.

But there's a reason why household staples have lagged behind other kinds of products in online sales. Such goods have long been deemed too bulky or too cheap to justify the high shipping costs involved with Internet selling. To sell household staples profitably online, companies like Amazon and P&G must work together to streamline the distribution process and reduce costs. That's where Vendor Flex comes in.

Vendor Flex takes channel partnering to an entirely new level. Co-locating "in the same tent" creates advantages for both partners. For Amazon, Vendor Flex

reduces the costs of storing bulky items, such as diapers and toilet paper, in its own distribution centers, and it frees up space in Amazon's centers for more higher-margin goods. The sharing arrangement lets Amazon extend its consumer package goods selection without building more distribution center space. For example, the P&G warehouse also stocks other popular P&G household brands, from Gillette razors to Pantene shampoo to Tide laundry detergent. Finally, locating at the source guarantees Amazon immediate availability and facilitates quick delivery of P&G products to customers.

P&G also benefits from the Vendor Flex partnership. It saves money by cutting out the costs of transporting goods to Amazon's fulfillment centers, which in turn lets it charge more competitive prices to the e-commerce giant. And although P&G is a superb in-store brand marketer, it is still a relative newcomer to online selling, one of the company's top priorities. By partnering more closely with Amazon, P&G gets Amazon's expert help in moving its brands online.

Amazon considers household staples to be one of its next big frontiers for Internet sales. Its presence inside the P&G Pennsylvania warehouse is just the tip of the iceberg for Vendor Flex. Amazon and P&G quietly began sharing warehouse space three years ago, and the online merchant has set up shop inside at least seven other P&G distribution centers worldwide, including facilities in Japan and Germany. Amazon is also inside or talking with other major consumer goods suppliers—from Kimberly Clark to Georgia Pacific to Seventh Generation—about co-locating distribution facilities. Moreover, Amazon has invested heavily to build an infrastructure for profitably selling all kinds

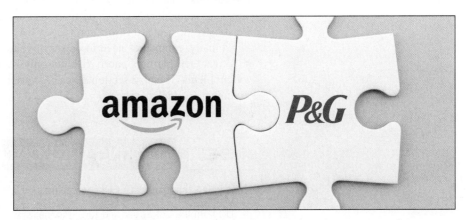

>> Partnering in the distribution channel: Under Amazon's Vendor Flex program, P&G and Amazon share warehouse facilities, creating distribution cost and delivery advantages for both partners.

Raywoo/Fotolia; Grzegorz Knec/Alamy; Grzegorz Knec/Alamy

of everyday household items to consumers online. For example, in late 2010, Amazon acquired Quidsi, the owner of Diapers.com and Soap.com, online retailers of baby products and household essentials. Since the Amazon acquisition, Quidsi has added a half-dozen new sites selling, among other things, toys (YoYo.com), pet supplies (Wag.com), premium beauty products (BeautyBar.com), and home products (Casa.com).

Vendor Flex looks like a win-win for everyone involved—Amazon, P&G, and final consumers. However, the close Amazon–P&G partnership has caused some grumbling among other important channel participants. For example, what about Walmart, P&G's largest customer by far? The giant store retailer is locked in a fierce online battle with Amazon, yet one of its largest suppliers appears to be giving Amazon preferential treatment. At the same time, Amazon's courtship of P&G may upset other important suppliers that compete with P&G on Amazon's site. Both P&G and Amazon must be careful that their close Vendor Flex relationship doesn't damage other important channel partnerships.

More broadly, some analysts assert that even with Vendor Flex, Amazon won't be able to sell products such as paper towels, detergent, or shaving cream profitably online. They reason that the margins on such items are simply too low to cover shipping costs. Amazon is already losing an estimated $1 billion to $2 billion annually on its Amazon Prime shipping program. And, they suggest, if there is money to be made by shipping a heavy jug of Tide or a bulky three-pack of Bounty

paper towels from P&G's warehouse to your front door, P&G would have been doing that long ago.

However, such doom-and-gloom predictions seem to overlook recent rapid changes in the distribution landscape, especially in online retailing. Mega-shippers like UPS and FedEx are continuing to drive down small-package delivery times and costs. And Amazon is moving aggressively toward same-day delivery in major market areas, including grocery and related items. The Vendor Flex program seems to align well with such distribution trends.

As for the Amazon–P&G Vendor Flex partnership, it looks like an ideal match for both companies. If P&G wants to be more effective in selling its brands online, what better partner could it have than Amazon, the undisputed master of online retailing? If Amazon wants to be more effective in selling household staples, what better partner could it have than P&G, the acknowledged master of consumer package goods marketing? Together, under Amazon's Vendor Flex, these respective industry leaders can flex their distribution muscles to their own benefit—and to the benefit of the consumers they jointly serve.

Sources: Serena Ng, "Soap Opera: Amazon Moves In with P&G," *Wall Street Journal*, October 15, 2013, p. A1; Andre Mouton, "Amazon Considers 'Co-Creation' with Procter & Gamble," *USA Today,* October 21, 2013, www.usatoday.com/story/tech/2013/10/21/amazon-proctor-gamble-products/3143773/; David Streitfeld, "Amazon to Raise Fees as Revenue Disappoints," *New York Times,* January 31, 2014, p. B1; and Bridget Bergin, "Amazon's Involvement with Manufacturing: When Is It Too Much?" *Manufacturing.net,* September 25, 2014, www.manufacturing.net/blogs/2014/09/amazon%E2%80%99s-involvement-with-manufacturing-when-is-it-too-much.

Evaluating Channel Members

The company must regularly check channel member performance against standards such as sales quotas, average inventory levels, customer delivery time, treatment of damaged and lost goods, cooperation in company promotion and training programs, and services to the customer. The company should recognize and reward intermediaries that are performing well and adding good value for consumers. Those that are performing poorly should be assisted or, as a last resort, replaced.

Finally, companies need to be sensitive to the needs of their channel partners. Those that treat their partners poorly risk not only losing their support but also causing some legal problems. The next section describes various rights and duties pertaining to companies and other channel members.

 LINKING THE CONCEPTS

Time for another pause. This time, compare the Caterpillar and KFC channel systems.

- Diagram the Caterpillar and KFC channel systems. How do they compare in terms of channel levels, types of intermediaries, channel member roles and responsibilities, and other characteristics? How well is each system designed?
- Assess how well Caterpillar and KFC have managed and supported their channels. With what results?

Public Policy and Distribution Decisions

For the most part, companies are legally free to develop whatever channel arrangements suit them. In fact, the laws affecting channels seek to prevent the exclusionary tactics of some companies that might keep another company from using a desired channel. Most channel law deals with the mutual rights and duties of channel members once they have formed a relationship.

Many producers and wholesalers like to develop exclusive channels for their products. When the seller allows only certain outlets to carry its products, this strategy is called *exclusive distribution*. When the seller requires that these dealers not handle competitors' products, its strategy is called *exclusive dealing*. Both parties can benefit from exclusive arrangements: The seller obtains more loyal and dependable outlets, and the dealers obtain a steady source of supply and stronger seller support. But exclusive arrangements also exclude other producers from selling to these dealers. This situation brings exclusive dealing contracts under the scope of the Clayton Act of 1914. They are legal as long as they do not substantially lessen competition or tend to create a monopoly and as long as both parties enter into the agreement voluntarily.

Exclusive dealing often includes *exclusive territorial agreements*. The producer may agree not to sell to other dealers in a given area, or the buyer may agree to sell only in its own territory. The first practice is normal under franchise systems as a way to increase dealer enthusiasm and commitment. It is also perfectly legal—a seller has no legal obligation to sell through more outlets than it wishes. The second practice, whereby the producer tries to keep a dealer from selling outside its territory, has become a major legal issue.

Producers of a strong brand sometimes sell it to dealers only if the dealers will take some or all of the rest of its line. This is called *full-line forcing*. Such *tying agreements* are not necessarily illegal, but they violate the Clayton Act if they tend to lessen competition substantially. The practice may prevent consumers from freely choosing among competing suppliers of these other brands.

Finally, producers are free to select their dealers, but their right to terminate dealers is somewhat restricted. In general, sellers can drop dealers "for cause." However, they cannot drop dealers if, for example, the dealers refuse to cooperate in a doubtful legal arrangement, such as exclusive dealing or tying agreements.

> **Author Comment**
> Marketers used to call this plain-old "physical distribution." But as these titles suggest, the topic has grown in importance, complexity, and sophistication.

Marketing Logistics and Supply Chain Management

In today's global marketplace, selling a product is sometimes easier than getting it to customers. Companies must decide on the best way to store, handle, and move their products and services so that they are available to customers in the right assortments, at the right time, and in the right place. Logistics effectiveness has a major impact on both customer satisfaction and company costs. Here we consider the nature and importance of logistics management in the supply chain, the goals of the logistics system, major logistics functions, and the need for integrated supply chain management.

Nature and Importance of Marketing Logistics

Marketing logistics (physical distribution)
Planning, implementing, and controlling the physical flow of goods, services, and related information from points of origin to points of consumption to meet customer requirements at a profit.

To some managers, marketing logistics means only trucks and warehouses. But modern logistics is much more than this. **Marketing logistics**—also called **physical distribution**—involves planning, implementing, and controlling the physical flow of goods, services, and related information from points of origin to points of consumption to meet customer requirements at a profit. In short, it involves getting the right product to the right customer in the right place at the right time profitably.

In the past, physical distribution planners typically started with products at the plant and then tried to find low-cost solutions to get them to customers. However, today's *customer-centered* logistics starts with the marketplace and works backward to the factory

>> Figure 10.5 Supply Chain
Management

                    **Inbound   Outbound
                    logistics   logistics**

| Suppliers | → | Company | → | Resellers | → | **Customers** |

Reverse logistics

Managing the supply chain calls for customer-centered thinking. Remember, it's also called the customer value delivery network.

Supply chain management
Managing upstream and downstream value-added flows of materials, final goods, and related information among suppliers, the company, resellers, and final consumers.

or even to sources of supply. Marketing logistics involves not only *outbound logistics* (moving products from the factory to resellers and ultimately to customers) but also *inbound logistics* (moving products and materials from suppliers to the factory) and *reverse logistics* (reusing, recycling, refurbishing, or disposing of broken, unwanted, or excess products returned by consumers or resellers). That is, it involves the entirety of **supply chain management**—managing upstream and downstream value-added flows of materials, final goods, and related information among suppliers, the company, resellers, and final consumers, as shown in >> **Figure 10.5**.

The logistics manager's task is to coordinate the activities of suppliers, purchasing agents, marketers, channel members, and customers. These activities include forecasting, information systems, purchasing, production planning, order processing, inventory, warehousing, and transportation planning.

Companies today are placing greater emphasis on logistics for several reasons. First, companies can gain a powerful competitive advantage by using improved logistics to give customers better service or lower prices. Second, improved logistics can yield tremendous cost savings to both a company and its customers. As much as 20 percent of an average product's price is accounted for by shipping and transport alone. This far exceeds the cost of advertising and many other marketing costs. >> American companies spend $1.39 trillion each year—about 8.2 percent of GDP—to wrap, bundle, load, unload, sort, reload, and transport goods. That's more than the total national GDPs of all but 12 countries worldwide.[16]

Shaving off even a small fraction of logistics costs can mean substantial savings. For example, Walmart is currently implementing a program of logistics improvements through more efficient sourcing, greater supply chain productivity, and better management of its more than $51 billion worth of owned inventory, and that will reduce supply chain costs by 5 to 15 percent over five years—that's a whopping $4 billion to $12 billion.[17]

Third, the explosion in product variety has created a need for improved logistics management. For example, in 1916 the typical Piggly Wiggly grocery store carried only 605 items. Today, a Piggly Wiggly carries a bewildering stock of between 20,000 and 35,000 items, depending on store size. A Walmart Supercenter store carries more than 140,000 products, 30,000 of which are grocery products.[18] Ordering, shipping, stocking, and controlling such a variety of products presents a sizable logistics challenge.

Improvements in information technology have also created opportunities for major gains in distribution efficiency. Today's companies are using sophisticated supply chain management software, Internet-based logistics systems, point-of-sale scanners, RFID tags, satellite tracking, and electronic transfer of order and payment data. Such technology lets them quickly and efficiently manage the flow of goods, information, and finances through the supply chain.

>> **Logistics: As this huge container ship suggests, American companies spent $1.39 trillion last year—8.2 percent of U.S. GDP—to wrap, bundle, load, unload, sort, reload, and transport goods.**
E.G.Pors/Shutterstock

Finally, more than almost any other marketing function, logistics affects the environment and a firm's environmental sustainability efforts. Transportation, warehousing, packaging, and other logistics functions are typically the biggest supply chain contributors to the company's environmental footprint. So many companies are now developing *green supply chains*.

Sustainable Supply Chains

Companies have many reasons for reducing the environmental impact of their supply chains. For one thing, if they don't green up voluntarily, a host of sustainability regulations enacted around the world will soon require them to. For another, many large customers—from Walmart and Nike to the federal government—are demanding it. Environmental sustainability has become an important factor in supplier selection and performance evaluation. But perhaps even more important than *having* to do it, designing sustainable supply chains is simply the *right* thing to do. It's one more way that companies can contribute to saving our world for future generations.

But that's all pretty heady stuff. As it turns out, companies have a more immediate and practical reason for turning their supply chains green. Not only are sustainable channels good for the world, they're also good for a company's bottom line. The very logistics activities that create the biggest environmental footprint—such as transportation, warehousing, and packaging—also account for a lion's share of logistics costs. Companies green up their supply chains through greater efficiency, and greater efficiency means lower costs and higher profits. In other words, developing a sustainable supply chain is not only environmentally responsible, it can also be profitable. Consider Nike:[19]

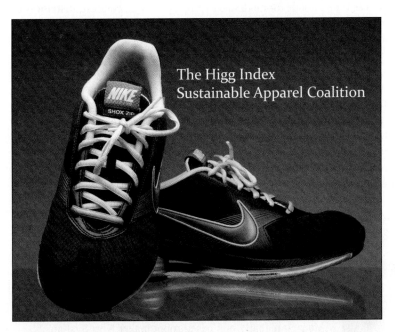

The Higg Index
Sustainable Apparel Coalition

Nike, the iconic sports shoe and apparel company, has developed a sweeping strategy for greening every phase of its supply chain. For example, Nike recently teamed with Levi's, REI, Target, and other members of the Sustainable Apparel Coalition to develop the Higg Index—a tool that measures how a single apparel product affects the environment across the entire supply chain. Nike uses the Higg Index to work with suppliers and distributors to reduce its supply chain's environmental footprint. For instance, during just the past three years, the more than 900 contract factories that make Nike footwear worldwide have reduced their carbon emissions by 6 percent, despite production increases of 20 percent. That's equivalent to an emissions savings equal to more than 1 billion car-miles.

Nike has found that even seemingly simple supply chain adjustments can produce big benefits. For example, the company sources its shoes in Asia, but most are sold in North America. Until about a decade ago, the shoes were shipped from factory to store by air freight. After analyzing distribution costs more carefully, Nike shifted a sizable portion of its cargo to ocean freight. That simple shoes-to-ships shift reduced emissions per product by 4 percent, making environmentalists smile. But it also put a smile on the faces of Nike's accountants by saving the company some $8 million a year in shipping costs.

>> **Green supply chains: Nike has developed a sweeping strategy for greening its supply chain. The Higg Index lets Nike work with suppliers and distributors to reduce the supply chain's environmental footprint while at the same time reducing its logistics costs.**

Sergio Azenha/Alamy

Goals of the Logistics System

Some companies state their logistics objective as providing maximum customer service at the least cost. Unfortunately, as nice as this sounds, no logistics system can *both* maximize customer service *and* minimize distribution costs. Maximum customer service implies rapid delivery, large inventories, flexible assortments, liberal returns policies, and other services—all of which raise distribution costs. In contrast, minimum distribution costs imply slower delivery, smaller inventories, and larger shipping lots—which represent a lower level of overall customer service.

The goal of marketing logistics should be to provide a *targeted* level of customer service at the least cost. A company must first research the importance of various distribution services to customers and then set desired service levels for each segment. The objective is to maximize *profits*, not sales. Therefore, the company must weigh the benefits of providing higher levels of service against the costs. Some companies offer less service than their competitors and charge a lower price. Other companies offer more service and charge higher prices to cover higher costs.

Major Logistics Functions

Given a set of logistics objectives, the company designs a logistics system that will minimize the cost of attaining these objectives. The major logistics functions are *warehousing, inventory management, transportation*, and *logistics information management*.

Warehousing

Production and consumption cycles rarely match, so most companies must store their goods while they wait to be sold. For example, Snapper, Toro, and other lawn mower manufacturers run their factories all year long and store up products for the heavy spring and summer buying seasons. The storage function overcomes differences in needed quantities and timing, ensuring that products are available when customers are ready to buy them.

A company must decide on *how many* and *what types* of warehouses it needs and *where* they will be located. The company might use either *storage warehouses* or *distribution centers*. Storage warehouses store goods for moderate to long periods. In contrast, **distribution centers** are designed to move goods rather than just store them. They are large and highly automated warehouses designed to receive goods from various plants and suppliers, take orders, fill them efficiently, and deliver goods to customers as quickly as possible.

For example, Amazon operates more than 50 giant distribution centers, called fulfillment centers, which fill online orders and handle returns. These centers are huge and highly automated. For example, the Amazon fulfillment center in Tracy, California, covers 1.2 million square feet (equivalent to 27 football fields). At the center, 4,000 employees control an inventory of 21 million items and ship out up to 700,000 packages a day to Amazon customers in Northern California and parts of the Pacific Northwest. During last year's Cyber Monday, Amazon's fulfillment center network filled customer orders at a rate of 426 items per second globally.[20]

Distribution center
A large, highly automated warehouse designed to receive goods from various plants and suppliers, take orders, fill them efficiently, and deliver goods to customers as quickly as possible.

Like almost everything else these days, warehousing has seen dramatic changes in technology in recent years. Outdated materials-handling methods are steadily being replaced by newer, computer-controlled systems requiring fewer employees. Computers and scanners read orders and direct lift trucks, electric hoists, or robots to gather goods, move them to loading docks, and issue invoices. For example, to improve efficiency in its massive fulfillment centers, Amazon recently purchased robot maker Kiva Systems:[21]

When you buy from Amazon, the chances are still good that your order will be plucked and packed by human hands. However, the humans in Amazon's fulfillment centers are increasingly being assisted by an army of squat, ottoman-size, day-glo orange robots. The Tracy, California, fulfillment center has 3,000 of them, "let out of their cage to scurry hither and yon bearing 6-foot-high...movable shelves." The robots bring racks of merchandise to workers, who in turn fill boxes. Dubbed the "magic shelf," racks of items simply materialize in front of workers, with red lasers pointing to items to be picked. The robots then drive off and new shelves appear. The super-efficient robots work tirelessly 16 hours a day, seven days a week. They

>> **High-tech distribution centers: Amazon employs teams of super-retrievers—day-glo orange Kiva robots—to keep its fulfillment centers humming.**

David Paul Morris/Bloomberg/Getty Images

never complain about the workload or ask for pay raises, and they are pretty much maintenance free. "When they run low on power, they head to battery-charging terminals," notes one observer, "or, as warehouse personnel say, 'They get themselves a drink of water.'"

Inventory Management

Inventory management also affects customer satisfaction. Here, managers must maintain the delicate balance between carrying too little inventory and carrying too much. With too little stock, the firm risks not having products when customers want to buy. To remedy this, the firm may need costly emergency shipments or production. Carrying too much inventory results in higher-than-necessary inventory-carrying costs and stock obsolescence. Thus, in managing inventory, firms must balance the costs of carrying larger inventories against resulting sales and profits.

Many companies have greatly reduced their inventories and related costs through *just-in-time* logistics systems. With such systems, producers and retailers carry only small inventories of parts or merchandise, often enough for only a few days of operations. New stock arrives exactly when needed rather than being stored in inventory until being used. Just-in-time systems require accurate forecasting along with fast, frequent, and flexible delivery so that new supplies will be available when needed. However, these systems result in substantial savings in inventory-carrying and inventory-handling costs.

Marketers are always looking for new ways to make inventory management more efficient. In the not-too-distant future, handling inventory might even become fully automated. For example, in Chapter 3 we discussed RFID or "smart tag" technology, by which small transmitter chips are embedded in or placed on products and packaging for everything from flowers and razors to tires. Such "smart" products could make the entire supply chain—which accounts for nearly 75 percent of a product's cost—intelligent and automated.

Companies using RFID know, at any time, exactly where a product is located physically within the supply chain. "Smart shelves" would not only tell them when it's time to reorder but also place the order automatically with their suppliers. Such exciting new information technology is revolutionizing distribution as we know it. Many large and resourceful marketing companies, such as Walmart, Macy's, P&G, Kraft, and IBM, are investing heavily to make the full use of RFID technology a reality.

Transportation

The choice of transportation carriers affects the pricing of products, delivery performance, and the condition of goods when they arrive—all of which will affect customer satisfaction. In shipping goods to its warehouses, dealers, and customers, the company can choose among five main transportation modes: truck, rail, water, pipeline, and air, along with an alternative mode for digital products—the Internet.

Trucks have increased their share of transportation steadily and now account for 40 percent of total cargo ton-miles (a ton of freight moved one mile) transported in the United States. U.S. trucks travel more than 397 billion miles a year—more than double the distance traveled 25 years ago—carrying 9.2 billion tons of freight. According to the U.S. Department of Transportation, 70 percent of all the freight tonnage moved in the United States goes on trucks. Trucks are highly flexible in their routing and time schedules, and they can usually offer faster service than railroads. They are efficient for short hauls of high-value merchandise. Trucking firms have evolved in recent years to become full-service providers of global transportation services. For example, large trucking firms now offer everything from satellite tracking, Internet-based shipment management, and logistics planning software to cross-border shipping operations.[22]

Railroads account for 26 percent of the total cargo ton-miles moved. They are one of the most cost-effective modes for shipping large amounts of bulk products—coal, sand, minerals, and farm and forest products—over long distances. In recent years, railroads have increased their customer services by designing new equipment to handle special categories of goods, providing flatcars for carrying truck trailers by rail (piggyback), and providing in-transit services such as the diversion of shipped goods to other destinations en route and the processing of goods en route.

Multimodal transportation
Combining two or more modes of transportation.

Water carriers, which account for 7 percent of the cargo ton-miles, transport large amounts of goods by ships and barges on U.S. coastal and inland waterways. Although the cost of water transportation is very low for shipping bulky, low-value, nonperishable products such as sand, coal, grain, oil, and metallic ores, water transportation is the slowest mode and may be affected by the weather. *Pipelines*, which account for 17 percent of the cargo ton-miles, are a specialized means of shipping petroleum, natural gas, and chemicals from sources to markets. Most pipelines are used by their owners to ship their own products.

Although *air* carriers transport less than 1 percent of the cargo ton-miles of the nation's goods, they are an important transportation mode. Airfreight rates are much higher than rail or truck rates, but airfreight is ideal when speed is needed or distant markets have to be reached. Among the most frequently airfreighted products are perishables (such as fresh fish, cut flowers) and high-value, low-bulk items (technical instruments, jewelry). Companies find that airfreight also reduces inventory levels, packaging costs, and the number of warehouses needed.

The *Internet* carries digital products from producer to customer via satellite, cable, phone wire, or wireless signal. Software firms, the media, music and video companies, and education all make use of the Internet to transport digital products. The Internet holds the potential for lower product distribution costs. Whereas planes, trucks, and trains move freight and packages, digital technology moves information bits.

>> Shippers also use **multimodal transportation**—combining two or more modes of transportation. Eight percent of the total cargo ton-miles are moved via multiple modes. *Piggyback* describes the use of rail and trucks; *fishyback*, water and trucks; *trainship*, water and rail; and *airtruck*, air and trucks. Combining modes provides advantages that no single mode can deliver. Each combination offers advantages to the shipper. For example, not only is piggyback cheaper than trucking alone, but it also provides flexibility and convenience. Numerous logistics companies provide single-source multi-modal transportation solutions.

Most logistics carriers now recognize the importance of multimodal transportation, regardless of their main line of activity. For example, Union Pacific, primarily a rail carrier, offers "door-to-door shipping" coordination for its business customers. According to one Union Pacific ad: "The end of the tracks is just the beginning of our capabilities. Every day, we coordinate rail, trucks, and ocean carriers for thousands of companies—many without tracks to their doors. That would be a challenge if we were just a railroad, but we're not. We're logistics experts."

>> Transportation: In shipping goods to their warehouses, dealers, and customers, companies can choose among many transportation modes, including truck, rail, water, pipeline, and air. Much of today's shipping requires multiple modes.

Thanapun/Shutterstock

Logistics Information Management

Companies manage their supply chains through information. Channel partners often link up to share information and make better joint logistics decisions. From a logistics perspective, flows of information, such as customer transactions, billing, shipment and inventory levels, and even customer data, are closely linked to channel performance. Companies need simple, accessible, fast, and accurate processes for capturing, processing, and sharing channel information.

Information can be shared and managed in many ways, but most sharing takes place through *electronic data interchange* (EDI), the digital exchange of data between organizations, which primarily is transmitted via the Internet. Walmart, for example, requires EDI links with its more than 100,000 suppliers through its Retail Link sales data system. If new suppliers don't have the required EDI capability, Walmart will work with them to find and implement the needed tools.[23]

In some cases, suppliers might actually be asked to generate orders and arrange deliveries for their customers. Many large retailers—such as Walmart and Home Depot—work closely with major suppliers such as P&G or Moen to set up *vendor-managed inventory (VMI)* systems or *continuous inventory replenishment* systems. Using VMI, the customer shares real-time data on sales and current inventory levels with the supplier. The supplier then takes full responsibility for managing inventories and deliveries. Some retailers even go so far as to shift inventory and delivery costs to the supplier. Such systems require close cooperation between the buyer and seller.

Integrated Logistics Management

Integrated logistics management
The logistics concept that emphasizes teamwork—both inside the company and among all the marketing channel organizations—to maximize the performance of the entire distribution system.

Today, more and more companies are adopting the concept of **integrated logistics management**. This concept recognizes that providing better customer service and trimming distribution costs require *teamwork*, both inside the company and among all the marketing channel organizations. Inside, the company's various departments must work closely together to maximize its own logistics performance. Outside, the company must integrate its logistics system with those of its suppliers and customers to maximize the performance of the entire distribution network.

Cross-Functional Teamwork inside the Company

Most companies assign responsibility for various logistics activities to many different departments—marketing, sales, finance, operations, and purchasing. Too often, each function tries to optimize its own logistics performance without regard for the activities of the other functions. However, transportation, inventory, warehousing, and information management activities interact, often in an inverse way. Lower inventory levels reduce inventory-carrying costs. But they may also reduce customer service and increase costs from stockouts, backorders, special production runs, and costly fast-freight shipments. Because distribution activities involve strong trade-offs, decisions by different functions must be coordinated to achieve better overall logistics performance.

The goal of integrated supply chain management is to harmonize all of the company's logistics decisions. Close working relationships among departments can be achieved in several ways. Some companies have created permanent logistics committees composed of managers responsible for different physical distribution activities. Companies can also create supply chain manager positions that link the logistics activities of functional areas. For example, P&G has created product supply managers who manage all the supply chain activities for each product category. Many companies have a vice president of logistics or a supply chain VP with cross-functional authority.

Finally, companies can employ sophisticated, system-wide supply chain management software, now available from a wide range of software enterprises large and small, from SAP and Oracle to Infor and Logility. ≫ For example, Oracle's supply chain management software solutions help companies to "gain sustainable advantage and drive innovation by transforming their traditional supply chains into integrated value chains." It coordinates every aspect of the supply chain, from value chain collaboration to inventory optimization to transportation and logistics management. The important thing is that the company must coordinate its logistics, inventory investments, demand forecasting, and marketing activities to create high market satisfaction at a reasonable cost.

≫ **Integrated logistics management: Oracle's supply chain management software solutions help companies to "gain sustainable advantage and drive innovation by transforming their traditional supply chains into integrated value chains."**

Oracle Corporation

Building Logistics Partnerships

Companies must do more than improve their own logistics. They must also work with other channel partners to improve whole-channel distribution. The members of a marketing channel are linked closely in creating customer value and building customer relationships. One company's distribution system is another company's supply system. The success of each channel member depends on the performance of the entire supply chain. For example, furniture retailer IKEA can create its stylish but affordable furniture and deliver the "IKEA lifestyle" only if its entire supply chain—consisting of thousands of merchandise designers and suppliers, transport companies, warehouses, and service providers—operates at maximum efficiency and with customer-focused effectiveness.

Smart companies coordinate their logistics strategies and forge strong partnerships with suppliers and customers to improve customer service and reduce channel costs. Many companies have created *cross-functional, cross-company teams*. For example, Nestlé's Purina pet food unit has a team of dozens of people working in Bentonville, Arkansas, the home base of Walmart. The Purina Walmart team members work jointly with their counterparts at Walmart to find ways to squeeze costs out of their distribution system. Working together benefits not only Purina and Walmart but also their shared, final consumers.

Other companies partner through *shared projects*. For example, many large retailers conduct joint in-store programs with suppliers. Home Depot allows key suppliers to use its stores as a testing ground for new merchandising programs. The suppliers spend time at Home Depot stores watching how their product sells and how customers relate to it. They then create programs specially tailored to Home Depot and its customers. Clearly, both the supplier and the customer benefit from such partnerships. The point is that all supply chain members must work together in the cause of bringing value to final consumers.

Third-Party Logistics

Third-party logistics (3PL) provider
An independent logistics provider that performs any or all of the functions required to get a client's product to market.

Although most big companies love to make and sell their products, many loathe the associated logistics "grunt work." They detest the bundling, loading, unloading, sorting, storing, reloading, transporting, customs clearing, and tracking required to supply their factories and get products to their customers. They hate it so much that many firms outsource some or all of their logistics to **third-party logistics (3PL) providers** such as Ryder, Penske Logistics, BAX Global, DHL Logistics, FedEx Logistics, and UPS Business Solutions.

For example, UPS knows that, for many companies, logistics can be a real nightmare. But logistics is exactly what UPS does best. To UPS, logistics is today's most powerful force for creating competitive advantage. "We ♥ logistics," proclaims UPS. "It makes running your business easier. It can make your customers happier. It's a whole new way of thinking." As one UPS ad concludes: "We love logistics. Put UPS to work for you and you'll love logistics too."

At one level, UPS can simply handle a company's package shipments. But on a deeper level, UPS can help businesses sharpen their own logistics systems to cut costs and serve customers better. At a still deeper level, companies can let UPS take over and manage part or all of their logistics operations. For example, consumer electronics maker Toshiba lets UPS handle its entire laptop PC repair process—lock, stock, and barrel. And UPS not only delivers packages for online shoe and accessories marketer Zappos, it also manages Zappos's important and complex order returns process in an efficient, customer-pleasing way.[24]

3PL providers like UPS can help clients tighten up sluggish, overstuffed supply chains; slash inventories; and get products to customers more quickly and reliably. According to one report, 86 percent of *Fortune* 500 companies use 3PL (also called *outsourced logistics* or *contract logistics*) services. General Motors, P&G, and Walmart each use 50 or more 3PLs.[25]

Companies use third-party logistics providers for several reasons. First, because getting the product to market is their main focus, using these providers makes the most sense, as they can often do it more efficiently and at lower cost. Outsourcing typically results in a 10 to 25 percent cost savings.[26] Second, outsourcing logistics frees a company to focus more intensely on its core business. Finally, integrated logistics companies understand increasingly complex logistics environments.

MyMarketingLab

If assigned by your instructor, complete the questions marked with the ⭐ from the EOC Discussion Questions section in the MyLab. To complete the Marketing by the Numbers problems found in this section, go to your Assignments in the MyLab.

REVIEWING AND EXTENDING THE CONCEPTS

CHAPTER REVIEW AND CRITICAL THINKING

Objectives Review

Some companies pay too little attention to their distribution channels; others, however, have used imaginative distribution systems to gain a competitive advantage. A company's channel decisions directly affect every other marketing decision. Management must make channel decisions carefully, incorporating today's needs with tomorrow's likely selling environment.

 OBJECTIVE 10-1 Explain why companies use marketing channels and discuss the functions these channels perform. (pp 300–303)

In creating customer value, a company can't go it alone. It must work within an entire network of partners—a value delivery network—to accomplish this task. Individual companies and brands don't compete; their entire value delivery networks do.

Most producers use intermediaries to bring their products to market. They forge a *marketing channel* (or *distribution channel*)—a set of interdependent organizations involved in the process of making a product or service available for use or consumption by the consumer or business user. Through their contacts, experience, specialization, and scale of operation, intermediaries usually offer the firm more than it can achieve on its own.

Marketing channels perform many key functions. Some help *complete transactions* by gathering and distributing *information* needed for planning and aiding exchange, developing and spreading persuasive *communications* about an offer, performing *contact* work (finding and communicating

with prospective buyers), *matching* (shaping and fitting the offer to the buyer's needs), and entering into *negotiation* to reach an agreement on price and other terms of the offer so that ownership can be transferred. Other functions help to *fulfill* the completed transactions by offering *physical distribution* (transporting and storing goods), *financing* (acquiring and using funds to cover the costs of the channel work), and *risk taking* (assuming the risks of carrying out the channel work.

 OBJECTIVE 10-2 Discuss how channel members interact and how they organize to perform the work of the channel. (pp 304–311)

The channel will be most effective when each member assumes the tasks it can do best. Ideally, because the success of individual channel members depends on overall channel success, all channel firms should work together smoothly. They should understand and accept their roles, coordinate their goals and activities, and cooperate to attain overall channel goals. By cooperating, they can more effectively sense, serve, and satisfy the target market.

In a large company, the formal organization structure assigns roles and provides needed leadership. But in a distribution channel composed of independent firms, leadership and power are not formally set. Traditionally, distribution channels have lacked the leadership needed to assign roles and manage conflict. In recent years, however, new types of channel organizations have appeared that provide stronger leadership and improved performance.

OBJECTIVE 10-3 **Identify the major channel alternatives open to a company. (pp 311–315)**

Channel alternatives vary from direct selling to using one, two, three, or more intermediary *channel levels*. Marketing channels face continuous and sometimes dramatic change. Three of the most important trends are the growth of *vertical, horizontal,* and *multichannel marketing systems*. These trends affect channel cooperation, conflict, and competition.

Channel design begins with assessing customer channel service needs and company channel objectives and constraints. The company then identifies the major channel alternatives in terms of the *types* of intermediaries, the *number* of intermediaries, and the *channel responsibilities* of each. Each channel alternative must be evaluated according to economic, control, and adaptive criteria. *Channel management* calls for selecting qualified intermediaries and motivating them. Individual channel members must be evaluated regularly.

 OBJECTIVE 10-4 **Explain how companies select, motivate, and evaluate channel members. (pp 315–319)**

Producers vary in their ability to attract qualified marketing intermediaries. Some producers have no trouble signing up channel members, whereas others have to work hard to line up enough qualified intermediaries. When selecting intermediaries, the company should evaluate each channel member's qualifications and select those that best fit its channel objectives.

Once selected, channel members must be continuously motivated to do their best. The company must sell not only *through* the intermediaries but also *with* them. It should forge strong partnerships with channel members to create a

marketing system that meets the needs of both the manufacturer *and* the partners.

 OBJECTIVE 10-5 **Discuss the nature and importance of marketing logistics and integrated supply chain management. (pp 319–326)**

Marketing logistics (or *physical distribution*) is an area of potentially high cost savings and improved customer satisfaction. Marketing logistics addresses not only *outbound logistics* but also *inbound logistics* and *reverse logistics*. That is, it involves the entire *supply chain management*—managing value-added flows between suppliers, the company, resellers, and final users. No logistics system can both maximize customer service and minimize distribution costs. Instead, the goal of logistics management is to provide a *targeted* level of service at the least cost. The major logistics functions are *warehousing, inventory management, transportation*, and *logistics information management*.

The *integrated supply chain management concept* recognizes that improved logistics requires teamwork in the form of close working relationships across functional areas inside the company and across various organizations in the supply chain. Companies can achieve logistics harmony among functions by creating cross-functional logistics teams, integrative supply manager positions, and senior-level logistics executive positions with cross-functional authority. Channel partnerships can take the form of cross-company teams, shared projects, and information-sharing systems. Today, some companies are outsourcing their logistics functions to third-party logistics (3PL) providers to save costs, increase efficiency, and gain faster and more effective access to global markets.

Key Terms

Objective 10-1
Value delivery network (p 300)
Marketing channel (distribution channel)
    (p 301)
Channel level (p 303)
Direct marketing channel (p 303)
Indirect marketing channel (p 303)

Objective 10-2
Channel conflict (p 304)
Conventional distribution channel
    (p 305)
Vertical marketing system (VMS)
    (p 305)

Corporate VMS (p 306)
Contractual VMS (p 306)
Franchise organization (p 306)
Administered VMS (p 307)
Horizontal marketing system (p 307)
Multichannel distribution system
    (p 308)
Disintermediation (p 308)

Objective 10-3
Marketing channel design (p 311)
Intensive distribution (p 313)
Exclusive distribution (p 313)
Selective distribution (p 313)

Objective 10-4
Marketing channel management
    (p 315)

Objective 10-5
Marketing logistics (physical
    distribution) (p 319)
Supply chain management (p 320)
Distribution center (p 322)
Multimodal transportation (p 324)
Integrated logistics management
    (p 325)
Third-party logistics (3PL) provider
    (p 326)

Discussion Questions

10-1. Compare and contrast upstream and downstream partners in a company's supply chain. Explain why *value delivery network* might be a better term to use than *supply chain*. (AACSB: Communication)

⭐ **10-2.** Compare direct marketing channels and indirect marketing channels. Name the various types of resellers in marketing channels. (AACSB: Communication)

10-3. Name and describe the three strategies available when determining the number of marketing intermediaries. (AACSB: Communication; Reflective Thinking)

10-4. List and briefly describe the major logistics functions. Provide an example of a decision a logistics manager would make for each major function. (AACSB: Communication; Reflective Thinking)

10-5. What are third-party logistics providers, and why do companies use them? (AACSB: Communication)

Critical Thinking Exercises

10-6. The most common type of contractual vertical marketing system is the franchise organization. Visit the International Franchise Association at www.franchise.org and find a franchise that interests you. Write a report describing the franchise. Identify what type of franchise it represents and research the market opportunities for that product or service. (AACSB: Communication; Use of IT; Reflective Thinking)

⭐ **10-7.** Form a small group and research the distribution challenges faced by companies expanding into emerging international markets such as China, Africa, and India.

Develop a multimedia presentation on how one company overcame these challenges. (AACSB: Communication; Reflective Thinking; Use of IT)

10-8. The term *last mile* is often used in the telecommunications industry. Research what is going on in this industry and how the *last mile* has evolved in recent years, and then predict where it is heading in the future. What companies are major players in the *last mile,* and how does the concept of *net neutrality* fit in? (AACSB: Communication; Reflective Thinking)

MINICASES AND APPLICATIONS

Online, Mobile, and Social Media Marketing   Self-Publishing

Do you think that you have what it takes to write a best-selling novel? In the past, authors had to go through traditional publishing houses to print and distribute their work, but technology has turned the publishing industry on its head. Although aspiring authors could always self-publish a book, selling it through the traditional channels—bookstores—was only a pipe dream for most. But that has all changed thanks to the Internet and social media. Amazon's Kindle Direct Publishing is a popular platform for self-publishers, but others such as Smashwords, Author Solutions, and Fast-Pencil offer similar services with hundreds of thousands of authors and titles. For example, Amanda Hocking's self-published e-book sales caught the attention of a publisher, and now the former social worker is a millionaire. Self-published books have grown nearly 300 percent in less than 10 years, with the majority being e-books. Almost 40 percent of readers now own e-readers, such as Kindles and iPads. That creates

opportunities for anyone wanting to distribute their works to these avid readers. For example, after being turned away by traditional publishers, author Christine Bronstein created her own online social network to promote her book, *Nothing but the Truth, So Help Me God: 51 Women Reveal the Power of Positive Female Connection*, which launched on Amazon and Barnes & Noble sites.

10-9. Visit a self-publishing site such as Amazon's Kindle Direct (https://kdp.amazon.com) and create a presentation to give to aspiring authors about distributing their works this way. (AACSB: Communication; Use of IT; Reflective Thinking)

⭐ **10-10.** What other industries' channels of distribution have been affected dramatically by online, mobile, and social media? (AACSB: Communication; Reflective Thinking)

Marketing Ethics   Trucker Rest Rules

Large trucks are an important piece of the logistics chain. However, there were 333,000 large truck crashes in 2012, resulting in almost 3,800 fatalities, the majority being drivers or passengers of other vehicles, not the truck driver. One accident in 2014 caused a public uproar when a Walmart truck driver fell asleep at the wheel after being awake for 24 hours and crashed into another car, killing one person and critically injuring others, one being a well-known comedian. The U.S. Department of Transportation's Federal Motor Carrier Safety Administration enacted tougher hours-of-service rules that went into effect in July 2013. One report claimed that the industry would lose $1 billion in lost productivity as a result of these rules, while another concluded the industry would realize

almost $500 million in benefit from reduced driver mortality. The new rules have caused considerable controversy and have caused hardships for drivers. As one driver put it, "If the wheels aren't turning, you're not earning."

10-11. Research the DOT's trucker hours-of-service rules and write a brief report outlining the rules. What is the current status of the 2013 rules? (AACSB: Communication; Reflective Thinking)

10-12. Do you think it is ethical that the trucking industry wants the rules repealed? Explain why or why not. (AACSB: Communication; Reflective Thinking; Ethical Reasoning)

Marketing by the Numbers   Tyson Expanding Distribution

Tyson Foods is the largest U.S. beef and chicken supplier, processing more than 100,000 head of cattle and 40-plus million chickens weekly. Primary distribution channels are supermarket meat departments. However, the company is now expanding distribution into convenience stores. There are almost 150,000 gas stations and convenience stores where the company would like to sell hot Buffalo chicken bites near the checkout. This is a promising channel, as sales are growing considerably at these retail outlets and profit margins on prepared foods are higher than selling raw meat to grocery stores. Tyson will have to hire 10 more sales representatives at a salary of $45,000 each to expand into this distribution channel because many of these types of stores are

independently owned. Each convenience store is expected to generate an average of $50,000 in revenue for Tyson. Refer to Appendix 3: Marketing by the Numbers to answer the following questions.

10-13. If Tyson's contribution margin is 30 percent on this product, what increase in sales will it need to break even on the increase in fixed costs to hire the new sales reps? (AACSB: Communication; Analytical Reasoning)

10-14. How many new retail accounts must the company acquire to break even on this tactic? What average number of accounts must each new rep acquire? (AACSB: Communication; Analytical Reasoning)

Video Case   Progressive

Progressive has attained top-tier status in the insurance industry by focusing on innovation. Progressive was the first company to offer drive-in claims service, installment payment of premiums, and 24/7 customer service. But perhaps Progressive's most innovative moves involve its channels of distribution. Whereas most insurance companies distribute via intermediary agents or direct-to-consumer methods, Progressive was one of the first to see value in doing both. In the late 1980s, it augmented its agency distribution with a direct 800-number channel.

Two decades ago, Progressive moved into the digital future by becoming the first major insurer to launch a Web site. Soon after, it allowed customers to buy auto insurance policies online in real time. Today, customers can use Progressive's

Web site to do everything from managing their own account information to reporting claims directly. Progressive even offers one-stop concierge claim service.

After viewing the Progressive video segment, answer the following questions about marketing channels.

10-15. Apply the concept of the supply chain to Progressive.

10-16. Using the model of consumer and business channels found in the chapter, sketch out as many channels for Progressive as you can. How does each of these channels meet distinct customer needs?

10-17. Discuss the various ways that Progressive has had an impact on the insurance industry.

Company Cases   10 Apple Pay/15 7-Eleven

See Appendix 1 for cases appropriate for this chapter. **Case 10, Apple Pay: Taking Moble Payments Mainstream.** In the past, Apple has disrupted marketing channels with revolutionary products. With Apple Pay, Apple is proving once again that it can deliver. **Case 15, 7-Eleven: Adapting to The World's Many Cultures.** Just a convenience store in the U.S., 7-Eleven has a strong global presence by catering to different distribution strategies throughout the world.

MyMarketingLab

If assigned by your instructor, complete these writing sections from your Assignments in the MyLab.

10-18. Why does channel conflict occur? Name and describe the various types of channel conflict. (AACSB: Communication)

10-19. Should retailers be responsible for safety conditions in garment supplier factories in other countries? Discuss. (AACSB: Written and Oral Communication; Reflective Thinking; Ethical Understanding and Reasoning)

11 Retailing and Wholesaling

CHAPTER ROAD MAP | Objective Outline

OBJECTIVE 11-1 Explain the role of retailers in the distribution channel and describe the major types of retailers. Retailing (334–340)

OBJECTIVE 11-2 Describe the major retailer marketing decisions. Retailer Marketing Decisions (341–348)

OBJECTIVE 11-3 Discuss the major trends and developments in retailing. Retailing Trends and Developments (348–354)

OBJECTIVE 11-4 Explain the major types of wholesalers and their marketing decisions. Wholesaling (355–360)

Previewing the Concepts

We now look more deeply into the two major intermediary marketing channel functions: retailing and wholesaling. You already know something about retailing—retailers of all shapes and sizes serve you every day, both in stores and online. However, you probably know much less about the hoard of wholesalers working behind the scenes. In this chapter, we examine the characteristics of different kinds of retailers and wholesalers, the marketing decisions they make, and trends for the future.

When it comes to retailers, you have to start with Walmart. This megaretailer's phenomenal success has resulted from an unrelenting focus on bringing value to its customers. Day in and day out, Walmart lives up to its promise: "Save money. Live better." That focus on customer value has made Walmart the world's largest retailer, the world's largest company. Yet, despite its huge success, Walmart still faces plenty of fresh opportunities and some daunting challenges as well.

First Stop

Walmart: The World's Largest *Retailer*—the World's Largest *Company*

Walmart is almost unimaginably big. It's the world's largest retailer—the world's largest *company*. It rang up an incredible $487 billion in sales last year—more than double the sales of competitors Costco, Target, Macy's, Sears, Kmart, JCPenney, and Kohl's *combined*.

Walmart is the number-one seller in many categories of consumer products, including groceries, clothing, toys, and pet care products. It sells nearly 2.7 times as many groceries as Kroger, the leading grocery-only food retailer, and its clothing and shoe sales alone exceed the total revenues of Macy's Inc., parent of both Macy's and Bloomingdale's department stores. Incredibly, Walmart sells an estimated 30 percent of the disposable diapers purchased in the United States each year, 30 percent of the hair care products, 30 percent of all health and beauty products, 26 percent of the toothpaste, 25 percent of all groceries, and 20 percent of the pet food. On average, worldwide, Walmart serves more than 250 million customers per week through more than 11,000 stores in 27 countries and online in 10 countries.

It's also hard to fathom Walmart's impact on the U.S. economy. It's the nation's largest employer—one out of every 246 men, women, and children in the United States is a Walmart associate. The chain's average profit is $3.1 million per *hour*. If Walmart were a separate country, it would be the world's 26th largest economy. By one estimate, through its own low prices and impact on competitors' prices, Walmart saves the average American household $2,500 each year, equivalent to more than six months' worth of groceries for the average family.

What's behind this spectacular success? First and foremost, Walmart is passionately dedicated to its long-time, low-price value proposition and what its low prices mean to customers: "Save money. Live better." To accomplish this mission, Walmart offers a broad selection of goods at "unbeatable low prices," day in and day out. No other retailer has come nearly so close to mastering the concepts of everyday low prices and one-stop shopping. Sam Walton himself summed up Walmart's mission best when he said, "If we work together, we'll lower the cost of living for everyone … we'll give the world an opportunity to see what it's like to save and have a better life."

How does Walmart make money with such low prices? Walmart is a lean, mean distribution machine—it has the lowest cost structure in the industry. Low costs let the giant retailer charge lower prices while remaining profitable. Lower prices attract more shoppers, producing more sales, making the company more efficient, and enabling it to lower prices even more.

Walmart's low costs result from superior operations management, sophisticated information technology, and good-old "tough buying." Its huge, fully automated distribution centers supply stores efficiently. It employs an information technology system that the U.S. Department of Defense would envy, giving managers around the world instant access to sales and operating information. And Walmart is known for using its massive scale to wring low prices from suppliers. "Don't expect a greeter and don't expect friendly," said one supplier's sales executive after a visit to Walmart's buying offices. "Once you

» At Walmart: "Save money. Live better." Says Walmart's CEO, "We're obsessed with delivering value to customers."
Beth Hall/Bloomberg/Getty Images

are ushered into one of the spartan little buyers' rooms, expect a steely eye across the table and be prepared to cut your price. They are very, very focused people, and they use their buying power more forcefully than anyone else in America."

Despite its incredible success over the past five decades, mighty Walmart faces some weighty challenges ahead. Having grown so big, the maturing giant is having difficulty maintaining the rapid growth rates of its youth. Think about this: To grow just 7 percent next year, Walmart will have to add more than $33 billion in new sales. That's a sales *increase* greater than the *total* sales of all but the top 96 companies on the *Fortune* 500, including companies such as McDonald's, Macy's, American Express, Xerox, Goodyear, Nike, or nearly three JCPenneys. The bigger Walmart gets, the harder it is to maintain a high rate of growth.

To keep growing, Walmart has pushed into new, faster-growing product and service lines, including organic foods, store brands, in-store health clinics, and consumer financial services. To combat trendier competitors such as Target, Walmart even gave itself a modest image face-lift. It spruced up its stores with a cleaner, brighter, more open look and less clutter to make them more shopper friendly. In search of broader appeal, it has added new, higher-quality products. Many Walmart stores now carry a selection of higher-end consumer electronics products, from Samsung ultra-thin televisions to Dell and Toshiba laptops to Apple iPhones and iPads.

> Day in and day out, giant Walmart lives up to its promise: "Save money. Live better." Its obsession with customer value has made Walmart not only the world's largest retailer but also the world's largest *company*.

Despite its massive presence, Walmart still has room to expand geographically. Believe it or not, there are plenty of places in the United States that still don't have a Walmart. And the giant retailer is expanding rapidly in international markets, where sales grew to nearly 19 percent of total sales at $136 billion. Walmart also faces substantial growth opportunities—and challenges—in online, mobile, and social media commerce (see the Chapter 9 opening story on Walmart versus Amazon). Its online sales of an estimated $14 billion account for only about 2.7 percent of total sales, making it a distant online also-ran next to Amazon.com, which last year topped $89 billion in online sales. Walmart lists "winning in global e-commerce" as one of its top priorities for the future.

As Walmart continues to adapt and grow, however, one thing seems certain. The giant retailer may add new product lines and services. It might go digital and global. It might brush up its look and image. But Walmart has no intention of ever giving up its core low-price value proposition. After all, Walmart is and always will be a discounter. "I don't think Walmart's ... ever going to be edgy," says a Walmart marketer. "I don't think that fits our brand. Our brand is about saving people money" so that they can live better.[1]

T he Walmart story sets the stage for examining the fast-changing world of today's resellers. This chapter looks at *retailing* and *wholesaling*. In the first section, we look at the nature and importance of retailing, the major types of store and non-store retailers, the decisions retailers make, and the future of retailing. In the second section, we discuss these same topics as they apply to wholesalers.

Retailing

Retailing
All the activities involved in selling products or services directly to final consumers for their personal, nonbusiness use.

Retailer
A business whose sales come *primarily* from retailing.

Shopper marketing
Focusing the entire marketing process on turning shoppers into buyers as they approach the point of sale, whether during in-store, online, or mobile shopping.

What is retailing? We all know that Costco, Home Depot, Macy's, and Target are retailers, but so are Amazon.com, the local Hampton Inn, and a doctor seeing patients. **Retailing** includes all the activities involved in selling products or services directly to final consumers for their personal, nonbusiness use. Many institutions—manufacturers, wholesalers, and retailers—do retailing. But most retailing is done by **retailers**, businesses whose sales come *primarily* from retailing. Retailing plays a very important role in most marketing channels. Last year, retailers accounted for more than $5 trillion of sales to final consumers.[2]

Retailing: Connecting Brands with Consumers

Retailers connect brands with consumers in the final phases of the buying process and at the point of purchase. In fact, many marketers are now embracing the concept of **shopper marketing**, focusing the entire marketing process—from product and brand development to logistics, promotion, and merchandising—toward turning shoppers into buyers as they approach the point of sale. Of course, every well-designed marketing effort focuses on customer buying behavior. What differentiates the concept of shopper marketing is the suggestion that these efforts should be coordinated around the shopping process itself.

Shopper marketing builds around what P&G calls the "First Moment of Truth"—the critical three to seven seconds that a shopper considers a product on a store shelf.[3]
>> However, the dramatic growth of online and mobile shopping has added new dimensions to shopper marketing. The retailing "moment of truth" no longer takes place only in stores. Instead, Google defines a "zero moment of truth," when consumers begin the buying process by searching for and learning about products online.

Today's consumers are increasingly *omni-channel buyers,* who make little distinction between in-store and online shopping and for whom the path to a retail purchase runs across multiple channels. For these buyers, a particular purchase might consist of researching a product online and buying it from an online retailer, without ever setting foot in a retail store. Alternatively, they might use a smartphone to research a purchase on the fly, or even while in retail store aisles. For example, it's common to see a consumer examining an item

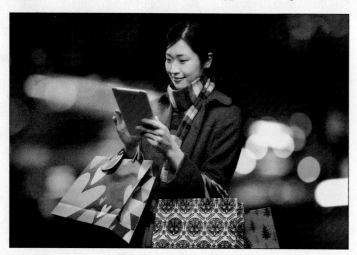

>> Shopper marketing: The dramatic growth in online and mobile shopping has added new dimensions to "point of purchase." Influencing consumers' buying decisions as they shop now involves omni-channel efforts aimed at integrating in-store, online, and mobile shopping.

Betsie Van der Meer/Getty Images

on a shelf at Target while at the same time using a mobile app to look for coupons or check product reviews and prices at Amazon.com.

Thus, these days, shopper marketing and the "point of purchase" go well beyond in-store buying. They involve consumers working across multiple channels as they shop. Influencing consumers' buying decisions calls for **omni-channel retailing**, creating a seamless cross-channel buying experience that integrates in-store, online, and mobile shopping.[4]

Although most retailing is still done in retail stores, in recent years direct and online retailing have been growing much faster than store retailing. We discuss direct, online, and omni-channel retailing in detail later in this chapter and in Chapter 14. For now, we will focus on store retailing.

Omni-channel retailing
Creating a seamless cross-channel buying experience that integrates in-store, online, and mobile shopping.

Types of Retailers

Retail stores come in all shapes and sizes—from your local hairstyling salon or family-owned restaurant to national specialty chain retailers such as REI or Williams-Sonoma to megadiscounters such as Costco or Walmart. The most important types of retail stores are described in ≫ Table 11.1 and discussed in the following sections. They can be classified in terms of several characteristics, including the *amount of service* they offer, the breadth and depth of their *product lines*, the *relative prices* they charge, and how they are *organized*.

Amount of Service
Different types of customers and products require different amounts of service. To meet these varying service needs, retailers may offer one of three service levels: self-service, limited service, and full service.

≫ Table 11.1	Major Store Retailer Types	
Type	**Description**	**Examples**
Specialty store	A store that carries a narrow product line with a deep assortment, such as apparel stores, sporting-goods stores, furniture stores, florists, and bookstores.	REI, Sunglass Hut, Sephora, Williams-Sonoma
Department store	A store that carries several product lines—typically clothing, home furnishings, and household goods—with each line operated as a separate department managed by specialist buyers or merchandisers.	Macy's, Sears, Neiman Marcus
Supermarket	A relatively large, low-cost, low-margin, high-volume, self-service operation designed to serve the consumer's total needs for grocery and household products.	Kroger, Safeway, SuperValu, Publix
Convenience store	A relatively small store located near residential areas, open 24/7, and carrying a limited line of high-turnover convenience products at slightly higher prices.	7-Eleven, Circle K, Speedway, Sheetz
Discount store	A store that carries standard merchandise sold at lower prices with lower margins and higher volumes.	Walmart, Target, Kohl's
Off-price retailer	A store that sells merchandise bought at less-than-regular wholesale prices and sold at less than retail. These include *factory outlets* owned and operated by manufacturers; *independent off-price retailers* owned and run by entrepreneurs or by divisions of larger retail corporations; and *warehouse (or wholesale) clubs* selling a limited selection of goods at deep discounts to consumers who pay membership fees.	Mikasa (factory outlet); TJ Maxx (independent off-price retailer); Costco, Sam's Club, BJ's (warehouse clubs)
Superstore	A very large store that meets consumers' total needs for routinely purchased food and nonfood items. This includes *supercenters*, combined supermarket and discount stores, and *category killers*, which carry a deep assortment in a particular category.	Walmart Supercenter, SuperTarget, Meijer (discount stores); Best Buy, Petco, Staples, Bed Bath & Beyond (category killers)

Self-service retailers serve customers who are willing to perform their own *locate-compare-select* process to save time or money. Self-service is the basis of all discount operations and is typically used by retailers selling convenience goods (such as supermarkets) and nationally branded, fast-moving shopping goods (such as Target or Kohl's). *Limited-service retailers*, such as Sears or JCPenney, provide more sales assistance because they carry more shopping goods about which customers need information. Their increased operating costs result in higher prices.

Full-service retailers, such as high-end specialty stores (for example, Tiffany or Williams-Sonoma) and first-class department stores (such as Nordstrom or Neiman Marcus) assist customers in every phase of the shopping process. Full-service stores usually carry more specialty goods for which customers need or want assistance or advice. They provide more services, which results in much higher operating costs. These higher costs are passed along to customers as higher prices.

Product Line

Retailers can also be classified by the length and breadth of their product assortments. Some retailers, such as **specialty stores**, carry narrow product lines with deep assortments within those lines. Today, specialty stores are flourishing. The increasing use of market segmentation, market targeting, and product specialization has resulted in a greater need for stores that focus on specific products and segments.

By contrast, **department stores** carry a wide variety of product lines. In recent years, middle-market department stores have been squeezed between more focused and flexible specialty stores on the one hand and more efficient, lower-priced discounters on the other. In response, many have added promotional pricing to meet the discount threat. Others have stepped up the use of store brands and single-brand *designer shops* to compete with specialty stores. Still others are trying direct and online selling. Service remains the key differentiating factor. Retailers such as Nordstrom, Saks, Neiman Marcus, and other high-end department stores are doing well by emphasizing exclusive merchandise and high-quality service.

Supermarkets are the most frequently visited type of retail store. Today, however, they are facing slow sales growth because of slower population growth and an increase in competition from discounters (Walmart, Costco, and Dollar General) on the one hand and specialty food stores (Whole Foods Market, Trader Joe's, ALDI, Sprouts) on the other. Supermarkets' share of U.S. packaged foods sales slipped from 53 percent in 1998 to 37 percent in 2012.[5] Supermarkets also have been hit hard by the rapid growth of out-of-home eating over the past two decades.

In the battle for "share of stomachs," some supermarkets have moved upscale, providing improved store environments and higher-quality food offerings, such as from-scratch bakeries, gourmet deli counters, natural foods, and fresh seafood departments. Others, however, are competing head-on with large discounters such as Costco and Walmart by cutting costs, establishing more-efficient operations, and lowering prices. ❯❯ WinCo, a fast-growing regional discount-grocery chain in the western United States, has done this successfully:[6]

> You probably haven't heard of WinCo yet. But you can bet that Walmart and Costco are keeping a close eye on the small discount-grocery chain. In fact, according to one supermarket-retailing expert, WinCo is fast becoming "Walmart's worst nightmare." In its markets, WinCo (short for "Winning Company") positions itself directly against mighty Walmart as "The Supermarket Low Price Leader." And that's more than just a slogan—WinCo doesn't just match Walmart's prices; it often undercuts them. WinCo keeps prices low through low-cost, efficient operations. The chain often cuts out distributors and buys goods at lower costs directly from farms and factories. Its large, efficient, no-frills stores carry a limited assortment of basic fast-moving merchandise. WinCo's customers help to keep costs down by bagging their own groceries and paying cash (no credit cards accepted). Finally, the employee-owned chain has a reputation for treating its

Specialty store
A retail store that carries a narrow product line with a deep assortment within that line.

Department store
A retail store that carries a wide variety of product lines, each operated as a separate department managed by specialist buyers or merchandisers.

Supermarket
A large, low-cost, low-margin, high-volume, self-service store that carries a wide variety of grocery and household products.

❯❯ In the battle for "share of stomach," regional supermarket chain WinCo successfully competes head-on with large discounters such as Costco and Walmart. It's rapidly becoming "Walmart's worst nightmare."
WinCo Foods, Inc.

employees right in terms of pay, benefits, and pensions. The result is a cheerful, highly motivated, productive workforce that genuinely contributes to the company's low-cost success. Why should Walmart and Costco worry about WinCo? The rapidly growing chain expects to double in size every five to seven years. According to the retailing expert, "WinCo is really unstoppable at this point."

Convenience store

A small store, located near a residential area, that is open long hours seven days a week and carries a limited line of high-turnover convenience goods.

Convenience stores are small stores that carry a limited line of high-turnover convenience goods. After several years of stagnant sales, these stores are now experiencing growth. Many convenience store chains have tried to expand beyond their primary market of young, blue-collar men by redesigning their stores to attract female shoppers. They are shedding the image of a "truck stop" where men go to buy gas, beer, cigarettes, or shriveled hotdogs on a roller grill and are instead offering freshly prepared foods and cleaner, safer, more-upscale environments.

For example, consider 7-Eleven, long known as a haven for Slurpees, Big Gulps, hot dogs spinning on a roller, self-serve nachos, smokes, beer, and bags of chips. The convenience chain now employs a team of culinary and food science experts who are stocking its shelves with an expanding menu of healthier snack and meal items under 400 calories, such as yogurt parfaits, salads, bags of carrots and celery, fresh subs, Smart turkey sandwiches on whole wheat bread, and a Bistro Snack Protein Pack—carrots, hummus, pita rounds, cheddar cheese, and grapes in a meal-to-go box. The chain is also resizing and single-sizing existing products. Over the next three years, 7-Eleven plans to boost its sales of high-margin fresh foods to 20 percent, twice the current level.[7]

Superstore

A store much larger than a regular supermarket that offers a large assortment of routinely purchased food products, nonfood items, and services.

Superstores are much larger than regular supermarkets and offer a large assortment of routinely purchased food products, nonfood items, and services. Walmart, Target, Meijer, and other discount retailers offer *supercenters*, very large combination food and discount stores. Whereas a traditional grocery store brings in about $482,000 a week in sales, a supercenter brings in about $1.4 million a week. Walmart, which opened its first supercenter in 1988, now has more than 3,400 supercenters in the United States and is opening new ones at a rate of about 120 per year.[8]

Category killer

A giant specialty store that carries a very deep assortment of a particular line.

Recent years have also seen the rapid growth of superstores that are actually giant specialty stores, the so-called **category killers** (for example, Best Buy, Home Depot, Petco, and Bed Bath & Beyond). They feature stores the size of airplane hangars that carry a very deep assortment of a particular line. Category killers are found in a wide range of categories, including electronics, home-improvement products, books, baby gear, toys, home goods, party goods, sporting goods, and even pet supplies.

Service retailer

A retailer whose product line is actually a service; examples include hotels, airlines, banks, colleges, and many others.

Finally, for many retailers, the product line is actually a service. **Service retailers** include hotels and motels, banks, airlines, restaurants, colleges, hospitals, movie theaters, tennis clubs, bowling alleys, repair services, hair salons, and dry cleaners. Service retailers in the United States are growing faster than product retailers.

Relative Prices

Retailers can also be classified according to the prices they charge (see Table 11.1). Most retailers charge regular prices and offer normal-quality goods and customer service. Others offer higher-quality goods and service at higher prices. Retailers that feature low prices are discount stores and "off-price" retailers.

Discount store

A retail operation that sells standard merchandise at lower prices by accepting lower margins and selling at higher volume.

Discount Stores. A **discount store** (for example, Target, Kohl's, or Walmart) sells standard merchandise at lower prices by accepting lower margins and selling at higher volume. The early discount stores cut expenses by offering few services and operating in warehouse-like facilities in low-rent, heavily traveled districts. Today's discounters have improved their store environments and increased their services while at the same time keeping prices low through lean, efficient operations.

Leading "big-box" discounters, such as Walmart and Target, now dominate the retail scene. However, even "small-box" discounters are thriving in the current economic environment. For example, dollar stores are now today's fastest-growing retail format. Back in the day, dollar stores sold mostly odd-lot assortments of novelties, factory overruns, closeouts, and outdated merchandise—most priced at $1. Not anymore. Dollar General, the

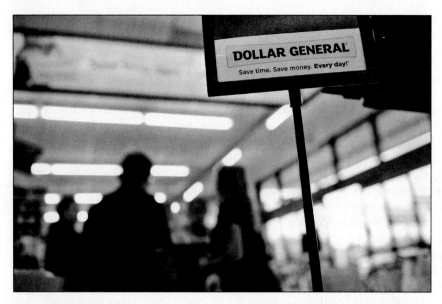

>> Discounter Dollar General, the nation's largest small-box discount retailer, makes a powerful value promise for the times: "Save time. Save money. Every day."

Daniel Acker/Bloomberg/Getty Images

nation's largest small-box discount retailer, makes a powerful value promise for the times: "Save time. Save money. Every day":[9]

>> Dollar General's slogan isn't just for show. It's a careful statement of the store's value promise. The retailer's goal is to keep shopping simple by offering only a selected assortment of popular brands at everyday low prices in small and convenient locations. Dollar General's slimmed-down product line and smaller stores (you could fit more than 25 Dollar General stores inside the average Walmart supercenter) add up to a quick trip—the average customer is in and out of the store in less than 10 minutes. And its prices on the popular brand name products it carries are an estimated 20 to 40 percent lower than grocery store prices. Put it all together, and things are sizzling right now at Dollar General. Moreover, the fast-growing retailer is well positioned for the future. We "see signs of a new consumerism," says Dollar General's CEO, "as people shift where they shop, switch to lower-cost brands, and stay generally more frugal." Convenience and low prices, it seems, never go out of style.

Off-price retailer

A retailer that buys at less-than-regular wholesale prices and sells at less than retail.

Independent off-price retailer

An off-price retailer that is independently owned and operated or a division of a larger retail corporation.

Factory outlet

An off-price retailing operation that is owned and operated by a manufacturer and normally carries the manufacturer's surplus, discontinued, or irregular goods.

Off-Price Retailers. As the major discount stores traded up, a new wave of **off-price retailers** moved in to fill the ultralow-price, high-volume gap. Ordinary discounters buy at regular wholesale prices and accept lower margins to keep prices down. By contrast, off-price retailers buy at less-than-regular wholesale prices and charge consumers less than retail. Off-price retailers can be found in all areas, from food, clothing, and electronics to no-frills banking and discount brokerages.

The three main types of off-price retailers are *independents, factory outlets*, and *warehouse clubs*. **Independent off-price retailers** either are independently owned and run or are divisions of larger retail corporations. Although many off-price operations are run by smaller independents, most large off-price retailer operations are owned by bigger retail chains. >> Examples include store retailers such as TJ Maxx, Marshalls, and HomeGoods, all owned by TJX Companies, and online sellers such as Overstock.com. TJ Maxx promises brand name and designer fashions for 20 to 60 percent off department store prices. How does it fulfill this promise? Its buyers are constantly on the lookout for deals. "So when a designer overproduces and department stores overbuy," says the company, "we swoop in, negotiate the lowest possible price, and pass the savings on."[10]

Factory outlets—manufacturer-owned and operated stores by firms such as J.Crew, Gap, Levi Strauss, and others—sometimes group together in *factory outlet malls* and *value-retail centers*. At these centers, dozens of outlet stores offer prices as much as 50 percent below retail on a wide range of mostly surplus, discounted, or irregular goods. Whereas outlet malls consist primarily of manufacturers' outlets, value-retail centers combine manufacturers' outlets with off-price retail stores and department store clearance outlets.

These malls in general are now moving upscale—and even dropping *factory* from their descriptions. A growing number of outlet malls now feature luxury brands such as Coach, Polo Ralph Lauren, Dolce & Gabbana, Giorgio Armani, Burberry, and Versace. As consumers become more value-minded, even upper-end retailers are accelerating their factory outlet strategies, placing more emphasis on outlets such as Nordstrom Rack, Neiman Marcus Last Call, Bloomingdale's Outlets, and Saks Off 5th. Many companies now regard outlets not simply as a way of disposing of problem merchandise but as an additional way of gaining business for fresh merchandise. For example, 90 percent of the merchandise sold in Neiman Marcus's Last Call outlets is made specifically for those stores.[11] The combination of highbrow brands and lowbrow prices found at outlets provides powerful shopper appeal, especially in thriftier times.

>> **Off-price retailers: Independent off-price retailer TJX Companies negotiates the lowest prices on brand name goods and passes the savings on to customers.**

Matthew Staver/Bloomberg/Getty Images

Warehouse club

An off-price retailer that sells a limited selection of brand name grocery items, appliances, clothing, and other goods at deep discounts to members who pay annual membership fees.

Corporate chains

Two or more outlets that are commonly owned and controlled.

Warehouse clubs (also known as *wholesale clubs* or *membership warehouses*), such as Costco, Sam's Club, and BJ's, operate in huge, drafty, warehouse-like facilities and offer few frills. However, they offer ultralow prices and surprise deals on selected branded merchandise. Warehouse clubs have grown rapidly in recent years. These retailers appeal not only to low-income consumers seeking bargains on bare-bones products but also to all kinds of customers shopping for a wide range of goods, from necessities to extravagances.

Consider Costco, now the world's second-largest retailer, behind only Walmart. Low price is an important part of Costco's equation, but what really set Costco apart are the products it carries and the sense of urgency that it builds into the Costco shopper's store experience:[12]

> Costco is a retail treasure hunt, where both low-end and high-end products meet deep-discount prices. Alongside the gallon jars of peanut butter and 2,250-count packs of Q-Tips, Costco offers an ever-changing assortment of high-quality products—even luxuries—all at tantalizingly low margins. Last year, Costco sold more than 109 million hot dog and soda combinations (still only $1.50, as they have been for more than 27 years). At the same time, it sold more than 100,000 carats of diamonds. It is the nation's biggest baster of poultry (nearly 70,000 rotisserie chickens a year at $4.99) but also the country's biggest seller of fine wines (including the likes of a Chateau Cheval Blanc Premier Grand Cru Classe at $1,750 a bottle).
>
> Each Costco store is a theater of retail that creates buying urgency and excitement. Mixed in with its regular stock of staples, Costco features a glittering, constantly shifting array of one-time specials, such as discounted Prada bags, Calloway golf clubs, or Kenneth Cole bags—deals you just won't find anywhere else. In fact, of the 3,600 items that Costco carries, 1,000 are designated as "treasure items" (Costco's words). The changing assortment and great prices keep people of all kinds coming back, wallets in hand. There was a time when only the great, unwashed masses shopped at off-price retailers, but Costco has changed all that. Now, even people who don't have to pinch pennies shop there.

Organizational Approach

Although many retail stores are independently owned, others band together under some form of corporate or contractual organization. >> **Table 11.2** describes four major types of retail organizations—*corporate chains, voluntary chains, retailer cooperatives*, and *franchise organizations*.

Corporate chains are two or more outlets that are commonly owned and controlled. They have many advantages over independents. Their size allows them to buy in large quantities at lower prices and gain promotional economies. They can hire specialists to deal with areas such as pricing, promotion, merchandising, inventory control, and sales forecasting.

>> Table 11.2   Major Types of Retail Organizations

Type	Description	Examples
Corporate chain	Two or more outlets that are commonly owned and controlled. Corporate chains appear in all types of retailing but they are strongest in department stores, discount stores, food stores, drugstores, and restaurants.	Macy's (department stores), Target (discount stores), Kroger (grocery stores), CVS (drugstores)
Voluntary chain	Wholesaler-sponsored group of independent retailers engaged in group buying and merchandising.	Independent Grocers Alliance (IGA), Western Auto (auto supply), True Value (hardware)
Retailer cooperative	Group of independent retailers who jointly establish a central buying organization and conduct joint promotion efforts.	Associated Grocers (groceries), Ace Hardware (hardware)
Franchise organization	Contractual association between a franchisor (a manufacturer, wholesaler, or service organization) and franchisees (independent businesspeople who buy the right to own and operate one or more units in the franchise system).	McDonald's, Subway, Pizza Hut, Jiffy Lube, Meineke Mufflers, 7-Eleven

Franchise
A contractual association between a manufacturer, wholesaler, or service organization (a franchisor) and independent businesspeople (franchisees) who buy the right to own and operate one or more units in the franchise system.

The great success of corporate chains caused many independents to band together in one of two forms of contractual associations. One is the *voluntary chain*—a wholesaler-sponsored group of independent retailers that engages in group buying and common merchandising. Examples include the Independent Grocers Alliance (IGA), Western Auto, and True Value hardware stores. The other type of contractual association is the *retailer cooperative*—a group of independent retailers that bands together to set up a jointly owned, central wholesale operation and conduct joint merchandising and promotion efforts. Examples are Associated Grocers and Ace Hardware. These organizations give independents the buying and promotion economies they need to meet the prices of corporate chains.

Another form of contractual retail organization is a **franchise**. The main difference between franchise organizations and other contractual systems (voluntary chains and retail cooperatives) is that franchise systems are normally based on some unique product or service; a method of doing business; or the trade name, goodwill, or patent that the franchisor has developed. Franchising has been prominent in fast-food restaurants, motels, health and fitness centers, auto sales and service dealerships, and real estate agencies.

However, franchising covers a lot more than just burger joints and fitness centers. Franchises have sprung up to meet just about any need. For example, Mad Science Group franchisees put on science programs for schools, scout troops, and birthday parties. H&R Block provides tax-preparation services, and Supercuts offers affordable, anytime, walk-in haircuts. Mr. Handyman provides repair services for homeowners, while Merry Maids tidies up their houses. And Soccer Shots offers programs that give kids ages two to eight an introduction to basic soccer skills at daycare centers, schools, and parks.

Franchises now command about 45 percent of all retail sales in the United States. These days, it's nearly impossible to stroll down a city block or drive on a city street without seeing a McDonald's, Subway, Jiffy Lube, or Holiday Inn. One of the best-known and most successful franchisers, McDonald's, now has more than 36,000 stores in more than 100 countries, including more than 14,000 in the United States. It serves 70 million customers a day and racks up more than $98 billion in annual system-wide sales. More than 80 percent of McDonald's restaurants worldwide are owned and operated by franchisees. Gaining fast is Subway, one of the fastest-growing franchise restaurants, with system-wide sales of $18.8 billion and more than 43,000 shops in 110 countries, including more than 27,000 in the United States.[13]

>> **Franchising covers a lot more than just burger joints and fitness centers. For example, Soccer Shots franchisees offer programs that give kids ages two to eight an introduction to basic soccer skills.**
Soccer Shots Franchising

LINKING THE CONCEPTS

Pause here and think about all the different kinds of retailers you deal with regularly, many of which overlap in the products they carry.

● Pick a familiar product: a camera, microwave oven, lawn tool, or something else. Shop for this product at two very different store types, say, a discount store or category killer on the one hand and a department store or smaller specialty store on the other. Then shop for it online. Compare the three shopping outlets on product assortment, services, and prices. If you were going to buy the product, where would you buy it and why?

● What does your shopping trip suggest about the futures of the competing store formats that you sampled?

Retailer Marketing Decisions

Retailers are always searching for new marketing strategies to attract and hold customers. In the past, retailers attracted customers with unique product assortments and more or better services. Today, the assortments and services of various retailers are looking more and more alike. You can find most consumer brands not only in department stores but also in mass-merchandise discount stores, off-price discount stores, and all over the Internet. Thus, it's now more difficult for any one retailer to offer exclusive merchandise.

Service differentiation among retailers has also eroded. Many department stores have trimmed their services, whereas discounters have increased theirs. In addition, customers have become smarter and more price sensitive. They see no reason to pay more for identical brands, especially when service differences are shrinking. For all these reasons, many retailers today are rethinking their marketing strategies.

As shown in >> Figure 11.1, retailers face major marketing decisions about *segmentation and targeting, store differentiation and positioning*, and the *retail marketing mix*.

Segmentation, Targeting, Differentiation, and Positioning Decisions

Retailers must first segment and define their target markets and then decide how they will differentiate and position themselves in these markets. Should they focus on upscale, midscale, or downscale shoppers? Do target shoppers want variety, depth of assortment, convenience, or low prices? Until they define and profile their markets, retailers cannot make consistent decisions about product assortment, services, pricing, advertising, store décor, online and mobile site design, or any of the other decisions that must support their positions.

Too many retailers, even big ones, fail to clearly define their target markets and positions. For example, what market does Sears target? For what is the department store known? What is its value proposition versus, say, Walmart on one hand and Macy's or Nordstrom on the other? If you're having trouble answering those questions, you're not alone—so is Sears's management:

> For well over a century, Sears was America's iconic retailer. Its well-known slogan, "Where America Shops," was more than just an advertising tagline—it was a meaningful positioning statement. Almost every American relied on Sears for everything from basic apparel and home goods to appliances and tools. But during the past two decades, once-mighty Sears has lost its way. Squeezed between lower-priced big-box discount stores on the one hand and trendier, more targeted upscale department and specialty stores on the other, Sears has gotten lost in the murky middle. Its old "Where America Shops" positioning has

>> Figure 11.1 Retailer Marketing Strategies

As with other types of marketers, the name of the game for retailers is to find the customer value-driven marketing strategy and mix that will let them create value for customers and capture value in return. Think of Target's "Expect More. Pay Less." value proposition. And Olive Garden's "When you're here, you're family."

little meaning these days for a store with little more than one-twentieth the sales of competitor Walmart. It seems that about the only thing Sears has going for it these days is that everything it sells is always on sale. However, price is not a convincing value proposition for Sears, which has trouble matching the low prices of competitors such as Walmart, Target, or Kohl's. Now in a financial tailspin, some analysts even predict that once-dominant Sears will soon disappear entirely. To once again position Sears as the place "Where America Shops," the retailer must first answer the question "Why should people shop at Sears?"

By contrast, successful retailers define their target markets well and position themselves strongly. For example, Trader Joe's has established its "cheap gourmet" value proposition. Walmart is powerfully positioned on low prices and what those always-low prices mean to its customers. And highly successful outdoor products retailer Bass Pro Shops positions itself strongly as being "as close to the Great Outdoors as you can get indoors!"

With solid targeting and positioning, a retailer can compete effectively against even the largest and strongest competitors. For example, compare little Which Wich Superior Sandwiches to giant Subway. Which Wich has only about 300 stores and $175 million in sales; Subway has nearly 43,000 stores worldwide and system-wide sales of $18.8 billion. How does Which Wich compete with one of the world's largest franchise chains? It doesn't—at least not directly. >> Which Wich succeeds by carefully positioning itself *away* from Subway:[14]

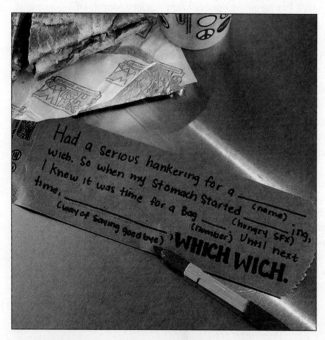

>> Retail targeting and positioning: Which Wich Superior Sandwiches succeeds by positioning itself strongly *away* from larger competitors. It offers more than 50 varieties of unique customizable "wiches" and a "positive energy" from being in the store—both unlike anything you'll find at Subway.

Courtesy of Which Wich® Superior Sandwiches. www.WhichWich.com

Sandwiches are where it's at these days. If you're craving something between two slices of bread, you have no end of choices, from a basic Subway sub to more exotic creations from Panera Bread, McAlister's Deli, Au Bon Pain, or Potbelly Sandwich Shop. But Which Wich Superior Sandwiches stands out from the pack as the ultimate "have it your way" sandwich place. Which Wich invites you to "Crave something interesting." It offers more than 50 varieties of customizable "wiches"—unlike anything you'll find at Subway—from the signature Wicked (loaded with five meats and three cheeses) to unique items such as the Thank You Turkey (with stuffing and cranberry sauce) and the Elvis Wich (peanut butter, bacon, sweet honey, and fresh banana). Customers use red Sharpies to mark up preprinted menus on sandwich bags, starting with one of the 50 sandwich bases and customizing it with their choices of everything from breads to mustards to veggies. The possibilities for personalization are endless. And instead of standing in a cafeteria-style line as you would at Subway, at Which Wich you hand your bag to the cashier, grab a drink and chips, have a seat, and wait to hear your name called. While you're eating, use the red Sharpie to draw on your bag, then hang your "artwork" on the community wall. It's not just the food that sets Which Wich apart, says the company, "it's a feeling, that positive energy you get from being in our store."

So, Which Wich can't match Subway's massive economies of scale, incredible volume purchasing power, ultraefficient logistics, and low prices. But then again, it doesn't even try. By positioning itself away from Subway and other large competitors, Which Wich has become one of the nation's fastest-growing fast-casual restaurant chains.

Product Assortment and Services Decision

Retailers must decide on three major product variables: product assortment, services mix, and store atmosphere.

The retailer's *product assortment* should differentiate it while matching target shoppers' expectations. One strategy is to offer a highly targeted product assortment: Lane Bryant carries plus-size clothing, Brookstone offers an unusual assortment of gadgets and gifts, and BatteryDepot.com offers about every imaginable kind of replacement battery. Alternatively, a retailer can differentiate itself by offering merchandise that no other competitor carries, such as store brands or national brands on which it holds exclusive rights. For example, Kohl's gets exclusive rights to carry well-known labels such as Simply Vera by Vera Wang and a Food Network-branded line of kitchen tools, utensils, and appliances. Kohl's also offers its own private-label lines, such as Sonoma, Croft & Barrow, Candies, and Apt. 9.

The *services mix* can also help set one retailer apart from another. For example, some retailers invite customers to ask questions or consult service representatives in person or via phone or keyboard. Home Depot offers a diverse mix of services to do-it-yourselfers, from "how-to" classes and "do-it-herself" and kid workshops to a proprietary credit card. Nordstrom delivers top-notch service and promises to "take care of the customer, no matter what it takes."

The *store's atmosphere* is another important element in the reseller's product arsenal. Retailers want to create a unique store experience, one that suits the target market and moves customers to buy. Many retailers practice *experiential retailing.* >> For example, L.L.Bean has turned its flagship retail store in Freeport, Maine, into an adventure center where customers can experience the store's goods before buying them:[15]

Customers don't just shop at L.L.Bean's flagship store in Freeport; they *experience* it. Sure, the company's several stores on the Freeport campus offer a full assortment of outdoor apparel and gear. But more than that, they create outdoor experiences. For example, along with selling camping, fishing, hiking, boating, home furnishings, and other goods, L.L.Bean offers a slate of free in-store, hands-on clinics in which knowledgeable experts share tips and techniques to help customers prepare for their own outdoor adventures. Clinics cover everything from tying knots and fishing flies to roadside bike repair to compass navigation and even stargazing. Customers seeking more depth can sign up for one of L.L.Bean's Outdoor Discovery Schools programs in snowshoeing, cross-country skiing, stand-up paddleboarding, fly fishing, biking, birdwatching, canoeing, hunting, or any of a dozen other outdoor activities.

L.L.Bean has turned the Freeport campus into a full-fledged outdoor adventure center, where customers can hike, bike, golf, kayak, or even go seal watching or fishing at nearby Cisco Bay. The adventure center pulls in more customers, who in turn buy more goods. L.L.Bean's flagship store and Freeport campus attract more than 3 million visitors a year, making them Maine's second-most popular tourist destination behind Acadia National Park. In addition, the Freeport campus has become a model for additional L.L.Bean adventure centers in other states from Vermont to Illinois.

>> **Experiential retailing: L.L.Bean has turned its flagship retail store in Freeport, Maine, into an adventure center where customers can experience goods before buying them.**

Photos courtesy of L.L.Bean

Today's digital technologies present many new challenges and opportunities for shaping retail experiences. The surge in online and mobile shopping has changed retail customer behaviors and expectations. As a result, a wide range of store retailers—from high-tech sellers such as AT&T to high-touch sellers like Audi and Build-A-Bear—are digitizing the in-store experience. They are merging the physical and digital worlds to create new-age experiential retailing environments (see Marketing at Work 11.1).

Successful retailers carefully orchestrate virtually every aspect of the consumer store experience. The next time you step into a retail store—whether it sells consumer electronics, hardware, or high fashion—stop and carefully consider your surroundings. Think about the store's layout and displays. Listen to the background music. Check out the colors. Smell the smells. Chances are good that everything in the store, from the layout and lighting to the music and even the colors and smells, has been carefully orchestrated to help shape the customers' shopping experiences—and open their wallets.

For example, retailers choose the colors in their logos and interiors carefully: Black suggests sophistication, orange is associated with fairness and affordability, white signifies

MARKETING AT WORK   11.1

Digitizing the In-Store Retail Experience

There's a flashy new store on Michigan Avenue in downtown Chicago's high-end retail district known as the Magnificent Mile. The store is bright and inviting, with sights and sounds designed to pull people in and get them to linger longer. Customers sit at any of dozens of stations, sampling the latest phone apps and electronic gadgetry. Enthusiastic, iPad-wielding associates mingle with customers, talking tech and dispensing hands-on help and advice. With 130 digital screens and an 18-foot video wall, every aspect of the open space is designed to engage customers about future wireless technologies and services. It feels more like a techy neighborhood hangout than a place to buy products.

A gleaming new Apple store? Think again. This is AT&T's new flagship store. But the resemblance to Apple's ground-breaking retail concept is no mistake. Dozens of diverse retail chains—from high-tech sellers like AT&T to high-touch merchants such as Audi and Build-A-Bear—are remaking their stores in the image of Apple's open marketplace prototypes. But even more, with the surge in digital, online, and mobile technologies invading the retail space, these store chains are blazing new ground. They are digitizing in-store retail—transforming the traditional in-store experience by infusing digital and online technologies into their physical store environments. It's the future of store retailing, but it's already happening.

When they first walk into AT&T's new store, customers quickly realize that it's like nothing they've seen before. "One of my favorite comments from a recent patron … was that it was like walking into a Web site," says AT&T's president of retail. Organized into zones and stations, the store's technology immerses customers in multimedia and interpersonal experiences. In the Explorer Lounge, customers can play with and learn about the latest apps. At the App Bar, "apptenders" give one-on-one or group demos, which are displayed on the Apps Wall for others to follow along. The 18-foot-high Connect Wall features a giant interactive video screen that displays customer interactions with content and product information, visible to the entire store and to passersby outside. Lifestyle Boutiques organize products, apps, and accessories by customer needs, such as Get Fit, Be Productive, and Share Your Life. At the Experience Platform, customers can interact with AT&T products for home security and automation, entertainment, music, and automobiles.

Although it might seem that the store is all about products and technologies, the real focus is on the customer experience. The store is designed to let customers interact with devices and services, understand how they work, and experience the impact the devices can have on their lives. In one store area, for example, customers can experience how Jawbone's Up Bracelet

integrates with a smartphone app to monitor health and fitness by tracking sleep, eating, and movement patterns. In another, a Nissan Leaf is set up to interactively demonstrate various auto-based apps that help customers solve problems, such as monitoring how fast their teenagers are driving. The store is a physical manifestation of AT&T's "It's what you do with what we do" marketing campaign. "We used to sell phones," says the AT&T executive. "Now we've shifted to offering solutions."

Digitizing in-store retail is an obvious fit for a technology retailer like AT&T. But companies in a wide range of other industries are also pioneering the concept. Take German auto-maker Audi, for instance. In the lead-up to the XXX Summer Olympics in London, Audi threw open the doors to its first Audi City, a stunningly innovative digitized showroom in London's busy Piccadilly Circus area.

Rather than displaying a sea of shiny new vehicles, the Audi City showroom contains very few actual cars, and future Audi showrooms may have none at all. Instead, Audi City is all-digital. Prospective customers use touchscreens and Kinect-style cameras to design and manipulate virtual, life-size cars of their dreams displayed on massive screens surrounding the showroom space. When they've finished, a video shows the car they've designed in action, complete with the exact sound of the chosen engine in full stereo fidelity. The car is then loaded onto a memory stick that the customer can take for later remembering and sharing.

The idea of buying a car without actually seeing it flies in the face of auto retailing tradition. But these car-buying times are anything but traditional. Audi sees digitization as a way to fit showrooms into smaller urban settings and to overcome the limitations of physical dealerships. With 12 different models, each

>> Digitizing in-store retail: AT&T's flagship Chicago showroom infuses digital and online technologies into a physical store environment to let customers experience the impact of its devices and services on their lives. It's "like walking into a Web site."

with up to six different trim levels, all with numerous options, no physical dealership can have every possible model on hand. Virtual showrooms, however, can present every model in Audi's extensive portfolio in every possible permutation. Moreover, customers can call them up instantly and make changes on the fly.

So far, the Audi City virtual experience is producing very real-world results. Audi City showrooms in London, Beijing, and Dubai are outselling their traditional counterparts by 70 percent, with an average increase in margin per vehicle of 30 percent. And the digitized auto lounges are bringing more new customers through the doors. Ninety percent of Audi City visitors are new to the brand.

The digitized showroom is finding its way into every industry imaginable. Consider Build-A-Bear Workshop. No stranger to retail innovation, Build-A-Bear revolutionized the in-store experience when it burst into America's malls almost 20 years ago with unique stores that were part showroom, part factory, and part theme park. With the original Build-A-Bear format, children moved from station to station, constructing and customizing their stuffed bears and watching them come to life before their very eyes.

But as smartphones, tablets, and other digital devices changed the way children play, Build-A-Bear saw its sales decline and losses mount. Now, however, rather than fighting digital-age developments, Build-A-Bear is deploying them. Today's Build-A-Bear stores are designed to engage the new generation of digitally adept children. A large video screen at the front of the store uses movement technology to greet children, engage them with interactive games, and introduce store features. From there, each of the eight stations in the bear-building process is enhanced by touchscreens and digital features that give young bear-builders more hands-on involvement and more design options. Kids can even give their finished bear a virtual bath before fluffing it with real air.

For AT&T, Audi, and Build-A-Bear, retailing is nothing new. Each has been in brick-and-mortar retailing for years, with hundreds of showrooms worldwide. But these forward-looking retailers are now betting on a digitized in-store future. AT&T plans to roll out six or seven elements of its Michigan Avenue store to each of its 2,300 other stores. Audi plans to open 20 more Audi City showrooms within a year. And Build-A-Bear has already updated each of its more than 400 stores with its new digital workstations. As AT&T's president of retail points out, digitization is more than just electronic whizbang. "It's all about creating [relevant customer experiences and] interactions rather than just transactions."

Sources: *Jacqueline Renfrow, "AT&T Turns Michigan Avenue Flagship into a Museum," Fierce Retail, March 11, 2015,* www.fierceretail.com/story/att-turns-michigan-avenue-flagship-museum/2015-03-11; Christopher Heine, "The Store of the Future Has Arrived," *Adweek,* June 3, 2013, www.adweek.com/print/149900; Nicole Giannopoulos, "A 'Magnificent' In-Store Experience," *Retail Info Systems News,* June 10, 2013, http://risnews.edgl.com/magazine/June-2013/A-Magnificent-In-Store-Experience86772; Elizabeth Olson, "Build-A-Bear Goes High Tech," *New York Times,* September 27, 2012, p. B3; Rajesh Setty, "Re-Imagining the Retail Experience: The Audi City Store," *Huffington Post,* December 29, 2013, www.huffingtonpost.com/rajesh-setty/re-imagining-the-retail-e_b_4514046.html; and www.callison.com/projects/att-%E2%80%93-michigan-avenue and www.youtube.com/watch?v=GDdPN6mVLPM, accessed October 2015.

simplicity and purity (think Apple stores), and blue connotes trust and dependability (financial institutions use it a lot). And most large retailers have developed signature scents that you smell only in their stores:[16]

> Anytime Fitness pipes in "Inspire," a eucalyptus-mint fragrance to create a uniform scent from store to store and mask that "gym" smell. Bloomingdale's uses different essences in different departments: the soft scent of baby powder in the baby store, coconut in the swimsuit area, lilacs in intimate apparel, and sugar cookies and evergreen scent during the holiday season. Luxury men's fashion brand Hugo Boss chose a signature smooth, musky scent for all of its stores. "We wanted it to feel like coming home," says a Hugo Boss marketer. Scents can subtly reinforce a brand's imagery and positioning. For example, the Hard Rock Café Hotel in Orlando added a scent of the ocean in its lobby to help guests imagine checking into a seaside resort (even though the hotel is located an hour from the coast). To draw customers into the hotel's often-overlooked downstairs ice cream shop, the hotel put a sugar cookie aroma at the top of the stairs and a whiff of waffle cone at the bottom. Ice cream sales jumped 45 percent in the following six months.

Such *experiential retailing* confirms that retail stores are much more than simply assortments of goods. They are environments to be experienced by the people who shop in them.

Price Decision

A retailer's price policy must fit its target market and positioning, product and service assortment, the competition, and economic factors. All retailers would like to charge high markups and achieve high volume, but the two seldom go together. Most retailers seek *either* high markups on lower volume (most specialty stores) *or* low markups on higher volume (mass merchandisers and discount stores).

Thus, 110-year-old Bergdorf Goodman caters to the upper crust by selling apparel, shoes, and jewelry created by designers such as Chanel, Prada, Hermes, and Jimmy Choo. The upmarket retailer pampers its customers with services such as a personal shopper and in-store showings of the upcoming season's trends with cocktails and hors d'oeuvres. By contrast, TJ Maxx sells brand name clothing at discount prices aimed at middle-class Americans. As it stocks new products each week, the discounter provides a treasure hunt for bargain shoppers. "No sales. No gimmicks." says the retailer. "Just brand name and designer fashions for you ... for up to 60 percent off department store prices."

Retailers must also decide on the extent to which they will use sales and other price promotions. Some retailers use no price promotions at all, competing instead on product and service quality rather than on price. For example, it's difficult to imagine Bergdorf Goodman holding a two-for-the-price-of-one sale on Chanel handbags, even in a tight economy. Other retailers—such as Walmart, Costco, ALDI, and Family Dollar—practice *everyday low pricing (EDLP)*, charging constant, everyday low prices with few sales or discounts.

Still other retailers practice *high-low pricing*—charging higher prices on an everyday basis coupled with frequent sales and other price promotions to increase store traffic, create a low-price image, or attract customers who will buy other goods at full prices. Recent tighter economic times caused a rash of high-low pricing, as retailers poured on price cuts and promotions to coax bargain-hunting customers into their stores. Which pricing strategy is best depends on the retailer's overall marketing strategy, the pricing approaches of its competitors, and the economic environment.

Promotion Decision

Retailers use various combinations of the five promotion tools—advertising, personal selling, sales promotion, public relations, and direct and social media marketing—to reach consumers. They advertise in newspapers and magazines and on radio and television. Advertising may be supported by newspaper inserts and catalogs. Store salespeople greet customers, meet their needs, and build relationships. Sales promotions may include in-store demonstrations, displays, sales, and loyalty programs. PR activities, such as new-store openings, special events, newsletters and blogs, store magazines, and public service activities, are also available to retailers.

Most retailers also interact digitally with customers using Web sites and digital catalogs, online ads and video, social media, mobile ads and apps, blogs, and email. Almost every retailer, large or small, maintains a full social media presence. For example, giant Walmart leads the way with a whopping 35 million Facebook Likes, 41,000 Pinterest followers, 664,000 Twitter followers, and 66,000 YouTube subscribers. By contrast, Fairway Market, the small but fast-growing metropolitan New York grocery chain that carries a huge product assortment—from "sky-high piles" of produce to overflowing bins of fresh seafood to hand-roasted coffee—has only 114,000 Facebook Likes. But Fairway isn't complaining—that's twice as many Facebook Likes per million dollars of sales as mighty Walmart.[17]

Digital promotions let retailers reach individual customers with carefully targeted messages. »For example, to compete more effectively against rivals online, CVS distributes personalized versions of its weekly circulars to the chain's ExtraCare loyalty program members. Called myWeekly Ad, customers can view their circulars by logging into their personal accounts at CVS.com on computers, tablets, or smartphones. Based on ExtraCare members' characteristics and previous purchases, the personalized promotions highlight sales items and special offers of special interest to each specific customer. With the myWeekly Ad program, "We're trying to get people to change

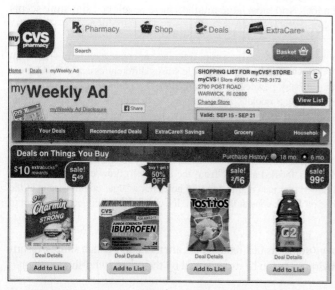

» **Retailer promotion: Most retailers interact digitally with customers using Web sites and digital catalogs, mobile and social media, and other digital platforms. CVS's myWeekly Ad program distributes personalized versions of its weekly circulars to the chain's ExtraCare loyalty program members.**

CVS Caremark Corporation

their behavior," says the CVS marketer heading up the effort, "going online for a much more personalized experience" rather than checking weekly circulars.[18]

Place Decision

Retailers often point to three critical factors in retailing success: location, location, and location! It's very important that retailers select locations that are accessible to the target market in areas that are consistent with the retailer's positioning. For example, Apple locates its stores in high-end malls and trendy shopping districts—such as the Magnificent Mile on Chicago's Michigan Avenue or Fifth Avenue in Manhattan—not low-rent strip malls on the edge of town. By contrast, to keep costs down and support its "cheap gourmet" positioning, Trader Joe's places its stores in lower-rent, out-of-the-way locations. Small retailers may have to settle for whatever locations they can find or afford. Large retailers, however, usually employ specialists who use advanced methods to select store locations.

Most stores today cluster together to increase their customer pulling power and give consumers the convenience of one-stop shopping. Central business districts were the main form of retail cluster until the 1950s. Every large city and town had a central business district with department stores, specialty stores, banks, and movie theaters. When people began moving to the suburbs, however, many of these central business districts, with their traffic, parking, and crime problems, began to lose business. In recent years, many cities have joined with merchants to revive downtown shopping areas, generally with only mixed success.

Shopping center

A group of retail businesses built on a site that is planned, developed, owned, and managed as a unit.

A **shopping center** is a group of retail businesses built on a site that is planned, developed, owned, and managed as a unit. A *regional shopping center*, or *regional shopping mall*, the largest and most dramatic shopping center, has from 50 to more than 100 stores, including two or more full-line department stores. It is like a covered mini-downtown and attracts customers from a wide area. A *community shopping center* contains between 15 and 50 retail stores. It normally contains a branch of a department store or variety store, a supermarket, specialty stores, professional offices, and sometimes a bank. Most shopping centers are *neighborhood shopping centers* or *strip malls* that generally contain between 5 and 15 stores. These centers, which are close and convenient for consumers, usually contain a supermarket, perhaps a discount store, and several service stores—dry cleaner, drugstore, hardware store, local restaurant, or other stores.[19]

A newer form of shopping center is the so-called power center. *Power centers* are huge unenclosed shopping centers consisting of a long strip of retail stores, including large, freestanding anchors such as Walmart, Home Depot, Costco, Best Buy, Michaels, PetSmart, and Office Depot. Each store has its own entrance with parking directly in front for shoppers who wish to visit only one store.

In contrast, *lifestyle centers* are smaller, open-air malls with upscale stores, convenient locations, and nonretail activities, such as a playground, skating rink, hotel, dining establishments, and a movie theater complex. The most recent lifestyle centers often consist of *mixed-use* developments, with ground-floor retail establishments and apartments or condominiums above, combining shopping convenience with the community feel of a neighborhood center. Meanwhile, traditional regional shopping malls are adding lifestyle elements—such as fitness centers, common areas, and multiplex theaters—to make themselves more social and welcoming. In all, today's centers are more like places to hang out rather than just places to shop. "The line between shopping, entertainment, and community building has blurred," says one analyst. "Shopping centers aren't just places to buy things. They're social centers, places for entertainment, and employment hubs."[20]

The past few years have brought hard times for shopping centers. Many experts suggest that the country has long been "overmalled." Not surprisingly, the Great Recession and its aftermath hit shopping malls hard. Consumer spending cutbacks forced many retailers—small and large—out of business, and vacancy rates at the nation's enclosed malls soared.[21] Power centers were also hard hit as their big-box retailer tenants such as Circuit City, Borders, Mervyns, and Linens N Things went out of business and others such as Best Buy, Barnes & Noble, and Office Depot reduced the number or size of their stores. Some of the pizzazz has also gone out of lifestyle centers, whose upper-middle-class shoppers suffered most during the recession.

As the economy has improved, however, malls of all types have rebounded a bit. Many power centers, for example, are filling their empty space with a broader range of retailers, from the likes of Ross Dress for Less, Boot Barn, Nordstrom Rack, and other off-price retailers to dollar stores, warehouse grocers, and traditional discounters like Walmart and Target.

Retailing Trends and Developments

Retailers operate in a harsh and fast-changing environment, which offers threats as well as opportunities. Consumer demographics, lifestyles, and spending patterns are changing rapidly, as are retailing technologies. To be successful, retailers need to choose target segments carefully and position themselves strongly. They need to take the following retailing developments into account as they plan and execute their competitive strategies.

Tighter Consumer Spending

Following many years of good economic times for retailers, the Great Recession of 2008–2009 turned many retailers' fortunes from boom to bust. Even as the economy has recovered, retailers will feel the effects of changed consumer spending patterns well into the future.

Some retailers actually benefit from a down economy. For example, as consumers cut back and looked for ways to spend less on what they bought, big discounters such as Costco scooped up new business from bargain-hungry shoppers. And price-oriented and off-price retailers such as ALDI, Dollar General, and TJ Maxx have attracted greater shares of more frugal buyers.

For other retailers, however, tighter consumer spending meant tough times. During and following the recession, several large and familiar retailers declared bankruptcy or closed their doors completely—including household names such as Linens N Things, Circuit City, KB Toys, Borders Books, and Sharper Image, to name a few. Other retailers, from Macy's and Home Depot to Starbucks, laid off employees, cut their costs, and offered deep price discounts and promotions aimed at luring cash-strapped customers back into their stores.

As the economy has improved and as consumers have retained their more frugal spending ways, many retailers have added new value pitches to their positioning. For example, Home Depot replaced its older "You can do it. We can help." theme with a thriftier one: "More saving. More doing." And retailers ranging from Walmart to Macy's to Kroger and Whole Foods Market are boosting their emphasis on more economical private-label brands.

>> Value positioning: Facing tighter consumer spending, Home Depot adopted a thriftier theme: "More saving. More doing."

iofoto/Shutterstock; The Home Depot, Inc.

When reacting to economic difficulties, retailers must be careful that their short-run actions don't damage their long-run images and positions. For example, drastic price discounting can increase immediate sales but damage brand loyalty. One analyst calls this "death by discount" and suggests that "virtually every retailer—at both the high and the low end—has fallen so deeply into the trap that discounting has become an expectation of customers rather than a bonus."[22] A stroll through your local shopping mall confirms this assessment. However, instead of relying on cost-cutting and price reductions, retailers should focus on building greater customer value within their long-term store positioning strategies.

New Retail Forms, Shortening Retail Life Cycles, and Retail Convergence

New retail forms continue to emerge to meet new situations and consumer needs, but the life cycle of new retail forms is getting shorter. Department stores took about 100 years to reach the mature stage of the life cycle; more recent forms, such as warehouse stores, reached maturity in about 10 years. In such an environment, seemingly solid retail positions can crumble quickly. Of the top 10 discount retailers in 1962 (the year that the first Walmart, Kmart, Target, and Kohl's stores opened), not one still exists today. Even the most successful retailers can't sit back with a winning formula. To remain successful, they must keep adapting.

>> **New retail forms: Many retailers, such as Brazilian sandal maker Havaianas, use temporary pop-up shops to promote their brands to seasonal shoppers and create buzz in busy areas.**

Havaianas

New retail forms are always emerging. The most recent blockbuster retailing trend is the advent of online retailing, by both online-only and store retailers, via Web sites, mobile apps, and social media. But lesser innovations occur regularly. >> For example, many retailers are now using limited-time *pop-up stores* that let them promote their brands to seasonal shoppers and create buzz in busy areas. During an NBA All-Star weekend at the Barclays Center in Brooklyn, New York, Nike opened a Jordan-themed pop-up shop across the street. Brazilian sandal maker Havaianas is known for opening temporary seasonal pop-up shops at beaches, festivals, and other summer hot spots around the world.[23]

The online and mobile equivalent is *flash sales* sites, such as Nordstrom's HauteLook and Amazon's MyHabit, which host time-limited sales events on top fashion and lifestyle brands. Similarly, Gilt.com flashes member-only, 70 percent discounts on designer-label clothing; and Groupon offers flash deals on travel through Groupon Getaways. Zulily flashes sales on products for moms, babies, and kids, offering limited-time sales "events" that quickly "scoot away to make room for new events." Flash sales add excitement and urgency to buying. Says Zulily, "Shopping here is like opening a new treasure chest every day. You never know exactly what you'll uncover, but you know gems are waiting."[24]

Today's retail forms appear to be converging. Increasingly, different types of retailers now sell the same products at the same prices to the same consumers. For example, you can buy brand name home appliances at department stores, discount stores, home-improvement stores, off-price retailers, electronics superstores, and a slew of online sites that all compete for the same customers. If you can't find the microwave oven you want at Sears, you can step across the street and find one for a better price at Lowe's or Best Buy—or just order one online from Amazon.com or even RitzCamera.com. This merging of consumers, products, prices, and retailers is called *retail convergence*. Such convergence means greater competition for retailers and greater difficulty in differentiating the product assortments of different types of retailers.

The Rise of Megaretailers

The rise of huge mass merchandisers and specialty superstores, the formation of vertical marketing systems, and a rash of retail mergers and acquisitions have created a core of superpower megaretailers. With their size and buying power, these giant retailers can offer better merchandise selections, good service, and strong price savings to consumers. As a result, they grow even larger by squeezing out their smaller, weaker competitors.

The megaretailers have shifted the balance of power between retailers and producers. A small handful of retailers now controls access to enormous numbers of consumers, giving them the upper hand in their dealings with manufacturers. For example, you may never have heard of specialty coatings and sealants manufacturer RPM International, but you've probably used one or more of its many familiar do-it-yourself brands—such as Rust-Oleum paints, Plastic Wood and Dap fillers, Mohawk and Watco finishes, and Testors hobby cements and paints—all of which you can buy at your local Home Depot store. Home Depot is a very important customer to RPM, accounting for a significant share of its consumer sales. However, Home Depot's sales of $78 billion are almost 20 times RPM's sales of $4.3 billion. As a result, the giant retailer can, and often does, use this power to wring concessions from RPM and thousands of other smaller suppliers.[25]

Growth of Direct, Online, Mobile, and Social Media Retailing

Most consumers still make a majority of their purchases the old-fashioned way: They go to a store, find what they want, plunk down their cash or credit cards, and bring home the goods. However, consumers now have a broad array of nonstore alternatives, including direct and digital shopping via Web sites, mobiles apps, and social media. As we'll discuss in Chapter 14, direct and digital marketing are currently the fastest-growing forms of marketing.

Today, thanks to advanced technologies, easier-to-use and enticing online sites and mobile apps, improved online services, and the increasing sophistication of search technologies, online retailing is thriving. In fact, although it currently accounts for only about 7 percent of total U.S. retail sales, online buying is growing at a much brisker pace than retail buying as a whole. Last year's U.S. online retail sales grew 117 percent over the previous year versus a 4 percent increase in overall retail sales.[26]

Retailer online sites, mobile apps, and social media also influence a large amount of in-store buying. An estimated 52 percent of total U.S. retail sales were either transacted directly or influenced by online research. An estimated 15 percent of all online sales now take place on mobile devices, a number that will grow to 25 percent by 2017. Retailers of all kinds rely on social media to engage their buyer communities. For example, whereas Walmart leads among retailers in Facebook Likes, L.L.Bean is tops in Pinterest followers. Victoria's Secret leads in Twitter followers, but H&M comes in a close second. And Victoria's Secret has the most YouTube subscribers.[27]

The spurt in online, mobile, and social media retailing is both a blessing and a curse to store retailers. Although it gives them new channels for engaging and selling to customers, it also creates more competition from online-only retailers. To the dismay of some store retailers, many shoppers now check out merchandise at physical-store showrooms but then buy it online using a computer or mobile device, sometimes while in the store—a process called **showrooming.** ≫ These days, 75 percent of smartphone-carrying shoppers use their phones while shopping in stores. And as many as half of all shoppers who buy products online check them out first at a traditional store.[28] Store retailers such as Target, Walmart, Best Buy, Bed Bath & Beyond, and Toys "R" Us have been hit hard by showrooming.

Today, however, many store retailers are developing effective strategies to counter showrooming. Others are even embracing it as an opportunity to highlight the advantages of shopping in stores versus online-only retailers. The flip side of showrooming is *webrooming,* by which consumers first check out merchandise online, then buy it in a store. The key for store retailers is to convert showrooming shoppers into buyers when they visit the store.

However, it's no longer a matter of customers deciding whether to shop in a store *or* shop online. The Internet and digital devices have spawned a whole new breed of shopper and way of shopping. Today's omni-channel buyers shift seamlessly across online and in-store channels during the buying process. They've gotten used to researching and buying anywhere, anytime—whether it's in the store, online, on the go, or even online while in the store. To meet the needs of these omni-channel buyers, store retailers must master *omni-channel retailing,* integrating store and online channels into a single shopper experience (see Marketing at Work 11.2).

An increasing share of the growth in online sales is being captured by omni-channel retailers who successfully merge the virtual and physical worlds. In a recent ranking of the top 10 online retailers, five were store-based retail chains. Another study showed that, among the top 500 online retailers, online sales by store chains were growing 8 percent faster than those of online-only retailers and 40 percent faster than overall e-commerce.[29]

For example, thanks largely to rapid growth in online sales, upscale home products retailer Williams-Sonoma now captures more than half of its total revenues from its direct-to-consumer channel. Like many retailers, Williams-Sonoma has discovered that many of its best customers visit and shop both online and offline. Beyond just offering online shopping, the retailer engages customers through its Web site, online communities, social media, mobile apps, a blog, and special online programs. "The Internet has changed the way

Showrooming
The shopping practice of coming into retail store showrooms to check out merchandise and prices but instead buying from an online-only rival, sometimes while in the store.

≫ Showrooming: The now-common practice of viewing products in stores but buying them online presents serious challenges to store retailers. But rather than fighting showrooming, retailers are now embracing it as a way to showcase their omni-channel strengths.

Kumar Sriskandan/Alamy

MARKETING AT WORK | 11.2

Omni-Channel Retailing: Creating a Seamless Shopping Experience

The shopping process has changed radically in recent years. Not all that long ago, shopping consisted mostly of going store to store—or perhaps flipping through catalogs—to gather product information, make price comparisons, and purchase goods. That was then. Now—in this age of the Internet, computers, smartphones, and other digital devices—shopping typically involves a dazzling array of channels and platforms.

Today's omni-channel consumers readily research products and prices online, shopping digitally from home, from work, in stores, or anywhere in between. They scour retailer Web sites and social media for buying ideas, inspiration, and advice. They might see products in stores and order them online, see products online then buy them in stores, or even buy goods online for in-store pickup. This massive shift in how people shop calls for massive changes in how store retailers operate. Omni-channel *buying* calls for omni-channel *retailing*, integrating all available shopping channels and devices into a seamless customer shopping experience.

At first, as online and mobile shopping caught fire, store retailers worried about *showrooming*—smartphone-wielding customers researching products online while examining them in stores, then jumping ship to catch lower online prices. But most store retailers have now adjusted to the showrooming threat with price-matching and other in-store tactics. In fact, smart retailers now see phone-toting customers not as a threat but as an opportunity.

For example, Best Buy has found that omni-channel shoppers have a higher-than-average propensity to purchase. One study showed that shoppers who use mobile devices in stores are almost twice as likely to purchase from the same retailer in-store or online than to buy elsewhere. "We love being used as the Internet's showroom," says Best Buy's CEO. Where Best Buy once fought showrooming, the chain now facilitates the process, converting showroomers into buyers. Best Buy sales associates are trained to proactively cross-check prices against both their own and other retailer's online offers, including online retailers like Amazon. Employees can then price-match competitors, putting the price question to rest and letting associates focus on areas where Best Buy has the advantage—such as personal advice and service, immediacy, convenient locations, and easy returns. Best Buy's new tagline highlights this strategy: "Best Buy: Expert Service. Unbeatable Prices."

Retailers have learned that shoppers with smartphones are doing far more than just checking online prices. More often, they are filling in the information gap. "The consumer has never been more informed, and that information comes from their phone," says a senior marketer at outdoor-gear retailer REI. "We love when someone enters the store holding their phone saying, 'I want this tent. I want this bike. Help me find this.'" This type of activity shows how digital and store retailing can come together to make a sale, even without cutting price.

But omni-channel retailing goes way beyond just helping in-store customers as they cross-shop on digital devices. It requires carefully integrating the entire range of available shopping channels, both in-store and out, from discovery to purchase in the buying process. For example, most large retailers are now boosting their own online and digital selling options and linking them with stores. One popular way to do that is by letting customers order online and pick up in the store. The "click-and-collect" experience merges the attractions of digital and in-store shopping. For example, Walmart has upped its emphasis on in-store pickups. It tells customers that they can order from its Walmart.com site, often pick up items on the same day, avoid shipping fees, and easily return items to the store if not satisfied. Customers now pick up half of all Walmart.com purchases in stores, often buying additional merchandise during the visit.

Some customers even use mobile devices to place online orders with a given retailer while visiting that retailer's store. Ten percent of Walmart purchases via mobile devices are made from inside a Walmart store. GAP Inc.—which operates the GAP, Old Navy, and Banana Republic chains—actively promotes in-store online ordering. Sales associates with tablets help customers search company-wide store and online inventories to find out-of-stock items. "It gives the team in the store the full capability

>> Foot Locker has mastered omni-channel retailing. It skillfully integrates its in-store environment, high-powered Web sites, and extensive social media presence to create the seamless, anytime-anywhere, omni-channel shopping experience that today's customers seek.

Luke Sharrett/Bloomberg/Getty Images

to ... meet your needs without you having to go home and do it yourself," says a Banana Republic marketer.

In addition to Web sites, omni-channel retailers are integrating other digital shopping channels. Walmart, Target, Macy's, and other major retailers offer handy mobile apps that pull customers to both their Web sites and stores, let them prepare shopping lists, help them locate merchandise inside stores, and, in Target's case, received daily alerts and exclusive discounts sent to their phones. Macy's uses Shopkick's shopBeacon technology, by which in-store sensors detect opted-in customers as they enter a Macy's store, welcome them via the Macy's app on their phones, and pass along personalized shopping information and "only-for-you" deals.

Social media also play an important part in omni-channel retailing. Thirty percent of shoppers made purchases via social media last year, 44 percent discovered new products via social networks, and 49 percent made purchases based on referrals from social media. In turn, most large store retailers now use social media extensively to engage customers, build community, and link buyers to their Web sites and stores.

But simply creating a digital-friendly store, high-powered Web site, and extensive social media presence doesn't constitute good omni-channel retailing. The key is to integrate these elements to create that critical seamless, anywhere-anytime, omni-channel shopping experience that today's customers seek. Consider athletic footwear and apparel giant Foot Locker, which operates several chains, including Foot Locker and Champs Sports:

> Foot Locker has mastered omni-channel retailing. It now gets 12 percent of its sales online, half of that from mobile buying, and its online sales are growing at an eye-popping 40 percent annually. Its online and mobile efforts link seamlessly with store operations, offering options such as "buy online, ship from store" and "buy

online, reserve in store" for pickup. And you'll find Foot Locker everywhere in social media, with more than 150 million total followers across Instagram, Facebook, Snapchat, Twitter, YouTube, and Pinterest, where it builds customer community and pulls customers to its online and store locations.

Foot Locker's omni-channel prowess comes to life inside its Foot Locker, Champs Sports, and other stores. The chain gives sales associates the same mobile research capabilities that customers have. Tablets in hand, using online information about products and competitor offers, associates work with and educate customers. Foot Locker trains store employees to go beyond prices and engage customers in ways that add value through personal touches. With 3,500 stores and Foot Locker's own substantial online presence, the store retailer can help customers to shape almost any kind of shopping experience, including a broad choice of service, payment, and delivery options not available from online-only retailers. Thanks to its omni-channel mastery, whereas other shoe and apparel retailers have had trouble fending off Web-only sellers like online star Zappos, Foot Locker is thriving in the new omni-channel shopping environment. Over the past four years, the retailer's sales have zoomed 40 percent and profits have tripled.

Sources: Tim Simmons, "The Keys to Unlocking the Retail Omni-Channel Advantage," *Forbes*, January 2, 2015, www.forbes.com/sites/teradata/2015/01/02/the-keys-to-unlocking-the-retail-omni-channel-advantage/; Sarah Halzack, "Online or In-Store? How about a Little of Both?", *Washington Post*, November 28, 2014, p. A01; Christine Birkner, "Good Tidings for Retail," *Marketing News,* December 2014, p. 14; Kyle Stock, "Does Foot Locker Have Too Many Nikes?" *Bloomberg Businessweek,* March 7, 2014, www.bloomberg.com/bw/articles/2014-03-07/does-foot-locker-have-too-many-nikes; Laura Heller, "How Foot Locker Is Using Mobile to Reach Millennials," *FierceMobileRetail*, August 4, 2014, www.fierceretail.com/mobileretail/story/how-foot-locker-using-mobile-reach-millennials/2014-08-04; Brian Sozzi, "Foot Locker Transforming Its Stores as It Seeks to Keep Sales on Fire," *TheStreet,* March 17, 2015, www.thestreet.com/story/13081277/1/foot-locker-transforming-its-stores-as-it-seeks-to-keep-sales-on-fire.html; and www.footlocker-inc.com and www.footlocker.com, accessed October 2015.

our customers shop," says Williams-Sonoma CEO Laura Alber, "and the online brand experience has to be inspiring and seamless."[30]

Growing Importance of Retail Technology

Retail technologies have become critically important as competitive tools. Progressive retailers are using advanced information technology and software systems to produce better forecasts, control inventory costs, interact electronically with suppliers, send information between stores, and even sell to customers within stores. They have adopted sophisticated systems for checkout scanning, RFID inventory tracking, merchandise handling, information sharing, and customer interactions.

Perhaps the most startling advances in retail technology concern the ways in which retailers are connecting with consumers. Increasingly, retailers are bringing online and digital technologies into their physical stores. Many retailers now routinely use technologies ranging from touchscreen kiosks and handheld shopping assistants to interactive dressing-room mirrors and virtual sales associates. Macy's uses Shopkick's shopBeacon indoor positioning system to engage customers digitally as they shop around its stores. ≫ When opted-in customers enter a Macy's store, a Bluetooth signal wakes up the shopBeacon app on their smartphone or tablet, which welcomes them and alerts them to location-specific rewards, deals, discounts, and personalized product recommendations within the store. The technology can also link in-store and at-home browsing; if the customer "likes" a specific product online, shopBeacon can remind them where to find it in the store, pop up a brief product video, and maybe pass along a for-you-only deal. The goal of

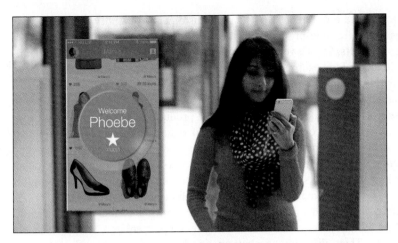

>> Retail technology: Macy's uses Shopkick's shopBeacon to engage consumers in the store and personalize their shopping experiences.

Shopkick, Inc.

shopBeacon is to engage Macy's tech-savvy and social customers as a trusted companion and to personalize their in-store shopping experience.[31]

The future of technology in retailing is to blend the new technologies with traditional services. For example, Walmart's goal is to merge in-store and online, social media, and mobile innovations to give customers an enhanced shopping experience:

> To augment in-store shopping, Walmart formed @ WalmartLabs, which develops mobile and social media platforms that make shopping easier, more accessible, and more fun. For example, the retailer's Walmart Gifts gift-finder app applies data from users' Facebook Likes, comments, status updates, and other data to recommend the best products for customers and gifts for their friends. The retailer's feature-rich mobile apps let customers create smart shopping lists, scan barcodes and check prices, access product information, and scan coupons in real time—all from a smartphone or tablet, at home, at work, in the store, or anywhere in between. Walmart's "Savings Catcher" app lets customers scan their store receipt to compare prices at competing stores—if the app finds cheaper prices elsewhere, shoppers get money back in the form of a gift card. And Walmart customers will soon be able to use their smartphones in self-checkout lines. The Walmart SocialStore team at @WalmartLabs is exploring other new in-store social media, mobile, and kiosk technologies that will both assist customers as they shop and help stores get to know and serve their customers better.[32]

Green Retailing

Today's retailers are increasingly adopting environmentally sustainable practices. They are greening up their stores and operations, promoting more environmentally responsible products, launching programs to help customers be more responsible, and working with channel partners to reduce their environmental impact.

At the most basic level, most large retailers are making their stores more environmentally friendly through sustainable building design, construction, and operations. >> For example, under its "People & Planet Positive" sustainability strategy, home furnishings retailer IKEA's long-term goal is to become 100 sustainable:[33]

PEOPLE & PLANET POSITIVE

IKEA Group Sustainability Direction for 2020

>> Green retailing: Under its "People & Planet Positive" sustainability strategy, IKEA's long-term goal is to become 100 sustainable.

Used with the permission of Inter IKEA Systems B.V

> The "People & Planet Positive" strategy begins with making IKEA's 315 giant stores in 27 countries more energy independent and efficient. To power its stores, IKEA has committed to owning and operating 224 wind turbines and has installed 700,000 solar panels—90 percent of its U.S. stores have solar panels. By 2020, IKEA will generate as much energy as it uses from renewable sources. Inside its stores, IKEA uses only energy-efficient LED lighting. Most stores also sort food waste from in-store customer restaurants for composting or send it to treatment centers where it is turned into animal feed or biogas to fuel cars and buses. Some IKEAs offer customer recycling centers for products such as plastic, paper, CFL light bulbs, batteries, and even end-of-life appliances.

Retailers are also greening up their product assortments. For example, IKEA now sells only LED lighting products in its stores, and a growing proportion of the home furnishing products it sells are made from sustainable and renewable cotton, wood, and other resources. IKEA suppliers must adhere the retailer's IWAY supplier code of conduct sustainability standards. IKEA's goal is have all of its home furnishings made from renewable, recyclable, or recycled materials. "At IKEA, sustainability is central to our business," says the company, "to ensure that we have a positive impact on people and the planet."

Many retailers have also launched programs that help consumers make more environmentally responsible decisions. Staples's Easy on the Planet program "makes it easier to make a difference" by helping customers to identify green products sold in its stores and to recycle printer cartridges, mobile phones, computers, and other office technology products. Staples recycles some 30 million printer cartridges and 10 million pounds of old technology each year.[34]

Finally, many large retailers are joining forces with suppliers and distributors to create more sustainable products, packaging, and distribution systems. For example, Amazon .com works closely with the producers of many of the products it sells to reduce and simplify their packaging. And beyond its own substantial sustainability initiatives, Walmart wields its huge buying power to urge its army of suppliers to improve their environmental impact and practices. The retailer has even developed a worldwide Sustainable Product Index by which it rates suppliers. It plans to translate the index into a simple rating for consumers to help them make more sustainable buying choices.

Green retailing yields both top- and bottom-line benefits. Sustainable practices lift a retailer's top line by attracting consumers looking to support environmentally friendly sellers and products. They also help the bottom line by reducing costs. For example, Amazon.com's reduced-packaging efforts increase customer convenience and eliminate "wrap rage" while at the same time saving packaging costs. And IKEA's more energy-efficient buildings not only appeal to customers and help save the planet but also cost less to operate.

Global Expansion of Major Retailers

Retailers with unique formats and strong brand positions are increasingly moving into other countries. Many are expanding internationally to escape saturated home markets. Over the years, some giant U.S. retailers, such as McDonald's, have become globally prominent as a result of their marketing prowess. Others, such as Walmart, are rapidly establishing a global presence. Walmart, which now operates more than 6,100 stores in 26 non-U.S. markets, sees exciting global potential. Its international division alone last year racked up sales of more than $136 billion, almost 86 percent more than rival Target's *total* sales of $73 billion.[35]

However, most U.S. retailers are still significantly behind Europe and Asia when it comes to global expansion. Although nine of the world's top 20 retailers are U.S. companies, only four of these retailers have set up stores outside North America (Walmart, Home Depot, Costco, and Best Buy). Of the 12 non-U.S. retailers in the world's top 20, eight have stores in at least 10 countries. Foreign retailers that have gone global include France's Carrefour, Groupe Casino, and Auchan chains; Germany's Metro, Lidl, and ALDI chains; Britain's Tesco; and Japan's Seven & I.[36]

International retailing presents challenges as well as opportunities. Retailers can face dramatically different retail environments when crossing countries, continents, and cultures. Simply adapting the operations that work well in the home country is usually not enough to create success abroad. Instead, when going global, retailers must understand and meet the needs of local markets.

 ## LINKING THE CONCEPTS

Time out! So-called experts have long predicted that online retailing eventually will replace store retailing as our primary way to shop. What do you think?

- Shop for a good book at the Barnes & Noble Web site (www.bn.com), taking time to browse the site and see what it has to offer. Next, shop at a nearby Barnes & Noble or other bookstore. Compare the two shopping experiences. Where would you rather shop? On what occasions? Why?
- A Barnes & Noble store creates an ideal "community" where people can "hang out." How does its Web site compare on this dimension?
- Do Barnes & Noble's various social media efforts create community for the retailer and its customers? For example, see www.facebook.com/barnesandnoble, https://twitter.com/bnbooks, and http://pinterest.com/barnesandnoble/followers/.

Author Comment
Whereas retailers primarily sell goods and services directly to final consumers for personal use, wholesalers sell primarily to those buying for resale or business use. Because wholesalers operate behind the scenes, they are largely unknown to final consumers. But they are very important to their business customers.

Wholesaling
All the activities involved in selling goods and services to those buying for resale or business use.

Wholesaler
A firm engaged *primarily* in wholesaling activities.

Wholesaling

Wholesaling includes all the activities involved in selling goods and services to those buying them for resale or business use. Firms engaged *primarily* in wholesaling activities are called **wholesalers**.

Wholesalers buy mostly from producers and sell mostly to retailers, industrial consumers, and other wholesalers. As a result, many of the nation's largest and most important wholesalers are largely unknown to final consumers. For example, Sysco is a huge $46 billion wholesale food distribution company that operates behind the scenes to supply boxes of seafood, chicken, pasta, vegetables, baked goods, condiments, napkins, and other goods to more than 425,000 restaurants, schools, hospitals, colleges, and other commercial customers that prepare meals away from home. Wholesaler Arrow Electronics supplies $23 billion worth of computer chips, capacitors, and other electronics and computer components annually to more than 100,000 original equipment manufacturers and commercial customers through a global network of more than 460 locations in 56 countries. ≫And you may never have heard of a company called Grainger, even though it is very well known and much valued by its more than 2 million business and institutional customers in more than 150 countries:[37]

Grainger may be the biggest market leader you've never heard of. It's a $10 billion business that offers more than 1.4 million maintenance, repair, and operating (MRO) products from more than 4,500 manufacturers to over 2 million active customers. Through its branch network, service centers, sales reps, catalog, and online and social media sites, Grainger links customers with the supplies they need to keep their facilities running smoothly and their people safe—everything from lightbulbs, cleaners, and display cases to nuts and bolts, motors, valves, power tools, test equipment, and safety supplies. Grainger's nearly 700 branches, 33 strategically located distribution centers, more than 23,700 employees, and innovative Web sites handle more than 115,000 transactions a day. Grainger's customers include organizations ranging from factories, garages, and grocers to schools and military bases.

Grainger operates on a simple value proposition: to make it easier and less costly for customers to find and buy MRO supplies. It starts by acting as a one-stop shop for products needed to maintain facilities. On a broader level, it builds lasting relationships with customers by helping them find *solutions* to their overall MRO problems. Acting as consultants, Grainger sales reps help buyers with everything from improving their supply chain management to reducing inventories and streamlining warehousing operations.

So, how come you've never heard of Grainger? Perhaps it's because the company operates in the not-so-glamorous world of MRO supplies, which are important to every business but not so important to consumers. More likely, it's because Grainger is a wholesaler. And like most wholesalers, it operates behind the scenes, selling mostly to other businesses.

Why are wholesalers important to sellers? For example, why would a producer use wholesalers rather than selling directly to retailers or consumers? Simply put, wholesalers add value by performing one or more of the following channel functions:

- *Selling and promoting.* Wholesalers' sales forces help manufacturers reach many small customers at a low cost. The wholesaler has more contacts and is often more trusted by the buyer than the distant manufacturer.
- *Buying and assortment building.* Wholesalers can select items and build assortments needed by their customers, thereby saving much work.
- *Bulk breaking.* Wholesalers save their customers money by buying in carload lots and breaking bulk (breaking large lots into small quantities).
- *Warehousing.* Wholesalers hold inventories, thereby reducing the inventory costs and risks of suppliers and customers.

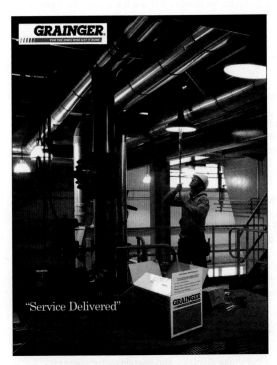

≫ **Wholesaling: Many of the nation's largest and most important wholesalers—like Grainger—are largely unknown to final consumers. But they are very well known and much valued by the business customers they serve.**

W. W. Grainger, Inc.

- *Transportation.* Wholesalers can provide quicker delivery to buyers because they are closer to buyers than are producers.
- *Financing.* Wholesalers finance their customers by giving credit, and they finance their suppliers by ordering early and paying bills on time.
- *Risk bearing.* Wholesalers absorb risk by taking title and bearing the cost of theft, damage, spoilage, and obsolescence.
- *Market information.* Wholesalers give information to suppliers and customers about competitors, new products, and price developments.
- *Management services and advice.* Wholesalers often help retailers train their salesclerks, improve store layouts and displays, and set up accounting and inventory control systems.

Types of Wholesalers

Merchant wholesaler
An independently owned wholesale business that takes title to the merchandise it handles.

Wholesalers fall into three major groups (see **≫ Table 11.3**): *merchant wholesalers, brokers and agents,* and *manufacturers' and retailers' branches and offices.* **Merchant wholesalers** are the largest single group of wholesalers, accounting for roughly 50 percent of all wholesaling. Merchant wholesalers include two broad types: full-service wholesalers and limited-service wholesalers. *Full-service wholesalers* provide a full set of services, whereas the various *limited-service wholesalers* offer fewer services to their suppliers and customers. The different types of limited-service wholesalers perform varied specialized functions in the distribution channel.

≫ Table 11.3 Major Types of Wholesalers

Type	Description
Merchant wholesalers	Independently owned businesses that take title to all merchandise handled. There are full-service wholesalers and limited-service wholesalers.
Full-service wholesalers	Provide a full line of services: carrying stock, maintaining a sales force, offering credit, making deliveries, and providing management assistance. Full-service wholesalers include wholesale merchants and industrial distributors.
Wholesale merchants	Sell primarily to retailers and provide a full range of services. General merchandise wholesalers carry several merchandise lines, whereas general line wholesalers carry one or two lines in great depth. Specialty wholesalers specialize in carrying only part of a line.
Industrial distributors	Sell to manufacturers rather than to retailers. Provide several services, such as carrying stock, offering credit, and providing delivery. May carry a broad range of merchandise, a general line, or a specialty line.
Limited-service wholesalers	Offer fewer services than full-service wholesalers. Limited-service wholesalers are of several types:
Cash-and-carry wholesalers	Carry a limited line of fast-moving goods and sell to small retailers for cash. Normally do not deliver.
Truck wholesalers (or truck jobbers)	Perform primarily a selling and delivery function. Carry a limited line of semiperishable merchandise (such as milk, bread, snack foods), which is sold for cash as deliveries are made to supermarkets, small groceries, hospitals, restaurants, factory cafeterias, and hotels.
Drop shippers	Do not carry inventory or handle the product. On receiving an order, drop shippers select a manufacturer, who then ships the merchandise directly to the customer. Drop shippers operate in bulk industries, such as coal, lumber, and heavy equipment.
Rack jobbers	Serve grocery and drug retailers, mostly in nonfood items. Rack jobbers send delivery trucks to stores, where the delivery people set up toys, paperbacks, hardware items, health and beauty aids, or other items. Rack jobbers price the goods, keep them fresh, set up point-of-purchase displays, and keep inventory records.
Producers' cooperatives	Farmer-owned members that assemble farm produce for sale in local markets. Producers' cooperatives often attempt to improve product quality and promote a co-op brand name, such as Sun-Maid raisins, Sunkist oranges, or Diamond nuts.
Mail-order or Web wholesalers	Send catalogs to or maintain Web sites for retail, industrial, and institutional customers featuring jewelry, cosmetics, specialty foods, and other small items. Its primary customers are businesses in small outlying areas.

Brokers and agents	Do not take title to goods. The main function is to facilitate buying and selling, for which they earn a commission on the selling price. Generally specialize by product line or customer type.
Brokers	Bring buyers and sellers together and assist in negotiation. Brokers are paid by the party who hired the broker and do not carry inventory, get involved in financing, or assume risk. Examples include food brokers, real estate brokers, insurance brokers, and security brokers.
Agents	Represent either buyers or sellers on a more permanent basis than brokers do. There are four types:
Manufacturers' agents	Represent two or more manufacturers of complementary lines. Often used in such lines as apparel, furniture, and electrical goods. A manufacturer's agent is hired by small manufacturers who cannot afford their own field sales forces and by large manufacturers who use agents to open new territories or cover territories that cannot support full-time salespeople.
Selling agents	Have contractual authority to sell a manufacturer's entire output. The selling agent serves as a sales department and has significant influence over prices, terms, and conditions of sale. Found in product areas such as textiles, industrial machinery and equipment, coal and coke, chemicals, and metals.
Purchasing agents	Generally have a long-term relationship with buyers and make purchases for them, often receiving, inspecting, warehousing, and shipping the merchandise to buyers. Purchasing agents help clients obtain the best goods and prices available.
Commission merchants	Take physical possession of products and negotiate sales. Used most often in agricultural marketing by farmers who do not want to sell their own output. Take a truckload of commodities to a central market, sell it for the best price, deduct a commission and expenses, and remit the balance to the producers.
Manufacturers' and retailers' branches and offices	Wholesaling operations conducted by sellers or buyers themselves rather than operating through independent wholesalers. Separate branches and offices can be dedicated to either sales or purchasing.
Sales branches and offices	Set up by manufacturers to improve inventory control, selling, and promotion. Sales branches carry inventory and are found in industries such as lumber and automotive equipment and parts. Sales offices do not carry inventory and are most prominent in the dry goods and notions industries.
Purchasing offices	Perform a role similar to that of brokers or agents but are part of the buyer's organization. Many retailers set up purchasing offices in major market centers, such as New York and Chicago.

Broker
A wholesaler who does not take title to goods and whose function is to bring buyers and sellers together and assist in negotiation.

Agent
A wholesaler who represents buyers or sellers on a relatively permanent basis, performs only a few functions, and does not take title to goods.

Manufacturers' and retailers' branches and offices
Wholesaling by sellers or buyers themselves rather than through independent wholesalers.

Brokers and *agents* differ from merchant wholesalers in two ways: They do not take title to goods, and they perform only a few functions. Like merchant wholesalers, they generally specialize by product line or customer type. A **broker** brings buyers and sellers together and assists in negotiation. **Agents** represent buyers or sellers on a more permanent basis. *Manufacturers' agents* (also called *manufacturers' representatives*) are the most common type of agent wholesaler. The third major type of wholesaling is that done in **manufacturers' and retailers' branches and offices** by sellers or buyers themselves rather than through independent wholesalers.

Wholesaler Marketing Decisions

Wholesalers now face growing competitive pressures, more-demanding customers, new technologies, and more direct-buying programs on the part of large industrial, institutional, and retail buyers. As a result, they have taken a fresh look at their marketing strategies. As with retailers, their marketing decisions include choices of segmentation and targeting, differentiation and positioning, and the marketing mix—product and service assortments, price, promotion, and distribution (see >> **Figure 11.2**).

Segmentation, Targeting, Differentiation, and Positioning Decisions

Like retailers, wholesalers must segment and define their target markets and differentiate and position themselves effectively—they cannot serve everyone. They can choose a target group by size of customer (for example, large retailers only), type of customer (convenience stores only), the need for service (customers who need credit), or other factors. Within the target

>> Figure 11.2 Wholesaler Marketing Strategies

group, they can identify the more profitable customers, design stronger offers, and build better relationships with them. They can propose automatic reordering systems, establish management-training and advisory systems, or even sponsor a voluntary chain. They can discourage less-profitable customers by requiring larger orders or adding service charges to smaller ones.

Marketing Mix Decisions

Like retailers, wholesalers must decide on product and service assortments, prices, promotion, and place. Wholesalers add customer value though the *products and services* they offer. They are often under great pressure to carry a full line and stock enough for immediate delivery. But this practice can damage profits. Wholesalers today are cutting down on the number of lines they carry, choosing to carry only the more profitable ones. They are also rethinking which services count most in building strong customer relationships and which should be dropped or paid for by the customer. The key for companies is to find the mix of services most valued by their target customers.

Price is also an important wholesaler decision. Wholesalers usually mark up the cost of goods by a standard percentage—say, 20 percent. Expenses may run 17 percent of the gross margin, leaving a profit margin of 3 percent. In grocery wholesaling, the average profit margin is often less than 2 percent. The recent recession put heavy pressure on wholesalers to cut their costs and prices. As their retail and industrial customers face sales and margin declines, these customers turn to wholesalers, looking for lower prices. Wholesalers may, in turn, cut their margins on some lines to keep important customers. They may also ask suppliers for special price breaks in cases when they can turn them into an increase in the supplier's sales.

Although *promotion* can be critical to wholesaler success, most wholesalers are not promotion minded. They use largely scattered and unplanned trade advertising, sales promotion, personal selling, and public relations. Many are behind the times in personal selling; they still see selling as a single salesperson talking to a single customer instead of as a team effort to sell, build, and service major accounts. Wholesalers also need to adopt some of the nonpersonal promotion techniques used by retailers. They need to develop an overall promotion strategy and make greater use of supplier promotion materials and programs. Digital and social media are playing an increasingly important role. For example, Grainger maintains an active presence on Facebook, YouTube, Twitter, LinkedIn, and Google+. It also provides a feature-rich mobile app. On its YouTube channel, Grainger lists more than 500 videos on topics ranging from the company and its products and services to keeping down inventory costs.

Finally, *distribution* (location) is important. Wholesalers must choose their locations, facilities, and Web locations carefully. There was a time when wholesalers could locate in low-rent, low-tax areas and invest little money in their buildings, equipment, and systems. Today, however, as technology zooms forward, such behavior results in outdated systems for material handling, order processing, and delivery.

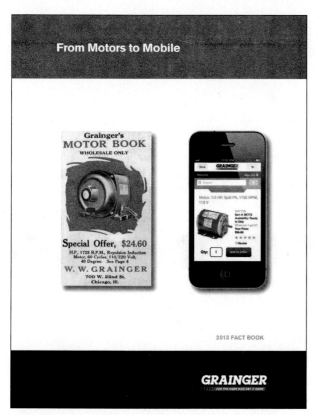

From Motors to Mobile

Grainger's
MOTOR BOOK
WHOLESALE ONLY

Special Offer, $24.60
H.P., 1725 R.P.M., Repulsion Induction
Motor, 60 Cycles, 110/220 Volt,
40 Degree. See Page 4
W. W. GRAINGER
700 W. 22nd St.
Chicago, Ill.

2013 FACT BOOK

GRAINGER

≫ **Wholesaler marketing: Progressive wholesalers like Grainger maintain an active presence in online, mobile, and social media. For example, online and mobile purchasing now account for 80 percent of Grainger's total sales.**

W. W. Grainger, Inc.

Instead, today's large and progressive wholesalers have reacted to rising costs by investing in automated warehouses and IT systems. Orders are fed from the retailer's information system directly into the wholesaler's, and the items are picked up by mechanical devices and automatically taken to a shipping platform where they are assembled. Most large wholesalers use technology to carry out accounting, billing, inventory control, and forecasting. Modern wholesalers are adapting their services to the needs of target customers and finding cost-reducing methods of doing business. ≫ They are also transacting more business online. For example, e-commerce is Grainger's fastest-growing sales channel, making Grainger the 13th-largest online seller in the United States and Canada. Online and mobile purchasing now account for 36 percent of the wholesaler's total sales.[38]

Trends in Wholesaling

Today's wholesalers face considerable challenges. The industry remains vulnerable to one of its most enduring trends—the need for ever-greater efficiency. Recent tighter economic conditions have led to demands for even lower prices and the winnowing out of suppliers who are not adding value based on cost and quality. Progressive wholesalers constantly watch for better ways to meet the changing needs of their suppliers and target customers. They recognize that their only reason for existence comes from adding value, which occurs by increasing the efficiency and effectiveness of the entire marketing channel.

As with other types of marketers, the goal is to build value-adding customer relationships. McKesson provides an example of progressive, value-adding wholesaling. The company is a diversified health-care-services provider and the nation's leading wholesaler of pharmaceuticals, health and beauty care, home health-care, and medical supply and equipment products. To survive, especially in a tight economic environment, McKesson has to be more cost effective than manufacturers' sales branches. Thus, the company has built efficient automated warehouses, established direct computer links with drug manufacturers, and created extensive online supply management and accounts receivable systems for customers. It offers retail pharmacists a wide range of online resources, including supply management assistance, catalog searches, real-time order tracking, and an account management system. It has also created solutions such as automated pharmaceutical-dispensing machines that assist pharmacists by reducing costs and improving accuracy. Retailers can even use the McKesson systems to maintain prescription histories and medical profiles on their customers.

McKesson's medical-surgical supply and equipment customers receive a rich assortment of online solutions and supply management tools, including an online order management system and real-time information on products and pricing, inventory availability, and order status. According to McKesson, it adds value in the channel by providing "supply, information, and health care management products and services designed to reduce costs and improve quality across healthcare."[39]

The distinction between large retailers and large wholesalers continues to blur. Many retailers now operate formats such as wholesale clubs and supercenters that perform many wholesale functions. In return, some large wholesalers are setting up their own retailing operations. For example, SuperValu is the nation's largest food wholesaler, and it's also one of the country's largest food retailers. About half of the company's sales come from its Cub Foods, Save-A-Lot, Farm Fresh, Hornbacher's, Shop 'n Save, and Shoppers stores. In fact, SuperValu now bills itself as "America's neighborhood grocer."[40]

Wholesalers will continue to increase the services they provide to retailers—retail pricing, cooperative advertising, marketing and management information services, accounting services, online transactions, and others. However, both the more value-focused environment and the demand for increased services have put the squeeze on wholesaler profits. Wholesalers that do not find efficient ways to deliver value to their customers will soon drop by the wayside. Fortunately, the increased use of computerized, automated, and Internet-based systems will help wholesalers contain the costs of ordering, shipping, and inventory holding, thus boosting their productivity.

MyMarketingLab

If assigned by your instructor, complete the questions marked with the ⭐ from the EOC Discussion Questions section in the MyLab. To complete the Marketing by the Numbers problems found in this section, go to your Assignments in the MyLab.

REVIEWING AND EXTENDING THE CONCEPTS

CHAPTER REVIEW AND CRITICAL THINKING

Objectives Review

Retailing and wholesaling consist of many organizations bringing goods and services from the point of production to the point of use. In this chapter, we examined the nature and importance of retailing, the major types of retailers, the decisions retailers make, and the future of retailing. We then examined these same topics for wholesalers.

 OBJECTIVE 11-1 Explain the role of retailers in the distribution channel and describe the major types of retailers. (pp 334–340)

Retailing includes all the activities involved in selling goods or services directly to final consumers for their personal, nonbusiness use. Retailers play an important role in connecting brands to consumers in the final phases of the buying process. *Shopper marketing* involves focusing the entire marketing process on turning shoppers into buyers as they approach the point of sale. These days, shopper marketing and the "point of purchase" go well beyond in-store buying. Today's buyers are omni-channel consumers who work across multiple channels as they shop. Thus, influencing consumers' buying decisions calls for *omni-channel retailing*, creating a seamless cross-channel buying experience that integrates in-store, online, and mobile shopping.

Retail stores come in all shapes and sizes, and new retail types keep emerging. Store retailers can be classified by the *amount of service* they provide (self-service, limited service, or full service), *product line sold* (specialty stores, department stores, supermarkets, convenience stores, superstores, and service businesses), and *relative prices* (discount stores and off-price retailers). Today, many retailers are banding together in corporate and contractual *retail organizations* (corporate chains, voluntary chains, retailer cooperatives, and franchise organizations).

OBJECTIVE 11-2 Describe the major retailer marketing decisions. (pp 341–348)

Retailers are always searching for new marketing strategies to attract and hold customers. They face major marketing decisions about segmentation and targeting, store differentiation and positioning, and the retail marketing mix.

Retailers must first segment and define their target markets and then decide how they will differentiate and position themselves in these markets. Those that try to offer "something for everyone" end up satisfying no market well. By contrast, successful retailers define their target markets well and position themselves strongly.

Guided by strong targeting and positioning, retailers must decide on a retail marketing mix—product and services assortment, price, promotion, and place. Retail stores are much more than simply an assortment of goods. Beyond the products and services they offer, today's successful retailers carefully orchestrate virtually every aspect of the consumer store experience. A retailer's price policy must fit its target market and positioning, products and services assortment, and competition. Retailers use various combinations of the five promotion tools—advertising, personal selling, sales promotion, PR, and direct marketing—to reach consumers. Online, mobile, and social media tools are playing an ever-increasing role in helping retailers to engage customers. Finally, it's very important that retailers select locations that are accessible to the target market in areas that are consistent with the retailer's positioning.

OBJECTIVE 11-3 Discuss the major trends and developments in retailing. (pp 348–354)

Retailers operate in a harsh and fast-changing environment, which offers threats as well as opportunities. Following years of good economic times, retailers have now adjusted to the new economic realities and more thrift-minded consumers. New retail forms continue to emerge. At the same time, however, different types of retailers are increasingly serving similar customers with the same products and prices (retail convergence), making differentiation more difficult. Other trends in retailing include the rise of megaretailers; the rapid growth of direct, online, mobile, and social media retailing; the growing importance of retail technology; a surge in green retailing; and the global expansion of major retailers.

 OBJECTIVE 11-4 Explain the major types of wholesalers and their marketing decisions. (pp 355–360)

Wholesaling includes all the activities involved in selling goods or services to those who are buying for the purpose of resale or business use. Wholesalers fall into three groups. First, *merchant wholesalers* take possession of the goods. They include *full-service*

wholesalers (wholesale merchants and industrial distributors) and *limited-service wholesalers* (cash-and-carry wholesalers, truck wholesalers, drop shippers, rack jobbers, producers' cooperatives, and mail-order wholesalers). Second, *brokers* and *agents* do not take possession of the goods but are paid a commission for aiding companies in buying and selling. Finally, *manufacturers' and retailers' branches and offices* are wholesaling operations conducted by non-wholesalers to bypass the wholesalers.

Like retailers, wholesalers must target carefully and position themselves strongly. And, like retailers, wholesalers must decide on product and service assortments, prices, promotion, and place. Progressive wholesalers constantly watch for better ways to meet the changing needs of their suppliers and target customers. They recognize that, in the long run, their only reason for existence comes from adding value, which occurs by increasing the efficiency and effectiveness of the entire marketing channel. As with other types of marketers, the goal is to build value-adding customer relationships.

Key Terms

Objective 11-1
Retailing (p 334)
Retailer (p 334)
Shopper marketing (p 334)
Omni-channel retailing (p 335)
Specialty store (p 336)
Department store (p 336)
Supermarket (p 336)
Convenience store (p 337)
Superstore (p 337)
Category killer (p 337)

Service retailer (p 337)
Discount store (p 337)
Off-price retailer (p 338)
Independent off-price retailer (p 338)
Factory outlet (p 338)
Warehouse club (p 339)
Corporate chains (p 339)
Franchise (p 340)

Objective 11-2
Shopping center (p 347)

Objective 11-3
Showrooming (p 350)

Objective 11-4
Wholesaling (p 355)
Wholesaler (p 355)
Merchant wholesaler (p 356)
Broker (p 357)
Agent (p 357)
Manufacturers' and retailers' branches and offices (p 357)

Discussion Questions

11-1. Define the concept of *shopper marketing* and explain why it has grown in prominence. (AACSB: Communication)

11-2. Explain how retailers can be classified based by the amount of service offered and discuss an example of each retailer type. (AACSB: Communication; Reflective Thinking)

11-3. Name and describe the three types of off-price retailers. How do off-price retailers differ from discount stores? (AACSB: Communication)

11-4. Name and describe the three major groups of wholesalers. (AACSB: Communication; Reflective Thinking)

11-5. Compare and contrast brokers and agents with merchant wholesalers. (AACSB: Communication; Reflective Thinking)

Critical Thinking Exercises

11-6. In a small group, present a plan for a new retail store. Who is the target market? Describe the merchandise, atmospherics, price points, services provided, location, and how you would promote your retail store. Describe how you will differentiate your store from competitors. (AACSB: Communication; Reflective Thinking)

11-7. Visit a local mall and evaluate five stores. What type of retailer is each of these stores? What is the target

market for each? How is each store positioned? Do the retail atmospherics of each store enhance this positioning effectively to attract and satisfy the target market? (AACSB: Communication; Reflective Thinking)

11-8. Identify a retailer that is currently struggling. Discuss why it is having difficulties and suggest ways to turn things around. (AACSB: Communication; Reflective Thinking)

MINICASES AND APPLICATIONS

Online, Mobile, and Social Media Marketing   Local Retailers

It seems you can't get away from the buzz of online, mobile, and social media marketing from the likes of Amazon, Walmart, Nordstrom, and other large retailers. But what about the small independent retailers? Are they also getting on the online, mobile, and social media bandwagon? Some independent retailers are using these tools. For example, a convenience store owner in Miami Tweets a picture to 7,000 followers of a new beer he just stocked that morning, and by late afternoon customers come streaming in to check it out. Emerson Salon in Seattle sources 75 percent of its business from Facebook, Twitter, and its blog. Butter Lane cupcake bakery in New York City has found success using social media as well. Although these retailers have embraced online, mobile, and social media marketing, to most small retailers, using Facebook, Twitter,

Pinterest, Tumblr, Groupon, Instagram, Yelp, Foursquare, and other digital media can seem downright intimidating.

11-9. Find an example of a local retailer in your community that uses online, mobile, and social media marketing. Interview the owner of the store or restaurant and ask about the challenges and successes they've experienced when implementing this strategy. (AACSB: Communication; Use of IT; Reflective Thinking)

11-10. Create a presentation to give to local retailers explaining how they can effectively use online, mobile, and social media marketing to engage customers and enhance their business. (AACSB: Communication; Reflective Thinking)

Marketing Ethics   Lilly for Target

The Lilly Pulitzer brand of brightly colored dresses and resort-themed designer items is the uniform of the preppy, Palm Beach set. Indeed, only select young women belonging to certain sororities in certain communities are allowed discounts on the $100 to $500 items. But Target created a buying frenzy by debuting its Lilly for Target collection in April 2015. Target's Pulitzer line was composed of 250 items, such as Lilly dresses at $40, which sold out within minutes of launch, crashed the store's Web site, and created a firestorm of negative online comments from customers. The long lines outside stores caused one manager to name the event "Preppy Black Friday," likening it to the frenzied shopping day after Thanksgiving known as Black Friday. Most shoppers went home empty-handed because others scooped up as much as they could, emptying the racks within minutes. Items then sold on eBay for much higher prices. This type of launch is not new for Target. In 2011, the retailer launched a line of Missoni items priced at $30 to $40.

Missoni's distinctive zigzag and geometric-patterned knitwear, shoes, and houseware items normally sell for hundreds of dollars at retailers such as Bloomingdale's and Saks Fifth Avenue. During the Missoni event, shoppers grabbed goods by the armload, even poaching items from other shoppers' carts. While some shoppers went away happy, many more were not. In both merchandise promotions, Target officials announced the sold-out items would not be replenished.

11-11. Is it ethical for retailers to create a promotion but not have sufficient merchandise for all shoppers who want to buy the items? (AACSB: Communication; Ethical Reasoning)

11-12. Is it smart for Target to create such shopping frenzies even though some customers are dissatisfied? Explain why or why not. (AACSB: Communication; Reflective Thinking)

Marketing by the Numbers   Stockturn Rate

Retailers need merchandise to make sales. In fact, a retailer's inventory is its biggest asset. Not stocking enough merchandise can result in lost sales, but carrying too much inventory increases costs and lowers margins. Both circumstances reduce profits. One measure of a reseller's inventory management effectiveness is its *stockturn rate* (also called *inventory turnover rate* for manufacturers). The key to success in retailing is realizing a large volume of sales on as little inventory as possible while maintaining enough stock to meet customer demands.

11-13. Refer to Appendix 3: Marketing by the Numbers, and determine the stockturn rate of a retailer carrying an average inventory at cost of $850,000, with a cost of goods sold of $1,800,000. (AACSB: Communication; Analytical Reasoning)

11-14. If this company's stockturn rate was 4.5 last year, is the stockturn rate calculated above better or worse? Explain. (AACSB: Communication; Reflective Thinking)

Video Case Kmart

Once the leader in discount retailing, Kmart long ago took a back seat to Walmart, Target, and others discount chains. But recent efforts to provide value to customers through innovation show that the veteran retailer may still have its edge. To gain a competitive one-up, Kmart started a unique program that combined the benefits of online and brick-and-mortar shopping. When an item that customers wanted to purchase was not in stock at one of its stores, Kmart would ship the item to the customer's home for free.

To launch this program, Kmart unveiled an ad campaign that illustrated an uncharacteristic relevance to younger, tech-savvy customers. With the slight-of-mouth message that customers could "ship their pants" (or any of the other 65 million items in Kmart's inventory) for free, the ad went viral. As a result, Kmart got its message out in spades, entertaining many while offending a few along the way.

After viewing the video featuring Kmart, answer the following questions:

11-15. Consider the retail marketing mix. How did Kmart differentiate itself from other retailers with its free shipping program?

11-16. What kind of customer does the "Ship My Pants" campaign target? How is this significant?

11-17. Discuss what will be the ultimate effects of this Kmart campaign.

Company Cases 11 Sears/14 Alibaba/15 7-Eleven

See Appendix 1 for cases appropriate for this chapter. **Case 11, Sears: Why Should You Shop There?** Once "Where America Shops", the former leading retailer now has customers scratching their heads. **Case 14, Alibaba: The World's Largest E-Tailer Is Not Amazon.** Hardly known in the U.S., Alibaba has become the fastest growing e-tailer in the world by expanding into just about every consumer business imaginable. **Case 15, 7-Eleven: Adapting to The World's Many Cultures.** Just a convenience store in the U.S., 7-Eleven has a strong global presence by adapting its retail marketing mix to fit the unique needs of consumers worldwide.

MyMarketingLab

If assigned by your instructor, complete these writing sections from your Assignments in the MyLab.

11-18. Describe the types of shopping centers and identify specific examples in your community or a nearby city. (AACSB: Communication; Reflective Thinking)

11-19. The atmosphere in a retail store is carefully crafted to influence shoppers. Select a retailer that has both a physical store and an online store. Describe the elements of the physical store's atmosphere, such as the colors, lighting, music, scents, and décor. What image is the store's atmosphere projecting? Is that image appropriate given the merchandise assortment and target market of the store? Which elements of the physical store's atmosphere are part of its online store atmosphere? Does the retailer integrate the physical store's atmosphere with its online presence? Explain. (AACSB: Written and Oral Communication; Information Technology; Reflective Thinking)

12

Engaging Consumers and Communicating Customer Value
Advertising and Public Relations

CHAPTER ROAD MAP Objective Outline

▶ **OBJECTIVE 12-1** **Define the five promotion mix tools for communicating customer value.** The Promotion Mix (366–367)

▶ **OBJECTIVE 12-2** **Discuss the changing communications landscape and the need for integrated marketing communications.** Integrated Marketing Communications (367–374)

▶ **OBJECTIVE 12-3** **Describe and discuss the major decisions involved in developing an advertising program.** Advertising (375–392)

▶ **OBJECTIVE 12-4** **Explain how companies use public relations to communicate with their publics.** Public Relations (392–394)

Previewing the Concepts

In this and the next two chapters, we'll examine the last of the marketing mix tools—promotion. Companies must do more than just create customer value. They must also clearly and persuasively communicate that value. Promotion is not a single tool but rather a mix of several tools. Ideally, under the concept of *integrated marketing communications,* a company will carefully coordinate these promotion elements to engage customers and build a clear, consistent, and compelling message about an organization and its products. We'll begin by introducing the various promotion mix tools. Next, we'll examine the rapidly changing communications environment—especially the addition of digital, mobile, and social media—and the need for integrated marketing communications. Finally, we'll look more closely at two of the promotion tools—advertising and public relations. In the next chapter, we'll visit two other promotion mix tools—sales promotion and personal selling. Then, in Chapter 14, we'll explore direct, online, mobile, and social media marketing.

Let's start by looking at an outstanding advertising campaign. Two decades ago, GEICO was a little-known nicher in the U.S. auto-insurance industry. But now, thanks in large part to an industry-changing, big-budget advertising program, featuring an enduring tagline and a likeable but unlikely spokes-lizard, GEICO has muscled its way to the number-two position in its ultra-competitive industry. The message: Good advertising really does matter. Here's the story.

First Stop

GEICO: From Bit Player to Behemoth through Good Advertising

Founded in 1936, GEICO initially targeted a select customer group of government employees and noncommissioned military officers with exceptional driving records. Unlike its competitors, GEICO had no agents. Instead, the auto insurer marketed directly to customers, keeping its costs low and passing on the savings in the form of lower premiums. For nearly 60 years, GEICO's marketing relied almost entirely on direct mail and telephone advertising.

In 1994, however, when GEICO decided to expand its customer base, it knew that it must also expand its marketing. So it entered the world of mass media, a shift that would dramatically change the face of insurance advertising. GEICO started slowly, spending a paltry $10 million to launch its first national TV, radio, and print ads. Then, in 1996, billionaire investor Warren Buffett bought the company and famously told the marketing group "money is no object" when it comes to growing the business, so "speed things up." Did it ever. Over the next 10 years, GEICO's ad spending jumped 50-fold, to more than $500 million a year.

By now, you know a lot about GEICO and its smooth-talking gecko. But at the start, the insurer faced a tough task—introducing a little-known brand with a funny name to a national audience. Like all good advertising, the GEICO campaign began with a simple but compelling theme, one that highlights the convenience and savings advantages of GEICO's direct-to-customers system. To this day, every single one of the hundreds of ads and other content pieces in the GEICO campaign has driven home the now-familiar pitch: "15 minutes could save you 15 percent or more on car insurance."

But what really set GEICO's advertising apart was the inspired way the company chose to bring its value proposition to life. At the time, competitors were using serious and sentimental pitches—"You're in good hands with Allstate" or "Like a good neighbor, State Farm is there." To make its advertising stand out, GEICO decided to deliver its punch line with humor. The creative approach worked, and sales began to climb.

In trying to grow the brand, it become apparent that customers had difficulty pronouncing the GEICO name (which stands for Government Employees Insurance Company). Too often, GEICO became "gecko." Enter the charismatic green lizard. In 1999, GEICO ran a 15-second spot in which the now-famous, British-accented gecko called a press conference and pleaded: "I am a gecko, not to be confused with GEICO, which could save you hundreds on car insurance. So stop calling me." The ad was supposed to be a one-time "throwaway," but consumers quickly flooded the company with calls and letters begging to see more of the gecko. The rest, as they say, is history.

Although the gecko remains GEICO's iconic spokesman, one lizard could take the company only so far. So over the years, to keep its pitch fresh and entertaining, GEICO has supplemented the gecko ads with a continuous flow of clever, buzzworthy new executions telling the brand's value story. Early on, when GEICO first went online, the campaign employed a clutch of cultured cavemen, insulted by the company's advertising slogan, "It's so easy to use GEICO.com, even a caveman could do it." Later, in response to the question, "Can switching to GEICO really save you 15 percent or more on car

insurance?," the "Rhetorical Questions" campaign responded, "Is Ed 'Too Tall' Jones too tall?," "Was Abe Lincoln honest?," and "Did the little piggy cry 'wee wee wee' all the way home?" That last ad introduced the world to Maxwell, the talking pig who went on to star in his own GEICO campaign, emphasizing GEICO's growing digital, social, and mobile advances.

Another ad series promoted yet another GEICO character to pop culture icon status—the wildly popular Caleb the Camel who struts through the office every Wednesday rejoicing "It's hump day," suggesting that GEICO customers are "Happier than a camel on hump day." The swaggering Caleb went on to star in other GEICO commercials and even appeared in a string of pre-game Super Bowl commercials with Terry Bradshaw. In GEICO's more recent "It's what you do" campaign, among another fresh batch of creative ads and characters, one episode features Caleb and a friend at the zoo, nonchalantly accepting the taunts of people imitating his best "it's hump day" lines from previous commercials. The ad concludes, "If you're a camel, you put up with this all the time. It's what you do. And if you want to save 15 percent or more on car insurance, you switch to GEICO. It's what you do."

> Thanks in large part to an industry-changing, big-budget advertising program, featuring an enduring tagline and a likeable but unlikely spokes-lizard, GEICO has muscled its way to the number-two position in its ultra-competitive industry.

"No matter how many GEICO ads you've seen over the years—and it's a bunch—they never seem to grow stale," observes one expert. The company's chief marketing officer explains, "We're trying to stay ever-present in the consumer's mind but not bore them and have them just tune out yet another GEICO ad." However, no matter how varied, each minicampaign has a distinctly GEICO flavor, and every single ad closes strongly with the crucial "15 minutes could save you 15 percent" tagline.

The GEICO tagline is now so well-recognized that in one minicampaign—"Did you know?"—the brand even poked a little fun at itself. The commercials showed one person reading a GEICO "15 percent" ad while a second person observed, "Everybody knows that." The first person then responded, "Well, did you know ..." followed by a humorous (though fictional) fact. For instance, after revealing that "Old MacDonald was a really bad speller," one ad showed a farmer participant being eliminated from a spelling bee when he spells *cow* "C-O-W ... E-I-E-I-O." Each ad concluded, "GEICO: 15 minutes could save you, well ... you know."

Along with fresh content, GEICO has also adapted its content delivery to the fast-changing digital times. The brand was one of the first in its industry to provide customers with mobile apps and options for obtaining quotes, buying policies, and managing their accounts. The company is also an acknowledged leader in the use of online and social media, ranking third in the insurance industry behind only full-line insurers Allstate and State Farm in social media performance and digital customer engagement. The company's ads and Web-only videos are heavily viewed favorites online.

GEICO continues to invest heavily in advertising and content marketing, outspending every other insurance company in measured media by a nearly two-to-one margin. Its annual advertising budget, now more than $1 billion, makes GEICO the third-most-advertised U.S. megabrand, ahead of big spenders such as McDonald's, Toyota, and Walmart. The brand's creative and relentless advertising messaging, plus its heavy investment, has paid big dividends. The once little-known GEICO brand now enjoys well over 90 percent awareness among insurance shoppers. And after years of double-digit market share gains, GEICO recently passed Allstate to move into second place in the ultra-competitive U.S. car-insurance market.

Moreover, beyond spurring GEICO's spectacular growth, the brand's advertising has changed the way the entire insurance industry markets its products. In what was once a yawn-provoking category, competitors ranging from Allstate (with "Mayhem") to Progressive (with "Flo") are now injecting humor and interest in their own advertising campaigns. "This strategy is absolutely working for GEICO," asserts one analyst. It's "a testament to how GEICO has used advertising to evolve from a bit player to a behemoth," says another.[1]

Author Comment

The promotion mix is the marketer's bag of tools for engaging and communicating with customers and other stakeholders. To deliver a clear and compelling message, each tool must be carefully coordinated under the concept of integrated marketing communications (IMC).

Building good customer relationships calls for more than just developing a good product, pricing it attractively, and making it available to target customers. Companies must also *engage* consumers and *communicate* their value propositions to customers, and what they communicate should not be left to chance. All communications must be planned and blended into carefully integrated programs. Just as good communication is important in building and maintaining any other kind of relationship, it is a crucial element in a company's efforts to engage customers and build profitable customer relationships.

The Promotion Mix

A company's total **promotion mix**—also called its **marketing communications mix**—consists of the specific blend of advertising, public relations, personal selling, sales promotion, and direct marketing tools that the company uses to engage consumers, persuasively communicate customer value, and build customer relationships. The five major promotion tools are defined as follows:[2]

Promotion mix (marketing communications mix)
The specific blend of promotion tools that the company uses to engage customers, persuasively communicate customer value, and build customer relationships.

Advertising
Any paid form of nonpersonal presentation and promotion of ideas, goods, or services by an identified sponsor.

Sales promotion
Short-term incentives to encourage the purchase or sale of a product or a service.

Personal selling
Personal customer interactions by the firm's sales force for the purpose of engaging customers, making sales, and building customer relationships.

- **Advertising**. Any paid form of nonpersonal presentation and promotion of ideas, goods, or services by an identified sponsor.
- **Sales promotion**. Short-term incentives to encourage the purchase or sale of a product or service.
- **Personal selling**. Personal customer interactions by the firm's sales force for the purpose of engaging customers, making sales, and building customer relationships.
- **Public relations (PR)**. Building good relations with the company's various publics by obtaining favorable publicity, building up a good corporate image, and handling or heading off unfavorable rumors, stories, and events.
- **Direct and digital marketing**. Engaging directly with carefully targeted individual consumers and customer communities to both obtain an immediate response and build lasting customer relationships.

Each category involves specific promotional tools that are used to communicate with customers. For example, *advertising* includes broadcast, print, online, mobile, outdoor, and other forms. *Sales promotion* includes discounts, coupons, displays, and demonstrations. *Personal selling* includes sales presentations, trade shows, and incentive programs. *Public relations* includes press releases, sponsorships, events, and Web pages. And *direct and digital marketing* includes direct mail, catalogs, online and social media, mobile marketing, and more.

At the same time, marketing communication goes beyond these specific promotion tools. The product's design, its price, the shape and color of its package, and the stores that sell it—*all* communicate something to buyers. Thus, although the promotion mix is the company's primary engagement and communications activity, the entire marketing mix—promotion, *and* product, price, and place—must be coordinated for greatest impact.

Integrated Marketing Communications

In past decades, marketers perfected the art of mass marketing: selling highly standardized products to masses of customers. In the process, they developed effective mass-media communication techniques to support these strategies. Large companies now routinely invest millions or even billions of dollars in television, magazine, or other mass-media advertising, reaching tens of millions of customers with a single ad. Today, however, marketing managers face some new marketing communications realities. Perhaps no other area of marketing is changing so profoundly as marketing communications, creating both exciting and challenging times for marketing communicators.

The New Marketing Communications Model

Several major factors are changing the face of today's marketing communications. First, *consumers* are changing. In this digital, wireless age, consumers are better informed and more communications empowered. Rather than relying on marketer-supplied information, they can use the Internet, social media, and other technologies to find information on their own. They can connect easily with other consumers to exchange brand-related information or even create their own brand messages and experiences.

Second, *marketing strategies* are changing. As mass markets have fragmented, marketers are shifting away from mass marketing. More and more, they are developing focused marketing programs designed to engage customers and build customer relationships in more narrowly defined micromarkets.

Finally, sweeping advances in *digital technology* are causing remarkable changes in the ways companies and customers communicate with each other. The digital age has spawned a host of new information and communication tools—from smartphones and tablets to satellite and cable television systems to the many faces of the Internet (brand Web sites, email, blogs, social media and online communities, the mobile Web, and so much more). Just as mass marketing once gave rise to a new generation of mass-media communications, the new digital and social media have given birth to a more targeted, social, and engaging marketing communications model.

Although network television, magazines, newspapers, and other traditional mass media remain very important, their dominance is declining. In their place, advertisers are now adding a broad selection of more-specialized and highly targeted media to engage smaller customer communities with more personalized, interactive content. The new media range from specialty cable television channels and made-for-the-Web videos to online ads, email and texting, blogs, mobile catalogs and coupons, and a burgeoning list of social media. Such new media have taken marketing by storm.

Public relations (PR)
Building good relations with the company's various publics by obtaining favorable publicity, building up a good corporate image, and handling or heading off unfavorable rumors, stories, and events.

Direct and digital marketing
Engaging directly with carefully targeted individual consumers and customer communities to both obtain an immediate response and build lasting customer relationships.

Some advertising industry experts even predict that the old mass-media communications model will eventually become obsolete. Mass-media costs are rising, audiences are shrinking, ad clutter is increasing, and viewers are gaining control of message exposure through technologies such as video streaming or DVRs that let them skip disruptive television commercials. As a result, the skeptics suggest, marketers are shifting ever-larger portions of their marketing budgets away from old-media mainstays and moving them to online, social, mobile, and other new-age media.

In recent years, although TV still dominates as an advertising medium with a 38 percent share of U.S. ad spending, its growth has stagnated. Spending in magazines, newspapers, and radio has lost ground. Meanwhile, digital media have come from nowhere during the past several years to account for about 30 percent of U.S. advertising spending, second only to TV. By far the fastest-growing ad-spending category, digital's share is expected to grow to 36 percent by 2019. P&G, the world's biggest advertiser, now spends as much as one-third of its marketing budget on digital media. By one estimate, companies around the world now invest an average of 24 percent of their media budgets on digital.[3]

Some marketers now rely almost entirely on digital and social media. ≫ For example, eco-friendly household products maker Method employs a full but mostly digital promotional campaign themed "Clean happy":[4]

> Method is known for offbeat campaigns using slogans like "People against dirty" and "For the love of clean." But the most notable thing about the "Clean happy" campaign is that it at first used zero ads in traditional media like TV or magazines. Instead, the centerpiece of the campaign was brand videos aired only on YouTube and on the Method Facebook page. The campaign also employed online media ads as well as a major presence in social media that included, in addition to YouTube and Facebook, the Method Twitter feed and blogs. The "Clean happy" campaign fit both Method's personality and its budget. Method is the kind of grassroots brand that benefits from social media–type word of mouth. Moreover, "Clean happy" ran a first-year budget of only about $3.5 million, compared with the whopping $150 million or so that rival P&G might spend just to bring out a single new product, such as Tide Pods detergent packets.
>
> Method ran the digital-only campaign for a full year before beginning to bring it to TV. Even now, the "Clean happy" campaign relies heavily on digital and social media, supported only by carefully targeted regional cable TV in selected markets. More recent campaign installments include "Life's Messy Moments," a romantic comedy-style series of TV and online ads and other social media content that follow a young couple and their relatable messes from their first kiss to first kid to a clean, happy ending. To kick off the campaign on Facebook, Method hosted a photo contest called Clean Happy Awards, asking fans to submit their best pet, kid, and party messes. "We're embracing this grassroots movement," says a Method ad executive. "When you don't have 150 million bucks, that's what you have to do."

≫ The new marketing communications model: Method's successful and long-running "Clean happy" campaign began as an online-only effort and still relies heavily on digital and social media, supported only by carefully targeted regional cable TV ads in selected markets.
Method Products PBC

In the new marketing communications world, rather than using old approaches that interrupt customers and force-feed them mass messages, new media formats let marketers reach smaller communities of consumers in more engaging ways. For example, think about television viewing these days. Consumers can now watch their favorite programs on just about anything with a screen—on televisions but also laptops, smartphones, or tablets. And they can choose to watch programs whenever and wherever they wish, often without commercials. Increasingly, some programs, ads, and videos are being produced only for online viewing.

Despite the shift toward digital media, however, traditional mass media still capture a sizable share of the promotion budgets of most major marketing firms, a fact that probably won't change quickly. Thus, rather than the old-media model collapsing completely, most marketers foresee a shifting mix of both traditional mass media and online, mobile, and social media that engage more-targeted consumer communities in a more personalized way. In the end, regardless of the communications channel, the key is to integrate all of these media in a way that best engages customers, communicates the brand message, and enhances the customer's brand experiences.

As the marketing communications environment shifts, so will the role of marketing communicators. Rather than just creating and placing "TV ads" or "print ads" or "Snapchat branded story ads," many marketers now view themselves more broadly as **content marketing** managers. As such, they create, inspire, and share brand messages and conversations with and among customers across a fluid mix of *paid, owned, earned,* and *shared* communication channels. These channels include media that are both traditional and new as well as controlled and not controlled (see Marketing at Work 12.1).

Content marketing
Creating, inspiring, and sharing brand messages and conversations with and among consumers across a fluid mix of paid, owned, earned, and shared channels.

MARKETING AT WORK | 12.1

Just Don't Call It Advertising: It's Content Marketing

In the good old days, life seemed so simple for advertisers. When a brand needed an advertising campaign, everybody knew what that meant. The brand team and ad agency came up with a creative strategy, developed a media plan, produced and placed a set of TV commercials and magazine or newspaper ads, and maybe issued a press release to stir up some news. But in these digital times, the old practice of placing "advertisements" in well-defined "media" within the tidy framework of a carefully managed "advertising campaign" just doesn't work anymore.

Instead, the lines are rapidly blurring between traditional advertising and new digital content. To be relevant, today's brand messages must be social, mobile, interactively engaging, and multi-platformed. Says one industry insider: "Today's media landscape keeps getting more diverse—it's broadcast, cable, and streaming; it's online, tablet, and smartphone; it's video, rich media, social media, branded content, banners, apps, in-app advertising, and interactive technology products."

The new digital landscape has called into question the very definition of advertising. "What Is Advertising Anyway?" asks one provocative headline. Call it whatever you want, admonishes another, but "Just *Don't* Call It Advertising." Instead, according to many marketers these days, it's "content marketing," creating and distributing a broad mix of compelling content that engages customers, builds relationships with and among them, and moves them to action. To feed today's digital and social media machinery and to sustain "always-on" consumer conversations, brands need a constant supply of fresh content across a breadth of traditional and digital platforms.

Many advertisers and marketers now view themselves more broadly as *content marketing managers* who create, inspire, share, and curate marketing content—both their own content and that created by consumers and others. Rather than using traditional media breakdowns, they subscribe to a new framework that builds on how and by whom marketing content is created, controlled, and distributed. The new classification identifies four major types of media: paid, owned, earned, and shared (POES):

Paid media—promotional channels paid for by the marketer, including traditional media (such as TV, radio, print, or outdoor) and online and digital media (paid search ads, mobile ads, email marketing, or Web and social media display ads and sponsored content).

Owned media—promotional channels owned and controlled by the company, including company Web sites, corporate blogs, owned social media sites, proprietary brand communities, sales forces, and events.

Earned media—PR media channels, such as television, newspapers, blogs, online video sites, and other media not directly paid for or controlled by the marketer but that incorporate the content because of viewer, reader, or user interest.

Shared media—media shared by consumers with other consumers, such as social media, blogs, mobile media, and viral channels as well as traditional word of mouth.

In the past, advertisers have focused on traditional paid (broadcast, print) or earned (public relations) media. Now, however, content marketers are rapidly adding the new digital generation of owned (Web sites, blogs, brand communities) and shared (online social, mobile, email) media. Whereas a successful paid ad used to be an end in itself, marketers are now developing integrated marketing content that leverages the combined power of all the POES channels. Thus, many TV ads often aren't just TV ads anymore. They're "video content" you might see anywhere—on a TV screen but also on a tablet or phone. Other video content looks a lot like TV advertising but was never intended for TV, such as made-for-online videos posted on Web sites or social media. Similarly, printed brand messages and pictures no longer appear only in carefully crafted magazine ads or catalogs. Instead, such content, created by a variety of sources, pops up in anything from formal ads and online brand pages to mobile and social media and independent blogs.

>> Content marketing: Intel and Toshiba's award-winning "Inside" social media film series blurs the line between advertising, social media, and entertainment, creating high levels of customer–brand engagement for the two brands.

Courtesy Intel and Toshiba American Information Systems, Inc.

The new "content marketing" campaigns look a lot different from the old "advertising" campaigns. For example, to move beyond its long-running, traditional "Intel Inside" advertising, Intel recently teamed with computer maker Toshiba to produce an award-winning social media film series called "Inside." Enlisting the talents of Hollywood directors and actors, the engaging series blurs the lines between advertising, social media, and entertainment. One series, a comedy/sci-fi adventure called "The Power Inside," chronicled the efforts of a Scooby-Doo squad of 20-somethings to foil the plans of aliens intent on taking over the world by disguising themselves as mustaches and unibrows. Intel-powered Toshiba Ultrabooks play a central role, but the subtle product placement doesn't come across as an ad.

"The Power Inside" was released in six episodes on YouTube, with traffic driven through Facebook and Twitter (shared media), a dedicated microsite (owned media), and ads placed on Skype and Spotify (paid media). Awareness and popularity of the series were driven higher by mentions and articles in independent blogs and the press (earned media). "The Power Inside" earned even more publicity when its launch coincided perfectly with the awarding of a Daytime Emmy and the coveted Cannes Grand Prix award to the previous Intel/Toshiba series, "The Beauty Inside." In all, the integrated, multi-platform content marketing campaign created high levels of customer–brand engagement for the Intel and Toshiba brands. Based on the success of its partnership with Toshiba, Intel recently launched yet another social film series, "What Lives Inside," this time partnering with Dell.

Careful integration across the POES channels can produce striking communications results. Consider Samsung's "Life's a Photo. Take It." campaign to launch its Web-connected Galaxy Camera in 18 regions worldwide. To show how easily images taken by the camera can be shared instantly anytime, anyplace, Samsung chose 32 prominent Instagramers ("the world's most social photographers") and challenged them to use the new camera to prove that their cities—from London, Amsterdam, Berlin, Madrid, and Milan to Paris, Sydney, and San Francisco—were the most photogenic in the world. Their photos were uploaded to Tumblr, and fans voted for their favorites via Tumblr, Facebook, Twitter, and Pinterest. The winning city—Berlin—hosted a massive final event, where influencers invited from across Europe took photos with the connected camera and saw them projected onto giant, inflatable, 3D-projection cubes.

The "Life's a Photo. Take It." campaign, with its rich mix of marketing content, was an unqualified success. During its three-month run, the campaign reached more than 79 million people worldwide. Awareness of the Galaxy Camera rose 58 percent; purchase intent jumped 115 percent. The campaign won an Interactive Advertising Bureau MIXX award for content marketing, sparking a flurry of additional publicity. Finally, the social media campaign served as a foundation for a series of paid television ads. In the end, Samsung reignited a product category that many considered to be waning—dedicated digital cameras—and became the market leader in Web-connected digital imaging.

So, we can't just call it "advertising" anymore. Today's shifting and sometimes chaotic marketing communications environment calls for more than simply creating and placing ads in well-defined and controlled media spaces. Rather, today's marketing communicators must be marketing content strategists, creators, connectors, and catalysts who manage brand conversations with and among customers and help those conversations catch fire across a fluid mix of channels. That's a tall order, but with today's new thinking, anything is POES-ible!

Sources: Randall Rothenberg, "What Is Advertising Anyway?" *Ad Week*, September 16, 2013, p. 15; Joan Voight, "Intel and Toshiba Peddle Product Placement in Branded Film 'The Power Inside,'" *Ad Week*, July 29, 2013, www.adweek.com/print/151476; Patrick Darling, "Chip Shot: Dell and Intel Debut New Social Film 'What Lives Inside' on Hulu," March 23, 2015, http://newsroom.intel.com/community/intel_newsroom/blog/2015/03/23/chip-shot-dell-and-intel-debut-new-social-film-what-lives-inside-on-hulu; Peter Himler, "Paid, Earned & Owned: Revisited," *The Flack*, June 21, 2011, http://flatironcomm.com/2011/06/paid-earned-owned-revisited/; "Samsung's Galaxy Camera," 2013 AIB MIXX Awards Winners Gallery, www.iab.net/mixxawards/gallery2013/strategies-and-objectives/content-marketing.html; http:// samsungcamera.tumblr.com/latest; "Life's a Photo, Take It," Jam, www.spreadingjam.com/our-work/samsung/life-s-a-photo-take-it, accessed June 2015; and "'Life's a Photo. Take It'—Campaign Overview," *Vice*, www.vice.com/sgc/lifes-a-photo-take-it-campaign-overview, accessed October 2015.

The Need for *Integrated* Marketing Communications

The shift toward a richer mix of media and content approaches poses a problem for marketers. Consumers today are bombarded by brand messages from a broad range of sources. But all too often, companies fail to integrate their various communication channels. Mass-media ads say one thing, whereas company's Internet site, emails, social media pages, or videos posted on YouTube say something altogether different.

One problem is that marketing content often comes from different parts of the company. Advertising messages are prepared by the advertising department or an ad agency. Other company departments or agencies prepare public relations messages, sales promotion events, and online or social media content. However, consumers don't distinguish between content sources the way marketers do. In the consumer's mind, brand-related content from different sources—whether it's a Super Bowl ad, in-store display, mobile app, or friend's social media post—all merge into a single message about the brand or

Figure 12.1 Integrated Marketing Communications

Carefully blended mix of promotion tools

- Advertising
- Personal selling
- Sales promotion
- Public relations
- Direct and digital marketing

Consistent, clear, and compelling company and brand messages

Today's customers are bombarded by brand content from all directions. For example, think about all the ways you interact with companies such as Nike, Apple, or Coca-Cola. Integrated marketing communications means that companies must carefully coordinate all of these customer touch points to ensure clear brand messages.

company. Conflicting content from these different sources can result in confused company images, brand positions, and customer relationships.

Thus, the explosion of online, mobile, and social media marketing presents tremendous opportunities but also big challenges. It gives marketers rich new tools for understanding and engaging customers. At the same time, it complicates and fragments overall marketing communications. The challenge is to bring it all together in an organized way. To that end, more companies today are adopting the concept of **integrated marketing communications (IMC)**. Under this concept, as illustrated in ≫ **Figure 12.1**, the company carefully integrates and coordinates its many communication channels to deliver a clear, consistent, and compelling message about the organization and its brands.

Often, different media play unique roles in engaging, informing, and persuading consumers. For example, a recent study showed that more than two-thirds of advertisers and their agencies are planning video ad campaigns that stretch across multiple viewing platforms, such as traditional TV and digital, mobile, and social media. Such *video convergence*, as it's called, combines TV's core strength—vast reach—with digital's better targeting, interaction, and engagement.[5] These varied media and roles must be carefully coordinated under the overall integrated marketing communications plan.

One good example of a well-integrated marketing communications effort is home-improvement retailer Lowe's "Never Stop Improving" campaign, which integrates the clout of big-budget traditional media with the power of social media to create personalized, real-time customer engagement:[6]

To be sure, Lowe's runs a full slate of big-budget television spots and other traditional media ads that drive home its "Never Stop Improving" positioning. But in recent years, the company has added a rich flow of engaging, carefully integrated social media content that personalizes and enriches the Lowe's customer experience in ways that traditional media can't. Just one example is the Lowe's "Fix in Six" Vine video campaign. ≫ "Fix in Six" features dozens of clever six-second looping videos showing quick-fix solutions to home-improvement problems—everything from removing stripped screws to keeping squirrels away from plants. The award-winning series was a huge success from the start, generating 28,000 social media mentions within just the first week and earning millions of total campaign impressions to date.

Integrated marketing communications (IMC)
Carefully integrating and coordinating the company's many communications channels to deliver a clear, consistent, and compelling message about the organization and its brands.

LOWE'S VINE FIX IN SIX

Lowe's is the second largest home improvement retailer in the world and in the business of providing 'how to' tips. When Vine launched earlier this year, we saw an opportunity.

Using stop-motion techniques and the Vine application, we animated a dozen entertainingly useful six-second videos.

In the first campaign of its kind, we used the Vine platform as a way to bring useful tips to life. The campaign was recognized by the press and users alike for bringing meaning to a platform often associated with trivial curiosities, rather than compelling content.

≫ **Integrated marketing communications: The Lowe's "Never Stop Improving" campaign integrates the clout of big-budget traditional media with the power of social media to create personalized, real-time customer engagement.**

LOWE'S, the Gable Mansard Design, and NEVER STOP IMPROVING are trademarks or registered trademarks of LF, LLC.

Beyond Vine, the Lowe's "Never Stop Improving" campaign integrates a broad mix of social media, each playing its own unique role. Lowe's uses its heavily subscribed YouTube channel for longer DIY video tips and tutorials to supplement the quick hits on Vine. It uses Pinterest and Instagram to inspire customers' projects to life through high-impact imagery. Facebook provides a platform for engaging customers in dialogue—every Facebook comment gets an answer. Twitter serves for posting short comments or spreading the word about special offers. No matter what the platform, all content—from television spots to online videos to Facebook posts—is carefully coordinated under Lowe's "Never Stop Improving" mantra and its mission of helping customers find home-improvement solutions. According to one Lowe's marketer, the integrated marketing campaign is less about making the cash register ring and more about "making sure that customers … know that Lowe's is offering them value and [about keeping them] engaged with the brand."

Author Comment

In this section, we'll look at how marketers blend the various marketing communication tools into a smooth-functioning integrated promotion mix.

Shaping the Overall Promotion Mix

The concept of integrated marketing communications suggests that the company must blend the promotion tools carefully into a coordinated *promotion mix*. But how does it determine what mix of promotion tools to use? Companies within the same industry differ greatly in the design of their promotion mixes. For example, cosmetics maker Mary Kay spends most of its promotion funds on personal selling and direct marketing, whereas competitor CoverGirl spends heavily on consumer advertising. We now look at factors that influence the marketer's choice of promotion tools.

The Nature of Each Promotion Tool

Each promotion tool has unique characteristics and costs. Marketers must understand these characteristics in shaping the promotion mix.

Advertising. Advertising can reach masses of geographically dispersed buyers at a low cost per exposure, and it enables the seller to repeat a message many times. Television advertising can reach huge audiences. For example, more than 114 million Americans watched the most recent Super Bowl, and as many as 18 million avid fans tuned in each week for the latest season of NCIS. What's more, a popular TV ad's reach can be extended through online and social media. ▶ For example, consider Microsoft's inspiring and effective Super Bowl XLIX "Empowering" ad, featuring six-year-old Braylon O'Neill excelling on prosthetic legs and showing how technology empowers us all to make the impossible possible. In addition to 100-plus million TV viewers, the ad drew more than 6.2 million YouTube views during the ensuing two months. For companies that want to reach a mass audience, TV is the place to be.[7]

Beyond its reach, large-scale advertising says something positive about the seller's size, popularity, and success. Because of advertising's public nature, consumers tend to view advertised products as more legitimate. Advertising is also very expressive; it allows the company to dramatize its products through the artful use of visuals, print, sound, and color. On the one hand, advertising can be used to build up a long-term image for a product (such as Coca-Cola ads). On the other hand, advertising can trigger quick sales (as when Kohl's advertises weekend specials).

Advertising also has some shortcomings. Although it reaches many people quickly, mass-media advertising is impersonal and lacks the direct persuasiveness of company salespeople. For the most part, advertising can carry on only a one-way communication with an audience, and the audience does not feel that it has to pay attention or respond. In addition, advertising can be very costly. Although some advertising forms—such as newspaper, radio, or online advertising—can be done on smaller budgets, other forms,

▶ TV advertising has vast reach. Microsoft's inspiring Super Bowl XLIX "Empowering" ad—about how technology improves our lives—drew 100-plus million TV viewers and triggered millions of online views and shares.

Microsoft Corporation

such as network TV advertising, require very large budgets. For example, the one-minute Microsoft "Empowering" Super Bowl ad discussed above cost $9 million for media time alone, not counting the costs of producing the ad.

Personal Selling. Personal selling is the most effective tool at certain stages of the buying process, particularly in building up buyers' preferences, convictions, and actions. It involves personal interaction between two or more people, so each person can observe the other's needs and characteristics and make quick adjustments. Personal selling also allows all kinds of customer relationships to spring up, ranging from matter-of-fact selling relationships to personal friendships. An effective salesperson keeps the customer's interests at heart to build a long-term relationship by solving a customer's problems. Finally, with personal selling, the buyer usually feels a greater need to listen and respond, even if the response is a polite "No, thank you."

These unique qualities come at a cost, however. A sales force requires a longer-term commitment than does advertising—advertising can be turned up or down, but the size of a sales force is harder to change. Personal selling is also the company's most expensive promotion tool, costing companies on average $600 or more per sales call, depending on the industry.[8] U.S. firms spend up to three times as much on personal selling as they do on advertising.

Sales Promotion. Sales promotion includes a wide assortment of tools—coupons, contests, discounts, premiums, and others—all of which have many unique qualities. They attract consumer attention, engage consumers, offer strong incentives to purchase, and can be used to dramatize product offers and boost sagging sales. Sales promotions invite and reward quick response. Whereas advertising says, "Buy our product," sales promotion says, "Buy it now." Sales promotion effects can be short lived, however, and often are not as effective as advertising or personal selling in building long-run brand preference and customer relationships.

Public Relations. Public relations is very believable—news stories, features, sponsorships, and events seem more real and believable to readers than ads do. PR can also reach many prospects who avoid salespeople and advertisements—the message gets to buyers as "news and events" rather than as a sales-directed communication. And, as with advertising, public relations can dramatize a company or product. Marketers tend to underuse public relations or use it as an afterthought. Yet a well-thought-out public relations campaign used with other promotion mix elements can be very effective and economical.

Direct and Digital Marketing. The many forms of direct and digital marketing—from direct mail, catalogs, and telephone marketing to online, mobile, and social media—all share some distinctive characteristics. Direct marketing is more targeted: It's usually directed to a specific customer or customer community. Direct marketing is immediate and personalized: Messages can be prepared quickly—even in real time—and tailored to appeal to individual consumers or brand groups. Finally, direct marketing is interactive: It allows a dialogue between the marketing team and the consumer, and messages can be altered depending on the consumer's response. Thus, direct and digital marketing are well suited to highly targeted marketing efforts, creating customer engagement, and building one-to-one customer relationships.

Promotion Mix Strategies

Marketers can choose from two basic promotion mix strategies: *push* promotion or *pull* promotion. ≫**Figure 12.2** contrasts the two strategies. The relative emphasis given to the specific promotion tools differs for push and pull strategies. A **push strategy** involves "pushing" the product through marketing channels to final consumers. The producer directs its marketing activities (primarily personal selling and trade promotion) toward channel members to induce them to carry the product and promote it to final consumers. For example, John Deere does very little promoting of its lawn mowers, garden tractors, and other residential consumer products to final consumers. Instead, John Deere's sales force works with Lowe's, Home Depot, independent dealers, and other channel members, who in turn push John Deere products to final consumers.

Push strategy
A promotion strategy that calls for using the sales force and trade promotion to push the product through channels. The producer promotes the product to channel members who in turn promote it to final consumers.

In a push strategy, the company "pushes" the product to resellers, which in turn "push" it to consumers.

In a pull strategy, the company promotes directly to final consumers, creating a demand vacuum that "pulls" the product through the channel. Most companies use some combination of push and pull.

>> Figure 12.2 Push versus Pull Promotion Strategy

Pull strategy

A promotion strategy that calls for spending a lot on consumer advertising and promotion to induce final consumers to buy the product, creating a demand vacuum that "pulls" the product through the channel.

Using a **pull strategy**, the producer directs its marketing activities (primarily advertising, consumer promotion, and direct and digital media) toward final consumers to induce them to buy the product. For example, Unilever promotes its Axe grooming products directly to its young male target market using TV and print ads, Web and social media brand sites, and other channels. If the pull strategy is effective, consumers will then demand the brand from retailers such as CVS, Walgreens, or Walmart, which will in turn demand it from Unilever. Thus, under a pull strategy, consumer demand "pulls" the product through the channels.

Some industrial-goods companies use only push strategies; likewise, some direct marketing companies use only pull strategies. However, most large companies use some combination of both. For example, Unilever spends nearly $8 billion worldwide each year on consumer marketing and sales promotions to create brand preference and pull customers into stores that carry its products.[9] At the same time, it uses its own and distributors' sales forces and trade promotions to push its brands through the channels so that they will be available on store shelves when consumers come calling.

Companies consider many factors when designing their promotion mix strategies, including the type of product and market. For example, the importance of different promotion tools varies between consumer and business markets. Business-to-consumer companies usually pull more, putting more of their funds into advertising, followed by sales promotion, personal selling, and then public relations. In contrast, business-to-business marketers tend to push more, putting more of their funds into personal selling, followed by sales promotion, advertising, and public relations.

Now that we've examined the concept of integrated marketing communications and the factors that firms consider when shaping their promotion mixes, let's look more closely at the specific marketing communications tools.

LINKING THE CONCEPTS

Pause here for a few minutes. Flip back through and link the parts of the chapter you've read so far.

- How does the *integrated marketing communications (IMC)* concept relate to the *promotion mix* concept?
- How has the changing communications environment affected the ways in which companies communicate with you about their products and services? If you were in the market for a new car, where might you hear about various available models? Where would you *search* for information?

Advertising

Advertising can be traced back to the very beginnings of recorded history. Archaeologists working in countries around the Mediterranean Sea have dug up signs announcing various events and offers. The Romans painted walls to announce gladiator fights, and the Phoenicians painted pictures on large rocks to promote their wares along parade routes. During the golden age in Greece, town criers announced the sale of cattle, crafted items, and even cosmetics. An early "singing commercial" went as follows: "For eyes that are shining, for cheeks like the dawn/For beauty that lasts after girlhood is gone/For prices in reason, the woman who knows/Will buy her cosmetics from Aesclyptos."

Modern advertising, however, is a far cry from these early efforts. U.S. advertisers now run up an estimated annual bill of nearly $183 billion on measured advertising media; worldwide ad spending is an estimated $545 billion. P&G, the world's largest advertiser, spent more than $4.6 billion on U.S. advertising and $11.5 billion worldwide.[10]

Although advertising is used mostly by business firms, a wide range of not-for-profit organizations, professionals, and social agencies also use advertising to promote their causes to various target publics. In fact, the 39th-largest U.S. advertising spender is a not-for-profit organization—the U.S. government, which advertises in many ways. For example, its Centers for Disease Control spent $68 million on the third year of an anti-smoking advertising campaign titled "Tips from a Former Smoker," showing people who have paid dearly due to smoking-related diseases.[11] Advertising is a good way to engage, inform, and persuade, whether the purpose is to sell Coca-Cola worldwide, help smokers kick the habit, or educate people in developing nations on how to lead healthier lives.

Marketing management must make four important decisions when developing an advertising program (see ➤➤**Figure 12.3**): *setting advertising objectives, setting the advertising budget, developing advertising strategy (message decisions and media decisions), and evaluating advertising effectiveness.*

Setting Advertising Objectives

Advertising objective
A specific communication *task* to be accomplished with a specific *target* audience during a specific period of *time.*

The first step is to set *advertising objectives.* These objectives should be based on past decisions about the target market, positioning, and the marketing mix, which define the job that advertising must do in the total marketing program. The overall advertising objective is to help engage customers and build customer relationships by communicating customer value. Here, we discuss specific advertising objectives.

An **advertising objective** is a specific communication *task* to be accomplished with a specific *target* audience during a specific period of *time.* Advertising objectives can be classified by their primary purpose—to *inform, persuade,* or *remind.* ➤➤**Table 12.1** lists examples of each of these specific objectives.

➤➤ **Figure 12.3 Major Advertising Decisions**

>> Table 12.1 Possible Advertising Objectives

Informative Advertising

Communicating customer value	Suggesting new uses for a product
Building a brand and company image	Informing the market of a price change
Telling the market about a new product	Describing available services and support
Explaining how a product works	Correcting false impressions

Persuasive Advertising

Building brand preference	Persuading customers to purchase now
Encouraging switching to a brand	Creating customer engagement
Changing customer perceptions of product value	Building brand community

Reminder Advertising

Maintaining customer relationships	Reminding consumers where to buy the product
Reminding consumers that the product may be needed in the near future	Keeping the brand in a customer's mind during off-seasons

Informative advertising is used heavily when introducing a new product category. In this case, the objective is to build primary demand. Thus, early producers of HDTVs first had to inform consumers of the image quality and size benefits of the new product. *Persuasive advertising* becomes more important as competition increases. Here, the company's objective is to build selective demand. For example, once HDTVs became established, Samsung began trying to persuade consumers that *its* brand offered the best quality for their money. Such advertising wants to engage customers and create brand community.

Some persuasive advertising has become *comparative advertising* (or *attack advertising*), in which a company directly or indirectly compares its brand with one or more other brands. You see examples of comparative advertising in almost every product category, ranging from sports drinks and fast food to car rentals, credit cards, and wireless phone services. For example, Taco Bell's initial ads introducing its then-new breakfast menu took a direct poke at fast-food breakfast leader McDonald's. Taco Bell ads employed a slew of actual people named Ronald McDonald as Taco Bell spokespeople. "It's not surprising these guys are loving Taco Bell," says one ad. "What's surprising is who they are." An online "behind-the-scenes" video drew millions of YouTube views. Taco Bell has continued rubbing its breakfast fare in McDonald's face with new comparative ads introducing other breakfast items.[12]

Microsoft has run several recent ad campaigns featuring head-on comparisons with competitors Google and Apple. Its "Bing It On" campaign directly challenged users to make side-by-side comparisons of Microsoft's Bing search engine results to Google search results without knowing which results were from which search engine. Similarly, ads for Microsoft's Surface tablets directly challenge Apple's laptops. >> One recent Surface Pro video ad made a convincing side-by-side comparison of the Microsoft Surface Pro with the Apple MacBook Air, concluding that the Surface is "the tablet that can replace your laptop." A Surface Pro print ad proclaimed, "Powerful as a laptop, lighter than Air."[13]

Advertisers should use comparative advertising with caution. All too often, such ads invite competitor responses, resulting in an advertising war that neither competitor can win. Upset competitors might also take more drastic action, such as filing complaints with the self-regulatory National Advertising Division of the Council of Better Business Bureaus or even filing false-advertising lawsuits.

The tablet that can replace your laptop.

Surface Pro 3

surface.com

>> **Comparative advertising: Many Microsoft ads feature head-on comparisons with competitors like Apple. The above video compared the Microsoft Surface Pro with the Apple MacBook Air, concluding that the Surface is "the tablet that can replace your laptop."**
Microsoft Corporation

Advertising budget
The dollars and other resources allocated to a product or a company advertising program.

Affordable method
Setting the promotion budget at the level management thinks the company can afford.

Percentage-of-sales method
Setting the promotion budget at a certain percentage of current or forecasted sales or as a percentage of the unit sales price.

Reminder advertising is important for mature products; it helps to maintain customer relationships and keep consumers thinking about the product. Expensive Coca-Cola television ads primarily build and maintain the Coca-Cola brand relationship rather than inform consumers or persuade them to buy it in the short run.

Advertising's goal is to help move consumers through the buying process. Some advertising is designed to move people to immediate action. For example, a direct-response television ad by Weight Watchers urges consumers to go online and sign up right away, and a Best Buy newspaper insert for a weekend sale encourages immediate store visits. However, many ads focus on building or strengthening long-term customer relationships. For example, a Nike television ad in which well-known athletes work through extreme challenges in their Nike gear never directly asks for a sale. Instead, the goal is to engage customers and somehow change the way they think or feel about the brand.

Setting the Advertising Budget

After determining its advertising objectives, the company next sets its **advertising budget** for each product. Here, we look at four common methods used to set the total budget for advertising: the *affordable method*, the *percentage-of-sales method*, the *competitive-parity method*, and the *objective-and-task method*.

Affordable Method

Some companies use the **affordable method**: They set the promotion budget at the level they think the company can afford. Small businesses often use this method, reasoning that a company cannot spend more on advertising than it has. They start with total revenues, deduct operating expenses and capital outlays, and then devote some portion of the remaining funds to advertising.

Unfortunately, this method of setting budgets completely ignores the effects of promotion on sales. It tends to place promotion last among spending priorities, even in situations in which advertising is critical to the firm's success. It leads to an uncertain annual promotion budget, which makes long-range market planning difficult. Although the affordable method can result in overspending on advertising, it more often results in underspending.

Percentage-of-Sales Method

Other companies use the **percentage-of-sales method**, setting their promotion budget at a certain percentage of current or forecasted sales. Or they budget a percentage of the unit sales price. The percentage-of-sales method has advantages. It is simple to use and helps management think about the relationships between promotion spending, selling price, and profit per unit.

Despite these claimed advantages, however, the percentage-of-sales method has little to justify it. It wrongly views sales as the *cause* of promotion rather than as the *result*. Although studies have found a positive correlation between promotional spending and brand strength, this relationship often turns out to be effect and cause, not cause and effect. Stronger brands with higher sales can afford the biggest ad budgets.

Thus, the percentage-of-sales budget is based on availability of funds rather than on opportunities. It may prevent the increased spending sometimes needed to turn around falling sales. Because the budget varies with year-to-year sales, long-range planning is difficult. Finally, the method does not provide any basis for choosing a *specific* percentage, except what has been done in the past or what competitors are doing.

Competitive-parity method
Setting the promotion budget to match competitors' outlays.

Competitive-Parity Method

Still other companies use the **competitive-parity method**, setting their promotion budgets to match competitors' outlays. They monitor competitors' advertising or get industry promotion spending estimates from publications or trade associations and then set their budgets based on the industry average.

Two arguments support this method. First, competitors' budgets represent the collective wisdom of the industry. Second, spending what competitors spend helps prevent promotion wars. Unfortunately, neither argument is valid. There are no grounds for believing that the competition has a better idea of what a company should be spending on promotion than does the company itself. Companies differ greatly, and each has its own special promotion needs. Finally, there is no evidence that budgets based on competitive parity prevent promotion wars.

Objective-and-Task Method

Objective-and-task method
Developing the promotion budget by (1) defining specific promotion objectives, (2) determining the tasks needed to achieve these objectives, and (3) estimating the costs of performing these tasks. The sum of these costs is the proposed promotion budget.

The most logical budget-setting method is the **objective-and-task method**, whereby the company sets its promotion budget based on what it wants to accomplish with promotion. This budgeting method entails (1) defining specific promotion objectives, (2) determining the tasks needed to achieve these objectives, and (3) estimating the costs of performing these tasks. The sum of these costs is the proposed promotion budget.

The advantage of the objective-and-task method is that it forces management to spell out its assumptions about the relationship between dollars spent and promotion results. But it is also the most difficult method to use. Often, it is hard to figure out which specific tasks will achieve stated objectives. For example, suppose Microsoft wants 75 percent awareness for the latest version of its Surface tablet during the three-month introductory period. What specific advertising messages and media schedules should Microsoft use to attain this objective? How much would these messages and media schedules cost? Microsoft management must consider such questions, even though they are hard to answer.

No matter what method is used, setting the advertising budget is no easy task. John Wanamaker, the department store magnate, once said, "I know that half of my advertising is wasted, but I don't know which half. I spent $2 million for advertising, and I don't know if that is half enough or twice too much." >> For example, Coca-Cola spends hundreds of millions of dollars annually on advertising, but is that too little, just right, or too much?

As a result of such thinking, advertising is one of the easiest budget items to cut when economic times get tough. Cuts in brand-building advertising appear to do little short-term harm to sales. For example, in the wake of the recent Great Recession, U.S. advertising expenditures plummeted 12 percent over the previous year. In the long run, however, slashing ad spending risks long-term damage to a brand's image and market share. In fact, companies that can maintain or even increase their advertising spending while competitors are decreasing theirs can gain competitive advantage.

For example, during the Great Recession, while competitors were cutting back, car maker Audi actually increased its marketing and advertising spending. Audi "kept its foot on the pedal while everyone else is pulling back," said an Audi ad executive at the time. "Why would we go backwards now when the industry is generally locking the brakes and cutting spending?" As a result, Audi's brand awareness and buyer consideration reached record levels during the recession, outstripping those of BMW, Mercedes, and Lexus and positioning Audi strongly for the post-recession era. In the post-recession economy, Audi is now one of the hottest auto brands on the market.[14]

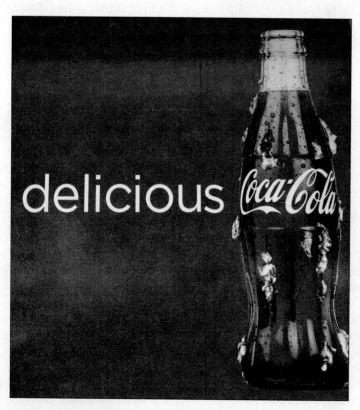

>> Setting the promotion budget is one of the hardest decisions facing a company. Coca-Cola spends hundreds of millions of dollars annually, but is that "half enough or twice too much"?
Migstock/Alamy

Developing Advertising Strategy

Advertising strategy
The strategy by which the company accomplishes its advertising objectives. It consists of two major elements: creating advertising messages and selecting advertising media.

Advertising strategy consists of two major elements: creating advertising *messages* and selecting advertising *media*. In the past, companies often viewed media planning as secondary to the message-creation process. After the creative department created good advertisements, the media department then selected and purchased the best media for carrying those advertisements to the desired target audiences. This often caused friction between creatives and media planners.

Today, however, soaring media costs, more-focused target marketing strategies, and the blizzard of new online, mobile, and social media have promoted the importance of the media-planning function. The decision about which media to use for an ad campaign—television, newspapers, magazines, video, a Web site, social media, mobile devices, or email—is now sometimes more critical than the creative elements of the campaign. Also, brand content is now often co-created through interactions with and among consumers. As a result, more and more advertisers are orchestrating a closer harmony between their messages and the media that deliver them. As discussed in the previous chapter, the goal is to create and manage brand content across a full range of media, whether they are paid, owned, earned, or shared.

Creating the Advertising Message and Brand Content

No matter how big the budget, advertising can succeed only if it engages consumers and communicates well. Good advertising messages and content are especially important in today's costly and cluttered advertising environment.

Today, the average household receives about TV 189 channels, and consumers have more than 7,200 magazines from which to choose.[15] Add in the countless radio stations and a continuous barrage of catalogs, direct mail, out-of-home media, email, and online, mobile, and social media exposures, and consumers are being bombarded with ads and brand content at home, work, and all points in between. For example, Americans are exposed to a cumulative 5.3 trillion online ad impressions each year and a daily diet of 500 million Tweets, 432,000 hours of uploaded YouTube video, 70 million photos shared on Instagram, 5 million article pins on Pinterest, and 4.75 billion pieces of shared content on Facebook.[16]

Breaking through the Clutter. If all this clutter bothers some consumers, it also causes huge headaches for marketers. Take the situation facing network television advertisers. They pay an average of $354,000 to produce a single 30-second commercial. Then, each time they show it, they pay an average of $112,100 for 30 seconds of advertising time during a popular primetime program. They pay even more if it's an especially popular program, such as *Sunday Night Football* ($627,000), *The Big Bang Theory* ($345,000), or a mega-event such as the Super Bowl (averaging $4.5 million per 30 seconds!). Then their ads are sandwiched in with a clutter of other commercials, network promotions, and other nonprogram material totaling as much as 20 minutes per primetime hour, with long commercial breaks coming every six minutes on average. Such clutter in television and other ad media has created an increasingly hostile advertising environment.[17]

Until recently, television viewers were pretty much a captive audience for advertisers. But today's digital wizardry has given viewers a rich new set of information and entertainment options—the Internet, video streaming, social and mobile media, tablets and smartphones, and others. Digital technology has also armed consumers with an arsenal of weapons for choosing what they watch or don't watch and when. ≫ Increasingly, thanks to the growth of DVR systems and digital streaming, consumers are choosing *not* to watch

≫ Advertising clutter: Today's consumers, armed with an arsenal of weapons, can choose what they watch and don't watch. Increasingly, they are choosing not to watch ads.

Piotr Marcinski/Shutterstock

ads. For example, 76 percent of U.S. homes have a DVR, subscribe to Netflix, or use video-on-demand from a cable or telecommunications provider. Forty-seven percent of American TV homes have DVRs, and two-thirds of DVR owners use the device to skip commercials.[18]

Thus, advertisers can no longer force-feed the same old cookie-cutter messages and content to captive consumers through traditional media. Simply interrupting or disrupting consumers no longer works. Unless ads provide content that is engaging, useful, or entertaining, many consumers will simply ignore or skip them.

Merging Advertising and Entertainment. To break through the clutter, many marketers have subscribed to a new merging of advertising and entertainment, dubbed "**Madison & Vine.**" You've probably heard of Madison Avenue, the New York City street that houses the headquarters of many of the nation's largest advertising agencies. You may also have heard of Hollywood & Vine, the intersection of Hollywood Avenue and Vine Street in Hollywood, California, long the symbolic heart of the U.S. entertainment industry. Now, Madison Avenue and Hollywood & Vine have come together to form a new intersection—Madison & Vine—that represents the merging of advertising and entertainment in an effort to create new avenues for reaching consumers with more engaging messages.[19]

This merging of advertising and entertainment takes one of two forms: advertainment or brand integrations. The aim of *advertainment* is to make ads and brand content themselves so entertaining, or so useful, that people *want* to watch them. There's no chance that you'd watch ads on purpose, you say? Think again. For example, the Super Bowl has become an annual advertainment showcase. Tens of millions of people tune in to the Super Bowl each year, as much to watch the entertaining ads as to see the game. And ads and related content posted online before and after the big game draw tens of millions of views. These days, it's common to see an entertaining ad on YouTube before you see it on TV.

Advertisers are also creating new content forms that look less like ads and more like short films or shows. A range of new brand messaging platforms—from Webisodes and blogs to online videos and social media posts—now blur the line between ads and other consumer content. For example, as part of its long-running, highly successful Campaign for Real Beauty, Unilever's Dove brand created a thought-provoking three-minute video, called "Dove Real Beauty Sketches," about how women view themselves. The video compares images of women drawn by an FBI-trained sketch artist based on their self-descriptions versus strangers' descriptions of them. Side-by-side comparisons show that the stranger-described images are invariably more accurate and more flattering, creating strong reactions from the women. The tagline concludes, "You're more beautiful than you think." Although the award-winning video was never shown on TV, it drew more than 163 million global YouTube views within just two months, making it the most-watched video ever.[20]

Marketers have tested all kinds of novel ways to break through today's clutter and engage consumers. For example, Hostess Brands—maker of those yummy Twinkies, Ho Hos, Ding Dongs, and cream-filled cupcakes—recently shared a Tweet celebrating the opening day of the Major League Baseball season. The Tweet contained a picture of baseball-decorated cupcakes but also the bold headline TOUCHDOWN. As expected, the Tweet grabbed plenty of attention, as droves of Twitter followers pounced to point out the mistake, just the reaction Hostess intended. "The 'touchdown' line was intentional," says the marketing director of Hostess Brands. "It's fun and aimed at young audiences who are in on the running joke." Other brands have also "tested the stupid waters," as one analyst puts it. ≫ For example, JCPenney once posted incoherent Tweets, grabbing widespread attention and leading to speculation that the retailer's social media person was either drunk or had been hacked. Instead, says JCPenney, the person was Tweeting with mittens on to promote its winter merchandise.[21]

Brand integrations (or *branded entertainment*) involve making the brand an inseparable part of some other form of entertainment or content. The most common form of brand integration is product placements—embedding brands as props within other programming. It might be a brief glimpse of Starbucks coffee products on *Morning Joe* on MSNBC or of Microsoft's Surface tablet and Bing search engine in episodes of *Elementary* or *Arrow*.

Madison & Vine
A term that has come to represent the merging of advertising and entertainment in an effort to break through the clutter and create new avenues for reaching customers with more engaging messages.

It might be scenes from *Captain America: The Winter Soldier* in which our superhero rides a Harley-Davidson Street 750.

Or the product placement might be scripted into an episode. For example, an entire episode of *Modern Family,* called "Lost Connection," was built around and told through character Claire Dunphy's Apple MacBook Pro. The episode was shot completely with Apple MacBook Pros, iPhones, and iPads and told using familiar Apple apps—such as FaceTime, Messaging, Safari, iTunes, Reminders, iPhoto, and the iCloud—all seamlessly integrated within the show's theme of searching for missing daughter Haley. Other *Modern Family* episodes have been built around products ranging from Oreos and Target to the Toyota Prius.[22]

>> **Branded entertainment: The highly acclaimed *The LEGO Movie* was pretty much a 100-minute product placement for iconic LEGO construction bricks, what one writer calls "product-placement perfection.**

Pictorial Press Ltd/Alamy

Originally created with TV in mind, brand integration has spread quickly into other sectors of the entertainment industry. If you look carefully, you'll see product placements in movies, video games, comic books, Broadway musicals, and even pop music. For example, last year's top 35 movies contained 464 identifiable brand placements.[23] >>The highly acclaimed film *The LEGO Movie* was pretty much a 100-minute product placement for iconic LEGO construction bricks. According to one writer, "The audience happily sits through a cinematic sales pitch ... that shows off the immense versatility of the product while placing it in a deeply personal context. The majority of the film is a breathtaking display of what LEGO bricks are capable of as creative tools, but the personal element is what really elevates this film to product-placement perfection." *The LEGO Movie* boosted The LEGO Group's sales by 11 percent in the six months after it opened.[24]

A related form of brand integration is so-called *native advertising,* advertising or other brand-produced online content that appears to be "native to" the Web or social media site in which it is placed. That is, the brand content looks in form and function like the other natural content surrounding it on a Web or social media platform. It might be an article on a Web site such as *The Huffington Post, BuzzFeed, Mashable,* or even *The New York Times* or *The Wall Street Journal* that is paid for, written by, and placed by an advertiser but uses the same format as articles written by the editorial staff. Or it might be brand-prepared videos, pictures, posts, or pages integrated into social media such as Facebook, YouTube, Instagram, Pinterest, or Twitter that match the form and feel of native content on those media. Examples include Twitter's promoted Tweets, Facebook's promoted stories, *BuzzFeed*'s sponsored posts, or Snapchat's "brand story" ads, branded posts that appear in the app's "Stories" feed. Native advertising is an increasingly popular form of brand content. It lets advertisers create relevant associations between brand and consumer content. According to a recent study by the Association of National Advertisers, "given today's media landscape, where consumers can avoid ads more than ever, advertisers are looking for new ways to get their messages noticed and acted upon."[25]

Thus, Madison & Vine is now the meeting place for advertising, brand content, and entertainment. The goal is to make brand messages a part of the broader flow of consumer content and conversation rather than an intrusion or interruption of it. As advertising agency JWT puts it, "We believe advertising needs to stop *interrupting* what people are interested in and *be* what people are interested in." However, advertisers must be careful that the new intersection itself doesn't become too congested. With all the new brand content formats and integration, Madison & Vine threatens to create even more of the very clutter that it was designed to break through. At that point, consumers might decide to take yet a different route.

Message and Content Strategy. The first step in creating effective advertising content is to plan a *message strategy*—the general message that will be communicated to consumers. The purpose of advertising is to get consumers to engage with or react to the product or company in a certain way. People will engage and react only if they believe they will benefit from doing so. Thus, developing an effective message strategy begins with identifying customer *benefits* that can be used as advertising appeals. Ideally, the message strategy will follow directly from the company's broader positioning and customer value-creation strategies.

Message strategy statements tend to be plain, straightforward outlines of benefits and positioning points that the advertiser wants to stress. The advertiser must next develop a compelling **creative concept**—or *big idea*—that will bring the message strategy to life in a distinctive and memorable way. At this stage, simple message ideas become great ad campaigns. Usually, a copywriter and an art director will team up to generate many creative concepts, hoping that one of these concepts will turn out to be the big idea. The creative concept may emerge as a visualization, a phrase, or a combination of the two.

The creative concept will guide the choice of specific appeals to be used in an advertising campaign. *Advertising appeals* should have three characteristics. First, they should be *meaningful*, pointing out benefits that make the product more desirable or interesting to consumers. Second, appeals must be *believable*. Consumers must believe that the product or service will deliver the promised benefits.

However, the most meaningful and believable benefits may not be the best ones to feature. Appeals should also be *distinctive*. They should tell how the product is better than competing brands. For example, the most meaningful benefit of a refrigerator is that it keeps foods cold. But GE sets its Café refrigerator apart as one that gives users an in-the-door filtered hot water dispenser and a Keurig K-Cup single-serve brewing system for making cups of coffee, tea, and other hot beverages at the fridge. It's "Brewing up the next big thing in refrigeration." Similarly, the most meaningful benefit of owning a wristwatch is that it keeps accurate time, yet few watch ads feature this benefit. Instead, watch advertisers might select any of a number of advertising themes. For years, Timex has been the affordable watch that "takes a licking and keeps on ticking." In contrast, Rolex ads talk about the brand's "obsession with perfection" and the fact that "Rolex has been the preeminent symbol of performance and prestige for more than a century."

Distinctive advertising appeals: GE sets its Café refrigerator apart as one that gives users an in-the-door filtered hot water dispenser and Keurig K-Cup single-serve brewing system. It's "Brewing up the next big thing in refrigeration."

Courtesy of General Electric

Creative concept
The compelling "big idea" that will bring an advertising message strategy to life in a distinctive and memorable way.

Execution style
The approach, style, tone, words, and format used for presenting an advertising message.

Message Execution. The advertiser now must turn the big idea into an actual ad execution that will capture the target market's attention and interest. The creative team must find the best approach, style, tone, words, and format for executing the message. The message can be presented in various **execution styles**, such as the following:

- *Slice of life.* This style shows one or more "typical" people using the product in a normal setting. For example, a Silk Soymilk "Rise and Shine" ad shows a young professional starting the day with a healthier breakfast and high hopes.
- *Lifestyle.* This style shows how a product fits in with a particular lifestyle. For example, an ad for Athleta active wear shows a woman in a complex yoga pose and states: "If your body is your temple, build it one piece at a time."
- *Fantasy.* This style creates a fantasy around the product or its use. For example, a Calvin Klein "Drive in to Fantasy" ad shows a woman floating blissfully above a surf-strewn beach at sunset in her Calvin Klein Nightwear.
- *Mood or image.* This style builds a mood or image around the product or service, such as beauty, love, intrigue, serenity, or pride. Few claims are made about the product or service except through suggestion. For example, Dodge Ram Truck's moving Super Bowl XLVII commercial—"To the Farmer in Us All"—added poignant pictures to radio-broadcast-legend Paul Harvey's "So God Made a Farmer"

speech, pulling down the number-two spot in *USA Today's* Ad Meter ratings that year. Except for a few brief frames and a closing picture, the two-minute ad never directly mentioned or showed sponsor Dodge Ram Trucks. However, it associated the brand with strong emotions and basic American values.

- *Musical.* This style shows people or cartoon characters singing about the product. For example, the M&M's "Love Ballad" ad, part of the Better with M campaign, featured Red singing Meat Loaf's "I'd Do Anything for Love," showcasing his commitment to actress Naya Rivera. Red has second thoughts, however, when Rivera can't resist adding Red to some of her favorite treats, including cookies, cake, and ice cream. To all of that, Red answers with the lyric, "But I won't do that … or that … or that … or that."
- *Personality symbol.* This style creates a character that represents the product. The character might be animated (Mr. Clean, the GEICO Gecko, or the Michelin Man) or real (perky Progressive Insurance spokeswoman Flo, Allstate's Mayhem, Ronald McDonald).
- *Technical expertise.* This style shows the company's expertise in making the product. Thus, Jim Koch of the Boston Beer Company tells about his many years of experience in brewing Samuel Adams beer.
- *Scientific evidence.* This style presents survey or scientific evidence that the brand is better or better liked than one or more other brands. For years, Crest toothpaste has used scientific evidence to convince buyers that Crest is better than other brands at fighting cavities.
- *Testimonial evidence or endorsement.* This style features a highly believable or likable source endorsing the product. It could be ordinary people saying how much they like a given product. For example, Whole Foods features a variety of real customers in its Values Matter marketing campaign. Or it might be a celebrity presenting the product, such as Beyoncé or Sofia Vergara speaking for Diet Pepsi.

The advertiser also must choose a *tone* for the ad. For example, P&G always uses a positive tone: Its ads say something very positive about its products. Other advertisers now use edgy humor to break through the commercial clutter. Bud Light commercials are famous for this.

The advertiser must use memorable and attention-getting *words* in the ad. For example, rather than just saying that its prescription sunglass lenses protect your eyes and look good at the same time, a LensCrafters ad announces, "Sunblock Never Looked So Good." Similarly, rather than claiming simply that its laundry detergent is "superconcentrated," Method asks customers, "Are you jug addicted?" The solution: "Our patent-pending formula that's so fricken' concentrated, 50 loads fits in a teeny bottle. … With our help, you can get off the jugs and get clean."

Finally, *format* elements make a difference in an ad's impact as well as in its cost. A small change in an ad's design can make a big difference in its effect. In a print or display ad, the *illustration* is the first thing the reader notices—it must be strong enough to draw attention. Next, the *headline* must effectively entice the right people to read the copy. Finally, the *copy*—the main block of text in the ad—must be simple but strong and convincing. Moreover, these three elements must effectively work *together* to engage customers and persuasively present customer value. However, novel formats can help an ad stand out from the clutter. ›› For example, in one striking ad from Volkswagen, the illustration does most of the work in catching relevant attention for the car maker's precision parking assist feature. It shows a porcupine "parked" in a tight space between goldfish in water-filled plastic bags. The small-print headline says only, "Precision Parking. Park Assist by Volkswagen." Enough said!

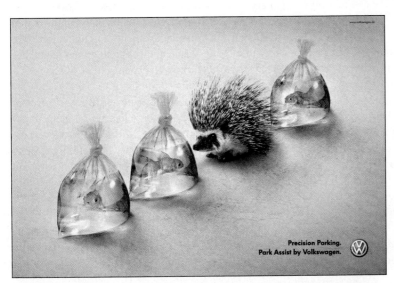

Precision Parking.
Park Assist by Volkswagen.

›› Novel formats can help an advertisement stand out. In this Volkswagen ad, the illustration does most of the work in illustrating the car maker's parking assist feature.

Used with permission of Volkswagen Aktiengesellschaft. Creative studio - The Operators

Consumer-Generated Content. Taking advantage of today's digital and social media technologies, many companies are now tapping consumers for marketing content, message ideas, or even actual ads and videos. Sometimes the results are outstanding; sometimes they are forgettable. If done well, however, user-generated content can incorporate the voice of the customer into brand messages and generate greater customer engagement.

Perhaps the best-known consumer-generated content effort is the long-running annual "Crash the Super Bowl Challenge" held annually by PepsiCo's Doritos brand. Doritos invites consumers to create their own 30-second video ads, and winners receive large cash awards and have their ads run during the Super Bowl. But brands across a wide range of industries—from automakers and fast-food chains to apparel brands and pet food marketers—are inviting customers to participate in generating marketing content.

For example, Chevrolet held an Oscars Program Video Contest last year that produced 72 imaginative ad videos for its Chevy Cruze model. The winner—a delightfully quirky one-minute video called "Speed Chaser"—was shot in an open field for only $4,000. Similarly, Purina conducted a video contest on its YouTube page, inviting owners of everyday dogs to submit videos showing "How is your dog great?" Using a compilation of clips from more than 500 submitted videos, Purina created a 60-second "How I'm Great" commercial and aired it during the broadcast of the Westminster Kennel Club Dog Show. And to help boost digital and social media engagement, >> Taco Bell invited YouTube stars and influencers to create video content for its new Fiery Doritos Locos Tacos. Taco Bell ended up choosing 65 video ads to distribute online through Twitter feeds and social networks and used one clever video—featuring a "3D Doritos Taco printer"—in subsequent paid online advertising.[26]

Consumer-generated content can make customers an everyday part of the brand conversation. Yogawear company Lululemon launched its #TheSweatLife campaign, in which it invited customers to Tweet or Instagram photos of themselves "getting their sweat on" in Lululemon gear. "Your perspiration is our inspiration," said the brand at its Web site. Within only a few months, the brand had received more than 7,000 photos, which it featured in a #TheSweatLife online gallery, quickly drawing more than 40,000 unique visitors. The user-generated content campaign created substantial customer engagement for Lululemon. "We created the program as a way to connect with our guests and showcase how they're authentically sweating in our product offline," says a Lululemon brand manager. "We see it as a unique way to bring their offline experiences into our online community."[27]

>> Consumer-generated content: Taco Bell boosted digital and social media coverage of the introduction of its Fiery Doritos Locos Tacos with consumer-generated videos distributed through Twitter feeds, social networks, and online advertising buys.
Taco Bell

Not all consumer-generated content efforts, however, are so successful. As many big companies have learned, ads and other content made by amateurs can be ... well, pretty amateurish. If done well, however, consumer-generated content efforts can produce new creative ideas and fresh perspectives on the brand from consumers who actually experience it. Such campaigns can boost consumer engagement and get customers talking and thinking about a brand and its value to them.

Selecting Advertising Media

Advertising media
The vehicles through which advertising messages are delivered to their intended audiences.

The major steps in **advertising media** selection are (1) determining *reach, frequency, impact,* and *engagement*; (2) choosing among major *media types*; (3) selecting specific *media vehicles*; and (4) choosing *media timing*.

Determining Reach, Frequency, Impact, and Engagement. To select media, the advertiser must determine the reach and frequency needed to achieve the advertising objectives. *Reach* is a measure of the *percentage* of people in the target market who are exposed to an ad campaign during a given period of time. For example, the advertiser might try to reach

70 percent of the target market during the first three months of a campaign. *Frequency* is a measure of how many *times* the average person in the target market is exposed to a message. For example, the advertiser might want an average exposure frequency of three.

But advertisers want to do more than just reach a given number of consumers a specific number of times. The advertiser also must determine the desired *media impact*—the *qualitative value* of message exposure through a given medium. For example, the same message in one magazine (say, *Time*) may be more believable than in another (say, the *National Enquirer*). For products that need to be demonstrated, television ads or online videos may have more impact than radio messages because they use sight, motion, *and* sound. Products for which consumers provide input on design or features might be better promoted at an interactive Web site or social media page than in a direct mailing.

More generally, an advertiser wants to choose media that will *engage* consumers rather than simply reach them. Using any medium, the relevance of ad content for its audience is often much more important than how many people it reaches. >> For example, when Mazda wanted to preannounce the sale of 100 25th-anniversary models of its iconic Mazda MX-5 Miata car at last year's New York International Auto show, it didn't use big-budget, high-reach media. Instead, it began churning out Facebook, Twitter, and Google+ posts directly to its large MX-5 Miata fan base, directing them to a microsite where they could preorder the sporty little car. Engaging the right audience in the right media worked well for Mazda. The microsite opened a month later to a flood of responses, and the limited-edition Miata model sold out within only 10 minutes.[28]

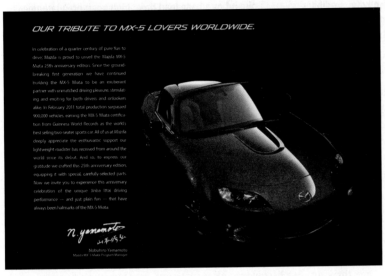

OUR TRIBUTE TO MX-5 LOVERS WORLDWIDE.

In celebration of a quarter century of pure fun to drive, Mazda is proud to unveil the Mazda MX-5 Miata 25th anniversary edition. Since the ground-breaking first generation we have continued building the MX-5 Miata to be an exuberant partner with unmatched driving pleasure, stimulating and exciting for both drivers and onlookers alike. In February 2011 total production surpassed 900,000 vehicles, earning the MX-5 Miata certification from Guinness World Records as the world's best selling two-seater sports car. All of us at Mazda deeply appreciate the enthusiastic support our lightweight roadster has received from around the world since its debut. And so, to express our gratitude we crafted this 25th anniversary edition, equipping it with special, carefully-selected parts. Now we invite you to experience this anniversary celebration of the unique Jinba Ittai driving performance — and just plain fun — that have always been hallmarks of the MX-5 Miata.

n. yamamoto

Nobuhiro Yamamoto
Mazda MX-5 Miata Program Manager

>> **Engaging the right consumers with the right media worked well for Mazda. Using a highly targeted digital campaign, it sold out 100 25th-anniversary models of its iconic Mazda MX-5 Miata car in only 10 minutes.**

Special thanks to those at Mazda North America Operations. Here's to 26 years of the MX-5 Miata and beyond. Long live the roadster.

Although Nielsen is beginning to measure *media engagement* levels for some television, radio, and social media, such measures are still hard to find in most cases. Current media measures are things such as ratings, readership, listenership, and click-through rates. However, engagement happens inside the consumer. It's hard enough to measure how many people are exposed to a given television ad, video, or social media post, let alone measuring the depth of engagement with that content. Still, marketers need to know how customers connect with an ad and brand idea as a part of the broader brand relationship.

Engaged consumers are more likely to act upon brand messages and even share them with others. Thus, rather than simply tracking *consumer impressions* for a media placement—how many people see, hear, or read an ad—Coca-Cola now also tracks the *consumer expressions* that result, such as a comment, a "Like," uploading a photo or video, or sharing brand content on social networks. Today's empowered consumers often generate more messages about a brand than a company can.

For example, Coca-Cola estimates that of the hundreds of millions of views of Coca-Cola–related content on YouTube each year, only about 18 percent are of content created by Coca-Cola. The other 82 percent are of content created by engaged consumers. So, many Coca-Cola marketing campaigns are aimed at sparking brand-related consumer expressions rather than just impressions. For example, the brand's recent "Ahh Effect" campaign called for teens to share the "ahh moments" they experience while drinking Coke at a www.AHH.com Web site and via social media using the hashtag #ThisisAHH. It then featured the user-generated personal expressions in "This is AHH" commercials on youth-oriented TV channels.[29]

Choosing among Major Media Types. As summarized in >> **Table 12.2**, the major media types are television; digital, mobile, and social media; newspapers; direct mail; magazines; radio; and outdoor. Each medium has its advantages and its limitations. Media planners want to choose a mix of media that will effectively and efficiently present the advertising message to target customers. Thus, they must consider each medium's impact, message effectiveness, and cost.

>> Table 12.2   Profiles of Major Media Types

Medium	Advantages	Limitations
Television	Good mass-marketing coverage; low cost per exposure; combines sight, sound, and motion; appealing to the senses	High absolute costs; high clutter; fleeting exposure; less audience selectivity
Digital, mobile, and social media	High selectivity; low cost; immediacy; engagement capabilities	Potentially low impact; high audience control of content and exposure
Newspapers	Flexibility; timeliness; good local market coverage; broad acceptability; high believability	Short life; poor reproduction quality; small pass-along audience
Direct mail	High audience selectivity; flexibility; no ad competition within the same medium; allows personalization	Relatively high cost per exposure; "junk mail" image
Magazines	High geographic and demographic selectivity; credibility and prestige; high-quality reproduction; long life and good pass-along readership	Long ad purchase lead time; high cost; no guarantee of position
Radio	Good local acceptance; high geographic and demographic selectivity; low cost	Audio only; fleeting exposure; low attention ("the half-heard" medium); fragmented audiences
Outdoor	Flexibility; high repeat exposure; low cost; low message competition; good positional selectivity	Little audience selectivity; creative limitations

As discussed earlier in the chapter, traditional mass media still dominate today's media mixes. However, as mass-media costs rise and audiences shrink, many companies are now adding digital, mobile, and social media that cost less, target more effectively, and engage consumers more fully. Today's marketers want to assemble a full mix of *paid, owned, earned, and shared media* that create and deliver engaging brand content to target consumers.

In addition to the explosion of online, mobile, and social media, cable and satellite television systems are thriving. Such systems allow narrow programming formats, such as all sports, all news, nutrition, arts, home improvement and gardening, cooking, travel, history, finance, and others that target select groups. Comcast and other cable operators are even testing systems that will let them target specific types of ads to TVs in specific neighborhoods or individually to specific types of customers. For example, ads for a Spanish-language channel would run in only Hispanic neighborhoods, or only pet owners would see ads from pet food companies.

Finally, in their efforts to find less costly and more highly targeted ways to reach consumers, advertisers have discovered a dazzling collection of *alternative media*. These days, no matter where you go or what you do, you will probably run into some new form of advertising:

>> Marketers have discovered a dazzling array of alternative media, like this heated Caribou Coffee bus shelter.
Caribou Coffee

Tiny billboards attached to shopping carts urge you to buy Pampers while ads roll by on the store's checkout conveyor touting your local Chevy dealer. Step outside and there goes a city trash truck sporting an ad for Glad trash bags or a school bus displaying a Little Caesar's pizza ad. A nearby fire hydrant is emblazoned with advertising for KFC's "fiery" chicken wings. You escape to the ballpark, only to find billboard-size video screens running Budweiser ads while a blimp with an electronic message board circles lazily overhead. >> In midwinter, you wait in a city bus shelter that looks like an oven—with heat coming from the coils—shouting out Caribou Coffee's lineup of hot breakfast sandwiches.

These days, you're likely to find ads—well—anywhere. Taxi cabs sport electronic messaging signs tied to GPS location sensors that can pitch local stores and restaurants wherever they roam. Ad space is being sold on parking-lot tickets, airline boarding passes, subway turnstiles, highway toll booth gates, ATMs, municipal garbage cans, and even police cars, doctors' examining tables, and church bulletins. One company even sells space on toilet paper furnished free to restaurants, stadiums, and malls—the paper carries advertiser logos, coupons, and codes you can scan with your smartphone to download digital coupons or link to advertisers' social media pages. Now that's a captive audience.

Such alternative media seem a bit far-fetched, and they sometimes irritate consumers who resent it all as "ad nauseam." But for many marketers, these media can save money and provide a way to hit selected consumers where they live, shop, work, and play.

Another important trend affecting media selection is the rapid growth in the number of *media multitaskers*, people who absorb more than one medium at a time. For example, it's not uncommon to find someone watching TV with a smartphone in hand, Tweeting, Snapchatting with friends, and chasing down product information on Google. One recent survey found that 35 percent of all screen time involves simultaneous use of TV and a digital device. Although some of this multitasking is related to TV viewing—such as looking up related product and program information—most multitasking involves tasks unrelated to the shows or ads being watched. Marketers need to take such media interactions into account when selecting the types of media they will use.[30]

Selecting Specific Media Vehicles. Media planners must also choose the best media vehicles—specific media within each general media type. For example, television vehicles include *Modern Family* and *ABC World News Tonight*. Magazine vehicles include *Time, Real Simple*, and *ESPN The Magazine*. Online and mobile vehicles include Twitter, Facebook, Instagram, and YouTube.

Media planners must compute the cost per 1,000 persons reached by a vehicle. For example, if a full-page, four-color advertisement in the U.S. national edition of *Forbes* costs $148,220 and *Forbes*'s readership is 900,000 people, the cost of reaching each group of 1,000 persons is about $164. The same advertisement in *Bloomberg Businessweek*'s Northeast U.S. regional edition may cost only $48,100 but reach only 155,000 people—at a cost per 1,000 of about $310.[31] The media planner ranks each magazine by cost per 1,000 and favors those magazines with the lower cost per 1,000 for reaching target consumers. In the previous case, if a marketer is targeting Northeast business managers, *Businessweek* might be the more cost-effective buy, even at a higher cost per thousand.

Media planners must also consider the costs of producing ads for different media. Whereas newspaper ads may cost very little to produce, flashy television ads can be very costly. Many online and social media ads cost little to produce, but costs can climb when producing made-for-the-Web video and ad series.

In selecting specific media vehicles, media planners must balance media costs against several media effectiveness factors. First, the planner should evaluate the media vehicle's audience quality. For a Huggies disposable diapers ad, for example, *Parents* magazine would have a high exposure value; men's lifestyle magazine *Maxim* would have a low exposure value. Second, the media planner should consider audience engagement. Readers of *Vogue*, for example, typically pay more attention to ads than do *Time* readers. Third, the planner should assess the vehicle's editorial quality. *Time* and *The Wall Street Journal* are more believable and prestigious than *Star* or the *National Enquirer*.

Deciding on Media Timing. An advertiser must also decide how to schedule the advertising over time. Suppose sales of a product peak in December and drop in March (for winter outdoor gear, for instance). The firm can vary its advertising to follow the seasonal pattern, oppose the seasonal pattern, or be the same all year. Most firms do some seasonal advertising. For example, Mars currently runs M&M's special ads for almost every holiday and "season," from Easter, Fourth of July, and Halloween to the Super Bowl season and the Oscar season. And weight-loss product and service marketers tend to heavy-up after the first of the year, targeting consumers who let their appetites get the better of them

>> **Media timing: Today's social media let advertisers respond to events in real-time. Arby's "Hey @Pharrell, can we have our hat back?" Tweet during the Grammy Awards earned the brand more than 75,000 re-Tweets and 40,000 Favorites.**

Kevin Winter/WireImage/Getty Images; Arby's Restaurant Group, Inc.

over the holiday season. Weight Watchers, for instance, spends more than a quarter of its annual advertising budget in January. Some marketers do *only* seasonal advertising: For instance, P&G advertises its Vicks NyQuil only during the cold and flu season.[32]

Today's online and social media let advertisers create ads that respond to events in real time. For example, Lexus recently introduced a new model through live streaming from the North American International Auto Show via Facebook's News Feed. Some 100,000 people watched the introduction live in only the first 10 minutes; another 600,000 viewed it online within the next few days. Oreos reacted in a timely way to a power outage during Super Bowl XLVII with an outage-related "You can still dunk in the dark" Tweet ad. The fast-reaction ad was re-Tweeted and Favorited thousands of times in only 15 minutes. Similarly, Arby's created big buzz during last year's Grammy Awards with a real-time Tweet responding to Pharrell Williams' infamous Vivienne Westwood hat, which looks a bit like the hat in the familiar Arby's logo. >> The Tweet "Hey @Pharrell, can we have our hat back?" earned more than 75,000 re-Tweets and 40,000 Favorites.[33]

Evaluating Advertising Effectiveness and the Return on Advertising Investment

Return on advertising investment
The net return on advertising investment divided by the costs of the advertising investment.

Measuring advertising effectiveness and the **return on advertising investment** has become a hot issue for most companies. Top management at many companies is asking marketing managers, "How do we know that we're spending the right amount on advertising?" and "What return are we getting on our advertising investment?"

Advertisers should regularly evaluate two types of advertising results: the communication effects and the sales and profit effects. Measuring the *communication effects* of an ad or ad campaign tells whether the ads and media are communicating the ad message well. Individual ads can be tested before or after they are run. Before an ad is placed, the advertiser can show it to consumers, ask how they like it, and measure message recall or attitude changes resulting from it. After an ad is run, the advertiser can measure how the ad affected consumer recall or product awareness, engagement, knowledge, and preference. Pre- and post-evaluations of communication effects can be made for entire advertising campaigns as well.

Advertisers have gotten pretty good at measuring the communication effects of their ads and ad campaigns. However, *sales and profit* effects of advertising and other content are often much harder to measure. For example, what sales and profits are produced by an ad campaign that increases brand awareness by 20 percent and brand preference by 10 percent? Sales and profits are affected by many factors other than advertising—such as product features, price, and availability.

One way to measure the sales and profit effects of advertising is to compare past sales and profits with past advertising expenditures. Another way is through experiments. For example, to test the effects of different advertising spending levels, Coca-Cola could vary the amount it spends on advertising in different market areas and measure the differences in the resulting sales and profit levels. More complex experiments could be designed to include other variables, such as differences in the ads or media used.

However, because so many factors affect advertising effectiveness, some controllable and others not, measuring the results of advertising spending remains an inexact science. For example, dozens of advertisers spend lavishly on high-profile Super Bowl ads each year. Although they sense that the returns are worth the sizable investment, few could actually measure or prove it (see Marketing at Work 12.2). Managers often must rely on large doses of judgment along with quantitative analysis when assessing advertising performance.

MARKETING AT WORK   12.2

The Super Bowl: The Mother of All Advertising Events—But Is It Worth the Price?

The Super Bowl is the mother of all advertising events. Each year, dozens of blue-chip advertisers showcase some of their best work to huge audiences around the world. But all this doesn't come cheap. Last year, major advertisers plunked down an average of $4.5 million per 30-second spot—that's $150,000 per second! Throw in ad production costs—which can run millions more per ad—and running even a single Super Bowl ad becomes a super-expensive proposition.

So each year, up pops the big debate: Is Super Bowl advertising worth all that money? Super Bowl stalwarts such as Anheuser-Busch, Doritos, Coca-Cola, and GM must think it's a good investment—they come back year after year. But for every big brand that invests in the Super Bowl, there are lots of others that just don't think the returns justify the costs.

The naysayers make some pretty good arguments. Super Bowl advertising is outrageously expensive. And, beyond the costs, the competition for attention during the Super Bowl is fierce. Every single ad represents the best efforts of a major marketer trying to design a knock-your-socks-off spectacular. Many advertisers feel they can get more for their dollar in venues that aren't so crowded with bigger-than-life commercials. For example, the cost of just one Super Bowl ad would buy more than 40 regular prime-time TV commercials, 6.4 million clicks on search ads, 50 million views on Facebook, a full week's worth of advertising on Snapchat, or a whopping 3.5 billion display ads across the Internet.

Still, the Super Bowl has much to offer advertisers. It plays to a huge and receptive audience. Super Bowl XLIV drew nearly 115 million U.S. viewers, making it the most-watched television event in history. What's more, during a typical Super Bowl, the ads draw as much or more viewership than the game. As a result, according to one study, the ROI for one Super Bowl ad can equal that of as many as 250 regular TV ads.

Perhaps more important, more and more these days, a Super Bowl ad itself is only the centerpiece of something much, much bigger. Long before the game begins and long after it ends, consumers, ad critics, media pundits, and advertisers are previewing, reviewing, sharing, rating, and rehashing the commercials. What used to be a one-time showing with some postgame "watercooler" chat is now a full eight- to 12-week experience.

In this digital, mobile, and social media age, rather than surprising viewers with their blockbuster ads during the game, most sponsors now flood online and social media channels weeks in advance with teasers or often entire ads. Weeks and days before the Super Bowl XLIX kick-off, ads posted by Budweiser, Doritos, BMW, Morphie, Snickers, Dove Men+Care, and many other brands had already grabbed hundreds of millions of online views. In fact, YouTube activity for Super Bowl XLIX ads and teaser videos produced 4 million hours of viewing before the game even started. Rather than stealing from a blockbuster ad, the previews seem to make them even more effective on game day. According to one study, 60 percent of the most-shared Super Bowl spots of all time were introduced before the game was broadcast. And on average, commercials uploaded to YouTube before the game generated 3.4 times more views than commercials released on game day.

Consider Anheuser-Busch's pregame activities for Super Bowl XLIX. The company released its Budweiser "Lost Dog" ad—a heartwarming tale featuring a lost Golden Retriever puppy rescued in the nick of time by the Clydesdales—on YouTube four days before the game. By game time, "Lost Dog" had already garnered 41.8 million YouTube views, 10 million more than the brand's ever-so-popular "Puppy Love" prequel the previous year. Aided by the previews, during the game, the endearing ad became the runaway leader in almost every major Super Bowl ad rating.

Super Bowl advertisers also work hard these days to create ads that engage consumers interactively during the game itself. Half of this year's Super Bowl ads incorporated hashtags, and many ads prominently mentioned Facebook, Twitter, YouTube, and other social media. All those digital nods made Super Bowl XLIX the most social Super Bowl ever. Viewers exchanged more than 28 million game-related Tweets during the event. Sixty-five million Facebook users generated 265 million actions, most related to the ads. Budweiser scored the big win—"Lost Dog" was shared more than 2 million times and inspired off nearly 200,000 Tweets during the game. Skittles, Nationwide, Doritos, and McDonald's rounded out the top-five most-talked-about ads on social media.

>> The Doritos Crash the Super Bowl contest and ads generate substantial consumer engagement before, during, and after the Big Game, extending the brand's return on its hefty Super Bowl advertising investment

Frito-Lay Inc.

Finally, for most Super Bowl advertisers, long after the game ends, the marketing content machine is still cranking. Next-day watercooler discussions about Super Bowl ads have been going on for decades. But digital, mobile, and social media have taken post-game buzz into the stratosphere. For days or even weeks following the game, online social channels hum with ad views and reviews, Likes, Shares, and comments. Becoming a part of all that online conversation and sharing can substantially extend a company's return on the game-day investment.

PepsiCo's Doritos brand begins its Super Bowl campaign each year a full four months prior to the event with its "Crash the Super Bowl" contest. Doritos invites consumers to submit their own 30-second commercials and, based on fan votes, runs the best ones during the game. The contest and ads ensure several months of heavy consumer involvement. Now in its ninth year, "Crash the Super Bowl" has produced numerous top-place finishers in the USA Today Ad Meter rankings. Last year's contest attracted 4,900 entries from 29 countries. The winner, "Middle Seat"—a clever ad about a man who uses a bag of Doritos to entice a pretty woman to sit next to him on a plane flight only to find that she has a fussy baby in tow —placed fifth in the Ad Meter rankings and earned its amateur creators a $1 million prize plus a "dream job" working at Universal Studios. The ad created buzz well beyond the actual game-day broadcast, as did the runner-up ad, "When Pigs Fly"—a chuckler in which a farm kid straps a rocket on a pig and makes the impossible happen in order to score a bag of Doritos.

So—back to the original question: Is Super Bowl advertising really worth the huge investment? The Super Bowl is certainly not for every brand. But for the right brands—and the brands that do it right—the answer is a resounding "yes." It's not just about running an ad or two during the big game. Instead, it's about consumers by the millions watching, streaming, sharing, commenting, debating, and buzzing about ads and brands before the game, in the moment, and after the main event. For the Super Bowl, says one marketing executive, "We are fundamentally playing a different game. [It's] no longer about 30 seconds [but] about a month long, really, really meaningful program." Says another Super Bowl regular: "Not only does the broadcast itself bring great value, but if you just look at the explosion in the social-media value and digital value in recent years, it's a terrific return on investment."

Sources: Julia Boorstin, "Who Won the Social Super Bowl," CNBC, February 2, 2015, www.cnbc.com/id/102389530; Drew Beechler, "Super Bowl XLIX Social Media Trends and Analysis #Infographic," *Salesforce.com*, February 2, 2015, www.salesforce.com/blog/2015/02/super-bowl-xlix-social-media-trends-and-analysis.html; Stuart Elliott, "Super Bowl Ads Get Their Own Pregame Show," *New York Times*, January 17, 2014; "Pepsi Alters Super Bowl Strategy, Takes Masterbrand Approach," *Advertising Age*, January 24, 2014, http://adage.com/print/291271; "How Marketers Can Bring Their A-Game to the Super Bowl," *Advertising Age*, November 4, 2013, http://adage.com/print/291177; John McDermott, "What the Cost of a Super Bowl Ad Can Buy Online," *Digiday*, January 30, 2015, http://digiday.com/platforms/cost-super-bowl-ad-can-buy-online/; and Jeanine Poggi, "Is the Super Bowl Worth the Price?" *Advertising Age*, February 9, 2015, p. 8.

Other Advertising Considerations

In developing advertising strategies and programs, the company must address two additional questions. First, how will the company organize its advertising function—who will perform which advertising tasks? Second, how will the company adapt its advertising strategies and programs to the complexities of international markets?

Organizing for Advertising

Different companies organize in different ways to handle advertising. In small companies, advertising might be handled by someone in the sales department. Large companies have advertising departments whose job it is to set the advertising budget, work with ad agencies, and handle other advertising not done by an agency. However, most large companies use outside advertising agencies because they offer several advantages.

Advertising agency
A marketing services firm that assists companies in planning, preparing, implementing, and evaluating all or portions of their advertising programs.

How does an **advertising agency** work? Advertising agencies originated in the mid- to late 1800s from salespeople and brokers who worked for the media and received a commission for selling advertising space to companies. As time passed, the salespeople began to help customers prepare their ads. Eventually, they formed agencies and grew closer to the advertisers than to the media.

Today's agencies employ specialists who can often perform advertising and brand content tasks better than the company's own staff can. Agencies also bring an outside point of view to solving the company's problems, along with lots of experience from working with different clients and situations. So, today, even companies with strong advertising departments of their own use advertising agencies.

Some ad agencies are huge; the largest U.S. agency, Y&R, has annual gross U.S. revenues of $1.69 billion. In recent years, many agencies have grown by gobbling up other agencies, thus creating huge agency holding companies. The largest of these megagroups, WPP, includes several large advertising, PR, digital, and promotion agencies with combined worldwide revenues of more than $17 billion.[34]

Most large advertising agencies have the staff and resources to handle all phases of an advertising campaign for their clients, from creating a marketing plan to developing ad and content campaigns and preparing, placing, and evaluating ads and content. Large brands commonly employ several agencies that handle everything from mass-media advertising campaigns to shopper marketing and social media content.

International Advertising Decisions

International advertisers face many complexities not encountered by domestic advertisers. The most basic issue concerns the degree to which global advertising should be adapted to the unique characteristics of various country markets.

Some advertisers have attempted to support their global brands with highly standardized worldwide advertising, with campaigns that work as well in Bangkok as they do in Baltimore. >> For example, McDonald's unifies its creative elements and brand presentation under the familiar "i'm lovin' it" theme in all its 100-plus markets worldwide. Visa coordinates its $500 million worldwide advertising efforts for its debit and credit cards under the "Everywhere you want to be" creative platform, which works as well in Korea as it does in the United States or Brazil.[35] And Snickers runs similar versions of its "You're not you when you're hungry" ads in 80 different countries, from the United States and the United Kingdom to Mexico, Australia, and even Russia. No matter what the country, the ads strike a common human emotion that everyone can relate to—people get out of sorts and do uncharacteristic things when they need nutrition. A Snickers bar can help them get back to being their real selves. Snickers let's local markets make adjustments for local languages and personalities. Otherwise, the ads are similar worldwide.[36]

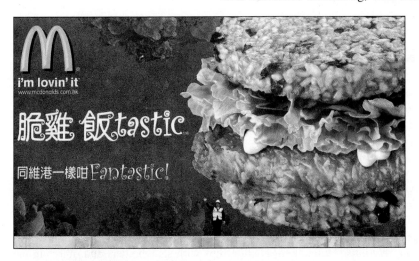

>> **International advertising: McDonald's unifies its global advertising under the familiar "i'm lovin' it" theme in all its 100-plus markets worldwide, here China.**

TED ALJIBE/AFP/Getty Images

In recent years, the increased popularity of online marketing and social media sharing has boosted the need for advertising standardization for global brands. Most big marketing and advertising campaigns include a large online presence. Connected consumers can now zip easily across borders via the Internet and social media, making it difficult for advertisers to roll out adapted campaigns in a controlled, orderly fashion. As a result, at the very least, most global consumer brands coordinate their Web sites internationally. For example, Coca-Cola Web sites around the world, from Australia and Argentina to France, Romania, and Russia, are surprisingly uniform. All feature splashes of familiar Coke red, iconic Coke bottle shapes, and Coca-Cola's music and "open happiness" themes.

Standardization produces many benefits—lower advertising costs, greater global advertising coordination, and a more consistent worldwide image. But it also has drawbacks. Most important, it ignores the fact that country markets differ greatly in their cultures, demographics, and economic conditions. Thus, most international advertisers "think globally but act locally." They develop global advertising *strategies* that make their worldwide efforts more efficient and consistent. Then they adapt their advertising *programs* to make them more responsive to consumer needs and expectations within local markets. For example, although Visa employs its "Everywhere you want to be" theme globally, ads in specific locales employ local language and inspiring local imagery that make the theme relevant to the local markets in which they appear.

Global advertisers face several special problems. For instance, advertising media costs and availability differ vastly from country to country. Countries also differ in the extent to which they regulate advertising practices. Many countries have extensive systems of laws restricting how much a company can spend on advertising, the media used, the nature of advertising claims, and other aspects of the advertising program. Such restrictions often require advertisers to adapt their campaigns from country to country.

Thus, although advertisers may develop global strategies to guide their overall advertising efforts, specific advertising programs must usually be adapted to meet local cultures and customs, media characteristics, and regulations.

LINKING THE CONCEPTS

Think about what goes on behind the scenes for the ads we all tend to take for granted.

● Pick a favorite print or television ad. Why do you like it? Do you think that it's effective? Can you think of an ad that people like that may not be effective?

● Dig a little deeper and learn about the campaign *behind* your ad. What are the campaign's objectives? What is its budget? Assess the campaign's message and media strategies. What other brand content does the campaign contain? Looking beyond your own feelings about the ad, is the campaign likely to be effective?

Author Comment

Not long ago, public relations was considered a marketing stepchild because of its limited marketing use. That situation is changing fast, however, as more marketers recognize PR's brand-building, customer engagement, and social power.

Public Relations

Another major mass-promotion tool, public relations, consists of activities designed to engage and build good relations with the company's various publics. PR departments may perform any or all of the following functions:[37]

● **Press relations or press agency.** Creating and placing newsworthy information in the news media to attract attention to a person, product, or service.
● **Product publicity.** Publicizing specific products.
● **Public affairs.** Building and maintaining national or local community relationships.
● **Lobbying.** Building and maintaining relationships with legislators and government officials to influence legislation and regulation.
● **Investor relations.** Maintaining relationships with shareholders and others in the financial community.
● **Development.** Working with donors or members of nonprofit organizations to gain financial or volunteer support.

Public relations is used to promote products, people, places, ideas, activities, organizations, and even nations. Companies use PR to build good relations with consumers, investors, the media, and their communities. Trade associations have used PR to rebuild interest in commodities, such as eggs, apples, potatoes, onions, and even chocolate milk. For example, the Milk Processor Education Program (MilkPEP), known for its successful "Got Milk?" campaign in previous years, created a strong PR campaign to promote the health benefits and boost consumption of chocolate milk:[38]

MilkPEP launched an extensive, integrated PR campaign to reposition chocolate milk—the traditional children's favorite—as a post-workout, sports recovery beverage for adults. Backed by more than 20 research studies that support the refueling benefits of chocolate milk, MilkPEP's "Built With Chocolate Milk" campaign enlists important influencers—such as athletes, sports nutritionists, fitness bloggers, and health researchers—to help change perceptions of chocolate milk from just a kid's drink to a legitimate sports drink, one that's "Trusted by Athletes. Backed by Science." ≫Ads and social media content feature both everyday and well-known athletes, such as 12-time swimming medalist Dara Torres, pro hockey's Zach Parise, Ironman World Champions Chris Lieto and Mirinda Carfrae, and NBA basketball star Carmelo Anthony. For example, MilkPEP sponsored Pittsburgh Steelers football player Hines Ward to train and compete in the Ironman. The chocolate milk team followed Hines through workouts and meetings with dieticians, showing the science behind chocolate milk as a recovery drink, then posted videos and other accounts on YouTube, Twitter, and Facebook. Hines's experience with chocolate milk inspired both fans and fellow athletes to try the beverage. Beyond working with professional athletes, MilkPEP also participates in hundreds of local events across the country, such as California's Big

≫ MilkPEP's "Built With Chocolate Milk" public relations campaign is repositioning chocolate milk as a sports recovery "after" beverage for both everyday and well-known adults, here Ironman World Champion Chris Lieto.

Bob Levey/WireImage/Getty images

Sur Marathon, passing out free chocolate milk at finish lines. Thanks to strong PR, chocolate milk is now making a comeback, with 6 to 12 percent sales increases among targeted adults.

The Role and Impact of PR

Public relations can have a strong impact on public awareness at a much lower cost than advertising can. When using public relations, the company does not pay for the space or time in the media. Rather, it pays for a staff to develop and circulate information and manage events. If the company develops an interesting story or event, it could be picked up by several different media and have the same effect as advertising that would cost millions of dollars. What's more, public relations has the power to engage consumers and make them a part of the brand story and its telling.

PR results can sometimes be spectacular. Consider the launch of Apple's iPad:[39]

Apple's iPad was one of the most successful new product launches in history. The funny thing: Whereas most big product launches are accompanied by huge prelaunch advertising campaigns, Apple pulled this one off with no advertising. None at all. Instead, it simply fed the PR fire. It built buzz months in advance by distributing iPads for early reviews, feeding the offline and online press with tempting tidbits and offering fans an early online peek at thousands of new iPad apps that would be available. At launch time, it fanned the flames with a cameo on the TV sitcom *Modern Family*, a flurry of launch-day appearances on TV talk shows, and other launch-day events. In the process, through PR alone, the iPad launch generated unbounded consumer excitement, a media frenzy, and long lines outside retail stores on launch day. Apple sold more than 300,000 of the sleek gadgets on the first day alone and more than 2 million in the first two months—even as demand outstripped supply. Apple repeated the feat a year later with the equally successful launch of iPad 2, which sold close to 1 million devices the weekend of its launch.

Despite its potential strengths, public relations is occasionally described as a marketing stepchild because of its sometimes limited and scattered use. The PR department is often located at corporate headquarters or handled by a third-party agency. Its staff is so busy dealing with various publics—stockholders, employees, legislators, and the press—that PR programs to support product marketing objectives may be ignored. Moreover, marketing managers and PR practitioners do not always speak the same language. Whereas many PR practitioners see their jobs as simply communicating, marketing managers tend to be much more interested in how advertising and PR affect brand building, sales and profits, and customer engagement and relationships.

This situation is changing, however. Although public relations still captures only a small portion of the overall marketing budgets of many firms, PR can be a powerful brand-building tool. Especially in this digital age, the lines between advertising, PR, and other content are becoming more and more blurred. For example, are brand Web sites, blogs, brand videos, and social media activities advertising, PR, or something else? All are marketing content. And as the use of earned and shared digital content grows rapidly, PR may play a bigger role in marketing content management. More than any other department, PR has always been responsible for creating relevant marketing content that draws consumers to a brand rather than pushing messages out. "PR pros are an organization's master story-tellers. In a word, they *do* content," says one expert. "The rise of social media [is] moving public relations professionals from the backroom, crafting press releases and organizing events, to the forefront of brand development and customer engagement," says another.[40] The point is that PR should work hand in hand with advertising within an integrated marketing communications program to help build customer engagement and relationships.

Major Public Relations Tools

Public relations uses several tools. One of the major tools is *news*. PR professionals find or create favorable news about the company and its products or people. Sometimes news stories occur naturally; sometimes the PR person can suggest events or activities that would create news. Another common PR tool is *special events*, ranging from news conferences and speeches, brand tours, and sponsorships to laser light shows, multimedia presentations, or educational programs designed to reach and interest target publics.

Public relations people also prepare *written materials* to reach and influence their target markets. These materials include annual reports, brochures, articles, and company newsletters and magazines. *Audiovisual materials*, such as DVDs and online videos, are being used increasingly as communication tools. *Corporate identity materials* can also help create a corporate identity that the public immediately recognizes. Logos, stationery, brochures, signs, business forms, business cards, buildings, uniforms, and company cars and trucks all become marketing tools when they are attractive, distinctive, and memorable. Finally, companies can improve public goodwill by contributing money and time to *public service activities*.

As previously discussed, the Web and social media are also important PR channels. Web sites, blogs, and social media such as YouTube, Facebook, Instagram, Snapchat, Pinterest, and Twitter are providing new ways to reach and engage people. As noted, storytelling and engagement are core PR strengths, and that plays well into the use of online, mobile, and social media.

As with the other promotion tools, in considering when and how to use product public relations, management should set PR objectives, choose the PR messages and vehicles, implement the PR plan, and evaluate the results. The firm's PR should be blended smoothly with other promotion activities within the company's overall integrated marketing communications effort.

MyMarketingLab

If assigned by your instructor, complete the questions marked with the ⭐ from the EOC Discussion Questions section in the MyLab. To complete the Marketing by the Numbers problems found in this section, go to your Assignments in the MyLab.

REVIEWING AND EXTENDING THE CONCEPTS

CHAPTER REVIEW AND CRITICAL THINKING

Objectives Review

In this chapter, you've learned how companies use integrated marketing communications (IMC) to engage customers and communicate customer value. You've also explored two of the major marketing communications mix elements—advertising and public relations. Modern marketing calls for more than just creating customer value by developing a good product, pricing it attractively, and making it available to target customers. Companies also must clearly and persuasively *communicate* that value to current and prospective customers. To do this, they must blend five communication mix tools, guided by a well-designed and implemented integrated marketing communications strategy.

 OBJECTIVE 12-1 Define the five promotion mix tools for communicating customer value. (pp 366–367)

A company's total *promotion mix*—also called its *marketing communications mix*—consists of the specific blend of *advertising, personal selling, sales promotion, public relations,* and *direct and digital marketing* tools that the company uses to engage customers, persuasively communicate customer value, and build customer relationships. Advertising includes any paid form of nonpersonal presentation and promotion of ideas, goods, or services by an identified sponsor. In contrast, public relations focuses on building good relations with the company's various publics. Personal selling

is personal presentation by the firm's sales force for the purpose of making sales and building customer relationships. Firms use sales promotion to provide short-term incentives to encourage the purchase or sale of a product or service. Finally, firms seeking immediate response from targeted individual consumers and consumer communities use direct, digital, and social media marketing tools to engage consumers and cultivate relationships with them.

OBJECTIVE 12-2 Discuss the changing communications landscape and the need for integrated marketing communications. (pp 367–374)

The explosive developments in communications technology and changes in marketer and customer communication strategies have had a dramatic impact on marketing communications. The new digital and social media have given birth to a more targeted, social, and engaging marketing communications model. Along with traditional media, advertisers are now adding a broad selection of more-specialized and highly targeted media to engage smaller customer segments with more-personalized, interactive content. As they adopt richer but more fragmented media and promotion mixes to reach their diverse markets, however, they risk creating a communications hodgepodge for consumers. To prevent this, companies are adopting the concept of *integrated marketing communications (IMC)*. Guided by an overall IMC strategy, the company works out the roles that the various promotional tools will play and the extent to which each will be used. It carefully coordinates the promotional activities and the timing of when major campaigns take place.

media decisions must be closely coordinated for maximum campaign effectiveness. Finally, *evaluation* calls for evaluating the communication and sales effects of advertising and other brand content before, during, and after it is placed and measuring advertising return on investment.

 OBJECTIVE 12-3 **Describe and discuss the major decisions involved in developing an advertising program. (pp 375–392)**

Advertising—the use of paid, owned, earned, and shared media by a seller to inform, persuade, and remind about its products or organization—is a strong promotion tool that takes many forms and has many uses. *Advertising decision making* involves decisions about the objectives, the budget, the message, the media, and, finally, the evaluation of results. Advertisers should set clear *objectives* as to whether the advertising is supposed to inform, persuade, or remind buyers. The advertising *budget* can be based on what is affordable, on sales, on competitors' spending, or on advertising objectives and tasks. The *message decision* calls for planning a creative concept (or "big idea") and message strategy and executing it effectively. The *media decision* involves defining reach, frequency, impact, and engagement goals; choosing major media types; selecting media vehicles; and deciding on media timing. Message and

 OBJECTIVE 12-4 **Explain how companies use public relations to communicate with their publics. (pp 392–394)**

Public relations involves building good relations with the company's various publics. Its functions include *press agency, product publicity, public affairs, lobbying, investor relations,* and *development*. Public relations can have a strong impact on public awareness at a much lower cost than advertising can, and PR results can sometimes be spectacular. Despite its potential strengths, however, PR sometimes sees only limited and scattered use. Public relations tools include *news, special events, written materials, audiovisual materials, corporate identity materials,* and *public service activities*. A company's Web site and online social media can be good PR vehicles. In considering when and how to use product PR, management should set PR objectives, choose the PR messages and vehicles, implement the PR plan, and evaluate the results. Public relations should be blended smoothly with other promotion activities within the company's overall integrated marketing communications effort.

Key Terms

Objective 12-1
Promotion mix (marketing communications mix) (p 366)
Advertising (p 366)
Sales promotion (p 366)
Personal selling (p 366)
Public relations (PR) (p 366)
Direct and digital marketing (p 366)
Content marketing (p 368)

Objective 12-2
Integrated marketing communications (IMC) (p 371)
Push strategy (p 373)
Pull strategy (p 374)

Objective 12-3
Advertising objective (p 375)
Advertising budget (p 377)
Affordable method (p 377)

Percentage-of-sales method (p 377)
Competitive-parity method (p 378)
Objective-and-task method (p 378)
Advertising strategy (p 379)
Madison & Vine (p 380)
Creative concept (p 382)
Execution style (p 382)
Advertising media (p 384)
Return on advertising investment (p 388)
Advertising agency (p 390)

Discussion Questions

12-1. Name and describe the five major promotion tools used in marketing. (AASCB: Communication)

12-2. What is integrated marketing communications (IMC), and how does a company go about implementing it? (AACSB: Communication)

12-3. Compare and contrast push and pull promotion strategies and discuss the factors marketers consider when

deciding which one to use. (AACSB: Communication; Reflective Thinking)

12-4. What are the role and functions of public relations within an organization? (AACSB: Communication)

12-5. Discuss the major public relations tools and the roles played by the Internet and social media. (AACSB: Communication)

Critical Thinking Exercises

12-6. Marketers use Q Scores to determine a celebrity's appeal to their target audience. Research Q Scores and write a report on a specific celebrity's Q Score for the past several years. If the score changed considerably, what could be the reason? What other types of Q Scores are there

besides scores for celebrities? (AACSB: Communication; Reflective Thinking)

12-7. Find three examples of advertisements that incorporate socially responsible marketing in their messages. Some companies are criticized for exploiting social issues or organizations by promoting them for their own gain. Do the examples you found do that? Explain. (AACSB: Communication; Ethical Reasoning; Reflective Thinking)

12-8. The Public Relations Society of America (PRSA) awards the best public relations campaigns with Silver Anvil Awards. Visit www.prsa.org/Awards/Search and review several case reports on previous winners. What does the field of public relations encompass? Write a report on one of the award winners focusing on marketing-related activities. (AACSB: Communication; Use of IT; Reflective Thinking)

MINICASES AND APPLICATIONS

Online, Mobile, and Social Media Marketing   Native Advertising

Marketers have always advertised in traditional media such as newspapers, television, and magazines, but today they are increasingly creating content for the online platforms of these media through *native advertising*, also called sponsored content. This form of promotion is not new. It dates back to the late 1880s as "reading notices" that placed information about brands and companies in news stories, usually without indicating sponsorship. However, sponsorship of today's native advertising is often clearly labeled. Native advertising is growing quickly. It is now offered by 73 percent of online publishers, and more than 40 percent of brands now use it. For example, *Forbes*'s BrandVoice lets companies such as IBM and CenturyLink place content both in the print magazine and on its digital platform at Forbes.com. Readers can learn from CenturyLink about how big data will change travel marketing or from Samsung about how to close the gender gap in science, technology, engineering, and math (STEM) education. Other publisher sites, such as *The Huffington Post*, help marketers create sponsored content. Its HuffPost Partner Studio provides writers, designers, and editors who assist business partners in creating relevant content about their brands in the familiar HuffPost voice. Fiber One tells readers "11 Diet 'Rules' You Can Absolutely Break," IBM explains how businesses can use social media, and Cottonelle tells readers how to fix the mistakes they are making in the bathroom. Social media are also getting in on the action. For example, Facebook reaped more than $1 billion in mobile native advertising alone in just one quarter. The rapid growth of native advertising has also caught the attention of the Federal Trade Commission. The FTC recently held a conference, "Blurred Lines: Advertising or Content? An FTC Workshop on Native Advertising" to discuss the issues of blending advertising with news and other content, leaving some to wonder if further regulations are forthcoming.

12-9. Find examples of native advertising on various publishers' Web and mobile sites. Create a presentation with screenshots showing the content and how it is identified. Has the content been shared with others via social media? (AACSB: Communication; Use of IT)

12-10. Debate whether the FTC's current regulations and guidelines regarding online advertising are adequate for this nature of advertising promotions. Will the FTC likely issue new guidelines or regulations? (AACSB Communication; Reflective Thinking)

Marketing Ethics   Amazon's Dronerama

On the eve of the biggest e-commerce shopping day of the year in 2013, Amazon's normally secretive founder and CEO, Jeff Bezos, scored a public relations home run by going on CBS's *60 Minutes* program to unveil the company's Prime Air unmanned aircraft project to deliver packages to consumers' doorsteps. Forget that it couldn't be implemented because the Federal Aviation Administration does not allow such use of drones and that it will likely be 2026 before drone delivery might even be possible. The interview set off "Dronerama," as some have called it. The next morning—Cyber Monday—the media were abuzz about drone delivery, with news organizations and Internet sites replaying the video of Amazon's cool drone delivering a package. The normally hard-hitting *60 Minutes* interview has been criticized because the interviewer, the famous Charlie Rose, seemed to gush all over Bezos and ignore other controversial issues, such as working conditions at Amazon. Rose further gushed over Amazon during the *60 Minutes Overtime* digital supplement to the show. Critics believe the normally unattainable Bezos called the shots in return for appearing on the show. "Dronerama" not only got Amazon on every cyber shoppers' lips on that all-important online shopping day, it seemed to take some of the wind out of the sails of a recently released book critical of Bezos at a time when Amazon needed customers the most.

12-11. Watch the *60 Minutes* interview at www.cbsnews.com/news/amazons-jeff-bezos-looks-to-the-future/. Is it ethical for companies to use the media in this way to gain favorable exposure? Did Jeff Bezos acknowledge the fact that drones were not feasible at the time of the interview? (AACSB: Communication; Ethical Reasoning; Reflective Thinking)

12-12. Create a presentation on the publicity Amazon received as a result of the *60 Minutes* interview and continues to receive over drone delivery. Would you judge this campaign a success or failure? (AACSB: Communication; Use of IT; Reflective Thinking)

Marketing by the Numbers   Advertising-to-Sales Ratios

Using the percent-of-sales method, an advertiser sets its advertising budget at a certain percentage of current or forecasted sales. However, determining what percentage to use is not always clear. Many marketers look at industry averages and competitor spending for comparisons. Web sites and trade publications publish data regarding industry averages to guide marketers in setting the percentage to use. For example, firms competing in the toy and apparel industries spend 10 percent or more of sales on advertising, whereas firms competing in the mortgage servicing and insulation industries spend less than 1 percent of sales on advertising. You read about GEICO at the beginning of the chapter. It is the number-two auto insurer with $17 billion in revenue last year. It spent $1.1 billion on advertising that year and plans to continue spending the same percentage of sales on advertising next year. The average advertising-to-sales ratio for the insurance industry is 0.1 percent of sales.

12-13. If GEICO projects $19 billion in sales next year, using the percentage-of-sales method of advertising budgeting, how much will the company budget for advertising if basing it on projected sales? (AACSB: Communication; Analytical Reasoning; Reflective Thinking)

12-14. How much would GEICO budget if the company based its advertising spending on the industry advertising-to-sales ratio? Is GEICO consistent with average industry ad spending? (AACSB: Communication; Analytical Reasoning; Reflective Thinking)

Video Case   Kmart

On the heels of its wildly popular "Ship My Pants" ads, Kmart struck again with an ad that was considered hilarious by some, offensive by others, and a stroke of genius by advertising critics. Its latest ad, "Big Gas Savings," was launched on YouTube prior to airing on television. And like its "Ship My Pants" predecessor, the ad also went viral.

In addition to relying on potty humor to pull its sales out of the toilet, Kmart struck a very timely note in the tune of customer value—saving money on gasoline. Customers could save 30 cents a gallon on gas by spending $50 or more in its stores.

Millions of customers took advantage of the offer, driving traffic into Kmart stores.

After viewing the video featuring Kmart, answer the following questions:

12-15. What is the advertising message in the Kmart "Big Gas Savings" ad?

12-16. Why did Kmart choose to air this video on YouTube?

12-17. Is this Kmart ad effective? Explain.

Company Cases   12 Allstate/5 GoldieBlox

See Appendix 1 for cases appropriate for this chapter. **Case 12, Allstate: Bringing Mayhem to the Auto Insurance Advertising Wars**. With an endlessly flexible advertising mascot, Allstate is driving its message to consumers and keeping competitors on their toes. **Case 5, GoldieBlox: Swimming**

Upstream Against Consumer Perceptions. A new toy company, GoldieBlox is out to change how people think of toys for girls with the message that success comes not from playing with dollhouses, but from building them.

MyMarketingLab

If assigned by your instructor, complete these writing sections from your Assignments in the MyLab.

12-18. Name and describe the various execution styles for presenting messages and provide an example of each style different from the ones in the chapter. (AACSB: Communication)

12-19. Discuss the major advertising objectives and describe an advertisement that is attempting to achieve each objective. (AACSB: Written and Oral Communication; Reflective Thinking)

13 Personal Selling and Sales Promotion

CHAPTER ROAD MAP | Objective Outline

▶ **OBJECTIVE 13-1** **Discuss the role of a company's salespeople in creating value for customers and building customer relationships.** Personal Selling (400–402)

▶ **OBJECTIVE 13-2** **Identify and explain the six major sales force management steps.** Managing the Sales Force (402–410); Social Selling: Online, Mobile, and Social Media Tools (410–413)

▶ **OBJECTIVE 13-3** **Discuss the personal selling process, distinguishing between transaction-oriented marketing and relationship marketing.** The Personal Selling Process (414–417)

▶ **OBJECTIVE 13-4** **Explain how sales promotion campaigns are developed and implemented.** Sales Promotion (417–424)

Previewing the Concepts

In the previous two chapters, you learned about engaging customers and communicating customer value through integrated marketing communications (IMC) and two elements of the promotion mix: advertising and public relations. In this chapter, we examine two more IMC elements: personal selling and sales promotion. Personal selling is the interpersonal arm of marketing communications, in which the sales force engages customers and prospects to build relationships and make sales. Sales promotion consists of short-term incentives to encourage the purchase or sale of a product or service. Although this chapter presents personal selling and sales promotion as separate tools, they must be carefully integrated with the other elements of the promotion mix.

First, let's look at a real-life sales force. When you think of salespeople, perhaps you think of pushy retail sales clerks, "yell and sell" TV pitchmen, or the stereotypical glad-handing "used-car salesman." But such stereotypes don't fit the reality of most of today's salespeople—sales professionals who succeed not by taking advantage of customers but by listening to their needs and helping to forge solutions. Consider Salesforce—the industry leader in customer relationship management solutions. Salesforce not only produces market-leading sales management software, it also excels at practicing what it preaches—effective personal selling.

First Stop

Salesforce: You Need a Great Sales Force to Sell Salesforce

Salesforce is way out in front of the $20 billion market for customer relationship management (CRM) solutions. The Salesforce logo, set inside the image of a puffy cloud, underscores Salesforce's highly successful cloud-based computing model (no software to install or own). Cloud-based systems are common today, but they were state-of-the-art when Salesforce pioneered the concept more than 15 years ago. Since then, the company has established itself as a leading innovator, constantly finding new ways to help client companies connect with customers and achieve greater sales force effectiveness using the latest online, mobile, social, and cloud technologies.

Salesforce helps businesses to "supercharge their sales." It supplies what it calls a "Customer Success Platform," a wide array of cloud-based sales force automation and customer relationship management tools that gather, organize, analyze, and disseminate in-depth data about a company's customers, sales, and individual sales rep and overall sales force performance. From its home in the cloud, Salesforce makes all these data and analysis readily available anytime, from anywhere, on any device with online access—desktops, laptops, tablets, or smartphones. Salesforce also integrates with major social media, providing tools for social media monitoring and real-time customer engagement and collaboration on its Salesforce Chatter platform, a kind of Facebook for enterprises.

Salesforce's innovative products have made it the world's number-one and fastest-growing CRM platform, ahead of blue-chip competitors such as Microsoft, Oracle, SAP, and IBM. The company's revenues hit $5.4 billion last year, up an impressive 32 percent over the previous year and more than triple what they were just four years ago. Salesforce has been named by *Forbes* as the World's Most Innovative Company in any industry for four straight years.

Innovative products and platforms have played a major role in Salesforce's stunning success. But even the best products don't sell themselves. You need a great sales force to sell Salesforce, and the company excels at practicing what it preaches—effective personal selling. Like the companies that buy its services, Salesforce has its own army of experienced, well-trained, highly motivated sales reps who take the company's products to customers. In many respects, Salesforce's own sales force serves as a model for the products and services it sells—not just for using the Salesforce cloud but more generally for achieving the "supercharged" sales force results that the company promises its clients.

At Salesforce, developing an outstanding sale force starts with recruiting and hiring top-notch salespeople. Salesforce's aggressive but highly selective recruiting program skims the cream off the top of the global sales rep candidate pool. Last year, Salesforce hired only 4.5 percent of the more than 100,000 candidates who applied. Experience counts. Salesforce expects a minimum of two years of prior sales experience for small-business sales reps and up to two decades of experience for sales execs assigned to major accounts. To find such experienced candidates, Salesforce freely raids rival companies for new hires, counting on its high-energy culture and strong compensation packages to lure successful salespeople into the Salesforce fold.

>> Salesforce's cloud-based "Customer Success Platform" provides a wide array of customer relationship management tools that help its customers "supercharge their sales."

webpics/Alamy

Once hired, as you might expect, Salesforce salespeople have access to all the latest high-tech selling tools. In fact, the first major assignment of new hires is to study 20 hours of at-home video that teaches them the ins and outs of the Salesforce technologies that they won't be just selling but also using. But Salesforce would be the first to tell you that, although its cloud wizardry can help to optimize customer contact and the selling process, it doesn't take the place of good personal selling skills. So in training and fine-tuning its own sales force, the company starts by preaching tried-and-true selling fundamentals, tempered by its own modern twists.

The first fundamental of good selling at Salesforce is to *listen and learn*. As new recruits go through Salesforce's week-long selling boot camp, taught at the company's Salesforce U, they learn that they should begin building customer relationships by asking probing questions and getting customers to talk, seeking to understand everything they can about a customer's situation and needs. "Eighty-five percent of salespeople don't slow down enough to really understand their customer's business," says a senior Salesforce sales executive.

> Salesforce leads the market in sales force automation and customer relationship management solutions. But even Salesforce's innovative products won't sell themselves. The company knows that it needs a great sales force to sell Salesforce.

Understanding the customer leads to a second selling fundamental: *empathize*—let customers know that you understand their issues and feel their pain. Empathy builds rapport and trust, an important step toward closing sales and building long-term customer relationships. Listening, learning, and empathizing are important first steps, but more is needed. "If all you are is responsive and helpful, then all you are is an administrative assistant," says the Salesforce sales executive.

So the next important step is to *offer solutions*—to show how Salesforce's cloud-based solutions will help clients make their sales forces more effective and productive in connecting with and selling to customers. Salesforce believes that the best way to offer solutions is by telling good stories that highlight other customers' successes with its products. "Storytelling is very, very important," says Salesforce's sales productivity manager. "It can be the foundation of things like the corporate pitch and your interactions with your customers and prospects." When it comes to handling objections—such as "I don't trust putting our data in the cloud," or "My current system is working fine," or "It costs too much"—Salesforce tells its salespeople that stories can be the most powerful tools they have. "When faced with objections, we always relate it back to a customer story," says a Salesforce marketing manager. "We're not the hero in our customer's stories," says another manager. "It's how the customer succeeded, not how we saved them."

When it comes to competitors, Salesforce's salespeople are ferocious. But Salesforce reps are trained to take the high road—to sell Salesforce's strengths, not competitors' weaknesses. "Internally, we have these posters: Crush Microsoft and Obliterate Oracle," says the Salesforce marketing manager. But, he adds "when you go out to your customers, you have to be careful that you're guiding them and not just stepping on Microsoft. Even though we all want to."

Thus, effective professional selling is about much more than glad-handing and back-slapping on the one hand or plying high-tech CRM tools and data analytics on the other. Even though Salesforce boasts the best sales and customer connection tools in the business, backed by big data and combined with plenty of new-school techniques, its sales reps stay focused on old-school selling principles. At Salesforce—or anywhere else—good selling starts with the fundamentals of engaging and listening to customers, understanding and empathizing with their problems, and building relationships by offering meaningful solutions for mutual gain. That's how you build an incredibly successful sales force and Salesforce.[1]

I n this chapter, we examine two more promotion mix tools: *personal selling* and *sales promotion*. Personal selling consists of interpersonal interactions with customers and prospects to make sales and maintain customer relationships. Sales promotion involves using short-term incentives to encourage customer purchasing, reseller support, and sales force efforts.

Author Comment
Personal selling is the interpersonal arm of the promotion mix. A company's sales force creates and communicates customer value by personally engaging customers and building customer relationships.

Personal Selling

Robert Louis Stevenson once noted, "Everyone lives by selling something." Companies around the world use sales forces to sell products and services to business customers and final consumers. But sales forces are also found in many other kinds of organizations. For example, colleges use recruiters to attract new students, and churches use membership committees to attract new members. Museums and fine arts organizations use fundraisers to contact donors and raise money. Even governments use sales forces. The U.S. Postal Service, for instance, uses a sales force to sell Express Mail and other shipping and mailing solutions to corporate customers. In the first part of this chapter, we examine personal selling's role in the organization, sales force management decisions, and the personal selling process.

The Nature of Personal Selling

Personal selling

Personal presentations by the firm's sales force for the purpose of engaging customers, making sales, and building customer relationships.

Personal selling is one of the oldest professions in the world. The people who do the selling go by many names, including salespeople, sales representatives, agents, district managers, account executives, sales consultants, and sales engineers.

People hold many stereotypes of salespeople—including some unfavorable ones. *Salesman* may bring to mind the image of Dwight Schrute, the opinionated Dunder Mifflin paper salesman from the old TV show *The Office*, who lacks both common sense and social skills. Or they may think of the real-life "yell-and-sell" TV pitchmen, who hawk everything from the Flex Seal to the FOCUS T25 Workout and the Ove Glove in infomercials. However, the majority of salespeople are a far cry from these unfortunate stereotypes.

As the opening Salesforce story shows, most salespeople are well-educated and well-trained professionals who add value for customers and maintain long-term customer relationships. They listen to their customers, assess customer needs, and organize

>> **Professional selling: It takes more than fast talk and a warm smile to sell expensive airplanes. Boeing's real challenge is to win business by building partnerships—day-in, day-out, year-in, year-out—with its customers.**

Kin Cheung/AP Images

the company's efforts to solve customer problems. The best salespeople are the ones who work closely with customers for mutual gain. >> Consider Boeing, the aerospace giant competing in the rough-and-tumble worldwide commercial aircraft market. It takes more than fast talk and a warm smile to sell expensive airplanes:

Selling high-tech aircraft at $150 million or more a copy is complex and challenging. A single big sale to an airline, air-freight carrier, government, and military customer can easily run into billions of dollars. Boeing salespeople head up an extensive team of company specialists—sales and service technicians, financial analysts, planners, engineers—all dedicated to finding ways to satisfy a large customer's needs. On the customer side, buying a batch of jetliners involves dozens or even hundreds of decision-makers from all levels of the buying organization and layer upon layer of subtle and not-so-subtle buying influences. The selling process is nerve-rackingly slow—it can take two or three years from the first sales presentation to the day the sale is announced. After getting the order, salespeople then must stay in almost constant touch to keep track of the account's equipment needs and to make certain the customer stays satisfied. The real challenge is to win buyers' business by building day-in, day-out, year-in, year-out partnerships with them based on superior products and close collaboration.

Salesperson
An individual who represents a company to customers by performing one or more of the following activities: prospecting, communicating, selling, servicing, information gathering, and relationship building.

The term **salesperson** covers a wide range of positions. At one extreme, a salesperson might be largely an *order taker*, such as the department store salesperson standing behind the counter. At the other extreme are *order getters*, whose positions demand *creative selling, social selling,* and *relationship building* for products and services ranging from appliances, industrial equipment, and airplanes to insurance and IT services. In this chapter, we focus on the more creative types of selling and the process of building and managing an effective sales force.

The Role of the Sales Force

Personal selling is the interpersonal arm of the promotion mix. It involves interpersonal interactions and engagement between salespeople and individual customers—whether face to face, by phone, via email or social media, through video or online conferences, or by other means. Personal selling can be very effective in complex selling situations. Salespeople can probe customers to learn more about their problems and then adjust the marketing offer and presentation to fit each customer's special needs.

The role of personal selling varies from company to company. Some firms have no salespeople at all—for example, companies that sell only online, or companies that sell through manufacturers' reps, sales agents, or brokers. In most firms, however, the sales force plays a major role. In companies that sell business products and services, such as IBM, DuPont, or Boeing, salespeople work directly with customers. In consumer product companies such as P&G or Nike, the sales force plays an important behind-the-scenes role. It works with wholesalers and retailers to gain their support and help them be more effective in selling the company's products to final buyers.

Linking the Company with Its Customers

The sales force serves as a critical link between a company and its customers. In many cases, salespeople serve two masters—the seller and the buyer. First, they *represent the company to customers*. They find and develop new customers and communicate information about

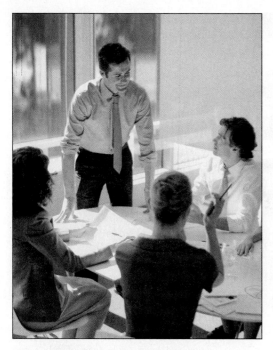

>> **Salespeople link the company with its customers. To many customers, the salesperson is the company.**

Tim Robbins/Mint Images Limited/Alamy

Sales force management
Analyzing, planning, implementing, and controlling sales force activities.

Author Comment
Here's another definition of sales force management: "planning, organizing, leading, and controlling personal contact programs designed to achieve profitable customer relationships." Once again, the goal of every marketing activity is to create customer value, engage customers, and build profitable customer relationships.

the company's products and services. They sell products by engaging customers, presenting their offerings, answering objections, negotiating prices and terms, closing sales, servicing accounts, and maintaining account relationships.

At the same time, salespeople *represent customers to the company*, acting inside the firm as "champions" of customers' interests and managing the buyer–seller relationship. Salespeople relay customer concerns about company products and actions back inside to those who can handle them. They learn about customer needs and work with other marketing and nonmarketing people in the company to develop greater customer value.

>> In fact, to many customers, the salesperson *is* the company—the only tangible manifestation of the company that they see. Hence, customers may become loyal to salespeople as well as to the companies and products they represent. This concept of *salesperson-owned loyalty* lends even more importance to the salesperson's customer-relationship-building abilities. Strong relationships with the salesperson will result in strong relationships with the company and its products. Conversely, poor salesperson relationships will probably result in poor company and product relationships.

Coordinating Marketing and Sales

Ideally, the sales force and other marketing functions (marketing planners, brand managers, marketing content managers, and researchers) should work together closely to jointly create value for customers. Unfortunately, however, some companies still treat sales and marketing as separate functions. When this happens, the separate sales and marketing groups may not get along well.

When things go wrong, marketers blame the sales force for its poor execution of what they see as an otherwise splendid strategy. In turn, the sales team blames the marketers for being out of touch with what's really going on with customers. Neither group fully values the other's contributions. However, if not repaired, such disconnects between marketing and sales can damage customer relationships and company performance.

A company can take several actions to help bring its marketing and sales functions closer together. At the most basic level, it can increase communications between the two groups by arranging joint meetings and spelling out communication channels. It can create opportunities for salespeople and marketers to work together. Brand managers and researchers can tag along on sales calls or sit in on sales planning sessions. In turn, salespeople can sit in on marketing planning sessions and share their firsthand customer knowledge.

A company can also create joint objectives and reward systems for sales and marketing teams or appoint marketing–sales liaisons—people from marketing who "live with the sales force" and help coordinate marketing and sales force programs and efforts. Finally, it can appoint a high-level marketing executive to oversee both marketing and sales. Such a person can help infuse marketing and sales with the common goal of creating value for customers to capture value in return.[2]

Managing the Sales Force

We define **sales force management** as analyzing, planning, implementing, and controlling sales force activities. It includes designing sales force strategy and structure as well as recruiting, selecting, training, compensating, supervising, and evaluating the firm's salespeople. These major sales force management decisions are shown in >> **Figure 13.1** and discussed in the following sections.

Designing the Sales Force Strategy and Structure

Marketing managers face several sales force strategy and design questions. How should salespeople and their tasks be structured? How big should the sales force be? Should salespeople sell alone or work in teams with other people in the company? Should they sell in the field, by phone, or using online and social media? We address these issues next.

>> Figure 13.1 Major Steps in Sales Force Management

| Designing sales force strategy and structure | Recruiting and selecting salespeople | Training salespeople | Compensating salespeople | Supervising salespeople | Evaluating salespeople |

> The goal of this process? You guessed it! The company wants to build a skilled and motivated sales team that will help to create customer value, engage customers, and build strong customer relationships.

The Sales Force Structure

A company can divide sales responsibilities along any of several lines. The structure decision is simple if the company sells only one product line to one industry with customers in many locations. In that case the company would use a *territorial sales force structure*. However, if the company sells many products to many types of customers, it might need a *product sales force structure*, a *customer sales force structure*, or a combination of the two.

In the **territorial sales force structure**, each salesperson is assigned to an exclusive geographic area and sells the company's full line of products or services to all customers in that territory. This organization clearly defines each salesperson's job and fixes accountability. It also increases the salesperson's desire to build local customer relationships that, in turn, improve selling effectiveness. Finally, because each salesperson travels within a limited geographic area, travel expenses are relatively small. A territorial sales organization is often supported by many levels of sales management positions. For example, individual territory sales reps may report to area managers, who in turn report to regional managers who report to a director of sales.

If a company has numerous and complex products, it can adopt a **product sales force structure**, in which the sales force specializes along product lines. For example, GE employs different sales forces within different product and service divisions of its major businesses. Within GE Infrastructure, for instance, the company has separate sales forces for aviation, energy, transportation, and water processing products and technologies. No single salesperson can become expert in all of these product categories, so product specialization is required. Similarly, GE Healthcare employs different sales forces for diagnostic imaging, life sciences, and integrated IT products and services. In all, a company as large and complex as GE might have dozens of separate sales forces serving its diverse product and service portfolio.

Using a **customer (or market) sales force structure**, a company organizes its sales force along customer or industry lines. Separate sales forces may be set up for different industries, serving current customers versus finding new ones, and serving major accounts versus regular accounts. Organizing the sales force around customers can help a company build closer relationships with important customers. Many companies even have special sales forces to handle the needs of individual large customers. For example, GE Aviation has a special Boeing sales team. >> And appliance maker Whirlpool assigns individual teams of salespeople to big retail customers such as Sears, Lowe's, Best Buy, and Home Depot. Each Whirlpool sales team aligns with the large customer's buying team.

When a company sells a wide variety of products to many types of customers over a broad geographic area, it often employs a *complex sales force structure*, which combines several types of organization. Salespeople can be specialized by customer and territory; product and territory; product and customer; or territory, product, and customer. For example, Whirlpool specializes its sales force by customer (with different sales teams for Sears, Lowe's, Best Buy, Home Depot, and smaller independent retailers) *and* by territory for each key customer group (territory representatives, territory managers, regional managers, and so on). No

Territorial sales force structure
A sales force organization that assigns each salesperson to an exclusive geographic territory in which that salesperson sells the company's full line.

Product sales force structure
A sales force organization in which salespeople specialize in selling only a portion of the company's products or lines.

Customer (or market) sales force structure
A sales force organization in which salespeople specialize in selling only to certain customers or industries.

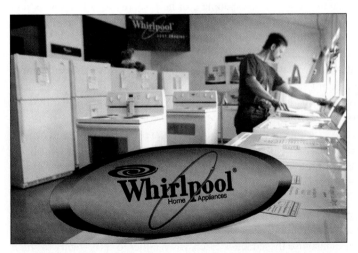

>> Sales force structure: Whirlpool specializes its sales force by customer and by territory for each key customer group.

Paul Sancya/AP Images

single structure is best for all companies and situations. Each company should select a sales force structure that best serves the needs of its customers and fits its overall marketing strategy.

Sales Force Size

Once the company has set its structure, it is ready to consider *sales force size*. Sales forces may range in size from only a few salespeople to tens of thousands. Some sales forces are huge—for example, in the United States, PepsiCo employs 36,000 salespeople; American Express, 23,400; GE, 16,400; and Cisco Systems, 14,000.[3] Salespeople constitute one of the company's most productive—and most expensive—assets. Therefore, increasing their numbers will increase both sales and costs.

A company might use some form of *workload approach* to set sales force size. Using this approach, a company first groups accounts into different classes according to size, account status, or other factors related to the amount of effort required to maintain the account. It then determines the number of salespeople needed to call on each class of accounts the desired number of times.

The company might think as follows: Suppose we have 1,000 A-level accounts and 2,000 B-level accounts. A-level accounts require 36 calls per year, and B-level accounts require 12 calls per year. In this case, the sales force's *workload*—the number of calls it must make per year—is 60,000 calls [(1,000 × 36) + (2,000 × 12) = 36,000 + 24,000 = 60,000]. Suppose our average salesperson can make 1,000 calls a year. Thus, we need 60 salespeople (60,000 ÷ 1,000).

Other Sales Force Strategy and Structure Issues

Sales management must also determine who will be involved in the selling effort and how various sales and sales-support people will work together.

Outside sales force (or field sales force)
Salespeople who travel to call on customers in the field.

Inside sales force
Salespeople who conduct business from their offices via telephone, online and social media interactions, or visits from buyers.

Outside and Inside Sales Forces. A company may have an **outside sales force (or field sales force)**, an **inside sales force**, or both. Outside salespeople travel to call on customers in the field. In contrast, inside salespeople conduct business from their offices via telephone, online and social media interactions, or visits from buyers. The use of inside sales has grown in recent years as a result of increased outside selling costs and the surge in online, mobile, and social media technologies.

Some inside salespeople provide support for the outside sales force, freeing them to spend more time selling to major accounts and finding new prospects. For example, *technical sales-support people* provide technical information and answers to customers' questions. *Sales assistants* provide research and administrative backup for outside salespeople. They track down sales leads, call ahead and confirm appointments, follow up on deliveries, and answer customers' questions when outside salespeople cannot be reached. Using such combinations of inside and outside salespeople can help serve important customers better. The inside rep provides daily access and support, whereas the outside rep provides face-to-face collaboration and relationship building.

Other inside salespeople do more than just provide support. *Telemarketers* and *online sellers* use the phone, Internet, and social media to find new leads, learn about customers and their business, and sell and service accounts directly. Telemarketing and online selling can be very effective, less costly ways to sell to smaller, harder-to-reach customers. Depending on the complexity of the product and customer, for example, a telemarketer can make from 20 to 33 decision-maker contacts a day, compared with the average of four that an outside salesperson can make. In addition, whereas the cost of a business-to-business (B-to-B) field sales call can average close to $600, a routine industrial telemarketing or online contact might average only $20 to $30.[4]

Although the federal government's Do Not Call Registry put a dent in telephone sales to consumers, telemarketing remains a vital tool for most B-to-B marketers. For some smaller companies, telephone and online selling may be the primary sales approaches. However, most of the larger companies also use these tactics extensively, either to sell directly to small and midsize customers or to assist their sales forces in selling to larger ones.

In addition to costs savings, in today's digital, mobile, and social media environments, many buyers are more receptive to—or even prefer—phone and online contact versus the high level of face-to-face contact once required. Today's customers are more inclined to gather their own information online—one study showed that a typical buyer reports contacting a sales rep only after independently completing about 60 percent of the buying process. Then buyers routinely use the phone, online meetings, and social media interactions to engage sellers and close deals. "With virtual meeting software such as GoToMeeting.com and WebEx, communications tools such as Skype, and social media sites such as Twitter, Facebook, and LinkedIn, it's become easier to sell with few if any face-to-face meetings," says an inside sales consultant.[5]

As a result of these trends, telephone and online selling are growing much faster than in-person selling. One recent study found that inside sales positions are growing 300 times faster than outside sales positions. Another study also notes the emergence of the "hybrid sales rep," a modern cross between a field sales rep and an inside rep, who often works from a remote location. Some 41 percent of outside sales activity is now done over the phone or a mobile device, from either a home office or a company office or on the go.[6]

For many types of products and selling situations, >> phone or online selling can be as effective as a personal sales call:[7]

Climax Portable Machining and Welding Systems Company, which manufactures portable maintenance tools for the metal cutting industry, has proven that telephone and online marketing can save money and still lavish attention on buyers. Under the old system, Climax sales engineers spent one-third of their time on the road, training distributor salespeople and accompanying them on calls. They could make about four contacts a day. Now, each sales engineers on Climax's inside sales team calls about 30 prospects a day, following up on leads generated by ads, emails, and the company's Facebook, LinkedIn, Twitter, YouTube, and other social media sites. Because it takes about five calls to close a sale, the sales engineers update a prospect's profile after each contact, noting the degree of commitment, requirements, next call date, and personal comments. "If anyone mentions he's going on a fishing trip, our sales engineer enters that in the sales information system and uses it to personalize the next call," says Climax's president, noting that this is one way to engage customers and build good relations.

Another is that the first contact with a prospect includes the sales engineer's business card with his or her picture on it. Climax's customer sales system also gives inside reps instant access to customer information entered by the outside sales force and service people. Armed with all the information, inside reps can build surprisingly strong and personal customer relationships. Of course, it takes more than friendliness to sell $15,000 machine tools without face-to-face contact (special orders may run $200,000), but the telephone and online approach works well. When Climax customers were asked, "Do you see the sales engineer often enough?" the response was overwhelmingly positive. Obviously, many people didn't realize that the only contact they had with Climax had been on the phone or Internet.

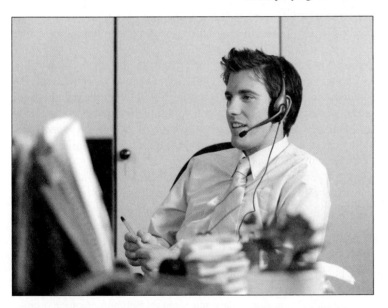

>> **For many types of selling situations, phone or Web selling can be as effective as a personal sales call. At Climax Portable Machine Tools, phone reps build surprisingly strong and personal customer relationships.**

Image Source/Getty Images

Team selling

Using teams of people from sales, marketing, engineering, finance, technical support, and even upper management to service large, complex accounts.

Team Selling. As products become more complex and as customers grow larger and more demanding, a single salesperson simply can't handle all of a large customer's needs. Instead, most companies now use **team selling** to service large, complex accounts. Sales teams can unearth problems, solutions, and sales opportunities that no individual salesperson could. Such teams might include experts from any area or level of the selling firm—sales, marketing, technical and support services, research and development, engineering, operations, finance, and others.

In many cases, the move to team selling mirrors similar changes in customers' buying organizations. Many large customer companies have implemented team-based purchasing, requiring marketers to employ equivalent team-based selling. When dealing with large, complex accounts, one salesperson can't be an expert in everything the customer needs. Instead, selling is done by strategic account teams, quarterbacked by senior account managers or customer business managers.

Some companies, such as IBM and P&G, have used teams for a long time. P&G sales reps are organized into Customer Business Development (CBD) teams. Each CBD team is assigned to a major P&G customer, such as Walmart, Safeway, or CVS Health. The CBD organization places the focus on serving the complete needs of each major customer. It lets P&G "grow business by working as a 'strategic partner' with our accounts," not just as a supplier.[8]

Team selling does have some pitfalls, however. For example, salespeople are by nature competitive and have often been trained and rewarded for outstanding individual performance. Salespeople who are used to having customers all to themselves may have trouble learning to work with and trust others on a team. In addition, selling teams can confuse or overwhelm customers who are used to working with only one salesperson. Finally, difficulties in evaluating individual contributions to the team-selling effort can create some sticky compensation issues.

Recruiting and Selecting Salespeople

At the heart of any successful sales force operation is the recruitment and selection of good salespeople. The performance difference between an average salesperson and a top salesperson can be substantial. In a typical sales force, the top 30 percent of the salespeople might bring in 60 percent of the sales. Thus, careful salesperson selection can greatly increase overall sales force performance. Beyond the differences in sales performance, poor selection results in costly turnover. When a salesperson quits, the costs of finding and training a new salesperson—plus the costs of lost sales—can be very high. One sales consulting firm calculates the total costs of a bad sales hire at a whopping $616,000.[9] Also, a sales force with many new people is less productive, and turnover disrupts important customer relationships and sales team morale.

What sets great salespeople apart from all the rest? In an effort to profile top sales performers, Gallup Consulting, a division of the well-known Gallup polling organization, has interviewed hundreds of thousands of salespeople. Its research suggests that the best salespeople possess four key talents: intrinsic motivation, a disciplined work style, the ability to close a sale, and, perhaps most important, the ability to build relationships with customers.[10]

Super salespeople are motivated from within—they have an unrelenting drive to excel. Some salespeople are driven by money, a desire for recognition, or the satisfaction of competing and winning. Others are driven by the desire to provide service and build relationships. The best salespeople possess some of each of these motivations. However, another analysis found that the best salespeople are driven by a strong sense of purpose: "The salespeople who sold with noble purpose, who truly want to make a difference to customers, consistently outsold the salespeople focused on sales goals and money." Selling with such a sense of customer-related purpose is not only more successful, it's also more profitable and more satisfying to salespeople.[11]

Super salespeople also have a disciplined work style. They lay out detailed, organized plans and then follow through in a timely way. But motivation and discipline mean little unless they result in closing more sales and building better customer relationships. Super salespeople build the skills and knowledge they need to get the job done. ≫ Perhaps most important, top salespeople are excellent customer problem solvers and relationship builders. They understand their customers' needs. Talk to sales executives and they'll describe top performers in these terms: good listeners, empathetic, patient, caring, and responsive. Top performers can put themselves on the buyer's side of the desk and see the world through their customers' eyes. They don't want just to be liked; they want to add value for their customers.

That said, there is no one right way to sell. Each successful salesperson uses a different approach, one that best applies his or her unique strengths and talents. For example, some salespeople enjoy the thrill of a harder sell in confronting challenges and winning people over. Others

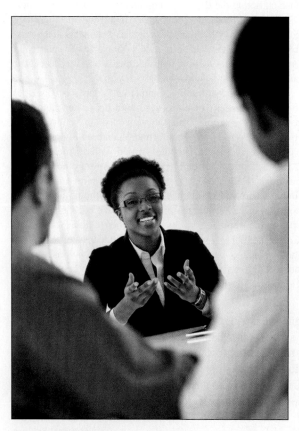

≫ **Great salespeople: The best salespeople possess intrinsic motivation, a disciplined work style, the ability to close a sale, and, perhaps most important, the ability to build relationships with customers.**

Paul Bradbury/OJO Images Ltd/Alamy

might apply "softer" talents to reach the same goal. "The truth is, no two great sales reps are alike," says one sales consultant. "You might thrive on fierce competition, while a colleague wins by being a super-analytical problem solver. Or maybe you have a tremendous talent for building relationships, while your fellow top performer is a brilliant strategist. What's most important is that you win business your way."[12]

When recruiting, a company should analyze the sales job itself and the characteristics of its most successful salespeople to identify the traits needed by a successful salesperson in their industry. Then it must recruit the right salespeople. The human resources department looks for applicants by getting names from current salespeople, using employment agencies, searching the Internet and online social media, posting ads and notices on its Web site and industry media, and working through college placement services. Another source is to attract top salespeople from other companies. Proven salespeople need less training and can be productive immediately.

Recruiting will attract many applicants from which the company must select the best. The selection procedure can vary from a single informal interview to lengthy testing and interviewing. Many companies give formal tests to sales applicants. Tests typically measure sales aptitude, analytical and organizational skills, personality traits, and other characteristics. But test scores provide only one piece of information in a set that includes personal characteristics, references, past employment history, and interviewer reactions.

Training Salespeople

New salespeople may spend anywhere from a few weeks or months to a year or more in training. After the initial training ends, most companies provide continuing sales training via seminars, sales meetings, and online learning throughout the salesperson's career. According to one source, American firms spent approximately $15 billion on sales training each year. Although training can be expensive, it can also yield dramatic returns. For instance, one recent study showed that sales training conducted by ADP, an administrative services firm, resulted in a return on investment of nearly 340 percent in only 90 days.[13]

Training programs have several goals. First, salespeople need to know about customers and how to build relationships with them. Therefore, the training program must teach them about different types of customers and their needs, buying motives, and buying habits. It must also teach them how to sell effectively and train them in the basics of the selling process. Salespeople also need to know and identify with the company, its products, and its competitors. Therefore, an effective training program teaches them about the company's objectives, organization, products, and the strategies of major competitors.

Today, many companies are adding digital e-learning to their sales training programs. Online training may range from simple text- and video-based product training and Internet-based sales exercises that build sales skills to sophisticated simulations that re-create the dynamics of real-life sales calls. One of the most basic forms is virtual instructor-led training (VILT). Using this method, a small group of salespeople at remote locations logs on to an online conferencing site, where a sales instructor leads training sessions using online video, audio, and interactive learning tools.

>> Training online instead of on-site can cut travel and other training costs, and it takes up less of a salesperson's selling time. It also makes on-demand training available to salespeople, letting them train as little or as much as needed, whenever and wherever needed. Although most e-learning is Web-based, many companies now offer on-demand training from anywhere via almost any mobile digital device.

>> **E-training can make sales training more efficient—and more fun. Bayer HealthCare Pharmaceuticals' role-playing video game—Rep Race—helped improve sales rep effectiveness by 20 percent.**

Concentric Pharma Advertising

Many companies are now using imaginative and sophisticated e-learning techniques to make sales training more efficient—and sometimes even more fun. For example, Bayer HealthCare Pharmaceuticals worked with Concentric Pharma Advertising, a health-care marketing agency, to create a role-playing simulation video game to train its sales force on a new drug marketing program:[14]

Most people don't usually associate fast-paced rock music and flashy graphics with online sales training tools. But Concentric Pharma Advertising's innovative role-playing video game—Rep Race: The Battle for Office Supremacy—has all that and a lot more. Rep Race gives Bayer sales reps far more entertainment than the staid old multiple-choice skills tests it replaces. The game was created to help breathe new life into a mature Bayer product—Betaseron, an 18-year-old multiple sclerosis (MS) therapy treatment. The aim was to find a fresh, more active way to help Bayer sales reps apply the in-depth information they learned about Betaseron to actual selling and objections-handling situations. Bayer also wanted to increase rep engagement through interactive learning and feedback through real-time results. Bayer reps liked Rep Race from the start. According to Bayer, when the game was first launched, reps played it as many as 30 times. In addition to its educational and motivational value, Rep Race allowed Bayer to measure sales reps' individual and collective performance. In the end, Bayer calculated that the Rep Race simulation helped improve the Betaseron sales team's effectiveness by 20 percent.

Compensating Salespeople

To attract good salespeople, a company must have an appealing compensation plan. Compensation consists of four elements: a fixed amount, a variable amount, expenses, and fringe benefits. The fixed amount, usually a salary, gives the salesperson some stable income. The variable amount, which might be commissions or bonuses based on sales performance, rewards the salesperson for greater effort and success.

A sales force compensation plan can both motivate salespeople and direct their activities. ≫ Compensation should direct salespeople toward activities that are consistent with the overall sales force and marketing objectives.[15] For example, if the strategy is to acquire new business, grow rapidly, and gain market share, the compensation plan might include a larger commission component, coupled with a new-account bonus to encourage high sales performance and new account development. In contrast, if the goal is to maximize current account profitability, the compensation plan might contain a larger base-salary component with additional incentives for current account sales or customer satisfaction.

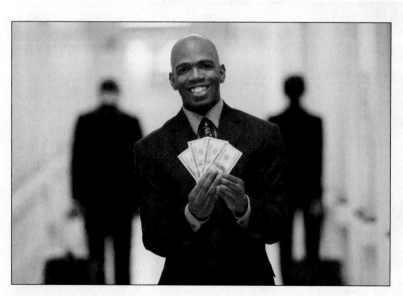

≫ **Sales force compensation: A good compensation plan both motivates salespeople and directs their activities.**

Amble Design/Shutterstock

In fact, more and more companies are moving away from high-commission plans that may drive salespeople to make short-term grabs for business. They worry that a salesperson who is pushing too hard to close a deal may ruin the customer relationship. Instead, companies are designing compensation plans that reward salespeople for building customer relationships and growing the long-run value of each customer.

When times get tough economically, some companies are tempted to cut costs by reducing sales compensation. However, although some cost-cutting measures make sense when business is sluggish, cutting sales force compensation across the board is usually an action of last resort. Top salespeople are always in demand, and paying them less might mean losing them at a time when they are most needed. Thus, short-changing key salespeople can result in short-changing important customer relationships. If the company must reduce its compensation expenses, rather than making across-the-board cuts, companies should continue to pay top performers well while turning loose low performers.

Supervising and Motivating Salespeople

New salespeople need more than a territory, compensation, and training—they need supervision and motivation. The goal of *supervision* is to help salespeople "work smart" by doing the right things in the right ways. The goal of *motivation* is to encourage salespeople to "work hard" and energetically toward sales force goals. If salespeople work smart and work hard, they will realize their full potential—to their own and the company's benefit.

Supervising Salespeople

Companies vary in how closely they supervise their salespeople. Many help salespeople identify target customers and set call objectives. Some may also specify how much time the sales force should spend prospecting for new accounts and set other time management priorities. One tool is the weekly, monthly, or annual *call plan* that shows which customers and prospects to call on and which activities to carry out. Another tool is *time-and-duty analysis*. In addition to time spent selling, the salesperson spends time traveling, waiting, taking breaks, and doing administrative chores.

≫ **Figure 13.2** shows how salespeople spend their time. On average, active selling time accounts for only 37 percent of total working time.[16] Companies are always looking for ways to save time—simplifying administrative duties, developing better sales-call and routing plans, supplying more and better customer information, and using phone, email, online, or mobile conferencing instead of traveling.

Many firms have adopted *sales force automation systems*: computerized, digitized sales force operations that let salespeople work more effectively anytime, anywhere. Companies now routinely equip their salespeople with laptops or tablets, smartphones, wireless connections, videoconferencing technologies, and customer-contact and relationship management software. Armed with these technologies, salespeople can more effectively and efficiently profile customers and prospects, analyze and forecast sales, engage customers, make presentations, prepare sales and expense reports, and manage account relationships. The result is better time management, improved customer service, lower sales costs, and higher sales performance. In all, technology has reshaped the ways in which salespeople carry out their duties and engage customers.

Motivating Salespeople

Beyond directing salespeople, sales managers must also motivate them. Some salespeople will do their best without any special urging from management. To them, selling may be the most fascinating job in the world. But selling can also be frustrating. Salespeople often work alone, and they must sometimes travel away from home. They may also face aggressive competing salespeople and difficult customers. Therefore, salespeople often need special encouragement to do their best.

Management can boost sales force morale and performance through its organizational climate, sales quotas, and positive incentives. *Organizational climate* describes the feeling that salespeople have about their opportunities, value, and rewards for a good performance. Some companies treat salespeople as if they are not very important, so performance suffers accordingly. Other companies treat their

≫ **Figure 13.2 How Salespeople Spend Their Time**

Source: "2014 Sales Performance Optimization Study," *CSO Insights*, www.csoinsights.com. Used with permission.

13.9% Meetings, administrative

17.1% Post-sales tasks

10% Travel, training

21.7% Researching accounts, pursuing leads

37.1% **Active selling (face to face or phone)**

This is far too little. Companies need to free up salespeople to spend much more face-to-face time with customers and prospects. For example, GE wants its salespeople to "spend four days a week in front of the customer and one day a week for all the admin stuff."

Sales quota
A standard that states the amount a salesperson should sell and how sales should be divided among the company's products.

salespeople as valued contributors and allow virtually unlimited opportunity for income and promotion. Not surprisingly, these companies enjoy higher sales force performance and less turnover.

Many companies motivate their salespeople by setting **sales quotas**—standards stating the amount they should sell and how sales should be divided among the company's products. Compensation is often related to how well salespeople meet their quotas. Companies also use various *positive incentives* to increase the sales force effort. *Sales meetings* provide social occasions, breaks from the routine, chances to meet and talk with "company brass," and opportunities to air feelings and identify with a larger group. Companies also sponsor *sales contests* to spur the sales force to make a selling effort above and beyond what is normally expected. Other incentives include honors, merchandise and cash awards, trips, and profit-sharing plans.

Evaluating Salespeople and Sales Force Performance

We have thus far described how management communicates what salespeople should be doing and how it motivates them to do it. This process requires good feedback, which means getting regular information about salespeople to evaluate their performance.

Management gets information about its salespeople in several ways. The most important source is *sales reports*, including weekly or monthly work plans and longer-term territory marketing plans. Salespeople also write up their completed activities on *call reports* and turn in *expense reports* for which they are partly or wholly reimbursed. The company can also monitor the sales and profit performance data in the salesperson's territory. Additional information comes from personal observation, customer surveys, and talks with other salespeople.

Using various sales force reports and other information, sales management evaluates the members of the sales force. It evaluates salespeople on their ability to "plan their work and work their plan." Formal evaluation forces management to develop and communicate clear standards for judging performance. It also provides salespeople with constructive feedback and motivates them to perform well.

On a broader level, management should evaluate the performance of the sales force as a whole. Is the sales force accomplishing its customer relationship, sales, and profit objectives? Is it working well with other areas of the marketing and company organization? Are sales force costs in line with outcomes? As with other marketing activities, the company wants to measure its *return on sales investment*.

Author Comment
Like just about everything else these days, digital technologies have affected selling big time. Today's sales forces are mastering the use of online, mobile, and social media tools to engage business customers, build relationships, and make sales.

Social selling
Using online, mobile, and social media to engage customers, build stronger customer relationships, and augment sales performance.

Social Selling: Online, Mobile, and Social Media Tools

The fastest-growing sales trend is the explosion in **social selling**—the use of online, mobile, and social media to engage customers, build stronger customer relationships, and augment sales performance. New digital sales force technologies are creating exciting new avenues for connecting with and engaging customers in the digital and social media age. Some analysts even predict that the Internet will mean the death of person-to-person selling, as salespeople are ultimately replaced by Web sites, online social media, mobile apps, video and conferencing technologies, and other tools that allow direct customer contact. "Don't believe it," says one sales expert. "There may be less face-to-face selling," says another. "But on the seller's side, there needs to be someone in charge of that (customer) interaction. That will remain the role of the salesperson" (see Marketing at Work 13.1).[17] Thus, online and social media technologies won't likely make salespeople obsolete. Used properly, however, they will make salespeople more productive and effective.

The new digital technologies are providing salespeople with powerful tools for identifying and learning about prospects, engaging customers, creating customer value, closing sales, and nurturing customer relationships. Social selling technologies can produce big organizational benefits for sales forces. They help conserve salespeople's valuable time, save travel dollars, and give salespeople new vehicles for selling and servicing accounts.

MARKETING AT WORK | 13.1

B-to-B Salespeople: In This Digital and Social Media Age, Who Needs Them Anymore?

It's hard to imagine a world without salespeople. But according to some analysts, there will be a lot fewer of them a decade from now. With the explosion of the Internet, mobile devices, social media, and other technologies that link customers directly with companies, they reason, who needs face-to-face selling anymore? According to the doubters, salespeople are rapidly being replaced by Web sites, email, blogs, mobile apps, video sharing, virtual trade shows, social media such as LinkedIn and Facebook, and a host of other digital-age interaction tools.

Research firm Forrester predicts a 22 percent decline in the number of B-to-B sales reps in the United States over the next five years. That means that one in five sales reps will be out of a job by 2020. "The world no longer needs salespeople," one doomsayer boldly proclaims. "Sales is a dying profession and soon will be as outmoded as oil lamps and the rotary phone." Says another, "If we don't find and fill a need faster than a computer, we won't be needed."

So, is business-to-business selling really dying? Will the Internet, mobile technologies, and social media replace the age-old art of selling face to face? To answer these questions, *SellingPower* magazine called together a panel of sales experts and asked them to weigh in on the future of B-to-B sales. The panel members agreed that technology is radically transforming the selling profession. Today's revolutionary changes in how people communicate are affecting every aspect of business, and selling is no exception.

But is B-to-B selling dead in this digital and social media age? Don't believe it, says the *SellingPower* panel. Technology and the Internet won't soon be replacing person-to-person buying and selling. Selling has changed, agrees the panel, and the technology can greatly enhance the selling process. But it can't replace many of the functions that salespeople perform. "The Internet can take orders and disseminate content, but what it can't do is discover customer needs," says one panelist. "It can't build relationships, and it can't prospect on its own." Adds another panelist, "Someone must define the company's value proposition and unique message and communicate it to the market, and that person is the sales rep."

What is dying, however, is what one panelist calls the account-maintenance role—the order taker who stops by the customer's office on Friday and says, "Hey, got anything for me?" Likewise, there's not much of a future for explainers, reps who simply convey product and service information that can be obtained more quickly and easily online. Such salespeople are not creating value and can easily be replaced by automation. However, salespeople who excel at new customer acquisition, relationship management, problem solving, and account growth with existing customers will always be in high demand.

There's no doubt about it—technology is transforming the selling profession. Instead of relying on salespeople for basic information and education, customers can now do much of their own prepurchase research via Web sites, online searches, phone apps, social media contacts, and other venues. Many customers now start the sales process online and do their homework about problems, competing products, and suppliers before the first sales meeting ever takes place. They don't need basic information or product education; they need solutions and new insights. According to one recent survey, business buyers are at least 57 percent of the way through the buying process by the time they reach out to a vendor. So today's salespeople need "to move into the discovery and relationship-building phase, uncovering pain points and focusing on the prospect's business," says a panelist. In fact, jobs for such consultant-type sales reps are expected to increase by one-half million during the next five years.

Rather than replacing salespeople, technology is augmenting them. Today's salespeople aren't really doing anything fundamentally new. They've always done customer research and social networking. Today, however, they are doing it on steroids, using a new kit of high-tech digital tools and applications.

For example, many companies have moved rapidly into online-community-based selling. Case in point: Enterprise-software company SAP, which six years ago set up EcoHub, its

>> Online selling tools, such as SAP's EcoHub and SAP Store online community-based marketplaces, can help to build customer engagement and generate buying interest and sales. But rather than replacing salespeople, such efforts extend their reach and effectiveness.

©2015 SAP SE

own online, community-powered social media and mobile marketplace consisting of customers, SAP software experts, partners, and almost anyone else who wanted to join. The EcoHub community grew quickly to more than 2 million users in 200 countries, extending across a broad online spectrum—a dedicated Web site, mobile apps, Twitter channels, LinkedIn groups, Facebook and Google+ pages, YouTube channels, and more. EcoHub grew to more than 600 "solution storefronts," where visitors could "discover, evaluate, and buy" software solutions and services from SAP and its partners. EcoHub also let users rate and share the solutions and advice they got from other community members.

SAP was surprised to learn that what it had originally seen as a place for customers to discuss issues, problems, and solutions turned into a significant point of sale. The information, give-and-take discussions, and conversations at the site drew in customers, even for big-ticket sales of $20 to $30 million or more. In fact, EcoHub has now evolved into SAP Store, a gigantic SAP marketplace where customers can engage with SAP, its partners, and each other to share information, post comments and reviews, discover problems, and evaluate and buy SAP solutions.

However, although the SAP Store draws in new potential customers and takes them through many of the initial stages of product discovery and evaluation, it doesn't replace SAP's or its partners' salespeople. Instead, it extends their reach and effectiveness. Its real value is the flood of sales leads it creates for the SAP and partner sales forces. Once prospective customers have discovered, discussed, and evaluated SAP solutions online, SAP invites them to initiate contact, request a proposal, or start the negotiation process. That's where the person-to-person selling begins.

All this suggests that B-to-B selling isn't dying, it's just changing. The tools and techniques may be different as sales forces leverage and adapt to selling in the digital and social media age. But the panelists agree strongly that B-to-B marketers will never be able to do without strong sales teams. Salespeople who can engage customers, discover customer needs, solve customer problems, and build relationships will be needed and successful, regardless of what else changes. Especially for those big-ticket B-to-B sales, "all the new technology may make it easier to sell by building strong ties to customers even before the first sit-down, but when the signature hits the dotted line, there will be a sales rep there."

Sources: Based on information from Tom Pisello, "Death of a Salesman? Forrester Says Yes (at Least 1 in 5 at Risk)!" *Alinean,* March 12, 2015, http://blog .alinean.com/2015/03/death-of-salesman-forrester-says-yes.html; Tony J. Hughes, "Back to the Future of Sales in 2015," *LinkedIn,* December 27, 2014, www .linkedin.com/pulse/back-future-sales-2015-tony-j-hughes; Lain Chroust Ehmann, "Sales Up!" *SellingPower,* January/February 2011, p. 40; Paul Nolan, "Mapping the Buyer's Journey," *Sales and Marketing Management,* March 27, 2015, www .salesandmarketing.com/content/mapping-buyer's-journey; "Getting Started with SAP EcoHub," http://ecohub.sap.com/getting-started, accessed June 2015; "SAP EcoHub to the SAP Store: The Evolution of the Online Channel at SAP," YouTube, www.youtube.com/watch?v=WADFf6k34V8, accessed June 2015; and https:// store.sap.com/ and https://scn.sap.com, accessed September 2015.

Social selling hasn't really changed the fundamentals of selling. Sales forces have always taken the primary responsibility for reaching out to and engaging customers and managing customer relationships. Now, more of that is being done digitally. However, online and social media are dramatically changing the customer buying process. As a result, they are also changing the selling process. In today's digital world, many customers no longer rely as much as they once did on information and assistance provided by salespeople. Instead, they carry out more of the buying process on their own—especially the early stages. Increasingly, they use online and social media resources to analyze their own problems, research solutions, get advice from colleagues, and rank buying options before ever speaking to a salesperson. A recent study of business buyers found that 92 percent of buyers start their searches online and that, on average, buyers completed nearly 60 percent of the buying process before contacting a supplier.[18]

Thus, today's customers have much more control over the sales process than they had in the days when brochures, pricing, and product advice were available only from a sales rep. Customers can now browse corporate Web sites, blogs, and YouTube videos to identify and qualify sellers. They can hobnob with other buyers on social media such as LinkedIn, Google+, Twitter, or Facebook to share experiences, identify solutions, and evaluate products they are considering. As a result, if and when salespeople do enter the buying process, customers often know almost as much about a company's products as the salespeople do. And when customers do call in salespeople, they are more often doing it digitally, with the expectation of real-time engagement.

In response to this new digital buying environment, sellers are reorienting their selling processes around the new customer buying process. They are "going where customers are"—social media, Web forums, online communities, blogs—in order to engage customers earlier. They are engaging customers not just where and when they are buying but also where and when they are learning about and evaluating what they will buy.

Salespeople now routinely use digital tools that monitor customer social media exchanges to spot trends, identify prospects, and learn what customers would like to buy, how they feel about a vendor, and what it would take to make a sale. They generate lists of prospective customers from online databases and social networking sites, such as

InsideView, Hoovers, and LinkedIn. They create dialogues when prospective customers visit their Web and social media sites through live chats with the sales team. They use Internet conferencing tools such as WebEx, Zoom, GoToMeeting, or TelePresence to talk live with customers about products and services. They provide videos and other information on their YouTube channels and Facebook pages.

Today's sales forces are also ramping up their own use of social media to engage customers throughout the buying process. A recent survey of business-to-business marketers found that, although they have recently cut back on traditional media and event spending, they are investing more in social media, ranging from proprietary online customer communities to Webinars and social media and mobile applications.[19] »Consider industrial and consumer products giant GE:[20]

GE complements its sales force efforts through a wide variety of digital and social media that inform and engage business customers, connect them with GE salespeople, and promote customer purchasing and relationships. For example, GE's various divisions—from GE Aviation to GE Healthcare and GE Energy—offer dozens of industry-specific Web sites, containing thousands of individual site areas and tens of thousands of pages that provide B-to-B customers with purchasing solutions, product overviews, detailed technical information, online videos and Webinars, live chats, and real-time customer support. GE also builds brand awareness and helps its sales force engage business customers deeply through a comprehensive presence in major social media, such as Facebook, Twitter, LinkedIn, Google+, Salesforce.com, and even Instagram, Pinterest, and Vine. "We have a core belief that business is social," says GE's chief marketing officer. "If you're in business you need social because it's going to get you closer to your customers. We want to get our sales team 100 percent digitized."

 Social selling: GE complements its sales force efforts through a wide variety of social media that inform and engage business customers, connect them with GE salespeople, and promote customer purchasing and relationships. "We want to get our sales team 100 percent digitized."

GE

Ultimately, social selling technologies are helping to make sales forces more efficient, cost-effective, and productive. The technologies help salespeople do what good salespeople have always done—build customer relationships by solving customer problems—but do it better, faster, and cheaper.

However, social selling also has some drawbacks. For starters, it's not cheap. In addition, such systems can intimidate low-tech salespeople or clients. Even more, there are some things you just can't present or teach via the Internet—things that require personal engagement and interaction. For these reasons, some high-tech experts recommend that sales executives use online and social media technologies to spot opportunities, provide information, maintain customer contact, and make preliminary client sales presentations but resort to old-fashioned, face-to-face meetings when the time draws near to close a big deal.

LINKING THE CONCEPTS

Take a break and reexamine your thoughts about salespeople and sales management.

- Again, when someone says "salesperson," what image comes to mind? Have your perceptions of salespeople changed after what you've read in the chapter so far? If so, how? Be specific.
- Find and talk with someone employed in professional sales. Ask about and report on how this salesperson's company designs its sales force and recruits, selects, trains, compensates, supervises, and evaluates its salespeople. Would you like to work as a salesperson for this company?

Author Comment
So far, we've examined how sales management develops and implements overall sales force strategies and programs. In this section, we'll look at how individual salespeople and sales teams sell to customers and build relationships with them.

The Personal Selling Process

We now turn from designing and managing a sales force to the personal selling process. The **selling process** consists of several steps that salespeople must master. These steps focus on the goal of getting new customers and obtaining orders from them. However, most salespeople spend much of their time maintaining existing accounts and building long-term customer relationships. We will discuss the relationship aspect of the personal selling process in a later section.

Steps in the Selling Process

As shown in ≫ **Figure 13.3**, the selling process consists of seven steps: prospecting and qualifying, preapproach, approach, presentation and demonstration, handling objections, closing, and follow-up.

Prospecting and Qualifying

The first step in the selling process is **prospecting**—identifying qualified potential customers. Approaching the right customers is crucial to selling success. Salespeople don't want to call on just any potential customers. They want to call on those who are most likely to appreciate and respond to the company's value proposition—those the company can serve well and profitably.

A salesperson must often approach many prospects to get only a few sales. Although the company supplies some leads, salespeople need skill in finding their own. The best source is referrals. Salespeople can ask current customers for referrals and cultivate other referral sources, such as suppliers, dealers, noncompeting salespeople, and online or social media contacts. They can also search for prospects in directories or on the Internet and track down leads using the telephone, email, and social media. Or, as a last resort, they can drop in unannounced on various offices (a practice known as *cold calling*).

Salespeople also need to know how to *qualify* leads—that is, how to identify the good ones and screen out the poor ones. Prospects can be qualified by looking at their financial ability, volume of business, special needs, location, and possibilities for growth.

Preapproach

Before calling on a prospect, the salesperson should learn as much as possible about the organization (what it needs, who is involved in the buying) and its buyers (their characteristics and buying styles). This step is known as **preapproach**. A successful sale begins long before the salesperson makes initial contact with a prospect. Preapproach begins with good research and preparation. The salesperson can consult standard industry and online sources, acquaintances, and others to learn about the company. He or she can scour the prospect's Web and social media sites for information about its products, buyers, and buying processes. Then the salesperson must apply the research gathered to develop a customer strategy.

Selling process
The steps that salespeople follow when selling, which include prospecting and qualifying, preapproach, approach, presentation and demonstration, handling objections, closing, and follow-up.

Prospecting
The sales step in which a salesperson or company identifies qualified potential customers.

Preapproach
The sales step in which a salesperson learns as much as possible about a prospective customer before making a sales call.

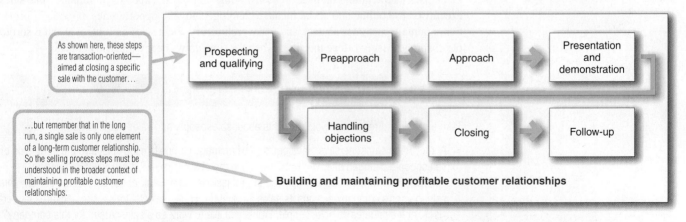

≫ **Figure 13.3 Steps in the Selling Process**

The salesperson should set *call objectives*, which may be to qualify the prospect, gather information, or make an immediate sale. Another task is to determine the best approach, which might be a personal visit, a phone call, an email, or a text or Tweet. The ideal timing should be considered carefully because many prospects are busiest at certain times of the day or week. Finally, the salesperson should give thought to an overall sales strategy for the account.

Approach

Approach
The sales step in which a salesperson meets the customer for the first time.

During the **approach** step, the salesperson should know how to meet and greet the buyer and get the relationship off to a good start. The approach might take place offline or online, in-person or via digital conferencing or social media. This step involves the salesperson's appearance, opening lines, and follow-up remarks. The opening lines should be positive to build goodwill from the outset. This opening might be followed by some key questions to learn more about the customer's needs or by showing a display or sample to attract the buyer's attention and curiosity. As in all stages of the selling process, listening to the customer is crucial.

Presentation and Demonstration

Presentation
The sales step in which a salesperson tells the "value story" to the buyer, showing how the company's offer solves the customer's problems.

During the **presentation** step of the selling process, the salesperson tells the "value story" to the buyer, showing how the company's offer solves the customer's problems. The *customer-solution approach* fits better with today's relationship marketing focus than does a hard sell or glad-handing approach.

The goal should be to show how the company's products and services fit the customer's needs. Buyers today want insights and solutions, not smiles; results, not razzle-dazzle. Moreover, buyers don't want just products; they want to know how those products will add value to their businesses. They want salespeople who listen to their concerns, understand their needs, and respond with the right products and services.

But before salespeople can *present* customer solutions, they must *develop* solutions to present. The solutions approach calls for good listening and problem-solving skills. The qualities that buyers *dislike most* in salespeople include being pushy, late, deceitful, unprepared, disorganized, or overly talkative. The qualities they *value most* include good listening, empathy, honesty, dependability, thoroughness, and follow-through. >> Great salespeople know how to sell, but more important, they know how to listen and build strong customer relationships. According to an old sales adage, "You have two ears and one mouth. Use them proportionally." A classic ad from office products maker Boise Cascade makes the listening point. It shows a Boise salesperson with huge ears drawn on. "With Boise, you'll notice a difference right away, especially with our sales force," says the ad. "At Boise … our account representatives have the unique ability to listen to your needs."

Finally, salespeople must also plan their presentation methods. Good interpersonal communication skills count when it comes to engaging customers and making effective sales presentations. However, the current media-rich and cluttered communications environment presents many new challenges for sales presenters. Today's information-overloaded customers demand richer presentation experiences. For their part, presenters now face multiple distractions during presentations from mobile phones, text messages, and other digital competition. As a result, salespeople must deliver their messages in more engaging and compelling ways.

Thus, today's salespeople are employing advanced presentation technologies that allow for full multimedia presentations to only one or a few people. The venerable old sales presentation flip chart has been replaced with tablets, sophisticated presentation software, online presentation technologies, interactive whiteboards, and digital projectors.

>> **Great salespeople know how to sell, but more important, they know how to listen and build strong customer relationships.**

Tony Garcia/The Image Bank/Getty Images

Handling objections
The sales step in which a salesperson seeks out, clarifies, and overcomes any customer objections to buying.

Handling Objections

Customers almost always have objections during the presentation or when asked to place an order. The objections can be either logical or psychological, and they are often unspoken. In **handling objections**, the salesperson should use a positive approach, seek out hidden objections, ask the buyer to clarify any objections, take objections as opportunities to provide more information, and turn the objections into reasons for buying. Every salesperson needs training in the skills of handling objections.

Closing

Closing
The sales step in which a salesperson asks the customer for an order.

After handling the prospect's objections, the salesperson next tries to close the sale. However, some salespeople do not get around to **closing** or don't handle it well. They may lack confidence, feel guilty about asking for the order, or fail to recognize the right moment to close the sale. Salespeople should know how to recognize closing signals from the buyer, including physical actions, comments, and questions. For example, the customer might sit forward and nod approvingly or ask about prices and credit terms.

Salespeople can use any of several closing techniques. They can ask for the order, review points of agreement, offer to help write up the order, ask whether the buyer wants this model or that one, or note that the buyer will lose out if the order is not placed now. The salesperson may offer the buyer special reasons to close, such as a lower price, an extra quantity at no charge, or additional services.

Follow-Up

Follow-up
The sales step in which a salesperson follows up after the sale to ensure customer satisfaction and repeat business.

The last step in the selling process—**follow-up**—is necessary if the salesperson wants to ensure customer satisfaction and repeat business. Right after closing, the salesperson should complete any details on delivery time, purchase terms, and other matters. The salesperson then should schedule a follow-up call after the buyer receives the initial order to make sure proper installation, instruction, and servicing occur. This visit would reveal any problems, assure the buyer of the salesperson's interest, and reduce any buyer concerns that might have arisen since the sale.

Personal Selling and Managing Customer Relationships

The steps in the just-described selling process are *transaction oriented*—their aim is to help salespeople close a specific sale with a customer. But in most cases, the company is not simply seeking a sale. Rather, it wants to engage the customer over the long haul in a mutually profitable *relationship*. The sales force usually plays an important role in customer relationship building. Thus, as shown in Figure 13.3, the selling process must be understood in the context of building and maintaining profitable customer relationships. Moreover, as discussed in a previous section, today's buyers are increasingly moving through the early stages of the buying process themselves, before ever engaging sellers. Salespeople must adapt their selling process to match the new buying process. That means discovering and engaging customers on a relationship basis rather than a transaction basis.

Successful sales organizations recognize that winning and keeping accounts requires more than making good products and directing the sales force to close lots of sales. If the company wishes only to close sales and capture short-term business, it can do this by simply slashing its prices to meet or beat those of competitors. Instead, most companies want their salespeople to practice *value selling*—demonstrating and delivering superior customer value and capturing a return on that value that is fair for both the customer and the company.

Unfortunately, in the heat of closing sales, salespeople too often take the easy way out by cutting prices rather than selling value. ❯❯ Sales management's challenge is to transform salespeople from customer advocates for price cuts into company advocates for value. Here's how Rockwell Automation sells value and relationships rather than price:[21]

Under pressure from Walmart to lower its prices, a condiment producer asked several competing supplier representatives—including Rockwell Automation sales rep Jeff Policicchio—to help it find ways to reduce its operating costs. After spending a day in the customer's plant,

>> **Value selling: Sales management's challenge is to transform salespeople from customer advocates for price cuts into company advocates for value.**

Almagami/123rf

Policicchio quickly put his finger on the major problem: Production was suffering because of down time due to poorly performing pumps on the customer's 32 large condiment tanks. Quickly gathering cost and usage data, Policicchio used his Rockwell Automation laptop value-assessment tool to develop an effective solution for the customer's pump problem.

The next day, as he and competing reps presented their cost-reduction proposals to plant management, Policicchio offered the following value proposition: "With this Rockwell Automation pump solution, through less downtime, reduced administrative costs in procurement, and lower spending on repair parts, your company will save at least $16,268 per pump—on up to 32 pumps—relative to our best competitor's solution." Compared with competitors' proposals, Policicchio's solution carried a higher initial price. However, no competing rep offered more than fuzzy promises about possible cost savings. Most simply lowered their prices.

Impressed by Policicchio's value proposition—despite its higher initial price—the plant managers opted to buy and try one Rockwell Automation pump. When the pump performed even better than predicted, the customer ordered all of the remaining pumps. By demonstrating tangible value rather than simply selling on price, Policicchio not only landed the initial sale but also earned a loyal future customer.

Thus, value selling requires listening to customers, understanding their needs, and carefully coordinating the whole company's efforts to create lasting relationships based on customer value.

Sales promotion
Short-term incentives to encourage the purchase or sale of a product or a service.

Sales Promotion

Personal selling and advertising often work closely with another promotion tool: sales promotion. **Sales promotion** consists of short-term incentives to encourage the purchase or sales of a product or service. Whereas advertising offers reasons to buy a product or service, sales promotion offers reasons to buy *now*.

>> Examples of sales promotions are found everywhere. A freestanding insert in the Sunday newspaper contains a coupon offering $1 off Meow Mix Tender Centers food for your cat. A Sunday newspaper ad from your local Orange Leaf frozen yogurt store offers "Buy 1 Get 1 Free" and "20% off your next purchase." The end-of-the-aisle display in the local supermarket tempts impulse buyers with a wall of Coca-Cola cases—four 12-packs for $12. Buy a new Samsung tablet and get a free memory upgrade. A hardware store chain receives a 10 percent discount on selected Stihl power lawn and garden tools if it agrees to advertise them in local newspapers. Sales promotion includes a wide variety of promotion tools designed to stimulate earlier or stronger market response.

The Rapid Growth of Sales Promotion

Sales promotion tools are used by most organizations, including manufacturers, distributors, retailers, and not-for-profit institutions. They are targeted toward final buyers (*consumer promotions*), retailers and wholesalers (*trade promotions*), business customers (*business promotions*), and members of the sales force (*sales force promotions*). Today, in the average consumer packaged-goods company, sales promotion accounts for 60 percent of all marketing budgets.[22]

Several factors have contributed to the rapid growth of sales promotion, particularly in consumer markets. First, inside the company, product managers face greater pressures to increase current sales, and they view promotion as an effective short-run sales tool. Second, externally, the company faces more competition, and competing brands are less differentiated. Increasingly, competitors are using sales promotion to help differentiate their offers. Third, advertising efficiency has declined because of rising costs, media clutter, and legal restraints.

>> **Sales promotions are found everywhere. For example, your Sunday newspaper or favorite magazine is loaded with offers like this one that promote a strong and immediate response.**

Orange Leaf Frozen Yogurt

Finally, consumers have become more deal oriented. In the current economy, consumers are demanding lower prices and better deals. Sales promotions can help attract today's more thrift-oriented consumers.

The growing use of sales promotion has resulted in *promotion clutter*, which is similar to advertising clutter. With so many products being sold on deal these days, a given promotion runs the risk of being lost in a sea of other promotions, weakening its ability to trigger an immediate purchase. Manufacturers are now searching for ways to rise above the clutter, such as offering larger coupon values, creating more dramatic point-of-purchase displays, or delivering promotions through new digital media—such as the Internet or mobile phones. According to one study, 88 percent of retailers now see digital promotions— such as mobile coupons, shopper emails, and online deals—as an important part of their shopper marketing efforts.[23]

In developing a sales promotion program, a company must first set sales promotion objectives and then select the best tools for accomplishing these objectives.

Sales Promotion Objectives

Sales promotion objectives vary widely. Sellers may use *consumer promotions* to urge short-term customer buying or boost customer–brand engagement. Objectives for *trade promotions* include getting retailers to carry new items and more inventory, buy ahead, or promote the company's products and give them more shelf space. *Business promotions* are used to generate business leads, stimulate purchases, reward customers, and motivate salespeople. For the sales force, objectives include getting more sales force support for current or new products and getting salespeople to sign up new accounts.

Sales promotions are usually used together with advertising, personal selling, direct marketing, or other promotion mix tools. Consumer promotions must usually be advertised and can add excitement and pulling power to ads and other marketing content. Trade and business sales promotions support the firm's personal selling process.

When the economy tightens and sales lag, it's tempting to offer deep promotional discounts to spur consumer spending. In general, however, rather than creating only short-term sales or temporary brand switching, sales promotions should help to reinforce the product's position and build long-term customer relationships. If properly designed, every sales promotion tool has the potential to build both short-term excitement and long-term consumer engagement and relationships. Marketers should avoid "quick fix," price-only promotions in favor of promotions that are designed to build brand equity. Examples include the various *frequency marketing programs* and loyalty cards that have mushroomed in popularity in recent years. Most hotels, supermarkets, and airlines offer frequent-guest/buyer/flier programs that give rewards to regular customers to keep them coming back. Such promotional programs can build loyalty through added value rather than discounted prices.

>> **Customer loyalty programs: Bloomingdale's Loyallist program works well because of its simplicity. "Become a Loyallist," says the company. "It's better on the list."**

Bloomingdale's, Inc.

>> For example, department store Bloomingdale's offers its Loyallist program for loyal shoppers. Loyallist members earn points for every dollar they spend, in-store or online, no matter how they pay. They also receive special opportunities to earn double, triple, or even quadruple points at special times, along with free shipping and a

$25 Bloomingdale's gift card every time they reach 5,000 points. Loyallists can use any of a variety of apps to access their cards and balances wherever they are. The Loyallist program's success lies in its simplicity. According to one analyst, the program "is winning because it delivers well on the main goal of all loyalty programs: when members spend money, they are rewarded by points that they can turn around and use like money, which incentivizes future purchases for happy shoppers to spend—you guessed it—more money."[24]

Major Sales Promotion Tools

Many tools can be used to accomplish sales promotion objectives. Descriptions of the main consumer, trade, and business promotion tools follow.

Consumer Promotions

Consumer promotions include a wide range of tools—from samples, coupons, refunds, premiums, and point-of-purchase displays to contests, sweepstakes, and event sponsorships.

Samples are offers of a trial amount of a product. Sampling is the most effective—but most expensive—way to introduce a new product or create new excitement for an existing one. Some samples are free; for others, the company charges a small amount to offset its cost. The sample might be sent by mail, handed out in a store or at a kiosk, attached to another product, or featured in an ad, email, or mobile offer. Samples are sometimes combined into sample packs, which can then be used to promote other products and services. Sampling can be a powerful promotional tool. For example, a bevy of big-name food marketers—from Papa John's Pizza and Pizza Hut to Campbell Soup and PepsiCo—descended upon Super Bowl XLVIII–related events in New York and New Jersey, handing out free samples. Pizza Hut handed out more than 10,000 slices of its hand-tossed pizza. "It's a massive opportunity to sample our new product," said a Pizza Hut marketer.[25]

Coupons are certificates that save buyers money when they purchase specified products. Most consumers love coupons. U.S. consumer packaged goods companies distributed 310 billion coupons with an average face value of $1.72 last year. Consumers redeemed more than 2.75 billion of them for a total savings of about $3.6 billion.[26] Coupons can promote early trial of a new brand or stimulate sales of a mature brand. However, to combat the increase in coupon clutter, most major consumer goods companies are issuing fewer coupons and targeting them more carefully.

Marketers are also cultivating new outlets for distributing coupons, such as supermarket shelf dispensers, electronic point-of-sale coupon printers, and online and mobile coupon programs. Digital coupons represent today's fastest-growing coupon segment. Digital coupons can be individually targeted and personalized in ways that print coupons can't. Digital coupons accounted for nearly 11 percent of all coupons redeemed last year; about 7 percent were printed from a computer at home, and 4 percent were redeemed via smartphone or other mobile devices. According to one study, an estimate 40 percent of smartphone users will redeem a mobile coupon this year.[27]

As mobile phones become appendages that many people can't live without, businesses are increasingly eyeing them as prime real estate for coupons, offers, and other marketing messages. ≫ For example, drugstore chain Walgreens makes coupons available to its customers through several mobile channels:[28]

> Using the Walgreens smartphone app, customers can instantly download coupons ranging in value from 50 cents to $5, good toward anything from health and beauty products to everyday essentials such as diapers. The coupons are conveniently scannable—no clipping or printing required. Customers simply pull up the coupons on the Walgreens app and cashiers scan them straight from the customer's phone. Walgreens also Tweets mobile coupons to customers who check in to any of its 8,100 stores nationwide using check-in apps such as Foursquare, Yelp, or Shopkick. Walgreens has mobile scanning capabilities available at all of its stores, giving it the nation's largest retail mobile coupon program. Through its mobile app, "Walgreens is using technology to go above and beyond," says one analyst. "They're thinking about the customer."

Rebates (or *cash refunds*) are like coupons except that the price reduction occurs after the purchase rather than at the retail outlet. The customer sends proof of purchase to the

Consumer promotions
Sales promotion tools used to boost short-term customer buying and engagement or enhance long-term customer relationships.

≫ **Coupons:** Drugstore chain Walgreens makes coupons available to customers through numerous channels, including its weekly ads, Web site, and mobile app.
Courtesy of Walgreen Co.

manufacturer, who then refunds part of the purchase price by mail. For example, Toro ran a clever preseason promotion on some of its snowblower models, offering a rebate if the snowfall in the buyer's market area turned out to be below average. Competitors were not able to match this offer on such short notice, and the promotion was very successful.

Price packs (also called *cents-off deals*) offer consumers savings off the regular price of a product. The producer marks the reduced prices directly on the label or package. Price packs can be single packages sold at a reduced price (such as two for the price of one) or two related products banded together (such as a toothbrush and toothpaste). Price packs are very effective—even more so than coupons—in stimulating short-term sales.

Premiums are goods offered either free or at low cost as an incentive to buy a product, ranging from toys included with kids' products to phone cards and DVDs. A premium may come inside the package (in-pack), outside the package (on-pack), or through the mail. For example, over the years, McDonald's has offered a variety of premiums in its Happy Meals—from *My Little Pony* characters to Beanie Boos and LEGO hologram drink cups. Customers can visit www.happymeal.com to play games, read e-books, and watch commercials associated with the current Happy Meal sponsor.[29]

Advertising specialties, also called *promotional products*, are useful articles imprinted with an advertiser's name, logo, or message that are given as gifts to consumers. Typical items include T-shirts and other apparel, pens, coffee mugs, calendars, key rings, tote bags, coolers, golf balls, and caps. U.S. marketers spent nearly $20 billion on advertising specialties last year. Such items can be very effective. The "best of them stick around for months, subtly burning a brand name into a user's brain," notes a promotional products expert.[30]

Point-of-purchase (POP) promotions include displays and demonstrations that take place at the point of sale. Think of your last visit to the local Costco, Walmart, or Bed Bath & Beyond. Chances are good that you were tripping over aisle displays, promotional signs, "shelf talkers," or demonstrators offering free tastes of featured food products. Unfortunately, many retailers do not like to handle the hundreds of displays, signs, and posters they receive from manufacturers each year. Manufacturers have therefore responded by offering better POP materials, offering to set them up, and tying them in with television, print, or online messages.

Contests, sweepstakes, and *games* give consumers the chance to win something, such as cash, trips, or goods, by luck or through extra effort. A *contest* calls for consumers to submit an entry—a jingle, guess, suggestion—to be judged by a panel that will select the best entries. A *sweepstakes* calls for consumers to submit their names for a drawing. A *game* presents consumers with something—bingo numbers, missing letters—every time they buy, which may or may not help them win a prize.

All kinds of companies use sweepstakes and contests to create brand attention and boost consumer involvement. For example, Google's "Doodle 4 Google" contest invites kids to design a Google logo based on the theme "If I could invent one thing to make the world a better place … ," with prizes ranging from T-shirts and tablets to a $30,000 college scholarship. The "OXO I Do Sweepstakes" invites soon-to-be-married couples to "Like" OXO's Facebook page and earn a chance to win $500 toward their Amazon wedding registry. Enter the Coleman Camping Kit Giveaway and you win a gear prize pack worth more than $1,000. And if your recipe wins the annual Pillsbury Bake-Off, you could take home a $1 million prize.

Event marketing (or event sponsorships)
Creating a brand-marketing event or serving as a sole or participating sponsor of events created by others.

Finally, marketers can promote their brands through **event marketing** (or **event sponsorships**). They can create their own brand-marketing events or serve as sole or participating sponsors of events created by others. The events might include anything from mobile brand tours to festivals, reunions, marathons, concerts, or other sponsored gatherings. Event marketing is huge, and it may be the fastest-growing area of promotion. Effective event marketing links events and sponsorships to a brand's value proposition. And with the social sharing power of today's digital media, even local events can have far-reaching impact. For example, P&G's recent "Everyday Effect" takeover event in Manhattan illustrates how companies are now blending old-school promotional techniques with new-school social sharing technologies to enhance the impact of both (see Marketing at Work 13.2).

All kinds of brands now hold events. One week, it might be the National Football League (NFL) filling the southern tip of Times Square with NFL players to promote new

MARKETING AT WORK   13.2

P&G's "Everyday Effect" Event: A Great Marriage between Old-School Promotions and New-School Social Sharing

It was a hot, sunny June day in Manhattan, and pedestrians bustled along at 33rd Street and 7th Avenue near Madison Square Garden. But on this day, something special happened. In the middle of the sidewalk stood a glass shower stall, emblazoned with colorful Old Spice signage, causing even normally jaded New York City passersby to take notice. An Old Spice brand rep handed out samples of Old Spice bar soap and extended an unusual invitation—jump in the shower and give it a try. Surprisingly, many people accepted, including a well-dressed executive who lathered up while still in his finely tailored business suit.

Just another sales promotion gimmick? Not this time. The Old Spice Constant Shower was just one small piece of a live mega-promotion—P&G's "Everyday Effect" event—in which brand representatives and celebrities handed out more than 50,000 samples of 25 different P&G brands at multiple Manhattan locations in a single day. With street teams and exhibits all over town, the Everyday Effect takeover extravaganza was by far the biggest "consumer experience" event in P&G's 175-year history.

Visitors to the Gillette Man Cave "experience box" in Washington Square Park were pampered with free shaves and visits from actor Laz Alonso and New York Jets center Nick Mangold. At the Covergirl Beauty box near Times Square, *Fast and Furious* actress Jordana Brewster helped with free beauty and nail touch-ups. The Iam's Loving Home box at Riverside Park on the Upper West Side featured *Dancing with the Stars* heartthrob Val Chmerkovskiy posing for photos with pets and handing out Iam's product samples. And in Harlem, P&G's "My Black Is Beautiful" reps served up beauty tips and free mini-makeovers. All day long, brand ambassadors and characters such as the Charmin Bears fanned out across city streets giving out product samples, high-value coupons, advice, and even special P&G pedicab rides. They dispensed Scope mouthwash samples to coffee drinkers, Febreze car vent clips to taxi drivers, and personal care products to barber shops and salons.

By itself, the massive Manhattan giveaway produced substantial benefits for P&G in terms of brand trial and experience. "Simply getting someone to try a product remains the holy grail for consumer-goods companies," says one analyst. The event also reinforced P&G's broader, ongoing Everyday Effect campaign showcasing the effects of its products on the lives of real people. "We're making a deliberate effort to demonstrate to consumers how our brands improve their everyday life in small yet meaningful ways," says P&G's North American group president. "That's what we call the P&G 'Everyday Effect.'"

However, some experts question whether the returns on such a massive—and expensive—local event could ever justify the investment. Beyond the costs of product samples, P&G had to rent pricy Manhattan real estate, employ hundreds of reps, erect expensive facilities and props, provide incentives for celebrities, and put a sizable security detail in place to keep things orderly.

But the impact of the Everyday Effect event went far beyond the city limits of New York City. What made the event extra special was the skillful way that P&G used social media channels to turbocharge consumer engagement, not just in Manhattan but around the nation and world. Throughout the day, video of live events was streamed across P&G brand and social media sites. Nearly every element of the event was hashtagged, and visitors to event sites were given incentives to upload photos to their personal feeds. Followers of PGEveryday on Twitter and Facebook had opportunities to win Visa and Amazon gift cards. Participating celebrities not only helped draw coverage from more than 100 media outlets, they also reached out personally to their own fans through Twitter, Facebook, Instagram, and other social media.

"We chose New York as the world's largest stage," says a P&G brand executive. "At the end of the day, [we wanted to reach] as many New Yorkers as possible [but also] touch consumers we couldn't physically reach that day." Mission accomplished. By evening, the Everyday Effect event had scored some impressive social sharing results. The opt-in rate at the PGEveryday.com coupon and sampling site jumped 20 percent;

>> **P&G's star-studded Everyday Effect event blended old-school live event marketing with new-school social sharing. Visitors to the Gillette Man Cave box were pampered with free shaves and visits from actor Laz Alonso and New York Jets center Nick Mangold. At the CoverGirl Beauty box, actress Jordana Brewster helped with free beauty and nail touch-ups. Such celebrities helped draw substantial social and traditional media coverage.**

Everett Collection/Newscom (left); Dennis Van Tine/ABACAUSA.COM/Newscom (right) the engagement rate for visitors to the PGEveryday Facebook page soared 151 percent. And the social media were abuzz with pictures and posts of the day's happenings. #EverydayEffect became the day's number-two trending topic on Twitter.

P&G's Everyday Effect event is an example of how companies these days are blending old-school promotion techniques, such as samples and pop-ups, with new-school social sharing technologies to enhance the impact of both. Increasingly, the two promotional approaches form an important symbiotic relationship: A live event creates special face-to-face brand engagements that generate needed social media content. In turn, the social media help amplify and extend the event's impact.

"On the one hand, social is extending the reach of events to intensify their impact beyond those in attendance," says one event marketing expert. "On the other, events are becoming crucial content sources for brands' Facebook, Twitter,

and Instagram feeds." Says another expert, "Social media in isolation is sort of like a long distance relationship; the human contact piece is missing." In contrast, an "experiential [event], as a deep engagement thing, can be very satisfying but you can't get scale behind it." His conclusion: "Together they're a great marriage."

Sources: Stuart Feil, "All the World Is a Stage," *Adweek*, July 22, 2013, www .adweek.com/print/151231; Kyle Stock, "The Logic behind P&G's Old-School Manhattan Giveaway," *Businessweek*, June 19, 2013, www.businessweek.com/ articles/2013-06-19/the-logic-behind-p-and-gs-old-school-manhattan-give-away; Barry Silverstein, "P&G Hosts Massive Everyday Effect Giveaway Event in New York City," *Brand Channel*, June 19, 2013, www.brandchannel.com/ home/post/2013/06/19/PG-Everyday-Effect-Event-061913.aspx; "Tweeting the #EverydayEffect," www.pgeveryday.com/beauty/get-the-look/article/tweeting-the-everydayeffect, accessed June 2015; and "Everyday Effect," *P&G Newsroom,* http://news.pg.com/category/tags/everyday-effectandwww.pgeveryday.com/tag/ everydayeffect, accessed September 2015.

>> **Event marketing: Red Bull hosts hundreds of events each year in dozens of sports around the world, designed to bring the high-octane world of Red Bull to its community of enthusiasts.**

Max Rossi/Reuters

NFL jersey designs. The next week, it's a mob of Russian models on the northern triangle of Times Square (called Duffy Square), using it as a fashion runway for Maybelline. But according to one business reporter, energy drink maker Red Bull is the "mother of all event marketers":[31]

Event pioneer Red Bull holds hundreds of events each year in dozens of sports around the world. >> Each event features off-the-grid experiences designed to bring the high-octane world of Red Bull to its community of enthusiasts. The brand even hosts a "Holy S**t" tab on its Web site, featuring videos of everything from 27-meter ocean cliff dives at its Cliff Diving Series event in Grimstad, Norway, to daredevil freeskiing feats at its Red Bull Cold Rush event in the Colorado mountain peaks to absolutely breathtaking wing suit flights at Red Bull events staged in exotic locations from Monterrey, Mexico, to Hunan Province, China. The Red Bull Final Descent series is a mountain biking challenge that pushes riders to the brink and back, over some of the most technically challenging terrain in North America. Red Bull events draw large crowds and plenty of media coverage. But it's about more than just the events—it's about customer engagement. It's about creating face-to-face experiences in which customers can actually feel the excitement and live the brand. "It's about deepening and enhancing relationships," says one analyst.

Trade Promotions

Trade promotions

Sales promotion tools used to persuade resellers to carry a brand, give it shelf space, promote it in advertising, and push it to consumers.

Manufacturers direct more sales promotion dollars toward retailers and wholesalers (79 percent of all promotions dollars) than to final consumers (21 percent).[32] **Trade promotions** can persuade resellers to carry a brand, give it shelf space, promote it in advertising, and push it to consumers. Shelf space is so scarce these days that manufacturers often have to offer price-offs, allowances, buy-back guarantees, or free goods to retailers and wholesalers to get products on the shelf and, once there, to keep them on it.

Manufacturers use several trade promotion tools. Many of the tools used for consumer promotions—contests, premiums, displays—can also be used as trade promotions. Or the manufacturer may offer a straight *discount* off the list price on each case purchased during a stated period of time (also called a *price-off, off-invoice,* or *off-list*). Manufacturers also may offer an *allowance* (usually so much off per case) in return for the retailer's agreement to feature the manufacturer's products in some way. For example, an advertising allowance compensates retailers for advertising the product, whereas a display allowance compensates them for using special displays.

Manufacturers may offer *free goods*, which are extra cases of merchandise, to resellers who buy a certain quantity or who feature a certain flavor or size. They may also offer *push money*—cash or gifts to dealers or their sales forces to "push" the manufacturer's goods. Manufacturers may give retailers free *specialty advertising items* that carry the company's name, such as pens, calendars, memo pads, flashlights, and tote bags.

Business Promotions

Business promotions

Sales promotion tools used to generate business leads, stimulate purchases, reward customers, and motivate salespeople.

Companies spend billions of dollars each year on promotion geared toward industrial customers. **Business promotions** are used to generate business leads, stimulate purchases, reward customers, and motivate salespeople. Business promotions include many of the same tools used for consumer or trade promotions. Here, we focus on two additional major business promotion tools: conventions and trade shows and sales contests.

Many companies and trade associations organize *conventions and trade shows* to promote their products. Firms selling to the industry show their products at the trade show. Vendors at these shows receive many benefits, such as opportunities to find new sales leads, contact customers, introduce new products, meet new customers, sell more to present customers, and educate customers with publications and audiovisual materials. Trade shows also help companies reach many prospects that are not reached through their sales forces.

Some trade shows are huge. For example, at this year's International Consumer Electronics Show, 3,673 exhibitors attracted some 165,000 professional visitors. >> Even more impressive, at the Bauma mining and construction equipment trade show in Munich, Germany, more than 3,400 exhibitors from 57 countries presented their latest product innovations to more than 530,000 attendees from more than 200 countries. Total exhibition space equaled about 6.1 million square feet (more than 127 football fields).[33]

A *sales contest* is a contest for salespeople or dealers to motivate them to increase their sales performance over a given period. Sales contests motivate and recognize good company performers, who may receive trips, cash prizes, or other gifts. Some companies award points for performance, which the receiver can turn in for any of a variety of prizes. Sales contests work best when they are tied to measurable and achievable sales objectives (such as finding new accounts, reviving old accounts, or increasing account profitability).

>> **Some trade shows are huge. At this year's Bauma mining and construction equipment trade show in Munich, Germany, more than 3,400 exhibitors from 57 countries presented their latest product innovations to more than 530,000 attendees from more than 200 countries.**

Messe Munchen

Developing the Sales Promotion Program

Beyond selecting the types of promotions to use, marketers must make several other decisions in designing the full sales promotion program. First, they must determine the *size of the incentive*. A certain minimum incentive is necessary if the promotion is to succeed; a larger incentive will produce more sales response. The marketer also must set *conditions for participation*. Incentives might be offered to everyone or only to select groups.

Marketers must determine how to *promote and distribute the promotion* program itself. For example, a $2-off coupon could be given out in a package, in an advertisement, at the store, via the Internet, or in a mobile download. Each distribution method involves a different level of reach and cost. Increasingly, marketers are blending several media into a total campaign concept. The *length of the promotion* is also important. If the sales promotion period is too short, many prospects (who may not be buying during that time) will miss it. If the promotion runs too long, the deal will lose some of its "act now" force.

Evaluation is also very important. Marketers should work to measure the returns on their sales promotion investments, just as they should seek to assess the returns on other marketing activities. The most common evaluation method is to compare sales before, during, and after a promotion. Marketers should ask: Did the promotion attract new customers or more purchasing from current customers? Can we hold onto these new customers and purchases? Will the long-run customer relationship and sales gains from the promotion justify its costs?

Clearly, sales promotion plays an important role in the total promotion mix. To use it well, the marketer must define the sales promotion objectives, select the best tools, design the sales promotion program, implement the program, and evaluate the results. Moreover, sales promotion must be coordinated carefully with other promotion mix elements within the overall IMC program.

MyMarketingLab

If assigned by your instructor, complete the questions marked with the ⭐ from the EOC Discussion Questions section in the MyLab. To complete the Marketing by the Numbers problems found in this section, go to your Assignments in the MyLab.

REVIEWING AND EXTENDING THE CONCEPTS

CHAPTER REVIEW AND CRITICAL THINKING

Objectives Review

This chapter is the second of three chapters covering the final marketing mix element—promotion. The previous chapter dealt with overall integrated marketing communications and with advertising and public relations. This chapter investigated personal selling and sales promotion. Personal selling is the interpersonal arm of the communications mix. Sales promotion consists of short-term incentives to encourage the purchase or sale of a product or service.

 OBJECTIVE 13-1 Discuss the role of a company's salespeople in creating value for customers and building customer relationships. (pp 400–402)

Most companies use salespeople, and many companies assign them an important role in the marketing mix. For companies selling business products, the firm's sales force works directly with customers. Often, the sales force is the customer's only direct contact with the company and therefore may be viewed by customers as representing the company itself. In contrast, for consumer product companies that sell through intermediaries, consumers usually do not meet salespeople or even know about them. The sales force works behind the scenes, dealing with wholesalers and retailers to obtain their support and helping them become more effective in selling the firm's products.

As an element of the promotion mix, the sales force is very effective in achieving certain marketing objectives and carrying out such activities as prospecting, communicating, selling and servicing, and information gathering. But with companies becoming more market oriented, a customer-focused sales force also works to produce both customer satisfaction and company profit. The sales force plays a key role in engaging customers and developing and managing profitable customer relationships.

 OBJECTIVE 13-2 Identify and explain the six major sales force management steps. (pp 402–413)

High sales force costs necessitate an effective sales management process consisting of six steps: designing sales force strategy and structure, recruiting and selecting, training, compensating, supervising, and evaluating salespeople and sales force performance.

In designing a sales force, sales management must address various issues, including what type of sales force structure will work best (territorial, product, customer, or complex structure), sales force size, who will be involved in selling, and how various salespeople and sales-support people will work together (inside or outside sales forces and team selling).

Salespeople must be recruited and selected carefully. In recruiting salespeople, a company may look to the job duties and the characteristics of its most successful salespeople to suggest the traits it wants in new salespeople. It must then look for applicants through recommendations of current salespeople, ads, and the Internet and social media as well as college recruitment/placement centers. After the selection process is complete, training programs familiarize new salespeople not only with the art of selling but also with the company's history, its products and policies, and the characteristics of its customers and competitors.

The sales force compensation system helps to reward, motivate, and direct salespeople. In addition to compensation, all salespeople need supervision, and many need continuous encouragement because they must make many decisions and face many frustrations. Periodically, the company must evaluate their performance to help them do a better job. In evaluating salespeople, the company relies on information gathered from sales reports, personal observations, customer surveys, and conversations with other salespeople.

The fastest-growing sales trend is the explosion in social selling—using online, mobile, and social media in selling. The new digital technologies are providing salespeople with powerful tools for identifying and learning about prospects, engaging customers, creating customer value, closing sales, and nurturing customer relationships. Many of today's customers no longer rely as much on assistance provided by salespeople. Instead, increasingly, they use online and social media resources to analyze their own problems, research solutions, get advice from colleagues, and rank buying options before ever speaking to a salesperson. In response, sellers are reorienting their selling processes around the new customer buying process. They are using social media, mobile devices, Web forums, online communities, blogs, and other digital tools to engage customers earlier and more fully. Ultimately, online, mobile, and social media technologies are helping to make sales forces more efficient, cost-effective, and productive.

 OBJECTIVE 13-3 **Discuss the personal selling process, distinguishing between transaction-oriented marketing and relationship marketing. (pp 414–417)**

Selling involves a seven-step process: prospecting and qualifying, preapproach, approach, presentation and demonstration, handling objections, closing, and follow-up. These steps help marketers close a specific sale and, as such, are transaction oriented. However, a seller's dealings with customers should be guided by the larger concept of relationship marketing. The company's sales force should help to orchestrate a whole-company effort to develop profitable long-term relationships with key customers based on superior customer value and satisfaction.

 OBJECTIVE 13-4 **Explain how sales promotion campaigns are developed and implemented. (pp 417–424)**

Sales promotion campaigns call for setting sales promotion objectives (in general, sales promotions should be *consumer relationship building*); selecting tools; and developing and implementing the sales promotion program by using *consumer promotion tools* (from coupons, refunds, premiums, and point-of-purchase promotions to contests, sweepstakes, and events), *trade promotion tools* (from discounts and allowances to free goods and push money), and *business promotion tools* (conventions, trade shows, and sales contests) as well as determining such things as the size of the incentive, the conditions for participation, how to promote and distribute the promotion package, and the length of the promotion. After this process is completed, the company must evaluate its sales promotion results.

Key Terms

Objective 3-1
Personal selling (p 400)
Salesperson (p 401)

Objective 3-2
Sales force management (p 402)
Territorial sales force structure (p 403)
Product sales force structure (p 403)
Customer (or market) sales force structure (p 403)
Outside sales force (or field sales force) (p 404)

Inside sales force (p 404)
Team selling (p 405)
Sales quota (p 410)
Social selling (p 410)

Objective 3-3
Selling process (p 414)
Prospecting (p 414)
Preapproach (p 414)
Approach (p 415)
Presentation (p 415)

Handling objections (p 416)
Closing (p 416)
Follow-up (p 416)

Objective 3-4
Sales promotion (p 417)
Consumer promotions (p 419)
Event marketing (or event sponsorships) (p 420)
Trade promotions (p 422)
Business promotions (p 423)

Discussion Questions

13-1. Describe the roles that a salesperson and the sales force perform in marketing. (AASCB: Communication; Reflective Thinking)

13-2. What traits and behaviors should an ethical salesperson possess? What role does the sales manager play in ethical selling behavior? (AACSB: Ethical Understanding and Reasoning)

13-3. Name and describe the four sales compensation elements. What are the various compensation combinations, and

how can they be used to achieve the company's marketing objectives? (AACSB: Communication; Reflective Thinking)

13-4. Define *sales promotion* and discuss its objectives. (AACSB: Communication)

13-5. Discuss the different types of trade sales promotions and distinguish these types of promotions from business promotions. (AACSB: Communication)

Critical Thinking Exercises

13-6. There are considerable free sales training resources available on the Internet. Search "free sales training" to find some of these resources and access one of them. Create a presentation highlighting what you learned. (AACSB: Communication; Use of IT; Reflective Thinking)

13-7. Select a product or service and role-play a sales call—from the approach to the close—with another student. Have one member of the team act as the salesperson with the other member acting as the customer, raising at least three objections. Select another product or service and perform this exercise again with your roles reversed. (AACSB: Communication; Reflective Thinking)

13-8. In a small group, design a sales promotion campaign using online, social media, and mobile marketing for a small business or organization in your community. Develop a presentation to pitch your campaign to the business or organization and incorporate what you've learned about the selling process. (AACSB: Communication; Reflective Thinking)

MINICASES AND APPLICATIONS

Online, Social Media, and Mobile Marketing   Snap It and Redeem It!

More than 300 billion coupons are distributed each year, with more than 90 percent of them printed on paper. Consumers redeem only about 1 percent of coupons distributed, often because they clip them but forget to use them in the store. SnipSnap has a solution for consumers. Hailed as the Best Shopping App by About.com and winning Media Post's Apply Awards for Best Finance App, this app has mobilized those paper coupons for consumers. SnipSnap now boasts 4 million users and more than 50 national retail partners. The app allows consumers to snap a photo of retailers' paper coupons and redeem them at the store. Users can share with friends on Facebook and Twitter and follow others' couponing. SnipSnap is the first mobile app that scans the text, images, logos, and barcodes in printed coupons and creates a mobile coupon. It also sends expiration date reminders and location-based notifications. Retailer Lord & Taylor installed iBeacon technology and partnered with SnipSnap to send shoppers targeted coupons based on where they are in the store. So if you want a good deal on a Michael Kors purse, it knows you are looking at the item and might send you a coupon through the app.

SnipSnap employees noticed consumers were snapping pictures of "coupons" they created to send to friends and family that were good for some special treatment, so the company created a spin-off app called GoodFor. Now, if you want to send a special someone a coupon good for a 30-minute massage or your kid a "get out of chores free" coupon, GoodFor allows you to do it!

13-9. Research other types of apps that rely on smartphone cameras to redeem a sales promotion offer. Explain how they work and how they are similar to and different from SnipSnap. (AACSB: Communication; Use of IT; Reflective Thinking)

13-10. The profitable growth potential for SnipSnap is in the enterprise market where it provides mobile promotion services to retailers. SnipSnap is working with retailers to create and manage geo-conquesting campaigns. Research what this is and create a presentation explaining how it works. (AACSB: Communication; Use of IT; Reflective Thinking)

Marketing Ethics   "Dollars for Docs"?

The pharmaceutical industry is innovating at a dizzying pace, but it is getting more difficult for pharmaceutical sales reps to reach doctors to inform them of new or improved products. One option is to host educational seminars. However, many educational seminars are held at lavish restaurants or destinations underwritten by pharmaceutical companies, and doctors providing the education are paid consulting and speaking fees to the tune of more than $2 billion since 2009. In some cases, speakers are given scripts developed by the pharmaceutical company, leading to the criticism that this is company-scripted marketing and the distinguished speaker is merely a "paid parrot" selling drugs for the company. Critics also claim that such promotion results in needlessly increased prescriptions for expensive branded drugs that are no better than generic alternatives. Many drug makers are reducing expenditures for such product promotions because of the Physician Payment Sunshine Act, a provision of the Affordable Care Act of 2010. *Pro Publica* has a "Dollars for Docs" searchable database, and as part of the Sunshine Act, a searchable government Web site is available to the public to shed light on pharmaceutical sales practices.

13-11. Is it wrong for pharmaceutical companies to explain the benefits of their products to physicians this way? Suggest other alternatives for reaching doctors to inform them of the benefits of a company's products. (AACSB: Communication; Ethical Reasoning; Reflective Thinking)

⭐ **13-12.** Learn about the Physician Payment Sunshine Act. Search *Pro Publica's* "Dollars for Docs" database (http://projects .propublica.org/docdollars/) for local physicians to see if they have received payments from pharmaceutical companies. Search the government's Web site (https:// openpaymentsdata.cms.gov/) and compare your findings with those of *Pro Publica's* database. Write a report on what you found. (AACSB: Communication; Use of IT; Reflective Thinking)

Marketing by the Numbers   Salesforce Analysis

Wheels, Inc. manufactures bicycles sold through retail bicycle shops in the southeastern United States. The company has two salespeople that do more than just sell the products— they manage relationships with the bicycle shops to enable them to better meet consumers' needs. The company's sales reps visit the shops several times per year, often for hours at a time. The owner of Wheels is considering expanding to the rest of the country and would like to have distribution through 1,000 bicycle shops. To do so, however, the company would have to hire more salespeople. Each salesperson earns $40,000 plus 2 percent commission on all sales annually. Another alternative is to use the services of sales agents instead of its own sales force. Sales agents would be paid 5 percent of sales.

13-13. Refer to Appendix 3 to answer this question. Determine the number of salespeople Wheels needs if it has 1,000 bicycle shop accounts that need to be called on four times per year. Each sales call lasts approximately 2.5 hours, and each sales rep has approximately 1,250 hours per year to devote to customers. (AACSB: Communication; Analytical Reasoning)

13-14. At what level of sales would it be more cost efficient for Wheels to use to sales agents compared with its own sales force? To determine this, consider the fixed and variable costs for each alternative. What are the pros and cons of using a company's own sales force versus independent sales agents? (AACSB: Communication; Analytical Reasoning; Reflective Thinking)

Video Case   First Flavor

First Flavor is a start-up company with a unique product. It manufactures great-tasting edible film that can replicate the flavor of just about anything, from an eight-topping pizza to an alcoholic beverage. If you're wondering why a company would make such a product, think of the endless possibilities it allows for consumers to sample the taste of a food or beverage before purchasing it.

Although First Flavor first replicated flavors on thin film in order to market the product as a new method for product sampling, the company is now evaluating many other applications of the technology. This video demonstrates how one product can be marketed in multiple ways.

After viewing the video featuring First Flavor, answer the following questions:

13-15. Classify First Flavor's core business as a sales promotion element.

13-16. Brainstorm a list of the ways that First Flavor's edible film might be used to sample products.

13-17. Can First Flavor successfully in pursue consumer product opportunities in addition to its promotional services? Explain.

Company Cases   13 Sungard/8 3M

See Appendix 1 for cases appropriate for this chapter. **Case 13, Sungard: Building Sustained Growth by Selling the SunGard Way.** Consistently one of the top companies to sell for, Sungard is out to stay that way through a complete transformation of its sales force model. **Case 8, 3M: Where Innovation Is a Way of Life.** Although it has many consumer products, 3M is truly a B2B company that relies on a strong sales force.

MyMarketingLab

If assigned by your instructor, complete these writing sections from your Assignments in the MyLab.

13-18. What is social selling, and how is it affecting the sales function in organizations? (AACSB: Communication; Reflective Thinking)

13-19. What is team selling, and why has it become more important? Are there any pitfalls to this approach? (AACSB: Communication; Reflective Thinking)

14

Direct, Online, Social Media, and Mobile Marketing

CHAPTER ROAD MAP   Objective Outline

▶ **OBJECTIVE 14-1**   **Define *direct and digital marketing* and discuss their rapid growth and benefits to customers and companies.** Direct and Digital Marketing (430–432)

▶ **OBJECTIVE 14-2**   **Identify and discuss the major forms of direct and digital marketing.** Forms of Direct and Digital Marketing (432–433); Digital and Social Media Marketing (433)

▶ **OBJECTIVE 14-3**   **Explain how companies have responded to the Internet and the digital age with various online marketing strategies.** Marketing, the Internet, and the Digital Age (433–434); Online Marketing (434–439)

▶ **OBJECTIVE 14-4**   **Discuss how companies use social media and mobile marketing to engage consumers and create brand community.** Social Media Marketing (439–443); Mobile Marketing (443–447)

▶ **OBJECTIVE 14-5**   **Identify and discuss the traditional direct marketing forms and overview public policy and ethical issues presented by direct marketing.** Traditional Direct Marketing Forms (447–451); Public Policy Issues in Direct and Digital Marketing (451–453)

Previewing the Concepts

In the previous two chapters, you learned about engaging consumers and communicating customer value through integrated marketing communication, and about four elements of the marketing communications mix: advertising, publicity, personal selling, and sales promotion. In this chapter, we examine direct marketing and its fastest-growing form: digital marketing (online, social media, and mobile marketing). Today, spurred by the surge in Internet usage and buying as well as rapid advances in digital technologies—from smartphones, tablets, and other digital devices to the spate of online mobile and social media—direct marketing has undergone a dramatic transformation. As you read this chapter, remember that although direct and digital marketing are presented as separate tools, they must be carefully integrated with each other and with other elements of the promotion and marketing mixes.

Let's start by looking at Amazon, a company that markets *only* directly and digitally. In little over 20 years, Amazon has blossomed from an obscure dot-com upstart into one of the most powerful names on the Internet. According to one estimate, an incredible 30 percent of all online shoppers research Amazon.com first before buying. How has Amazon become such an incredibly successful direct and online marketer in such a short time? It's all about creating customer engagement, value, and relationships through personal and satisfying online customer experiences. Few online marketers do that as well as Amazon.com.

First Stop

Amazon.com: The Poster Child for Direct and Digital Marketing

When you think of shopping online, chances are good that you think first of Amazon. The online pioneer first opened its virtual doors in 1995, selling books out of founder Jeff Bezos's garage in suburban Seattle. Amazon still sells books—lots and lots of books. But it now sells just about everything else as well, from music, electronics, tools, housewares, apparel, and groceries to fashions, loose diamonds, and Maine lobsters. Most analysts view Amazon as *the* model for direct marketing in the digital age.

From the start, Amazon has grown explosively. Its annual sales have rocketed from a modest $150 million in 1997 to $89 billion today. During just the past five years, Amazon's revenues have more than tripled. On last year's Cyber Monday alone, Amazon.com sold 37 million items to its 270 million active customers worldwide—that's 428 items per second. Amazon's revenues will likely reach $100 billion within the next year, faster to that mark than any other company in history (it took Walmart 34 years). That would make it the nation's second-largest retailer, trailing only Walmart.

What has made Amazon such an amazing success story? Founder and CEO Bezos puts it in three simple words: "Obsess over customers." To its core, the company is relentlessly customer driven. "The thing that drives everything is creating genuine value for customers," says Bezos. Amazon believes that if it does what's good for customers, profits will follow. So the company starts with the customer and works backward. Rather than asking what it can do with its current capabilities, Amazon first asks: Who are our customers? What do they need? Then it develops whatever capabilities are required to meet those customer needs.

At Amazon, every decision is made with an eye toward improving the Amazon.com customer experience. In fact, at many Amazon meetings, the most influential figure in the room is "the empty chair"— literally an empty chair at the table that represents the all-important customer. At times, the empty chair isn't empty but is occupied by a "Customer Experience Bar Raiser," an employee who is specially trained to represent customers' interests.

Amazon's obsession with serving the needs of its customers drives the company to take risks and innovate in ways that other companies don't. For example, when it noted that its book-buying customers needed better access to e-books and other digital content, Amazon developed the Kindle e-reader, its first-ever original product. The Kindle took more than four years and a whole new set of skills to develop. But Amazon's start-with-the-customer thinking paid off handsomely. The Kindle is one of the company's best-selling products, and Amazon.com now sells more e-books than hardcovers and paperbacks combined. What's more, the company's growing line of Kindle Fire tablets now leads the market for low-priced tablet computers. Thus, what started as an effort to improve the customer experience now gives Amazon a powerful presence in the burgeoning world of digital, mobile, and social media. Not only does the Kindle allow access to e-books, music, videos, and apps sold by Amazon, it

>> Amazon does much more than just sell goods online. It engages customers and creates direct, personalized, and highly satisfying customer online buying experiences.

Philippe Huguen/AFP/Getty Images

makes interacting online with the digital giant easier than ever. Customers use their Kindle tablets to shop at Amazon.com and interact with the company on its blogs and social media pages.

Amazon wants to deliver a special online experience to every customer. Most Amazon.com regulars feel a surprisingly strong relationship with the company, especially given the almost complete lack of actual human interaction. Amazon obsesses over making each customer's experience uniquely personal. For example, the Amazon.com site greets customers with their very own home pages, complete with personalized recommendations. Amazon was the first company to sift through each customer's past purchases and browsing histories and the purchasing patterns of customers with similar profiles to come up with personalized site content. Amazon wants to personalize the shopping experience for each individual customer. If it has 270 million customers, it reasons, it should have 270 million stores.

Visitors to Amazon.com receive a unique blend of benefits: huge selection, good value, low prices, and convenience. But it's the "discovery" factor that makes the buying experience really special. Once on the Amazon.com site, you're compelled to stay for a while—looking, learning, and discovering. To create even greater selection and discovery for customers, Amazon allows competing retailers—from mom-and-pop operations to Marks & Spencer—to sell their products on Amazon.com through the Amazon Marketplace, creating a virtual shopping mall of incredible proportions. The broader selection attracts more customers, and everyone benefits. Last year, Amazon customers bought more than 2 billion items from 2 million third-party

> Amazon's deep-down passion for creating superb online customer experiences has made it one of the most powerful names on the Internet. Amazon is *the* model for successful direct and digital marketing.

Amazon Marketplace sellers worldwide, accounting for 40 percent of Amazon's unit sales.

Amazon also makes the order delivery experience a whiz with its Amazon Prime service. For $99 a year, Prime members can receive free two-day shipping for all eligible purchases plus unlimited streaming of movies and TV shows with Prime Instant Video and access to borrowing e-books from the Kindle Owners' Lending Library. Amazon is moving rapidly toward same-day delivery. It recently launched Prime Now, which offers speedy two-*hour* free delivery of tens of thousands of items in several large metropolitan areas (or one-hour delivery for a $7.99 fee). "In the past six weeks my husband and I have made an embarrassing number of orders through Amazon Prime Now," says one excited customer. "It's cheap, easy, and insanely fast."

More than just a place to buy things, Amazon.com has become a kind of online community in which customers can browse for products, research purchase alternatives, share opinions and reviews with other visitors, and chat online with authors and experts. In this way, Amazon does much more than just sell goods online. It engages customers and creates direct, personalized customer relationships and satisfying online experiences. Year after year, Amazon places at or near the top of almost every customer satisfaction ranking, regardless of industry.

Based on its powerful growth, many analysts have speculated that Amazon will become the Walmart of the Web. In fact, some argue, it already is. Although Walmart's total sales of $487 billion dwarf Amazon's $89 billion in sales, Amazon's online sales are 7.5 times greater than Walmart's. So online, it's Walmart that's chasing Amazon. Put another way, Walmart wants to become the Amazon of the Web, not the other way around. However, despite its mammoth proportions, to catch Amazon online, Walmart will have to match the superb Amazon.com online customer experience, and that won't be easy.

Thus, Amazon has become the poster child for direct and digital marketing. "The reason I'm so obsessed with ... the customer experience is that I believe [our success] has been driven exclusively by that experience," says Jeff Bezos. It all starts with customer value. If Amazon creates superior value for customers, it will earn their business and loyalty, and success will follow in terms of company sales and returns. As Bezos puts it, "When things get complicated, we simplify them by asking, 'What's best for the customer?' We believe that if we do that, things will work out in the long term."[1]

M any of the marketing and promotion tools that we've examined in previous chapters were developed in the context of *mass marketing*: targeting broad markets with standardized messages and offers distributed through intermediaries. Today, however, with the trend toward narrower targeting and the surge in digital and social media technologies, many companies are adopting *direct marketing*, either as a primary marketing approach or as a supplement to other approaches. In this section, we explore the exploding world of direct marketing and its fastest-growing form—digital marketing using online, social media, and mobile marketing channels.

Direct and Digital Marketing

Direct and digital marketing
Engaging directly with carefully targeted individual consumers and customer communities to both obtain an immediate response and build lasting customer relationships.

Direct and digital marketing involve engaging directly with carefully targeted individual consumers and customer communities to both obtain an immediate response and build lasting customer relationships. Companies use direct marketing to tailor their offers and content to the needs and interests of narrowly defined segments or individual buyers. In this way, they build customer engagement, brand community, and sales.

For example, Amazon.com interacts directly with customers via its Web site or mobile app to help them discover and buy almost anything and everything online. Similarly, GEICO interacts directly with customers—by telephone, through its Web site or smartphone app, or on its Facebook, Twitter, and YouTube pages—to build individual brand relationships, give insurance quotes, sell policies, or service customer accounts.

The New Direct Marketing Model

Early direct marketers—catalog companies, direct mailers, and telemarketers—gathered customer names and sold goods mainly by mail and telephone. Today, however, spurred by the surge in Internet usage and buying, and by rapid advances in digital technologies—from smartphones, tablets, and other digital devices to the spate of online social and mobile media—direct marketing has undergone a dramatic transformation.

In previous chapters, we discussed direct marketing as direct distribution—as marketing channels that contain no intermediaries. We also included direct and digital marketing elements of the promotion mix—as an approach for engaging consumers directly and creating brand community. In actuality, direct marketing is both of these things and much more.

Most companies still use direct marketing as a supplementary channel or medium. Thus, most department stores, such as Sears or Macy's, sell the majority of their merchandise off their store shelves, but they also sell through direct mail, online catalogs, and social media pages. Pepsi's Mountain Dew brand markets heavily through mass-media advertising and its retail partners' channels. However, it also supplements these channels with a heavy dose of direct marketing. Mountain Dew's marketing mix consists of 55 percent television advertising and 45 percent digital. It uses its several brand Web sites and a long list of social media to engage its digitally connected customer community in everything from designing their own Mountain Dew lifestyle pages to deciding which limited-edition flavors should be launched or retired. Through such direct interactions, Mountain Dew has created one of the most passionately loyal fan bases of any brand, who in turn have made it the nation's fourth-largest soft drink brand.[2]

However, for many companies today, direct and digital marketing are more than just supplementary channels or advertising media—they constitute a complete model for doing business. Firms employing this direct model use it as the only approach. Companies such as Amazon, Google, Facebook, eBay, Netflix, GEICO, and Priceline.com have successfully built their entire approach to the marketplace around direct and digital marketing. ≫ For example, Priceline.com, the online travel company, sells its services exclusively through online, mobile, and social media channels. Priceline.com and other online travel agency competitors such as Expedia and Orbitz have pretty much driven traditional offline travel agencies to extinction.[3]

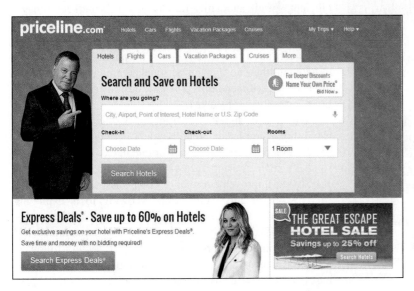

≫ **The new direct marketing model: Online travel agency Priceline.com sells its services exclusively through online, mobile, and social media channels. Along with other online competitors, Priceline.com has pretty much driven traditional offline travel agencies to extinction.**

Priceline.com

Rapid Growth of Direct and Digital Marketing

Direct and digital marketing have become the fastest-growing form of marketing. According to one source, U.S. companies spent an estimated $157 billion on direct and digital marketing last year, up more than 11 percent over the previous year. As a result, direct-marketing-driven sales now amount to more than $2 trillion, accounting for 12 percent of the U.S. economy.[4]

Direct marketing continues to become more Internet-based, and digital direct marketing is claiming a surging share of marketing spending and sales. For example, U.S. marketers spent an estimated $64 billion on digital advertising alone last year, up a blistering 26 percent over the previous year. Total digital advertising spending—including online display and search advertising, social media, mobile, video, email, and other—now accounts for the second-largest share of media spending, behind only television, which it's expected to overtake by 2018. And as consumers spend more and more time on their tablets and smartphones, spending on mobile advertising is exploding. Next year alone, mobile ad spending is expected to grow by 50 percent, and by 2018 it will account for an expected 25 percent of all U.S. ad spending.[5]

Benefits of Direct and Digital Marketing to Buyers and Sellers

For buyers, direct and digital marketing are convenient, easy, and private. They give buyers anywhere, anytime access to an almost unlimited assortment of goods and a wealth of product and buying information. For example, on its Web site and mobile app, Amazon.com offers more information than most of us can digest, ranging from top 10 product lists, extensive product descriptions, and expert and user product reviews to recommendations based on customers' previous searches and purchases. Through direct marketing, buyers can interact with sellers by phone or on the seller's Web site or mobile

>> **Direct and digital marketing lets brands create immediate and timely customer engagement, as when GE celebrated last year's National Inventors' Day by asking Twitter followers for offbeat invention ideas, then created illustrations of the best ones.**
GE

app to create exactly the configuration of information, products, or services they want and then order them on the spot. Finally, for consumers who want it, digital marketing through online, mobile, and social media provides a sense of brand engagement and community—a place to share brand information and experiences with other brand fans.

For sellers, direct marketing often provides a low-cost, efficient, speedy alternative for reaching their markets. Today's direct marketers can target small groups or individual customers. Because of the one-to-one nature of direct marketing, companies can interact with customers by phone or online, learn more about their needs, and personalize products and services to specific customer tastes. In turn, customers can ask questions and volunteer feedback.

Direct and digital marketing also offer sellers greater flexibility. They let marketers make ongoing adjustments to prices and programs or create immediate, timely, and personal engagement and offers. For example, last Fourth of July, home-improvement retailer Lowe's issued a stop-motion "Happy 4th of July" Vine video showing tools exploding into fireworks, a nice supplement to its ongoing Vine series of "Fix in Six" do-it-yourself videos. >>GE celebrated last year's National Inventors' Day by asking its Twitter followers for offbeat invention ideas, then created illustrations of the best ones, such as a "hand-holding robot."

Especially in today's digital environment, direct marketing provides opportunities for *real-time marketing* that links brands to important moments and trending events in customers' lives. It is a powerful tool for moving customers through the buying process and for building customer engagement, community, and personalized relationships.

Author Comment
Direct marketing is rich in tools, from traditional favorites such as direct mail and catalogs to dazzling new digital tools—online, mobile, and social media.

Forms of Direct and Digital Marketing

The major forms of direct and digital marketing are shown in >>**Figure 14.1**. Traditional direct marketing tools include face-to-face selling, direct-mail marketing, catalog marketing, telemarketing, direct-response television marketing, and kiosk marketing. In recent years, however, a dazzling new set of digital direct marketing tools has burst onto the marketing scene, including online marketing (Web sites, online ads and promotions, email, online videos, and blogs), social media marketing, and mobile marketing. We'll begin by examining the new direct digital and social media marketing tools that have received so much attention lately. Then we'll look at the still heavily used and very important traditional direct marketing tools. As always, however, it's important to remember that all of these tools—both the new digital and the more traditional forms—must be blended into a fully integrated marketing communications program.

We'll begin with the exciting new digital forms of direct marketing. But remember that the traditional forms are still heavily used and that the new and old must be integrated for maximum impact.

Digital and social media marketing
Online marketing
(Web sites, online advertising,
email, online videos, blogs)
Social media marketing
Mobile marketing

Build direct customer engagement and community

Traditional direct marketing
Face-to-face selling
Direct-mail marketing
Catalog marketing
Telemarketing
Direct-response TV marketing
Kiosk marketing

>> **Figure 14.1 Forms of Direct and Digital Marketing**

🔗 LINKING THE CONCEPTS

Hold up a moment and think about the impact of direct and digital marketing on your life.

● When was last time that you bought something via direct or digital marketing? What did you buy, and why did you buy it direct? When was the last time that you *rejected* a direct or digital marketing offer? Why did you reject it? Based on these experiences, what advice would you give to direct marketers?

● For the next week, keep track of all the direct and digital marketing offers that come your way via direct mail and catalogs, email and mobile ads, online and social media marketing offers, and others. Then analyze the offers by type, source, and what you liked or disliked about each offer and the way it was delivered. Which offer best hit its target (you)? Which missed by the widest margin?

Author Comment
Direct digital and social media marketing is surging and grabbing all the headlines these days, so we'll start with it. But the traditional direct marketing tools are still heavily used. We'll dig into them later in the chapter.

Digital and Social Media Marketing

As noted earlier, **digital and social media marketing** is the fastest-growing form of direct marketing. It uses digital marketing tools such as Web sites, online video, email, blogs, social media, mobile ads and apps, and other digital platforms to directly engage consumers anywhere, anytime via their computers, smartphones, tablets, Internet-ready TVs, and other digital devices. The widespread use of the Internet and digital technologies is having a dramatic impact on both buyers and the marketers who serve them.

Digital and social media marketing
Using digital marketing tools such as Web sites, social media, mobile apps and ads, online video, email, and blogs to engage consumers anywhere, anytime via their digital devices.

Marketing, the Internet, and the Digital Age

Much of the world's business today is carried out over digital networks that connect people and companies. These days, people connect digitally with information, brands, and each other at almost any time and from almost anywhere. The digital age has fundamentally changed customers' notions of convenience, speed, price, product information, service, and brand interactions. As a result, it has given marketers a whole new way to create customer value, engage customers, and build customer relationships.

Digital usage and impact continues to grow steadily. More than 87 percent of all U.S. adults use the Internet, and the average U.S. Internet user spends almost six hours a day using digital media, primarily via mobile devices. Worldwide, 40 percent of the population has Internet access. And 23 percent has access to the mobile Internet, a number that's expected to double over the next five years as mobile becomes an ever-more-popular way to get online.[6]

As a result, more than half of all U.S. households now regularly shop online, and digital buying continues to grow at a healthy double-digit rate. U.S. online retail sales were an estimated $305 billion last year, 6.5 percent of total retail sales. By 2018 as consumers continue to shift their spending from physical to digital stores, that number is expected to grow to almost $500 billion (8.9 percent of total retail sales). Perhaps even more important, it's estimated that nearly half of all U.S. retail sales were either transacted directly online or influenced by Internet research.[7] As today's omni-channel consumers become more and more adept at blending online and in-store shopping, digital channels will come into play for an ever-larger proportion of their purchases.

To reach this burgeoning market, most companies now market online. Some companies operate *only* online. They include a wide array of firms, from *e-tailers* such as Amazon and Expedia.com that sell products and services directly to final buyers via the Internet to *search engines and portals* (such as Google, Yahoo!, Bing, and DuckDuckGo), *transaction sites* (eBay, Craigslist), *content sites* (the *New York Times* on the Web, ESPN.com, and *Encyclopædia Britannica*), and *online social media* (Facebook, Twitter, YouTube, Pinterest, Instragram, and Snapchat).

Today, however, it's hard to find a company that doesn't have a substantial online presence. Even companies that have traditionally operated offline have now created their own

Omni-channel retailing
Creating a seamless cross-channel buying experience that integrates in-store, online, and mobile shopping.

online sales, marketing, and brand community channels. In fact, **omni-channel retailing** companies are having as much online success as their online-only competitors. A recent ranking of the nation's 10 largest online retail sites contained only three online-only retailers (Amazon.com, which was ranked number one, Netflix, and Liberty Interactive). Number two was a manufacturer—Apple. All of the rest were omni-channel retailers.[8]

For example, number three on the list of online retail sites is Staples, the $22 billion office supply retailer. Staples operates more than 1,675 North American superstores. ➤➤But you might be surprised to learn that almost half of Staples's sales are generated online from its Web site and mobile app; its presence on social media such as Facebook, Google+, Twitter, YouTube, and LinkedIn; and its own Staples.com community.[9]

➤➤ **Multichannel marketing: Almost half of Staples's sales come from its online marketing operations, including its Web site and mobile app, its presence on social media, and its own Staples.com community.**

Courtesy of Staples the Office Superstore, LLC & Staples, Inc.

Selling online lets Staples build deeper, more personalized relationships with customers large and small. A large customer, such as GE or P&G, can create lists of approved office products at discount prices and then let company departments or even individuals do their own online and mobile purchasing. This reduces ordering costs, cuts through the red tape, and speeds up the ordering process for customers. At the same time, it encourages companies to use Staples as a sole source for office supplies. Even the smallest companies and individual consumers find 24/7 online ordering via the Web, Staples mobile app, or social media sites easier and more efficient.

In addition, Staples' online, mobile, and social media efforts complement store sales by engaging customers, enlarging product assortments, offering hot deals, and helping customers find a local store and check stock and prices. In return, local stores promote online buying through in-store kiosks. If customers don't find what they need on the shelves, they can quickly order it via the kiosk. Thus, Staples backs its "make more happen" positioning by offering a full range of contact points and delivery modes—online, social media, mobile, catalogs, phone, and in the store. No online-only or store-only seller can match that kind of call, click, or visit convenience and support. "We're offering more products, more ways to buy, and more great value," summarizes Staples's vice president of global marketing.

Direct digital and social media marketing takes any of the several forms shown in Figure 14.1. These forms include online marketing, social media marketing, and mobile marketing. We discuss each in turn, starting with online marketing.

Online Marketing

Online marketing
Marketing via the Internet using company Web sites, online ads and promotions, email, online video, and blogs.

Online marketing refers to marketing via the Internet using company Web sites, online advertising and promotions, email marketing, online video, and blogs. Social media and mobile marketing also take place online and must be closely coordinated with other forms of digital marketing. However, because of their special characteristics, we discuss the fast-growing social media and mobile marketing approaches in separate sections.

Web Sites and Branded Web Communities

Marketing Web site
A Web site that engages consumers to move them closer to a direct purchase or other marketing outcome.

For most companies, the first step in conducting online marketing is to create a Web site. Web sites vary greatly in purpose and content. Some Web sites are primarily **marketing Web sites**, designed to engage consumers and move them closer to a direct purchase or other marketing outcome.

For example, GEICO operates a marketing Web site at www.geico.com. Once a potential customer clicks in, GEICO wastes no time trying to turn the inquiry into a sale and then into a long-term relationship. ➤➤A bold headline urges potential customers to "Get a quote," and the site provides all the information and tools needed to do just that, complete with an auto insurance calculator to help buyers estimate the right insurance

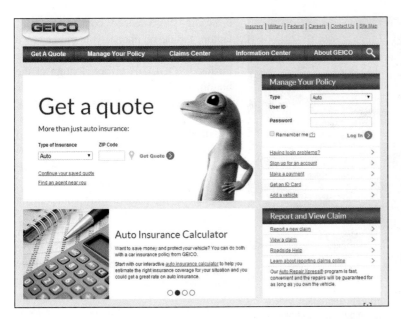

>> **Marketing Web sites: Once a potential customer clicks in, GEICO's Web site wastes no time trying to turn the inquiry into a sale and then into a long-term relationship.**

GEICO

Branded community Web site
A Web site that presents brand content that engages consumers and creates customer community around a brand.

coverage, rates, and savings. The straightforward site also makes it easy for current customers to manage their accounts and policies, add or replace vehicles, and make and view claims, all under the watchful eye of the familiar GEICO Gecko. Customers can also use GEICO's mobile app to access the brand's mobile Web site, where they can pay bills, get account and coverage information, view their ID cards, and even watch the latest GEICO ads and chat with Lily, their GEICO insurance voice assistant.

In contrast, **branded community Web sites** don't try to sell anything at all. Instead, their primary purpose is to present brand content that engages consumers and creates customer–brand community. Such sites typically offer a rich variety of brand information, videos, blogs, activities, and other features that build closer customer relationships and generate engagement with and between the brand and its customers.

For example, consider ESPN's Web site. You can't buy anything at ESPN.com. Instead, the site creates a vast branded sports community:[10]

At ESPN.com, sports fans can access an almost overwhelming repository of sports information, statistics, and game updates. They can customize site content by sport, team, players, and authors to match their own special sports interests and team preferences. The site engages fans in contests and fantasy games (everything from fantasy football, baseball, basketball, and hockey to poker). Sports fans from around the world can participate in discussions with other fans and celebrities before, during, and after sporting events. They can friend and message other users and post comments on message boards and blogs. By downloading various widgets and apps, fans can customize their ESPN experience and carry it with them wherever they go. In all, ESPN's Web site creates a virtual brand community without walls, a must-have experience that keeps fans coming back again and again.

Creating a Web site is one thing; getting people to *visit* the site is another. To attract visitors, companies aggressively promote their Web sites in offline print and broadcast advertising and through ads and links on other sites. But today's Web users are quick to abandon any Web site that doesn't measure up. The key is to create enough engaging and valued content to get consumers to come to the site, stick around, and come back again.

At the very least, a Web site should be easy to use and visually appealing. Ultimately, however, Web sites must also be *useful*. When it comes to online browsing and shopping, most people prefer substance over style and function over flash. For example, ESPN's site isn't all that flashy, and it's pretty heavily packed and congested. But it connects customers quickly and effectively to all the sports information and involvement they are seeking. Thus, effective Web sites contain deep and useful information, interactive tools that help find and evaluate content of interest, links to other related sites, changing promotional offers, and entertaining features that lend relevant excitement.

Online Advertising

Online advertising
Advertising that appears while consumers are browsing online, including display ads and search-related ads.

As consumers spend more and more time online, companies are shifting more of their marketing dollars to **online advertising** to build brand sales or attract visitors to their Internet, mobile, and social media sites. Online advertising has become a major promotional medium. The main forms of online advertising are display ads and search-related ads. Together, display and search-related ads account for the largest portion of firms' digital marketing budgets.

Online display ads might appear anywhere on an Internet user's screen and are often related to the information being viewed. Such display ads have come a long way in recent years in terms of engaging consumers and moving them along the path to purchase. Today's *rich media* ads incorporate animation, video, sound, and interactivity. For example, while

Online display advertising: Today's dynamic rich media ads incorporate animation, video, sound, and interactivity, engaging consumers and moving them along the path to purchase.

The Procter & Gamble Company

browsing sports-related content on your laptop, tablet, or phone, you might see a bright blue and green banner ad for Gillette Fusion PROGLIDE razors floating at the bottom of the page, with the provocative headline "Our Gentlest Shave." >> A click on the banner expands it into a full interactive display ad, complete with an embedded 15-second demonstration video plus click-throughs to the Gillette Fusion PROGLIDE microsite and a buy-now link. Similarly, while perusing your favorite backpacking site, you might see an attention-grabbing video ad from The North Face. Roll over the brand logo and up pops an interactive ad panel, with the video continuing in the upper right corner alongside information on featured products and real-time links to The North Face Web site and a store locator. Such dynamic ads can engage consumers and deliver substantial impact.[11]

Using *search-related ads* (or *contextual advertising*), text- and image-based ads and links appear atop or alongside search engine results on sites such as Google, Yahoo!, and Bing. For example, search Google for "LCD TVs." At the top and side of the resulting search list, you'll see inconspicuous ads for 10 or more advertisers, ranging from Samsung and Panasonic to Best Buy, Amazon.com, Walmart.com, Crutchfield, and CDW. Almost 90 percent of Google's $66 billion in revenues last year came from ad sales. Search is an always-on kind of medium, and the results are easily measured.[12]

A search advertiser buys search terms from the search site and pays only if consumers click through to its site. For instance, type "Coke" or "Coca-Cola" or even just "soft drinks" or "rewards" into your search engine and almost without fail "My Coke Rewards" comes up as one of the top options, perhaps along with a display ad and link to Coca-Cola's official Google+ page. This is no coincidence. Coca-Cola supports its popular online loyalty program largely through search buys. The soft drink giant started first with traditional TV and print advertising but quickly learned that search was the most effective way to bring consumers to its www.mycokerewards.com Web site to register. Now, any of dozens of purchased search terms will return mycokerewards.com at or near the top of the search list.

Email Marketing

Email marketing
Sending highly targeted, tightly personalized, relationship-building marketing messages via email.

Email marketing remains an important and growing digital marketing tool. "Social media is the hot new thing," says one observer, "but email is still the king."[13] By one estimate, 91 percent of all U.S. consumers use email every day. What's more, email is no longer limited to PCs and workstations; 66 percent of all emails are now opened on mobile devices. Not surprisingly, then, a recent study found that email is 40 times more effective at capturing customers than Facebook and Twitter combined.

According to one recent survey, during the latest holiday season, 90 percent of marketers said that their holiday campaigns included email marketing. U.S. companies spent $2.3 billion on email marketing last year, up from only $243 million 12 years earlier. Despite all the email clutter, thanks to its low costs, email marketing still brings one of the highest marketing returns on investment. According to the Direct Marketing Association, marketers get a return of $42 on every $1 they spend on email.[14]

When used properly, email can be the ultimate direct marketing medium. Email lets these marketers send highly targeted, tightly personalized, relationship-building messages. And today's emails are anything but the staid, text-only messages of the past. Instead, they are colorful, inviting, personalized, and interactive. >> For example, one recent CVS Pharmacy email, sent to the chain's ExtraCare Rewards Program members

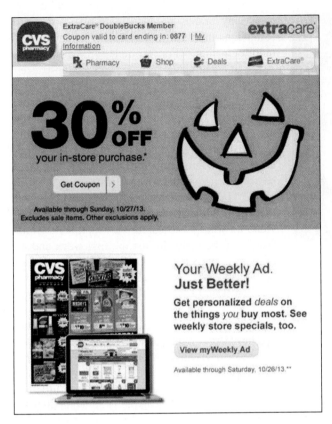

>> **Email marketing: Today's emails are colorful, inviting, personalized, and interactive, like the CVS Pharmacy "Prepare for the Scare" email coupon offer.**

CVS Caremark Corporation

Spam
Unsolicited, unwanted commercial email messages.

Viral marketing
The digital version of word-of-mouth marketing: videos, ads, and other marketing content that is so infectious that customers will seek it out or pass it along to friends.

prior to Halloween, contained a colorful, attention-getting coupon offering 30 percent off an in-store purchase. Clicking the "Get Coupon" button gave customers a choice of printing the coupon or simply having it zapped onto their loyalty cards for later automatic redemption. The CVS "Prepare for the Scare" email also contained a "View myWeekly Ad" button, by which ExtraCare members could link through to a Web page loaded with personalized deals based on things they buy most. Thus, the much-viewed email promoted both immediate store visits and customer loyalty.

But there's a dark side to the growing use of email marketing. The explosion of **spam**—unsolicited, unwanted commercial email messages that clog up our email boxes—has produced consumer irritation and frustration. According to one research company, spam now accounts for 64 percent of the billions of emails sent worldwide each day, almost two out of every three emails. Workers in American businesses send and receive nearly 109 billion emails per day and spend nearly one-third of their workweek managing email.[15] Email marketers walk a fine line between adding value for consumers and being intrusive and annoying.

To address these concerns, most legitimate marketers now practice *permission-based email marketing*, sending email pitches only to customers who "opt in." Many companies use configurable email systems that let customers choose what they want to get. Amazon.com targets opt-in customers with a limited number of helpful "we thought you'd like to know" messages based on their expressed preferences and previous purchases. Few customers object, and many actually welcome such promotional messages. Amazon.com benefits through higher return rates and by avoiding alienating customers with emails they don't want.

Online Videos

Another form of online marketing is posting digital video content on brand Web sites or on social media sites such as YouTube, Facebook, Vine, and others. Some videos are made specifically for the Web and social media. Such videos range from "how-to" instructional videos and public relations (PR) pieces to brand promotions and brand-related entertainment. Other videos are ads that a company makes primarily for TV and other media but posts online before or after an advertising campaign to extend their reach and impact.

Good online videos can engage consumers by the tens of millions. The online video audience is soaring, with more than 60 percent of the U.S. population now streaming video.[16] Marketers hope that some of their videos will go viral. **Viral marketing**, the digital version of word-of-mouth marketing, involves creating videos, ads, and other marketing content that are so infectious that customers will seek them out or pass them along to their friends. Because customers find and pass along the message or promotion, viral marketing can be very inexpensive. And when a video or other information comes from a friend, the recipient is much more likely to view or read it.

All kinds of videos can go viral, producing engagement and positive exposure for a brand. For example, in one simple but honest McDonald's video, the director of marketing at McDonald's Canada answered an online viewer's question about why McDonald's products look better in ads than in real life by conducting a behind-the-scenes tour of how a McDonald's ad is made. The award-winning three-and-a-half-minute video pulled almost 15 million views and 15,000 shares, earning the company praise for its honesty and transparency. As another example, P&G's Always brand launched an inspiring #LikeAGirl video campaign, which set out to replace the negative connotations of what it means "to do something like a girl" with the message "Let's make #LikeAGirl mean amazing things." The initial three-minute video was an instant viral hit, garnering 8 million YouTube views in the first week alone and more than 57 million views to date.[17]

>> Viral marketing: adidas's recent "Take It" campaign featuring famous adidas athletes (here international soccer star Lionel Messi) gutting it out in practice and on game day began on TV but quickly zoomed to the top of the viral charts.

adidas

Blogs

Online forums where people and companies post their thoughts and other content, usually related to narrowly defined topics.

Many brands produce multi-platform video campaigns that bridge traditional TV, online, and mobile media. >> For example, Adidas's recent "Take It" campaign—a series of action-packed 60-second video ads featuring famous Adidas athletes gutting it out in practice and on game day—began on TV but quickly zoomed to the top of the viral charts. The campaign drove home a captivating motivational message: "Do something, and be remembered. Or do nothing, and be forgotten. No one owns today. Take it." The initial "Take It" ad broke during NBA All-Star Weekend, but that was only the beginning. The video ad went on to capture a whopping 21 million YouTube views in just the first week and 40 million in the first two months. Additional videos in the ad series grabbed millions more views, making "Take It" one of the most successful viral campaigns of the decade.[18]

Despite these viral successes, it's important to note that marketers usually have little control over where their viral messages end up. They can seed content online, but that does little good unless the message itself strikes a chord with consumers. Says one creative director, "You hope that the creative is at a high enough mark where the seeds grow into mighty oaks. If they don't like it, it ain't gonna move. If they like it, it'll move a little bit; and if they love it, it's gonna move like a fast-burning fire through the Hollywood hills."[19]

Blogs and Other Online Forums

Brands also conduct online marketing through various digital forums that appeal to specific special-interest groups and brand communities. **Blogs** (or Web logs) are online forums where people and companies post their thoughts and other content, usually related to narrowly defined topics. Blogs can be about anything, from politics or baseball to haiku, car repair, brands, or the latest television series. Many bloggers use social networks such as Twitter, Facebook, Tumblr, and Instagram to promote their blogs, giving them huge reach. Such reach can give blogs—especially those with large and devoted followings—substantial influence.

Most marketers are now tapping into the blogosphere with their own brand-related blogs that reach customer communities. For example, on the Coca-Cola Unbottled blog, Coke fans and company insiders can "look at what's beyond the bottle," sharing posts on everything from new products and sustainability initiatives to fun and inspiring "what's bubbling" fan stories about "spreading happiness." On the Netflix Blog, members of the Netflix team (themselves rabid movie fans) tell about the latest Netflix features, share tricks for getting the most out of the Netflix experience, and collect feedback from subscribers. >> And the creative Nuts About Southwest blog, written by Southwest Airline employees, fosters a two-way dialogue that gives customers a look inside the company's culture and operations. At the same time, it lets Southwest engage customers directly and get feedback from them.

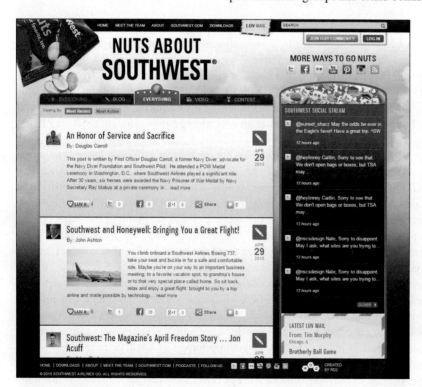

>> Tapping into blogs: The creative Nuts About Southwest blog, written by Southwest employees, fosters a two-way dialogue that gives customers a look inside the company's culture and operations.

Southwest Airlines Co.

Beyond their own brand blogs, many marketers use third-party blogs to help get their messages out. For example, McDonald's systematically reaches out to key "mommy bloggers," those who influence the nation's homemakers, who in turn influence their families' eating-out choices:[20]

> McDonald's recently hosted 15 influential bloggers on an all-expenses-paid tour of its headquarters in Oak Brook, Illinois. The bloggers toured the facilities (including the company's test kitchens), met McDonald's USA president, and had their pictures taken with Ronald at a nearby Ronald McDonald House. McDonald's knows that these mommy bloggers have loyal followings and talk a lot about McDonald's in their blogs. So it's turning the bloggers into believers by giving them a behind-the-scenes view. McDonald's doesn't try to tell the bloggers what to say in their posts about the visit. It simply asks them to write one honest recap of their trip. However, the resulting posts (each acknowledging the blogger's connection with McDonald's) were mostly very positive. Thanks to this and other such efforts, mommy bloggers around the country are now more informed about and connected with McDonald's. "I know they have smoothies and they have yogurt and they have other things that my kids would want," says one prominent blogger. "I really couldn't tell you what Burger King's doing right now," she adds. "I have no idea."

As a marketing tool, blogs offer some advantages. They can offer a fresh, original, personal, and cheap way to enter into consumer online and social media conversations. However, the blogosphere is cluttered and difficult to control. And although companies can sometimes leverage blogs to engage customers in meaningful relationships, blogs remain largely a consumer-controlled medium. Whether or not they actively participate in the blogs, companies should monitor and listen to them. Marketers can use insights from consumer online conversations to improve their marketing programs.

Social Media Marketing

As we've discussed throughout the text so far, the surge in Internet usage and digital technologies and devices has spawned a dazzling array of online **social media** and digital communities. Countless independent and commercial social networks have arisen where people congregate to socialize and share messages, opinions, pictures, videos, and other content. These days, it seems, almost everyone is buddying up on Facebook or Google+, checking in with Twitter, tuning into the day's hottest videos at YouTube, pinning images on social scrapbooking site Pinterest, or sharing photos with Instagram and Snapchat. And, of course, wherever consumers congregate, marketers will surely follow.

Most marketers are now riding the huge social media wave. According to one survey, 92 percent of U.S. companies now claim that social media marketing is important for their businesses.[21] Interestingly, just as marketers are now learning how to use social media to engage customers, the social media themselves are learning how to make their communities a suitable platform for marketing content, in a way that benefits both social media users and brands. Most social media, even the most successful ones, still face a monetization issue: How can they profitably tap the marketing potential of their massive communities to make money without driving off loyal users (see Marketing at Work 14.1)?

Using Social Media

Marketers can engage in social media in two ways: They can use existing social media or they can set up their own. Using existing social media seems the easiest. Thus, most brands—large and small—have set up shop on a host of social media sites. Check the Web sites of brands ranging from Coca-Cola, Nike, and Victoria's Secret to the Chicago Bulls or even the U.S. Forest Service and you'll find links to each brand's Facebook, Google+, Twitter, YouTube, Flickr, Instagram, or other social media pages. Such social media can create substantial brand communities. For example, the Bulls have more the 17 million Facebook fans; Coca-Cola has an eye-popping 90 million Facebook fans.

Some of the major social networks are huge. Nearly 1.4 billion people access Facebook every month, nearly 4.4 times the population of the United States. Similarly, Twitter has more than 288 million active monthly users. And YouTube's more than 1 billion users upload 300 hours of video every minute of every day. The list goes on: Google+ has 359 million active users, Instagram 300 million, LinkedIn 187 million, and Pinterest 40 million.[22]

Author Comment

As in about every other area of our lives, social media and mobile technologies have taken the marketing world by storm. They offer some amazing marketing possibilities. But truth be told, many marketers are still sweating over how to use them most effectively.

Social media
Independent and commercial online social networks where people congregate to socialize and share messages, opinions, pictures, videos, and other content.

MARKETING AT WORK   14.1

Social Media Monetization: Making Money without Driving Fans Away

As the world has rapidly gone social and mobile, social media have played a huge role. Whether it's on massive networks such as Facebook, Twitter, YouTube, Instagram, and Snapchat or lesser-known niche sites such as Blurty, Dogster, and Reddit, it's common to see people everywhere these days, heads down with devices in hand, connecting, posting, and sharing. On Facebook alone, every day, a mind-blowing 936 million of the network's 1.4 billion active users worldwide upload 350 million photos, generate 4.5 billion "Likes," and share 4.75 billion pieces of content.

However, although social media networks have achieved incredible success in terms of numbers of users, sheer volume of content and activity, and even company valuations, a nagging problem still plagues them. It's called *monetization*. How can social media profitably tap the marketing potential of their massive communities to make money without driving off their legions of loyal users? Most social media still struggle to make a profit, and even the most popular ones are only beginning to tap their full financial potential.

The first and best bet for converting the social-sharing potential of a social network's gigantic user community into real dollars is online advertising. For marketers, the targeting and customer engagement potential of social media is a dream come true, and advertisers willingly pay for access via ads and other paid brand content. However, placing commercial content in social media is still in its infancy, for both marketers and the social media networks. Successfully injecting brand content alongside user content can be tricky and risky. Social media users often cherish the free (and commercial-free) sharing cultures of their online communities. If not well conceived, commercial content becomes an unwelcome intrusion that can alienate users and potentially drive them away.

Thus, although social media have exploded in popularity, most are still having trouble making money. Even Facebook—far and away the most financially successful social network, which earned $2.9 billion in profits on $12.5 billion in revenues last year—has yet to scratch the surface of its vast financial potential.

To illustrate the monetization difficulties that social media face, let's dig deeper into one of today's most successful ones, Snapchat, the wildly popular messaging app. Snapchat serves a fast-growing community of more than 100 million users, heavily weighted toward young Millennials. As on other social media, Snapchat users share pictures or videos—known as Snaps—with friends and family. But unlike images shared on other networks, Snaps disappear without a trace in only seconds.

Snapchat exploded onto the scene only about five years ago. By the end of its first year, 1 billion photos had been shared through Snapchat's servers; after only two years, the Snapchat community was sharing 700 million photos every single day. As Snapchat's popularity soared, so did its valuation. Two years in, Facebook made Snapchat's founders a startling $3 billion buyout

offer; the founders politely declined. A year later, Snapchat had raised more than $200 million in venture capital funding and was valued at $10 billion. Yet in its rise to glory, Snapchat had yet to make even a dime of revenues or profits.

Snapchat's financial story is typical for successful social media: modest beginnings as a start-up, followed by meteoric growth in popularity and use, leading to outrageously high valuation—all with little or no income. Then comes that difficult question: How can they monetize their massive user bases to make profits and sustain themselves? For Snapchat, that's especially difficult. The very feature that makes Snapchat unique and so popular—content lasting only seconds—means that it can't track and analyze users for targeting purposes, a turnoff to marketers. "In an era where big data rules, how does Snapchat, which collects no data on the user, sell itself to marketers?" asks one online advertiser. Snapchat's challenge is to persuade marketers that the benefits of reaching its young Millennials community outweigh user anonymity and lack of pinpoint targeting potential.

Careful not to ruffle its community's sensitivities or disrupt the user experience, Snapchat didn't introduce its first advertising platform until October 2014. Called Brand Stories, the platform let marketers share brand-related photo and video posts with users via its sponsored Stories feed, at rates of up to $750,000 per ad unit. The first client was Universal Pictures, which sent a 20-second video trailer for its upcoming fright film *Ouija*. A growing number of other brands—from Taco Bell and frozen-yogurt chain 16 Handles to the New Orleans Saints—soon began creating Snapchat handles and dabbling with Snaps to users. Although advertisers seemed eager to pay for the ad units, Snapchat halted Brand Stories after only six

» Wildly popular messaging app Snapchat and other social media face a nagging *monetization* issue: How can they profitably tap the marketing potential of their massive communities to make money without driving off their legions of loyal users?

Jens Büttner/AP Images

months, apparently concerned about the feature's impact on the Snapchat user experience. The company suggested that it might reintroduce the feature later in a new form.

Meanwhile, Snapchat has focused on two other advertising formats: a magazine-like platform called "Discover" and a sponsored feeds platform dubbed "Our Story." Discover is a Snapchat content area where publishers ranging from ESPN, CNN, Comedy Central, and Food Channel to *Cosmopolitan, National Geographic,* and *People* post daily collections of their best content. Snapchat users can share Discover news stories and video with personalized comments or emoji. Advertisers pay as much as $100,000 a day to advertise alongside the Discover content.

Snapchat's Our Story feeds are TV-like streams of an event such as New Year's Eve, March Madness, an important football game, or the Macy's Thanksgiving Parade, featuring user-generated content curated by Snapchat. Advertisers can buy sponsorship rights for an Our Story feed for $400,000 to $500,000, which includes a brand mention in the opening title as well as branded snaps interspersed throughout the feed. For example, Macy's sponsors the Macy's Thanksgiving Parade feed, weaving its own brand content in with user content. Advertisers can also pay $100,000 for a single 10-second brand snap woven into a feed. Our Story feeds garner an estimated 20 million daily views within the Snapchat community.

All this leaves Snapchat's revenue model in a state of constant flux, as it tinkers to find the best monetization formula. In fact, features like Discover and Our Story may well have morphed into something else by the time you read this story. For example, word leaked recently that Snapchat would soon change the name of its Our Story feature to Live Story, Live Event, or even just Live,

more in line with the evolving nature of the platform. "Snapchat, like social platforms before it, is making the bumpy transition from startup to big media company," says an analyst. "Ad products—and the clients who love them—are often affected by that change."

In its quest to monetize, Snapchat has a lot at stake. Will increased advertising and brand content alienate avid Snapchat fans? If they're done right, probably not. Studies show that social media users readily accept—even welcome—well-targeted brand content. A recent Snapchat survey found that 60 percent of Snapchat users actually like Our Story ads.

But that's the catch—doing it right. Like its own disappearing photo feature, Snapchat's soaring popularity could vanish quickly if overly aggressive monetization causes resentment within its highly mobile and typically fickle fan base. Snapchat must move forward carefully. As one Snapchat marketer concludes, "We're always fine tuning to ensure we deliver the best possible experience for our community."

Sources: Julia Greenberg, "Snapchat Allows Users to (Finally!) Share News," *Wired,* May 5, 2015, www.wired.com/2015/05/snapchat-news-business-discover-share/; "By the Numbers: 200+ Amazing Facebook User Statistics," http://expandedramblings.com/index.php/by-the-numbers-17-amazing-facebook-stats/#.U2F1gtxH38u, accessed June 2015; Kurt Wagner, "Snapchat Is No Longer Selling Its Original Ad Unit, Brand Stories," *re/code,* April 13, 2015, http://recode.net/2015/04/13/snapchat-is-no-longer-selling-its-original-ad-unit-brand-stories/; Jessi Hempel and Adam Lashinsky, "Countdown to the Snapchat Revolution," *Fortune,* January 1, 2014, pp. 82–87; James O'Toole, "Could Snapchat Really Be Worth $10 billion?" *CNNMoney,* August 1, 2014, http://money.cnn.com/2014/08/01/technology/social/snapchat-10-billion/index.html; Garrett Sloane, "Snapchat Persuades Brands to Go Vertical with Their Video," *Adweek,* April 27, 2015, pp. 20–22; and Tim Peterson, "With Snapchat's First Ad Format on Hold, Focus Shifts to Live Event Feeds," *Advertising Age,* April 16, 2015, www.adage.com/print/298082.

Although these large social media networks grab most of the headlines, countless niche social media have also emerged. Niche online social networks cater to the needs of smaller communities of like-minded people, making them ideal vehicles for marketers who want to target special interest groups. There's at least one social media network for just about every interest, hobby, or group. Kaboodle.com is for shopaholics, »whereas moms share advice and commiseration at CafeMom.com. FarmersOnly.com provides online dating for down-to-earth "country folks" who enjoy "blue skies, living free and at peace in wide open spaces, raising animals, and appreciating nature"—"because city folks just don't get it." At Birdpost.com, avid bird watchers can keep an online list of birds they've seen and share bird sightings with other members using modern satellite maps.[23]

Beyond these independent social media, many companies have created their own online brand communities. For example, in Nike's Nike+ running community—consisting of more than 20 million runners who together have logged more than 1 billion running miles worldwide—members join together online to upload, track, and compare their performances. Due to its success, Nike has expanded Nike+ to both basketball and general training, each with its own unique community site, app, and corresponding products.[24]

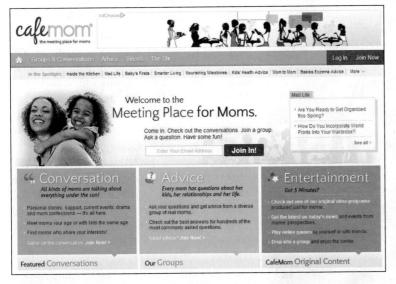

» **Countless niche social media have emerged, catering to needs of smaller communities of like-minded people. CafeMom is a "Meeting Place for Moms," where they can share conversations, advice, and entertainment.**

CafeMom.com

Social Media Marketing Advantages and Challenges

Using social media presents both advantages and challenges. On the plus side, social media are *targeted* and *personal*—they allow marketers to create and share tailored brand content with individual consumers and customer communities. Social media are *interactive*, making them ideal for starting and participating in customer conversations and listening to customer feedback. For example, Whole Foods Market hosts regular Thursday evening Twitter chats using the #WFMDish hashtag hosted by the @wholefoods account. The chats bring together the Whole Foods community of health-minded eaters to discuss themes such as what to eat during the winter months or how to host a healthy (but tasty) Super Bowl party. Chat participants share recipes, ideas, and opinions, while Whole Foods tweets links to blog posts and multimedia content.[25]

Social media are also *immediate* and *timely*. They can be used to reach customers anytime, anywhere with timely and relevant marketing content regarding brand happenings and activities. As discussed earlier in the chapter, the rapid growth in social media usage has caused a surge in *real-time marketing*, allowing marketers to create and join consumer conversations around situations and events as they occur. Marketers can now watch what's trending and create content to match.

Social media can be very *cost-effective*. Although creating and administering social media content can be costly, many social media are free or inexpensive to use. Thus, returns on social media investments are often high compared with those of expensive traditional media such as television or print. The low cost of social media puts them within easy reach of even small businesses and brands that can't afford the high costs of big-budget marketing campaigns.

Perhaps the biggest advantage of social media is their *engagement and social sharing capabilities*. Social media are especially well suited to creating customer engagement and community—for getting customers involved with the brand and with each other. More than any other channels, social media can involve customers in shaping and sharing brand content, experiences, information, and ideas.

>> For example, consider Etsy—the online craft marketplace that's "Your place to buy and sell all things handmade." Etsy uses its Web and mobile sites and a host of social media to create an Etsy lifestyle community, where buyers congregate to learn about, explore, exchange, and share ideas about handmade and vintage products and related topics. In addition to its active Facebook, Twitter, and YouTube pages, Etsy engages 334,000 brand followers on photo-sharing site Instagram, where the Etsy community shares photos of creative ideas and projects. It also engages 580,000 followers on social scrapbooking site Pinterest, with 113 boards on topics ranging from "DIY Projects," "Entertaining," and "Stuff We Love" to "Etsy Weddings" and even "Yum! Recipes to Share," where the community posts favorite recipes. Etsy sells few of the ingredients that go into the recipes, but it's all part of the Etsy lifestyle. Through its extensive online and social media presence, Etsy has created an active and engaged worldwide community of 19.8 million buyers and 1.4 million sellers worldwide in what it calls "The marketplace we make together."[26]

Social media marketing also presents challenges. First, many companies are still experimenting with how to use them effectively, and results are hard to measure. Second, such social networks are largely user controlled. The company's goal in using social media is to make the brand a part of consumers' conversations and their lives. However, marketers can't simply muscle their way into consumers' digital interactions—they need to earn the right to be there. Rather than intruding, marketers must become a valued part of the online experience by developing a steady flow of engaging content.

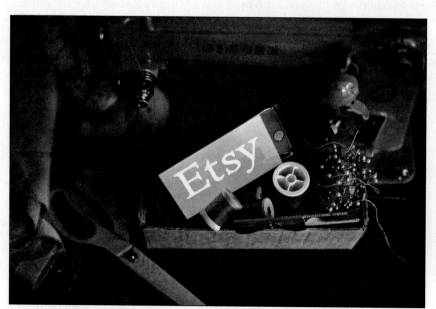

>> Through its extensive online and social media presence, Etsy has created an active and engaged worldwide brand community of buyers and sellers in what it calls "The marketplace we make together."

Etsy, Inc.

Because consumers have so much control over social media content, even the seemingly most harmless social media campaign can backfire. For example, Frito-Lay recently launched an annual Do Us a Flavor contest, in which it asks people to come up with new potato chip flavors, submit them to its Web or Facebook site, and design bag art for their creations. Many consumers take the annual contest (and the $1 million grand prize) seriously, submitting flavors that people would truly want to eat. However, others recently hijacked the contest by submitting sometimes hilarious but completely bogus flavors, ranging from Crunchy Frog and Blue Cheese, Toothpaste and Orange Juice, and 7th Grade Locker Room to Bandaid in a Public Pool and "90% Air and Like 4 Chips." Unfortunately, for each submission, no matter how bogus, the Web site responded cheerfully with a colorful rendition of the bag and flavor name, along with a message like the following: "7th Grade Locker Room? That does sound yummy as a chip! Keep those tasty ideas coming for your next chance to win $1 million."

Frito-Lay and its customers took the hijacking with good humor, and the Do Us a Flavor contest continues on its successful way. However, there's a clear message. With social media, "you're going into the consumer's backyard. This is their place," warns one social marketer. "Social media is a pressure cooker," says another. "The hundreds of thousands, or millions, of people out there are going to take your idea, and they're going to try to shred it or tear it apart and find what's weak or stupid in it."[27]

Integrated Social Media Marketing

Using social media might be as simple as posting some messages and promotions on a brand's Facebook or Twitter pages or creating brand buzz with videos or images on YouTube, Vine, or Pinterest. However, most large companies are now designing full-scale social media efforts that blend with and support other elements of a brand's marketing content strategy and tactics. More than making scattered efforts and chasing "Likes" and Tweets, companies that use social media successfully are integrating a broad range of diverse media to create brand-related social sharing, engagement, and customer community.

Managing a brand's social media efforts can be a major undertaking. For example, Starbucks, one of the most successful social media marketers, manages 51 Facebook pages (including 43 in other countries), 31 Twitter handles (19 of them international), and 22 Instagram names (14 international) plus Google+, Pinterest, YouTube, and Foursquare accounts. Managing and integrating all that social media content is challenging, but the results are worth the investment. Customers can and do engage with Starbucks by the tens of millions digitally, without ever setting foot in a store.

But more than just creating online engagement and community, Starbucks' social media presence also drives customers into its stores. For example, in its first big social media promotion six years ago, Starbucks offered a free pastry with a morning drink purchase. A million people showed up. Its more recent "Tweet-a-Coffee" promotion, which let customers give a $5 gift card to a friend by putting both #tweetacoffee and the friend's handle in a Tweet, resulted in $180,000 in purchases within little more than one month. Social media "are not just about engaging and telling a story and connecting," says Starbucks's head of global digital marketing. "They can have a material impact on the business."[28]

Mobile Marketing

Mobile marketing
Marketing messages, promotions, and other marketing content delivered to on-the-go consumers through mobile phones, smartphones, tablets, and other mobile devices.

Mobile marketing features marketing messages, promotions, and other marketing content delivered to on-the-go consumers through their mobile devices. Marketers use mobile marketing to engage customers anywhere, anytime during the buying and relationship-building processes. The widespread adoption of mobile devices and the surge in mobile Web traffic have made mobile marketing a must for most brands.

With the recent proliferation of mobile phones, smartphones, and tablets, mobile device penetration is now greater than 100 percent in the United States (many people possess more than one mobile device). Almost 40 percent of U.S. households are currently mobile-only households with no landline phone. About 65 percent of people in the United States own a smartphone, and more than 60 percent of smartphone users use them to access the mobile Internet. They not only browse the mobile Internet but are also avid mobile app users. The mobile apps market has exploded globally: There are more than 2 million apps available, and the average smartphone has 26 apps installed on it.[29]

Most people love their phones and rely heavily on them. According to one study, nearly 90 percent of consumers who own smartphones, tablets, computers, and TVs would give up all of those other screens before giving up their phones. On average, Americans check their phones 150 times a day—once every six-and-a-half minutes—and spend two hours and 51 minutes a day on their smartphones and other mobile devices talking, texting, and visiting Web sites. Thus, although TV is still a big part of people's lives, mobile is rapidly becoming their "first screen." Away from home, it's their only screen.[30]

For consumers, a smartphone or tablet can be a handy shopping companion. It can provide on-the-go product information, price comparisons, advice and reviews from other consumers, and access to instant deals and digital coupons. One recent study by Google found that 87 percent of mobile device owners use mobile to pre-shop and research purchases before getting to a store, and 75 percent of smartphone-toting shoppers use their phones in-store.[31] Not surprisingly, then, mobile devices provide a rich platform for engaging consumers more deeply as they move through the buying process with tools ranging from mobile ads, coupons, and texts to apps and mobile Web sites.

Mobile advertising spending in the United States is surging; it more than doubled last year alone and is expected to double again by next year. Almost every major marketer—from P&G and Macy's to your local bank or supermarket to nonprofits such as the ASPCA—is now integrating mobile marketing into its direct marketing programs. Such efforts can produce very positive outcomes. For example, 49 percent of mobile users search for more information after seeing a mobile ad.[32]

Companies use mobile marketing to stimulate immediate buying, make shopping easier, enrich the brand experience, or all of these. It lets marketers provide consumers with information, incentives, and choices at the moment they are expressing an interest or when they are in a position to make a buying choice. For example, McDonald's uses mobile marketing to promote new menu items, announce special promotions, and drive immediate traffic at its restaurants. One recent interactive ad on Pandora's mobile app read "Taste buds. Any size soft drink or sweet tea for $1. Tap to visit site." A tap on the mobile ad took customers to a mobile site promoting McDonald's ongoing summer promotion. Another McDonald's mobile campaign used a word scrabble game to entice customers to try the fast feeder's dollar menu items. Such efforts create both customer engagement and store traffic. Using a game "inside a mobile campaign is all about finding and maintaining engagement," says a McDonald's marketer.[33]

Today's rich-media mobile ads can create substantial engagement and impact. For example, JetBlue recently created a voice-activated mobile ad that interacts with customers and talks back. It starts with a JetBlue mobile banner ad that says, "Click here to learn how to speak pigeon." A click expands the ad, which then instructs users by voice to repeat words on the screen, such as "coo, coo, coo." When they've completed two full sentences in pigeon, users receive a virtual medal and the option to play again. Hitting "Learn more" takes users to the JetBlue Landing Perch, where they can explore and send messages to friends via digital carrier pigeons. The mobile ad is part of JetBlue's "Air on the Side of Humanity" campaign, which features pigeons—the ultimate frequent fliers. Rather than making direct sales pitches, the voice ad aims simply to enrich the JetBlue experience. The airline hopes people will "watch the ads, play with the pigeons, and remember us when they want to book tickets," says JetBlue's advertising manager.[34]

Retailers can use mobile marketing to enrich the customer's shopping experience at the same time that they stimulate buying. For example, Macy's built its recent "Brasil: A Magical Journey" promotion around a popular and imaginative smartphone app. The campaign featured apparel from Brazilian designers and in-store experiences celebrating Brazilian culture. By using their smartphones to scan codes throughout the store, shoppers could learn about featured fashions and experience Brazilian culture through virtual tours, such as a trip to the Amazon, a visit to Rio de Janeiro during Carnival, or attending a Brazilian soccer match.

Many marketers have created their own mobile online sites, optimized for specific phones and mobile service providers. Others have created useful or entertaining mobile apps to engage customers with their brands and help them shop (see Marketing at Work 14.2).

| MARKETING AT WORK | 14.2 |

Mobile Marketing: Smartphones Are Changing How People Live—and How They Buy

Armed only with a smartphone or other mobile device, you can learn, do, or buy almost anything these days, from anywhere, and at any time. Google's Waze app does more than just help you navigate—it pinpoints traffic jams, accidents, speed traps, and gas prices in real time, all updated by members of the Waze community. Is that Redbox kiosk too slow? Download the Redbox app—it lets you find and reserve a DVD using your mobile device and have it waiting for you at the kiosk. REI's Snow Report app, with its snowy fresh look and feel, gives you ski slope information for locations throughout the United States and Canada, such as snow conditions, number of open lifts, trail maps, and Webcam views. The app even helps you share resort information with friends via Twitter and Facebook, and it links you to "Shop REI" for times "when you decide you can't live without a new set of K2 skis or a two-man Hubba Hubba tent."

Welcome to the world of mobile marketing. Today's smartphones and other mobile devices are changing how people live, becoming indispensable hubs for communication, information, and entertainment. They are also revolutionizing the way people shop and buy, giving marketers new opportunities to engage customers in more effective and satisfying ways.

Marketers are responding to the huge growth in mobile access and use. Mobile ad spending has skyrocketed by more than 400 percent in the past three years and is expected to double in the next three. And the mobile app market has outright exploded. Just six years ago, Apple's App Store had a then-astounding 10,000 apps. But by last year, it boasted 1.2 million apps; Android's Google Play took the lead with more than 1.3 million apps. Mobile has become today's brave new marketing frontier, especially for brands courting younger consumers. Mobile devices are very personal, ever-present, and always on. That makes them an ideal medium for obtaining quick responses to individualized, time-sensitive offers.

Some marketers are still just warming up to mobile, and most are still learning how to use it effectively. Successful mobile marketing goes beyond just giving people a coupon and a link to buy. Instead, it enhances brand engagement and creates a "frictionless" buying experience. For example, with Amazon's mobile app—thanks to "1-click" purchasing, Prime membership, and other features—customers located anywhere, anytime can have products delivered to practically any location in less than 24 hours with nothing more than a smartphone, a simple search or scan, and the click of a button.

Consumers have come to expect such frictionless mobile buying experiences from marketing giants like Amazon. But with recent rapid advances in mobile capabilities, from location-based technologies to mobile payment systems, more and more companies are becoming the Amazons of their industries. Consider mobile app-based car-sharing service Getaround.

In the United States alone, personal cars sit idle for 6 billion car-hours every day. Peer-to-peer car-sharing service Getaround lets car owners earn money by sharing those unused hours with others in the Getaround community for a fee. The young company has already developed a fast-growing base of 25,000 car-sharing owners, who receive 60 percent of the rental fees—an average of $500 to $1,000 per month depending on the car. Getaround takes care of everything—customer contact and support, insurance, roadside assistance, and payment. To use Getaround, you just download the mobile app and supply credit card and driver's license information. Then you can use the app to search among and view thousands of cars available in the neighborhood and rent one by the hour or day, right when you need it. You locate the car with your phone's GPS, unlock it with the app, and get in and drive it away. Pay with a credit card on file or using Apple Pay with a single tap. It's that simple. The Getaround app even provides trip management tools for planning getaways on the go.

Mobile marketing can do much more than simply ease the buying process. It can also take ads, coupons, and other promotions to new levels. Mobile marketers can personalize promotions and weave them into relevant everyday customer experiences. For example, Kiip, a mobile reward network, specializes in helping brands provide customers with just the right reward at just the right time based on their everyday activities. The agency started by embedding its technology into video game apps such as Zombie Farm and Mega Jump. Gamers who

» Mobile marketing: Mobile promotions agency Kiip helps client brands link mobile offers to relevant customer experiences and positive moments. "We want to capitalize on happiness," says Kiip's CEO.

Kiip, inc.

reach a new game level or meet some other goal get a coupon to one of their favorite retailers, such as American Apparel.

Kiip now boasts a network of 2,500 apps and 60 million users across games, fitness, productivity, music, and cooking categories. It showcases more than 500 million reward moments every month for clients like McDonald's, Propel, Sour Patch Kids, P&G, and MasterCard. For fitness apps like MapMyRun and productivity apps like Any.do, Kiip ties rewards to real-life achievements. When users cross things off their to-do lists or achieve a running goal, they get a reward from a relevant brand. For example, P&G's Secret deodorant recently rewarded female MapMyRun users with free song downloads for their workout playlists. And snack giant Mondelez rewarded Any.do users with free packs of Trident when they set new personal records.

Kiip helps marketers reach targeted users at positive moments with rewards relevant to their real-time doings and accomplishments. Readers who finish a certain number of pages in a reading app receive a free magazine subscription. People using a couple's app to stay in touch receive credits toward a purchase from 1-800-Flowers. Kiip is even working with connected-car company Mojio, whose 4G telematic device plugs into a car's diagnostic port, tracks information about the car's status, and keeps the owner connected to favorite people, places, and things. Through Mojio, Kiip helps clients—from insurance companies and car repair shops to parking meter and garage operators— provide rewards tied to specific driver locations and behaviors.

Unlike typical banner ads, pop-ups, or emails, Kiip offers enhance a user's regular activities rather than interrupting them. According to Kiip's founder and CEO, Kiip "is less about real-time marketing and more about real-time-needs addressing." In fact, he asserts, Kiip isn't really in the mobile ad business at all—it's in the happiness business. "We want to capitalize on happiness," he says. "Everything's better when you're happy." Mobile timeliness, relevance, and happiness pay off in terms of consumer response. Users redeem Kiip's mobile promotions at a 22-percent clip, compared with the 0.3 percent for typical app ad engagement. Kiip's offers also increase mobile app revisits by 30 percent and more than double average app length of use.

Many consumers are initially skeptical about mobile marketing. But they often change their minds if mobile offers deliver useful brand and shopping information, entertaining content, or timely coupons and discounted prices. Most mobile efforts target only consumers who voluntarily opt in or download apps. In the increasingly cluttered mobile marketing space, customers just won't do that unless they see real value in it. The challenge for marketers: develop valued mobile offers, ads, and apps that make customers come calling.

Sources: Robert Hof, "Mobile Ads Will Smash $100 Billion Mark Worldwide in 2016," *Forbes,* April 2, 2015, www.forbes.com/sites/roberthof/2015/04/02/mobile-ads-will-smash-100-billion-mark-worldwide-in-2016/; Lindsay Harrison, "Kiip: For Making Mobile Ads That People Want," *Fast Company,* February 11, 2013, www.fastcompany.com/most-innovative-companies/2013/kiip; Christina Chaey, "How Kiip Ties Brand Rewards to Game and Life Achievements to Make Mobile Ads Engaging," *Fast Company,* July 23, 2012, www.fastcocreate.com/1681287; Neil Undgerleider, "Advertisers Are about to Enter Your Connected Car," *Fast Company,* April 11, 2014, www.fastcompany.com/3028744/most-innovative-companies/advertisers-are-about-to-enter-your-connected-car; Jason Ankeny, "Young Millionaires: How These Entrepreneurs under 30 Are Changing the World," *Entrepreneur,* August 20, 2014, www.entrepreneur.com/article/236621; and www.kiip.com/me, www.getaround.com/mobile, www.getaround.com/tour, and www.getaround.com/tour/benefits, accessed September 2015.

» **Mobile marketing: The Benjamin Moore Color Capture app engages customers and helps them shop.**

Benjamin Moore, Color Capture and the triangle "M" are registered trademarks licensed to Benjamin Moore & Co.

» For example, the Benjamin Moore Color Capture app lets customers take photos of colorful objects, then match them to any of 3,500 Benjamin Moore paint colors. Starbucks's mobile app lets customers use their phones as a Starbucks card to make fast and easy purchases. And Charles Schwab's mobile apps let customers get up-to-the-minute investment news, monitor their accounts, and make trades at any time from any location—it helps you "stay connected with your money."

As with other forms of direct marketing, however, companies must use mobile marketing responsibly or risk angering already ad-weary consumers. Most people don't want to be interrupted regularly by advertising, so marketers must be smart about how they engage people on mobile devices. The key is to provide genuinely useful information and offers that will make consumers want to engage. And many marketers target mobile ads on an opt-in-only basis.

In all, digital direct marketing—online, social media, and mobile marketing—offers both great promise and many challenges for the future. Its most ardent apostles still envision a time when the Internet and digital marketing will replace magazines, newspapers, and even stores as sources for information, engagement, and buying. Most marketers, however, hold a more realistic view. For most companies, digital and social media marketing will remain just one important approach to the marketplace that works alongside other approaches in a fully integrated marketing mix.

Although the fast-growing digital marketing tools have grabbed most of the headlines lately, traditional direct marketing tools are very much alive and still heavily used. We now examine the traditional direct marketing approaches shown on the right side of Figure 14.1.

 LINKING THE CONCEPTS

Stop now and think about how online, social media, and mobile marketing affect your brand buying behavior and preferences.

● How much of your product research, shopping, and actual buying take place online? How much of that is conducted on a mobile device? How and how much do your digital and in-store buying activities interact?

● How much and what kinds of online, social media, and mobile marketing do you encounter? Do you benefit from such marketing, or is it more of an unwelcome intrusion? In what ways?

● Do you engage directly with any brands or brand communities through online sites, social media, or phone apps? Do your online, social media, or mobile interactions influence your brand preferences and buying? Discuss.

> **Author Comment**
> Again, although online, social media, and mobile direct marketing seem to be getting much of the attention these days, traditional direct media still carry a lot of the direct marketing freight. Just think about your often overstuffed mailbox.

Direct-mail marketing
Marketing that occurs by sending an offer, announcement, reminder, or other item directly to a person at a particular address.

Traditional Direct Marketing Forms

The major traditional forms of direct marketing—as shown in Figure 14.1—are face-to-face or personal selling, direct-mail marketing, catalog marketing, telemarketing, direct-response television (DRTV) marketing, and kiosk marketing. We examined personal selling in depth in Chapter 13. Here, we look into the other forms of traditional direct marketing.

Direct-Mail Marketing

Direct-mail marketing involves sending an offer, announcement, reminder, or other item directly to a person at a particular address. Using highly selective mailing lists, direct marketers send out millions of mail pieces each year—letters, catalogs, ads, brochures, samples, videos, and other "salespeople with wings." U.S. marketers spent an estimated $46 billion on direct mail last year (including both catalog and noncatalog mail), which accounted for 29 percent of all direct marketing spending. According to the Direct Mail Marketing Association, every dollar spent on direct mail generates $12.53 in sales.[35]

Direct mail is well suited to direct, one-to-one communication. It permits high target-market selectivity, can be personalized, is flexible, and allows the easy measurement of results. Although direct mail costs more per thousand people reached than mass media such as television or magazines, the people it reaches are much better prospects. Direct mail has proved successful in promoting all kinds of products, from books, insurance, travel, gift items, gourmet foods, clothing, and other consumer goods to industrial products of all kinds. Charities also use direct mail heavily to raise billions of dollars each year.

Some analysts predict a decline in the use of traditional forms of direct mail in the coming years as marketers switch to newer digital forms, such as email and online, social media, and mobile marketing. The newer digital direct marketing approaches deliver messages at incredible speeds and lower costs compared to the U.S. Post Office's "snail mail" pace.

However, even though new digital forms of direct marketing are bursting onto the scene, traditional direct mail is still heavily used by most marketers. Mail marketing offers some distinct advantages over digital forms. It provides something tangible for people to hold and keep, and it can be used to send samples. "Mail makes it real," says one analyst. It "creates an emotional connection with customers that digital cannot. They hold it, view it, and engage with it in a manner entirely different from their [digital] experiences." In contrast, email and other digital forms are easily filtered or trashed. "[With] spam filters and spam folders

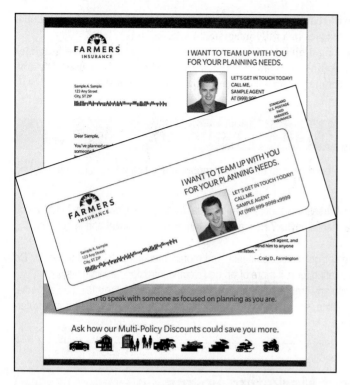

>> **Direct mail marketing: Insurance companies like Farmers Insurance rely heavily on TV advertising to establish broad customer awareness. However, they also use lots of good old direct mail to communicate with consumers in a more direct and personalized way.**

Farmers Group, Inc.

Catalog marketing
Direct marketing through print, video, or digital catalogs that are mailed to select customers, made available in stores, or presented online.

to keep our messaging away from consumers' inboxes," says a direct marketer, "sometimes you have to lick a few stamps."[36]

Traditional direct mail can be an effective component of a broader integrated marketing campaign. For example, most large insurance companies rely heavily on TV advertising to establish broad customer awareness and positioning. However, the insurance companies also use lots of good old direct mail to break through the glut of insurance advertising on TV. Whereas TV advertising talks to broad audiences, direct mail communicates in a more direct and personal way. **>>** "Mail is a channel that allows all of us to find the consumer with a very targeted, very specific message that you can't do in broadcast," says John Ingersoll, vice president of marketing communications for Farmers Insurance. And "most people are still amenable to getting marketing communications in their mailbox, which is why I think direct mail will grow."[37]

Direct mail may be resented as *junk mail* if sent to people who have no interest in it. For this reason, smart marketers are targeting their direct mail carefully so as not to waste their money and recipients' time. They are designing permission-based programs that send direct mail only to those who want to receive it.

Catalog Marketing

Advances in technology, along with the move toward personalized, one-to-one marketing, have resulted in exciting changes in **catalog marketing**. *Catalog Age* magazine used to define a *catalog* as "a printed, bound piece of at least eight pages, selling multiple products, and offering a direct ordering mechanism." Today, the definition must be revamped to meet the changing times.

With the stampede to the Internet and digital marketing, more and more catalogs are going digital. A variety of online-only catalogers have emerged, and most print catalogers have added Web-based catalogs and smartphone catalog shopping apps to their marketing mixes. For example, apps such as Catalog Spree put a mall full of classic catalogs from retailers such as Macy's, Anthropologie, L.L. Bean, Hammacher Schlemmer, Coldwater Creek, or West Elm only a swipe of the finger away on a smartphone or tablet. And days before the latest Eddie Bauer catalog arrives in the mail, customers can access it digitally on a laptop or mobile device at eddiebauer.com or catch highlights via social media outlets such as Pinterest. Eddie Bauer's mobile catalog gives customers the convenience of on-the-go browsing and purchasing.

Digital catalogs eliminate printing and mailing costs. And whereas space is limited in a print catalog, online catalogs can offer an almost unlimited amount of merchandise. They also offer a broader assortment of presentation formats, including search and video. Finally, online catalogs allow real-time merchandising; products and features can be added or removed as needed, and prices can be adjusted instantly to match demand. Customers can carry digital catalogs anywhere they go, even when shopping at physical stores.

Despite the advantages of digital catalogs, however, as your overstuffed mailbox may suggest, printed catalogs are still thriving. U.S. direct marketers mailed out some 12 billion catalogs last year—more than 97 per American household.[38] Why aren't companies ditching their old-fashioned paper catalogs in this new digital era? For one thing, printed catalogs are one of the best ways to drive online and mobile sales, making them more important than ever in digital time. According to one study, about 58 percent of online shoppers browse physical catalogs for ideas, and 31 percent have a retailer's catalog with them when they make a purchase online. Catalog users look at more than double the number of online pages per visit to the company's site than the average visitor and spend twice the amount of time there.[39]

But beyond their ability to drive immediate sales, paper catalogs create emotional connections with customers. Somehow, turning actual catalog pages engages consumers in a way that digital images simply can't. And many sellers are revamping their

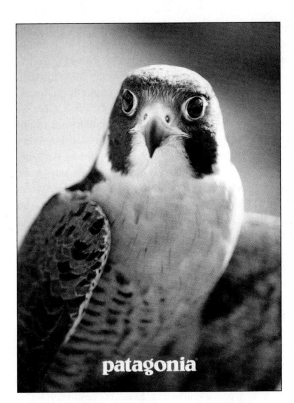

Telemarketing
Using the telephone to sell directly to customers.

Direct-response television (DRTV) marketing
Direct marketing via television, including direct-response television advertising (or infomercials) and interactive television (iTV) advertising.

catalogs, making them much more than just big books full of product pictures and prices. For example, Anthropologie calls its catalogs "journals" and fills them with lifestyle images. "Of course we're trying to sell clothes and accessories," says Anthropologie's CMO, "but it's more to inspire and engage." Similarly, in addition to the 10 or so traditional catalogs that it publishes each year, Patagonia sends out other catalogs built around themes. >> One recent catalog featured falconry, with images of children with condors in Chile and wildlife volunteers in California releasing rehabilitated red-tailed hawks. The catalog included only a handful of products, placed on the last four pages of the 43-page book. Such catalogs are "a way we're speaking to our closest friends and people who know the brand really well," says a Patagonia marketer. "Years ago, [a catalog] was a selling tool, and now it's become an inspirational source," says another direct marketer. "We know our customers love a tactile experience."[40]

Telemarketing

Telemarketing involves using the telephone to sell directly to consumers and business customers. U.S. marketers spent an estimated $43 billion on telemarketing last year, almost as much as on direct mail.[41] We're all familiar with telephone marketing directed toward consumers, but business-to-business (B-to-B) marketers also use telemarketing extensively. Marketers use *outbound* telephone marketing to sell directly to consumers and businesses. They also use *inbound* toll-free numbers to receive orders from television and print ads, direct mail, or catalogs.

Properly designed and targeted telemarketing provides many benefits, including purchasing convenience and increased product and service information. However, the explosion in unsolicited outbound telephone marketing over the years annoyed many consumers, who objected to the almost daily "junk phone calls." In 2003, U.S. lawmakers responded with the National Do Not Call Registry, which is managed by the Federal Trade Commission (FTC). The legislation bans most telemarketing calls to registered phone numbers (although people can still receive calls from nonprofit groups, politicians, and companies with which they have recently done business). Consumers responded enthusiastically. To date, more than 217 million home and mobile phone numbers have been registered at www.donotcall.gov or by calling 888-382-1222.[42] Businesses that break do-not-call laws can be fined up to $16,000 per violation. As a result, the program has been very successful.

Do-not-call legislation has hurt parts of the consumer telemarketing industry. However, two major forms of telemarketing—inbound consumer telemarketing and outbound B-to-B telemarketing—remain strong and growing. Telemarketing also remains a major fundraising tool for nonprofit and political groups. Interestingly, do-not-call regulations appear to be helping some direct marketers more than they're hurting them. Rather than making unwanted calls, many of these marketers are developing "opt-in" calling systems, in which they provide useful information and offers to customers who have invited the company to contact them by phone or email. The opt-in model provides better returns for marketers than the formerly invasive one.

Direct-Response Television Marketing

Direct-response television (DRTV) marketing takes one of two major forms: direct-response television advertising and interactive TV (iTV) advertising. Using *direct-response television advertising*, direct marketers air television spots, often 60 or 120 seconds in length, which persuasively describe a product and give customers a toll-free number or an online site for ordering. It also includes full 30-minute or longer advertising programs, called *infomercials*, for a single product.

Successful direct-response television advertising campaigns can ring up big sales. For example, little-known infomercial maker Guthy-Renker has helped propel its Proactiv

Solution acne treatment and other "transformational" products into power brands that pull in $1.8 billion in sales annually to 5 million active customers (compare that to only about $150 million in annual drugstore sales of acne products in the United States). Guthy-Renker now combines DRTV with social media campaigns using Facebook, Pinterest, Google+, Twitter, and YouTube to create a powerful integrated direct marketing channel that builds consumer involvement and buying.[43]

DRTV ads are often associated with somewhat loud or questionable pitches for cleaners, stain removers, kitchen gadgets, and nifty ways to stay in shape without working very hard at it. For example, over the past few years yell-and-sell TV pitchmen like Anthony Sullivan (Swivel Sweeper, Awesome Auger) and Vince Offer (ShamWow, SlapChop) have racked up billions of dollars in sales of "As Seen on TV" products. Brands like OxiClean, ShamWow, and the Snuggie (a blanket with sleeves) have become DRTV cult classics. And direct marketer Beachbody brings in more than $32 million annually via an army of workout videos—from P90X and T-25 to Insanity and Hip Hop Abs—that it advertises on TV using before-and-after stories, clips of the workout, and words of encouragement from the creators.

In recent years, however, a number of large companies—from P&G, Disney, Revlon, and Apple to Toyota, Coca-Cola, Anheuser-Busch, and even the U.S. Navy—have begun using infomercials to sell their wares, refer customers to retailers, recruit members, or attract buyers to their online, mobile, and social media sites.

A more recent form of direct-response television marketing is *interactive TV (iTV)*, which lets viewers interact with television programming and advertising. Thanks to technologies such as interactive cable systems, Internet-ready smart TVs, and smartphones and tablets, consumers can now use their TV remotes, phones, or other devices to obtain more information or make purchases directly from TV ads. For example, fashion retailer H&M recently ran ads that let viewers with certain Samsung smart TVs use their remotes to interact directly with the commercials. A small pop-up menu, shown as the ads ran, offered product information, the ability to send that information to another device, and the option to buy directly.[44]

Also, increasingly, as the lines continue to blur between TV screens and other video screens, interactive ads and infomercials are appearing not just on TV, but also on mobile, online, and social media platforms, adding even more TV-like interactive direct marketing venues.

Kiosk Marketing

As consumers become more and more comfortable with digital and touchscreen technologies, many companies are placing information and ordering machines—called *kiosks* (good old-fashioned vending machines but so much more)—in stores, airports, hotels, college campuses, and other locations. Kiosks are everywhere these days, from self-service hotel and airline check-in devices, to unmanned product and information kiosks in malls, to in-store ordering devices that let you order merchandise not carried in the store. Many modern "smart kiosks" are now wireless-enabled. And some machines can even use facial recognition software that lets them guess gender and age and make product recommendations based on that data.

In-store Kodak, Fuji, and HP kiosks let customers transfer pictures from memory cards, mobile phones, and other digital storage devices; edit them; and make high-quality color prints. Seattle's Best kiosks in grocery, drug, and mass merchandise stores grind and brew fresh coffee beans and serve coffee, mochas, and lattes to on-the-go customers around the clock. ≫ Redbox operates more than 42,000 DVD rental kiosks in McDonald's, Walmart, Walgreens, CVS, Family Dollar, and other retail outlets—customers make their selections on a touchscreen, then swipe a credit or debit card to rent DVDs for less than $2 a day.

ZoomSystems creates small, free-standing kiosks called ZoomShops for retailers ranging from Apple, Sephora, and The Body Shop to Macy's and Best Buy. For example, 100 Best Buy Express ZoomShop kiosks across the country—conveniently located in airports, busy malls, military bases, retail stores, and resorts—automatically dispense an assortment of portable media

≫ **Kiosk marketing: Redbox operates more than 42,000 DVD rental kiosks in supermarkets, fast-food restaurants, and other retail outlets.**
Images-USA/Alamy

players, digital cameras, gaming consoles, headphones, phone chargers, travel gadgets, and other popular products. According to ZoomSystems, today's automated retailing "offers [consumers] the convenience of online shopping with the immediate gratification of traditional retail."[45]

Author Comment
Although we mostly benefit from direct and digital marketing, like most other things in life, they have a dark side as well. Marketers and customers alike must guard against irritating or harmful direct and digital marketing practices.

Public Policy Issues in Direct and Digital Marketing

Direct marketers and their customers usually enjoy mutually rewarding relationships. Occasionally, however, a darker side emerges. The aggressive and sometimes shady tactics of a few direct marketers can bother or harm consumers, giving the entire industry a black eye. Abuses range from simple excesses that irritate consumers to instances of unfair practices or even outright deception and fraud. The direct marketing industry has also faced growing privacy concerns, and online marketers must deal with Internet and mobile security issues.

Irritation, Unfairness, Deception, and Fraud

Direct marketing excesses sometimes annoy or offend consumers. For example, most of us dislike direct-response TV commercials that are too loud, long, and insistent. Our mailboxes fill up with unwanted junk mail, our email inboxes bulge with unwanted spam, and our computer, phone, and tablet screens flash with unwanted online or mobile display ads, pop-ups, or pop-unders.

Beyond irritating consumers, some direct marketers have been accused of taking unfair advantage of impulsive or less-sophisticated buyers. Television shopping channels, enticing Web sites, and program-long infomercials targeting television-addicted shoppers seem to be the worst culprits. They feature smooth-talking hosts, elaborately staged demonstrations, claims of drastic price reductions, "while they last" time limitations, and unequaled ease of purchase to inflame buyers who have low sales resistance.

Fraudulent schemes, such as investment scams or phony collections for charity, have also multiplied in recent years. *Internet fraud*, including identity theft and financial scams, has become a serious problem. >> According to the Internet Crime Complaint Center, since 2005, Internet scam complaints have more than tripled to almost 300,000 per year. Last year, the monetary loss of scam complaints exceeded $800 million.[46]

One common form of Internet fraud is *phishing*, a type of identity theft that uses deceptive emails and fraudulent online sites to fool users into divulging their personal data. For example, consumers may receive an email, supposedly from their bank or credit card company, saying that their account's security has been compromised. The sender asks them to log on to a provided Web address and confirm their account number, password, and perhaps even their Social Security number. If they follow the instructions, users are actually turning this sensitive information over to scam artists. Although many consumers are now aware of such schemes, phishing can be extremely costly to those caught in the net. It also damages the brand identities of legitimate online marketers who have worked to build user confidence in Web, email, and other digital transactions.

Many consumers also worry about *online and digital security*. They fear that unscrupulous snoopers will eavesdrop on their online transactions and social media postings, picking up personal information or intercepting credit and debit card numbers. Although online shopping has grown rapidly, one recent study indicated that 70 percent of participants were still concerned about identity theft.[47]

Another Internet marketing concern is that of *access by vulnerable or unauthorized groups*. For example, marketers of adult-oriented materials and sites have found it difficult to restrict access by minors. Although Facebook allows no children under age 13 to have a profile, it has an estimated 5.6 million underage accounts. It removed some 800,000 underage accounts last year. And it's not just Facebook. Young users are logging onto social media

FBI FRAUD ALERT

IF YOU ANSWER "YES" TO ANY OF THE FOLLOWING QUESTIONS, YOU MAY BE GETTING SCAMMED!

Are you about to cash a check from an item you sold on the Internet, such as a car, boat, jewelry, etc?
- Is it the result of communicating with someone by email?
- Did it arrive via an overnight delivery service?
- Is it from a business or individual account that is different from the person buying your item or product?
- Is the amount for more than the item's selling price?

Are you sending money overseas?
- Did you win an international lottery you didn't enter?
- Have you been asked to pay money to receive an inheritance from another country?
- Are you receiving a commission for accepting money transfers through your bank and/or PayPal account?

To report an online crime, go to: www.IC3.gov

DON'T BE A VICTIM OF IDENTITY THEFT!

>> Internet fraud has multiplied in recent years. The FBI's Internet Crime Complaint Center provides consumers with a convenient way to alert authorities to suspected violations.
FBI

such as Formspring, Tweeting their locations to the Web, and making friends with strangers on Disney and other game sites. Concerned state and national lawmakers are currently debating bills that would help better protect children online. Unfortunately, this requires the development of technology solutions, and as Facebook puts it, "That's not so easy."[48]

Consumer Privacy

Invasion of privacy is perhaps the toughest public policy issue now confronting the direct marketing industry. Consumers often benefit from database marketing; they receive more offers that are closely matched to their interests. However, many critics worry that marketers may know *too* much about consumers' lives and that they may use this knowledge to take unfair advantage of consumers. At some point, they claim, the extensive use of databases intrudes on consumer privacy. Consumers, too, worry about their privacy. Although they are now much more willing to share personal information and preferences with marketers via digital and social media, they are still nervous about it. One recent survey found that 92 percent of U.S. Internet users worry about their privacy online. Another found that more than 90 percent of Americans feel they have lost control over the collection and use by companies of their personal data and information they share on social media sites.[49]

In these days of "big data," it seems that almost every time consumers post something on social media or send a Tweet, visit a Web site, enter a sweepstakes, apply for a credit card, or order products by phone or online, their names are entered into some company's already bulging database. Using sophisticated big data analytics, direct marketers can mine these databases to "microtarget" their selling efforts. Most marketers have become highly skilled at collecting and analyzing detailed consumer information both online and offline. Even the experts are sometimes surprised by how much marketers can learn. Consider this account by one *Advertising Age* reporter:[50]

> I'm no neophyte when it comes to targeting—not only do I work at *Ad Age*, but I cover direct marketing. Yet even I was taken aback when, as an experiment, we asked the database-marketing company to come up with a demographic and psychographic profile of me. Was it ever spot-on. Using only publicly available information, it concluded my date of birth, home phone number, and political-party affiliation. It gleamed that I was a college graduate, that I was married, and that one of my parents had passed away. It found that I have several bank, credit, and retail cards at "low-end" department stores. It knew not just how long I've lived at my house but how much it cost, how much it was worth, the type of mortgage that's on it, and—within a really close ballpark guess—how much is left to pay on it. It estimated my household income—again nearly perfectly—and determined that I am of British descent.
>
> But that was just the beginning. The company also nailed my psychographic profile. It correctly placed me into various groupings such as: someone who relies more on their own opinions than the recommendations of others when making a purchase; someone who is turned off by loud and aggressive advertising; someone who is family-oriented and has an interest in music, running, sports, computers, and is an avid concert-goer; someone who is never far from an Internet connection, generally used to peruse sports and general news updates; and someone who sees health as a core value. Scary? Certainly.

Some consumers and policy makers worry that the ready availability of information may leave consumers open to abuse. For example, they ask, should online sellers be allowed to plant cookies in the browsers of consumers who visit their sites and use tracking information to target ads and other marketing efforts? Should credit card companies be allowed to make data on their millions of cardholders worldwide available to merchants who accept their cards? Or is it right for states to sell the names and addresses of driver's license holders, along with height, weight, and gender information, allowing apparel retailers to target tall or overweight people with special clothing offers?

A Need for Action

To curb direct marketing excesses, various government agencies are investigating not only do-not-call lists but also do-not-mail lists, do-not-track-online lists, and Can Spam legislation. In response to online privacy and security concerns, the federal government has considered numerous legislative actions to regulate how online, social media, and mobile operators obtain and use consumer information. For example, Congress is drafting legislation that would give consumers more control over how online information is used. In addition, the FTC is taking a more active role in policing online privacy.

All of these concerns call for strong actions by marketers to monitor and prevent privacy abuses before legislators step in to do it for them. For example, to head off increased government regulation, six advertiser groups—the American Association of Advertising Agencies, the American Advertising Federation, the Association of National Advertisers, the Direct Marketing Association, the Interactive Advertising Bureau, and the Network Advertising Initiative—recently issued a set of online advertising principles through the Digital Advertising Alliance. Among other measures, the self-regulatory principles call for online marketers to provide transparency and choice to consumers if online viewing data are collected or used for targeting interest-based advertising. ≫ The ad industry uses an *advertising option icon*—a little "i" inside a triangle—that it adds to behaviorally targeted online ads to tell consumers why they are seeing a particular ad and allowing them to opt out.[51]

Of special concern are the privacy rights of children. In 2000, Congress passed the Children's Online Privacy Protection Act (COPPA), which requires online operators targeting children to post privacy policies on their sites. They must also notify parents about any information they're gathering and obtain parental consent before collecting personal information from children under age 13. With the subsequent advent of online social media, mobile phones, and other digital technologies, Congress in 2013 extended COPPA to include "identifiers such as cookies that track a child's activity online, as well as geolocation information, photos, videos, and audio recordings." The main concern is the amount of data mined by third parties from social media as well as social media's own hazy privacy policies.[52]

≫ Consumer privacy: The ad industry has agreed on an *advertising option icon* that will tell consumers why they are seeing a particular ad and allow them to opt out.

Digital Advertising Alliance

Many companies have responded to consumer privacy and security concerns with actions of their own. Still others are taking an industry-wide approach. For example, TRUSTe, a nonprofit self-regulatory organization, works with many large corporate sponsors, including Microsoft, Yahoo!, AT&T, Facebook, Disney, and Apple, to audit privacy and security measures and help consumers navigate the Internet safely. According to the company's Web site, "TRUSTe believes that an environment of mutual trust and openness will help make and keep the Internet a free, comfortable, and richly diverse community for everyone." To reassure consumers, the company lends its TRUSTe privacy seal to Web sites, mobile apps, email marketing, and other online and social media channels that meet its privacy and security standards.[53]

The direct marketing industry as a whole is also addressing public policy issues. For example, in an effort to build consumer confidence in shopping direct, the Direct Marketing Association—the largest association for businesses practicing direct, database, and interactive marketing, including nearly half of the *Fortune* 100 companies—launched a "Privacy Promise to American Consumers." The Privacy Promise requires that all DMA members adhere to a carefully developed set of consumer privacy rules. Members must agree to notify customers when any personal information is rented, sold, or exchanged with others. They must also honor consumer requests to opt out of receiving further solicitations or having their contact information transferred to other marketers. Finally, they must abide by the DMA's Preference Service by removing the names of consumers who do not wish to receive mail, phone, or email offers.[54]

Direct marketers know that, if left untended, such direct marketing abuses will lead to increasingly negative consumer attitudes, lower response and engagement rates, and calls for more restrictive state and federal legislation. Most direct marketers want the same things that consumers want: honest and well-designed marketing offers targeted only toward consumers who will appreciate and respond to them. Direct marketing is just too expensive to waste on consumers who don't want it.

MyMarketingLab

If assigned by your instructor, complete the questions marked with the ⭐ from the EOC Discussion Questions section in the MyLab. To complete the Marketing by the Numbers problems found in this section, go to your Assignments in the MyLab.

REVIEWING AND EXTENDING THE CONCEPTS

CHAPTER REVIEW AND CRITICAL THINKING

Objectives Review

This chapter is the last of three chapters covering the final marketing mix element—promotion. The previous chapters dealt with advertising, public relations, personal selling, and sales promotion. This one investigates the burgeoning field of direct and digital marketing, including online, social media, and mobile marketing.

 OBJECTIVE 14-1 Define *direct and digital marketing* and discuss their rapid growth and benefits to customers and companies. (pp 430–432)

Direct and digital marketing involve engaging directly with carefully targeted individual consumers and customer communities to both obtain an immediate response and build lasting customer relationships. Companies use direct marketing to tailor their offers and content to the needs and interests of narrowly defined segments or individual buyers to build direct customer engagement, brand community, and sales. Today, spurred by the surge in Internet usage and buying and by rapid advances in digital technologies—from smartphones, tablets, and other digital devices to the spate of online social and mobile media—direct marketing has undergone a dramatic transformation.

For buyers, direct and digital marketing are convenient, easy to use, and private. They give buyers anywhere, anytime access to an almost unlimited assortment of products and buying information. Direct marketing is also immediate and interactive, allowing buyers to create exactly the configuration of information, products, or services they desire and then order them on the spot. Finally, for consumers who want it, digital marketing through online, mobile, and social media provides a sense of brand engagement and community—a place to share brand information and experiences with other brand fans. For sellers, direct and digital marketing are powerful tools for building customer engagement and close, personalized, interactive customer relationships. They also offer greater flexibility, letting marketers make ongoing adjustments to prices and programs or make immediate, timely, and personal announcements and offers.

 OBJECTIVE 14-2 Identify and discuss the major forms of direct and digital marketing. (pp 432–433)

The main forms of direct and digital marketing include traditional direct marketing tools and the new digital marketing tools. Traditional direct approaches are face-to-face personal selling, direct-mail marketing, catalog marketing, telemarketing, DRTV marketing, and kiosk marketing. These traditional tools are still heavily used and very important in most firms' direct marketing efforts. In recent years, however, a dazzling new set of direct

digital marketing tools has burst onto the marketing scene, including online marketing (Web sites, online ads and promotions, email, online videos, and blogs), social media marketing, and mobile marketing. The chapter first discusses the fast-growing new digital direct marketing tools and then examines the traditional tools.

 OBJECTIVE 14-3 Explain how companies have responded to the Internet and the digital age with various online marketing strategies. (pp 433–439)

The Internet and digital age have fundamentally changed customers' notions of convenience, speed, price, product information, service, and brand interactions. As a result, they have given marketers a whole new way to create customer value, engage customers, and build customer relationships. The Internet now influences a staggering 50 percent of total sales—including sales transacted online plus those made in stores but encouraged by online research. To reach this burgeoning market, most companies now market online.

Online marketing takes several forms, including company Web sites, online advertising and promotions, email marketing, online video, and blogs. Social media and mobile marketing also take place online. But because of their special characteristics, we discuss these fast-growing digital marketing approaches in separate sections. For most companies, the first step in conducting online marketing is to create a Web site. The key to a successful Web site is to create enough value and engagement to get consumers to come to the site, stick around, and come back again.

Online advertising has become a major promotional medium. The main forms of online advertising are display ads and search-related ads. Email marketing is also an important form of digital marketing. Used properly, email lets marketers send highly targeted, tightly personalized, relationship-building messages. Another important form of online marketing is posting digital video content on brand Web sites or social media. Marketers hope that some of their videos will go viral, engaging consumers by the tens of millions. Finally, companies can use blogs as effective means of reaching customer communities. They can create their own blogs and advertise on existing blogs or influence content there.

 OBJECTIVE 14-4 Discuss how companies use social media and mobile marketing to engage consumers and create brand community. (pp 439–447)

In the digital age, countless independent and commercial social media have arisen that give consumers online places to congregate, socialize, and exchange views and information. Most marketers are now riding this huge social media wave. Brands can use existing social media or they can set up their own. Using existing social media seems the easiest. Thus, most brands—large and small—have set up shop on a host of social media sites. Some of the major social networks are huge; other niche social media cater to the needs of smaller communities of like-minded people. Beyond these independent social media, many companies have created their own online brand communities. More than making just scattered efforts and chasing "Likes" and Tweets, most companies are integrating a broad range of diverse media to create brand-related social sharing, engagement, and customer community.

Using social media presents both advantages and challenges. On the plus side, social media are targeted and personal, interactive, immediate and timely, and cost-effective. Perhaps the biggest advantage is their engagement and social sharing capabilities, making them ideal for creating customer community. On the down side, consumers' control over social media content makes social media difficult to control.

Mobile marketing features marketing messages, promotions, and other content delivered to on-the-go consumers through their mobile devices. Marketers use mobile marketing to engage customers anywhere, anytime during the buying and relationship-building processes. The widespread adoption of mobile devices and the surge in mobile Web traffic have made mobile marketing a must for most brands, and almost every major marketer is now integrating mobile marketing into its direct marketing programs. Many marketers have created their own mobile online sites. Others have created useful or entertaining mobile apps to engage customers with their brands and help them shop.

 OBJECTIVE 14-5 **Identify and discuss the traditional direct marketing forms and overview the public policy and ethical issues presented by direct marketing. (pp 447–453)**

Although the fast-growing digital marketing tools have grabbed most of the headlines lately, traditional direct marketing tools are very much alive and still heavily used. The major forms are face-to-face or personal selling, direct-mail marketing, catalog marketing, telemarketing, direct-response television (DRTV) marketing, and kiosk marketing.

Direct-mail marketing consists of the company sending an offer, announcement, reminder, or other item to a person at a specific address. Some marketers rely on catalog marketing—selling through catalogs mailed to a select list of customers, made available in stores, or accessed online. Telemarketing consists of using the telephone to sell directly to consumers. DRTV marketing has two forms: direct-response advertising (or infomercials) and interactive television (iTV) marketing. Kiosks are information and ordering machines that direct marketers place in stores, airports, hotels, and other locations.

Direct marketers and their customers usually enjoy mutually rewarding relationships. Sometimes, however, direct marketing presents a darker side. The aggressive and sometimes shady tactics of a few direct marketers can bother or harm consumers, giving the entire industry a black eye. Abuses range from simple excesses that irritate consumers to instances of unfair practices or even outright deception and fraud. The direct marketing industry has also faced growing concerns about invasion-of-privacy and Internet security issues. Such concerns call for strong action by marketers and public policy makers to curb direct marketing abuses. In the end, most direct marketers want the same things that consumers want: honest and well-designed marketing offers targeted only toward consumers who will appreciate and respond to them.

Key Terms

Objective 14-1
Direct and digital marketing (p 430)

Objective 14-2
Digital and social media marketing (p 433)

Objective 14-3
Omni-channel retailing (p 434)
Online marketing (p 434)
Marketing Web site (p 434)

Branded community Web site (p 435)
Online advertising (p 435)
Email marketing (p 436)
Spam (p 437)
Viral marketing (p 437)
Blogs (p 438)

Objective 14-4
Social media (p 439)
Mobile marketing (p 443)

Objective 14-5
Direct-mail marketing (p 447)
Catalog marketing (p 448)
Telemarketing (p 449)
Direct-response television (DRTV)
  marketing (p 449)

Discussion Questions

14-1. Discuss the benefits of direct and digital marketing to buyers and sellers. (AACSB: Communication)

14-2. What are blogs, and how are marketers using them to market their products and services? What advantages and disadvantages do blogs pose for marketers? (AACSB: Communication)

14-3. Discuss the advantages and challenges of social media marketing. (AASCB: Communication)

14-4. List and briefly describe the major traditional forms of direct marketing. (AACSB: Communication)

14-5. What is phishing, and how does it affect Internet marketing? (AACSB: Communication; Reflective Thinking)

Critical Thinking Exercises

14-6. In a small group, design and deliver a direct response television (DRTV) ad for a national brand not normally associated with this type of promotion, such as an athletic shoe, automobile, or food product. (AACSB: Communication; Reflective Thinking)

⭐ **14-7.** Review the Telephone Consumer Protection Act and discuss a recent case in which a marketer was fined for violating the act. (AACSB: Communication; Use of IT; Reflective Thinking)

14-8. Although mobile advertising makes up a small percentage of online advertising, it is one of the fastest-growing advertising channels. But one obstacle is measuring return on investment in mobile advertising. How are marketers doing so? Develop a presentation suggesting metrics marketers should use to measure effectiveness of mobile advertising. (AACSB: Communication; Use of IT; Reflective Thinking)

MINICASES AND APPLICATIONS

Online, Social Media, and Mobile Marketing   "Buy" Buttons

Amazon is the big gun in e-commerce that has disrupted traditional retailing. But now, it seems, Amazon is in for some disruptive competition itself. With global e-commerce sales expected to reach almost $2 trillion a year, Google and social media sites such as Facebook, Twitter, Pinterest, and Instagram want to get in on the action. Several social media sites are experimenting with "Buy" buttons on their sites that let consumers purchase directly through the social medium. Google is experimenting with "Buy" buttons on search results to counter the almost 40 percent of consumers who now start their shopping searches on Amazon instead of search engines like Google. The biggest game changer, however, might be Pinterest. Pinterest started in 1999 as a sharable bulletin board where participants "pin" pictures of things they like. It is now a multibillion-dollar company with 70 million monthly visitors who have saved more than 50 billion objects on a billion Pinterest bulletin boards. Lots of people would like to be able to buy some of those pinned objects, so Pinterest has added a "Buy" button to its mobile app. Users had already been able to click through to a marketer's Web site, but

now they can purchase any of more than 2 million products from retailers such as Macy's, Bloomingdales, and Nordstrom directly through Pinterest without leaving the site. Payments are processed through Pinterest's partners Stripe, Brainstorm, or Apply Pay, but the seller provides the order fulfillment. In the future, Pinterest users may see an appetizing recipe, click the "Buy" button to order the ingredients from Fresh Direct, and have them delivered to their homes in less than an hour.

14-9. What competitive advantage does Pinterest (www.pinterest.com) have over other social media that might make its "Buy" button more successful? (AACSB: Communication; Reflective Thinking)

14-10. Discuss advantages and disadvantages of "Buy" buttons for social media sites like Pinterest and search engines like Google. What are the advantages and disadvantages for marketers making their goods available through "Buy" buttons on these sites? (AACSB Communication; Reflective Thinking)

Marketing Ethics   Tracking in "Meat Space"

By now, you know about behavioral targeting—marketers tracking consumers' online behavior in cyberspace to send them targeted advertising. Krux Digital reports that the average visit to a Web page generated 56 instances of data collection, a fivefold increase in just one year. An investigation by *The Wall Street Journal* found that the 50 most popular U.S. Web sites installed more than 3,000 tracking files on the computer used in the study. The total was even higher—4,123 tracking files—for the top 50 sites that are popular with children and teens. Many sites installed more than 100 tracking tools each during the tests. Tracking tools include files placed on users'

computers and on Web sites. Marketers use this information to target online advertisements. But now, wearable and mobile devices allow marketers to track consumer movements in the physical world. The term *meat space* refers to the physical world in which our bodies move and do things, and marketers are using information obtained from wearable and mobile devices to personalize offers while consumers move around their space. With the growing trend in smartphone tracking and wearable technology such as smartwatches, fitness bands, and smart garments that are part of the "Internet of Things," tracking consumers in meat space is only going to grow.

14-11. Debate whether it is ethical to track consumers' physical movements, especially children's movements. (AACSB: Communication; Ethical Reasoning)

14-12. Discuss other ways marketers can track consumers in meat space. (AACSB: Communication; Reflective Thinking)

Marketing by the Numbers   Field Sales versus Telemarketing

Many companies are realizing the efficiency of telemarketing in the face of soaring sales force costs. Whereas a business-to-business sales call by an outside salesperson on average costs $600, the cost of a telemarketing sales call can be as little as $20 to $30. And telemarketers can make 20 to 33 decision-maker contacts per day to a salesperson's four per day. This has gotten the attention of many business-to-business marketers, where telemarketing can be very effective.

14-13. Refer to Appendix 3: Marketing by the Numbers to determine the marketing return on sales (marketing ROS) and return on marketing investment (marketing ROI) for company A and company B in the chart below. Which company is performing better? Explain.

(AACSB: Communication; Analytical Reasoning; Reflective Thinking)

	Company A (sales force only)	Company B (telemarketing only)
Net sales	$1,000,000	$850,000
Cost of goods sold	$500,000	$425,000
Sales expenses	$300,000	$100,000

⭐ **14-14.** Should all companies consider reducing their sales forces in favor of telemarketing? Discuss the pros and cons of this action. (AACSB: Communication; Reflective Thinking)

Video Case   Nutrisystem

You've probably heard of Nutrisystem, a company that produced $800 million in revenues last year by selling weight-loss products. What started as a small effort based on an e-commerce marketing plan has evolved into a multipronged marketing campaign that not only has expanded the business but also provides substantial return-on-investment potential.

The key to Nutrisystem's efforts is its direct-to-consumer platform. Using various advertising outlets, from magazines to television, Nutrisystem's promotions all have one thing in common—they let customers make direct contact with the company. Inserting a unique URL or 800 number in every ad also lets Nutrisystem track the success of each and every effort.

After viewing the video featuring Nutrisystem, answer the following questions:

14-15. In what different ways does Nutrisystem engage in direct marketing?

14-16. What advantages does Nutrisystem's marketing campaign have over selling through intermediary channels?

14-17. In addition to its direct-to-consumer distribution and promotional efforts, what is essential to the success of Nutrisystem?

Company Cases   14 Alibaba/10 Apple Pay/11 Sears

See Appendix 1 for cases appropriate for this chapter. **Case 14, Alibaba: The World's Largest E-Tailer Is Not Amazon**. Selling more than Amazon and EBay combined, Alibaba's rapid growth may keep it out in front for good. **Case 10, Apple Pay: Taking Mobile Payments Mainstream.** Apple may succeed where Google, Paypal, Visa, and others have failed in making mobile payments the go-to way to pay. **Case 11, Sears: Why Should You Shop There?** Formerly the leading retailer, Sears struggles for survival by trying everything, including building an ecommerce presence.

MyMarketingLab

If assigned by your instructor, complete these writing sections from your Assignments in the MyLab.

14-18. Compare and contrast a marketing Web site and a branded community Web site. (AACSB: Communication)

14-19. Review the FTC's guidelines on disclosure in online, social media, and mobile advertisements at www.ftc.gov/os/2013/03/130312dotcomdisclosures.pdf. Will the FTC's requirements regarding ads and endorsements make Twitter less effective as an advertising medium?

15 The Global Marketplace

CHAPTER ROAD MAP Objective Outline

Previewing the Concepts

You've now learned the fundamentals of how companies develop competitive marketing strategies to engage customers, create customer value, and build lasting customer relationships. In this chapter, we extend these fundamentals to global marketing. Although we've discussed global topics in each previous chapter—it's difficult to find an area of marketing that doesn't contain at least some international elements—here we'll focus on special considerations that companies face when they market their brands globally. Advances in communication, transportation, and digital technologies have made the world a much smaller place. Today, almost every firm, large or small, faces international marketing issues. In this chapter, we will examine six major decisions marketers make in going global.

To start our exploration of global marketing, let's look at L'Oréal, the French cosmetics and beauty care giant. L'Oréal and its brands are truly global in scope and appeal. But the company's outstanding international success comes from achieving a global–local balance, one that adapts and differentiates L'Oréal's well-known brands to meet local needs while also integrating them across world markets to optimize their global impact. You can think of L'Oréal as a kind of "United Nations of beauty."

First Stop

L'Oréal: "The United Nations of Beauty"

How does a French company successfully market an American version of a Korean skin-beautifier under a French brand name in Australia? Ask L'Oréal, which sells more than $25 billion worth of cosmetics, hair care products, skin care concoctions, and fragrances each year in 130 countries, making it the world's biggest cosmetics marketer. L'Oréal sells its brands globally by understanding how they appeal to varied cultural nuances of beauty in specific local markets. Then it finds the best balance between standardizing its brands for global impact and adapting them to meet local needs and desires.

L'Oréal is as global as a company gets. With offices spread across 130 nations and more than half of its sales coming from markets outside Europe and North America, the company no longer has a clearly defined home market. L'Oréal's well-known brands originated in a half dozen or more different cultures, including French (L'Oréal Paris, Garnier, Lancôme), American (Maybelline, Kiehl's, SoftSheen-Carson, Ralph Lauren, Urban Decay, Clarisonic, Redken), British (The Body Shop), Italian (Giorgio Armani), and Japanese (Shu Uemura). With these and many other well-known brands, the master global marketer is the uncontested world leader in makeup, skin care, and hair coloring and second only to P&G in hair care.

L'Oréal's global mastery starts with a corps of highly multicultural managers. The company is famous for building global brand teams around managers who have deep backgrounds in several cultures. L'Oréal managers around the world bring diverse cultural perspectives to their brands as if they were, say, German or American or Chinese—or all three at once. As explained by one Indian-American-French manager of a team that launched a men's skin care line in Southeast Asia: "I cannot think about things one way. I have a stock of references in different languages: English, Hindi, and French. I read books in three different languages, meet people from different countries, eat food from different [cultures], and so on."

For example, a French-Irish-Cambodian skin care manager noticed that, in Europe, face creams tended to be either "tinted" (and considered makeup) or "lifting" (considered skin care). In Asia, however, many face creams combine both traits. Recognizing the growing popularity of Asian beauty trends in Europe, the manager and his team developed a tinted lifting cream for the French market, a product that proved highly successful.

L'Oréal digs deep to understand what beauty means to consumers in different parts of the world. It outspends all major competitors on R&D, painstakingly researching beauty and personal care behaviors unique to specific locales. L'Oréal has set up R&D centers all over the world, perfecting a local observation approach it calls "geocosmetics." This science is fueled with insights gained through everything from in-home visits to observations made in "bathroom laboratories" equipped with high-tech gadgetry. L'Oréal's research produces precise information about regional beauty and hygiene rituals and about local conditions and constraints that affect the use of its products, such as humidity and temperature:

> How many minutes does a Chinese woman devote to her morning beauty routine? How do people wash their hair in Bangkok? How many

>> **Global–local balance: Cosmetics and beauty care giant L'Oréal balances local brand responsiveness and global brand impact, making it "The United Nations of Beauty."**

Marc Piasecki/Stringer/Getty images

brush strokes does a Japanese woman or a French woman use to apply mascara? These beauty rituals, repeated thousands of times, are inherently cultural. Passed on by tradition, influenced by climate and by local living conditions, they strive to achieve an ideal of perfection that is different from one country and from one continent to the next. They provide an incredibly rich source of information for L'Oréal. Behind these rituals, there are physiological realities: fine, straight, and short eyelashes cannot be made up the same way as thick, curled, and long lashes.

L'Oréal uses such detailed insights to create products and positioning for brands in local markets. "Beauty is less and less one size fits all," says a L'Oréal executive in China. "You have to have an answer for very different needs." For example, more than 260 scientists now work in L'Oréal's Shanghai research center, tailoring products ranging from lipstick to herbal cleaners to cucumber toners for Chinese tastes.

At the same time that understanding the minute details of local customer behavior helps L'Oréal be responsive to specific market needs, it also lets the company achieve global scale by integrating brands across world cultures. For example, consider Elséve Total Reparação, a hair care line initially developed at L'Oréal's labs in Rio de Janeiro to address specific hair problems described by Brazilian women. In Brazil, more than half of all women have long, dry, dull, and very curly hair, resulting from the humid Brazilian climate, exposure to the sun, frequent washing, and smoothing and straightening treatments. Elséve Total Reparação was an immediate hit in Brazil, and L'Oréal quickly rolled it out to other South American and Latin American markets. The company then tracked down other global locales with

> Cosmetic and beauty care giant L'Oréal and its brands are truly global. But the company's huge international success comes from a global–local balance that adapts brands to local markets while optimizing their impact globally.

climate characteristics and hair care rituals similar to those faced by Brazilian women. Subsequently, L'Oréal launched the brand as Elséve Total Repair in numerous European, Indian, and other South East Asian markets, where consumers greeted it with similar enthusiasm.

Such adaptation often plays out across multiple L'Oréal brands—which takes us back to that Korean skin-beautifier sold under a French brand in Australia mentioned in the opening paragraph. Blemish Balm Cream (BB Cream) was originally created by L'Oréal dermatologists in Korea to soothe skin and hide minor blemishes. It quickly became a high-flying Korean brand. However, applying their deep knowledge of skin colors, treatments, and makeup worldwide, L'Oréal researchers developed a successful new-generation BB Cream adapted to conditions and skin colors in U.S. markets (where BB stands for "beauty balm") and launched it under the Maybelline New York brand. Still not finished, L'Oréal created yet another local version for Europe under the Garnier brand, which it also introduced in other world markets, including Australia.

L'Oréal doesn't just adapt its product formulations globally. It also adapts brand positioning and marketing to international needs and expectations. For example, more than 20 years ago, the company bought stodgy American makeup producer Maybelline. To reinvigorate and globalize the brand, it moved the unit's headquarters from Tennessee to New York City and added "New York" to the label. The resulting urban, street-smart, Big Apple image played well with the midprice positioning of the workaday makeup brand globally. The makeover soon earned Maybelline a 20 percent market share in its category in Western Europe. The young urban positioning also hit the mark in Asia, where few women realized that the trendy "New York" Maybelline brand belonged to French cosmetics giant L'Oréal.

Thus, L'Oréal and its brands are truly global. But the company's huge international success comes from achieving a global–local balance that adapts and differentiates brands in local markets while optimizing their impact across global markets. L'Oréal is one of few companies that have achieved both local brand responsiveness and global brand integration. "We respect the differences among our consumers around the world," says L'Oréal's CEO. "We have global brands, but we need to adapt them to local needs." When a former CEO once addressed a UNESCO conference, nobody batted an eyelid when he described L'Oréal as "The United Nations of Beauty."[1]

I n the past, U.S. companies paid little attention to international trade. If they could pick up some extra sales via exports, that was fine. But the big market was at home, and it teemed with opportunities. The home market was also much safer. Managers did not need to learn other languages, deal with strange and changing currencies, face political and legal uncertainties, or adapt their products to different customer needs and expectations. Today, however, the situation is much different. Organizations of all kinds, from Coca-Cola and Nike to Google, MTV, and even the NBA, have gone global.

Author Comment
The rapidly changing global environment provides both opportunities and threats. It's difficult to find a marketer today that isn't affected in some way by global developments.

Global Marketing Today

The world is shrinking rapidly with the advent of faster digital communication, transportation, and financial flows. Products developed in one country— McDonald's hamburgers, Netflix video service, Samsung electronics, Zara fashions, Caterpillar construction equipment, German BMWs, Facebook social networking—have found enthusiastic acceptance in other countries. It would not be surprising to hear about a German businessman wearing an Italian suit meeting an English friend at a Japanese restaurant who later returns home to drink Russian vodka while watching *The Big Bang Theory* on TV and checking Facebook posts from friends around the world.

International trade has boomed over the past three decades. Since 1990, the number of multinational corporations in the world has more than doubled to more than 65,000. Some of these multinationals are true giants. In fact, of the largest 150 economies in the world, only 88 are countries. The remaining 62 are multinational corporations. Walmart, the world's largest company (based on a weighted average of sales, profits, assets, and market value), has annual revenues greater than the gross domestic product (GDP) of all but the world's 27 largest countries.[2] Despite a dip in world trade caused by the recent worldwide recession, the world trade of products and services last year was valued at nearly $19 trillion, about 24 percent of GDP worldwide.[3]

Many U.S. companies have long been successful at international marketing: Coca-Cola, McDonald's, Starbucks, Nike, GE, IBM, Apple, Google, Colgate, Caterpillar, Boeing, and dozens of other American firms have made the world their market. In the United States, non-American brands such as Toyota, Samsung, Nestlé, IKEA, Canon, and adidas have become household words. Other products and services that appear to be American

>> **Many American companies have now made the world their market. Nearly 60 percent of Apple's sales come from outside the Americas.**

Prakash Singh/AFP/Getty Images

Global firm

A firm that, by operating in more than one country, gains R&D, production, marketing, and financial advantages in its costs and reputation that are not available to purely domestic competitors.

are, in fact, produced or owned by foreign companies, such as Ben & Jerry's ice cream, Budweiser beer, Purina pet foods, 7-Eleven, GE and RCA televisions, Carnation milk, Universal Studios, and Motel 6. Michelin, the oh-so-French tire manufacturer, now does 35 percent of its business in North America and Mexico; J&J, the maker of quintessentially all-American products such as BAND-AIDs and Johnson's Baby Shampoo, does 53 percent of its business abroad. America's own Caterpillar belongs more to the wider world, with 62 percent of its sales coming from outside the United States. And with more than 3,500 products worldwide, American favorite Coca-Cola now sells "moments of happiness" more than 1.9 billion times a day in more than 200 countries.[4]

But as global trade grows, global competition is also intensifying. Foreign firms are expanding aggressively into new international markets, and home markets are no longer as rich in opportunity. Few industries are currently safe from foreign competition. If companies delay taking steps toward internationalizing, they risk being shut out of growing markets in Western and Eastern Europe, China and the Pacific Rim, Russia, India, Brazil, and elsewhere. Firms that stay at home to play it safe might not only lose their chances to enter other markets but also risk losing their home markets. Domestic companies that never thought about foreign competitors suddenly find these competitors in their own backyards.

Ironically, although the need for companies to go abroad is greater today than in the past, so are the risks. Companies that go global may face highly unstable governments and currencies, restrictive government policies and regulations, and high trade barriers. The recently dampened global economic environment has also created big global challenges. In addition, corruption is an increasing problem; officials in several countries often award business not to the best bidder but to the highest briber.

A **global firm** is one that, by operating in more than one country, gains marketing, production, research and development (R&D), and financial advantages that are not available to purely domestic competitors. Because the global company sees the world as one market, it minimizes the importance of national boundaries and develops global brands. The global company raises capital, obtains materials and components, and manufactures and markets its goods wherever it can do the best job.

For example, U.S.-based Otis Elevator, the world's largest elevator maker, is headquartered in Farmington, Connecticut. However, it offers products in more than 200 countries and achieves 83 percent of its sales from outside the United States. It gets elevator door systems from France, small geared parts from Spain, electronics from Germany, and special motor drives from Japan. It operates manufacturing facilities in the Americas, Europe, and Asia and engineering and test centers in the United States, Austria, Brazil, China, Czech Republic, France, Germany, India, Italy, Japan, Korea, and Spain. In turn, Otis Elevator is a wholly owned subsidiary of global commercial and aerospace giant United Technologies Corporation.[5] Many of today's global corporations—both large and small—have become truly borderless.

This does not mean, however, that every firm must operate in dozens of countries to succeed. Smaller firms can practice global niching. But the world is becoming smaller, and every company operating in a global industry—whether large or small—must assess and establish its place in world markets.

The rapid move toward globalization means that all companies will have to answer some basic questions: What market position should we try to establish in our country, in

>> **Figure 15.1 Major International Marketing Decisions**

| Looking at the global marketing environment | → | Deciding whether to go global | → | Deciding which markets to enter | → | Deciding how to enter the market | → | Deciding on the global marketing program | → | Deciding on the global marketing organization |

It's a big and beautiful but threatening world out there for marketers! Most large American firms have made the world their market. For example, once all-American McDonald's now captures 66 percent of its sales from outside the United States.

our economic region, and globally? Who will our global competitors be, and what are their strategies and resources? Where should we produce or source our products? What strategic alliances should we form with other firms around the world?

As shown in >> **Figure 15.1**, a company faces six major decisions in international marketing. We discuss each decision in detail in this chapter.

> **Author Comment**
> As if operating within a company's own borders wasn't difficult enough, going global adds many layers of complexities. For example, Coca-Cola markets its products in hundreds of countries around the globe. It must understand the varying trade, economic, cultural, and political environments in each market.

Looking at the Global Marketing Environment

Before deciding whether to operate internationally, a company must understand the international marketing environment. That environment has changed a great deal in recent decades, creating both new opportunities and new problems.

The International Trade System

U.S. companies looking abroad must start by understanding the international *trade system*. When selling to another country, a firm may face restrictions on trade between nations. Governments may charge *tariffs* or *duties*, taxes on certain imported products designed to raise revenue or protect domestic firms. Tariffs and duties are often used to force favorable trade behaviors from other nations.

For example, the European Union (EU) recently placed import duties on Chinese solar panels after determining that Chinese companies were selling the panels in EU countries at under-market prices. To retaliate, the very next day, the Chinese government placed duties on EU wine exports to China. The duties targeted the wines of Spain, France, and Italy but spared Germany, which had taken China's side in the solar panel dispute. The disputes were resolved when Chinese solar panel producers agreed to a minimum price in Europe and Europe agreed to help China develop its own wine industry in return for promoting European wines there.[6]

Countries may set *quotas*, limits on the amount of foreign imports that they will accept in certain product categories. The purpose of a quota is to conserve on foreign exchange and protect local industry and employment. Firms may also encounter *exchange controls*, which limit the amount of foreign exchange and the exchange rate against other currencies.

A company also may face *nontariff trade barriers*, such as biases against its bids, restrictive product standards, or excessive host-country regulations or enforcement. >> For example, Walmart recently suspended its once-ambitious plans to expand into India's huge but fragmented retail market by opening hundreds of Walmart superstores there. Beyond difficult market conditions, such as spotty electricity and poor roads, India is notorious for throwing up nontariff obstacles to protect the nation's own predominately mom-and-pop retailers, which control 96 percent of India's $500 billion in retail sales. One such obstacle is a government regulation requiring foreign retailers in India to buy 30 percent of the merchandise they sell from local small

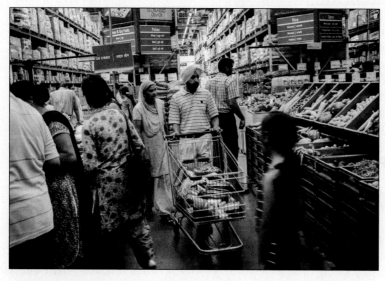

>> **Nontariff trade barriers: Because of nontariff obstacles, Walmart recently suspended its once-ambitious plans to expand into India's huge but fragmented retail market.**
Prakash Singh/Bloomberg/Getty Images

>> **The WTO promotes trade by reducing tariffs and other international trade barriers. It also imposes international trade sanctions and mediates global trade disputes.**

(left) Stockbyte/Getty Images; (right) Donald Stampfli/AP Images

Economic community
A group of nations organized to work toward common goals in the regulation of international trade.

businesses. Such a requirement is nearly impossible for Walmart because small suppliers can't produce the quantities of goods needed by the giant retailer. Further, India's few large domestic retailers are not bound by the same rule, making it difficult for Walmart to compete profitably. Walmart is now looking for a domestic partner that can help it crack the mammoth Indian market.[7]

At the same time, certain other forces can *help* trade between nations. Examples include the World Trade Organization (WTO) and various regional free trade agreements.

The World Trade Organization

The General Agreement on Tariffs and Trade (GATT), established in 1947 and modified in 1994, was designed to promote world trade by reducing tariffs and other international trade barriers. >> It established the World Trade Organization (WTO), which replaced GATT in 1995 and now oversees the original GATT provisions. WTO and GATT member nations (currently numbering 161) have met in eight rounds of negotiations to reassess trade barriers and establish new rules for international trade. The WTO also imposes international trade sanctions and mediates global trade disputes. Its actions have been productive. The first seven rounds of negotiations reduced the average worldwide tariffs on manufactured goods from 45 percent to just 5 percent.[8]

The most recently completed negotiations, dubbed the Uruguay Round, dragged on for seven long years before concluding in 1994. The benefits of the Uruguay Round will be felt for many years, as the accord promoted long-term global trade growth, reduced the world's remaining merchandise tariffs by 30 percent, extended the WTO to cover trade in agriculture and a wide range of services, and toughened the international protection of copyrights, patents, trademarks, and other intellectual property. A new round of global WTO trade talks, the Doha Round, began in Doha, Qatar, in late 2001 and was set to conclude in 2005; however, the discussions still continued through 2015.[9]

Regional Free Trade Zones

Certain countries have formed *free trade zones* or **economic communities**. These are groups of nations organized to work toward common goals in the regulation of international trade. One such community is the *European Union (EU)*. Formed in 1957, the EU set out to create a single European market by reducing barriers to the free flow of products, services, finances, and labor among member countries and developing policies on trade with nonmember nations. Today, the EU represents one of the world's largest single markets. >> Currently, it has 28 member countries containing more than half a billion consumers and accounting for almost 16 percent of the world's imports and exports.[10] The EU offers tremendous trade opportunities for U.S. and other non-European firms.

Over the past decade and a half, 19 EU member nations have adopted the euro as a common currency. Widespread adoption of the euro has decreased much of the currency risk associated with doing business in Europe, making member countries with previously weak currencies more attractive markets. However, the adoption of a common currency has also caused problems, as European economic powers such as Germany and France have had to step in recently to prop up weaker economies such as those of Greece, Portugal, and Cyprus. This recent ongoing "euro crisis" has led some analysts to predict the possible breakup of the euro zone as it is now set up.[11]

>> **Economic communities: The European Union represents one of the world's single largest markets. Its current member countries contain more than half a billion consumers and account for 20 percent of the world's exports.**

Europian Union, 2015

It is unlikely that the EU will ever go against 2,000 years of tradition and become the "United States of Europe." A community with more than two dozen different languages and cultures will always have difficulty coming together and acting as a single entity. Still, with a combined annual GDP of more than \$18 trillion, the EU has become a potent economic force.[12]

In 1994, the *North American Free Trade Agreement (NAFTA)* established a free trade zone among the United States, Mexico, and Canada. The agreement created a single market of 474 million people who produce and consume \$20.5 trillion worth of goods and services annually. Over the past 20 years, NAFTA has eliminated trade barriers and investment restrictions among the three countries. Total trade among the NAFTA countries nearly tripled from \$288 billion in 1993 to more than \$1.1 trillion a year.[13]

Following the apparent success of NAFTA, in 2005 the Central American Free Trade Agreement (CAFTA-DR) established a free trade zone between the United States and Costa Rica, the Dominican Republic, El Salvador, Guatemala, Honduras, and Nicaragua. Other free trade areas have formed in Latin America and South America. For example, the Union of South American Nations (UNASUR), modeled after the EU, was formed in 2004 and formalized by a constitutional treaty in 2008. Consisting of 12 countries, UNASUR makes up the largest trading bloc after NAFTA and the EU, with a population of more than 387 million and a combined economy of more than \$4.1 trillion. Similar to NAFTA and the EU, UNASUR aims to eliminate all tariffs between nations by 2019.[14]

Each nation has unique features that must be understood. A nation's readiness for different products and services and its attractiveness as a market to foreign firms depend on its economic, political-legal, and cultural environments.

Economic Environment

The international marketer must study each country's economy. Two economic factors reflect the country's attractiveness as a market: its industrial structure and its income distribution.

The country's *industrial structure* shapes its product and service needs, income levels, and employment levels. The four types of industrial structures are as follows:

- **Subsistence economies.** In a subsistence economy, the vast majority of people engage in simple agriculture. They consume most of their output and barter the rest for simple goods and services. These economies offer few market opportunities. Many African countries fall into this category.
- **Raw material exporting economies.** These economies are rich in one or more natural resources but poor in other ways. Much of their revenue comes from exporting these resources. Some examples are Chile (tin and copper) and the Democratic Republic of the Congo (copper, cobalt, and coffee). These countries are good markets for large equipment, tools and supplies, and trucks. If there are many foreign residents and a wealthy upper class, they are also a market for luxury goods.
- **Emerging economies (industrializing economies).** In an emerging economy, fast growth in manufacturing results in rapid overall economic growth. Examples include the BRIC countries—Brazil, Russia, India, and China. As manufacturing increases, the country needs more imports of raw textile materials, steel, and heavy machinery and fewer imports of finished textiles, paper products, and automobiles. Industrialization typically creates a new rich class and a growing middle class, both demanding new types of imported goods. As more developed markets stagnate and become increasingly competitive, many marketers are now targeting growth opportunities in emerging markets.
- **Industrial economies.** Industrial economies are major exporters of manufactured goods, services, and investment funds. They trade goods among themselves and also export them to other types of economies for raw materials and semifinished goods. The varied manufacturing activities of these industrial nations and their large middle class make them rich markets for all sorts of goods. Examples include the United States, Japan, and Norway.

The second economic factor is the country's *income distribution*. Industrialized nations may have low-, medium-, and high-income households. In contrast, countries with subsistence economies consist mostly of households with very low family incomes. Still other countries may have households with either very low or very high incomes. Even poor or emerging economies may be attractive markets for all kinds of goods. In recent years, as the weakened global economy has slowed growth in both domestic and emerging markets, many companies are shifting their sights to include a new target—the so-called "bottom of the economic pyramid," the vast untapped market consisting of the world's poorest consumers (see Marketing at Work 15.1).

These days, companies in a wide range of industries—from cars to computers to soft drinks—are increasingly targeting middle-income or low-income consumers in emerging economies. For example, as soft drink sales growth has lost its fizz in North America and Europe, Coca-Cola has had to look elsewhere to meet its ambitious growth goals. So the company has set its sights on Africa, with its promising though challenging long-term growth opportunities. Many Western companies view Africa as an untamed final frontier, plagued by poverty, political instability, unreliable transportation, and shortages of fresh water and other essential resources. But Coca-Cola sees plenty of opportunity to justify the risks. The African continent has a growing population of more than 1.1 billion people, a just-emerging middle class, and $2.4 trillion of GDP and spending power. Six of the world's 10 fastest-growing markets are in Africa: [15]

Coca-Cola has operated in Africa since 1929 and holds a dominant 29 percent market share in Africa and the Middle East, compared with Pepsi's 15 percent share. However, there's still plenty of room for Coca-Cola to grow there. For example, annual per capita consumption of Coke and other soft drinks is about 13 times less in Africa than in North America. Still, marketing in Africa is very different from marketing in more developed regions. Beyond just marketing through traditional channels in larger African cities, Coca-Cola is now invading smaller communities with more grassroots tactics.

>> Small stores play a big role in helping Coca-Cola to grow in Africa. In countless poor neighborhoods across the continent, crowded streets are lined with shops painted Coke red, selling low-priced Coca-Cola products by the bottle out of Coke-provided, refrigerated coolers. Such shops are supplied by a rudimentary but effective network of Coca-Cola distributors, whose crews often deliver crates of Coke products by hand-pulled trolleys or even a crate at a time carried on their heads. Because of the poor roads crowded with traffic, moving drinks by hand is often the best method. The company's first rule is to get its products "cold and close." "If they don't have roads to move products long distances on trucks, we will use boats, canoes, or trolleys," says the president of Coca-Cola South Africa. For example, in Nigeria's Makako district—a maze of stilt houses on the Lagos lagoon—women crisscross the waterways in canoes selling Coca-Cola directly to residents.

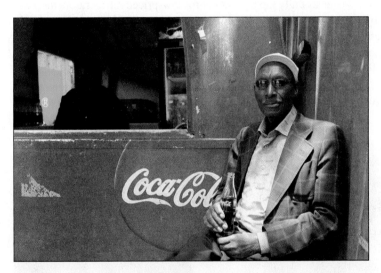

>> With sales stagnating in its mature markets, Coca-Cola is looking to emerging markets—such as Africa—to meet its ambitious growth goals. Its African distribution network is rudimentary but effective.

Marco Di Lauro/Getty Images

Political-Legal Environment

Nations differ greatly in their political-legal environments. In considering whether to do business in a given country, a company should consider factors such as the country's attitudes toward international buying, government bureaucracy, political stability, and monetary regulations.

Some nations are very receptive to foreign firms; others are less accommodating. For example, India has tended to bother foreign businesses with import quotas, currency restrictions, and other limitations that make operating there a challenge. In contrast, neighboring Asian countries, such as Singapore and Thailand, court foreign investors and shower them with incentives and favorable operating conditions. Political and regulatory stability is another

MARKETING AT WORK   15.1

International Marketing: Targeting the Bottom of the Economic Pyramid

Many companies are now waking up to a shocking statistic. Of the roughly 7 billion people on this planet, 4 billion of them (that's 57 percent) live in poverty. Known as the "bottom of the pyramid," the world's poor might not seem like a promising market. However, despite their paltry incomes, as a group, these consumers represent an eye-popping $5 trillion in annual purchasing power. Moreover, this vast segment is largely untapped. The world's poor often have little or no access to even the most basic products and services taken for granted by more affluent consumers. As the weakened global economy has flattened domestic markets and slowed the growth of emerging middle-class markets, companies are increasingly looking to the bottom of the pyramid for fresh growth opportunities.

But how can a company sell profitably to consumers with incomes below the poverty level? For starters, the *price* has got to be right. And in this case, says one analyst, "right" means "lower than you can imagine." With this in mind, many companies have made their products more affordable simply by offering smaller package sizes or lower-tech versions of current products. For example, in Nigeria, P&G sells a Gillette razor for 23 cents, a 1-ounce package of Ariel detergent for about 10 cents, and a 10-count pack of one-diaper-a-night Pampers for $2.30. Although there isn't much margin on products selling for pennies apiece, P&G is succeeding through massive volume.

Consider Pampers: Nigeria alone produces some 6 million newborns each year, almost 50 percent more than the United States, a country with twice the population. Nigeria's astounding birthrate creates a huge, untapped market for Pampers diapers, P&G's top-selling brand. However, the typical Nigerian mother spends only about 5,000 naira a month, about $30, on all household purchases. P&G's task is to make Pampers affordable to this mother and to convince her that Pampers are worth some of her scarce spending. To keep costs and prices low in markets like Nigeria, P&G invented an absorbent diaper with fewer features. Although much less expensive, the diaper still functions at a high level. When creating such affordable new products, says an R&D manager at P&G, "Delight, don't dilute." That is, the diaper needs to be priced low, but it also has to do what other cheap diapers don't—keep a baby comfortable and dry for 12 hours.

Even with the right diaper at the right price, selling Pampers in Nigeria presents a challenge. In the West, babies typically go through numerous disposable diapers a day. In Nigeria, however, most babies are in cloth diapers. To make Pampers more acceptable and even more affordable for

Nigerians, P&G markets the diapers as a one-a-day item. According to company ads, "One Pampers equals one dry night." The campaign tells mothers that keeping babies dry at night helps them to get a good night's sleep, which in turn helps them to grow and achieve. The message taps into a deep sentiment among Nigerians, unearthed by P&G researchers, that their children will have a better life than they do. Thus, thanks to affordable pricing, a product that meets customers' needs, and relevant positioning, Pampers sales are booming. In Nigeria, the name Pampers is now synonymous with diapers.

As P&G has learned, in most cases, selling profitably to the bottom of the pyramid takes much more than just developing single-use packets and pennies-apiece pricing. It requires broad-based innovation that produces not just lower prices but also new products that give people in poverty more for their money, not less. As another example, consider how Indian appliance company Godrej & Boyce used customer-driven innovation to successfully tap the market for low-priced refrigerators in India:

Because of their high cost to both buy and operate, traditional compressor-driven refrigerators had penetrated only 18 percent of the Indian market. But rather than just produce a cheaper, stripped-down version of its higher-end refrigerators, Godrej assigned a team to study the needs of Indian consumers with poor or no refrigeration. The semi-urban and rural people the team observed typically earned 5,000 to 8,000 rupees (about $125 to $200) a month,

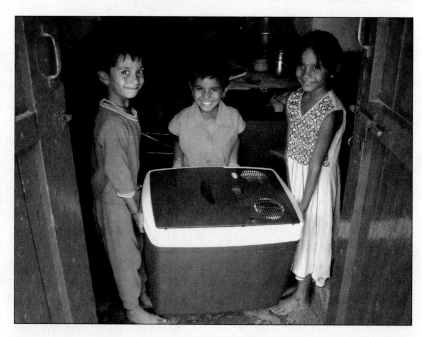

» Selling to the world's poor: At only $69, Godrej's ChotuKool ("little cool") does a better job of meeting the needs of low-end Indian consumers at half the price of even the most basic conventional refrigerator.

Courtesy of Godrej & Boyce Mfg. Co. Ltd.

lived in single-room dwellings with four or five family members, and changed residences frequently. Unable to afford conventional refrigerators, these consumers were making do with communal, usually second-hand ones. But even the shared fridges usually contained only a few items. Their users tended to shop daily and buy only small quantities of vegetables and milk. Moreover, electricity was unreliable, putting even the little food they wanted to keep cool at risk.

Godrej concluded that the low-end segment had little need for a conventional high-end refrigerator; it needed a fundamentally new product. So Godrej invented the ChotuKool ("little cool"), a candy red, top-opening, highly portable, dorm-size unit that has room for the few items users want to keep fresh for a day or two. Rather than a compressor and refrigerant, the miserly little unit uses a chip that cools when current is applied, and its top-opening design keeps cold air inside when the lid is opened. In all, the ChotuKool uses less than half the energy of a conventional refrigerator and can run on a battery during the power outages common in rural villages. The best part: At only $69, "little cool" does a better job of meeting the needs of low-end consumers at half the price of even the most basic traditional refrigerator.

Thus, the bottom of the pyramid offers huge untapped opportunities to companies that can develop the right products at the right prices. And companies such as P&G are moving aggressively to capture these opportunities. P&G has set lofty goals for acquiring new customers, moving the company's emphasis from the developed West, where it currently gets most of its revenue, to the developing economies of Asia and Africa.

But successfully tapping these new developing markets will require more than just shipping out cheaper versions of existing products. "Our innovation strategy is not just diluting the top-tier product for the lower-end consumer," says P&G's CEO. "You have to discretely innovate for every one of those consumers on that economic curve, and if you don't do that, you'll fail."

Sources: See Erik Simanis and Duncan Duke, "Profits at the Bottom of the Pyramid, *Harvard Business Review,* October 2014, pp. 87–93; Matthew J. Eyring, Mark W. Johnson, and Hari Nair, "New Business Models in Emerging Markets," *Harvard Business Review,* January–February 2011, pp. 89–95; Mya Frazier, "How P&G Brought the Diaper Revolution to China," *CBS News,* January 7, 2010, www.cbsnews.com/8301-505125_162-51379838/; David Holthaus, "Health Talk First, Then a Sales Pitch," April 17, 2011, *Cincinnati .com,* http://news.cincinnati.com/article/20110417/BIZ01/104170344/; Lisa Jones Christensen, Enno Siemsen, and Sridhar Balasubramanian, "Consumer Behavior Change at the Base of the Pyramid: Bridging the Gap between For-Profit and Social Responsibility Strategies," *Strategic Management Journal,* February 2015, pp. 307–317; and "The State of Consumption Today," *Worldwatch Institute,* www .worldwatch.org/node/810, accessed September 2015.

issue. For example, Russia is consumed by corruption and governmental red tape, which the government finds difficult to control. The country's recent geopolitical conflicts with Europe, the United States, and other countries have made doing business in Russia difficult and risky.[16]

Companies must also consider a country's monetary regulations. Sellers want to take their profits in a currency of value to them. Ideally, the buyer can pay in the seller's currency or in other world currencies. Short of this, sellers might accept a blocked currency—one whose removal from the country is restricted by the buyer's government—if they can buy other goods in that country that they need or can sell elsewhere for a needed currency. In addition to currency limits, a changing exchange rate also creates high risks for the seller.

Most international trade involves cash transactions. Yet many nations have too little hard currency to pay for their purchases from other countries. They may want to pay with other items instead of cash. *Barter* involves the direct exchange of goods or services. For example, Venezuela regularly barters oil, which it produces in surplus quantities, for food on the international market—rice from Guyana; coffee from El Salvador; sugar, coffee, meat, and more from Nicaragua; and beans and pasta from the Dominican Republic. Venezuela has even struck a deal to supply oil to Cuba in exchange for Cuban doctors and medical care for Venezuelans.[17]

Cultural Environment

Each country has its own folkways, norms, and taboos. When designing global marketing strategies, companies must understand how culture affects consumer reactions in each of its world markets. In turn, they must also understand how their strategies affect local cultures.

The Impact of Culture on Marketing Strategy

Sellers must understand the ways that consumers in different countries think about and use certain products before planning a marketing program. There are often surprises. For example, the average French man uses almost twice as many cosmetics and grooming aids as his wife. The Germans and the French eat more packaged, branded spaghetti than Italians do. Some 49 percent of Chinese eat on the way to work. Most American women let down their hair and take off makeup at bedtime, whereas 15 percent of Chinese women style their hair at bedtime and 11 percent put *on* makeup.[18]

Companies that ignore cultural norms and differences can make some very expensive and embarrassing mistakes. Here are two examples:

Nike inadvertently offended Chinese officials when it ran an ad featuring LeBron James crushing a number of culturally revered Chinese figures in a kung fu–themed television ad. The Chinese government found that the ad violated regulations to uphold national dignity and respect the "motherland's culture" and yanked the multimillion-dollar campaign. With egg on its face, Nike released a formal apology. Burger King made a similar mistake when it created in-store ads in Spain showing Hindu goddess Lakshmi atop a ham sandwich with the caption "a snack that is sacred." Cultural and religious groups worldwide objected strenuously—Hindus are vegetarian. Burger King apologized and pulled the ads.[19]

Business norms and behaviors also vary from country to country. For example, American executives like to get right down to business and engage in fast and tough face-to-face bargaining. However, Japanese and other Asian businesspeople often find this behavior offensive. They prefer to start with polite conversation, and they rarely say no in face-to-face conversations. As another example, firm handshakes are a common and

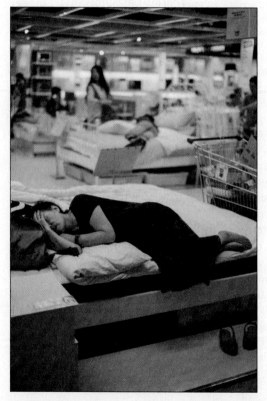

expected greeting in most Western countries; in some Middle Eastern countries, however, handshakes might be refused if offered. Microsoft founder Bill Gates once set off a flurry of international controversy when he shook the hand of South Korea's president with his right hand while keeping his left hand in his pocket, something that Koreans consider highly disrespectful. In some countries, when being entertained at a meal, not finishing all the food implies that it was somehow substandard. In other countries, in contrast, wolfing down every last bite might be taken as a mild insult, suggesting that the host didn't supply enough quantity.[20] American business executives need to understand these kinds of cultural nuances before conducting business in another country.

By the same token, companies that understand cultural nuances can use them to their advantage in the global markets. For example, furniture retailer IKEA's stores are a big draw for up-and-coming Chinese consumers. ≫ But IKEA has learned that customers in China want a lot more from its stores than just affordable Scandinavian-designed furniture:[21]

In Chinese, IKEA is known as Yi Jia. Translated, it means "comfortable home," a concept taken literally by the millions of consumers who visit one of IKEA's 18 huge Chinese stores each year. "Customers come on family outings, hop into display beds and nap, pose for snapshots with the décor, and hang out for hours to enjoy the air conditioning and free soda refills," notes one observer. On a typical Saturday afternoon, for example, display beds and other furniture in a huge Chinese IKEA store are occupied with customers of all ages lounging or even fast asleep. One Chinese IKEA has even hosted several weddings. IKEA managers encourage such behavior, figuring that familiarity with the store will result in later purchasing when shoppers' incomes eventually rise to match their aspirations. "Maybe if you've been visiting IKEA, eating meatballs, hot dogs, or ice cream for 10 years, then maybe you will consider IKEA when you get yourself a sofa," says the company's Asia-Pacific president. Thanks to such cultural understandings coupled with competitively low prices, China was IKEA's fastest-growing market last year. What do Chinese consumers think of Swedish meatballs? "They love them," says IKEA China's marketing director.

≫ **The impact of culture on marketing strategy: IKEA customers in China want a lot more from its stores than just affordable Scandinavian-designed furniture.**

ZUMA Press, Inc./Alamy

Thus, understanding cultural traditions, preferences, and behaviors can help companies not only avoid embarrassing mistakes but also take advantage of cross-cultural opportunities.

The Impact of Marketing Strategy on Cultures

Whereas marketers worry about the impact of global cultures on their marketing strategies, others may worry about the impact of marketing strategies on global cultures. For example, social critics contend that large American multinationals, such as McDonald's, Coca-Cola, Starbucks, Nike, Google, Disney, and Facebook, aren't just globalizing their brands; they are Americanizing the world's cultures. Other elements of American culture have become pervasive worldwide. For instance, more people now study English in China than speak it in the United States. If you assemble businesspeople from Brazil, Germany, and China, they'll likely transact in English. And the thing that binds the world's teens together in a kind of global community, notes one observer, "is American culture—the music, the Hollywood fare, the electronic games, Google, Facebook, American consumer brands. The ... rest of the world is becoming [evermore] like us—in ways good and bad."[22]

"Today, globalization often wears Mickey Mouse ears, eats Big Macs, drinks Coke or Pepsi, and does its computing with Windows," says Thomas Friedman in his book *The Lexus and the Olive Tree: Understanding Globalization.* "Some Chinese kids' first English word [is] Mickey," notes another writer.[23]

Critics worry that, under such "McDomination," countries around the globe are losing their individual cultural identities. Teens in Turkey watch MTV, connect with others globally through Facebook and Twitter, and ask their parents for more Westernized clothes and other symbols of American pop culture and values. Grandmothers in small European villas no longer spend each morning visiting local meat, bread, and produce markets to gather the ingredients for dinner. Instead, they now shop at Walmart. Women in Saudi Arabia see American films, question their societal roles, and shop at any of the country's growing number of Victoria's Secret boutiques. In China, most people never drank coffee before Starbucks entered the market. Now Chinese consumers rush to Starbucks stores because it symbolizes a new kind of lifestyle. Similarly, in China, where McDonald's operates more than 80 restaurants in Beijing alone, nearly half of all children identify the chain as a domestic brand.

Such concerns have sometimes led to a backlash against American globalization. Well-known U.S. brands have become the targets of boycotts and protests in some international markets. As symbols of American capitalism, companies such as Coca-Cola, McDonald's, Nike, and KFC have been singled out by protestors and governments in hot spots around the world, especially when anti-American sentiment peaks. For example, following Russia's annexation of Crimea and the resulting sanctions by the West, Russian authorities initiated a crackdown on McDonald's franchises (even though most were Russian-owned), forcing some to close for uncertain reasons. The three McDonald's in Crimea were shuttered, with at least one becoming a nationalist chain outlet called Rusburger, serving "Czar Cheeseburgers" where Quarter Pounders once flowed.[24]

Despite such problems, defenders of globalization argue that concerns of Americanization and the potential damage to American brands are overblown. U.S. brands are doing very well internationally. In the most recent Millward Brown BrandZ brand value survey of global consumer brands, 19 of the top 25 global brands were American owned, including megabrands such as Google, Apple, IBM, Microsoft, McDonald's, Coca-Cola, GE, Amazon.com, and Walmart.[25]

Many iconic American brands are soaring globally. For example, most international markets covet American fast food. Consider KFC in Japan. On the day that KFC introduced its outrageous Double Down sandwich—bacon, melted cheese, and a "secret sauce" between two deep-fried chicken patties—in one of its restaurants in Japan, fans formed long lines and slept on the sidewalks outside to get a taste. "It was like the iPhone," says the CMO of KFC International, "people [were] crazy." The U.S. limited-time item has since become a runaway success worldwide, from Canada to Australia, the Philippines, and Malaysia. ≫ More broadly, KFC has become its own cultural institution in Japan. For instance, the brand has long been one of Japan's leading Christmas dining traditions, with the iconic Colonel Sanders standing in as a kind of Japanese Father Christmas:[26]

≫ **American brands in other cultures:** KFC has become one of Japan's leading Christmas dining traditions, with the iconic Colonel Sanders standing in as a kind of Japanese Father Christmas.

Anthea Freshwater

Japan's KFC Christmas tradition began more than 40 years ago when the company unleashed a "Kentucky for Christmas" advertising campaign in Japan to help the brand get off the ground. Now, eating Kentucky Fried Chicken has become one of the country's most popular holiday traditions. Each KFC store displays a life-size Colonel Sanders statue, adorned in a traditional fur-trimmed red suit and Santa hat. A month in advance, Japanese customers order their special Christmas meal—a special bucket of fried chicken with wine and cake for about US $40. Those who don't preorder risk standing in lines that snake around the block or having to go without KFC's coveted blend of 11 herbs and spices altogether. Christmas Eve is KFC's most successful sales day of the year in Japan, and December monthly sales run as much as 10 times greater than sales in other months.

More fundamentally, the cultural exchange goes both ways: America gets as well as gives cultural influence. True, Hollywood dominates the global movie market, but British TV originated the programming that was Americanized into such hits as *House of Cards* and *Dancing with the Stars*. Although Chinese and Russian youth are donning NBA superstar jerseys, the increasing popularity of soccer in America has deep international roots.

Even American childhood has been increasingly influenced by European and Asian cultural imports. Most kids know all about imports such as Hello Kitty, the Bakugan Battle Brawler, or any of a host of Nintendo or Sega game characters. And J. K. Rowling's so-very-British Harry Potter books shaped the thinking of a generation of American youngsters, not to mention the millions of American oldsters who fell under their spell as well. For the moment, English remains the dominant language of the Internet, and having Web and mobile access often means that third-world youth have greater exposure to American popular culture. Yet these same technologies let Eastern European students studying in the United States hear Webcast news and music from Poland, Romania, or Belarus.

Thus, globalization is a two-way street. If globalization has Mickey Mouse ears, it is also talking on a Samsung smartphone, buying furniture at IKEA, driving a Toyota Camry, and watching a British-inspired show on a Panasonic LED TV.

Deciding Whether to go Global

Not all companies need to venture into international markets to survive. For example, most local businesses need to market well only in their local marketplaces. Operating domestically is easier and safer. Managers don't need to learn another country's language and laws. They don't have to deal with unstable currencies, face political and legal uncertainties, or redesign their products to suit different customer expectations. However, companies that operate in global industries, where their strategic positions in specific markets are affected strongly by their overall global positions, must compete on a regional or worldwide basis to succeed.

Any of several factors might draw a company into the international arena. For example, global competitors might attack the company's home market by offering better products or lower prices. The company might want to counterattack these competitors in their home markets to tie up their resources. The company's customers might be expanding abroad and require international servicing. Or, most likely, international markets might simply provide better opportunities for growth. For example, as note previously, Coca-Cola has emphasized international growth in recent years to offset stagnant or declining U.S. soft drink sales. Today, non-U.S. sales account for 57 percent of Coca-Cola's total revenues and 83 percent of its net income, and the company is making major pushes into 90 emerging markets, such as China, India, and the entire African continent.[27]

Before going abroad, the company must weigh several risks and answer many questions about its ability to operate globally. Can the company learn to understand the preferences and buyer behavior of consumers in other countries? Can it offer competitively attractive products? Will it be able to adapt to other countries' business cultures and deal effectively with foreign nationals? Do the company's managers have the necessary international experience? Has management considered the impact of regulations and the political environments of other countries?

Deciding Which Markets to Enter

Before going abroad, the company should try to define its international *marketing objectives and policies*. It should decide what *volume* of foreign sales it wants. Most companies start small when they go abroad. Some plan to stay small, seeing international sales as a small part of their business. Other companies have bigger plans, however, seeing international business as equal to—or even more important than—their domestic business.

The company also needs to choose in *how many* countries it wants to market. Companies must be careful not to spread themselves too thin or expand beyond their capabilities by operating in too many countries too soon. Next, the company needs to decide on the *types* of countries to enter. A country's attractiveness depends on the product, geographical factors, income and population, political climate, and other considerations. In recent years, many major new markets have emerged, offering both substantial opportunities and daunting challenges.

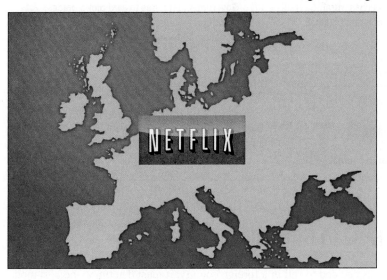

>> **Entering new global markets: Netflix's decision to expand into new European markets seems like a no-brainer. But despite its huge market potential, Europe presents Netflix with some formidable challenges.**

PSL Images/Alamy (logo)/Abstract images/Alamy (map)

After listing possible international markets, the company must carefully evaluate each one. It must consider many factors. >> For example, Netflix's decision to expand into European markets such as Germany, France, Austria, and Switzerland seems like a no-brainer. Netflix needs to grow its subscriber base to cover rapidly rising content costs, and Europe offers huge opportunities. Western Europe boasts 134 million broadband homes, compared with 94 million in the United States. The as-yet-largely-untapped European video-services market is expected to grow by 67 percent to more than $1.1 billion by 2017. Netflix has already entered the UK and the Nordic nations and is the leading video service in Sweden after only two years.[28]

However, as Netflix considers expanding into new European markets, it must ask some important questions. Can it compete effectively on a country-by-country basis with local competitors? Can it master the varied cultural and buying differences of European consumers? Will it be able to meet environmental and regulatory hurdles in each country? For example, Netflix's expansion has been slow and difficult in Latin America, where e-commerce is less established.

In entering new European markets, Netflix will face many challenges. For example, Europe is now crowded with formidable competitors. More than a dozen local Netflix-like rivals have sprung up there during the past few years—services such as Snap in Germany, Infinity in Italy, and CanalPlay in France have been busy locking in subscribers and content rights. And Amazon.com's Prime Instant Video is already the leading streaming service in Germany.

Content is another major consideration. Although Netflix is building its own portfolio of international content rights, European competitors already own exclusive in-country rights to many popular U.S. and non-U.S. shows. Netflix may also encounter local regulatory obstacles. Regulations in France, for instance, restrict services like Netflix from airing films until three years after they open nationally in theaters, and video services there are usually required to invest in film production in the country. Despite these challenges, however, Netflix CEO Reed Hastings seems unfazed. "We can still build a very successful business [in these new markets]," he says. Wherever Netflix goes, "I think the key is having unique content, a great reputation, and a good value proposition," things at which Netflix excels.

Possible global markets should be ranked on several factors, including market size, market growth, the cost of doing business, competitive advantage, and risk level. The goal is to determine the potential of each market, using indicators such as those shown in >> Table 15.1. Then the marketer must decide which markets offer the greatest long-run return on investment.

≫ Table 15.1 | Indicators of Market Potential

Demographic Characteristics	Sociocultural Factors
Education	Consumer lifestyles, beliefs, and values
Population size and growth	Business norms and approaches
Population age composition	Cultural and social norms
	Languages

Geographic Characteristics	Political and Legal Factors
Climate	National priorities
Country size	Political stability
Population density—urban, rural	Government attitudes toward global trade
Transportation structure and market accessibility	Government bureaucracy
	Monetary and trade regulations

Economic Factors

GDP size and growth
Income distribution
Industrial infrastructure
Natural resources
Financial and human resources

Author Comment

A company has many options for entering an international market, from simply exporting its products to working jointly with foreign companies to setting up its own foreign-based operations.

Deciding How to Enter the Market

Once a company has decided to sell in a foreign country, it must determine the best mode of entry. Its choices are *exporting, joint venturing*, and *direct investment*. ≫Figure 15.2 shows the three market entry strategies along with the options each one offers. As the figure shows, each succeeding strategy involves more commitment and risk but also more control and potential profits.

Exporting

Exporting
Entering foreign markets by selling goods produced in the company's home country, often with little modification.

The simplest way to enter a foreign market is through **exporting**. The company may passively export its surpluses from time to time, or it may make an active commitment to expand exports to a particular market. In either case, the company produces all its goods in its home country. It may or may not modify them for the export market. Exporting involves the least change in the company's product lines, organization, investments, or mission.

≫ Figure 15.2 Market Entry Strategies

Companies typically start with *indirect exporting*, working through independent international marketing intermediaries. Indirect exporting involves less investment because the firm does not require an overseas marketing organization or network. It also involves less risk. International marketing intermediaries bring know-how and services to the relationship, so the seller normally makes fewer mistakes. Sellers may eventually move into *direct exporting*, whereby they handle their own exports. The investment and risk are somewhat greater in this strategy, but so is the potential return.

Joint Venturing

Joint venturing

Entering foreign markets by joining with foreign companies to produce or market products or services.

A second method of entering a foreign market is by **joint venturing**—joining with foreign companies to produce or market products or services. Joint venturing differs from exporting in that the company joins with a host country partner to sell or market abroad. It differs from direct investment in that an association is formed with someone in the foreign country. There are four types of joint ventures: *licensing, contract manufacturing, management contracting*, and *joint ownership*.

Licensing

Licensing

Entering foreign markets through developing an agreement with a licensee in the foreign market.

Licensing is a simple way for a manufacturer to enter international marketing. The company enters into an agreement with a licensee in the foreign market. For a fee or royalty payments, the licensee buys the right to use the company's manufacturing process, trademark, patent, trade secret, or other item of value. The company thus gains entry into a foreign market at little risk; at the same time, the licensee gains production expertise or a well-known product or name without having to start from scratch.

In Japan, Budweiser beer flows from Kirin breweries, and Mizkan produces Sunkist lemon juice, drinks, and dessert items. ≫Tokyo Disney Resort is owned and operated by Oriental Land Company under license from The Walt Disney Company. The 45-year license gives Disney licensing fees plus a percentage of admissions and food and merchandise sales. And Coca-Cola markets internationally by licensing bottlers around the world and supplying them with the syrup needed to produce the product. Its global bottling partners range from the Coca-Cola Bottling Company of Saudi Arabia to Europe-based Coca-Cola Hellenic, which bottles and markets 136 Coca-Cola brands to 589 million people in 28 countries, from Italy and Greece to Nigeria and Russia.[29]

Licensing has potential disadvantages, however. The firm has less control over the licensee than it would over its own operations. Furthermore, if the licensee is very successful, the firm has given up these profits, and if and when the contract ends, it may find it has created a competitor.

≫ **International licensing: The Tokyo Disney Resort is owned and operated by Oriental Land Company (a Japanese development company) under license from The Walt Disney Company.**

David Harding/Alamy

Contract Manufacturing

Contract manufacturing

A joint venture in which a company contracts with manufacturers in a foreign market to produce its product or provide its service.

Another option is **contract manufacturing**, in which the company makes agreements with manufacturers in the foreign market to produce its product or provide its service. For example, P&G serves 650 million consumers across India with the help of nine contract manufacturing sites there. And Volkswagen contracts with Russia's largest auto manufacturer, GAZ Group, to make Volkswagen Jettas for the Russian market as well as its Škoda (VW's Czech Republic subsidiary) Octavia and Yeti models sold there.[30] The drawbacks of contract manufacturing are decreased control over the manufacturing process and loss of potential profits on manufacturing. The benefits are the chance to start faster, with less risk, and the later opportunity either to form a partnership with or buy out the local manufacturer. Contract manufacturing can also reduce plant investment, transportation, and tariff costs while at the same time helping to meet the host country's local manufacturing requirements.

Management contracting

A joint venture in which the domestic firm supplies the management know-how to a foreign company that supplies the capital; the domestic firm exports management services rather than products.

Management Contracting

Under **management contracting**, the domestic firm provides the management know-how to a foreign company that supplies the capital. In other words, the domestic firm exports management services rather than products. Hilton uses this arrangement in managing hotels around the world. For example, the hotel chain operates DoubleTree by Hilton hotels in countries ranging from the UK and Italy to Peru and Costa Rica to China, Russia, and Tanzania. The properties are locally owned, but Hilton manages the hotels with its world-renowned hospitality expertise.[31]

Management contracting is a low-risk method of getting into a foreign market, and it yields income from the beginning. The arrangement is even more attractive if the contracting firm has an option to buy some share in the managed company later on. The arrangement is not sensible, however, if the company can put its scarce management talent to better uses or if it can make greater profits by undertaking the whole venture. Management contracting also prevents the company from setting up its own operations for a period of time.

Joint Ownership

Joint ownership

A cooperative venture in which a company creates a local business with investors in a foreign market who share ownership and control.

Joint ownership ventures consist of one company joining forces with foreign investors to create a local business in which they share possession and control. A company may buy an interest in a local firm, or the two parties may form a new business venture. Joint ownership may be needed for economic or political reasons. For example, the firm may lack the financial, physical, or managerial resources to undertake the venture alone. Alternatively, a foreign government may require joint ownership as a condition for entry.

Often, companies form joint ownership ventures to merge their complementary strengths in developing a global marketing opportunity. >> For example, to increase its presence and local influence in China's mobile phone and tablets markets, chipmaker Intel recently paid $1.5 billion for 20 percent ownership in China's state-run Tsinghua Unigroup, which controls two domestic mobile chipmakers. The joint ownership investment will help Intel to better understand Chinese consumers. It may also help to earn more favorable treatment from Chinese regulators. So far, Intel has gone untouched by China's recent crackdown on foreign technology companies such as competitor Qualcomm and software makers Microsoft and Symantec.[32]

Joint ownership has certain drawbacks, however. The partners may disagree over investment, marketing, or other policies. Whereas many U.S. firms like to reinvest earnings for growth, local firms often prefer to take out these earnings; whereas U.S. firms emphasize the role of marketing, local investors may rely on selling.

>> Joint ownership and direct investment: To increase its understanding and influence in China's huge mobile device market, Intel has invested heavily there in joint ownership ventures and its own manufacturing facilities.

Jing Wei/Imaginechina/AP Images

Direct Investment

Direct investment

Entering a foreign market by developing foreign-based assembly or manufacturing facilities.

The biggest involvement in a foreign market comes through **direct investment**—the development of foreign-based assembly or manufacturing facilities. For example, in addition to joint ownership ventures in China, Intel has also made substantial investments in its own manufacturing and research facilities there. It recently spent $1.6 billion upgrading its decade-old chip factory in the central Chinese city of Chengdu and another $2.5 billion to build a shiny new fabrication plant in Dalian, a port city in China's northeast. "China is our fastest-growing major market," says Intel's CEO, "and we believe it's critical that we invest in markets that will provide for future growth to better serve our customers."[33]

If a company has gained experience in exporting and if the foreign market is large enough, foreign production facilities offer many advantages. The firm may have lower costs in the form of cheaper labor or raw materials, foreign government investment incentives, and freight savings. The firm may also improve its image in the host country because it creates jobs. Generally, a firm develops a deeper relationship with the government, customers, local suppliers, and distributors, allowing it to adapt its products to the local market better.

Finally, the firm keeps full control over the investment and therefore can develop manufacturing and marketing policies that serve its long-term international objectives.

The main disadvantage of direct investment is that the firm faces many risks, such as restricted or devalued currencies, falling markets, or government changes. In some cases, a firm has no choice but to accept these risks if it wants to operate in the host country.

LINKING THE CONCEPTS

Slow down here and think about McDonald's global marketing issues.

- To what extent can McDonald's standardize for the Chinese market? What marketing strategy and program elements can be similar to those used in the United States and other parts of the Western world? Which ones must be adapted? Be specific.
- To what extent can McDonald's standardize its strategy, products, and programs for the Canadian market? What elements can be standardized, and which must be adapted?
- To what extent are McDonald's "globalization" efforts contributing to "Americanization" of countries and cultures around the world? What are the positives and negatives of such cultural developments?

<table>
<tr><td>

Author Comment

The major global marketing decision usually boils down to this: How much, if at all, should a company adapt its marketing strategy and programs to local markets? How might the answer differ for Boeing versus McDonald's?

</td><td>

Deciding on the Global Marketing Program

Companies that operate in one or more foreign markets must decide how much, if at all, to adapt their marketing strategies and programs to local conditions. At one extreme are global companies that use **standardized global marketing**, essentially using the same marketing strategy approaches and marketing mix worldwide. At the other extreme is **adapted global marketing**. In this case, the producer adjusts the marketing strategy and mix elements to each international target market, resulting in more costs but hopefully producing a larger market share and return.

</td></tr>
</table>

Standardized global marketing
A global marketing strategy that basically uses the same marketing strategy and mix in all of the company's international markets.

Adapted global marketing
A global marketing approach that adjusts the marketing strategy and mix elements to each international target market, which creates more costs but hopefully produces a larger market share and return.

The question of whether to adapt or standardize the marketing strategy and program has been much debated over the years. On the one hand, some global marketers believe that technology is making the world a smaller place, and consumer needs around the world are becoming more similar. This paves the way for global brands and standardized global marketing. Global branding and standardization, in turn, result in greater brand power and reduced costs from economies of scale.

On the other hand, the marketing concept holds that marketing programs will be more engaging if tailored to the unique needs of each targeted customer group. If this concept applies within a country, it should apply even more across international markets. Despite global convergence, consumers in different countries still have widely varied cultural backgrounds. They still differ significantly in their needs and wants, spending power, product preferences, and shopping patterns. Because these differences are hard to change, most marketers today adapt their products, prices, channels, and promotions to fit consumer desires in each country.

However, global standardization is not an all-or-nothing proposition. It's a matter of degree. Most international marketers suggest that companies should "think globally but act locally." They should seek a balance between standardization and adaptation, leveraging global brand recognition but adapting their marketing, products, and operations to specific markets. For example, as discussed in the story at the start of this chapter, cosmetics and beauty care giant L'Oréal and its brands are truly global. But the company's outstanding international success comes from achieving a global–local balance that adapts and differentiates brands to make them responsive to local needs while also integrating them across world markets to optimize their global impact.

Collectively, local brands still account for the overwhelming majority of consumer purchases. Most consumers, wherever they live, lead very local lives. So a global brand must engage consumers at a local level, respecting the culture and becoming a part of it. Starbucks operates this way. The company's overall brand strategy provides global strategic direction. Then regional or local units focus on adapting the strategy and brand to

Straight product extension
Marketing a product in a foreign market without making significant changes to the product.

Product adaptation
Adapting a product to meet local conditions or wants in foreign markets.

specific local markets. >> For example, when Starbucks entered China in 1998, given the strong Chinese tea-drinking culture, few observers expected success. But Starbucks quickly proved the doubters wrong:[34]

> Starbucks's success in China results from building on its global brand identity and values while at the same time adapting its brand strategy to the unique characteristics of Chinese consumers. Rather than forcing U.S. products on the Chinese, Starbucks developed new flavors—such as green tea–flavored coffee drinks—that appeal to local tastes. Rather than just charging U.S.-style premium prices in China, Starbucks boosted prices even higher, positioning the brand as a status symbol for the rapidly growing Chinese middle and upper classes. And rather than pushing takeout orders, which account for most of its U.S. revenues, Starbucks promoted dine-in services—making its stores the perfect meeting place for Chinese professionals and their friends. Whereas U.S. locations do about 70 percent of their business before 10 am, China stores do more than 70 percent of their business in the afternoon and evening. "It's a lifestyle to the Chinese," says the head of Starbucks's China and Asia Pacific operations. "It's much more of a gathering place for social occasions." Under this adapted strategy, Starbucks China is thriving. China is now Starbucks's largest market outside of the United States, with more than 1,700 current stores and 1,700 more stores in 70 cities planned by 2020. "We're trying to build a different kind of company in China and are mindful of how we grow while maintaining the heart and soul of what Starbucks stands for," says the Starbucks executive.

Product

Five strategies are used for adapting product and marketing communication strategies to a global market (see >>**Figure 15.3**).[35] We first discuss the three product strategies and then turn to the two communication strategies.

Straight product extension means marketing a product in a foreign market without making significant changes to the product. Top management tells its marketing people, "Take the product as is and find customers for it." The first step, however, should be to find out whether foreign consumers use that product and what form they prefer.

Straight extension has been successful in some cases and disastrous in others. Apple iPads, Gillette razors, Black & Decker tools, and even 7-Eleven Slurpees are all sold successfully in about the same form around the world. But when General Foods introduced its standard powdered JELL-O in the British market, it discovered that British consumers prefer a solid wafer or cake form. Likewise, Philips began to make a profit in Japan only after it reduced the size of its coffeemakers to fit into smaller Japanese kitchens and its shavers to fit smaller Japanese hands. And Panasonic's refrigerator sales in China surged 10-fold in a single year after it shaved the width of its appliances by 15 percent to fit smaller Chinese kitchens.[36] Straight extension is tempting because it involves no additional product development costs, manufacturing changes, or new promotion. But it can be costly in the long run if products fail to satisfy consumers in specific global markets.

Product adaptation involves changing the product to meet local requirements, conditions, or wants. For example, McDonald's operates in more than 100 countries, with sometimes widely varying local food preferences. So although you'll find its

>> **Figure 15.3 Five Global Product and Communications Strategies**

The real question buried in this figure is this: How much should a company standardize or adapt its products and marketing across global markets?

	Product		
Communications	**Don't change** product	**Adapt** product	**Develop new** product
Don't change communications	Straight extension	Product adaptation	Product invention
Adapt communications	Communication adaptation	Dual adaptation	

signature burgers and fries in most locations around the world, the chain has added menu items that meet the unique taste buds of customers in local markets. McDonald's serves salmon burgers in Norway, mashed-potato burgers in China, shrimp burgers in Japan, a Samurai Pork Burger in Thailand, chicken porridge in Malaysia, and Spam and eggs in Hawaii. In a German McDonald's, you'll find the Nürnburger (three large bratwurst on a soft roll with lots of mustard, of course); in Israel, there's the McFalafel (chickpea fritters, tomatoes, cucumber, and cheese topped with tahini and wrapped in lafa). And menus in Turkey feature a chocolate orange fried pie (Brazil adds banana, Egypt taro, and Hawaii pineapple).

In many major global markets, McDonald's adapts more than just its menu. It also adjusts its restaurant design and operations. For example, McDonald's France has redefined itself as a French company that adapts to the needs and preferences of French consumers:[37]

"France—the land of haute cuisine, fine wine, and cheese—would be the last place you would expect to find a thriving [McDonald's]," opines one observer. Yet the fast-food giant has turned France into its second-most-profitable world market. Although a McDonald's in Paris might at first seem a lot like one in Chicago, McDonald's has carefully adapted its French operations to the preferences of local customers. At the most basic level, although a majority of revenues still come from burgers and fries, McDonald's France has changed its menu to please the French palate. For instance, it offers up burgers with French cheeses such as chevre, cantel, and bleu, topped off with whole-grain French mustard sauce. And French consumers love baguettes, so McDonald's bakes them fresh in its restaurants and sells them in oh-so-French McBaguette sandwiches.

But perhaps the biggest difference isn't in the food, but in the design of the restaurants themselves, which have been adapted to suit French lifestyles. For example, French meal times tend to be longer, with more food consumed per sitting. So McDonald's has refined its restaurant interiors to create a comfortable, welcoming environment where customers want to linger and perhaps order an additional coffee or dessert. McDonald's even provides table-side service. As a result, the average French McDonald's customer spends about four times what an American customer spends per visit.

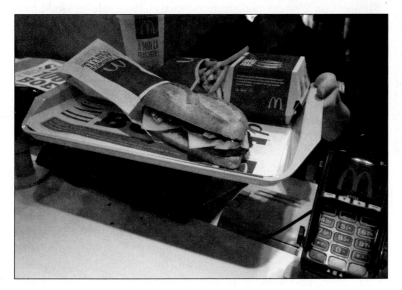

>> **Product adaptation:** By leveraging the power of its global brand but constantly adapting to the needs and preferences of French consumers and their culture, McDonald's has turned France into its second-most-profitable world market.

AFP/Getty Images

Product invention
Creating new products or services for foreign markets.

Product invention consists of creating something new to meet the needs of consumers in a given country. As markets have gone global, companies ranging from appliance manufacturers and carmakers to candy and soft drink producers have developed products that meet the special purchasing needs of low-income consumers in developing economies.

For example, Chinese appliance producer Haier developed sturdier washing machines for rural users in emerging markets, where it found that lighter-duty machines often became clogged with mud when farmers used them to clean vegetables as well as clothes. And solar lighting manufacturer d.light Solar has developed affordable solar-powered home lighting systems for the hundreds of millions of people in the developing world who don't have access to reliable power. d.light's hanging lamps and portable lanterns require no energy source other than the sun and can last up to 15 hours on one charge. The company has already reached 49 million users, is adding 1 million users per month and plans to reach 100 million users by 2020.[38]

Promotion

Companies can either adopt the same communication strategy they use in the home market or change it for each local market. Consider advertising messages. Some global companies use a standardized advertising theme around the world. For example, Chevrolet recently

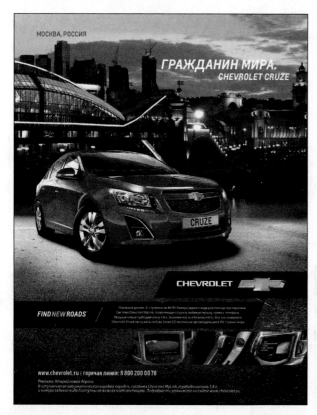

МОСКВА, РОССИЯ

ГРАЖДАНИН МИРА.
CHEVROLET CRUZE

CRUZE

CHEVROLET

FIND NEW ROADS

www.chevrolet.ru | горячая линия: 8 800 200 00 76

>> **Communication standardization:** With nearly two-thirds of its sales now outside the United States, Chevy recently switched to a new, more global "Find New Roads" positioning and advertising theme that has meaning in all markets worldwide, here Russia.

General Motors, LLC

Communication adaptation
A global communication strategy of fully adapting advertising messages to local markets.

swapped out its previous, American-focused "Chevy Runs Deep" positioning and advertising theme with a more global "Find New Roads" theme. >> The new theme is one "that works in all markets," says a GM marketing executive. "The theme has meaning in mature markets like the U.S. as well as emerging markets like Russia and India, where the potential for continued growth is the greatest." The time is right for a more globally consistent Chevy brand message. Chevrolet sells cars in more than 140 countries, and nearly two-thirds of its sales are now outside the United States, compared with only about one-third a decade ago.[39]

Of course, even in highly standardized communications campaigns, some adjustments might be required for language and cultural differences. For example, ads for Pepsi's youthful "Live for Now" campaign have a similar look worldwide but are adapted in different global markets to feature local consumers, languages, and events. Similarly, in Western markets, fast-casual clothing retailer H&M runs fashion ads with models showing liberal amounts of bare skin. But in the Middle East, where attitudes toward public nudity are more conservative, the retailer runs the same ads digitally adapted to better cover its models.

Global companies often have difficulty crossing the language barrier, with results ranging from mild embarrassment to outright failure. Seemingly innocuous brand names and advertising phrases can take on unintended or hidden meanings when translated into other languages. For example, Interbrand of London, the firm that created household names such as Prozac and Acura, recently developed a brand name "hall of shame" list, which contained these and other foreign brand names you're never likely to see inside the local Kroger supermarket: Krapp toilet paper (Denmark), Plopp chocolate (Scandinavia), Crapsy Fruit cereal (France), Poo curry powder (Argentina), and Pschitt lemonade (France). Similarly, advertising themes often lose—or gain—something in the translation. In Chinese, the KFC slogan "finger-lickin' good" came out as "eat your fingers off." And Motorola's Hellomoto ringtone sounds like "Hello, Fatty" in India.

Marketers must be watchful to avoid such mistakes, taking great care when localizing their brand names and messages to specific global markets. In important but culturally different markets such as China, finding just the right name can make or break a brand (see Marketing at Work 15.2).

Rather than standardizing their advertising globally, other companies follow a strategy of **communication adaptation**, fully adapting their advertising messages to local markets. For example, in the United States and most Western countries, where running is accepted as a positive, healthful activity, Nike advertising focuses on products and personal performance. In China, however, running is viewed as a boring sport or even a punishment—something rigorous and painful. It's not something that most people in Asia's polluted cities choose to do, especially on streets jammed with pedestrians, bicycles, cars, and even rickshaws. "The joke is that when there's a person running in the city (and it's often a Westerner), people turn to see who's chasing him," quips one observer.

However, China is the largest footwear market in the world, offering huge untapped potential for Nike. So, in China, rather than pushing products and performance, Nike's advertising focuses on just trying to get more Chinese to put on running shoes. Ads and social media feature ordinary people who choose to run on city streets, letting them relate their reasons in their own words. "I run to make the hidden visible," says one young woman. "I run to get lost," says another. Salad—a stressed-out office worker who lives and runs in Shanghai—relates: "The city is always noisy and busy. This adds even more pressure to my day. I guess for me, running is about shutting down the noise." To make running a more social activity, Nike also sponsors nighttime "Lunar Runs" in big cities like Beijing and marathons in Shanghai, featuring fitness instructors, live music, and

MARKETING AT WORK 15.2

Localizing Chinese Brand Names: Very Important but Notoriously Tricky

After a long day's work, an average upscale Beijinger can't wait to dash home, lace on a comfortable pair of Enduring and Persevering, pop the top on a refreshing can of Tasty Fun, then hop into his Dashing Speed and head to the local tavern for a frosty glass of Happiness Power with friends. Translation? In China, those are the brand-name meanings for Nike, Coca-Cola, Mercedes, and Heineken, respectively.

To Westerners, such names sound pretty silly, but to brands doing business in China, the world's biggest and fastest-growing consumer market, they are no laughing matter. Perhaps more than anywhere else in the world, brand names in China take on deep significance. Finding just the right name can make or break a brand. "Often, a company's most important marketing decision in China is localizing its name," asserts one global branding analyst. "It's also a notoriously tricky one."

Ideally, to maintain global consistency, the Chinese name should sound similar to the original, while at the same time conveying the brand's benefits in meaningful symbolic terms. Nike's Chinese brand name, Nai ke, does this well. Not only does it sound the same when pronounced in Chinese, its "Enduring and Persevering" meaning powerfully encapsulates the "Just Do It" essence of the Nike brand the world over. Similarly, P&G's Tide is Taizi in China, which translates to "gets out the dirt," a perfect moniker for a tough-acting detergent. Coca-Cola's Chinese name—Ke kou ke le—dates all the way back to 1928. It not only sounds much like the English name, the Chinese symbols convey happiness in the mouth, a close fit to Coca-Cola's current "open happiness" positioning. Other names that wear well on Chinese ears while also conveying a brand's essence include Lay's snack foods—Le shi ("happy things"); Reebok—Rui bu ("quick steps"); and Colgate—Gau lu jie ("revealing superior cleanliness").

Chinese brand names can convey subtle meanings that might not be apparent to Western sensibilities. For example, "Dashing Speed" seems appropriate enough for an upscale automobile brand like Mercedes. So does BMW's name—Bao Ma—which translates to "Precious Horse." However, in China, "precious" has a feminine connotation, whereas "dashing speed" is more masculine. This works out well for both car makers, which target different genders among China's upper crust. For instance, BMW is a market leader among affluent Chinese women.

Some brand names translate naturally. For example, when Garnier introduced its Clear shampoo in China, it lucked out. The Chinese word for "clear"—Qing—is one of a select few Chinese words with unusually positive associations that are used in many brand names. Garnier added the word *yang*, which means "flying" or "scattering to the wind." According to the director of Garnier's brand consultancy, the Qing Yang brand name connotes "very light, healthy, and happy—think of hair in the air," just what the brand intends. Other universally positive Chinese words commonly found in brand names include "le" and "xi" (happy), "li" (strength or power), "ma" (horse), and "fu" (lucky). Thus, Kia sells one model in China named Qian li ma, or "thousand kilometer horse," suggesting unusual strength.

There was a time when Western companies entering China simply created a brand name that was phonetically similar to the domestic name, even if it had no meaning in the Chinese language. In fact, such obviously foreign-looking and sounding names often communicated a sense of Western cache. For example, Cadillac went with Ka di la ke—a meaningless group of sounds that gave status to the luxury brand. And McDonald's got away with Mai dang lao, a term that sounds

>> **Brand names in China take on deep significance. Coca-Cola's Chinese name, when pronounced, sounds much like the English name, and the Chinese symbols convey "tasty fun" or "happiness in the mouth," a close fit to Coca-Cola's current worldwide "open happiness" positioning.**

Zhang Peng/Getty Images

like the English version but whose characters translate into gibberish—"wheat," "should," and "labor." Other global companies with short names such as IBM or Gap simply expect consumers to learn their Western names.

Today, however, with so many foreign brands entering the crowded Chinese market, most companies expect more of their Chinese brand names. If Chinese consumers can't pronounce a name or don't know what it stands for, they are much less likely to buy it or talk about it with others, in person or in social media. Instead, with some work, companies can come up with names that will engage and inspire buyers. In China, it's not Subway, it's Sai bai wei—"better than 100 tastes." It's not Marriott but Wan Hao, or "10,000 wealthy elites."

However, finding the right names and characters can be a daunting challenge. Brand name development in China has become more of a science than an art, involving global branding consultants, computer software, linguistic analysis, and extensive consumer testing. Some global names require careful recrafting. For example, Microsoft had to rethink the introduction of its Bing search engine in China, where the most common translations of the character pronounced "bing" are words like "defect" or "virus," not good

associations for a digital product. Microsoft changed the name of its product in China to Bi ying, which means "very certain to respond." Still, the brand is having difficulty shaking the resemblance to the original name.

Similarly, S.C. Johnson belatedly renamed its popular Mr. Muscle line of cleaners to Mr. Powerful (Weimeng xiansheng) in China, where Mr. Muscle had a less compelling second meaning—"Mr. Chicken Meat." And French automaker Peugeot thought it had a winning brand name with Biao zhi, only to learn too late that it was too close to biaozi, slang for prostitute. It's no surprise that the brand generated more off-color jokes than sales.

Sources: "Lost in Translation? Pick Your Chinese Brand Name Carefully," *Shanghalist*, March 28, 2014, http://shanghaiist.com/2014/03/28/hutong-school-pick-your-chinese-brand-name-carefully.php; Michael Wines, "Picking Brand Names in China Is a Business Itself," *New York Times*, November 12, 2011, p. A4; Carly Chalmers, "12 Amazing Translations of Chinese Brand Names," *todaytranslations*, August 27, 2013, www.todaytranslations.com/blog/12-amazing-translations-of-chinese-brand-names/; Angela Doland, "Why Western Companies Like LinkedIn Need Chinese Brand Names," *Advertising Age*, March 5, 2014, www.adage.com/print/291960/; and Alfred Maskeroni, "Can You Identify All These Famous Logos Redesigned by an Artist into Chinese?" *Adweek*, February 10, 2015, www.adweek.com/print/162867.

celebrities to introduce Chinese students and young professionals to running as a fun and rewarding after-class or after-work activity. The goal is to get more people to at least give running a try. But changing basic perceptions of the sport won't be easy. "It's a very long road for us," says a Nike China marketer.[40]

Media also need to be adapted internationally because media availability and regulations vary from country to country. TV advertising time is very limited in Europe, for instance, ranging from four hours a day in France to none in Scandinavian countries. Advertisers must buy time months in advance, and they have little control over airtimes. However, mobile phone ads are much more widely accepted in Europe and Asia than in the United States. Magazines also vary in effectiveness. For example, magazines are a major medium in Italy but a minor one in Austria. Newspapers are national in the United Kingdom but only local in Spain.[41]

Price

Companies also face many considerations in setting their international prices. For example, how might Makita price its power tools globally? It could set a uniform price globally, but this amount would be too high of a price in poor countries and not high enough in rich ones. It could charge what consumers in each country would bear, but this strategy ignores differences in the actual costs from country to country. Finally, the company could use a standard markup of its costs everywhere, but this approach might price Makita out of the market in some countries where costs are high.

Regardless of how companies go about pricing their products, their foreign prices probably will be higher than their domestic prices for comparable products. An Apple iPad Air that sells for $499 in the United States goes for $609 in the United Kingdom. Why? Apple faces a *price escalation* problem. It must add the cost of transportation, tariffs, importer margin, wholesaler margin, and retailer margin to its factory price. Depending on these added costs, a product may have to sell for two to five times as much in another country to make the same profit.

To overcome this problem when selling to less-affluent consumers in developing countries, many companies make simpler or smaller versions of their products that

International pricing: Lenovo's Motorola division developed the ultra-cheap Moto G smartphone intended primarily for emerging markets where consumers want low-cost phones.

ChinaFotoPress/Getty Images

can be sold at lower prices. Others have introduced new, more affordable brands for global markets. ≫ For example, Lenovo's Motorola division developed the ultra-cheap Moto G smartphone. Although not a flashy, high-tech gadget, the full-function device sells for only $179.99 in the United States with no contract. Motorola first introduced the phone in Brazil, one of the largest and fastest-growing emerging markets, then in other parts of South America, the Middle East, India, and more of Asia. Intended primarily for emerging markets where consumers want low-cost phones, the Moto G may also sell well to cost-conscious consumers in major developed markets, such as the United States and Europe. The Moto G phone puts pressure on Apple, which has focused on selling older models at reduced prices rather than developing cheaper models. The extremely affordable Moto G is now the most popular smartphone in Brazil, where it holds a sizable 18 percent market share, making Motorola the country's second-largest smartphone maker. The low-end phone also helped catapult a then-flagging Motorola into the number-four position in the huge Indian smartphone market.[42]

Recent economic and technological forces have had an impact on global pricing. For example, the Internet is making global price differences more obvious. When firms sell their wares over the Internet, customers can see how much products sell for in different countries. They can even order a given product directly from the company location or dealer offering the lowest price. This is forcing companies toward more standardized international pricing.

Distribution Channels

Whole-channel view

Designing international channels that take into account the entire global supply chain and marketing channel, forging an effective global value delivery network.

An international company must take a **whole-channel view** of the problem of distributing products to final consumers. ≫ **Figure 15.4** shows the two major links between the seller and the final buyer. The first link, *channels between nations*, moves company products from points of production to the borders of countries within which they are sold. The second link, *channels within nations*, moves products from their market entry points to the final consumers. The whole-channel view takes into account the entire global supply chain and marketing channel. It recognizes that to compete well internationally, the company must effectively design and manage an entire *global value delivery network*.

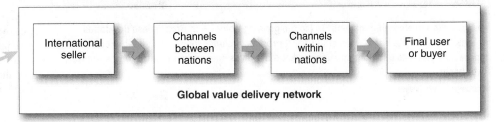

Distribution channels can vary dramatically around the world. For example, in the U.S., Coca-Cola distributes products through sophisticated retail channels. In less-developed countries, it delivers Coke using everything from push carts to delivery donkeys

International seller → Channels between nations → Channels within nations → Final user or buyer

Global value delivery network

≫ **Figure 15.4 Whole-Channel Concept for International Marketing**

Channels of distribution within countries vary greatly from nation to nation. There are large differences in the numbers and types of intermediaries serving each country market and in the transportation infrastructure serving these intermediaries. For example, whereas large-scale retail chains dominate the U.S. scene, most of the retailing in other countries is done by small, independent retailers. In India or Indonesia, millions of retailers operate tiny shops or sell in open markets.

Even in world markets containing similar types of sellers, retailing practices can vary widely. For example, you'll find plenty of Walmarts, Carrefours, Tescos, and other retail superstores in major Chinese cities. But whereas consumer brands sold in such stores in Western markets rely largely on self-service, brands in China hire armies of uniformed in-store promoters—called "promoter girls" or "push girls"—to dispense samples and pitch their products person to person. In a Beijing Walmart, on any given weekend, you'll find 100 or more such promoters acquainting customers with products from Kraft, Unilever, P&G, Johnson & Johnson, and a slew of local competitors. "Chinese consumers know the brand name through media," says the director of a Chinese retail marketing service, "but they want to feel the product and get a detailed understanding before they make a purchase."[43]

When selling in emerging markets, companies must often overcome distribution infrastructure and supply challenges. For example, in Nigeria, Domino's Pizza has had to dig wells and install water-treatment plants behind many of its restaurants to obtain clean water. And after having difficulty sourcing quality beef in South Africa, rather than buying scarce beef from scrawny cattle raised by local herdsmen, Burger King finally invested $5 million in its own local cattle ranch.[44]

Brazil's northeast region is its poorest, and many residents there lack access to basics such as roads and running water. But as it happens, northeast Brazil is also the region with the greatest growth in household income. So marketers are finding innovative ways to meet the distribution challenges in these regions to capture the growing potential there. Consider Nestlé:[45]

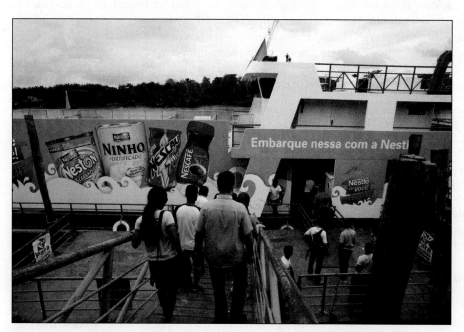

>> Marketing in emerging markets: To tap the growing potential in Brazil's less developed regions, Nestlé's "Ate Voce" ("Reaching You") program includes innovative distribution approaches, such as this floating supermarket that serves customers in the country's Amazon River basin.

Bloomberg via Getty Images

To tap the potential in less-developed regions of Brazil, Nestlé developed its "até Você" ("Reaching You") program, by which its reps go door to door with push carts—a method residents find very appealing—selling "kits" full of dairy products, cookies, yogurt, and desserts. More than just selling products, these Nestlé vendors are trained to serve as nutrition consultants, helping customers to develop healthier diets. >> To serve consumers in northeast Brazil's Amazon River basin, which lacks a solid network of roads and highways, Nestlé has even launched a floating supermarket that takes goods directly to consumers. Setting sail from Belem, Brazil's biggest city along the Amazon, the boat serves 1.5 million consumers in 27 riverside towns with 300 different Nestlé products. It spends one day at each stop. Customers can check the floating store's schedule at nestleatevoce.com.br, call a toll-free number, or text for more information and plan their shopping accordingly. This and other innovative até Você marketing initiatives are paying off for Nestlé. "Demand for our products has more than doubled in the north and northeast compared to other Brazilian regions," says Nestlé's marketing manager in Brazil.

Deciding on the Global Marketing Organization

Author Comment
Many large companies, regardless of their "home country," now think of themselves as truly *global* organizations. They view the entire world as a single borderless market. For example, although headquartered in Chicago, Boeing is as comfortable selling planes to Lufthansa or Air China as to American Airlines.

Companies manage their international marketing activities in at least three different ways: Most companies first organize an export department, then create an international division, and finally become a global organization.

A firm normally gets into international marketing by simply shipping out its goods. If its international sales expand, the company will establish an *export department* with a sales manager and a few assistants. As sales increase, the export department can expand to include various marketing services so that it can actively go after business. If the firm moves into joint ventures or direct investment, the export department will no longer be adequate.

Many companies get involved in several international markets and ventures. A company may export to one country, license to another, have a joint ownership venture in a third, and own a subsidiary in a fourth. Sooner or later it will create *international divisions* or subsidiaries to handle all its international activity.

International divisions are organized in a variety of ways. An international division's corporate staff consists of marketing, manufacturing, research, finance, planning, and personnel specialists. It plans for and provides services to various operating units, which can be organized in one of three ways. They can be *geographical organizations*, with country managers who are responsible for salespeople, sales branches, distributors, and licensees in their respective countries. Or the operating units can be *world product groups*, each responsible for worldwide sales of different product groups. Finally, operating units can be *international subsidiaries*, each responsible for their own sales and profits.

Many firms have passed beyond the international division stage and are truly *global organizations*. For example, as discussed in the chapter-opening story, despite its French origins, L'Oréal no longer has a clearly defined home market. Nor does it have a home-office staff. Instead, multicultural managers operate out of facilities located all around the world, bringing diverse cultural perspectives to their brands and operations.

Global organizations don't think of themselves as national marketers that sell abroad but as global marketers. The top corporate management and staff plan worldwide manufacturing facilities, marketing policies, financial flows, and logistical systems. The global operating units report directly to the chief executive or the executive committee of the organization, not to the head of an international division. Executives are trained in worldwide operations, not just domestic *or* international operations. Global companies recruit management from many countries, buy components and supplies where they cost the least, and invest where the expected returns are greatest.

Today, major companies must become more global if they hope to compete. As foreign companies successfully invade their domestic markets, companies must move more aggressively into foreign markets. They will have to change from companies that treat their international operations as secondary to companies that view the entire world as a single borderless market.

MyMarketingLab

If assigned by your instructor, complete the questions marked with the ⭐ from the EOC Discussion Questions section in the MyLab. To complete the Marketing by the Numbers problems found in this section, go to your Assignments in the MyLab.

REVIEWING AND EXTENDING THE CONCEPTS

CHAPTER REVIEW AND CRITICAL THINKING

Objectives Review

Companies today can no longer afford to pay attention only to their domestic market, regardless of its size. Many industries are global industries, and firms that operate globally achieve lower costs and higher brand awareness. At the same time, global marketing is risky because of variable exchange rates, unstable governments, tariffs and trade barriers, and several other factors. Given the potential gains and risks of international marketing, companies need a systematic way to make their global marketing decisions.

 OBJECTIVE 15-1 Discuss how the international trade system and the economic, political-legal, and cultural environments affect a company's international marketing decisions. (pp 460–472)

A company must understand the *global marketing environment*, especially the international trade system. It should assess each foreign market's *economic, political-legal*, and *cultural characteristics*. The company can then decide whether it wants to go abroad and consider the potential risks and benefits. It must decide on the volume of international sales it wants, how many countries it wants to market in, and which specific markets it wants to enter. These decisions call for weighing the probable returns against the level of risk.

 OBJECTIVE 15-2 Describe three key approaches to entering international markets. (pp 472–475)

The company must decide how to enter each chosen market—whether through *exporting, joint venturing*, or *direct investment*. Many companies start as exporters, move to joint ventures, and finally make a direct investment in foreign markets. In *exporting*, the company enters a foreign market by sending and selling products through international marketing intermediaries (indirect exporting) or the company's own department, branch, or sales representatives or agents (direct exporting). When establishing a *joint venture*, a company enters foreign markets by joining with foreign companies to produce or market a product or service. In *licensing*, the company enters a foreign market by contracting with a licensee in the foreign market and offering the right to use a manufacturing process, trademark, patent, trade secret, or other item of value for a fee or royalty.

 OBJECTIVE 15-3 Explain how companies adapt their marketing strategies and mixes for international markets. (pp 475–482)

Companies must also decide how much their marketing strategies and their products, promotion, price, and channels should be adapted for each foreign market. At one extreme, global companies use *standardized global marketing* worldwide. Others use *adapted global marketing*, in which they adjust the marketing strategy and mix to each target market, bearing more costs but hoping for a larger market share and return. However, global standardization is not an all-or-nothing proposition. It's a matter of degree. Most international marketers suggest that companies should "think globally but act locally"—that they should seek a balance between globally standardized strategies and locally adapted marketing mix tactics.

 OBJECTIVE 15-4 Identify the three major forms of international marketing organization. (p 483)

The company must develop an effective organization for international marketing. Most firms start with an *export department* and graduate to an *international division*. Large companies eventually become *global organizations*, with worldwide marketing planned and managed by the top officers of the company. Global organizations view the entire world as a single, borderless market.

Key Terms

Objective 15-1
Global firm (p 461)
Economic community (p 463)

Objective 15-2
Exporting (p 472)
Joint venturing (p 473)
Licensing (p 473)

Contract manufacturing (p 473)
Management contracting (p 474)
Joint ownership (p 474)
Direct investment (p 474)

Objective 15-3
Standardized global marketing (p 475)
Adapted global marketing (p 475)

Straight product extension (p 476)
Product adaptation (p 476)
Product invention (p 477)
Communication adaptation (p 478)
Whole-channel view (p 481)

Discussion Questions

15-1. Explain what is meant by the term *global firm* and list the major decisions involved in international marketing. (AASCB: Communication)

⭐ **15-2.** Discuss the four types of country industrial structures and the opportunities each offers to international marketers. (AACSB: Communication)

15-3. What factors do companies consider when deciding on possible global markets to enter? (AACSB: Communication; Reflective Thinking)

15-4. Name and describe the four types of joint ventures as methods for entering another country. How does joint venturing differ from other methods of entering a foreign market? (AACSB: Communication; Reflective Thinking)

15-5. Explain what is meant by a whole-channel view and why it is important in international marketing. (AACSB: Communication; Reflective Thinking)

Critical Thinking Exercises

⭐ **15-6.** Visit www.transparency.org and find the most recent Corruption Perceptions Index (CPI) report. What is the most recent CPI for the following countries: Argentina, Denmark, Jamaica, Myanmar, New Zealand, Somali, and the United States? What are the implications of this index for U.S.-based companies doing business in these countries? (AACSB: Communication; Use of IT; Reflective Thinking)

15-7. In a small group, identify and research an environmental threat—such as a regulatory threat, a cultural threat, or and economic threat—posed to global marketers.

Analyze the issues related to this threat, discuss how affected companies are reacting, and make recommendations regarding how these companies should address the threat. (AACSB: Communication; Reflective Thinking)

15-8. One way to analyze the cultural differences among countries is to conduct a Hofstede analysis. Visit www.geert-hofstede.com/ to learn what this analysis involves. Develop a presentation explaining how three countries of your choice differ from the United States. (AACSB: Communication; Use of IT; Reflective Thinking)

MINICASES AND APPLICATIONS

Online, Mobile, and Social Media Marketing   Russian E-commerce

Russia is emerging as the next big e-commerce frontier with a population of 143 million, 70 million of whom are Internet users. Although online sales in Russia are not has high as U.S. online sales, they have grown rapidly in the past few years. That fact has caught the attention of global e-commerce firms such as the U.S.'s Amazon and eBay and China's equivalent of Amazon, Alibaba. The leading local online retailer in Russia is Ozon Group, often referred to as "Russia's Amazon." Ozon's sales last year were close to $500 million, an almost 70 percent increase in just two years. There are obstacles to e-commerce in Russia, however. The majority of consumers do not have credit cards because many do not trust them to pay for purchases online or offline, making Russia a heavily cash-based marketplace. Delivery is another problem. To combat these barriers, Ozon developed its own courier system, and drivers

not only collect cash payments, they even offer style advice on apparel orders when delivered. Russian consumers ordering items from international e-commerce sites such as Amazon may never receive their packages. In fact, officials at Moscow airport reported having 500 metric tons of unprocessed packages in one month alone. Seeing an opportunity for revenue, Russia's Customs Service is considering import duties on packages ordered from foreign Web sites.

15-9. What types of barriers are present in Russia that might slow the expansion of international e-commerce there? (AACSB: Communication; Reflective Thinking)

15-10. Suggest the best ways companies such as eBay and Amazon can enter this market. (AACSB: Communication; Reflective Thinking)

Marketing Ethics   Global Safety Standards

India is home to some of the world's deadliest roads. However, international automobile makers do not provide standard safety features in entry-level cars sold in India that are required in other developed countries. India's death toll on the roads has ranked top in the world for eight straight years, exceeding 130,000 fatalities a year. Despite this, automakers strip safety features such as air bags and antilock brakes out of the cars most people in India drive. They argue that Indian consumers cannot afford or are not willing to pay for safety features that could increase the cost of the car by 30 percent or more. Some manufacturers have begun to offer more safety features as standard in their models. But other producers are offering them only as an option, and some are not offering them at all to maintain price competitiveness.

⭐ **15-11.** Is it right for manufacturers to include product safety features that are known to save lives in countries that require them but not to include such features in a country where they are not specifically required? (AACSB: Communication; Ethical Reasoning)

15-12. Discuss world organizations that assist companies in developing and abiding by global standards to protect consumers worldwide. (AACSB: Communication; Reflective Thinking)

Marketing by the Numbers   Netflix Global Expansion

Video streaming service Netflix is expanding rapidly around the globe. It is currently available in 50 countries with the goal of expanding to 200 countries by the end of 2016. Netflix's international slogan is "Have content, will travel." There are challenges to international expansion for this type of service, such as inadequate disposable household income and a low percentage of households with high-speed Internet needed to stream videos. And even though almost half of France's TV-owning households have Internet-connected TVs, cultural restrictions limit English-language program content, requiring Netflix to invest in local content for French customers. The next countries to get Netflix are Italy, Spain, and Portugal. Similar to Netflix's other European offerings, service will be offered at a price of €7.99 per month, which converts to U.S. $8.97 during the time of expansion.

euros and U.S. dollars. There are 18,217,300 television households in Spain, with 75 percent having high-speed Internet. Assume 50 percent of the households are willing and able to purchase the service and would purchase one subscription at an average price of €7.99 per month ($8.97). (AACSB: Communication; Analytical Reasoning; Reflective Thinking)

15-14. Calculate the market sales potential using the current exchange rate between euros and U.S. dollars (see www.xe.com/currencyconverter/). Is the dollar currently strong or weak compared with the euro? Why are U.S.-based international companies concerned when the U.S. dollar is strong compared to other currencies? (AACSB: Communication; Analytic Reasoning; Reflective Thinking)

15-13. Refer to Appendix 3: Marketing by the Numbers to calculatethe annual market sales potential for Spain in

Video Case   Monster Worldwide

Monster.com is one of the most visited employment sites in the United States and one of the largest in the world. Now a part of parent company Monster Worldwide, Monster.com pioneered job recruiting on the Internet. Today, it is the only online recruitment provider that can service job seekers and job posters on a truly global basis. With a presence in 50 countries around the world, Monster has unparalleled international reach. Even through tough economic times, Monster continued to invest heavily in order to maintain and expand its global presence.

Monster's international expansion included the purchase of ChinaHR.com, giving it a strong presence in the world's largest country. Monster already gets about 45 percent of its annual revenue of $1.3 billion from outside the United States.

But it expects to become even more global in the coming years. To back that geographic expansion, Monster is also investing heavily in search technologies and Web design in order to appeal to clients everywhere.

After viewing the video featuring Monster Worldwide, answer the following questions:

15-15. Which of the five strategies for adapting products and promotion for global markets does Monster employ?

15-16. Which factors in the global marketing environment have challenged Monster's global marketing activities most? How has Monster met those challenges?

Company Cases   15 7-Eleven/14 Alibaba/16 Adidas

See Appendix 1 for cases appropriate for this chapter. **Case 15, 7-Eleven: Adapting to The World's Many Cultures.** Just a convenience store in the U.S., 7-Eleven has a strong global presence by adapting its model to fit the unique needs of consumers worldwide. **Case 14, Alibaba: The World's Largest E-Tailer Is Not Amazon.** Alibaba quickly became the world's largest e-tailer by selling to the world's largest consumer market. Now, as the company sets it sights on growth outside of China, there may be no stopping it. **Case 16, Adidas: Athletic Apparel With Purpose.** A strategy of sustainability may just give Adidas the global edge that it is looking for.

MyMarketingLab

If assigned by your instructor, complete these writing sections from your Assignments in the MyLab.

15-17. What is the World Trade Organization? What is its purpose, and what has it accomplished? (AACSB: Communication)

15-18. Visit www.ikea.com and compare a catalog from one country to that of another. Note the prices of some of the products. Convert some of the foreign prices to U.S. dollars and compare them to the prices in the U.S. catalog. Are the prices equivalent? Are they consistently higher or lower? (AACSB: Written and Oral Communication; Reflective Thinking)

16 Sustainable Marketing
Social Responsibility and Ethics

CHAPTER ROAD MAP Objective Outline

▶ **OBJECTIVE 16-1** Define *sustainable marketing* and discuss its importance. Sustainable Marketing (490–492)

▶ **OBJECTIVE 16-2** Identify the major social criticisms of marketing. Social Criticisms of Marketing (492–499)

▶ **OBJECTIVE 16-3** Define *consumerism* and *environmentalism* and explain how they affect marketing strategies. Consumer Actions to Promote Sustainable Marketing (499–506)

▶ **OBJECTIVE 16-4** Describe the principles of sustainable marketing. Business Actions Toward Sustainable Marketing (506–510)

▶ **OBJECTIVE 16-5** Explain the role of ethics in marketing. Marketing Ethics (510–513); The Sustainable Company (513)

Previewing the Concepts

In this final chapter, we'll examine the concept of sustainable marketing, meeting the needs of consumers, businesses, and society—now and in the future—through socially and environmentally responsible marketing actions. We'll start by defining sustainable marketing and then look at some common criticisms of marketing as it affects individual consumers as well as public actions that promote sustainable marketing. Finally, we'll see how companies themselves can benefit from proactively pursuing sustainable marketing practices that bring value to not only individual customers but also society as a whole. Sustainable marketing actions are more than just the right thing to do; they're also good for business.

First, let's look at an example of sustainable marketing in action at Patagonia, a company founded on a mission of inspiring business solutions to environmental problems. The company donates 1 percent of its revenue annually to environmental causes and adheres fiercely to a "Five *R*s" mantra: "reduce, repair, reuse, recycle, and reimagine." But Patagonia recently took sustainability to a whole new level, telling its customers, "Don't buy our products."

First Stop

Patagonia: "Conscious Consumption"—Telling Consumers to Buy *Less*

Patagonia—the high-end outdoor clothing and gear company—was founded on a mission of using business to help save the planet. More than 40 years ago, mountain-climber entrepreneur Yvon Chouinard started the company with this enduring mission: "Build the best product, cause no unnecessary harm, use business to inspire and implement solutions to the environmental crisis." Now, Chouinard and Patagonia are taking that mission to new extremes. They're actually telling consumers, "Don't buy our products."

It started a few years ago with a full-page *New York Times* ad on Black Friday, the day after Thanksgiving and busiest shopping day of the year, showing Patagonia's best-selling R2 jacket and pronouncing "Don't Buy This Jacket." Patagonia backed the ad with messaging in its retail stores and at its Web site and social media pages. To top things off, Patagonia customers received a follow-up email prior to Cyber Monday—the season's major online shopping day—reasserting the brand's buy less message. Here's part of what it said:

> Because Patagonia wants to be in business for a good long time—and leave a world inhabitable for our kids—we want to do the opposite of every other business today. We ask you to buy less and to reflect before you spend a dime on this jacket or anything else.
>
> The environmental cost of everything we make is astonishing. Consider the R2 Jacket shown, one of our best sellers. To make it required 135 liters of water, enough to meet the daily needs (three glasses a day) of 45 people. Its journey from its origin as 60% recycled polyester to our Reno warehouse generated nearly 20 pounds of carbon dioxide, 24 times the weight of the finished product. This jacket left behind, on its way to Reno, two-thirds its weight in waste. And this is a 60% recycled polyester jacket, knit and sewn to a high standard. But, as is true of all the things we can make and you can buy, this jacket comes with an environmental cost higher than its price.
>
> There is much to be done and plenty for us all to do. Don't buy what you don't need. Think twice before you buy anything. [Work with us] to reimagine a world where we take only what nature can replace.

A for-profit firm telling its customers to buy *less*? It sounds crazy. But that message is right on target with Patagonia's reason for being. Founder Chouinard contends that capitalism is on an unsustainable path. Today's companies and customers are wasting the world's resources by making and buying low-quality goods that they buy mindlessly and throw away too quickly. Instead, Chouinard and his company are calling for *conscious consumption,* asking customers to think before they buy and to stop consuming for consumption's sake.

Coming from Patagonia, a company that spends almost nothing on traditional advertising, the paradoxical "Don't Buy This Jacket" ad had tremendous impact. The Internet was soon ablaze with comments from online journalists, bloggers, and customers regarding the meaning and motivation behind Patagonia's message. Analysts speculated about whether the ad would help or harm sales—whether it would engage customers and build loyalty or be perceived as little more than a cheap marketing gimmick.

》 Sense-of-mission marketing: A for-profit company telling consumers to buy less sounds crazy. But it's right on target with Patagonia's conscious consumption mission.

Property of Patagonia, Inc. Used with permission.

But to Patagonia, far from a marketing gimmick, the campaign expressed the brand's deeply held philosophy of sustainability. The purpose was to increase awareness of and participation in the Patagonia Common Threads Initiative, which urges customers to take a pledge to work together with the company to consume more responsibly. Common Threads rests on five Rs of joint action toward sustainability:

> Patagonia was founded on a mission of using business to help save the planet. Recently, the company has taken its sustainability mission to new extremes, actually telling customers, "Don't buy our products."

Reduce: **WE** make useful gear that lasts a long time. **YOU** don't buy what you don't need.

Repair: **WE** help you repair your Patagonia gear. **YOU** pledge to fix what's broken.

Reuse: **WE** help find a home for Patagonia gear you no longer need. **YOU** sell or pass it on.

489

Recycle: **WE** take back your Patagonia gear that is worn out. **YOU** pledge to keep your stuff out of the landfill and incinerator.

Reimagine: **TOGETHER** we reimagine a world where we take only what nature can replace.

So Patagonia's conscious consumption solution seems pretty simple. Making, buying, repairing, and reusing higher-quality goods results in less consumption, which in turn uses fewer resources and lowers costs for everyone. Patagonia has always been committed to the idea of quality as a cure for overconsumption. It makes durable products with timeless designs, products that customers can keep and use for a long time. Then, through programs like its Worn Wear Initiative, Patagonia uses social media to let customers share stories about their long-lasting gear and to inspire people to keep their clothing in circulation for as long as possible. In Patagonia's words:

> At the end of the day, we can tinker with our supply chain, improve sourcing, use all-recycled fabrics, and give away millions of dollars to environmental organizations until the cows come in, but nothing is more important and impactful than keeping our clothing in use for as long as possible.

So on that Black Friday weekend, while other companies were inundating customers with promotions that encouraged them to "buy, buy, buy," Patagonia stood on its founding principles. It said, "Hey, look: Only purchase what you need," explains Rob BonDurant, vice president of marketing and communications at Patagonia. "The message, 'Don't buy this jacket,' is obviously super counterintuitive to what a for-profit company would say, especially on a day like Black Friday, but honestly [it] is what we really were after, [communicating] this idea of evolving capitalism and conscious consumption that we wanted to effect."

Not just any company can pull off something like this—such a message can only work if it is real. Patagonia didn't just suddenly stick an ad in the *New York Times* on Black Friday. It had been sending—and living—this message for decades. Can other companies follow Patagonia's lead? "If it is [just] a marketing campaign, no," says BonDurant. "If it is a way they live their lives and do their business, absolutely. You can't just apply it to your messaging or to a particular window of time. It has to be done 24 hours a day, 365 days a year."

Pushing conscious consumption doesn't mean that Patagonia wants customers to stop buying its products. To the contrary, like other for-profit brands, Patagonia really does care about doing well on Black Friday and the rest of the holiday season. As a company that sells products mostly for cold-weather activities, Patagonia reaps a whopping 40 percent of its revenues during the final two months of the year. But to Patagonia, business is about more than making money. And according to BonDurant, the "Don't Buy This Jacket" campaign has more than paid for itself with the interest and involvement it created for the Common Threads Initiative. As an added bonus, however, the campaign also boosted sales. During the first year of the campaign, Patagonia's sales surged by almost a third.

"It is not enough just to make good products anymore," says BonDurant. "There also has to be a message that people can buy into, that people feel they are a part of, that they can be solutions-based. That is what [Patagonia's "buy only what you need"] communication efforts are really all about." But what's good for customers and the planet is also good for Patagonia. Says founder Chouinard, "I know it sounds crazy, but every time I have made a decision that is best for the planet, I have made money. Our customers know that—and they want to be part of that environmental commitment."[1]

R esponsible marketers discover what consumers want and respond with market offerings that create value for buyers and capture value in return. The *marketing concept* is a philosophy of customer value and mutual gain. Its practice leads the economy by an invisible hand to satisfy the many and changing needs of consumers.

Not all marketers follow the marketing concept, however. In fact, some companies use questionable marketing practices that serve their own rather than consumers' interests. Moreover, even well-intentioned marketing actions that meet the current needs of some consumers may cause immediate or future harm to other consumers or the larger society. Responsible marketers must consider whether their actions are sustainable in the longer run.

This chapter examines sustainable marketing and the social and environmental effects of private marketing practices. First, we address the question: What is sustainable marketing, and why is it important?

Sustainable marketing
Socially and environmentally responsible marketing that meets the present needs of consumers and businesses while also preserving or enhancing the ability of future generations to meet their needs.

Sustainable Marketing

Author Comment
Marketers must think beyond immediate customer satisfaction and business performance toward sustainable strategies that preserve the world for future generations.

Sustainable marketing calls for socially and environmentally responsible actions that meet the present needs of consumers and businesses while also preserving or enhancing the ability of future generations to meet their needs. **>>Figure 16.1** compares the sustainable marketing concept with marketing concepts we studied in earlier chapters.

The *marketing concept* recognizes that organizations thrive by determining the current needs and wants of target customers and fulfilling them more effectively and efficiently than competitors do. It focuses on meeting the company's short-term sales, growth, and profit needs by engaging customers and giving them what they want now.

The marketing concept means meeting the current needs of both customers and the company. But that can sometimes mean compromising the future of both.

Sustainable marketing means meeting current needs in a way that preserves the rights and options of future generations of consumers and businesses.

>> **Figure 16.1 Sustainable Marketing**

However, satisfying consumers' immediate needs and desires doesn't always serve the future best interests of either customers or the business.

For example, McDonald's early decisions to market tasty but fat- and salt-laden fast foods created immediate satisfaction for customers as well as sales and profits for the company. However, critics assert that McDonald's and other fast-food chains contributed to a longer-term national obesity epidemic, damaging consumer health and burdening the national health system. In turn, many consumers began looking for healthier eating options, causing a slump in the sales and profits of the fast-food industry. Beyond issues of ethical behavior and social welfare, McDonald's was also criticized for the sizable environmental footprint of its vast global operations, everything from wasteful packaging and solid waste creation to inefficient energy use in its stores. Thus, McDonald's strategy was not sustainable in the long run in terms of either consumer or company benefit.

Whereas the *societal marketing concept* identified in Figure 16.1 considers the future welfare of consumers and the *strategic planning concept* considers future company needs, the *sustainable marketing concept* considers both. Sustainable marketing calls for socially and environmentally responsible actions that meet both the immediate and future needs of customers and the company.

For example, for more than a dozen years, McDonald's has responded to these challenges with a more sustainable "Plan to Win" strategy of diversifying into salads, fruits, grilled chicken, low-fat milk, and other healthy fare. The company also sponsored a major multifaceted education campaign—called "it's what i eat and what i do ... i'm lovin' it"—to help consumers better understand the keys to living balanced, active lifestyles. >> And it recently announced a list of "Commitments to Offer Improved Nutrition Choices," including a continuing commitment to children's well-being, expanded and improved nutritionally balanced menu choices, and increased consumer and employee access to nutrition information. McDonald's points out that 80 percent of the items on its national menu fall into its "favorites under 400 calories" category—from a basic cheeseburger to products such as Fruit & Maple Oatmeal and the Egg White Delight McMuffin, made with eight grams of whole grain, 100 percent egg whites, and extra-lean Canadian bacon.[2]

The McDonald's "Plan to Win" strategy also addresses environmental issues. For example, it calls for food-supply sustainability, reduced and environmentally sustainable packaging, reuse and recycling, and more responsible store designs. McDonald's has even developed an environmental scorecard that rates its suppliers' performance in areas

>> **Sustainable marketing: Under its "Plan to Win" strategy, McDonald's has created sustainable value for both customers and the company. Now, 80 percent of the chain's menu is under 400 calories, including this Egg White Delight McMuffin, which weighs in with eight grams of whole grain against only 250 calories and five grams of fat.**

Michael Neelon/Alamy

such as water use, energy use, and solid waste management. Thus, McDonald's is now well positioned for a sustainably profitable future.

Truly sustainable marketing requires a smooth-functioning marketing system in which consumers, companies, public policy makers, and others work together to ensure socially and environmentally responsible marketing actions. Unfortunately, however, the marketing system doesn't always work smoothly. The following sections examine several sustainability questions: What are the most frequent social criticisms of marketing? What steps have private citizens taken to curb marketing ills? What steps have legislators and government agencies taken to promote sustainable marketing? What steps have enlightened companies taken to carry out socially responsible and ethical marketing that creates sustainable value for both individual customers and society as a whole?

Author Comment

In most ways, we all benefit greatly from marketing activities. However, like most other human endeavors, marketing has its flaws. Here we present both sides of some of the most common criticisms of marketing.

Social Criticisms of Marketing

Marketing receives much criticism. Some of this criticism is justified; much is not. Social critics claim that certain marketing practices hurt individual consumers, society as a whole, and other business firms.

Marketing's Impact on Individual Consumers

Consumers have many concerns about how well the American marketing system serves their interests. Surveys usually show that consumers hold mixed or even slightly unfavorable attitudes toward marketing practices. Consumer advocates, government agencies, and other critics have accused marketing of harming consumers through high prices, deceptive practices, high-pressure selling, shoddy or unsafe products, planned obsolescence, and poor service to disadvantaged consumers. Such questionable marketing practices are not sustainable in terms of long-term consumer or business welfare.

High Prices

Many critics charge that the American marketing system causes prices to be higher than they would be under more "sensible" systems. Such high prices are hard to swallow, especially when the economy gets tight. Critics point to three factors—*high costs of distribution, high advertising and promotion costs*, and *excessive markups*.

A long-standing charge is that greedy marketing channel members mark up prices beyond the value of their services. As a result, distribution costs too much, and consumers pay for these excessive costs in the form of higher prices. Resellers respond that intermediaries do work that would otherwise have to be done by manufacturers or consumers. Their prices reflect services that consumers want—more convenience, larger stores and assortments, more service, longer store hours, return privileges, and others. In fact, they argue, retail competition is so intense that margins are actually quite low. And discounters such as Walmart, Costco, and others pressure their competitors to operate efficiently and keep their prices down.

Modern marketing is also accused of pushing up prices to finance unneeded advertising, sales promotion, and packaging. ≫ For example, a heavily promoted national brand sells for much more than a virtually identical store-branded product. Critics charge that much of this promotion and packaging adds only psychological, not functional, value. Marketers respond that although advertising adds to product costs, it also adds value by informing potential buyers of the availability and merits of a brand. Brand name products may cost more, but branding assures

≫ A heavily promoted national brand sells for much more than a virtually identical non-branded or store-branded product. Critics charge that promotion adds only psychological value to the product rather than functional value.

Keri Miksza

buyers of consistent quality. Moreover, although consumers can usually buy functional versions of products at lower prices, they *want* and are willing to pay more for products that also provide psychological benefits—that make them feel wealthy, attractive, or special.

Critics also charge that some companies mark up goods excessively. They point to the drug industry, where a pill costing five cents to make may cost the consumer $2 to buy, and to the high charges for auto repairs and other services. Marketers respond that most businesses try to price fairly to consumers because they want to build customer relationships and repeat business. Also, they assert, consumers often don't understand the reasons for high markups. For example, pharmaceutical markups help cover the costs of making and distributing existing medicines plus the high costs of developing and testing new medicines. As pharmaceuticals company GlaxoSmithKline has stated in its ads, "Today's medicines finance tomorrow's miracles."

Deceptive Practices

Marketers are sometimes accused of deceptive practices that lead consumers to believe they will get more value than they actually do. Deceptive practices fall into three groups: promotion, packaging, and pricing. *Deceptive promotion* includes practices such as misrepresenting the product's features or performance or luring customers to the store for a bargain that is out of stock. *Deceptive packaging* includes exaggerating package contents through subtle design, using misleading labeling, or describing size in misleading terms.

Deceptive pricing includes practices such as falsely advertising "factory" or "wholesale" prices or a large price reduction from a phony high retail list price. For example, Overstock.com was recently fined $6.8 million by a California court as a result of a fraudulent pricing lawsuit filed by the attorneys general of eight California counties. The suit charged that the online giant routinely advertised its prices as lower than fabricated "list prices." It recites one example in which Overstock sold a patio set for $449 while claiming that the list price was $999. When the item was delivered, the customer found that it had a Walmart sticker stating a price of $247.[3]

>> **Deceptive practices: Marketers of the popular caffeine-charged 5-Hour Energy drink were recently sued by the Attorneys Generals in three U.S. states, whose suits alleged that the brand's advertising was deceptive and misleading**

ZUMA Press, Inc/Alamy

Deceptive practices have led to legislation and other consumer protection actions. For example, in 1938 Congress enacted the Wheeler-Lea Act, which gave the Federal Trade Commission (FTC) power to regulate "unfair or deceptive acts or practices." The FTC has since published several guidelines listing deceptive practices. Despite regulations, however, some critics argue that deceptive claims are still common, even for well-known brands. For example, the FTC recently charged Gerber Products with falsely advertising that its Good Start Gentle baby formula could reduce or prevent the risk of allergies, a claim that Gerber insists is backed by extensive science. The FTC also slapped Nissan's hands for a misleading TV ad showing a Nissan Frontier pickup truck dramatically pushing a stranded dune buggy up a steep sand dune—both vehicles were dragged by cables that viewers couldn't see. And Skechers paid $55 million in consumer refunds to resolve allegations by the FTC and attorneys general in 44 states that it made false advertising claims that its rocker-bottom Shapeups and other toning shoes would help customers tone muscles and lose weight.[4]

Living Essentials, marketer of the popular caffeine-charged 5-Hour Energy drink, was recently sued by the attorneys general of three U.S. states, who alleged in separate suits that the brand's advertising was deceptive and misleading. >> The suits asserted that the brand's ads claimed that 5-Hour Energy contains a unique combination of ingredients to boost energy and focus, whereas the product contains only a concentrated dose of caffeine. The suits also took issue with 5-Hour Energy's advertising and packaging claims "Hours of energy now—No crash later," which suggested that a user would not experience a crash like the one that often follows a caffeine high. Although the company denies any wrongdoing, it also faces civil suits claiming false and deceptive advertising.[5]

The toughest problem often is defining what is "deceptive." For instance, an advertiser's claim that its chewing gum will "rock your world" isn't intended to be taken literally. Instead, the advertiser might claim, it is "puffery"—innocent exaggeration for effect. However, others claim that puffery and alluring imagery can harm consumers in subtle ways. Think about the popular and long-running MasterCard Priceless commercials that once painted pictures of consumers fulfilling their priceless dreams despite the costs. The ads suggested that your credit card could make it happen. But critics charge that such imagery by credit card companies encouraged a spend-now-pay-later attitude that caused many consumers to *over*use their cards.

Marketers argue that most companies avoid deceptive practices. Because such practices harm a company's business in the long run, they simply aren't sustainable. Profitable customer relationships are built on a foundation of value and trust. If consumers do not get what they expect, they will switch to more reliable products. In addition, consumers usually protect themselves from deception. Most consumers recognize a marketer's selling intent and are careful when they buy, sometimes even to the point of not believing completely true product claims.

High-Pressure Selling

Salespeople are sometimes accused of high-pressure selling that persuades people to buy goods they had no thought of buying. It is often said that insurance, real estate, and used cars are *sold*, not *bought*. Salespeople are trained to deliver smooth, canned talks to entice purchases. They sell hard because sales contests promise big prizes to those who sell the most. Similarly, TV infomercial pitchmen use "yell and sell" presentations that create a sense of consumer urgency that only those with strong willpower can resist.

But in most cases, marketers have little to gain from high-pressure selling. Although such tactics may work in one-time selling situations for short-term gain, most selling involves building long-term relationships with valued customers. High-pressure or deceptive selling can seriously damage such relationships. For example, imagine a P&G account manager trying to pressure a Walmart buyer or an IBM salesperson trying to browbeat an information technology manager at GE. It simply wouldn't work.

Shoddy, Harmful, or Unsafe Products

Another criticism concerns poor product quality or function. One complaint is that, too often, products and services are not made well or do not perform well. A second complaint concerns product safety. Product safety has been a problem for several reasons, including company indifference, increased product complexity, and poor quality control. A third complaint is that many products deliver little benefit or may even be harmful.

For example, think about the soft drink industry. Many critics blame the plentiful supply of sugar-laden, high-calorie soft drinks for the nation's rapidly growing obesity epidemic. Studies show that more than two-thirds of American adults are either obese or overweight. In addition, almost one-third of American children are obese.[6] This national weight issue continues despite repeated medical studies showing that excess weight brings increased risks for heart disease, diabetes, and other maladies, even cancer. The critics are quick to fault what they see as greedy beverage marketers cashing in on vulnerable consumers, turning us into a nation of Big Gulpers. ≫ New York City's mayor once even tried to pass a ban on soft drinks 16 ounces and larger, and the New York City Department of Health and Mental Hygiene (NYC Health) has fielded a "Pouring on the Pounds" ad campaign highlighting the risks of drinking too many sugary drinks for both children and adults.[7]

Is the soft drink industry being socially irresponsible by aggressively promoting overindulgence to ill-informed or unwary consumers? Or is it simply serving the wants of customers by offering products that ping consumer taste buds while letting consumers make their own consumption choices? Is it the industry's job to police public tastes? As in many matters of social responsibility, what's right and wrong may be a matter of opinion. Whereas some analysts criticize the industry, others suggest that responsibility lies with consumers. "Soft drinks have unfairly become the whipping boy of most anti-obesity campaigns," suggests one business reporter. "Maybe friends shouldn't give friends Big Gulps,

Harmful products: NYC Health asks, "Are you pouring on the pounds?" Is the soft drink industry being irresponsible by promoting overindulgence, or is it simply serving the wants of customers by offering products that ping their taste buds while letting them make their own consumption choices?

New York Department of Health and Mental Hygiene

but to my knowledge, no one's ever been forced to buy and drink one. There's an element of personal responsibility and control that [needs to be addressed]."[8]

Most manufacturers *want* to produce quality goods. After all, the way a company deals with product quality and safety problems can harm or help its reputation. Companies selling poor-quality or unsafe products risk damaging conflicts with consumer groups and regulators. Unsafe products can result in product liability suits and large awards for damages. More fundamentally, consumers who are unhappy with a firm's products may avoid future purchases and talk other consumers into doing the same. In today's social media and online review environment, word of poor quality can spread like wildfire. Thus, quality missteps are not consistent with sustainable marketing. Today's marketers know that good quality results in customer value and satisfaction, which in turn create sustainable customer relationships.

Planned Obsolescence

Critics also have charged that some companies practice *planned obsolescence*, causing their products to become obsolete before they actually should need replacement. They accuse some producers of using materials and components that will break, wear, rust, or rot sooner than they should. And if the products themselves don't wear out fast enough, other companies are charged with *perceived obsolescence*—continually changing consumer concepts of acceptable styles to encourage more and earlier buying. An obvious example is the fast-fashion industry with its constantly changing clothing fashions, which some critics claim creates a wasteful disposable clothing culture. "Too many garments end up in landfill sites," bemoans one designer. "They are deemed aesthetically redundant and get discarded at the end of the season when there are often years of wear left."[9]

Still others are accused of introducing planned streams of new products that make older models obsolete, turning consumers into "serial replacers." Critics claim that this occurs in the consumer electronics industries. If you're like most people, you probably have a drawer full of yesterday's hottest technological gadgets—from mobile phones and cameras to iPods and flash drives—now reduced to the status of fossils. It seems that anything more than a year or two old is hopelessly out of date.

Marketers respond that consumers *like* style changes; they get tired of the old goods and want a new look in fashion. Or they *want* the latest high-tech innovations, even if older models still work. No one has to buy a new product, and if too few people like it, it will simply fail. Finally, most companies do not design their products to break down earlier because they do not want to lose customers to other brands. Instead, they seek constant improvement to ensure that products will consistently meet or exceed customer expectations.

Much of the so-called planned obsolescence is the working of the competitive and technological forces in a free society—forces that lead to ever-improving goods and services. For example, if Apple produced a new iPhone or iPad that would last 10 years, few consumers would want it. Instead, buyers want the latest technological innovations. "Obsolescence isn't something companies are forcing on us," confirms one analyst. "It's progress, and it's something we pretty much demand. As usual, the market gives us exactly what we want."[10]

Poor Service to Disadvantaged Consumers

Finally, the American marketing system has been accused of poorly serving disadvantaged consumers. For example, critics claim that the urban poor often have to shop in smaller

Serving underserved consumers: Many national food chains, such as Whole Foods Market, are opening stores in underserved communities ignored by other sellers.

ZUMA Press, Inc/Alamy

stores that carry inferior goods and charge higher prices. The presence of large national chain stores in low-income neighborhoods would help to keep prices down. However, the critics accuse major chain retailers of *redlining*, drawing a red line around disadvantaged neighborhoods and avoiding placing stores there.

For example, the nation's poor areas have 30 percent fewer supermarkets than affluent areas do. As a result, many low-income consumers find themselves in *food deserts*, which are awash with small markets offering frozen pizzas, Cheetos, Moon Pies, and Cokes but where fruits and vegetables or fresh fish and chicken are out of reach. Currently, some 23.5 million Americans—including 6.5 million children—live in low-income areas that lack stores selling affordable and nutritious foods. What's more, 2.3 million households have no access to a car but live more than a mile from a supermarket, forcing them to shop at convenience stores where expensive processed food is the only dietary choice. In turn, the lack of access to healthy, affordable fresh foods has a negative impact on the health of underserved consumers in these areas. Many national chains, such as Walmart, Walgreens, SuperValu, and even Whole Foods Market, have recently agreed to open or expand more stores that bring nutritious and fresh foods to underserved communities. >> Whole Foods has recently been opening stores in disadvantaged parts of cities such as Detroit, Chicago, and New Orleans, "trying to serve the needs of communities that others ignore completely."[11]

Clearly, better marketing systems must be built to service disadvantaged consumers. In fact, many marketers profitably target such consumers with legitimate goods and services that create real value. In cases in which marketers do not step in to fill the void, the government likely will. For example, the FTC has taken action against sellers that advertise false values, wrongfully deny services, or charge disadvantaged customers too much.

GⱭ LINKING THE CONCEPTS

Hold up for a moment. Few marketers *want* to abuse or anger consumers—it's simply not good business. Still, some marketing abuses do occur.

- Think back over the past three months or so and list any instances in which you've suffered a marketing abuse such as those just discussed. Analyze your list: What kinds of companies were involved? Were the abuses intentional? What did the situations have in common?
- Pick one of the instances you listed and describe it in detail. How might you go about righting this wrong? Write out an action plan and then do something to remedy the abuse. If we all took such actions when wronged, there would be far fewer wrongs to right!

Marketing's Impact on Society as a Whole

The American marketing system has been accused of adding to several "evils" in American society at large, such as creating too much materialism, too few social goods, and a glut of cultural pollution.

False Wants and Too Much Materialism

Critics have charged that the marketing system urges too much interest in material possessions, and that America's love affair with worldly possessions is not sustainable. Too often, people are judged by what they *own* rather than by who they *are*. The critics do not view this interest in material things as a natural state of mind but rather as a matter of false wants created by marketing. Marketers, they claim, stimulate people's desires for goods and create materialistic models of the good life. Thus, marketers have created an endless

What does More Fun Less Stuff mean to you?

Tell us at: newdream.org/less-stuff

MORE FUN! LESS stuff

>> Materialism: A marketing campaign by the Center for a New American Dream urges people to reject "buy more" messages and instead say "More fun! Less stuff!"

Center for a New American Dream

cycle of mass consumption based on a distorted interpretation of the "American Dream."

In this view, marketing's purpose is to promote consumption, and the inevitable outcome of successful marketing is unsustainable *over*consumption. According to the critics, more is not always better. Some groups have taken their concerns straight to the public. >> For example, the Center for a New American Dream is a nonprofit organization founded on a mission to "help Americans to reduce and shift their consumption to improve quality of life, protect the environment, and promote social justice." Through educational videos and marketing campaigns such as "More fun! Less stuff!" the organization works with individuals, institutions, communities, and businesses to help conserve natural resources, counter the commercialization of culture, and promote positive changes in the way goods are produced and consumed.[12]

Marketers respond that such criticisms overstate the power of business to create needs. They claim people have strong defenses against advertising and other marketing tools. Marketers are most effective when they appeal to existing wants rather than when they attempt to create new ones. Furthermore, people seek information when making important purchases and often do not rely on single sources. Even minor purchases that may be affected by advertising messages lead to repeat purchases only if the product delivers the promised customer value. Finally, the high failure rate of new products shows that companies are not able to control demand.

On a deeper level, our wants and values are influenced not only by marketers but also by family, peer groups, religion, cultural background, and education. If Americans are highly materialistic, these values arose out of basic socialization processes that go much deeper than business and marketing could produce alone.

Moreover, consumption patterns and attitudes are also subject to larger forces, such as the economy. As discussed in Chapter 1, the recent Great Recession put a damper on materialism and conspicuous spending. Additionally, today's consumers are more supportive of environmental and social sustainability efforts by companies. As a result, instead of encouraging today's more sensible and conscientious consumers to overspend their means or spend wastefully, most marketers are working to help them find greater value with less and to share their material prosperity with the less fortunate.

An example is the "Shwopping" movement started by British retailing giant Marks & Spencer, by which it urges customers to exchange an old item of clothing, even if it's not from M&S, each time they buy something new. Shwopped items go to Oxfam International, a nonprofit organization that resells, recycles, or forwards them to raise money and help people around the world overcome poverty. "We hope to collect as many clothes as we sell and change the way we all shop forever," says Marks & Spencer.[13]

Too Few Social Goods

Business has been accused of overselling private goods at the expense of public goods. As private goods increase, they require more public services that are usually not forthcoming. For example, private automobile ownership (private good) requires highways, traffic control, parking spaces, and police services (public goods). The overselling of private goods results in social costs. For cars, some of the social costs include traffic congestion, gasoline shortages, and air pollution. For example, American travelers lose, on average, 38 hours a year in traffic jams, costing the United States more than $120 billion a year—$820 per commuter. In the process, they waste 2.9 billion gallons of fuel (enough to fill the New Orleans Superdome four times) and emit 56 billion tons of greenhouse gases.[14]

A way must be found to restore a balance between private and public goods. One option is to make producers bear the full social costs of their operations. For example, the government is requiring automobile manufacturers to build cars with more efficient engines and better pollution-control systems. Automakers will then raise their prices to cover the extra costs. If buyers find the price of some car models too high, however, these models will disappear. Demand will then move to those producers that can support the sum of the private and social costs.

A second option is to make consumers pay the social costs. For example, many cities around the world are now charging congestion tolls in an effort to reduce traffic congestion. To decrease rush hour traffic on the Bay Bridge between Oakland and San Francisco, California, the Metropolitan Transportation Commission charges a $6 toll during peak commute hours versus $4 at other times. The charge reduced the flow of drivers during peak hours, cutting the average 32-minute wait time some bridges approach in half.[15]

Cultural Pollution

Critics charge the marketing system with creating *cultural pollution*. They feel our senses are being constantly assaulted by marketing and advertising. >> Commercials interrupt serious programs; pages of ads obscure magazines; billboards mar beautiful scenery; spam fills our email inboxes; flashing display ads intrude on our online and mobile screens. What's more, the critics claim, these interruptions continually pollute people's minds with messages of materialism, sex, power, or status. Some critics call for sweeping changes.

Marketers answer the charges of commercial noise with these arguments: First, they hope that their ads primarily reach the target audience. But because of mass-communication channels, some ads are bound to reach people who have no interest in the product and are therefore bored or annoyed. People who buy magazines they like or who opt in to email, social media, or mobile marketing programs rarely complain about the ads because they involve products and services of interest.

Second, because of ads, many television, radio, online, and social media sites are free to users. Ads also help keep down the costs of magazines and newspapers. Many people think viewing ads is a small price to

>> Cultural pollution: People's senses are sometimes assaulted by a clutter of commercial messages and noise.
Christian Science Monitor/Getty Images

pay for these benefits. In addition, consumers find many television commercials entertaining and seek them out; for example, ad viewership during the Super Bowl usually equals or exceeds game viewership. Finally, today's consumers have alternatives. For example, they can zip or zap TV commercials on recorded programs or avoid them altogether on many paid cable, satellite, and online channels. Thus, to hold consumer attention, advertisers are making their ads more entertaining and informative.

Marketing's Impact on Other Businesses

Critics also charge that a company's marketing practices can harm other companies and reduce competition. They identify three problems: acquisitions of competitors, marketing practices that create barriers to entry, and unfair competitive marketing practices.

Critics claim that firms are harmed and competition is reduced when companies expand by acquiring competitors rather than by developing their own new products. The large number of acquisitions and the rapid pace of industry consolidation over the past several decades have caused concern that vigorous young competitors will be absorbed, thereby reducing competition. In virtually every major industry—retailing, entertainment, financial services, utilities, transportation, automobiles, telecommunications, health care—the number of major competitors is shrinking.

Acquisition is a complex subject. In some cases, acquisitions can be good for society. The acquiring company may gain economies of scale that lead to lower costs and lower prices. In addition, a well-managed company may take over a poorly managed company and improve its efficiency. An industry that was not very competitive might become more competitive after the acquisition. But acquisitions can also be harmful and therefore are closely regulated by the government.

Critics have also charged that marketing practices bar new companies from entering an industry. Large marketing companies can use patents and heavy promotion spending or tie up suppliers or dealers to keep out or drive out competitors. Those concerned with antitrust regulation recognize that some barriers are the natural result of the economic advantages of doing business on a large scale. Existing and new laws can challenge other barriers. For example, some critics have proposed a progressive tax on advertising spending to reduce the role of selling costs as a major barrier to entry.

Finally, some firms have, in fact, used unfair competitive marketing practices with the intention of hurting or destroying other firms. They may set their prices below costs, threaten to cut off business with suppliers, discourage the buying of a competitor's products, or use their size and market dominance to unfairly damage rivals. Although various laws work to prevent such predatory competition, it is often difficult to prove that the intent or action was really predatory. It's often difficult to differentiate predatory practices from effective competitive strategy and tactics.

In recent years, search giant Google has been accused of using predatory practices at the expense of smaller competitors. >> For example, the European Commission recently accused Google of abusing its Web-search dominance, harming both competitors and consumers in European Union markets.[16] The commission also began investigating antitrust issues related to Google's Android mobile operating system. Google's Web-search engine claims a commanding 92 percent European market share; the Android operating system dominates with a 71 percent share.

The European Commission formally accused Google of manipulating its search-engine results to favor its own shopping services at the expense of rivals. According to the commission, such "conduct may therefore artificially divert traffic from rival comparison shopping services and hinder their ability to compete, to the detriment of consumers, as well as stifling innovation." The commission's future antitrust investigations could expand beyond Google's shopping services into areas such as online and mobile searches for travel services and restaurants. For its part, however, Google contends that its Web-search and mobile operations constitute fair and effective competition that serves the best interests of consumers. If the antitrust charges stand, the European Commission could hit Google with billions of dollars in fines.

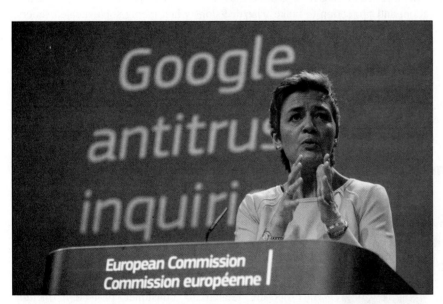

>> Competitive marketing practices: The European Commission recently accused Google of abusing its Web-search dominance, harming both competitors and consumers in European Union markets. Google claims that its practices constitute fair and effective competition.

Virginia Mayo/AP Images

Author Comment
Sustainable marketing isn't something that only businesses and governments do. Through consumerism and environmentalism, consumers themselves can play an important role.

Consumer Actions to Promote Sustainable Marketing

Sustainable marketing calls for more responsible actions by both businesses and consumers. Because some people view businesses as the cause of many economic and social ills, grassroots movements have arisen from time to time to keep businesses in line. Two major movements have been *consumerism* and *environmentalism*.

Consumerism

Consumerism
An organized movement of citizens and government agencies to improve the rights and power of buyers in relation to sellers.

Consumerism is an organized movement of citizens and government agencies to improve the rights and power of buyers in relation to sellers. Traditional *sellers' rights* include the following:

- The right to introduce any product in any size and style, provided it is not hazardous to personal health or safety, or, if it is, to include proper warnings and controls
- The right to charge any price for the product, provided no discrimination exists among similar kinds of buyers
- The right to spend any amount to promote the product, provided it is not defined as unfair competition
- The right to use any product message, provided it is not misleading or dishonest in content or execution
- The right to use buying incentive programs, provided they are not unfair or misleading

Traditional *buyers' rights* include the following:

- The right not to buy a product that is offered for sale
- The right to expect the product to be safe
- The right to expect the product to perform as claimed

In comparing these rights, many believe that the balance of power lies on the seller's side. True, the buyer can refuse to buy. But critics feel that the buyer has too little information, education, and protection to make wise decisions when facing sophisticated sellers. Consumer advocates call for the following additional consumer rights:

- The right to be well informed about important aspects of the product
- The right to be protected against questionable products and marketing practices
- The right to influence products and marketing practices in ways that will improve "quality of life"
- The right to consume now in a way that will preserve the world for future generations of consumers

>> Consumer desire for more information led to package labels with useful facts, from ingredients and nutrition facts to recycling and country of origin information.
Spauln/E+/Getty Images

Each proposed right has led to more specific proposals by consumerists and consumer protection actions by the government. >> The right to be informed includes the right to know the true interest on a loan (truth in lending), the true cost per unit of a brand (unit pricing), the ingredients in a product (ingredient labeling), the nutritional value of foods (nutritional labeling), product freshness (open dating), and the true benefits of a product (truth in advertising).

Proposals related to consumer protection include strengthening consumer rights in cases of business fraud and financial protection, requiring greater product safety, ensuring information privacy, and giving more power to government agencies. Proposals relating to quality of life include controlling the ingredients that go into certain products and packaging and reducing the level of advertising "noise." Proposals for preserving the world for future consumption include promoting the use of sustainable ingredients, recycling and reducing solid wastes, and managing energy consumption.

Sustainable marketing applies not only to businesses and governments but also to consumers. Consumers have not only the *right* but also the *responsibility* to protect themselves instead of leaving this function to the government or someone else. Consumers who believe they got a bad deal have several remedies available, including contacting the company;

making their case through the media or social media; contacting federal, state, or local agencies; and going to small-claims courts. Consumers should also make good consumption choices, rewarding companies that act responsibly while punishing those that don't. Ultimately, the move from irresponsible consumption to sustainable consumption is in the hands of consumers.

Environmentalism

Environmentalism
An organized movement of concerned citizens, businesses, and government agencies designed to protect and improve people's current and future living environment.

Whereas consumerists consider whether the marketing system is efficiently serving consumer wants, environmentalists are concerned with marketing's effects on the environment and the environmental costs of serving consumer needs and wants. **Environmentalism** is an organized movement of concerned citizens, businesses, and government agencies designed to protect and improve people's current and future living environment.

Environmentalists are not against marketing and consumption; they simply want people and organizations to operate with more care for the environment. They call for doing away with what sustainability advocate and Unilever CEO Paul Polman calls "mindless consumption." According to Polman, "The road to well-being doesn't go via reduced consumption. It has to be done via more responsible consumption."[17] The marketing system's goal, environmentalists assert, should not be to maximize consumption, consumer choice, or consumer satisfaction but rather to maximize life quality. Life quality means not only the quantity and quality of consumer goods and services but also the quality of the environment, now and for future generations.

Environmentalism is concerned with damage to the ecosystem caused by global warming, resource depletion, toxic and solid wastes, litter, the availability of fresh water, and other problems. Other issues include the loss of recreational areas and the increase in health problems caused by bad air, polluted water, and chemically treated food.

Over the past several decades, such concerns have resulted in federal and state laws and regulations governing industrial commercial practices affecting the environment. Some companies have strongly resented and resisted such environmental regulations, claiming that they are too costly and have made their industries less competitive. These companies responded to consumer environmental concerns by doing only what was required to avert new regulations or keep environmentalists quiet.

Environmental sustainability
A management approach that involves developing strategies that both sustain the environment and produce profits for the company.

In recent years, however, most companies have accepted responsibility for doing no harm to the environment. They have shifted from protest to prevention and from regulation to responsibility. More and more companies are now adopting policies of **environmental sustainability**. Simply put, environmental sustainability is about generating profits while helping to save the planet. Today's enlightened companies are taking action not because someone is forcing them to or to reap short-run profits but because it's the right thing to do—because it's for their customers' well-being, the company's well-being, and the planet's environmental future. For example, consumer products giant Unilever has successfully built its core mission around environmental sustainability—its aim is to "make sustainable living commonplace" (see Marketing at Work 16.1).

» **Figure 16.2** shows a grid that companies can use to gauge their progress toward environmental sustainability. It includes both internal and external *greening* activities that will pay off for the firm and environment in the short run and *beyond greening* activities that will pay off in the longer term. At the most basic level, a company can

» **Figure 16.2 Environmental Sustainability and Sustainable Value**

Source: Based on Stuart L. Hart, "Sustainable Value," www.stuartlhart.com/sustainablevalue.html, July 2015.

	Today: Greening	**Tomorrow: Beyond Greening**
Internal	**Pollution prevention** Eliminating or reducing waste before it is created	**New clean technology** Developing new sets of environmental skills and capabilities
External	**Product stewardship** Minimizing environmental impact throughout the entire product life cycle	**Sustainability vision** Developing a strategy framework for creating sustainable value

This framework addresses more than just natural environmental challenges. It also points to opportunities for creating sustainable value for markets and the firm through environmentally sustainable strategies and practices.

MARKETING AT WORK   16.1

Sustainability at Unilever: Creating a Better Future Every Day

When Paul Polman took over as CEO of Unilever a half-dozen years ago, the foods, home, and personal care products company was a slumbering giant. Despite its stable of star-studded brands—including the likes of Dove, Axe, Noxzema, Sunsilk, OMO, Hellmann's, Knorr, Lipton, and Ben & Jerry's—Unilever had experienced a decade of stagnant sales and profits. The company needed renewed energy and purpose. "To drag the world back to sanity, we need to know why we are here," said Polman.

To answer the "why are we here" question and find a more energizing mission, Polman looked beyond the usual corporate goals of growing sales, profits, and shareholder value. Instead, he asserted, growth results from accomplishing a broader social and environmental mission. Unilever exists "for consumers, not shareholders," he said. "If we are in sync with consumer needs and the environment in which we operate, and take responsibility for our [societal impact], then the shareholder will also be rewarded."

Evaluating and working on sustainability impact are nothing new at Unilever. Prior to Polman taking the reins, the company already had multiple programs in place to manage the impact of its products and operations. But the existing programs and results—while good—simply didn't go far enough for Polman. So in late 2010 Unilever launched its Sustainable Living Plan—an aggressive long-term plan that takes capitalism to the next level. Under the plan, the company set out to "create a better future every day for people around the world: the people who work for us, those we do business with, the billions of people who use our products, and future generations whose quality of life depends on the way we protect the environment today." According to Polman, Unilever's long-run commercial success depends on how well it manages the social and environmental impact of its actions.

The Sustainable Living Plan sets out three major social and environmental objectives to be accomplished by 2020: "(1) To help more than one billion people take action to improve their health and well-being; (2) to halve the environmental footprint of the making and use of our products; and (3) to enhance the livelihoods of millions of people as we grow our business." The Sustainable Living Plan pulls together all of the work Unilever had already been doing and sets ambitious new sustainability goals. These goals span the entire value chain, from how the company sources raw materials to how consumers use and dispose of its products. "Our aim is to make our activities more sustainable and also encourage our customers, suppliers, and others to do the same," says the company.

On the "upstream supply side," more than half of Unilever's raw materials come from agriculture, so the company is helping suppliers develop sustainable farming practices that meet its own high expectations for environmental and social impact. Unilever assesses suppliers against two sets of standards. The

first is the Unilever Supplier Code, which calls for socially responsible actions regarding human rights, labor practices, product safety, and care for the environment. Second, specifically for agricultural suppliers, the Unilever Sustainable Agriculture Code details Unilever's expectations for sustainable agriculture practices so that it and its suppliers "can commit to the sustainability journey together."

But Unilever's Sustainable Living Plan goes far beyond simply creating more responsible supply and distribution chains. Approximately 68 percent of the total greenhouse gas footprint of Unilever's products and 50 percent of the water footprint occur during consumer use. So Unilever is also working with its consumers to improve the environmental impact of its products in use. About 2 billion people in 190 markets worldwide use a Unilever product on any given day. Therefore, small everyday consumer actions can add up to a big difference. Unilever sums it up with this equation: "Unilever brands $\times$ small everyday actions $\times$ billions of consumers = big difference."

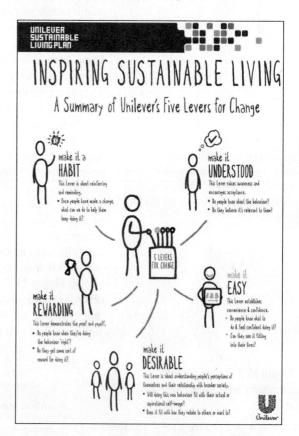

>> **As part of its Sustainable Living Plan, Unilever is working with its more than 2 billion customers worldwide to improve the social and environmental impact of its products in use. "Small actions. Big difference."**

Reproduced with kind permission of Unilever PLC and group companies.

For example, almost one-third of households worldwide use Unilever laundry products to do their washing—approximately 125 billion washes every year. Therefore, under its Sustainable Living Plan, Unilever is both creating more eco-friendly laundry products and motivating consumers to improve their laundry habits.

Around the world, for instance, Unilever is encouraging consumers to wash clothes at lower temperatures and use the correct dosage of detergent. Unilever products such as OMO and Persil Small & Mighty concentrated laundry detergents use less packaging, making them cheaper and less polluting to transport. More important, they've been reformulated to wash efficiently at lower temperatures, using less energy and water. Unilever estimates that these changes have achieved a 15 percent reduction in greenhouse gas emissions. Another Unilever product, Comfort One Rinse fabric conditioner, was created for hand washing clothes in developing and emerging markets where water is often in short supply. The innovative product requires only one bucket of water for rinsing rather than three, saving consumers time, effort, and 30 liters of water per wash.

Such energy and water savings don't show up on Unilever's income statement, but they will be extremely important to the people and the planet. "Ultimately," says the company, "we will only succeed if we inspire people around the world to take small, everyday actions that can add up to a big difference for the world." To meet this objective, Unilever has identified "Five Levers for Change"—things that its marketers can do to inspire people to adopt specific sustainable behaviors. The model helps marketers identify the barriers and triggers for change. The levers for change are: make it understood, make it easy, make it desirable, make it rewarding, and make it a habit.

Will Unilever's Sustainable Living Plan produce results for the company? So far, so good. Unilever is making excellent progress on its overall mission of "making sustainable living commonplace" and on its 79 aggressive Sustainable Living Plan goals. The company has already achieved 13 specific targets, is right on pace with 57 more, and is making good progress on the other nine. And despite volatility in its global markets, Unilever's profits continue to grow.

The sustainability plan is not just the right thing to do for people and the environment, claims Polman, it's also right for Unilever. The quest for sustainability saves money by reducing energy use and minimizing waste. It fuels innovation, resulting in new products and new consumer benefits. And it creates new market opportunities: More than half of Unilever's sales are from developing countries, the very places that face the greatest sustainability challenges.

In all, Polman predicts, the sustainability plan will help Unilever double in size while also creating a better future for billions of people without increasing the environmental footprint. "We do not believe there is a conflict between sustainability and profitable growth," he concludes. "The daily act of making and selling consumer goods drives economic and social progress. There are billions of people around the world who deserve the better quality of life that everyday products like soap, shampoo, and tea can provide. Sustainable living is not a pipedream. It can be done, and there is very little downside."

Sources: Based on quotes and other information from Andrew Saunders, "Paul Polman of Unilever," *Management Today,* March 2011, pp. 42–47; Adi Ignatius, "Captain Planet," *Harvard Business Review,* June 2012, pp. 2–8; "Unilever: Key Trends to Watch in 2015," *Forbes,* March 5, 2015, www.forbes.com/sites/greatspeculations/2015/03/05/unilever-key-trends-to-watch-in-2015/; and www.unilever.com/sustainable-living/the-sustainable-living-plan/, accessed September 2015.

---

practice *pollution prevention.* This involves more than pollution control—cleaning up waste after it has been created. Pollution prevention means eliminating or minimizing waste *before* it is created. Companies emphasizing prevention have responded with internal green marketing programs—designing and developing ecologically safer products, recyclable and biodegradable packaging, better pollution controls, and more energy-efficient operations.

For example, Nike makes shoes out of "environmentally preferred materials," recycles old sneakers, and educates young people about conservation, reuse, and recycling. Its revolutionary woven Flyknit shoes are lightweight, comfortable, and durable but produce 66 percent less material waste in production—the material wasted making each pair of Flyknits weighs only as much as a sheet of paper.

≫ SC Johnson—maker of familiar household brands ranging from Windex, Pledge, Shout, and Scrubbing Bubbles to Ziploc, OFF!, and Raid—sells concentrated versions of most of its household cleaners in recyclable bottles, helping to reduce the number of empty trigger bottles from landfills. The company has undertaken ten renewable energy initiatives to help create a smaller carbon footprint. Using renewable energy sources, its largest global manufacturing facility—the size of 36 football fields—is now able to generate most of its electrical energy onsite. The company's trademarked Greenlist process helped develop lighter weight Windex bottles that reduced consumer waste by one million pounds annually. What's more, these Windex bottles are now made from 100 percent post-consumer-recycled plastic. SC Johnson boasts a commitment to "creating winning products, ensuring less waste, reducing our carbon footprint, and helping make life better for families around the globe."[18]

Minimizing Our Greenhouse Gas Emissions

With three years of our current five-year environmental targets completed, this year SC Johnson achieved our greenhouse gas emissions goal for 2016. We aimed to reduce greenhouse gas emissions from our global manufacturing sites 48 percent versus our 2000 baseline, when indexed to production. In 2013, we reached a 50.5 percent reduction.

GLOBAL GREENHOUSE GAS REDUCTION

GOAL: By 2016, reduce greenhouse gas emissions from global manufacturing sites 48% versus our 2000 baseline.

WE NOW HAVE 10 RENEWABLE ENERGY INITIATIVES AROUND THE GLOBE TO HELP REDUCE OUR GREENHOUSE GAS EMISSIONS.

SMALLER FOOTPRINT

34 THE CHOICES WE MAKE | 2014 SUSTAINABILITY REPORT   WWW.SCJOHNSON.COM

≫ **Environmental sustainability:** Though sustainability initiatives such as using renewable energy sources, SC Johnson is committed to "creating winning products, ensuring less waste, reducing our carbon footprint, and helping make life better for families around the globe."

Image courtesy of SC Johnson

At the next level, companies can practice *product stewardship*—minimizing not only pollution from production and product design but also all environmental impacts throughout the full product life cycle while at the same time reducing costs. Many companies have adopted *design for environment (DFE)* and *cradle-to-cradle* practices. This involves thinking ahead to design products that are easier to recover, reuse, recycle, or safely return to nature after usage, thus becoming part of the ecological cycle. DFE and cradle-to-cradle practices not only help to sustain the environment, but they can also be highly profitable for the company.

For example, more than a decade ago, IBM started a business—IBM Global Asset Recovery Services—designed to reuse and recycle parts from returned mainframe computers and other equipment. Last year, IBM processed more than 54.3 million pounds of end-of-life products and product waste worldwide, stripping down old equipment to recover chips and valuable metals. Since 2002 it has processed more than 1.09 billion pounds of machines, parts, and material. IBM Global Asset Recovery Services finds uses for more than 99 percent of what it takes in, sending less than 1 percent to landfills and incineration facilities. What started out as an environmental effort has now grown into a multibillion-dollar IBM business that profitably recycles electronic equipment at 22 sites worldwide.[19]

Today's *greening* activities focus on improving what companies already do to protect the environment. The *beyond greening* activities identified in Figure 16.2 look to the future. First, internally, companies can plan for *new clean technology*. Many organizations that have made good sustainability headway are still limited by existing technologies. To create fully sustainable strategies, they will need to develop innovative new technologies.

For example, by 2020, Coca-Cola has committed to reclaiming and recycling the equivalent of all the packaging it uses around the world. It has also pledged to dramatically reduce its overall environmental footprint. To accomplish these goals, the company invests heavily in new clean technologies that address a host of environmental issues, such as recycling, resource usage, and distribution:[20]

> First, to attack the solid waste problem caused by its plastic bottles, Coca-Cola invested heavily to build the world's largest state-of-the-art plastic-bottle-to-bottle recycling plant. As a more permanent solution, Coke is researching and testing new bottles made from aluminum, corn, or bioplastics. It has been steadily replacing its PET plastic bottles with PlantBottle packaging, which incorporates 30 percent plant-based materials. The company is also designing more eco-friendly distribution alternatives. Currently, some 10 million vending machines and refrigerated coolers gobble up energy and use potent greenhouse gases called hydrofluorocarbons (HFCs) to keep Cokes cold. To eliminate them, the company invested $40 million in research and began installing sleek new HFC-free coolers that use 30 to 40 percent less energy—so far 1 million have been installed. Coca-Cola has even developed a line of "eKOCool" solar-powered coolers that not only conserve energy resources but are also functional in rural areas of emerging economies such as India, where conventional power sources are often unreliable. Coca-Cola also aims to become "water neutral" by researching ways to help its bottlers add back all the fresh water they extract during the production of Coca-Cola beverages.

Finally, companies can develop a *sustainability vision*, which serves as a guide to the future. It shows how the company's products and services, processes, and policies must evolve and what new technologies must be developed to get there. This vision of sustainability provides a framework for pollution control, product stewardship, and new environmental technology for the company and others to follow. It addresses not just challenges in the natural environment but also strategic opportunities for using environmental strategies to create sustainable value for the firm and its markets.

Most companies today focus on the upper-left quadrant of the grid in Figure 16.2, investing most heavily in pollution prevention. Some forward-looking companies practice product stewardship and are developing new environmental technologies. However, emphasizing only one or two quadrants in the environmental sustainability grid can be shortsighted. Investing only in the left half of the grid puts a company in a good position today but leaves it vulnerable in the future. In contrast, a heavy emphasis on the right half suggests that a company has good environmental vision but lacks the skills needed to implement it. Thus, companies should work at developing all four dimensions of environmental sustainability.

The North Face, for example, is doing just that through its own environmental sustainability actions and its impact on the actions of suppliers and consumers:[21]

>> **Sustainability vision: At The North Face, sustainability is about more than just doing the right thing—it also makes good business sense. Sustainability efforts such as its "Clothes the Loop" program are good for the company, its customers, *and* the planet.**

VF Corporation

The North Face's new headquarters building in Alameda, California, comes complete with solar panels and wind turbines that generate more electricity than the building uses. The building employs an evaporating cooling system that eliminates the need for emissions-heavy coolants. The company's other regional head-quarters and distribution centers also incorporate solar or water-saving features. In manufacturing, The North Face works closely with suppliers to achieve its goal to use polyester—which makes up 80 percent of its clothing lines—from 100 percent recycled content by 2016. The North Face also partners with suppliers to reduce waste and chemical, water, and energy usage in their mills. Since 2010, The North Face's suppliers have removed more than 100 tanker trucks of chemicals and more than 230 Olympic swimming pools of water from their manufacturing processes.

In addition, The North Face has dedicated itself to inspiring customers to reduce the waste generated by today's fast-fashion era. The company's lifetime apparel and gear warranty results in the return and repair of more than 80,000 products annually. >> The North Face also runs a program called "Clothes the Loop," by which it collects worn-out or unwanted used clothing of any brand from customers for recycling or renewal. Items dropped in its collection bins are sent to a recycling center where they are carefully sorted, then repurposed for reuse to extend their life or recycled into raw materials for use in making other products. Proceeds from the program benefit the Conservation Alliance, which funds community-based campaigns to protect shared wilderness and recreation areas.

For The North Face, being environmentally sustainable is about more than just doing the right thing. It also makes good business sense. More efficient operations and less wasteful products not only are good for the environment but also save The North Face money, helping it to deliver more value to customers. It's a winning combination. "At the heart of The North Face is a mission to inspire a global movement of outdoor exploration and conservation," says The North Face's president. We believe the success of our business is fundamentally linked to having a healthy planet."[22]

Public Actions to Regulate Marketing

Citizen concerns about marketing practices will usually lead to public attention and legislative proposals. Many of the laws that affect marketing were identified in Chapter 3. The task is to translate these laws into a language that marketing executives understand as they make decisions about competitive relations, products, price, promotion, and distribution channels. >> **Figure 16.3** illustrates the major legal issues facing marketing management.

Business Actions Toward Sustainable Marketing

At first, many companies opposed consumerism, environmentalism, and other elements of sustainable marketing. They thought the criticisms were either unfair or unimportant. But by now, most companies have grown to embrace sustainability principles as a way to create both immediate and future customer value and strengthen customer relationships.

Sustainable Marketing Principles

Under the sustainable marketing concept, a company's marketing should support the best long-run performance of the marketing system. It should be guided by five sustainable marketing principles: *consumer-oriented marketing, customer value marketing, innovative marketing, sense-of-mission marketing,* and *societal marketing.*

Consumer-Oriented Marketing

Consumer-oriented marketing
A company should view and organize its marketing activities from the consumer's point of view.

Consumer-oriented marketing means that the company should view and organize its marketing activities from the consumer's point of view. It should work hard to sense, serve, and satisfy the needs of a defined group of customers—both now and in the future. The good marketing companies that we've discussed throughout this text have had this in common: an all-consuming passion for delivering superior value to carefully chosen customers. Only by seeing the world through its customers' eyes can the company build sustainable and profitable customer relationships.

Customer Value Marketing

Customer value marketing
A company should put most of its resources into customer value-building marketing investments.

According to the principle of **customer value marketing**, the company should put most of its resources into customer value-building marketing investments. Many things marketers

>> **Figure 16.3 Major Marketing Decision Areas That May Be Called into Question under the Law**

Source: (photo) Wavebreakmedia/Shutterstock

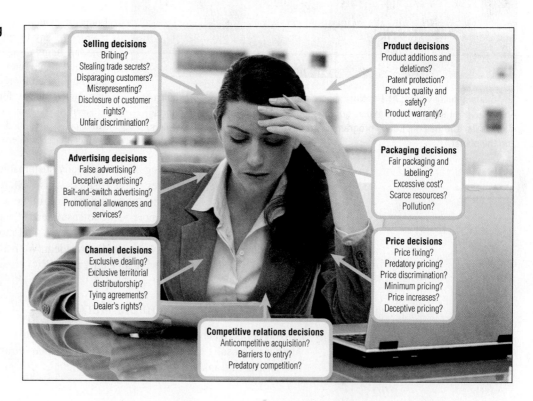

Selling decisions
Bribing?
Stealing trade secrets?
Disparaging customers?
Misrepresenting?
Disclosure of customer rights?
Unfair discrimination?

Product decisions
Product additions and deletions?
Patent protection?
Product quality and safety?
Product warranty?

Advertising decisions
False advertising?
Deceptive advertising?
Bait-and-switch advertising?
Promotional allowances and services?

Packaging decisions
Fair packaging and labeling?
Excessive cost?
Scarce resources?
Pollution?

Channel decisions
Exclusive dealing?
Exclusive territorial distributorship?
Tying agreements?
Dealer's rights?

Price decisions
Price fixing?
Predatory pricing?
Price discrimination?
Minimum pricing?
Price increases?
Deceptive pricing?

Competitive relations decisions
Anticompetitive acquisition?
Barriers to entry?
Predatory competition?

do—one-shot sales promotions, cosmetic product changes, direct-response advertising—may raise sales in the short run but add less *value* than would actual improvements in the product's quality, features, or convenience. Enlightened marketing calls for building long-run consumer engagement, loyalty, and relationships by continually improving the value consumers receive from the firm's market offering. By creating value *for* consumers, the company can capture value *from* consumers in return.

Innovative Marketing

Innovative marketing
A company should seek real product and marketing improvements.

The principle of **innovative marketing** requires that the company continuously seek real product and marketing improvements. The company that overlooks new and better ways to do things will eventually lose customers to another company that has found a better way. Think back to the Nike story in Chapter 1:[23]

>> **Innovative marketing: New products, such as the Nike FuelBand and Flyknit Racer, along with its innovative social media marketing efforts recently earned Nike the title as *Fast Company*'s number-one most innovative marketer.**

Rodrigo Reyes Marin/AFLO/Newscom

For nearly 50 years, through innovative marketing, Nike has built the ever-present swoosh into one of the world's best-known brand symbols. When sales languished in the late 1990s and new competitors made gains, Nike knew it had to reinvent itself via product and marketing innovation. "One of my fears is being this big, slow, constipated, bureaucratic company that's happy with its success," says Nike CEO Mark Parker. Instead, over the past few years, a hungry Nike has unleashed a number of highly successful new products. >> For example, with the relatively recent launch of the Nike Flyknit Racer, Nike has now reinvented the very way that shoes are manufactured. The featherweight Flyknit feels more like a sock with a sole. Woven not sewn, the Flyknit is super comfortable and durable, more affordable to make, and more environmentally friendly than traditional sneakers. Top off Nike's new products with a heavy investment in social media content and Nike remains the world's largest sports apparel company, 44 percent larger than closest rival adidas. Both *Forbes* and *Fast Company* recently anointed Nike as the world's number-one most innovative company.

Sense-of-Mission Marketing

Sense-of-mission marketing
A company should define its mission in broad *social* terms rather than narrow *product* terms.

Sense-of-mission marketing means that the company should define its mission in broad *social* terms rather than narrow *product* terms. When a company defines a social mission, employees feel better about their work and have a clearer sense of direction. Brands linked with broader missions can serve the best long-run interests of both the brand and consumers.

For example, successful home furnishings retailer IKEA has a deeply ingrained sense of mission—called The IKEA Way—to create a better everyday life for people by "offering well-designed, functional home furnishing products at prices so low that as many people as possible will be able to afford them." Johnson & Johnson's flagship Johnson's Baby brand dedicates itself to a mission of understanding babies and the special nurturing they require, then uses that knowledge to provide parents with safe and effective baby care products. The company's recently launched "Our Promise" advertising and social media campaign—which will include some 40 videos featuring and shared by Johnson's Baby brand employees—assures parents that "It's a responsibility we take seriously as we continue to apply our knowledge and research to bring you safe, innovative products that live up to our pure, mild, and gentle promise." The first "Our Promise" states that "We are moms and dads just like you. We'll always listen and be here for you. Promise." Sense-of-mission marketing has made Johnson's Baby the world's leading baby care brand, with a nearly 25 percent worldwide market share.[24]

Some companies define their overall corporate missions in broad societal terms. For example, under its buy-one-give-one model, TOMS seeks both profits and to make the world a better place. Thus, at TOMS, "doing good" and "doing well" go hand in hand. To achieve its social-change mission, TOMS has to make money. At the same time, the brand's social mission gives customers a powerful reason to buy (see Marketing at Work 16.2).

MARKETING AT WORK | 16.2

TOMS: "*Be* the Change You Want to See in the World"

If the world were a village of 100 people, 14 of the 100 would be illiterate, 20 would be malnourished, 23 would drink polluted water, 25 would have no shelter, 33 would have no electricity, and 40 would have no shoes. About a decade ago, these stark facts, especially the last one, struck Blake Mycoskie up close and personally as he visited Argentina to learn how to play polo, practice his tango, and do some community service work. While there, the sight of barefooted children, too poor to have shoes, stunned him.

So Mycoskie launched TOMS Shoes with $300,000 of his own money. The founding concept was this: For every pair of TOMS shoes that customers bought, the company would donate another pair of shoes to a child in need around the world. Mycoskie had previously started five successful strictly for-profit businesses. "But I was ready to do something more meaningful," says Mycoskie. "I always knew I wanted to help others. Now, it was time to do something that wasn't just for profit." Mycoskie remembered Mahatma Gandhi's saying: "*Be the change you want to see in the world.*"

"Doing good" is an important part of TOMS's mission. But so is "doing well"—the company is very much a for-profit venture. At TOMS, the two missions go hand in hand. Beyond being socially admirable, the buy-one-give-one-away concept is also a good business proposition. To achieve social change, TOMS has to make money—lots of it. At the same time, the social mission gives customers a powerful reason to buy.

With all these "do good" and "do well" goals swirling in his head, Mycoskie returned home from his Argentina trip, hired an intern, and set about making 250 pairs of shoes in the loft of his Santa Monica, California, home. Stuffing the shoes into three duffel bags, he made the fledgling company's first of many "Shoe Drop" tours, returning to the Argentine village and giving one pair of shoes to each child. Mycoskie arrived back home to find an article about his project on the front page of the *Los Angeles Times* Calendar section. TOMS had been in business for only two weeks, but by that very afternoon, he had orders for 2,200 pairs of shoes on his Web site.

True to the company's one-for-one promise, Mycoskie undertook a second TOMS Shoe Drop tour. Consistent with his new title, "Chief Shoe Giver of TOMS Shoes," he led 15 employees and volunteers back to Argentina, where they went from school to school, village to village, and gave away another 10,000 pairs of shoes. "We [didn't] just drop the shoes off, as the name might imply," says Mycoskie. "We [placed] the shoes on each child's feet so that we [could] establish a connection, which is such an important part of our brand. We want to give the children the feeling of love, and warmth, and experience. But *we* also get those feelings as we give the shoes."

Today, TOMS Shoes is, in fact, both "doing good" *and* "doing well." TOMS has given away more than 35 million

pairs of shoes in more than 70 countries. Under its one-for-one model, that means TOMS has also *sold* more than 35 million pairs of shoes, ringing up an estimated $300 million in annual revenues. Retailers such as Nordstrom, Neiman-Marcus, Urban Outfitters, Amazon.com, and even Whole Foods Market now offer TOMS shoes in locations across America. And the company just keeps growing. Says an optimistic Mycoskie, "I had no idea it would ever get this big."

TOMS's rapid growth is the result of purchases by caring customers who then tell the TOMS story to their friends. Although strongly represented on Facebook, Twitter, Pinterest, Instagram, YouTube, and other social media, TOMS spends almost nothing on traditional advertising and promotion. Instead, loyal TOMS disciples promote the brand with evangelical zeal. "Ultimately, it is our customers who drive our success," says Mycoskie. "Giving not only makes you feel good, but it actually is a very good business strategy, especially in this day and age. Your customers become your marketers."

Riding this success, TOMS and Mycoskie are now looking for even more ways to make the world a better place. Beyond the one-for-one shoes program (The Gift of Shoes), TOMS has already expanded its lines to include TOMS-branded eyewear and coffee. For each pair of TOMS glasses purchased, the company donates a free pair (The Gift of Sight); for each bag of TOMS coffee bought, the company donates a week of clean water to a person in need (The Gift of Water).

In fact, Mycoskie asserts, TOMS isn't just a shoe seller anymore—the company has even detached the word "Shoes" from its brand. Instead, he envisions TOMS as a lifestyle brand

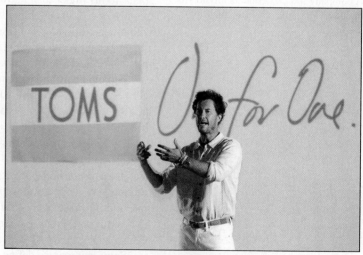

» **Founder Blake Mycoskie launched TOMS on a "one for one" model and a mission that seeks both company profits and to make the world a better place. At TOMS, "doing well" and "doing good" go hand in hand.**
ZUMA Press, Inc./Alamy

that sells many different products and uses the proceeds to fund social initiatives. "I want to show people that one-for-one is not just for the lifestyle-fashion space," Mycoskie says. "It can even be for everyday products."

How far might TOMS expand? Mycoskie isn't telling yet, but in addition to trademarking the term "One for One" for the shoe, eyewear, and coffee categories, TOMS has also sought to extend that trademark to a host of other beverages, from beer and mineral water to fruit drinks. And TOMS's parent company, Mycoskie LLC, has registered more than 200 Internet domain names, including tomswine.com, tomscreditcard.com, ticket-togive.com, and tomsmortgage.com. Mycoskie even envisions a chain of TOMS café-stores where people can not only buy TOMS shoes, glasses, or a bag of whole bean coffee, they can order a coffee beverage Starbucks style.

All this sounds pretty far-reaching. But, Mycoskie explains, TOMS's target customers are already seeking ways to consume responsibly. They're shopping at farmers markets, buying organic food and clothing, giving up their birthdays to raise money for charity, and buying TOMS shoes. Through expansion, TOMS is "taking them along this path where they can integrate giving," says Mycoskie. Customers who buy TOMS products are buying into doing something positive with their consumer dollars. Confirms the head of retail marketing for TOMS, "We're about empowering people, inspiring people, helping them to see the life they could live differently."

More than affecting how consumers buy and see life, TOMS is also out to change the way companies do business. "I believe what we're doing is affecting the way businesses will be built for hundreds of years to come," says Mycoskie grandly. If the number of copycats is any indication, that change is already underway. Dozens of companies have now adopted the one-for-one model pioneered by TOMS, from Warby Parker (eyewear), KNO Clothing (clothes for the homeless), and LSTN (headphones for hearing restoration) to One World Futbol (soccer balls), Smile Squared (toothbrushes), Soapbox Soaps (bar and liquid soaps), and Open Happiness (baby outfits and blankets—"one to love, one to give").

"My thinking was that TOMS would show that entrepreneurs no longer had to choose between earning money or making a difference in the world," says Mycoskie. "Business and charity or public service don't have to be mutually exclusive. In fact, when they come together, they can be very powerful."

Sources: Stephanie Strom, "Turning Coffee into Water to Expand Business Model," *New York Times*, March 12, 2014, B3; Stacy Perman, "Making a Do-Gooder's Business Model Work," *BusinessWeek Online,* January 26, 2009, www .businessweek.com/smallbiz/content/jan2009/sb20090123_ 264702.htm; Cotton Timberlake, "Compassionate Consumerism Draws Copycats," *Businessweek*, August 2, 2012, www.businessweek.com/articles/2012-08-02/compassionate-consumerism-draws-copycats; Jeff Chu and Jessica Weiss, "The Cobbler's Conundrum," *Fast Company*, July/August 2013, pp. 98–112; Christopher Marquis and Andrew Park, "Inside the Buy-One Give-One Model," *Stanford Social Innovation Review,* Winter 2014, pp. 28–33; Marco della Cava, "Toms Uses Instagram to Give Away a Million Shoes," *USA Today,* May 5, 2015, www .usatoday.com/story/tech/2015/05/04/toms-using-instagram-to-try-and-give-away-a-million-shoes/26892739/; and www.toms.com/about-toms#companyInfo and www.toms.com/one-for-one-en, accessed September 2015.

However, having a *double bottom line* of values and profits isn't easy. Over the years, brands such as Ben & Jerry's, Timberland, The Body Shop, and Burt's Bees—all known and respected for putting "principles before profits"—have at times struggled with less-than-stellar financial returns. In recent years, however, a new generation of social entrepreneurs has emerged, well-trained business managers who know that to *do good*, they must first *do well* in terms of profitable business operations. Moreover, today, socially responsible business is no longer the sole province of small, socially conscious entrepreneurs. Many large, established companies and brands—from Walmart and Nike to Starbucks and Coca-Cola—have adopted substantial social and environmental responsibility missions.

Societal Marketing

Following the principle of **societal marketing**, a company makes marketing decisions by considering consumers' wants, the company's requirements, consumers' long-run interests, and society's long-run interests. Companies should be aware that neglecting consumer and societal long-run interests is a disservice to consumers and society. Alert companies view societal problems as opportunities.

Sustainable marketing calls for products that are not only pleasing but also beneficial. The difference is shown in >> **Figure 16.4**. Products can be classified according to their degree of immediate consumer satisfaction and long-run consumer benefit.

Deficient products, such as bad-tasting and ineffective medicine, have neither immediate appeal nor long-run benefits. **Pleasing products** give high immediate satisfaction but may hurt consumers in the long run. Examples include cigarettes and junk food. **Salutary products** have low immediate appeal but may benefit consumers in the long run, for instance, bicycle helmets or some insurance products. **Desirable products** give both high immediate satisfaction and high long-run benefits, such as a tasty *and* nutritious breakfast food.

Societal marketing
A company should make marketing decisions by considering consumers' wants, the company's requirements, consumers' long-run interests, and society's long-run interests.

Deficient products
Products that have neither immediate appeal nor long-run benefits.

Pleasing products
Products that give high immediate satisfaction but may hurt consumers in the long run.

Salutary products
Products that have low immediate appeal but may benefit consumers in the long run.

Desirable products
Products that give both high immediate satisfaction and high long-run benefits.

>> **Figure 16.4 Societal Classification of Products**

Immediate Satisfaction

	Low	High
High Long-run Consumer Benefit	Salutary products	**Desirable products**
Low	Deficient products	Pleasing products

The goal? Create desirable products—those that create both immediate customer satisfaction and long-run benefit. For example, Vapur Anti-Bottles are highly functional but also convenient, stylish, and environmentally friendly.

Examples of desirable products abound. >> For example, Vapur makes a line of reusable, lightweight, collapsible water bottles that are highly functional and also more convenient, stylish, and environmentally friendly than either the disposable plastic bottles or rigid water bottles they replace. When full, pliable Vapur Anti-Bottles can be easily stuffed in pockets or backpacks; when empty, they can be rolled, folded, or flattened and easily tucked away. At the same time, the bottles require less energy to make and transport than rigid bottles, and unlike disposable plastic bottles, they don't clog landfills or require recycling. Vapur also donates portions of its sales to organizations such as Leave No Trace and The Conservation Alliance, and its Drops of Hope program annually donates thousands of Vapur bottles to charitable organizations around the world.[25]

>> **Desirable products:** Vapur Anti-Bottles' reusable, collapsible water bottles are highly functional and also more convenient, stylish, and environmentally friendly than either the disposable plastic bottles or rigid water bottles they replace.
Vapur, Inc.

Companies should try to turn all of their products into desirable products. The challenge posed by pleasing products is that they sell very well but may end up hurting the consumer. The product opportunity, therefore, is to add long-run benefits without reducing the product's pleasing qualities. The challenge posed by salutary products is to add some pleasing qualities so that they will become more desirable in consumers' minds.

For example, PepsiCo hired a team of "idealistic scientists," headed by a former director of the World Health Organization, to help the company create attractive new healthy product options while "making the bad stuff less bad." PepsiCo wants healthy products to be a $30 billion business for the company by 2020. The group of physicians, PhDs, and other health advocates, under the direction of PepsiCo's vice president for global health policy, looks for healthier ingredients that can go into multiple products as well as reductions of sugar, salt, and fat while maintaining the same flavor in its familiar products. For example, since forming the team, PepsiCo's Frito-Lay unit has cut the salt in all of its potato chips by 25 percent. To help cut calories, the company now uses a zero-calorie sweetener, Pure Via, in its Tropicana Trop50 orange juice and Gatorade G2 brands. And it recently replaced artificial sweetener aspartame in its Diet Pepsi with natural, no-calorie sucralose. PepsiCo's nutrition business revenue now represents 20 percent of its annual net revenue—more than $13 billion a year.[26]

Marketing Ethics

Good ethics are a cornerstone of sustainable marketing. In the long run, unethical marketing harms customers and society as a whole. Further, it eventually damages a company's reputation and effectiveness, jeopardizing its very survival. Thus, the sustainable marketing goals of long-term consumer and business welfare can be achieved only through ethical marketing conduct.

Conscientious marketers face many moral dilemmas. The best thing to do is often unclear. Because not all managers have fine moral sensitivity, companies need to develop *corporate marketing ethics policies*—broad guidelines that everyone in the organization must follow. These policies should cover distributor relations, advertising standards, customer service, pricing, product development, and general ethical standards.

The finest guidelines cannot resolve all the difficult ethical situations the marketer faces. **≫ Table 16.1** lists some difficult ethical issues marketers could face during their careers. If marketers choose immediate-sales-producing actions in all of these cases, their marketing behavior might well be described as immoral or even amoral. If they refuse to go along with *any* of the actions, they might be ineffective as marketing managers and unhappy because of the constant moral tension. Managers need a set of principles that will help them figure out the moral importance of each situation and decide how far they can go in good conscience.

But *what* principle should guide companies and marketing managers on issues of ethics and social responsibility? One philosophy is that the free market and the legal system should decide such issues. Under this principle, companies and their managers are not responsible for making moral judgments. Companies can in good conscience do whatever the market and legal systems allow.

However, history provides an endless list of examples of company actions that were legal but highly irresponsible. A second philosophy puts responsibility not on the system but in the hands of individual companies and managers. This more enlightened philosophy suggests that a company should have a social conscience. Companies and managers should apply high standards of ethics and morality when making corporate decisions, regardless of "what the system allows."

Each company and marketing manager must work out a philosophy of socially responsible and ethical behavior. Under the societal marketing concept, each manager must look beyond what is legal and allowed and develop standards based on personal integrity, corporate conscience, and long-run consumer welfare.

Dealing with issues of ethics and social responsibility in a proactive, open, and forthright way helps to build and maintain strong customer relationships based on honesty and trust. For example, think again about SC Johnson, maker of familiar home-products

---

≫ Table 16.1 | Some Morally Difficult Situations in Marketing

1. Your R&D department has slightly changed one of your company's products. It is not really "new and improved," but you know that putting this statement on the package and in advertising will increase sales. What would you do?

2. You have been asked to add a stripped-down model to your line that could be advertised to pull customers into the store. The product won't be very good, but salespeople will be able to switch buyers who come into the store up to higher-priced units. You are asked to give the green light for the stripped-down version. What would you do?

3. You are thinking of hiring a product manager who has just left a competitor's company. She would be more than happy to tell you all the competitor's plans for the coming year. What would you do?

4. One of your top dealers in an important territory recently has had family troubles, and his sales have slipped. It looks like it will take him a while to straighten out his family troubles. Meanwhile, you are losing many sales. Legally, on performance grounds, you can terminate the dealer's franchise and replace him. What would you do?

5. You have a chance to win a big account in another country that will mean a lot to you and your company. The purchasing agent hints that a "gift" would influence the decision. Such gifts are common in that country, and some of your competitors will probably make one. What would you do?

6. You have heard that a competitor has a new product feature that will make a big difference in sales. The competitor will demonstrate the feature in a private dealer meeting at the annual trade show. You can easily send a snooper to this meeting to learn about the new feature. What would you do?

7. You have to choose between three advertising and social media campaigns outlined by your agency. The first (a) is a soft-sell, honest, straight-information campaign. The second (b) uses sex-loaded emotional appeals and exaggerates the product's benefits. The third (c) involves a noisy, somewhat irritating commercial that is sure to gain audience attention. Pretests show that the campaigns are effective in the following order: c, b, and a. What would you do?

8. You are interviewing a capable female applicant for a job as salesperson. She is better qualified than the men who have been interviewed. Nevertheless, you know that in your industry some important customers prefer dealing with men, and you will lose some sales if you hire her. What would you do?

brands such as Pledge, Shout, Windex, Ziploc, and Saran Wrap. SC Johnson believes deeply that "Integrity is part of our DNA. It's been our family way since 1886." Based on that belief, the company has a long tradition of doing what's right, even at the expense of sales. Just one example involves Saran Wrap, a longtime market leader and one of SC Johnson's best-known and biggest brands:[27]

> For more than 50 years, Saran Wrap was made with polyvinylidene chloride (PVDC), an ingredient responsible for the product's two major differentiating features: impenetrable odor barrier qualities and superior microwavability. Without PVDC, Saran Wrap would have been no better than competing wraps by Glad and Reynolds, which did not contain PVDC. In the early 2000s, however, regulators, environmentalists, and consumers began to voice concerns about materials containing chlorine, specifically polyvinyl chloride (PVC). In fact, SC Johnson's own Greenlist analysis—by which it rates product ingredients based on their impact on environmental and human health—confirmed the hazards of PVCs, and the company quickly pledged to eliminate them from its products and packaging.
>
> But SC Johnson took things a step further. In 2004, it also eliminated PVDCs, even though that important ingredient had not yet come under scrutiny. The company developed a PVDC-free polyethylene version of Saran Wrap, an admittedly less effective product. Sure enough, Saran Wrap's market share dropped from 18 percent in 2004 to only 11 percent today. Over the years, however, even though such decisions have sometimes hurt sales, they have helped SC Johnson to earn and keep the trust of customers. "I don't regret the decision," says SC Johnson's CEO. "Despite the cost, it was the right thing to do, and ... I sleep better at night because of it. We gained a surer sense of who we are as a company and what we want SC Johnson to represent."

As with environmentalism, the issue of ethics presents special challenges for international marketers. Business standards and practices vary a great deal from one country to the next. For example, bribes and kickbacks are illegal for U.S. firms, and various treaties against bribery and corruption have been signed and ratified by more than 60 countries. Yet these are still standard business practices in many countries. The World Bank estimates that bribes totaling more than $1 trillion per year are paid out worldwide. One study showed that the most flagrant bribe-paying firms were from Indonesia, Mexico, China, and Russia. Other countries where corruption is common include Sierra Leone, Kenya, and Yemen. The least corrupt were companies from Australia, Denmark, Finland, and Japan.[28] The question arises as to whether a company must lower its ethical standards to compete effectively in countries with lower standards. The answer is no. Companies should make a commitment to a common set of shared standards worldwide.

Many industrial and professional associations have suggested codes of ethics, and many companies are now adopting their own codes. For example, the American Marketing Association, an international association of marketing managers and scholars, developed a code of ethics that calls on marketers to adopt the following ethical norms:[29]

- *Do no harm.* This means consciously avoiding harmful actions or omissions by embodying high ethical standards and adhering to all applicable laws and regulations in the choices we make.
- *Foster trust in the marketing system.* This means striving for good faith and fair dealing so as to contribute toward the efficacy of the exchange process as well as avoiding deception in product design, pricing, communication, and delivery or distribution.
- *Embrace ethical values.* This means building relationships and enhancing consumer confidence in the integrity of marketing by affirming these core values: honesty, responsibility, fairness, respect, transparency, and citizenship.

Companies are also developing programs to teach managers about important ethical issues and help them find the proper responses. They hold ethics workshops and seminars and create ethics committees. Furthermore, most major U.S. companies have appointed high-level ethics officers to champion ethical issues and help resolve ethics problems and concerns facing employees. And most companies have established their own codes of ethical conduct.

>> **Marketing ethics: Google's Code of Conduct is the mechanism by which the company puts its well-known "Don't be evil" motto into practice.**

Pearson Education

Google is a good example. >> Its official Google Code of Conduct is the mechanism by which the company puts its well-known "Don't be evil" motto into practice. The detailed code's core message is simple: Google employees (known inside as "Googlers") must earn users' faith and trust by holding themselves to the highest possible standards of ethical business conduct. The Google Code of Conduct is "about providing our users unbiased access to information, focusing on their needs, and giving them the best products and services that we can. But it's also about doing the right thing more generally—following the law, acting honorably, and treating each other with respect."

Google requires all Googlers—from board members to the newest employee—to take personal responsibility for practicing both the spirit and letter of the code and encouraging other Googlers to do the same. It urges employees to report violations to their managers, to human resources representatives, or using an Ethics & Compliance hotline. "If you have a question or ever think that one of your fellow Googlers or the company as a whole may be falling short of our commitment, don't be silent," states the code. "We want—and need—to hear from you."[30]

Still, written codes and ethics programs do not ensure ethical behavior. Ethics and social responsibility require a total corporate commitment. They must be a component of the overall corporate culture. As the Google Code of Conduct concludes: "It's impossible to spell out every possible ethical scenario we might face. Instead, we rely on one another's good judgment to uphold a high standard of integrity for ourselves and our company. Remember ... don't be evil. If you see something that isn't right, speak up!"

The Sustainable Company

At the foundation of marketing is the belief that companies that fulfill the needs and wants of customers will thrive. Companies that fail to meet customer needs or that intentionally or unintentionally harm customers, others in society, or future generations will decline.

Says one observer, "Sustainability is an emerging business megatrend, like electrification and mass production, that will profoundly affect companies' competitiveness and even their survival." Says another, "increasingly, companies and leaders will be assessed not only on immediate results but also on ... the ultimate effects their actions have on societal wellbeing. This trend has been coming in small ways for years but now is surging. So pick up your recycled cup of fair-trade coffee, and get ready."[31]

Sustainable companies are those that create value for customers through socially, environmentally, and ethically responsible actions. Sustainable marketing goes beyond caring for the needs and wants of today's customers. It means having concern for tomorrow's customers in ensuring the survival and success of the business, shareholders, employees, and the broader world in which they all live. It means pursuing the mission of a triple bottom line: people, planet, profits. Sustainable marketing provides the context in which companies can build profitable customer relationships by creating value *for* customers in order to capture value *from* customers in return—now and in the future.

MyMarketingLab

If assigned by your instructor, complete the questions marked with the ⭐ from the EOC Discussion Questions section in the MyLab. To complete the Marketing by the Numbers problems found in this section, go to your Assignments in the MyLab.

REVIEWING AND EXTENDING THE CONCEPTS

CHAPTER REVIEW AND CRITICAL THINKING

Objectives Review

In this chapter, we addressed many of the important *sustainable marketing* concepts related to marketing's sweeping impact on individual consumers, other businesses, and society as a whole. Sustainable marketing requires socially, environmentally, and ethically responsible actions that bring value to not only present-day consumers and businesses but also future generations and society as a whole. Sustainable companies are those that act responsibly to create value for customers in order to capture value from customers in return—now and in the future.

▶ OBJECTIVE 16-1   Define *sustainable marketing* and discuss its importance. (pp 490–492)

Sustainable marketing calls for meeting the present needs of consumers and businesses while preserving or enhancing the ability of future generations to meet their needs. Whereas the marketing concept recognizes that companies thrive by fulfilling the day-to-day needs of customers, sustainable marketing calls for socially and environmentally responsible actions that meet both the immediate and future needs of customers and the company. Truly sustainable marketing requires a smooth-functioning marketing system in which consumers, companies, public policy makers, and others work together to ensure responsible marketing actions.

▶ OBJECTIVE 16-2   Identify the major social criticisms of marketing. (pp 492–499)

Marketing's *impact on individual consumer welfare* has been criticized for its high prices, deceptive practices, high-pressure selling, shoddy or unsafe products, planned obsolescence, and poor service to disadvantaged consumers. Marketing's *impact on society* has been criticized for creating false wants and too much materialism, too few social goods, and cultural pollution. Critics have also denounced marketing's *impact on other businesses* for harming competitors and reducing competition through acquisitions, practices that create barriers to entry, and unfair competitive marketing practices. Some of these concerns are justified; some are not.

▶ OBJECTIVE 16-3   Define *consumerism* and *environmentalism* and explain how they affect marketing strategies. (pp 499–506)

Concerns about the marketing system have led to citizen action movements. *Consumerism* is an organized social movement intended to strengthen the rights and power of consumers relative to sellers. Alert marketers view it as an opportunity to serve consumers better by providing more consumer information, education, and protection. *Environmentalism* is an organized social movement seeking to minimize the harm done to the environment and quality of life by marketing practices. Most companies are now accepting responsibility for doing no environmental harm. They are adopting policies of *environmental sustainability*—developing strategies that both sustain the environment and produce profits for the company. Both consumerism and environmentalism are important components of sustainable marketing.

▶ OBJECTIVE 16-4   Describe the principles of sustainable marketing. (pp 506–510)

Many companies originally resisted these social movements and laws, but most now recognize a need for positive consumer information, education, and protection. Under the sustainable marketing concept, a company's marketing should support the best long-run performance of the marketing system. It should be guided by five sustainable marketing principles: *consumer-oriented marketing, customer value marketing, innovative marketing, sense-of-mission marketing*, and *societal marketing*.

▶ OBJECTIVE 16-5   Explain the role of ethics in marketing. (pp 510–513)

Increasingly, companies are responding to the need to provide company policies and guidelines to help their managers deal with questions of *marketing ethics*. Of course, even the best guidelines cannot resolve all the difficult ethical decisions that individuals and firms must make. But there are some principles from which marketers can choose. One principle states that the free market and the legal system should decide such issues. A second and more enlightened principle puts responsibility not on the system but in the hands of individual companies and managers. Each firm and marketing manager must work out a philosophy of socially responsible and ethical behavior. Under the sustainable marketing concept, managers must look beyond what is legal and allowable and develop standards based on personal integrity, corporate conscience, and long-term consumer welfare.

Key Terms

Objective 16-1
Sustainable marketing (p 490)

Objective 16-3
Consumerism (p 500)
Environmentalism (p 501)
Environmental sustainability (p 501)

Objective 16-4
Consumer-oriented marketing (p 506)
Customer value marketing (p 506)
Innovative marketing (p 507)
Sense-of-mission marketing (p 507)

Societal marketing (p 509)
Deficient products (p 509)
Pleasing products (p 509)
Salutary products (p 509)
Desirable products (p 509)

Discussion Questions

16-1. What is sustainable marketing? Explain how the sustainable marketing concept differs from the marketing concept and the societal marketing concept. (AASCB: Communication)

16-2. What is planned obsolescence? How do marketers respond to this criticism? (AACSB: Communication; Reflective Thinking)

16-3. How can marketers respond to the criticism that marketing creates false wants and encourages materialism? (AACSB: Communication)

16-4. How can marketing practices create barriers to entry that potentially harm other firms? Are these barriers helpful or harmful to consumers? (AACSB: Communication; Reflective Thinking)

16-5. What is environmental sustainability? How should companies gauge their progress toward achieving it? (AACSB: Communication)

Critical Thinking Exercises

16-6. The chapter discusses McDonald's responses to social responsibility criticisms. Find other examples of how marketers have responded to social criticisms of their products or marketing practices. (AACSB: Communication; Reflective Thinking)

16-7. Deceptive advertising hurts consumers and competitors alike, and the Federal Trade Commission has stepped up efforts to combat it. Discuss a recent example of decep-

tive advertising investigated by the FTC and one investigated by the industry self-regulatory body, the National Advertising Division (NAD). (AACSB: Communication; Use of IT; Reflective Thinking)

16-8. In a small group, discuss each of the morally difficult situations in marketing presented in Table 16.1. Which ethics philosophy is guiding your decision in each situation? (AACSB: Communication; Ethical Reasoning)

MINICASES AND APPLICATIONS

Online, Mobile, and Social Media Marketing

Facebook changed its policy and now allows teens' posts to become public. Before the change, Facebook would allow 13- to 17-year-old users' posts to be seen only by their "friends" and "friends of friends." Now, however, their posts can be seen by anyone on the network if teens choose to make their posts "public." Twitter, another social medium gaining popularity with teens, has always let users, including teens, share Tweets publicly. But because of Facebook's vast reach, privacy advocates are very concerned about this latest development, particularly when it comes to children's safety. Online predators and bullying are real safety issues facing youth. Other criticisms of Facebook's decision boil down to money—some argue that the change was just about monetizing kids. Facebook can offer a younger demographic to advertisers wanting to reach them.

Teens and Social Media

Facebook defended its actions, saying the change in policy is due to teenagers wanting the ability to post publicly, primarily for fundraising and promoting extracurricular activities such as sports and other school student organizations. Facebook has added precautions, such as a pop-up warning before teens can post publicly and making "seen only by friends" as the default that must be changed if the teen desires posts to be public.

16-9. Is Facebook acting responsibly or merely trying to monetize kids as critics claim? (AACSB: Communication; Ethical Reasoning)

16-10. Come up with creative ways marketers can reach this demographic on Facebook without alienating parents. (AACSB: Communication; Reflective Thinking)

Marketing Ethics   Pricey Deal?

Kmart offers a lease-to-own program targeted to low-income consumers and is taking some heat over it. Rent-to-own is not new—chains such as Aaron's and Rent-A-Center have been around for years—but it is new that a mainstream retailer has moved into this market. Kmart's parent corporation, Sears Holdings, launched a similar program, and according to a company executive, it is satisfying the unmet needs of new customers. Some critics say that it is just encouraging instant gratification and exploiting disadvantaged consumers. These types of customers don't qualify for credit and don't have enough cash to purchase desired products outright, such as televisions and other big-ticket items. However, a $300 TV purchased through Kmart's program ends up costing consumers $415 if purchased at the end of the lease. If customers make just minimum payments over the course of the lease, one expert calculated, that it is equivalent to charging a 117 percent annual interest rate. Sears spokespeople defend their service as being better for consumers compared with other rent-to-own options because the retailer does not mark up the price of the product beyond the normal retail markup and limits the lease period to 18 months, whereas other national rental chains' prices are much higher and leases can run two to four years.

16-11. Are Sears and Kmart exploiting disadvantaged consumers? Explain why or why not. (AACSB: Communication; Ethical Reasoning)

16-12. Low-income consumers often don't have bank accounts and credit cards. Describe how some financial institutions are trying to meet the needs of these "unbanked" consumers. (AACSB: Communication; Reflective Thinking)

Marketing by the Numbers   The Cost of Sustainability

Kroger, the country's leading grocery-only chain, added a line of private-label organic and natural foods call Simple Truth to its stores. If you've priced organic foods, you know they are more expensive. For example, a dozen conventionally farmed Grade A eggs at Kroger costs consumers $1.70, whereas Simple Truth eggs are priced at $3.50 per dozen. One study found that, overall, the average price of organic foods is 85 percent more than that of conventional foods. However, if prices get too high, consumers will not purchase the organic options. One element of sustainability is organic farming, which costs much more than conventional farming, and those higher costs are passed on to consumers. Suppose that a conventional egg farmer's average fixed costs per year for conventionally farmed eggs are $1 million, but an organic egg farmer's fixed costs are three times that amount. Further assume that the organic farmer's variable costs of $1.80 per dozen are twice as much as a conventional farmer's variable costs. Refer to Appendix 3: Marketing by the Numbers to answer the following questions.

16-13. Most large egg farmers sell eggs directly to retailers. Using Kroger's prices, what is the farmer's price per dozen to the retailer for conventional and organic eggs if Kroger's margin is 20 percent based on its retail price? (AACSB: Communication; Analytical Reasoning)

16-14. How many dozen eggs does a conventional farmer need to sell to break even? How many does an organic farmer need to sell to break even? (AACSB: Communication; Analytical Reasoning)

Video Case: Honest Tea

Honest Tea, the Coca-Cola brand that produced $130 million in global revenues last year, got its start because cofounder Seth Goldman didn't like the options in the beverage coolers at convenience stores. So with the help of a former professor, he launched Honest Tea—the nation's first fully organic bottled tea.

But the company's drive for success was not based not as much on profits as on a desire to change the world. With social responsibility steeped deep into its business model, Honest Tea set out to help develop the economic structure of impoverished nations. Honest Tea purchased raw ingredients from Native American and South African farmers and invested in its supplier-farmers to help them become self-reliant. Although Honest Tea has been a wholly owned subsidiary of the Coca-Cola Company since 2011, it continues to operate on the principles of social responsibility established by its founders.

After viewing the video featuring Honest Tea, answer the following questions:

16-15. List as many examples as you can showing how Honest Tea defies the common social criticisms of marketing.

16-16. How does Honest Tea practice sustainable marketing?

16-17. With all its efforts to do good, can Honest Tea continue to do well? Explain.

Company Cases   16 Adidas/5 GoldieBlox

See Appendix 1 for cases appropriate for this chapter. **Case 16, Adidas: Athletic Apparel With Purpose.** While it has been fighting for global dominance in athletic footwear and apparel, adidas has been quietly establishing itself as one of the most sustainable corporations in the world. **Case 5, GoldieBlox:**

Swimming Upstream Against Consumer Perceptions. A new toy company, GoldieBlox is out to change how people think of toys for girls with the message that success comes not from playing with dollhouses, but from building them.

MyMarketingLab

If assigned by your instructor, complete these writing sections from your Assignments in the MyLab.

16-18. What is consumerism? What rights do consumers have, and why do some critics feel buyers need more protection? (AACSB: Communication)

16-19. Discuss the philosophies that might guide marketers facing ethical issues. (AACSB: Written and Oral Communication)

Appendix 1 Company Cases

Company Case 1

FedEx: Making Every Customer Experience Outstanding

When you have a package that absolutely must arrive at a distant location within 24 hours, what's the first company that comes to mind? More than likely, it's FedEx. Just as Google is used as a verb for Internet search, FedEx is often synonymous with overnight shipping, as in "I'll FedEx it to you." From its humble beginnings in 1971, FedEx has grown into a $46-billion-a-year global giant. Every day, 325,000 FedEx employees deliver 11 million packages via 673 aircraft and 100,000 motor vehicles, connecting more than 99 percent of world's GDP. How did FedEx become so successful? Through its single-minded focus on the customer experience.

Starting with a Customer Need

Even in this era when Internet start-ups get all the press for amazing entrepreneurial stories, FedEx still stands as one of the greatest business success stories of the past 40 years. It all started in the 1960s when Fred Smith, FedEx's founder and current chairman and CEO, was an undergraduate student at Yale, paying his way through school working as a charter pilot. As he crossed paths with corporate pilots, the young Smith saw a trend emerging. Computers and other high-tech components were rapidly finding their way into the business world. But when those things broke down, companies had difficulty getting urgently needed parts to the right places quickly. There were no services for regional or national overnight shipping. In fact, companies often used their own corporate planes as internal courier systems—at great expense—to cart around parts in an effort to minimize downtime.

Smith wrote a paper for an economics class at Yale, proposing the idea of a national overnight-delivery service (reportedly, the professor gave him a C on the paper, calling the idea infeasible). But it wasn't until after college and a tour of duty in the Marine Corps that Smith decided to actually do something about the idea. Smith knew that the need for businesses to move packages fast would only grow with time. With that insight, the FedEx Corporation (Federal Express back then) was born, with eight aircraft providing overnight delivery service to 35 cities.

Putting the Customer First

More than just a good idea at the right time, one thing has kept FedEx growing and thriving over the past four decades. From the beginning, FedEx was built on a foundation of obsessive customer focus. "If people were going to use FedEx in lieu of having incalculable amounts of money tied up in inventories, it 'absolutely, positively' had to be there when promised," said Smith in a recent interview. Hence came FedEx's first positioning slogan—FedEx: When it absolutely, positively has to be there overnight.

To ensure that FedEx could deliver on that promise, Smith pursued the goal with a "no holds barred" vigor. He began FedEx with a nationwide clearinghouse infrastructure and its own fleet of planes and trucks, giving the company complete control. But while complex and expensive, those attributes were conventional. It was the unconventional elements that characterized the boundless pursuit of customer service that formed the core of the FedEx brand.

For example, when FedEx first started shipping packages, no one had ever printed "multiform, sequentially numbered" labels that could be attached to items and machine-read. And no other shipper had even contemplated using small, hand-held computers with barcode-scanning capabilities to communicate shipping information on a real-time basis. No company was tracking inventory on the move, let alone coordinating it with stationary inventory. It was these kinds of innovative capabilities that allowed Smith and FedEx to reliably move packages from one city to another in such a short time. These technologies not only made FedEx's service possible, they also gave rise to companies such as Walmart, Dell, and countless others.

The tenacious pursuit of fulfilling customer needs in FedEx's early days led to what is known at the company today as the "Purple Promise," a promise committed to memory by every FedEx employee: "I will make every FedEx experience outstanding." Fulfilling this promise requires elements of good service, such as treating "customers in a professional, competent, polite, and caring manner" and handling "every customer transaction with the precision required to achieve the highest quality service." But the Purple Promise goes far beyond traditional service. It requires all employees, regardless of their job titles, to recognize that what they do affects how customers perceive the FedEx brand.

Consider how FedEx fixed the problem of its "leaning tower of packages." For years, FedEx management thought of the majority of customers at its World Service Centers and FedEx Office locations as "Frisbees"—customers who step in, drop off packages, and step back out as quickly as possible. Management also thought it was doing a good job of serving these customers. However, recently, company satisfaction surveys began to reveal that not all customers were pleased with their experiences when dropping off packages.

FedEx quickly commissioned a study, which revealed that only about 10 percent of its drop-off customers were, in fact,

"Frisbees." The other 90 percent fell evenly into three different behavioral groups. The most intriguing of these groups was the "Confirmers." In a word, Confirmers were "uneasy." They entered a FedEx location well-prepared, with packages wrapped and ready to go. They had a clear sense of how much shipments would cost and how long they would take to deliver. Still, as they dropped off packages, they were filled with worry that something could go wrong with the shipment. That worry was compounded by the "leaning tower of packages"—FedEx-speak for the piles of packages already stacked behind the counter. For employees, there was no concern in the world that these packages would reach their destination on time. For the Confirmers, however, seemingly haphazard piles of packages sent a visual cue that something in the process was broken, increasing the chances that their packages might get lost. These uneasy customers were on the verge of taking their shipping business elsewhere.

FedEx's Purple Promise drove the company to make a simple, system-wide change that put the minds of Confirmers at ease. The company placed a wall behind the counter with five presort windows. Employees were then trained to thank the customer, turn around, and slip the package through the window that corresponded to the type of service the customer had purchased. For the Confirmers, this careful and organized processing of packages was a visible confirmation that packages were safely on their way.

The Purple Promise Today

A customer-centric culture requires that a company be flexible and dynamic, modifying its strategies and tactics to fit consumer trends. One example of how FedEx remains open to customer-centered change is the degree to which it has embraced social media. At FedEx, the customer service function is responsible for delighting customers through excellent and timely service. Given the omnipresence of mobile devices and social media in consumers' lives these days, the customer service function at FedEx often pursues the goal of delighting customers through social channels, including social networks such as Facebook and Twitter, blogs, and live chat.

Marketing through social and mobile media is all the rage these days. But at FedEx, it's more action than talk. And FedEx goes beyond just listening to customers; it engages them and helps solve their problems. Take the example of Nicole Snow, a now-loyal FedEx customer who owns a small business in Maine called "Darn Good Yarn."

[Nicole Snow] is in a remote area with few shipping options, and extreme weather makes running her home business more difficult. One day she reached out to FedEx on social networks and asked for help in getting her supply chain set up. The team responded immediately and helped her solve the problem.

Snow's story is fascinating. She hires women in India and Nepal to make yarn out of reclaimed materials like silk. She is nurturing a supply chain that reaches halfway across the globe as well as sourcing from local businesses in Maine. She is highly engaged in the community through activities like teaching knitting classes. "I take materials that otherwise would be thrown out in India and Nepal and import them into Maine and then FedEx

them all over the world to my customers. I know that I can get something from India and to my house in the middle of Maine in three days. That's amazing!" Snow is now a huge FedEx fan and advocate. She shares stories of excellent FedEx support everywhere she goes.

Chinks in the Armor

Despite FedEx's obsessive customer focus, with 11 million packages flying all over the planet every day, there are bound to be some glitches now and then. And while social media have been a tremendous blessing, they can also be a curse. In the past few years, FedEx has had its share of videos go viral showing employees mishandling packages. For example, there's the one of a Maryland FedEx driver, captured by the resident's security camera, throwing a package onto a front porch from a distance of about 20 feet. Then there's the FedEx truck driving down a Colorado highway two days before Christmas with its rear door wide open and packages falling out onto the highway. And who can forget the FedEx driver who tossed a package containing a Samsung computer monitor over a six-foot iron fence onto a customer's driveway, with the FedEx truck clearly visible in the background.

As if employees caught on video aren't bad enough, a Philadelphia FedEx driver was caught stealing iPhones out of customers' packages. He was charged, tried, and found guilty to the tune of $40,000 worth of stolen merchandise. On a corporate level, FedEx was caught overcharging some business customers by as much as $3 per package over a three-year period. The company settled the ensuing lawsuit for $21.5 million.

Although none of these actions are justifiable, the fallout would have been far worse had it not been for similar bad press for competitor UPS, including videos of drivers throwing packages, making obscene gestures at a security camera, and even stealing iPads off porches (delivered by FedEx, no less). In FedEx's case, the company took responsibility when it needed to, fired offending employees, and made restitution for damages. In the case of the Samsung monitor–throwing incident, the aggrieved customer even received a personal visit and apology from FedEx's senior vice president of operations. "This goes directly against all FedEx values," declared the executive.

Today, FedEx continues to focus on its goal to "make every FedEx experience outstanding." According to one recent company statement, "Everyone at FedEx is committed to placing customer needs at the center of everything we do." The pledge seems to receive more than just lip service. FedEx routinely ranks among the top 10 of both *MSN Money*'s "Customer Service Hall of Fame" and *Fortune*'s "World's Most Admired Companies." With founder Fred Smith still at the helm after more than 40 years, it appears that FedEx intends to be around for the long haul by putting customers first.

Questions for Discussion

1. Give examples of needs, wants, and demands that FedEx customers demonstrate, differentiating these three concepts.

2. Describe FedEx in terms of the value it provides customers. How does FedEx engage customers?

3. Evaluate FedEx's performance relative to customer expectations. What is the outcome of this process?

4. Which of the five marketing management orientations best applies to FedEx?

5. With increased competition today, how can FedEx continue to be competitive?

Sources: Christopher Tkaczyk, "World's Most Admired Companies," *Fortune*, March 1, 2015, pp. 97–104; "Driver Alerts FedEx Delivery Man to Packages Spilling from Open Truck," *CBS Local*, December 23, 2014, http://denver.cbslocal.com/2014/12/22/driver-alerts-fedex-delivery-man-to-packages-spilling-from-open-truck/; Karen Aho, "2013 Customer Service Hall of Fame," *MSN Money*, http://money.msn.com/investing/2013-customer-service-hall-of-fame; Ekaterina Walter, "The Big Brand Theory: How FedEx Achieves Social Customer Service Success," *Social Media Today*, May 27, 2013, www.socialmediatoday.com/ekaterinawalter/1494726/big-brand-theory-how-fedex-achieves-social-customer-service-success; Harley Manning and Kerry Bodine, "How FedEx Revamped Its Brand by Fixing Its 'Leaning Tower of Packages,'" *Fast Company*, August 21, 2012, www.fastcompany.com/3000554/how-fedex-revamped-its-brand-fixing-its-leaning-tower-packages; "Online Extra: Fred Smith on the Birth of FedEx," *Business Week*, September 19, 2004, www.businessweek.com/stories/2004-09-19/online-extra-fred-smith-on-the-birth-of-fedex; and http://about.van.fedex.com, September 2015.

Company Case 2

Samsung: A Strategic Plan for Success

You're probably familiar with Samsung. Maybe you have one of the company's hot new Galaxy smartphones or tablets that track your eye movements to help you navigate the screen. You might be doing your homework on one of its cutting-edge laptops. Or perhaps you've seen one of its dazzling new ultra-high-definition curved-screen smart TVs with Nano-crystal technology.

Chances are good that you or someone you know owns a Samsung product. After all, Samsung is the world's largest consumer electronics manufacturer, producing "gotta have" products in just about every electronics category, including TVs, DVD players, home theaters, digital cameras and camcorders, mobile devices, smartwatches, home appliances, laptops, printers, and LED lighting.

But only 20 years ago, Samsung was little known, and it was anything but cutting-edge. Back then, Samsung was a Korean copycat brand that you bought off a shipping pallet at Costco if you couldn't afford a Sony, then the world's most coveted consumer electronics brand. However, in 1993 Samsung made an inspired decision. It turned its back on cheap knock-offs and set out to overtake rival Sony. At the time, no one outside of Samsung believed that was possible. But the Korean manufacturer passed Sony in just 10 years, and Samsung has been widening the gap that separates it from the former market leader ever since.

The New Management Strategy

How did Samsung move so far so fast? The dramatic shift came about as a result of a top-down mandate to reform Samsung's business model and culture. In 1993, CEO Lee Kun-hee unveiled a new strategy. The goal: Dethrone Sony as the biggest and most desirable consumer electronics brand in the world. Turn Samsung into a premier brand and a trailblazing

product leader. To that end, the company hired a crop of fresh, young designers and managers who unleashed a torrent of new products—not humdrum, me-too products, but sleek, bold, and beautiful products targeted to high-end users. Samsung called them "lifestyle works of art." Every new product had to pass the "Wow!" test: If it didn't get a "Wow!" reaction during market testing, it went straight back to the design studio.

Beyond just seeking cutting-edge technology and stylish designs, Samsung put the customer at the core of this innovation movement. "Put simply, our differentiation is centered on producing innovative technology that brings genuine change to people's lives," said Sue Shim, Samsung's chief marketing officer. "We do this by bringing a relentless focus on consumer experience and product innovation in everything we do."

With its fresh customer-centered focus, Samsung made quick work of surpassing Sony. Today, Samsung's annual revenues of $196 billion are more than two and a half times Sony's $75 billion. And over the past five years, as Samsung's sales and profits have seen double-digit growth, Sony's revenues have declined and losses have compounded. According to brand tracker Interbrand, Samsung is now the world's seventh most valuable brand—ahead of megabrands like Disney, Pepsi, Nike, and Toyota—and one of the fastest-growing brands in the world. And Sony? It has fallen from grace as the value of its brand has declined as dramatically as Samsung's has risen.

But more than growth, Samsung has achieved the new product Wow! factor it sought. As evidence, Samsung is a dominant force at the annual International Design Excellence Awards (IDEA) presentations—the Academy Awards of the design world—which judge new products based on appearance, functionality, and inspirational thinking. Year after year, Samsung emerges as the top corporate winner. Last year, Samsung claimed 10 awards, more than three times as many as the runners-up.

When New Becomes Old

Good companies achieve their strategic goals. Great companies modify their strategic plans as goals are met, always looking to the future and positioning themselves to remain in front. After Lee was named top CEO of the Decade by *Fortune Korea*, he announced that the "new management" plan was old news. After 17 years of remarkable success, Lee admitted that Samsung's main products would likely become obsolete within the next 10 years. He then unveiled the underpinnings of a new strategic direction based on the Chinese axiom *mabuljungje*—meaning "horse that does not stop." In a memo to Samsung employees, Lee said, "The 'new management' doctrine for the past 17 years helped catapult the company into being one of the world's best electronics makers. Now is not a time to be complacent but a time to run."

Although Samsung doesn't claim to know what will replace today's products as they become obsolete, it is investing heavily to ensure that it is the company that develops them. Even with its new product systems in place, CEO Lee stresses the need for Samsung to completely overhaul its business model or risk losing market share. Fortunately for Samsung, profits have been so good that it has the funds to support its quest to remain at the top of the innovation heap. Year after year, Samsung boosts its innovation investment budget to record highs, even as its competition makes cuts. Its most recent research and development expense of $13.4 billion was second only to Volkswagen's $13.5 billion and more than double that of Amazon, IBM, or Cisco. Sony, Toshiba, Sharp, and Hitachi—Samsung's more traditional competitors in the past—didn't even come close.

The folks at Samsung know that future success will require much more than flashy hardware gadgets. For that reason, Samsung isn't really paying attention to Sony anymore. Samsung knows that it cannot thrive in the long term by merely offering sharper colors, better sound quality, or even "Wow!" designs. Over the past half-decade, Samsung has focused on competing with the likes of Apple for dominance of the mobile device market and for the content and advertising that go along with such devices.

That focus has paid off, and Samsung has surged to the top of the smartphone market. Just a few years ago, Samsung's goal was to double its share of the smartphone market from 5 percent to 10 percent. But the success of the Galaxy line catapulted Samsung into the position of market leader, besting Apple with a global market share of more than 30 percent. And although Apple has the jump on controlling content with more than 100 billion downloads through its App Store, Samsung's Galaxy App Store is holding its own.

The Internet of Things

Despite its indisputable success in smartphones, Samsung knows that that success can be short-lived. Although it still maintains the lead in the market, Samsung's fortunes have waned in the past year as the latest rendition of the iPhone cut its market share in China in half, reducing its global market share to 25 percent. In a saturated and cut-throat market, Samsung knows that future growth will not come from a bigger, better smartphone.

Rather, Samsung is again shifting its strategic direction. Samsung wants to take the lead in "the Internet of Things"— a global environment where all electronic devices, appliances, vehicles, and even static items such as clothing will be digitally connected with each other, with the people who use them, and with the companies that make them.

In recent years, Samsung has quietly gone about creating a foundation for establishing an interconnective web between all of its products and linking them with the rest of the world. It already makes products in just about every imaginable category of home devices. Not many years ago, it dove into semiconductors, a business that has been growing rapidly for the company in terms of size, innovation, and profitability. And last year, it purchased SmartThings, a smart-home start-up company.

But at the recent Internet of Things World event in San Francisco, Young Sohn, Samsung's chief strategy officer, blew things wide open. He unveiled a plan that makes Samsung's intentions clear. The company is committing a funding pool of $100 million to start-ups that want to help build the ecosystem. Committing to a policy of openness and collaboration, Sohn unveiled a new line of semiconductor chips—state-of-the-art processors that combine hardware and software—that are now available for sale, helping companies large and small quickly and easily build Internet-connected devices. And to meet what it expects will be enormous demand for these and future chips, Samsung is investing $14 billion in a massive semiconductor manufacturing complex.

To accomplish its goal of becoming a leader in the Internet of Things market, Samsung is taking on its biggest challenge yet. For starters, this shift in strategy broadens Samsung's list of competitors from an already daunting set to one that includes just about every company in every field of high technology and even some beyond that. Adding to that challenge, there are no common standards for technologies required to connect the many devices of the world—technologies that involve networking, software, and hardware. As a result, there are thousands of companies—from Google and Apple to myriad start-ups— trying to move their products toward interconnectivity but not getting much closer to a state of universal compatibility.

To add to this challenge, the many participants in the Internet of Things game don't see eye to eye, a competitive dynamic that makes the process much more difficult. As the many players work toward compatibility, they employ numerous and often incompatible approaches. And whereas Samsung and many others have committed to collaboration and an open ecosystem, others intend to go it alone and develop their own systems. For example, Apple is developing its HomeKit platform—a proprietary system that allows users to command the devices in their homes through Apple TV using Siri. Remember "Intel Inside"? Picture a "Made for iPhone" logo on devices that would ensure shoppers of interoperability under the Apple system.

But these challenges are not dousing Samsung's fire. The company's motivations go beyond greater financial performance. According to Alex Hawkinson, CEO for SmartThings, Samsung is trying to lead by example and trying to "do what is right by the customers" by giving them more choice and flexibility. "We will focus on creating amazing experiences in both software and hardware, and win through the power of our innovation rather than trying to win by locking others out or limiting choice," Hawkinson says.

So far as the Internet of Things goes, the ultimate goal is to build artificial intelligence technology that can gather data from smart homes, cars, and wearable devices and turn them into useful insights. That might sounds just a little too Big Brother-ish, but the wheels are already in motion. According to one conservative estimate, the number of networked devices will surge from about a billion today to 26 billion by 2020, representing a $3 trillion market. By that time, Samsung claims that 100 percent of the products it makes will be Internet-connected.

Twenty years ago, few people would have predicted that Samsung could have transformed itself so quickly and completely from a low-cost copycat manufacturer into a world-leading innovator of stylish, high-performing, premium products. But through savvy strategic planning, that's exactly what Samsung has done. And not so long ago, few if any would have predicted that Samsung would be one of the driving forces behind creating a world that is entirely interconnected. Yet, while that much remains to be seen, Samsung certainly seems to have all the right ingredients. And, based on it record of success, Yoon may have waxed prophetic as he unveiled Samsung's new strategic direction: "We have to show consumers what's in it for them and what the Internet of Things can achieve—to transform our economy, society, and how we live our lives."

Questions for Discussion

1. How was Samsung able to go from a copycat brand to an innovation leader?

2. In recent years, how has Samsung achieved its goals in markets where it had little presence, such as smartphones?

3. What challenges does Samsung face with such a diverse product portfolio? What benefits?

4. Is Samsung's current and future strategy customer focused? Why or why not?

5. Will Samsung be successful in achieving its goal of becoming a leader in the Internet of Things market?

Sources: Jared Newman, "Samsung's $100 Million Internet of Things Bet Is Even Crazier Than You Think," *Fast Company*, January 28, 2015, www.fastcompany.com/3041104/app-economy/samsungs-100-million-internet-of-things-bet-is-even-crazier-than-you-think; Parmy Olson, "Samsung Set to Unveil New Chips to Power Internet of Things," *Forbes*, May 12, 2015, www.forbes.com/sites/parmyolson/2015/05/12/samsung-artik-system-on-a-chip-internet-of-things/; Brian X. Chen, "Samsung Emerges as a Potent Rival to Apple's Cool," *New York Times*, February 11, 2013, p. B1; Laurie Burkitt, "Samsung Courts Consumers, Marketers," *Forbes*, June 7, 2010, p. 27; Choi He-suk, "Samsung Renews Resolve to Reform," *Korea Herald*, June 8, 2010, www.koreaherald.com/view.php?ud=20100607001598; Max Chafkin, "Samsung: For Elevating Imitation to an Art Form," *Fast Company*, March 2013, p. 108; Shara Tibken, "Samsung Launches Artik Chips for the Internet of Things," *CNet*, May 12, 2015, www.cnet.com/news/samsung-launches-artik-chips-for-internet-of-things/; and information from www.samsung.com, accessed September 2015.

Company Case 3

Sony: Battling the Marketing Environment's "Perfect Storm"

With all the hype these days about companies such as Apple, Google, Amazon, and Samsung, it's hard to remember that companies like Sony once ruled. In fact, not all that long ago, Sony was a high-tech rock star, a veritable merchant of cool. Not only was it the world's largest consumer electronics company, its history of innovative products—such as Trinitron TVs, Walkman portable music players, Handycam video recorders, and PlayStation video game consoles—had revolutionized entire industries. Sony's innovations drove pop culture, earned the adoration of the masses, and made money for the company. The Sony brand was revered as a symbol of innovation, style, and high quality.

Today, however, Sony is more a relic than a rock star, lost in the shadows of today's high-fliers. While Sony is still an enormous company with extensive global reach, Samsung overtook the former market leader as the world's largest consumer electronics company more than a decade ago and has been pulling away ever since. Likewise, Apple has pounded Sony with one new product after another. "When I was young, I had to have a Sony product," summarizes one analyst, "but for the younger generation today it's Apple." The company's latest slogan is "Be Moved." But that seems only to be pointing to the migration of Sony's customers to other brands.

Sony's declining popularity among consumers is reflected in its financial situation. For the most recent year, Samsung and Apple each tallied revenues exceeding $180 billion—more than double Sony's top line. Samsung's profits have surged in recent years while Sony's losses reached catastrophic levels. And whereas stock prices and brand values have skyrocketed for competitors, Sony's have reached new lows. Adding insult to injury, Moody's Investors Service recently cut Sony's credit rating to "junk" status.

How did Sony fall so hard so fast? The answer is a complex one. Sony never lost the capabilities that made it great. In fact, throughout the past decade, Sony was poised to sweep the markets for mp3 players, smartphones, online digital stores, and many other hit products that other companies have marketed successfully. But Sony was caught in the middle of a perfect storm of environmental forces that inhibited its growth and success. Some factors were beyond Sony's control. However, at the core of it all, Sony took its eye off the market, losing sight of the future by failing to adapt to important changes occurring all around it.

Hit on All Sides

For starters, Sony fell behind in technology. The company built its once-mighty empire based on the innovative engineering and design of standalone electronics—TVs, CD players, and video game consoles. However, as Internet and digital technologies surged, creating a more connected and mobile world, standalone hardware was rapidly replaced by new connecting technologies, media, and content. As the world of consumer entertainment gave way to digital downloads and shared content accessed through PCs, iPods, smartphones, tablets, and Internet-ready TVs, Sony was late to adapt.

Behaving as though its market leadership could never be challenged, an arrogant Sony clung to successful old technologies rather than embracing new ones. For example, for three years prior to the launch of Apple's first iPod in 2001, Sony had been selling devices that could download and play digital music files. Sony had everything it needed to create an iPod/iTunes-type world, including its own recording company. But it passed up that idea in favor of continued emphasis on its then-highly successful CD business. "[Apple's] Steve Jobs figured it out, we figured it out, we didn't execute," said Sir Howard Stringer, former Sony CEO. "The music guys didn't want to see the CD go away."

Similarly, as the world's largest TV producer, Sony clung to its cherished Trinitron cathode-ray-tube technology. Meanwhile, Samsung, LG, and other competitors were moving rapidly ahead with flat screens. Sony eventually responded. But today, both Samsung and LG sell more TVs than Sony. Sony's TV business, once its main profit center, has lost $8 billion over the last 11 years. In an effort to get back on its feet, Sony spun off its TV division into a standalone unit. But it faces a daunting uphill battle in a competitive landscape that is far different from the one in Sony's heyday. Not only does Sony continue to lose market share to Samsung and LG, but Chinese TV makers such as Haier, Hisense, and TCL are producing cutting-edge flat-panel offerings with a cost advantage that significantly undercuts Sony.

It was a similar story for Sony's PlayStation consoles, once the undisputed market leader and accounting for one-third of Sony's profits. Sony yawned when Nintendo introduced its innovative motion-sensing Nintendo Wii, dismissing it as a "niche game device." Instead, Sony engineers loaded up the PS3 with pricey technology that produced a loss of $300 per unit sold. Wii became a smash hit and the best-selling game console; the PS3 lost billions for Sony, dropping it from first place to third.

Even as a money loser, the PlayStation system, with its elegant blending of hardware and software, had all the right ingredients to make Sony a leader in the new world of digital entertainment distribution and social networking. Executives inside Sony even recognized the PlayStation platform as the "epitome of convergence," with the potential to create "a fusion of computers and entertainment." In other words, Sony could have made a strong competitive response to Apple's iTunes. But that vision never materialized, and Sony has lagged in the burgeoning business of connecting people to digital entertainment.

There are plenty of other examples of Sony's failure to capitalize on market trends despite the fact that it had the products to do so. Consider the Sony MYLO (or MY Life Online), a clever device released a year before the first iPhone that had the essence of everything that would eventually define the smartphone—a touch screen, Skype, a built-in camera, even apps. Or how about the long line of Sony Reader devices, the first of which was released a year before Amazon took the world by storm with its first Kindle.

The Turnaround

As Sony awoke to the reality of flattening revenues and plummeting profits, it made efforts to turn things around. In 2005, then-CEO Stringer moved in to put Sony back on track. To his credit, Stringer made a credible effort to reignite company, developing a turnaround plan aimed at changing the Sony mindset and moving the company into the new connected and mobile digital age. Stringer's efforts were slow to take root, meeting resistance within Sony's hardware-worshipping culture. "Whenever I mentioned content," he says, "people would roll their eyes because, 'This is an electronics company, and content is secondary.'" But even with its rigid structure and inflexible culture working against it, Sony's strengths kept it in the game. In fact, just a few years into Stringer's tenure, the once-great consumer electronics giant began to show signs of life, as Sony's profits jumped 200 percent to $3.3 billion on rising revenue.

But if Sony didn't already have enough challenges, this uptick occurred just as the Great Recession hit. A year later, Sony was right back where it started with a billion-dollar loss. Stringer was quick to point out that if not for the global financial collapse and the yen trading near a post-war high, Sony would have been comfortably profitable. After a few more years of negative profits, Sony was again poised for success. Its best batch of new products in more than a decade was heading for store shelves. Perhaps more important, the company was ready to launch the Sony Entertainment Network—an iTunes-like global network that would finally combine Sony's strengths in movies, music, and video games with all its televisions, PCs, phones, and tablets. Analysts forecasted a profit of $2 billion.

But on March 11, 2011, Stringer received a text message at 4:30 am, after having just arrived in New York City. Eastern Japan had been devastated by an earthquake and tsunami. Nobody at Sony was hurt. In fact, Sony's employees dove into rescue efforts, fashioning rescue boats from foam shipping containers to assist in saving victims and ferrying supplies. But in the aftermath of the destruction, Sony shuttered 10 plants, disrupting the flow of Blu-ray discs, batteries, and many other Sony items.

In the wake of the extreme economic and natural disasters, Sony's miseries had only just begun. A month later, a hacking attack invaded the company's Internet entertainment services. In what was determined to be the second-largest online data breach in U.S. history, Sony was forced to shut down the PlayStation Network. A short four months later, fires set by rioters in London destroyed a Sony warehouse and an estimated 25 million CDs and DVDs, gutting the inventory of 150 independent labels. And to round out the year, floods in Thailand shut down component plants, disrupting production and distribution of Sony cameras.

Sony's big comeback turned out to be big all right, but for all the wrong reasons. The projected $2 billion profit ended up as a $3.1 billion loss, marking a three-year losing streak. As Stringer prepared to fade away into retirement, Kazuo Hirai, Sony's emerging CEO, began speaking publicly of Sony's "sense of crisis." Indeed, Sony entered the record books the following year with a net loss of $6 billion—its biggest ever.

Assessing the Damage

So, in the end, just what is it that has caused Sony's dramatic fall from grace? Was it an addiction to hardware, an uncompetitive cost structure, the global financial crisis, natural disasters, computer hacking, or riots? In retrospect, all these elements of the marketing environment combined to deliver blow after blow. Sony's encounter with a perfect storm of environmental forces illustrates the havoc such forces can wreak—whether unforeseeable natural and economic events or more predictable turns in technology.

Throughout Sony's recent turbulent existence, a few things remain clear. Sony is a company with a long history and strong legacy that refuses to give up. Even now, CEO Hirai and others at Sony are firmly resolved to save the company. In addition to spinning off the TV division, Hirai sold Sony's Vaio PC operation and cut thousands of jobs as part of a restructuring plan with the purpose of cutting costs and making Sony profitable again. But as revenues continue to slide and seven-figure annual losses continue to mount, there are few lifelines in sight. Sony hasn't had a breakout product in more than a decade. Even now, the most innovative items in development are a mobile payment device and smart glasses, products that competitors have already brought to the market. With its existing portfolio of products and the Sony Entertainment Network, the company still has all the ingredients needed to become a total entertainment provider in today's connected market. But so far, Sony doesn't seem to be making the kinds of changes needed to bring those ingredients together. And even if it does, can the Sony brand regain the allure that will bring consumers calling?

Questions for Discussion

1. What microenvironmental factors have affected Sony's performance since 2000?

2. What macroenvironmental factors have affected Sony's performance during that period?

3. What stands in the way of Sony's success today?

4. Given Sony's current situation, what recommendations would you make to Hirai for the future of the company?

Sources: Ewan Spence, "Sony's Lost Confidence Will Doom the Xperia Z4," *Forbes,* April 24, 2015, www.forbes.com/sites/ewanspence/2015/04/24/sony-xperia-z4-pr-fail/; Will Ripley and Charles Riley, "Can Anything Save Sony?" *CNNMoney,* October 31, 2014, http://money.cnn.com/2014/10/30/technology/sony/; James McQuivey, "Sony Should Have Been a Digital Contender," *Forbes,* February 6, 2014, www.forbes.com/sites/forrester/2014/02/06/sony-should-have-been-a-digital-contender/; Cliff Edwards and Mariko Yasu, "Sony's Search for Cool. The Old-Fashioned Way," *Bloomberg Businessweek,* February 24, 2013, pp. 20–21; and information from www.sony.net, accessed September 2015.

Company Case 4

Campbell Soup Company: Watching What You Eat

You might think that a well-known, veteran consumer products company like the Campbell Soup Company has it made. After all, when people think of soup, they think of Campbell's. Selling products under such an iconic brand name should be a snap. But if you ask Denise Morrison, CEO of Campbell, she'll tell you a different story. Just a few years ago, when Morrison took over as head of the world's oldest and best-known soup company, she faced a big challenge—reverse the declining market share of a 144-year-old brand in a mature, low-growth, and fickle market characterized by shifting consumer preferences, ever-expanding tastes, and little tolerance for price increases. Turning things around would require revitalizing the company's brands in a way that would attract new customers without alienating the faithful who had been buying Campbell products for decades.

Morrison had a plan. A core element of that plan was to maintain a laser-like focus on consumers. "The consumer is our boss," Morrison said. "[Maintaining a customer focus] requires a clear, up-to-the-minute understanding of consumers in order to create more relevant products." Morrison's plan involved transforming the traditional stagnant culture of a corporate dinosaur into one that embraces creativity and flexibility. But it also involved employing innovative methods that would allow brand managers and product developers to establish the customer understanding that was so desperately needed. In other words, marketing research at the Campbell Soup Company was about to change.

Reading Consumers' Minds

Soup is a well-accepted product found in just about everyone's pantry in the United States. However, not long ago, Campbell researchers discovered that marketing soups presents unique problems. People don't covet soup. Sure, a steaming bowl of savory soup really hits the spot after coming in out of a bitingly cold rain. But soup is not a top-of-mind meal or snack choice, and it's typically a prelude to a more interesting main course. The bottom line—consumers don't really think much about soup, making meaningful marketing research difficult.

For years, Campbell researchers relied on good old paper-and-pencil surveys and traditional interviews to gain consumer insights for making ads, labels and packaging, and the products themselves more effective. But Campbell's experience with such traditional marketing research showed that traditional methods failed to capture important subconscious thoughts, emotions, and behaviors that consumers experience when shopping for soup.

So instead, to get closer to what was really going on inside consumers' hearts and minds, Campbell researchers began employing state-of-the-art neuroscience methods. They outfitted shoppers with special vests that measured skin-moisture levels, heart rates, depth and pace of breathing, and postures. Sensors tracked eye movements and pupil width. Then, to aid interpretation, such biometric data was combined with interviews and videos that captured each shopper's experiences.

The high-tech research produced some startling insights. Campbell knew that people hold strong emotions associated with eating soup. After all, who doesn't remember getting a hot bowl of soup from Mom when they were sick or cold? But the new biometric testing revealed that all that warmth and those positive emotions evaporated when consumers confronted the sea of nearly identical red and white Campbell's cans found on a typical grocery store soup aisle.

In the past, the top of a typical store shelf display featured a large Campbell's logo with a bright-red background. But the new research showed that such signs made all varieties of Campbell's Soup blend together, creating an overwhelming browsing situation and causing shoppers to spend less time at the aisle. The biometric research methods also revealed that the soup can labels themselves were lacking—the big bowl of soup on a Campbell's label was not perceived warmly, and the large spoon filled with soup provoked no emotional response.

Bases on these research insights, in an attempt to prompt and preserve important consumer emotions surrounding soup consumption, Campbell's began evaluating specific aspects of its displays, labels, and packaging. This led to seemingly small but important changes. For starters, the Campbell's logo is now smaller and lower on the shelf, minimizing the overwhelming "sea of cans" effect. To further encourage browsing, can labels now fall into different categories, each with distinguishing visual cues. Varieties like Beef Broth and Broccoli Cheese, which are typically used as ingredients in recipes, feature a narrow blue swath across the middle of the can with a "Great for Cooking" label. A green swath and the label "98% Fat Free" characterize reduced-fat varieties. Tomato Chipotle & Olive Oil, part of Campbell's "Latin Inspired" line, features a black background rather than the traditional white. And top-sellers such as Chicken Noodle, Tomato, and Cream of Mushroom feature the plain traditional label with the center medallion, immortalized by Andy Warhol's larger-than-life recreations of Campbell's soup cans. As for bringing out those warm emotions, Campbell's labels are now adorned with steam rising off a larger, more vibrant picture of the featured soup in a more modern white bowl. The nonemotional spoons are gone as well.

Can such minor label changes make a real difference? Yes, they can. Campbell's claims that its sales of condensed soups are up by 2 percent since making the changes. That may not sound like much, but even a small sales bump applied to a $2 billion consumer brand means real money. The sales jump also indicates that consumers are receiving greater value through a more fulfilling shopping experience.

Diving Deeper for Insights

Although the insights from Campbell's biometric marketing research have proven valuable, it will take more to capture the attention of a new generation of customers and stay attuned to the changing nature of consumer food tastes and preferences. Additionally, the Campbell Soup Company makes and markets much more than just soup these days. Over the years, the company has added or created such brands as Pepperidge Farms, Swanson, Pace, Prego, V8, Bolthouse Farms, and Plum Organics. Today, Campbell's house of packaged food brands includes something for just about everyone. With that kind of product portfolio, maintaining and creating relevant products based on a clear, up-to-the-minute understanding of consumers is an especially daunting proposition.

To capture clear and contemporary customer insights, Campbell's researchers turn to deep dive marketing research—qualitative methods employed in the fields of anthropology and other social sciences for up-close-and-personal study. Campbell's researchers and marketers dive in and spend time with consumers on their own turf. "We're in their homes," says Charles Vila, Campbell's vice president of consumer and customer insights. "We are cooking with them; we're eating with them; we're shopping with them." By spending hours at a time with consumers and observing them in their natural environments, researchers can unlock deep consumer insights of which customers themselves are often not aware.

By employing deep dive marketing research methods, Campbell researchers have identified six different consumer groups, each with an extensive profile. For each of these groups, Campbell has created six fully equipped kitchens at its Camden, New Jersey, headquarters, each designed to mirror the homes of consumers in the six groups. Each kitchen has a unique design, with different appliances, different features, and, most importantly, different food in the cabinets and refrigerators.

At one end of the spectrum is the group called "Uninvolved Quick Fixers." These are individuals and families who are not acquainted with or into cooking. Their kitchens are strewn with pizza boxes, and collections of takeout menus adorn their fridges. Their stoves and ovens often look like they've never been touched. "They're doing a lot of microwaving and frozen foods," explains the manager of Campbell's test facilities.

At the other end of the spectrum is group six, the "Passionate Kitchen Masters." Their kitchens tend to be filled with well-used, high-end appliances. Their refrigerators are stuffed with fresh produce, dairy, and meats. Gourmet sauces and artisanal breads and pastas are complemented by a wide variety of spices.

Such levels of detail help Campbell marketers discover and understand existing and developing trends in each consumer group as well as in the general market. For example, ginger is in. Only a few years ago, this herb was something found only in ethnic restaurants or in obscure recipes. But now its popularity is soaring. Campbell expects that it will soon be an important ingredient for each of the six consumer segments, a valuable insight for developing new products.

Another conclusion from Campbell's deep dive is that although Passionate Kitchen Masters consume far fewer prepared and packaged foods than other consumers, they still buy a lot of ingredients—such as broth. Broth flies under the radar of most consumers. But for people who like to cook, it's a sturdy component of soups, sauces, and braised meats.

Under both the Campbell's and Swanson brands, broth is also a $400 million business for the Campbell Soup Company. Applying the 2 percent sales boost resulting from the label changes discussed earlier translates to $8 million sales gains in broth alone. That's why Campbell's researchers are so interested in consumer trends, big and small.

The main goal is to enhance the customer's food experience. For example, Thai dishes are becoming more popular for foodies. But coming up with key ingredients like lemongrass is both time consuming and expensive. "Even for confident cooks, to bring those together, to go and purchase them, and actually blend them in such a way that it actually works, that's not easy," says Campbell's vice president Dale Clemiss, who oversees the Swanson and other Campbell brands. Add that to other insights that Campbell's research has uncovered, and a new broth is born—Swanson Thai Ginger, a broth "infused with flavors of lime, soy sauce, coconut, lemongrass, cilantro, and ginger—a simple way to make delicious restaurant inspired global dishes at home."

Every marketing research method has pitfalls. So Campbell combines multiple research methods. In addition to neuroscience and deep dive research, the company still employs traditional methods of surveys and interviews. The triangulation of data across methods allows for greater accuracy as well as the ability to cover larger consumer samples.

In the packaged foods business, every little bit helps. It's all about staying in tune with consumers and keeping up with the changes—large and small—in consumer preferences. That philosophy has worked well for the Campbell Soup Company in the past. And as Campbell has dug deeper through multiple marketing research methods, the proof is in the pudding. Last year, Campbell's corporate revenues were up 2.4 percent, following a 5.1 percent increase the year before. Net profits are steady at 8 to 10 percent. Campbell's stock price has also increased by nearly 50 percent in the past few years. As the company Web site states, "For generations, people have trusted Campbell to provide authentic, flavorful, and readily available foods and beverages that connect them to each other, to warm memories, and to what's important today." With the help of Campbell's marketing research program, it looks like consumers will continue to trust Campbell for generations to come.

Questions for Discussion

1. What are the strengths and weaknesses of the Campbell Soup Company's marketing information system?

2. What objectives does Campbell have for the marketing research efforts described in this case?

3. Compare the effectiveness of Campbell's biometric research with its deep dive research.

4. Describe how traditional marketing research could be integrated with Campbell's research efforts from this case.

Sources: Mark Garrison, "How Food Companies Watch What You Eat," *Marketplace*, December 2, 2013, www.marketplace.org/topics/business/how-food-companies-watch-what-you-eat; Ilan Brat, "The Emotional Quotient of Soup Shopping," *Wall Street Journal*, February 17, 2010, p. B1; Bonnie Marcus, "Campbell Soup CEO Denise Morrison Stirs the Pot to Create Cultural Change," *Forbes*, April 25, 2015, www.forbes.com/sites/bonniemarcus/2014/04/25/campbell-soup-ceo-denise-morrison-stirs-the-pot-to-create-cultural-change/; and information from www.campbellsoupcompany.com/about-campbell/, accessed September 2015.

Company Case 5

GoldieBlox: Swimming Upstream against Consumer Perceptions

When Debbie Sterling was in high school, her math teacher recognized her quantitative talent and suggested she pursue engineering as a college major. At the time, Sterling couldn't figure out why her teacher thought she should drive trains for a living. But the suggestion was enough to get her started down the right path. After four years at Stanford, Sterling graduated with a degree in mechanical engineering. But throughout the course of her studies, Sterling noticed the lack of women in her engineering program—a characteristic phenomenon in field where men outnumber women 86 percent to 14 percent. This observation ignited an obsession in Sterling. She set out on a mission to inspire a future generation of female engineers by disrupting the pink aisle in toy stores.

During the past few years, Sterling has been named *Time*'s "Person of the Moment" and one of *Business Insider*'s "30 Women Who Are Changing the World" among other accolades. Why? Because Sterling is the founder and CEO of GoldieBlox, a toy company that is making Sterling's mission a reality.

A Different Kind of Toy Company

After graduating, Sterling started researching everything from childhood development to gender roles. One of her findings was that in order to gain interest in and pursue a given field, a person must be exposed to the right inputs at an early age. This fact became particularly bothersome as Sterling became more and more familiar with the contents of the average toy aisle in stores. Toys for girls are in the pink aisle, dominated by dolls, stuffed animals, and princesses, whereas toys for boys are found in the blue aisle, filled with macho action figures, various toy weapons, and a huge variety of building block sets. Most experts agree that the toys served up to young girls do little to encourage an interest in science, technology, engineering, and math (STEM) subjects. This knowledge led Sterling to develop a plan to create a different kind of toy for girls.

As she began developing ideas for toys, another research finding struck her—girls possess stellar verbal skills and tend to learn better by interacting with stories. That insight was instrumental in the creation of the GoldieBlox line of construction sets. Part Erector Set and part storybook, the combination was designed to engage girls through their verbal skills and encourage them to build through narratives that feature the adventures of Goldie, a freckled-faced blonde girl donning overalls and a tool belt. Although Goldie comes off as a bit of a tomboy, she's still girlish. Skinny, blonde, and cute, she favors pinks and purples. The toys and stories feature animals and ribbons, and characters are more likely to help others than to succeed on their own.

After her innovative toy sets received little interest at the American International Toy Fair in New York City, Sterling started her own company. That decision sparked more interest than she could have ever imagined. To raise the $150,000 needed for the first round of production, Sterling launched a Kickstarter crowd-sourced funding campaign. Her funding goal was reached in just four days, and the funding topped out at $285,000.

With little to spend on traditional advertising, Sterling first promoted her inventive toys with some YouTube ads, including "Princess Machine," featuring young girls who take their stereotypically girly toys and create a sophisticated Rube Goldberg device. That video went viral to the tune of 8 million views in little more than a week. Shortly thereafter, GoldieBlox's first two products became Amazon's top two selling toys during the industry's busiest month of December. And if all that wasn't enough, GoldieBlox beat out 15,000 contenders in Intuit's "Small Business Big Game" Super Bowl ad contest, winning a $4 million spot during the big game.

Today, less than three years after the launch of its first product, GoldieBlox's toys are sold at Target, Toys "R" Us, Amazon, and 6,000 other retailers worldwide. The brand features more than a dozen play sets, the Bloxtown interactive Web site and app, a Goldie action figure, a "More Than Just a Princess" line of T-shirts and hoodies, and an original music video. GoldieBlox has won numerous industry awards, and its toys have succeeded in raising awareness about the lack of women in technical and scientific fields as well as the issues associated with the traditional pink aisle.

All That Glitters Is Not Goldie

With all this success, you would think that GoldieBlox would be heralded by anyone and everyone wanting to change gender-based stereotypes in toys. But GoldieBlox has sparked substantial debate over whether it is really helping the cause it claims to be serving. The opposition, led by many feminist voices, claims that GoldieBox's approach is little more than window dressing. The debate got really ugly after the launch of GoldieBlox and the Parade Float, a construction set based on a new challenge faced by Goldie and her friends—to create a float to transport the winner of a beauty pageant. "You cannot create a toy meant to break down stereotypes when you start off with the ideal that 'we know all girls love princesses,'" argues author Melissa Atkins Wardy. Those in the opposition camp call for toys that are gender-neutral. "When we use princess culture, pinkification, and beauty norms to sell STEM toys to girls and fool ourselves that we are amazing and progressive and raising an incredible generation of female engineers, we continue to

sell our girls short." Additionally, while the toys are designed to stir interest in girls by having them build and create, critics have raised concerns that GoldieBlox toys are too simplistic.

But Sterling is quick to respond to all such arguments and show that GoldieBlox isn't just trying to hook parents with a gimmick that doesn't deliver. "There's nothing wrong with being a princess," says the 32-year-old entrepreneur. "We just think girls can build their own castles too." This idea is backed by many advocates who recognize that to disrupt the pink aisle, you can't start out by trying to obliterate it.

To influence through play the types of hobbies and academic fields that women pursue, a company first must penetrate a very competitive market. Creating toys that are void of things that girls find appealing will only send girls scrambling for the nearest Bratz doll or Disney princess. GoldieBlox toys may incorporate traditional gender stereotypes, but they tweak and reframe them. GoldieBlox spent years researching gender differences, seeking significant input from Harvard neuroscientists, and observing children's play patterns. "Our stories leverage girls' advanced verbal skills to help develop and build self-confidence in their spatial skills," says Sterling with confidence.

Whether or not these two sides will resolve their differences in trying to achieve the same goal, there is no question that GoldieBlox has taken the toy industry by storm. And Sterling is far from finished. While clearly motivated to put an end to the stereotypes that have been generated by the toy and entertainment industries, she makes it clear that the goal is to become a multi-platform character brand à la Disney. "We want to be the brand that kids are whining for."

If the next three years are anything like GoldieBlox's first three, it's easy to envision a new kind of toy aisle at the local supercenter—one that heavily features Goldieblox's multi-platform brand.

Questions for Discussion

1. Of the factors that influence consumer behavior, which category or categories (cultural, social, personal, or psychological) best explain the existence of a blue toy aisle and a pink toy aisle? Why?

2. Choose the specific factor (for example, culture, family, occupation, attitudes) that you think most accounts for the blue/pink toy aisle phenomenon. Explain the challenges faced by GoldieBlox in attempting to market toys that "swim against the stream" or push back against the forces of that factor.

3. To what degree is GoldieBlox bucking the blue/pink toy aisle system?

4. If GoldieBlox succeeds at selling lots of its toys, will that accomplish the mission of increasing the presence of females in the field of engineering?

Sources: Lisa Wirthman, "4 Innovation Lessons Entrepreneurs Can Learn from GoldieBox," *Forbes*, March 2, 2015, www.forbes.com/ sites/northwesternmutual/2015/03/02/disrupting-pink-how-goldieblox-changes-the-way-girls-think-about-toys/; Katy Waldman, "GoldieBlox: Great for Girls? Terrible for Girls? Or Just Selling Toys?" *Slate*,

November 26, 2013, www.slate.com/blogs/xx_factor/2013/11/26/goldieblox_disrupting_the_pink_aisle_or_just_selling_toys.html; Jennifer Reingold, "Watch Out Disney: This Toy Startup's Coming for You," *Fortune*, November 26, 2014, http://fortune.com/2014/11/26/ goldieblox-toy-startup/; "Meet the Toymaker Who Is Disrupting the Pink Aisle," *American Association of University Women*, February 26, 2015, www.nccwsl.org/2015/02/26/debbie-sterling/; and information from www.goldieblox.com, accessed September 2015.

Company Case 6

Virgin America: Flight Service for the Tech Savvy

After an exceptionally frustrating day at the office, Jessica set out to unwind in one of her favorite third places. The mood lighting immediately brought her blood pressure down as she walked in and took a deep, relaxing breath. She was happy that her favorite spot was available—a comfy leather chair in the back corner of the room, where she used the touchscreen at the table in front of her to order her favorite drink. Then, putting on a set of noise-canceling headphones, Jessica began catching up on her favorite TV show with her own personal entertainment portal.

If this sounds like a local Starbucks or trendy nightclub, think again. Jessica had just boarded a flight on Virgin America, one of the youngest airlines in the United States. It's also the hottest airline, besting all competition in various industry and customer surveys. And after just six years in business, Virgin America is also profitable—one of the fastest launch-to-profitability postings in all of airdom.

How does a start-up airline break into one of the most competitive industries in the world, notorious for barriers to entry? For Virgin America, the answer is twofold—by putting customers first and by targeting the right customer segment.

Targeting the Right Customers

Virgin America first took to the skies in 2007. This wouldn't be the first shot at starting an airline for Richard Branson—founder of parent company Virgin Group. Virgin's international airline, Virgin Atlantic, had been crossing the pond between the United States and Europe since 1984. But Virgin America would be an entirely independent enterprise. And while Branson and other Virgin Group executives make no day-to-day decisions at Virgin America, the unorthodox Virgin culture—fun, creative, even whacky—is unmistakable.

One of Branson's core values that permeates Virgin America is this: Take care of your people first and profits will follow. In an industry characterized by customer complaints about service, it would seem that a customer-centric approach would be enough to gain a foothold in the market. But when Virgin started air service in the United States, at least a few other airlines had already established themselves based on a "customer first" mantra, including industry leader Southwest Airlines. And Virgin America knew that it could not expect to succeed by playing the low-price game. Not only was Southwest the reigning champion on value, but the bulk of airline competitors were already beating each other up for low-price dominance.

Virgin America found a different competitive hook. It targeted a segment of frequent fliers who were young, savvy, influential, and willing to pay just a little bit more for an airline that would take care of them—the Silicon Valley faction. By providing exceptional service and amenities that appeal to this particular slice of airline customers, Virgin America has been able to charge slightly higher fares and still establish a growing base of fiercely loyal patrons.

Honing In on the Details

Offering unique amenities in the airline business is a challenge for any company. But from the beginning, the Virgin America experience was designed with its target customer in mind. Its fleet consists of 53 Airbus A320s, each brand new when it went into service, minimizing the unexpected delays due to maintenance and repairs. Custom-designed leather seats are roomier and more comfortable than average coach seating. And that mood lighting? Not only does it bathe the aircraft cabin in an appealing purplish glow, it automatically adjusts to one of 12 different shades based on outside light.

To appeal to tech gurus, Virgin America focused on equipping its planes with the latest hardware and software. From day one, Virgin was the only domestic carrier to offer fleetwide inflight WiFi—a distinction that it maintains to this day, even as it has stayed ahead of the competition by upgrading the network to ensure the fastest in-flight speeds available. Every seat has its own power outlet, USB port, and nine-inch video touchscreen with a QWERTY keyboard/remote control.

That touchscreen provides access to the most advanced entertainment and information system in U.S. skies. Virgin America's proprietary Red system allows each guest to choose on-demand movies, TV programs, music, or video games. Red also allows patrons to track their flight on interactive Google Maps, engage in seat-to-seat chat with other customers, and order food and drinks for themselves or anyone else on board. It's a system designed to give passengers a feeling of control during an experience that is otherwise mostly out of their control.

Many of these ideas came by way of Virgin America's techy clientele. It's no accident that the company's headquarters are located in Burlingame, California, just a few short miles from the San Francisco airport. In fact, Virgin America is the only airline based in Silicon Valley. Not only is the company constantly experimenting with every aspect of the business, it has made strong efforts to involve Silicon Valley entrepreneurs and executives in the process, helping Virgin to think like its disruptive clientele. "We see ourselves as more of an incubator," says Luanne Calvert, Virgin America's chief marketing officer.

Take VX Next, for example—a group of 30 or so frequent fliers who act as a brain trust for Virgin America, generating ideas for the company at no charge. Among other winning ideas, this group was instrumental in developing the company's recent interactive promotional campaign. At the center of the campaign is a slick cinematic site that provides viewers with a virtual tour of a Virgin America flight. Demonstrating the airline's in-flight perks are founders and CEOs of companies such as Pandora, Gilt, and Pitchfork. As part of the tour, visitors to the site discover that several of the passengers on board are Virgin America frequent fliers and Silicon Valley celebrities who have made creative contributions to the airline's services with things such as curating in-flight music and menu items.

Virgin America's home-brewed tech panel was also instrumental in creating the company's latest safety video. When the company started operations, it delighted customers with a safety video like none other—an animated short featuring a techie nun and a matador with his bull. Posted online as well, the video racked up millions of views and cemented Virgin America's image as a company that could find creative alternatives to just about anything, even a federally mandated reminder to wear seatbelts. That image has carried over to Virgin America's new safety video—one created by a top Hollywood director and world-class choreographers that features 10 *So You Think You Can Dance* alums, two former Olympians, and one *American Idol* finalist. Debuting in Times Square and getting plenty of coverage from the press, the new safety video racked up 6 million views in less than two weeks.

Above the Clouds

Although there is plenty of anecdotal evidence that Virgin America's customers are thrilled with its service, it's the industry quality ratings that count. Virgin America is coming through with flying colors there as well. In the most recent annual Airline Quality Report—a survey that ranks airlines based on mishandled baggage, customer complaints, denied boardings, and on-time percent—Virgin America was number one. Virgin America is also in the top spot for customer satisfaction on *Consumer Reports*. In fact, Virgin America came away with the highest score achieved by any U.S. airline in many years.

Not to get too cocky, Virgin knows that maintaining such high rankings will be a challenge. In the coming years, the airline will expand service to more cities with cold climates, a factor that will increase the likelihood of canceled or delayed flights. It will also increase the number of passengers on flights, which will lead to longer boarding and deplaning times, affecting multiple customer service metrics. And with Virgin's techy and connected clientele, any screwup is likely to be texted, Tweeted, or otherwise broadcast for all the world to see.

Playing the features and amenities game is also problematic. Things that delight customers today become ho hum tomorrow, especially when competitors are constantly trying to improve their offerings.

That's why Virgin America views its operations as a work in progress, continually changing and improving, no matter how good current operations are. "If we stand still, they'll catch us," says David Cush, Virgin America's CEO. And Virgin America sees all those Tweeting customers as an opportunity to address customer service issues in real time, not to mention a powerful source of word of mouth.

With all its success, after six years, Virgin America still had not achieved an annual profit. With still-skeptical experts looking on, however, the company has now crossed that threshold, posting net profits for the past two years. For the most recent year, Virgin America achieved $84 million in profit—the highest ever for a young airline—on $1.5 billion in revenues. The company also went public in the second-largest airline IPO in history. Although the company is far from being out of the woods, Virgin America will continue to slowly expand its services by doing what it has done for its first eight years—wow every customer with exceptional service while giving the tech community a little something extra. It's a formula that Virgin aims to keep applying, even after it grows up.

Questions for Discussion

1. Using the full spectrum of segmentation variables, describe how Virgin America segments and targets the market for airline services.

2. Which market targeting strategy is Virgin America following? Justify your answer.

3. Write a positioning statement for Virgin America.

4. Will Virgin America succeed in the long run? Why or why not?

Sources: Lauren Schwartzberg, "Most Innovative Companies: 2015, Virgin America," *Fast Company*, March, 2015, pp. 135–137; Joe Berkowitz, "Silicon Valley Celebs Star in New Virgin America Campaign," *Fast Company*, September 5, 2012, www.fastcocreate.com/1681551/silicon-valley-celebs-star-in-new-virgin-america-campaign; Grant Martin, "America's Best Airlines," *Forbes*, April 15, 2015, www.forbes.com/sites/grantmartin/2015/04/15/americas-best-airlines/; Matt Richtel, "At Virgin America, a Fine Line between Pizazz and Profit," *New York Times*, September 8, 2013, p. BU1; Charisse Jones, "Virgin America Posts Record Profit for 2014," *USA Today*, February 18, 2015, www.usatoday.com/story/money/2015/02/18/virgin-america-posts-record-profit/23608205/; and information from www.virginamerica.com/cms/about-our-airline/corporate-facts.html, accessed September 2015.

Company Case 7

Target: Where Store Brands Offer More Than Low Prices

When it comes to discount retailing, Target doesn't need to make many excuses. In little more than 50 years, the Minnesota-based company has dotted the United States and Canada with more than 1,800 stores bearing the famous red-and-white bull's-eye. With $72 billion in annual sales, Target plays second fiddle in the U.S. discount retail market only to Walmart—the world's biggest corporation. And although it is only one-seventh Walmart's size, Target has managed to keep its much larger rival on its toes with a "cheap chic" image that has revolutionized discount retailing with heavy doses of style and fashion.

Throughout the past decade, however, Target has experienced its share of ups and downs. Whereas it outpaced Walmart in growth during the early 2000s, that growth has cooled as even the trendiest value shoppers have been drawn to the more-low-price positioning of Walmart and dollar stores. Through several years of changes that have included cost-cutting, store remodeling, and inventory restructuring, Target has better positioned itself strategically to fulfill its mission to deliver "outstanding value, continuous innovation and exceptional guest experiences by consistently fulfilling our 'Expect More. Pay Less.' brand promise."

One of the ways Target is carrying out this mission is through a strong portfolio of private brands. Although store brands are nothing new for Target, it has sought not only to expand its portfolio of store brands but also to raise the perceived value of those brands in the minds of consumers. Target still sells plenty of national brands. But as customers snatch up dozens of owned and exclusive brands that can be found only in Target stores, the chain has set a benchmark for retailers of every stripe to follow when it comes to executing a store-brand strategy.

Bringing Designer Labels to Discount Retail

Not that long ago, store brands everywhere carried a "low quality" and "bland" stigma. With those less-than-attractive perceptions, such brands were purchased primarily because they were priced much lower than comparable name-brand products. Perhaps more than any other retailer, Target has fought to establish its exclusive brands as anything but traditional. In fact, Target has clung to two mission-supporting corporate values to guide store brand development: "design and innovation" and "value as more for less."

As part its private-brand strategy, Target is forging collaborative relationships with high-end designers to create exclusive product lines. Since 1999, when it introduced design partners Michael Graves and Sonia Kashuk, Target has covered just about every category of goods with designer labels. It has signed more than 50 different designers to Target-exclusive agreements, from Graves's housewares line to Mulberry for Target handbags to Isaac Mizrahi's lines of clothing, accessories, bedding, and pet products. In the last year alone, Target introduced collections by Adam Lippes (plaid apparel, accessories, home furnishings, and pet goods), Eddie Borgo (jewelry and wall art), and Lilly Pulitzer (outdoor and beach apparel, shoes, and accessories).

With these alliances, everybody benefits. The designers get tremendous exposure, a large customer base, and the power and deep pockets of a mass retailer. Target gets brand cachet that enhances the chicness of its image, and customers get style at affordable prices. As products with a designer label that might normally adorn goods with a three- or four-figure price tag, Target's designer items have been huge hits. Tales have circulated of Target customers fighting over apparel items and filling their carts to the brim on days when new items go on sale. Sellouts are common, and Target's designer labels have been known to show up on eBay with significantly higher prices.

Setting a High Bar for Store Brands

As popular as Target's designer lines have been, they represent the smaller portion of the company's exclusive store brand efforts. Rather, Target has applied its value philosophy and design expertise to creating more than a dozen store brands. The most pervasive of these is "Up & Up," which replaced the main "Target" store brand a few years ago. Instead of the familiar bull's-eye, the Up & Up lines come in white packages with big, colorful, upward-pointing arrows. With more than 800 different products in more than 50 different categories, the Up & Up brand can be found in every department of a Target store.

While Up & Up follows the more traditional approach of store brands that provide budget-friendly basics, Target has taken great care to match the quality levels of national brands wherever possible. For certain basics such as hand sanitizer ($1.74 versus $2.69 for Purell), napkins ($2.66 versus $2.99 for Bounty), and cotton swabs ($2.99 versus $4.79 for Q-tips), it's tough to tell the difference. And even when customers can see a difference, the savings are worth it. On average, Up & Up products are priced about 30 percent lower than comparable name-brand products.

But as with its designer labels, Target does not pursue a singularly low-price positioning for its store brands. This is perhaps most evident in grocery aisles, where Target now has not one but three distinct in-house food brands. Like Up & Up, Target's own Market Pantry brand covers basic staples such as cheese, milk, eggs, baking ingredients, juices, snacks, and prepared meal options. And like Up & Up, the positioning is also similar to national brands—the same quality and taste but for a lot less money.

Target's other two food brands, however, go beyond just offering customers a lower-priced option. Archer Farms is a "healthier" choice that promises no artificial flavors, artificial sweeteners, or trans fats. And although it is a "budget-friendly" brand, that budget friendliness is relative only to the types of foods that carry the Archer Farms label—items that would typically interest food snobs and gourmets. To that end, Archer Farms products are noticeably fancier.

For example, why settle for a basic variety of trail mix from Planters when you can get Caramel Cashew, Sunny Cranberry, Tex Mex, or Cinnamon Raisin Nut Breakfast from Archer Farms? As with many Archer Farms categories, Target offers far more varieties with its store brands than it does with national brands. It also focuses on flavors that consumers won't find anywhere else. "One of the best-selling Archer Farms' chips is a blue corn chip with flax seed," says Annette Miller, who oversees Target's grocery business. "One of our best-selling Archer Farms pizzas is a goat cheese, potato, and spinach pizza." Priced 10 to 30 percent lower than name brands, Archer Farms products are still cheaper. And with options such as Key Lime Cookie Straws and organic milk, Archer Farms is very much in keeping with Target's "cheap chic" image.

If Archer Farms products still aren't fancy enough for some shoppers, Target has them covered with its third and latest food brand, Simply Balanced—a mostly organic line of more than 250 products originally launched as an Archer Farms sub-brand. Claiming 40 percent organic content, Simply Balanced also claims to be mostly free of genetically modified organisms. This newest Target brand is hardly cheap, but its prices compare favorably with those of other organic upscale brands that Target doesn't even stock.

With its food brands, Target focuses on products that customers are more inclined to try, such as snacks, coffee, and dairy. Especially with its two upper-tier brands, Target's store brand foods are expected to be at least as good if not better than those made by national brands. To keep costs down and maintain quality, Target focuses on developing its own food products rather than sourcing them out to other companies. In its Minneapolis test kitchens, Target employees prepare, cook, and taste-test every product before it makes it onto Target's grocery shelves.

Capitalizing on Trends

The fact that Target pushes three separate in-house food brands clearly indicates that store brands have come a long way. Similar to trends for store brands in general, Target's brands are benefiting from—if not contributing to—a national trend in acceptance and consumption of private-label foods. According to recent studies, store brands are increasingly found in U.S. kitchens. Fewer consumers feel that they are sacrificing when they purchase store food brands, and fewer consumers indicate an intention to purchase fewer store brands in the future. In fact, a surprisingly high 80 percent of all shoppers believe that private-label brands are equal to or better than national brands in terms of quality. "I'll buy Target brand and not have any qualms about the product," said one budget-minded college student. "It is a bit cheaper, and it's still really good quality." And it's not just lower-income consumers who are turning to store brands. Fortunately for Target, the greatest surge in store-brand purchases is among more affluent shoppers.

Similar to the path that Target has pursued with its private-label food brands, the company has covered many other product

categories as well. Target's Cherokee brand offers "classically cool kidswear at prices that make moms and dads everywhere smile." The Xhilaration brand helps juniors to "stay on top of the latest trends." Mossimo Supply Co. "boasts funkier, more laid-back casual looks for both women and men," and Merona is "Modern classic style … shoes, accessories, and separates." Circo covers infants and children, and Gilligan & O'Malley has women's sleepwear and lingerie covered. When it comes to furniture and household accessories, RE (Room Essentials) appeals to the needs of young adults, whereas Threshold's claim of "quality & design" is more for the established household.

In many ways, Target's store-brand strategy is paying off. About one-third of Target's sales volume comes from its private brands, and that number is rising. "We've grown our own brand foods faster than our total food growth over the past five years, as we've continued to expand our product offering into new product categories that we hadn't developed before," says Target's Miller. Additionally, 10 of Target's private-label brands generate more than $1 billion a year. Not one to rest on its laurels, Target recently extended the return window for many of its private-label brands from 90 days to one year, a bold move that signals confidence in brand quality.

But Target continues to face a tough battle in the highly competitive discount retail sector. Net revenues have remained flat over the past few years, while Walmart's have been increasing by low single digits. Target's net profits have languished as well. This tepid financial performance seems to be despite Target's store-brand efforts rather than because of them. As Target deals with various factors in the marketing environment in its struggles to get financials back on track, its store brands have staved off higher losses and provide promise for the future. If general growth trends of store brands continue, you will likely see more and more Target brands on the retailer's shelves. Fortunately for Target, it is far better prepared for such developments than many of its competitors.

Questions for Discussion

1. What benefits does Target receive from its store brands?

2. Is Target's store brand strategy working? Explain.

3. What could Target do in the future to further develop its strengths in store brands?

4. What potential problems does Target face in continuing its focus on store brands?

Sources: Paul Ziobro, "Target Extends Return Window for Private-Label Brands," *Wall Street Journal*, March 18, 2015, www.wsj.com/articles/target-extends-return-window-for-private-label-brands-1426692941; Brad Tuttle, "The Rise of the Swanky No-Name Brand," *Time*, June 11, 2013, http://business.time.com/2013/06/11/the-rise-of-the-swanky-no-name-brand/; Martin Moylan, "Target Benefits from Popularity of Store Brands," *MPR News*, November 19, 2010, www.mprnews.org/story/2010/11/19/store-brands; and additional information from www.corporate.target.com/about/design-innovation/owned-brands/# and www.corporate.target.com/about/mission-values, accessed September 2015.

Company Case 8

3M: Where Innovation Is a Way of Life

In recent years, companies topping the world's "most innovative" lists are typically high-tech leaders such as Google, Apple, Samsung, and Amazon. When thinking of companies that set the world on fire with one revolutionary product after another, the image of a stodgy company that originated in the mining industry more than 100 years ago is hardly the icon. But while 3M may not be as flashy as today's high-tech headliners, it's anything but stodgy.

3M—the Minnesota Mining and Manufacturing Company—is a multinational powerhouse with more than $31 billion in annual sales. Year after year, with machine-like precision, 20 percent of 3M's sales filter down as operating profits, allowing the company to increase its dividend to shareholders—something it has done every year for the past 57 years.

3M sells more than 50,000 products in nearly 200 countries across dozens of industries, including office products, construction, telecommunications, electronics, health care, aerospace, and automotive. Among its products are some of the world's most recognizable consumer brands, such as Scotch Tape, Nexcare first aid products, Filtrete home filtration products, Command mounting products, and Post-it Notes. But 3M's portfolio is also packed with hundreds of brands that most people have never heard of—like Peltor hearing protection equipment or Pruven waste bags for picking up dog poop.

The unusual breadth of 3M's product portfolio is both a blessing and a curse for the company. Having a hand in so many industries shields the company from overreliance on any given market. Even when multiple industries are down, many more are doing just fine. That explains 3M's financial strength. But it also explains why 3M has a hard time thrilling Wall Street. Even a hit new product doesn't make much of a difference in 3M's steady but unspectacular growth rate—one that is consistently in the low single digits.

Like 3M, the company's current CEO, Inge Thulin, is methodical and understated. He keeps a long-term focus and places strong emphasis on maintaining 3M's reliable profitability. But Thulin is also interested in stoking the fire just a bit, to put a little more heat under sales growth. One of the first things Thulin did when he took over as CEO a few years ago was to trim 3M's annual sales growth goal from 7 or 8 percent—a goal the company consistently missed—to between 4 and 6 percent. Then, as the world watched, 3M's organic sales growth grew to 5.8 percent. And under Thulin's leadership, 3M is now on track to maintain that stronger growth rate.

How did Thulin do it? By doing the same thing 3M has been doing it for decades. At the core of 3M's success is its business model—organic growth comes from innovation and the creation of market-changing products. Such market-changing products have at times created entirely new industries. 3M has sustained this type of innovation decade after decade by fostering a deep culture of innovation, encouraging collaboration, and maintaining a dedication to research and development.

Culture of Innovation

From its earliest days, 3M created a culture of innovation by allowing team members to take risks in a protected environment. 3M knows that it must try thousands of product ideas to hit the new product jackpot. One well-worn slogan at 3M is "You have to kiss a lot of frogs to find a prince." "Kissing frogs" often means making mistakes, but 3M accepts blunders and dead ends as a normal part of creativity and innovation. In fact, its philosophy seems to be "If you aren't making mistakes, you probably aren't doing anything."

As it turns out, "blunders" have turned into some of 3M's most successful products. Old-timers at 3M love to tell the story about the chemist who accidentally spilled a new chemical on her sneakers. Some days later, she noticed that the spots hit by the chemical had not gotten dirty—an attractive benefit. It was that discovery that eventually led to the creation of Scotchgard fabric protector. They tell about the early 3M scientist who had a deathly fear of shaving with a straight razor. So he invented a very fine, waterproof sandpaper, which he used to sand the stubble from his face each morning. Although this invention never caught on as a shaving solution, it became one of 3M's best-selling products—wet-dry sandpaper, now used for a wide variety of commercial and industrial applications.

And then there's the one about 3M scientist Spencer Silver. Silver started out to develop a super-strong adhesive; instead he came up with one that didn't stick very well at all. He sent the apparently useless substance on to other 3M researchers to see whether they could find something to do with it. Nothing happened for several years. Then 3M scientist Arthur Fry had an idea. As a choir member in a local church, Mr. Fry was having trouble marking places in his hymnal—the little scraps of paper he used kept falling out. He tried dabbing some of Mr. Silver's weak glue on one of the scraps. It stuck nicely and later peeled off without damaging the book. Thus were born 3M's Post-it Notes, a product that is now one of the top-selling office supply products in the world.

One of the ways 3M fosters a culture of innovation is by encouraging everyone to look for new products. The company's renowned "15 percent rule" allows all employees to spend up to 15 percent of their time "bootlegging"—working on projects of personal interest whether those projects directly benefit the company or not. And yet there is a vibe throughout the company regarding these precious six hours a week. Who knows where the next Post-it Note will come from? "It's one of the things that sets 3M apart as an innovative company … giving every one of our employees the ability to follow their instincts to take advantage of opportunities for the company," says Kurt Beinlich, a technical director who oversees a 70-person lab team. "It's really shaped what and who 3M is."

Encouraging Collaboration

Although 3M's 15 percent program has inspired other companies to follow suit (both Google and HP apply their own versions), it's a rare perk in the corporate world. Not only is it an expense, but to be successful it takes a lot more than simply giving employees the time. Experts suggest that this kind of program works best at companies where there is a high level of collaboration across employees and departments.

3M has created that collaboration in spades. One example is an annual event that is simple but has a huge impact. The event resembles a middle school science fair, as employees from dozens of 3M divisions make cardboard posters describing their 15-percent-time project. Employees hang out next to their posters, await feedback, and look for potential collaborators. Wayne Maurer, an R&D manager in 3M's abrasives division, refers to it as a chance for people to unhinge their "inner geek." "For technical people, it's the most passionate and engaged event we have at 3M."

The event is more than just an opportunity to show off; it has actually moved projects through the development phase to commercialization. Past projects that have made it to market include clear bandages, optical films that reflect light, and painter's tape that prevents bleeding. The event has even put new life in projects that have sat on a back burner for years.

One employee had an idea for creating a sandpaper with reshaped grit particles that wouldn't dull so quickly. But after playing around with the idea for a while, he shelved it and moved on to other things. Fifteen years later, the employee resurrected the project during his 15 percent time and made a poster in hopes of getting some ideas that would move the project along. With the help of new employees and new technology, 3M discovered that a particle's sharp, pyramid-like shape became more durable with a change in the mixing order of the ingredients. That discovery led to the launch of Cubitron II, sandpaper that acts more like a cutting tool. On the market since 2009, it still stumps other companies trying to create copycat products.

Emphasis on R&D

Few companies provide more support for research and development than 3M. For years, 3M invested 6 percent of sales every year in R&D. But in recent years, that spending had been cut to just 5.5 percent—a small difference on paper, but one that Thulin believes is significant. "Those long-term investments are needed to get the growth engine up and going." If such investments are reduced, Thulin believes, "you will kill the business." That's why 3M's R&D expenditures are once again up to 6 percent. Thulin believes R&D "is the heartbeat of this company and it's a competitive advantage for us." By comparison, the average of R&D expenses across corporations is about 3 percent. For the most recent year, Apple spent $4.5 billion on R&D, a company record that still amounted to only 2.6 percent of sales.

But it isn't just the amount of money invested that is important for a successful R&D program. It's how the money is used. In addition to increasing 3M's R&D allotment, Thulin is putting more priority on the 3M technologies that have the most potential for growth. Among these technologies are films designed to protect everything from smartphones to kitchen appliances and a construction wrap that will outperform DuPont's Tyvek as a weather-resistant barrier for homes and buildings.

But Thulin's plan for allocating R&D funds also includes eliminating 3M units with poor financial performance or those that aren't a good fit with the company's core strengths. For Thulin, it's nothing personal; it's strictly business. Over the past two years, 3M sold Scientific Anglers—which makes fishing line and other related products—and its Static Control business. Thulin believed there was little symbiosis between developments in the product lines of these two divisions and other 3M technologies.

Although Thulin's plan focuses on high-tech areas, it also recognizes the importance of a broad portfolio that includes low-tech items—such as doggie doo bags. In fact, 3M is committed to a broad range of pet care supplies. "You cannot have only high-tech in every category because then you will not get space in the shops," says Thulin, recognizing that mass retailers want to purchase full lines of products within and across categories from manufacturers.

This is all reflected in 3M's first promotional campaign in more than 25 years, "3M Science. Applied to Life." This global campaign is a fully digital promotional effort designed to showcase 3M's technologies and the ways that they improve everyday life. The company hopes that the campaign will bring greater exposure to many of its products that have become ubiquitous. "Like any great company, we're looking at how we can improve and continue to invest in our strengths," says Jesse Singh, 3M's senior VP of marketing and sales. "We are continuing to invest in R&D, and likewise we felt it important that we continue to take steps to emphasize the brand."

3M will likely never have growth rates matching those of Apple, Facebook, or even Microsoft in its heyday. But it will also likely never experience the potential downturns that even the biggest companies eventually face. That's why 3M's net profits hum along at about 15 percent of sales year after year. It's also why 3M's stock price has doubled over the past four years. 3M's long-term dedication to innovative new products and technologies has sustained the company for decades, and there's no reason to expect that this will change. Who knows—the next "big thing" may just have "3M" stamped on it instead of "Apple."

Questions for Discussion

1. Based on concepts discussed in Chapter 8, describe the factors that have contributed to 3M's new product success.

2. Is 3M's product development process customer centered? Why or why not?

3. Considering the product life cycle, what challenges does 3M face in managing its product portfolio?

4. Are there limits to how broad 3M's product portfolio can grow? Explain.

5. Is it possible for 3M to maintain steady growth and profitability *and* raise that growth to much higher levels?

Sources: Jennifer Rooney, "Inside 3M's First Global Brand Campaign in More than 25 Years," *Forbes*, March 11, 2015, www.forbes.com/sites/jenniferrooney/2015/03/11/inside-3ms-first-global-brand-campaign-in-more-than-25-years/; "Here Is Why We Think 3M Is Worth $140," *Forbes*, March 6, 2014, www.forbes.com/sites/greatspeculations/2014/03/06/here-is-why-we-think-3m-is-worth-140/; James R. Hagerty, "50,000 Products but 3M Still Searching for Growth," *Wall Street Journal*, November 18, 2013, p. B1; Kaomi Goetz, "How 3M Gave Everyone Days Off and Created an Innovation Dynamo," *Fast Company*, February 1, 2011, www.fastcodesign.com/1663137/how-3m-gave-everyone-days-off-and-created-an-innovation-dynamo; and additional information from www.3m.com/3M/en_US/company-us/, accessed September, 2015.

Company Case 9

Coach: Riding the Wave of Premium Pricing

Victor Luis stood looking out the window of his office on 34th Street in Manhattan's Hell's Kitchen neighborhood. It had been just over a year since he had taken over as CEO of Coach, Inc., a position that had previously been held by Lewis Frankfort for 28 years. Under Frankfort's leadership, it seemed Coach could do no wrong. Indeed, over the previous decade, the 73-year-old company had seen its revenues skyrocket from about $1 billion to more than $5 billion as its handbags became one of the most coveted luxury items for women in the United States and beyond. On top of that, the company's $1 billion bottom line—a 20 percent net margin—was a common annual outcome. Coach's revenues made it the leading handbags seller in the nation. The brand's premium price and profit margins made the company a Wall Street darling.

Right around the time Luis took over, however, Coach's fortunes had begun to stumble. Although the company had experienced promising results with expansion into men's lines and international markets, it had just recorded the fourth straight quarter of declining revenues in the United States, a market that accounts for 70 percent of its business. North American comparable sales were down by a whopping 21 percent over the previous year. Once the trendsetter, Coach lost market share to younger and more nimble competitors for two years in a row. Investors were jittery, causing Coach's stock price to drop nearly 50 percent during that time. After years of success, it now seemed that Coach could do little right.

Artisanal Origins

In a Manhattan loft in 1941, six artisans formed a partnership called Gail Leather Products and ran it as a family-owned business. Employing skills handed down from generation to generation, the group handcrafted a collection of leather goods, primarily wallets and billfolds. Five years later, the company hired Miles and Lillian Cahn—owners of a leather handbag manufacturing firm—and by 1950, Miles was running things.

As the business grew, Cahn took particular interest in the distinctive properties of the leather in baseball gloves. The gloves were stiff and tough when new, but with use they became soft and supple. Cahn developed a method that mimicked the wear-and-tear process, making a leather that was stronger, softer, and more flexible. As an added benefit, the worn leather also absorbed dye to a greater degree, producing deep, rich tones. When Lillian Cahn suggested that the company add women's handbags to the company's low-margin line of wallets, the Coach brand was born.

Over the next 20 years, Coach's uniquely soft and feminine cowhide bags developed a reputation for durability. Coach bags also became known for innovative features and bright colors rather than the usual browns and tans. As the Coach brand expanded into shoes and accessories, it also became known for attractive integrated hardware pieces—particularly the silver toggle that remains an identifying feature of the Coach brand today. In 1985, the Cahns sold Coach to the Sara Lee Corporation, which housed the brand within its Hanes Group. Frankfort became Coach's director and took the brand into a new era of growth and development.

Under Frankfort's leadership, Coach grew from a relatively small company to a widely recognized global brand. This growth included not only new designs for handbags and new product lines but a major expansion of outlets as well. When Frankfort assumed the top position, Coach had only six boutiques located within department stores and a flagship Coach store on Madison Avenue. By the time Frankfort stepped down, there were more than 900 Coach stores in North America, Asia, and Europe, with hundreds of Coach boutiques in department stores throughout those same markets as well as in Latin America, the Middle East, and Australia. In addition to the brick-and-mortar outlets, Coach had developed a healthy stream of online sales through its Web sites.

High Price Equals High Sales

With the expansion in Coach's product lines and distribution outlets, women everywhere were drawn to the brand's quality and style. But perhaps more than anything, they were attracted to the brand as a symbol of luxury, taste, and success. Over the years, Coach had taken great care to find an optimal price point, well above that of ordinary department store brands. Whereas stores that carried Coach products also sold mid-tier handbag brands for moderate prices, Coach bags were priced as much as five times higher.

It might seem that such a high price would scare buyers off. To the contrary. As Coach's reputation grew, women aspired to own its products. And although the price of a Coach bag is an extravagance for most buyers, it is still within reach for even middle-class women who want to splurge once in a while. And with comparable bags from Gucci, Fendi, or Prada priced five to ten times higher, a Coach bag is a relative bargain.

With its image as an accessible status symbol, Coach was one of the few luxury brands that maintained steady growth and profits throughout the Great Recession. And it did so without discounting its prices. Fearing that price cuts would damage the brand's image, Coach instead introduced its "Poppy" line at prices about 30 percent lower than regular Coach bags. Coach concentrated on its factory stores in outlet malls. And it maintained an emphasis on quality to drive perceptions of value. As a result, Coach's devoted customer base remained loyal throughout the tough times.

At about the same time, Coach also invested in new customers. It opened its first men's-only store, stocked with small leather goods, travel accessories, footwear, jewelry, and swimsuits. Coach also expanded men's collections in other stores. As a result, its revenue from men's products doubled in one year. The company saw similar success with international customers, pressing hard into Europe, China, and other Asian markets.

But just as it seemed that Coach was untouchable, the brand showed signs of frailty. Coach's U.S. handbag business started slowing down. During Luis's first year on the job, Coach's share of the U.S. handbag market fell from 19 percent to 17.5 percent—the second straight year for such a loss. During that same period, Michael Kors, Coach's biggest competitive threat, saw its market share increase from 4.5 percent to 7 percent. Up-and-comers Kate Spade and Tory Burch also saw increases. Because the U.S. market accounted for such a large portion of the company's business, overall revenue took a dip despite the brand's growth in new markets.

What's the Problem?

Many factors could be blamed for Coach's U.S. decline. During the most recent holiday season, Coach had to contend with the same problem many other retailers faced—less traffic in shopping malls. But Kate Spade and Michael Kors, which operate their own stores and sell through department stores in malls just as Coach does, experienced double-digit gains during the same period. Coach's performance also ran counter to the dynamics of the handbag and accessory market as a whole, which grew by nearly 10 percent over the previous year.

The differences in sales trends between Coach and its competitors have led some analysts to speculate that the long-time leader has lost its eye for fashion. "These guys are definitely losing share," said analyst Brian Yarbrough. "Fashion-wise, they're missing the beat." Yarbrough isn't alone. Many others assert that, under the same creative direction for 17 years, Coach's designs have grown stale.

Then there is the issue of Coach's price structure—in short, Coach may have taken the premium price point too far. "Coach tried to eliminate coupon promotions tied directly to its discount outlets, which are the company's biggest source of revenue, and which attract customers looking to stretch their dollars," said one luxury retail expert. "The number of people willing and able to pay a premium for luxury brands, like Coach, is getting small as this weak economy continues." However, price alone would not explain why Coach's business slid at the same time

that sales by comparably priced competitors rose. Additionally, while Coach's North American revenues were down last year, sales of its high-end handbags (priced above $400) actually increased.

Some analysts have also questioned the effect of Coach's popularity on its image of exclusivity. A luxury brand's image and customer aspirations often rest on the fact that not everyone can afford it. But Coach has become so accessible, anyone that wants a Coach product can usually find a way to buy one. This availability has been fostered by Coach's outlet stores—company-owned stores that carry prior season merchandise, seconds, and lower-quality lines at much lower prices. With the number of customers drawn in by low prices, Coach's outlet stores now account for a sizable 60 percent of revenues and an even higher percentage of unit sales. Outlet sales, combined with a healthy secondary market through eBay and other Web sites, mean that Coach products are no longer as exclusive as they once were.

Although new as CEO, Luis has been with Coach for the past eight years and oversaw Coach's international expansion. And although Frankfort has stepped down, he is still involved as chairman of the board. Led by these seasoned fashion executives, Coach has a turnaround plan. For starters, the company hired a new creative director. Stuart Vevers brings to Coach the same magic that he worked for brands like Louis Vuitton, Givenchy, Bottega Veneta, and Mulberry. According to Luis, Vevers is "providing a fashion relevance for the brand like we have never had."

In addition to the creative and design changes, Coach is rebalancing its product portfolio. To win back shoppers, Coach will be positioned as a lifestyle brand with greater expansion into footwear, clothing, and accessories. Additionally, the company will increase the number of handbag offerings priced at $400 or more, a move that could raise the average price point of Coach's handbags.

The initial fruit of Coach's turnaround plan appears promising. The first lines under Vevers's direction show evidence of a complete transformation while still remaining true to the core elements of the brand. Bold new shapes and colors abound in the handbag lines. But the real changes are apparent in Coach's other lines—black leather biker jackets festooned with pins and zippers, suede coats and parkas, and urban hiker boots, all accented liberally with shearling pieces. Vevers was going for "a Coach approach to luxury, even an American approach to luxury—not too precious . . . not too perfect." Based on reviews from the fashion world and the public, Vevers seems to have dialed in the right combination. "Coach is cool again, and not in a way that's appealing only to fashion insiders," says Lauren Indvik, editor in chief of *Fashionista*.

Every company gets things wrong now and then. What distinguishes good companies from bad ones is the fact that good companies are able to see their mistakes and correct them. It's clear that those in charge at Coach have recognized their mistakes. But it remains to be seen if the turnaround plan is the antidote. With all that Coach has at stake, Luis, Frankfort, and the others will not give up easily. The question is, will the new strategy restore Coach to its former glory days?

Questions for Discussion

1. What challenges does Coach face in pricing its vast product line?

2. Based on principles from the chapter, explain how price affects customer perceptions of the Coach brand.

3. How has increased competition at Coach's price points affected the brand's performance?

4. Will the plan proposed by current Coach's leadership be successful in reversing the brand's slide in market share? Why or why not?

5. What recommendations would you make to Coach?

Sources: Lauren Indvik, "Stuart Vevers Is Creating Luxury That's 'Not Too Precious' for Coach," *Fashionista*, February 13, 2015, http://fashionista .com/2015/02/coach-fall-2015; Andrew Marder, "Coach, Inc. Can't Get It Together," *Motley Fool*, April 30, 2014, www.fool.com/investing/ general/2014/04/30/coach-inc-cant-get-it-together.aspx; Phil Wahba, "Coach Sales in North America Plummet as Market Share Erodes," *Reuters*, January 22, 2014, http://in.reuters.com/article/2014/01/22/ coach-results-idINL3N0KW3V920140122; and additional information taken from www.coach.com/aboutus?contentObject=about-us, accessed September, 2015.

Company Case 10

Apple Pay: Taking Mobile Payments Mainstream

After leaving his office in Manhattan, Tag stopped at a nearby Panera to grab a Frontega Chicken Panini and Green Passion Power Smoothie as a quick dinner on his way to see some friends in Soho. Upon ordering, he held his Apple Watch to the contactless reader near the register, gently pressed his finger to the TouchID fingerprint sensor on the small screen, and let Apple Pay do the rest.

Wanting to get across town as soon as possible, Tag used his Uber app to summon an UberX car. During the car ride, he remembered that he needed a couple of new dress shirts. With a few quick clicks on his watch, he selected the shirts through his Macy's app. With a simple tap, he used Apple Pay to seamlessly complete the transaction. As he neared his destination, Tag added a tip to the bill for the ride through the Uber app, which he'd already configured to use Apple Pay as the default. With one simple press of his finger to TouchID on his watch, he exited the cab.

Three purchases—offline, online, and, well, sort of in between—no wallet required. No traditional wallet, that is. This new reality—one that many early adopters are already living—is rapidly expanding toward what some experts predict will become the future for everyone. Folks like Tag don't even carry traditional wallets anymore, only their mobile devices and perhaps an ID and a backup credit card for retailers that don't accept mobile payments—yet. After years of predictions that mobile payments would replace cash and credit cards, there are finally signs that it might actually be happening. And Apple is leading the way.

Hardly New

The ability to pay for transactions with a mobile device is hardly new. In fact, the first technology for mobile payments was invented by Sony way back in 1989. It was first put into use in Hong Kong's subway system in 1997 and began taking root in Japan in 2001. The tech-savvy Japanese warmed to the idea quickly, and mobile wallet apps were being used on mobile phones throughout Japan by 2004. Ever since, more than 245 million Japanese mobile phones have been equipped with the capability to make mobile payments, and Japanese consumers use mobile payments for everything from transportation to food and household purchases.

So it seems odd that a similar system has not taken root in the United States, although it hasn't been for lack of trying. Companies have been experimenting with different approaches for years. PayPal was the first to take advantage of the smartphone revolution by creating a payment app that gave just about every smartphone the potential for mobile payments. About a year later, Google entered the mobile payment game with the launch of Google Wallet. In the past five years, numerous other companies, from small start-ups to electronics and retailing giants, have tried to gain market acceptance in mobile payments. They include the likes of Samsung, Square, and CurrentC, a mobile wallet app backed by a consortium of U.S. retailers (with Walmart leading the way) that hope to cut credit card companies and their fees out of the buying loop.

But none of these players—individually or together—have made much of a dent in replacing traditional credit cards and cash as a form of payment in the multi-trillion-dollar U.S. retail market. Although the mobile payments concept may seem like a no-brainer for convenience-loving American consumers, numerous barriers on both the buyer and seller sides have kept the concept from gaining momentum. With its recent launch of Apple Pay, Apple is clearly a market follower. But it's a feat that the innovative company has performed to perfection time and again—take a new technology, make it better than any of the initial offerings, then watch the market explode as the Apple version becomes the runaway market leader.

Overcoming Negative Consumer Perceptions

As with every new technology that involves paying for things, consumers have concerns about the security of mobile payments. Paypal, Google, and the others took significant measures to design secure systems. However, most consumers just weren't comfortable with the idea that their phone might be used as a portal to their credit cards and bank accounts if it fell into the wrong hands. Never mind that the same could be said of a wallet or handbag, far less secure devices.

Recognizing consumer reluctance to place digital versions of their financial devices in one app, Apple took security to a higher level. Requiring a fingerprint makes the process much more secure than the more common safeguard of entering a passcode. And if a mobile device is ever lost or stolen, the owner can use its Find My iPhone feature to immediately lock down Apple Pay or even wipe the device completely clean.

Additionally, every compatible Apple device is assigned a unique Device Account Number. This is encrypted and securely stored in a dedicated security chip on the device. That and a transaction-specific security code are the only numbers that Apple transmits to merchants. In fact, the merchant doesn't even need to know the customer's name. Credit and debit card numbers are stored only on the local device, not on Apple servers. This makes Apple Pay even more secure and more private than paying by credit card.

Beyond consumer security concerns, previous adoption of mobile payment apps has been slowed by perceptions of a clunky user experience. If convenience is the biggest draw for consumers, then anything more arduous than the already convenient swipe of a credit card simply won't cut it. Setting up any of the existing mobile payment apps takes time and effort. Using such apps at the point of purchase is far from seamless, especially if the technology isn't working quite right. "I don't want to be that guy holding up the line while we fumble around to get it all to work," says one business columnist, "just like I don't want to be the guy who holds up the line boarding an airplane because his mobile boarding pass can't be read." Mobile apps that hit the market prior to Apple Pay required entering a passcode and—in some cases—hitting multiple buttons. That took longer than the traditional swipe of the card, even if everything worked as intended.

With Apple Pay, users still need to configure the app. But Apple already has 800 million credit cards on file with its existing iTunes store. Not only can this facilitate a set up that is already streamlined compared with existing apps, it's a sign that iTunes users may be more comfortable with using the app given that they have already given their credit card information to Apple. And with the TouchID sensor, Apple has the transaction down to a one-touch process. That's quicker than swiping a card and going through the typical menu, not to mention quicker than inputting a passcode.

Establishing Points of Acceptance

For mobile payments to penetrate the market, consumer acceptance is necessary. But companies face a twofold challenge in making such a technology successful. Consumers won't adopt it if retailers don't accept it, and retailers won't invest the resources necessary to accept it unless there is sufficient consumer demand. And the lack of consumer demand is the biggest factor that has kept retailers from jumping onto the mobile payments bandwagon. As a result, there are currently too few retailers that accept mobile payments to convince people that they can leave their credit cards at home.

But thanks to Apple, that situation is changing rapidly. It may be because of Apple's clout or because of the company's massive and loyal user base. But in less than a year, Apple has signed up far more retailers than all the previous mobile payment providers combined. "You need so many points of acceptance to make mobile payments work," says a mobile payments analyst for Forrester Research. "Apple has made that happen, striking partnerships with top national brands across a variety of categories that will give consumers plenty of opportunity to use the service." Apple has also signed up enough credit card issuing banks and credit unions to cover 83 percent of charge volume. In fact, Apple Pay has gained enough steam that Best Buy and Meijer will soon be accepting the payment app, despite having signed exclusivity agreements as part of the CurrentC consortium.

But Apple still faces many challenges. For example, even though Apple Pay is now technically accepted at more than 700,000 U.S. retail outlets, many of those outlets don't yet have the hardware installed that will recognize Apple's app. That fact can be discouraging to early adopters, hurting repeat usage. One recent survey showed that 66 percent of iPhone 6 owners had signed up for Apple Pay, but nearly half of them had visited a store listed as an Apple Pay merchant only to find that the location wasn't set up yet to process mobile payments through the app. Additionally, although Apple's penetration of the market far exceeds that of the competition and continues to grow each month, the mobile payments leader has a long way to go before reaching critical mass with 8 million retail outlets. And this doesn't even take into account online and in-app payments.

Still, Apple remains confident. "We are more convinced than ever that 2015 will be the year of Apple Pay," says Tim Cook, Apple's CEO. While there are still plenty of doubters that mobile payments will replace plastic as the go-to method for purchasing goods and services, there are also plenty of believers. And while Apple is clearly ahead in this game, its success also bodes well for the competition. As the concept catches on and technologies become more compatible, demand among non-Apple users will increase as well.

There is no shortage of options in the mobile payments field. And improvements designed to make the apps more convenient are being made continually, including the integration of loyalty cards and other promotional mechanisms. But even as other companies' offerings get better, expect Apple to be more competitive than ever. After all, nothing is stopping it from creating Apple Pay for Android devices.

Questions for Discussion

1. As completely as possible, sketch the value delivery network for Apple Pay.

2. With respect to Apple Pay, is Apple a producer, a consumer, or an intermediary? Explain.

3. Identify all the reasons why Apple's partnerships are essential to the success of Apple Pay.

4. With respect to marketing channels, what are some threats to Apple Pay's future?

Sources: Robert Hof, "Apple Pay Starts to Take Off, Leaving Competition in the Dust," *Forbes*, January 27, 2015, www.forbes.com/sites/roberthof/2015/01/27/apple-pay-starts-to-take-off-leaving-competition-in-the-dust/; Robert Hof, "Apple Pay Momentum Keeps Growing Despite Challenges in Stores," *Forbes*, April 27, 2015, www.forbes.com/sites/roberthof/2015/04/27/apple-pay-momentum-keeps-growing-despite-challenges-in-stores/; Cade Metz, "How Apple Pay Will Destroy the Online-Offline Shopping Divide," *Wired*, September 10, 2014, www.wired.com/2014/09/how-apple-pay-will-become-the-easy-way-to-buy-everything/; and information from www.apple.com/apple-pay/, accessed September 2015.

Company Case 11

Sears: Why Should You Shop There?

After working late one evening, Joan stopped off at Sears to return some items she had purchased online from Lands' End—a Sears-affiliated brand since 2002. She couldn't remember the last time she'd set foot in a Sears store, instead usually shopping at other department stores or discount retailers. As she walked in, she noticed that the store felt old and a bit run-down. She also noticed that she was one of few people in the entire store. The store seemed to stock a hodgepodge of products and brands, arranged in a pedestrian way. On her way out of the store, she wondered to herself, "Who shops at Sears? Why?"

Younger shoppers might find it hard to believe, but until the 1980s, Sears was America's largest retailer—the Walmart of its day. It's once-famous slogan, "Where America Shops," wasn't just a clever tagline conjured up by Madison Avenue. It was a positioning statement with power. Sears catered to all, selling merchandise in just about every category to just about every customer segment.

But the once-dominant Sears has since fallen so hard and fast that some analysts are now predicting its complete demise within the next few years. Its once-famous slogan seems almost comical now, as its stores are often deserted, even during peak times. What caused this decline? Sears lost its focus. Whereas many retail brands have forged strong positioning strategies targeting specific segments, Sears no longer stands for much of anything. Mention Walmart and people think "Save money. Live better." Bring up Target and they know to "Expect more. Pay less." At Macy's you get "the magic of Macy's," and Nordstrom promises to "take care of customers no matter what it takes." But say Sears and most customers draw a blank. The chain has neither an image nor an apparent value proposition that gives people a compelling reason to shop at its stores.

The Fall of an Icon

Founded in 1886, during the next century, Sears grew to become America's iconic retailer. It began as a mail-order catalog company in the 1880s, grew into a national chain of urban department stores during the early to mid-1900s, and became an important anchor store in the fast-growing suburban malls of the 1960s and 1970s. Through the 1980s, Sears was the nation's largest retail chain. Almost every American relied on Sears for everything from basic apparel and home goods to appliances and tools. But during the past two decades, as the retail landscape has shifted, once-mighty Sears has lost its way. Sears has failed to refresh its positioning to make itself relevant in today's marketplace.

A look at Sears advertising or a visit to the Sears Web site testifies to the retailer's almost complete lack of current positioning. Headlines scream "Buy more, save more on appliances," "50% off your favorite apparel brands," "Lowest prices on Craftsman lawn and garden," and "Big brand sale: great values, top brands." It seems that about the only thing Sears has going for it these days is that everything it sells is always on sale. However, price is not a convincing value proposition for Sears, which has trouble matching the low prices of competitors such as Walmart, Target, or Kohl's.

In 2005, a struggling Sears merged with an even more distressed Kmart to become Sears Holding Corporation. The merger of the two failing retailers left analysts scratching their heads and customers even more confused about the value propositions of the respective chains. Following the merger, the corporation jumped from one questionable tactic to another. For example, Kmart stores began carrying well-known Sears brands such as Craftsman tools, Kenmore appliances, and Diehard batteries, diluting one of Sears's only remaining differentiating assets.

Sears Holding has also tried a variety of store formats. For instance, it converted 400 Kmart stores to Sears Essentials stores, which it later changed to Sears Grand stores—Walmart-like outlets that carry regular Sears merchandise plus everything from health and beauty brands, toys, and baby products to party supplies and groceries. It has also dabbled with a confusing assortment of other formats carrying the Sears name, such as Sears Hometown stores (a franchised smaller version of full-sized Sears stores), Sears Hardware stores, Sears Home Appliance Showrooms, Sears Outlet stores, and Sears Auto Centers.

Despite the variety of store formats, Sears has done little to refresh its positioning. "A lot of traditional department stores have reinvigorated themselves through merchandising. You haven't seen that from Sears," says one analyst. To make matters worse, whereas most competing retailers have invested heavily to spruce up their stores, Sears has spent less than one-quarter of the industry average on store maintenance and renovation, leaving many of its outlets looking old and shabby. "There's no reason to shop at Sears," concludes a retailing expert. "It offers a depressing shopping experience and uncompetitive prices."

Once a Retailer, Now a Hedge Fund

Many critics place the blame for Sears's lack of sound marketing and positioning on Sears Holding Company chairman Edward Lampert, a hedge fund manager and the driving force behind the Sears/Kmart merger. Lampert and his funds own about 60 percent of Sears Holding's stock. Critics claim that since the 2005 merger, Lampert has run the company more as a portfolio of financial assets than as a retail chain. A fierce advocate of free-market economics, Lampert restructured Sears into approximately 40 business units, each set up to operate as an independent business with its own set of c-suite officers, boards of directors, and profit-and-loss statements. The intention was for the decentralized structure to foster independence and competitiveness and to make each part of the corporation more accountable.

It had other, less appealing effects. For example, because the appliance unit could make more money selling products manufactured by outside brands, it began featuring brands like LG over Sears's own Kenmore. A similar problem arose when the Sears Craftsman brand unit proposed a tool co-branded with the Sears DieHard brand. But under the new structure, Craftsman would have had to pay DieHard royalties, making the cost of the item prohibitive. Craftsman tools and Kenmore appliances still lead their categories, and the DieHard brand of automotive batteries remains strong. But the infighting has had a negative effect on the market positions and fortunes of these and other Sears brands.

The decentralized structure also created barriers to pricing Sears and Kmart products competitively relative to competing chains. After studying the company's prices, a newly appointed president of retail services surmised that Kmart's food and drugs were more expensive than those at Walmart and Target. He proposed reducing prices on these product lines, bringing them in line with competitors. The presidents of various business units agreed with the proposal. But no unit was willing to cough up the $2 million needed to fund the project. Corporate headquarters rejected a request for a loan. So prices remained at uncompetitive levels.

As day-to-day operations played out, cooperation and collaboration gave way to a "warring tribes" culture that made the lack of a solid marketing message even worse. As chief marketing officers fought over advertising space in the weekly Sears circular, the circular turned into what one former executive referred to as a "Frankenstein" promotion—a hodgepodge of product combinations with no overall cohesion. Screwdrivers were advertised next to lingerie, and lawnmowers sat next to ladies' shoes. For the cover of one Mother's Day circular, the sporting-goods unit purchased space for a Doodle Bug minibike—an item popular with young boys.

All of this speaks to a lack of leadership at the top. Since the 2005 merger, Lampert has hired four CEOs, not a single one with any retailing experience. After the last CEO left more than a year ago, Lampert assumed CEO responsibilities himself. But "being a successful hedge fund manager doesn't make you a good retailer," says one Sears watcher.

The Only Hope?

There are a few signs of a prosperous future for the nation's once-greatest retailer. To streamline operations and free up cash, Sears is selling off parts of the company. Last year, Sears Holdings spun off Sears Hometown and Sears Outlet stores. Lampert also facilitated the sale of a portion of Sears's stake in Sears Canada. Most recently, the company sold Lands' End—now an independent company, although still located within Sears—in a transaction that put more than $1 billion in Sears's coffers. Lampert is eying similar deals for other Sears businesses. Although some see this as a way to strengthen the company by focusing on its core business, others see it as little more than "continuing to burn the furniture to stay warm."

One potential bright spot for Sears is online sales. As the company's revenues continued to drop, its online sales have been on the uptick. With a strategy to become a fully integrated omni-channel retailer, revenue from e-commerce has been growing by an average of 10 percent over the past few years. In fact, Sears is the sixth-largest online retailer in the United States. This is no accident. Lampert is a believer in selling online. In a recent statement that accompanied a financial update to the press, Lampert came as close as he ever has to issuing a statement of corporate strategy. "We are transitioning from a business that has historically focused on running a store network into a business that provides and delivers value by serving its members in the manner most convenient for them: whether in stores, at home, or through digital devices."

To support this assertion, Sears has developed the Shop Your Way loyalty program—a hybrid between Amazon and Facebook that allows customers to accumulate and spend rewards online or off. Sears has also experimented with a store pickup service, MyGofer—an initiative that essentially turns Kmart stores into a same-day pickup location for all Sears and Kmart brands and merchandise ordered online. With the omni-channel model very much in vogue, this strategy seems to put Sears right on target in terms of where the retail industry is headed.

But while Sears is apparently investing in the digital side of its business, it is neglecting the brick-and-mortar side. The chain hasn't opened a new store in years. In fact, it's selling off locations—235 this year alone. "Our stores are often in the wrong place and are often too large for our needs" was all that Lampert could say when questioned about the high rate of store closures. And Sears's remaining stores are progressively becoming less appealing. One retail analyst, once a big Sears fan, remembers growing up in Chicago at a time when his family wouldn't think of shopping anywhere but Sears. Now things are different. "I shopped for back-to-school clothes at a store [that's] now so dark and depressing, I can't bear to go in," he says, "even though it's [just] blocks from my home—a home that sits on a street that shares a name with an iconic Sears brand."

Although Lampert and his team continue to claim that turnaround efforts will soon bear fruit, things don't look promising for Sears. The lack of customer thinking and marketing strategy has taken a devastating toll. Sears Holding Corporation's revenues have fallen for 29 consecutive quarters. Total sales for the most recent year were $31.2 billion, down 14 percent from the previous year and a far cry from a peak of $53 billion just eight years prior. Profits also paint a grim picture—the company lost $1.7 billion last year, more than it made from selling off Lands' End. As a result, Sears's stock price has fallen nearly 80 percent since 2007.

In a letter to shareholders after the release of the most recent year's financials, Lampert boasted of his e-commerce plan, saying that otherwise, "we would be stuck on the same path that has claimed Circuit City, Borders, Radio Shack, and others," all iconic retailers that have gone out of business. And yet, with no cogent marketing plan and seemingly no way out of its financial tailspin, many analysts predict that once-dominant Sears will soon follow the same fate and disappear entirely.

Questions for Discussion

1. According to the principles of retail strategy, how did Sears once become the nation's biggest retailer?

2. According to those same principles, how did Sears lose its once-commanding market position?

3. What is the relationship between the current Sears corporate strategy and its marketing struggles?

4. Assess Sears' efforts to become a true bricks-and-clicks retailer.

5. Can anything save Sears? Support your position.

Sources: James Covert, "Sears Posts $548 million loss, Plans to Close 235 Stores," *New York Post*, December 4, 2014, http://nypost.com/2014/12/04/sears-posts-wider-q3-loss-on-13-revenue-drop/; Phil Wahba, "Eddie Lampert's Incredible Shrinking Empire," *Fortune*, February 26, 2015, http://fortune.com/2015/02/26/sears-earnings/; Lauren Coleman-Lochner and Carol Hymowitz, "A Money Man's Trials in Retailing," *Bloomberg Businessweek*, January 5, 2012, pp. 24–25; and various pages at www.sears.com, accessed September 2015.

Company Case 12

Allstate: Bringing Mayhem to the Auto Insurance Advertising Wars

In the spring of 1950, the teenage daughter of Allstate general sales manager Davis Ellis was stricken with hepatitis shortly before she was to graduate from high school. The worried executive arrived home from work one evening just as his wife returned from the hospital where their daughter was admitted. As he met her at the front door, his wife reported, "The hospital said not to worry ... we're in good hands with the doctor."

Later that year, Ellis became part of a team charged with developing the first major national advertising campaign for the Allstate Insurance Company. As the team discussed the message they wanted the brand to convey, Ellis recalled his wife's "we're in good hands" remark and how good it made him feel. The phrase projected security, reassurance, and responsibility, exactly the traits the team wanted customers to associate with Allstate. Thus was born the slogan "You're in good hands with Allstate."

By the early 2000s, a study by Northwestern University found that the long-standing Allstate catchphrase was the most recognized slogan in the United States. For years, Allstate held the position as the second-largest personal lines insurer, trailing only State Farm. In 2003, Allstate hired actor Dennis Haysbert as the brand's spokesperson. After starring in dozens of Allstate commercials—each culminating with the question "Are you in good hands?—Haysbert's deep voice became a comforting familiarity to television viewers. Today, the "Good Hands" slogan is the oldest surviving slogan for a paid campaign.

An Advertising Shakeup

Although Allstate's advertising served it well for decades, by the late 1990s, the company had fallen into the same routine as the rest of its industry. Big auto insurance companies were spending modestly on sleepy ad campaigns featuring touchy-feely, reassuring messages such as Allstate's "You're in good hands" or State Farm's "Like a good neighbor." In an industry characterized by low budgets and even lower-key ads, no brand's marketing stood out.

However, the advertising serenity ended with the first appearance of the now-iconic GEICO Gecko in 1999, backed by a big budget and pitching direct sales and low prices. That single GEICO ad campaign sparked a frenzy of ad spending and creativity in the insurance industry that quickly escalated into a full-scale advertising war. Once-conservative car insurance ads became creative showstoppers, as edgy and creative as ads found in any industry. Here are a few highlights:

- *GEICO:* GEICO got the auto insurance advertising wars rolling when it was acquired by billionaire Warren Buffet's Berkshire-Hathaway company in 1996 and given a blank check to aggressively increase market share. That led to an onslaught of advertising the likes of which the auto insurance industry had never seen. A string of creative GEICO campaigns featured everything from civilized cavemen to cash with googly eyes. But it was the GEICO Gecko that had the biggest impact. With his signature English accent, the Gecko made GEICO's simple message clear—"15 minutes can save you 15 percent or more on car insurance." More than any other industry spokesperson, the Gecko lent personality and pizzazz to the previously sleepy insurance industry and its staid brands.

- *Progressive:* Following GEICO's lead, in 2008 Progressive created its own perky and endearing personality—Flo. Progressive created the ever-upbeat, ruby-lipped salesclerk to help convince consumers who are already in the market that they can get an even better price deal from Progressive. Flo helped put Progressive hot on the heels of rising GEICO as the fourth-largest auto insurer. Flo assists people when they are ready to shop. Progressive later introduced a complementary campaign featuring the Messenger—the mustachioed, leather-jacket-wearing stranger—and Brad—the easy-going, self-assured man with an absurdly funny sense of self-esteem who refers to himself only in the third person.

Like the GEICO Gecko, Flo, the Messenger, and Brad pitch price savings as their primary appeal.

- *State Farm:* As GEICO and Progressive shook up the industry with their direct, low-price, high-profile selling models, conventional agent-based auto insurers were forced to respond. Ninety-year-old State Farm, the long-time industry leader, was hardly a stranger to advertising. Like Allstate, State Farm had a long-standing, widely recognized slogan—"Like a good neighbor, State Farm is there"—a jingle written by pop music icon Barry Manilow in 1971. Sensing the threat from the rising newcomers, State Farm fought back vigorously with a new campaign centered on its enduring jingle. In its "magic jingle" campaign, State Farm agents magically appear when summoned with the jingle by young drivers in trouble—including the likes of LeBron James. The campaign's goal—to convince consumers that they still need the services of one of State Farm's 18,000 agents. To help make the point more forcefully, State Farm doubled its ad budget.

"Good Hands" Meets Mayhem

Amid this surge in competition and advertising creativity, Allstate struggled just to hold its own, let alone to grow. In the wake of the Gecko and Flo, Allstate had lost market share for two years running, even with Haysbert's presence as company pitchman. The brand needed its own over-the-top personality. So Allstate brought mayhem to life—literally. With the new creepy Mayhem character played by actor Dean Winters, Allstate created a villainous counterpart to Haysbert's soothing hero. The campaign's goal: to convince consumers that there is more to buying car insurance than just price. Put more bluntly, says an ad agency executive involved with the campaign, "We wanted to kick Flo's ass."

Mayhem portrays all of the unlikely events that can lead to a major auto insurance claim. As a deer, he jumps into the path of a moving car at night "because that's what we deer do." As a torrential downpour, he loves leaky sunroofs. As a malfunctioning GPS, he sends a driver swerving into another car. As snow, he weighs down the roof of a garage until it collapses, smashing the car within. Each quirky ad ends with the statement and question "If you have cut-rate insurance, you could be paying for this yourself. Are you in good hands?"

Through such clever ads, Allstate's creative and award-winning "Mayhem. It's Everywhere." campaign has put a contemporary, attention-grabbing twist on the company's long-standing "You're in good hands with Allstate" slogan, helping to position the brand as a superior alternative to price-oriented competitors. Even with its long-standing "Good Hands" campaign, Allstate needed something unconventional. In fact, mayhem didn't just describe the Allstate campaign—it characterized the entire world of auto insurance advertising.

The Mayhem campaign quickly won many top ad industry awards. But perhaps a bigger indication of the campaign's impact is the extent to which the character has become ingrained in the pop culture. Although Mayhem has just more than a third of Flo's 4.9 million Facebook fans, he commands an engagement score nearly eight times that of Progressive's perky spokeswoman. And when the character's creator recently saw a Mayhem-costumed trick-or-treater walking down her street, she called it "a career highlight that gave her chills."

More than just popular, Mayhem is right on message. At the end of each ad, he warns, "If you've got cut-rate insurance, you could be paying for this yourself." Then a reassuring Haysbert provides the solution: "Are you in good hands?" he asks. "Get Allstate. You can save money and be better protected from Mayhem." This "worth-paying-a-little-more" message puts Allstate back at the top in terms of customer value.

Mayhem Redux

Allstate's ads were not only creative, they were effective. After a few years of Mayhem ads complementing Haysbert's Good Hands ads, Allstate's unaided brand awareness of 74 percent trailed State Farm's by only a slight margin, despite State Farm's 60 percent greater ad spending. And for a time, the Mayhem campaign halted Allstate's market share slide. According to Allstate CEO Thomas Wilson, "It's working. If you look at our quotes and our new business, it's way up." All this prompted Allstate to extend the campaign, including the introduction of Mayhem's Hispanic cousin, Mala Suerte (bad luck), aimed at Hispanic consumers.

In extending the campaign, Allstate took Mayhem to the next level, giving the character his own Twitter account. Seemingly late to the Twitter party, Allstate executives indicated that the delay was intentional. "We've been very careful about not overdoing Mayhem and not overexposing [him]," said Jennifer Egeland, Allstate's director of advertising. "[We wanted] the right idea for launching him in the Twitter space."

The right idea was to conform to Mayhem's persona. As a recent football season dawned, Mayhem polled followers about what he should portray in the next ad—a charcoal grill or a cheap bungee cord. Consumers voted for the cord. Mayhem disobeyed, Tweeting: "Too bad I'm a tailgate grill. Who's got a light?" He followed that up with Vine videos of a car set on fire from a grill mishap. Allstate then released two new Mayhem ads—"Tailgate Grill Fire" and "Cheap Bungee Cord," making everyone happy. Similar antics ensued for the ensuing March Madness kickoff of the NCAA playoffs, helping drive more than 61,000 followers to the @Mayhem Twitter account.

With all this activity and public response, Allstate thought it had a surefire weapon for maintaining its market position. But the all-out auto insurance advertising war illustrates just how critical it is to stay one step ahead of the competition. For the most recent year, Allstate increased its ad budget to $887 million, outdoing even market leader State Farm's $802 million effort. However, both companies were eclipsed by GEICO's eye-popping $1.1 billion advertising spending. Today, no fewer than 11 car insurance brands are running national TV advertising campaigns. Combined, the auto insurers now spend more than $6 billion each year to get their messages out. That makes things confusing for consumers, who struggle under the deluge of clever ads for the respective brands.

The intense competition, big budgets, and focus on consumer advertising have kept industry market share dynamic. In fact, in the last year, GEICO moved into the number-two spot behind State Farm and is pulling away with a 10.8 percent share of the auto insurance market to Allstate's 10.0 percent. Allstate has grown its auto insurance business in recent years. But GEICO's growth has been consistently stronger. With that development, Allstate is left to reconsider the value that it is getting out of its advertising investments and just how it might slow GEICO down GEICO and retake its number-two market position.

Questions for Discussion

1. Why has Allstate's "good hands" slogan withstood the test of time to become advertising's longest-running slogan?

2. Analyze Mayhem ads based on the process of creating an advertising message as outlined in the text (for Mayhem ads, check out www.allstate.com/mayhem-is-everywhere.aspx).

3. Discuss issues of selecting advertising media for the Mayhem campaign. How might this process differ from that of campaigns for other companies?

4. Based on the information in this case, how might Allstate measure the effectiveness of the Mayhem campaign?

5. Has the Mayhem campaign been effective? Support your answer.

Sources: Ashley Rodriguez, "How Allstate's Mayhem Disrupted the Chatter around Insurance," *Advertising Age*, June 10, 2015, http://adage.com/print/298779; Steve Daniels, "GEICO Overtakes Allstate as No. 2 Auto Insurer," *Advertising Age*, March 3, 2014, http://adage.com/print/291947; E.J. Schultz, "Allstate's Mayhem Joins Twitter … Now What," *Advertising Age*, October 14, 2013, p. 28; Anthony Crup, "Allstate's Marketing Boss Talks Up 'March Mayhem,'" *Ad Week*, March 25, 2014, www.adweek.com/print/156471; and advertisements and other information accessed at www.allstatenewsroom.com and www.allstate.com/mayhem-is-everywhere.aspx, accessed September 2015.

Company Case 13

SunGard: Building Sustained Growth by Selling the SunGard Way

If asked what company topped the most recent *Selling Power* magazine list of "50 Best Companies to Sell For," you'd probably guess IBM, P&G, or maybe Xerox, companies long known for their outstanding sales forces. But number one on this year's list is a company you probably know less about—software and technology services company SunGard.

What makes SunGard such a good place to work as a salesperson? For starters, SunGard has strong name recognition and a solid reputation in its industry. SunGard has long provided excellent compensation and training to its salespeople. And the company has consistently delivered strong customer growth and retention. However, although SunGard has long been good in these areas, what has made it outstanding and put it at the top of *Selling Power*'s list is a recent complete transformation of SunGard's sales force model.

Pioneering a New Industry

In the late 1970s, the computer services division of the Sun Oil Company (today Sunoco) pioneered a service now considered indispensable by virtually every company in the world. Sun and 20 other Philadelphia-area companies entered an agreement to act as backups for each others' data systems. To create the needed capacity, the group developed a designated disaster recovery backup center. But when member companies were slow to pay their shares of the expenses, Sun Oil took over the backup operation and began selling computer services. In 1983, Sun Oil spun off the computer division and SunGard was born.

Since then, with the help of a few acquisitions, SunGard has grown steadily. It's now one of the world's leading software and technology services companies, with nearly $3 billion in annual revenues. SunGard now provides processing solutions for the financial services industry, K–12 education, and public sector organizations. It serves 16,000 customers in more than 70 countries. As a business-to-business service provider, that requires a substantial sales force.

Good, but Not Great

When Russell Fradin took over as the CEO of SunGard in 2011, business was good. But the company faced some issues of concern. For starters, the Internet increasingly provided SunGard clients and potential clients with the information they needed to solve their own problems. For both its private and public sector businesses, compliance with government regulations was also increasing. And increasing globalization made it more and more challenging for SunGard's sales reps to meet client needs. SunGard was not alone in facing these issues. But that just added to the pressure—any company finding effective ways to meet these challenges would gain considerable strategic advantage.

SunGard also faced plenty of internal issues. The company sold multiple product lines, and Fradin felt that the SunGard sales force wasn't achieving its potential in terms of selling the optimal mix of products. The company's thousands of sales reps spent most of their time and effort selling licensed software rather than developing broader solutions to customer problems. Moreover, with multiple divisions and product lines and a fragmented go-to-market approach, SunGard often had multiple sales reps pursuing the same clients, sapping productivity and even driving some customers away.

Based on these assessments, Fradin asked himself, "How can SunGard make its sales force—one of the company's biggest and most important investments—perform more effectively?" SunGard had decent systems in place for recruiting, hiring, and training its salespeople. And SunGard's sales executives did a reasonable job of making incremental changes. But Fradin felt that the company needed to do more in order to improve its growth and performance. If more drastic changes weren't made, the mounting challenges would likely limit future sales and profits. To Fradin's thinking, SunGard needed a complete sales force transformation.

According to a report by global sales consulting firm ZA Associates, companies that move sales force effectiveness from good to excellent by virtue of a sales force transformation can increase profitable growth by as much as 20 percent. But that kind of transformation would require a major effort, many months to plan and execute, and even longer to take hold. It would demand nothing less than a total commitment from everyone in the organization—those at the lowest rung on the corporate ladder up to senior management and executives. It would also require that everyone have a clear vision of the benefits, for both themselves and for the organization as a whole. Disruptions from implementing such a sweeping change would likely mean losing good people and clients. It might also result in a short-term dip in performance before the benefits began to kick in.

Setting Transformation in Motion

In early 2012, Fradin hired Jim Neve and Ken Powell to head up SunGard's global sales efforts. The two-person team had worked on other successful large-scale sales force transformations, and they planned to carry out the same process at SunGard. "We needed to maximize our channels, sell the broadest set of solutions possible, and go to market in a coordinated manner," said Powell. "We needed to build a sustainable growth engine."

Neve and Powell branded the sales force transformation initiative as "Selling the SunGard Way." More than just a fancy title, "Selling the SunGard Way" was a philosophy defined by specific goals and characteristics. First and foremost, the transformation would shift the basic sales approach from selling based on meeting customer needs to selling based on insights. SunGard reps needed to thoroughly understand the client buying decision process, anticipate needs before even customers themselves were aware of them, and tailor the client relationship to meet shifting concerns. Focusing on product functionality and price just wouldn't cut it anymore. And sales interactions would need to draw from technology and services across all SunGard business units, not just within specific divisions or product lines. In order to achieve these skills, SunGard's sales personnel would need greater knowledge and expertise of the full line of company products as well as the nature of each client's business.

After thoroughly surveying the needs of SunGard sales associates, Neve and Powell drafted a detailed transformation plan. Sales reps needed better training, detailed competitive analyses, and more effective sales campaigns. They needed better data, fewer administrative tasks, and a simplified interface for its Salesforce CRM sales management tool. To achieve such goals, Neve and Powell set out to overhaul SunGard's core sales

functions, including recruiting, training, managing, and compensating sales force personnel.

This transformation would take time and effort, and it would cost millions. But by the time the plan was revealed, there was support throughout the company. "The whole organization gravitated toward change," said Powell. "[Everyone] knew it had to happen." To help cover costs, the company shifted budgets, reallocating funds from ineffective programs to the transformation project.

On the recruiting front, SunGard adopted a new talent-assessment tool that defined ideal job profiles and evaluated skills and performance patterns of potential hires. The company also hired a team of sales development managers, charged with increasing the productivity of first-year sales reps. It was their job to make sure that new sales reps received all the training and exposure necessary to understand the company's structure, strategic plans, products, and sales tools. That relieved front-line sales managers of these tasks, letting them focus more on selling. Sales development manager compensation hinged on the performance of first-year sales reps.

For existing sales personnel, SunGard revised procedures, metrics, training, and tools to make them consistent across the organization. It also made major revisions to its Salesforce CRM and sales management tool, with an eye toward providing salespeople with all the information they needed for every aspect of the sales process. The important tool now provided easy and immediate access to content such as case studies, customer information, and market data. Additional tools were made available to guide people through the necessary steps of effectively closing a sale.

But to improve effectiveness for both new and existing sales personnel, SunGard needed to make even more changes in how performance was measured and tracked. For example, prior to the transformation, the company tracked incentives and commissions manually, and they were not readily accessible by relevant stakeholders. Under the new scheme, metrics such as individual goals and forecasts, as well as how often sales were made or lost, became part of an automated system, accessible by sales reps and managers via mobile interface at any time. They could even run "what-if" scenarios to determine potential earnings of different situations. This capability motivated sales reps by increasing accountability and promoting a competitive spirit.

From Transformation to Results

As the new sales structure and tools took root, it wasn't long before they began to bear fruit. "There was a tremendous product suite that had yet to capture its full market share," says Todd Albright, who joined SunGard as senior vice president of sales for the Americas after the transformation was under way. That market share will soon be achieved. "There were tremendous assets locked up at SunGard," Neve summarizes. "We put a road map in place to unlock those assets, translating them into new sales and revenue growth."

With its billion-dollar sales plan now in place, SunGard is on target. As one example, consider the productivity improvements for first-year reps. Prior to the transformation, about

75 percent of new reps booked their first sale before the end of their first year at an average of about $400,000. Through the new policies, that sales productivity will soon double, adding an incremental $30 to $40 million to annual sales.

If boosting sales force effectiveness was easy, every company would achieve optimal sales force productivity. SunGard was willing to pay the price. In the first year following the implementation of the transformation, as expected, SunGard revenues decreased over the previous year—down by about 16 percent. However, profits rose by nearly 35 percent, thanks in part to reduced costs from more efficient operations. By the end of the second year, revenues were back on the rise. Fradin was notably pleased. "Clients are responding positively to these initiatives, knowing that our offerings help their businesses be more competitive. We [are] particularly pleased with our sales momentum and our organic revenue growth."

Importantly, SunGard's sales force is now much more coordinated and collaborative. It's better trained and equipped to sell based on insights. Its products and services are bundled across product lines rather than within lines. And reps are developing partnerships with customers, assisting them in streamlining operations, accelerating growth, and complying with regulations. By transforming its sales force to "Selling the SunGard Way," SunGard is on a path to sustainable, organic growth for years to come.

Questions for Discussion

1. Compare SunGard's sales force structure before and after the transformation.

2. What are the positive and negative aspects of SunGard's new sales force structure?

3. How would the challenges faced by SunGard have affected sales productivity had the company not initiated its transformational plan?

4. Identify specific ways SunGard's transformational plan addresses the different steps of managing the sales force.

5. Will "Selling the SunGard Way" really work? Why or why not?

Sources: Henry Canaday, "Selling the New SunGard Way," *Selling Power,* www.sellingpower.com/content/article/?a=10217/selling-the-new-sungard-way&page=1, accessed June 2015; "50 Companies to Sell For in 2014," *Selling Power,* www.sellingpower.com/2014/50-best-companies-to-sell-for/, accessed June 2015; Andris Zoltners, P. K. Sinha, and Sally Lorimer, "Improving Your Sales Force: Fine-tune or Transform?" *Harvard Business Review,* November 13, 2012, http://blogs.hbr.org/2012/11/improving-your-sales-force-fin/; and information from www.sungard.com/about-us and www.sungard.com/financials, accessed September 2015.

Company Case 14

Alibaba: The World's Largest E-tailer Is Not Amazon

There's a new king of e-commerce, and it dwarfs Amazon. Introducing Alibaba, the China-based behemoth that racked up $420 billion in revenues last year and is rapidly building an online empire that will include businesses ranging from a traditional online marketplace to online investment services. With annual sales that already place it much closer to Walmart ($487 billion) than to Amazon ($89 billion), Alibaba is growing so rapidly that by the end of the year it will comfortably pass Walmart to become the world's largest company. How is this Chinese upstart pulling off such a startling Internet feat? Let's start by taking a look at Alibaba's founder, Jack Ma.

Unlikely Beginnings

Jack Ma is an unlikely figure to be atop of one of the world's most powerful companies. Time and again, U.S. tech start-ups have emerged from California garages. However, perhaps none of those start-ups were founded by individuals as seemingly unprepared as Ma. Growing up in Shanghai, Ma did poorly in school. He failed the college entrance exam twice before getting in and completing a teaching degree. He learned to speak English by hanging out around tourists and listening to radio broadcasts. Ma was rejected for a number of jobs—including

being a manager for KFC—before finally landing a job teaching English for $12 a month.

But Ma was animated and energetic, and he had lofty goals and ambitions, a combination that earned him the nickname "Crazy Jack." During China's export boom in the 1990s, Ma started a translation company. On a business trip to the United States, he was exposed to the World Wide Web and was surprised to find almost no Chinese content. After a failed attempt at starting an Internet company in China, Ma corralled 17 friends in his apartment in 1999 and set out to build an online marketplace. Substituting vision and charisma for coding skills, Ma started Alibaba.com, only a few years after legendary e-commerce marketers Amazon and eBay got their starts.

Feeding the Masses

It's difficult to examine Alibaba without making comparisons to the more globally familiar online sellers. In fact, Alibaba is often referred to as the "Amazon of China." But it's the differences between Alibaba and the Amazons, eBays, Googles, Walmarts, Costcos, Sears, and thousands of other successful e-tailers that explain how the Chinese company has grown so big and will grow so much bigger in the future.

For starters, consider the respective domestic markets. Amazon and the others got their starts in the United States, home to roughly 320 million people. This market serves up the most developed retail industry and the highest standard of living in the world. As the tech boom took off, numerous ambitious upstarts competed fiercely to transfer America's retail businesses into the quickly developing space. Tech-savvy U.S.

consumers scrambled to convert some of their buying from brick-and-mortar stores to online purchases.

Contrast this with China. With 1.3 billion people and the fastest-growing economy in the world, the Chinese market has tremendous power and potential. But perhaps more important, China's retail sector was still in the Dark Ages when Alibaba got its start. "E-commerce in the U.S. is like a dessert. It's just supplementary to your main business," Ma said recently. "In China, because the infrastructure of [traditional retail] commerce is [so] bad, e-commerce becomes the main course."

As many Chinese move from poverty to middle-class status, their exposure to buying online coincided with their exposure to any kind of buying. Relative to the U.S. market, there were relatively few competitors. The size and nature of China's market have Alibaba boasting of 300 million registered customers, a base that comfortably exceeds the size of the entire purchasing population of the United States. And Internet penetration in China is still only 47 percent, compared with the much more saturated 87 percent in the United States, providing enormous growth potential.

In adapting traditional retail to an online environment, Amazon and the other U.S. e-tailers operate a "managed marketplace"—they own their own distribution centers, sell a majority of their products directly, and even market their own brands, all characteristics that mimic traditional retail structures. This allows U.S. e-tailers to benefit from established distribution channels and to maintain a great deal of control over their operations. But it also requires massive investments in infrastructure and armies of employees, both of which result in wafer-thin profit margins. In fact, for two of the past four years, Amazon has lost money. For the other two years, the biggest profit it could muster was only 1.3 percent of sales. Walmart's profit margin percentages for both online and offline sales are typically in the low single digits.

But Alibaba does not own or operate massive distribution centers. It doesn't own the items sold on its sites. And it only employs about 25,000 people, a fraction of Amazon's 132,000 employees. Instead, Alibaba's open market platform simply connects buyers with sellers. That might sound like an eBay approach, but Ma insists that it is not. "Amazon and eBay are e-commerce companies, and Alibaba is not an e-commerce company," Ma said recently. "Alibaba helps others to do e-commerce. We do not sell things." While this gives Alibaba less control over the customer experience, Ma sleeps easier at night without the burden of obsessing over keeping prices low. As market forces work to set price points, Alibaba sits back and watches the cash pour in. Its profit margin over the past two years averaged almost 40 percent.

A Little of Everything

The continuous influx of cash has allowed Alibaba to invest in just about every kind of business imaginable. In its infancy, Alibaba.com primarily matched Chinese exporters with businesses throughout the rest of the world. But the company quickly shifted focus, catering to the growing purchase power of its domestic market. Unlike its Western counterparts, Alibaba developed and acquired different online sites and established major divisions. For example, Taobao.com is a site that helps small businesses and private parties sell merchandise to customers. But unlike eBay's commission structure, Taobao sellers pay only for the

advertised promotion. From a shopping standpoint, Alibaba's Tmall.com is more similar Amazon, pairing customers with big corporations, including many global corporations such as Nike, P&G, Apple, and even retailers like Costco.

But Alibaba's development has taken it down numerous other paths as well. And although it may seem that the surging Chinese conglomerate is simply playing copycat, Ma's vision plays out creatively in every case. For example, Alipay is similar to PayPal. But starved for investment opportunities in an environment dominated by state-run banks, Alipay customers have access to financial products that pay attractive returns. In the first year of making such options available, Alipay customers tucked away $82 billion.

In another example of "follow-the-Silicon-Valley-guru," the soon-to-be-launched Tmall Box Office—or TBO—"aims to become [the equivalent] of Netflix in the U.S.," including plans to run original content produced by Alibaba's own Alibaba Pictures. But in an environment where TV viewers aren't accustomed to the pay-to-watch model, Alibaba is a true pioneer. And that pioneering effort extends to a crowd-sourced film investment fund, a model that threatens to upend traditional film financing in China by allowing regular folks to become producers with less risk.

During the past six months alone, Alibaba has spent $8 billion investing in start-up firms. Today, the Alibaba Group spreads out over a constellation of services, including music, gaming, blogs, social networks (the company just dropped $200 million on Snapchat), event ticket sales, shipping, ridesharing, and smartphones.

As Alibaba's list of businesses grows, Ma's vision and innovation seem unbounded. After all, how many U.S. Internet veterans can say they started their own holiday? Just six years ago, Ma enthusiastically launched Singles Day on November 11. What started as a sort of anti-Valentine's Day for single people is now one of the biggest blockbuster sales holidays in the world. Last year, it resulted in $9.3 billion in sales in a 24-hour period, almost double what fanatical U.S. residents spent during the five-day Thanksgiving shopping spree across all companies combined.

As Alibaba continues to grow, one frontier looms large—global expansion. Although China's biggest dot.com success certainly has global ambitions, it has so far chosen to focus on the massive potential of its home market. That will certainly change. "We plan to invest more in [the U.S. and U.K. markets] to get more traffic and ... build brand awareness," says Joe Yan, director of international B2C at Alibaba's export division. "Our biggest advantage is abundance, with 100 million products, we have more options for customers who can buy our products cheaper and at high quality." And while it remains to be seen how Alibaba will attack global markets, one analyst recently predicted a future marriage down the road of Alibaba and eBay.

At the same time, U.S. companies like Netflix and Amazon are exploring ways to expand their small presence in China. However, although the massive markets on both sides of the pond represent opportunities too tempting to pass up, only time will tell whether any of these successful U.S. companies can export the models they have applied so successfully in their home markets.

As U.S. competitors try to counter Alibaba, they will face one more particularly big hurdle. The Chinese love Jack Ma. For their own part, U.S. tech founders such as Bezos, Zuckerberg, Brin and Page, and certainly the late Steve Jobs are considered visionaries who have shaped the world's digital eco-system. But the Chinese revere Mr. Ma, the man who turned a local underdog into a dominant giant with revenues bigger than Amazon, Facebook, Google, and Apple combined. Those kinds of patriotic emotions will be tough to crack.

Questions for Discussion

1. As a digital retailer, how does Alibaba provide value to Chinese consumers? What sets of values are unique to the Chinese market?

2. Given that Alibaba does not own or distribute any of the merchandise exchanged on its sites, describe what factors had to develop for the company to succeed.

3. Analyze Alibaba's business model relative to all the different forms of digital and online marketing covered in this chapter.

4. Can Alibaba succeed in countries outside of China? Why or why not?

Sources: Aaron Back, "Alibaba Dreams of E-commerce Globally but Acts Locally," *Wall Street Journal (Eastern Edition)*, June 24, 2015, p. C12; "Alibaba Plans Subscription Video Service," *Wall Street Journal*, June 14, 2015, www.wsj.com/articles/alibaba-plans-subscription-video-service-1434310742; Jillian D'Onfro, "How Jack Ma Went from Being a Poor School Teacher to Turning Alibaba into a $160 Billion Behemoth," *Business Insider*, September 14, 2014, www.businessinsider.com/the-story-of-jack-ma-founder-of-alibaba-2014-9#ixzz3dqFm4M9B; Angela Doland, "Five Takeaways from Alibaba's Record-Busting $9.3 Billion Shopping Fest," *Advertising Age*, November 11, 2014, http://adage.coverleaf.com/advertisingage/20141117?pg=42#pg42; Julie Makinen, "Alibaba: For Helping Consumers Save, Spend, and Be Entertained," www.fastcompany.com/3039571/most-innovative-companies-2015/alibaba; Charles Riley, "Alibaba Is Not the Amazon of China," *CNNMoney*, September 16, 2014, http://money.cnn.com/2014/09/15/investing/alibaba-amazon-china/; and Mohanbir Sawhney and Sanjay Khosla, "Alibaba vs. Amazon: Who Will Win the Global E-commerce War?" *Forbes*, September 22, 2014, www.forbes.com/sites/forbesleadershipforum/2014/09/22/alibaba-vs-amazon-who-will-win-the-global-e-commerce-war/.

Company Case 15

7-Eleven: Adapting to the World's Many Cultures

Americans love convenience stores. There's one on every corner, or so it seems. They open early and stay open late. And while you can't get everything at a convenience store, you can get what matters most—gas, beer, cigarettes … and lots of snack foods! Snickers, Twinkies, Mountain Dew, Funyuns, Slim Jim, or Good Humor—the list goes on. Although new convenience store designs are serving up made-to-order hot meals for breakfast, lunch, and dinner, the presentation of America's favorite snack foods has risen to shrine-like status.

In an age of national brands, convenience store chains remain somewhat regional in the United States. At the same time, the top chains represent some of the country's biggest retailers—Circle K, Speedway, Casey's, QuikTrip, and Sheetz. Or maybe you prefer the small chains like Nebraska-based Bucky's, Moto-Mart in Illinois, or Minnesota's own Pump 'N Munch. While there is still no U.S. convenience store chain that comes close to covering all 50 states, there are hundreds of chains and more than 150,000 convenience store locations. Given the regional nature of domestic convenience store chains, it's hard to imagine any of them as global brands akin to Nike, McDonald's, or Coca-Cola. And because nearly all U.S.-based convenience stores adhere so closely to a prescribed formula, it's hard to imagine a convenience store being anything else.

But one convenience store chain is sweeping the planet. 7-Eleven, America's largest convenience store chain with more than 10,000 U.S. stores in 34 states, is also the world's biggest, with more than 55,000 stores in 16 countries, including North America, Asia, and Europe. That number grows every year. And as 7-Eleven expands, it provides a great example of how to adapt a successful business model to differences across global markets.

It All Started with Ice

In 1927, "Uncle Johnny" Jefferson Green started selling milk, bread, and eggs from the dock of the Southland Ice Company where he worked, often on Sundays and evenings when regular grocery stores were closed. Trying to make a little extra money, Uncle Johnny had no idea that he was inventing what would become one of the biggest and longest-standing retail concepts. His boss, Joe C. Thompson Jr., took notice. Within 10 years, Thompson's Southland Ice Company had 60 such retail outlets that sold the basic staples—everything from canned goods to cold watermelon. As the chain slowly grew, the convenience store concept took root—a small store (2,000 to 3,000 square feet) carrying 2,500 high-demand products, convenient locations, fair prices, speedy transactions, and friendly service.

Thompson's chain continued to grow and innovate. In 1946, the chain boldly established longer business hours than any other store had yet dared. Open from 7 a.m. to 11 p.m., the company changed its name to cement the convenience of its long hours into its brand image. In 1963, the first 7-Eleven open 24/7 emerged, and another revolution began. When the chain reached 1,500 locations in the mid-1960s, it unleashed a brain-freeze plague on the nation with the introduction of the Slurpee. Coffee-to-go, the 32-ounce Big Gulp, and the larger-than-normal Big Bite hot dog are among other innovations that would quickly become convenience store staples. But in 1969, 7-Eleven would launch another first that would become the template for its future. It was the first convenience store chain to begin opening outlets in other countries—first Canada, then Mexico, and soon Japan and other Asian markets.

Keeping up with such rapid expansion is challenging for any company. Shortly before it opened its first international store, 7-Eleven adopted a franchise model that would allow it to grow at a breakneck pace by requiring franchisees to shoulder some of the financial and operational burdens. The company also gave franchisees flexibility, within certain parameters, to customize product offerings in any given store in order to cater to local tastes, what 7-Eleven today refers to as "retailer initiative." The chain considers local initiative to be an important competitive advantage.

That idea of catering to local tastes would become the cornerstone of 7-Eleven's international expansion. Certain aspects of the corporate marketing mix would remain standard—such as the small-store format and the concept of selling products and services that local customers want most and most often. But as the company opened more international stores, it became obvious that each market possessed differences that changed the meaning of convenience.

The Japanese Invasion

Consider Japan, one of 7-Eleven's first international markets. U.S. tourists visiting Japan today notice a stark contrast between 7-Eleven stores in the Land of the Rising Sun and those they are familiar with at home. For starters, the stores are everywhere. There are more than 17,000 7-Eleven stores in Japan, 2,300 in Tokyo alone. That makes Japan by far the company's largest market.

But the large number of stores is only the beginning. The reason there are so many 7-Elevens in Japan is that the chain has become the country's most popular eatery. Around mealtime, the aisles at every 7-Eleven are packed and the lines are long. But the Japanese aren't lining up for potato chips and Slurpees. Instead, in Japan, 7-Eleven patrons are treated to some of the finest prepared foods in the world. Typical offerings include salmon on rice with butter and soy sauce, hashed beef doria in a red wine demi-glace, and ground chicken with ginger and a side of spinach coleslaw. Fresh sushi abounds, the ongiri (rice balls with seaweed) is wrapped in a way that keeps the seaweed crispy and the rice moist, and a perfectly cooked unshelled boiled egg somehow has an already salted yoke. 7-Eleven also offers a wide selection of beverages, including soft drinks, beer, sake, champagne, single-malt scotch, wine, and more than 20 varieties of iced coffee. This is not your typical U.S. 7-Eleven.

But it isn't just the selection of food that sets Japan's 7-Elevens apart. Stores receive two to five deliveries of food goods per day, keeping shelves stocked, making the food fresh, and ensuring that everything is made locally. Open display cases—both cold and hot—serve food in a manner that is more Trader Joe's than convenience store. And if all those stores aren't convenient enough, Japanese customers can order food and groceries online and have them delivered by a single-seat electric car.

If all this sounds too good to be true, there's more. Japan's number-one convenience store chain is also designed to meet the service needs of locals. At 7-Eleven, customers can pay their phone or utility bills, pick up their mail and parcel deliveries, and even buy baseball tickets from the copy machine.

For 7-Eleven, Japan represents far more than just a booming international market. Since the early 1990s, Japan has become 7-Eleven's domestic market. That's right. When Dallas-based 7-Eleven, Inc. went bankrupt in 1991, its own Japanese subsidiary bailed it out, buying a majority stake, debt and all. In 2005, Seven & I Holdings was created and the remaining shares of 7-Eleven, Inc. were acquired. Then, in a case of the student becoming the master, the directives were reversed as the new parent corporation increased investment in merchandising, store renovation,

distribution and logistics systems, and information systems. What 7-Eleven Japan had mastered over the previous 40 years was used to strengthen "retailer initiative" in the U.S. division.

The Third Place of Convenience Stores

While it wouldn't be the first time that a Japanese company took a U.S. business concept, perfected it, then brought it back to the United States (think Honda automobiles, Sony televisions, or Toshiba computers), the core strategy remained the same—give the people what they want in every market. Many features established in 7-Eleven Japan worked well in other rapidly expanding Asian markets, including Taiwan, Singapore, China, and the Philippines. But the new parent company continues to adapt the model masterfully.

Nowhere is that more apparent than in one of 7-Eleven's newest markets, Indonesia. Picture this—on a Saturday night, thousands of young Indonesians gather at one of 200 7-Eleven stores to sip coffee or beer at sidewalk tables, listen to live music, and engage in their newest passion—the Internet. If that sounds more like Starbucks, it's no accident. As Seven & I Holdings analyzed the Indonesian market, certain insights became apparent.

For starters, Indonesia has a growing economy and a population of 240 million people. Until a few years ago, however, the country had largely been overlooked by global corporations. This meant that as consumer buying power began to increase, there were few options to satisfy local needs. That made Indonesia one of the world's most attractive international growth opportunities.

Although certain things in the Indonesian culture were common to other countries, the market also exhibited unique traits. For starters, hanging out and doing nothing—something the locals refer to as "nongkrong"—is a favorite pastime. People gather at street markets, roadside food stalls, and Western fast-food outlets simply to pass the time and share stories. But the demand for hangouts exceeded the supply, and few options provided wireless connectivity, an ever-increasing need.

In response, the concept for 7-Eleven stores in Indonesia focused more on the "third place" concept pioneered by Starbucks than on the convenience store concept found elsewhere. The chain still offers basic convenience store products, such as inexpensive ready-made food, snacks, and a variety of popular beverages. And 24-hour operations are perfect for a culture not bound by time. But to drive traffic into stores, 7-Eleven Indonesia also provides hassle-free parking (a premium feature in the traffic-choked island nation), a venue for local bands (the bands sometimes pay a fee for the privilege of playing), air-conditioning, free wireless connectivity, and lots of space to hang out. The target customer is between 18 and 35. And rather than putting stores on every corner, the target for locations is on big hubs in the country that consists of 17,000 islands.

The 7-Eleven local initiative formula is working once again. Even as the company strategically applies the 7-Eleven concept to each global market, franchisees and managers customize the offerings in each store to get even closer to fulfilling local consumer needs. As the company Website points out, "At 7-Eleven, our purpose and mission is to make life a little easier for our guests by being where they need us, whenever they need us." While it still has a way to go before conquering the world, 7-Eleven is accomplishing its mission well in markets where it does business.

Questions for Discussion

1. Of the five global product and communications strategies, which best describes 7-Eleven's approach?

2. On a scale of one to five, to what degree does 7-Eleven adapt its offering in each global market? Support your answer.

3. Which strategy does 7-Eleven employ for entering a new market? How does the company benefit from this approach?

4. Will 7-Eleven continue to succeed in Indonesia? How about the rest of the markets where it does business? Why or why not?

Sources: Taryn Stenvei, "What 7-Elevens in Tokyo Taught Me about Japan," *AWOL*, September 11, 2014, http://awol.com.au/what-7-elevens-in-tokyo-taught-me-about-japan/98; Justin Moyer, "In Honor of 7/11: How Japan Slurped Up 7-Eleven," *Washington Post*, July 11, 2014, www.washingtonpost.com/news/morning-mix/wp/2014/07/11/in-honor-of-711-how-japan-slurped-up-7-eleven/; Margot Huber, "Hang-out Haven," *Business Today*, May 26, 2013, http://businesstoday.intoday.in/story/london-business-school-case-study-on-7-eleven/1/194769.html; and information from http://corp.7-eleven.com/corp/7-eleven-profile, accessed September 2015.

Company Case 16

Adidas: Athletic Apparel with Purpose

As CEO of the adidas Group for the past 14 years, Herbert Hainer has made quite a mark. Although the global athletic footwear and apparel giant has established itself as a leader in just about every sport, Hainer's legacy might stand in an area that has little to do with basketball, baseball, or even soccer. Under Hainer's influence, adidas has emerged as one of the global leaders in sustainable practices. Last year, the Germany-based sports giant ranked third among the Global 100 Most Sustainable Corporations.

A Marathon, Not a Sprint

Some companies have sustainability built in to their DNA. Companies such as Patagonia, Ben & Jerry's, and Method were founded by folks who were more driven to created socially responsible products, companies, and business practices than to make money. But companies such as Unilever, BMW, and adidas—all current sustainability leaders—discovered over time that they could succeed financially in their respective industries while at the same time being kind to the environment and providing better working conditions. In fact, these companies contend that a sound strategic plan built on sustainable practices makes them better financial performers than they might be otherwise.

Adidas came to that realization nearly 20 years ago. In 1998, the company issued its first official environmental statement. In the years that followed, it tracked its performance against social and environmental goals and made its progress transparent in an annual report. But in 2008, the company revised its sustainability strategy, making it more comprehensive and ambitious than ever before.

These days, just about every company makes claims about reducing its carbon footprint. But adidas's sustainability path stands as a model to any company that truly wants to make a difference. In short, making a difference when it comes to the health and well-being of the planet and its inhabitants takes more than just lip service. For a company to make an impact, sustainability must be ingrained in its organizational culture.

At adidas, such a cultural commitment is apparent in the degree to which the company has woven sustainability into its core business. Using a sports analogy, adidas's sustainability statement describes its efforts to become more sustainable and socially responsible as a marathon, not a sprint. "It's about preparedness and setting the right pace, having both the drive and the stamina to make it the distance. And most of all, it is about endurance: overcoming setbacks and difficulties, keeping the finishing line always in the forefront of our minds."

Some time ago, adidas established a set of core values that have shaped its corporate culture: performance, passion, integrity, and diversity. If these were just words on the wall at corporate headquarters, they wouldn't amount to much. But at adidas, these values "commit us to playing by the rules that society expects of a responsible company." Such values create the cultural infrastructure that drives "designing products that are environmentally sound … reducing the environmental impacts of our day-to-day operations and in our supply chain … setting workplace standards for our suppliers to meet … looking after the well-being and careers of our employees … and making a positive contribution to the communities where we operate."

The Four *P*s of Sustainability

To translate this culture into action, adidas sticks to the four *P*s—but not the same four *P*s that make up the marketing mix. Rather, adidas frames and reviews its sustainability goals and performance within the context of four pillars—people, product, planet, and partnership. It's what adidas calls its "Fair Play Framework."

People. "We positively influence the lives of our employees, factory workers, and people living in the communities where we have a business presence." To achieve a more positive impact on the lives of people, adidas involves itself in hundreds of community projects either with financial support or by providing employees as volunteers. But the "people" pillar also teaches common sense in doing the right thing.

When the owners of an apparel factory in Indonesia promptly closed and abandoned the factory just six months after being unable to resolve differences with adidas regarding its operations, hundreds of workers were left without jobs. Adidas was there to ensure the workers were taken care of. This included millions of dollars in humanitarian aid, placement services, and direct advocacy with the Indonesian government to improve workers' rights. These efforts had a direct and positive impact on the lives of people who had been working to make adidas products.

Product. "We find better ways to create our products—mainly through efficiencies, increased use of more sustainable materials, and innovation." Among the product targets are specific goals, such as reducing the number of colors used in products by 50 percent, reducing product samples to intermediaries through virtualization, and increasing the use of sustainable materials in footwear and apparel. As the company focuses on these and other initiatives, compliance can be tracked, as can the impact on such factors as water usage, carbon emissions, and volume of product being disposed of in landfills.

For example, adidas's virtualization project has reduced the demand for samples by 1.5 million items over a three-year period. Its initiative to source 100 percent of its cotton as "sustainable cotton" takes into account the use of water, health of the soil, and quality of the fiber. Adidas is 23 percent of the way to its goal and ahead of schedule. And increasing the use of innovative fabrics has saved 50 million liters of water by reducing the amount needed to launder such items.

Planet. "We reduce the environmental footprint of both our own operations and our suppliers' factories." In addition to product actions that reduce environmental impact, adidas also sets goals targeting operational facilities and human behavior. One of the main initiatives for this pillar is the ISO 14001 certification of company and supplier facilities. To move office buildings, factories, and distribution plants toward the international standards for certification, adidas sets specific goals and provides employees with specific directives.

For example, the company has a goal to reduce energy consumption by 20 percent. Some directives include turning off computers when they are not in use and turning off lights when people leave a room or their office. To achieve a goal of 50 percent reduction in paper use, employees are encouraged to "think before printing" and "reuse paper for notes."

Partnership. "We engage with critical stakeholders and collaborate with partners to improve our industry." The partnership pillar provides direction and motivation to seek out supplier, distributor, and relationships with other organizations that are trying to achieve the same sustainability goals as adidas. This includes working with partners to help them develop strategies whereby they can get on track and make progress. As one example, the Adidas Group is an active participant of the Sustainable Apparel Coalition, a trade association that has worked to develop an index for measuring and tracking the comprehensive environmental and social impact of products across the value chain.

Doing Well by Doing Good?

These are just a few examples of how adidas is putting sustainable concepts into action and achieving sustainability results. Not only is adidas achieving results, it is being recognized for them. Its recent third-place ranking is not its first time on the Global 100 Index list—it the company's 10th appearance. Adidas has also garnered Gold Class status and Sector Leader awards from RobecoSam—a well-known investment firm that focuses on sustainability investing. And adidas has been included in the Dow Jones Sustainability Indexes for each of the past 14 years.

Although adidas is clearly succeeding at implementing sustainable practices, one big question remains: Does all this do-gooding translate into sound financial performance as many companies claim? Many adidas stakeholders have asked that question. During Hainer's watch, superstar Nike has risen to such global dominance that adidas's financial performance is suffering. While Nike's revenues have shown strong gains year over year, adidas's have flattened. In fact, last year its sales dropped by 10 percent. Not only has Nike been outperforming adidas in the United States, last year Nike bested adidas in sales growth on its home turf in Europe by a factor of two. Nike is even stealing adidas's thunder in soccer, a sport where the German company has long been the leader.

But adidas continues to press forward in its efforts to make the company and the world better places. In Hainer's own words, "We are not perfect and we do not always get it right. But as we go about our work, we aim to honor the spirit of 'fair play' in everything we do. Therefore, let me assure you that we continue to take serious responsibility for our actions. And we continue to integrate sustainability into our business strategy."

Questions for Discussion

1. Give as many examples as you can for how adidas defies the common social criticisms of marketing.

2. Of the five sustainable marketing principles discussed in the text, which one best describes adidas's approach?

3. Analyze adidas's business according to the societal classification of products (Figure 16.4).

4. Would Adidas be more financially successful if it were not so focused on social responsibility? Explain.

Sources: Andrew Burger, "'Fair Play': Adidas Reports Progress across Four Pillars of Sustainability," *Triplepundit.com*, May 6, 2014, www.triplepundit.com/2014/05/fair-play-adidas-reports-progress-across-four-pillars-sustainability/; Michael Yow, "2015 Global 100 Results," *Corporate Knights*, January 21, 2015, www.corporateknights.com/reports/global-100/2015-global-100-results-14218559/; and information from www.adidas-group.com/en/sustainability/managing-sustainability/general-approach/#/our-sustainability-strategy/, accessed September 2015.

Appendix 2: Marketing Plan

The Marketing Plan: An Introduction

As a marketer, you will need a good marketing plan to provide direction and focus for your brand, product, or company. With a detailed plan, any business will be better prepared to launch a new product or build sales for existing products. Nonprofit organizations also use marketing plans to guide their fundraising and outreach efforts. Even government agencies put together marketing plans for initiatives such as building public awareness of proper nutrition and stimulating area tourism.

The Purpose and Content of a Marketing Plan

Unlike a business plan, which offers a broad overview of the entire organization's mission, objectives, strategy, and resource allocation, a marketing plan has a more limited scope. It serves to document how the organization's strategic objectives will be achieved through specific marketing strategies and tactics, with the customer as the starting point. It is also linked to the plans of other departments within the organization. Suppose, for example, a marketing plan calls for selling 200,000 units annually. The production department must gear up to make that many units, the finance department must arrange funding to cover the expenses, the human resources department must be ready to hire and train staff, and so on. Without the appropriate level of organizational support and resources, no marketing plan can succeed.

Although the exact length and layout will vary from company to company, a marketing plan usually contains the sections described in Chapter 2. Smaller businesses may create shorter or less formal marketing plans whereas corporations frequently require highly structured marketing plans. To guide implementation effectively, every part of the plan must be described in considerable detail. Sometimes a company will post its marketing plans on an intranet site, which allows managers and employees in different locations to consult specific sections and collaborate on additions or changes.

The Role of Research

Marketing plans are not created in a vacuum. To develop successful strategies and action programs, marketers need up-to-date information about the environment, the competition, and the market segments to be served. Often, analysis of internal data is the starting point for assessing the current marketing situation, supplemented by marketing intelligence and research investigating the overall market, the competition, key issues, and threats and opportunities. As the plan is put into effect, marketers use a variety of research techniques to measure progress toward objectives and identify areas for improvement if results fall short of projections.

Finally, marketing research helps marketers learn more about their customers' requirements, expectations, perceptions, and satisfaction levels. This deeper understanding provides a foundation for building competitive advantage through well-informed segmenting, targeting, differentiating, and positioning decisions. Thus, the marketing plan should outline what marketing research will be conducted and how the findings will be applied.

The Role of Relationships

The marketing plan shows how the company will engage customers and build profitable customer relationships. In the process, however, it also shapes a number of internal and external relationships. First, it affects how marketing personnel work with each other and with other departments to deliver value and satisfy customers. Second, it affects how the company works with suppliers, distributors, and strategic alliance partners to achieve the objectives listed in the plan. Third, it influences the company's dealings with other stakeholders, including government regulators, the media, and the community at large. All of these relationships are important to the organization's success, so they should be considered when a marketing plan is being developed.

From Marketing Plan to Marketing Action

Companies generally create yearly marketing plans, although some plans cover a longer period. Marketers start planning well in advance of the implementation date to allow time for marketing research, thorough analysis, management review, and coordination between departments. Then, after each action program begins, marketers monitor ongoing results, compare them with projections, analyze any differences, and take corrective steps as needed. Some marketers also prepare contingency plans for implementation if certain conditions emerge. Because of inevitable and sometimes unpredictable environmental changes, marketers must be ready to update and adapt marketing plans at any time.

For effective implementation and control, the marketing plan should define how progress toward objectives will be measured. Managers typically use budgets, schedules, and performance standards for monitoring and evaluating results. With budgets, they can compare planned expenditures with actual expenditures for a given week, month, or other period. Schedules allow management to see when tasks were supposed to be completed—and when they were actually completed. Performance standards track the outcomes of marketing programs to see whether the company is moving toward its objectives. Some examples of performance standards are market share, sales volume, product profitability, and customer satisfaction.

Sample Marketing Plan: Chill Beverage Company

Executive Summary

The Chill Beverage Company is preparing to launch a new line of vitamin-enhanced water called NutriWater. Although the bottled water market is maturing, the vitamin-enhanced water category is still growing. NutriWater will be positioned by the slogan "Expect more"—indicating that the brand offers more in the way of desirable product features and benefits at a competitive price. Chill Beverage is taking advantage of its existing experience and brand equity among its loyal current customer base of Millennials who consume its Chill Soda soft drink. NutriWater will target similar Millennials who are maturing and looking for an alternative to soft drinks and high-calorie sugared beverages.

The primary marketing objective is to achieve first-year U.S. sales of $35 million, roughly 2 percent of the enhanced water market. Based on this market share goal, the company expects to sell more than 20 million units the first year and break even in the final period of the year.

Current Marketing Situation

The Chill Beverage Company was founded in 2007 by an entrepreneur who had successfully built a company that primarily distributed niche and emerging products in the beverage industry. Its Chill Soda soft drink brand hit the market with six unique flavors in glass bottles. A few years later, the Chill Soda brand introduced an energy drink as well as a line of natural juice drinks. The company now markets dozens of Chill Soda flavors, many unique to the brand. Chill Beverage has grown its business every year since it was founded. In the most recent year, it achieved $185 million in revenue and net profits of $14.5 million. As part of its future growth strategy, Chill Beverage is currently preparing to enter a new beverage category with a line of vitamin-enhanced waters.

For years, U.S. consumers drank more carbonated soft drinks than any other beverage. But recently, water once again became the number-one beverage of choice as concerns over health and obesity caused the soda market to go flat. On average, people in the U.S. drink 58 gallons of water each year compared with 44 gallons of soda. While those water numbers include tap water, bottled water consumption has grown tremendously since the 1990s. Currently, the average person in the United States consumes more than 34 gallons of bottled water every year, more than double the figure just 15 years prior. Bottled water consumption is second only to soft drink consumption, ahead of milk, beer, and coffee. As a beverage category, bottled water is growing at a robust rate of 5 to 7 percent annually, a figure that is expected to increase in years to come. Most other beverage categories have experienced declines. In the most recent year, 10.8 billion gallons of bottled water were sold in the United States with a value of approximately $13 billion.

Competition is more intense now than ever as demand slows, industry consolidation continues, and new types of bottled water emerge. The U.S. market is dominated by three global corporations. With a portfolio of 12 brands (including Poland Spring, Nestlé Pure Life, Arrowhead, Deer Park, and Ice Mountain), Nestlé leads the market for "plain" bottled water. However, when all subcategories of bottled water are included (enhanced water, flavored water, and so on), Coca-Cola leads the U.S. market with a 22.9 percent share. Nestlé markets only plain waters but is number two at 21.5 percent of the total bottled water market. PepsiCo is third with 16.2 percent of the market.

To break into this market, dominated by huge global corporations and littered with dozens of other small players, Chill Beverage must carefully target specific segments with features and benefits valued by those segments.

Market Description

The bottled water market consists of many different types of water. Varieties of plain water include spring, purified, mineral, and distilled. Although these different types of water are sold as consumer products, they also serve as the core ingredient for other types of bottled waters including enhanced water, flavored water, sparkling water, or any combination of those categories.

Although some consumers may not perceive much of a difference between brands, others are drawn to specific product features and benefits provided by different brands. For example, some consumers may perceive spring water as healthier than other types of water. Some may look for water that is optimized for hydration. Others seek additional nutritional benefits claimed by bottlers that enhance their brands with vitamins, minerals, herbs, and other additives. Still other consumers make selections based on flavor. The industry as a whole has positioned bottled water of all kinds as a low-calorie, healthy alternative to soft drinks, sports drinks, energy drinks, and other types of beverages.

Bottled water brands also distinguish themselves by size and type of container, multipacks, and refrigeration at point-of-sale. Chill Beverage's market for NutriWater consists of consumers of single-serving-sized bottled beverages who are looking for a healthy yet flavorful alternative. "Healthy" in this context means both low-calorie and enhanced nutritional content. This market includes traditional soft drink consumers who want to improve their health as well as non-soft-drink consumers who want an option other than plain bottled water. Specific segments that Chill Beverage will target during the first year include athletes, the health conscious, the socially responsible, and Millennials who favor independent corporations. The Chill Soda brand has established a strong base of loyal customers, primarily among Millennials. This generational segment is becoming a prime target as it matures and seeks alternatives to full-calorie soft drinks. **>> Table A2.1** shows how NutriWater addresses the needs of targeted consumer segments.

Product Review

Chill Beverage's new line of vitamin-enhanced water—called NutriWater—offers the following features:

- Six new-age flavors including Peach Mango, Berry Pomegranate, Kiwi Dragonfruit, Mandarin Orange, Blueberry Grape, and Key Lime.
- Single-serving size, 20-ounce, PET recyclable bottles.
- Formulated for wellness, replenishment, and optimum energy.
- Full Recommended Daily Allowance (RDA) of essential vitamins and minerals (including electrolytes).

>> Table A2.1   Segment Needs and Corresponding Features/Benefits of NutriWater

Targeted Segment	Customer Need	Corresponding Features/Benefits
Athletes	• Hydration and replenishment of essential minerals • Energy to maximize performance	• Electrolytes and carbohydrates • B vitamins, carbohydrates
Health conscious	• Maintain optimum weight • Optimize nutrition levels • Avoid harmful chemicals and additives • Desire to consume a tastier beverage than water	• Half the calories of fully sugared beverages • Higher levels of vitamins A, B, C, E, Zinc, Chromium, and Folic Acid than other products; vitamins unavailable in other products • All natural ingredients • Six new-age flavors
Socially conscious	• Support causes that help solve world's social problems	• 25-cent donation from each purchase to Vitamin Angels
Millennials	• Aversion to mass-media advertising/technologically savvy • Counter-culture attitude • Diet enhancement due to fast-paced lifestyle	• Less-invasive online and social networking promotional tactics • Small, privately held company • Full RDA levels of essential vitamins and minerals

- Higher vitamin concentration—vitamin levels are two to ten times higher than market-leading products, with more vitamins and minerals than any other brand.
- Additional vitamins—vitamins include A, E, and B2 as well as folic acid—none of which are contained in the market-leading products.
- All natural—no artificial flavors, colors, or preservatives.
- Sweetened with pure cane sugar and Stevia, a natural zero-calorie sweetener.
- Twenty-five cents from each purchase will be donated to Vitamin Angels, a nonprofit organization with a mission to prevent vitamin deficiency in at-risk children.

Competitive Review

As sales of bottled waters entered a strong growth phase in the 1990s, the category began to expand. In addition to the various types of plain water, new categories emerged. These included flavored waters—such as Aquafina's Flavorsplash—as well as enhanced waters. Enhanced waters emerged to bridge the gap between soft drinks and waters, appealing to people who knew they should drink more water and fewer soft drinks but still wanted flavor. Initially, development of brands for this product variation occurred primarily in start-up and boutique beverage companies like Sobe and Glacéau, creator of Vitaminwater. In the 2000s, major beverage corporations acquired the most successful smaller brands, providing the bigger firms with a solid market position in this category and diversification in bottled waters in general. At that point, enhanced waters grew at a rate that exceeded that of plain water.

To demonstrate the strength of the enhanced water segment, Coca-Cola's Vitaminwater became the fourth-largest bottled water brand, behind plain water brands Nestlé Pure Life, Coca-Cola's Dasani, and Pepsi's Aquafina. In recent years, vitamin-enhanced waters have taken a hit in the wake of some bad press focusing on the low amount of vitamins and high amount of sugar contained in most brands. Nonetheless, enhanced water sales account for approximately 13 percent of the total bottled water market, and industry insiders expect sales to return to a growth trajectory in coming years.

The fragmentation of this category, combined with domination by the market leaders, has created a severely competitive environment. Although there is indirect competition posed by all types of bottled waters and even other types of beverages (soft drinks, energy drinks, juices, teas, and flavor drops), this competitive analysis focuses on direct competition from enhanced water brands. For the purposes of this analysis, enhanced water is bottled water with additives that are intended to provide health and wellness benefits. The most common additives include vitamins, minerals (including electrolytes), and herbs. Most commonly, enhanced waters are sweetened, flavored, and colored. This definition distinguishes enhanced water from sports drinks that have the primary purpose of maximizing hydration by replenishing electrolytes.

Enhanced water brands are typically sweetened with a combination of some kind of sugar and a zero-calorie sweetener, resulting in about half the sugar content, carbohydrates, and calories of regular soft drinks and other sweetened beverages. The types of sweeteners used create a point of differentiation. Many brands, including the market leaders, sell both regular and zero-calorie varieties.

Pricing for this product is consistent across brands and varies by type of retail outlet, with convenience stores typically charging more than grocery stores. The price for a 20-ounce bottle ranges from $1.00 to $1.89, with some niche brands costing slightly more. Key competitors to Chill Beverage's NutriWater line include the following:

- *Vitaminwater:* Created in 2000 as a new product for Energy Brands' Glacéau, which was also the developer of Smartwater (distilled water with electrolytes). Coca-Cola purchased Energy Brands for $4.1 billion in 2007. Vitaminwater is sold in regular and zero-calorie versions. With 19 bottled varieties—11 regular and 8 zero-calorie—as well as availability in fountain form and drops, Vitaminwater offers more options than any brand on the market. Whereas Vitaminwater varieties are distinguished by flavor, they are named to evoke perceptions of benefits such as Essential, Defense, Focus, and Revive. The brand's current slogan is "Hydrate the Hustle." Vitaminwater is vapor distilled, deionized, and/or filtered and is sweetened with crystalline fructose (corn syrup) and erythritol all-natural sweetener. Vitaminwater exceeds $700 million in annual sales and commands 63 percent of the enhanced water market.
- *Propel:* Gatorade created Propel in 2000, just one year prior to PepsiCo's purchase of this leading sports drink marketer. Marketed as "The Workout Water," Propel was originally available in regular and zero-calorie varieties. However, it is now available only as a zero-calorie beverage. Propel comes in nine flavors, each containing the same blend of B vitamins, vitamin C, vitamin E, antioxidants, and electrolytes. It is sweetened with sucralose. Propel is available in a wide variety of sizes, with 16.9-, 20-, and 24-ounce PET bottles and multipacks. Propel is also marketed in powder form and as a liquid enhancer to be added to bottled water. With $171 million in revenues, Propel is the number-two enhanced water brand with a 15 percent share of the enhanced water market.
- *SoBe Lifewater:* PepsiCo bought SoBe in 2000. SoBe introduced Lifewater in 2008 with a hit Super Bowl ad as an answer to Coca-Cola's Vitaminwater. The Lifewater line includes 13 regular and zero-calorie varieties. Each variety is infused with a formulation of vitamins, minerals, and herbs designed to provide a claimed benefit. Sweetened with a combination of sugar and erythritol, Lifewater makes the claim to be "all natural." It contains no artificial flavors or colors. However, some analysts debate the "natural" designation for erythritol. Lifewater is sold in 20-ounce PET bottles and multipacks as well as one-liter PET bottles. With more than $200 million in annual revenues, Lifewater is the number-three enhanced water brand with a 12 percent share.
- *Niche brands:* The market for enhanced waters includes at least four companies that market their wares on a small scale through independent retailers: Assure, Ex Aqua Vitamins, Ayala Herbal Water, and Skinny Water. Some brands feature exotic additives and/or artistic glass bottles.

Despite the strong competition, NutriWater believes it can create a relevant brand image and gain recognition among the targeted segments. The brand offers strong points of differentiation with higher and unique vitamin content, all-natural ingredients, and support for a relevant social cause. With other strategic assets, Chill Beverage is confident that it can establish a competitive advantage that will allow NutriWater to grow in the market. ≫ **Table A2.2** shows a sample of competing products.

Channels and Logistics Review

With the three main brands now owned by Coca-Cola and PepsiCo, there is a huge hole in the independent distributor system. NutriWater will be distributed through an independent distributor to a network of retailers in the United States. This strategy will avoid some of the head-on competition for shelf space with the Coca-Cola and PepsiCo brands and will

>> Table A2.2 — Sample of Competitive Products

Competitor	Brand	Features
Coca-Cola	Vitaminwater	Regular and zero-calorie versions; 15 varieties; each flavor provides a different function based on blend of vitamins and minerals; vapor distilled, deionized, and/or filtered; sweetened with crystalline fructose and erythritol; 20-ounce single-serve or multipack, fountain, and drops.
PepsiCo	Propel	Zero-calorie only; seven flavors; fitness positioning based on "Replenish + Energize + Protect"; B vitamins, vitamin C, vitamin E, antioxidants, and electrolytes; sweetened with sucralose; 16.9-ounce, 20-ounce, and 24-ounce PET bottles and multipacks; powdered packets; liquid enhancer.
PepsiCo	SoBe Lifewater	Regular and zero-calorie versions; 15 varieties; six different functional categories; vitamins, minerals, and herbs; Pure—mildly flavored, unsweetened water; sweetened with sugar and erythritol; "all natural"; 20-ounce single-serve and multipacks as well as one-liter bottles.

also directly target likely NutriWater customers. As with the rollout of the core Chill Soda brand, this strategy will focus on placing coolers in retail locations that will exclusively hold NutriWater. These retailers include:

- *Grocery chains:* Regional grocery chains such as HyVee in the Midwest, Wegman's in the East, and WinCo in the West.
- *Health and natural food stores:* Chains such as Whole Foods Market as well as local health food co-ops.
- *Fitness centers:* National fitness center chains such as 24 Hour Fitness, Gold's Gym, and other regional chains.

As the brand gains acceptance, channels will expand into larger grocery chains, convenience stores, and unique locations relevant to the target customer segment.

Strengths, Weaknesses, Opportunities, and Threats Analysis

NutriWater has several powerful strengths on which to build, but its major weakness is lack of brand awareness and image. Major opportunities include a growing market and consumer trends targeted by NutriWater's product traits. Threats include barriers to entry posed by limited retail space as well as image issues for the bottled water industry. >> **Table A2.3** summarizes NutriWater's main strengths, weaknesses, opportunities, and threats.

Strengths

NutriWater can rely on the following important strengths:

1. *Superior quality:* NutriWater boasts the highest levels of added vitamins of any enhanced water, including full RDA levels of many vitamins. It is all natural with no artificial flavors, colors, or preservatives. It is sweetened with both pure cane sugar and the natural zero-calorie sweetener Stevia.
2. *Expertise in alternative beverage marketing:* The Chill Soda brand went from nothing to a successful and rapidly growing soft drink brand with fiercely loyal customers in a matter of only one decade. This success was achieved by starting small and focusing on gaps in the marketplace.
3. *Social responsibility:* Every customer will have the added benefit of helping malnourished children throughout the world. Although the price of NutriWater is in line with other competitors, low promotional costs allow for the substantial charitable donation of 25 cents per bottle while maintaining profitability.
4. *Antiestablishment image:* The big brands have decent products and strong distribution relationships. But they also carry the image of the large, corporate establishments. Chill Beverage has achieved success with an underdog image while remaining privately held. Vitaminwater and SoBe were built on this same image, but both are now owned by major multinational corporations.

» Table A2.3 | **NutriWater's Strengths, Weaknesses, Opportunities, and Threats**

Strengths	Weaknesses
• Superior quality	• Lack of brand awareness
• Expertise in alternative beverage marketing	• Limited budget
• Social responsibility	
• Antiestablishment image	

Opportunities	Threats
• Market growth	• Limited shelf space
• Gap in the distribution network	• Image of enhanced waters
• Health trends	• Environmental issues
• Antiestablishment image	

Weaknesses

1. *Lack of brand awareness:* As an entirely new brand, NutriWater will enter the market with limited or no brand awareness. The affiliation with Chill Soda will be kept at a minimum in order to prevent associations between NutriWater·and soft drinks. This issue will be addressed through promotion and distribution strategies.
2. *Limited budget:* As a smaller company, Chill Beverage has much smaller funds available for promotional and research activities.

Opportunities

1. *Market growth:* Bottled water as a category is growing at a rate of about 7 percent annually. While the enhanced water subcategory has decreased in overall sales, that is expected to reverse as the enhanced water brands move past the negative associations of the past. Of the top six beverage categories, soft drinks, beer, milk, and fruit drinks experienced declines. The growth for coffee was less than 1 percent.
2. *Gap in the distribution network:* The market leaders distribute directly to retailers. This gives them an advantage in large national chains. However, no major enhanced water brands are currently being sold through independent distributors.
3. *Health trends:* Weight and nutrition continue to be issues for consumers in the United States. The country has the highest obesity rate for developed countries at 34 percent, with well over 60 percent of the population officially "overweight." Those numbers continue to rise. Additionally, Americans get 21 percent of their daily calories from beverages, a number that has tripled in the last three decades. Consumers still desire flavored beverages but look for lower-calorie alternatives.
4. *Antiestablishment image:* Millennials (born between 1977 and 2000) maintain a higher aversion to mass marketing messages and global corporations than do Gen Xers and baby boomers.

Threats

1. *Limited shelf space:* Whereas competition is generally a threat for any type of product, competition in retail beverages is particularly high because of limited retail space. Carrying a new beverage product requires retailers to reduce shelf or cooler space already occupied by other brands.
2. *Image of enhanced waters:* The image of enhanced waters took a hit as Coca-Cola recently fought a class-action lawsuit accusing it of violating FDA regulations by promoting the health benefits of Vitaminwater. The lawsuit exposed the number-one bottled water brand as basically sugar water with minimal nutritional value. Each of the major brands is strengthening its zero-calorie lines. They no longer promote health benefits on the labels. While this is potentially a threat, it is also an opportunity for Chill to exploit.

3. *Environmental issues:* Environmental groups continue to educate the public on the environmental costs of bottled water, including landfill waste, carbon emissions from production and transportation, and harmful effects of chemicals in plastics.

Objectives and Issues

Chill Beverage has set aggressive but achievable objectives for NutriWater for the first and second years of market entry.

First-Year Objectives

During the initial year on the market, Chill Beverage aims for NutriWater to achieve a 2 percent share of the enhanced water market, or approximately $35 million in sales, with break-even achieved in the final period of the year. With an average retail price of $1.69, that equates with a sales goal of 20,710,059 bottles.

Second-Year Objectives

During the second year, Chill Beverage will unveil additional NutriWater flavors, including zero-calorie varieties. The second-year objective is to double sales from the first year, to $70 million.

Issues

In launching this new brand, the main issue is the ability to establish brand awareness and a meaningful brand image based on positioning that is relevant to target customer segments. Chill Beverage will invest in nontraditional means of promotion to accomplish these goals and to spark word of mouth. Establishing distributor and retailer relationships will also be critical in order to make the product available and provide point-of-purchase communications. Brand awareness and knowledge will be measured in order to adjust marketing efforts as necessary.

Marketing Strategy

NutriWater's marketing strategy will involve developing a "more for the same" positioning based on extra benefits for the price. The brand will also establish channel differentiation, as it will be available in locations where major competing brands are not. The primary target segment is Millennials. This segment is composed of late teens (15 to 18) and young adults (19 to 38). NutriWater will focus specifically on the young adult market. Subsets of this generational segment include athletes, the health conscious, and the socially responsible.

Positioning

NutriWater will be positioned on an "Expect more" value proposition. This will allow for differentiating the brand based on product features (expect more vitamin content and all-natural ingredients), desirable benefits (expect greater nutritional benefits), and values (do more for a social cause). Marketing will focus on conveying that NutriWater is more than just a beverage: It gives customers much more for their money in a variety of ways.

Product Strategy

NutriWater will be sold with all the features described in the Product Review section. As awareness takes hold and retail availability increases, more varieties will be made available. A zero-calorie version will be added to the product line, providing a solid fit with the health benefits sought by consumers. Chill Beverage's considerable experience in brand building will be applied as an integral part of the product strategy for NutriWater. All aspects of the marketing mix will be consistent with the brand.

Pricing

There is little price variation in the enhanced waters category, particularly among leading brands. For this reason, NutriWater will follow a competition-based pricing strategy. Given that NutriWater claims superior quality, it must be careful not to position itself as a lower-cost alternative. Manufacturers do not quote list prices on this type of beverage, and prices vary considerably based on type of retail outlet and whether the product is refrigerated. Regular prices for single 20-ounce bottles of competing products are as low as $1.00 in discount-retailer stores and as high as $1.89 in convenience stores. Because NutriWater will not be targeting discount retailers and convenience stores initially, this will allow Chill Beverage to set prices at the average to higher end of the range for similar products in the same outlets. For grocery chains, this should be approximately $1.49 per bottle, with that price rising to $1.89 at health food stores and fitness centers, where prices tend to be higher.

Distribution Strategy

NutriWater will employ a selective distribution strategy with well-known regional grocers, health and natural food stores, and fitness centers. This distribution strategy will be executed through a network of independent beverage distributors, as there are no other major brands of enhanced water following this strategy. Chill Beverage gained success for its core Chill Soda soft drink line using this method. It also placed coolers with the brand logo in truly unique venues such as skate, surf, and snowboarding shops; tattoo and piercing parlors; fashion stores; and music stores—places that would expose the brand to target customers. Then the soft drink brand expanded by getting contracts with retailers such as Panera, Barnes & Noble, Target, and Starbucks. This same approach will be taken with NutriWater by starting small, then expanding into larger chains. NutriWater will not target all the same stores used originally by Chill Soda, as many of those outlets were unique to the positioning and target customer for the Chill Soda soft drink brand.

Marketing Communication Strategy

As with the core Chill Soda brand, the marketing communication strategy for NutriWater will not follow a strategy based on traditional mass-communication advertising. Initially, there will be no broadcast or print advertising. Promotional resources for NutriWater will focus on three areas:

- *Online and mobile marketing:* The typical target customer for NutriWater spends more time online than with traditional media channels. A core component for this strategy will be building Web and mobile brand sites and driving traffic to those sites by creating a presence on social networks, including Facebook, Google+, and Twitter. The NutriWater brand will also incorporate location-based services by Foursquare and Facebook to help drive traffic to retail locations. A mobile phone ad campaign will provide additional support to the online efforts.
- *Trade promotions:* Like the core Chill Soda brand, NutriWater's success will rely on relationships with retailers to create product availability. Primary incentives to retailers will include point-of-purchase displays, branded coolers, and volume incentives and contests. This push marketing strategy will combine with the other pull strategies.
- *Event marketing:* NutriWater will deploy teams in brand-labeled RVs to distribute product samples at events such as skiing and snowboarding competitions, golf tournaments, and concerts.

Marketing Research

To remain consistent with the online promotional approach as well as using research methods that will effectively reach target customers, Chill Beverage will monitor online discussions via services such as Radian6. In this manner, the company will gauge customer perceptions of the brand, the products, and general satisfaction. For future development of the product and new distribution outlets, crowdsourcing methods will be utilized.

Action Programs

NutriWater will be introduced in February. The following are summaries of action programs that will be used during the first six months of the year to achieve the stated objectives.

January: Chill Beverage representatives will work with both independent distributors and retailers to educate them on the trade promotional campaign, incentives, and advantages for selling NutriWater. Representatives will also ensure that distributors and retailers are educated on product features and benefits as well as instructions for displaying point-of-purchase materials and coolers. The brand Web site and other sites such as Facebook will present teaser information about the product as well as availability dates and locations. Buzz will be enhanced by providing product samples to selected product reviewers, opinion leaders, influential bloggers, and celebrities.

February: On the date of availability, product coolers and point-of-purchase displays will be placed in retail locations. The full brand Web site and social network campaign will launch with full efforts on Facebook, Google+, and Twitter. This campaign will drive the "Expect more" slogan as well as illustrate the ways that NutriWater delivers more than expected on product features, desirable benefits, and values by donating to Vitamin Angels and the social cause of battling vitamin deficiency in children.

March: To enhance the online and social marketing campaign, location-based services Foursquare and Facebook Places will be employed to drive traffic to retailers. Point-of-purchase displays and signage will be updated to support these efforts and to continue supporting retailers. The message of this campaign will focus on all aspects of "Expect more."

April: A mobile phone ad campaign will provide additional support, driving Web traffic to the brand Web site and social network sites as well as driving traffic to retailers.

May: A trade sales contest will offer additional incentives and prizes to the distributors and retailers that sell the most NutriWater during a four-week period.

June: An event marketing campaign will mobilize a team of NutriWater representatives in NutriWater RVs to concerts and sports events. This will provide additional visibility for the brand as well as give customers and potential customers the opportunity to sample products.

Budgets

Chill Beverage has set a first-year retail sales goal of $35 million with a projected average retail price of $1.69 per unit for a total of 20,710,059 units sold. With an average wholesale price of 85 cents per unit, this provides revenues of $17.6 million. Chill Beverage expects to break even during the final period of the first year. A break-even analysis assumes per-unit wholesale revenue of 85 cents per unit, a variable cost per unit of 14 cents, and estimated first-year fixed costs of $12,500,000. Based on these assumptions, the break-even calculation is:

$$\frac{\$12,500,000}{\$0.85/\text{unit} - \$0.14/\text{unit}} = 17,605,634$$

Controls

Chill Beverage is planning tight control measures to closely monitor product quality, brand awareness, brand image, and customer satisfaction. This will enable the company to react quickly in correcting any problems that may occur. Other early warning signals that will be monitored for signs of deviation from the plan include monthly sales (by segment and channel) and monthly expenses. Given the market's volatility, contingency plans are also in place to address fast-moving environmental changes such as shifting consumer preferences, new products, and new competition.

Sources: "Channel Check," *Bevnet,* January/February 2015, p. 18; "Channel Check," *Bevnet,* July/August 2015, p. 26; "The Heat Is On for U.S. Bottled Water Market," *PR Newswire,* July 21, 2015, www .prnewswire.com/news-releases/report-the-heat-is-on-for-us-bottled-water-market-300115888.html; Jeffrey Klineman, "Restoring an Icon," *Beverage Spectrum Magazine,* December 2010, pp. 16–18; Matt Casey, "Enhanced Options Divide a Category," *Beverage Spectrum Magazine,* December 2008, p. 74; "Water Becomes America's Favorite Drink Again," *USA Today,* March 11, 2013, www .usatoday.com/story/news/nation/2013/03/11/water-americas-favorite-drink/1978959/; and product and market information obtained from www.sobe.com, www.vitaminwater.com, and www.nestle-waters .com, accessed September 2015.

Appendix 3 Marketing by the Numbers

Marketing managers are facing increased accountability for the financial implications of their actions. This appendix provides a basic introduction to measuring marketing financial performance. Such financial analysis guides marketers in making sound marketing decisions and in assessing the outcomes of those decisions.

The appendix is built around a hypothetical manufacturer of consumer electronics products—HD. The company is introducing a device that plays videos and television programming streamed over the Internet on multiple devices in a home, including high-definition televisions, tablets, and mobile phones. In this appendix, we will analyze the various decisions HD's marketing managers must make before and after the new product launch.

The appendix is organized into *three sections*. The *first section* introduces pricing, break-even, and margin analysis assessments that will guide the introduction of HD's new product. The *second section* discusses demand estimates, the marketing budget, and marketing performance measures. It begins with a discussion of estimating market potential and company sales. It then introduces the marketing budget, as illustrated through a *pro forma* profit-and-loss statement followed by the actual profit-and-loss statement. Next, we discuss marketing performance measures, with a focus on helping marketing managers to better defend their decisions from a financial perspective. In the *third section,* we analyze the financial implications of various marketing tactics.

Each of the three sections ends with a set of quantitative exercises that provide you with an opportunity to apply the concepts you learned to situations beyond HD.

Pricing, Break-Even, and Margin Analysis

Pricing Considerations

Determining price is one of the most important marketing mix decisions. The limiting factors are demand and costs. Demand factors, such as buyer-perceived value, set the price ceiling. The company's costs set the price floor. In between these two factors, marketers must consider competitors' prices and other factors such as reseller requirements, government regulations, and company objectives.

Most current competing Internet streaming products sell at retail prices between $100 and $500. We first consider HD's pricing decision from a cost perspective. Then we consider consumer value, the competitive environment, and reseller requirements.

Determining Costs

Fixed costs

Costs that do not vary with production or sales level.

Variable costs

Costs that vary directly with the level of production.

Total costs

The sum of the fixed and variable costs for any given level of production.

Recall from Chapter 9 that there are different types of costs. **Fixed costs** do not vary with production or sales level and include costs such as rent, interest, depreciation, and clerical and management salaries. Regardless of the level of output, the company must pay these costs. Whereas total fixed costs remain constant as output increases, the fixed cost per unit (or average fixed cost) will decrease as output increases because the total fixed costs are spread across more units of output. **Variable costs** vary directly with the level of production and include costs related to the direct production of the product (such as costs of goods sold—COGS) and many of the marketing costs associated with selling it. Although these costs tend to be uniform for each unit produced, they are called variable because their total varies with the number of units produced. **Total costs** are the sum of the fixed and variable costs for any given level of production.

HD has invested $10 million in refurbishing an existing facility to manufacture the new video streaming product. Once production begins, the company estimates that it will incur fixed costs of $20 million per year. The variable cost to produce each device is estimated to be $125 and is expected to remain at that level for the output capacity of the facility.

Setting Price Based on Costs

Cost-plus pricing (or markup pricing)
A standard markup to the cost of the product.

HD starts with the cost-based approach to pricing discussed in Chapter 9. Recall that the simplest method, **cost-plus pricing (or markup pricing)**, simply adds a standard markup to the cost of the product. To use this method, however, HD must specify expected unit sales so that total unit costs can be determined. Unit variable costs will remain constant regardless of the output, but *average unit fixed costs* will decrease as output increases.

To illustrate this method, suppose HD has fixed costs of $20 million, variable costs of $125 per unit, and expects unit sales of 1 million players. Thus, the cost per unit is given by:

$$\text{Unit cost} = \text{variable cost} + \frac{\text{fixed costs}}{\text{unit sales}} = \$125 + \frac{\$20,000,000}{1,000,000} = \$145$$

Relevant costs
Costs that will occur in the future and that will vary across the alternatives being considered.

Note that we do *not* include the initial investment of $10 million in the total fixed cost figure. It is not considered a fixed cost because it is not a *relevant* cost. **Relevant costs** are those that will occur in the future and that will vary across the alternatives being considered. HD's investment to refurbish the manufacturing facility was a one-time cost that will not reoccur in the future. Such past costs are *sunk costs* and should not be considered in future analyses.

Break-even price
The price at which total revenue equals total cost and profit is zero.

Also notice that if HD sells its product for $145, the price is equal to the total cost per unit. This is the **break-even price**—the price at which total revenue equals total cost and profit is zero.

Suppose HD does not want to merely break even but rather wants to earn a 25% markup on sales. HD's markup price is:[1]

$$\text{Markup price} = \frac{\text{unit cost}}{(1 - \text{desired return on sales})} = \frac{\$145}{1 - .25} = \$193.33$$

This is the price at which HD would sell the product to resellers such as wholesalers or retailers to earn a 25% profit on sales.

Return on investment (ROI) pricing (or target-return pricing)
A cost-based pricing method that determines price based on a specified rate of return on investment.

Another approach HD could use is called **return on investment (ROI) pricing (or target-return pricing)**. In this case, the company *would* consider the initial $10 million investment, but only to determine the dollar profit goal. Suppose the company wants a 30% return on its investment. The price necessary to satisfy this requirement can be determined by:

$$\text{ROI price} = \text{unit cost} + \frac{\text{ROI} \times \text{investment}}{\text{unit sales}} = \$145 + \frac{0.3 \times \$10,000,000}{1,000,000} = \$148$$

That is, if HD sells its product for $148, it will realize a 30% return on its initial investment of $10 million.

In these pricing calculations, unit cost is a function of the expected sales, which were estimated to be 1 million units. But what if actual sales were lower? Then the unit cost would be higher because the fixed costs would be spread over fewer units, and the realized percentage markup on sales or ROI would be lower. Alternatively, if sales are higher than the estimated 1 million units, unit cost would be lower than $145, so a lower price would produce the desired markup on sales or ROI. It's important to note that these cost-based pricing methods are *internally* focused and do not consider demand, competitors' prices, or reseller requirements. Because HD will be selling this product to consumers through wholesalers and retailers offering competing brands, the company must consider markup pricing from this perspective.

Setting Price Based on External Factors

Whereas costs determine the price floor, HD also must consider external factors when setting price. HD does not have the final say concerning the final price of its product to consumers—retailers do. So it must start with its suggested retail price and work back. In doing so, HD must consider the markups required by resellers that sell the product to consumers.

Markup

The difference between a company's selling price for a product and its cost to manufacture or purchase it.

In general, a dollar **markup** is the difference between a company's selling price for a product and its cost to manufacture or purchase it. For a retailer, then, the markup is the difference between the price it charges consumers and the cost the retailer must pay for the product. Thus, for any level of reseller:

$$\text{Dollar markup} = \text{selling price} - \text{cost}$$

Markups are usually expressed as a percentage, and there are two different ways to compute markups—on *cost* or on *selling price*:

$$\text{Markup percentage on cost} = \frac{\text{dollar markup}}{\text{cost}}$$

$$\text{Markup percentage on selling price} = \frac{\text{dollar markup}}{\text{selling price}}$$

To apply reseller margin analysis, HD must first set the suggested retail price and then work back to the price at which it must sell the product to a wholesaler. Suppose retailers expect a 30% margin and wholesalers want a 20% margin based on their respective selling prices. And suppose that HD sets a manufacturer's suggested retail price (MSRP) of $299.99 for its product.

Value-based pricing

Offering just the right combination of quality and good service at a fair price.

HD selected the $299.99 MSRP because it is lower than most competitors' prices but is not so low that consumers might perceive it to be of poor quality. And the company's research shows that it is below the threshold at which more consumers are willing to purchase the product. By using buyers' perceptions of value and not the seller's cost to determine the MSRP, HD is using **value-based pricing**. For simplicity, we will use an MSRP of $300 in further analyses.

Markup chain

The sequence of markups used by firms at each level in a channel.

To determine the price HD will charge wholesalers, we must first subtract the retailer's margin from the retail price to determine the retailer's cost ($300 − ($300 × 0.30) = $210). The retailer's cost is the wholesaler's price, so HD next subtracts the wholesaler's margin ($210 − ($210 × 0.20) = $168). Thus, the **markup chain** representing the sequence of markups used by firms at each level in a channel for HD's new product is:

Suggested retail price:	$300
minus retail margin (30%):	−$ 90
Retailer's cost/wholesaler's price:	$210
minus wholesaler's margin (20%):	−$ 42
Wholesaler's cost/HD's price:	$168

By deducting the markups for each level in the markup chain, HD arrives at a price for the product to wholesalers of $168.

Break-Even and Margin Analysis

The previous analyses derived a value-based price of $168 for HD's product. Although this price is higher than the break-even price of $145 and covers costs, that price assumed a demand of 1 million units. But how many units and what level of dollar sales must HD achieve to break even at the $168 price? And what level of sales must be achieved to realize various profit goals? These questions can be answered through break-even and margin analysis.

Determining Break-Even Unit Volume and Dollar Sales

Based on an understanding of costs, consumer value, the competitive environment, and reseller requirements, HD has decided to set its price to wholesalers at $168. At that price, what sales level will be needed for HD to break even or make a profit on its product? **Break-even analysis** determines the unit volume and dollar sales needed to be profitable given a particular price and cost structure. At the break-even point, total revenue equals total costs and profit is zero. Above this point, the company will make a profit; below it, the company will lose money. HD can calculate break-even volume using the following formula:

Break-even analysis
Analysis to determine the unit volume and dollar sales needed to be profitable given a particular price and cost structure.

$$\text{Break-even volume} = \frac{\text{fixed costs}}{\text{price} - \text{unit variable cost}}$$

The denominator (price – unit variable cost) is called **unit contribution** (sometimes called contribution margin). It represents the amount that each unit contributes to covering fixed costs. Break-even volume represents the level of output at which all (variable and fixed) costs are covered. In HD's case, break-even unit volume is:

Unit contribution
The amount that each unit contributes to covering fixed costs—the difference between price and variable costs.

$$\text{Break-even volume} = \frac{\text{fixed cost}}{\text{price} - \text{variable cost}} = \frac{\$20,000,000}{\$168 - \$125} = 465,116.2 \, \text{units}$$

Thus, at the given cost and pricing structure, HD will break even at 465,117 units.

To determine the break-even dollar sales, simply multiply unit break-even volume by the selling price:

$$\text{BE sales} = \text{BE}_{vol} \times \text{price} = 465,117 \times \$168 = \$78,139,656$$

Another way to calculate dollar break-even sales is to use the percentage contribution margin (hereafter referred to as **contribution margin**), which is the unit contribution divided by the selling price:

Contribution margin
The unit contribution divided by the selling price.

$$\text{Contribution margin} = \frac{\text{price} - \text{variable cost}}{\text{price}} = \frac{\$168 - \$125}{\$168} = 0.256 \text{ or } 25.6\%$$

Then,

$$\text{Break-even sales} = \frac{\text{fixed costs}}{\text{contribution margin}} = \frac{\$20,000,000}{0.256} = \$78,125,000$$

Note that the difference between the two break-even sales calculations is due to rounding.

Such break-even analysis helps HD by showing the unit volume needed to cover costs. If production capacity cannot attain this level of output, then the company should not launch this product. However, the unit break-even volume is well within HD's capacity. Of course, the bigger question concerns whether HD can sell this volume at the $168 price. We'll address that issue a little later.

Understanding contribution margin is useful in other types of analyses as well, particularly if unit prices and unit variable costs are unknown or if a company (say, a retailer) sells many products at different prices and knows the percentage of total sales variable costs represent. Whereas unit contribution is the difference between unit price and unit variable costs, total contribution is the difference between total sales and total variable costs. The overall contribution margin can be calculated by:

$$\text{Contribution margin} = \frac{\text{total sales} - \text{total variable costs}}{\text{total sales}}$$

Regardless of the actual level of sales, if the company knows what percentage of sales is represented by variable costs, it can calculate contribution margin. For example, HD's unit variable cost is $125, or 74% of the selling price ($125 ÷ $168 = 0.74). That means for every $1 of sales revenue for HD, $0.74 represents variable costs, and the difference ($0.26) represents contribution to fixed costs. But even if the company doesn't know its unit price and unit variable cost, it can calculate the contribution margin from total sales and total variable costs or from knowledge of the total cost structure. It can set total sales equal to 100% regardless of the actual absolute amount and determine the contribution margin:

$$\text{Contribution margin} = \frac{100\% - 74\%}{100\%} = \frac{1 - 0.74}{1} = 1 - 0.74 = 0.26 \text{ or } 26\%$$

Note that this matches the percentage calculated from the unit price and unit variable cost information. This alternative calculation will be very useful later when analyzing various marketing decisions.

Determining "Break-even" for Profit Goals

Although it is useful to know the break-even point, most companies are more interested in making a profit. Assume HD would like to realize a $5 million profit in the first year. How many must it sell at the $168 price to cover fixed costs and produce this profit? To determine this, HD can simply add the profit figure to fixed costs and again divide by the unit contribution to determine unit sales:

$$\text{Unit volume} = \frac{\text{fixed cost} + \text{profit goal}}{\text{price} - \text{variable cost}} = \frac{\$20,000,000 + \$5,000,000}{\$168 - \$125} = 581,395.3 \text{ units}$$

Thus, to earn a $5 million profit, HD must sell 581,396 units. Multiply by price to determine dollar sales needed to achieve a $5 million profit:

$$\text{Dollar sales} = 581,396 \text{ units} \times \$168 = \$97,674,528$$

Or use the contribution margin:

$$\text{Sales} = \frac{\text{fixed cost} + \text{profit goal}}{\text{contribution margin}} = \frac{\$20,000,000 + \$5,000,000}{0.256} = \$97,656,250$$

Again, note that the difference between the two break-even sales calculations is due to rounding.

As we saw previously, a profit goal can also be stated as a return on investment goal. For example, recall that HD wants a 30% return on its $10 million investment. Thus, its absolute profit goal is $3 million ($10,000,000 × 0.30). This profit goal is treated the same way as in the previous example:[ii]

$$\text{Unit volume} = \frac{\text{fixed cost} + \text{profit goal}}{\text{price} - \text{variable cost}} = \frac{\$20,000,000 + \$3,000,000}{\$168 - \$125} = 534,884 \text{ units}$$

$$\text{Dollar sales} = 534,884 \text{ units} \times \$168 = \$89,860,512$$

Or

$$\text{Dollar sales} = \frac{\text{fixed cost} + \text{profit goal}}{\text{contribution margin}} = \frac{\$20,000,000 + \$3,000,000}{0.256} = \$89,843,750$$

Finally, HD can express its profit goal as a percentage of sales, which we also saw in previous pricing analyses. Assume HD desires a 25% return on sales. To determine the unit and sales volume necessary to achieve this goal, the calculation is a little different from the previous two examples. In this case, we incorporate the profit goal into the unit contribution as an additional variable cost. Look at it this way: If 25% of each sale must go toward profits, that leaves only 75% of the selling price to cover fixed costs. Thus, the equation becomes:

$$\text{Unit volume} = \frac{\text{fixed cost}}{\text{price} - \text{variable cost} - (0.25 \times \text{price})} \text{ or } \frac{\text{fixed cost}}{(0.75 \times \text{price}) - \text{variable cost}}$$

So,

$$\text{Unit volume} = \frac{\$20,000,000}{(0.75 \times \$168) - \$125} = 20,000,000 \text{ units}$$

$$\text{Dollar sales necessary} = 20,000,000 \text{ units} \times \$168 = \$3,360,000,000$$

Thus, HD would need more than $3 billion in sales to realize a 25% return on sales given its current price and cost structure! Could it possibly achieve this level of sales? The major point is this: Although break-even analysis can be useful in determining the level of sales needed to cover costs or to achieve a stated profit goal, it does not tell the company whether it is *possible* to achieve that level of sales at the specified price. To address this issue, HD needs to estimate demand for this product.

Before moving on, however, let's stop here and practice applying the concepts covered so far. Now that you have seen pricing and break-even concepts in action as they relate to HD's new product, here are several exercises for you to apply what you have learned in other contexts.

Marketing by the Numbers Exercise Set One

Now that you've studied pricing, break-even, and margin analysis as they relate to HD's new product launch, use the following exercises to apply these concepts in other contexts.

1.1 Elkins, a manufacturer of ice makers, realizes a cost of $250 for every unit it produces. Its total fixed costs equal $5 million. If the company manufactures 500,000 units, compute the following:
a. unit cost
b. markup price if the company desires a 10% return on sales
c. ROI price if the company desires a 25% return on an investment of $1 million

1.2 A gift shop owner purchases items to sell in her store. She purchases a chair for $125 and sells it for $275. Determine the following:
a. dollar markup
b. markup percentage on cost
c. markup percentage on selling price

1.3 A consumer purchases a coffee maker from a retailer for $90. The retailer's markup is 30%, and the wholesaler's markup is 10%, both based on selling price. For what price does the manufacturer sell the product to the wholesaler?

1.4 A lawn mower manufacturer has a unit cost of $140 and wishes to achieve a margin of 30% based on selling price. If the manufacturer sells directly to a retailer who then adds a set margin of 40% based on selling price, determine the retail price charged to consumers.

1.5 Advanced Electronics manufactures DVDs and sells them directly to retailers who typically sell them for $20. Retailers take a 40% margin based on the retail selling price. Advanced's cost information is as follows:

DVD package and disc	$2.50/DVD
Royalties	$2.25/DVD
Advertising and promotion	$500,000
Overhead	$200,000

Calculate the following:
a. contribution per unit and contribution margin
b. break-even volume in DVD units and dollars
c. volume in DVD units and dollar sales necessary if Advanced's profit goal is 20% profit on sales
d. net profit if 5 million DVDs are sold

Demand Estimates, the Marketing Budget, and Marketing Performance Measures

Market Potential and Sales Estimates

HD has now calculated the sales needed to break even and to attain various profit goals on its new product. However, the company needs more information regarding demand in order to assess the feasibility of attaining the needed sales levels. This information is also needed for production and other decisions. For example, production schedules need to be developed, and marketing tactics need to be planned.

Total market demand
The total volume that would be bought by a defined consumer group in a defined geographic area in a defined time period in a defined marketing environment under a defined level and mix of industry marketing effort.

The **total market demand** for a product or service is the total volume that would be bought by a defined consumer group in a defined geographic area in a defined time period in a defined marketing environment under a defined level and mix of industry marketing effort. Total market demand is not a fixed number but a function of the stated conditions. For example, next year's total market demand for this type of product will depend on how much other producers spend on marketing their brands. It also depends on many environmental factors, such as government regulations, economic conditions, and the level of consumer confidence in a given market. The upper limit of market demand is called **market potential**.

Market potential
The upper limit of market demand.

One general but practical method that HD might use for estimating total market demand uses three variables: (1) the number of prospective buyers, (2) the quantity purchased by an average buyer per year, and (3) the price of an average unit. Using these numbers, HD can estimate total market demand as follows:

$$Q = n \times q \times p$$

where
Q = total market demand
n = number of buyers in the market
q = quantity purchased by an average buyer per year
p = price of an average unit

Chain ratio method
Estimating market demand by multiplying a base number by a chain of adjusting percentages.

A variation of this approach is the **chain ratio method**. This method involves multiplying a base number by a chain of adjusting percentages. For example, HD's product is designed to stream high-definition video on high-definition televisions as well as play other video content streamed from the Internet to multiple devices in a home. Thus, consumers who do not own a high-definition television will not likely purchase this player. Additionally, only households with broadband Internet access will be able to use the product. Finally, not all HDTV-owning Internet households will be willing and able to purchase this product. HD can estimate U.S. demand using a chain of calculations like the following:

Total number of U.S. households
× The percentage of HDTV-owning U.S. households with broadband Internet access
× The percentage of these households willing and able to buy this device

The U.S. Census Bureau estimates that there are approximately 115 million households in the United States.[iii] HD's research indicates that 60 percent of U.S. households own at least one HDTV and have broadband Internet access. Finally, the company's research also reveals that 30 percent of households possess the discretionary income needed and are willing to buy a product such as this. Then the total number of households willing and able to purchase this product is:

$$115 \text{ million households} \times 0.60 \times 0.30 = 20.7 \text{ million households}$$

Households need to purchase only one device because it can stream content to other devices throughout the household. Assuming the average retail price across all brands is $350 for this product, the estimate of total market demand is as follows:

$$20.7 \text{ million households} \times 1 \text{ device per household} \times \$350 = \$7,245,000,000$$

This simple chain of calculations gives HD only a rough estimate of potential demand. However, more detailed chains involving additional segments and other qualifying factors would yield more accurate and refined estimates. Still, these are only *estimates* of market potential. They rely heavily on assumptions regarding adjusting percentages, average quantity, and average price. Thus, HD must make certain that its assumptions are reasonable and defendable. As can be seen, the overall market potential in dollar sales can vary widely given the average price used. For this reason, HD will use unit sales potential to determine its sales estimate for next year. Market potential in terms of units is 20.7 million (20.7 million households × 1 device per household).

Assuming that HD forecasts it will have a 3.6% market share in the first year after launching this product, then it can forecast unit sales at 20.7 million units × 0.036 = 745,200 units. At a selling price of $168 per unit, this translates into sales of $125,193,600 (745,200 units × $168 per unit). For simplicity, further analyses will use forecasted sales of $125 million.

This unit volume estimate is well within HD's production capacity and exceeds not only the break-even estimate (465,117 units) calculated earlier but also the volume necessary to realize a $5 million profit (581,396 units) or a 30% return on investment (534,884 units). However, this forecast falls well short of the volume necessary to realize a 25% return on sales (20 million units!) and may require that HD revise expectations.

To assess expected profits, we must now look at the budgeted expenses for launching this product. To do this, we will construct a pro forma profit-and-loss statement.

The Profit-and-Loss Statement and Marketing Budget

All marketing managers must account for the profit impact of their marketing strategies. A major tool for projecting such profit impact is a **pro forma** (or projected) **profit-and-loss statement** (also called an **income statement** or **operating statement**). A pro forma statement shows projected revenues less budgeted expenses and estimates the projected net profit for an organization, product, or brand during a specific planning period, typically a year. It includes direct product production costs, marketing expenses budgeted to attain a given sales forecast, and overhead expenses assigned to the organization or product. A profit-and-loss statement typically consists of several major components (see **>> Table A3.1**):

Pro forma (or projected) profit-and-loss statement (or income statement or operating statement)
A statement that shows projected revenues less budgeted expenses and estimates the projected net profit for an organization, product, or brand during a specific planning period, typically a year.

- *Net sales*—gross sales revenue minus returns and allowances (for example, trade, cash, quantity, and promotion allowances). HD's net sales for 2016 are estimated to be $125 million, as determined in the previous analysis.
- *Cost of goods sold*—(sometimes called *cost of sales*)—the actual cost of the merchandise sold by a manufacturer or reseller. It includes the cost of inventory, purchases, and other costs associated with making the goods. HD's cost of goods sold is estimated to be 50% of net sales, or $62.5 million.
- *Gross margin (or gross profit)*—the difference between net sales and cost of goods sold. HD's gross margin is estimated to be $62.5 million.
- *Operating expenses*—the expenses incurred while doing business. These include all other expenses beyond the cost of goods sold that are necessary to conduct

>> Table A3.1	Pro Forma Profit-and-Loss Statement for the 12-Month Period Ended December 31, 2016

			Percent of Sales
Net Sales		$125,000,000	100%
Cost of Goods Sold		62,500,000	50%
Gross Margin		$ 62,500,000	50%
Marketing Expenses			
Sales expenses	$17,500,000		
Promotion expenses	15,000,000		
Freight	12,500,000	45,000,000	36%
General and Administrative Expenses			
Managerial salaries and expenses	$2,000,000		
Indirect overhead	3,000,000	5,000,000	4%
Net Profit before Income Tax		$12,500,000	10%

business. Operating expenses can be presented in total or broken down in detail. Here, HD's estimated operating expenses include *marketing expenses* and *general and administrative expenses*.

Marketing expenses include sales expenses, promotion expenses, and distribution expenses. The new product will be sold through HD's sales force, so the company budgets $5 million for sales salaries. However, because sales representatives earn a 10% commission on sales, HD must also add a variable component to sales expenses of $12.5 million (10% of $125 million net sales), for a total budgeted sales expense of $17.5 million. HD sets its advertising and promotion to launch this product at $10 million. However, the company also budgets 4% of sales, or $5 million, for cooperative advertising allowances to retailers who promote HD's new product in their advertising. Thus, the total budgeted advertising and promotion expenses are $15 million ($10 million for advertising plus $5 million in co-op allowances). Finally, HD budgets 10% of net sales, or $12.5 million, for freight and delivery charges. In all, total marketing expenses are estimated to be $17.5 million + $15 million + $12.5 million = $45 million.

General and administrative expenses are estimated at $5 million, broken down into $2 million for managerial salaries and expenses for the marketing function and $3 million of indirect overhead allocated to this product by the corporate accountants (such as depreciation, interest, maintenance, and insurance). Total expenses for the year, then, are estimated to be $50 million ($45 million marketing expenses + $5 million in general and administrative expenses).

- *Net profit before taxes*—profit earned after all costs are deducted. HD's estimated net profit before taxes is $12.5 million.

In all, as Table A3.1 shows, HD expects to earn a profit on its new product of $12.5 million in 2016. Also note that the percentage of sales that each component of the profit-and-loss statement represents is given in the right-hand column. These percentages are determined by dividing the cost figure by net sales (that is, marketing expenses represent 36% of net sales determined by $45 million ÷ $125 million). As can be seen, HD projects a net profit return on sales of 10% in the first year after launching this product.

Marketing Performance Measures

Profit-and-loss statement (or income statement or operating statement)
A statement that shows actual revenues less expenses and net profit for an organization, product, or brand during a specific planning period, typically a year.

Now let's fast-forward a year. HD's product has been on the market for one year, and management wants to assess its sales and profit performance. One way to assess this performance is to compute performance ratios derived from HD's **profit-and-loss statement** (or **income statement** or **operating statement**).

Whereas the pro forma profit-and-loss statement shows *projected* financial performance, the statement given in **≫ Table A3.2** shows HD's *actual* financial performance based on actual sales, cost of goods sold, and expenses during the past year. By comparing the profit-and-loss statement from one period to the next, HD can gauge performance against goals, spot favorable or unfavorable trends, and take appropriate corrective action.

The profit-and-loss statement shows that HD lost $1 million rather than making the $12.5 million profit projected in the pro forma statement. Why? One obvious reason is that net sales fell $25 million short of estimated sales. Lower sales translated into lower variable costs associated with marketing the product. However, both fixed costs and the cost of goods sold as a percentage of sales exceeded expectations. Hence, the product's contribution margin was 21% rather than the estimated 26%. That is, variable costs represented 79% of sales (55% for cost of goods sold, 10% for sales commissions, 10% for freight, and 4% for co-op allowances). Recall that contribution margin can be calculated by subtracting that fraction from one $(1 - 0.79 = 0.21)$. Total fixed costs were $22 million, $2 million more than estimated. Thus, the sales that HD needed to break even given this cost structure can be calculated as:

$$\text{Break-even sales} = \frac{\text{fixed costs}}{\text{contribution margin}} = \frac{\$22,000,000}{0.21} = \$104,761,905$$

If HD had achieved another $5 million in sales, it would have earned a profit.

Market share
Company sales divided by market sales.

Although HD's sales fell short of the forecasted sales, so did overall industry sales for this product. Overall industry sales were only $2.5 billion. That means that HD's **market share** was 4% ($100 million ÷ $2.5 billion = 0.04 = 4%), which was higher than forecasted. Thus, HD attained a higher-than-expected market share, but the overall market sales were not as high as estimated.

≫ Table A3.2 Profit-and-Loss Statement for the 12-Month Period Ended December 31, 2016

			Percent of Sales
Net Sales		$100,000,000	100%
Cost of Goods Sold		55,000,000	55%
Gross Margin		$ 45,000,000	45%
Marketing Expenses			
Sales expenses	$15,000,000		
Promotion expenses	14,000,000		
Freight	10,000,000	39,000,000	39%
General and Administrative Expenses			
Managerial salaries and expenses	$2,000,000		
Indirect overhead	5,000,000	7,000,000	7%
Net Profit before Income Tax		−$1,000,000	−1%

Analytic Ratios

Operating ratios
The ratios of selected operating statement items to net sales.

The profit-and-loss statement provides the figures needed to compute some crucial **operating ratios**—the ratios of selected operating statement items to net sales. These ratios let marketers compare the firm's performance in one year to that in previous years (or with industry standards and competitors' performance in that year). The most commonly used operating ratios are the gross margin percentage, the net profit percentage, and the operating expense percentage. The inventory turnover rate and return on investment (ROI) are often used to measure managerial effectiveness and efficiency.

Gross margin percentage
The percentage of net sales remaining after cost of goods sold—calculated by dividing gross margin by net sales.

The **gross margin percentage** indicates the percentage of net sales remaining after cost of goods sold that can contribute to operating expenses and net profit before taxes. The higher this ratio, the more a firm has left to cover expenses and generate profit. HD's gross margin ratio was 45%:

$$\text{Gross margin percentage} = \frac{\text{gross margin}}{\text{net sales}} = \frac{\$45,000,000}{\$100,000,000} = 0.45 = 45\%$$

Note that this percentage is lower than estimated, and this ratio is seen easily in the percentage of sales column in Table A3.2. Stating items in the profit-and-loss statement as a percent of sales allows managers to quickly spot abnormal changes in costs over time. If there was previous history for this product and this ratio was declining, management should examine it more closely to determine why it has decreased (that is, because of a decrease in sales volume or price, an increase in costs, or a combination of these). In HD's case, net sales were $25 million lower than estimated, and cost of goods sold was higher than estimated (55% rather than the estimated 50%).

Net profit percentage
The percentage of each sales dollar going to profit—calculated by dividing net profits by net sales.

The **net profit percentage** shows the percentage of each sales dollar going to profit. It is calculated by dividing net profits by net sales:

$$\text{Net profit percentage} = \frac{\text{net profit}}{\text{net sales}} = \frac{-\$1,000,000}{\$100,000,000} = -0.01 = -1.0\%$$

This ratio is easily seen in the percent of sales column. HD's new product generated negative profits in the first year, not a good situation given that before the product launch net profits before taxes were estimated at more than $12 million. Later in this appendix, we will discuss further analyses the marketing manager should conduct to defend the product.

Operating expense percentage
The portion of net sales going to operating expenses—calculated by dividing total expenses by net sales.

The **operating expense percentage** indicates the portion of net sales going to operating expenses. Operating expenses include marketing and other expenses not directly related to marketing the product, such as indirect overhead assigned to this product. It is calculated by:

$$\text{Operating expense percentage} = \frac{\text{total expenses}}{\text{net sales}} = \frac{\$46,000,000}{\$100,000,000} = 0.46 = 46\%$$

This ratio can also be quickly determined from the percent of sales column in the profit-and-loss statement by adding the percentages for marketing expenses and general and administrative expenses (39% + 7%). Thus, 46 cents of every sales dollar went for operations. Although HD wants this ratio to be as low as possible, and 46% is not an alarming amount, it is of concern if it is increasing over time or if a loss is realized.

Inventory turnover rate (or stockturn rate)
The number of times an inventory turns over or is sold during a specified time period (often one year)—calculated based on costs, selling price, or units.

Another useful ratio is the **inventory turnover rate** (also called **stockturn rate** for resellers). The inventory turnover rate is the number of times an inventory turns over or is sold during a specified time period (often one year). This rate tells how quickly a business is moving inventory through the organization. Higher rates indicate that lower investments in inventory are made, thus freeing up funds for other investments. It may be computed on a cost, selling price, or unit basis. The formula based on cost is:

$$\text{Inventory turnover rate} = \frac{\text{cost of goods sold}}{\text{average inventory at cost}}$$

Assuming HD's beginning and ending inventories were $30 million and $20 million, respectively, the inventory turnover rate is:

$$\text{Inventory turnover rate} = \frac{\$55,000,000}{(\$30,000,000 + \$20,000,000)/2} = \frac{\$55,000,000}{\$25,000,000} = 2.2$$

That is, HD's inventory turned over 2.2 times in 2016. Normally, the higher the turnover rate, the higher the management efficiency and company profitability. However, this rate should be compared with industry averages, competitors' rates, and past performance to determine if HD is doing well. A competitor with similar sales but a higher inventory turnover rate will have fewer resources tied up in inventory, allowing it to invest in other areas of the business.

Companies frequently use **return on investment (ROI)** to measure managerial effectiveness and efficiency. For HD, ROI is the ratio of net profits to total investment required to manufacture the new product. This investment includes capital investments in land, buildings, and equipment (here, the initial $10 million to refurbish the manufacturing facility) plus inventory costs (HD's average inventory totaled $25 million), for a total of $35 million. Thus, HD's ROI for this product is:

$$\text{Return on investment} = \frac{\text{net profit before taxes}}{\text{investment}} = \frac{-\$1,000,000}{\$35,000,000} = -.0286 = -2.86\%$$

ROI is often used to compare alternatives, and a positive ROI is desired. The alternative with the highest ROI is preferred to other alternatives. HD needs to be concerned with the ROI realized. One obvious way HD can increase ROI is to increase net profit by reducing expenses. Another way is to reduce its investment, perhaps by investing less in inventory and turning it over more frequently.

Marketing Profitability Metrics

Given the above financial results, you may be thinking that HD should drop this new product. But what arguments can marketers make for keeping or dropping this product? The obvious arguments for dropping the product are that first-year sales were well below expected levels and the product lost money, resulting in a negative return on investment.

So what would happen if HD did drop this product? Surprisingly, if the company drops the product, the profits for the total organization will decrease by $4 million! How can that be? Marketing managers need to look closely at the numbers in the profit-and-loss statement to determine the *net marketing contribution* for this product. In HD's case, the net marketing contribution for the product is $4 million, and if the company drops this product, that contribution will disappear as well. Let's look more closely at this concept to illustrate how marketing managers can better assess and defend their marketing strategies and programs.

Net Marketing Contribution

Net marketing contribution (NMC), along with other marketing metrics derived from it, measures *marketing* profitability. It includes only components of profitability that are controlled by marketing. Whereas the previous calculation of net profit before taxes from the profit-and-loss statement includes operating expenses not under marketing's control, NMC does not. Referring back to HD's profit-and-loss statement given in Table A3.2, we can calculate net marketing contribution for the product as:

$$\text{NMC} = \text{net sales} - \text{cost of goods sold} - \text{marketing expenses}$$
$$= \$100 \text{ million} - \$55 \text{ million} - \$41 \text{ million} = \$4 \text{ million}$$

The marketing expenses include sales expenses ($15 million), promotion expenses ($14 million), freight expenses ($10 million), and the managerial salaries and expenses of the marketing function ($2 million), which total $41 million.

Thus, the product actually contributed $4 million to HD's profits. It was the $5 million of indirect overhead allocated to this product that caused the negative profit. Further, the amount allocated was $2 million more than estimated in the pro forma profit-and-loss statement. Indeed, if only the estimated amount had been allocated, the product would have earned a *profit* of $1 million rather than losing $1 million. If HD drops the product, the $5 million in fixed overhead expense will not disappear—it will simply have to be allocated elsewhere. However, the $4 million in net marketing contribution *will* disappear.

Marketing Return on Sales and Investment

To get an even deeper understanding of the profit impact of marketing strategy, we'll now examine two measures of marketing efficiency—*marketing return on sales* (marketing ROS) and *marketing return on investment* (marketing ROI).[iv]

Marketing return on sales (or **marketing ROS**) shows the percent of net sales attributable to the net marketing contribution. For our product, ROS is:

$$\text{Marketing ROS} = \frac{\text{net marketing contribution}}{\text{net sales}} = \frac{\$4,000,000}{\$100,000,000} = 0.04 = 4\%$$

Thus, out of every $100 of sales, the product returns $4 to HD's bottom line. A high marketing ROS is desirable. But to assess whether this is a good level of performance, HD must compare this figure to previous marketing ROS levels for the product, the ROSs of other products in the company's portfolio, and the ROSs of competing products.

Marketing return on investment (or **marketing ROI**) measures the marketing productivity of a marketing investment. In HD's case, the marketing investment is represented by $41 million of the total expenses. Thus, marketing ROI is:

$$\text{Marketing ROI} = \frac{\text{net marketing contribution}}{\text{marketing expenses}} = \frac{\$4,000,000}{\$41,000,000} = 0.0976 = 9.76\%$$

As with marketing ROS, a high value is desirable, but this figure should be compared with previous levels for the given product and with the marketing ROIs of competitors' products. Note from this equation that marketing ROI could be greater than 100%. This can be achieved by attaining a higher net marketing contribution and/or a lower total marketing expense.

In this section, we estimated market potential and sales, developed profit-and-loss statements, and examined financial measures of performance. In the next section, we discuss methods for analyzing the impact of various marketing tactics. However, before moving on to those analyses, here's another set of quantitative exercises to help you apply what you've learned to other situations.

Marketing by the Numbers Exercise Set Two

2.1 Determine the market potential for a product that has 20 million prospective buyers who purchase an average of two per year and price averages $50. How many units must a company sell if it desires a 10% share of this market?

2.2 Develop a profit-and-loss statement for the Westgate division of North Industries. This division manufactures light fixtures sold to consumers through home-improvement and hardware stores. Cost of goods sold represents 40% of net sales. Marketing expenses include selling expenses, promotion expenses, and freight. Selling expenses include sales salaries totaling $3 million per year and sales commissions (5% of sales). The company spent $3 million on advertising last year, and freight costs were 10% of sales. Other costs include $2 million for managerial salaries and expenses for the marketing function and another $3 million for indirect overhead allocated to the division.
a. Develop the profit-and-loss statement if net sales were $20 million last year.
b. Develop the profit-and-loss statement if net sales were $40 million last year.
c. Calculate Westgate's break-even sales.

Marketing return on sales (or marketing ROS)
The percent of net sales attributable to the net marketing contribution—calculated by dividing net marketing contribution by net sales.

Marketing return on investment (or marketing ROI)
A measure of the marketing productivity of a marketing investment—calculated by dividing net marketing contribution by marketing expenses.

2.3 Using the profit-and-loss statement you developed in question 2.2b and assuming that Westgate's beginning inventory was $11 million, ending inventory was $7 million, and total investment was $20 million including inventory, determine the following:
a. gross margin percentage
b. net profit percentage
c. operating expense percentage
d. inventory turnover rate
e. return on investment (ROI)
f. net marketing contribution
g. marketing return on sales (marketing ROS)
h. marketing return on investment (marketing ROI)
i. Is the Westgate division doing well? Explain your answer.

Financial Analysis of Marketing Tactics

Although the first-year profit performance for HD's new product was less than desired, management feels that this attractive market has excellent growth opportunities. Although the sales of HD's product were lower than initially projected, they were not unreasonable given the size of the current market. Thus, HD wants to explore new marketing tactics to help grow the market for this product and increase sales for the company.

For example, the company could increase advertising to promote more awareness of the new product and its category. It could add salespeople to secure greater product distribution. HD could decrease prices so that more consumers could afford its product. Finally, to expand the market, HD could introduce a lower-priced model in addition to the higher-priced original offering. Before pursuing any of these tactics, HD must analyze the financial implications of each.

Increase Advertising Expenditures

HD is considering boosting its advertising to make more people aware of the benefits of this device in general and of its own brand in particular. What if HD's marketers recommend increasing national advertising by 50% to $15 million (assume no change in the variable cooperative component of promotional expenditures)? This represents an increase in fixed costs of $5 million. What increase in sales will be needed to break even on this $5 million increase in fixed costs?

A quick way to answer this question is to divide the increase in fixed cost by the contribution margin, which we found in a previous analysis to be 21%:

$$\text{Increase in sales} = \frac{\text{increase in fixed cost}}{\text{contribution margin}} = \frac{\$5,000,000}{0.21} = \$23,809,524$$

Thus, a 50% increase in advertising expenditures must produce a sales increase of almost $24 million to just break even. That $24 million sales increase translates into an almost 1 percentage point increase in market share (1% of the $2.5 billion overall market equals $25 million). That is, to break even on the increased advertising expenditure, HD would have to increase its market share from 4% to 4.95% ($123,809,524 ÷ $2.5 billion = 0.0495, or 4.95% market share). All of this assumes that the total market will not grow, which might or might not be a reasonable assumption.

Increase Distribution Coverage

HD also wants to consider hiring more salespeople in order to call on new retailer accounts and increase distribution through more outlets. Even though HD sells directly to wholesalers, its sales representatives call on retail accounts to perform other functions in addition to selling, such as training retail salespeople. Currently, HD employs 60 sales reps who earn an average of $50,000 in salary plus 10% commission on sales. The product is currently sold to consumers through 1,875 retail outlets. Suppose HD wants to increase that number of outlets to 2,500, an increase of 625 retail outlets. How many additional salespeople will HD need, and what sales will be necessary to break even on the increased cost?

One method for determining what size sales force HD will need is the **workload method**. The workload method uses the following formula to determine the salesforce size:

$$NS = \frac{NC \times FC \times LC}{TA}$$

where
    NS = number of salespeople
    NC = number of customers
    FC = average frequency of customer calls per customer
    LC = average length of customer call
    TA = time an average salesperson has available for selling per year

HD's sales reps typically call on accounts an average of 20 times per year for about two hours per call. Although sales reps work 2,000 hours per year (50 weeks per year × 40 hours per week), they spent about 15 hours per week on nonselling activities such as administrative duties and travel. Thus, the average annual available selling time per sales rep per year is 1,250 hours (50 weeks × 25 hours per week). We can now calculate how many sales reps HD will need to cover the anticipated 2,500 retail outlets:

$$NS = \frac{2,500 \times 20 \times 2}{1,250} = 80 \text{ salespeople}$$

Therefore, HD will need to hire 20 more salespeople. The cost to hire these reps will be $1 million (20 salespeople × $50,000 salary per salesperson).

What increase in sales will be required to break even on this increase in fixed costs? The 10% commission is already accounted for in the contribution margin, so the contribution margin remains unchanged at 21%. Thus, the increase in sales needed to cover this increase in fixed costs can be calculated by:

$$\text{Increase in sales} = \frac{\text{increase in fixed cost}}{\text{contribution margin}} = \frac{\$1,000,000}{0.21} = \$4,761,905$$

That is, HD's sales must increase almost $5 million to break even on this tactic. So, how many new retail outlets will the company need to secure to achieve this sales increase? The average revenue generated per current outlet is $53,333 ($100 million in sales divided by 1,875 outlets). To achieve the nearly $5 million sales increase needed to break even, HD would need about 90 new outlets ($4,761,905 ÷ $53,333 = 89.3 outlets), or about 4.5 outlets per new rep. Given that current reps cover about 31 outlets apiece (1,875 outlets ÷ 60 reps), this seems very reasonable.

Decrease Price

HD is also considering lowering its price to increase sales revenue through increased volume. The company's research has shown that demand for most types of consumer electronics products is elastic—that is, the percentage increase in the quantity demanded is greater than the percentage decrease in price.

What increase in sales would be necessary to break even on a 10% decrease in price? That is, what increase in sales will be needed to maintain the total contribution that HD realized at the higher price? The current total contribution can be determined by multiplying the contribution margin by total sales:[v]

Current total contribution = contribution margin × sales = .21 × $100 million = $21 million

Price changes result in changes in unit contribution and contribution margin. Recall that the contribution margin of 21% was based on variable costs representing 79% of sales.

Therefore, unit variable costs can be determined by multiplying the original price by this percentage: $168 \times 0.79 = 132.72 per unit. If price is decreased by 10%, the new price is $151.20. However, variable costs do not change just because price decreased, so the contribution and contribution margin decrease as follows:

	Old	New (Reduced 10%)
Price	$168	$151.20
− Unit variable cost	$132.72	$132.72
= Unit contribution	$35.28	$18.48
Contribution margin	$35.28/$168 = 0.21 or 21%	$18.48/$151.20 = 0.12 or 12%

So a 10% reduction in price results in a decrease in the contribution margin from 21% to 12%.[vi] To determine the sales level needed to break even on this price reduction, we calculate the level of sales that must be attained at the new contribution margin to achieve the original total contribution of $21 million:

$$\text{New contribution margin} \times \text{new sales level} = \text{original total contribution}$$

So,

$$\text{New sales level} = \frac{\text{original contribution}}{\text{new contribution margin}} = \frac{\$21,000,000}{0.12} = \$175,000,000$$

Thus, sales must increase by $75 million ($175 million − $100 million) just to break even on a 10% price reduction. This means that HD must increase market share to 7% ($175 million ÷ $2.5 billion) to achieve the current level of profits (assuming no increase in the total market sales). The marketing manager must assess whether or not this is a reasonable goal.

Extend the Product Line

As a final option, HD is considering extending its product line by offering a lower-priced model. Of course, the new, lower-priced product would steal some sales from the higher-priced model. This is called **cannibalization**—the situation in which one product sold by a company takes a portion of its sales from other company products. If the new product has a lower contribution than the original product, the company's total contribution will decrease on the cannibalized sales. However, if the new product can generate enough new volume, it is worth considering.

To assess cannibalization, HD must look at the incremental contribution gained by having both products available. Recall that in the previous analysis we determined that unit variable costs were $132.72 and unit contribution was just over $35. Assuming costs remain the same next year, HD can expect to realize a contribution per unit of approximately $35 for every unit of the original product sold.

Assume that the first model offered by HD is called HD1 and the new, lower-priced model is called HD2. HD2 will retail for $250, and resellers will take the same markup percentages on price as they do with the higher-priced model. Therefore, HD2's price to wholesalers will be $140 as follows:

Retail price:	$250
minus retail margin (30%):	−$ 75
Retailer's cost/wholesaler's price:	$175
minus wholesaler's margin (20%):	−$ 35
Wholesaler's cost/HD's price	$140

If HD2's variable costs are estimated to be $120, then its contribution per unit will equal $20 ($140 − $120 = $20). That means for every unit that HD2 cannibalizes from HD1, HD will *lose* $15 in contribution toward fixed costs and profit (that is, contribution$_{HD2}$

Cannibalization
The situation in which one product sold by a company takes a portion of its sales from other company products.

– contribution$_{HD1}$ = $20 − $35 = −$15). You might conclude that HD should not pursue this tactic because it appears as though the company will be worse off if it introduces the lower-priced model. However, if HD2 captures enough *additional* sales, HD will be better off even though some HD1 sales are cannibalized. The company must examine what will happen to *total* contribution, which requires estimates of unit volume for both products.

Originally, HD estimated that next year's sales of HD1 would be 600,000 units. However, with the introduction of HD2, it now estimates that 200,000 of those sales will be cannibalized by the new model. If HD sells only 200,000 units of the new HD2 model (all cannibalized from HD1), the company would lose $3 million in total contribution (200,000 units × −$15 per cannibalized unit = −$3 million)—not a good outcome. However, HD estimates that HD2 will generate the 200,000 of cannibalized sales plus an *additional* 500,000 unit sales. Thus, the contribution on these additional HD2 units will be $10 million (i.e., 500,000 units × $20 per unit = $10 million). The net effect is that HD will gain $7 million in total contribution by introducing HD2.

The following table compares HD's total contribution with and without the introduction of HD2:

	HD1 only	HD1 and HD2
HD1 contribution	600,000 units × $35 = $21,000,000	400,000 units × $35 = $14,000,000
HD2 contribution	0	700,000 units × $20 = $14,000,000
Total contribution	$21,000,000	$28,000,000

The difference in the total contribution is a net gain of $7 million ($28 million − $21 million). Based on this analysis, HD should introduce the HD2 model because it results in a positive incremental contribution. However, if fixed costs will increase by more than $7 million as a result of adding this model, then the net effect will be negative and HD should not pursue this tactic.

Now that you have seen these marketing tactic analysis concepts in action as they relate to HD's new product, here are several exercises for you to apply what you have learned in this section in other contexts.

Marketing by the Numbers Exercise Set Three

3.1 Alliance, Inc. sells gas lamps to consumers through retail outlets. Total industry sales for Alliance's relevant market last year were $100 million, with Alliance's sales representing 5% of that total. Contribution margin is 25%. Alliance's sales force calls on retail outlets and each sales rep earns $50,000 per year plus 1% commission on all sales. Retailers receive a 40% margin on selling price and generate average revenue of $10,000 per outlet for Alliance.

    a. The marketing manager has suggested increasing consumer advertising by $200,000. By how much would dollar sales need to increase to break even on this expenditure? What increase in overall market share does this represent?

    b. Another suggestion is to hire two more sales representatives to gain new consumer retail accounts. How many new retail outlets would be necessary to break even on the increased cost of adding two sales reps?

    c. A final suggestion is to make a 10% across-the-board price reduction. By how much would dollar sales need to increase to maintain Alliance's current contribution? (See endnote 6 to calculate the new contribution margin.)

    d. Which suggestion do you think Alliance should implement? Explain your recommendation.

3.2 PepsiCo sells its soft drinks in approximately 400,000 retail establishments, such as supermarkets, discount stores, and convenience stores. Sales representatives call on each retail account weekly, which means each account is called on by a sales rep 52 times per year. The average length of a sales call is 75 minutes (or 1.25 hours).

An average salesperson works 2,000 hours per year (50 weeks per year × 40 hours per week), but each spends 10 hours a week on nonselling activities, such as administrative tasks and travel. How many salespeople does PepsiCo need?

3.3 Hair Zone manufactures a brand of hairstyling gel. It is considering adding a modified version of the product—a foam that provides stronger hold. Hair Zone's variable costs and prices to wholesalers are:

	Current Hair Gel	New Foam Product
Unit selling price	2.00	2.25
Unit variable costs	.85	1.25

Hair Zone expects to sell 1 million units of the new styling foam in the first year after introduction, but it expects that 60% of those sales will come from buyers who normally purchase Hair Zone's styling gel. Hair Zone estimates that it would sell 1.5 million units of the gel if it did not introduce the foam. If the fixed cost of launching the new foam will be $100,000 during the first year, should Hair Zone add the new product to its line? Why or why not?

Appendix 4 Careers in Marketing

You may have decided you want to pursue a marketing career because it offers constant challenge, stimulating problems, the opportunity to work with people, and excellent advancement opportunities. But you still may not know which part of marketing best suits you—marketing is a very broad field offering a wide variety of career options.

This appendix helps you discover what types of marketing jobs best match your special skills and interests, shows you how to conduct the kind of job search that will get you the position you want, describes marketing career paths open to you, and suggests other information resources.

Marketing Careers Today

The marketing field is booming, with nearly a third of all working Americans now employed in marketing-related positions. Marketing salaries may vary by company, position, and region, and salary figures change constantly. In general, entry-level marketing salaries usually are only slightly below those for engineering and chemistry but equal or exceed starting salaries in economics, finance, accounting, general business, and the liberal arts. Moreover, if you succeed in an entry-level marketing position, it's likely that you will be promoted quickly to higher levels of responsibility and salary. In addition, because of the consumer and product knowledge you will gain in these jobs, marketing positions provide excellent training for the highest levels in an organization.

Overall Marketing Facts and Trends

In conducting your job search, consider the following facts and trends that are changing the world of marketing:

Focus on customers. More and more, companies are realizing that they win in the marketplace only by creating superior value for customers. To capture value from customers, they must first find new and better ways to solve customer problems and improve customer brand experiences. This increasing focus on the customer puts marketers at the forefront in many of today's companies. As the primary customer-facing function, marketing's mission is to get all company departments to "think customer."

Technology. Technology is changing the way marketers work. For example, Internet, social media, mobile, and other digital technologies are rapidly changing the ways marketers interact with and service customers. They are also changing everything from the ways marketers create new products and advertise them to how marketers access information and recruit personnel. Whereas advertising firms have traditionally recruited "generalists" in account management, *generalist* has now taken on a whole new meaning—advertising account executives must now have both broad and specialized knowledge.

Diversity. The number of women and minorities in marketing continues to grow, and women and minorities also are advancing rapidly into marketing management. For example, women now outnumber men by nearly two to one as advertising account executives. As marketing becomes more global, the need for diversity in marketing positions will continue to increase, opening new opportunities.

Global. Companies such as Coca-Cola, McDonald's, Google, IBM, Walmart, and Procter & Gamble have become multinational, with manufacturing and marketing operations in hundreds of countries. Indeed, such companies often make more profit from sales outside the United States than from within. And it's not just the big companies that are involved in international marketing. Organizations of all sizes have moved into the global arena. Many new marketing opportunities and careers will be directly linked to the expanding global marketplace. The globalization of business also means that you will need more cultural, language, and people skills in the marketing world of the twenty-first century.

Not-for-profit organizations. Increasingly, colleges, arts organizations, libraries, hospitals, and other not-for-profit organizations are recognizing the need for effectively marketing their "products" and services to various publics. This awareness has led to new marketing positions—with these organizations hiring their own marketing directors and marketing vice presidents or using outside marketing specialists.

Looking for a Job in Today's Marketing World

To choose and find the right job, you will need to apply the marketing skills you've learned in this course, especially marketing analysis and planning. Follow these eight steps for marketing yourself: (1) conduct a self-assessment and seek career counseling; (2) examine job descriptions; (3) explore the job market, follow up, and assess opportunities; (4) develop search strategies; (5) prepare résumés; (6) write a cover letter and assemble supporting documents; (7) interview for jobs; and (8) take a follow-up interview.

Conduct a Self-Assessment and Seek Career Counseling

If you're having difficulty deciding what kind of marketing position is the best fit for you, start out by doing some self-testing or seeking career counseling. Self-assessments require that you honestly and thoroughly evaluate your interests, strengths, and weaknesses. What do you do well (your best and favorite skills) and not so well? What are your favorite interests? What are your career goals? What makes you stand out from other job seekers?

The answers to such questions may suggest which marketing careers you should seek or avoid. For help in completing an effective self-assessment, look for the following books in your local bookstore or online: Nicholas Lore, *The Pathfinder: How to Choose or Change Your Career for a Lifetime of Satisfaction and Success* (Touchstone, 2012), and Richard Bolles, *What Color Is Your Parachute? 2016* (Ten Speed Press, 2015; also see www.eparachute.com). Many online sites also offer self-assessment tools, such as the Keirsey Temperament Theory and the Temperament Sorter, a free but broad assessment available at Keirsey.com. For a more specific evaluation, CareerLeader.com offers a complete online business career self-assessment program designed by the Directors of MBA Career Development at Harvard Business School. You can use this for a fee.

For help in finding a career counselor to guide you in making a career assessment, Richard Bolles's *What Color Is Your Parachute? 2016* contains a useful state-by-state sampling. CareerLeader.com also offers personal career counseling. (Some counselors can help you in your actual job search, too.) You can also consult the career counseling, testing, and placement services at your college or university.

Examine Job Descriptions

After you have identified your skills, interests, and desires, you need to see which marketing positions are the best match for them. Two U.S. Labor Department publications available in your local library or online—the *Occupation Outlook Handbook* (www.bls.gov/ooh) and the *Dictionary of Occupational Titles* (www.occupationalinfo.org)—describe the duties involved in various occupations, the specific training and education needed, the availability of jobs in each field, possibilities for advancement, and probable earnings.

Your initial career shopping list should be broad and flexible. Look for different ways to achieve your objectives. For example, if you want a career in marketing management, consider the public as well as the private sector, and local and regional as well as national and international firms. Be open initially to exploring many options, then focus on specific industries and jobs, listing your basic goals as a way to guide your choices. Your list might include "a job in a start-up company, near a big city on the West Coast, doing new-product planning with a computer software firm."

Explore the Job Market, Follow Up, and Assess Opportunities

At this stage, you need to look at the market and see what positions are actually available. You do not have to do this alone. Any of the following may assist you.

Career Development Centers

Your college's career development center and its Web site are excellent places to start. For example, the Web sites of the undergraduate career services center provide lists of career links that can help to focus your job search. Most schools also provide career coaches and career education courses. Also check the National Association of Colleges and Employers Web site (www.naceweb.org). It publishes a national forecast of hiring intentions of employers as they relate to new college graduates (search "job outlook").

In addition, find out everything you can about the companies that interest you by consulting company Web sites, business magazine articles and online sites, annual reports, business reference books, faculty, career counselors, and others. Try to analyze the industry's and the company's future growth and profit potential, advancement opportunities, salary levels, entry positions, travel time, and other factors of significance to you.

Job Fairs

Career development centers often work with corporate recruiters to organize on-campus job fairs. You might also use the Internet to check on upcoming career fairs in your region. For example, visit National Career Fairs at www.nationalcareerfairs.com or Coast to Coast Career Fairs listings at www.coasttocoastcareerfairs.com.

Networking

Networking—asking for job leads from friends, family, people in your community, and career centers—is one of the best ways to find a marketing job. Studies estimate that 60 to 90 percent of jobs are found through networking. The idea is to spread your net wide, contacting anybody and everybody.

Internships

An internship is filled with many benefits, such as gaining experience in a specific field of interest and building up a network of contacts. The biggest benefit: the potential of being offered a job shortly before or soon after graduation. According to a recent survey by the National Association of Colleges and Employers, employers converted 51.2 percent of last year's interns into full-time hires. In addition, 63 percent of the seniors who had paid internship experience and applied for a job received at least one job offer. Conversely, only 35.2 percent of seniors without internship experience who applied for a job received an offer. In addition, survey results show that the median accepted salary offer for seniors with a paid internship was 40 percent higher than the median accepted salary offered to non-intern seniors.

Many company Internet sites have separate internship areas. For example, check out Internships.com, InternshipPrograms.com, MonsterCollege (college.monster.com/education), CampusCareerCenter.com, InternJobs.com, and GoAbroad.com (www.goabroad.com/intern-abroad). If you know of a company for which you wish to work, go to that company's corporate Web site, enter the human resources area, and check for internships. If none are listed, try emailing the human resources department, asking if internships are offered.

Job Hunting on the Internet

A constantly increasing number of sites on the Internet deals with job hunting. You can also use the Internet to make contacts with people who can help you gain information on and research companies that interest you. The Riley Guide offers a great introduction to what jobs are available (www.rileyguide.com). CareerBuilder.com and Monster.com are good general sites for seeking job listings. Other helpful sites are Disability.gov and Diversity.com, which contain information on opportunities for African Americans, Hispanic Americans, Asian Americans, and Native Americans.

Most companies have their own online sites on which they post job listings. This may be helpful if you have a specific and fairly limited number of companies that you are keeping your eye on for job opportunities. But if this is not the case, remember that to find out what interesting marketing jobs the companies themselves are posting, you may have to visit hundreds of corporate sites.

Professional Networking Sites

Many companies have now begun to take advantage of social networking sites to find talented applicants. From LinkedIn to Facebook to Google+, social networking has become professional networking. For example, companies ranging from P&G to BASF have career pages on LinkedIn (www.linkedin.com/company/procter-&-gamble/careers and www.linkedin.com/company/basf/careers) to find potential candidates for entry-level positions. And companies ranging from Walmart (www.facebook.com/walmartcareers) to Marriott (www.facebook.com/marriottjobsandcareers) have career listings pages on Facebook in addition to LinkedIn. For job seekers, online professional networking offers more efficient job targeting and reduces associated costs as compared with traditional interaction methods such as traveling to job fairs and interviews, printing résumés, and other expenses.

However, although the Internet offers a wealth of resources for searching for the perfect job, be aware that it's a two-way street. Just as job seekers can search the Internet to find job opportunities, employers can search for information on job candidates. Jobs searches can sometimes be derailed by information mined by potential employers from online social networking sites that reveals unintended or embarrassing anecdotes and photos. Internet searches can sometimes also reveal inconsistencies and résumé inflation. A recent study found that more than half of recruiters surveyed have reconsidered a candidate based on his or her social profile.

Develop Search Strategies

Once you've decided which companies you are interested in, you need to contact them. One of the best ways is through on-campus interviews. However, not every company you are interested in will visit your school. In such instances, you can write, email, or phone the company directly or ask marketing professors or school alumni for contacts.

Prepare Résumés

A résumé is a concise yet comprehensive written summary of your qualifications, including your academic, personal, and professional achievements, that showcases why you are the best candidate for the job. Because an employer will spend on average only 15 to 20 seconds reviewing your résumé, you want to be sure that you prepare a good one.

In preparing your résumé, remember that all information on it must be accurate and complete. Résumés typically begin with the applicant's full name, telephone number, and mail and email addresses. A simple and direct statement of career objectives generally appears next, followed by work history and academic data (including awards and internships), and then by personal activities and experiences applicable to the job sought.

The résumé sometimes ends with a list of references the employer may contact (at other times, references may be listed separately). If your work or internship experience is limited, nonexistent, or irrelevant, then it is a good idea to emphasize your academic and nonacademic achievements, showing skills related to those required for excellent job performance.

There are three main types of résumés. *Reverse chronological* résumés, which emphasize career growth, are organized in reverse chronological order, starting with your most recent job. They focus on job titles within organizations, describing the responsibilities and accomplishments for each job. *Functional* résumés focus less on job titles and work history and more on assets and achievements. This format works best if your job history is scanty or discontinuous. *Mixed,* or *combination,* résumés take from each of the other two formats. First, the skills used for a specific job are listed, then the job title is stated. This format works best for applicants whose past jobs are in other fields or seemingly unrelated to the position. For further explanation and examples of these types of résumés, see the Résumé Resource format page (www.resume-resource.com/format.html).

Many books can assist you in developing your résumé. A popular guide is Martin Yate, *Knock 'Em Dead: Secrets and Strategies for First-Time Job Seekers* (Adams Media: 2013). Software programs such as RésuméMaker (www.ResumeMaker.com) provide hundreds of sample résumés and ready-to-use phrases while guiding you through the résumé preparation process. CareerOneStop (www.careeronestop.org/resumeguide/introduction.aspx) offers a step-by-step résumé tutorial, and Monster (http://career-advice.monster.com) offers résumé advice and writing services. Finally, you can even create your own personalized online résumé at sites such as optimalresume.com.

Online Résumés

The Internet is now a widely used job-search environment, so it's a good idea to have your résumé ready for the online environment. You can forward it to networking contacts or recruiting professionals through email. You can also post it in online databases with the hope that employers and recruiters will find it.

Successful Internet-ready résumés require a different strategy than that for paper résumés. For instance, when companies search résumé banks, they search key words and industry buzz words that describe a skill or the core work required for each job, so nouns are much more important than verbs. Two good resources for preparing Internet-ready résumés are Susan Ireland's Résumé Site (www.gcflearnfree.org/resumewriting/9/print) and the Riley Guide (www.rileyguide.com/eresume.html).

After you have written your Internet-ready résumé, you need to post it. The following sites may be good locations to start: Monster (www.monster.com), LinkedIn (www.linkedin.com/job/home), and CareerBuilder.com (www.careerbuilder.com/jobseeker/postnewresume.aspx). However, use caution when posting your résumé on various sites. In this era of identity theft, you need to select sites with care so as to protect your privacy. Limit access to your personal contact information, and don't use sites that offer to "blast" your résumé into cyberspace.

Résumé Tips

- Communicate your worth to potential employers in a concrete manner, citing examples whenever possible.
- Be concise and direct.
- Use active verbs to show you are a doer.
- Do not skimp on quality or use gimmicks. Spare no expense in presenting a professional résumé.
- Have someone critique your work. A single typo can eliminate you from being considered.
- Customize your résumé for specific employers. Emphasize your strengths as they pertain to your targeted job.
- Keep your résumé compact, usually one page.
- Format the text to be attractive, professional, and readable. Times New Roman is often the font of choice. Avoid too much "design" or gimmicky flourishes.

Write a Cover Letter, Follow Up, and Assemble Supporting Documents

Cover Letter

You should include a cover letter informing the employer that a résumé is enclosed. But a cover letter does more than this. It also serves to summarize in one or two paragraphs the contents of the résumé and explains why you think you are the right person for the position. The goal is to persuade the employer to look at the more detailed résumé. A typical cover letter is organized as follows: (1) the name and position of the person you are contacting; (2) a statement identifying the position you are applying for, how you heard of the vacancy, and the reasons for your interest; (3) a summary of your qualifications for the job; (4) a description of what follow-ups you intend to make, such as phoning in two weeks to confirm that the résumé has been received; and (5) an expression of gratitude for the opportunity of being a candidate for the job. CareerOneStop (www.careeronestop .org/ResumeGuide/Writeeffectivecoverletters.aspx) offers a step-by-step tutorial on how to create a cover letter, and Susan Ireland's Web site contains more than 50 cover letter samples (susanireland.com/ letter/cover-letter-examples). Another popular guide is Jeremy Schifeling, *Get It Done: Write a Cover Letter* (Jeremy Schifeling, 2012).

Follow Up

Once you send your cover letter and résumé to prospective employers via the method they prefer—email, their Web site, or regular mail—it's often a good idea to follow up. In today's market, job seekers can't afford to wait for interviews to find them. A quality résumé and an attractive cover letter are crucial, but a proper follow-up may be the key to landing an interview. However, before you engage your potential employer, be sure to research the company. Knowing about the company and understanding its place in the industry will help you shine. When you place a call, send an email, or mail a letter to a company contact, be sure to restate your interest in the position, check on the status of your résumé, and ask employers about any questions they may have.

Letters of Recommendation

Letters of recommendation are written references by professors, former and current employers, and others that testify to your character, skills, and abilities. Some companies may request letters of recommendation, to be submitted either with the résumé or at the interview. Even if letters of recommendation aren't requested, it's a good idea to bring them with you to the interview. A good reference letter tells why you would be an excellent candidate for the position. In choosing someone to write a letter of recommendation, be confident that the person will give you a good reference. In addition, do not assume the person knows everything about you or the position you are seeking. Rather, provide the person with your résumé and other relevant data. As a courtesy, allow the reference writer at least a month to complete the letter and enclose a stamped, addressed envelope with your materials.

In the packet containing your résumé, cover letter, and letters of recommendation, you may also want to attach other relevant documents that support your candidacy, such as academic transcripts, graphics, portfolios, and samples of writing.

Interview for Jobs

As the old saying goes, "The résumé gets you the interview; the interview gets you the job." The job interview offers you an opportunity to gather more information about the organization while at the same time allowing the organization to gather more information about you. You'll want to present your best self. The interview process consists of three parts: before the interview, the interview itself, and after the interview. If you pass through these stages successfully, you will be called back for the follow-up interview.

Before the Interview

In preparing for your interview, do the following:

1. Understand that interviewers have diverse styles, including the "chitchat," let's-get-to-know-each-other style; the interrogation style of question after question; and the tough-probing "why, why, why" style, among others. So be ready for anything.
2. With a friend, practice being interviewed and then ask for a critique. Or make a video of yourself in a practice interview so that you can critique your own performance. Your college placement service may also offer "mock" interviews to help you.

3. Prepare at least five good questions whose answers are not easily found in the company literature, such as "What is the future direction of the firm?" "How does the firm differentiate itself from competitors?" or "Do you have a new-media division?"

4. Anticipate possible interview questions, such as "Why do you want to work for this company?" or "Why should we hire you?" Prepare solid answers before the interview. Have a clear idea of why you are interested in joining the company and the industry to which it belongs.

5. Avoid back-to-back interviews—they can be exhausting, and it is unpredictable how long each will last.

6. Prepare relevant documents that support your candidacy, such as academic transcripts, letters of recommendation, graphics, portfolios, and samples of writing. Bring multiple copies to the interview.

7. Dress conservatively and professionally. Be neat and clean.

8. Arrive 10 minutes early to collect your thoughts and review the major points you intend to cover. Check your name on the interview schedule, noting the name of the interviewer and the room number. Be courteous and polite to office staff.

9. Approach the interview enthusiastically. Let your personality shine through.

During the Interview

During the interview, do the following:

1. Shake hands firmly in greeting the interviewer. Introduce yourself, using the same form of address that the interviewer uses. Focus on creating a good initial impression.

2. Keep your poise. Relax, smile when appropriate, and be upbeat throughout.

3. Maintain eye contact and good posture, and speak distinctly. Don't clasp your hands or fiddle with jewelry, hair, or clothing. Sit comfortably in your chair.

4. Along with the copies of relevant documents that support your candidacy, carry extra copies of your résumé with you.

5. Have your story down pat. Present your selling points. Answer questions directly. Avoid both one-word and too-wordy answers.

6. Let the interviewer take the initiative, but don't be passive. Find an opportunity to direct the conversation to things about yourself that you want the interviewer to hear.

7. To end on a high note, make your most important point or ask your most pertinent question during the last part of the interview.

8. Don't hesitate to "close." You might say, "I'm very interested in the position, and I have enjoyed this interview."

9. Obtain the interviewer's business card or address and phone number so that you can follow up later.

A tip for acing the interview: Before you open your mouth, find out *what it's like* to be a brand manager, sales representative, market researcher, advertising account executive, or other position for which you're interviewing. See if you can find a "mentor"—someone in a position similar to the one you're seeking, perhaps with another company. Talk with this mentor about the ins and outs of the job and industry.

After the Interview

After the interview, do the following:

1. Record the key points that arose. Be sure to note who is to follow up and when a decision can be expected.

2. Analyze the interview objectively, including the questions asked, the answers to them, your overall interview presentation, and the interviewer's responses to specific points.

3. Immediately send a thank-you letter or email, mentioning any additional items and your willingness to supply further information.

4. If you do not hear from the employer within the specified time, call, email, or write the interviewer to determine your status.

Follow-Up Interview

If your first interview takes place off-site, such as at your college or at a job fair, and if you are successful with that initial interview, you will be invited to visit the organization. The in-company interview will probably run from several hours to an entire day. The organization will examine your interest, maturity, enthusiasm, assertiveness, logic, and company and functional knowledge. You should ask questions about issues of importance to you. Find out about the working environment, job role, responsibilities, opportunities for advancement, current industrial issues, and the company's personality. The company wants to discover if you are the right person for the job, whereas you want to find out if it is the right job for you. The key is to determine if the right *fit* exists between you and the company.

Marketing Jobs

This section describes some of the key marketing positions.

Advertising

Advertising is one of the most exciting fields in marketing, offering a wide range of career opportunities.

Job Descriptions

Key advertising positions include copywriter, art director, production manager, account executive, account planner, and media planner/buyer.

- *Copywriters* write advertising copy and help find the concepts behind the written words and visual images of advertisements.
- *Art directors,* the other part of the creative team, help translate the copywriters' ideas into dramatic visuals called "layouts." Agency artists develop print layouts, package designs, television and video layouts (called "storyboards"), corporate logotypes, trademarks, and symbols.
- *Production managers* are responsible for physically creating ads, either in-house or by contracting through outside production houses.
- *Account development executives* research and understand clients' markets and customers and help develop marketing and advertising strategies to affect them.
- *Account executives* serve as liaisons between clients and agencies. They coordinate the planning, creation, production, and implementation of an advertising campaign for the account.
- *Account planners* serve as the voice of the consumer in the agency. They research consumers to understand their needs and motivations as a basis for developing effective ad campaigns.
- *Media planners (or buyers)* determine the best mix of television, radio, newspaper, magazine, digital, and other media for the advertising campaign.

Skills Needed, Career Paths, and Typical Salaries

Work in advertising requires strong people skills in order to interact closely with an often-difficult and demanding client base. In addition, advertising attracts people with strong skills in planning, problem solving, creativity, communication, initiative, leadership, and presentation. Advertising involves working under high levels of stress and pressure created by unrelenting deadlines. Advertisers frequently have to work long hours to meet deadlines for a presentation. But work achievements are very apparent, with the results of creative strategies observed by thousands or even millions of people.

Positions in advertising sometimes require an MBA. But most jobs only require a business, graphic arts, or liberal arts degree. Advertising positions often serve as gateways to higher-level management. Moreover, with large advertising agencies opening offices all over the world, there is the possibility of eventually working on global campaigns.

Starting advertising salaries are relatively low compared with those of some other marketing jobs because of strong competition for entry-level advertising jobs. Compensation will increase quickly as you move into account executive or other management positions. For more facts and figures, see the online pages of *Advertising Age,* a key ad industry publication (www.adage.com, click on the Jobs link), and the American Association of Advertising Agencies (www.aaaa.org).

Brand and Product Management

Brand and product managers plan, direct, and control business and marketing efforts for their products. They are involved with research and development, packaging, manufacturing, sales and distribution, advertising, promotion, market research, and business analysis and forecasting.

Job Descriptions

A company's brand management team consists of people in several positions:

- *Brand managers* guide the development of marketing strategies for a specific brand.
- *Assistant brand managers* are responsible for certain strategic components of the brand.
- *Product managers* oversee several brands within a product line or product group.
- *Product category managers* direct multiple product lines in the product category.
- *Market analysts* research the market and provide important strategic information to the project managers.
- *Project directors* are responsible for collecting market information on a marketing or product project.
- *Research directors* oversee the planning, gathering, and analyzing of all organizational research.

Skills Needed, Career Paths, and Typical Salaries

Brand and product management requires high problem-solving, analytical, presentation, communication, and leadership skills as well as the ability to work well in a team. Product management requires long hours and involves the high pressure of running large projects. In consumer goods companies, the newcomer—who usually needs an MBA—joins a brand team as an assistant and learns the ropes by doing numerical analyses and assisting senior brand people. This person eventually heads the team and later moves on to manage a larger brand, then several brands.

Many industrial goods companies also have product managers. Product management is one of the best training grounds for future corporate officers. Product management also offers good opportunities to move into international marketing. Product managers command relatively high salaries. Because this job category encourages or requires a master's degree, starting pay tends to be higher than in other marketing categories such as advertising or retailing.

Sales and Sales Management

Sales and sales management opportunities exist in a wide range of profit and not-for-profit organizations and in product and service organizations, including financial, insurance, consulting, and government organizations.

Job Descriptions

Key jobs include consumer sales, industrial sales, national account managers, service support, sales trainers, and sales management

- *Consumer sales* involves selling consumer products and services through retailers.
- *Industrial sales* involves selling products and services to other businesses.
- *National account managers (NAMs)* oversee a few very large accounts.
- *Service support* personnel support salespeople during and after the sale of a product.

- *Sales trainers* train new hires and provide refresher training for all sales personnel.
- *Sales management* includes a sequence of positions ranging from district manager to vice president of sales.

Salespeople enjoy active professional lives, working outside the office and interacting with others. They manage their own time and activities. And successful salespeople can be very well paid. Competition for top jobs can be intense. Every sales job is different, but some positions involve extensive travel, long workdays, and working under pressure. You can also expect to be transferred more than once between company headquarters and regional offices. However, most companies are now working to bring good work–life balance to their salespeople and sales managers.

Skills Needed, Career Paths, and Typical Salaries

Selling is a people profession in which you will work with people every day, all day long. In addition to people skills, sales professionals need sales and communication skills. Most sales positions also require strong problem-solving, analytical, presentation, and leadership abilities as well as creativity and initiative. Teamwork skills are increasingly important.

Career paths lead from salesperson to district, regional, and higher levels of sales management and, in many cases, to the top management of the firm. Today, most entry-level sales management positions require a college degree. Increasingly, people seeking selling jobs are acquiring sales experience in an internship capacity or from a part-time job before graduating. Sales positions are great springboards to leadership positions, with more CEOs starting in sales than in any other entry-level position. This might explain why competition for top sales jobs is intense.

Starting base salaries in sales may be moderate, but compensation is often supplemented by significant commission, bonus, or other incentive plans. In addition, many sales jobs include a company car or car allowance. Successful salespeople are among most companies' highest paid employees.

Other Marketing Jobs

Retailing

Retailing provides an early opportunity to assume marketing responsibilities. Key jobs include store manager, regional manager, buyer, department manager, and salesperson. *Store managers* direct the management and operation of an individual store. *Regional managers* manage groups of stores across several states and report performance to headquarters. *Buyers* select and buy the merchandise that the store carries. The *department manager* acts as store manager of a department, such as clothing, but on the department level. The *salesperson* sells merchandise to retail customers. Retailing can involve relocation, but generally there is little travel, unless you are a buyer. Retailing requires high people and sales skills because retailers are constantly in contact with customers. Enthusiasm, willingness, and communication skills are very helpful for retailers, too.

Retailers work long hours, but their daily activities are often more structured than in some types of marketing positions. Starting salaries in retailing tend to be low, but pay increases as you move into management or a retailing specialty job.

Marketing Research

Marketing researchers interact with managers to define problems and identify the information needed to resolve them. They design research projects, prepare questionnaires and samples, analyze data, prepare reports, and present their findings and recommendations to management. They must understand statistics, consumer behavior, psychology, and sociology. As more and more marketing research goes digital, they must also understand the ins and outs of obtaining and managing online information. A master's degree helps. Career opportunities exist with manufacturers, retailers, some wholesalers, trade and industry associations, marketing research firms, advertising agencies, and governmental and private nonprofit agencies.

New Product Planning

People interested in new product planning can find opportunities in many types of organizations. They usually need a good background in marketing, marketing research, and sales forecasting; they need organizational skills to motivate and coordinate others; and they may need a technical background. Usually, these people work first in other marketing positions before joining the new product department.

Marketing Logistics (Physical Distribution)

Marketing logistics, or physical distribution, is a large and dynamic field, with many career opportunities. Major transportation carriers, manufacturers, wholesalers, and retailers all employ logistics specialists. Increasingly, marketing teams include logistics specialists, and marketing managers' career paths include marketing logistics assignments. Coursework in quantitative methods, finance, accounting, and marketing will provide you with the necessary skills for entering the field.

Public Relations

Most organizations have a public relations staff to anticipate problems with various publics, handle complaints, deal with media, and build the corporate image. People interested in public relations should be able to speak and write clearly and persuasively, and they should have a background in journalism, communications, or the liberal arts. The challenges in this job are highly varied and very people-oriented.

Not-for-Profit Services

The key jobs in not-for-profits include marketing director, director of development, event coordinator, publication specialist, and intern/volunteer. The *marketing director* is in charge of all marketing activities for the organization. The *director of development* organizes, manages, and directs the fundraising campaigns that keep a not-for-profit in existence. An *event coordinator* directs all aspects of fundraising events, from initial planning through implementation. The *publication specialist* oversees publications designed to promote awareness of the organization.

Although typically an unpaid position, the *intern/volunteer* performs various marketing functions, and this work can be an important step to gaining a full-time position. The not-for-profit sector is typically not for someone who is money-driven. Rather, most not-for-profits look for people with a strong sense of community spirit and the desire to help others. Therefore, starting pay is usually lower than in other marketing fields. However, the bigger the not-for-profit, the better your chance of rapidly increasing your income when moving into upper management.

Other Resources

Professional marketing associations and organizations are another source of information about careers. Marketers belong to many such societies. You may want to contact some of the following in your job search:

Advertising Women of New York, 28 West 44th Street, Suite 912, New York, NY 10036. (212) 221-7969 (www.awny.org)

American Advertising Federation, 1101 Vermont Avenue, NW, Washington, DC 20005. (202) 898-0089 (www.aaf.org)

American Marketing Association, 311 South Wacker Drive, Suite 5800, Chicago, IL 60606. (800) AMA-1150 (www.marketingpower.com)

The Association of Women in Communications, 3337 Duke Street, Alexandria, VA 22314. (703) 370-7436 (www.womcom.org)

Market Research Association, 1156 15th Street NW, Suite 302, Washington, DC 20005. (202) 800-2545 (www.marketingresearch.org)

National Association of Sales Professionals, 555 Friendly Street, Bloomfield Hills, MI 48341. (866) 365-1520 (www.nasp.com)

National Management Association, 2210 Arbor Boulevard, Dayton, OH 45439. (937) 294-0421 (www.nma1.org)

National Retail Federation, 1101 New York Ave NW, Washington, DC 20005. (800) 673-4692 (www.nrf.com)

Product Development and Management Association, 330 Wabash Avenue, Suite 2000, Chicago, IL 60611. (312) 321-5145 (www.pdma.org)

Public Relations Society of America, 33 Maiden Lane, Eleventh Floor, New York, NY 10038. (212) 460-1400 (www.prsa.org)

Sales and Marketing Executives International, PO Box 1390, Sumas, WA, 98295. (312) 893-0751 (www.smei.org)

Glossary

Adapted global marketing   A global marketing approach that adjusts the marketing strategy and mix elements to each international target market, which creates more costs but hopefully produces a larger market share and return.

Administered VMS   A vertical marketing system that coordinates successive stages of production and distribution through the size and power of one of the parties.

Adoption process   The mental process through which an individual passes from first hearing about an innovation to final adoption.

Advertising   Any paid form of nonpersonal presentation and promotion of ideas, goods, or services by an identified sponsor.

Advertising agency   A marketing services firm that assists companies in planning, preparing, implementing, and evaluating all or portions of their advertising programs.

Advertising budget   The dollars and other resources allocated to a product or a company advertising program.

Advertising media   The vehicles through which advertising messages are delivered to their intended audiences.

Advertising objective   A specific communication task to be accomplished with a specific target audience during a specific period of time.

Advertising strategy   The strategy by which a company accomplishes its advertising objectives. It consists of two major elements: creating advertising messages and selecting advertising media.

Affordable method   Setting the promotion budget at the level management thinks the company can afford.

Age and life-cycle segmentation   Dividing a market into different age and life-cycle groups.

Agent   A wholesaler who represents buyers or sellers on a relatively permanent basis, performs only a few functions, and does not take title to goods.

Allowance   Promotional money paid by manufacturers to retailers in return for an agreement to feature the manufacturer's products in some way.

Approach   The sales step in which a salesperson meets the customer for the first time.

Attitude   A person's relatively consistent favorable or unfavorable evaluations, feelings, and tendencies toward an object or idea.

Baby boomers   The 78 million people born during the years following World War II and lasting until 1964.

Behavioral segmentation   Dividing a market into segments based on consumer knowledge, attitudes, uses of a product, or responses to a product.

Behavioral targeting   Using online consumer tracking data to target advertisements and marketing offers to specific consumers.

Belief   A descriptive thought that a person holds about something.

Benefit segmentation   Dividing a market into segments according to the different benefits that consumers seek from the product.

Big data   The huge and complex data sets generated by today's sophisticated information generation, collection, storage, and analysis technologies.

Blogs   Online forums where people and companies post their thoughts and other content, usually related to narrowly defined topics.

Brand   A name, term, sign, symbol, design, or a combination of these that identifies the products or services of one seller or group of sellers and differentiates them from those of competitors.

Brand equity   The differential effect that knowing the brand name has on customer response to the product and its marketing.

Brand extension   Extending an existing brand name to new product categories.

Brand value   The total financial value of a brand.

Branded community Web site   A Web site that presents brand content that engages consumers and creates customer community around a brand.

Break-even analysis   Analysis to determine the unit volume and dollar sales needed to be profitable given a particular price and cost structure.

Break-even pricing (target return pricing)   Setting price to break even on the costs of making and marketing a product or setting price to make a target return.

Broker   A wholesaler who does not take title to goods and whose function is to bring buyers and sellers together and assist in negotiation.

Business analysis   A review of the sales, costs, and profit projections for a new product to find out whether these factors satisfy the company's objectives.

Business buyer behavior   The buying behavior of organizations that buy goods and services for use in the production of other products and services that are sold, rented, or supplied to others.

Business buying process   The process by which business buyers determine which products and services their organizations need to purchase and then find, evaluate, and choose among alternative suppliers and brands.

Business portfolio   The collection of businesses and products that make up the company.

Business promotions   Sales promotion tools used to generate business leads, stimulate purchases, reward customers, and motivate salespeople.

Buying center   All the individuals and units that play a role in the purchase decision-making process.

By-product pricing   Setting a price for by-products in order to make the main product's price more competitive.

Cannibalization   The situation in which one product sold by a company takes a portion of its sales from other company products.

Captive-product pricing   Setting a price for products that must be used along with a main product, such as blades for a razor and games for a video-game console.

Catalog marketing   Direct marketing through print, video, or digital catalogs that are mailed to select customers, made available in stores, or presented online.

Category killer   A giant specialty store that carries a very deep assortment of a particular line.

Causal research   Marketing research to test hypotheses about cause-and-effect relationships.

Chain ratio method   Estimating market demand by multiplying a base number by a chain of adjusting percentages.

Channel conflict   Disagreements—among marketing channel members on goals, roles, and rewards—who should do what and for what rewards.

Channel level   A layer of intermediaries that performs some work in bringing the product and its ownership closer to the final buyer.

Closing   The sales step in which a salesperson asks the customer for an order.

Co-branding   The practice of using the established brand names of two different companies on the same product.

Cognitive dissonance   Buyer discomfort caused by postpurchase conflict.

Commercialization   Introducing a new product into the market.

Communication adaptation   A global communication strategy of fully adapting advertising messages to local markets.

Competition-based pricing   Setting prices based on competitors' strategies, prices, costs, and market offerings.

Competitive advantage   An advantage over competitors gained by offering greater customer value, either by having lower prices or providing more benefits that justify higher prices.

Competitive marketing intelligence   The systematic monitoring, collection, and analysis of publicly available information about consumers, competitors, and developments in the marketplace.

Competitive-parity method   Setting the promotion budget to match competitors' outlays.

Concentrated (niche) marketing   A market-coverage strategy in which a firm goes after a large share of one or a few segments or niches.

Concept testing   Testing new product concepts with a group of target consumers to find out if the concepts have strong consumer appeal.

Consumer buyer behavior   The buying behavior of final consumers—individuals and households that buy goods and services for personal consumption.

Consumer market   All the individuals and households that buy or acquire goods and services for personal consumption.

Consumer product   A product bought by final consumers for personal consumption.

Consumer promotions   Sales promotion tools used to boost short-term customer buying and engagement or enhance long-term customer relationships.

Consumer-generated marketing   Brand exchanges created by consumers themselves-both invited and uninvited-by which consumers are playing an increasing role in shaping their own brand experiences and those of other consumers.

Consumer-oriented marketing   A company should view and organize its marketing activities from the consumer's point of view.

Consumerism   An organized movement of citizens and government agencies to improve the rights and power of buyers in relation to sellers.

Content marketing   Creating, inspiring, and sharing brand messages and conversations with and among consumers across a fluid mix of paid, owned, earned, and shared channels.

Contract manufacturing   A joint venture in which a company contracts with manufacturers in a foreign market to produce its product or provide its service.

Contractual VMS   A vertical marketing system in which independent firms at different levels of production and distribution join together through contracts.

Contribution margin   The unit contribution divided by the selling price.

Convenience product   A consumer product that customers usually buy frequently, immediately, and with minimal comparison and buying effort.

Convenience store   A small store, located near a residential area, that is open long hours seven days a week and carries a limited line of high-turnover convenience goods.

Conventional distribution channel   A channel consisting of one or more independent producers, wholesalers, and retailers, each a separate business seeking to maximize its own profits, perhaps even at the expense of profits for the system as a whole.

Corporate chains   Two or more outlets that are commonly owned and controlled.

Corporate VMS   A vertical marketing system that combines successive stages of production and distribution under single ownership—channel leadership is established through common ownership.

Cost-based pricing   Setting prices based on the costs of producing, distributing, and selling the product plus a fair rate of return for effort and risk.

Cost-plus pricing (markup pricing)   Adding a standard markup to the cost of the product.

Creative concept   The compelling "big idea" that will bring an advertising message strategy to life in a distinctive and memorable way.

Crowdsourcing   Inviting broad communities of people-customers, employees, independent scientists and researchers, and even the public at large-into the new product innovation process.

Cultural environment   Institutions and other forces that affect a society's basic values, perceptions, preferences, and behaviors.

Culture   The set of basic values, perceptions, wants, and behaviors learned by a member of society from family and other important institutions.

Customer-perceived value   The customer's evaluation of the difference between all the benefits and all the costs of a marketing offer relative to those of competing offers.

Customer (or market) sales force structure   A sales force organization in which salespeople specialize in selling only to certain customers or industries.

Customer equity   The total combined customer lifetime values of all of the company's current and potential customers.

Customer insights   Fresh marketing information-based understandings of customers and the marketplace that become the basis for creating customer value, engagement, and relationships.

Customer lifetime value   The value of the entire stream of purchases a customer makes over a lifetime of patronage.

Customer relationship management   The overall process of building and maintaining profitable customer relationships by delivering superior customer value and satisfaction.

Customer relationship management (CRM)   Managing detailed information about individual customers and carefully managing customer touch points to maximize customer loyalty.

Customer satisfaction   The extent to which a product's perceived performance matches a buyer's expectations.

Customer value marketing   A company should put most of its resources into customer value-building marketing investments.

Customer value-based pricing   Setting price based on buyers' perceptions of value rather than on the seller's cost.

Customer-centered new product development   New product development that focuses on finding new ways to solve customer problems and create more customer-satisfying experiences.

Customer-engagement marketing   Making the brand a meaningful part of consumers' conversations and lives by fostering direct and continuous customer involvement in shaping brand conversations, experiences, and community.

Customer-perceived value The customer's evaluation of the difference between all the benefits and all the costs of a market offering relative to those of competing offers.

Decline stage The PLC stage in which a product's sales fade away.

Deficient products Products that have neither immediate appeal nor long-run benefits.

Demand curve A curve that shows the number of units the market will buy in a given time period at different prices that might be charged.

Demands Human wants that are backed by buying power.

Demographic segmentation Dividing the market into segments based on variables such as age, life-cycle stage, gender, income, occupation, education, religion, ethnicity, and generation.

Demography The study of human populations in terms of size, density, location, age, gender, race, occupation, and other statistics.

Department store A retail store that carries a wide variety of product lines, each operated as a separate department managed by specialist buyers or merchandisers.

Derived demand Business demand that ultimately comes from (derives from) the demand for consumer goods.

Descriptive research Marketing research to better describe marketing problems, situations, or markets, such as the market potential for a product or the demographics and attitudes of consumers.

Desirable products Products that give both high immediate satisfaction and high long-run benefits.

Differentiated (segmented) marketing A market-coverage strategy in which a firm decides to target several market segments and designs separate offers for each.

Differentiation Actually differentiating the market offering to create superior customer value.

Digital and social media marketing Using digital marketing tools such as Web sites, social media, mobile apps and ads, online video, email, and blogs to engage consumers anywhere, at any time, via their digital devices.

Direct and digital marketing Engaging directly with carefully targeted individual consumers and customer communities to both obtain an immediate response and build lasting customer relationships.

Direct investment Entering a foreign market by developing foreign-based assembly or manufacturing facilities.

Direct marketing channel A marketing channel that has no intermediary levels.

Direct-mail marketing Marketing that occurs by sending an offer, announcement, reminder, or other item directly to a person at a particular address.

Direct-response television (DRTV) marketing Direct marketing via television, including direct-response television advertising (or infomercials) and interactive television (iTV) advertising.

Discount A straight reduction in price on purchases during a stated period of time or of larger quantities.

Discount store A retail operation that sells standard merchandise at lower prices by accepting lower margins and selling at higher volume.

Disintermediation The cutting out of marketing channel intermediaries by product or service producers or the displacement of traditional resellers by radical new types of intermediaries.

Distribution center A large, highly automated warehouse designed to receive goods from various plants and suppliers, take orders, fill them efficiently, and deliver goods to customers as quickly as possible.

Diversification Company growth through starting up or acquiring businesses outside the company's current products and markets.

Dynamic pricing Adjusting prices continually to meet the characteristics and needs of individual customers and situations.

E-procurement Purchasing through electronic connections between buyers and sellers–usually online.

Economic community A group of nations organized to work toward common goals in the regulation of international trade.

Economic environment Economic factors that affect consumer purchasing power and spending patterns.

Email marketing Sending highly targeted, tightly personalized, relationship-building marketing messages via email.

Environmental sustainability Developing strategies and practices that create a world economy that the planet can support indefinitely.

Environmental sustainability A management approach that involves developing strategies that both sustain the environment and produce profits for the company.

Environmentalism An organized movement of concerned citizens, businesses, and government agencies designed to protect and improve people's current and future living environment.

Ethnographic research A form of observational research that involves sending trained observers to watch and interact with consumers in their "natural environments."

Event marketing (or event sponsorships) Creating a brand-marketing event or serving as a sole or participating sponsor of events created by others.

Exchange The act of obtaining a desired object from someone by offering something in return.

Exclusive distribution Giving a limited number of dealers the exclusive right to distribute the company's products in their territories.

Execution style The approach, style, tone, words, and format used for presenting an advertising message.

Experimental research Gathering primary data by selecting matched groups of subjects, giving them different treatments, controlling related factors, and checking for differences in group responses.

Exploratory research Marketing research to gather preliminary information that will help define problems and suggest hypotheses.

Exporting Entering foreign markets by selling goods produced in the company's home country, often with little modification.

Factory outlet An off-price retailing operation that is owned and operated by a manufacturer and normally carries the manufacturer's surplus, discontinued, or irregular goods.

Fad A temporary period of unusually high sales driven by consumer enthusiasm and immediate product or brand popularity.

Fashion A currently accepted or popular style in a given field.

Fixed costs (overhead) Costs that do not vary with production or sales level.

Focus group interviewing Personal interviewing that involves inviting small groups of people to gather for a few hours with a trained interviewer to talk about a product, service, or organization. The interviewer "focuses" the group discussion on important issues.

Follow-up The sales step in which a salesperson follows up after the sale to ensure customer satisfaction and repeat business.

Franchise A contractual association between a manufacturer, wholesaler, or service organization (a franchisor) and independent business-people (franchisees) who buy the right to own and operate one or more units in the franchise system.

Franchise organization A contractual vertical marketing system in which a channel member, called a franchisor, links several stages in the production-distribution process.

Gender segmentation Dividing a market into different segments based on gender.

Generation X The 49 million people born between 1965 and 1976 in the "birth dearth" following the baby boom.

Generation Z People born after 2000 (although many analysts include people born after 1995) who make up the kids, tweens, and teens markets.

Geographic segmentation Dividing a market into different geographical units, such as nations, states, regions, counties, cities, or even neighborhoods.

Global firm A firm that, by operating in more than one country, gains R&D, production, marketing, and financial advantages in its costs and reputation that are not available to purely domestic competitors.

Good-value pricing Offering just the right combination of quality and good service at a fair price.

Gross margin percentage The percentage of net sales remaining after cost of goods sold—calculated by dividing gross margin by net sales.

Group Two or more people who interact to accomplish individual or mutual goals.

Growth stage The PLC stage in which a product's sales start climbing quickly.

Growth-share matrix A portfolio-planning method that evaluates a company's strategic business units (SBUs) in terms of market growth rate and relative market share.

Handling objections The sales step in which a salesperson seeks out, clarifies, and overcomes any customer objections to buying.

Horizontal marketing system A channel arrangement in which two or more companies at one level join together to follow a new marketing opportunity.

Idea generation The systematic search for new product ideas.

Idea screening Screening new product ideas to spot good ones and drop poor ones as soon as possible.

Income segmentation Dividing a market into different income segments.

Independent off-price retailer An off-price retailer that is independently owned and operated or a division of a larger retail corporation.

Indirect marketing channel A marketing channel containing one or more intermediary levels.

Individual marketing Tailoring products and marketing programs to the needs and preferences of individual customers.

Industrial product A product bought by individuals and organizations for further processing or for use in conducting a business.

Innovative marketing A company should seek real product and marketing improvements.

Inside sales force Salespeople who conduct business from their offices via telephone, online and social media interactions, or visits from buyers.

Integrated logistics management The logistics concept that emphasizes teamwork-both inside the company and among all the marketing channel organizations-to maximize the performance of the entire distribution system.

Integrated marketing communications (IMC) Carefully integrating and coordinating the company's many communications channels to deliver a clear, consistent, and compelling message about the organization and its brands.

Intensive distribution Stocking the product in as many outlets as possible.

Interactive marketing Training service employees in the fine art of interacting with customers to satisfy their needs.

Intermarket (cross-market) segmentation Forming segments of consumers who have similar needs and buying behaviors even though they are located in different countries.

Internal databases Collections of consumer and market information obtained from data sources within the company network.

Internal marketing Orienting and motivating customer-contact employees and supporting service employees to work as a team to provide customer satisfaction.

Introduction stage The PLC stage in which a new product is first distributed and made available for purchase.

Inventory turnover rate (or stockturn rate) The number of times an inventory turns over or is sold during a specified time period (often one year)—calculated based on costs, selling price, or units.

Joint ownership A cooperative venture in which a company creates a local business with investors in a foreign market who share ownership and control.

Joint venturing Entering foreign markets by joining with foreign companies to produce or market products or services.

Learning Changes in an individual's behavior arising from experience.

Licensing Entering foreign markets through developing an agreement with a licensee in the foreign market.

Lifestyle A person's pattern of living as expressed in his or her activities, interests, and opinions.

Line extension Extending an existing brand name to new forms, colors, sizes, ingredients, or flavors of an existing product category.

Local marketing Tailoring brands and marketing to the needs and wants of local customer segments-cities, neighborhoods, and even specific stores.

Macroenvironment The larger societal forces that affect the microenvironment-demographic, economic, natural, technological, political, and cultural forces.

Madison & Vine A term that has come to represent the merging of advertising and entertainment in an effort to break through the clutter and create new avenues for reaching customers with more engaging messages.

Management contracting A joint venture in which the domestic firm supplies the management know-how to a foreign company that supplies the capital; the domestic firm exports management services rather than products.

Manufacturers' and retailers' branches and offices Wholesaling by sellers or buyers themselves rather than through independent wholesalers.

Market The set of all actual and potential buyers of a product or service.

Market development Company growth by identifying and developing new market segments for current company products.

Market offerings Some combination of products, services, information, or experiences offered to a market to satisfy a need or want.

Market penetration Company growth by increasing sales of current products to current market segments without changing the product.

Market potential The upper limit of market demand.

Market segment A group of consumers who respond in a similar way to a given set of marketing efforts.

Market segmentation Dividing a market into distinct groups of buyers who have different needs, characteristics, or behaviors and who might require separate marketing strategies or mixes.

Market share Company sales divided by market sales.

Market targeting (targeting) Evaluating each market segment's attractiveness and selecting one or more segments to serve.

Market-penetration pricing Setting a low price for a new product in order to attract a large number of buyers and a large market share.

Market-skimming pricing (price skimming) Setting a high price for a new product to skim maximum revenues layer by layer from the segments willing to pay the high price; the company makes fewer but more profitable sales.

Marketing The process by which companies engage customers, build strong customer relationships, and create customer value in order to capture value from customers in return.

Marketing analytics The analysis tools, technologies, and processes by which marketers dig out meaningful patterns in big data to gain customer insights and gauge marketing performance.

Marketing channel (distribution channel) A set of interdependent organizations that help make a product or service available for use or consumption by the consumer or business user.

Marketing channel design Designing effective marketing channels by analyzing customer needs, setting channel objectives, identifying major channel alternatives, and evaluating those alternatives.

Marketing channel management Selecting, managing, and motivating individual channel members and evaluating their performance over time.

Marketing concept A philosophy in which achieving organizational goals depends on knowing the needs and wants of target markets and delivering the desired satisfactions better than competitors do.

Marketing control Measuring and evaluating the results of marketing strategies and plans and taking corrective action to ensure that the objectives are achieved.

Marketing environment The actors and forces outside marketing that affect marketing management's ability to build and maintain successful relationships with target customers.

Marketing implementation Turning marketing strategies and plans into marketing actions to accomplish strategic marketing objectives.

Marketing information system (MIS) People and procedures dedicated to assessing information needs, developing the needed information, and helping decision makers to use the information to generate and validate actionable customer and market insights.

Marketing intermediaries Firms that help the company to promote, sell, and distribute its products to final buyers.

Marketing logistics (physical distribution) Planning, implementing, and controlling the physical flow of goods, services, and related information from points of origin to points of consumption to meet customer requirements at a profit.

Marketing management The art and science of choosing target markets and building profitable relationships with them.

Marketing mix The set of tactical marketing tools-product, price, place, and promotion-that the firm blends to produce the response it wants in the target market.

Marketing myopia The mistake of paying more attention to the specific products a company offers than to the benefits and experiences produced by these products.

Marketing research The systematic design, collection, analysis, and reporting of data relevant to a specific marketing situation facing an organization.

Marketing return on investment (or marketing ROI) The net return from a marketing investment divided by the costs of the marketing investment.

Marketing return on sales (or marketing ROS) The percent of net sales attributable to the net marketing contribution—calculated by dividing net marketing contribution by net sales.

Marketing strategy The marketing logic by which the company hopes to create customer value and achieve profitable customer relationships.

Marketing strategy development Designing an initial marketing strategy for a new product based on the product concept.

Marketing Web site A Web site that engages consumers to move them closer to a direct purchase or other marketing outcome.

Maturity stage The PLC stage in which a product's sales growth slows or levels off.

Merchant wholesaler An independently owned wholesale business that takes title to the merchandise it handles.

Microenvironment The actors close to the company that affect its ability to engage and serve its customers-the company, suppliers, marketing intermediaries, customer markets, competitors, and publics.

Micromarketing Tailoring products and marketing programs to the needs and wants of specific individuals and local customer segments; it includes local marketing and individual marketing.

Millennials (or Generation Y) The 83 million children of the baby boomers born between 1977 and 2000.

Mission statement A statement of the organization's purpose-what it wants to accomplish in the larger environment.

Mobile marketing Marketing messages, promotions, and other marketing content delivered to on-the-go consumers through mobile phones, smartphones, tablets, and other mobile devices.

Modified rebuy A business buying situation in which the buyer wants to modify product specifications, prices, terms, or suppliers.

Motive (drive) A need that is sufficiently pressing to direct the person to seek satisfaction.

Multichannel distribution system A distribution system in which a single firm sets up two or more marketing channels to reach one or more customer segments.

Multimodal transportation Combining two or more modes of transportation.

Natural environment The physical environment and the natural resources that are needed as inputs by marketers or that are affected by marketing activities.

Needs States of felt deprivation.

Net marketing contribution (NMC) A measure of marketing profitability that includes only components of profitability controlled by marketing.

Net profit percentage The percentage of each sales dollar going to profit—calculated by dividing net profits by net sales.

New product A good, service, or idea that is perceived by some potential customers as new.

New product development The development of original products, product improvements, product modifications, and new brands through the firm's own product development efforts.

New task A business buying situation in which the buyer purchases a product or service for the first time.

Objective-and-task method Developing the promotion budget by (1) defining specific promotion objectives, (2) determining the tasks needed to achieve these objectives, and (3) estimating the costs of performing these tasks. The sum of these costs is the proposed promotion budget.

Observational research Gathering primary data by observing relevant people, actions, and situations.

Occasion segmentation   Dividing a market into segments according to occasions when buyers get the idea to buy, actually make their purchase, or use the purchased item.

Off-price retailer   A retailer that buys at less-than-regular wholesale prices and sells at less than retail.

Omni-channel retailing   Creating a seamless cross-channel buying experience that integrates in-store, online, and mobile shopping.

Online advertising   Advertising that appears while consumers are browsing online, including display ads and search-related ads.

Online focus groups   Gathering a small group of people online with a trained moderator to chat about a product, service, or organization and gain qualitative insights about consumer attitudes and behavior.

Online marketing   Marketing via the Internet using company Web sites, online ads and promotions, email, online video, and blogs.

Online marketing research   Collecting primary data online through Internet surveys, online focus groups, Web-based experiments, or tracking of consumers' online behavior.

Online social networks   Online communities-blogs, social networking Web sites, and other online communities-where people socialize or exchange information and opinions.

Operating expense percentage   The portion of net sales going to operating expenses—calculated by dividing total expenses by net sales.

Operating ratios   The ratios of selected operating statement items to net sales.

Opinion leader   A person within a reference group who, because of special skills, knowledge, personality, or other characteristics, exerts social influence on others.

Optional-product pricing   The pricing of optional or accessory products along with a main product.

Outside sales force (or field sales force)   Salespeople who travel to call on customers in the field.

Packaging   The activities of designing and producing the container or wrapper for a product.

Partner relationship management   Working closely with partners in other company departments and outside the company to jointly bring greater value to customers.

Percentage-of-sales method   Setting the promotion budget at a certain percentage of current or forecasted sales or as a percentage of the unit sales price.

Perception   The process by which people select, organize, and interpret information to form a meaningful picture of the world.

Personal selling   Personal customer interactions by the firm's sales force for the purpose of engaging customers, making sales, and building customer relationships.

Personality   The unique psychological characteristics that distinguish a person or group.

Pleasing products   Products that give high immediate satisfaction but may hurt consumers in the long run.

Political environment   Laws, government agencies, and pressure groups that influence or limit various organizations and individuals in a given society.

Portfolio analysis   The process by which management evaluates the products and businesses that make up the company.

Positioning   Arranging for a market offering to occupy a clear, distinctive, and desirable place relative to competing products in the minds of target consumers.

Positioning statement   A statement that summarizes company or brand positioning using this form: To (target segment and need) our (brand) is (concept) that (point of difference).

Preapproach   The sales step in which a salesperson learns as much as possible about a prospective customer before making a sales call.

Presentation   The sales step in which a salesperson tells the "value story" to the buyer, showing how the company's offer solves the customer's problems.

Price   The amount of money charged for a product or service, or the sum of the values that customers exchange for the benefits of having or using the product or service.

Price elasticity   A measure of the sensitivity of demand to changes in price.

Primary data   Information collected for the specific purpose at hand.

Product   Anything that can be offered to a market for attention, acquisition, use, or consumption that might satisfy a want or need.

Product adaptation   Adapting a product to meet local conditions or wants in foreign markets.

Product bundle pricing   Combining several products and offering the bundle at a reduced price.

Product concept   The idea that consumers will favor products that offer the most quality, performance, and features; therefore, the organization should devote its energy to making continuous product improvements.

Product concept   A detailed version of the new product idea stated in meaningful consumer terms.

Product development   Company growth by offering modified or new products to current market segments.

Product development   Developing the product concept into a physical product to ensure that the product idea can be turned into a workable market offering.

Product invention   Creating new products or services for foreign markets.

Product life cycle (PLC)   The course of a product's sales and profits over its lifetime.

Product line   A group of products that are closely related because they function in a similar manner, are sold to the same customer groups, are marketed through the same types of outlets, or fall within given price ranges.

Product line pricing   Setting the price steps between various products in a product line based on cost differences between the products, customer evaluations of different features, and competitors' prices.

Product/market expansion grid   A portfolio-planning tool for identifying company growth opportunities through market penetration, market development, product development, or diversification.

Product mix (or product portfolio)   The set of all product lines and items that a particular seller offers for sale.

Product position   How a product is defined by consumers on important attributes—the place a product occupies in consumers' minds relative to competing products.

Product quality   The characteristics of a product or service that bear on its ability to satisfy stated or implied customer needs.

Product sales force structure   A sales force organization in which salespeople specialize in selling only a portion of the company's products or lines.

Production concept The idea that consumers will favor products that are available and highly affordable; therefore, the organization should focus on improving production and distribution efficiency.

Pro forma (or projected) profit-andloss statement (or income statement or operating statement) A statement that shows projected revenues less budgeted expenses and estimates the projected net profit for an organization, product, or brand during a specific planning period, typically a year.

Promotion mix (marketing communications mix) The specific blend of promotion tools that the company uses to engage customers, persuasively communicate customer value, and build customer relationships.

Promotional pricing Temporarily pricing products below the list price, and sometimes even below cost, to increase short-run sales.

Prospecting The sales step in which a salesperson or company identifies qualified potential customers.

Psychographic segmentation Dividing a market into different segments based on social class, lifestyle, or personality characteristics.

Psychological pricing Pricing that considers the psychology of prices and not simply the economics; the price is used to say something about the product.

Public Any group that has an actual or potential interest in or impact on an organization's ability to achieve its objectives.

Public relations (PR) Building good relations with the company's various publics by obtaining favorable publicity, building up a good corporate image, and handling or heading off unfavorable rumors, stories, and events.

Pull strategy A promotion strategy that calls for spending a lot on consumer advertising and promotion to induce final consumers to buy the product, creating a demand vacuum that "pulls" the product through the channel.

Push strategy A promotion strategy that calls for using the sales force and trade promotion to push the product through channels. The producer promotes the product to channel members who in turn promote it to final consumers.

Reference prices Prices that buyers carry in their minds and refer to when they look at a given product.

Relevant costs Costs that will occur in the future and that will vary across the alternatives being considered.

Retailer A business whose sales come primarily from retailing.

Retailing All the activities involved in selling products or services directly to final consumers for their personal, nonbusiness use.

Return on advertising investment The net return on advertising investment divided by the costs of the advertising investment.

Return on investment (ROI) A measure of managerial effectiveness and efficiency—net profit before taxes divided by total investment.

Return on investment (ROI) pricing (or target-return pricing) A cost-based pricing method that determines price based on a specified rate of return on investment.

Sales force management Analyzing, planning, implementing, and controlling sales force activities.

Sales promotion Short-term incentives to encourage the purchase or sale of a product or a service.

Sales promotion Short-term incentives to encourage the purchase or sale of a product or a service.

Sales quota A standard that states the amount a salesperson should sell and how sales should be divided among the company's products.

Salesperson An individual who represents a company to customers by performing one or more of the following activities: prospecting, communicating, selling, servicing, information gathering, and relationship building.

Salutary products Products that have low immediate appeal but may benefit consumers in the long run.

Sample A segment of the population selected for marketing research to represent the population as a whole.

Secondary data Information that already exists somewhere, having been collected for another purpose.

Segmented pricing Selling a product or service at two or more prices, where the difference in prices is not based on differences in costs.

Selective distribution The use of more than one but fewer than all of the intermediaries that are willing to carry the company's products.

Selling concept The idea that consumers will not buy enough of the firm's products unless the firm undertakes a large-scale selling and promotion effort.

Selling process The steps that salespeople follow when selling, which include prospecting and qualifying, preapproach, approach, presentation and demonstration, handling objections, closing, and follow-up.

Sense-of-mission marketing A company should define its mission in broad *social* terms rather than narrow *product* terms.

Service An activity, benefit, or satisfaction offered for sale that is essentially intangible and does not result in the ownership of anything.

Service inseparability Services are produced and consumed at the same time and cannot be separated from their providers.

Service intangibility Services cannot be seen, tasted, felt, heard, or smelled before they are bought.

Service perishability Services cannot be stored for later sale or use.

Service profit chain The chain that links service firm profits with employee and customer satisfaction.

Service retailer A retailer whose product line is actually a service; examples include hotels, airlines, banks, colleges, and many others.

Service variability The quality of services may vary greatly depending on who provides them and when, where, and how they are provided.

Share of customer The portion of the customer's purchasing that a company gets in its product categories.

Shopper marketing Focusing the entire marketing process on turning shoppers into buyers as they approach the point of sale, whether during in-store, online, or mobile shopping.

Shopping center A group of retail businesses built on a site that is planned, developed, owned, and managed as a unit.

Shopping product A consumer product that the customer, in the process of selecting and purchasing, usually compares on such attributes as suitability, quality, price, and style.

Showrooming The shopping practice of coming into retail store showrooms to check out merchandise and prices but instead buying from an online-only rival, sometimes while in the store.

Social class Relatively permanent and ordered divisions in a society whose members share similar values, interests, and behaviors.

Social marketing Using traditional business marketing concepts and tools to create behaviors that will create individual and societal well-being.

Social media Independent and commercial online social networks where people congregate to socialize and share messages, opinions, pictures, videos, and other content.

Social selling Using online, mobile, and social media to engage customers, build stronger customer relationships, and augment sales performance.

Societal marketing A company should make marketing decisions by considering consumers' wants, the company's requirements, consumers' long-run interests, and society's long-run interests.

Societal marketing concept The idea that a company's marketing decisions should consider consumers' wants, the company's requirements, consumers' long-run interests, and society's long-run interests.

Spam Unsolicited, unwanted commercial email messages.

Specialty product A consumer product with unique characteristics or brand identification for which a significant group of buyers is willing to make a special purchase effort.

Specialty store A retail store that carries a narrow product line with a deep assortment within that line.

Standardized global marketing A global marketing strategy that basically uses the same marketing strategy and mix in all of the company's international markets.

Store brand (or private brand) A brand created and owned by a reseller of a product or service.

Straight product extension Marketing a product in a foreign market without making significant changes to the product.

Straight rebuy A business buying situation in which the buyer routinely reorders something without any modifications.

Strategic planning The process of developing and maintaining a strategic fit between the organization's goals and capabilities and its changing marketing opportunities.

Style A basic and distinctive mode of expression.

Subculture A group of people with shared value systems based on common life experiences and situations.

Supermarket A large, low-cost, low-margin, high-volume, self-service store that carries a wide variety of grocery and household products.

Superstore A store much larger than a regular supermarket that offers a large assortment of routinely purchased food products, non-food items, and services.

Supplier development Systematic development of networks of supplier-partners to ensure a dependable supply of products and materials for use in making products or reselling them to others.

Supply chain management Managing upstream and downstream value-added flows of materials, final goods, and related information among suppliers, the company, resellers, and final consumers.

Survey research Gathering primary data by asking people questions about their knowledge, attitudes, preferences, and buying behavior.

Sustainable marketing Socially and environmentally responsible marketing that meets the present needs of consumers and businesses while also preserving or enhancing the ability of future generations to meet their needs.

SWOT analysis An overall evaluation of the company's strengths (S), weaknesses (W), opportunities (O), and threats (T).

Systems selling (or solutions selling) Buying a complete solution to a problem from a single seller, thus avoiding all the separate decisions involved in a complex buying situation.

Target costing Pricing that starts with an ideal selling price, then targets costs that will ensure that the price is met.

Target market A set of buyers sharing common needs or characteristics that the company decides to serve.

Team selling Using teams of people from sales, marketing, engineering, finance, technical support, and even upper management to service large, complex accounts.

Team-based new product development New product development in which various company departments work closely together, overlapping the steps in the product development process to save time and increase effectiveness.

Technological environment Forces that create new technologies, creating new product and market opportunities.

Telemarketing Using the telephone to sell directly to customers.

Territorial sales force structure A sales force organization that assigns each salesperson to an exclusive geographic territory in which that salesperson sells the company's full line.

Test marketing The stage of new product development at which the product and its proposed marketing program are tested in realistic market settings.

Third-party logistics (3PL) provider An independent logistics provider that performs any or all of the functions required to get a client's product to market.

Total costs The sum of the fixed and variable costs for any given level of production.

Total market demand The total volume that would be bought by a defined consumer group in a defined geographic area in a defined time period in a defined marketing environment under a defined level and mix of industry marketing effort.

Total market strategy Integrating ethnic themes and cross-cultural perspectives within a brand's mainstream marketing, appealing to consumer similarities across subcultural segments rather than differences.

Trade promotions Sales promotion tools used to persuade resellers to carry a brand, give it shelf space, promote it in advertising, and push it to consumers.

Undifferentiated (mass) marketing A market-coverage strategy in which a firm decides to ignore market segment differences and go after the whole market with one offer.

Unit contribution The amount that each unit contributes to covering fixed costs—the difference between price and variable costs.

Unsought product A consumer product that the consumer either does not know about or knows about but does not normally consider buying.

Value-added pricing Attaching value-added features and services to differentiate a company's offers and charging higher prices.

Value-based pricing Offering just the right combination of quality and good service at a fair price.

Value chain The series of internal departments that carry out value-creating activities to design, produce, market, deliver, and support a firm's products.

Value delivery network A network composed of the company, suppliers, distributors, and, ultimately, customers who partner with each other to improve the performance of the entire system in delivering customer value.

Value proposition The full positioning of a brand-the full mix of benefits on which it is differentiated and positioned.

Value-added pricing Attaching value-added features and services to differentiate a company's offers and charging higher prices.

Variable costs Costs that vary directly with the level of production.

Vertical marketing system (VMS) A channel structure in which producers, wholesalers, and retailers act as a unified system. One channel member owns the others, has contracts with them, or has so much power that they all cooperate.

Viral marketing The digital version of word-of-mouth marketing: videos, ads, and other marketing content that is so infectious that customers will seek it out or pass it along to friends.

Wants The form human needs take as they are shaped by culture and individual personality.

Warehouse club An off-price retailer that sells a limited selection of brand name grocery items, appliances, clothing, and other goods at deep discounts to members who pay annual membership fees.

Whole-channel view Designing international channels that take into account the entire global supply chain and marketing channel, forging an effective global value delivery network.

Wholesaler A firm engaged primarily in wholesaling activities.

Wholesaling All the activities involved in selling goods and services to those buying for resale or business use.

Word-of-mouth influence The impact of the personal words and recommendations of trusted friends, family, associates, and other consumers on buying behavior.

Workload method An approach to determining sales force size based on the workload required and the time available for selling.

References

Chapter 1

1. Mark Fidelman, "Nike Is Dominating the World Cup—Here's Why," *Forbes*, July 1, 2014, www.forbes.com/sites/markfidelman/2014/07/01/nike-is-dominating-the-world-cup-heres-why/; Grace Chung, "Non-Sponsor Nike Trounces Adidas for World Cup Video Views," *Advertising Age*, July 14, 2014, http://adage.com/print/294114/; Scott Cendrowski, "Nike's New Marketing Mojo," *Fortune*, February 13, 2012, http://fortune.com/2012/02/13/nikes-new-marketing-mojo/; Mary Lisbeth D'Amico, "Report Sends Nike and Adidas to Head of Digital Marketing Class," *Clickz*, September 25, 2012, www.clickz.com/clickz/news/2208172/report-sends-nike-and-adidas-to-head-of-digital-marketing-class; Daniel Newman, "Risk Everything: Nike Does for World Cup 2014, and Wins!" *Forbes*, June 9, 2014, www.forbes.com/sites/danielnewman/2014/06/09/risk-everything-nike-does-for-world-cup-2014-and-wins/; "Top Ad Campaigns of the 21st Century: 2—Nike+," *Advertising Age*, http://adage.com/lp/top15/#nikeplus, accessed June 2015; and http://investors.nikeinc.com/Investors and https://secure-nikeplus.nike.com/plus/, accessed September 2015.
2. See "Leading Social Networks Worldwide," www.statista.com/statistics/272014/global-social-networks-ranked-by-number-of-users/, accessed June 2015; Justin Fox, "Still Sweet on Coke and Pepsi?" *Bloomberg View*, January 15, 2015, www.bloombergview.com/articles/2015-01-21/still-sweet-on-coke-and-pepsi; and "Top 250 Global Retailers, 2015," *National Retail Federation*, https://nrf.com/2015/global250-table.
3. See Philip Kotler and Kevin Lane Keller, *Marketing Management*, 15th ed. (Hoboken, NJ: Pearson Education, 2016), p. 5.
4. The American Marketing Association offers the following definition: "Marketing is the activity, set of institutions, and processes for creating, communicating, delivering, and exchanging offerings that have value for customers, clients, partners, and society at large." See www.marketingpower.com/_layouts/Dictionary.aspx?dLetter=M, accessed September 2015.
5. See Daniel P. Smith, "Keep in Touch," *QSR Magazine*, July 2013, www.qsrmagazine.com/executive-insights/keep-touch; and Phil Wahba, "Back on Target," *Fortune*, March 1, 2015, p. 86–94.
6. See Samantha Shankman, "The Simple Message behind San Diego's $9 Million Ad Campaign," *Skift*, February 5, 2015, http://skift.com/2015/02/05/the-simple-message-behind-san-diegos-9-million-ad-campaign/; and http://stoptextsstopwrecks.org/#home, accessed September 2015.
7. See Theodore Levitt's classic article, "Marketing Myopia," *Harvard Business Review*, July–August 1960, pp. 45–56. For more recent discussions, see Minette E. Drumright and Mary C. Gentile, "The New Marketing Myopia," *Journal of Public Policy & Marketing*, Spring 2010, pp. 4–11; Roberto Friedmann, "What Business Are You In?" *Marketing Management*, Summer 2011, pp. 18–23; and Al Ries, "'Marketing Myopia' Revisited: Perhaps a Narrow Vision Is Better Business," *Advertising Age*, December 4, 2013, http://adage.com/print/245511.
8. See www.americangirl.com/stores/, accessed September 2015.
9. See https://play.google.com/store/apps/details?id=co.vine.android, accessed September 2015.
10. "The Difference in Creating Companies and Categories," *happycustomer*, March 4, 2014, http://happycustomer.stellaservice.com/2014/03/04/column-the-difference-in-creating-companies-and-categories/.
11. See Michael E. Porter and Mark R. Kramer, "Creating Shared Value," *Harvard Business Review*, January–February 2011, pp. 63–77; Marc Pfitzer, Valerie Bockstette, and Mike Stamp, "Innovating for Shared Value," *Harvard Business Review*, September 2013, pp. 100–107; "About Shared Value," *Shared Value Initiative*, http://sharedvalue.org/about-shared-value, accessed September 2015; and "Shared Value," www.fsg.org, accessed September 2015.
12. Michael Krauss, "Evolution of an Academic: Kotler on Marketing 3.0," *Marketing News*, January 30, 2011, p. 12; and Simon Mainwaring, "Marketing 3.0 Will Be Won by Purpose-Driven, Social Brands," *Forbes*, July 16, 2013, www.forbes.com/sites/simonmainwaring/2013/07/16/marketing-3-0-will-be-won-by-purpose-driven-social-brands-infographic/.
13. See Scott Campbell, "Lush Defies the Christmas Retail Slump," *The Telegraph*, January 6, 2014, www.telegraph.co.uk/finance/newsbysector/retailandconsumer/10554068/Lush-defies-the-Christmas-retail-slump.html; and "Lush Life: We Believe," www.lushusa.com/on/demandware.store/Sites-Lush-Site/en_US/AboutUs-OurStoryShow?cid=we-believe, accessed September 2015.
14. Based on information from Keenan Mayo, "A Cooler Fit for the Apocalypse," *Bloomberg Businessweek*, October 28–November 3, 2013, p. 62, and http://store.yeticoolers.com/, accessed September 2015.
15. See Stuart Elliott, "Putting on the Ritz, Six Words at a Time," *New York Times*, May 29, 2015, p. B11; Michael Bush, "Why You Should Be Putting on the Ritz," *Advertising Age*, June 21, 2010, p. 1; http://corporate.ritzcarlton.com/en/About/Awards.htm, accessed June 2015; and "Stories That Stay with You," www.ritzcarlton.com/en/StoriesThatStay.htm, accessed September 2015.
16. "Delighting the Customer Doesn't Pay," *Sales & Marketing Management*, November 11, 2013, http://salesandmarketing.com/content/delighting-customers-doesnt-pay.
17. See www.walgreens.com/Balance, accessed September 2015.
18. For more information, see www.apple.com/usergroups/ and www.webernation.com, accessed September 2015.
19. See Gordon Wyner, "Getting Engaged," *Marketing Management*, Fall 2012, pp. 4–9; David Aponovich, "Powered by People, Fueled by Optimism," *Fast Company*, July 18, 2012, www.fastcompany.com/1842834/life-good-powered-people-fueled-optimism; Celia Brown, "Life is good Redefines Retailing through Joy," *Forbes*, January 17, 2014, www.forbes.com/sites/sap/2014/01/17/life-is-good-redefines-retail-through-joy/; and www.lifeisgood.com and www.lifeisgood.com/good-vibes/, accessed September 2015.
20. See http://mystarbucksidea.force.com, accessed September 2015.
21. "2014 USA Today Ad Meter," http://admeter.usatoday.com/, accessed February 2015; "How a $2,000 Doritos Super Bowl Ad Became a Million-Dollar Sensation," *Washington Post*, February 4, 2015, www.washingtonpost.com/news/grade-point/wp/2015/02/04/how-a-2000-doritos-super-bowl-ad-became-a-million-dollar-sensation/; and www.doritos.com/, accessed September 2015.
22. See "#Bashtag: Avoiding User Outcry in Social Media," *WordStream*, March 8, 2013, www.wordstream.com/blog/ws/2013/03/07/bashtag-avoiding-social-media-backlash; and "What Is Hashtag Hijacking?" *Small Business Trends*, August 18, 2013, http://smallbiztrends.com/2013/08/what-is-hashtag-hijacking-2.html.
23. See www.stewleonards.com/about-us/company-story, accessed September 2015.
24. See Mai Erne, "Calculating Customer Lifetime Value," HaraPartners, www.harapartners.com/blog/calculating-lifetime-value/, accessed September 2015.
25. See Timothy Stenovec, "Amazon Prime Members Spend an Astonishing $1,500 a Year, Survey Says," *Huffington Post*, January 27, 2015, www.huffingtonpost.com/2015/01/27/amazon-prime-spending_n_6556374.html; Brad Stone, "What's in the Box? Instant Gratification, *Bloomberg Businessweek*, November 29–December 5, 2010, pp. 39–40; and www.amazon.com/gp/prime/ref=footer_prime, accessed September 2015.
26. For more discussions on customer equity, see Roland T. Rust, Valerie A. Zeithaml, and Katherine N. Lemon, *Driving Customer Equity* (New York: Free Press, 2000); Roland T. Rust, Katherine N. Lemon, and Valerie A. Zeithaml, "Return on Marketing: Using Customer Equity to Focus Marketing Strategy," *Journal of Marketing*, January 2004, pp. 109–127; Christian Gronroos and Pekka Helle, "Return on Relationships: Conceptual Understanding and Measurement of Mutual Gains from Relational Business Engagements," *Journal of Business & Industrial Marketing*, Vol. 27, No. 5, 2012, pp. 344–359; and Peter C. Verhoef and Katherine N. Lemon, "Successful Customer Value Management: Key Lessons and Emerging Trends," *European Management Journal*, February 2013, p. 1.
27. This example is based on one found in Rust, Lemon, and Zeithaml, "Where Should the Next Marketing Dollar Go?" *Marketing Management*, September–October 2001, pp. 24–28; with information from Grant McCracken, "Provocative Cadillac, Rescuing the Brand from Bland," *Harvard Business Review*, March 4, 2014, http://blogs.hbr.org/2014/03/provocative-cadillac-rescuing-the-brand-from-bland/; Robert Klara. "Cadillac's Image Gets a Tune-Up," *Adweek*, February 23, 2015, p. 13; and www.dare-greatly.com, accessed September 2015.

28. Based on Werner Reinartz and V. Kumar, "The Mismanagement of Customer Loyalty," *Harvard Business Review*, July 2002, pp. 86–94. Also see Chris Lema, "Not All Customers Are Equal—Butterflies & Barnacles," April 18, 2013, http://chrislema.com/not-all-customers-are-equal-butterflies-barnacles/; Jill Avery, Susan Fournier, and John Wittenbraker, "Unlock the Mysteries of Your Customer Relationships," *Harvard Business Review*, July–August 2014, pp. 72–81, and "Telling Customers 'You're Fired,'" *Sales and Marketing.com*, September/October 2014, p. 8.

29. See "Internet Usage Statistics, *Inernet World Stats*, www.internetworldstats.com/stats.htm; accessed June 2015; and "Mobile Technology Fact Sheet," www.pewinternet.org/fact-sheets/mobile-technology-fact-sheet/, accessed September 2015.

30. "Digital Set to Surpass TV in Time Spent with US Media," *eMarketer*, August 1, 2013, www.emarketer.com/Article/Digital- Set-Surpass-TV-Time-Spent-with-US-Media/1010096; and Marla Schimke, "Mobile as Marketing's Savior," *Adweek*, December 15, 2014, p. 19.

31. Chris Gayomali, "Brands Are Wasting Their Time and Money on Facebook and Twitter, Report Says," *Fast Company*, November 19, 2014, www.fastcompany.com/3038801; "Greatness Awaits: Sony PlayStation PS4 Launch," *Empowered*, http://groundswelldiscussion.com/groundswell/awards/detail.php?id=1174, accessed June 2015; Roger Katz, "2015 Will Be the Year of the Brand Community—Here's Why," *ClickZ*, January 23, 2015, www.clickz.com/clickz/column/2391666/2015-will-be-the-year-of-the-brand-community-here-s-why; and https://community.petco.com/, http://community.sephora.com/, and http://greatnessawaits.playstation.com/en-us/, accessed September 2015.

32. See Stuart Feil, "How to Win Friends and Influence People," *Adweek*, September 12, 2013, pp. S1–S7; and Salesforce.com "Just Published: 2015 State of Marketing Report," January 13, 2015, http://blogs.salesforce.com/company/2015/01/2015-state-of-marketing.html.

33. See Calla Cofield, "Social Media: NASA's Not So Secret Weapon for the Orion Test Flight," *Space*, December 3, 2014, www.space.com/27912-nasa-orion-spacecraft-social-media-blitz.html; Laura Nichols, "NASA Soars on Social Media with Orion Spacecraft," *PRWeek*, December 18, 2015, www.prweek.com/article/1327011; "By the Letters EFT: Sesame Street Muppets Count Down to NASA Launch," *Collect Space*, November 24, 2014, www.collectspace.com/news/news-112514a-orion-eft1-muppets-countdown.html; and www.nasa.gov, accessed September 2015.

34. Michael Applebaum, "Mobile Magnetism," *Adweek*, June 25, 2012, pp. S1–S9; and Bill Briggs, "M-Commerce Is Saturating the Globe," *Internet Retailer*, February 20, 2014, www.internetretailer.com/2014/02/20/m-commerce-saturating-globe.

35. "Mobile Marketing: How Redbox Drove 1.5 Million Texts and Added 200,000 Mobile Participants in 10 Days," *Marketing Sherpa*, October 6, 2011, www.marketingsherpa.com/article/case-study/how-redbox-drove-15-million; www.youtube.com/watch?v=c1nLbQeXAXc and www.redbox.com/textclub, accessed September 2015.

36. See John Gerzema, "How U.S. Consumers Are Steering the Spend Shift," *Advertising Age*, October 11, 2010, p. 26; Gregg Fairbrothers and Catalina Gorla, "The Decline and Rise of Thrift," *Forbes*, April 23, 2012, www.forbes.com/sites/greggfairbrothers/2012/04/23/the-decline-and-rise-of-thrift/.

37. See "Our Mission," https://corporate.target.com/about/mission-values, accessed June 2015.

38. See Lisa Wirthman, "How a Lemonade Stand Sparked a Movement to Cure Pediatric Cancer," *Forbes*, January 15, 2014; Jennifer Aaker and Andy Smith, "The Dragonfly Effect," *Stanford Social Innovation Review*," Winter 2011, pp. 31–35; and www.alexslemonade.org, accessed September 2015.

39. "100 Leading National Advertisers," *Advertising Age*, July 13, 2015, p. 15.

40. www.aboutmcdonalds.com/mcd and www.nikeinc.com, accessed September 2015.

41. See www.benjerry.com/values, www.benandjerrysfoundation.org and www.unilever.com/brands-in-action/detail/ben-and-jerrys/291995, accessed September 2015.

Chapter 2

1. David Kaplan, "Starbucks: The Art of Endless Transformation," *Inc.*, June, 2014, pp. 82–86+; Laura Lorenzetti, "Fortune's World's Most Admired Companies: Starbucks, Where Innovation Is Always Brewing," *Fortune*, October 30, 2014, http://fortune.com/2014/10/30/starbucks-innovation-cafe-to-classroom/; "Starbucks Corporation: Fiscal 2007 Annual Report," http://media.corporate-ir.net/media_files/irol/99/99518/2007AR.pdf; Julia Hanna, "Starbucks, Reinvented: A Seven-Year Study on Schultz, Strategy, and Reinventing a Brilliant Brand," *Forbes*, August 25, 2014, www.forbes.com/sites/hbsworkingknowledge/2014/08/25/starbucks-reinvented/; http://

roastery.starbucks.com, accessed March 2015; and Starbucks annual reports and other information accessed at www.starbucks.com, September 2015.

2. The NASA mission statement is from www.nasa.gov/about/highlights/what_does_nasa_do.html, accessed June 2015.

3. For more discussion of mission statements and examples, both good and bad, see Jack and Suzy Welch, "State Your Business; Too Many Mission Statements Are Loaded with Fatheaded Jargon. Play It Straight," *BusinessWeek*, January 14, 2008, p. 80; Setayesh Sattari et al., "How Readable Are Mission Statements? An Exploratory Study," *Corporate Communications*," 2011, p. 4; and www.missionstatements.com/fortune_500_mission_statements.html, accessed September 2015.

4. Based on information from Demitrios Kalogeropoulos, "3 Reasons Buffalo Wild Wings Can Keep Soaring in 2015," *The Motley Fool*, January 9, 2015, www.fool.com/investing/general/2015/01/09/3-reasons-why-buffalo-wild-wings-can-keep-soaring.aspx; "Buffalo Wild Wings," a 22SQUARED case study, www.22squared.com/work/project/buffalo-wild-wings, accessed June 2015; Brandon Southward, "The Crowd Goes Wild," *Fortune*, July 22, 2013, p. 18; Tanya Dua, "The Buffalo Wild Wings Recipe for the "Ultimate Sports Experience," *Digiday*, August 4, 2015, http://digiday.com/brands/buffalo-wild-wings-recipe-ultimate-sports-experience/; and www.buffalowildwings.com, accessed September 2015.

5. Information about CVS Health and its mission and activities from www.cvshealth.com/about-us, www.cvshealth.com/about-us/our-story-building-bridge-better-health, and www.cvshealth.com/our-businesses, accessed September 2015.

6. See "General Electric Co.," *Reuters*, www.reuters.com/finance/stocks/companyProfile?symbol=GE.N, accessed June 2015; and www.ge.com/ar2014/assets/pdf/GE_AR14.pdf and www.ge.com/products, accessed September 2015.

7. The following discussion is based in part on information found at www.bcg.com/documents/file13904.pdf, accessed September 2015.

8. See http://corporate.disney.go.com/investors/annual_reports.html, accessed September 2015.

9. H. Igor Ansoff, "Strategies for Diversification," *Harvard Business Review*, September–October 1957, pp. 113–124.

10. Information about Under Armour in this section is from Sarah Meehan, "Here's How Much Under Armour Spent on Marketing Last Year," *Business Journal*, February 24, 2015, www.bizjournals.com/baltimore/news/2015/02/24/heres-how-much-under-armour-spent-on-marketing.html?page=all; Bradley Seth McNew, "2 Ways Under Armour Inc Can Continue to Soar in 2015," *The Motley Fool*, December 15, 2014, www.fool.com/investing/general/2014/12/15/2-ways-under-armour-can-continue-soaring-in-2015.aspx; Nick Gardetto, "Under Armour: Growth at an Expensive Price," *Seeking Alpha*, July 31, 2014, http://seekingalpha.com/article/2364655; and various pages at www.underarmour.com and http://investor.underarmour.com, accessed September 2015.

11. See Michael E. Porter, *Competitive Advantage: Creating and Sustaining Superior Performance* (New York: Free Press, 1985); and Michael E. Porter, "What Is Strategy?" *Harvard Business Review*, November–December 1996, pp. 61–78. Also see "The Value Chain," www.quickmba.com/strategy/value-chain, accessed June 2015; and Philip Kotler and Kevin Lane Keller, *Marketing Management*, 15th ed. (Hoboken, NJ: Prentice Hall, 2016), Chapter 2.

12. Nirmalya Kumar, "The CEO's Marketing Manifesto," *Marketing Management*, November–December 2008, pp. 24–29; and Tom French and others, "We're All Marketers Now," *McKinsey Quarterly*, July 2011, www.mckinseyquarterly.com/Were_all_marketers_now_2834.

13. See www.gapinc.com/content/gapinc/html/aboutus/ourbrands/gap.html, accessed September 2015.

14. "100 Leading National Advertisers," *Advertising Age*, June 23, 2014, p. 16.

15. The four Ps classification was first suggested by E. Jerome McCarthy, *Basic Marketing: A Managerial Approach* (Homewood, IL: Irwin, 1960). The four As are discussed in Jagdish Sheth and Rajendra Sisodia, *The 4 A's of Marketing: Creating Value for Customer, Company and Society* (New York: Routledge, 2012); and Kotler and Keller, *Marketing Management*, p. 26.

16. Tim Dunn, "Is the Era of CMO Over?" *Adweek*, March 2, 2015, p. 14.

17. "Study Finds Marketers Don't Practice ROI They Preach," *Advertising Age*, March 11, 2012, http://adage.com/article/233243/; "Accountability Remains Senior Marketers' Top Concern," *Marketing Charts*, March 7, 2013, www.marketingcharts.com/wp/topics/branding/accountability-remains-senior-marketers-top-concern-27565/; "Quantitative Proof of Marketing Spend's ROI Still Eludes CMOs," *Marketing Charts*, February 21, 2014, www.marketingcharts.com/wp/traditional/quantitative-proof-of-marketing-spends-impact-still-eludes-cmos-40005/; and Christine Moorman, "From Marketing Spend to Marketing Accountability," *Marketing News*, May 2014, pp. 24–25.

18. For more on marketing dashboards and financial measures of marketing performance, see Ofer Mintz and Imran S. Currim, "What Drives Managerial Use of Marketing Financial Metrics and Does Metric Use Affect Performance of Marketing-Mix Activities?" *Journal of Marketing,* March 2013, pp. 17–40; and http://marketingnpv.com/dashboard-platform, accessed September 2015.

19. For a full discussion of this model and details on customer-centered measures of marketing return on investment, see Roland T. Rust, Katherine N. Lemon, and Valerie A. Zeithaml, "Return on Marketing: Using Customer Equity to Focus Marketing Strategy," *Journal of Marketing,* January 2004, pp. 109–127; Roland T. Rust, Katherine N. Lemon, and Das Narayandas, *Customer Equity Management* (Upper Saddle River, NJ: Prentice Hall, 2005); Roland T. Rust, "Seeking Higher ROI? Base Strategy on Customer Equity," *Advertising Age,* September 10, 2007, pp. 26–27; Andreas Persson and Lynette Ryals, "Customer Assets and Customer Equity: Management and Measurement Issues," *Marketing Theory,* December 2010, pp. 417–436; and Kirsten Korosec, "'Toma- to, Tomäto'? Not Exactly," *Marketing News,* January 13, 2012, p. 8.

Chapter 3

1. Devin Leonard, "Bad News in Cereal City," *Bloomberg Businessweek,* March 2–8, 2015, pp. 42-47; John Kell, "Decline In Cereal Sales Bites Into Kellogg's Results," *Fortune,* October 30, 2014, http://fortune.com/2014/10/30/kellogg-breakfast-sales-drop/; Jack Lanshi, "These 2 Charts Show the Biggest Change in America's Breakfast," *Time,* February 12, 2015, http://time.com/3705987/skipping-breakfast-cereal-kellogg/; and http://investor.kelloggs.com/investor-relations/annual-reports/default.aspx and www.kellogg.com, accessed September 2015.

2. Ginger Christ, "Supplier Relationships Key to Honda's Healthy Profit Margins," *Industry Week,* May 23, 2012, www.industryweek.com/blog/supplier-relationships-key-hondas-healthy-profit-margins; "2014 Annual Automotive OEM-Supplier Relations Study Shows Toyota and Honda on Top," *PR Newswire,* May 12, 2014; and www.hondainamerica.com/parts-and-suppliers and http://world.honda.com/profile/philosophy/, accessed September 2015.

3. Information from Robert J. Benes, Abbie Jarman, and Ashley Williams, "2007 NRA Sets Records," www.chefmagazine.com, accessed September 2007; "Thought Leadership Begins with Experience," *fishbowl,* www.fishbowl.com/coca-cola-offers-restaurant-customers-new-digital-marketing-solutions-powered-by-fishbowl/, accessed September 2015; and www.cokesolutions.com, accessed September 2015.

4. See http://officedepotfoundation.org/, http://officedepotfoundation.org/?page_id=428, http://officedepotfoundation.org/?page_id=164, and http://officedepotfoundation.org/?page_id=196, accessed June 2015. Listen Learn Care® is a registered trademark of Office Depot, Inc.

5. World POPClock, U.S. Census Bureau, at www.census.gov/popclock/, accessed June 2015. This Web site provides continuously updated projections of the U.S. and world populations.

6. U.S. Census Bureau projections and POPClock Projection, at www.census.gov/main/www/popclock.html, accessed September 2015.

7. Charles Kenny, "The Reproductive Recession," *Bloomberg Businessweek,* February 11, 2014, pp. 4–5.

8. See Tracy Sestili, "5 Reasons Why You Should Market to Baby Boomers," *Social Media Today,* January 27, 2014, http://socialmediatoday.com/tracy-sestili/2115511/5-reasons-why-you-should-market-to-baby-boomers-45-65-year-olds; and "50+ Facts and Fiction: Size, Wealth and Spending of 50+ Consumers," *Immersion Active,* March 9, 2015, www.immersionactive.com/resources/size-wealth-spending-50-consumers/.

9. "50+ Facts and Fiction: Mature Consumers Online," *Immersive Action,* March 8, 2015, www.immersionactive.com/resources/50-consumers-online/.

10. See "50+ Active & Healthy Living," www.amazon.com/gp/browse.html/?node=5856180011, accessed June 2015; and http://www.boomnc.com/wp-content/uploads/BOOM-media-kit.pdf, accessed September 2015.

11. For more discussion, see Penney Fox, "Gen X and Social Media: Stuck in the Middle," *Business2Community,* July 9, 2014, www.business2community.com/social-media/gen-x-social-media-stuck-middle-0939476; and "Generations Divided on Device Preferences," February 6, 2015, www.millwardbrown.com/global-navigation/news/press-releases/full-release/2015/02/06/generations-divided-on-device-preferences;

12. See Joe Ruiz, "How Lowe's Is Sustaining Customer Relationships," *Maximize Social Business,* January 27, 2014, http://maximizesocial business.com/lowes-sustaining-customer-relationships-12506/; and www.lowes.com/mobile, www.lowes.com, www.youtube.com/watch?v=zbFX7p6ZGTk, and www.pinterest.com/lowes/, accessed September 2015.

13. See Greg Petro, "Millennial Engagement and Loyalty—Make Them Part of the Process," *Forbes,* March 21, 2013, www.forbes.com/sites/gregpetro/2013/03/21/millennial-engagement-and-loyalty-make-them-part-of-the-process/; and "AT&T's Catherine Borda Spills the Secrets to Millennial Marketing," *Adweek,* March 3, 2015, www.adweek.com/print/163219.

14. Ellen Byron, "Marketing Decoder: Kitchen Appliances for 20-somethings," *Wall Street Journal,* June 25, 2013; Alan Wolf, "GE Develops Kitchen Line for Millennials," *Twice,* July 8, 2013, p. 44; and www.geappliances.com/products/artistry/, accessed September 2015.

15. See "Moxy Milan Malpensa Set to Open in September Followed by a Further Five Hotels in Europe by End of 2015," *Marriott New Center,* March 3, 2014, http://news.marriott.com/moxy-hotels/; "Moxy Hotels Looks to the Future in Europe," Marriott News Center, March 3, 2015, http://news.marriott.com/2015/03/moxy-hotels-looks-to-the-future-in-europe-150-hotels-and-25000-rooms-expected-by-2020.html; and http://moxy-hotels.marriott.com/, accessed September 2015.

16. See Julia Glum, "Marketing to Generation Z," *International Business Times,* January 13, 2015, www.ibtimes.com/marketing-generation-z-millennials-move-aside-brands-shift-focus-under-18-customers-1782220; and Ruth Bernstein, "Move Over Millennials—Here Comes Gen Z," *Advertising Age,* January 21, 2015, www.adage.com/article/cmo-strategy/move-millennials-gen-z/296577/.

17. See "GenZ: Digital in Their DNA"; Shannon Bryant, "'Generation Z' Children More Tech-Savvy; Prefer Gadgets, Not Toys," *Marketing Forecast,* April 3, 2013, www.ad-ology.com/tag/tech-savvy-children/#.U5d9avldV8E; and Brett Relander, "How to Market to Gen Z," *Entrpreneuer,* November 4, 2014, www.entrepreneur.com/article/238998.

18. Robert Klara, "It's Not Easy Being Tween," *Adweek,* June 27, 2012, www.adweek.com/print/141378; Tim Feran, "Retailer Justice Shedding Brothers Brand," *The Columbus Dispatch,* February 19, 2015, www.dispatch.com/content/stories/business/2015/02/18/justice-shedding-brothers-brand.html; and www.shopjustice.com, accessed September 2015.

19. For statistics on family composition, see U.S. Census Bureau, "Family Households," Table F1, www.census.gov/hhes/families/data/cps2014F.html; and U.S. Census Bureau, "Households by Type, Age of Members, Region of Residence, and Age of Householder: 2014," Table H2, www.census.gov/hhes/families/data/cps2014F.html, accessed September 2015.

20. See U.S. Census Bureau, "America's Families and Living Arrangements: 2013," Table FG1, www.census.gov/hhes/families/data/cps2014F.html, accessed June 2015; Claire Cain Miller and Liz Alderman, "The Flexibility Gap," *New York Times,* December 14, 2015, p. BU1; Bruce Horovitz, "Diversity Reaches New Levels in Honey Maid Ads," *USA Today,* March 10, 2014, www.usatoday.com/story/money/business/2014/03/10/honey-maid-mondelez-coca-cola-cheerios-diversity-commercials/6131151/; and U.S. Census Bureau, "Parents and Children in Stay at Home Parent Family Groups: 1994 to Present," Table SHP-1, www.census.gov/hhes/families/files/shp1.xls, accessed September 2015.

21. Based on information from Bruce Horovitz, "Diversity Reaches New Levels in Honey Maid Ads," *USA Today,* March 10, 2014, www.usatoday.com/story/money/business/2014/03/10/honey-maid-mondelez-coca-cola-cheerios-diversity-commercials/6131151/; and www.youtube.com/watch?v=2xeanX6xnRU, accessed September 2015.

22. U.S. Census Bureau, "Geographical Mobility/Migration," www.census.gov/population/www/socdemo/migrate.html, accessed September 2015.

23. See U.S. Census Bureau, "Metropolitan and Micropolitan Statistical Areas," www.census.gov/population/metro/data/index.html, accessed June 2015; U.S. Census Bureau, "Census Estimates Show New Patterns of Growth Nationwide," April 5, 2012, www.census.gov/newsroom/releases/archives/population/cb12-55.html; and "The 536 Micropolitan Statistical Areas of the United States of America," *Wikipedia,* http://en.wikipedia.org/wiki/List_of_Micropolitan_Statistical_Areas, accessed September 2015.

24. Mary C. Noonan and Jennifer L. Glass, "The Hard Truth about Telecommuting," *Monthly Labor Review,* June 2012, www.bls.gov/opub/mlr/2012/06/art3full.pdf; and "It's Unclearly Defined, but Telecommuting Is Fast on the Rise," *New York Times,* March 8, 2014, p. B5.

25. See "About WebEx," www.webex.com/why-webex/overview.html, accessed June 2015; www.gotomeeting.com, accessed June 2015; and "What Is Cloud Computing?" www.salesforce.com/cloudcomputing, accessed September 2015.

26. See http://nextspace.us/, http://grindspaces.com, and www.regus.com, accessed September 2015.

27. U.S. Census Bureau, "Educational Attainment," www.census.gov/hhes/socdemo/education/data/cps/2014/tables.html, accessed June 2015.

28. See U.S. Census Bureau, "The 2012 Statistical Abstract: Education," Tables 229 and 276, www.census.gov/compendia/statab/cats/education .html; and U.S. Department of Labor, "Employment Projections: 2012–2022 Summary," December 19, 2013, www.bls.gov/news.release/ecopro .nr0.htm.

29. See U.S. Census Bureau, "Projections of the Size and Composition of the U.S. Population: 2014 to 2060," March 2015, www.census.gov/ content/dam/Census/library/publications/2015/demo/p25-1143.pdf; and "Multicultural Consumers by the Numbers," *Advertising Age,* April 6, 2015, p. 20.

30. See "Ads Targeting Asian Americans in the U.S., Multicultural Marketing Resources, http://multicultural.com/multicultural_markets/asian-american, accessed June 2015; Marilyn Much, "More Firms Reach Out To Asian Americans," *Investors.com,* September 29, 2003, http://news.investors .com; and www.chineseparade.com/, www.southwest.com/asianoutreach/, access September 2015.

31. Witeck Communications, "America's LGBT 2013 Buying Power Estimated at $830 Billion," November 18, 2013, www.witeck.com/pressreleases/ lgbt-2013-buying-power.

32. For more discussion, see Stuart Elliott, "Commercials with a Gay Emphasis Are Moving to Mainstream Media," *New York Times,* June 26, 2013, p. B3; "Ad Campaigns Are Finally Reflecting Diversity of U.S.," *Advertising Age,* March 10, 2014, http://adage.com/print/292023; Kristina Monllos, "This Is Tiffany's First Engagement Ad to Feature a Same-Sex Couple," *Adweek,* January 12, 2015, www.adweek.com/print/162310; and www.aa.com/rainbow, www.facebook.com/AARainbowTeam, and http:// toddallthetime.com/Allstate-LGBT, accessed September 2015.

33. Witeck-Combs Communications, "America's Disability Market at a Glance," www.witeck.com/wp/files/Americas-Disability-Market-at-a-Glance-FINAL-5-25-2006.pdf; U.S. Census Bureau, "Nearly 1 in 5 People Have a Disability in the U.S., Census Bureau Reports," press release, July 25, 2012, www.census.gov/newsroom/releases/archives/miscellaneous/cb12-134 .html; and Christina Ng, "Huge Demographic Virtually Invisible in Media Wants to Be Seen," *ABC News,* May 29, 2013, http://abcnews.go.com/ Business/disabled-community-media-marketing/story?id=19143489.

34. "Ad of the Day: Paralympic Snowboarder Amy Purdy Perseveres in Toyota's Super Bowl Spot," *Adweek,* January 26, 2015, www.adweek.com/ print/162542.

35. See Rob Walker, "Tiffany & Co: At What Point Does Affordable Luxury Prove Costly?" *Euromonitor International,* June 25, 2014, http://blog .euromonitor.com/2014/06/tiffany-co-at-what-point-does-affordable-luxury-prove-costly.html; and "Tiffany Moves Down Market and Makes a Mint," *Bloomberg Businessweek,* May 21, 2014, www.bloomberg.com/ bw/articles/2014-05-21/tiffany-moves-down-market-and-makes-a-mint.

36. See U.S. Census Bureau, "Income and Poverty in the United States: 2013," Table 2, p. 17, September 2014, www.census.gov/content/dam/ Census/library/publications/2014/demo/p60-249.pdf.

37. Drew Harwell, "Meet the Secret Army of Meteorologists Who Keep Your Holiday Deliveries on Time," *The Washington Post,"* December 8, 2014, www.washingtonpost.com/business/economy/meet-the-secret-army-of-meteorologists-who-keep-your-holiday-deliveries-on-time/2014/12/08/ 2d9d3c82-759d-11e4-9d9b-86d397daad27_story.html.

38. The 2030 Water Resources Group, www.2030wrg.org, accessed June 2015; and "The World's Water," *Pacific Institute,* www.worldwater.org/ data.html, accessed September 2015.

39. Information from www.timberland.com, http://responsibility.timberland. com/, and http://community.timberland.com/earthkeeping/earthkeepers-collection, accessed June 2015.

40. See "Burberry Introduces Smart Personalization for Shoppers," *Integer,* March 25, 2013, http://shopperculture.integer.com/2013/03/ burberry-introduces-smart-personalization-for-shoppers.html; and "Tracking Customers' Shopping Data: RFIDs, Barcodes or QR Codes?" April 6, 2015, www.bigdata-madesimple.com/tracking-customers-shopping-data-rfids-barcodes-or-qr-codes/.

41. See "A $1 Billion Project to Remake the Disney World Experience, Using RFID," www.fastcodesign.com/1671616/a-1-billion-project-to-remake-the-disney-world-experience-using-rfid#1; Brooks Barnes, "At Disney Parks, a Bracelet Meant to Build Loyalty (and Sales), *New York Times,* January 7, 2013, p. B1; and Claire Swedberg, "MagicBands Bring Convenience, New Services to Walt Disney World," *RFID Journal,* June 16, 2014, www.rfidjournal.com/articles/view?11877.

42. See www.shakeshack.com/tag/great-american-shake-sale/ and www .itcanwait.com, accessed September 2015.

43. See "Warby Parker: Do Good," www.warbyparker.com/do-good/#home, accessed June 2015.

44. John Biggs, "Three Things Warby Parker Did to Launch a Successful Lifestyle Brand," *TechCrunch,* May 7, 2013, http://techcrunch .com/2013/05/07/the-three-things-warby-parker-did-to-launch-a-successful-lifestyle-brand/.

45. See "Statistics Every Cause Marketer Should Know," www .causemarketingforum.com/site/c.bkLUKcOTLkK4E/b.6448131/k.262B/ Statistics_Every_Cause_Marketer_Should_Know.htm, accessed September 2015.

46. See www.yogiproducts.com/ and www.yogiproducts.com/our-story/our-story/, accessed September 2015.

47. Sherry Turkle, "The Flight from Conversation," *New York Times,* April 22, 2012, p. SR1.

48. See Brent Snavely, "Chrysler Keeps 'Imported from Detroit' Tagline," *USA Today,* April 24, 2013; and "Apple Kicks Off 'Made in USA' Marketing Push with High-End Mac Pro," *Advertising Age,* December 19, 2013, http://adage.com/print/245765/.

49. See "Natural and Organic Foods and Beverages in the U.S., 4th Edition," *PR Newswire,* December 22, 2014, www.prnewswire.com/ news-releases/natural-and-organic-foods-and-beverages-in-the-us-4th-edition-300013041.html.

50. Based on information from various pages at www.annies.com, accessed September 2015.

51. The Pew Forum on Religion & Public Life, "Nones on the Rise," www .pewforum.org/Unaffiliated/nones-on-the-rise.aspx, accessed October 9, 2012; and http://religions.pewforum.org/, accessed September 2015.

52. For more discussion, see Diana Butler Bass, "The End of Church," *Huffington Post,* February 18, 2012, www.huffingtonpost.com/diana-butler-bass/the-end-of-church_b_1284954.html.

53. See Brad Tuttle, "McDonald's Made the Right Move in Response to Gross 'Pink Slime,'" *Time,* February 5, 2014, http://time.com/4680/ mcdonalds-made-the-right-move-in-response-to-gross-pink-slime/; www.youtube.com/watch?v=Ua5PaSqKD6k, accessed September 2015; Bruce Horovitz, "McDonald's to Customers: Ask about Food Quality," *USA Today,* October 13, 2014, www.usatoday.com/story/ money/business/2014/10/13/mcdonalds-fast-food-food-quality-restauants/17213145/; and www.mcdonalds.com/us/en/your_questions/ our_food.html, accessed September 2015.

Chapter 4

1. Jonathon Ringen, "When It Clicks, It Clicks," *Fast Company,* February 2015, pp. 72–78+; Jacob Davidson, "LEGO Is Now the Largest Toy Company in the World," *Money,* September 4, 2014, http://time.com/ money/3268065/lego-largest-toy-company-mattel/; Katarina Gustafsson, "Rebuilding LEGOs for Today's Kids," *Businessweek,* November 7, 2013, www.businessweek.com/printer/articles/166234; Andrew Jack, "How LEGO Took to Anthropology," *Financial Times,* February 26, 2014, www.ft.com/cms/s/0/b071990c-9d4c-11e3-a599-00144feab7de .html#axzz3N8u6XIPH; Roar Rude Trangbaek, "LEGO Friends Doubled Expectations for Sales in 2012," February 21, 2013, www.lego .com/en-us/aboutus/news-room/2013/february/lego-friends-doubled-expectations-for-sales-in-2012; Christian Madsbjerg and Mikkel B. Rasmussen, "An Anthropologist Walks into a Bar…," *Harvard Business Review,* March, 2014, pp. 80–88; Nicole Lee, "Lego Fusion Lets You Build Virtual Playground with Real-World Bricks," *engadget,* June 19, 2014, www.engadget.com/2014/06/19/lego-fusion/; and www.lego.com, September 2015. LEGO, MINDSTORMS, NINJAGO, and LEGENDS OF CHIMA are Trademarks of the LEGO Group of Companies, used here by permission. © 2015 The LEGO Group. All rights reserved.

2. See Craig Smith, "By the Numbers: 175 Amazing Pinterest Statistics," *Digital Marketing Ramblings,* January 2, 2015, http://expandedramblings .com/index.php/pinterest-stats/; and Kerry Flynn, "Get Ready to See More Ads on Pinterest in 2015," *Huffington Post,* December 29, 2014, www .huffingtonpost.com/2014/12/29/pinterest-ads_n_6390662.html.

3. See "Big Data," *Wikipedia,* http://en.wikipedia.org/wiki/Big_data, accessed February 2015; and Michael Lev-Ram, "What's the Next Big Thing in Big Data? Bigger Data," *Fortune,* June 16, 2014, pp. 233–240.

4. See a detailed description at "Customer Insights Analyst," http://jobs .geico.com/geico/customer-insights-analyst, accessed September 2015.

5. See www.walmartstores.com/Suppliers/248.aspx, accessed February 2015; and "Retail Link 2.0," *8th & Walton,* http://blog.8thandwalton .com/2014/08/retail-link-2-0/, accessed September 2015.

6. Based on information from "Macy's: 150+ Years of Customer Centricity," *Slideshare,* February 22, 2013, www.slideshare.net/imediaconnection/2013-

2brandmacys; Allison Schiff, "Macy's CMO Shares Loyalty Insights at NRF Big Show," *Direct Marketing News*, January 16, 2012, www.dmnews.com/macys-cmo-shares-loyalty-insights-at-nrf-big-show/article/223344/; Emily Heitkamp, "Macy's Strategic Customer Focus: Love Your Loyals," *loyalty360*, September 19, 2013, http://loyalty360.org/resources/article/macys-strategic-customer-focus-love-your-loyals; and "Macy's Focuses on the Customer; Builds Comprehensive View Across Touch Points," Acxiom Case Study, www.acxiom.com/resources/macys-focuses-customer-builds-comprehensive-view-across-touch-points/, accessed September 2015.

7. Example based on information from Michal Lev-Ram, "Samsung's Road to Mobile Domination," *Fortune*, February 4, 2013, pp. 99–101; Jason Gilbert, "Samsung Mocks iPhone 5, Apple Fanboys Again in New Galaxy S3 Commercial," *Huffington Post*, September 1, 2012, www.huffingtonpost.com/2012/09/20/samsung-mocks-iphone-5-commercial_n_1898443.html; Suzanne Vranica, "Tweets Spawn Ad Campaigns," *Wall Street Journal*, October 22, 2012, p. B5; and Luke Villapaz, "Samsung Mocks Apple iPhone 6 and Apple Watch in New Series of Ads," *International Business Times*, September 11, 2014, www.ibtimes.com/samsung-mocks-apple-iphone-6-apple-watch-new-series-ads-video-1685 612.

8. George Chidi, "Confessions of a Corporate Spy," *Inc.*, February 2013, pp. 72–77.

9. For more on research firms that supply marketing information, see Laurence N. Gold, "The 2015 AMA Gold Global Top 50 Report," *Marketing News*, August 2015. Other information from www.nielsen.com/us/en/solutions/measurement/retail-measurement.html and http://thefuturescompany.com/what-we-do/us-yankelovich-monitor, accessed February 2015.

10. See www.iriworldwide.com/SolutionsandServices/Detail.aspx?ProductID=181, accessed September 2015.

11. See www.fisher-price.com/en_US/ourstory/research-at-the-heart/index.html, accessed September 2015.

12. E. J. Schultz, "Tapping into the Secret Town," *Advertising Age*, June 17, 2013, pp. 12–13. For other discussions and examples of ethnographic research in marketing, see Madsbjerg and Rasmussen, "An Anthropologist Walks into a Bar…"; and Christine Birkner, "C'est La Vie," *Marketing News*, June 2014, pp. 23-27.

13. See Birkner, "C'est La Vie"; and "Landor Families," http://landor.com/#!/talk/articles-publications/articles/landor-families/, accessed September 2015.

14. See Rebecca Greenfield, "How the Deepest, Darkest Secrets of Moms Shape the Products in Aisle 6," *Fast Company*, December 19, 2014, www.fastcompany.com/3039798/most-creative-people/how-the-deepest-darkest-secrets-of-moms-shape-the-products-in-aisle-6?utm_source; and www.momcomplex.com, accessed September 2015.

15. Molly Soat, "Everything in Moderation," *Marketing News*, April 2014, pp. 36–46, here p. 38.

16. See "Pew Research Internet Project," *Pew Internet*, February 27, 2014, www.pewinternet.org/2014/02/27/part-1-how-the-internet-has-woven-itself-into-american-life/; and "Internet World Stats," www.internetworldstats.com/stats.htm, accessed September 2015.

17. For more information, see www.focusvision.com and www.youtube.com/watch?v=PG8RZl2dvNY, accessed September 2015.

18. See www.lexusadvisoryboard.com and www.nascarfancouncil.com, accessed September 2015.

19. For more discussion, see "Do-Not-Track Online Act of 2013," www.congress.gov/bill/113th-congress/senate-bill/418; Fred B. Campbell, Jr., "The Slow Death of 'Do Not Track,'" *New York Times*, December 27, 2014, p. A17; and "Do Not Track Legislation," http://en.wikipedia.org/wiki/Do_Not_Track_legislation, accessed September 2015.

20. See Clint Boulton, "Snack Maker Modernizes the Impulse Buy," *Wall Street Journal*, October 17, 2013, p. B4; Aaron Taube, "The Maker of Oreos Has Invented a Store Shelf that Spies on You While You're Shopping," *Business Insider*, October 18, 2013, www.businessinsider.com/mondelez-smart-shelf-technology-2013-10; and "Mondelez Smart Shelf," http://vimeo.com/96148396, accessed September 2015.

21. Based on information from Amy Chozick, "These Lab Specimens Watch 3-D Television," *New York Times*, January 25, 2012, p. B3; Sam Thielman, "Time Warner's Media Lab Knows What You Like to Watch," *Adweek*, February 4, 2013, www.adweek.com/news/technology/time-warner-s-media-lab-knows-what-you-watch-147045; and www.timewarnermedialab.com, accessed September 2015.

22. See Adam L. Penenberg, "NeuroFocus Uses Neuromarketing to Hack Your Brain," *FastCompany*, August 8, 2011, www.fastcompany.com/magazine/158/neuromarketing-intel-paypal; and Carmen Nobel, "Neuromarketing: Tapping into the 'Pleasure Center' of Consumers," *Forbes*, February 2, 2013,

www.forbes.com/sites/hbsworkingknowledge/2013/02/01/neuromarketing-tapping-into-the-pleasure-center-of-consumers/. For other examples and discussion, see Roger Dooley, "Is Starbucks Coffee Too Cheap?" *Forbes*, October 14, 2013, www.forbes.com/sites/rogerdooley/2013/10/14/is-starbucks-coffee-too-cheap/; and Thomas Zoega Ramsey, *Neuromarketing & Consumer Neuroscience* (Rorvig, Denmark: Neurons Inc, 2014).

23. See Jennifer Alsever, "Technology Is the Best Policy," *Fortune*, November 18, 2013; "Built in Record Time, the MetLife Wall Knocks Down Barriers to Great Customer Service," October 23, 2013, www.metlifegto.com/news/Built-in-record-time-the-MetL; and "5 Lessons Learned from the MetLife Wall," *Insurance Networking News*, www.insurancenetworking.com/gallery/5-lessons-learned-from-the-metlife-wall-34261-1.html, accessed September 2015.

24. Andrew Nusca, "Despite High Tech, the Future of Marketing Is Exactly the Same: Focus on Customers," *Fortune*, July 15, 2014, http://fortune.com/2014/07/15/big-data-future-marketing-customer-focus/; and Phani Nagarjuna, "Seven Steps to Understanding Your Business and Monetizing Analytics," *Sales & Marketing Management*, January 9, 2015, http://salesandmarketing.com/content/seven-steps-understanding-your-business-and-monetizing-analytics.

25. For more discussion, see Elizabeth A. Sullivan, "Analytics in Action," *Marketing News*, December 2014, pp. 24-33; and Jayson DeMers, "2014 Is the Year of Digital Marketing Analytics: What It Means for Your Company," *Forbes*, February 2, 2014, www.forbes.com/sites/jaysondemers/2014/02/10/2014-is-the-year-of-digital-marketing-analytics-what-it-means-for-your-company/.

26. Avi Dan, "How Data Nourishes Agile Marketing at Kraft," *Forbes*, October 26, 2014, www.forbes.com/sites/avidan/2014/10/26/how-data-nourishes-agile-marketing-at-kraft-foods/; and Jack Neff, "Kraft Says Content Delivers Four Times Better ROI than Ads," *Advertising Age*, September 15, 2014, p. 8.

27. "1-800-Flowers.com Customer Connection Blooms with SAS Business Analytics," www.sas.com/success/1800flowers.html, accessed September 2015.

28. See Daryl Travis, "The Best Omni-Channel Brands Look More Like a Cause than a Business," *The Hub*, August 2014, www.hubmagazine.com/the-hub-magazine/zappos-omnivalues-082014/; and https://zuul.zappos.com/zuul/login, accessed September 2015.

29. Based on information in Ann Zimmerman, "Small Business; Do the Research," *Wall Street Journal*, May 9, 2005, p. R3; with additional information and insights from John Tozzi, "Market Research on the Cheap," *BusinessWeek*, January 9, 2008, www.businessweek.com/smallbiz/content/jan2008/sb2008019_352779.htm; "Understanding the Basics of Small Business Market Research," *All Business*, www.allbusiness.com/marketing/market-research/2587-1.html#axzz2K8T92eOR, accessed February 2015; and www.bibbentuckers.com, accessed September 2015.

30. For some good advice on conducting market research in a small business, search "conducting market research" at www.sba.gov or see "Researching Your Market," *Entrepreneur*, www.entrepreneur.com/article/43024-1, accessed September 2015.

31. See "The 2015 AMA Gold Global Top 25 Report," *Marketing News*, August 2015, pp. 34+; and www.nielsen.com/us/en/about-us.html and www.nielsen.com/us/en.html?worldWideSelected=true, accessed August 2015.

32. For these and other examples, see "From Tactical to Personal: Synovate's Tips for Conducting Marketing Research in Emerging Markets," *Marketing News*, April 30, 2011, pp. 20–22. Internet stats are from http://data.worldbank.org/indicator/IT.NET.USER.P2, accessed September 2015.

33. Subhash C. Jain, *International Marketing Management*, 3rd ed. (Boston: PWS-Kent, 1990), p. 338. For more discussion on international marketing research issues and solutions, see Warren J. Keegan and Mark C. Green, *Global Marketing*, 8th ed. (Upper Saddle River, NJ: Prentice Hall, 2015), pp. 170–201.

34. Zach Miners, "Your Control of Your Personal Info Is All but Dead, Pew Respondents Fear," *PCWorld*, November 12, 2014, www.pcworld.com/article/2846855.

35. Based on information from Charles Duhigg, "Psst, You in Aisle 5," *New York Times*, February 19, 2012, p. MM30; and Kashmir Hill, "How Target Figured Out a Teen Girl Was Pregnant before Her Father Did," *Forbes*, February 16, 2012, www.forbes.com/sites/kashmirhill/2012/02/16/how-target-figured-out-a-teen-girl-was-pregnant-before-her-father-did/.

36. See Andrew Roberts, "In Some Stores, All Eyes Are on You," *Bloomberg Businessweek*, December 10, 2012, pp. 32–33; and "EyeSee Mannequin," www.almax-italy.com/en-US/ProgettiSpeciali/EyeSeeMannequin.aspx, accessed September 2014.

37. "ICC/ESOMAR International Code of Marketing and Social Research Practice," www.esomar.org/index.php/codes-guidelines.html, accessed

February 2015. Also see "Respondent Bill of Rights," www.mra-net.org/ga/billofrights.cfm, accessed September 2015.

38. "FTC Complaint Charges Deceptive Advertising by POM Wonderful," September 27, 2010, www.ftc.gov/opa/2010/09/pom.shtm; Ashley Post, "FTC Issues Final Ruling against POM Wonderful," *Inside Counsel. Break News*, January 17, 2013; and Brent Kendall, "Appeals Court Likely to Uphold FTC Ruling on Juice Maker Pom," *Wall Street Journal*, May 2, 2014, www.wsj.com/articles/SB1000142405270230367840457953812 3825242670.

39. Information at www.casro.org/?page=TheCASROCode&hhSearchTerms=%22code+and+standards%22, accessed September 2015.

Chapter 5

1. Quotes and other information from Ben Popkin, "How Harley-Davidson, Inc. Hopes to Gain Market Share," *The Motley Fool*, February 5, 2014, www.fool.com/investing/general/2014/02/05/how-harley-davidson-inc-hopes-to-gain-market-share.aspx; Susanna Hamner, "Harley, You're Not Getting Any Younger," *New York Times*, March 22, 2009, p. BU1; "Thousands of Thundering Motorcycles Rumble through Milwaukee for Harley-Davidson 110th Anniversary Parade," PRNewswire, August 31, 2013, www.prnewswire.com/news-releases/thousands-of-thundering-motorcycles-rumble-through-milwaukee-for-harley-davidson-110th-anniversary-parade-221946591.html; "Harley Owners Group," www.harley-davidson.com/content/h-d/en_US/home/owners/hog.html, accessed March 2014; and various pages at www.harley-davidson.com, accessed September 2015.

2. Consumer expenditure figures from www.cia.gov/library/publications/the-world-factbook/geos/us.html and "Household Final Consumption Expenditure," *The World Bank*, http://data.worldbank.org/indicator/NE.CON.PRVT.CD, accessed September 2015. Population figures from the World POPClock, U.S. Census Bureau, www.census.gov/main/www/popclock.html, accessed September 2015. This Web site provides continuously updated projections of U.S. and world populations.

3. See Danielle Britni, "African Americans Have $1.1 Trillion in Buying Power," *Clutch*, February 2014, www.clutchmagonline.com/2014/02/african-americans-1-1-trillion-dollars-buying-power-putting-good-use; U.S. Census Bureau, "U.S. Population Projections," www.census.gov/population/projections, accessed February 2015; and information from "Reaching Black Consumers," www.reachingblackconsumers.com, accessed September 2015.

4. "U.S. Forest Service and Ad Council Launch New Multimedia Public Service Advertising Effort to Encourage African American Families to Discover Nature," June 7, 2012, www.multivu.com/mnr/62047-us-forest-service-ad-council-psa-african-american-families-discover-nature; "US Forest Service Discover the Forest," National Environmental Justice Conference and Training Program, April 4, 2013, www.scribd.com/doc/134213528/US-Forest-Service-Discover-The-Forest#scribd; "Discovering Nature (African-American Market)," www.adcouncil.org/Our-Campaigns/Family-Community/Discovering-Nature-African-American-Market, accessed February 2015; and www.discovertheforest.org, accessed September 2015.

5. Advertising Age Hispanic Fact Pack, July 28, 2014, pp. 33–37; and "Population Projections," www.census.gov/population/projections/, accessed September 2015.

6. Lisa Gevelber, "Your Next Big Opportunity: The U.S. Hispanic Market," *thinkwithGoogle*, July 2014, www.thinkwithgoogle.com/articles/us-hispanic-market-digital.html; and Lee Vann, "5 Predictions for Hispanic Online Marketing in 2015," *MediaPost*, November 13, 2014, www.mediapost.com/publications/article/238136.

7. Based on information from Dale Buss, "Ram Redoubles Reach-Out to Hispanic Pickup-Truck Buyers," *Forbes*, October 23, 2012, www.forbes.com/sites/dalebuss/2012/10/23/ram-redoubles-reach-out-to-hispanic-pickup-truck-buyers/; Tanya Irwin, "Ram Truck Hispanic Effort 'Most Comprehensive,'" *Marketing Daily*, September 28, 2011, www.mediapost.com/publications/article/159482/?print; Michael D. Hernandez, "Big Brands Target Hispanic Consumers," *USA Today*, September 23, 2013, www.usatoday.com/story/money/business/2013/09/22/big-brands-target-hispanic-consumers/2845009/; and www.youtube.com/watch?v=-q3Ia1BXAg0 and www.ramtrucks-la.com/, accessed September 2015.

8. See Christine Birkner, "Asian-Americans in Focus," *Marketing News*, March 2013, p. 14; "Significant, Sophisticated and Savvy: The Asian American Consumer," December 3, 2013, www.nielsen.com/us/en/insights/reports/2013/significant-sophisticated-and-savvy-the-asian-american-consumer-report-2013.html; U.S. Census Bureau, "Facts for Features: Asian/Pacific American Heritage Month: May 2014," www.census.gov/newsroom/facts-for-features/2014/cb14-ff13.html; and U.S. Census Bureau,

"U.S. Population Projections," www.census.gov/population/projections, accessed September 2015.

9. See Liang Guo, "Crowdsourcing—AT&T and Wong Fu Productions 'Away We Happened,'" *Voices*, November 4, 2013, http://liyangnewmedia.wordpress.com/2013/11/04/crowdsourcing-att-and-wong-fu-productions-away-we-happened/; "Multicultural Media: Rezonate Media, AT&T, Away We Happened," December 28, 2012, www.mediapost.com/publications/article/190095/multicultural-media-rezonate-media-att-away-we.html; and AT&T "Away We Happened," www.effie.org/case_studies/case/2237, accessed September 2015.

10. See Don Ricker, "Swiffer Makes Sweeping Statement about What Makes a Family," *Huffington Post*, January 1, 2014, www.huffingtonpost.com/2014/01/22/swiffer-interracial-amputee-ad-inclusive_n_4639794.html; Stuart Elliott, "New Ad Organization to Promote Cross-Cultural Marketing," *New York Times*, August 30, 2013, www.nytimes.com/2013/08/31/business/media/new-ad-organization-to-promote-cross-cultural-marketing.html?_r=2&; and www.youtube.com/watch?v=Z01qH-jqGBY and www.youtube.com/watch?v=LKuQrKeGe6g, accessed September 2015.

11. Kimberly A. Whitler, "Why Word of Mouth Marketing Is the Most Important Social Media," *Forbes*, July 12, 2014, www.forbes.com/sites/kimberlywhitler/2014/07/17/why-word-of-mouth-marketing-is-the-most-important-social-media.

12. "Mercedes-Benz: Take the Wheel," http://industry.shortyawards.com/nominee/6th_annual/It/mercedes-benz-take-the-wheel, accessed March 2015; and "Take the Wheel," www.wommapedia.org/#section8, accessed September 2015.

13. Kate Taylor, "For McRib Fans, Search for the Sandwich Is Worth the Effort," *Entrepreneur*, November 21, 2013, www.entrepreneur.com//article/230063#; and http://mcriblocator.com, accessed September 2015.

14. Chris Slocumb, "Women Outspend Men 3 to 2 on Technology Purchases," *ClarityQuest*, January 3, 2013, www.clarityqst.com/women-outspend-men-3-to-2-on-technology-purchases/; Bryce Covert, "More Men Go Shopping and Do the Cooking," October 24, 2013, http://thinkprogress.org/economy/2013/10/24/2830121; Sarwant Singh, "Women in Cars: Overtaking Men on the Fast Lane," *Forbes*, May 23, 2014, www.forbes.com/sites/sarwantsingh/2014/05/23/women-in-cars-overtaking-men-on-the-fast-lane/; and D'Vera Cohn and Andrea Caumont, "7 Key Findings about Stay-at-Home Moms," *Fact Tank*, April 8, 2014, www.pewresearch.org/fact-tank/2014/04/08/7-key-findings-about-stay-at-home-moms/.

15. See E. J. Schultz, "Tale of Two Ads: Cheerios 'How to Dad' Campaign Makes U.S. Debut," *Advertising Age*, December 29, 2014, www.adage.com/print/296429; Jack Neff, "Move Over Mom, It's Dad's Turn," *Advertising Age*, January 26, 2014, p. 6; and www.youtube.com/watch?v=6GYxH2-WeZY, accessed September 2015.

16. See Bill Goodwin, "The Undeniable Influence of Kids," *Packaging Design*, October 16, 2013, www.packagingdigest.com/packaging-design/undeniable-influence-kids; "Kids Spending and Influencing Power: $1.2 Trillion Says Leading Ad Firm," Center for Digital Democracy, November 1, 2012, www.democraticmedia.org/kids-spending-and-influencing-power-12-trillion-says-leading-ad-firm; and Michael R. Solomon, *Consumer Behavior*, 10th ed. (Upper Saddle River, NJ: Pearson Publishing, 2013), Chapter 10.

17. For more on the Nielsen PRIZM, visit www.mybestsegments.com, accessed February 2015.

18. See "Microsoft-Nokia Launches Cheap Lumia Phones for Price Sensitive Consumers," *Forbes*, January 15, 2015, www.forbes.com/sites/greatspeculations/2015/01/15/microsoft-nokia-launches-cheap-lumia-phones-for-price-sensitive-consumers/; and "Apple Expected to Increase Marketing Presence Abroad with Low-Cost iPhone," *Advertising Age*, September 10, 2013, www.adage.com/print/244072.

19. See Christopher Heine, "Appliance Brands Are Diving into Digital This Summer," *Adweek*, July 12, 2013, www.adweek.com/news/technology/appliance-brands-are-diving-digital-summer-150989; "KitchenAid 'So Much More' TV Commercial," www.youtube.com/watch?v=tr9KQQL5lgQ, accessed March 2015; and http://blog.kitchenaid.com/, www.pinterest.com/kitchenaidusa/, and www.kitchenaid.com/about-kitchenaid/, accessed September 2015.

20. See Jennifer Aaker, "Dimensions of Measuring Brand Personality," *Journal of Marketing Research*, August 1997, pp. 347–356; and Philip Kotler and Kevin Lane Keller, *Marketing Management*, 15th ed. (Upper Saddle River, New Jersey: Pearson Publishing, 2016), Chapter 6.

21. See "Air on the Side of Humanity," September 17, 2013, www.mullen.com/air-on-the-side-of-humanity/; Shubhodeep Pal, "Inspiration for 2015: The Best Airline Marketing Campaigns from Last Year, *SimpliFlying*, January 8, 2015, http://simpliflying.com/2015/inspiration-2015-best-airline-marketing-2014/; and www.jetblue.com/corporate-social-responsibility/, accessed September 2015.

22. See Abraham H. Maslow, "A Theory of Human Motivation," *Psychological Review, 50* (1943), pp. 370–396. Also see Maslow, *Motivation and Personality*, 3rd ed. (New York: HarperCollins Publishers, 1987); and Michael R. Solomon, *Consumer Behavior,* 11th ed. (Upper Saddle River, NJ: Prentice Hall, 2014), pp. 132–134.

23. See Ellen Moore, "Letter to My Colleague: We Can Do Better," *Adweek,* December 22, 2010, www.adweek.com/news/advertising-branding/letter-my-colleagues-we-can-do-better-104084; and Kelsey Libert and Kristin Tynski, "Research: The Emotions That Make Marketing Campaigns Go Viral," *Harvard Business Review,* October 24, 2013, http://blogs.hbr.org/2013/10/research-the-emotions-that-make-marketing-campaigns-go-viral/.

24. Example based on information found in John Berman, "Shrek Boosts Vidalia Onion Sales," June 29, 2010, http://abcnews.go.com/WN/shrek-boosts-vidalia-onion-sales/story?id=11047273; and "Vidalia Onion Committee Cinches Triple Crown of National Marketing Awards," October 20, 2011, www.vidaliaonion.org/news/vidalia_onion_committee_cinches_triple_crown_of_national_-marketing_awards. Vidalia® is a registered certification mark of Georgia Department of Agriculture.

25. The following discussion draws from the work of Everett M. Rogers. See his *Diffusion of Innovations*, 5th ed. (New York: Free Press, 2003).

26. Based on Rogers, *Diffusion of Innovation*, p. 281. For more discussion, see http://en.wikipedia.org/wiki/Everett_Rogers, accessed September 2015.

27. See "Electric Car Use by Country," *Wikipedia,* http://en.wikipedia.org/wiki/Electric_car_use_by_country, accessed March 2015; and "Plug-In Vehicle Tracker: What's Coming, When," www.pluginamerica.org/vehicles, accessed September 2015.

28. See Corning Gorilla Glass 3 Featured in Micromax Smartphones," *Yahoo! Finance,* August 13, 2014, http://finance.yahoo.com/news/corning-gorilla-glass-3-featured-123101319.html; David Matthews, "Coming in 2015: A Stronger Gorilla Glass for Smartphone Screens," *Fast Company,* November 20, 2014, www.fastcompany.com/3038850; and www.corning.com/AdvancedGlass/GorillaGlass.aspx, accessed September 2015.

29. See "CSX Transportation Takes Delivery of 300th Evolution Series Locomotive from GE," *Bloomberg,* July 19, 2007, www.bloomberg.com/apps/news?pid=newsarchive&sid=a79WICjr0_RI; and www.getransportation.com/locomotives, accessed September 2015.

30. This classic categorization was first introduced in Patrick J. Robinson, Charles W. Faris, and Yoram Wind, *Industrial Buying Behavior and Creative Marketing* (Boston: Allyn & Bacon, 1967). Also see Kotler and Keller, *Marketing Management*, Chapter 7.

31. Based on information from "Six Flags Entertainment Corporation: Improving Business Efficiency with Enterprise Asset Management," July 12, 2012, www-01.ibm.com/software/success/cssdb.nsf/CS/LWIS-8W5Q84?OpenDocument&Site=default&cty=en_us; and www-01.ibm.com/software/tivoli/products/maximo-asset-mgmt/, accessed September 2015.

32. See Kate Maddox, "Seven B-to-B Marketing Trends That Will Shape 2015," *Advertising Age,* January 13, 2015, www.adage.com/print/296518; and "USG 'It's Your World. Build it,'" www.pinterest.com/gyroideasshop/usg-its-your-world-build-it/, accessed September 2015.

33. Robinson, Faris, and Wind, *Industrial Buying Behavior*, p. 14. Also see Kotler and Keller, *Marketing Management*, pp. 198–204.

34. For more ads in this series, see www.accenture.com/us-en/company/overview/advertising/Pages/brand-print-advertising.aspx, accessed September 2015.

35. See www.makino.com, www.youtube.com/user/MakinoMachineTools, www.facebook.com/MakinoMachine, and https://twitter.com/MakinoMachine, accessed September 2015.

Chapter 6

1. Quotes and other information from Christine Champagne and Teressa Iezzi, "Dunkin' Donuts and Starbucks: A Tale of Two Coffee Marketing Giants," *Fast Company,* August 21, 2014, www.fastcocreate.com/3034572; Leslie Patton, "Dunkin' Donuts Adds Jazz to Get Less Pit and More Stop," *Bloomberg Businessweek,* June 7, 2013, www.bloomberg.com/news/2013-06-07/dunkin-donuts-adds-jazz-to-get-less-pit-and-more-stop.html; Janet Adamy, "Battle Brewing: Dunkin' Donuts Tries to Go Upscale, but Not Too Far," *Wall Street Journal,* April 8, 2006, p. A1; "Dunkin' Donuts' Great Eight: Brand Keys Ranks Dunkin' Donuts Number One in Coffee Customer Loyalty for Eighth Straight Year," Dunkin' Donuts Newsroom, February 4, 2014, http://news.dunkindonuts.com; Khushbu Shah, "Starbucks or Dunkin' Donuts? Where America's Coffee Loyalty Lies," *Eater,* January 15, 2015, www.eater.com/2015/1/15/7551497/starbucks-dunkin-donuts-peets-coffee-spending-percent; and www.dunkindonuts.com and www.dunkinbrands.com, accessed March 2015.

2. Susan Berfield, "Can Target Find Its Place in the Big City?" *Bloomberg Businessweek,* January 13, 2014, pp. 18–20; and Rebecca Cooper, "Target Aiming TargetExpress Format at Washington, D.C. Area," *Washington Business Journal,* January 21, 2015, www.bizjournals.com/twincities/news/2015/01/21/target-targetexpress-washington-dc-arlington.html.

3. See "Macy's—Set for Healthy Performance in 2015," *Seeking Alpha,* January 21, 2015, http://seekingalpha.com/article/2836036; Cotton Timberlake, "With Stores Nationwide, Macy's Goes Local," *Bloomberg BusinessWeek,* October 4–10, 2010, pp. 21–22; and Jim Tierney, "Macy's Confident in My Macy's, Magic Selling Customer Engagement Strategies," *Loyalty 360,* August 15, 2013, http://loyalty360.org/resources/article/macys-confident-in-my-macys-magic-selling-customer-engagement-strategies.

4. See www.amazon.com/gp/feature.html?ie=UTF8&docId=1000863021, accessed March 2015.

5. See www.dovemencare.com/, accessed September 2015.

6. See Oliver Wainwright, "Meet GoldieBlox: The Toy Designed to Get Girls Interested in Engineering," *The Guardian,* October 16, 2012, www.theguardian.com/artanddesign/architecture-design-blog/2012/oct/16/goldieblox-toy-girls-engineering-gender; Caroline Bologna, "GoldieBlox Video Tells Parents to Encourage Daughters to Take Risks, Not Fear Failure," *Huffington Post,* December 17, 2014, www.huffingtonpost.com/2014/12/17/goldieblox-music-video-_n_6340660.html; and www.goldieblox.com/, accessed September 2015.

7. "Inside a Department Store's Secret Shopping Service," *Wall Street Journal,* August 11, 2011, www.wsj.com/articles/SB10001424053111904140604576498733634049992; Alanna Greco, "A Day at Saks: Getting Personal with Their Personal Stylists," *Luxe Me Now,* March 12, 2014, http://lmnonline.com/saks-interview/; and www.saksfifthavenue.com/Saks-Stylist, accessed September 2015.

8. See www.vfc.com/brands, accessed September 2015.

9. For more on brand tribes, see Tina Sharkey, "What's Your Tribe?" *Forbes,* January 25, 2012, www.forbes.com/sites/tinasharkey/2012/01/25/whats-your-tribe-tap-into-your-core-consumers-aspirations-like-nike-gatorade-babycenter-and-rei-do/; Seth Godin, *Tribes: We Need You to Lead Us* (Portfolio, 2008); "Brand Tribalism," *Wikipedia,* http://en.wikipedia.org/wiki/Brand_tribalism, accessed September 2015.

10. Lisa Fleisher, "Pumpkin Spice Latte, the Drink That Almost Wasn't," *Wall Street Journal,* August 30, 2013, http://blogs.wsj.com/corporate-intelligence/2013/08/30/pumpkin-spice-latte-the-drink-that-almost-wasnt/; "Everything You Need to Know about the Return of Starbucks Pumpkin Spice Latte," August 20, 2014, http://news.starbucks.com/news/everything-you-need-to-know-about-the-return-of-the-pumpkin-spice-lat; and www.starbucks.com/menu/drinks/espresso/pumpkin-spice-latte, accessed September 2015.

11. See Lisa Jennings, "CKE: Advertising, Turkey Burgers Drive Sales," *Restaurant News,* April 12, 2013, http://nrn.com/latest-headlines/cke-advertising-turkey-burgers-drive-sales; and "Introducing the New Big, Bold Texas BBQ Thickburger from Carl's Jr. and Hardee's," *Yahoo! Finance,* July 21, 2014, http://finance.yahoo.com/news/introducing-big-bold-texas-bbq-120000118.html.

12. See www.patagonia.com/us/ambassadors, accessed September 2015.

13. For this and other information on Experian's Mosaic USA system, see www.experian.com/marketing-services/consumer-segmentation.html and www.experian.com/assets/marketing-services/brochures/mosaic-brochure-october-2014.pdf, accessed September 2015.

14. See www.starbucksfs.com and http://starbucksocs.com/, accessed September 2015.

15. See Jay Moy, "Every Song Has a Place: Coca-Cola, Spotify Launch Groundbreaking Social Music App," June 11, 2013, www.coca-colacompany.com/coca-cola-music/every-song-has-a-place-coca-cola-spotify-launch-groundbreaking-social-music-app; "Coke Retools Teen Campaign in Second Year TV, Packaging Promotion Added to 'The Aah Effect,'" *Advertising Age,* March 26, 2014, www.adage.com/print/292314; and www.coca-cola.com/music, accessed September 2015.

16. See Michael Porter, *Competitive Advantage* (New York: Free Press, 1985), pp. 4–8, 234–236. For a more recent discussion, see Philip Kotler and Kevin Lane Keller, *Marketing Management*, 15th ed. (Upper Saddle River, NJ: Pearson, 2016), p. 221.

17. See Jack Neff, "Laundry Bounces Back by Playing Both Ends Against the Middle," *Advertising Age,* March 23, 2015, p. 28; Serena Ng, "New Tide Churns the Laundry Market," *Wall Street Journal,* September 26, 2013, http://online.wsj.com/news/articles/SB10001424052702304526204579099390487182058; Lauren Coleman-Lochner, "Laundry Detergent Maker Want More Suds," *Bloomberg Businessweek,* October 23, 2014, www.businessweek.com/articles/2014-10-23/laundry-detergent-sales-hurt-

by-water-saving-washing-machines; and www.pg.com/en_US/investors/ financial_reporting/annual_reports.shtml and www.pg.com/en_US/brands/ index.shtml, accessed September 2015.

18. Store information found at www.walmartstores.com, www.wholefoods market.com, and www.kroger.com, accessed September 2015.

19. Sapna Maheshwari, "Stitch Fix and the New Science behind What Women Want to Wear," *BuzzFeed,* September 24, 2014, www.buzzfeed .com/sapna/stitch-fix-and-the-new-science-behind-what-women-want-to-wea#.jcA81lEoW; Bridget Brennan, "The Retailer Redefining Personal Service in Ecommerce," *Forbes,* December 4, 2014, www.forbes.com/ sites/bridgetbrennan/2014/12/04/the-retailer-redefining-personal-service-in-ecommerce/; and www.stitchfix.com/referral/4097702 and www .stitchfix.com, accessed September 2015.

20. See Jay Moye, "The Next Big Thing: How Coke's Venturing & Emerging Brands Team Stays Ahead of Tomorrow's Thirsts," March 6, 2013, www.coca-colacompany.com/innovation/the-next-big-thing-how-cokes-venturing-emerging-brands-team-stays-a-step-ahead-of-tomorrows-thirsts.

21. See Joan Voight, "Marriott Chain Adds Some Local Flavor," *Adweek,* January 7, 2013, p. 9; "Renaissance Hotels Launches New Navigator Program to Help Guests Discover 'Hidden Gems' of Various Cities around the World," January 8, 2013, www.adweek.com/print/146321; and http:// renaissance-hotels.marriott.com/r-navigator, accessed September 2015.

22. See www.shopkick.com/partners and www.shopkick.com/about, accessed September 2015.

23. See www.mymms.com, www.jhaudio.com, http://factory.puma.com/en, and www.harley-davidson.com/content/h-d/en_US/home/hd1-customization .html, accessed September 2015.

24. Mike Shields, "Nike and AKQA Turn People's Running Data into 100,000 Unique Videos," *Wall Street Journal,* January 7, 2015, http://blogs .wsj.com/cmo/2015/01/07/nike-and-akqa-turn-peoples-running-data-into-100000-unique-videos/.

25. See Carolyn Kellogg, "McDonald's Brings Back Happy Meals with Books," *Los Angeles Time,* January 8, 2015, www.latimes.com/books/ jacketcopy/la-et-jc-mcdonalds-happy-meals-with-books-20150108-story .html.

26. Lucia Moses, "Kids and Ads," *Adweek,* March 18, 2014, p. 13.

27. Examples based on information from www.barbie.com/activities/fun_ games/#whats-hot and www.nick.com/club/, accessed September 2015.

28. See "IC3 2013 Internet Crime Report Released," May 2014, www.ic3 .gov/media/annualreports.aspx.

29. SUV sales data furnished by www.WardsAuto.com, accessed March 2015. Price data from www.edmunds.com, accessed September 2015.

30. See "Zappos Family Core Values," http://about.zappos.com/our-unique-culture/zappos-core-values; and http://about.zappos.com/, accessed September 2015.

31. David Rohde, "The Anti-Walmart: The Secret Sauce of Wegmans Is People," *The Atlantic,* March 23, 2012, www.theatlantic.com/business/ archive/2012/03/the-anti-walmart-the-secret-sauce-of-wegmans-is-people/254994/; and www.wegmans.com, accessed September 2015.

32. See www.heartsonfire.com/Learn-About-Our-Diamonds.aspx, accessed September 2015.

33. See Bobby J. Calder and Steven J. Reagan, "Brand Design," in Dawn Iacobucci, ed., *Kellogg on Marketing* (New York: John Wiley & Sons, 2001), p. 61. For more discussion, see Kotler and Keller, *Marketing Management*, Chapter 10.

Chapter 7

1. Based on information found in Leo Sun, "Will GoPro Stock Pop or Flop in 2015?" *The Motley Fool,* January 5, 2015, www.fool.com/investing/ general/2015/01/05/will-gopro-stock-pop-or-flop-in-2015.aspx; Marty Biancuzzo, "Why GoPro Is Set for a Strong Wall Street Debut," May 21, 2014, www.wallstreetdaily.com/2014/05/21/gopro-ipo/; Tom Foster, "The GoPro Army," *Inc.,* January 26, 2012, www.inc.com/magazine/201202/ the-gopro-army.html; Ryan Mac, "The Mad Billionaire behind GoPro: The World's Hottest Camera Company," *Forbes,* March 3, 2013, www .forbes.com/sites/ryanmac/2013/03/04/the-mad-billionaire-behind-gopro-the-worlds-hottest-camera-company/; Gregory S. McNeal, "GoPro CEO Talks Drones, Innovation and the Future at CES," *Forbes,* January 8, 2015, www.forbes.com/sites/gregorymcneal/2015/01/08/gopro-ceo-talks-drones-innovation-and-the-future-at-ces/; and www.gopro.com and http://-gopro.com/about-us/, accessed September 2015.

2. Based on information from Joshua Brustein, "Verizon Has a Class for You," *Bloomberg Businessweek,* November 20, 2013, www.businessweek .com/articles/2013-11-20/verizon-has-a-class-for-you; Paul Macchia,

"Verizon Wireless' Smart Stores—Enhancing the Customer Experience and Mobile Lifestyle through the Reinvention of Retail," September 8, 2014, www.verizonwireless.com/news/article/2014/09/verizon-wireless-smart-stores-enhancing-the-customer-experience-and-mobile-lifestyle-through-the-reinvention-of-retail.html; and Scott Charlston, "Seattle's U Village Showcases Verizon's Next-Gen Retail," January 27, 2015, www .verizonwireless.com/news/article/2015/01/seattles-u-village-showcases-verizons-next-gen-retail.html.

3. See "The B to B Best Awards 2015," *Advertising Age,* January 26, 2015, p. 28; and "Childlike Imagination—What My Mom Does at GE," www .ge.com/news/advertising, September 2015.

4. See www.neworleansonline.com and www.australia.com/campaigns/ nothinglike/us/index.html, accessed September 2015.

5. For more on social marketing, see Philip Kotler and Nancy Lee, *Social Marketing: Influencing Behaviors for Good,* 4th ed. (Thousand Oaks, CA: Sage Publications, 2011); and www.adcouncil.org and www.i-socialmarketing .org, accessed March 2015.

6. Quotes and definitions from Philip Kotler, *Marketing Insights from A to Z* (Hoboken, NJ: Wiley, 2003), p. 148; and www.asq.org/glossary/q.html, accessed September 2015.

7. See "Thumbs Up for Chick-fil-A," http://press.chick-fil-a.com/Pressroom/ Factsheets/Detail/thumbsup, accessed March 2015.

8. See Nathaniel Wice, "Sonos: The Best Wireless Speakers," *Barrons,* January 3, 2015, http://online.barrons.com/articles/sonos-the-best-wireless-speakers-1420260626; Tim Bradshaw, "Speaker Maker Sonos Raises $140m," *Financial Times,* December 3, 2014, www.ft.com/cms/s/0/ bcf5add4-7ab0-11e4-8646-00144feabdc0.html#axzz3QhVK6ky0; and www.sonos.com, accessed March 2015.

9. Based on information from Gene Weingarten, "Pearls before Breakfast," *Washington Post,* April 8, 2007, www.washingtonpost.com/wp-dyn/ content/article/2007/04/04/AR2007040401721.html; Jessica Contrera, "Joshua Bell's Metro Encore Draws a Crowd," *Washington Post,* September 30, 2014, www.washingtonpost.com/lifestyle/style/joshua-bells-metro-encore-draws-a-crowd/2014/09/30/c28b6c50-48d5-11e4-a046-120a8a855cca_story.html; and "Stop and Hear the Music," www .youtube.com/watch?v=hnOPu0_YWhw, accessed September 2015.

10. See http://cutieskids.com/what-is-a-cutie/, accessed March 2015.

11. See "3 in 4 Grocery Purchase Decisions Being Made In-Store," *MarketingCharts,* May 15, 2012, www.marketingcharts.com/direct/3-in-4-grocery-purchase-decisions-being-made-in-store-22094; "FMI—Supermarket Facts," www.fmi.org/research-resources/supermarket-facts, accessed April 2015; and "Our Retail Divisions," http://news.walmart .com/news-archive/2005/01/07/our-retail-divisions, accessed September 2015.

12. See Mary Mazzoni, "Amazon Continues Its Battle against 'Wrap Rage,'" *Triple Pundit,* December 9, 2013, www.triplepundit.com/2013/12/ amazon-continues-battle-against-wrap-rage/; and www.amazon.com/ b/?&node=5521637011, accessed September 2015.

13. See www.tiffany.com/WorldOfTiffany/TiffanyStory/Legacy/BlueBox.aspx, accessed March 2015.

14. Based on information from "Company Values," www.llbean.com/ customerService/aboutLLBean/company_values.html; www.llbean.com/ customerService/aboutLLBean/company_history.html?nav=s1-ln; and other pages at www.llbean.com, accessed September 2015.

15. See Anna Rose Welch, "Lowe's Leverages Mobile Initiatives to Improve Customer Experience," *Integrated Solutions for Retailers,* November 21, 2013, www.retailsolutionsonline.com/doc/lowe-s-leverages-mobile-initiatives-to-improve-customer-experience-0001; Vauhini Vara, "The Lowe's Robot and the Future of Service Work," *The New Yorker,* October 29, 2014, www.newyorker.com/business/currency/lowes-robot-future-service-work; and www.lowes.com/webapp/wcs/stores/servlet/ ContactUsLandingPageView, www.lowes.com/how-to-library, and https://twitter.com/LowesCares, accessed March 2015.

16. Information on The Clorox Company's product mix from www .thecloroxcompany.com/products/our-brands/, accessed September 2015.

17. Devika Krishna Kumar, ""P&G to Sell Up to 100 Brands to Revive Sales, Cut Costs," *Reuters,* August 1, 2014, www.reuters.com/ article/2014/08/01/procter-gamble-results-idUSL4N0Q745T20140801; and "All Eyes on P&G's Brand Consolidation Strategy as Currency Headwinds Weigh on Q2 Results," *Forbes,* January 26, 2015, www .forbes.com/sites/greatspeculations/2015/01/26/all-eyes-on-pgs-brand-consolidation-strategy-as-currency-headwinds-weigh-on-q2-results/; and Kevin Orland, "Coty Agrees to Buy P&G Beauty Brands for $12.5 Billion," *BloombergBusiness,* July 9, 2015, www.bloomberg.com/news/ articles/2015-07-09/p-g-accepts-coty-s-12-5-billion-offer-for-43-beauty-brands.

18. See CIA World FactBook, www.cia.gov/library/publications/the-world-factbook, accessed March 2015; and "List of Countries by GDP Sector Composition," http://en.wikipedia.org/wiki/List_of_countries_by_GDP_sector_composition, accessed September 2015.

19. Based on information from Leonard Berry and Neeli-Bendapudi, "Clueing In Customers," *Harvard Business Review*, February 2003, pp. 100–106; Jeff Hansel, "Mayo Hits the Blogosphere," *McClatchy-Tribune Business News*, January 22, 2009; "Mayo Clinic Model of Care," www.mayo.edu/pmts/mc4200-mc4299/mc4270.pdf, accessed September 2014; and www.mayoclinic.org, accessed September 2015.

20. See James L. Heskett, W. Earl Sasser, Jr., and Leonard A. Schlesinger, *The Service Profit Chain: How Leading Companies Link Profit and Growth to Loyalty, Satisfaction, and Value* (New York: Free Press, 1997); and Heskett, Sasser, and Schlesinger, *The Value Profit Chain: Treat Employees Like Customers and Customers Like Employees* (New York: Free Press, 2003). Also see John Marshall and Dave Mayer, "Activate a Brand Internally," *Marketing Management*, Winter 2012, pp. 37–44.

21. David Rohde, "The Anti-Walmart: The Secret Sauce of Wegmans Is People," *The Atlantic*, March 23, 2012, www.theatlantic.com/business/archive/2012/03/the-anti-walmart-the-secret-sauce-of-wegmans-is-people/254994/. Also see Carmine Gallo, "How Wegmans, Apple Store, and Ritz-Carlton Win Loyal Customers," *Forbes*, December 11, 2012, www.forbes.com/sites/carminegallo/2012/12/11/how-wegmans-apple-store-and-the-ritz-carlton-wins-loyal-customers/; and www.wegmans.com/careers, accessed September 2015.

22. See "United States: Prescription Drugs," www.statehealthfacts.org/profileind.jsp?sub=66&rgn=1&cat=5, accessed March 2015; and "Postal Facts," http://about.usps.com/who-we-are/postal-facts/welcome.htm, accessed September 2015.

23. See Terry Maxon, "Horrible Flight? Airlines' Apology Experts Will Make It Up to You," *McClatchy-Tribune News Service*, August 24, 2010; Katie Morell, "Lessons from Southwest Airlines' Stellar Customer Service," *ehotelier.com*, August 29, 2012, http://ehotelier.com/hospitality-news/item.php?id=23931_0_11_0M_C; and Micah Solomon, "Customer Service: What Southwest Knows and You Don't (Hint: Being Nice Isn't Enough)," *Forbes*, September 22, 2013, www.forbes.com/sites/micahsolomon/2013/09/22/not-hiring-jerks-isnt-enough-your-systems-have-to-love-your-customers-too/.

24. See Micah Solomon, "5 Social Media Customer Service Best Practices to Handle (or Prevent) Customer Complaints," *Forbes*, January 28, 2015, www.forbes.com/sites/micahsolomon/2015/01/28/5-best-practices-for-social-media-customer-service-how-to-handle-and-avoid-customer-complaints/.

25. See "McAtlas Shrugged," *Foreign Policy*, May–June 2001, pp. 26–37; and Philip Kotler and Kevin Lane Keller, *Marketing Management*, 15th ed. (Upper Saddle River: Pearson Publishing, 2016), p. 316.

26. See "For Sale: Hessian, A Brand without a Product," *Fast Company*, February 12, 2013, www.fastcodesign.com/1671819/for-sale-hessian-a-brand-without-a-product.

27. Pete Pachal, "Love Your Vespa? Now You Can Do It Officially on Social Media," *Mashable*, August 21, 2012, http://mashable.com/2012/08/21/la-vespa-vita/; and www.lavespavita.com/, accessed September 2015.

28. For more on BrandAsset Valuator, see Kotler and Keller, *Marketing Management*, Chapter 11; and "BrandAsset Valuator," www.yr.com/BAV, accessed September 2015.

29. See Millward Brown Optimor, "BrandZ Top 100 Most Valuable Global Brands," www.millwardbrown.com/docs/default-source/global-brandz-downloads/global/2014_BrandZ_Top100_Chart.pdf, accessed September 2015. Also see "Best Global Brands," www.bestglobalbrands.com/2014/ranking/, accessed September 2015.

30. See Scott Davis, *Brand Asset Management*, 2nd ed. (San Francisco: Jossey-Bass, 2002). For more on brand positioning, see Kotler and Keller, *Marketing Management*, Chapter 10.

31. See "For P&G, Success Lies in More Than Merely a Dryer Diaper," *Advertising Age*, October 15, 2007, p. 20; Jack Neff, "Just How Well-Defined Is Your Brand's Ideal?" *Advertising Age*, January 16, 2012, p. 4; and www.pampers.com, accessed September 2015.

32. See Aaron Ahuvia Rajeev and Richard P. Bagozzi, "Brand Love," *Journal of Marketing*, March 2012, pp. 1–16; Doug Grisaffe, "Feeling the Brand Love," *Marketing News*, February 2014, pp. 26-27; and www.saatchi.com/the_lovemarks_company and www.lovemarks.com, accessed October 2015.

33. See "Bing," *Wikipedia*, http://en.wikipedia.org/wiki/Bing, accessed March 2015.

34. "New Pricing Study Highlights Savings for Store Brands while the Winter Drags On," *PR Newswire*, February 19, 2014.

35. See Evan Clark, "UBS Sees Private-Label Goods Diminishing," *WWD*, November 26, 2013, www.wwd.com/retail-news/trends-analysis/ubs-sees-private-label-goods-diminishing-7291838; "Private Label Foods & Beverages in the U.S., 8th Edition," *PR Newswire*, October 29, 2014; and http://plma.com/storeBrands/marketprofile14a.html, accessed September 2015.

36. See Bonnie S. Benwick, "Store Brands, the (Now) Welcome Option," *Washington Post*, February 25, 2014, www.washingtonpost.com/lifestyle/food/store-brands-the-now-welcome-option/2014/02/24/be4808c6-99b0-11e3-80ac-63a8ba7f7942_story.html; Alexander Coolidge, "Kroger Using House Brands to Power Growth," *Cincinnati.com*, September 20, 2014, www.cincinnati.com/story/money/2014/09/20/kroger-using-house-brands-power-growth/15955797/; and Thad Rueter, "Amazon Powers Ahead to 2015," *Internet Retailer*, December 31, 2014, www.internetretailer.com/2014/12/31/amazon-powers-ahead-2015.

37. Stephanie Strom, "Groceries Are Cleaning Up in Store-Brand Aisles," *New York Times*, October 2, 2013, p. B1; and Deloitte, *The 2014 American Pantry Study*, www2.deloitte.com/content/dam/Deloitte/us/Documents/consumer-business/us-cp-aps-brochure.pdf.

38. See "Private Labels Use Branding to Increase Sales," *FHC Marketing*, January 29, 2014, www.fhcmarketing.com/private-labels-use-branding-increase-sales.

39. Lauren Coleman-Lochner, "Laundry Detergent Maker Want More Suds," *Bloomberg Businesseeek*, October 23, 2014, www.businessweek.com/articles/2014-10-23/laundry-detergent-sales-hurt-by-water-saving-washing-machines.

40. Matthew Daneman, "Kodak Brand Is Returning to Store Shelves," *USA Today*, December 26, 2014, www.usatoday.com/story/tech/2014/12/26/kodak-branding/20910231/.

41. "Top 150 Global Licensors," *Global License*, May 1, 2014, www.licensemag.com/license-global/top-150-global-licensors-0; and Felix Gillette, "SpongeBob Muscles Up," *Bloomberg Businessweek*, January 20, 2015, pp. 63–65.

42. See Devin Liddell, "3 Reasons Why Co-Making Is the Future of Branding," *Fast Company*, March 7, 2014, www.fastcodesign.com/3027047/3-reasons-why-co-making-is-the-future-of-branding; and www.tacobell.com/food/menuitem/Doritos-Locos-Tacos-Supreme, accessed September 2015.

43. Haley Peterson, "McDonald's Is Reportedly Cutting These Items from the Menu," *Business Insider*, January 23, 2015, www.businessinsider.com/mcdonalds-menu-cuts-2015-1.

44. See "The Brand That Launched 1000 Chips," *Bloomberg Businessweek*, October 3–9, 2011, p. 30; and www.fritolay.com/our-snacks/doritos.html, accessed September 2015.

45. See Michael Brown, "'Works with Nest' Program Gains Traction with 15 New Smart Device Integrations," *TechHive*, January 5, 2015, www.techhive.com/article/2864067/works-with-nest-program-explodes-with-15-new-smart-device-integrations.html.

46. For interesting lists of good and bad brand extension candidates, see Christina Austin, "See the 10 Worst Brand Extensions Currently on the Market," *Business Insider*, February 9, 2013, www.businessinsider.com/the-10-worst-brand-extensions-2013-2?op=1; and Brad Tuttle, "Why Some Brand Extensions Are Brilliant and Others Are Just Awkward," *Time*, February 7, 2013, http://business.time.com/2013/02/07/why-some-brand-extensions-are-brilliant-and-others-are-just-awkward/.

47. "100 Largest Global Marketers," *Advertising Age*, December 8, 2014, p. 26.

48. Stephen Cole, "Value of the Brand," *CA Magazine*, May 2005, pp. 39–40. Also see "The Power of Customer Service," *Fortune*, December 3, 2012, www.timeincnewsgroupcustompub.com/sections/121203_Disney.pdf; and "Customer Engagement," http://thewaltdisneycompany.com/citizenship/community/consumer-engagement, accessed September 2015.

Chapter 8

1. Based on information found in Jon Gertner, "The X Factor," *Fast Company*, May 2014, pp. 67–72; Miguel Helft, "The Most Ambitious CEO in the Universe," *Fortune*, December 1, 2014, pp. 140–150; Brad Stone, "Inside the Moonshot Factory," *Bloomberg Businessweek*, May 22, 2013, pp. 56–61; Chuck Salter, "Google: The Faces and Voices of the World's Most Innovative Company," *Fast Company*, March 2008, pp. 74–88; "The World's 50 Most Innovative Companies," *Fast Company*, www.fastcompany.com/section/most-innovative-companies-2015, accessed October 2015; "Google's U.S. Search Ex-Mobiles Drops Below 75% as Yahoo Makes More Firefox Gains," *TechCrunch*, February 15, 2015, http://techcrunch.com/2015/02/02/googles-u-s-search-ex-mobiles-drops-below-75-as-yahoo-makes-more-firefox-gains/; Nathan Ingraham, "YouTube abd Mobile Ads Drove Strong

Revenue Growth for Google Last Quarter," *The Verge,* July 16, 2015, www.theverge.com/2015/7/16/8981461/google-q2-2015-earnings; and www.google.com and http://investor.google.com/financial/tables.html, accessed October 2015.

2. Andrew Cunningham, "Apple's Q1 2015: Ridiculously High iPhone Sales, 18% Drop in iPad Sales," *ars technica,* January 27, 2015, http://arstechnica.com/apple/2015/01/apples-q1-2015-ridiculously-high-iphone-sales-18-drop-in-ipad-sales/.

3. David Meer, Edward C. Landry, and Samrat Sharma, "Creating What Consumers Want," *Forbes,* January 26, 2015, www.forbes.com/sites/strategyand/2015/01/26/creating-what-consumers-want/.

4. See Michael Martinez, "Ford Opens Silicon Valley Innovation Center," *The Detroit News,* January 22, 2015, www.detroitnews.com/story/business/autos/ford/2015/01/22/ford-silicon-valley/22165837/; and "Chick-fil-A Innovation," Matchstic, http://matchstic.com/work/case-studies/chick-fil-a-innovation, accessed October 2015.

5. For these and other examples, see Dan Schawbel, "Why Companies Want You to Become an Intrapreneur," *Forbes,* September 9, 2013, www.forbes.com/sites/danschawbel/2013/09/09/why-companies-want-you-to-become-an-intrapreneur/; and "Time to Think," http://solutions.3m.com/innovation/en_US/stories/time-to-think, accessed October 2015.

6. Kevin Scott, "The LinkedIn [in]cubator," December 7, 2012, http://blog.linkedin.com/2012/12/07/linkedin-incubator/; and www.linkedin.com/static?key=what_is_linkedin, accessed October 2015.

7. See Jonathan Ringen, "How LEGO Became the Apple of Toys," *Fast Company,* January 8, 2015, www.fastcompany.com/3040223/when-it-clicks-it-clicks; and https://ideas.lego.com, accessed October 2015.

8. "Samsung Is Fueling Its Future with Open Innovation," *InnoCentive,* October 23, 2103, www.innocentive.com/blog/2013/10/23/samsung-is-fueling-its-future-with-open-innovation/; and www.samsung.com/global/business/semiconductor/aboutus/business/open-innovation/overview, accessed October 2015.

9. See "Victorinox Success!" September 2012, www.jovoto.com/blog/2012/09/success-story-victorinox/; Bastian Unterberg et al., *Crowdstorm: The Future of Ideas, Innovation, and Problem Solving Is Collaboration* (Somerset, NJ: Wiley, 2013), pp. 175–177; and http://victorinox.jovoto.com and www.jovoto.com/clients, accessed October 2015.

10. Guido Jouret, "Inside Cisco's Search for the Next Big Idea," *Harvard Business Review,* September 2009, pp. 43–45; Geoff Livingston, "Real Challenges to Crowdsourcing for Social Good," *Mashable,* October 12, 2010, http://mashable.com/2010/10/12/social-good-crowdsourcing; and "Creating Business Opportunities to the Tune of $1 Billion Plus," *Brightidea,* www.brightidea.com/Brightidea-Case-Studies-Cisco.bix, accessed October 2015.

11. See George S. Day, "Is It Real? Can We Win? Is It Worth Doing?" *Harvard Business Review,* December 2007, pp. 110–120.

12. This example is based on Tesla Motors and information obtained from www.teslamotors.com, accessed April 2015, and Daniel Cooper, "Tesla's Long-Delayed Model X SUV Is Testing in California," *engadget,* January 13, 2015, www.engadget.com/2015/01/30/tesla-model-x-footage/. Also see Ryan Bradley, "Full Charge Ahead," *Fortune,* February 4, 2013, pp. 10–13; Leah Hunter, "How Tesla Protects the Romance of Driving while Disrupting the Industry," *Co.Design,* November 7, 2013, www.fastcodesign.com/3021312; "The Future of EV," www.chevrolet.com/culture/article/bolt-ev-concept-car.html, accessed October 2015; and "Electric Car," *Wikipedia,* http://en.wikipedia.org/wiki/Electric_car, accessed October 2015.

13. See www.carharttgroundbreakers.com and www.carhartt.com/GroundBreakersSignUpView?storeId=10201&langId=-1&catalogId=10551, accessed October 2015.

14. See Maureen Morrison, "Marketer of the Year: Taco Bell," *Advertising Age,* September 2, 2013, pp. 15–16; Susan Berfield, "Baristas, Patrons Steaming over Starbucks VIA," *Bloomberg BusinessWeek,* November 13, 2009; and Tamara Walsh, "Starbucks Makes a Big Bet on New Product Mix in 2014," *The Motley Fool,* January 8, 2014, www.fool.com/investing/general/2014/01/08/starbucks-makes-a-big-bet-on-new-product-mix-in-20.aspx.

15. Austin Carr, "Starbucks Leap of Faith," *Fast Company,* June 2013, pp. 46–48; and John Heggestuen, "An Inside Look at the Starbucks App, the Most Successful Mobile Payments System in the US," *Business Insider,* October 17, 2014, www.businessinsider.com/starbucks-mobile-payments-app-2014-9.

16. For information on BehaviorScan Rx, see www.iriworldwide.com/default.aspx?TabId=159&productid=75, accessed October 2015.

17. See Jack Neff, "P&G Reinvents Laundry with $150 Million Tide Pods Launch," *Advertising Age,* April 26, 2011, www.adage.com/print/227208/; and Sheila Shayon, "Microsoft Unleashes Global Marketing Blitz for Windows 8, New Devices," *BrandChannel,* October 25, 2012, www.brandchannel.com/home/post/2012/10/25/Microsoft-Global-Windows-8-Launch-102512.aspx.

18. "iPhone 6 & iPhone 6 Plus Arrive in 36 More Countries and Territories This Month," Apple press information, October 13, 2014, www.apple.com/pr/library/2014/10/13iPhone-6-iPhone-6-Plus-Arrive-in-36-More-Countries-and-Territories-This-Month.html.

19. See Robert G. Cooper, "Formula for Success," *Marketing Management,* March–April 2006, pp. 19–23; Christoph Fuchs and Martin Schreier, "Customer Empowerment in New Product Development," *Product Innovation Management,* January 2011, pp. 17–32; and Robert Safien, "The Lessons of Innovation," *Fast Company,* March 2012, p. 18.

20. See Chris O'Brien, "How Intuit became a Pioneer of 'Delight,'" *Los Angeles Times,* May 10, 2013; Brad Smith, "Intuit's CEO on Building a Design-Driven Company," *Harvard Business Review,* January–February 2015, pp. 35–38; and http://investors.intuit.com/financial-information/annual-reports/default.aspx and intuitlabs.com/innovation.html, accessed October 2015.

21. Based in part on information from Min-Jeong Lee, "Samsung Chases 'Wow' Moment," *Wall Street Journal,* March 12, 2013, http://online.wsj.com/news/articles/SB10001424127887324096404578355781939805000; Max Chafkin, "Samsung: For Elevating Imitation to an Art Form," *Fast Company,* March 2013, p. 108; Adam Lashinsky, "The Uncrowned King of Tech," *Fortune,* August 1, 2015, pp. 134-143; and information from www.sony.com, www.apple.com, and www.samsung.com, accessed October 2015.

22. This definition is based on one found in Bryan Lilly and Tammy R. Nelson, "Fads: Segmenting the Fad-Buyer Market," *Journal of Consumer Marketing,* Vol. 20, No. 3, 2003, pp. 252–265.

23. See Katya Kazakina and Robert Johnson, "A Fad's Father Seeks a Sequel," *New York Times,* May 30, 2004, www.nytimes.com; John Schwartz, "The Joy of Silly," *New York Times,* January 20, 2008, p. 5; "Drew Guarini, "11 Surprising Product Fads," *Huffington Post,* August 8, 2012, www.huffingtonpost.com/2012/08/22/product-fads_n_1819710.html#slide=1410262; and www.crazyfads.com, accessed October 2015.

24. Based on information from Stuart Elliott, "3M Says, 'Go Ahead, Make Something of It,'" *New York Times,* January 28, 2013, www.nytimes.com/2013/01/28/business/mutfund/3m-says-go-ahead-make-something-of-it.html?pagewanted=2&tntemail0=y&_r=3&emc=tnt; and "Post-it Brand. Go Ahead," www.youtube.com/watch?v=j_zUZb4EJTk, accessed October 2015.

25. See www.crayola.com/fashionshow/, accessed April 2015.

26. Tanzina Vega, "Quaker Oats Prepares to Court Younger, More Diverse Moms," *New York Times,* December 21, 2012, p. B3; E. J. Schultz, "The Quaker Man Is Growing a Milk Mustache," *Advertising Age,* September 8, 2014, www.adage.com/print/294857; and www.quakerup.com and www.quakeroats.com, accessed October2015.

27. See P&G Brand Divestitures Will Be Bigger Than Original Targets," *Advertising Age,* February 19, 2015, www.adage.com/print/297240.

28. For a more comprehensive discussion of marketing strategies over the course of the PLC, see Philip Kotler and Kevin Lane Keller, *Marketing Management,* 15th ed. (Upper Saddle River, NJ: Pearson Education, 2016), pp. 358+.

29. Jaclyn Trop, "Toyota Will Pay $1.6 Billion over Faulty Accelerator Suit," *New York Times,* July 20, 2013, p. 3B.

30. Based on information from "How PepsiCo Dreams Up New Products in China," *Advertising Age,* December 9, 2013, http://adage.com/print/245558; Louise Ho, "PepsiCo's Strategy Wins Market Share," *Global Times,* December 4, 2013, www.globaltimes.cn/content/829870.shtml#.Uu_5Q_ldV8F; Laurie Burkett, "PepsiCo Chips Away at China," *Wall Street Journal,* July 11, 2012, p. B3; and "PepsiCo's Greater China Region: Driving Growth and Innovation," *AmCahm China,* January 2014, www.amchamchina.org/article/12224.

31. Information from www.db.com, accessed October 2015.

32. Information from www.interpublic.com and www.mccann.com, accessed October 2015.

33. See "Global Powers of Retailing 2015," http://www2.deloitte.com/th/en/pages/consumer-business/articles/global-powers-retailing-2015.html; "Walmart Corporate International," http://corporate.walmart.com/our-story/locations, accessed October 2015; and information from www.walmart.com and www.carrefour.com, accessed October 2015.

Chapter 9

1. Based on information from Mike Shields, "Amazon Drives More Holiday Web Retail Traffic Than Biggest TV Ad Spender," *Wall Street Journal,* December 10, 2014, http://blogs.wsj.com/cmo/2014/12/10/amazon-drives-more-holiday-web-retail-traffic-than-biggest-tv-ad-spender/; Tom Gara, "When Elephants Fight: The Great Wal-Mart-Amazon War of 2013," *Wall Street Journal,* March 28, 2013, http://blogs.wsj.com/corporate-intelligence/2013/03/28/when-elephants-fight-the-great-wal-mart-amazon-war-of-2013; Shelly Banjo, "Walmart's E-Stumble with Amazon," *Wall Street Journal,* June 19, 2013, http://online.wsj.com/news/articles/SB10001424127887323566804578553301017702818; Sally Banjo, Suzanne Kapner, and Paul Ziobro, "Can Wal-Mart Clerks Ship as Fast as Amazon Robots?," *Wall Street Journal,* December 18, 2014, www.wsj.com/articles/can-wal-mart-clerks-ship-as-fast-as-amazon-robots-1418930087; "Walmart vs. Amazon Prime," *Advertising Age,* May 15, 2015, p. 6; and www.walmart.com and www.amazon.com, accessed October 2015.

2. For more on the importance of sound pricing strategy, see Thomas T. Nagle, John Hogan, and Joseph Zale, *The Strategy and Tactics of Pricing: A Guide to Growing More Profitably,* 5th ed. (Upper Saddle River, NJ: Prentice Hall, 2011), Chapter 1.

3. See Megan Willett, "How Swiss Watchmaker Patek Philippe Handcrafts Its Famous $500,000 Watches," *Business Insider,* July 12, 2013, www.businessinsider.com/how-a-patek-philippe-watch-is-made-2013-7; Stacy Perman, "Patek Philippe Crafts Its Future," *Fortune,* June 16, 2014, pp. 37–44; and www.patek.com/contents/default/en/values.html, accessed October 2015.

4. See Michael Johnsen, "Walmart Prepares to Expand Price First Launch," *Retailing Today,* August 21, 2014, www.retailingtoday.com/article/walmart-prepares-expand-price-first-nationwide; and www.mbusa.com/mercedes/vehicles/class/class-CLA/bodystyle-CPE, accessed October 2015.

5. See Maria Puente, "Theaters Turn Up the Luxury," *USA Today,* March 12, 2010, p. 1A; Dan Strack. "AMC Entertainment Set to Capitalize on a Strong 2015," *Seeking Alpha,* February 18, 2015, http://seekingalpha.com/article/2929046-amc-entertainment-set-to-capitalize-on-a-strong-2015; and information from http://dinein.amctheatres.com, accessed October 2015.

6. See www.traderjoes.com/our-story and www.traderjoes.com, accessed October 2015.

7. See Stan Schroeder, "Vertu's Luxury Android Smartphone Costs $10,000, *Mashable,* February 12, 2013, http://mashable.com/2013/02/12/vertu-ti/; Matt Vella, "The Ulter-Luxe Phone," *Fortune,* April 29, 2013, pp. 10–12; Lara O'Reilly, "Vertu Seeks to Broaden Appeal with Marketing," *Marketing Week,* October 13, 2013, www.marketingweek.co.uk/news/vertu-seeks-to-broaden-appeal-with-marketing/4008105.article; and www.vertu.com/us/en/discover-vertu/creating-extraordinary/ and www.vertu.com, accessed October 2015.

8. Based on information found in Joseph Weber, "Over a Buck for Dinner? Outrageous," *BusinessWeek,* March 9, 2009, p. 57; Tom Mulier and Matthew Boyle, "Dollar Dinners from ConAgra's Threatened by Costs," *Bloomberg Businessweek,* August 19, 2010, www.businessweek.com; and Barbara Soderlin, "ConAgra Tries to Change Consumers' Perceptions about Frozen Foods," *Omaha World-Herald,* May 20, 2013, www.omaha.com/money/conagra-tries-to-change-consumers-perceptions-about-frozen-foods/article_c9697b1b-e14a-5f31-a0a7-2675961eb70f.html.

9. For more information, see Annie Gasparro, "Whole Foods Aims to Alter 'Price Perception' as It Expands," *Wall Street Journal,* February 15, 2012; Julie Jargon, "Whole Foods' Battle for the Organic Shopper," *Wall Street Journal,* August 13, 2013, p. B1, http://online.wsj.com/news/articles/SB10001424127887323455104579015162135676136; and www.wholefoodsmarket.com/about-our-products/whole-deal, accessed October 2014.

10. See Stuart Elliott, "Whole Foods Asks Shoppers to Consider a Value Proposition," *New York Times,* October 20, 2014, p. B5; and Brad Stone, "Whole Foods, Half Off," *Bloomberg Businessweek,* January 25, 2015, pp. 45-49.

11. "Lower Cost Samsung GALAXY Unveiled in Kenya," *BiztechAfrica,* May 23, 2014, www.biztechafrica.com/article/lower-cost-samsung-samsung-galaxy-unveiled-kenya/2967/#.Uvo4bfIdV8F; Bruce Einhorn and others, "Samsung's China Problems Come to India," *Bloomberg Businessweek,* October 23, 2104, pp. 44–45; and "Samsung Galaxy Pocket Neo," www.mysmartprice.com/mobile/samsung-galaxy-pocket-neo-msp2810, accessed October 2015.

12. Karis Hustad, "Kindle Fire HDX Keeps Amazon's Low Price, Adds Extra Features," *Christian Science Monitor,* September 26, 2013, www.csmonitor.com/Innovation/2013/0926/Kindle-Fire-HDX-keeps-Amazon-s-low-price-adds-extra-features.

13. See information found at http://investor.keuriggreenmountain.com/annuals-proxies.cfm, accessed October 2015.

14. See Oliver Strand, "With Coffee, the Price of Individualism Can Be High," *New York Times,* February 8, 2012, p. D6; and "$51 per Pound: The Deceptive Cost of Single-Serve Coffee," *New York Times,* www.thekitchn.com/51-per-pound-the-deceptive-cost-of-single-serve-coffee-the-new-york-times-165712, accessed October 2015.

15. See Bill Campbell, "Cheese to the Rescue: Surprising Spray Melts Road Ice," NPR, January 21, 2014, www.npr.org/blogs/thetwo-way/2014/01/21/264562529/cheese-to-the-rescue-surprising-spray-melts-road-ice; and "Four Foods That Help Prevent Slippery Roads," *AccuWeater.com,* January 22, 2015, www.accuweather.com/en/weather-news/beet-cheese-and-potatoes-roads/22447484.

16. For this and other examples, see Peter Coy, "Why the Price Is Rarely Right," *Bloomberg Businessweek,* February 1 & 8, 2010, pp. 77–78.

17. See Anthony Allred, E. K. Valentin, and Goutam Chakraborty, "Pricing Risky Services: Preference and Quality Considerations," *Journal of Product and Brand Management,* Vol. 19, No. 1, 2010, p. 54; Kenneth C. Manning and David E. Sprott, "Price Endings, Left-Digit Effects, and Choice," *Journal of Consumer Research,* August 2009, pp. 328–336; Travis Nichols, "A Penny Saved: Psychological Pricing," *Gumroad,* October 18, 2013, http://blog.gumroad.com/post/64417917582/a-penny-saved-psychological-pricing; and Bouree Lam, "The Phychological Difference between $12.00 and $11.67," *The Atlantic,* January 30, 2015, www.theatlantic.com/business/archive/2015/01/the-psychological-difference-between-1200-and-1167/384993/.

18. See John Kell, "JCPenney to Close 33 Stores, Cut 2,000 Jobs," *Wall Street Journal,* January 14, 2014, p. B2; Kyle Stock, "Is JC Penney Giving Away the Store?," *Bloomberg Businessweek,* December 4, 2013, www.businessweek.com/articles/2013-12-04/is-jc-penney-giving-away-the-store; Brad Tuttle, "JCPenney Reintroduces Fake Prices," *Time,* May 2, 2013, http://business.time.com/2013/05/02/jc-penney-reintroduces-fake-prices-and-lots-of-coupons-too-of-course/; Natalie Zmuda, "JC Penney Reinvention Is Bold Bet, but Hardly Fail-Safe," *Advertising Age,* January 30, 2012, pp. 1, 22; Steve Denning, "JCPenney: Was Ron Johnson's Strategy Wrong?," *Forbes,* April 9, 2013, www.forbes.com/sites/stevedenning/2013/04/09/j-c-penney-was-ron-johnsons-strategy-wrong/; and http://ir.jcpenney.com/phoenix.zhtml?c=70528&p=irol-irHome, accessed October 2015.

19. See Justin D. Martin, "Dynamic Pricing: Internet Retailers Are Treating Us Like Foreign Tourists in Egypt," *Christian Science Monitor,* January 7, 2011; Patrick Rishe, "Dynamic Pricing: The Future of Ticket Pricing in Sports," *Forbes,* January 6, 2012, www.forbes.com/sites/prishe/2012/01/06/dynamic-pricing-the-future-of-ticket-pricing-in-sports/; and Mike Southon, "Time to Ensure the Price Is Right," *Financial Times,* January 21, 2012, p. 30.

20. See Natalie Zmuda, "Best Buy Tries to Co-Opt 'Showrooming' This Holiday Season," *Advertising Age,* October 29, 2013, http://adage.com/print/244993/; and Meredith Derby Berg, "Is Best Buy's 'Showrooming' Campaign Working?" *Advertising Age,* December 26, 2013, http://adage.com/print/245831/.

21. Liza Lin, "Shhh…Luxury Goods Are Discounted in China," *Bloomberg Businessweek,* August 21, 2014, pp. 28–29.

22. Matthew Boyle, "Unilever: Taking on the World, One Stall at a Time," *Bloomberg Businessweek,* January 7, 2013, pp. 18–20; and Martinne Geller, "Unilever Sticks with Emerging Markets as Sales Rebound," *Reuters,* January 21, 2014, http://uk.reuters.com/article/2014/01/21/uk-unilever-results-idUKBREA0K09A20140121.

23. See Serena Ng, "Toilet-Tissue 'Desheeting' Shrinks Rolls, Plumps Margins," *Wall Street Journal,* July 24, 2013, http://online.wsj.com/news/articles/SB10001424127887323971204578626223494483866; and Serena Ng, "At P&G, New Tide Comes In, Old Price Goes Up," *Wall Street Journal,* February 10, 2014, http://online.wsj.com/news/articles/SB10001424052702304450904579368852980301572.

24. For discussions of these issues, see Dhruv Grewel and Larry D. Compeau, "Pricing and Public Policy: A Research Agenda and Overview of the Special Issue," *Journal of Public Policy and Marketing,* Spring 1999, pp. 3–10; Walter L. Baker, Michael V. Marn, and Craig C. Zawada, *The Price Advantage* (Hoboken, NJ: John Wiley & Sons, 2010), Appendix 2; and Nagle, Hogan, and Zale, *The Strategy and Tactics of Pricing.*

25. See Tim Worstall, "Apple Fined $670,000 in Taiwan for Price Fixing," *Forbes,* December 25, 2013, www.forbes.com/sites/

timworstall/2013/12/25/apple-fined-670000-in-taiwan-for-price-fixing; and Lina Chan, "The Age of Amazon Is Upon Us," *Salon,* January 16, 2015, www.salon.com/2015/01/16/the_age_of_amazon_is_upon_us_how_one_court_battle_reveals_the_growing_threat_of_monopoly/.

26. Based on information found in Lynn Leary, "Publishers and Booksellers See a 'Predatory' Amazon," *NPR Books,* January 23, 2012, www.npr.org/2012/01/23/145468105; and Andrew Albanese, "At Apple Hearing, Amazon Called a 'Monopolist'" *Publishers Weekly,* December 15, 2014, www.publishersweekly.com/pw/by-topic/digital/content-and-e-books/article/65063-at-hearing-second-circuit-questions-e-book-case-against-apple.html.

27. "FTC Guides against Deceptive Pricing," www.ecfr.gov/cgi-bin/text-idx?c=ecfr&sid=dfafb89837c306cf5b010b5bde15f041&rgn=div5&view=text&node=16:1.0.1.2.16&idno=16, accessed October 2015.

Chapter 10

1. Jim Edwards, "Uber Has Changed My Life and as God Is My Witness I Will Never Take a Taxi Again" *Business Insider,* January 22, 2014, www.businessinsider.com/uber-has-changed-my-life-and-as-god-is-my-witness-i-will-never-take-a-taxi-again-where-available-2014-1#ixzz3TYF7ZY29; Brad Stone, "Invasion of the Taxi Snatchers: Uber Leads an Industry's Disruption," *Businessweek,* February 20, 2014, pp. 38–42; Om Malik, "Uber Is the New Google," *Fast Company,* June 2014, p. 50; Rebecca Borison, "Report: Uber Generates 12X More Revenue Than Lyft, Despite Charging More per Ride," *Business Insider,* September 11, 2014, www.businessinsider.com/uber-12x-revenue-over-lyft-2014-9; Douglas MacMillan, "How Sharp-Elbowed Uber Is Trying to Make Nice," *Wall Street Journal,* January 29, 2015, www.wsj.com/articles/hard-driving-uber-gives-compromise-a-try-1422588782; Alan Murray, "Uber-nomics," *Fortune,* January 2015, p. 6.

2. Based on information from Joe Cahill, "Mind Your Franchisees, Mayor McCheese," *Crain's Chicago Business,* April 26, 2013, www.chicagobusiness.com/article/20130426/BLOGS10/130429841; "McDonald's Customer Service Push Irritates Some Franchisees," *Chicago Business Journal,* April 17, 2014, www.bizjournals.com/chicago/news/2013/04/17/mcdonalds-riding-fine-line-franchisees.html; and "Is McDonald's Broken? Franchisees Are Furious," *Yahoo! Finance,* April 15, 2015, http://finance.yahoo.com/news/mcdonalds-broken-franchisees-furious-133644537.html.

3. See http://investors.sherwin-williams.com/; and "The Kroger Co. Fact Book," http://ir.kroger.com/CorporateProfile.aspx?iid=4004136, accessed October 2015.

4. See the Inditex Press Dossier, www.inditex.com/en/media/press_dossier, accessed April 2015.

5. Franchising facts from "The State of the Franchise Economy in 2013," http://franchiseeconomy.com/wp-content/uploads/2013/09/The-State-Of-The-Franchise-Economy-In-2013-9-17-13.pdf; www.azfranchises.com/franchisefacts.htm, accessed May 2013; and company sources, accessed June 2015. Also see "Franchise Business Economic Outlook for 2015," January 2015, http://emarket.franchise.org/FranchiseBizOutlook2015.pdf.

6. See "Two Men and a Truck Wraps Up Successful 2014, Fuels Future Expansion in 2015," January 29, 2015, www.twomenandatruck.com/details.aspx?p=1EC0C69A41A54054&ppid=59896&naid=C0CACB36C71828B8; and www.twomenandatruck.com/history-of-two-men-and-a-truck, accessed October 2015.

7. See Eric Platt, "22 Companies That Are Addicted to Walmart," June 13, 2012, *Business Insider,* www.businessinsider.com/22-companies-who-are-completely-addicted-to-walmart-2012-6#; and Dan Mitchell, "Say Goodbye to Your Supermarket," *Fortune,* March 14, 2014, http://fortune.com/2014/03/14/say-goodbye-to-your-supermarket/.

8. See "General Mills: Joint Ventures," www.generalmills.com/en/Company/Businesses/International/Joint_ventures.aspx, accessed October 2015.

9. "Barnes & Noble Abandons Plan to Spin Off Nook Business," *New York Post,* February 24, 2015, http://nypost.com/2015/02/26/barnes-noble-abandons-plan-to-spin-off-nook-business/.

10. Lawrence Frost, "Volvo to Launch Online Car Sales in Marketing Shift," *Reuters,* December 15, 2014, www.reuters.com/article/2014/12/15/us-volvo-internet-idUSKBN0JT0D020141215; and Diana Kuryiko, "Volvo Dealers Are Hungry for the Redesigned XC90," *Automotive News,* January 25, 2015, www.autonews.com/article/20150123/RETAIL06/301249995/volvo-dealers-are-hungry-for-the-redesigned-xc90.

11. See "Ace Town & Country Hardware: Recommended Reviews," *Yelp,* www.yelp.com/biz/ace-town-and-country-hardware-chapel-hill-2,

accessed April 2015; and www.acehardware.com/corp/index.jsp?page=about, accessed October 2015.

12. See http://new.pamperedchef.com/company-facts and www.stelladot.com/trunkshow, accessed October 2015.

13. See Grace Lavigne, "China Unveils Six-Year Plan to Cut Logistics," *Journal of Commerce,* October 7, 2014, www.joc.com/international-logistics/global-sourcing/china-unveils-six-year-plan-cut-logistics-costs_20141007.html; and Steven Butler, "Walmart China: Hitting Headwinds," *CNNMoney,* January 22, 2015, http://money.cnn.com/2015/01/22/news/economy/ozy-china-walmart/.

14. Based on information from Julie Jargon, "Asia Delivers for McDonald's," *Wall Street Journal,* December 13, 2011, http://online.wsj.com/article/SB10001424052970204397704577074982151549316.html; "Feel Like a Burger? Dial M for McDonald's Japan," *Asia Pulse,* January 23, 2012; and McDonald's annual reports, www.aboutmcdonalds.com/mcd/investors/annual_reports.html, accessed October 2015.

15. See Stephanie Strom, "CVS Vows to Quit Selling Tobacco Products," *New York Times,* February 5, 2014, p. B1; Bruce Japson, "CVS Health Kicks Smoking Habit and Still Has Record Sales," *Forbes,* February 20, 2015, www.forbes.com/sites/brucejapsen/2015/02/10/even-without-tobacco-revenue-cvs-reports-sales/; and http://info.cvscaremark.com/cvs-insights/cvs-quits, accessed October 2015.

16. See Rosalyn Wilson, "25th Annual State of Logistics Report: It's Complicated," July 1, 2014, www.logisticsmgmt.com/article/25th_annual_state_of_logistics_its_complicated.

17. William B. Cassidy, "Walmart Squeezes Costs from Supply Chain," *Journal of Commerce,* January 5, 2010; "Walmart to Save $150 Million Thanks to Sustainability Programs," *Triple Pundit,* October 16, 2012, www.triplepundit.com/2012/10/walmart-save-150-million-sustainability-programs/; and Phalguni Soni, "Walmart's Supply Chain and Distribution Model," *Market Realist,* February 18, 2015, http://marketrealist.com/2015/02/managing-walmarts-supply-chain-cross-docking-tools/.

18. Andy Brack, "Piggly Wiggly Center Offers Info-Packed Field Trip," *Charleston Currents,* January 4, 2010, www.charlestoncurrents.com/issue/10_issues/10.0104.htm; and information from http://en.wikipedia.org/wiki/Piggly_wiggly and http://news.walmart.com/news-archive/2005/01/07/our-retail-divisions, accessed October 2015.

19. Jessica Stillman, "Green Cred: Sustainability a Cost-Cutting Move for Suppliers," *Forbes,* December 11, 2012, www.forbes.com/sites/ups/2012/12/11/green-cred-sustainability-a-cost-cutting-move-for-suppliers/; and www.apparelcoalition.org/higgindex/, www.nikeresponsibility.com/, and www.nikeresponsibility.com/report/content/chapter/manufacturing, accessed October 2015.

20. Andrew S. Ross, "Forget the Elves; Amazon Turns to Robots This Holiday Season," SFGATE, December 21, 2014, www.sfgate.com/business/bottomline/article/Forget-the-elves-Amazon-turns-to-robots-this-5928294.php; and "Working at Amazon," January 2015, www.amazon.com/gp/help/customer/display.html?nodeId=200787540&view-type=stand-alone.

21. See Ross, "Forget the Elves"; Scott Kirsner, "Amazon Acquisition Puts Amazon Rivals in Awkward Spot," *Boston Globe,* December 1, 2013, www.bostonglobe.com/business/2013/12/01/will-amazon-owned-robot-maker-sell-tailer-rivals/FON7bVNKvfzS2sHnBHzfLM/story.html; Donna Tam, "Meet Amazon's Busiest Employee—the Kiva Robot," CNET, November 30, 2014, www.cnet.com/news/meet-amazons-busiest-employee-the-kiva-robot/; and www.kivasystems.com, accessed October 2015.

22. Bureau of Transportation Statistics, "Pocket Guide to Transportation 2015," January 2015, www.rita.dot.gov/bts/sites/rita.dot.gov.bts/files/publications/pocket_guide_to_transportation/2015; and American Trucking Association, www.trucking.org/News_and_Information_Reports_Industry_Data.aspx, accessed October 2015.

23. See Walmart's supplier requirements at http://corporate.walmart.com/suppliers, accessed April 2015.

24. For this and other UPS examples and information, see "Toshiba Laptop Repair," accessed at http://pressroom.ups.com/Video/Toshiba+Laptop+Repair, May 2013; and www.thenewlogistics.com and www.ups.com/content/us/en/about/facts/worldwide.html, accessed October 2015.

25. "3PL Customers Report Identifies Service Trends, 3PL Market Segment Sizes and Growth Rates," Armstrong & Associates, Inc., July 11, 2013, www.3plogistics.com/PR_3PL_Customers-2013.htm. Also see Robert C. Lieb, "25 Years of Third-Party Logistics Research & Studies," *Supply Chain 247,* December 31, 2014, http://www.supplychain247.com/article/25_years_of_third-party_logistics_research.

26. See John Langley Jr., "2014 Third-Party Logistics Study: The State of Logistics Outsourcing," Capgemini Consulting, www.capgemini.com/resource-file-access/resource/pdf/3pl_study_report_web_version.pdf., accessed May 2015.

Chapter 11

1. Based on information from "Fortune Global 500," *Fortune,* August 1, 2015, pp. F1-F6; Ashley Lutz and Mike Nudelman, "14 Facts about Wal-Mart That Will Blow Your Mind," *Business Insider,* October 17, 2013, www .businessinsider.com/facts-about-wal-mart-to-blow-your-mind-2013-10; John Huey, "Wal-Mart: Will It Take over the World?" *Fortune,* January 30, 1998, pp. 52–61; Michael Barbano and Stuart Elliott, "Clinging to Its Roots, Wal-Mart Steps Back from an Edgy, New Image," *New York Times,* December 10, 2006, www.nytimes.com/2006/12/10/business/ worldbusiness/10iht-walmart.3845671.html; "Top 250 Global Retailers, 2015," *National Retail Federation,* https://nrf.com/2015/global250-table; and annual reports and other information found at http://corporate .walmart.com/our-story/heritage/sam-walton, http://news.walmart.com/ walmart-facts/corporate-financial-fact-sheet, and www.walmartstores .com, accessed October 2015.

2. See "Monthly and Annual Retail Trade," U.S. Census Bureau, www .census.gov/retail/, accessed October 2015.

3. See "Just Released: P&G 2014 Annual Report," P&G Corporate Newsroom, August 20, 2014, http://news.pg.com/blog/company-strategy/ just-released-pg-2014-annual-report; and "Procter & Gamble," *Growth Champions,* March 2015, http://growthchampions.org/growth-champions/ procter-gamble/.

4. For more on digital aspects of shopper marketing and omni-channel retailing, see Tim Simmons, "The Keys to Unlocking the Retail Omni-Channel Advantage," *Forbes,* January 1, 2015, www.forbes.com/sites/ teradata/2015/01/02/the-keys-to-unlocking-the-retail-omni-channel-advantage/print/; Lisa R. Melsted, "Retailers Turn to Omnichannel Strategies to Remain Competitive," *Forbes,* February 9, 2015, www.forbes .com/sites/samsungbusiness/2015/02/09/retailers-turn-to-omnichannel-strategies-to-remain-competitive/print/; and www.shoppermarketingmag .com/home/, accessed May 2015; and "ZMOT," *Google Digital Services,* www.zeromomentoftruth.com/, accessed October 2015.

5. John Russell, "Grocery Wars Certain to Flair Up on North Side," *IndyStar,* January 27, 2015, www.indystar.com/story/news/2015/01/25/ grocery-wars-certain-flare-north-side/22125353/.

6. Jon Springer, "Pricing: WinCo Keeps Costs Down and Velocity High," *Supermarket News,* April 29, 2013, http://supermarketnews.com/ retail-amp-financial/pricing-winco-keeps-costs-down-and-velocity-high#ixzz2uLcJzlvN; Brad Tuttle, "Meet the Low-Key, Low-Cost Grocery Chain Being Called 'Walmart's Worst Nightmare,'" *Time,* August 7, 2013, http://business.time.com/2013/08/07/meet-the-low-key-low-cost-grocery-chain-being-called-wal-marts-worst-nightmare/; Justin Corr, "Learning about Retirement from WinCo's Millionaire Checkers," *KTVB.com,* February 3, 2015, www.ktvb.com/story/news/local/2015/02/03/winco-checkers-retirement/22793933/; and www.wincofoods.com, accessed October 2015.

7. See Jonathon Berr, "7-Eleven Goes on a Healthy Kick," *MSN Money,* September 13, 2013, http://money.msn.com/now/post-7-eleven-goes-on-a-health-kick; and http://corp.7-eleven.com, accessed October 2015.

8. http://corporate.walmart.com/our-story/our-business/locations/#/united-states, accessed June 2015; and "Supermarket Facts," www.fmi.org/ research-resources/supermarket-facts, accessed October 2015.

9. See "Dollar General Reports Record Fourth Quarter and Full Year 2014 Financial Results," March 12, 2015, http://newscenter.dollargeneral.com/ news/dollar-general-reports-record-fourth-quarter-and-full-year-2014-financial-results.htm; Christopher Matthews, "Will Dollar Stores Rule the Retail World?" *Time,* April 1, 2013, http://business.time.com/2013/04/01/ will-dollar-stores-rule-the-retail-world/; and http://investor.shareholder .com/dollar/financials.cfm, accessed October 2015.

10. Beth Kowitt, "Is T.J. Maxx the Best Retail Sore in the Land," *Fortune,* August 11, 2014, pp. 93-96; and "How We Do It," http://tjmaxx.tjx.com/ store/jump/topic/how-we-do-it/2400087, accessed October 2015.

11. Phil Wahba, "Macy's Mull Taking on T.J. Maxx, Nordstrom Rack in "Off-Price" Wars," *Fortune,* January 8, 2015, http://fortune.com/2015/01/08/ macys-outlet-off-price/.

12. Based on information from "Top 250 Global Retailers, 2015," *National Retail Federation,* https://nrf.com/2015/global250-table; Stan Laegreid, "The Choreography of Design, Treasure Hunts, and Hot Dogs That Have Made Costco So Successful," *Fast Company,* January 24, 2014, www .fastcompany.com/3025312; Susanna Kim, "7 Reasons Why People Can't Get Enough of Costco," *ABC News,* January 6, 2015, http://abcnews .go.com/Business/reasons-people-costco/story?id=26046572; and www .costco.com and http://www.costco.com/insider-guide-amazing-facts .html, accessed October 2015.

13. Company and franchising information from "2014 Franchise Times Top 200 Franchise Systems," *Franchise Times,* October 2014, www.franchisetimes .com/pdf/2014/Top200-2014.pdf, www.score.org/resources/should-i-buy-franchise; and http://www.aboutmcdonalds.com/mcd/our_company.html and www.subway.com/subwayroot/About_Us/default.aspx, accessed October 2015.

14. Numbers from "Top 200 Franchise Systems," *Franchise Times,* October 2014, www.franchisetimes.com/pdf/2014/Top200-2014.pdf. See also www.whichwich.com and www.whichwich.com/about_us, accessed October 2015.

15. Based on information from "How Do You See This Experiential Retailing Trend Working Its Way across Retail?" *Integrated Retailing,* www .integratedretailing.com/?p=131, accessed September 2014; and www .llbean.com, www.llbean.com/llb/shop/1000001692?nav=ftlink, and www.llbean.com/llb/shop/1000001704?page=campus-lander#, accessed October 2015.

16. See Justine Sharrock, "How Manufactured Smells Are Making People Shop Longer and Kill Better," *BuzzFeed,* March 15, 2013, www.buzzfeed .com/justinesharrock/how-manufactured-smells-are-making-people-shop-longer-and-ki; Alexandra Sifferlin, "My Nose Made Me Buy It," *Time,* December 16, 2013, http://healthland.time.com/2013/12/16/my-nose-made-me-buy-it-how-retailers-use-smell-and-other-tricks-to-get-you-to-spend-spend-spend/; Sarah Nassauer, "Using Scent as a Marketing Tool, Stores Hope It—and Shoppers—Will Linger," *Wall Street Journal,* May 20, 2014, www.wsj.com/articles/SB10001424052702303446870457 9573953132979382; and www.scentair.com/why-scentair-scent-studies/, accessed October 2015.

17. See various social media sites for Walmart and Fairway, accessed October 2015.

18. "CVS/pharmacy Revolutionizes the Way Customers Experience the Sales Circular with Launch of myWeekly Ad," October 17, 2013, http://info .cvscaremark.com/newsroom/press-releases/cvspharmacy-revolutionizes-way-customers-experience-sales-circular-launch; Stuart Elliott, "For CVS Regulars, Ads Tailored Just to Them," *New York Times,* October 10, 2013, www.nytimes.com/2013/10/11/business/media/for-cvs-regulars-ads-tailored-just-to-them.html?_r=0; and www.cvs.com, accessed June 2015.

19. For definitions of these and other types of shopping centers, see "Dictionary," *American Marketing Association,* www.marketingpower .com/_layouts/Dictionary.aspx, accessed October 2015.

20. See "Brick by Brick: The State of the Shopping Center," Nielsen, May 17, 2013, http://nielsen.com/us/en/reports/2013/brick-by-brick-the-state-of-the-shopping-center.html; "It's the End of the Mall as We Know It," *Real Estate Weekly,* February 22, 2013, www.rew-online.com/2013/02/22/ its-the-end-of-the-mall-as-we-know-it/; Judy Keen, "As Enclosed Malls Decline, 'Lifestyle Centers' Proliferate," MINNPOST, August 30, 2013, www.minnpost.com/cityscape/2013/08/enclosed-malls-decline-lifestyle-centers-proliferate; www.cvs.com/weeklyad/browse/browse-home.jsp#Browse; Jennifer Duell Popovec, "Existing Lifestyle Centers Thrive, but Developers Prefer Mixed-Use for New Projects," December 11, 2014, *National Real Estate Investor,* http://nreionline.com/retail/existing-lifestyle-centers-thrive-developers-prefer-mixed-use-new-projects.

21. Nelson D. Schwartz, "The Economics (and Naiostalgia) of Dead Malls," *New York Times,* January 3, 2015, www.nytimes.com/2015/01/04/ business/the-economics-and-nostalgia-of-dead-malls.html.

22. Jennifer Reingold and Phil Wahba, "Where Have All the Shopper Gone?" *Fortune,* September 3, 2014, http://fortune.com/2014/09/03/ where-have-all-the-shoppers-gone/.

23. See Rick Brockmann, "Nike to Open Pop-Up Shop Near Barclays for NBA's All-Star Weekend," *The Real Deal,* February 9, 2015.

24. See www.gilt.com and www.zulily.com, accessed October 2015.

25. See www.rpminc.com/leading-brands/consumer-brands, accessed October 2015.

26. Thad Rueter, "The Web's Influence on U.S. Retail Grows," *Internet Retailer,* July 25, 2014, www.internetretailer.com/2014/07/25/webs-influence-us-retail-grows; and U.S. Census Bureau News, "Quarterly Retail E-Commerce Sales, 4rd Quarter 2014," February 17, 2015, www .census.gov/retail/mrts/www/data/pdf/ec_current.pdf.

27. See Greg Sterling, "Mobile Devices: 30 Percent of Traffic, 15 Percent of Sales," *Marketing Land,* February 28, 2014, http://marketingland.com/mobile-devices-generate-30-pct-traffic-15-pct-e-sales-75498; and Thad Rueter, "The Web's Influence on U.S. Retail Grows," *Internet Retailer,* July 25, 2014, www.internetretailer.com/2014/07/25/webs-influence-us-retail-grows.

28. Lauren Johnson, "Target Turns Its Stores into One Big Mobile Game for the Holidays," *Adweek,* December 2, 2014, www.adweek.com/ print/161727.

29. "Store-Based Retailers Take the Early Lead among Top 500 Retailers in Online Sales Growth," *Internet Retailer,* February 18, 2014, www.internetretailer.com/2014/02/18/store-based-retailers-take-early-lead-among-top-500; and "Top 500 Guide," *Internet Retailer,* www.internetretailer.com/top500/top10/, accessed October 2015.

30. Paul Demery, "E-Commerce Becomes More Dominant at Williams-Sonoma," *Internet Retailer,* August 20, 2013, www.internetretailer.com/2013/08/30/e-commerce-becomes-more-dominant-williams-sonoma; Adam Blair, "Williams-Sonoma Invests $75M in Fast-Growing, Profitable E-Commerce," RIS, March 22, 2011, http://risnews.edgl.com/retail-best-practices/Williams-Sonoma-Invests-$75M-in-Fast-Growing,-Profitable-E-Commerce71523; and Laura Alber, "The CEO of Williams-Sonoma on Blending Instinct with Analysis," *Harvard Business Review,* September 2014, https://hbr.org/2014/09/the-ceo-of-williams-sonoma-on-blending-instinct-with-analysis.

31. Brad Tuttle, "The Creepy New Way Macy's Tempts You to Make Impulse Purchases," *Time,* September 26, 2015, http://time.com/money/3432693/macys-shopkick-ibeacon/.

32. See Lauren Johnson, "This $473 Billion Retailer Wants to Be the Next Ad-Tech Star," *Adweek,* November 18, 2014, www.adweek.com/print/161471; "Our Strategy: Winning in Global E-Commerce," *Walmart 2012 Annual Report,* www.walmartstores.com/sites/annual-report/2012/WalMart_AR.pdf, March 2013, pp. 12–13; and www.walmartlabs.com, accessed October 2015.

33. "Green MashUP: 7 Trends Transforming Retail Sustainability," *The Fifth Estate,* February 17, 2015, www.thefifthestate.com.au/business/trends/green-mashup-7-trends-transforming-retail-sustainability/71455; and "The IKEA Group Sustainability Report," www.ikea.com/ms/en_US/pdf/sustainability_report/sustainability_report_2014.pdf accessed October 2015.

34. See www.staples.com/sbd/cre/marketing/easy-on-the-planet/recycling-and-eco-services.html, accessed October 2015.

35. See http://news.walmart.com/walmart-facts/corporate-financial-fact-sheet, accessed October 2015.

36. See "Global Powers of Retailing 2015," Deloitte, January 2015, accessed at http://www2.deloitte.com/content/dam/Deloitte/global/Documents/Consumer-Business/gx-cb-global-powers-of-retailing.pdf.

37. Grainger facts and other information are from the "Grainger: Beyond the Box Fact Book," accessed at http://invest.grainger.com/phoenix.zhtml?c=76754&p=irol-irFactBook and www.grainger.com, accessed October 2015.

38. "Top 500 Guide," Internet Retailer, www.top500guide.com/top-500/the-top-500-list, accessed March 2014; and www.grainger.com, accessed October 2014.

39. Information from "About Us," www.mckesson.com; and "Supply Management Online," http://mckessonbop.com/solutions-services/mckesson-connect/, accessed October 2015.

40. Facts from "2014 Power 50," http://supermarketnews.com/2014-power-50-clickable-list, accessed June 2015; and www.supervalu.com, accessed October 2015.

Chapter 12

1. Quotes and other information from Dominique Mosbergen, "GEICO Creates 'Unskippable' Preroll YouTube Ads That You'll Want to Watch till the End," *Huffington Post,* March 2, 2015, www.huffingtonpost.com/2015/03/02/geico-unskippable-ad-youtube-preroll_n_6788894.html; E. J. Schultz, "Muscling Past Mayhem: GEICO Rides Giant Ad Budget Past Allstate," *Advertising Age,* July 8, 2013, www.adage.com/print/242980; "10 Most-Advertised Brands," *Advertising Age Marketing Fact Pack 2015,* December 29, 2014, pp. 7, 10; Michele Miller, "'Hump Day' GEICO Commercial: Creators Dish on Ad's Success, Its Development," *CBS News,* September 18, 2013, www.cbsnews.com/news/hump-day-geico-commercial-creators-dish-on-ads-success-its-development/; Andrea Paton-Ash, "Camels Return to the Spotlight in GEICO's Latest 'It's What You Do' Commercial," December 23, 2014, http://blog.geico.com/2014/12/23/camels-return-to-the-spotlight-in-geicos-latest-its-what-you-do-commercial/; and www.geico.com and www.youtube.com/user/GEICO, accessed October 2015.

2. For other definitions, see www.ama.org/resources/Pages/Dictionary.aspx, accessed October 2015.

3. "Ad Spending by Medium," *Advertising Age Marketing Fact Pack 2015,* December 29, 2014, p. 16; "Digital to Overtake TV Ad Spending in Two Years," *Advertising Age,* November 4, 2014, www.adage.com/print/295694; Natalie Tadena, "Magna Global: TV Will Remain Soft in 2015," *Wall Street Journal,* February 25, 2015, http://blogs.wsj.com/cmo/2015/02/25/magna-global-tv-ad-spending-will-remain-soft-in-2015/;

"P&G's Pritchard on Where Marketing, Media, and Metrics Are Going," *Advertising Age,* March 16, 2015, www.adage.com/print/297592; and Jack Neff and E. J. Schultz, "Overdose?," *Advertising Age,* February 9, 2015, pp. 14–15.

4. See Andrew Adam Newman, "With a French Accent, a Soap Brand Tells a Tale of Well-Scrubbed Lovers," *New York Times,* March 21, 2014, p. B4; Stuart Elliott, "Ad for Method Celebrates the Madness," *New York Times,* March 12, 2012, p. B1; and www.methodhome.com/cleanhappy/ and www.youtube.com/user/peopleagainstdirty, accessed October 2015.

5. See "Advertisers Blend Digital and TV for Well-Rounded Campaigns," *eMarketer,* March 12, 2014, www.emarketer.com/Article/Advertisers-Blend-Digital-TV-Well-Rounded-Campaigns/1010670.

6. See Troy Dreier, "How Lowe's and Vine Build Social Video Success," *Streaming Media,* May 2014, www.streamingmedia.com/Articles/Editorial/Featured-Articles/How-Lowes-and-Vine-Build-Social-Video-Success-96585.aspx; Alexxis Letozoa, "Lowe's Fix in Six," *–Ation,* December 1, 2014, http://ation.digitalmediauconn.org/lowes-fix-in-six/; https://vine.co/Lowes, www.youtube.com/user/Lowes, https://instagram.com/loweshomeimprovement/, www.pinterest.com/lowes/, and other Lowe's social media sites, accessed October 2015.

7. See Scott Collins, "Super Bowl 2015: Sunday's Game a Ratings Winner for NBC," *LA Times,* February 3, 2015; www.latimes.com/entertainment/tv/la-et-st-super-bowl-2015-ratings-20150203-story.html; Rick Kissell, "'NCIS' Has Become the World's Most-Watched TV Drama," *Variety,* June 11, 2014, http://variety.com/2014/tv/news/ncis-most-popular-drama-in-worldwatched-tv-drama-1201218492/; and www.youtube.com/watch?v=qaOvHKG0Tio, accessed October 2015.

8. See discussions at Mike Ishmael, "The Cost of a Sales Call," October 22, 2012, http://4dsales.com/the-cost-of-a-sales-call/; Jeff Green, "The New Willy Loman Survives by Staying Home," *Bloomberg Businessweek,* January 14–20, 2013, pp. 16–17; and "What Is the Real Cost of a B2B Sales Call?" www.marketing-playbook.com/sales-marketing-strategy/what-is-the-real-cost-of-a-b2b-sales-call, accessed October 2015.

9. "100 Largest Global Marketers," *Advertising Age,* December 8, 2014, p. 26.

10. For these and other advertising spending facts, see *Advertising Age Marketing Fact Pack 2015,* December 29, 2014, and "200 Leading National Advertisers," *Advertising Age,* July 13, 2015, pp. 14-23.

11. See "200 Leading National Advertisers," *Advertising Age,* July 13, 2015, p. 16; and "The CDC's Anti-Smoking Ads Now Include E-Cigarettes," *Bloomberg Businessweek,* March 26, 2015, www.bloomberg.com/news/articles/2015-03-26/the-cdc-s-anti-smoking-ads-now-include-e-cigarettes.

12. Bruce Horovitz, "Taco Bell Still Giving Ronald McDonald Grief," *USA Today,* April 3, 2014.

13. See "Microsoft Flips Famed PC vs. Mac Ads to Pitch Smartphones, Tablets," *Advertising Age,* August 12, 2014, www.adage.com/print/294551; and www.youtube.com/watch?v=yYC5dkQlQLA, accessed October 2015.

14. See Jean Halliday, "Thinking Big Takes Audi from Obscure to Awesome," *Advertising Age,* February 2, 2009, http://adage.com/print?article_id=134234; and "Audi U.S. Sales in February 2015 Rise to Record Level for 50th Consecutive Month," *Yahoo! Finance,* April 17, 2015, http://finance.yahoo.com/news/audi-u-sales-february-2015-170012501.html.

15. "Number of Magazines in the United States from 2002 to 2013," *Statistica,* www.statista.com/statistics/238589/number-of-magazines-in-the-united-states/, accessed June 2015; and Andrew Burger, "Nielsen: Despite Hundreds of Choices, Average Number of TV Channels Watched Is 17," *Telecompetitor,* May 9, 2014, www.telecompetitor.com/nielsen-average-number-of-tv-channels-watched-is-17/.

16. Kelsey Libert and Kristen Tynski, "Research: The Emotions That Make Marketing Campaigns Go Viral," *HBR Blog Network,* October 24, 2013, http://blogs.hbr.org/2013/10/research-the-emotions-that-make-marketing-campaigns-go-viral/; and data from YouTube, Facebook, Instagram, and Twitter from October 2015.

17. Steve McClellan, "4As Scraps Annual Ad Production Cost Survey," *Media Post,* February 11, 2014, www.mediapost.com/publications/article/219371/4as-scraps-annual-ad-production-cost-survey.html; Sam Thielman, "The New Hour Is 43 Minutes Long," *Adweek,* June 24, 2013, p. 12; Jeanine Poggi, "Football and 'Big Bang' Are Broadcast TV's Most Expensive Ad Buys," *AdAge,* September 25, 2014, http://adage.com/print/295130; and "What It Costs," *Advertising Age,* April 6, 2014, pp. 14–18.

18. See Anthony Grupi, "Are Nets Beating Back the Devil in the DVR?" *Advertising Age,* September 29, 2014, pp. 16–17; and Jeff Baumgartner, "76% of Homes Have DVR, Netflix or Use VOD: Study," *Multichannel News,* January 2, 2015, www.multichannel.com/news/technology/76-homes-have-dvr-netflix-or-use-vod-study/386584.

19. See Michael Sebastian, "Madison & Vine at 10," *Advertising Age,* May 12, 2014, pp. 18–19.

20. "Real Beauty Shines Through: Dove Wins Titanium Grand Prix, 163 Million Views on YouTube," *Google: Think Insights,* June2013, www .thinkwithgoogle.com/case-studies/dove-real-beauty-sketches.html; Nina Bahadur, "Dove 'Real Beauty' Campaign Turns 10: How a Brand Tried to Change the Conversation about Female Beauty," *Huffington Post,* February 6, 2014, www.huffingtonpost.com/2014/01/21/dove-real-beauty-campaign-turns-10_n_4575940.tml; "Powerful Dove Experiment Shows How Women Can Choose to Feel Beautiful," *Mashable,* April 7, 2015, http://mashable.com/2015/04/07/dove-video-doors-beautiful-average/; and www.youtube.com/watch?v=XpaOjMXyJGk, accessed October 2014.

21. See Seth Fiegerman, "The New Way Brands Like Hostess Use Social Media: Playing Dumb," *Mashable,* April 6, 2015, http://mashable.com/2015/04/06/brands-play-dumb/.

22. See Danny Sullivan, "Product Placement: The TV Ads Consumers Can't Skip or Hop," *Marketing Land,* May 28, 2013, http://marketingland .com/product-placement-tv-ads-45729; Jonathan Welsh, "Can 'Captain America' Help Harley-Davidson Sell Motorcycles?" *Wall Street Journal,* April 1, 2014, http://blogs.wsj.com/speakeasy/2014/04/01/can-captain-america-help-harley-davidson-sell-motorcycles/; and Jason Lynch, "'Modern Family's' Apple-centric Integration Is Product Integration at Its Best," *Quartz,* February 25, 2015, http://qz.com/350518/modern-familys-apple-centric-episode-is-product-placement-at-its-best-and-great-tv/.

23. Abe Sauer, "Announcing the 2015 Brandcameo Product Placement Awards," *BrandChannel,* February 20, 2015, www.brandchannel.com/home/post/150220-2015-Brandcameo-Product-Placement-Awards.aspx.

24. "Why *The Lego Movie* Is the Perfect Piece of Product Placement," *A.V. Club,* February 11, 2014, http://www.avclub.com/article/why-the-lego-movie-is-the-perfect-piece-of-product-201102; and Abe Sauer, "Announcing the 2015 Brandcameo Product Placement Awards," *BrandChannel,* February 20, 2015, http://brandchannel.com/2015/02/20/announcing-the-2015-brandcameo-product-placement-awards/.

25. Michael Sebastionm "Nearly Two-Thirds of Marketers Plan to Increase Native-Ad Spending in 2015," January 29, 2015, *Advertising Age,* www .adage.com/print/296887.

26. For these and other examples, see David Gianatasio, "Ad of the Day: Cute, Quirky Chevy Commercial on the Oscars Was Made for $4,000," *Adweek,* March 3, 2014, www.adweek.com/print/156071; "Purina Pro Plan Debuts New Consumer-Generated Ad during Westminster Kennel Club Dog Show," *PRNewswire,* February 11, 2013; "Taco Bell Commissions User-Generated YouTube Ads to Promote New Fiery Doritos Locos Taco," *Viral Gains,* www.viralgains.com/2013/08/taco-bell-commissions-user-generated-youtube-ads-promote-fiery-doritos-locos-taco/; and www.youtube.com/watch?v=g9EU1Fw-D2s and www .youtube.com/watch?v=swFZ3QJmqu8#t=20, accessed October 2015.

27. Quotes and other information from Lauren Drell, "User Generated Content: Lessons from 4 Killer Ad Campaigns," *American Express Open Forum,* January 28, 2013, www.openforum.com/articles/lessons-from-4-killer-ugc-campaigns/; and http://thesweatlife.lululemon.com/, accessed October 2015.

28. Lauren Johnson, "How Social and Email Helped Mazda's Limited-Edition Preorders Sell Out Crazy Fast," *Adweek,* May 28, 2014, www .adweek.com/print/157985.

29. See Anna Rudenko, "Coca-Cola USA Prompting Youngsters to Contribute Their "Ahh' Moments," POPSOP, March 24, 2014, http://popsop.com/2014/03/coca-cola-usa-prompting-youngsters-to-contribute-their-ahh-coke-moments/; and "Coca-Cola: The AHH Efect," *All Things Digital,* March 11, 2015, https://digitalcasestudies.wordpress .com/2015/03/11/coca-cola-the-ahh-effect/.

30. See Wayne Friedman, "Most Second-Screeners Don't Follow Ads," *Media Post,* December 16, 2014, www.mediapost.com/publications/article/240250/.

31. *Forbes* and *Bloomberg Businessweek* cost and circulation data found online at www.bloombergmedia.com/magazine/businessweek/rates/ and www.forbesmedia.com/forbes-magazine-rates/, accessed October 2015.

32. Natalie Tadena, "With the New Year Approaching, Weight Loss Ad Barrage Has Commenced," *Wall Street Journal,* December 30, 2014, http://blogs.wsj.com/cmo/2014/12/30/with-the-new-year-approaching-weight-loss-ad-barrage-has-commenced/.

33. For these and other examples, see Christopher Heine, "Lexus Nabs 100K Video Views on Facebook—in 10 Minutes," *Adweek,* January 23, 2013, www.adweek.com/news/technology/print/146726; Matt McGee, "Oreo, Audi, and Walgreens Newsjack Super Bowl 'Blackout Bowl,'" *Marketing Land,* February 3, 2013, http://marketingland.com/oreo-audi-walgreens-market-quickly-during-super-bowl-blackout-32407; and "Arby's Slayed the Grammys with This Tweet about Pharrell Williams' Hat," *Adweek,* January 27, 2014, www.adweek.com/print/155237.

34. Information on advertising agency revenues from "Agency Report," *Advertising Age,* April 28, 2014, pp. 8+; and *Advertising Age Marketing Fact Pack 2015,"* December 29, 2014, p. 26–29.

35. Stuart Elliott, "Visa Trims Slogan to Expand Meaning," *New York Times,* January 13, 2014, p. B6.

36. See E. J. Schultz, "Behind the Snickers Campaign That Launched a Global Comeback," *Advertising Age,* October 4, 2013, http://adage.com/print/244593; and http://adsoftheworld.com/media/outdoor/snickers_running and http://cargocollective.com/mirceaandronescu/SNICKERS-OOH, accessed September 2014.

37. Based on Glen Broom and Bey-Ling Sha, *Cutlip & Center's Effective Public Relations,* 11th ed. (Upper Saddle River, NJ: Prentice Hall, 2013), Chapter 1.

38. See Mark Fidelman, "8 of the Best Influencer Marketing Campaigns from 8 Hot Agencies," *Forbes,* August 6, 2013, www.forbes.com/sites/markfidelman/2013/08/06/8-of-the-best-influencer-marketing-campaigns-from-the-8-hottest-agencies; Melissa Malcolm, "Success Is Built with Chocolate Milk," *Dairy Foods,* February 2014, pp. 15–17; Polly Elmore, "Promoting Chocolate Milk as an Energy Drink," *PR Works,* February 3, 2014, http://prwrks.com/promoting-chocolate-milk-as-an-energy-drink; and http://gotchocolatemilk.com and http://gotmilksales.org/milk-sales-strategies/built-with-chocolate-milk/, accessed October 2015.

39. See Geoffrey Fowler and Ben Worthen, "Buzz Powers iPad Launch," *Wall Street Journal,* April 2, 2010; "Apple iPad Sales Top 2 Million since Launch," *Tribune-Review* (Pittsburgh), June 2, 2010; "PR Pros Must Be Apple's iPad as a True Game-Changer," *PRweek,* May 2010, p. 23; and "Apple Launches New iPad," March 7, 2012, www.apple.com/pr/library/2012/03/07Apple-Launches-New-iPad.html.

40. Quotes from Sarah Skerik, "An Emerging PR Trend: Content PR Strategy and Tactics," *PR Newswire,* January 15, 2013, http://blog .prnewswire.com/2013/01/15/an-emerging-pr-trend-content-pr-strategy-tactics/; and Mary Teresa Bitti, "The New Mad Men: How Publics Relations Firms Have Emerged from the Shadows," *Financial Post,* December 28, 2014, http://business.financialpost.com/entrepreneur/the-changing-role-of-public-relations-firms.

Chapter 13

1. Based on information from David Whitford, "Salesforce.com: The Software and the Story," *Inc.,* September 2014, pp. 113–117; Whitford, "Selling, the Story: Four Strategies Salesforce.com Uses to Stay on Top," *Inc.,* September 2014, p. 116; Heather Clancy, "Best Buyer for Salesforce?" *Fortune,* April 29, 2015, http://fortune.com/2015/04/29/best-buyer-for-salesforce/; "The World's Most Innovative Companies," *Forbes,* www.forbes.com/innovative-companies/list/, accessed June 2015; and www.salesforce.com and www.salesforce.com/company/, accessed September 2015.

2. See Chanin Ballance, "End Your Sales and Marketing Tug-of-War," *Sales & Marketing Management,* September 26, 2014, http://salesandmarketing .com/content/end-your-sales-and-marketing-tug-war; and Philip Kotler and Kevin Lane Keller, *Marketing Management,* 15th ed. (Hoboken, NJ: Prentice Hall, 2016), p. 644.

3. "Selling Power 500 Largest Sales Forces (2014)," *Selling Power,* www .sellingpower.com/content/article/index.php?a=10430/selling-power-500/largest-sales-forces/2014.

4. See discussions in Mike Ishmael, "The Cost of a Sales Call," October 22, 2012, http://4dsales.com/the-cost-of-a-sales-call/; Jeff Green, "The New Willy Loman Survives by Staying Home," *Bloomberg Businessweek,* January 14–20, 2013, pp. 16–17; and "What Is the Real Cost of a B2B Sales Call?" www.marketing-playbook.com/sales-marketing-strategy/what-is-the-real-cost-of-a-b2b-sales-call, accessed September 2015.

5. Green, "The New Willy Loman Survives by Staying Home"; Dave Stein, "The Evolution of Social Selling," *Sales & Marketing Management,* May/June 2013, p. 14; and Andris A. Zoltners, PK Sinha, and Sally E. Lorimer, "The Growing Power of Inside Sales," *Harvard Business Review,* July 29, 2013, https://hbr.org/2013/07/the-growing-power-of-inside-sa/.

6. Quote and facts from Jim Domanski, "Special Report: The 2012 B@B Tele-Sales Trend Report," www.salesopedia.com/downloads/2012%20B2B%20Tele-Sales%20Trend%20Special%20Reportl.pdf, accessed July 2013; and Kurt Shaver, "Why Inside Salespeople Make Great Social Sellers," November 12, 2014, http://blog.sellingpower.com/gg/2014/11/why-inside-salespeople-make-great-social-sellers.html.

7. See "Case Study: Climax Portable Machine Tools," www.selltis.com/productCaseStudiesClimaxPortableMachineTools.aspx, accessed June 2014; and www.climaxportable.com, accessed September 2015.

8. "Customer Business Development," http://we.experiencepg.com/home/customer_business_development_cbd_sales.html, accessed September 2015.

9. Scott Fuhr, "Good Hiring Makes Good Cents," *Selling Power,* July/August/September 2012, pp. 20–21; and "How Sales Rep Turnover Costs Your Company More Than You Think," *Insight Squared,* July 15, 2014, www.insightsquared.com/2014/07/how-sales-rep-turnover-costs-your-company-more-than-you-think/.

10. For this and more information and discussion, see www.gallupaustralia.com.au/consulting/118729/sales-force-effectiveness.aspx, accessed July 2012; Lynette Ryals and Iain Davies, "Do You Really Know Who Your Best Salespeople Are?" *Harvard Business Review,* December 2010, pp. 34–35; and Donal Daly, "6 Things Successful Salespeople Do," *Salesforce.com,* April 17, 2015, www.salesforce.com/blog/2015/04/6-things-successful-sellers-do-cso-gp.html.

11. See Steve Denning, "The One Thing the Greatest Salespeople All Have," *Forbes,* November 29, 2012, www.forbes.com/sites/stevedenning/2012/11/29/the-one-thing-the-greatest-salespeople-all-have/.

12. "Strengths Based Selling," www.gallup.com/press/176651/strengths-based-selling.aspx, accessed September 2015.

13. Corporate Visions, Inc., "ADP Case Study," http://corporatevisions.com/v5/documents/secure_downloads/CVI_caseStudy_ADP.pdf, accessed June 2015; and V. Kumar, Sarang Sundder, and Robert P. Leone, "Who's Your Most Valuable Salesperson?" *Harvard Business Review,* April 2015, pp. 62–66.

14. Based on information found in Sara Donnelly, "Staying in the Game," *Pharmaceutical Executive,* May 2008, pp. 158–159; Bayer Healthcare Pharmaceuticals, Inc., "Improving Sales Force Effectiveness: Bayer's Experiment with New Technology," 2008, www.icmrindia.org/casestudies/catalogue/Marketing/MKTG200.htm; Tanya Lewis, "Concentric," *Medical Marketing and Media,* July 2008, p. 59, www.hydraframe.com/mobile/project_reprace.htm, accessed July 2012; Andrew Tolve, "Pharma Sales: How Simulation Can Help Reps Sell," *Eye for Pharma,* March 28, 2012, http://social.eyeforpharma.com/sales/pharma-sales-how-simulation-can-help-reps-sell; and Krishna Depura, "Online Sales Training for Busy Sales Representatives," *MindTickle,* www.mindtickle.com/blog/online-sales-training-for-busy-sales-representative/#more-1474, accessed September 2015.

15. For more discussion, see Mark Roberge, "The Right Way to Use Compensation," *Harvard Business Review,* April 2015, pp. 70–75; and "Getting Beyond 'Show Me the Money,'" *Harvard Business Review,* April 2015, pp. 77–81.

16. See Louis Columbus, "Top-Five Focus Areas for Improving Sales Effectiveness Initiatives," *Accenture,* 2013, www.accenture.com/SiteCollectionDocuments/PDF/Accenture-Top-Five-Improvements-Sales-Effectiveness.pdf; and "2014 Sales Performance Optimization Study," CSO Insights, www.csoinsights.com/Publications/.

17. Lain Chroust Ehmann, "Sales Up!" *Selling Power,* January/February 2011, p. 40. Also see Pisello, "Death of a Salesman?"; Tony J. Hughes, "Back to the Future of Sales in 2015," *LinkedIn,* December 27, 2014, www.linkedin.com/pulse/back-future-sales-2015-tony-j-hughes; and "Getting Beyond 'Show Me the Money."

18. See Scott Gillum, "The Disappearing Sales Process," *Forbes,* January 7, 2013, www.forbes.com/sites/gyro/2013/01/07/the-disappearing-sales-process/; and Paul Nolan, "Mapping the Buyer's Journey," *Sales & Marketing Management,* March/April 2015, pp. 32–34.

19. Neil Davey, "Using Social Media Marketing in B2B Markets," *SmartInsights,* February 16, 2015, www.smartinsights.com/b2b-digital-marketing/b2b-social-media-marketing/b2bsocialmediamarketing/.

20. See "GE's Social Story," www.salesforcemarketingcloud.com/resources/videos/ges-social-story/, accessed June 2014; David Moth, "How General Electric Uses Facebook, Twitter, Pinterest and Google+," *Velocify,* May 2013, https://econsultancy.com/blog/62684-how-general-electric-uses-facebook-twitter-pinterest-and-google; and "GE Social Media," www.ge.com/news/social, accessed September 2015.

21. Example based on information from James C. Anderson, Nirmalya Kumar, and James A. Narus, "Become a Value Merchant," *Sales & Marketing Management,* May 6, 2008, pp. 20–23; and "Business Market Value Merchants," *Marketing Management,* March/April 2008, pp. 31+. For more discussion and examples, see Heather Baldwin, "Deeper Value Delivery," *Selling Power,* September/October 2010, p. 16; Thomas P. Reilly, "Value-Added Selling Is Smart," *Selling Power,* June 27, 2012, www.sellingpower.com/content/article.php?a=8917; and Ron Shapiro, "Selling While Holding Your Price," *Sales & Marketing Management,* January 5, 2015, www.salesandmarketing.com/content/selling-while-holding-your-price.

22. Kantar Retail, *Making Connections: Trade Promotion Integration across the Marketing Landscape* (Wilton, CT: Kantar Retail, July 2012), p. 5.

23. Ibid., p. 6.

24. See "Top 10 Retail Loyalty Programs," *BigDoor,* http://bigdoor.com/blog/2013/12/11/top-10-retail-loyalty-programs/, accessed June 2015; and www.bloomingdales.com/loyallist?cm_sp=FOOTER-_-BOTTOM_NAV-_-LOYALLIST, accessed September 2015.

25. Laura Petrecca, "Food Marketers Offer Super Samples before Super Bowl," *USA Today,* January 25, 2014, www.usatoday.com/story/money/business/2014/01/25/super-bowl-food-samples/4808625/.

26. NCH Marketing Services, "NCH Annual Topline U.S. CPG Coupon Facts Report for Year-End 2014," February 2015, www2.nchmarketing.com/ResourceCenter/assets/0/22/28/76/226/457/4bfe051da14f4f8f9e8bc7e48d9e510a.pdf.

27. See NCH Marketing Services, "NCH Annual Topline View: CPG Coupon Facts Report for Year-End 2014, https://www2.nchmarketing.com/resourcecenter/," accessed September 2015; and "One-Click Savings: A Quick Look at 2015 Mobile Coupon Statistics," *TrueShip,* March 24, 2015, www.trueship.com/blog/2015/03/24/one-click-savings-a-quick-look-at-2015-mobile-coupon-statistics/#.VS8RL2a-h5A.

28. Hilary Milnes, "Walgreens Uses Mobile Apps to Solve In-Store Headaches," *Digiday,* May 4, 2015, https://digiday.com/brands/walgreens-uses-mobile-apps-solve-store-headaches/; "Entering the New Era of Digital Coupons," *Adweek,* June 16, 2014, p. S7; and www.walgreens.com/topic/apps/learn_about_mobile_browser_app.jsp and www.walgreens.com/coupons, accessed September 2015.

29. See www.happymeal.com/en_US/, accessed September 2015.

30. See "The 2013 Estimate of Promotion Products Distributor Sales," *PPAI,* www.ppai.org/inside-ppai/research/Documents/2013%20SalesVolume%20Sheet.pdf; and "PPAI Distributor Quarterly Sales Barometer," www.ppai.org/inside-ppai/research/Documents/14SalesBarometerD-Q4.pdf, accessed September 2015.

31. Based on information found in Patrick Hanlon, "Face Slams: Event Marketing Takes Off," *Forbes,* May 9, 2012, www.forbes.com/sites/patrickhanlon/2012/05/09/face-slams-event-marketing-takes-off/; and www.redbull.com/us/en/events and www.redbull.com/cs/Satellite/en_INT/RedBull/HolyShit/011242745950125, accessed September 2015. The referenced wing suit flying video can be found at http://player.vimeo.com/video/31481531?autoplay=1.

32. Kantar Retail, *Making Connections,* p. 10.

33. See "CES Attendee Audit Summary Results," www.cesweb.org/Why-CES/2014-Attendee-Audit, accessed June 2015; "New Logo for Bauma Ahead of 2016 Trade Fair," *World Cement,* July 5, 2015, www.worldcement.com/europe-cis/07052014/Bauma_new_look_ahead_of_2016_show_145/.

Chapter 14

1. See Michael Ausien, "Cyber Monday Is Amazon's Busiest Day of the Year," *Indianapolis Star,* December 1, 2015, www.indystar.com/story/money/2014/12/01/cyber-monday-amazons-busiest-day-year/19749775/; Morten T. Hansen, Herminia Ibarra, and Urs Peyer, "The Best-Performing CEOs in the World," *Harvard Business Review,* January–February 2013, pp. 81–86; George Anders, "Jeff Bezos's Top 10 Leadership Lessons," *Forbes,* April 4, 2012, www.forbes.com/sites/georgeanders/2012/04/04/bezos-tips/; "Walmart vs. Amazon Prime," *Advertising Age,* May 15, 2015, p. 6; "Benchmarks by Company: Amazon," ACSI, www.theacsi.org/?option=com_content&view=article&id=149&catid=&Itemid=214&c=Amazon, accessed June 2015; "Number of Worldwide Active Amazon Customer Accounts from 1997 to 2014 (in Millions)," *Statistica,* www.statista.com/statistics/237810/number-of-active-amazon-customer-accounts-worldwide/, accessed June 2015; and annual reports and other information found at www.amazon.com, accessed September 2015.

2. Stan Phelps, "Three Lessons from Mountain Dew on Leveraging Events to Create an Authentic Brand Experience," *Forbes,* October 18, 2014, www.forbes.com/sites/stanphelps/2014/10/18/three-lessons-from-mountain-dew-on-leveraging-events-to-create-an-authentic-brand-experience/; Natalie Tadena, "Mountain Dew Ads Go Global with Return of 'Do the Dew,'" *Wall Street Journal,* March 29, 2015, http://blogs.wsj.com/cmo/2015/03/29/mountain-dew-ads-go-global-with-return-of-do-the-dew/; and www.mountaindew.com, accessed September 2015.

3. See "Priceline Profit Tops Estimates as Bookings Rise," *Reuters,* February 20, 2014, www.reuters.com/article/2014/02/21/us-priceline-results-idUSBREA1J26X20140221; and http://ir.pricelinegroup.com/financials.cfm, accessed September 2015.

4. For these and other direct marketing statistics in this section, see Direct Marketing Association, *The DMA Statistical Fact Book 2015*, 37th ed., May 2015; Dave Erlandson, "Direct Mail Ad Spending Forecast to Grow 1.1% in 2014," *PODi Insights*, January 23, 2014, http://blog.podi.org/direct-mail-ad-spending-forecast-to-grow-1-1-in-2014; Ginger Conlin, "Where Will Marketing Grow in 2015?" *Direct Marketing News*, January 9, 2015, www.dmnews.com/where-will-marketing-grow-in-2015/printarticle/391699/; and other information at www.thedma.org, accessed September 2015.

5. See "Worldwide Ad Spending," *eMarketer*, www.emarketer.com/adspendtool, accessed June 2015; "Total US Ad Spending to See Largest Increase Since 2004," *eMarketer*, July 2, 2014, www.emarketer.com/Article/Total-US-Ad-Spending-See-Largest-Increase-Since-2004/1010982; Erlandson, "Direct Mail Ad Spending Forecast to Grow 1.1% in 2014"; and Ginger Conlin, "Where Will Marketing Grow in 2015?" *Direct Marketing News*, January 9, 2015, .dmnews.com/where-will-marketing-grow-in-2015/printarticle/391699/.

6. See Pew Research Center's Internet & American Life Project, "Internet User Demographics," www.pewinternet.org/data-trend/internet-use/latest-stats/, accessed April 2015; "Mobile Continues to Steal Share of US Adults' Day Time Spent with Media," *eMarketer*, April 22, 2014, www.emarketer.com/Article/Mobile-Continues-Steal-Share-of-US-Adults-Daily-Time-Spent-with-Media/1010782; Aaron Smith, "U.S. Smartphone Use in 2015," Pew Research Center, April 1, 2015, www.pewinternet.org/2015/04/01/us-smartphone-use-in-2015/; "ITU Releases Annual Global ICT Data and ICT Development Index Country Rankings," November 24, 2014, www.itu.int/net/pressoffice/press_releases/2014/68.aspx#.VTRtbUthveI; "2 Billion Consumers Worldwide to Get Smartphones by 2016," *eMarketer*, December 11, 2014, www.emarketer.com/Article/2-Billion-Consumers-Worldwide-Smartphones-by-2016/1011694.

7. See "Retail Sales Worldwide Will Top $22 Trillion This Year," *eMarketer*, December 23, 2014, www.emarketer.com/Article/Retail-Sales-Worldwide-Will-Top-22-Trillion-This-Year/1011765; and "60% of U.S. Retail Sales Will Involve the Web by 2017," *Internet Retailer*, October 30, 2013, www.internetretailer.com/2013/10/30/60-us-retail-sales-will-involve-web-2017.

8. See "Internet Retailer: Top 500 Guide," www.top500guide.com/top-500/the-top-500-list, accessed June 2015; and "Amazon's Online Sales Dwarf the Competition," *Statista*, May 7, 2014, www.statista.com/chart/2214/10-largest-online-retailers/.

9. See "Staples Aims to Change Image with New Slogan," *Boston Globe*, January 3, 2014; Matt Linder, "Online Sales at Staples Grow 4.8% in Fiscal 2014, *Internet Retailer*, March 6, 2015, www.internetretailer.com/2015/03/06/online-sales-staples-grow-48-fiscal-2014; and annual reports and other information found at www.staples.com, accessed September 2015.

10. See Roger Katz. "2015 Will Be the Year of the Brand Community—Here's Why," *ClickZ*, January 23, 2015, www.clickz.com/clickz/column/2391666/2015-will-be-the-year-of-the-brand-community-here-s-why; ComBlu, "The State of Online Branded Communities," http://comblu.com/downloads/ComBlu_StateOfOnlineCommunities_2012.pdf, November 2012, p. 19; and www.espn.com, accessed September 2015.

11. For these and other examples of rich media ads, see "Rising Starts: Display," *Jivox*, www.jivox.com/ad-gallery.php, accessed June 2015; and "Best Rich Media Online Ad," www.iacaward.org/iac/winners_detail.asp?yr=all&award_level=best&medium=Rich%20media%20Online%20Ad, accessed September 2015.

12. Conlin, "Where Will Marketing Grow in 2015"; and Google annual reports, http://investor.google.com/proxy.html, accessed September 2015.

13. "Social Media Is the Hot New Thing, but Email Is Still the King," *Advertising Age*, September 30, 2013, p. 18.

14. See Greg Sterling, "Report: 66 Percent of Email Opens on Mobile, Mostly iOS Devices," *Marketing Land*, November 19, 2014, http://marketingland.com/report-66-percent-email-opens-mobile-devices-108420; Nora Aufreiter et al., "Why Marketers Should Keep Sending You Emails," McKinsey & Company, January 2014, www.mckinsey.com/insights/marketing_sales/why_marketers_should_keep_sending_you_emails; Suzanne Vranica, "You've Got Mail and More Is Coming," *Wall Street Journal*, November 14, 2014, http://blogs.wsj.com/cmo/2014/11/14/youve-got-mail-and-more-is-coming/, and "5 Ways to Optimize Email Marketing ROI," *CMO Essentials*, March 10, 2015, www.cmoessentials.com/5-ways-optimize-email-marketing-roi/#sthash.OjGWLbE0.dpbs.

15. Carol Stott, "2014 Estimated Global Email Spam Rate Is 64%," *Business2Community*, May 7, 2014, www.business2community.com/email-marketing/2014-estimated-global-email-spam-rate-64-thats-almost-2-3-emails-0875585; and "Email: Unloved, Unbreakable," *Fortune*, May 1, 2015, pp. 54–55.

16. Linda Moses, "Online Video Ads Have Higher Impact Than TV Ads," *Adweek*, May 1, 2013, www.adweek.com/print/148982; and "comScore Releases December 2013 U.S. Online Video Rankings," January 10, 2014, www.comscore.com/Insights/Press_Releases/2014/1/comScore_Releases_December_2013_US_Online_Video_Rankings.

17. For these and other examples, see "Samsung, Wieden & Kennedy Rule Ad Age's 2013 Viral Video Awards," *Advertising Age*, April 16, 2013, http://adage.com/article/240900/; and Alexandra Jardine, "Always Viral Ad 'Like a Girl' Cleans Up at Webby Awards," *Advertising Age*, April 27, 2015, http://adage.com/print/298258.

18. See "Top 10 Branded Videos: Adidas Racks Up 21 Million YouTube Views in One Week," *Adweek*, February 25, 2015, www.adweek.com/print/163145; and www.youtube.com/watch?v=uiQVkoDlBbQ, accessed September 2015.

19. Troy Dreier, "The Force Was Strong with This One," *Streaming Media Magazine*, April/May 2011, pp. 66–68; also see Thales Teixeira, "The New Science of Viral Ads," *Harvard Business Review*, March 2012, pp. 25–28; and Hilary Masell Oswald, "The Biology of a Marketplace Sensation," *Marketing News*, September 2013, pp. 31–35.

20. Based on information found in Keith O'Brien, "How McDonald's Came Back Bigger Than Ever," *New York Times*, May 6, 2012, p. MM44. Also see Jayson DeMers, "How to Get Mommy Bloggers to Bring Customers to Your Brand," *Huffington Post*, November 6, 2014, www.huffingtonpost.com/jayson-demers/how-to-get-mommy-bloggers_b_6109064.html.

21. Jason DeMers, "The Top 10 Benefits of Social Media Marketing," *Forbes*, August 11, 2014, www.forbes.com/sites/jaysondemers/2014/08/11/the-top-10-benefits-of-social-media-marketing.

22. See http://newsroom.fb.com/company-info; www.youtube.com/yt/press/statistics.html and www.statisticbrain.com/twitter-statistics/, accessed September 2015.

23. For these and other examples, see www.kaboodle.com, www.farmersonly.com, www.birdpost.com, and www.cafemom.com, all accessed September 2015.

24. See http://nikeinc.com/news/nike-coach-feature-motivates-runners-with-customized-training-plans and www.nikeplus.com, accessed September 2015.

25. "3 Brands That Are Doing Live Chat on Twitter Right," *Adly.com*, January 28, 2014, http://adly.com/blog/3-brands-doing-live-chat-right/; and https://twitter.com/hashtag/wfmdish, accessed September 2015.

26. See www.instagram.com/etsy/, www.pinterest.com/etsy/, and www.etsy.com/about, accessed September 2015.

27. Example and quotes from "Meme Watch: Lay's 'Do Us a Flavor' Crowdsourcing Hilariously Backfires," *Uproxx*, February 5, 2014, http://uproxx.com/gammasquad/2014/02/best-of-lays-do-us-a-flavor-parodies/?showall=true; Michael Bourne, "Sailing of 14 Social Cs," *Mullen Advertising*, February, 13, 2012, www.mullen.com/sailing-the-14-social-cs/; and Jenna Mullins, "The Submissions for New Lay's Chip Flavors Are Getting Out of Control (but We Love It)," *EOnline*, February 6, 2014, www.eonline.com/news/508137/the-submissions-for-new-lays-chip-flavors-are-getting-out-of-control-but-we-love-it; and www.dousaflavor.com/, accessed June 2015.

28. Melissa Allison, "Re-Creating the Coffee Klatch Online," *Raleigh News & Observer*," May 6, 2013, p. 1D; Todd Wassermann, *Mashable*, December 13, 2013, http://mashable.com/2013/12/05/starbuckss-tweet-a-coffee-180000/; and www.facebook.com/Starbucks and https://twitter.com/Starbucks, accessed June 2015.

29. Facts in this paragraph are from "Wireless Quick Facts," www.ctia.org/your-wireless-life/how-wireless-works/wireless-quick-facts, accessed June 2015; "Smartphones: So Many Apps, So Much Time," Nielsen, July 1, 2014, www.nielsen.com/us/en/insights/news/2014/smartphones-so-many-apps--so-much-time.html; and Pew Research Center's Internet & American Life Project, "Mobile Technology Fact Sheet," www.pewinternet.org/fact-sheets/mobile-technology-fact-sheet/, accessed September 2015.

30. Jonathan Nelson, "Voice: One Screen to Rule Them All," *Adweek*, February 13, 2013, p. 15; Stephen Willard, "Study: People Check Their Cell Phones Every Six Minutes, 150 Times a Day," *Elite Daily*, February 11, 2013, http://elitedaily.com/news/world/study-people-check-cell-phones-minutes-150-times-day/; and "Mobile Continues to Steal Share of US Adults' Daily Time Spent with Media," *eMarketer.com*, April 22, 2014, www.emarketer.com/Article/Mobile-Continues-Steal-Share-of-US-Adults-Daily-Time-Spent-with-Media/1010782.

31. Lauren Johnson, "Target Turns Its Stores into One Big Mobile Game for the Holidays," *Adweek*, December 2, 2014, www.adweek.com/print/161727.

32. "IAB Internet Advertising Revenue Report," September 2015, www.iab.net/research/industry_data_and_landscape/adrevenuereport; "The Mobile

Movement," accessed at www.thinkwithgoogle.com/insights/emea/library/studies/the-mobile-movement, May 2013; and "Mobile Advertising Fast Facts," *Advertising Age*, April 04, 2014, pp. 20+.

33. See Lauren Johnson, "McDonald's Beefs Up Advertising Strategy with Mobile Game," *Mobile Marketer*, March 28, 2013, www.mobilemarketer.com/cms/news/advertising/12447.html; and Rimma Kats, "McDonald's Beefs Up Mobile Efforts via Targeted Campaign," *Mobile Marketing*, August 16, 2013, www.mobilemarketer.com/cms/news/advertising/13553.html.

34. See Judith Acquino, "JetBlue Voice-Activated Ad Teaches People to Speak 'Pigeon,'" *Ad Exchanger*," September 26, 2013, www.adexchanger.com/online-advertising/jetblue-voice-activated-ads-teach-people-to-speak-pigeon/; and Lauren Johnson, "Top 10 Mobile Advertising Campaigns of 2013," December 24, 2013, www.mobilemarketer.com/cms/news/advertising/16847.html.

35. See "Direct Mail Marketing Essentials Guide 2014," *DMNews*, March 2014, http://media.dmnews.com/documents/64/eg_directmail_15763.pdf; Winterberry Group, "2015 Annual Outlook: What to Expect in Direct and Digital Marketing," January 2015, www.winterberrygroup.com/system/files/Winterberry%20Group–2015%20Annual%20Outlook–DMCNY%20Luncheon_1.8.14.pdf; Paul Vogel, "Marketers Are Rediscovering the Value of Mail," Postal Customer Council of Providence, June 27, 2014, http://providencepcc.org/marketers-are-rediscovering-the-value-of-mail/; and "Stats & Facts: Direct Marketing," *CMO Council*, www.cmocouncil.org/facts-stats-categories.php?view=all&category=direct-marketing, access September 2015.

36. Julie Liesse, "When Times Are Hard, Mail Works," *Advertising Age*, March 30, 2009, p. 14; and Lois Geller, "If Direct Mail Is Dying, It's Sure Taking Its Time about It," *Forbes*, December 4, 2013, www.forbes.com/sites/loisgeller/2013/12/04/if-direct-mail-is-dying-its-sure-taking-its-time-about-it/; and Craig Simpson, "4 Reasons to Use Direct Mail Marketing Instead of Email," *Entrepreneur*, February 17, 2015, www.entrepreneur.com/article/242731.

37. Bruce Britt, "Marketing Leaders Discuss the Resurgence of Direct Mail," *Deliver Magazine*, January 18, 2011, www.delivermagazine.com/2011/01/marketing-leaders-discuss-resurgence-of-direct-mail/. Also see Alex Palmer, "Insurance Marketers Leverage Targeted Marketing," *Direct Marketing*, February 1, 2012, www.dmnews.com/insurance-marketers-leverage-targeted-marketing/article/225127/; and Michele B. Peel, "4 Reasons Direct Mail Should Be Part of Your Plan to Acquire New Customers," *Insurance Journal*, March 9, 2015, www.insurancejournal.com/magazines/features/2015/03/09/359395.htm.

38. Rebecca R. Ruiz, "Catalogs, after Years of Decline, Are Revamped for Changing Times," *New York Times*, January 26, 2015, p. B1.

39. Kurt Solomon, "Is the Catalog Dead?" November 5, 2013, www.kurtsalmon.com/US/vertical-insight/Is-the-Catalog-Dead-?vertical=Retail&id=936&language=en-us#.UzTUVV5dCcC.

40. Ruiz, "Catalogs, after Years of Decline, Are Revamped for Changing Times."

41. Winterberry Group, "2015 Annual Outlook: What to Expect in Direct and Digital Marketing," January 2015, www.winterberrygroup.com/system/files/Winterberry%20Group–2015%20Annual%20Outlook–DMCNY%20Luncheon_1.8.14.pdf.

42. See Federal Trade Comission "FTC Issues FY 2014 National Do Not Call Registry Data," November 19, 2014, www.ftc.gov/news-events/press-releases/2014/11/ftc-issues-fy-2014-national-do-not-call-registry-data-book; and www.donotcall.gov, accessed September 2015.

43. See Rachel Brown, "Perry, Fischer, Lavigne Tapped for Proactiv," *WWD*, January 13, 2010, p. 3; Rahul Parikh, "Proactiv's Celebrity Shell Game," Salon.com, February 28, 2011, www.salon.com/2011/02/28/proactiv_celebrity_sham; "Guthy-Renker Honored with Nine Era Moxie Awards for Year's Best Direct Marketing Campaigns," *Marketing Weekly News*, October 19, 2013, p. 145; and www.proactiv.com, accessed September 2015.

44. Jeanine Poggi, "H&M Super Bowl Ad Lets You Buy Beckham Bodywear by Remote Control," *Advertising Age*, January 6, 2014, www.adage.com/print/290915.

45. "Best Buy: Consumer Electronics Retailing on the Go," www.zoomsystems.com/our-partners/partner-portfolio/; and www.zoomsystems.com/about-us, accessed September 2015.

46. See Internet Crime Complaint Center, www.ic3.gov, accessed September 2015.

47. See "Fear and Worry in America? Identity Theft and Cybercrime," *Huffington Post*, November 5, 2014, www.huffingtonpost.com/creditsesamecom/fear-and-worry-in-america_b_6102910.html.

48. See Susan Dominus, "Underage on Facebook," *MSN Living*, March 15, 2012, http://living.msn.com/family-parenting/underage-on-facebook-5;

Josh Wolford, "Facebook Still Has a Big Problem with Underage Users, and They Know It," *WebProNews*, January 24, 2013, www.webpronews.com/facebook-still-has-a-big-problem-with-underage-users-and-they-know-it-2013-01; and Samuel Gibbs, "Facebook Patent Reveals Plan for Children to Join the Social Network," *Guardian*, June 3, 2014, www.theguardian.com/technology/2014/jun/03/facebook-children-join-social-network.

49. See Zach Miners, "Your Control of Your Personal Info Is All but Dead, Pew Respondents Fear," *PCWorld*, November 12, 2014, www.pcworld.com/article/2846855; Hadley Malcolm, "Millennials Don't Worry about Online Privacy," *USA Today*, April 21, 2013; and "2015 TRUSTe US Consumer Confidence Index," *TRUSTe*, www.truste.com/resources/privacy-research/us-consumer-confidence-index-2015/.

50. Based on information from Michael Bush, "My Life, Seen through the Eyes of Marketers," *Advertising Age*, April 26, 2010, http://adage.com/print/143479.

51. See "Facebook to Make Targeted Ads More Transparent for Users," *Advertising Age*, February 4, 2013, http://adage.com/article/239564/; and www.aboutads.info/, accessed September 2015.

52. See Richard Byrne Reilly, "Feds to Mobile Marketers: Stop Targeting Kids, or Else," *Venture Beat*, March 27, 2014, http://venturebeat.com/2014/03/27/feds-to-mobile-marketers-stop-targeting-kids-or-else-exclusive/; and www.business.ftc.gov/privacy-and-security/childrens-privacy, accessed September 2015.

53. Information on TRUSTe at www.truste.com, accessed September 2015.

54. Information on the DMA Privacy Promise at www.the-dma.org/cgi/dispissue?article=129 and www.dmachoice.org/static/privacy_policy.php, accessed September 2015.

Chapter 15

1. Based on information from "Our Mission Is 'Beauty for All,' Says L'Oréal Global CEO Jean-Paul," *The Economic Times*," January 30, 2015, http://articles.economictimes.indiatimes.com/2015-01-30/news/58625572_1_l-oreal-loreal-jean-paul-agon; Hae-Jung Hong and Yves Doz, "L'Oréal Masters Multiculturalism," *Harvard Business Review*, June, 2013, pp. 114–119; Liza Lin, "L'Oréal Puts on a Happy Face in China," *Bloomberg Businessweek*, April 1–7, 2013, pp. 25–26; "A Worldwide Approach to Beauty Rituals," www.loreal.com/research-innovation/when-the-diversity-of-types-of-beauty-inspires-science/a-world-wide-approach-to-beauty-rituals.aspx, accessed September2015; and www.lorealusa.com/Article.aspx?topcode=CorpTopic_RI_CustomerInnovation, www.lorealusa.com/research-innovation/when-the-diversity-of-types-of-beauty-inspires-science/stories-of-multicultural-innovations.aspx, and www.loreal-finance.com/eng/annual-report, accessed September, 2015.

2. Data from "*Fortune* 500," *Fortune*, June 2015, http://money.cnn.com/magazines/fortune/fortune500/; Douglas B. Fay, "Multinational Customers: Are Their Needs Really Being Met?" www.globexintl.com/corporate/?p=82, accessed May 2015; and "List of Countries by GDP: List by the CIA World Factbook," *Wikipedia*, http://en.wikipedia.org/wiki/List_of_countries_by_GDP_(nominal), accessed September 2015.

3. "Modest Trade Recovery to Continue in 2015 and 2016 Following Three Years of Weak Expansion," WTO Press Release, April 14, 2015, www.wto.org/english/news_e/pres15_e/pr739_e.htm

4. Information from www.michelin.com/eng/finance/individual-shareholders/publications, www.jnj.com, and www.caterpillar.com, accessed September 2015.

5. See www.otisworldwide.com/d1-about.html; and UTC Annual Report, http://2014ar.utc.com/, accessed September 2015.

6. Rob Schmitz, "Trade Spat between China and EU Threatens Exports of Solar Panels, Wine," *Marketplace*, June 6, 2013, www.marketplace.org/topics/world/trade-spat-between-china-and-eu-threatens-exports-solar-panels-wine; Ben Blanchard and Francesco Guarascio, "EU, China End Wine Dispute Ahead of Xi's European Tour," *Reuters*, March 21, 2014, www.reuters.com/article/idUSBREA2K0QE20140321; and "EU to Benefit from China's 'New Normal' Economy: Ambassador," April 15, 2015, www.ecns.cn/voices/2015/04-15/161743.shtml.

7. Gardiner Harris, "Wal-Mart Drops Ambitious Expansion Plan for India," *New York Times*, October 10, 2013, p. B3; Paul Ausick, "Walmart Still Struggles in India," *247wallst*, April 8, 2014, http://247wallst.com/retail/2014/04/08/walmart-still-struggles-in-india/; Rhitu Chatterjee, "Indian Shopkeepers Greet Wal-Mart's Expansion Plans with Protests," *NPR*, November 20, 2014, www.npr.org/blogs/goatsandsoda/2014/11/20/365480337/; and "Budget 2015: Walmart See Increase in Domestic Consumption, Retail Growth in India," *The Economic Times*, March

15, 2015, http://economictimes.indiatimes.com/industry/services/retail/budget-2015-walmart-sees-increase-in-domestic-consumption-retail-growth-in-india/articleshow/46418646.cms.

8. "What Is the WTO?" www.wto.org/english/thewto_e/whatis_e/whatis_e.htm, accessed September 2015.

9. See "The Doha Round," www.wto.org/english/tratop_e/dda_e/dda_e.htm, accessed September 2015.

10. "The EU at a Glance," http://europa.eu/about-eu/index_en.htm; "EU Statistics and Opinion Polls," http://europa.eu/documentation/statistics-polls/index_en.htm; and "EU Position in World Trade, http://ec.europa.eu/trade/policy/eu-position-in-world-trade/, all accessed September 2015.

11. Jack Ewing, "European Banks Feel Heat in Crimea Crisis, with Austria Bearing Brunt," *New York Times,* March 28, 2014, p. B6; "France's Sapin: Euro's Weakening Phase Has Run Its Course," *Wall Street Journal,* April 17, 2015, www.wsj.com/articles/frances-sapin-euros-weakening-phase-has-run-its-course-1429300555; and "European Union: The Euro," http://europa.eu/about-eu/basic-information/money/euro/, accessed September 2015.

12. CIA, *The World Factbook,* https://www.cia.gov/library/publications/the-world-factbook, accessed September 2015.

13. Statistics and other information from CIA, *The World Factbook;* and NAFTANow.org, accessed May 2015.

14. See "Explainer: What Is UNASUR?" www.as-coa.org/articles/explainer-what-unasur and http://en.wikipedia.org/wiki/Union_of_South_American_Nations, accessed September 2015.

15. See Zeenat Moorad, "The Coca-Cola Company: Tapping Africa's Fizz," *Financial Mail,* May 4, 2015, www.financialmail.co.za/coverstory/2015/04/30/the-coca-cola-company-tapping-africas-fizz; Annaleigh Vallie, "Coke Turns 125 and Has Much Life Ahead," *Business Day,* May 16, 2011, www.businessday.co.za/articles/Content.aspx?id_142848; Andrew Cave, "Glaxo and Unilever Take Note: How General Electric and Coca-Cola Are Winning in Africa," *Forbes,* April 2, 2014, www.forbes.com/sites/andrewcave/2014/04/02/glaxo-and-unilever-take-note-how-general-electric-and-coca-cola-are-winning-in-africa/; and Coca-Cola annual reports and other information from www.thecoca-colacompany.com, accessed September 2015.

16. See "2014 Investment Climate Statement—Russia," U.S. Bureau of Economic and Business Affairs, June 2014, www.state.gov/e/eb/rls/othr/ics/2014/227933.htm; and "Welcome to the U.S. Commercial Service in Russia," http://export.gov/russia/, accessed September 2015.

17. Laurent Belsie, "What Will Venezuela Do with Its Oil?" *Christian Science Monitor,* March 6, 2013, www.csmonitor.com/Environment/2013/0307/What-will-Venezuela-do-with-its-oil-Top-five-energy-challenges-after-Chavez/Oil-bartering; John Paul Rathbone, "Venezuela: In Search of a Solution," *Financial Times,* March 2, 2014, www.ft.com/intl/cms/s/2/45c3cae4-a049-11e3-8557-00144feab7de.html#axzz2xgjEix7Y; and International Reciprocal Trade Association, www.irta.com/index.php/about/modern-trade-barter, accessed September 2015.

18. For these and other examples, see Emma Hall, "Do You Know Your Rites? BBDO Does," *Advertising Age,* May 21, 2007, p. 22.

19. Jamie Bryan, "The Mintz Dynasty," *Fast Company,* April 2006, pp. 56–61; Viji Sundaram, "Offensive Durga Display Dropped," *India-West,* February 2006, p. A1; and Emily Bryson York and Rupal Parekh, "Burger King's MO: Offend, Earn Media, Apologize, Repeat," *Advertising Age,* July 8, 2009, http://adage.com/print?article_id=137801. For other examples, see Chris Isidore, "Chevy Pulls Ad Offensive to Chinese," *CNNMoney,* May 1, 2013, www.money.cnn.com/2013/05/01/news/companies/offensive-chevy-ad/; Julia Lynn Rubin, "4 Offensive Ads You Won't Believe Are Real," *Contently,* September 5, 2014, http://contently.com/strategist/2014/09/05/4-of-the-most-offensive-ads-of-the-last-decade/; and "Misinterpretation or Culturally Insensitive," *IMC Hawk,* April 30, 2015, http://imcclass.com/.

20. For these and other examples, see Bill Chappell, "Bill Gates' Handshake with South Korea's Park Sparks Debate," *NPR,* April 23, 2013, www.npr.org/blogs/thetwo-way/2013/04/23/178650537/bill-gates-handshake-with-south-koreas-park-sparks-debate; "Managing Quality across the (Global) Organization, Its Stakeholders, Suppliers, and Customers," Chartered Quality Institute, www.thecqi.org/Knowledge-Hub/Knowledge-portal/Corporate-strategy/Managing-quality-globally, accessed September 2015.

21. Quotes and other information found in David Pierson, "Beijing Loves IKEA—but Not for Shopping," *Los Angeles Times,* August 25, 2009, http://articles.latimes.com/2009/aug/25/business/fi-china-ikea25; Michael Wei, "In IKEA's China Stores, Loitering Is Encouraged," *Bloomberg Businessweek,* November 1, 2010, pp. 22–23; Pan Kwan Yuk, "IKEA in China: Turning Gawkers into Customers," *BeyondBrics,* April 4, 2013, http://blogs.ft.com/beyond-brics/2013/04/04/ikea-in-china-turning-gawkers-into-consumers/?#axzz2SobYFh98; Emily Raulhala, "No, IKEA Hasn't Banned Customers from Sleeping in Its Chinese Stores," *Time,* April 10. 2015, http://time.com/3814935/ikea-china-customers-sleeping/; and "IKEA Group Yearly Summary FY2014," www.ikea.com/ms/en_US/pdf/yearly_summary/ikea-group-yearly-summary-fy14.pdf, accessed September 2015.

22. Andres Martinez, "The Next American Century," *Time,* March 22, 2010, p. 1.

23. Thomas L. Friedman, *The Lexus and the Olive Tree: Understanding Globalization* (New York: Anchor Books, 2000); and Michael Wei and Margaret Conley, "Global Brands: Some Chinese Kids' First Word: Mickey," *Bloomberg Businessweek,* June 19, 2011, pp. 24–25.

24. Adam Chandler, "How McDonald's Became a Target for Protest," *The Atlantic,* April 16, 2015, www.theatlantic.com/business/archive/2015/04/setting-the-symbolic-golden-arches-aflame/390708/.

25. "2015 BrandZ Top 100 Global Brands," Millward Brown, www.millwardbrown.com/mb-global/brand-strategy/brand-equity/brandz/top-global-brands/2015.

26. See Rachael Tepper, "Yum! Brands' International Product Strategy: How the Double Down Went Global," *Huffington Post,* March 11, 2013, www.huffingtonpost.com/2013/03/11/yum-brands-international-product-strategy_n_2814360.html; Molly Osberg, "How Colonel Sanders Became Father Christmas in Japan," *TPM,* December 23, 2014, http://talkingpointsmemo.com/theslice/kfc-christmas-in-japan-colonel-sanders-history-12-23-2014; and Jason Johnson, "KFC Christmas Tradition in Japan," *Brain Skewer,* May 2015, http://brainskewer.com/bs/20150506/kfc-christmas-tradition-japan.

27. See annual reports and other financial and review data from www.coca-colacompany.com/our-company/, accessed September 2015.

28. This Netflix example is based on information found in Sam Schechner, "Europe's Media Giants Prep for Netflix Landing," *Wall Street Journal,* January 29, 2014, http://online.wsj.com/news/articles/SB200014240527023032777045793487774128548520; and Joan E. Solsman, "Netflix Invades Europe: Why Expansion beyond the US Is So Critical," *CNET,* September 19, 2014, www.cnet.com/news/netflix-invades-europe-why-international-expansion-is-so-critical/.

29. See www.olc.co.jp/en/ and www.coca-colahellenic.com/aboutus/, accessed September 2015.

30. See "Škoda and Volkswagen Group Russia: One Year of Successful Production in Nizhny Novgorod," December 11, 2013, www.volkswagenag.com/content/vwcorp/info_center/en/news/2013/12/Nizhny_Novgorod.html; and www.pg.com/en_IN/company/pg-india.shtml, accessed September 2015.

31. See http://en.wikipedia.org/wiki/Doubletree, accessed September 2015.

32. Christina Larson, "Intel Buys Its Way Deeper into China," *Bloomberg Businessweek,* March 8, 2015, pp. 33–34.

33. "Intel in China," *iLook China,* May 28, 2010, http://ilookchina.net/2010/05/page/2/; and Christina Larson, "Intel Buys Its Way Deeper into China," *Bloomberg Businessweek,* March 8, 2015, pp. 33–34.

34. "A Tale of Two Countries: Starbucks in India and China," *Starbucks Newsroom,* March 27, 2014, http://news.starbucks.com/news/a-tale-of-two-countries-starbucks-growth-in-india-and-china; Anita Chong Beattie, "Can Starbucks Make China Love Joe?" *Advertising Age,* November 5, 2012, pp. 20–21; Bruce Horovitz, "China to Become No. 2 Marketing for Starbucks," *USA Today,* September 16, 2013, www.usatoday.com/story/money/business/2013/09/16/starbucks-china-flagship-stores/2820885/; and Rachael Lerman, "All the Tea in China: Starbucks' Biggest Market Isn't Where You Think," *Puget Sound Business Journal,* March 20, 2015, www.bizjournals.com/seattle/blog/2015/03/all-the-tea-in-china-starbucks-biggest-market-isnt.html?page=all.

35. See Warren J. Keegan and Mark C. Green, *Global Marketing,* 7th ed. (Upper Saddle River, NJ: Prentice Hall, 2013), pp. 303–308.

36. Toshiro Wakayama, Junjiro Shintaku, and Tomofumi Amano, "What Panasonic Learned in China," *Harvard Business Review,* December 2012, pp. 109–113.

37. Information on McDonald's menus and operations found in Lucy Fancourt, Bredesen Lewis, and Nicholas Majka, "Born in the USA, Made in France: How McDonald's Succeeds in the Land of Michelin Stars," Knowledge@Wharton, January 3, 2012, http://knowledge.wharton.upenn.edu/article.cfm?articleid=2906; Richard Vines and Caroline Connan, "McDonald's Wins Over French Chef with McBaguette Sandwich," *Bloomberg,* January 15, 2013, www.bloomberg.com/news/2013-01-15/mcdonald-s-wins-over-french-chef-with-mcbaguette-sandwich.html; Rob Wile, "The True Story of How McDonald's Conquered France," *Business Insider,* August 22, 2014, www.businessinsider.com/how-mcdonalds-conquered-

france-2014-8; and "McDonald's Food You Can't Get Here," *Chicago Tribune,* www.chicagotribune.com/business/ct-biz-mcdonalds-food-around-the-world,0,5168632.photogallery, accessed September 2015.

38. See Normandy Madden, "In China, Multinationals Forgo Adaptation for New-Brand Creation," *Advertising Age,* January 17, 2011, p. 10; Susan Adams, "The 10 Companies Considered 'Best for the World,'" *Forbes,* March 31, 2014, www.forbes.com/sites/susanadams/2014/03/31/10-companies-considered-best-for-the-world/; Meg Cichon, "Solar Making Big Strides to Power the Developing World," *Renewable Energy World,* May 7, 2014, www.renewableenergyworld.com/rea/news/article/2014/05/solar-making-big-strides-to-power-the-developing-world; and www.dlightdesign.com/, accessed September 2015.

39. Jeffrey N. Ross, "Chevrolet Will 'Find New Roads' as Brand Grows Globally: Aligns around the World behind Singular Vision," January 8, 2013, http://media.gm.com/media/us/en/gm/news.detail.html/content/Pages/news/us/en/2013/Jan/0107-find-new-roads.html; and Dale Buss, "Chevy Wins at Sochi by Giving Dimension to 'Find New Roads,'" *Forbes,* February 24, 2014, www.forbes.com/sites/dalebuss/2014/02/24/chevrolet-wins-at-sochi-as-find-new-roads-theme-gets-traction/.

40. "Nike Faces Ultimate Marketing Challenge in China: Make Running Cool," *Advertising Age,* October 31, 2011, pp. 1+; "Firms Help Spur a Running Craze in China," *China Sports News,* December 30, 2013, www.chinasportsbeat.com/2013/12/firms-help-spur-running-craze-in-china.html; and "Nike Faces Tough Competition in Europe and China," *Forbes,* March 4, 2014, www.forbes.com/sites/greatspeculations/2014/03/04/nike-faces-tough-competition-in-europe-and-china/.

41. See George E. Belch and Michael A. Belch, *Advertising and Promotion: An Integrated Marketing Communications Perspective*, 8th ed. (New York: McGraw Hill, 2011), Chapter 20; Shintero Okazaki and Charles R. Taylor, "What Is SMS Advertising and Why Do Multinationals Adopt It?" *Journal of Business Research,* January 2008, pp. 4–12; and Warren J. Keegan and Mark C. Green, *Global Marketing,* 7th ed. (Upper Saddle River, NJ: Prentice Hall, 2013), pp. 398–400.

42. See Brian X. Chen, "Motorola to Offer Moto G Smartphone Aimed at Emerging Markets," *New York Times,* November 14, 2013, p. B5; Nikhil Subramaniam, "Motorola Beats Nokia in India Smartphone Sales Thanks to Moto G, Moto E," *Tech 2,* August 4, 2014, http://tech.firstpost.com/news-analysis/motorola-beats-nokia-in-india-smartphone-sales-thanks-to-moto-g-moto-e-228420.html; and Luke Jones, "Motorola Moto G Brazil's Best-Selling Smartphone," *Mobile Burn,* March 29, 2015, www.mobileburn.com/24405/news/motorola-moto-g-brazils-best-selling-smartphone.

43. Anita Chang Beattie, "Catching the Eye of a Chinese Shopper," *Advertising Age,* December 10, 2013, pp. 20–21.

44. Drew Hinshaw, "Burgers Face a Tough Slog in Africa," *Wall Street Journal,* December 10, 2013, www.wsj.com/articles/SB10001424052702304607104579214133498585594.

45. See Claudia Penteado, "Brazil's Northeast Goes from 'Land of Laziness' to Next China," *Advertising Age,* June 13, 2011, http://adage.com/print/228070/; Richard Wallace, "Middle-Classes on the Up: Why Brazil Is Growing," *IGD,* September 15, 2011, www.igd.com/our-expertise/Retail/retail-outlook/4713/Middle-classes-on-the-up-why-Brazil-is-growing/; and www.nestle.com.br/portalnestle/nestleatevoce/abordo_sobre_projeto.aspx and http://nestleatevoce.com.br, accessed September 2015.

Chapter 16

1. Based on information from Danielle Sacks, "Any Fight Worth Fighting— That's the Attitude We Take," *Fast Company,* February 2015, pp. 34-36; Katherine Ling, "Walking the Talk," *Marketing News,* March 15, 2012, p. 24; Kyle Stock, "Patagonia's 'Buy Less' Plea Spurs More Buying," *Bloomberg Businessweek,* August 28, 2013, www.businessweek.com/printer/articles/147326-patagonias-buy-less-plea-spurs-more-buying; Daniela Walker, "Patagonia Truck Has Been Traveling across 50 States Mending Clothes," *PSFK,* May 6, 2015, www.psfk.com/2015/05/patagonia-truck-traveling-across-the-country-worn-wear-initiative.html; and www.patagonia.com/email/11/112811.html, www.patagonia.com/us/common-threads?src=112811_mt1, http://wornwear.patagonia.com/, and www.patagonia.com/us/environmentalism, accessed September 2015.

2. See "McDonald's Introduces Fresh, Whole Fruit Option in Happy Meals," December 1, 2014, http://news.mcdonalds.com/US/releases/McDONALD%E2%80%99S-INTRODUCES-FRESH,-WHOLE-FRUIT-OPTION-IN; and www.aboutmcdonalds.com/mcd/sustainability.html and www.mcdonalds.com/us/en/food/meal_bundles/favoritesunder400.html, accessed September 2015.

3. Tony T Liu, "Overstock.com Receives $6.8 Million Fine for False Advertising," *Orange Country Business Attorney Blog,* February 11, 2014, www.orangecountybusinessattorneyblog.com/2014/02/11/overstock-com-receives-6-8-million-fine-false-advertising/.

4. See "Challenging Deceptive Advertising and Marketing," www.ftc.gov/reports/annual-report-standard/ftc-2013/challenging-deceptive-advertising-and-marketing, accessed November 2013; Katy Bachman, "FTC Says 'No Way' to Nissan Frontier-Pushing Dune Buggy Ad," *Adweek,* January 23, 2014, www.adweek.com/print/155151; and Tennille Tracy, "FTC Says Gerber Falsely Advertised Baby Formula as Reducing Allergies," *Wall Street Journal,* October 30, 2015, www.wsj.com/articles/ftc-says-gerber-falsely-advertised-baby-formula-as-reducing-allergies-1414690530.

5. See Patience Haggin, "Three U.S. States Sue 5-Hour Energy Drink over Advertising," *Reuters,* July 17, 2014, www.reuters.com/article/2014/07/18/us-usa-energy-drink-lawsuit-idUSKBN0FN06N20140718; and Caroline Simson, "5-Hour Energy Makers Can't Dump False Ad MDL," *Law360,* January 23, 2015, www.law360.com/articles/614361/5-hour-energy-makers-can-t-dump-false-ad-mdl.

6. See "Overweight and Obesity in the U.S.," *FRAC,* http://frac.org/initiatives/hunger-and-obesity/obesity-in-the-us/, accessed September 2015; and "Overweight and Obesity," Centers for Disease Control and Prevention, www.cdc.gov/obesity/data/index.html, accessed September 2015.

7. See Chris Dolmetsch, "New York Big-Soda Ban Rejected by State's Highest Court," *Bloomberg Businessweek,* June 26, 2014, www.businessweek.com/news/2014-06-26/new-york-big-soda-ban-rejected-by-state-s-highest-court; and "Pouring on the Pounds Ad Campaign," *NYC Health,* www.nyc.gov/html/doh/html/living/sugarydrink-media.shtml, accessed September 2015.

8. Elena Ferretti, "Soft Drinks Are the Whipping Boy of Anti-Obesity Campaigns," *Fox News,* June 1, 2012, www.foxnews.com/leisure/2012/06/01/soda-ban/. Also see Natalie Zmuda and others, "Coca-Cola Would Like to Teach the World to Move," *Advertising Age,* September 11, 2013, http://adage.com/print/244077; and Mike Esterl, "Soda Producers Set Goals on Cutting U.S. Beverage Calories," *Wall Street Journal,* September 23, 2014, www.wsj.com/articles/soda-companies-set-goals-on-beverage-calories-1411493446.

9. Brian Clark Howard, "Planned Obsolescence: 8 Products Designed to Fail," *Popular Mechanics,* www.popularmechanics.com/technology/planned-obsole scence-460210#slide-5, accessed September 2015.

10. Rob Walker, "Replacement Therapy," *Atlantic Monthly,* September 2011, p. 38. For another interesting discussion, see Homa Khaleeli, "End of the Line for Stuff That's Built to Die?" *The Guardian,* March 3, 2015, www.theguardian.com/technology/shortcuts/2015/mar/03/has-planned-obsolesence-had-its-day-design.

11. See Kriston Capps, "Whole Foods Should Embrace Food Stamps," *Atlanta Citylab,* May 8, 2015, http://www.citylab.com/tech/2015/05/whole-foods-should-embrace-food-stamps/392804/; Spence Cooper, "National Food Chains Join First Lady to Reach 'Food Deserts,'" *Friends Eat,* July 25, 2011, http://blog.friendseat.com/michelle-obama-program-reaches-food-deserts; Matt Lerner, "Do You Live in a Food Desert?" *Walk Score,* March 26, 2014, http://blog.walkscore.com/2014/03/best-and-worst-u-s-food-deserts/; and U.S. Department of Agriculture, "Creating Access to Healthy, Affordable Food," http://apps.ams.usda.gov/fooddeserts, accessed September 2015.

12. See www.newdream.org/, www.newdream.org/about/mission, and www.newdream.org/blog/more-fun-less-stuff-photos, accessed September 2015.

13. See www.marksandspencer.com/s/plan-a-shwopping, accessed September 2015.

14. See Texas Transportation Institute, "Annual Urban Mobility Report," http://mobility.tamu.edu/ums/report/, accessed September 2015.

15. See Michael Cabanatuan, "Tolls Thin Traffic in Bay Bridge Carpool Lanes," *San Francisco Chronicle,* November 7, 2011, www.sfgate.com/news/article/Tolls-thin-traffic-in-Bay-Bridge-carpool-lanes-2323670.php#photo-1829296; and http://bata.mtc.ca.gov/tolls/schedule.htm, accessed September 2015. Also see "What Is Congestion Pricing?" http://ops.fhwa.dot.gov/publications/congestionpricing/sec2.htm, accessed September 2015.

16. For this and more information about the Google antitrust example, see Nathan Newman, "EU Antitrust Action Today Is Just the Beginning of Google's Troubles in Europe," *Huffington Post,* April 15, 2015, www.huffingtonpost.com/nathan-newman/eu-antitrust-action-today_b_7070568.html; and James Kanter and Mark Scott, "Europe Challenges Google, Seeing Violations of Its Antitrust Law," *New York Times,* April 16, 2015, p. B1.

17. See Philip Kotler, "Reinventing Marketing to Manage the Environmental Imperative," *Journal of Marketing*, July 2011, pp. 132–135; and Kai Ryssdal, "Unilever CEO: For Sustainable Business, Go against 'Mindless Consumption,'" *Marketplace,* June 11, 2013, www.marketplace.org/topics/sustainability/consumed/unilever-ceo-paul-polman-sustainble-business.

18. See Matt Townsend, "Is Nike's Flyknit the Swoosh of the Future?" *Bloomberg Businessweek,* March 19, 2012, pp. 31–32; "Sustainability," http://about.nike.com/pages/sustainability, accessed September 2015; and "SC Johnson Integrity," www.scjohnson.com/en/commitment/overview .aspx, accessed September 2015.

19. See Alan S. Brown, "The Many Shades of Green," *Mechanical Engineering*, January 2009, http://memagazine.asmc.org/Articles/2009/January/Many_Shades_Green.cfm; and www-03.ibm.com/financing/us/recovery/, accessed September 2015.

20. Based on information from "Local Insights Leasing to Globally Valid Innovations," Coca-Cola India, May 7, 2015, www.coca-colaindia .com/2015/05/07/local-insights-leading-globally-valid-innovations/; Simon Houpt, "Beyond the Bottle: Coke Trumpets Its Green Initiatives," *The Globe and Mail (Toronto)*, January 13, 2011; Marc Gunther, "Coca-Cola's Green Crusader," *Fortune,* April 28, 2008, p. 150; "Coca-Cola Installs 1 Millionth HFC-Free Cooler Globally, Preventing 5.25MM Metric Tons of CO2," January 22, 2014, www.coca-colacompany.com/press-center/press-releases/coca-cola-installs-1-millionth-hfc-free-cooler-globally-preventing-525mm-metrics-tons-of-co2; "Position Statement on Climate Protection," January 1, 2012, www.coca-colacompany .com/stories/position-statement-on-climate-protection; and www.coca-colacompany.com/stories/our-2020-environment-goals-infographic and www.coca-cola.com/content-store/en_US/SC/PlantBottle/, accessed September 2015.

21. Information from "The North Face 2014 Sustainability Report," http://neverstopexploring.com/2014/07/22/north-face-2014-corporate-responsibility-report/, accessed September 2015; Leon Kaye, "The North Face Sustainability Report," *Triple Pundit*, July 29, 2014, www.triplepundit .com/2014/07/the-north-face-sustainability/; and www.thenorthface.com/about-us/responsibility.html, accessed September 2015.

22. See www.thenorthface.com/about-us/responsibility.html, accessed September 2015.

23. See Austin Carr, "Nike: The No. 1 Most Innovative Company of 2013," *Fast Company*, March 2013, www.fastcompany.com/most-innovative-companies/2013/nike; Haydn Shaughnessy, "The World's Most Innovative Companies, A New View," *Forbes,* January 13, 2014, www .forbes.com/sites/haydnshaughnessy/2014/01/13/a-new-way-of-looking-at-the-worlds-most-innovative-companies/; and Pete Forester, "Why Nike Flyknit Is the Most Stylish and Innovative Sneaker Technology Today," *Complex*, April 2, 2015, www.complex.com/sneakers/2015/04/nike-flyknit-is-the-most-stylish-and-innovative-sneaker-technology-today.

24. See "Johnson & Johnson's Share of the Baby Care Market Worldwide from 2013 to 2021," *Statista*, www.statista.com/statistics/258429/johnson-und-johnsons-share-of-the-baby-care-market-worldwide/, accessed September 2015; Jack Neff, "Johnson's Baby Turns to Social-Media Transparency to Woo Millennial Moms," *Advertising Age,* July 30, 2014, www.adage.com/print/294376; "Our Promise," www.johnsonsbaby .com/difference/our-promise, accessed September 2015; and "The IKEA Way," www.ikea.com/ms/en_SA/about_ikea/the_ikea_way/index.html, accessed September 2015.

25. See http://vapur.us/about-vapur and http://vapur.us/cause, accessed September 2015. Vapur® and Anti-Bottle® are registered trademarks of Vapur, Inc.

26. Nanette Byrnes, "Pepsi Brings in the Health Police," *Bloomberg Businessweek*, January 25, 2010, pp. 50–51; Mike Esterl, "You Put What in This Chip?" *Wall Street Journal*, March 24, 2011, p. D1; and www.pepsico.com/Purpose/Human-Sustainability/Product-Choices and www.pepsico.com/Investors/Annual-Reports-and-Proxy-Information, accessed September 2015.

27. "SC Johnson's CEO on Doing the Right Thing, Even When It Hurts Business," *Harvard Business Review,* April 2015, pp. 33–36; and "We Commit to What Matters Most," http://scjohnson.com/en/commitment/overview.aspx, accessed September 2015.

28. See Transparency International, "Bribe Payers Index," www.transparency .org/research/bpi/overview; and "Global Corruption Barometer 2013," www.transparency.org/gcb2013. Also see Michael Montgomery, "The Cost of Corruption," American RadioWorks, http://americanradioworks .publicradio.org/features/corruption/, accessed September 2015.

29. See www.marketingpower.com/AboutAMA/Pages/Statement%20of%20 Ethics.aspx, accessed September 2015.

30. See http://investor.google.com/corporate/code-of-conduct.html, accessed June 2015.

31. David A. Lubin and Daniel C. Esty, "The Sustainability Imperative," *Harvard Business Review*, May 2010, pp. 41–50; and Roasbeth Moss Kanter, "It's Time to Take Full Responsibility," *Harvard Business Review*, October 2010, p. 42.

Appendix 3

i. This is derived by rearranging the following equation and solving for price: Percentage markup = (price − cost) ÷ price.

ii. Again, using the basic profit equation, we set profit equal to ROI × I: ROI × I = (P × Q) − TFC − (Q × UVC). Solving for Q gives Q = (TFC + (ROI × I)) ÷ (P − UVC).

iii. U.S. Census Bureau, available at http://quickfacts.census.gov/qfd/states/00000.html, June 13, 2014.

iv. See Roger J. Best, *Market-Based Management,* 4th ed. (Upper Saddle River, NJ: Prentice Hall, 2005).

v. Total contribution can also be determined from the unit contribution and unit volume: Total contribution = unit contribution × unit sales. Total units sold in 2016 were 595,238 units, which can be determined by dividing total sales by price per unit ($100 million ÷ $168). Total contribution = $35.28 contribution per unit × 595,238 units = $20,999,996.64 (difference due to rounding).

vi. Recall that the contribution margin of 21% was based on variable costs representing 79% of sales. Therefore, if we do not know price, we can set it equal to $1.00. If price equals $1.00, 79 cents represents variable costs and 21 cents represents unit contribution. If price is decreased by 10%, the new price is 90 cents. However, variable costs do not change just because price decreased, so the unit contribution and contribution margin decrease as follows:

	Old	New (Reduced 10%)
Price	$1.00	$0.90
− Unit variable cost	$0.79	$0.79
= Unit contribution	$0.21	$0.11
Contribution margin	$0.21/$1.00 = 0.21 or 21%	$0.11/$0.90 = 0.12 or 12%

Indexes

Brand, Name, and Organization Index

In this index *f* represents figures and *t* represents tables.

Subject Index

In this index *f* indicates figures, *p* indicates photos, and *t* indicates tables.